Cross✕Game

1

Story & Art by
Mitsuru Adachi

Contents Volume 1

Volume 1 ••••••••••••••••••••❖••••••••••••••••❖••••••••••••••••

Part I/The Season of Wakaba

Chapter 1: Four-Leaf Clover   3
Chapter 2: Since I Was Three   27
Chapter 3: Get Ready   45
Chapter 4: What Did You Draw?   64
Chapter 5: Just Barely Safe   83
Chapter 6: Yowch!   101
Chapter 7: Why, You—!   119
Chapter 8: Fireworks   137
Chapter 9: She Said by Evening   155
Chapter 10: It's Simple   173

Volume 2 ••••••••••••••••••••••••••••❖••••••••••••••••••••••

Part II

Chapter 1: I'm Free   195
Chapter 2: Just a Daily Routine   221
Chapter 3: I Hate Him!   239
Chapter 4: Change Pitchers!   257
Chapter 5: For Real?   275
Chapter 6: Scumbags   295
Chapter 7: Amazing Jr. High Student   313
Chapter 8: Who Was That?   331
Chapter 9: Secret Weapon   349
Chapter 10: Can I Borrow a Pot?   367

Volume 3 •••••••••❖•••••••••••••••••••••••••••••••❖••••••••••

Part II

Chapter 11: The First Spring of High School   389
Chapter 12: Why Did You Even Join the Baseball Team?   409
Chapter 13: Who Are You?   427
Chapter 14: A Good Dream   445
Chapter 15: Nope   463
Chapter 16: Aoba Tsukishima   481
Chapter 17: A Sucker for a Pretty Face   501
Chapter 18: We Think Alike   519
Chapter 19: Two of a Kind   537
Chapter 20: A Nightmare!   555

CHAPTER 1
FOUR-LEAF CLOVER

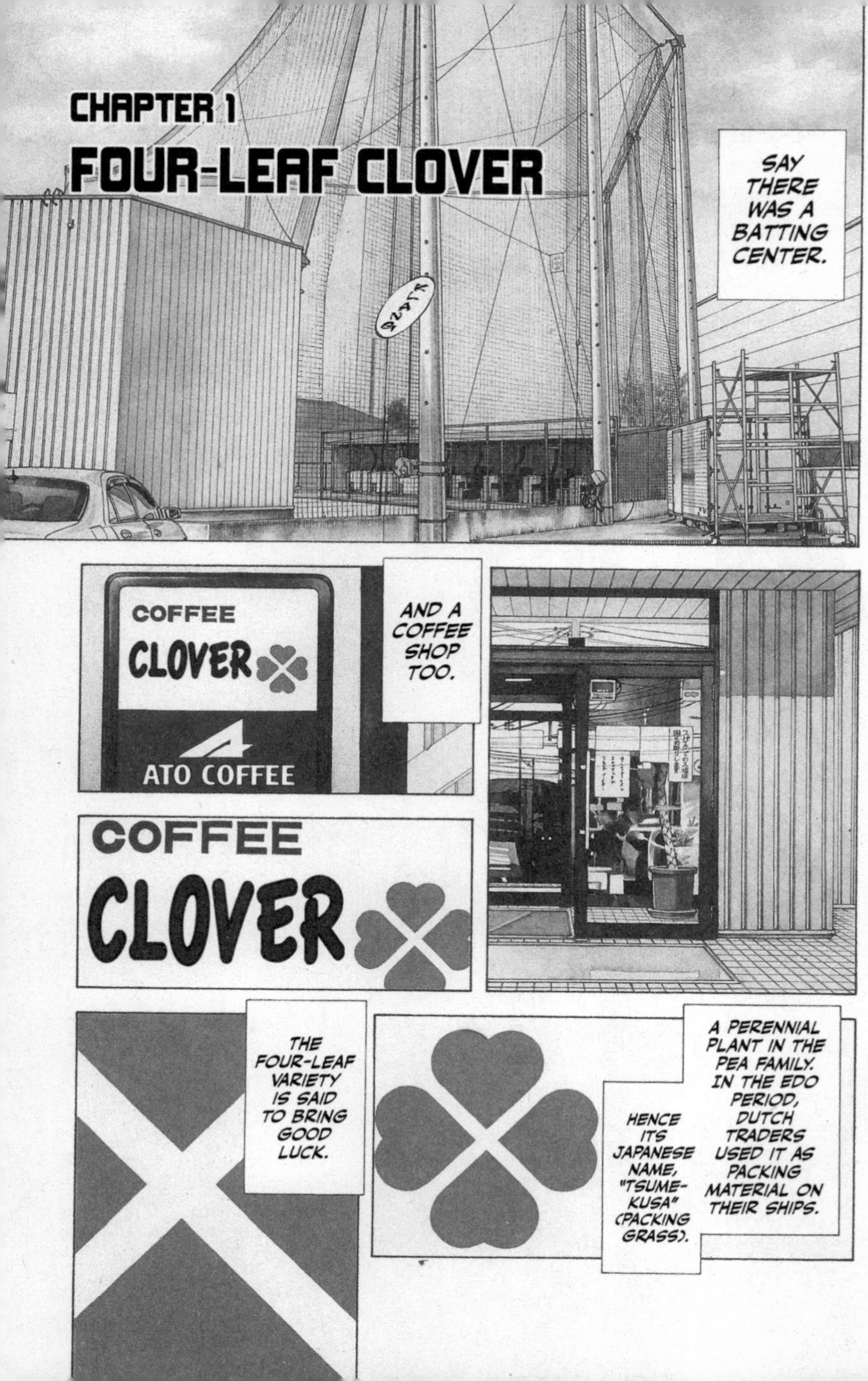
SAY THERE WAS A BATTING CENTER.
AND A COFFEE SHOP TOO.
COFFEE CLOVER
ATO COFFEE
COFFEE CLOVER
A PERENNIAL PLANT IN THE PEA FAMILY. IN THE EDO PERIOD, DUTCH TRADERS USED IT AS PACKING MATERIAL ON THEIR SHIPS.
HENCE ITS JAPANESE NAME, "TSUME-KUSA" (PACKING GRASS).
THE FOUR-LEAF VARIETY IS SAID TO BRING GOOD LUCK.

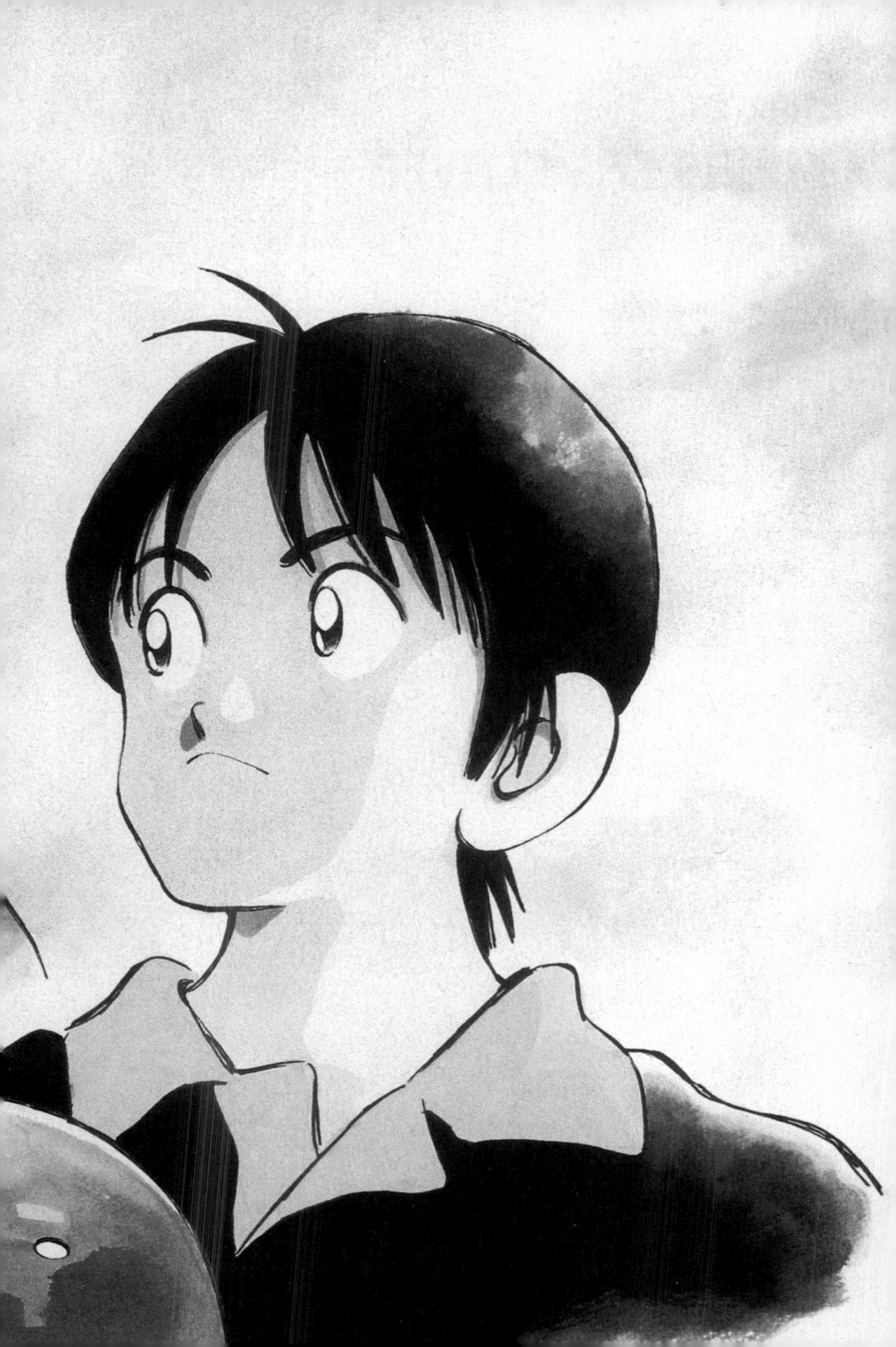

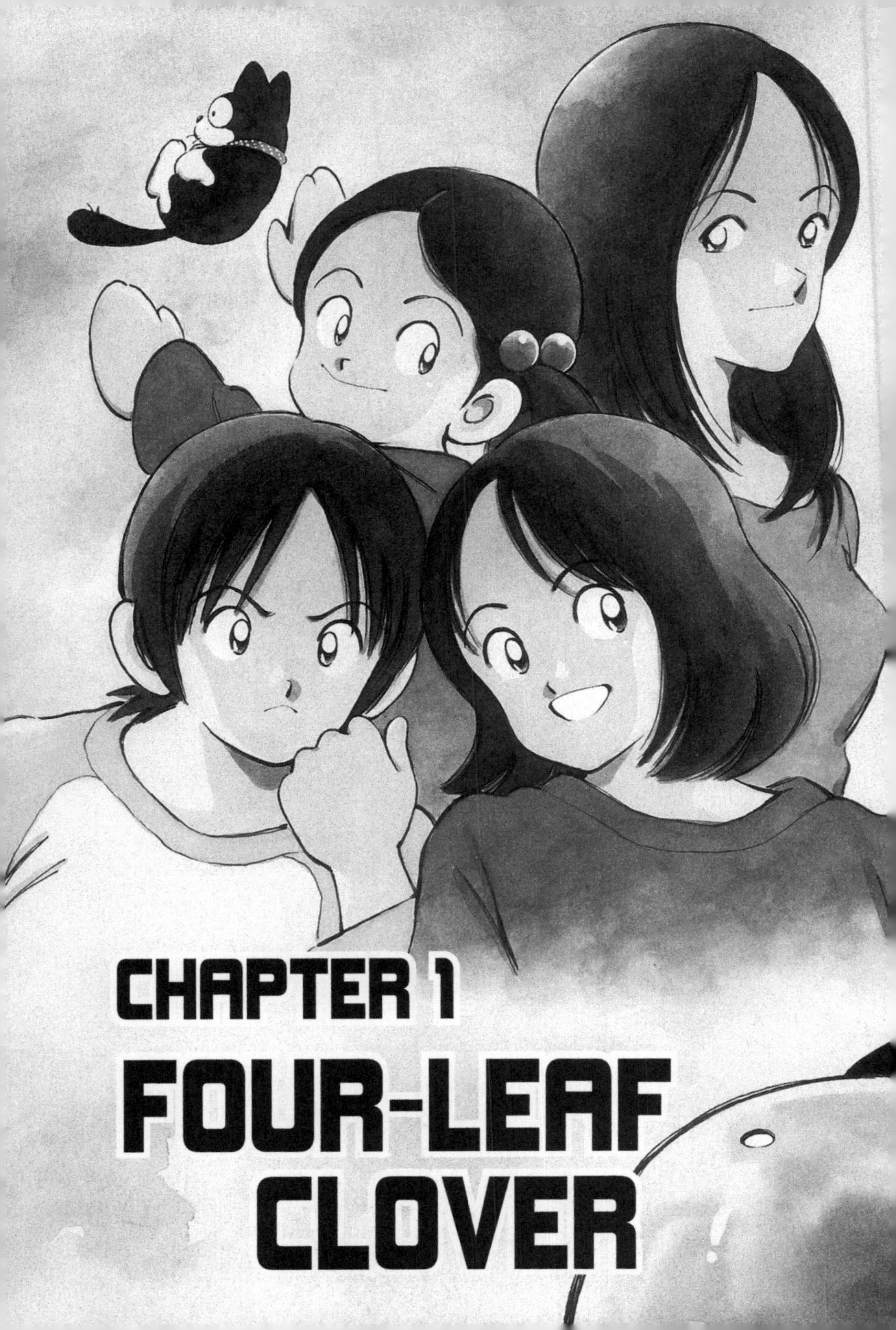
CHAPTER 1
FOUR-LEAF
CLOVER

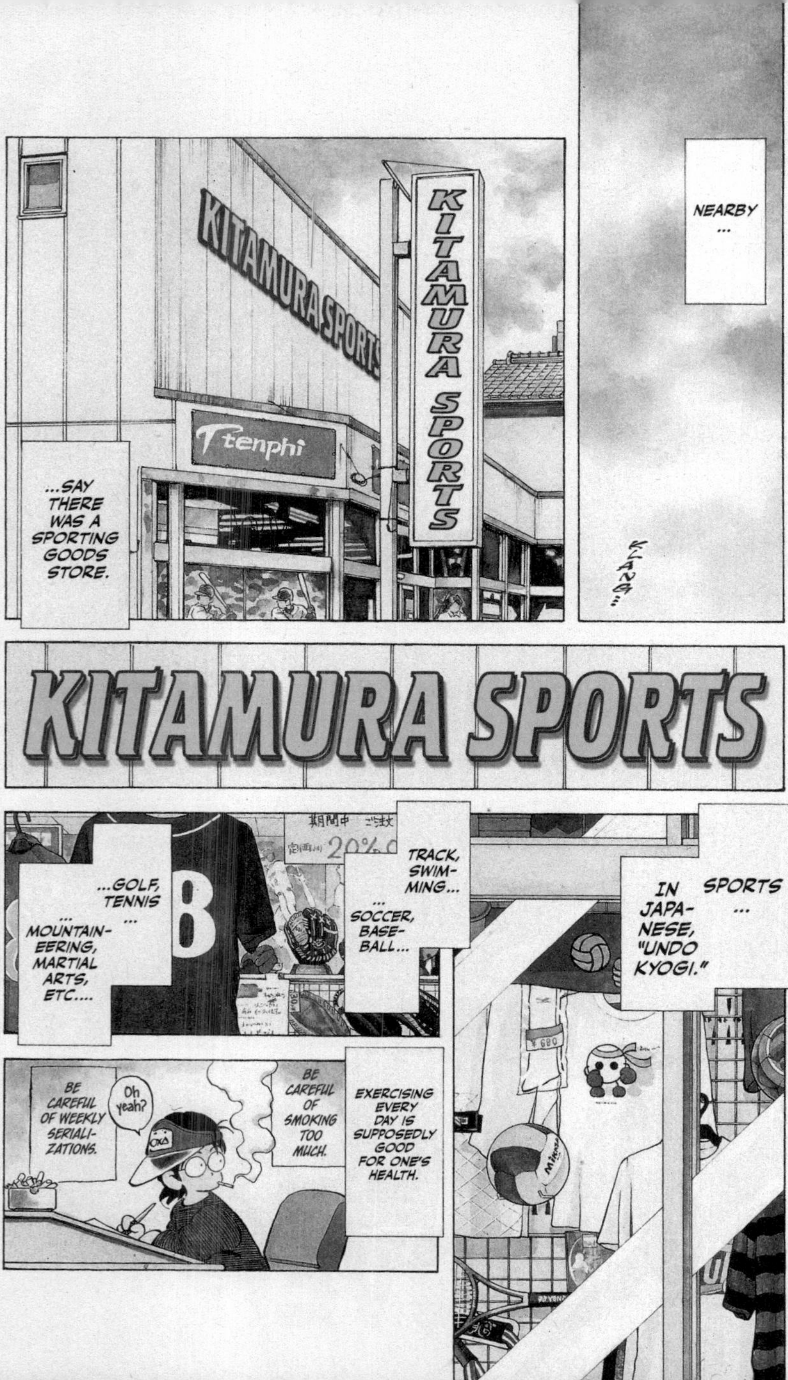
NEARBY ...
KLANG...
KITAMURA SPORTS
KITAMURA SPORTS
tenphi
...SAY THERE WAS A SPORTING GOODS STORE.
KITAMURA SPORTS
SPORTS ...
IN JAPANESE, "UNDO KYOGI."
TRACK, SWIMMING... ... SOCCER, BASEBALL...
...GOLF, TENNIS ... MOUNTAINEERING, MARTIAL ARTS, ETC....
期間中
EXERCISING EVERY DAY IS SUPPOSEDLY GOOD FOR ONE'S HEALTH.
BE CAREFUL OF SMOKING TOO MUCH.
Oh yeah?
BE CAREFUL OF WEEKLY SERIALIZATIONS.

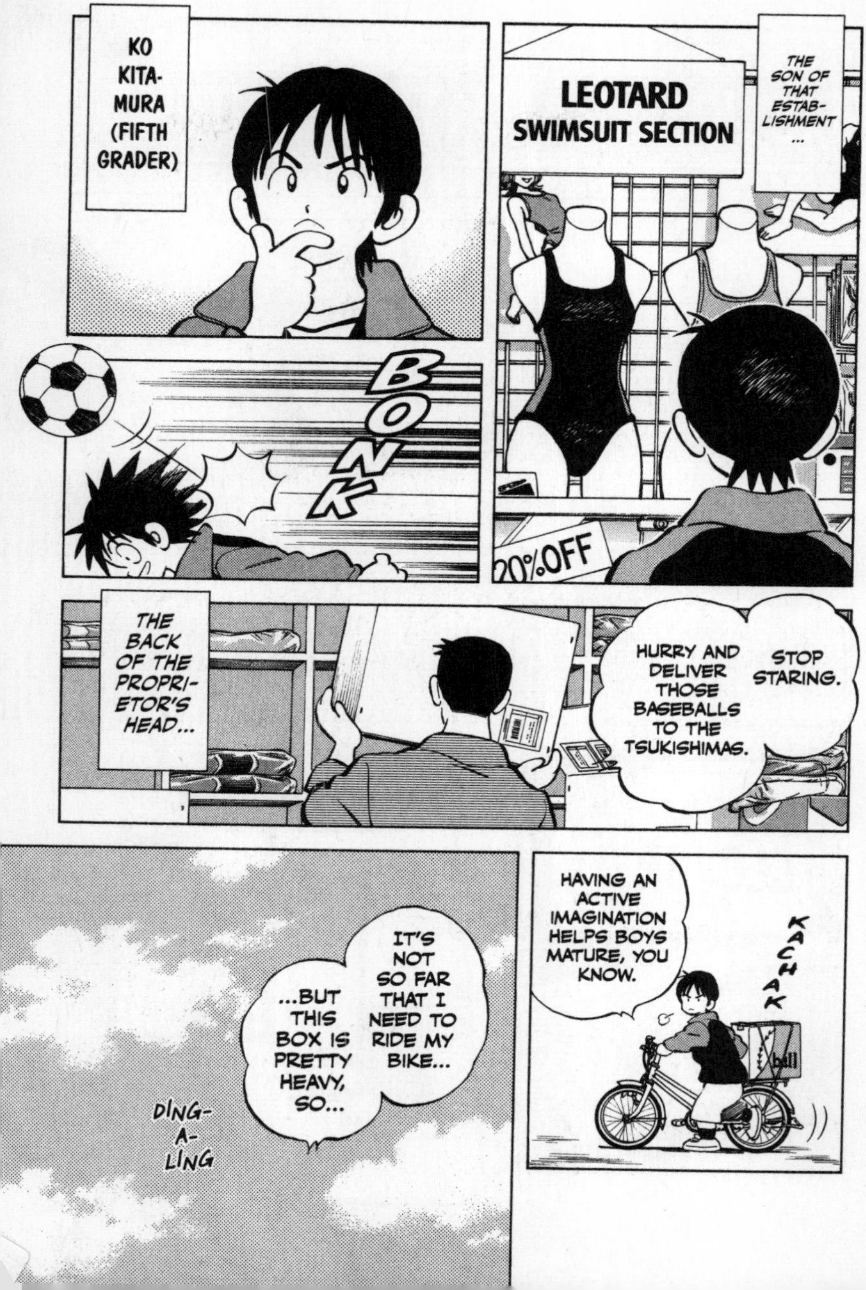
THE SON OF THAT ESTABLISHMENT ...
LEOTARD
SWIMSUIT SECTION
20%OFF
KO KITAMURA (FIFTH GRADER)
BONK
STOP STARING.
HURRY AND DELIVER THOSE BASEBALLS TO THE TSUKISHIMAS.
THE BACK OF THE PROPRIETOR'S HEAD...
HAVING AN ACTIVE IMAGINATION HELPS BOYS MATURE, YOU KNOW.
KACHAK
IT'S NOT SO FAR THAT I NEED TO RIDE MY BIKE...
...BUT THIS BOX IS PRETTY HEAVY, SO...
DING-A-LING

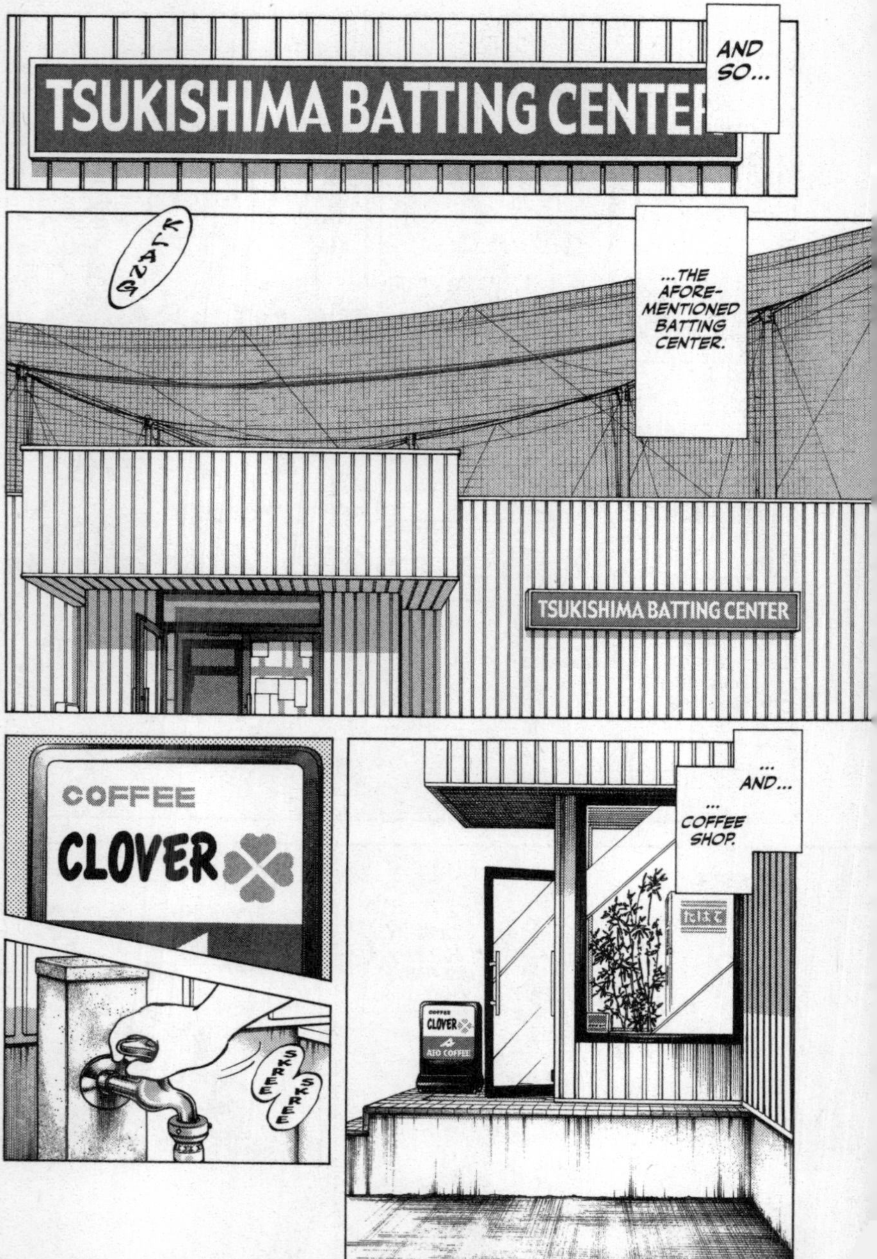
AND SO...
TSUKISHIMA BATTING CENTER
...THE AFORE-MENTIONED BATTING CENTER.
KLANG
TSUKISHIMA BATTING CENTER
... AND...
... COFFEE SHOP.
COFFEE CLOVER
AIO COFFEE
COFFEE
CLOVER
SKREE SKREE

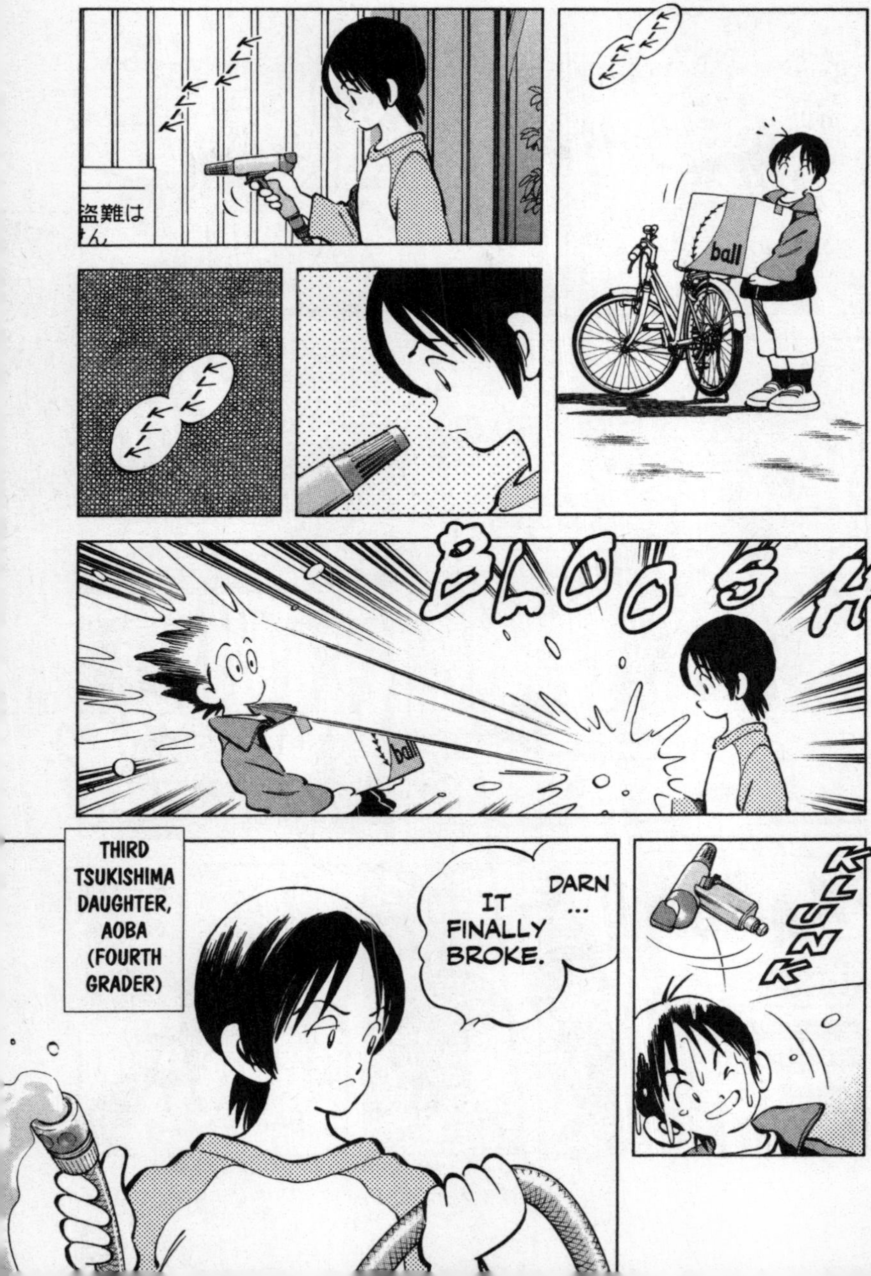
KLIK KLIK
KLIK KLIK
盗難は
KLIK KLIK
BLOOSH
KLUNK
DARN ... IT FINALLY BROKE.
THIRD TSUKISHIMA DAUGHTER, AOBA (FOURTH GRADER)

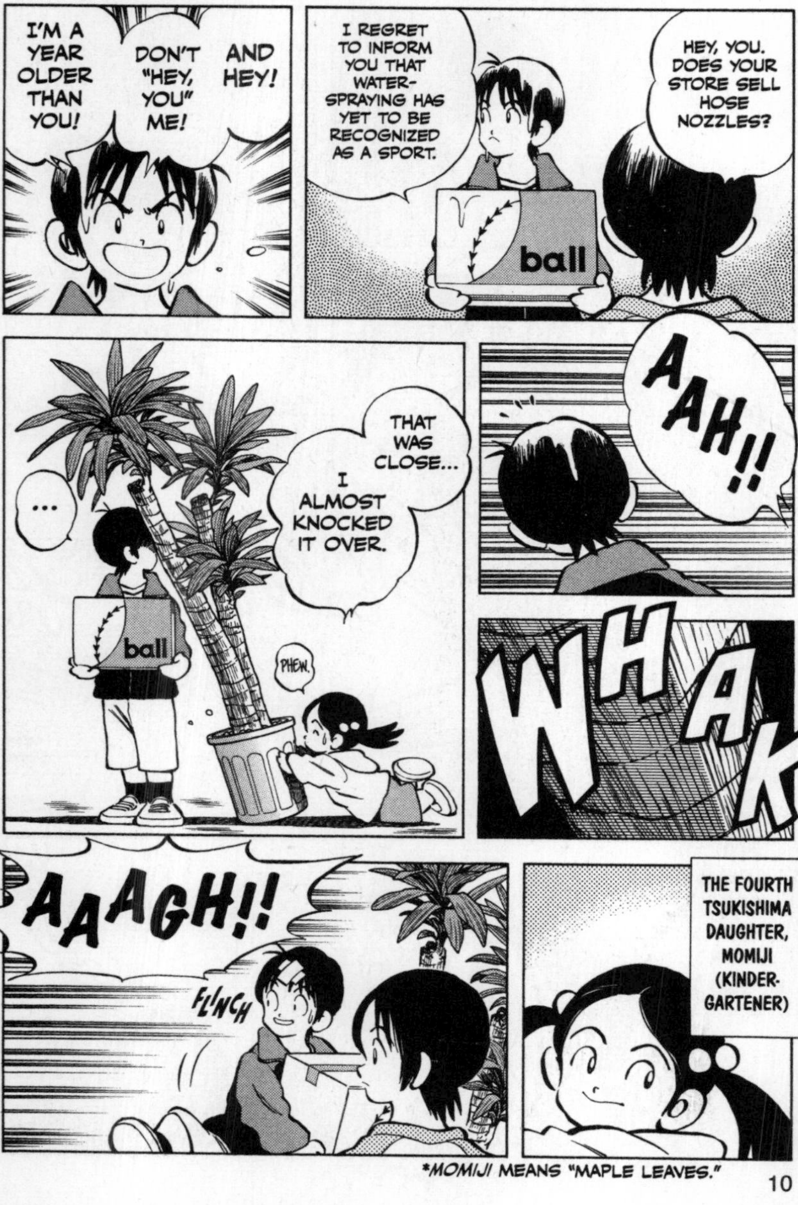
HEY, YOU. DOES YOUR STORE SELL HOSE NOZZLES?
I REGRET TO INFORM YOU THAT WATER-SPRAYING HAS YET TO BE RECOGNIZED AS A SPORT.
ball
AND HEY!
DON'T "HEY, YOU" ME!
I'M A YEAR OLDER THAN YOU!
AAH!!
WHAK
THAT WAS CLOSE...
I ALMOST KNOCKED IT OVER.
...
ball
PHEW.
THE FOURTH TSUKISHIMA DAUGHTER, MOMIJI (KINDER-GARTENER)
AAAGH!!
FLINCH

**MOMIJI* MEANS "MAPLE LEAVES."

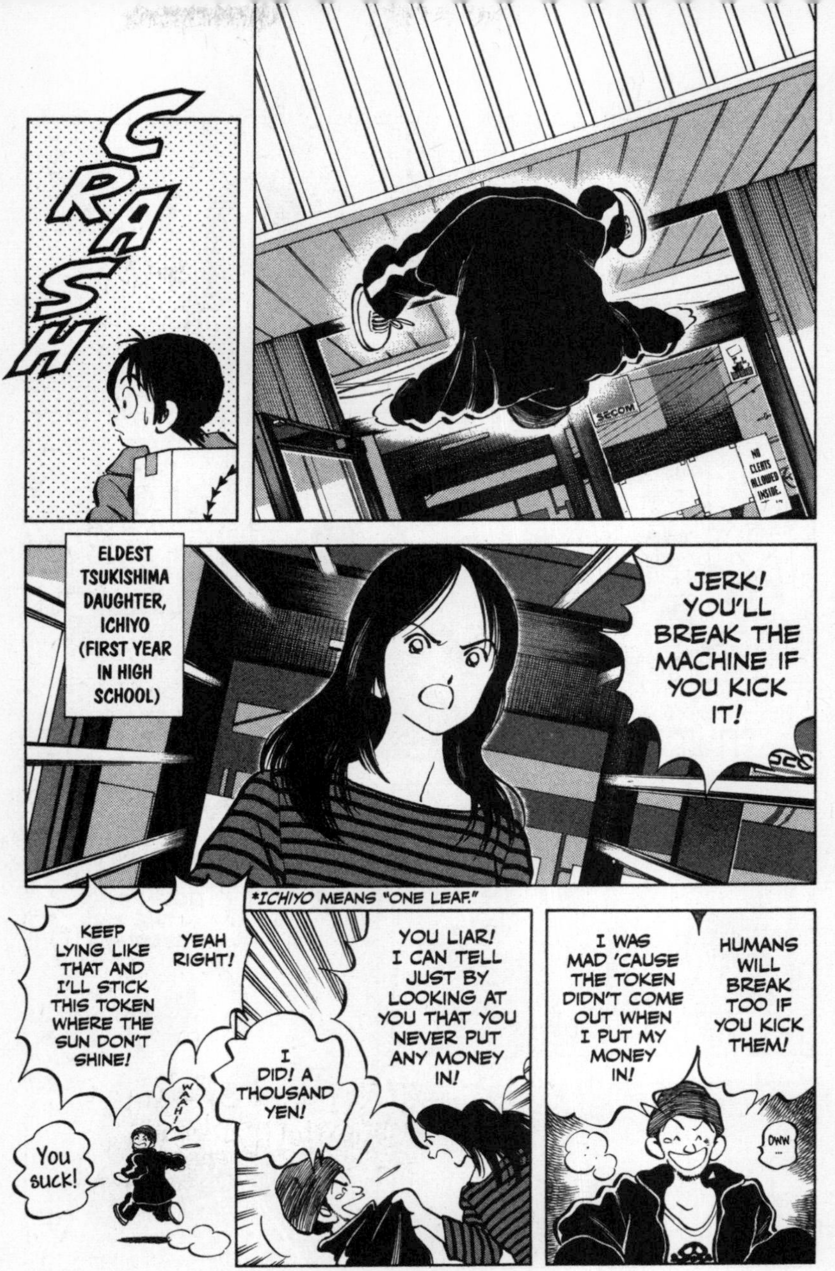
SECOM
NO CLEATS ALLOWED INSIDE.
CRASH
JERK! YOU'LL BREAK THE MACHINE IF YOU KICK IT!
ELDEST TSUKISHIMA DAUGHTER, ICHIYO (FIRST YEAR IN HIGH SCHOOL)
HUMANS WILL BREAK TOO IF YOU KICK THEM!
I WAS MAD 'CAUSE THE TOKEN DIDN'T COME OUT WHEN I PUT MY MONEY IN!
OWW...
YOU LIAR! I CAN TELL JUST BY LOOKING AT YOU THAT YOU NEVER PUT ANY MONEY IN!
I DID! A THOUSAND YEN!
YEAH RIGHT!
KEEP LYING LIKE THAT AND I'LL STICK THIS TOKEN WHERE THE SUN DON'T SHINE!
WAAH!
You suck!

*ICHIYO MEANS "ONE LEAF."

*ABOUT $10

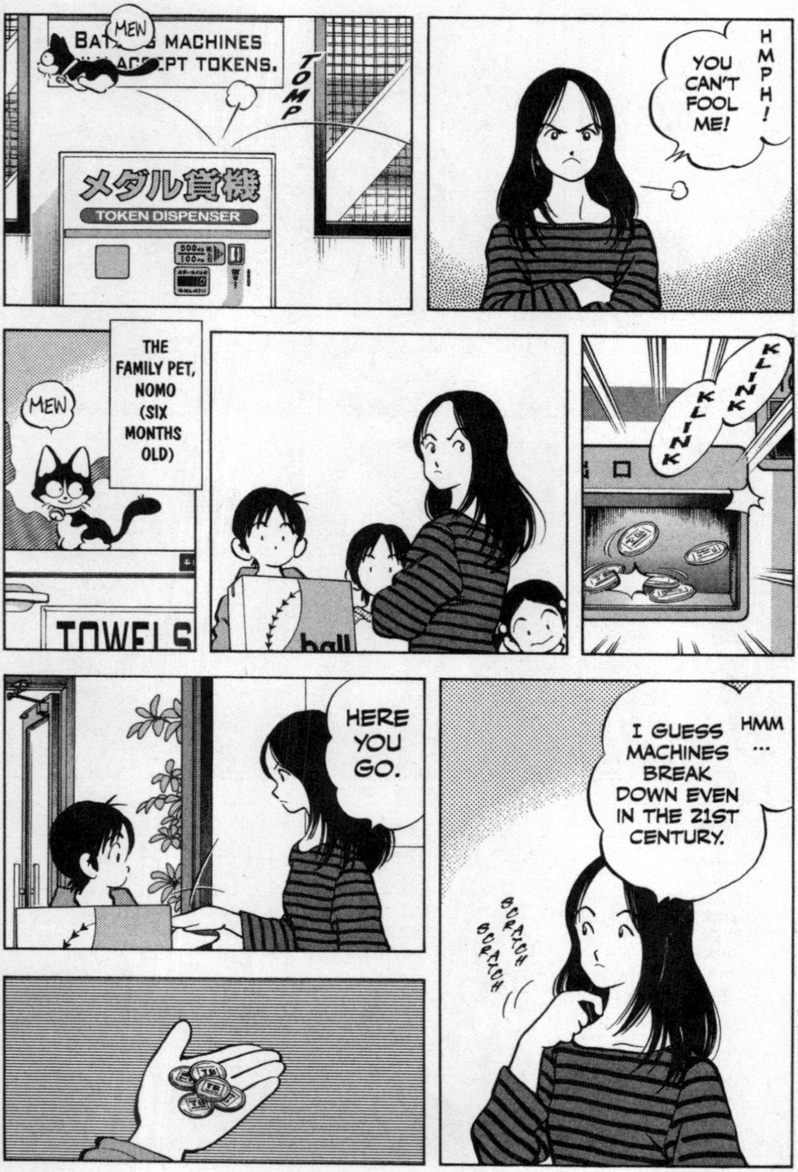
HMPH!
YOU CAN'T FOOL ME!
MEW
MACHINES
ACCEPT TOKENS.
TOMP
メダル貸機
TOKEN DISPENSER
KLINK
KLINK
THE FAMILY PET, NOMO (SIX MONTHS OLD)
MEW
TOWELS
ball
HMM...
I GUESS MACHINES BREAK DOWN EVEN IN THE 21ST CENTURY.
SCRATCH
SCRATCH
HERE YOU GO.

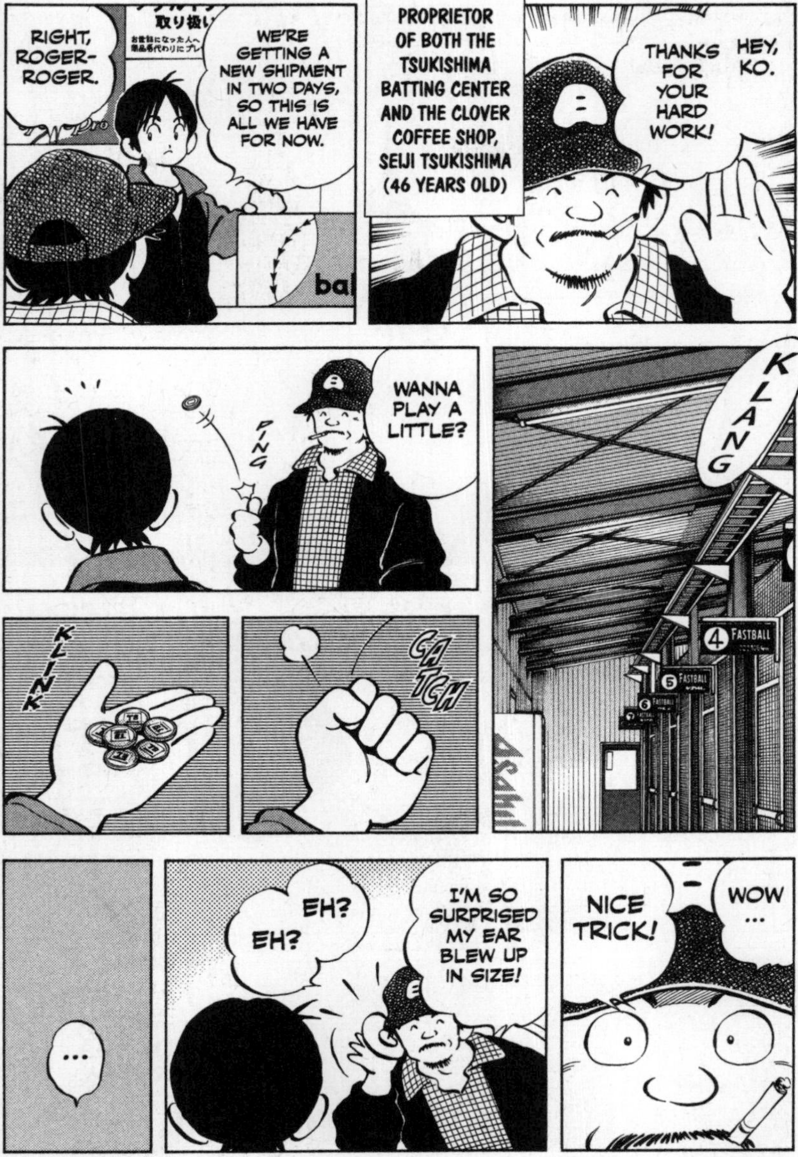
HEY, KO.
THANKS FOR YOUR HARD WORK!
PROPRIETOR OF BOTH THE TSUKISHIMA BATTING CENTER AND THE CLOVER COFFEE SHOP, SEIJI TSUKISHIMA (46 YEARS OLD)
取り扱い
WE'RE GETTING A NEW SHIPMENT IN TWO DAYS, SO THIS IS ALL WE HAVE FOR NOW.
RIGHT, ROGER-ROGER.
KLANG
4 FASTBALL
5 FASTBALL
WANNA PLAY A LITTLE?
PING
CATCH
KLINK
WOW ...
NICE TRICK!
I'M SO SURPRISED MY EAR BLEW UP IN SIZE!
EH?
EH?
...

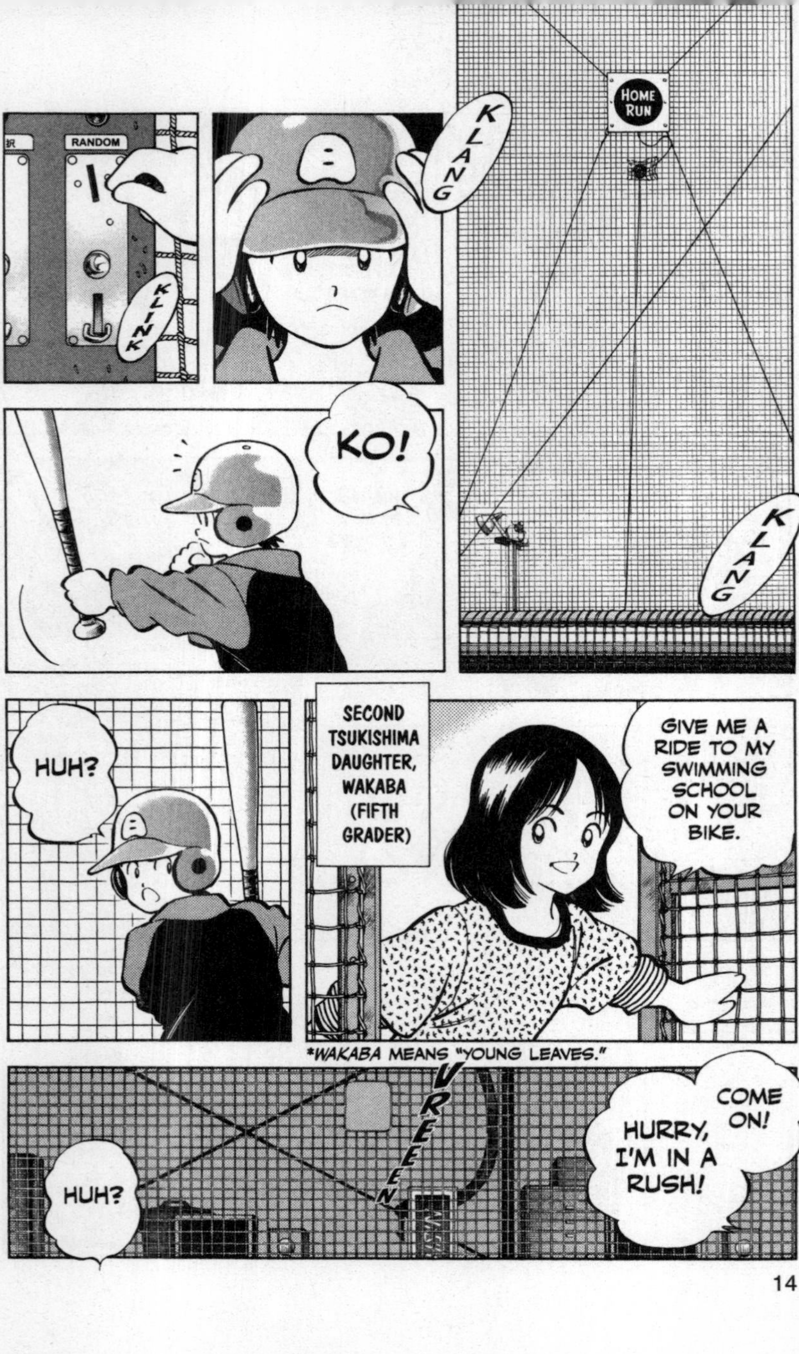

HOME RUN
KLANG
KLANG
RANDOM
KLINK
KO!
SECOND TSUKISHIMA DAUGHTER, WAKABA (FIFTH GRADER)
GIVE ME A RIDE TO MY SWIMMING SCHOOL ON YOUR BIKE.
HUH?
*WAKABA MEANS "YOUNG LEAVES."
COME ON!
HURRY, I'M IN A RUSH!
VREEEEN
HUH?

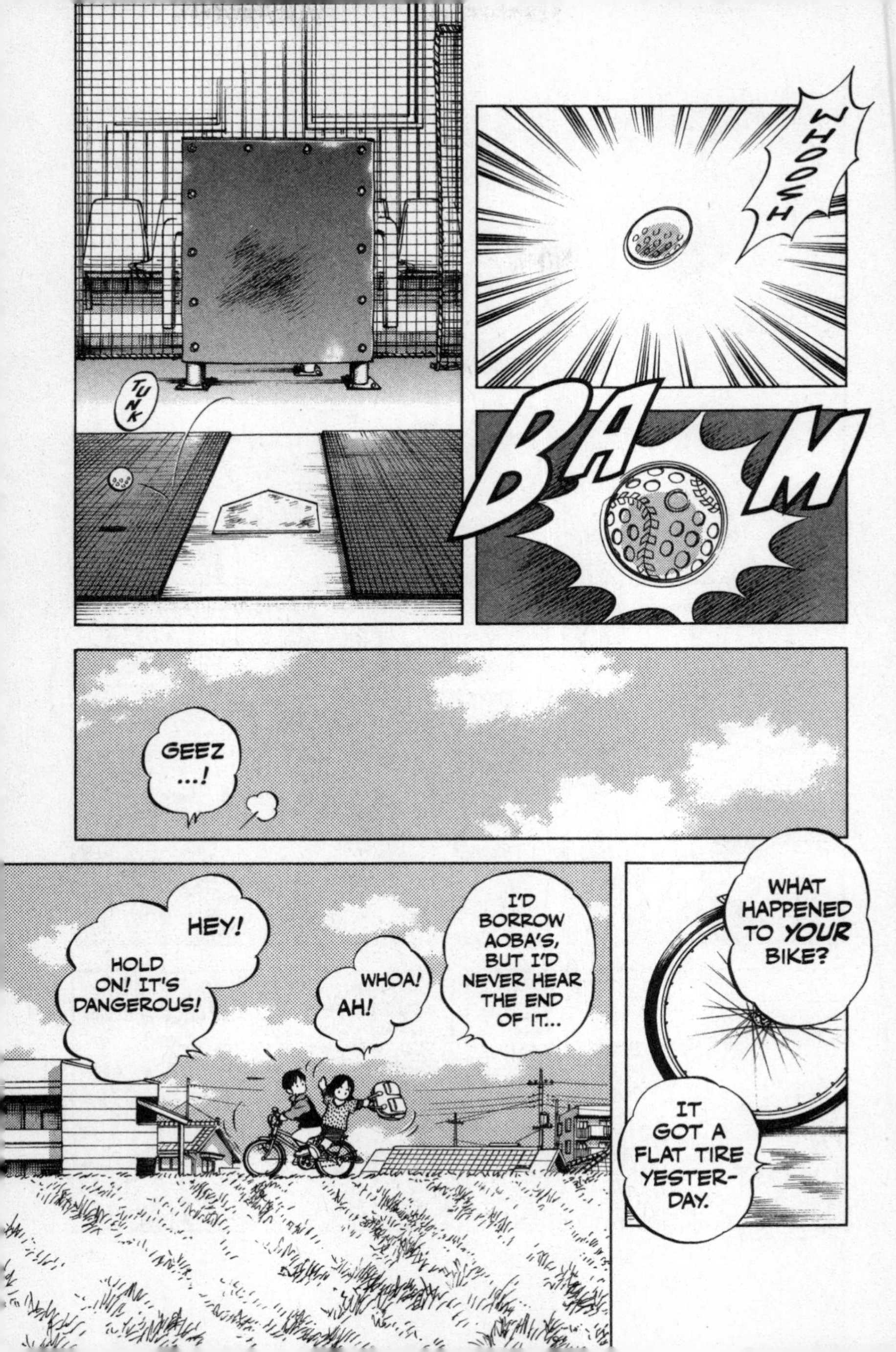
WHOOSH
BAM
TUNK
GEEZ ...!
WHAT HAPPENED TO *YOUR* BIKE?
IT GOT A FLAT TIRE YESTER-DAY.
I'D BORROW AOBA'S, BUT I'D NEVER HEAR THE END OF IT...
WHOA! AH!
HEY! HOLD ON! IT'S DANGEROUS!

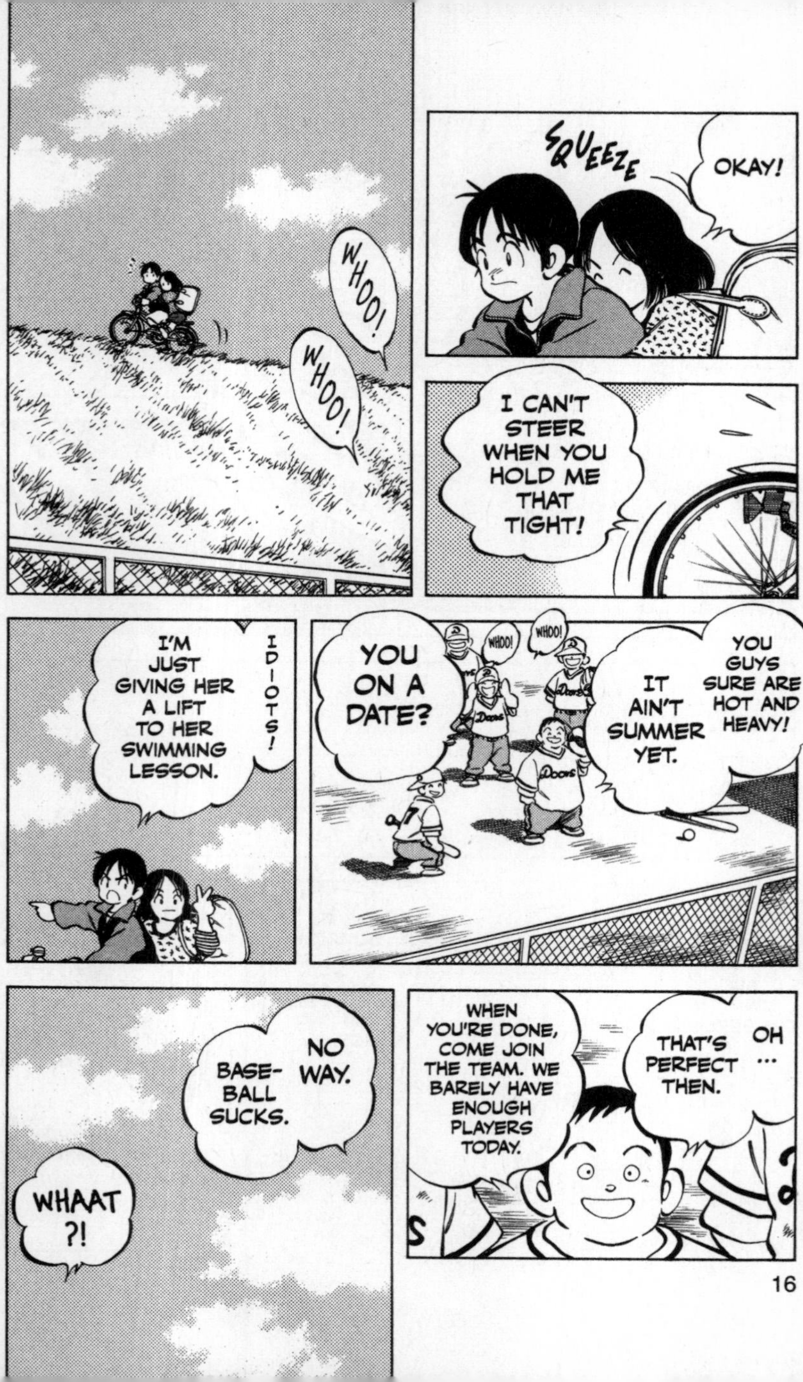
SQUEEZE
OKAY!
I CAN'T STEER WHEN YOU HOLD ME THAT TIGHT!
WHOO!
WHOO!
YOU GUYS SURE ARE HOT AND HEAVY!
IT AIN'T SUMMER YET.
WHOO!
WHOO!
YOU ON A DATE?
IDIOTS!
I'M JUST GIVING HER A LIFT TO HER SWIMMING LESSON.
OH ...
THAT'S PERFECT THEN.
WHEN YOU'RE DONE, COME JOIN THE TEAM. WE BARELY HAVE ENOUGH PLAYERS TODAY.
NO WAY.
BASE-BALL SUCKS.
WHAAT ?!

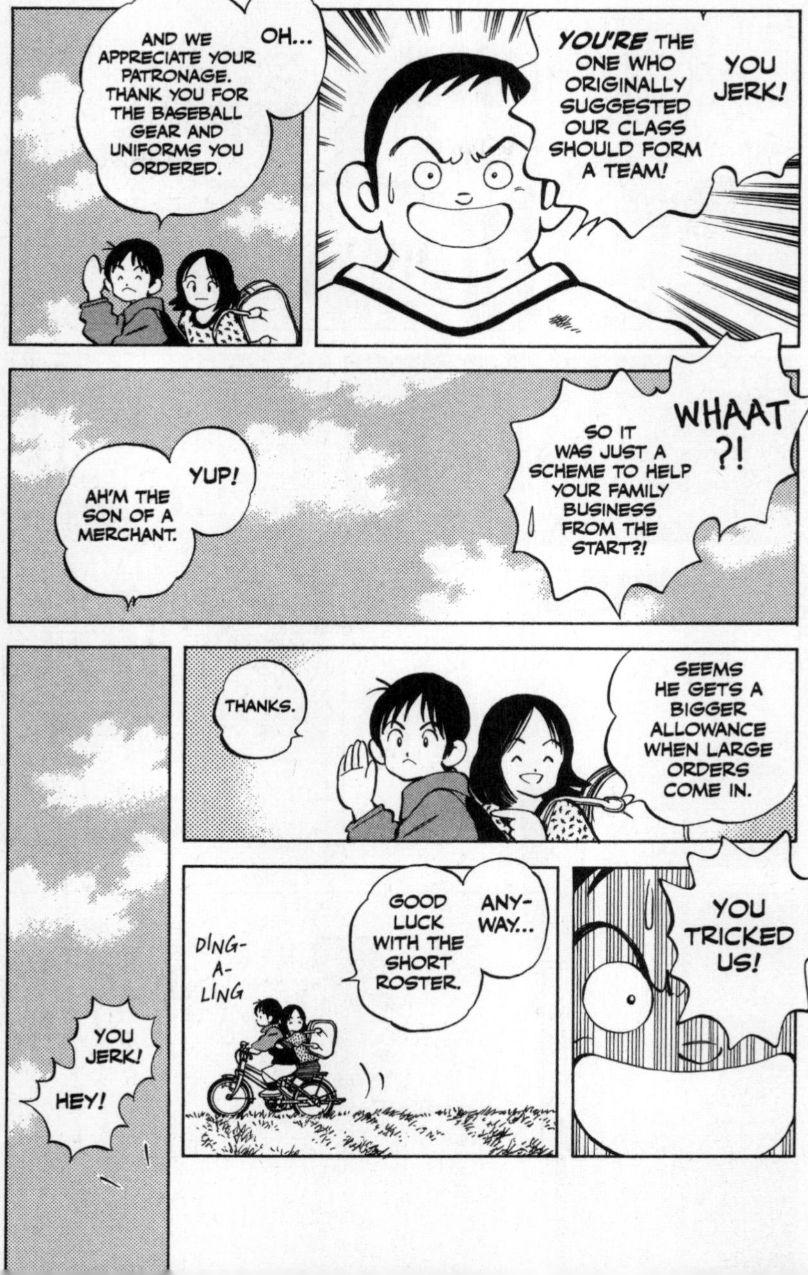
YOU JERK!
YOU'RE THE ONE WHO ORIGINALLY SUGGESTED OUR CLASS SHOULD FORM A TEAM!
OH...
AND WE APPRECIATE YOUR PATRONAGE. THANK YOU FOR THE BASEBALL GEAR AND UNIFORMS YOU ORDERED.
WHAAT ?!
SO IT WAS JUST A SCHEME TO HELP YOUR FAMILY BUSINESS FROM THE START?!
YUP!
AH'M THE SON OF A MERCHANT.
SEEMS HE GETS A BIGGER ALLOWANCE WHEN LARGE ORDERS COME IN.
THANKS.
YOU TRICKED US!
ANY-WAY...
GOOD LUCK WITH THE SHORT ROSTER.
DING-A-LING
YOU JERK!
HEY!

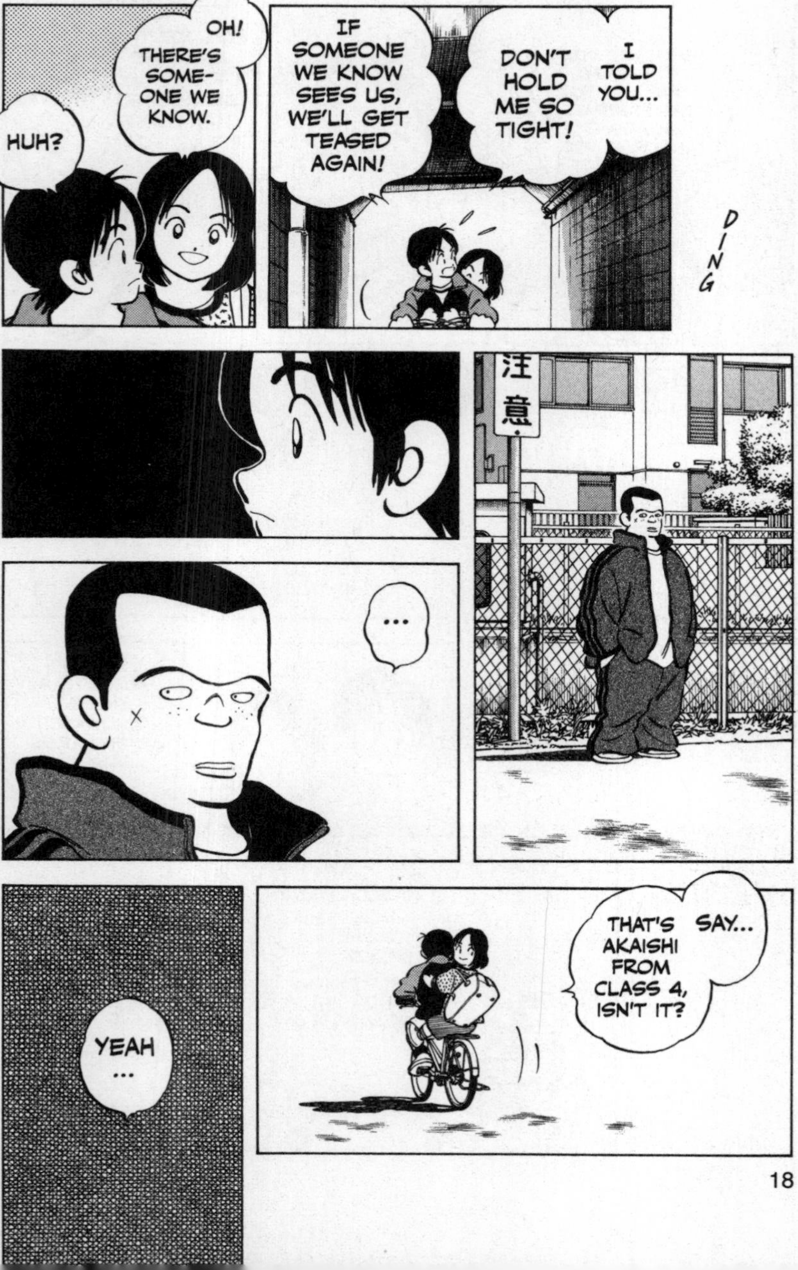
I TOLD YOU...
DON'T HOLD ME SO TIGHT!
IF SOMEONE WE KNOW SEES US, WE'LL GET TEASED AGAIN!
DING
OH! THERE'S SOME-ONE WE KNOW.
HUH?
注意
...
SAY...
THAT'S AKAISHI FROM CLASS 4, ISN'T IT?
YEAH ...

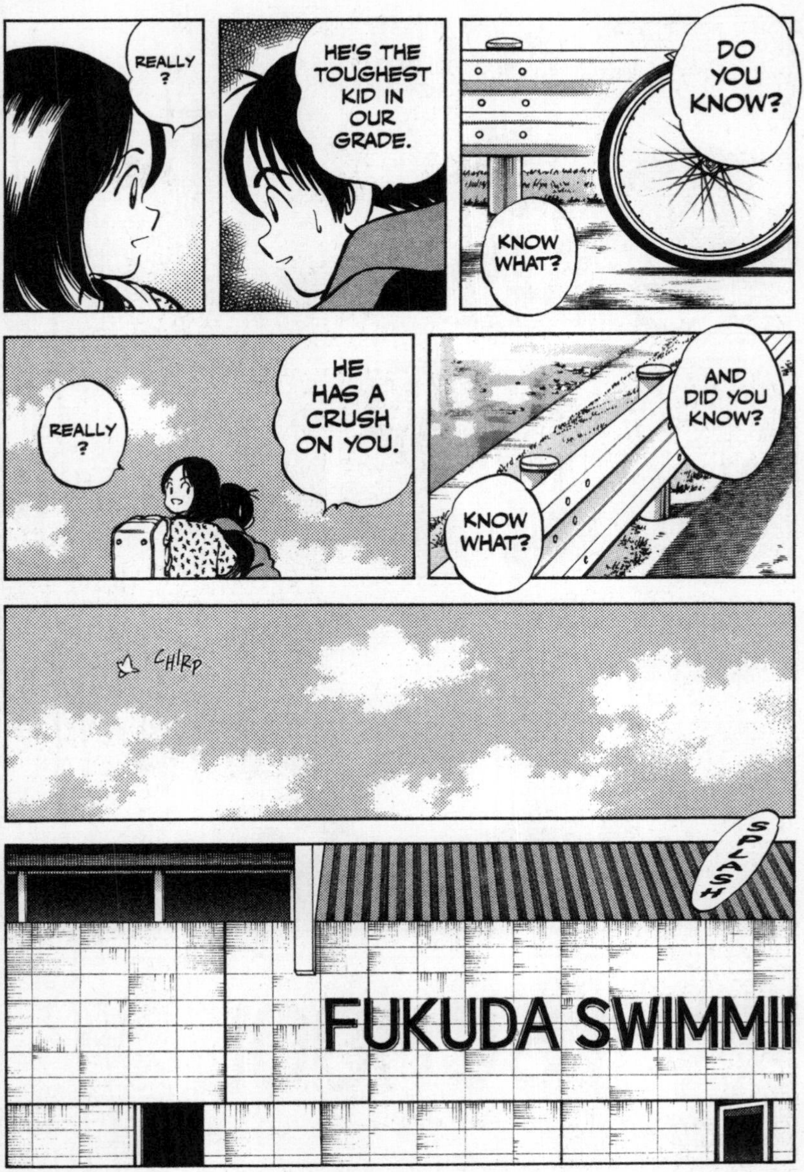
DO YOU KNOW?
KNOW WHAT?
HE'S THE TOUGHEST KID IN OUR GRADE.
REALLY ?
AND DID YOU KNOW?
KNOW WHAT?
HE HAS A CRUSH ON YOU.
REALLY ?
CHIRP
SPLASH
FUKUDA SWIMMI

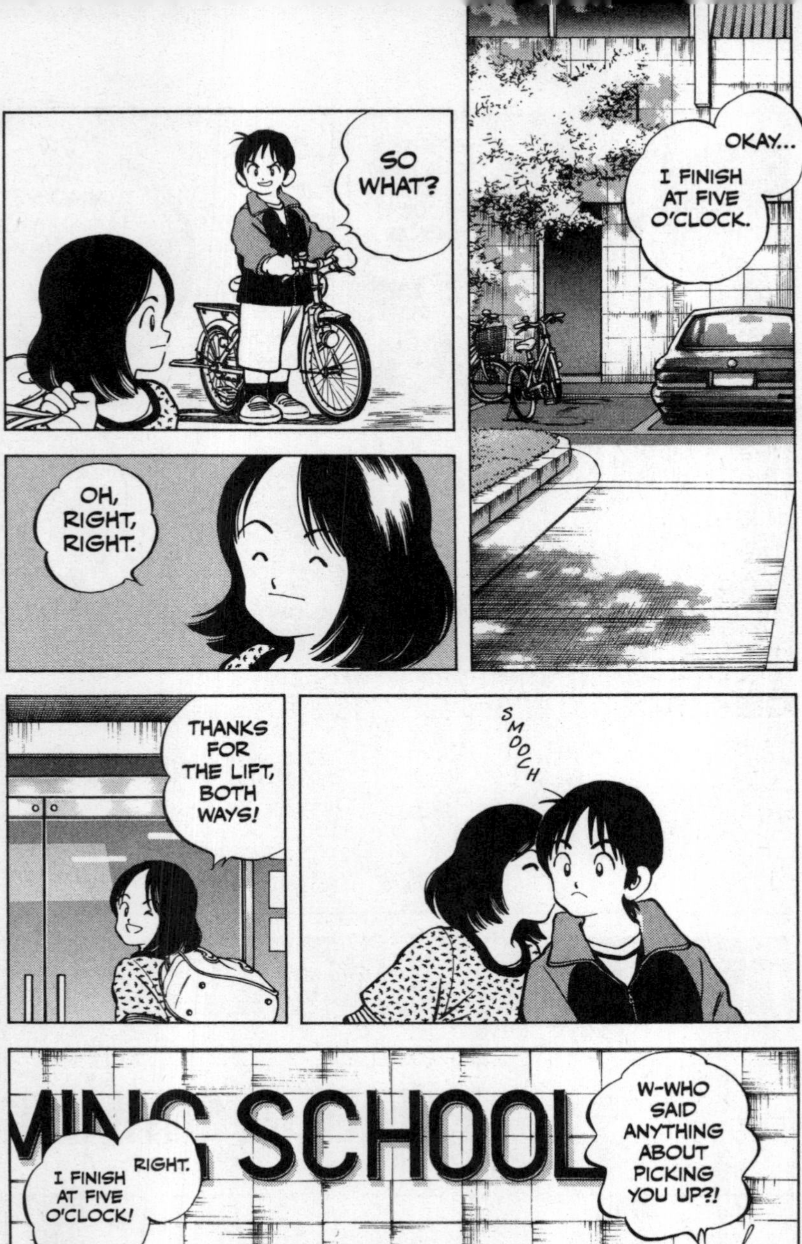
OKAY... I FINISH AT FIVE O'CLOCK.
SO WHAT?
OH, RIGHT, RIGHT.
SMOOCH
THANKS FOR THE LIFT, BOTH WAYS!
W-WHO SAID ANYTHING ABOUT PICKING YOU UP?!
SCHOOL
RIGHT. I FINISH AT FIVE O'CLOCK!

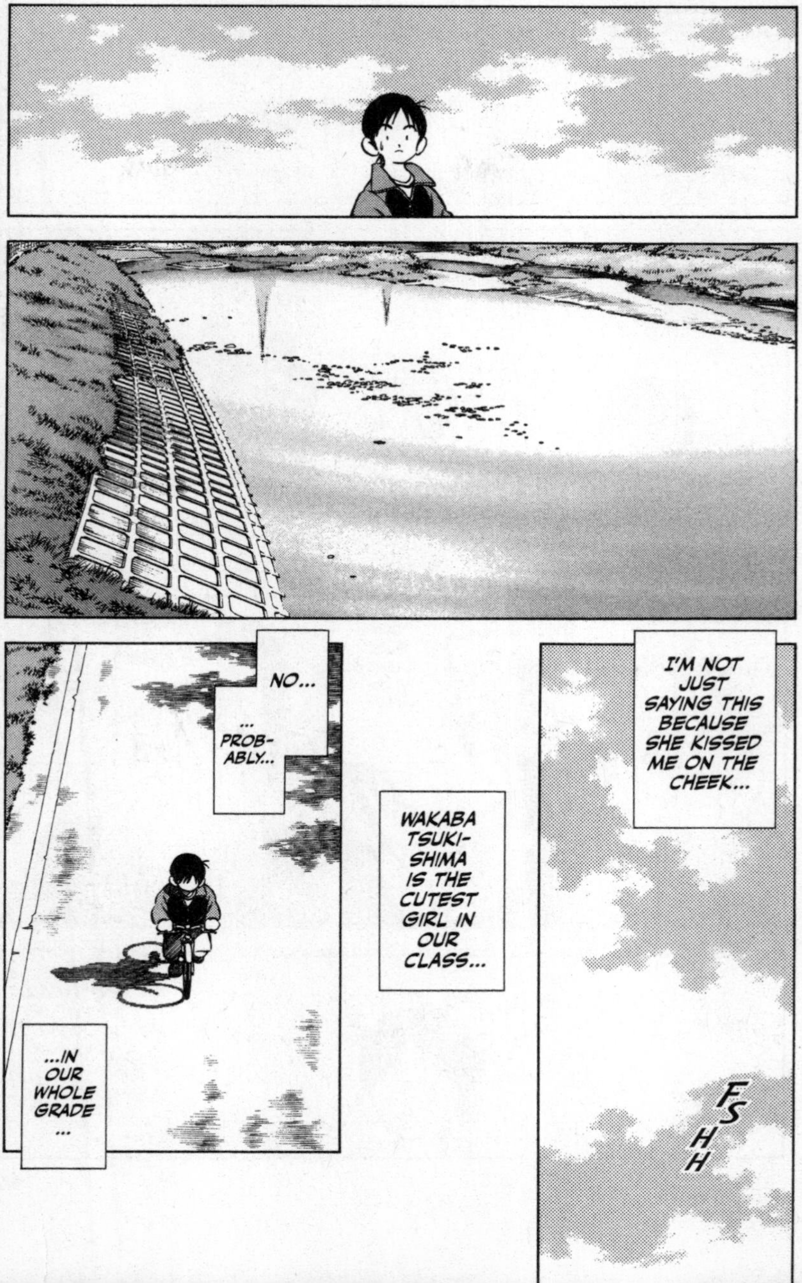
I'M NOT JUST SAYING THIS BECAUSE SHE KISSED ME ON THE CHEEK...
FSHH
WAKABA TSUKISHIMA IS THE CUTEST GIRL IN OUR CLASS...
NO...
...PROBABLY...
...IN OUR WHOLE GRADE...

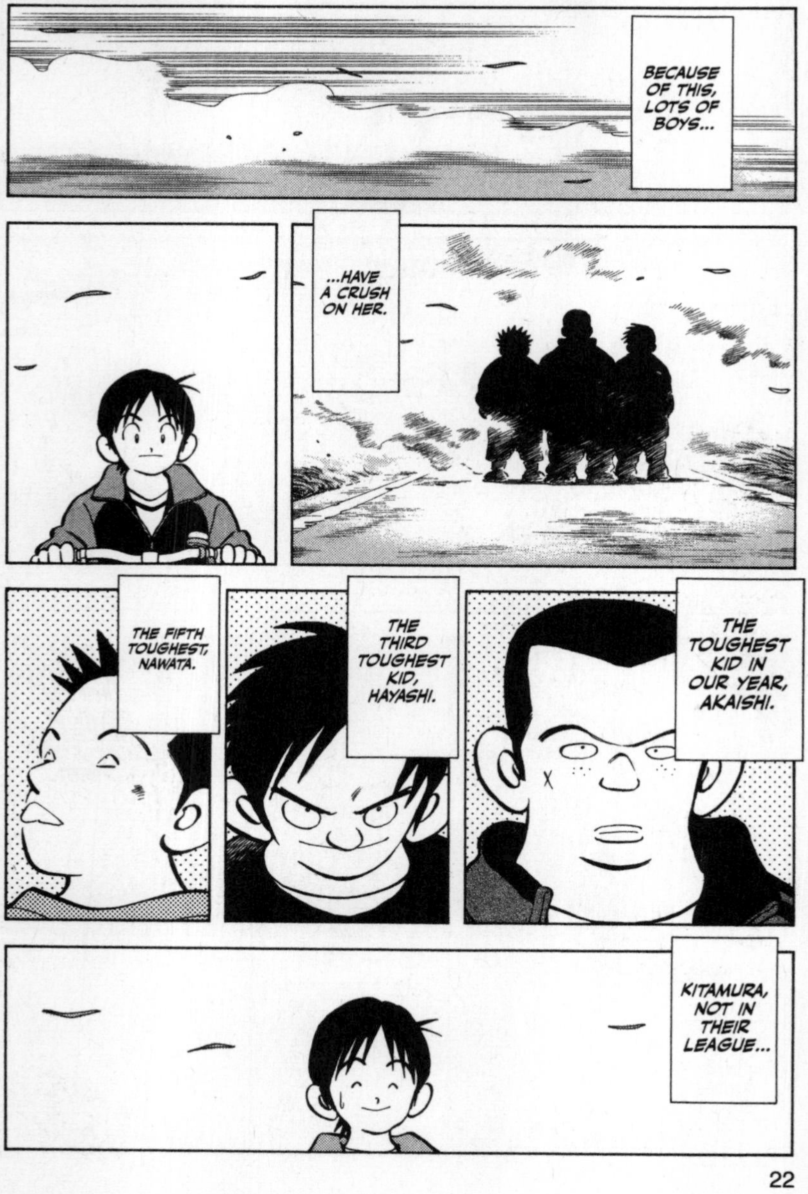
BECAUSE OF THIS, LOTS OF BOYS...
...HAVE A CRUSH ON HER.
THE TOUGHEST KID IN OUR YEAR, AKAISHI.
THE THIRD TOUGHEST KID, HAYASHI.
THE FIFTH TOUGHEST, NAWATA.
KITAMURA, NOT IN THEIR LEAGUE...

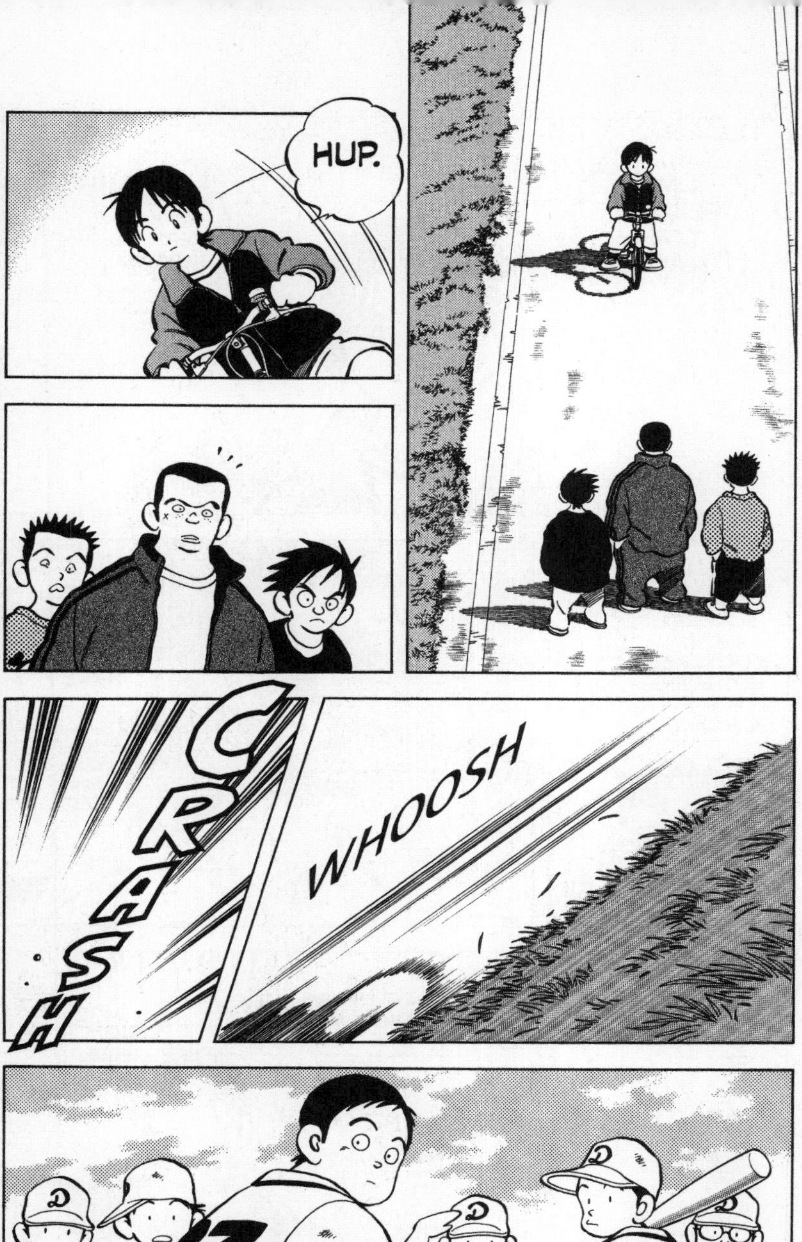
HUP.
WHOOSH
CRASH

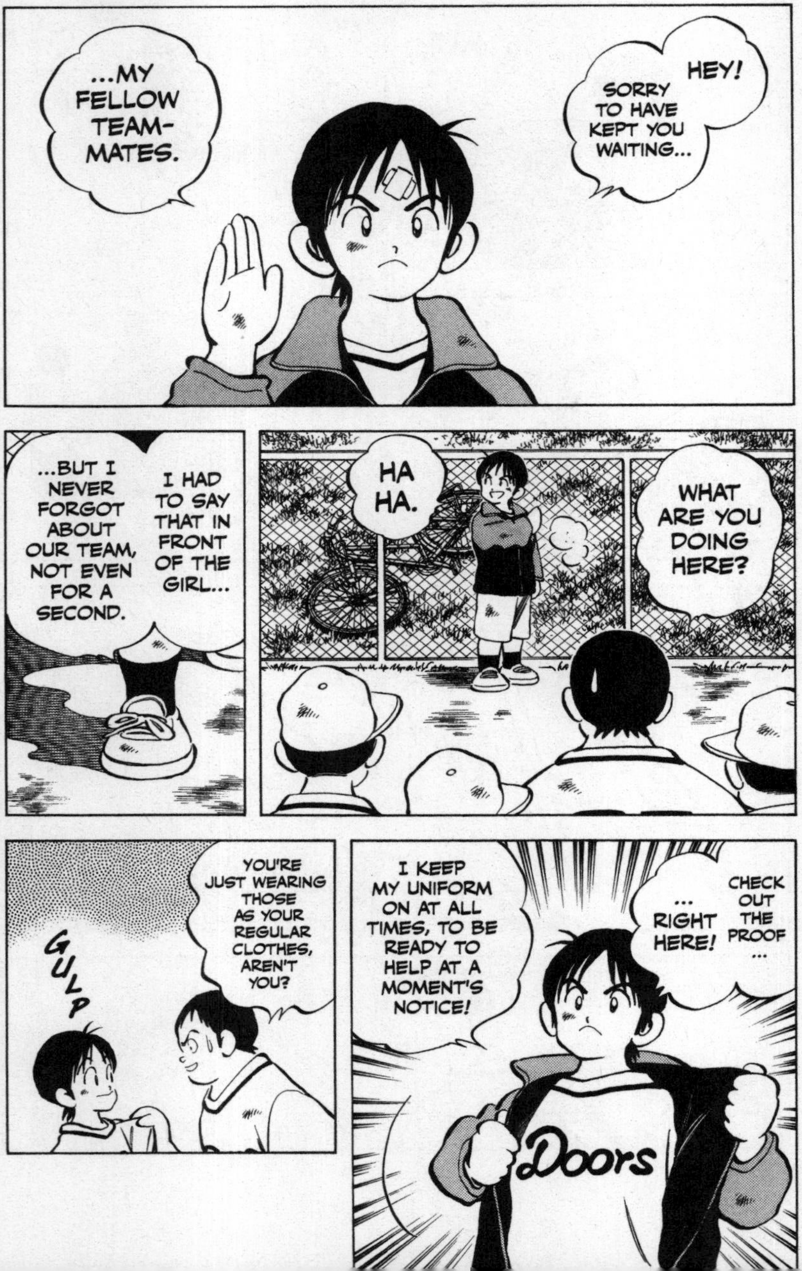
HEY!
SORRY TO HAVE KEPT YOU WAITING...
...MY FELLOW TEAM-MATES.
WHAT ARE YOU DOING HERE?
HA HA.
I HAD TO SAY THAT IN FRONT OF THE GIRL...
...BUT I NEVER FORGOT ABOUT OUR TEAM, NOT EVEN FOR A SECOND.
CHECK OUT THE PROOF ...
... RIGHT HERE!
I KEEP MY UNIFORM ON AT ALL TIMES, TO BE READY TO HELP AT A MOMENT'S NOTICE!
Doors
YOU'RE JUST WEARING THOSE AS YOUR REGULAR CLOTHES, AREN'T YOU?
GULP

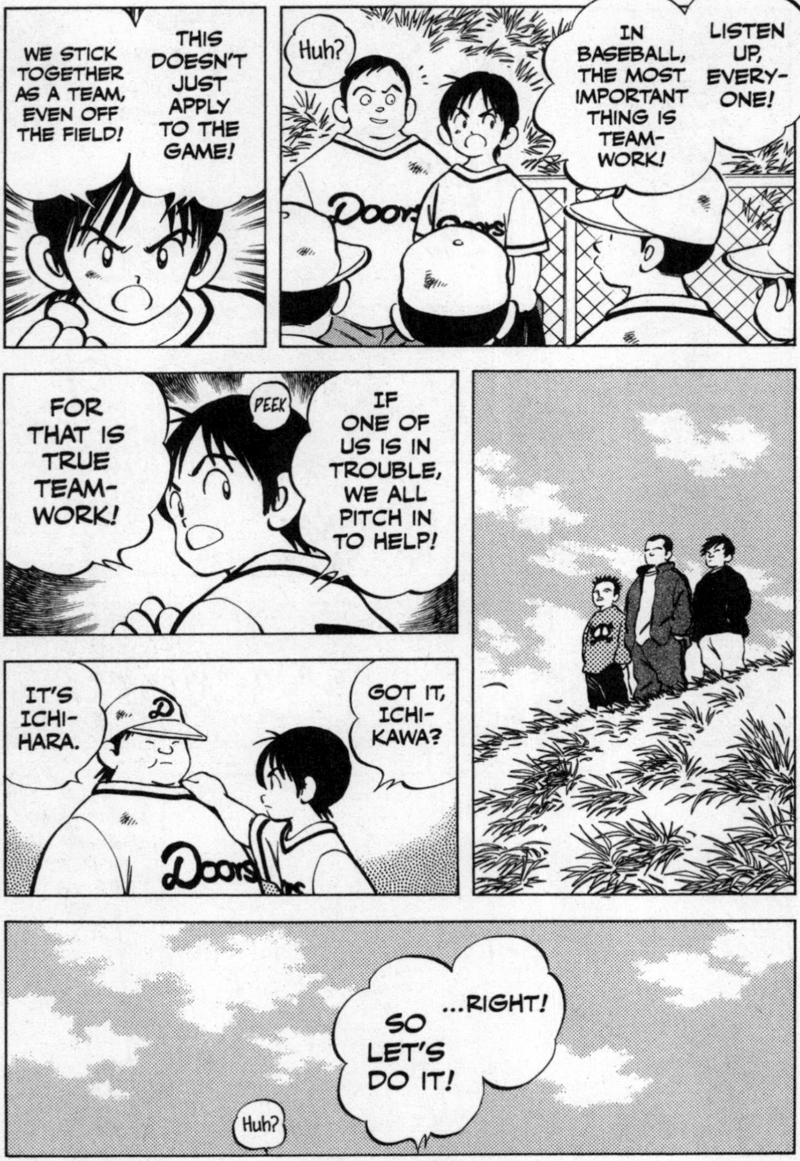
LISTEN UP, EVERY-ONE!
IN BASEBALL, THE MOST IMPORTANT THING IS TEAM-WORK!
Huh?
THIS DOESN'T JUST APPLY TO THE GAME!
WE STICK TOGETHER AS A TEAM, EVEN OFF THE FIELD!
IF ONE OF US IS IN TROUBLE, WE ALL PITCH IN TO HELP!
PEEK
FOR THAT IS TRUE TEAM-WORK!
GOT IT, ICHI-KAWA?
IT'S ICHI-HARA.
...RIGHT!
SO LET'S DO IT!
Huh?

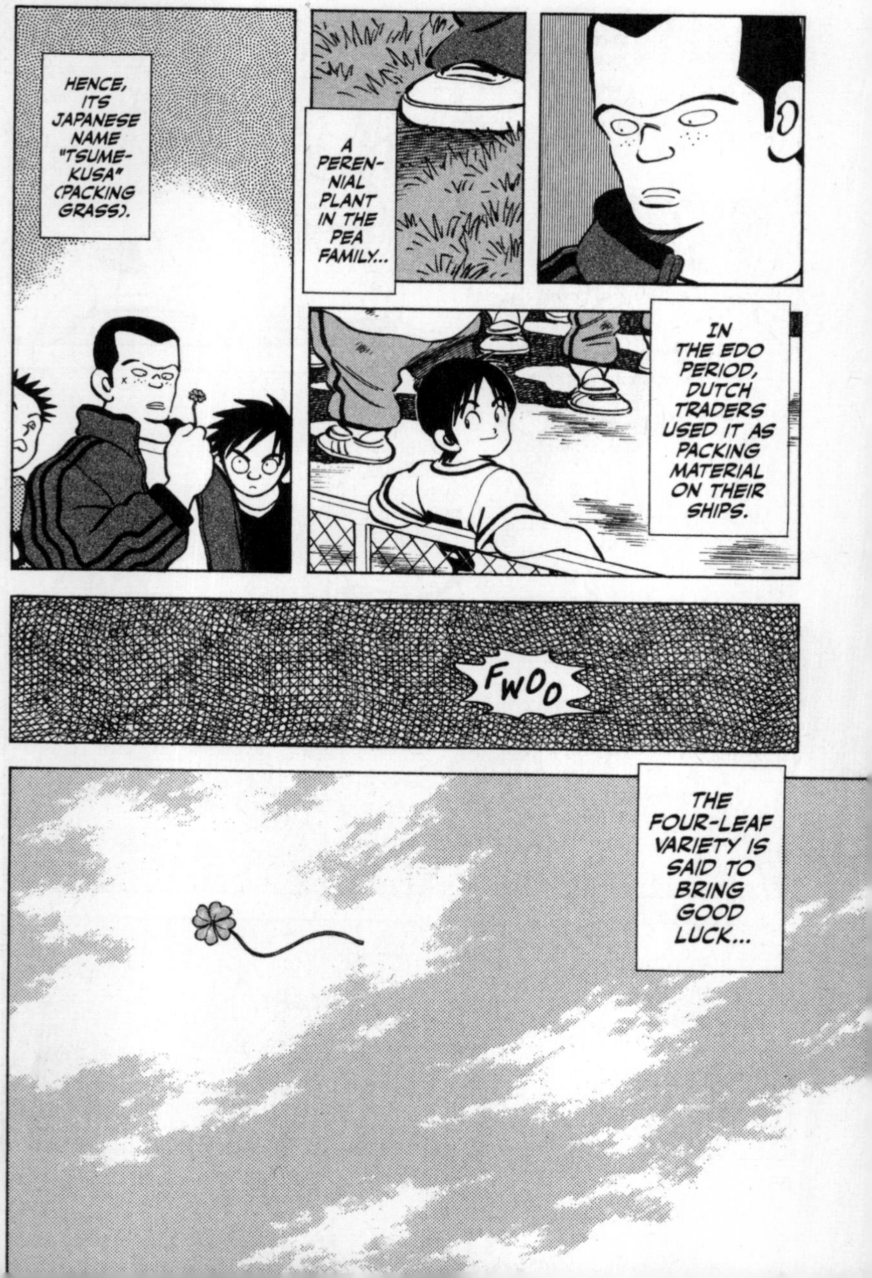
A PERENNIAL PLANT IN THE PEA FAMILY...
IN THE EDO PERIOD, DUTCH TRADERS USED IT AS PACKING MATERIAL ON THEIR SHIPS.
HENCE, ITS JAPANESE NAME "TSUME-KUSA" (PACKING GRASS).
FWOO
THE FOUR-LEAF VARIETY IS SAID TO BRING GOOD LUCK...

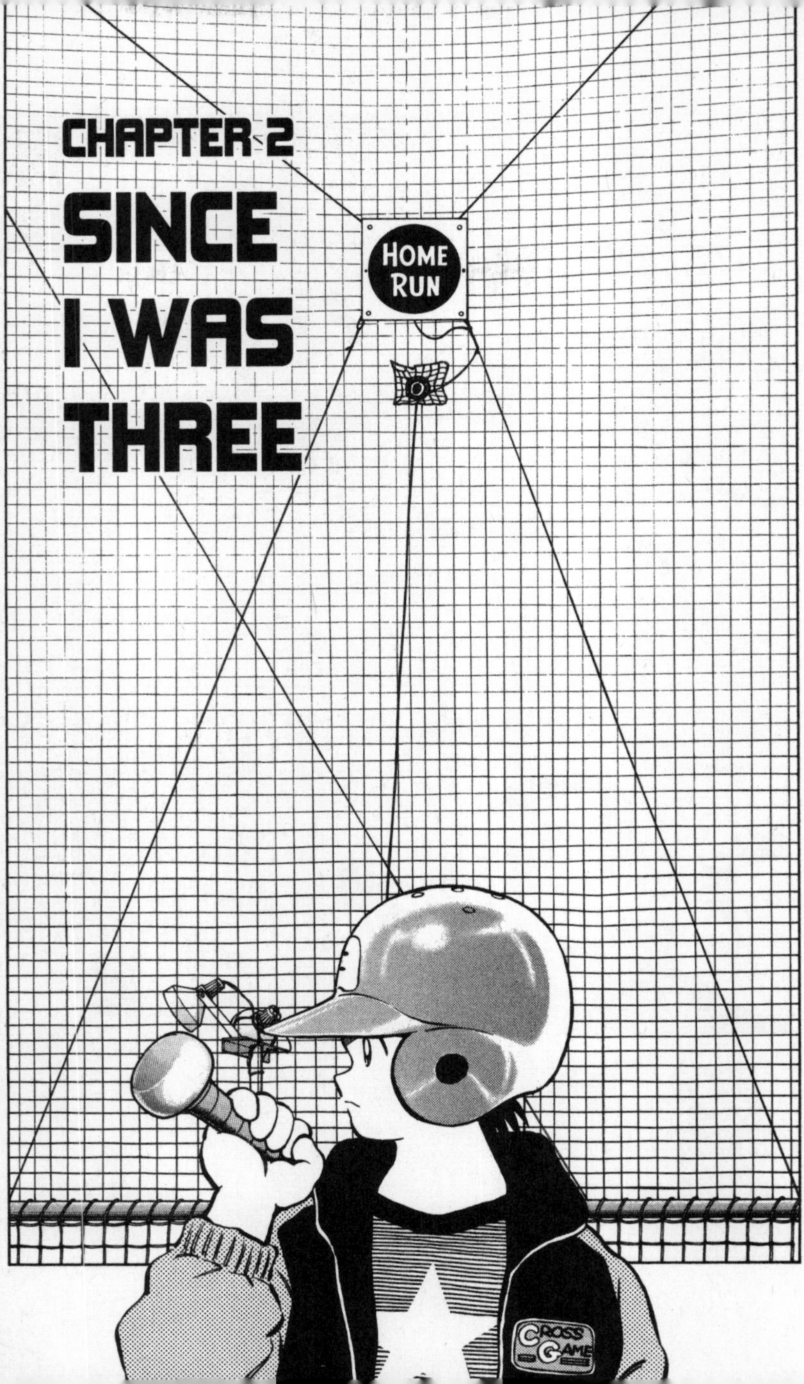
CHAPTER 2
SINCE I WAS THREE
HOME RUN
CROSS GAME

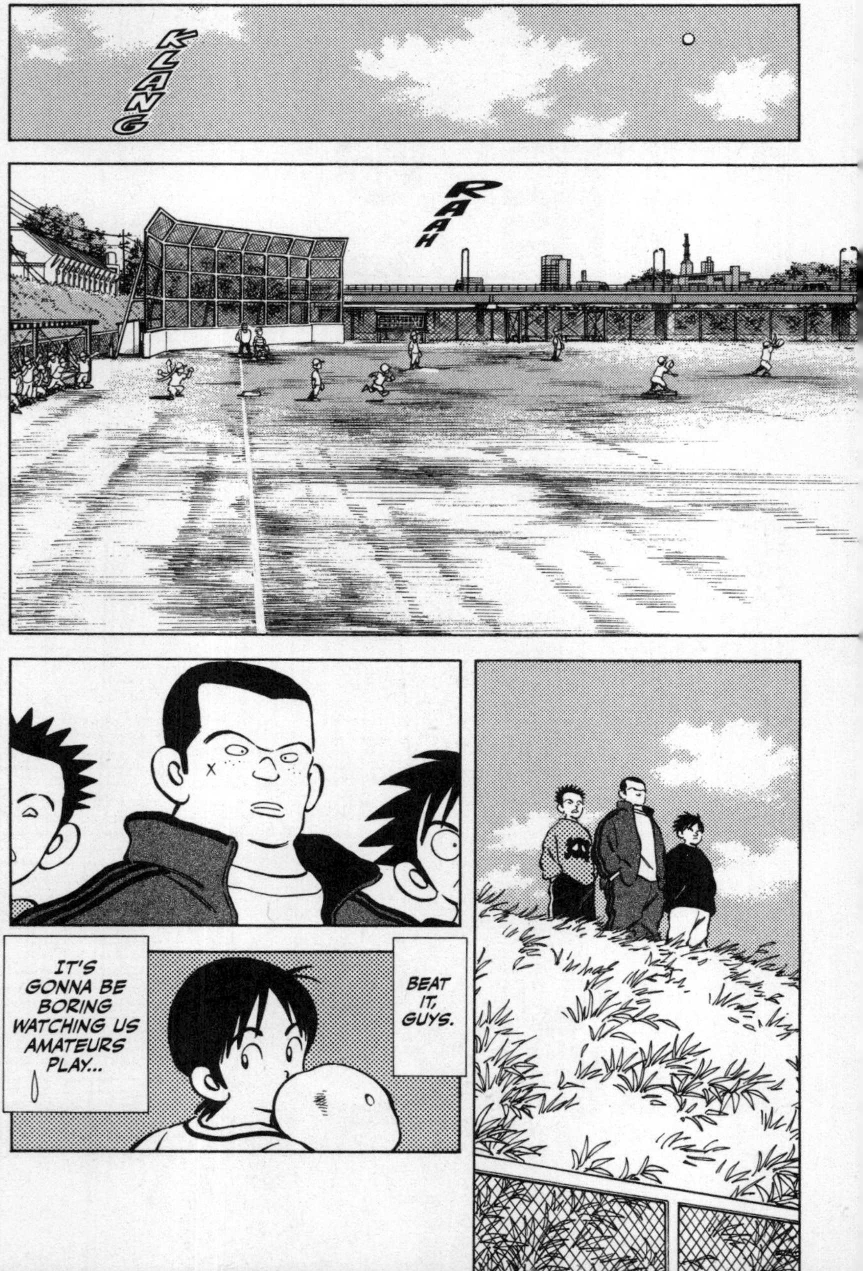
KLANG
RAAH
BEAT IT, GUYS.
IT'S GONNA BE BORING WATCHING US AMATEURS PLAY...

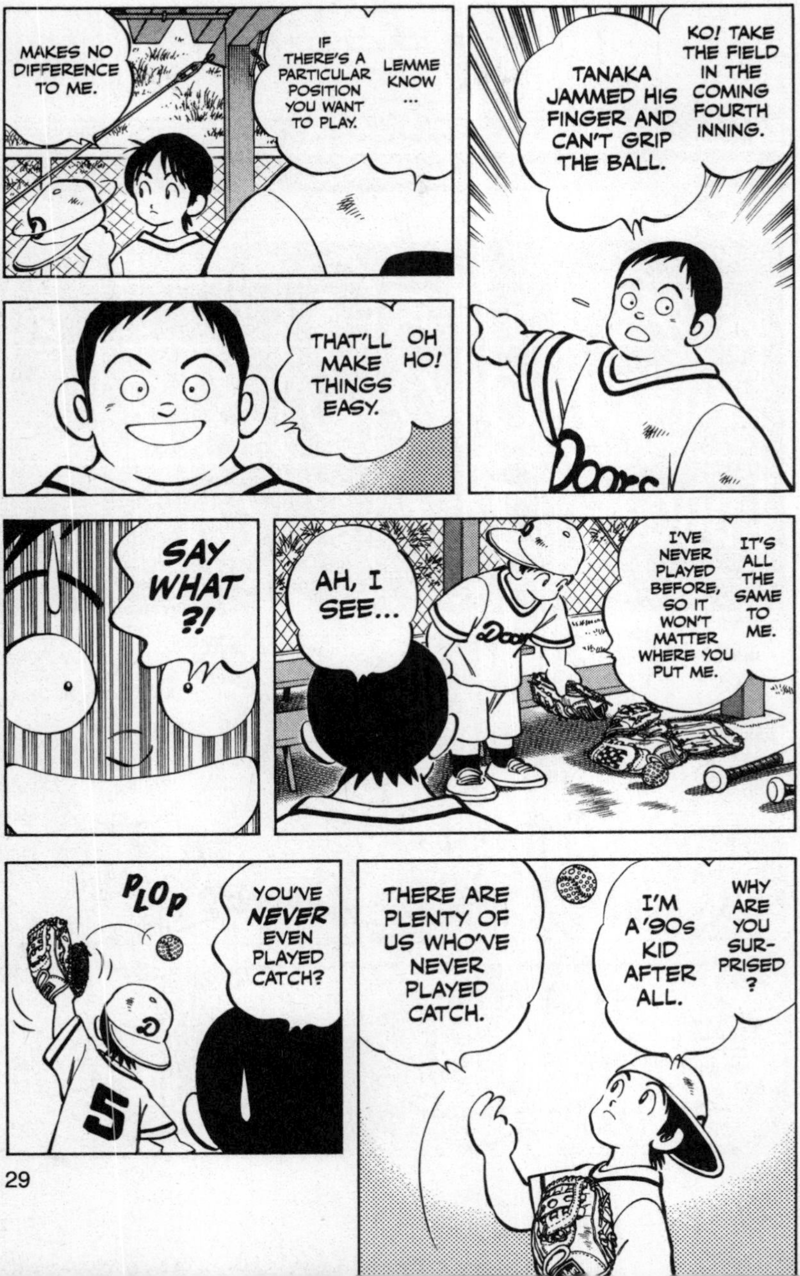
KO! TAKE THE FIELD IN THE COMING FOURTH INNING.
TANAKA JAMMED HIS FINGER AND CAN'T GRIP THE BALL.
LEMME KNOW ...
IF THERE'S A PARTICULAR POSITION YOU WANT TO PLAY.
MAKES NO DIFFERENCE TO ME.
OH HO!
THAT'LL MAKE THINGS EASY.
IT'S ALL THE SAME TO ME.
I'VE NEVER PLAYED BEFORE, SO IT WON'T MATTER WHERE YOU PUT ME.
AH, I SEE...
SAY WHAT?!
WHY ARE YOU SURPRISED?
I'M A '90s KID AFTER ALL.
THERE ARE PLENTY OF US WHO'VE NEVER PLAYED CATCH.
YOU'VE NEVER EVEN PLAYED CATCH?
PLOP

VROOOM
TEAM 1 2 3 4 5 6 7
PONZU 0 0 0 3 2
DOORS 2 1 2 0
MOVING RIGHT ALONG...
IT'S THE BOTTOM OF THE FIFTH, WITH THE DOORS COMING TO BAT.
HEY!
HOLD ON A MINUTE!
WE'RE MOVING ALONG TOO FAST!
Doors
WHY DON'T YOU EXPLAIN HOW I GAVE UP FIVE RUNS IN THE FIRST PLACE!
DOORS PITCHER DAIKI NAKANISHI (FIFTH GRADER)
IF YOU HADN'T MADE THOSE FOUR ERRORS...!
D
DON'T DWELL ON THE PAST.
WE SHOULD FOCUS ON THE PRESENT, AND WHAT'S TO COME.

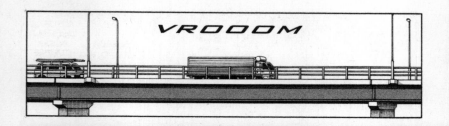

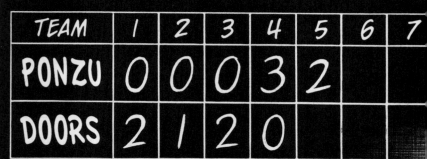

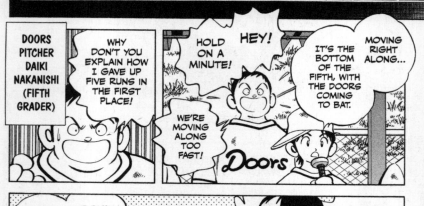

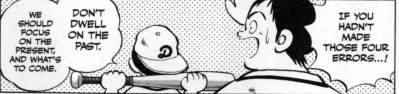

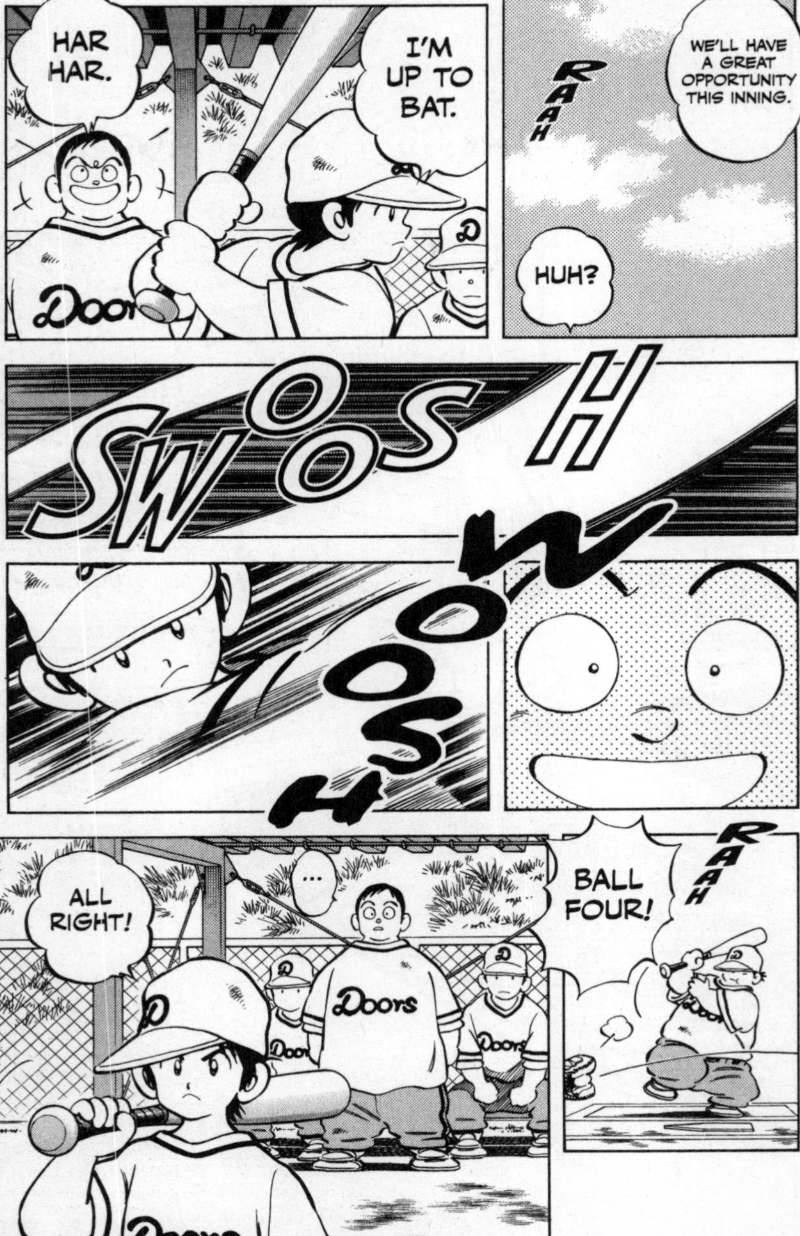
RAAH
WE'LL HAVE A GREAT OPPORTUNITY THIS INNING.
HUH?
I'M UP TO BAT.
HAR HAR.
SWOOSH
WOOSH
RAAH
BALL FOUR!
...
ALL RIGHT!
Doors

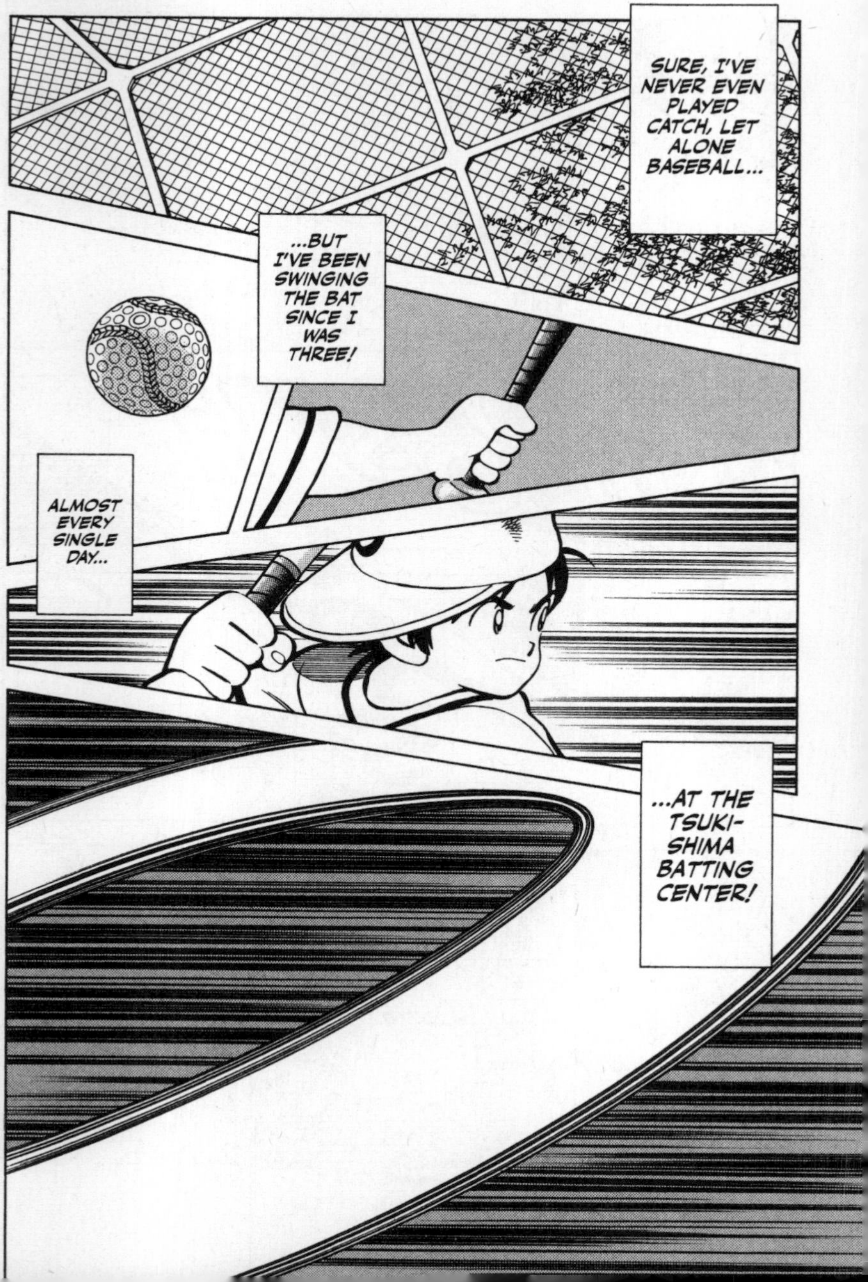
SURE, I'VE NEVER EVEN PLAYED CATCH, LET ALONE BASEBALL...
...BUT I'VE BEEN SWINGING THE BAT SINCE I WAS THREE!
ALMOST EVERY SINGLE DAY...
...AT THE TSUKI-SHIMA BATTING CENTER!

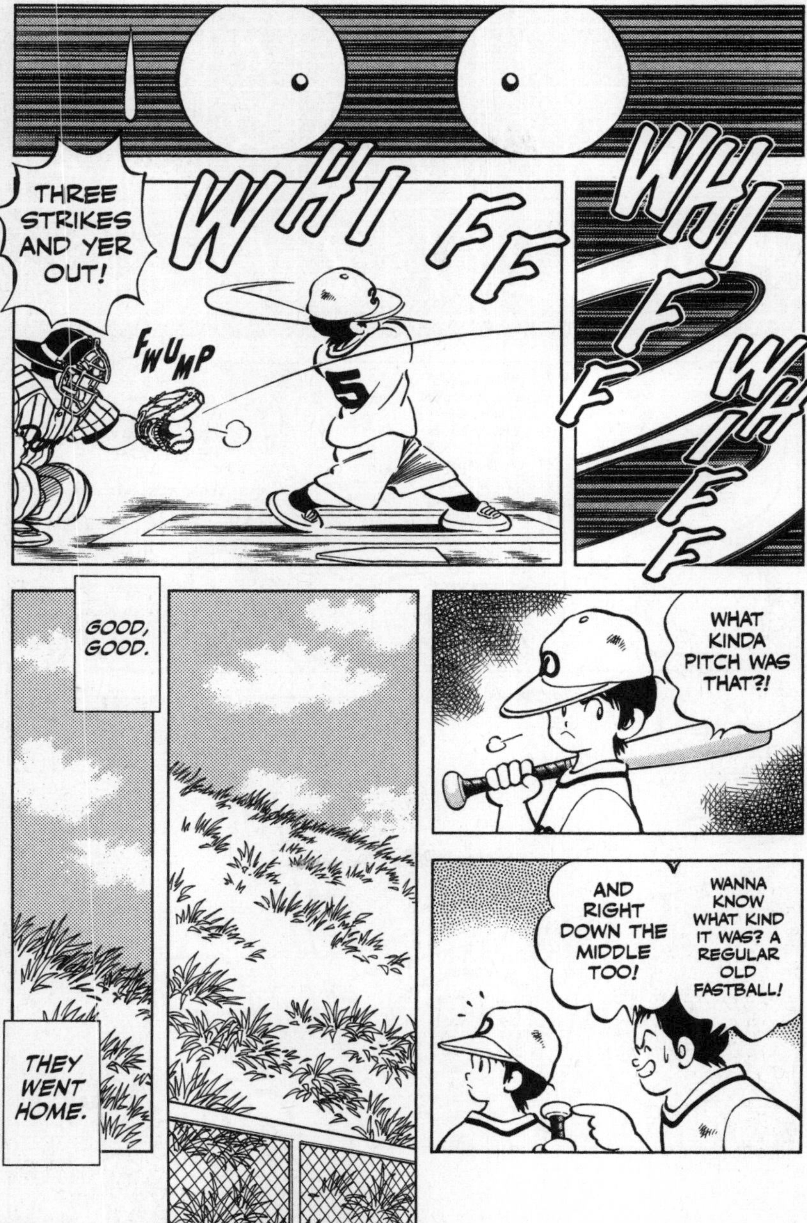
WHIFF
WHIFF
THREE STRIKES AND YER OUT!
WHIFF
FWUMP
WHAT KINDA PITCH WAS THAT?!
WANNA KNOW WHAT KIND IT WAS? A REGULAR OLD FASTBALL!
AND RIGHT DOWN THE MIDDLE TOO!
GOOD, GOOD.
THEY WENT HOME.

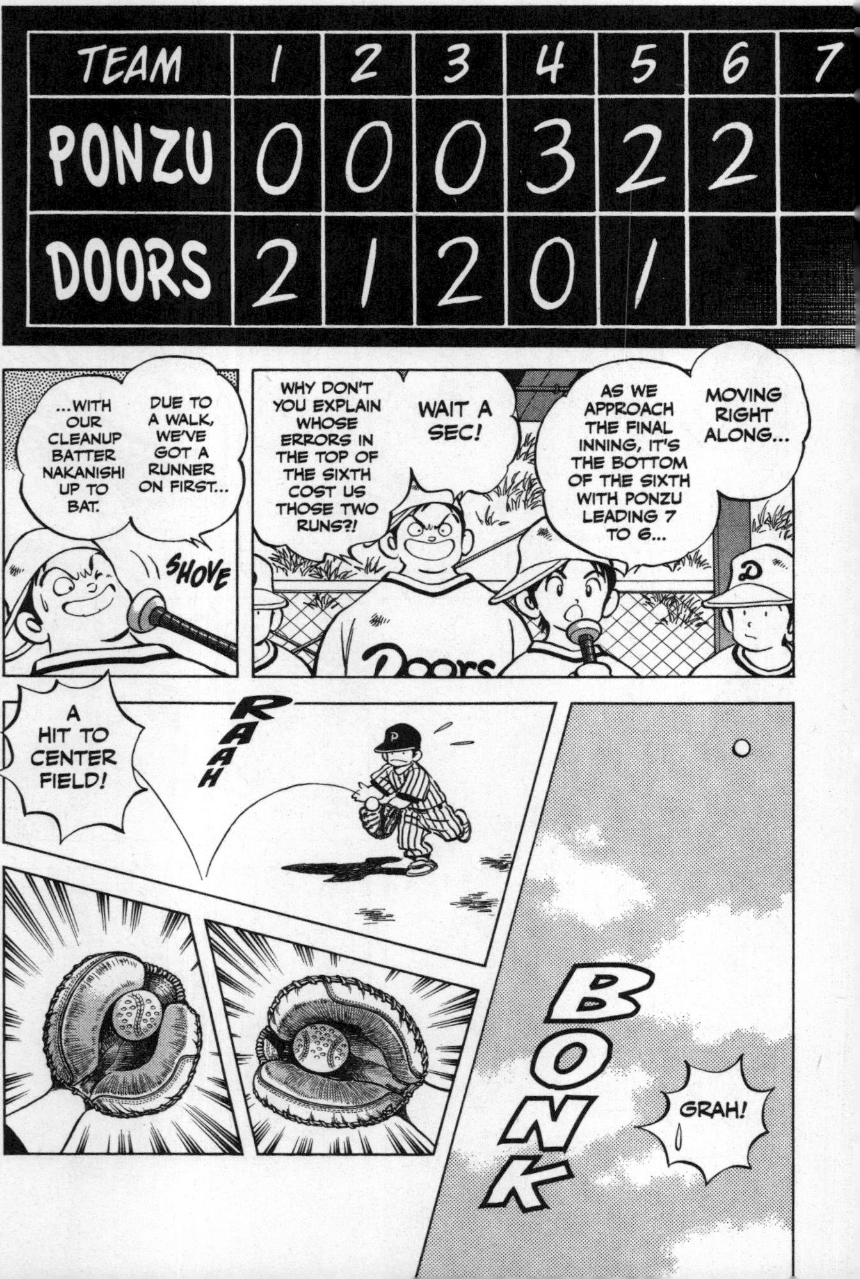
TEAM 1 2 3 4 5 6 7
PONZU 0 0 0 3 2 2
DOORS 2 1 2 0 1
MOVING RIGHT ALONG...
AS WE APPROACH THE FINAL INNING, IT'S THE BOTTOM OF THE SIXTH WITH PONZU LEADING 7 TO 6...
WAIT A SEC!
WHY DON'T YOU EXPLAIN WHOSE ERRORS IN THE TOP OF THE SIXTH COST US THOSE TWO RUNS?!
DUE TO A WALK, WE'VE GOT A RUNNER ON FIRST...
...WITH OUR CLEANUP BATTER NAKANISHI UP TO BAT.
SHOVE
BONK
GRAH!
RAAH
A HIT TO CENTER FIELD!

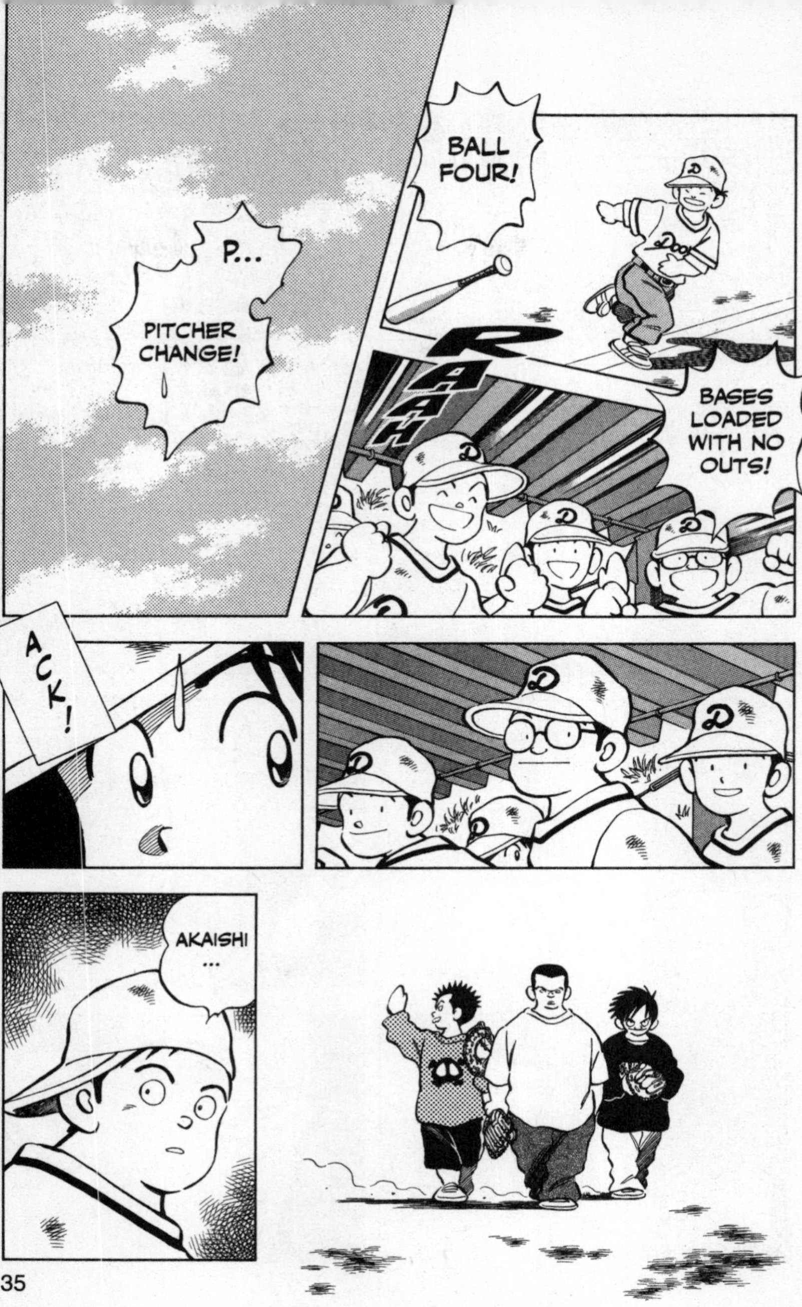
BALL FOUR!
RAAAH
BASES LOADED WITH NO OUTS!
P...
PITCHER CHANGE!
ACK!
AKAISHI ...

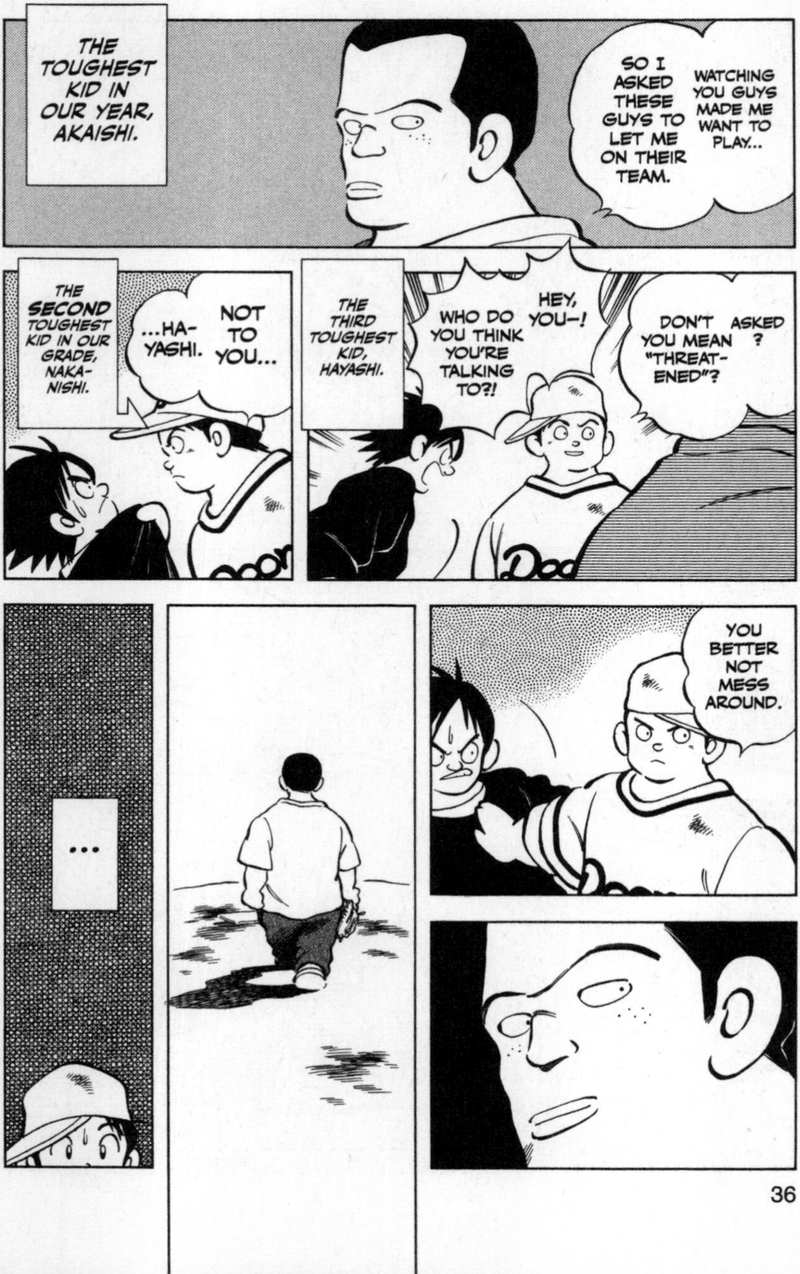
WATCHING YOU GUYS MADE ME WANT TO PLAY...
SO I ASKED THESE GUYS TO LET ME ON THEIR TEAM.
THE TOUGHEST KID IN OUR YEAR, AKAISHI.
ASKED ?
DON'T YOU MEAN "THREAT-ENED"?
HEY, YOU—!
WHO DO YOU THINK YOU'RE TALKING TO?!
THE THIRD TOUGHEST KID, HAYASHI.
NOT TO YOU...
...HA-YASHI.
THE SECOND TOUGHEST KID IN OUR GRADE, NAKA-NISHI.
YOU BETTER NOT MESS AROUND.
...

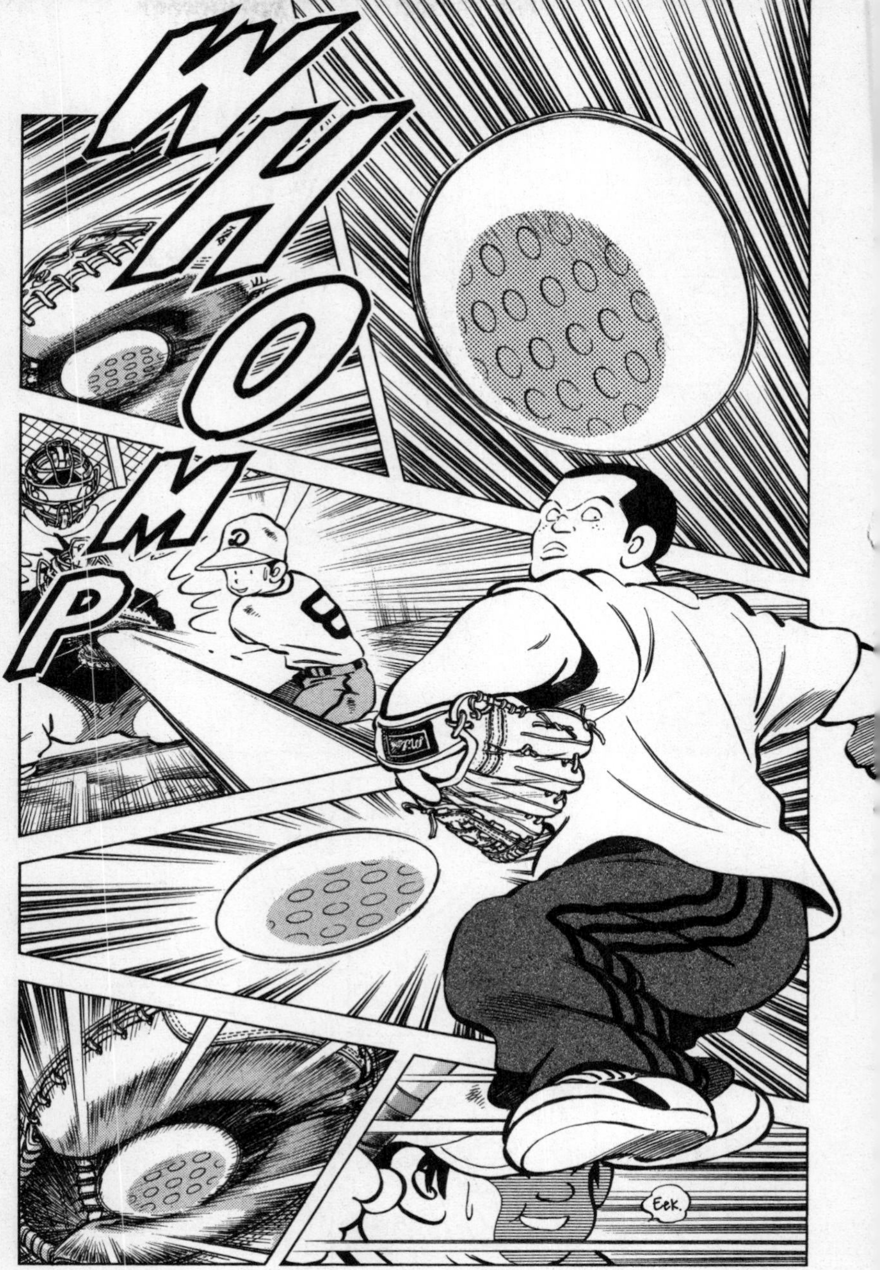
WHOMP
Eek.

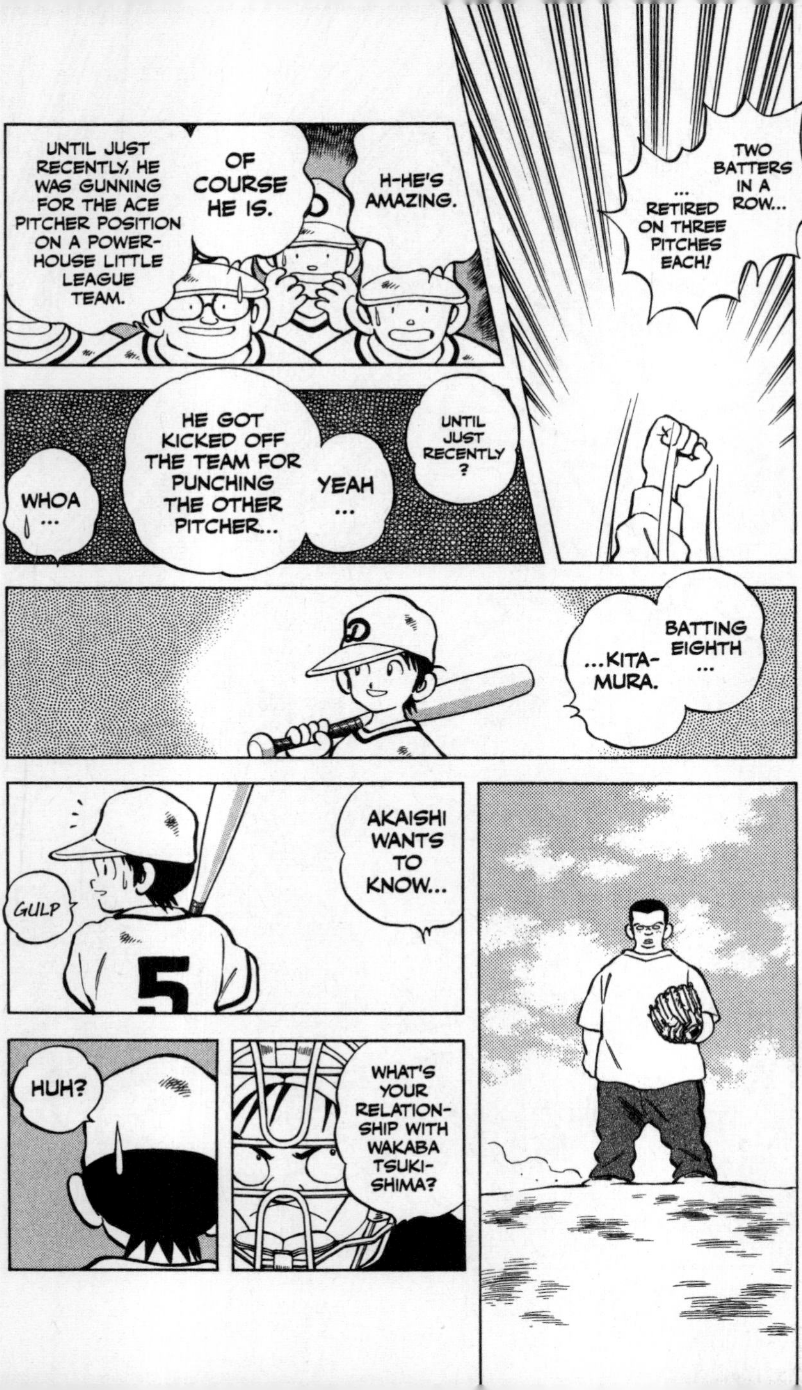
TWO BATTERS IN A ROW...
...RETIRED ON THREE PITCHES EACH!
H-HE'S AMAZING.
OF COURSE HE IS.
UNTIL JUST RECENTLY, HE WAS GUNNING FOR THE ACE PITCHER POSITION ON A POWER-HOUSE LITTLE LEAGUE TEAM.
UNTIL JUST RECENTLY?
YEAH...
HE GOT KICKED OFF THE TEAM FOR PUNCHING THE OTHER PITCHER...
WHOA...
BATTING EIGHTH...
...KITA-MURA.
AKAISHI WANTS TO KNOW...
GULP
WHAT'S YOUR RELATIONSHIP WITH WAKABA TSUKI-SHIMA?
HUH?

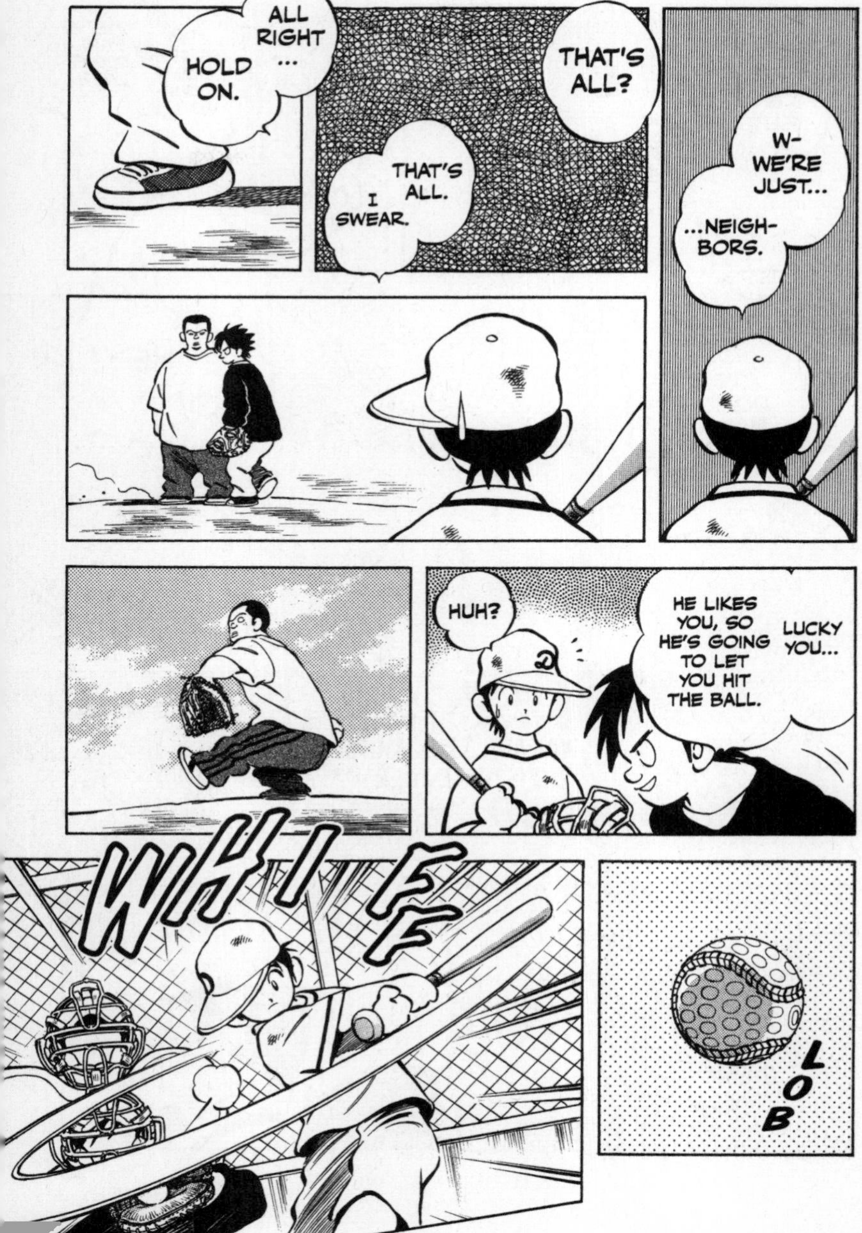
W- WE'RE JUST...
...NEIGHBORS.
THAT'S ALL?
THAT'S ALL. I SWEAR.
ALL RIGHT...
HOLD ON.
LUCKY YOU...
HE LIKES YOU, SO HE'S GOING TO LET YOU HIT THE BALL.
HUH?
LOB
WHIFF

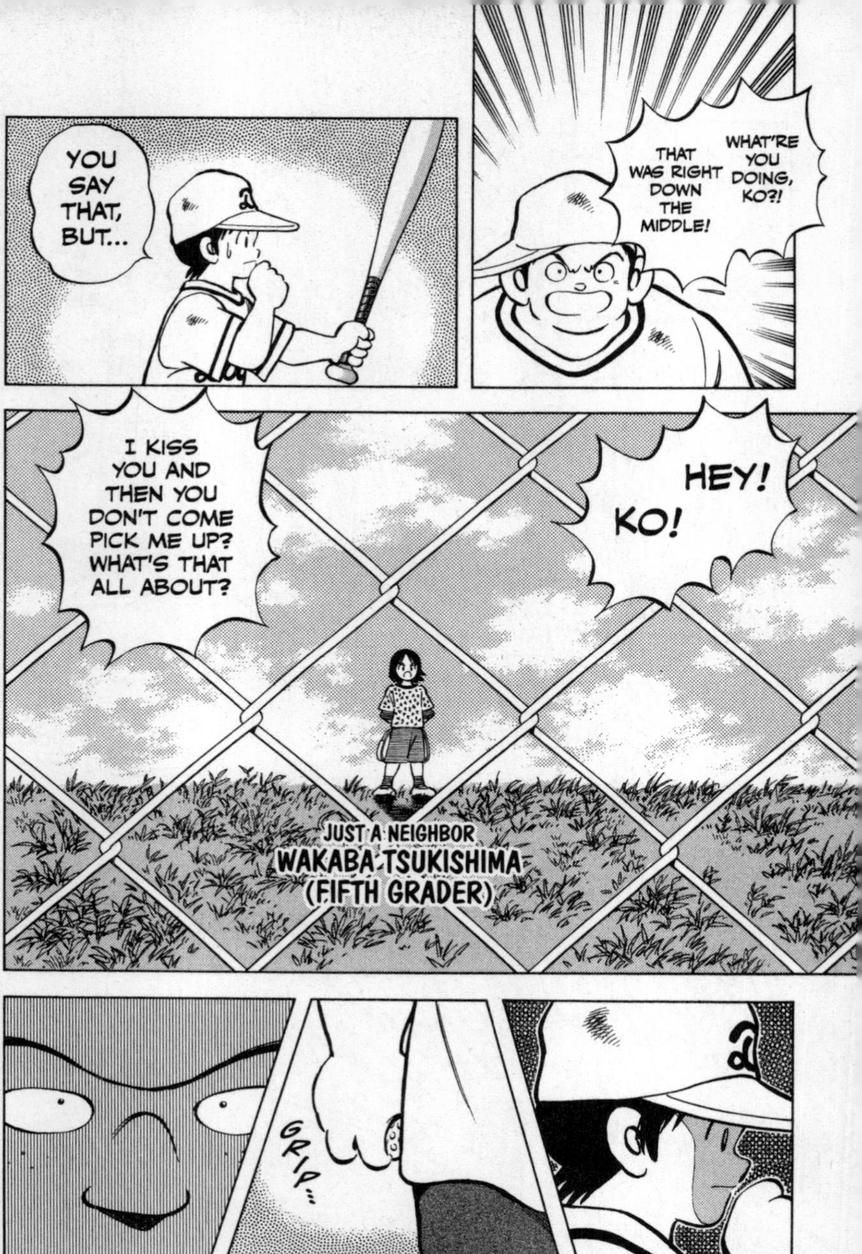
WHAT'RE YOU DOING, KO?!
THAT WAS RIGHT DOWN THE MIDDLE!
YOU SAY THAT, BUT...
HEY! KO!
I KISS YOU AND THEN YOU DON'T COME PICK ME UP? WHAT'S THAT ALL ABOUT?
JUST A NEIGHBOR
WAKABA TSUKISHIMA
(FIFTH GRADER)
GRIP...

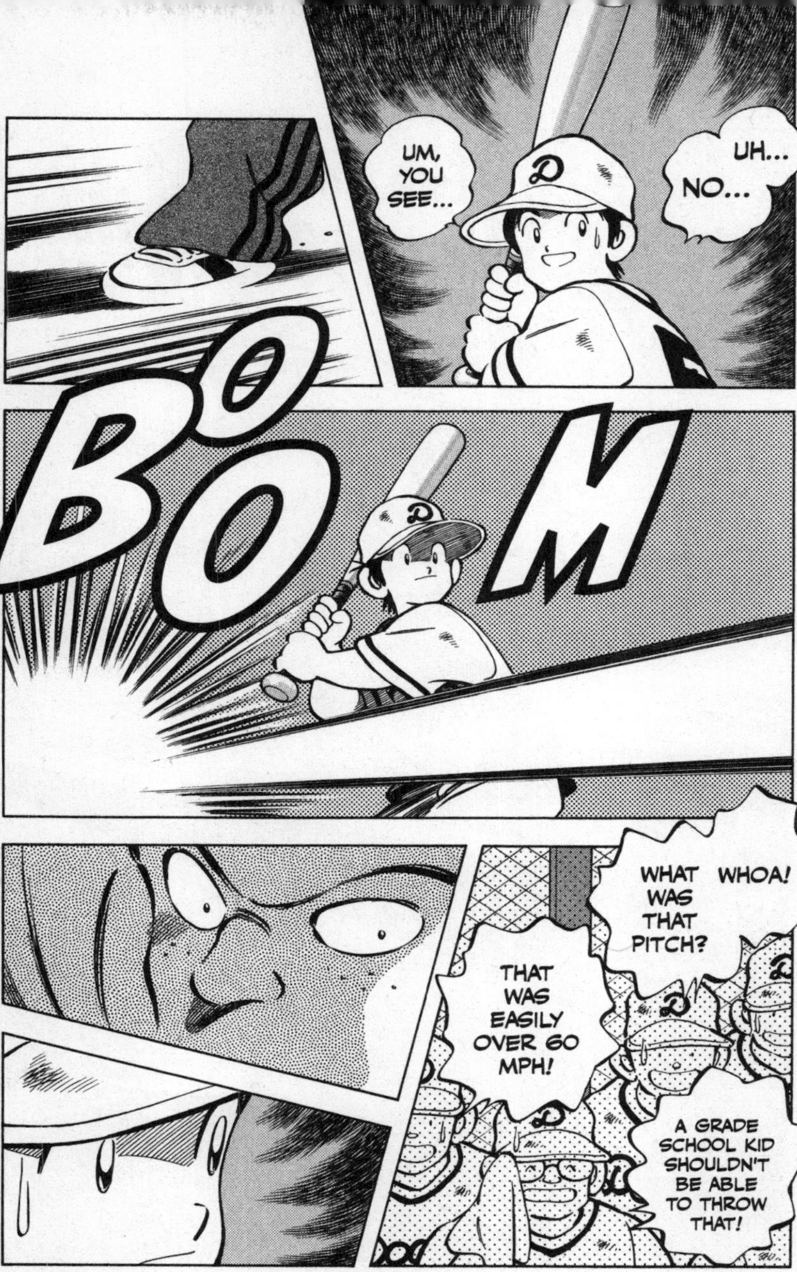
UH... NO...
UM, YOU SEE...
BOOM
WHOA!
WHAT WAS THAT PITCH?
THAT WAS EASILY OVER 60 MPH!
A GRADE SCHOOL KID SHOULDN'T BE ABLE TO THROW THAT!

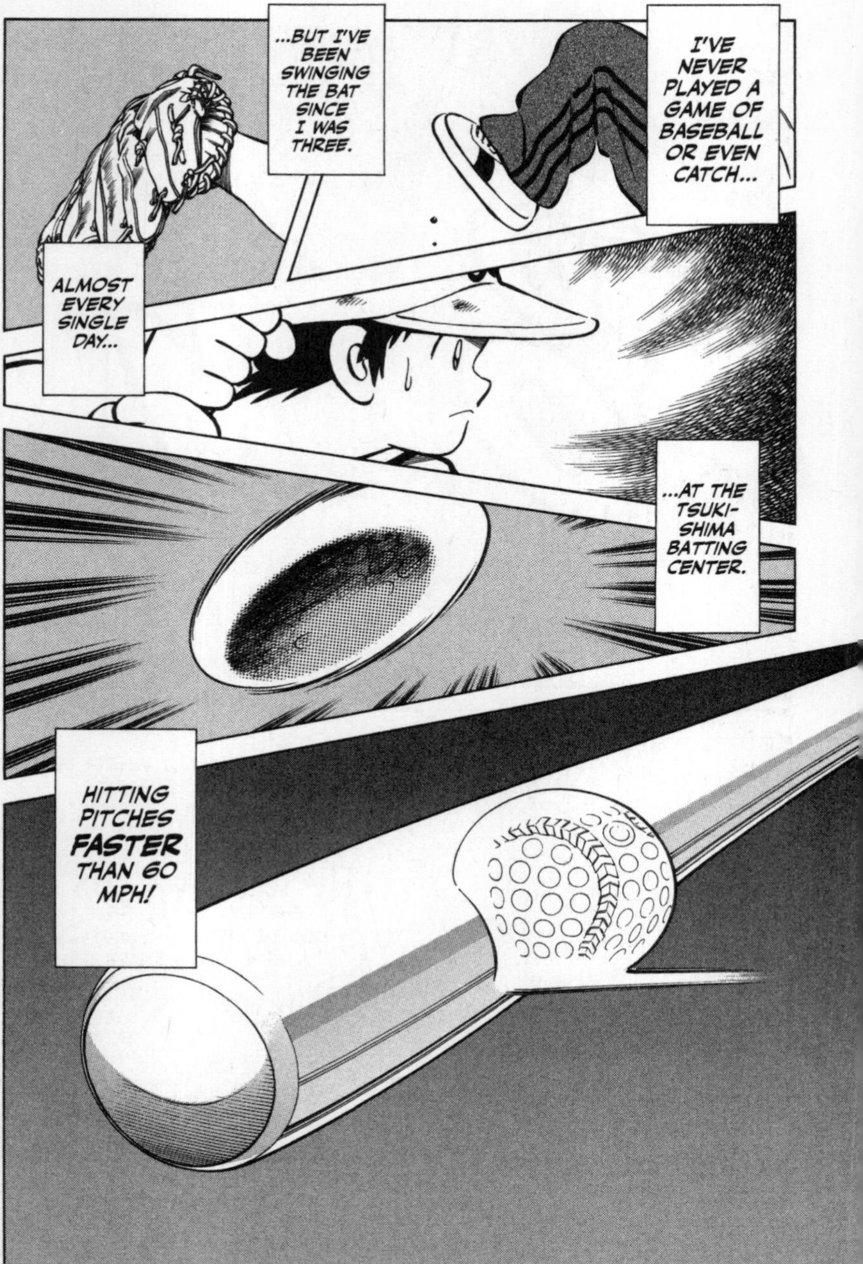
I'VE NEVER PLAYED A GAME OF BASEBALL OR EVEN CATCH...
...BUT I'VE BEEN SWINGING THE BAT SINCE I WAS THREE.
ALMOST EVERY SINGLE DAY...
...AT THE TSUKI-SHIMA BATTING CENTER.
HITTING PITCHES **FASTER** THAN 60 MPH!

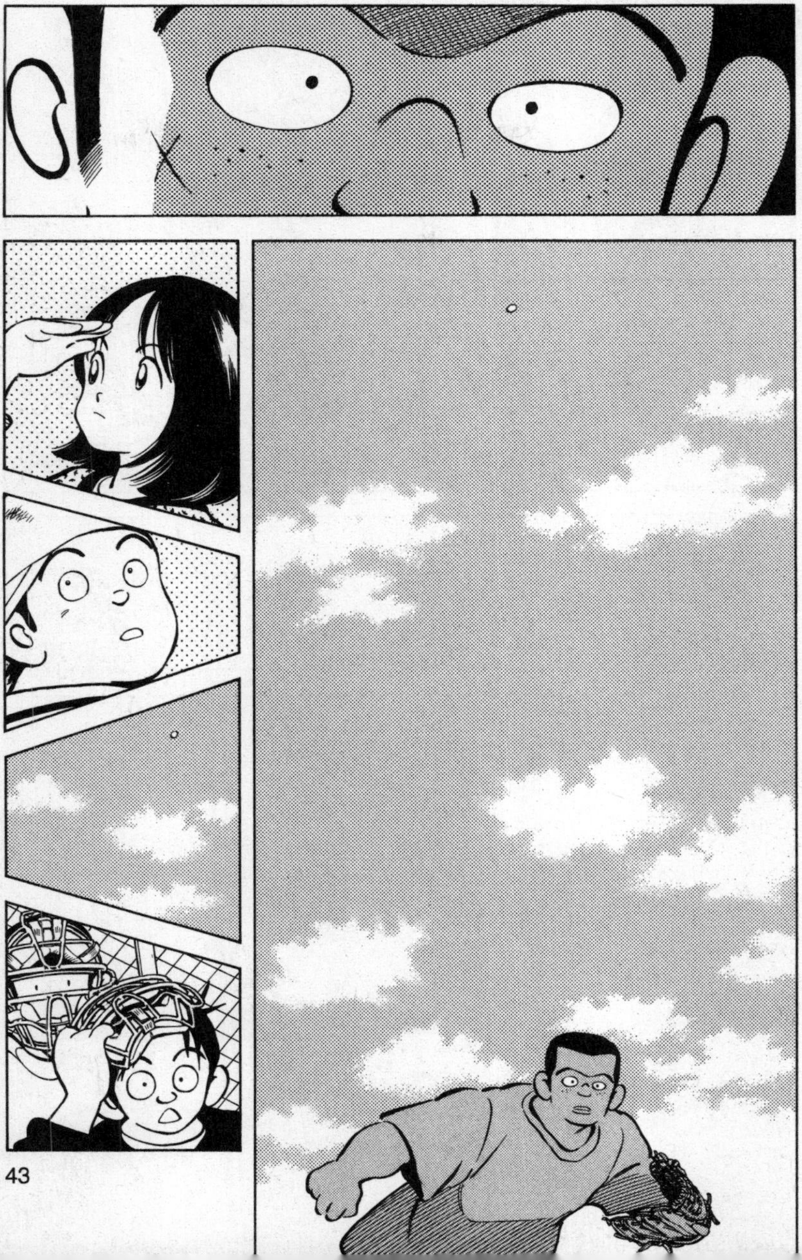

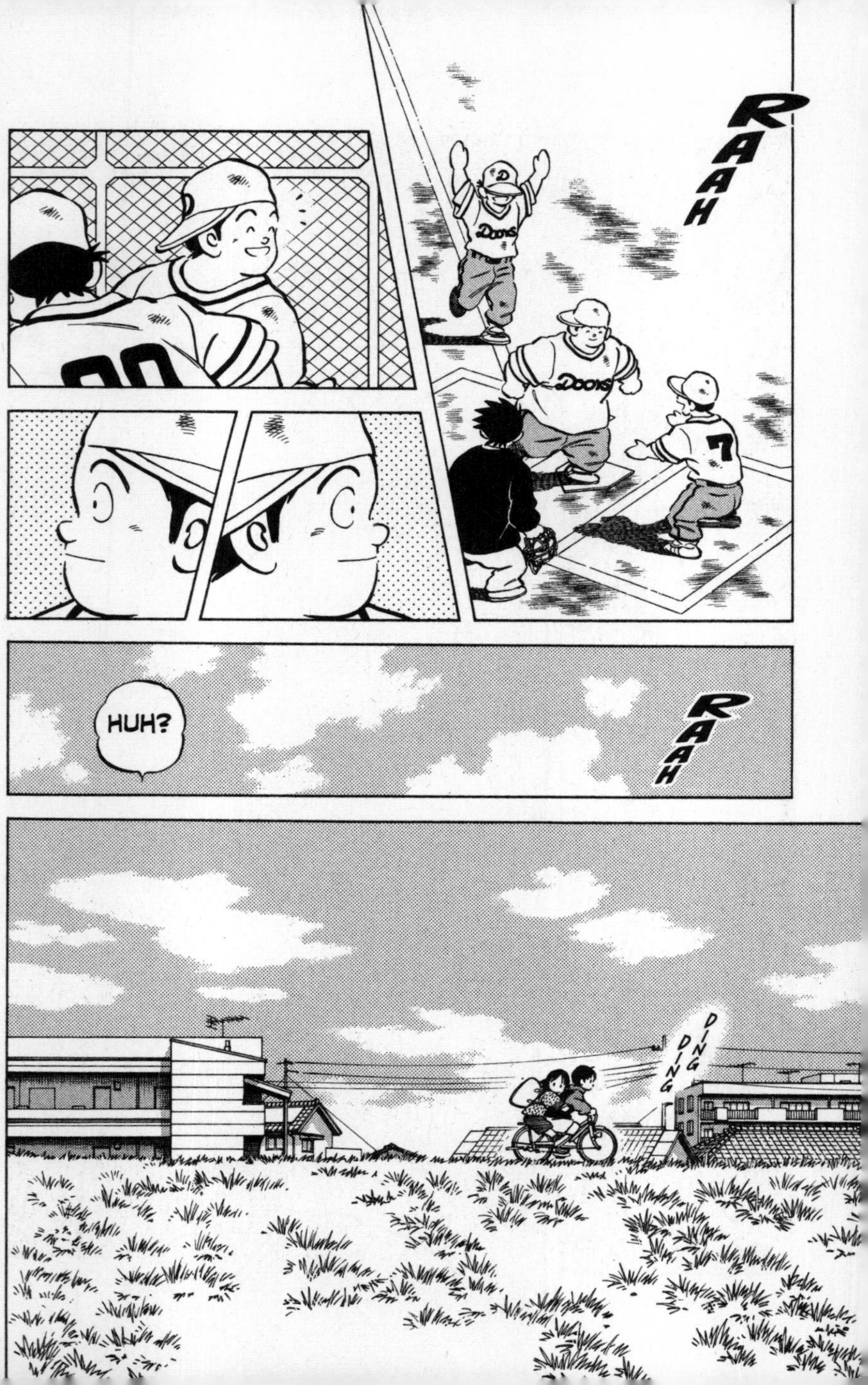
RAAH
HUH?
RAAH
DING DING

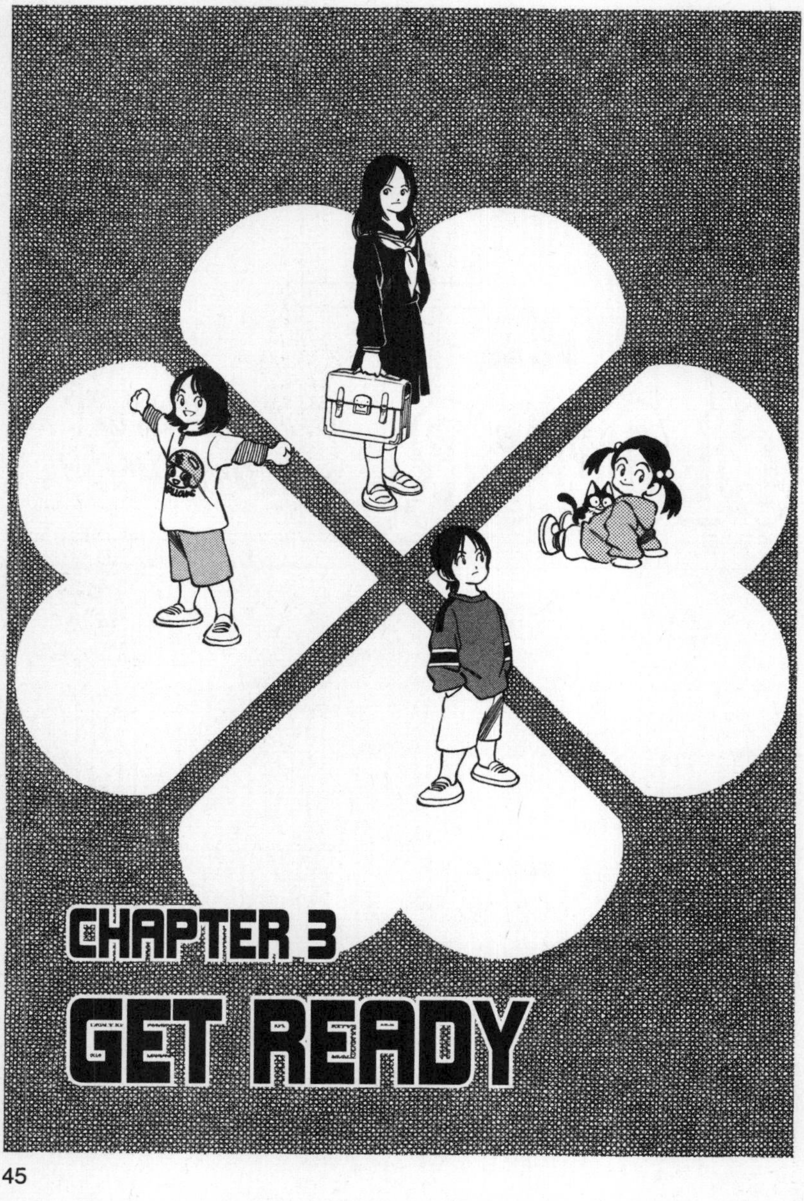
CHAPTER 3
GET READY

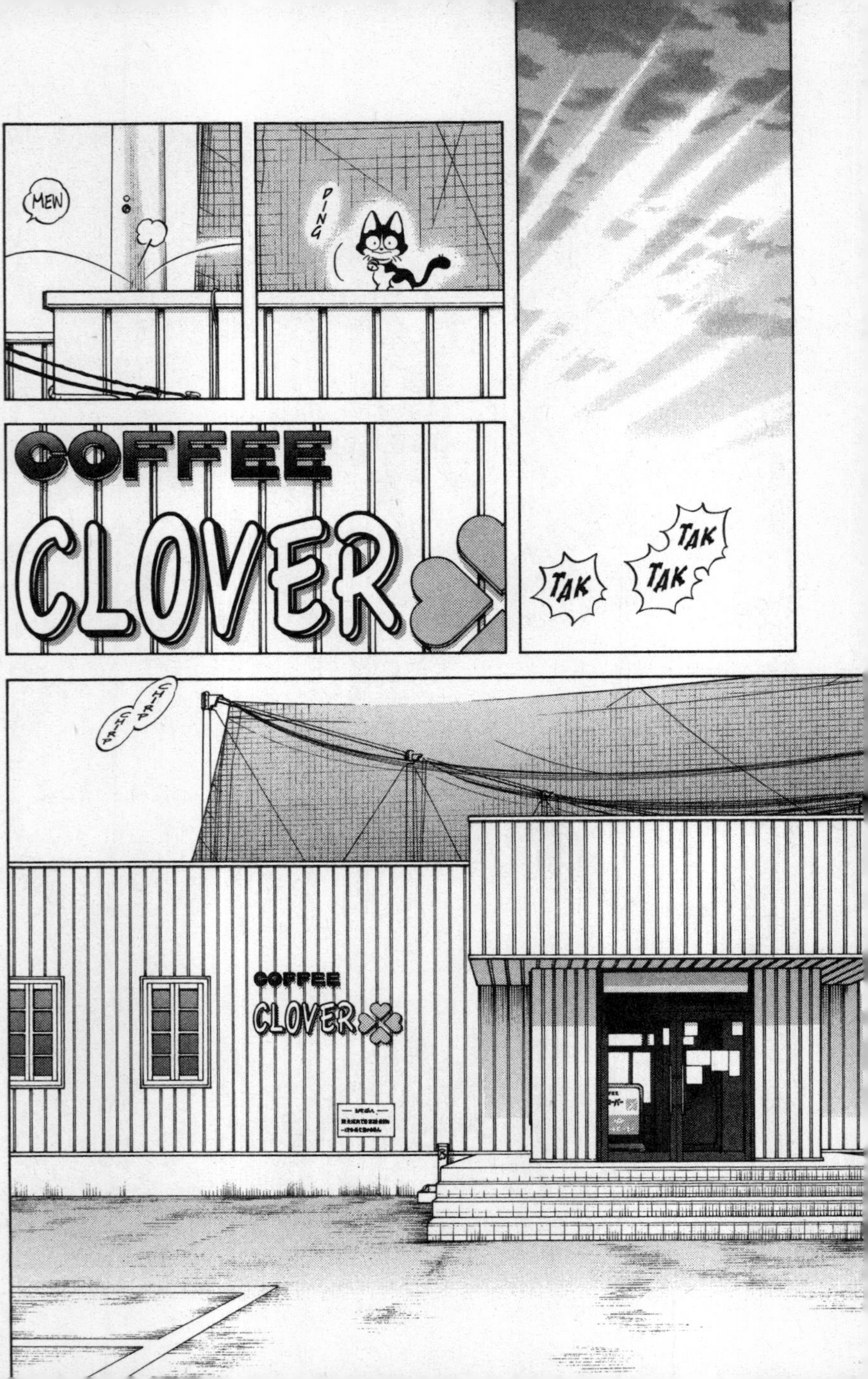
TAK
TAK
TAK
DING
MEW
COFFEE
CLOVER
CHIRP
CHIRP
COFFEE
CLOVER

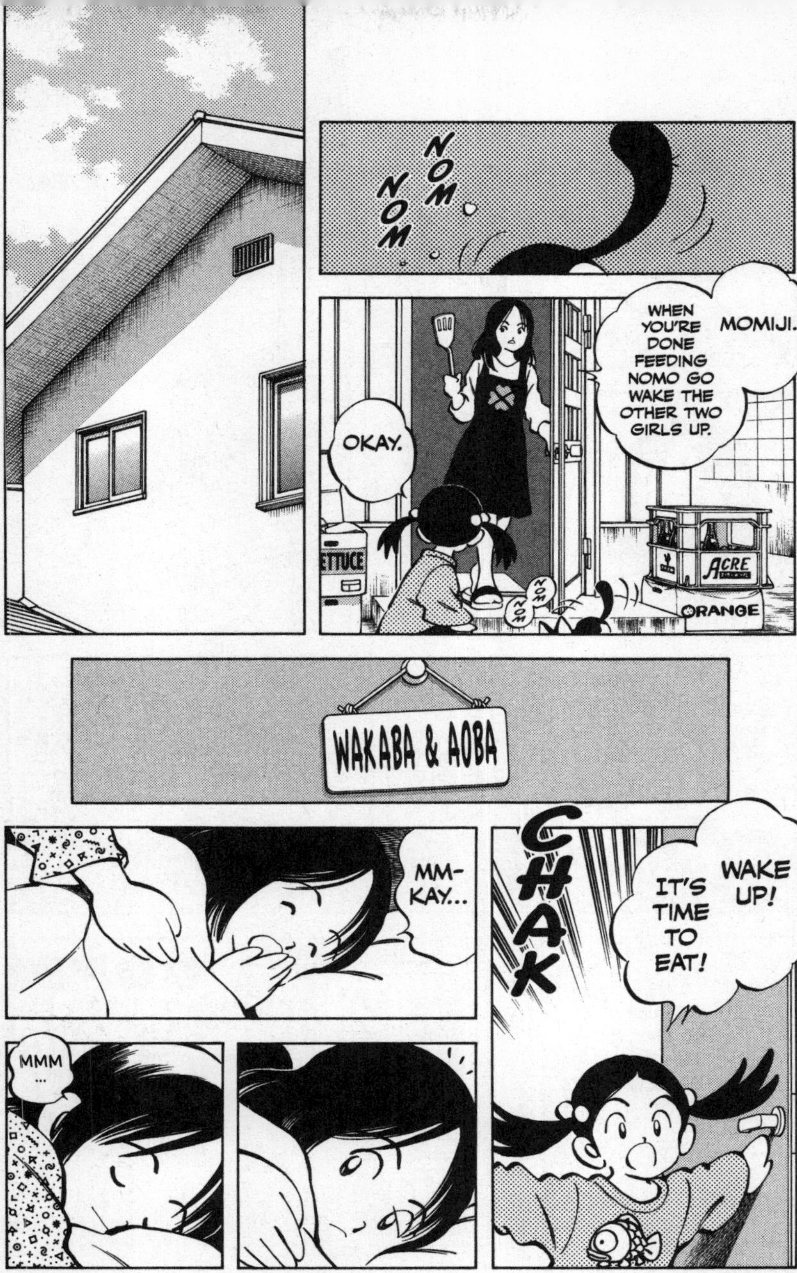
NOM NOM NOM
MOMIJI.
WHEN YOU'RE DONE FEEDING NOMO GO WAKE THE OTHER TWO GIRLS UP.
OKAY.
NOM NOM
ETTUCE
ACRE
ORANGE
WAKABA & AOBA
CHAK
WAKE UP!
IT'S TIME TO EAT!
MM-KAY...
MMM ...

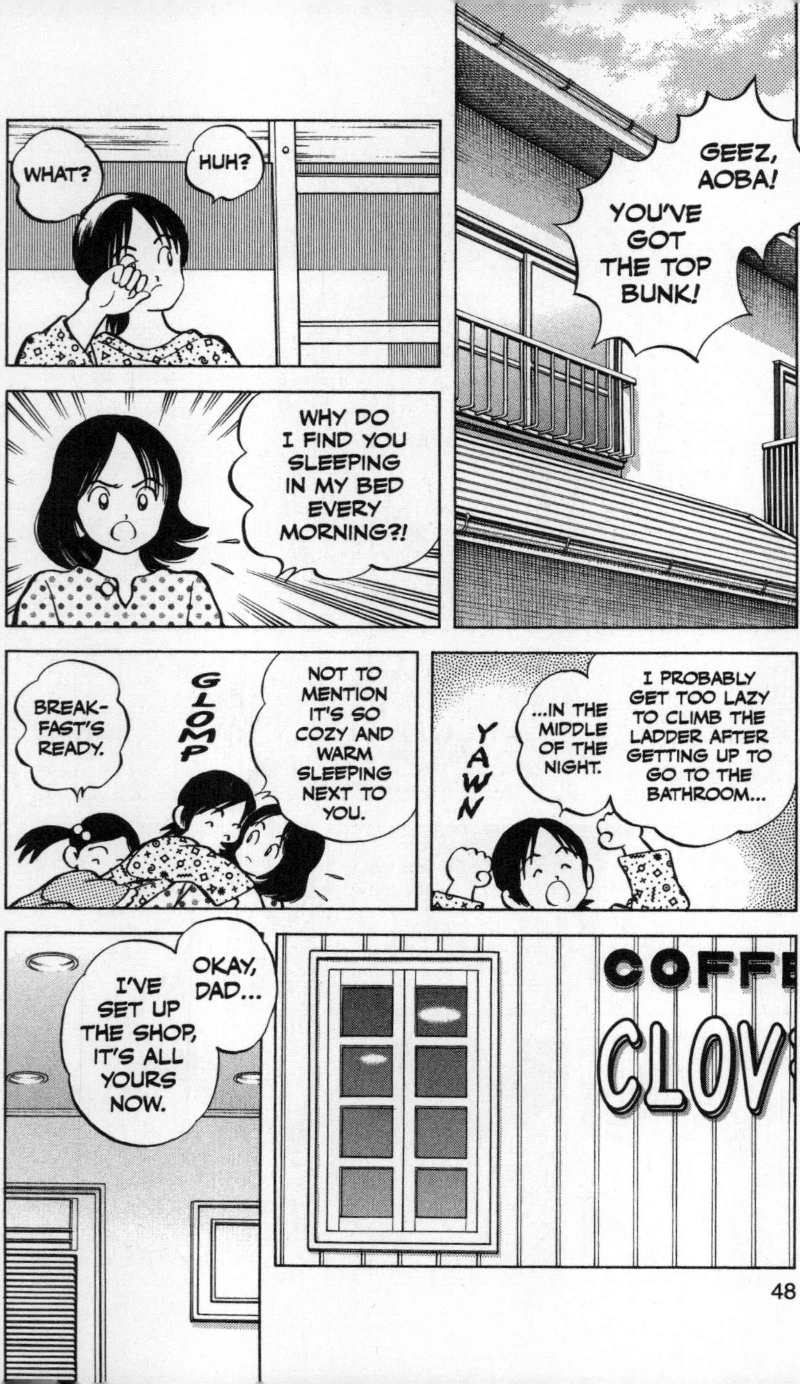
GEEZ, AOBA!
YOU'VE GOT THE TOP BUNK!
HUH?
WHAT?
WHY DO I FIND YOU SLEEPING IN MY BED EVERY MORNING?!
I PROBABLY GET TOO LAZY TO CLIMB THE LADDER AFTER GETTING UP TO GO TO THE BATHROOM...
...IN THE MIDDLE OF THE NIGHT.
YAWN
NOT TO MENTION IT'S SO COZY AND WARM SLEEPING NEXT TO YOU.
GLOMP
BREAK-FAST'S READY.
COFFE
CLOV
OKAY, DAD...
I'VE SET UP THE SHOP, IT'S ALL YOURS NOW.

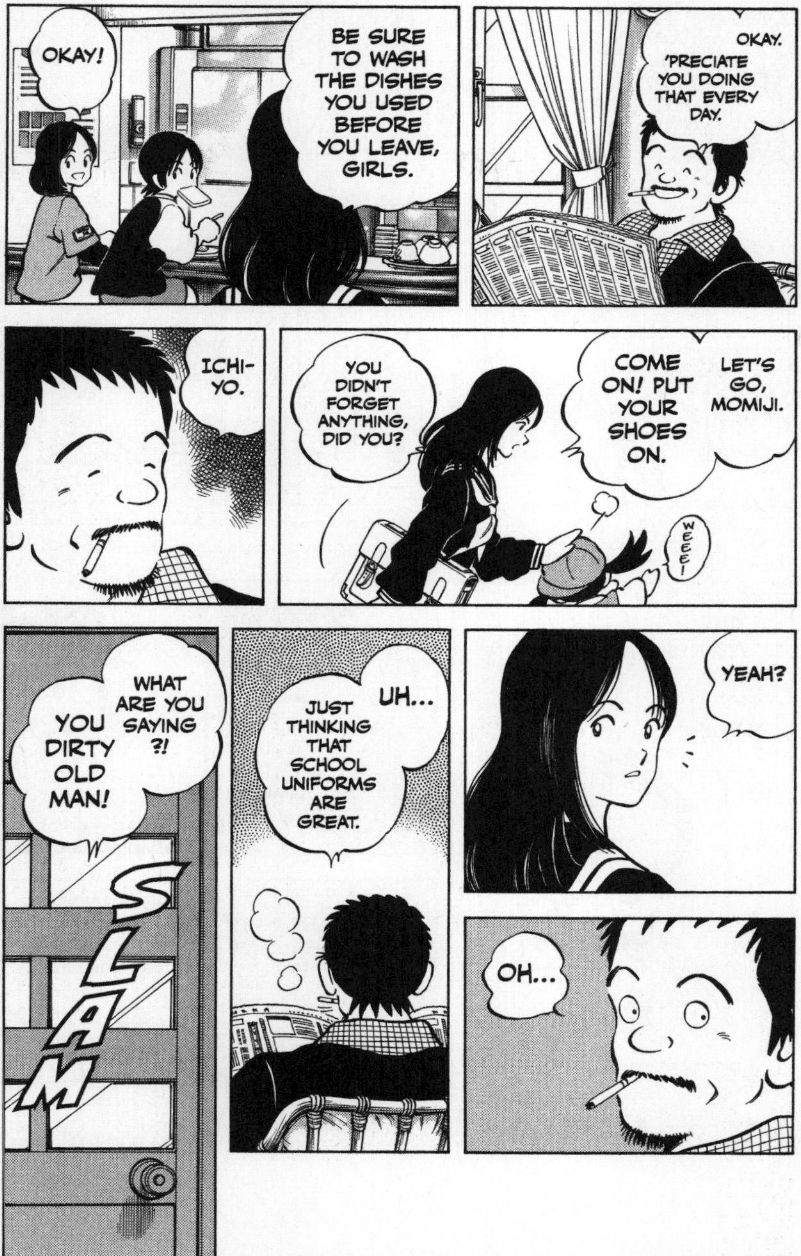
OKAY. 'PRECIATE YOU DOING THAT EVERY DAY.
BE SURE TO WASH THE DISHES YOU USED BEFORE YOU LEAVE, GIRLS.
OKAY!
LET'S GO, MOMIJI.
COME ON! PUT YOUR SHOES ON.
YOU DIDN'T FORGET ANYTHING, DID YOU?
WEEE!
ICHI-YO.
YEAH?
OH...
UH...
JUST THINKING THAT SCHOOL UNIFORMS ARE GREAT.
WHAT ARE YOU SAYING?!
YOU DIRTY OLD MAN!
SLAM

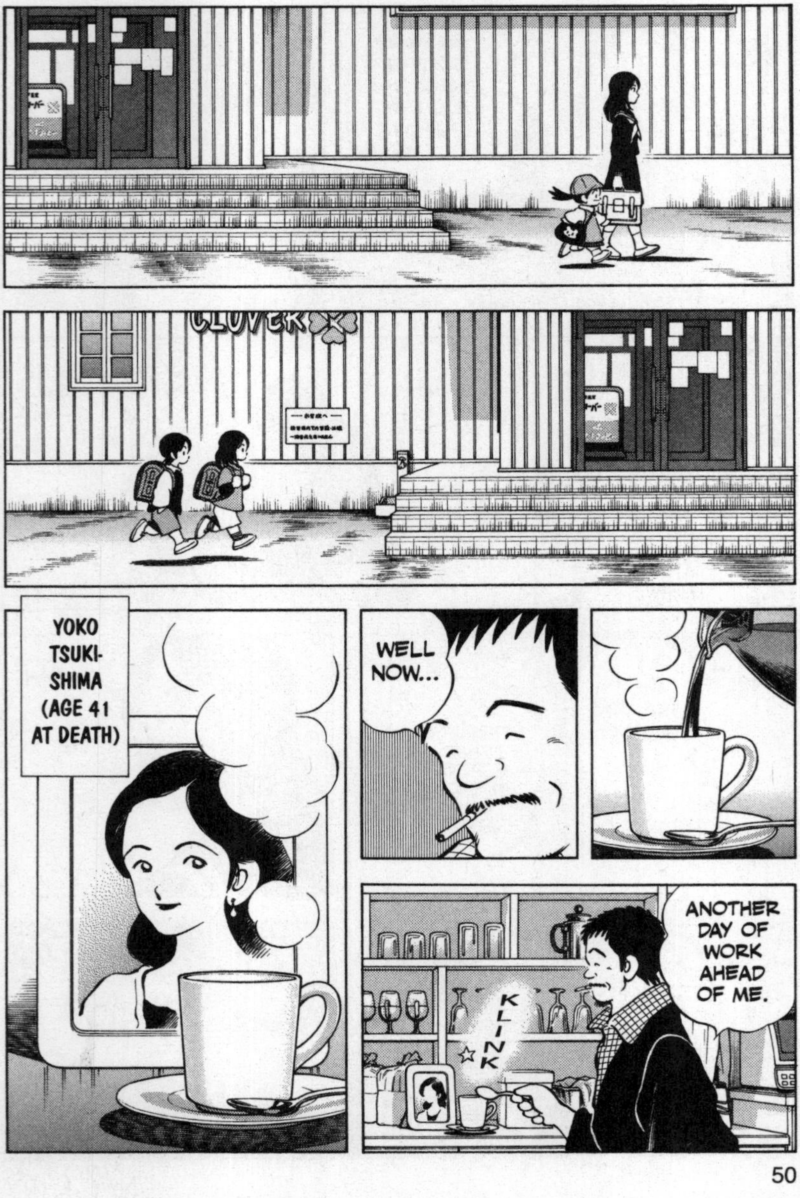
CLOVER
WELL NOW...
ANOTHER DAY OF WORK AHEAD OF ME.
KLINK
YOKO TSUKISHIMA (AGE 41 AT DEATH)

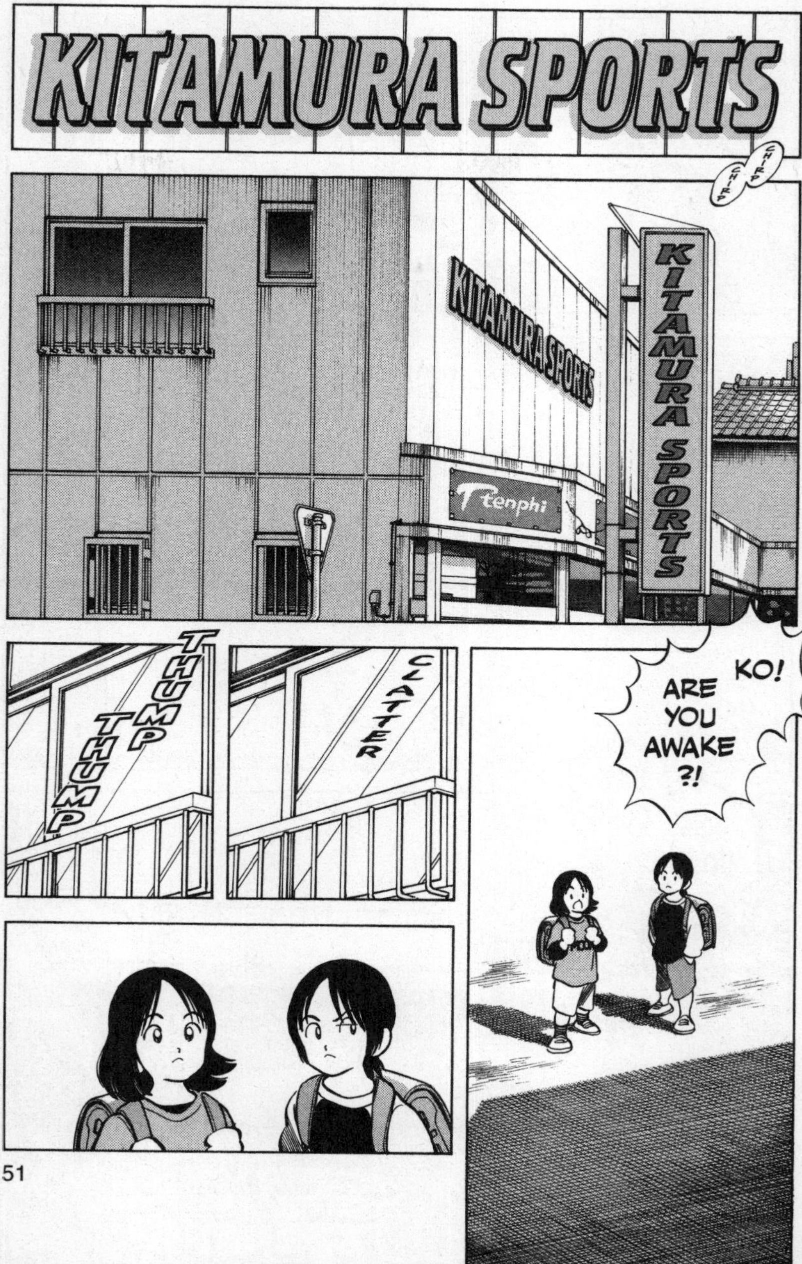
KITAMURA SPORTS
CHIRP CHIRP
KITAMURA SPORTS
KITAMURA SPORTS
Tenphi
KO! ARE YOU AWAKE?!
CLATTER
THUMP THUMP

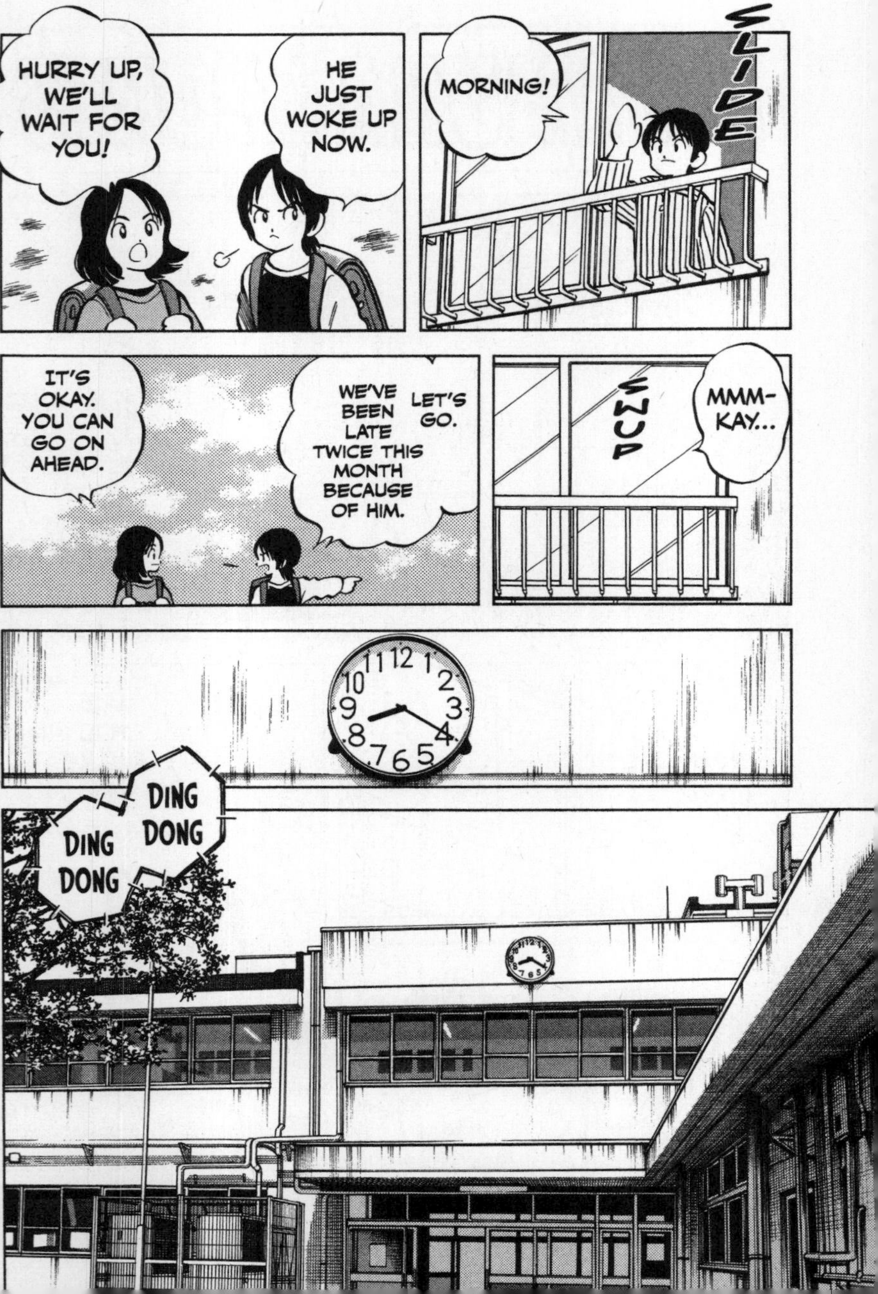
SLIDE
MORNING!
HE JUST WOKE UP NOW.
HURRY UP, WE'LL WAIT FOR YOU!
SWUP
MMM-KAY...
LET'S GO.
WE'VE BEEN LATE TWICE THIS MONTH BECAUSE OF HIM.
IT'S OKAY. YOU CAN GO ON AHEAD.
DING DONG
DING DONG

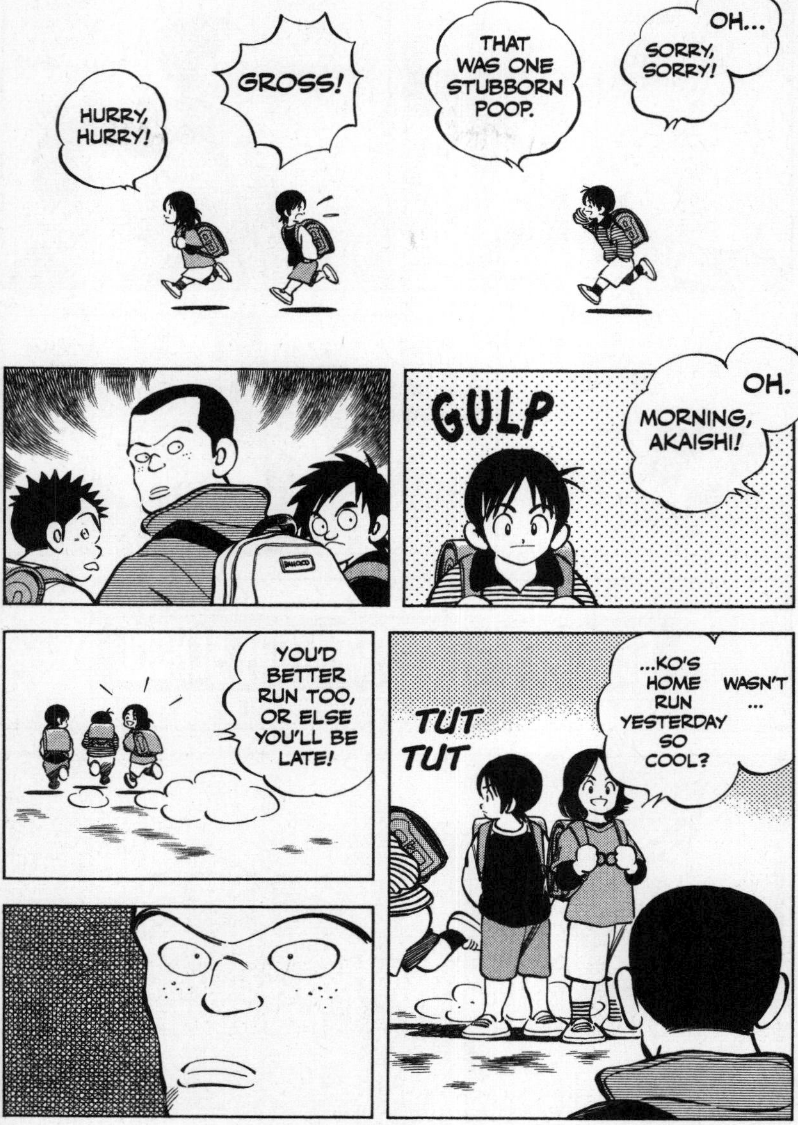
OH... SORRY, SORRY!
THAT WAS ONE STUBBORN POOP.
GROSS!
HURRY, HURRY!
GULP
OH. MORNING, AKAISHI!
TUT TUT
WASN'T ...
...KO'S HOME RUN YESTERDAY SO COOL?
YOU'D BETTER RUN TOO, OR ELSE YOU'LL BE LATE!

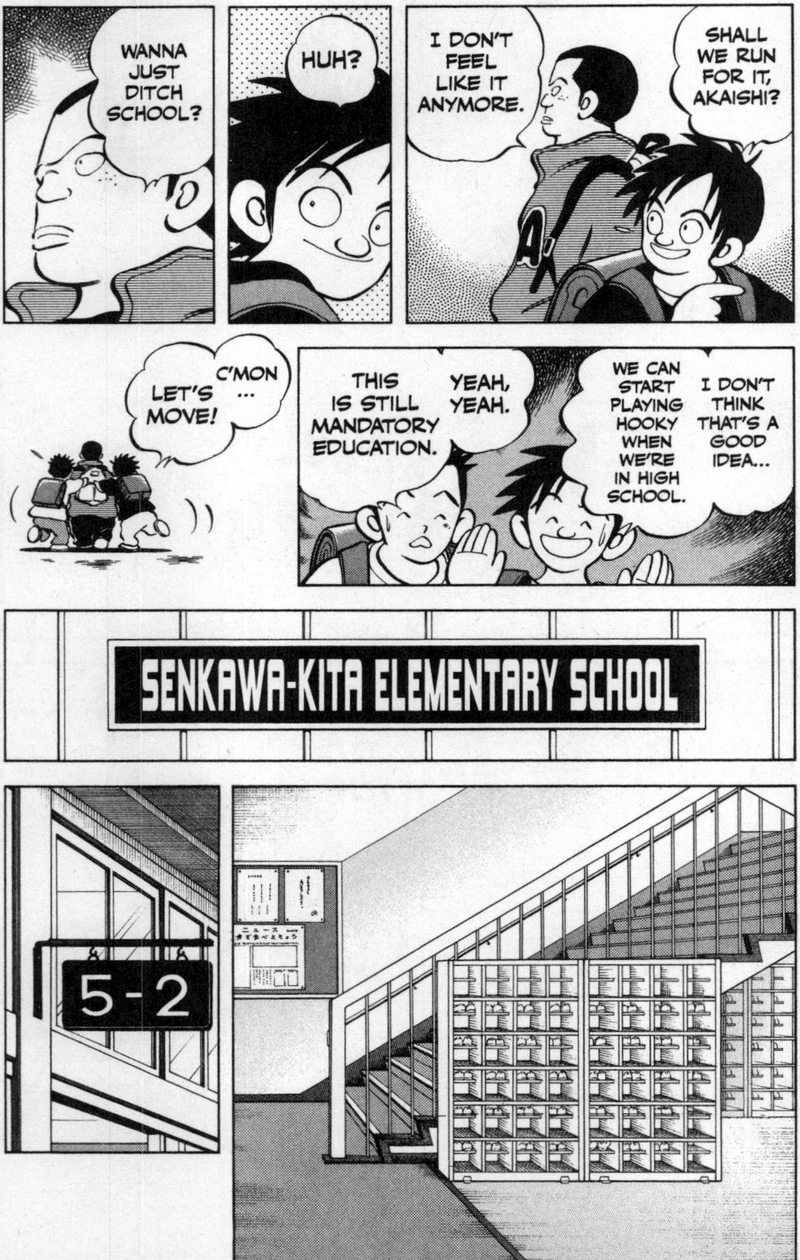
SHALL WE RUN FOR IT, AKAISHI?
I DON'T FEEL LIKE IT ANYMORE.
HUH?
WANNA JUST DITCH SCHOOL?
I DON'T THINK THAT'S A GOOD IDEA...
WE CAN START PLAYING HOOKY WHEN WE'RE IN HIGH SCHOOL.
YEAH, YEAH.
THIS IS STILL MANDATORY EDUCATION.
C'MON...
LET'S MOVE!
SENKAWA-KITA ELEMENTARY SCHOOL
ニュース
5-2

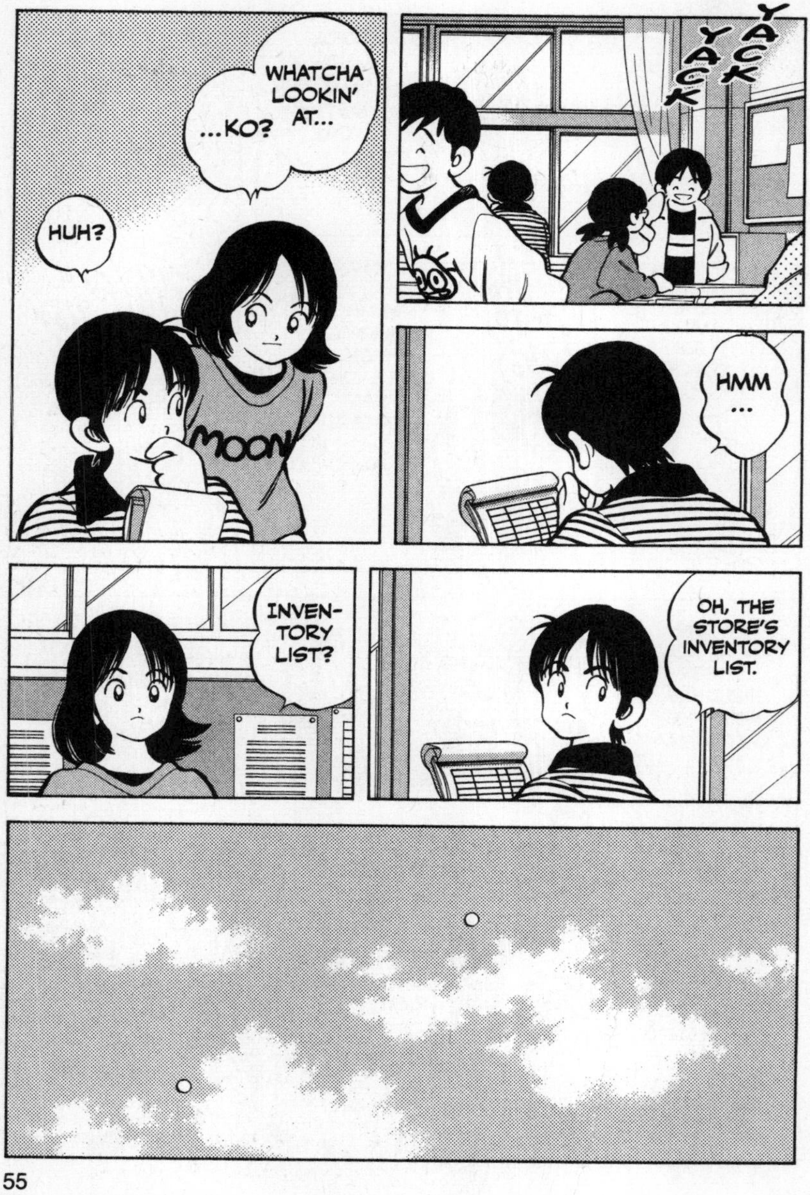
YACK YACK
HMM ...
WHATCHA LOOKIN' AT... ...KO?
HUH?
OH, THE STORE'S INVENTORY LIST.
INVEN-TORY LIST?

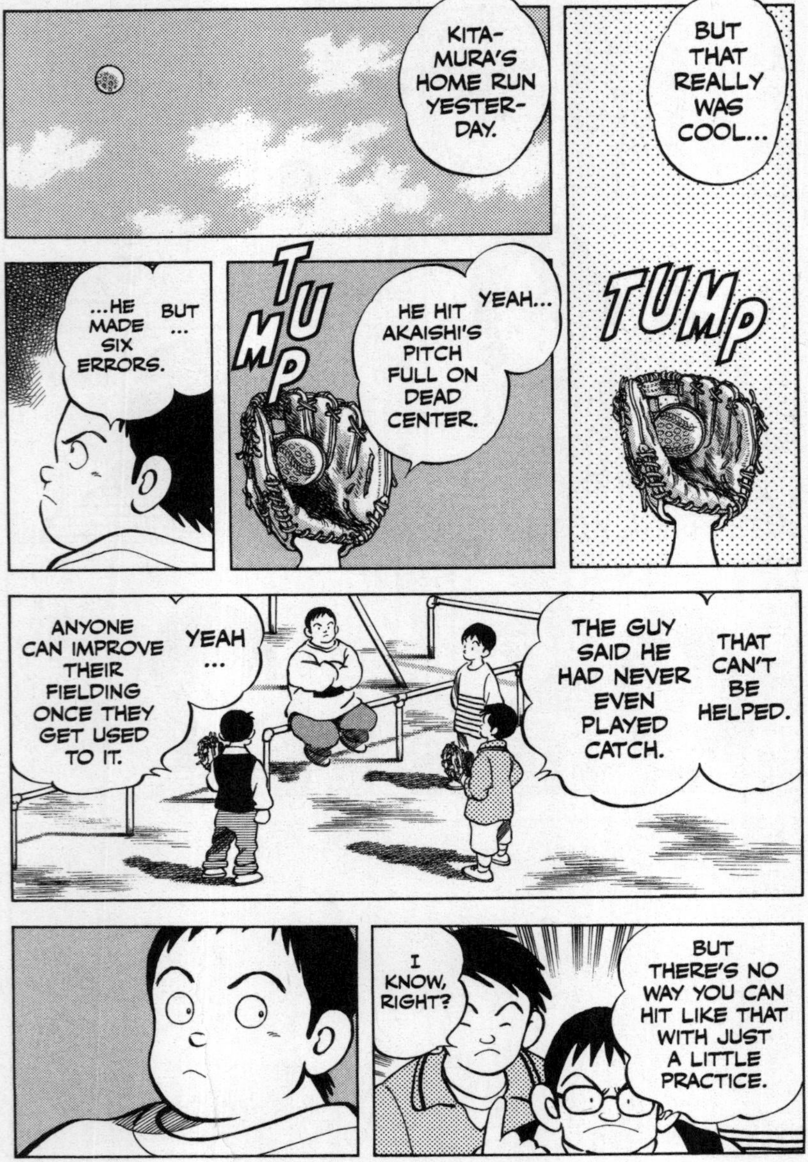
KITA-MURA'S HOME RUN YESTER-DAY.
BUT THAT REALLY WAS COOL...
TUMP
YEAH... HE HIT AKAISHI'S PITCH FULL ON DEAD CENTER.
TUMP
BUT ... ...HE MADE SIX ERRORS.
THAT CAN'T BE HELPED. THE GUY SAID HE HAD NEVER EVEN PLAYED CATCH.
YEAH ... ANYONE CAN IMPROVE THEIR FIELDING ONCE THEY GET USED TO IT.
BUT THERE'S NO WAY YOU CAN HIT LIKE THAT WITH JUST A LITTLE PRACTICE.
I KNOW, RIGHT?

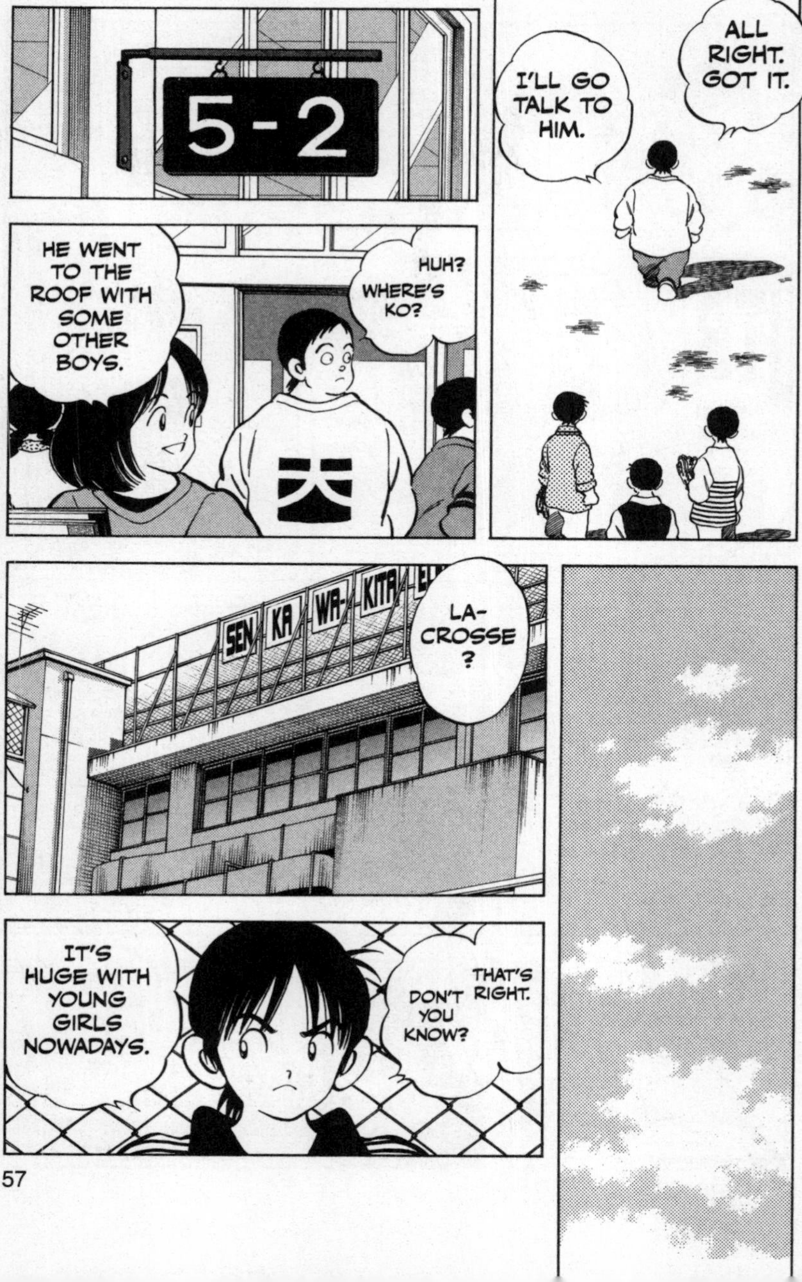
ALL RIGHT. GOT IT.
I'LL GO TALK TO HIM.
5-2
HUH? WHERE'S KO?
HE WENT TO THE ROOF WITH SOME OTHER BOYS.
SEN KA WA- KITA
LA-CROSSE?
THAT'S RIGHT.
DON'T YOU KNOW?
IT'S HUGE WITH YOUNG GIRLS NOWADAYS.

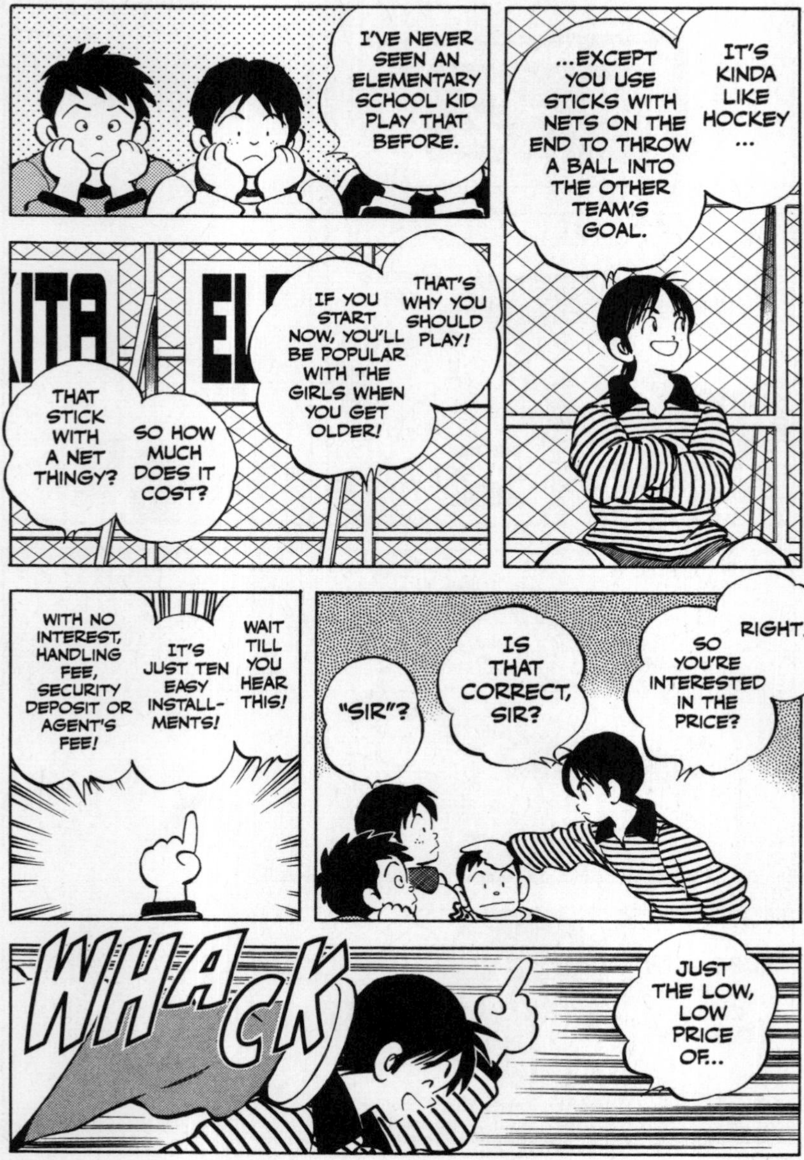
IT'S KINDA LIKE HOCKEY...
...EXCEPT YOU USE STICKS WITH NETS ON THE END TO THROW A BALL INTO THE OTHER TEAM'S GOAL.
I'VE NEVER SEEN AN ELEMENTARY SCHOOL KID PLAY THAT BEFORE.
THAT'S WHY YOU SHOULD PLAY!
IF YOU START NOW, YOU'LL BE POPULAR WITH THE GIRLS WHEN YOU GET OLDER!
SO HOW MUCH DOES IT COST?
THAT STICK WITH A NET THINGY?
RIGHT!
SO YOU'RE INTERESTED IN THE PRICE?
IS THAT CORRECT, SIR?
"SIR"?
WAIT TILL YOU HEAR THIS!
IT'S JUST TEN EASY INSTALL-MENTS!
WITH NO INTEREST, HANDLING FEE, SECURITY DEPOSIT OR AGENT'S FEE!
JUST THE LOW, LOW PRICE OF...
WHACK

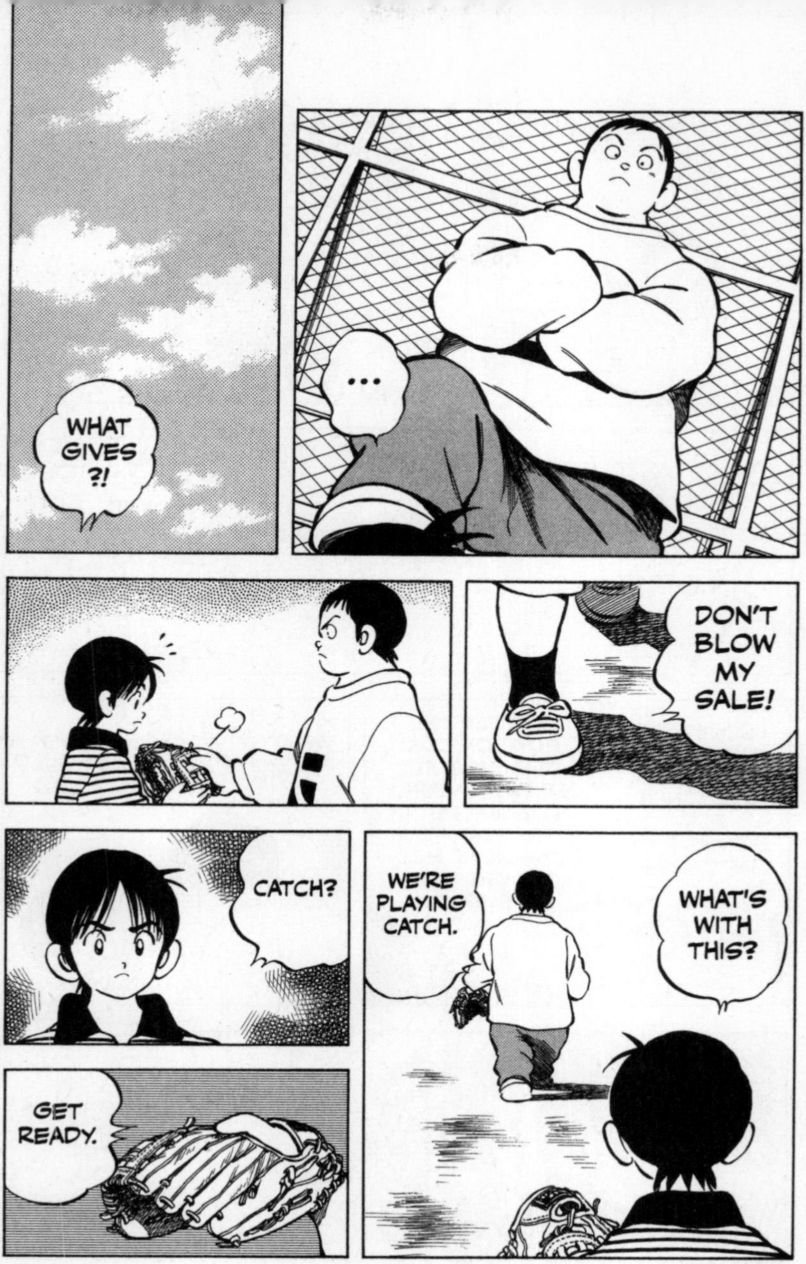
...
WHAT GIVES ?!
DON'T BLOW MY SALE!
WHAT'S WITH THIS?
WE'RE PLAYING CATCH.
CATCH?
GET READY.

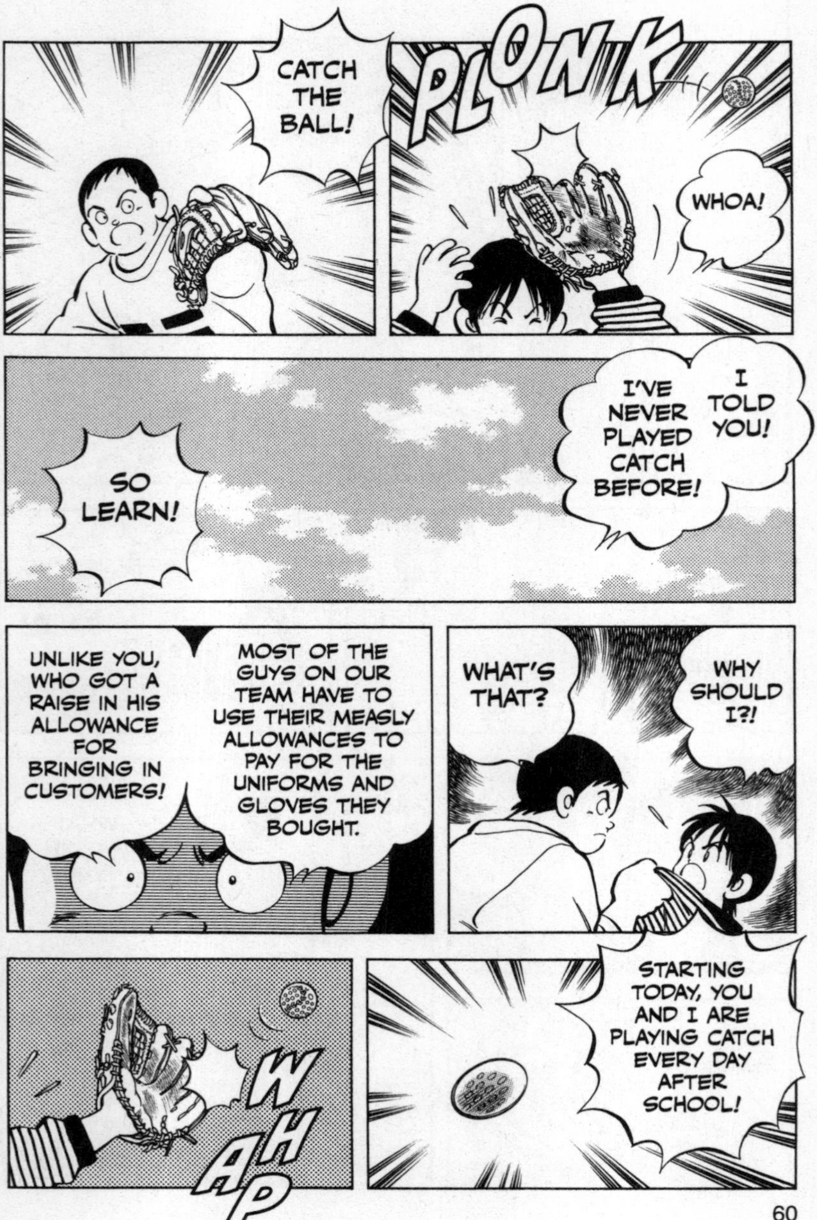
PLONK
WHOA!
CATCH THE BALL!
I TOLD YOU!
I'VE NEVER PLAYED CATCH BEFORE!
SO LEARN!
WHY SHOULD I?!
WHAT'S THAT?
MOST OF THE GUYS ON OUR TEAM HAVE TO USE THEIR MEASLY ALLOWANCES TO PAY FOR THE UNIFORMS AND GLOVES THEY BOUGHT.
UNLIKE YOU, WHO GOT A RAISE IN HIS ALLOWANCE FOR BRINGING IN CUSTOMERS!
STARTING TODAY, YOU AND I ARE PLAYING CATCH EVERY DAY AFTER SCHOOL!
WHAP

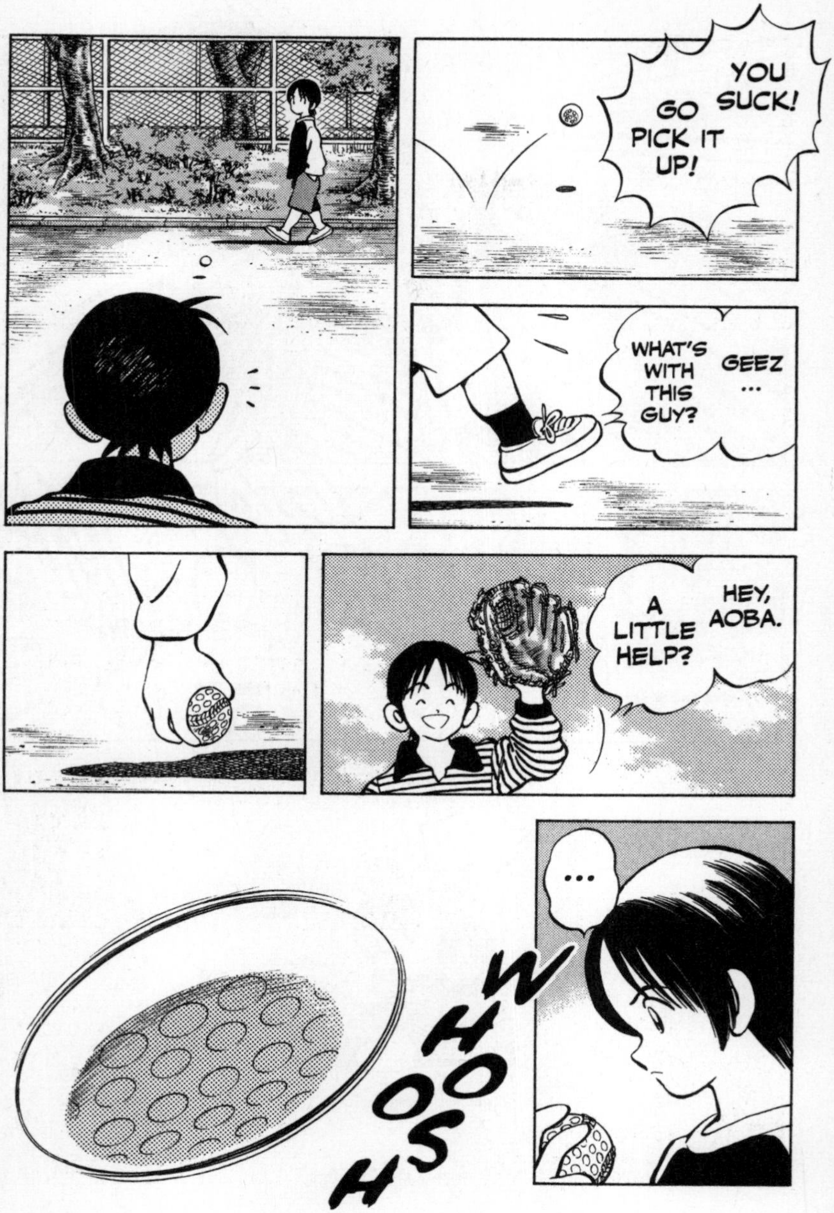
YOU SUCK! GO PICK IT UP!
GEEZ... WHAT'S WITH THIS GUY?
HEY, AOBA. A LITTLE HELP?
...
WHOOSH

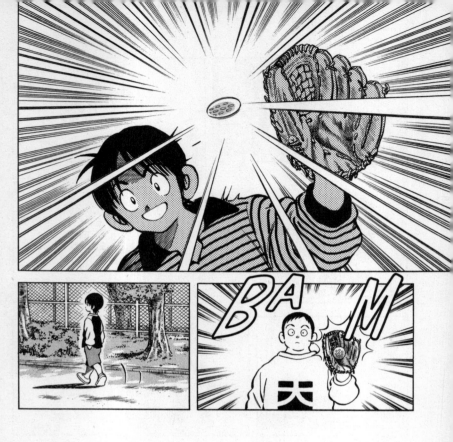

BAM

・・・

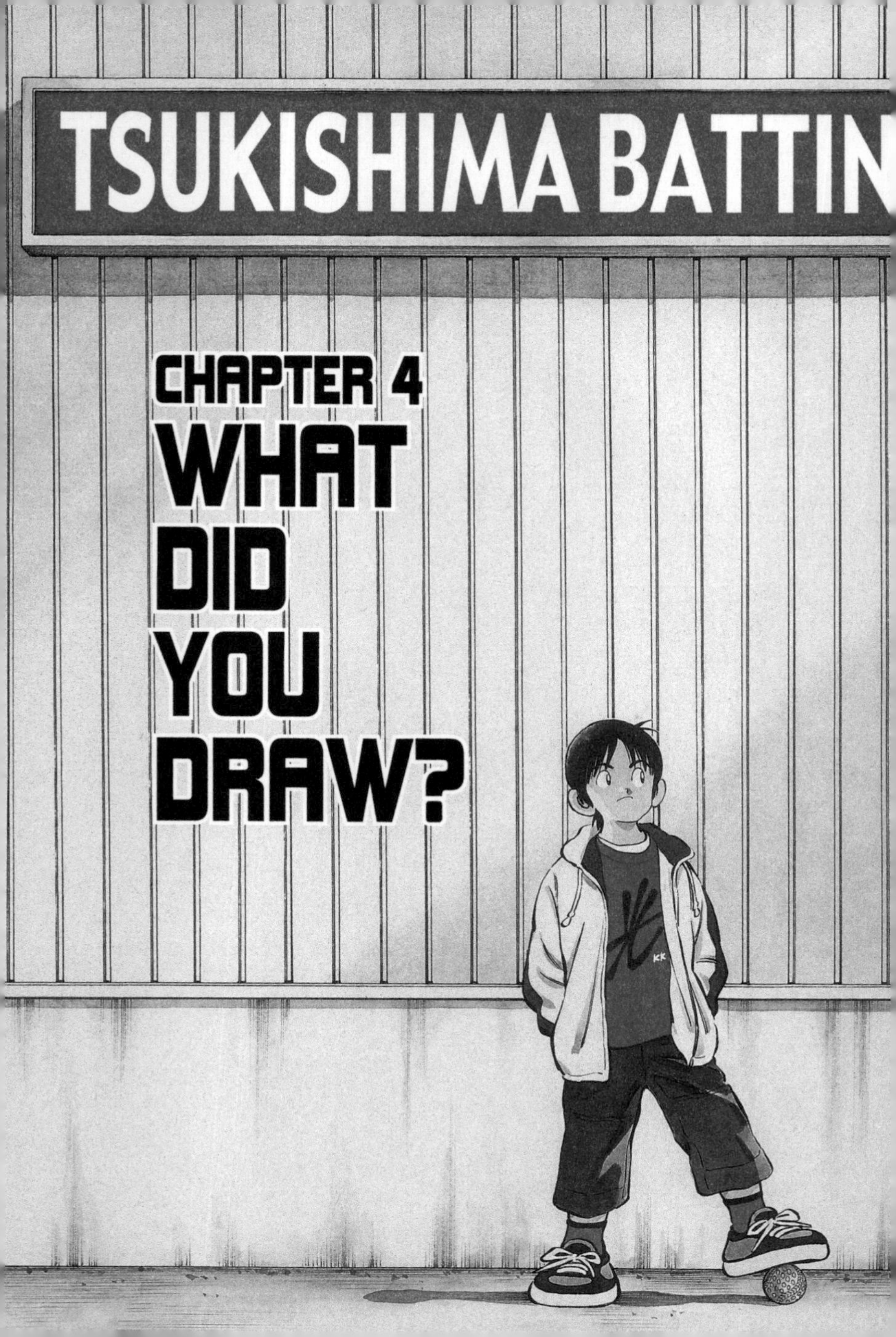
TSUKISHIMA BATTIN
CHAPTER 4
WHAT DID YOU DRAW?
KK

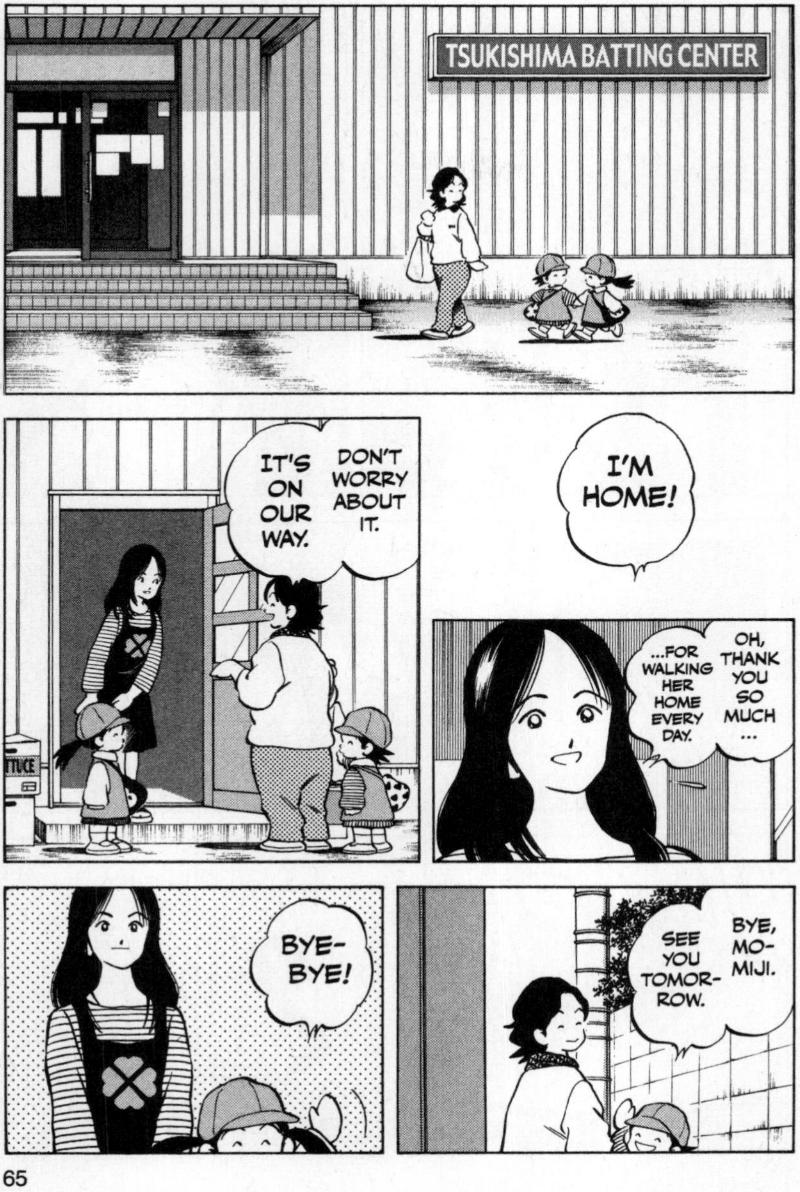
TSUKISHIMA BATTING CENTER
I'M HOME!
OH, THANK YOU SO MUCH...
...FOR WALKING HER HOME EVERY DAY.
DON'T WORRY ABOUT IT.
IT'S ON OUR WAY.
BYE, MO-MIJI.
SEE YOU TOMOR-ROW.
BYE-BYE!

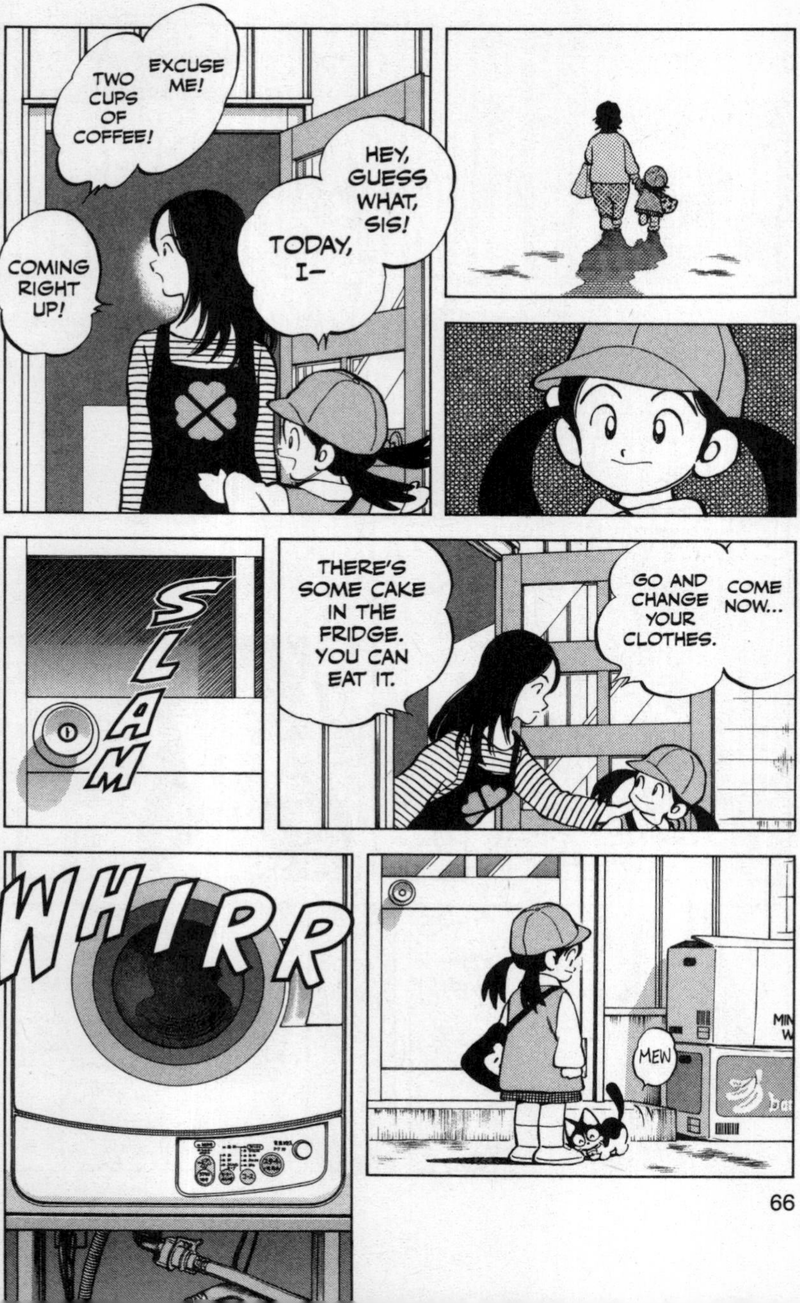
EXCUSE ME!
TWO CUPS OF COFFEE!
HEY, GUESS WHAT, SIS!
TODAY, I–
COMING RIGHT UP!
COME NOW...
GO AND CHANGE YOUR CLOTHES.
THERE'S SOME CAKE IN THE FRIDGE. YOU CAN EAT IT.
SLAM
MEW
WHIRR

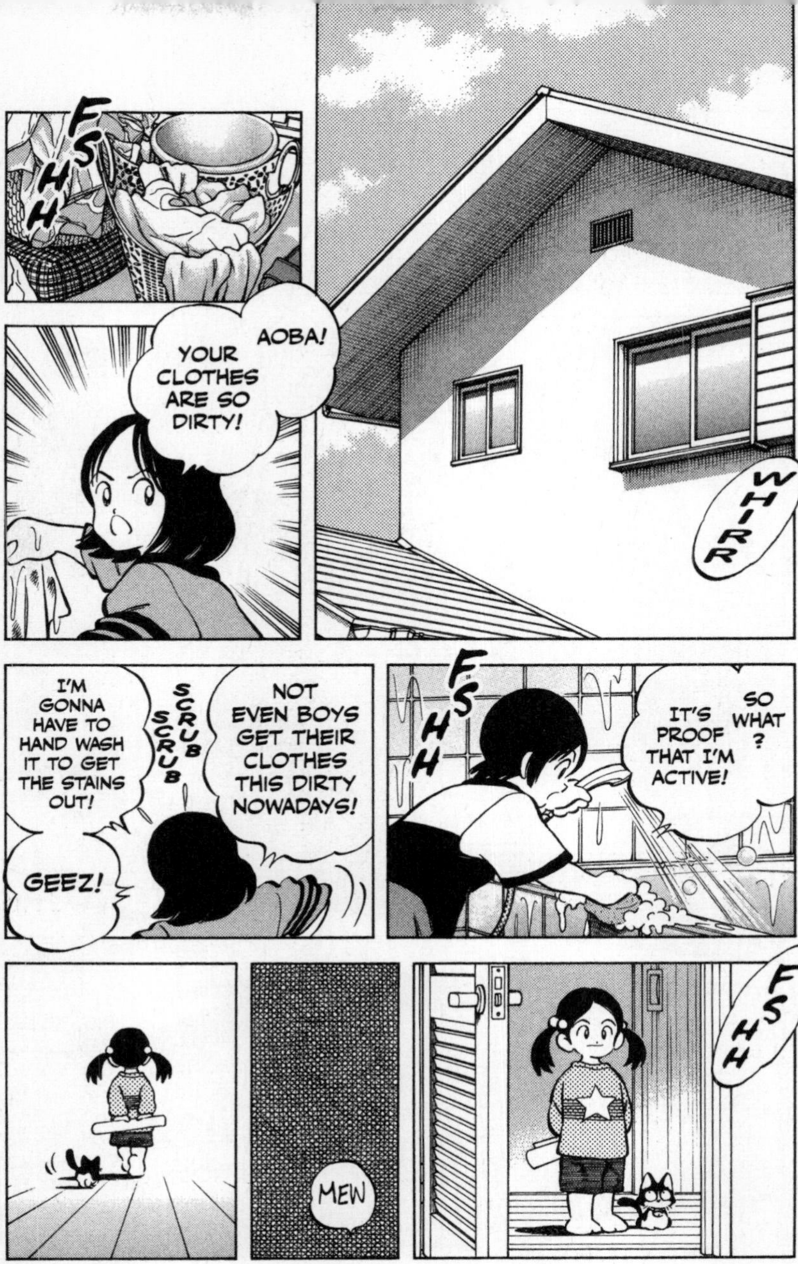
WHIRR
FSHH
AOBA! YOUR CLOTHES ARE SO DIRTY!
FSHH
SO WHAT? IT'S PROOF THAT I'M ACTIVE!
NOT EVEN BOYS GET THEIR CLOTHES THIS DIRTY NOWADAYS!
SCRUB SCRUB
I'M GONNA HAVE TO HAND WASH IT TO GET THE STAINS OUT!
GEEZ!
FSHH
MEW

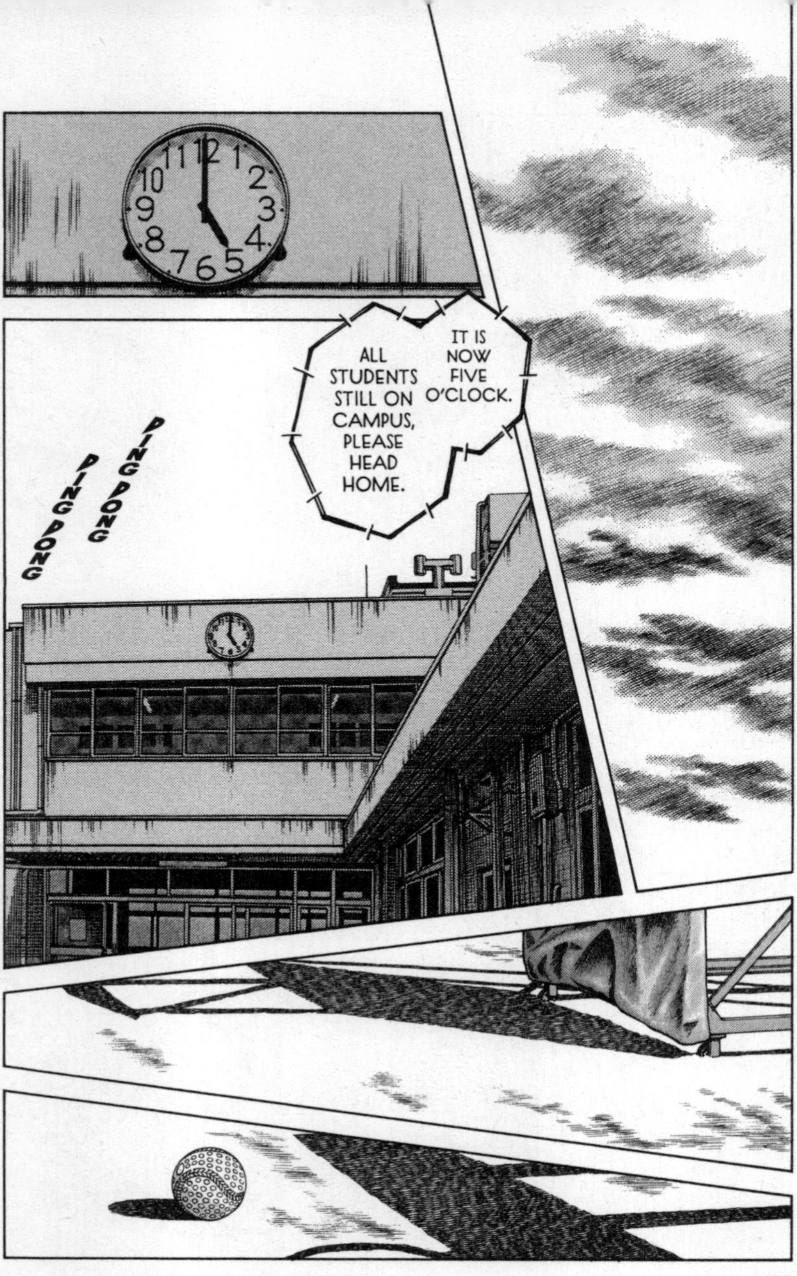
IT IS NOW FIVE O'CLOCK.
ALL STUDENTS STILL ON CAMPUS, PLEASE HEAD HOME.
DING DONG
DING DONG

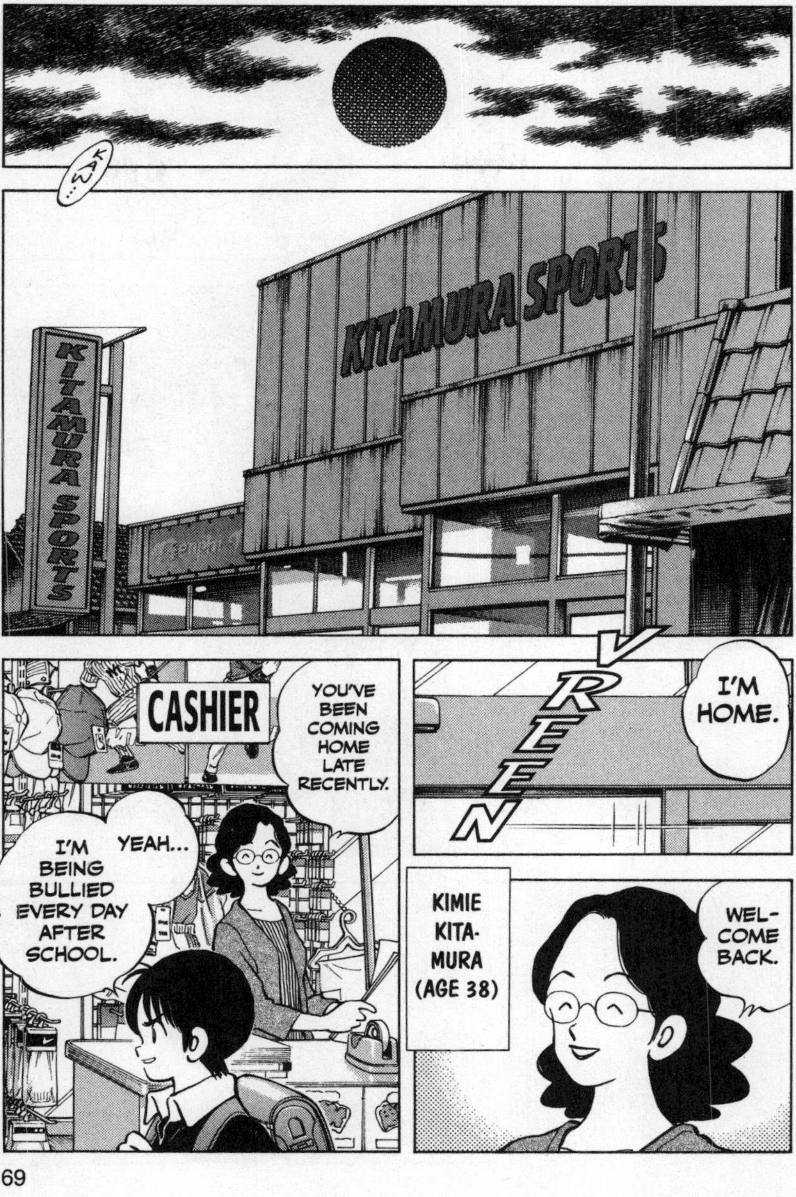
KAW...
KITAMURA SPORTS
KITAMURA SPORTS
VREEEN
I'M HOME.
KIMIE KITA-MURA (AGE 38)
WEL-COME BACK.
CASHIER
YOU'VE BEEN COMING HOME LATE RECENTLY.
YEAH...
I'M BEING BULLIED EVERY DAY AFTER SCHOOL.

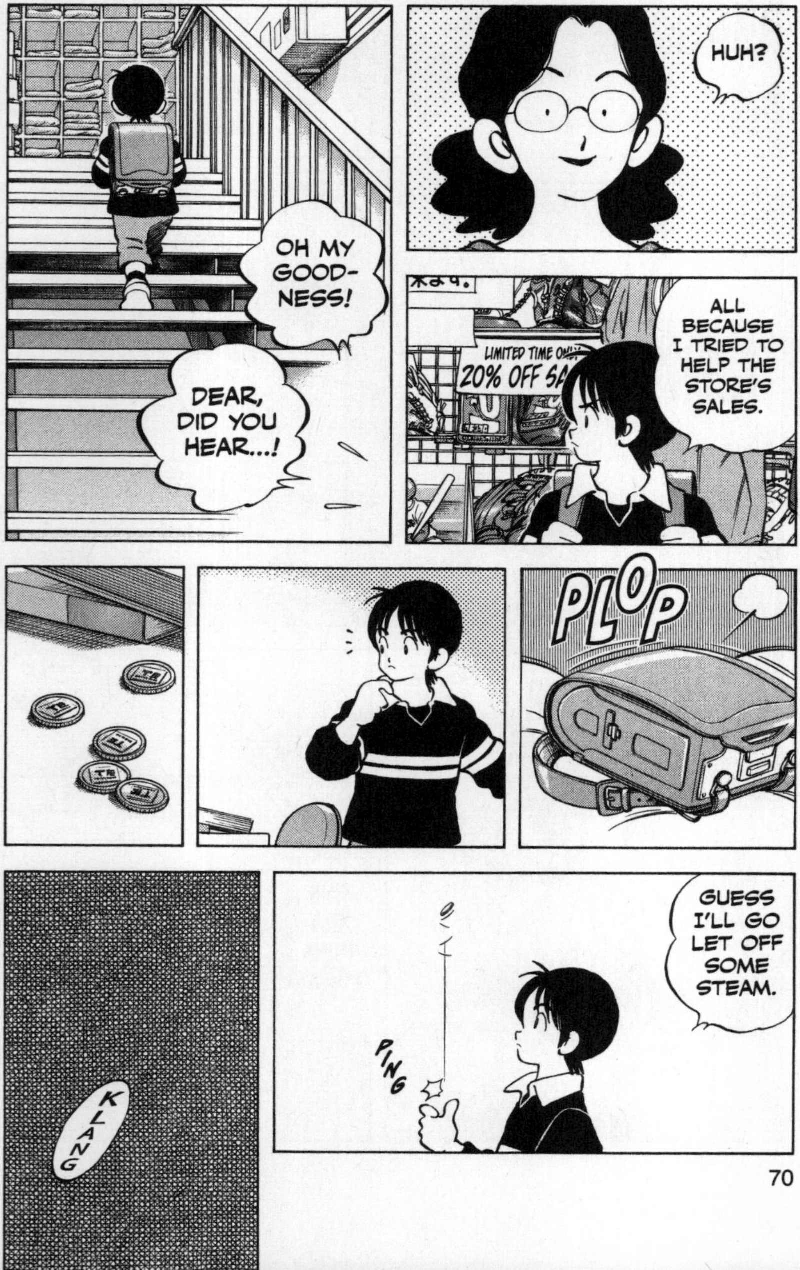
HUH?
ALL BECAUSE I TRIED TO HELP THE STORE'S SALES.
LIMITED TIME
20% OFF
OH MY GOODNESS!
DEAR, DID YOU HEAR...!
PLOP
GUESS I'LL GO LET OFF SOME STEAM.
PING
KLANG

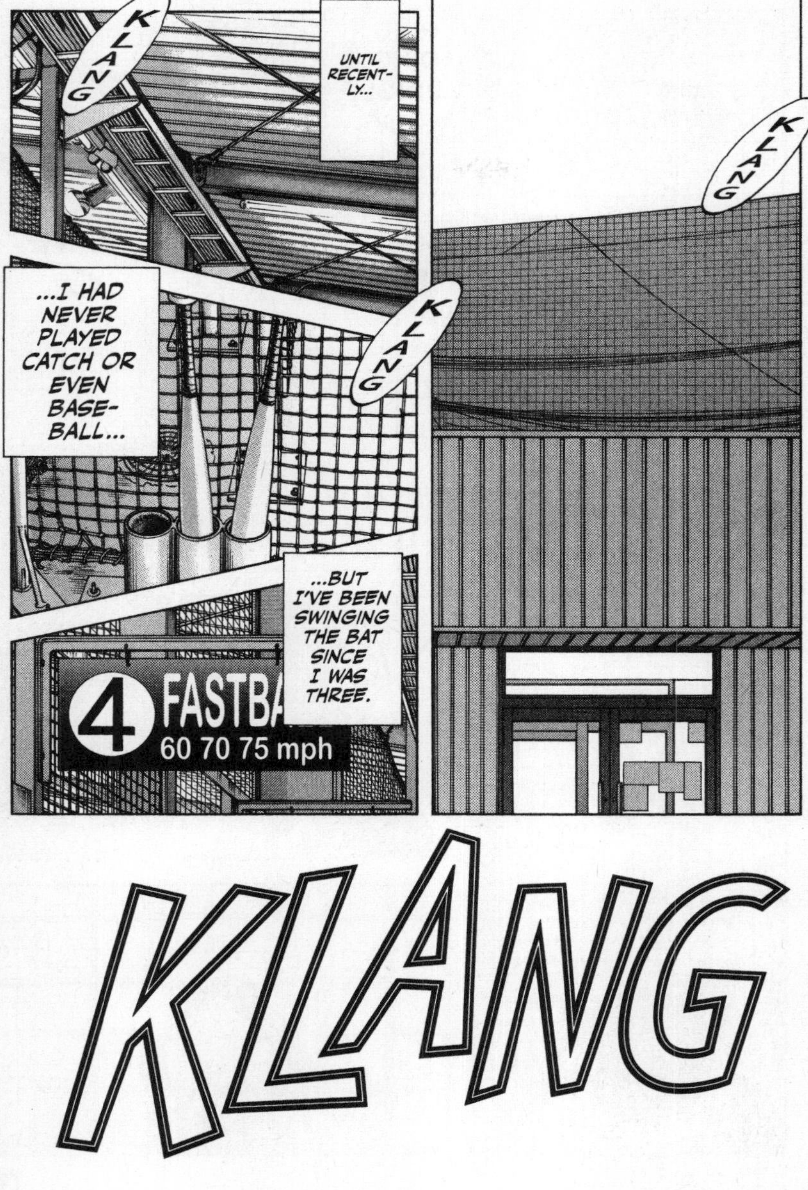
KLANG
KLANG
UNTIL RECENTLY...
KLANG
...I HAD NEVER PLAYED CATCH OR EVEN BASEBALL...
...BUT I'VE BEEN SWINGING THE BAT SINCE I WAS THREE.
4
60 70 75 mph
KLANG

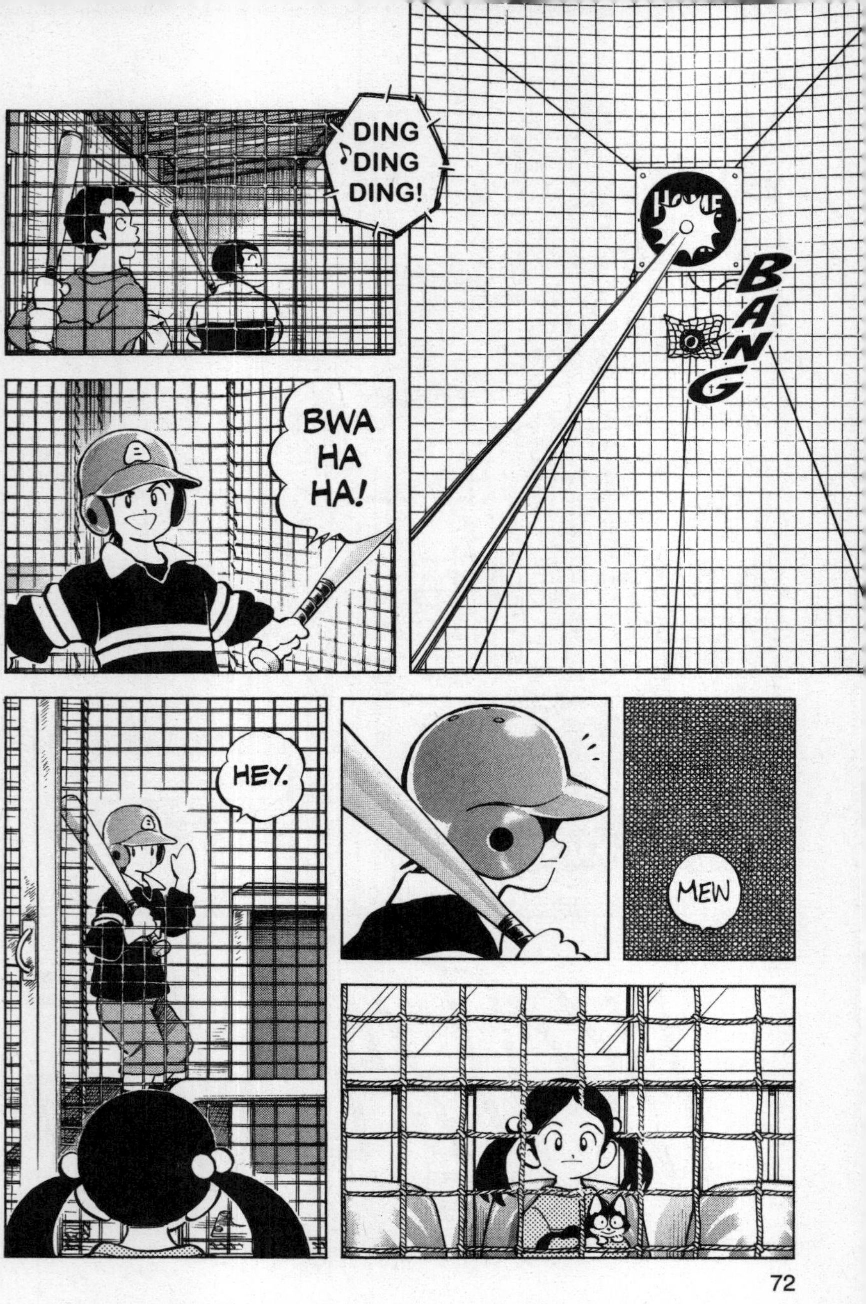
BANG
DING DING DING!
BWA HA HA!
MEW
HEY.

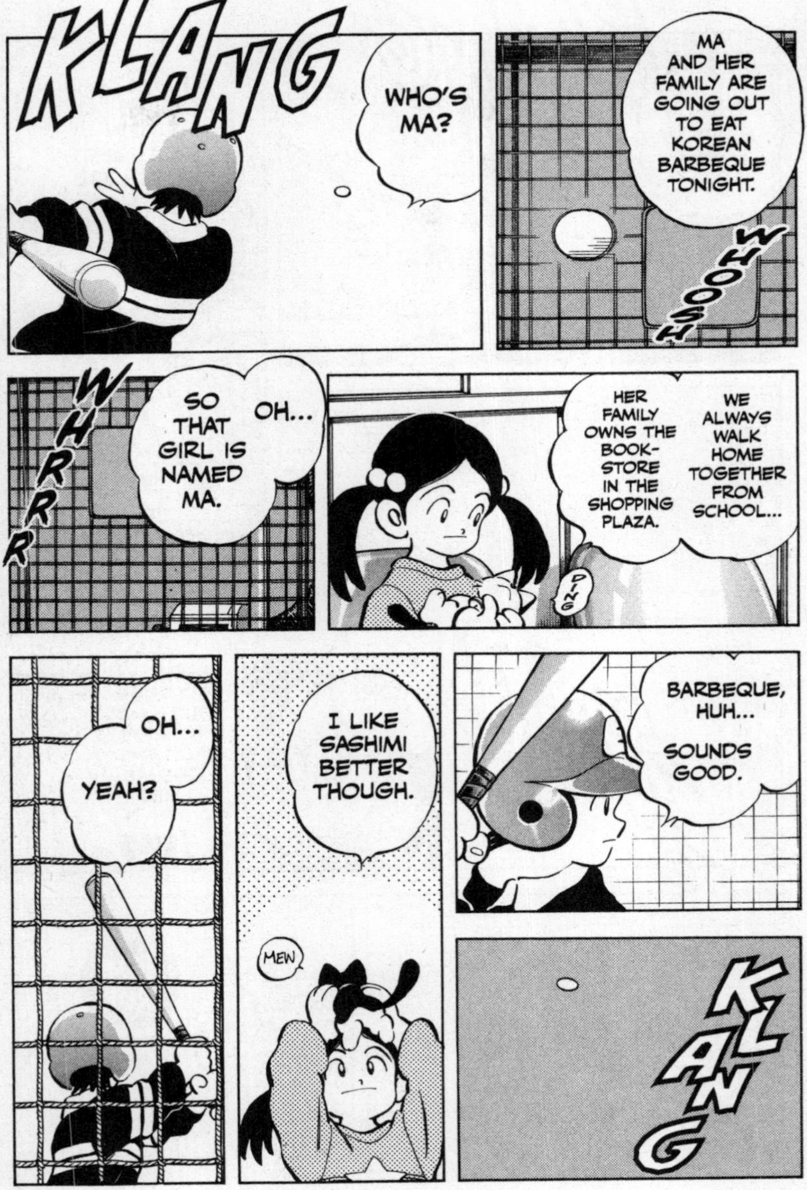
MA AND HER FAMILY ARE GOING OUT TO EAT KOREAN BARBEQUE TONIGHT.
WHOOSH
KLANG
WHO'S MA?
WE ALWAYS WALK HOME TOGETHER FROM SCHOOL...
HER FAMILY OWNS THE BOOK-STORE IN THE SHOPPING PLAZA.
DING
WHRRRR
OH...
SO THAT GIRL IS NAMED MA.
BARBEQUE, HUH...
SOUNDS GOOD.
KLANG
I LIKE SASHIMI BETTER THOUGH.
MEW
OH...
YEAH?

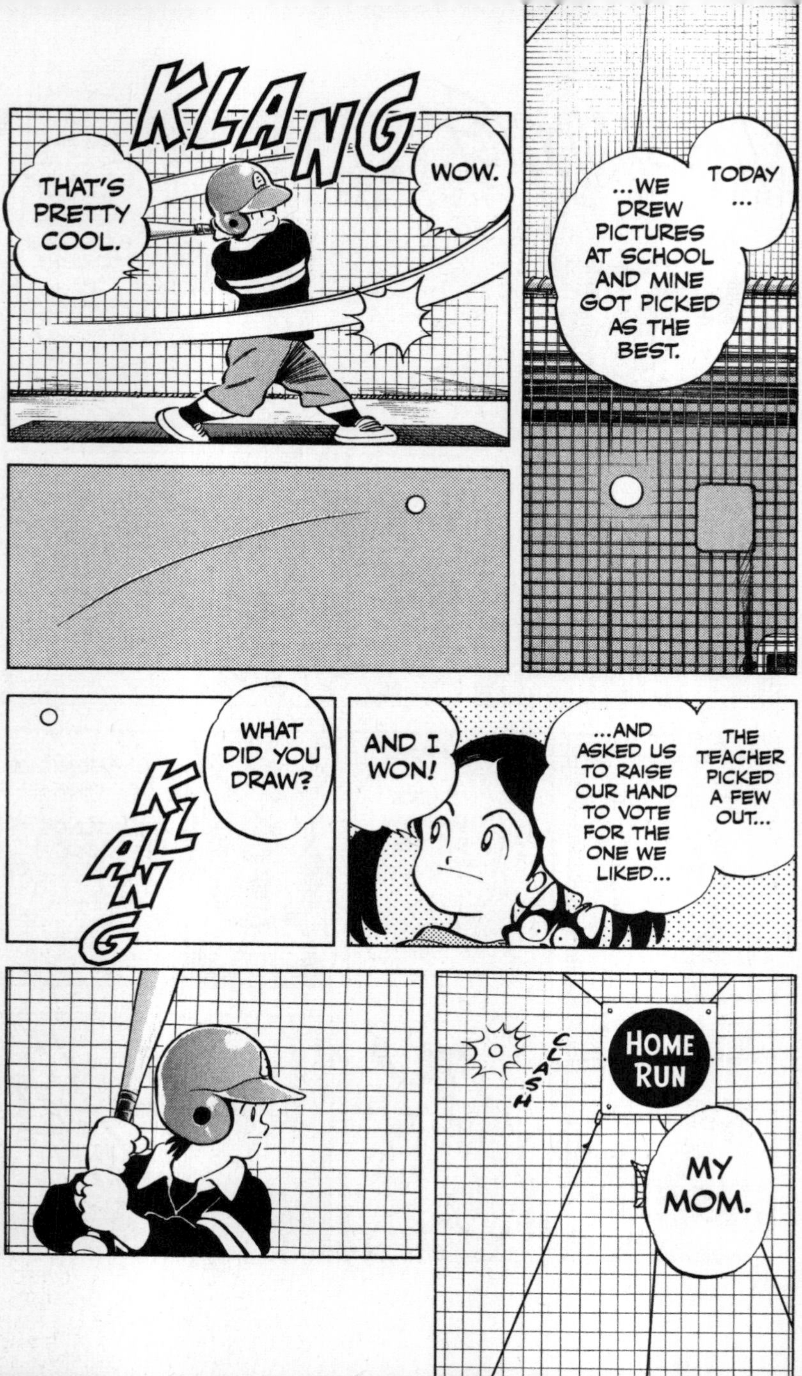
TODAY ...
...WE DREW PICTURES AT SCHOOL AND MINE GOT PICKED AS THE BEST.
KLANG
WOW.
THAT'S PRETTY COOL.
THE TEACHER PICKED A FEW OUT...
...AND ASKED US TO RAISE OUR HAND TO VOTE FOR THE ONE WE LIKED...
AND I WON!
WHAT DID YOU DRAW?
KLANG
HOME RUN
CLASH
MY MOM.

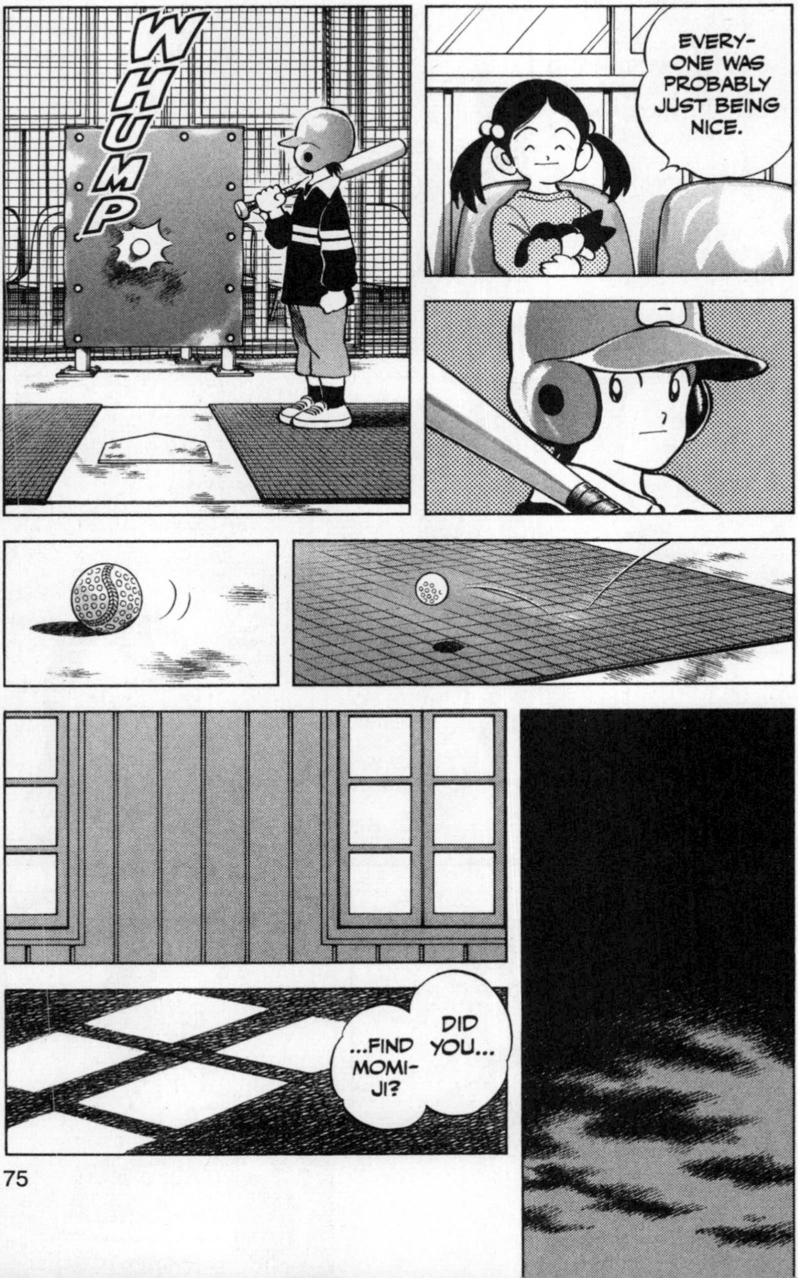
EVERY-ONE WAS PROBABLY JUST BEING NICE.
WHUMP
DID YOU...
...FIND MOMI-JI?

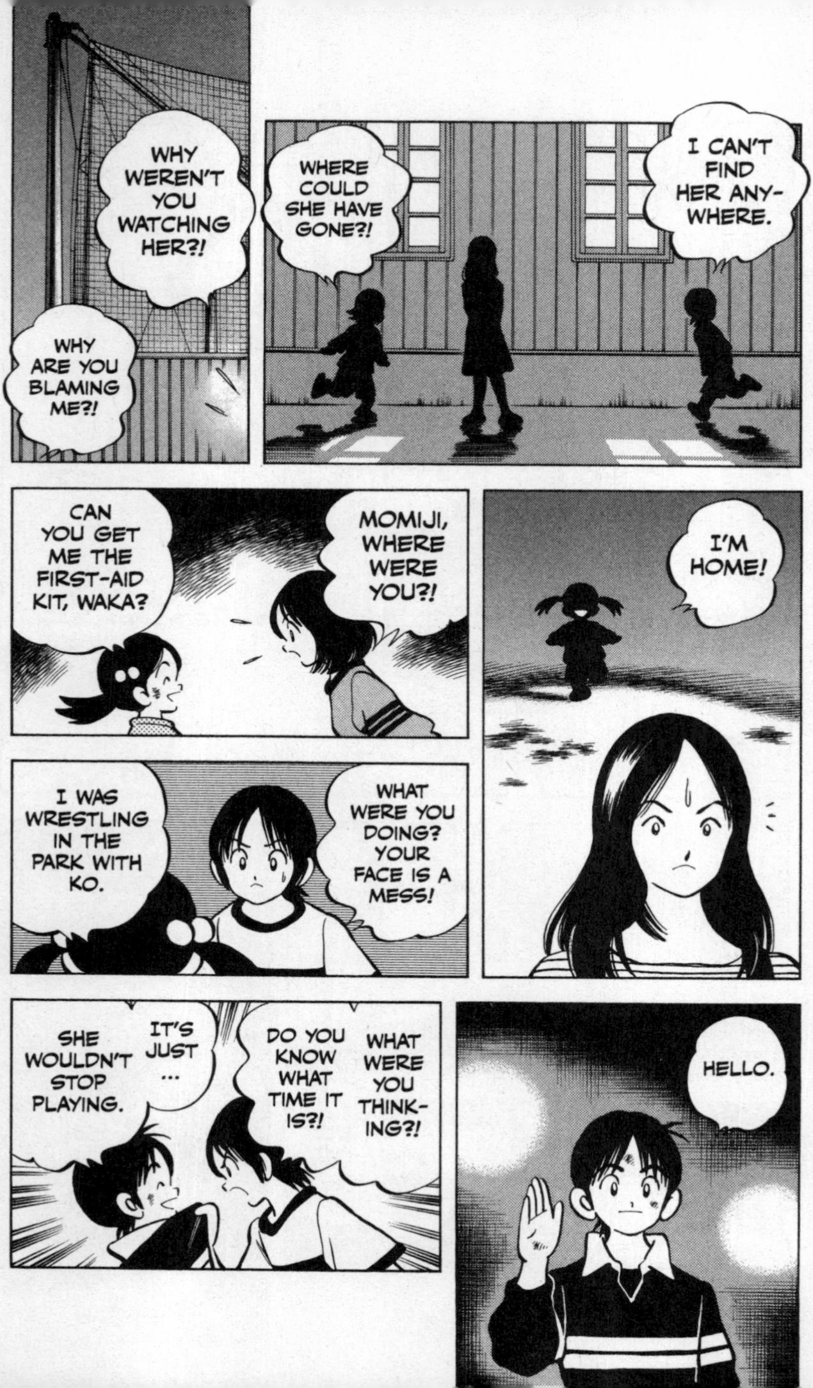
I CAN'T FIND HER ANY-WHERE.
WHERE COULD SHE HAVE GONE?!
WHY WEREN'T YOU WATCHING HER?!
WHY ARE YOU BLAMING ME?!
I'M HOME!
MOMIJI, WHERE WERE YOU?!
CAN YOU GET ME THE FIRST-AID KIT, WAKA?
WHAT WERE YOU DOING? YOUR FACE IS A MESS!
I WAS WRESTLING IN THE PARK WITH KO.
HELLO.
WHAT WERE YOU THINK-ING?!
DO YOU KNOW WHAT TIME IT IS?!
IT'S JUST ...
SHE WOULDN'T STOP PLAYING.

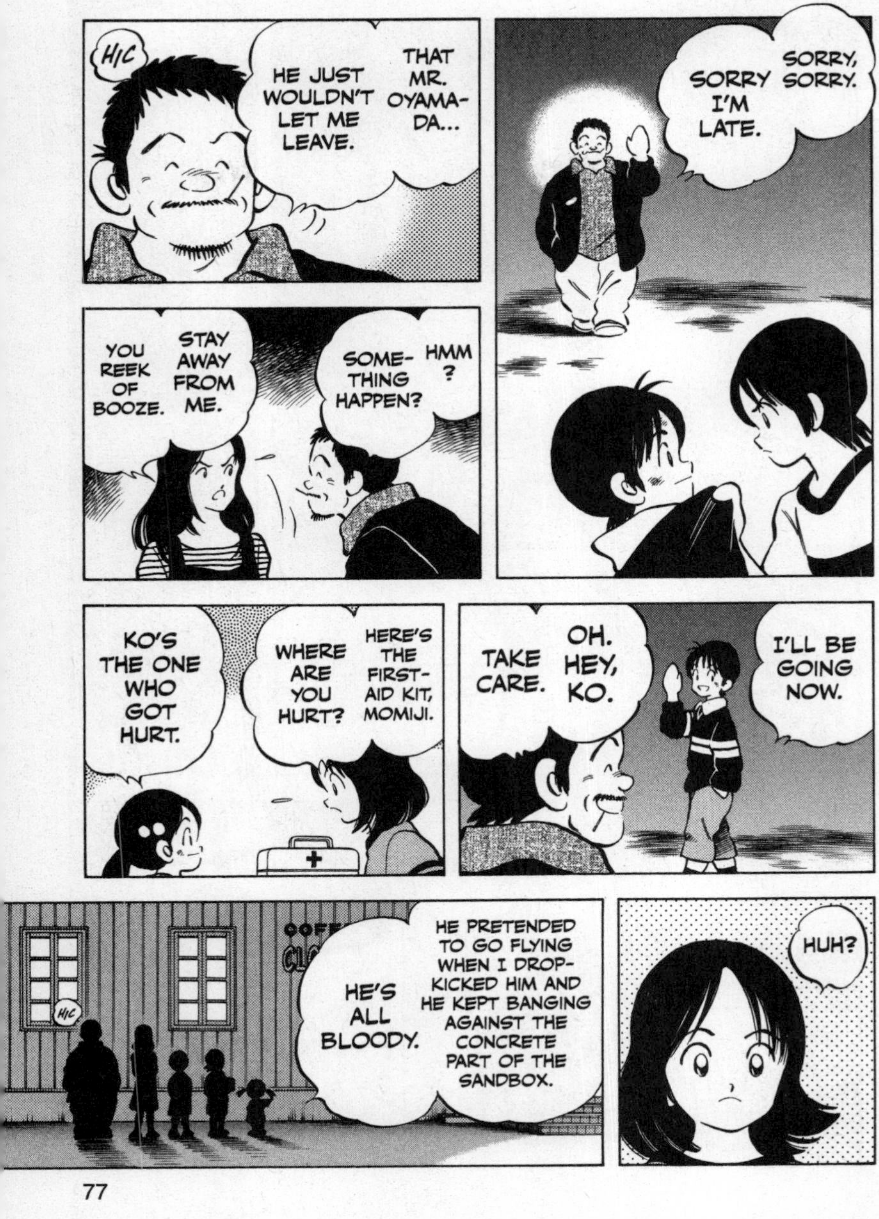
SORRY, SORRY. SORRY I'M LATE.
HIC
THAT MR. OYAMADA... HE JUST WOULDN'T LET ME LEAVE.
HMM? SOMETHING HAPPEN?
STAY AWAY FROM ME. YOU REEK OF BOOZE.
I'LL BE GOING NOW.
OH. HEY, KO. TAKE CARE.
HERE'S THE FIRST-AID KIT, MOMIJI. WHERE ARE YOU HURT?
KO'S THE ONE WHO GOT HURT.
HUH?
HE PRETENDED TO GO FLYING WHEN I DROP-KICKED HIM AND HE KEPT BANGING AGAINST THE CONCRETE PART OF THE SANDBOX.
HE'S ALL BLOODY.
HIC

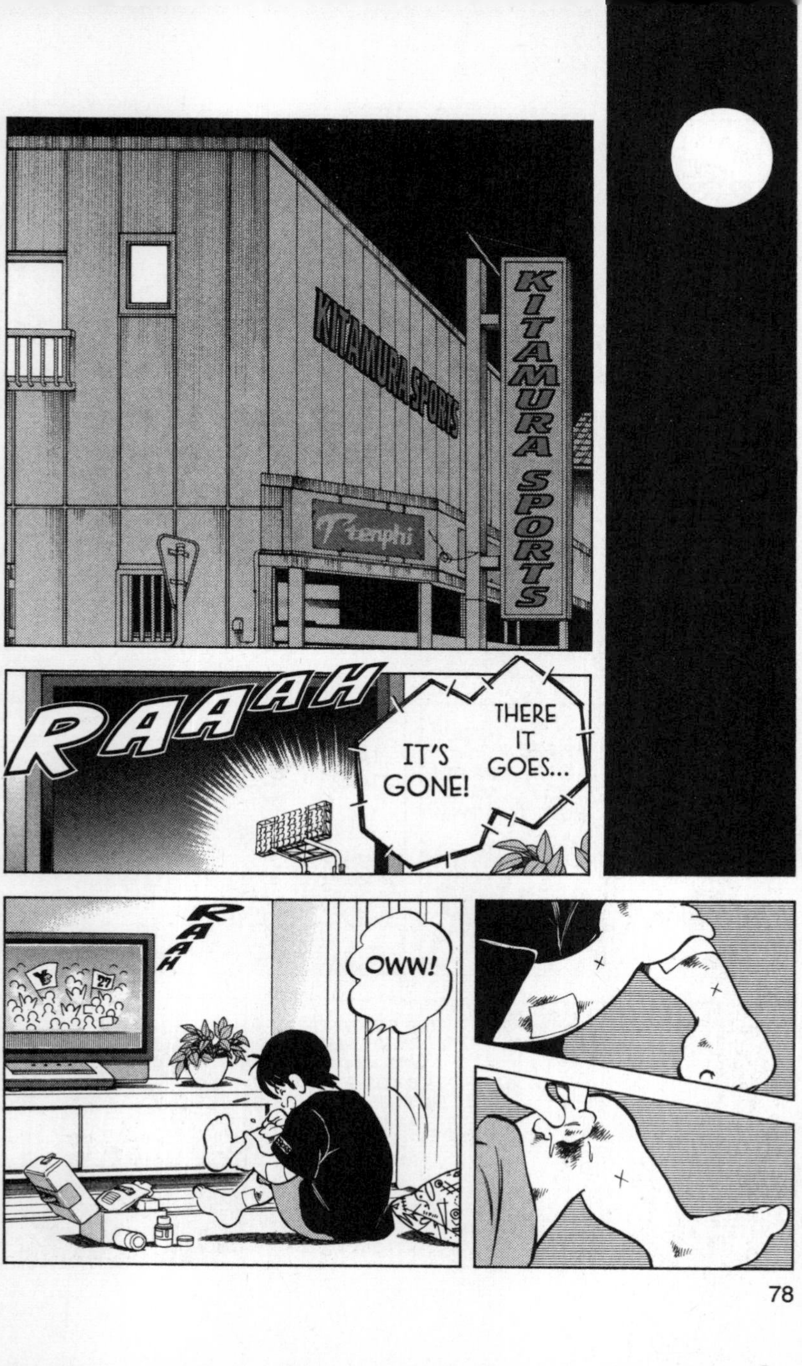
KITAMURA SPORTS
KITAMURA SPORTS
tenphi
RAAAAH
THERE IT GOES...
IT'S GONE!
RAAH
OWW!

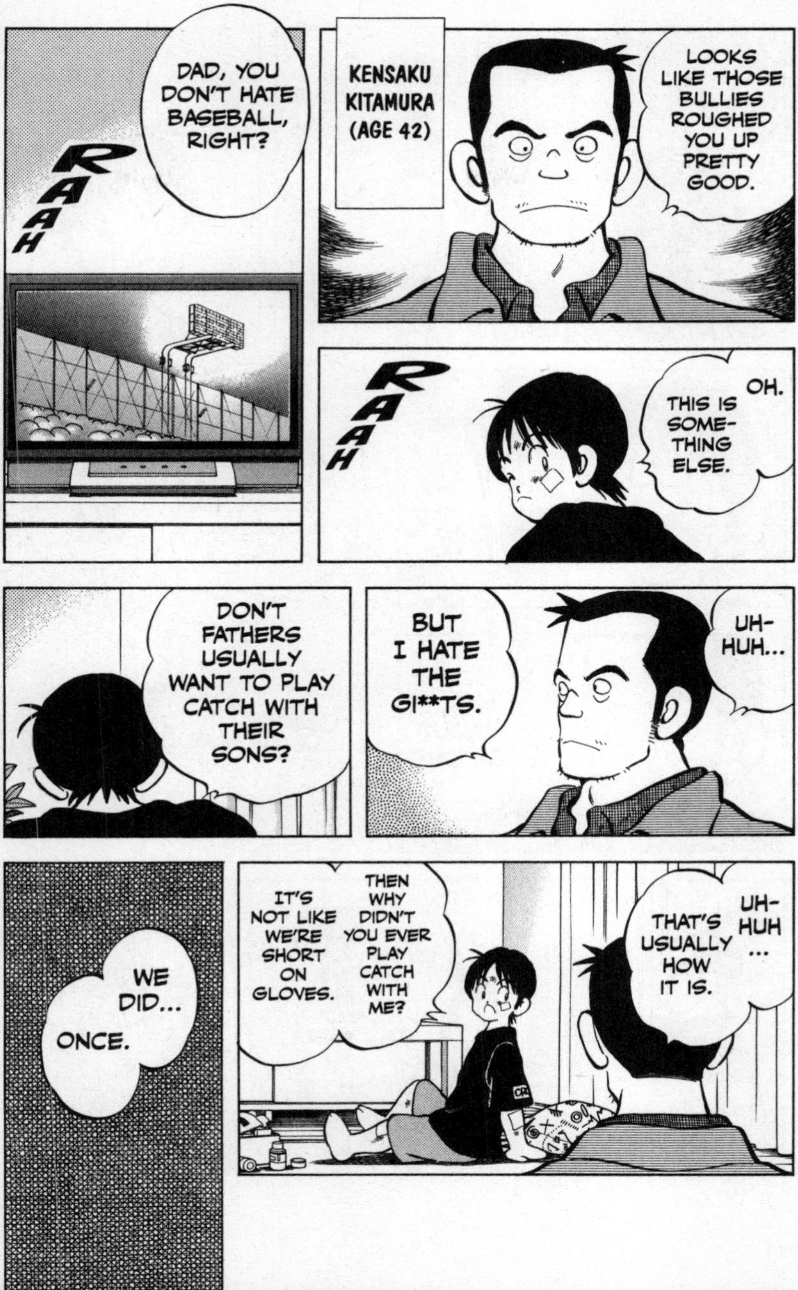
LOOKS LIKE THOSE BULLIES ROUGHED YOU UP PRETTY GOOD.
KENSAKU KITAMURA (AGE 42)
OH.
THIS IS SOMETHING ELSE.
RAAH
DAD, YOU DON'T HATE BASEBALL, RIGHT?
RAAH
UH-HUH...
BUT I HATE THE GI**TS.
DON'T FATHERS USUALLY WANT TO PLAY CATCH WITH THEIR SONS?
UH-HUH...
THAT'S USUALLY HOW IT IS.
THEN WHY DIDN'T YOU EVER PLAY CATCH WITH ME?
IT'S NOT LIKE WE'RE SHORT ON GLOVES.
WE DID...
ONCE.

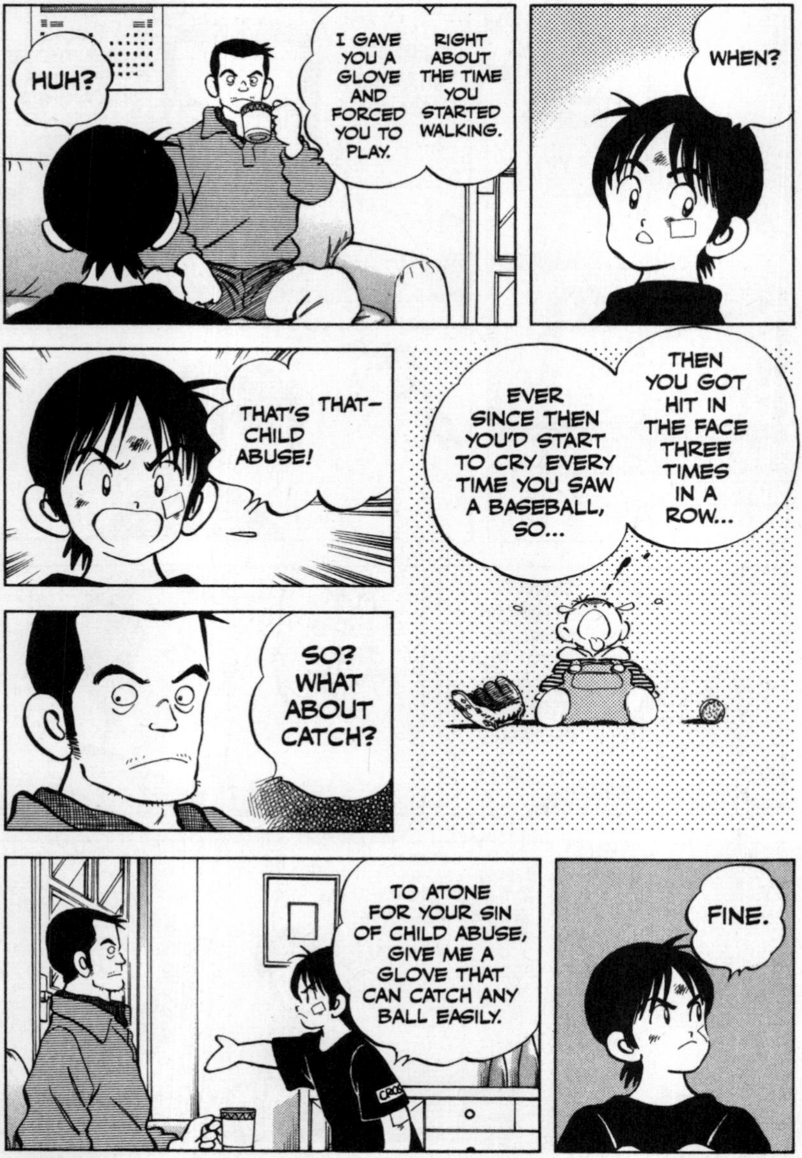
WHEN?
RIGHT ABOUT THE TIME YOU STARTED WALKING.
I GAVE YOU A GLOVE AND FORCED YOU TO PLAY.
HUH?
THEN YOU GOT HIT IN THE FACE THREE TIMES IN A ROW...
EVER SINCE THEN YOU'D START TO CRY EVERY TIME YOU SAW A BASEBALL, SO...
THAT— THAT'S CHILD ABUSE!
SO? WHAT ABOUT CATCH?
FINE.
TO ATONE FOR YOUR SIN OF CHILD ABUSE, GIVE ME A GLOVE THAT CAN CATCH ANY BALL EASILY.

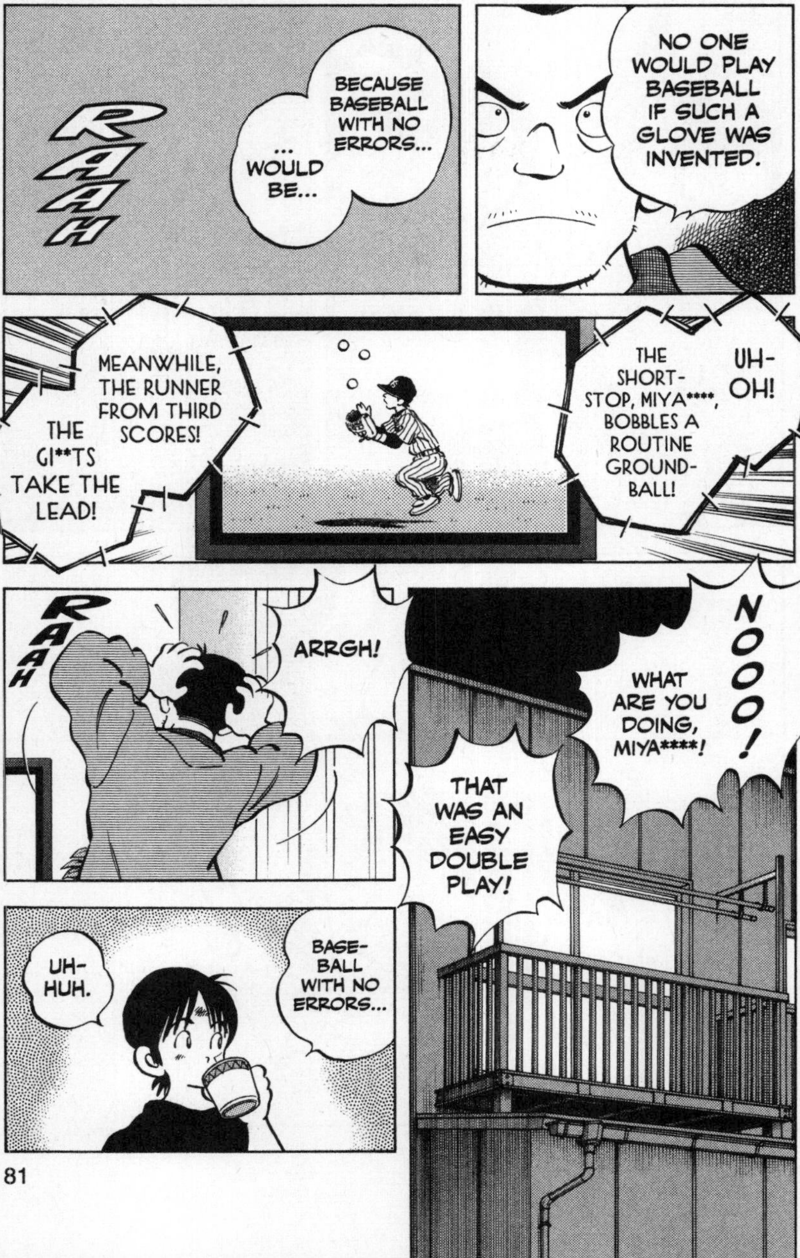
NO ONE WOULD PLAY BASEBALL IF SUCH A GLOVE WAS INVENTED.
BECAUSE BASEBALL WITH NO ERRORS...
... WOULD BE...
RAAAH
UH-OH!
THE SHORT-STOP, MIYA****, BOBBLES A ROUTINE GROUND-BALL!
MEANWHILE, THE RUNNER FROM THIRD SCORES!
THE GI**TS TAKE THE LEAD!
NOOOO!
WHAT ARE YOU DOING, MIYA****!
THAT WAS AN EASY DOUBLE PLAY!
ARRGH!
RAAAH
BASE-BALL WITH NO ERRORS...
UH-HUH.

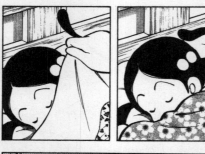

GREAT JOB!

MOMIJI TSUKI-SHIMA

MOM

CHAPTER 5
JUST BARELY SAFE

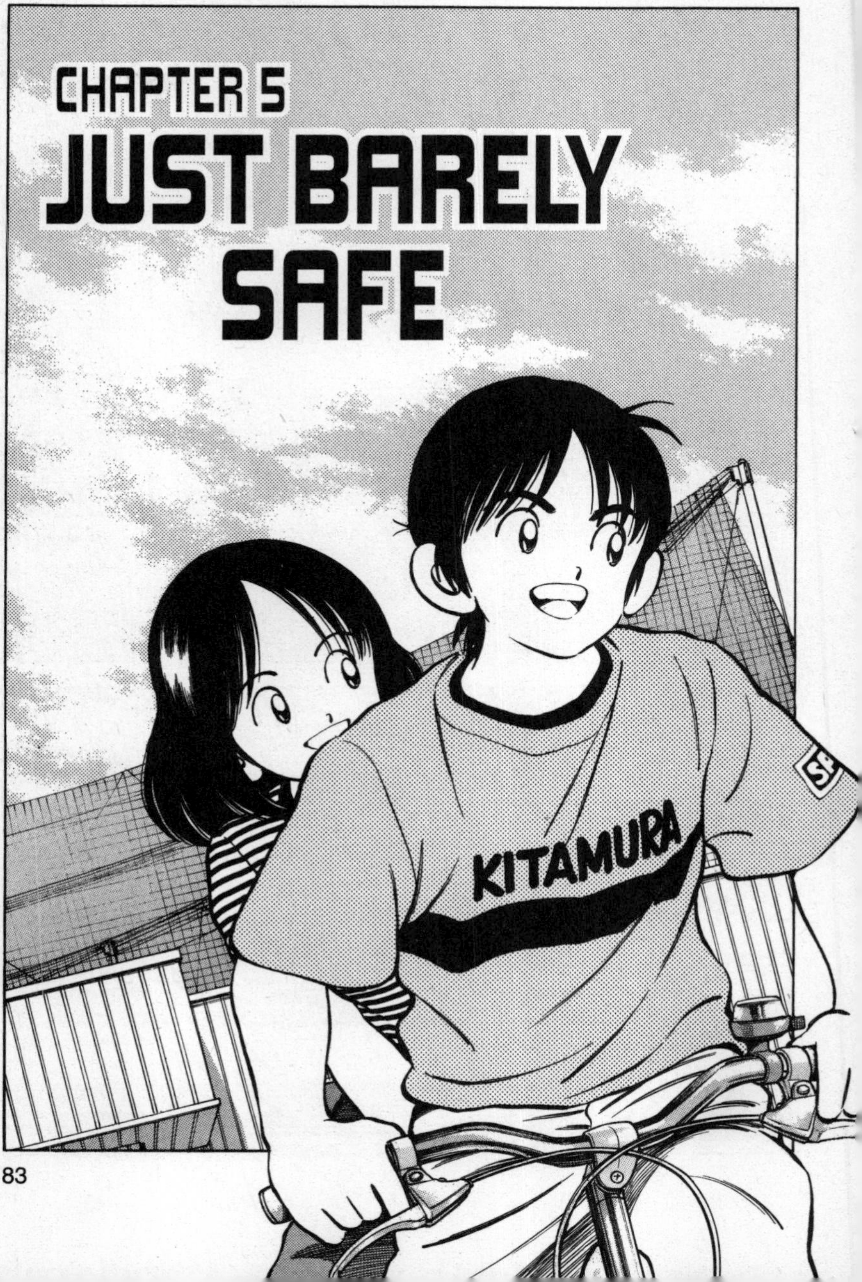

KITAMURA
SP

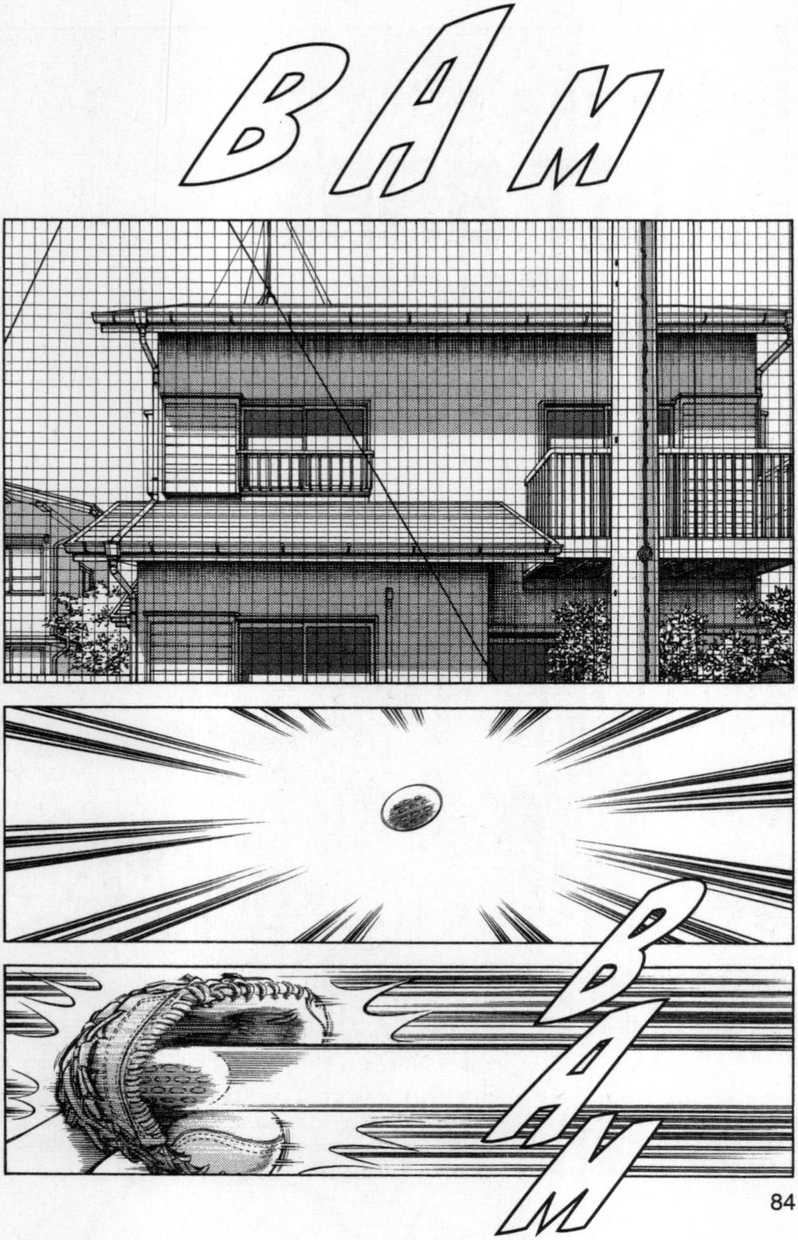
BAM
BAM

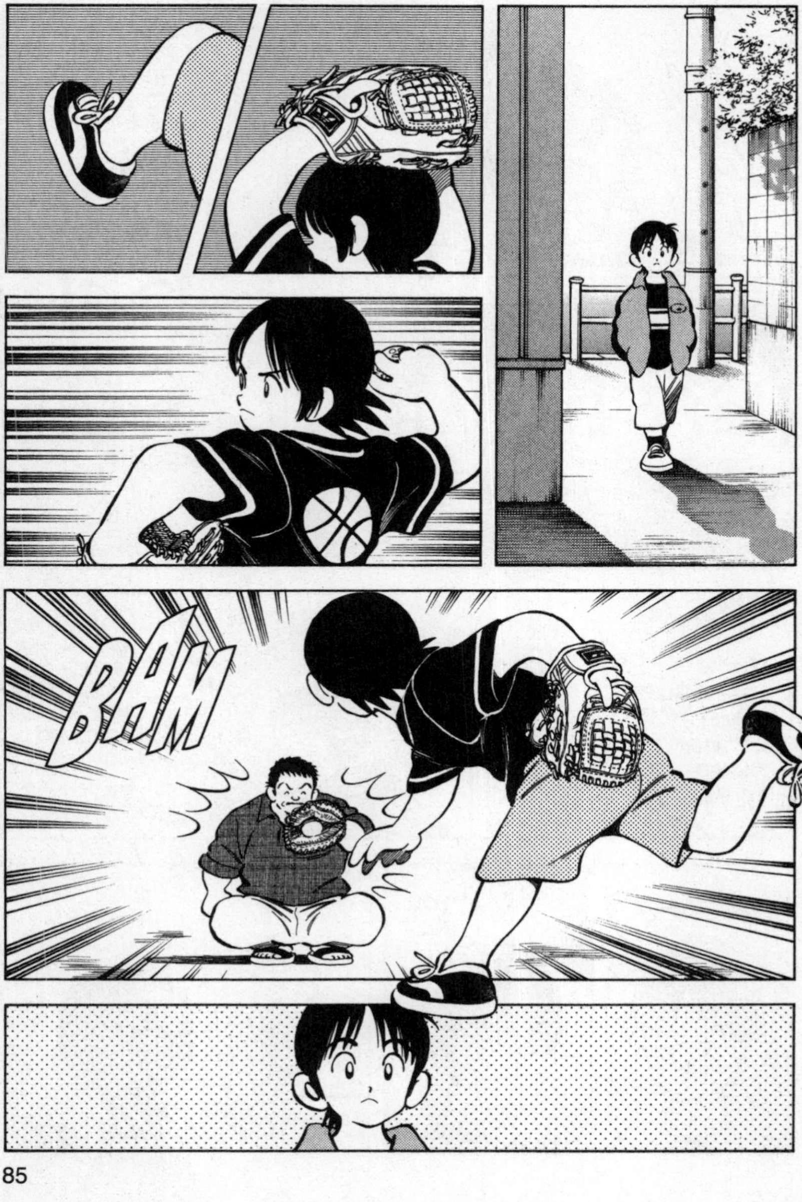
BAM

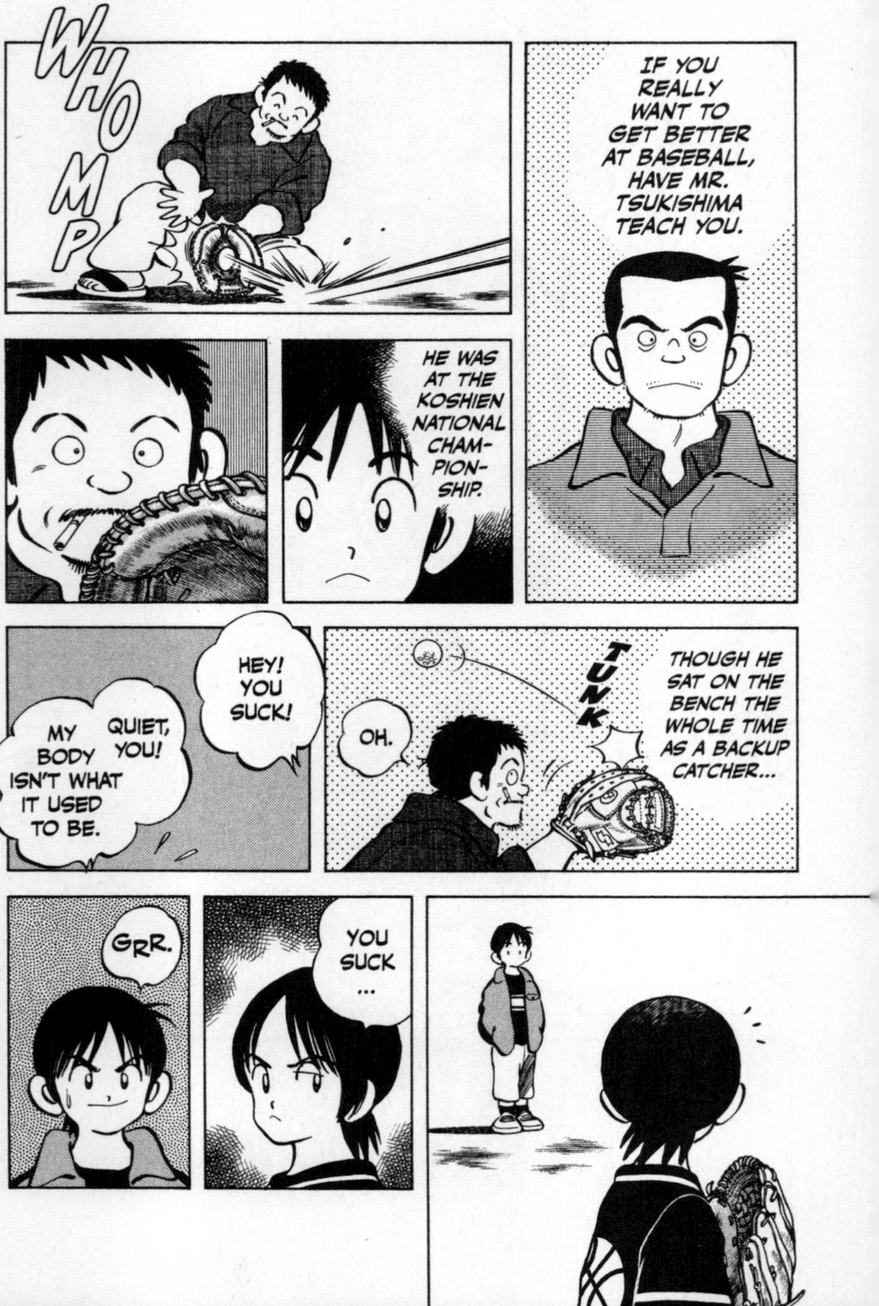
IF YOU REALLY WANT TO GET BETTER AT BASEBALL, HAVE MR. TSUKISHIMA TEACH YOU.
WHOMP
HE WAS AT THE KOSHIEN NATIONAL CHAMPIONSHIP.
THOUGH HE SAT ON THE BENCH THE WHOLE TIME AS A BACKUP CATCHER...
TUNK
OH.
HEY! YOU SUCK!
QUIET, YOU!
MY BODY ISN'T WHAT IT USED TO BE.
YOU SUCK ...
GRR.

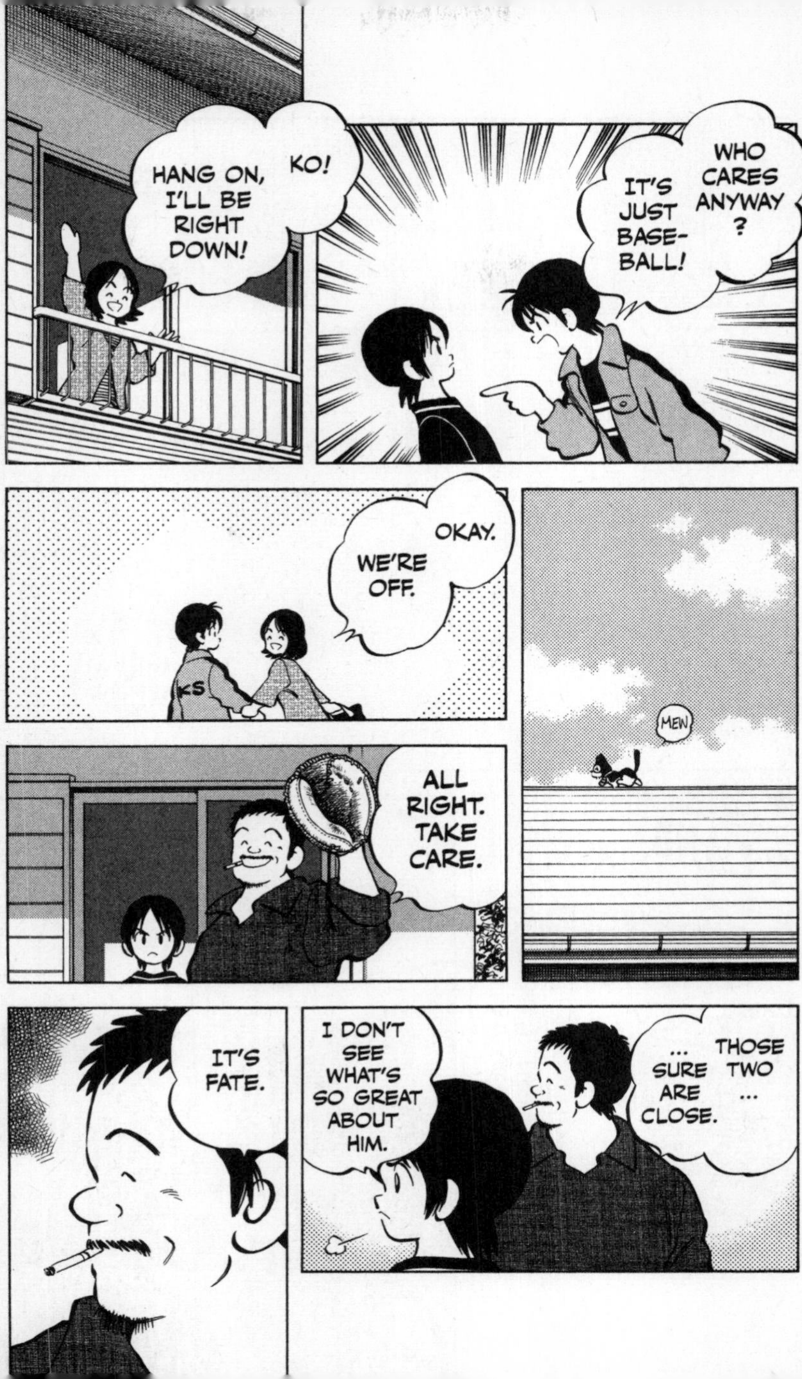
WHO CARES ANYWAY? IT'S JUST BASEBALL!
KO!
HANG ON, I'LL BE RIGHT DOWN!
MEW
OKAY.
WE'RE OFF.
ALL RIGHT. TAKE CARE.
THOSE TWO... ...SURE ARE CLOSE.
I DON'T SEE WHAT'S SO GREAT ABOUT HIM.
IT'S FATE.

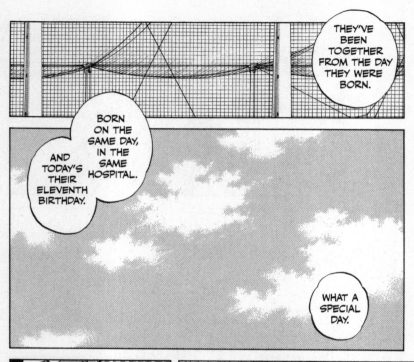

THEY'VE BEEN TOGETHER FROM THE DAY THEY WERE BORN.

BORN ON THE SAME DAY, IN THE SAME HOSPITAL.

AND TODAY'S THEIR ELEVENTH BIRTHDAY.

WHAT A SPECIAL DAY.

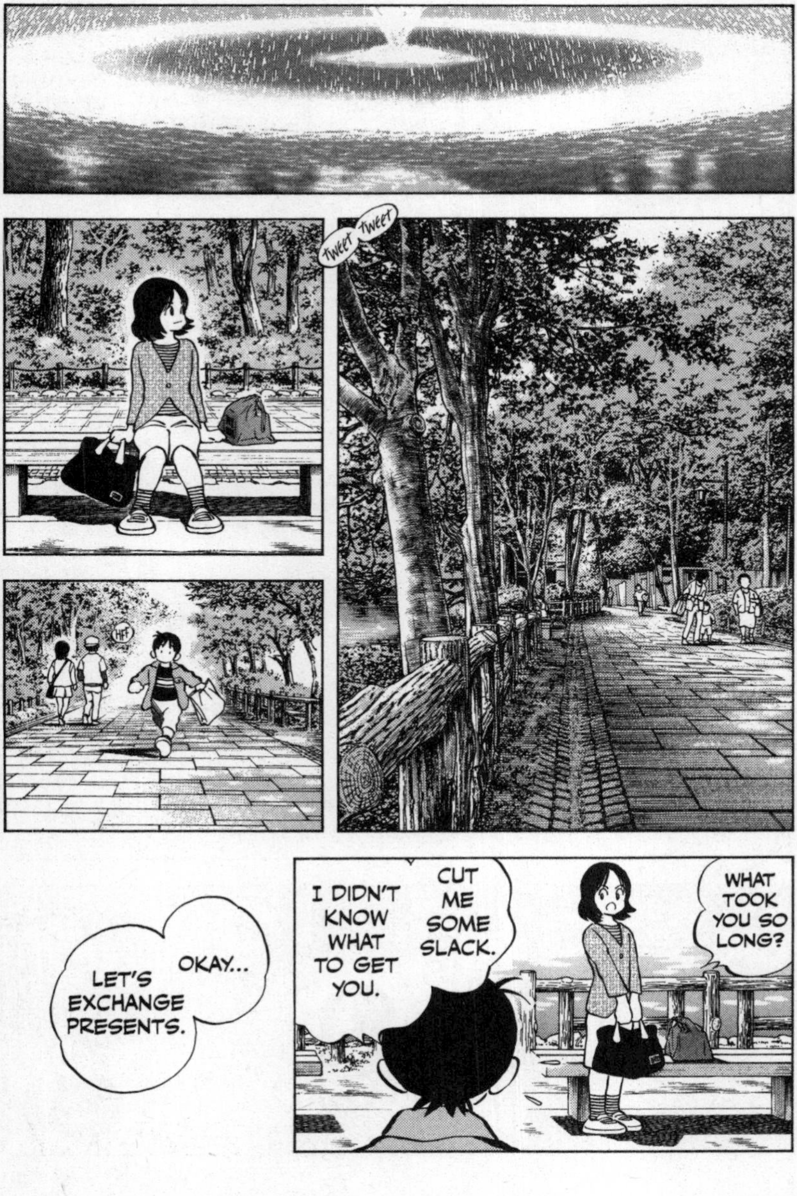
TWEET TWEET
HFF
WHAT TOOK YOU SO LONG?
CUT ME SOME SLACK.
I DIDN'T KNOW WHAT TO GET YOU.
OKAY...
LET'S EXCHANGE PRESENTS.

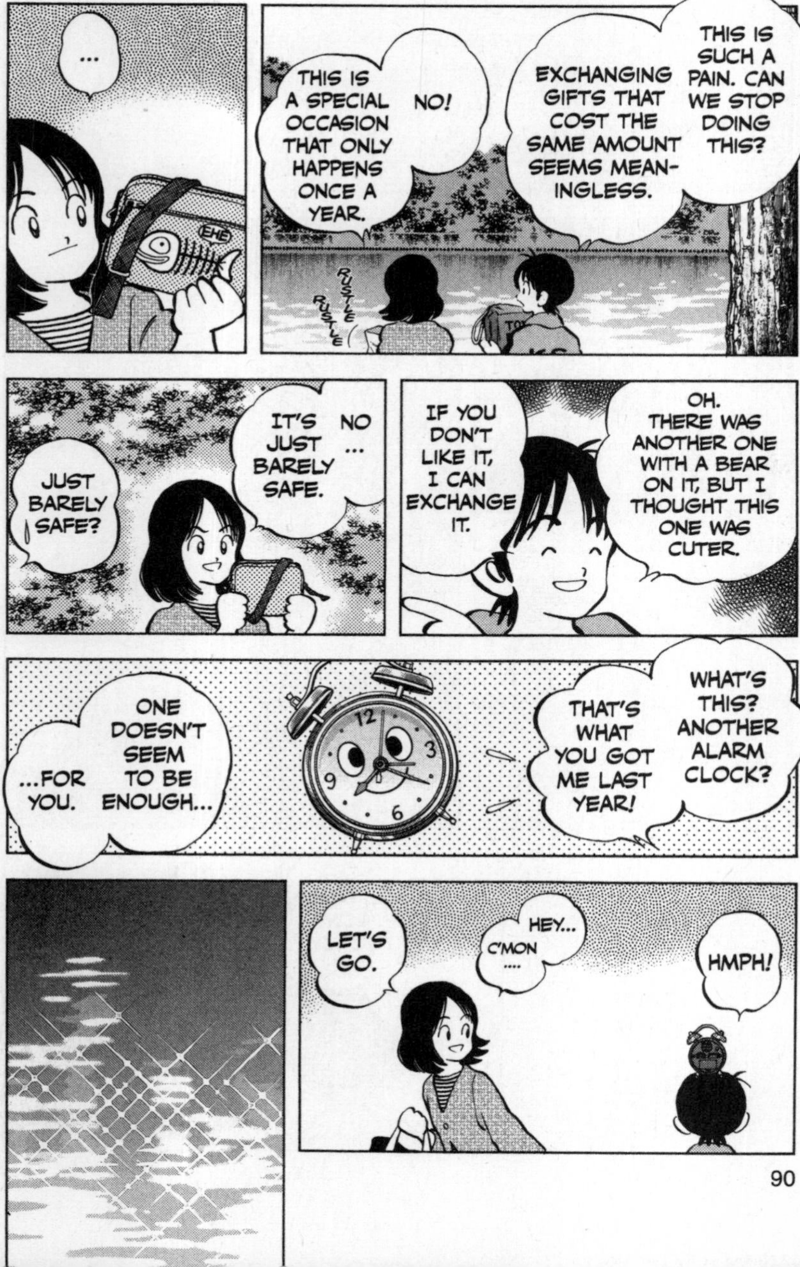
THIS IS SUCH A PAIN. CAN WE STOP DOING THIS?
EXCHANGING GIFTS THAT COST THE SAME AMOUNT SEEMS MEAN-INGLESS.
NO!
THIS IS A SPECIAL OCCASION THAT ONLY HAPPENS ONCE A YEAR.
RUSTLE RUSTLE
...
EHE
OH. THERE WAS ANOTHER ONE WITH A BEAR ON IT, BUT I THOUGHT THIS ONE WAS CUTER.
IF YOU DON'T LIKE IT, I CAN EXCHANGE IT.
NO ...
IT'S JUST BARELY SAFE.
JUST BARELY SAFE?
WHAT'S THIS? ANOTHER ALARM CLOCK?
THAT'S WHAT YOU GOT ME LAST YEAR!
ONE DOESN'T SEEM TO BE ENOUGH...
...FOR YOU.
HMPH!
HEY... C'MON ....
LET'S GO.

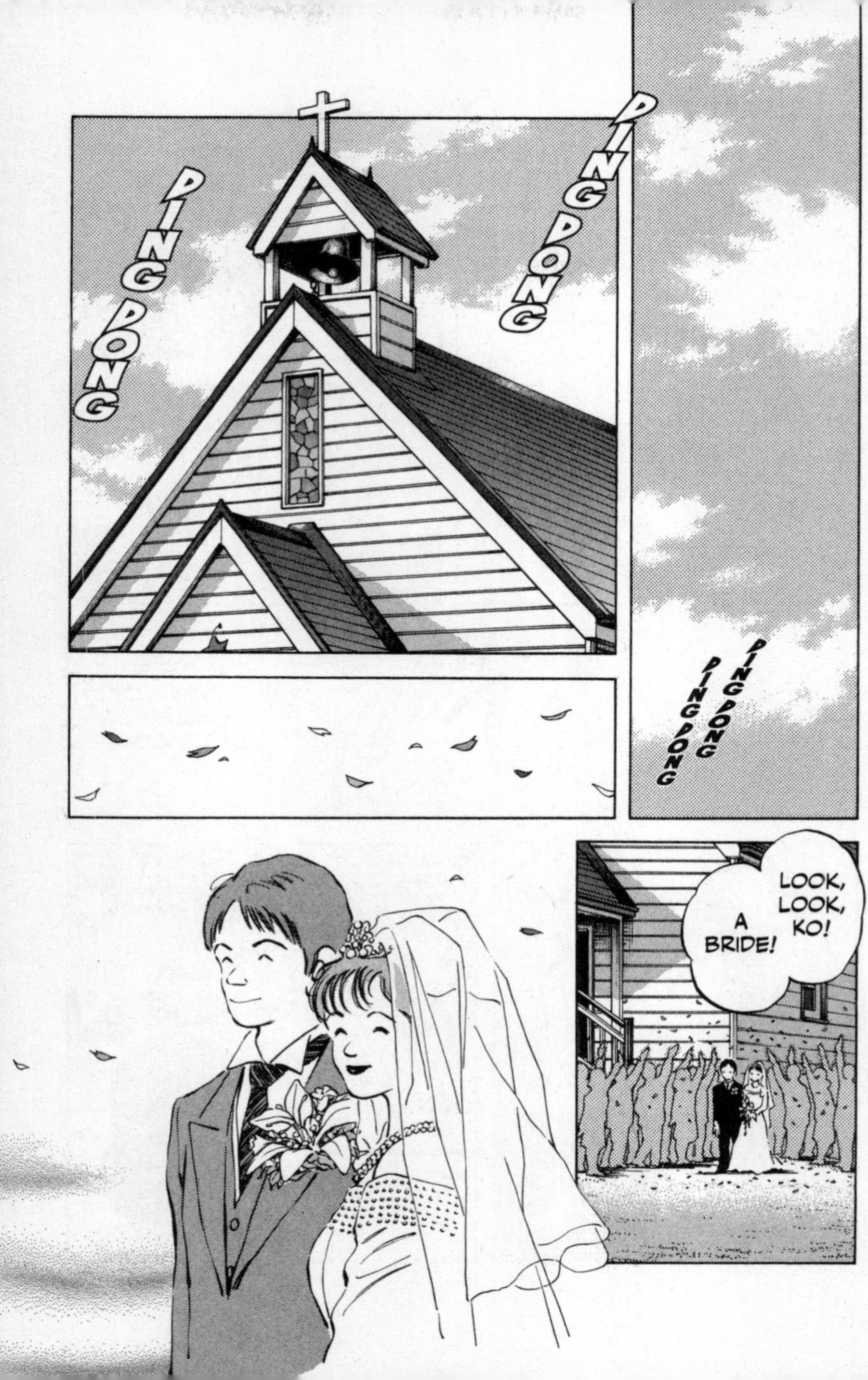
DING DONG
DING DONG
DING DONG
DING DONG
LOOK, LOOK, KO! A BRIDE!

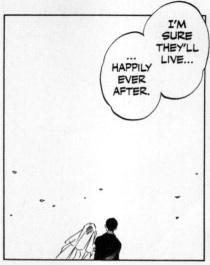

SHE'S SO PRETTY ...
YOU THINK?
SHE LOOKS AVERAGE TO ME.
I'M SURE THEY'LL LIVE...
... HAPPILY EVER AFTER.
AFTER ALL, THEY GOT MARRIED ON OUR BIRTHDAY.
...
HUH?
UH.
YEAH, SURE.

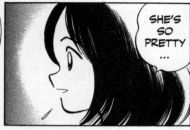

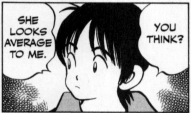

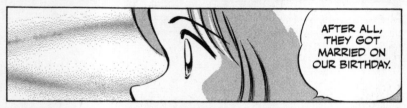

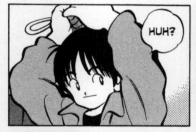

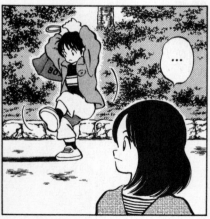

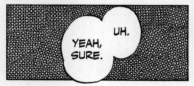

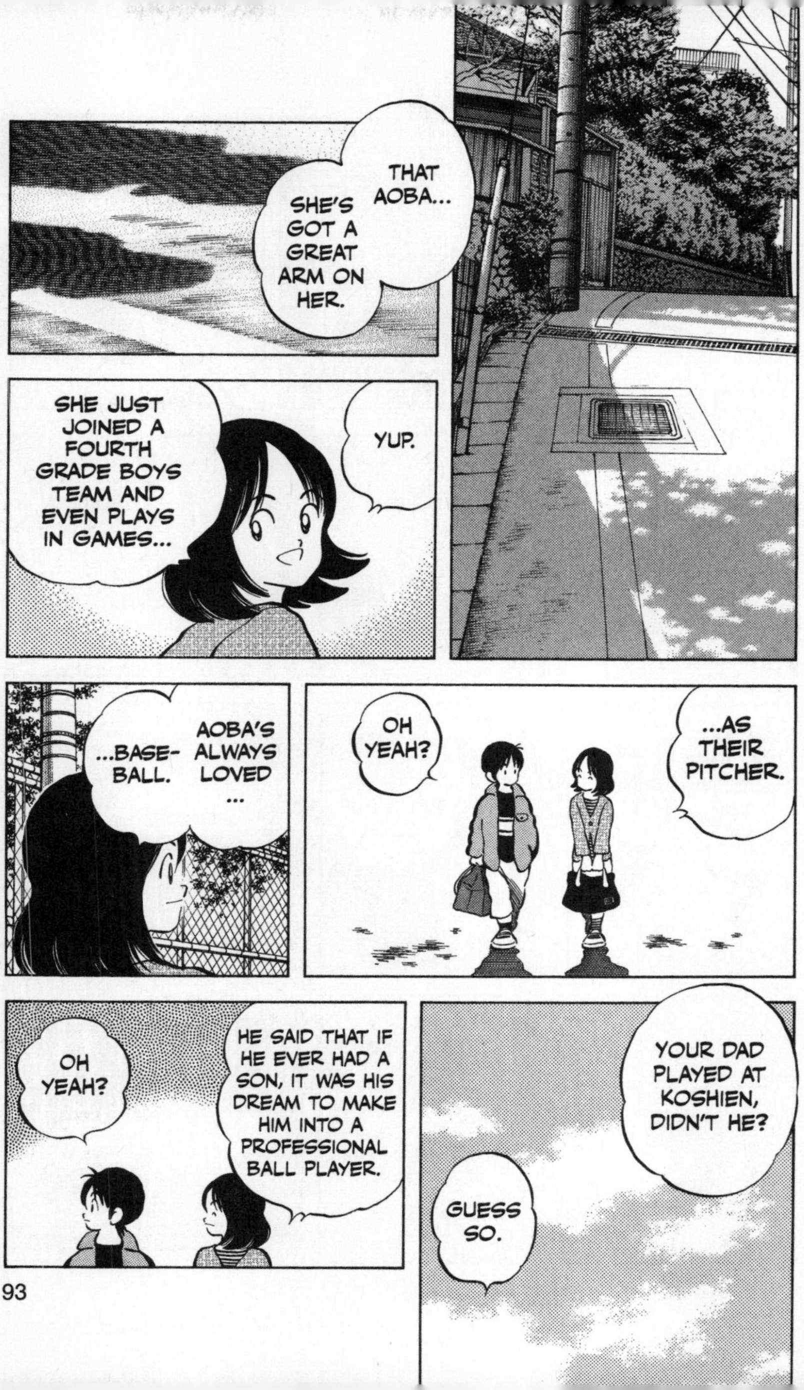
THAT AOBA... SHE'S GOT A GREAT ARM ON HER.
YUP.
SHE JUST JOINED A FOURTH GRADE BOYS TEAM AND EVEN PLAYS IN GAMES...
...AS THEIR PITCHER.
OH YEAH?
AOBA'S ALWAYS LOVED ...
...BASE-BALL.
YOUR DAD PLAYED AT KOSHIEN, DIDN'T HE?
GUESS SO.
HE SAID THAT IF HE EVER HAD A SON, IT WAS HIS DREAM TO MAKE HIM INTO A PROFESSIONAL BALL PLAYER.
OH YEAH?

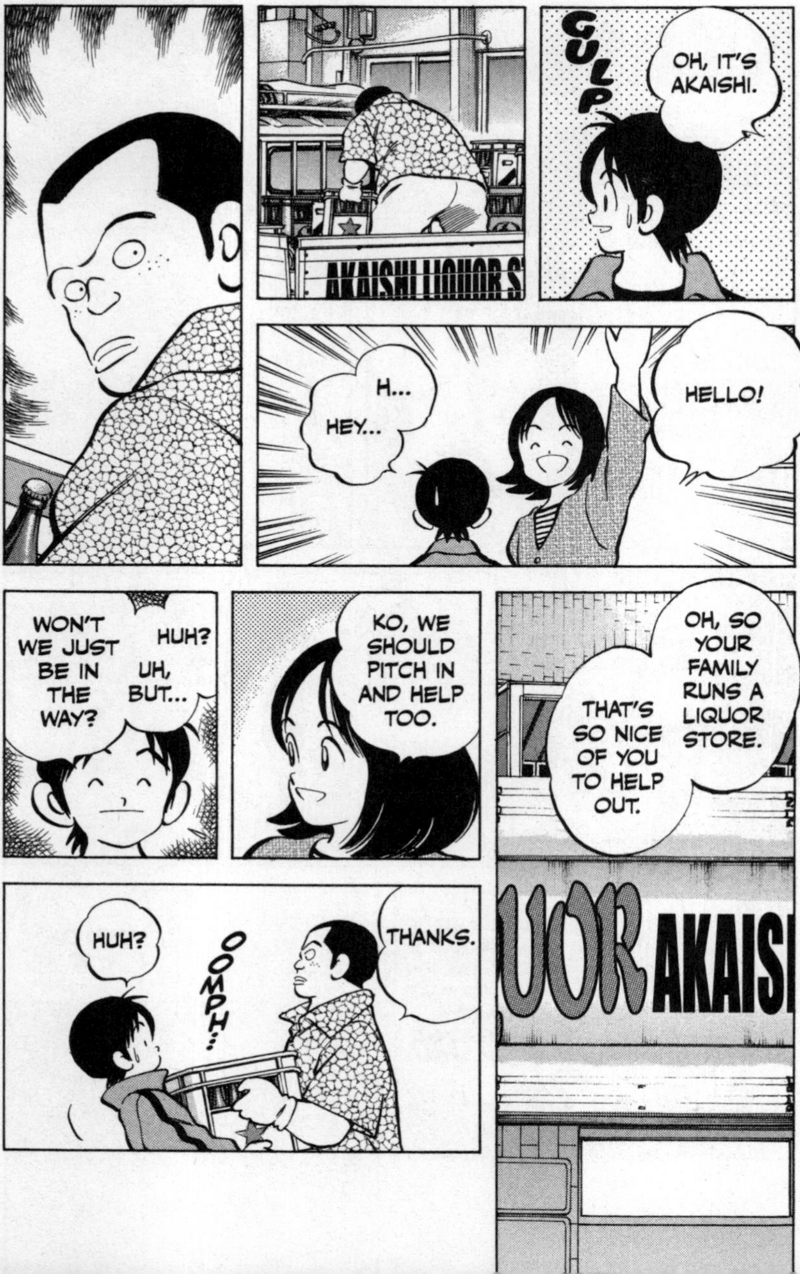
GULP
OH, IT'S AKAISHI.
AKAISHI LIQUOR S
HELLO!
H... HEY...
OH, SO YOUR FAMILY RUNS A LIQUOR STORE.
THAT'S SO NICE OF YOU TO HELP OUT.
UOR AKAISI
KO, WE SHOULD PITCH IN AND HELP TOO.
HUH? UH, BUT...
WON'T WE JUST BE IN THE WAY?
THANKS.
OOMPH...
HUH?

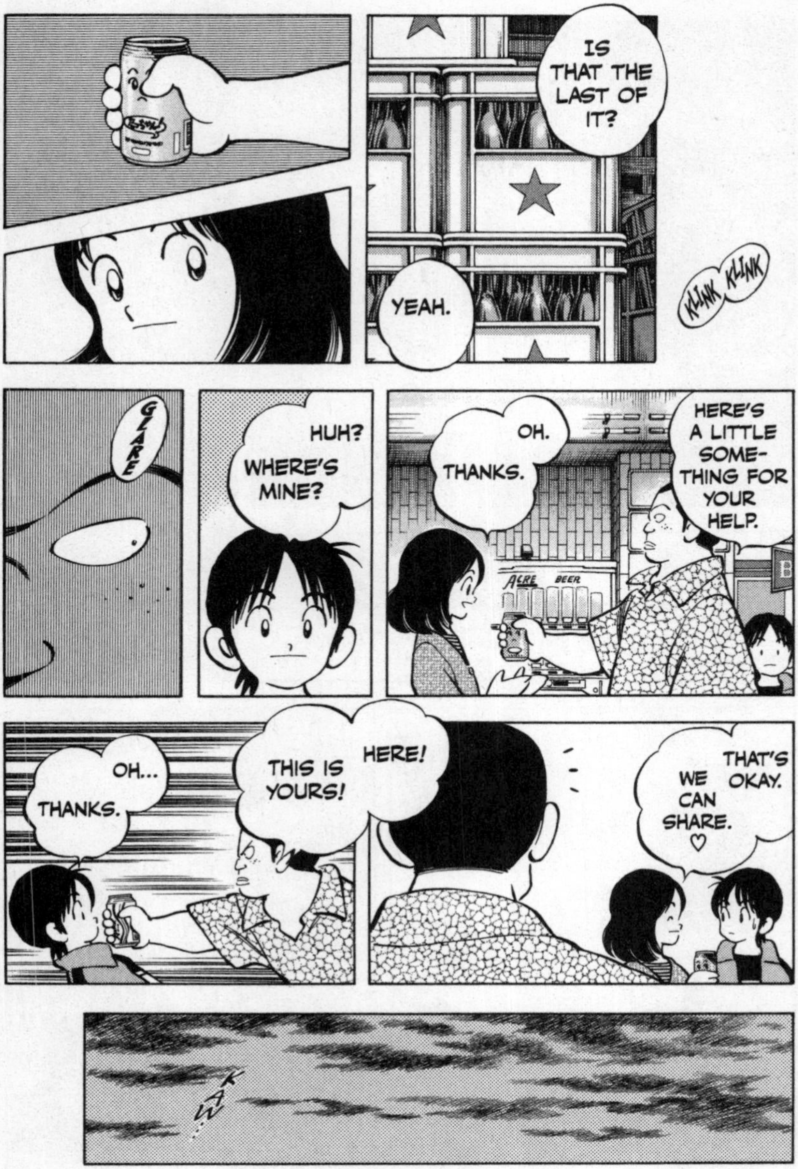
IS THAT THE LAST OF IT?
YEAH.
KLINK KLINK
HERE'S A LITTLE SOME-THING FOR YOUR HELP.
OH. THANKS.
ALE BEER
HUH? WHERE'S MINE?
GLARE
THAT'S OKAY. WE CAN SHARE. ♡
HERE! THIS IS YOURS!
OH... THANKS.
KAW...

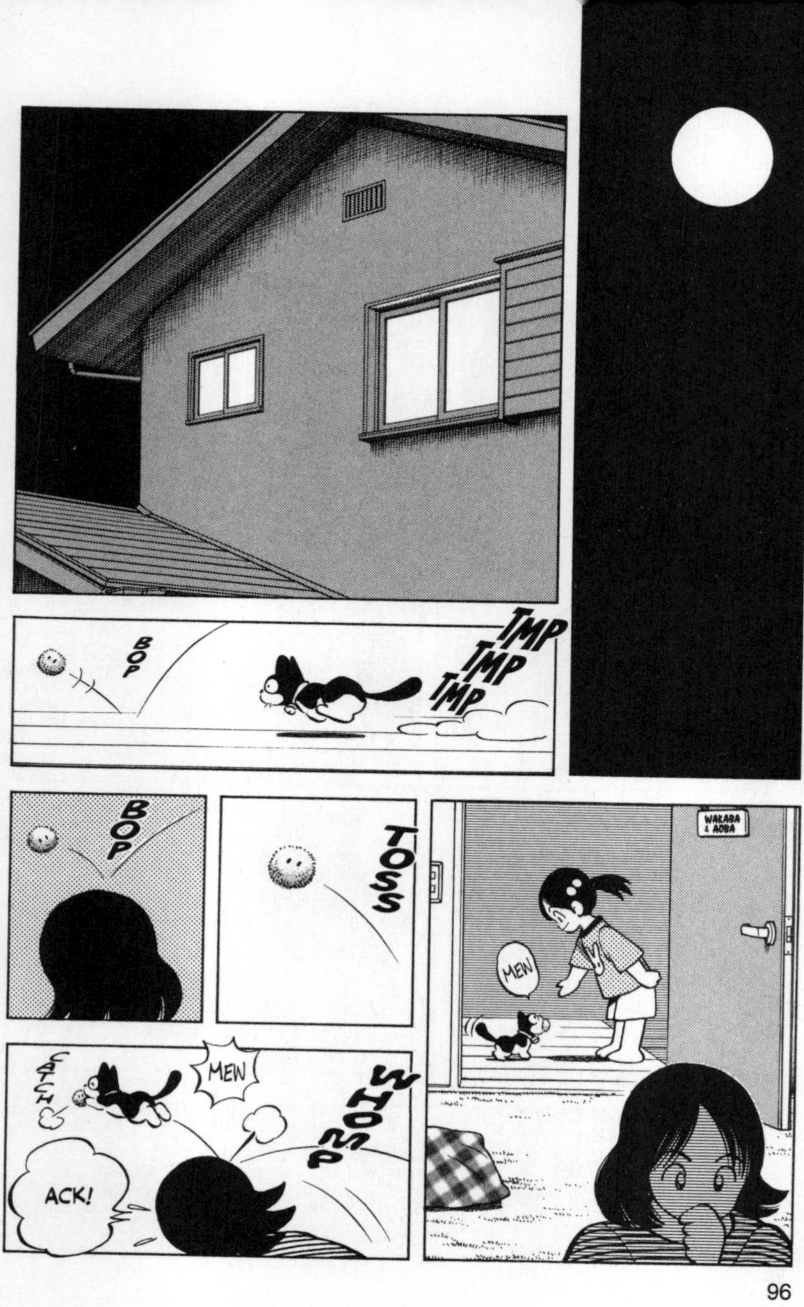

TMP TMP TMP
BOP
WAKABA & AOBA
MEW
TOSS
BOP
WHOMP
MEW
CATCH
ACK!

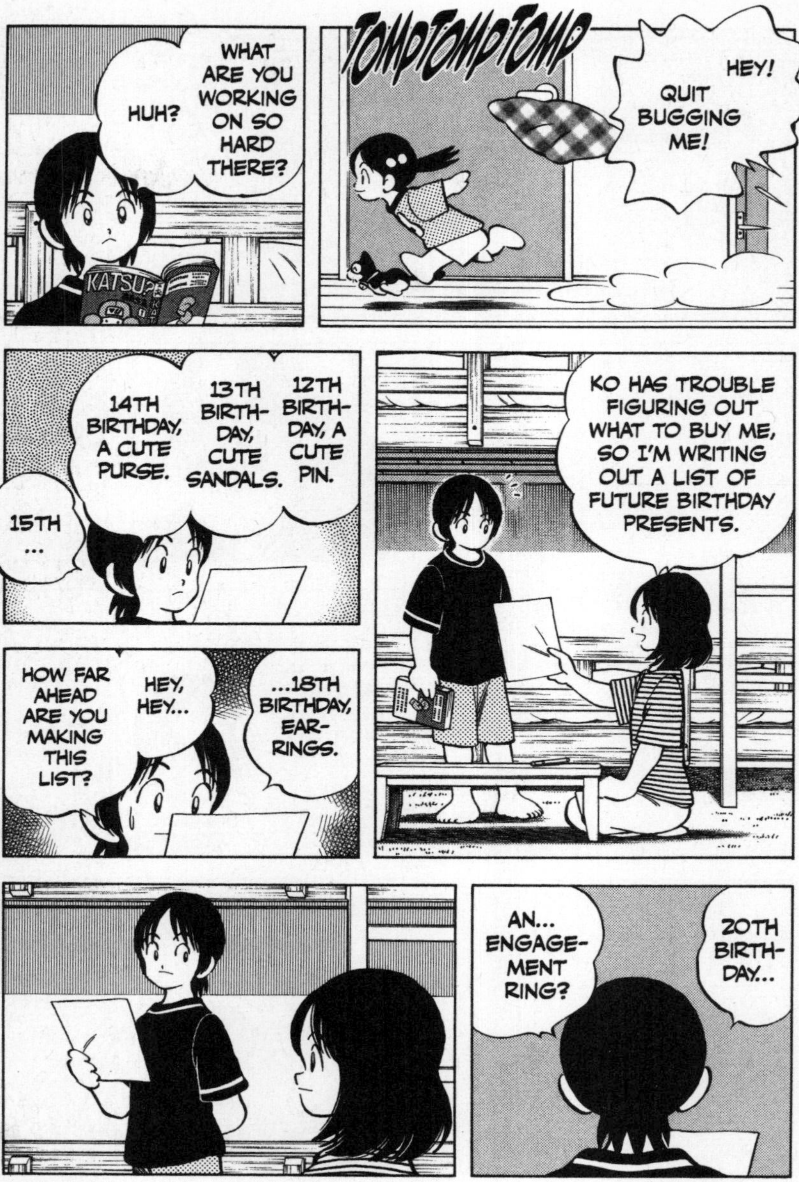
TOMP TOMP TOMP
HEY!
QUIT BUGGING ME!
WHAT ARE YOU WORKING ON SO HARD THERE?
HUH?
KO HAS TROUBLE FIGURING OUT WHAT TO BUY ME, SO I'M WRITING OUT A LIST OF FUTURE BIRTHDAY PRESENTS.
12TH BIRTH-DAY, A CUTE PIN.
13TH BIRTH-DAY, CUTE SANDALS.
14TH BIRTHDAY, A CUTE PURSE.
15TH ...
...18TH BIRTHDAY, EAR-RINGS.
HEY, HEY...
HOW FAR AHEAD ARE YOU MAKING THIS LIST?
20TH BIRTH-DAY...
AN... ENGAGE-MENT RING?

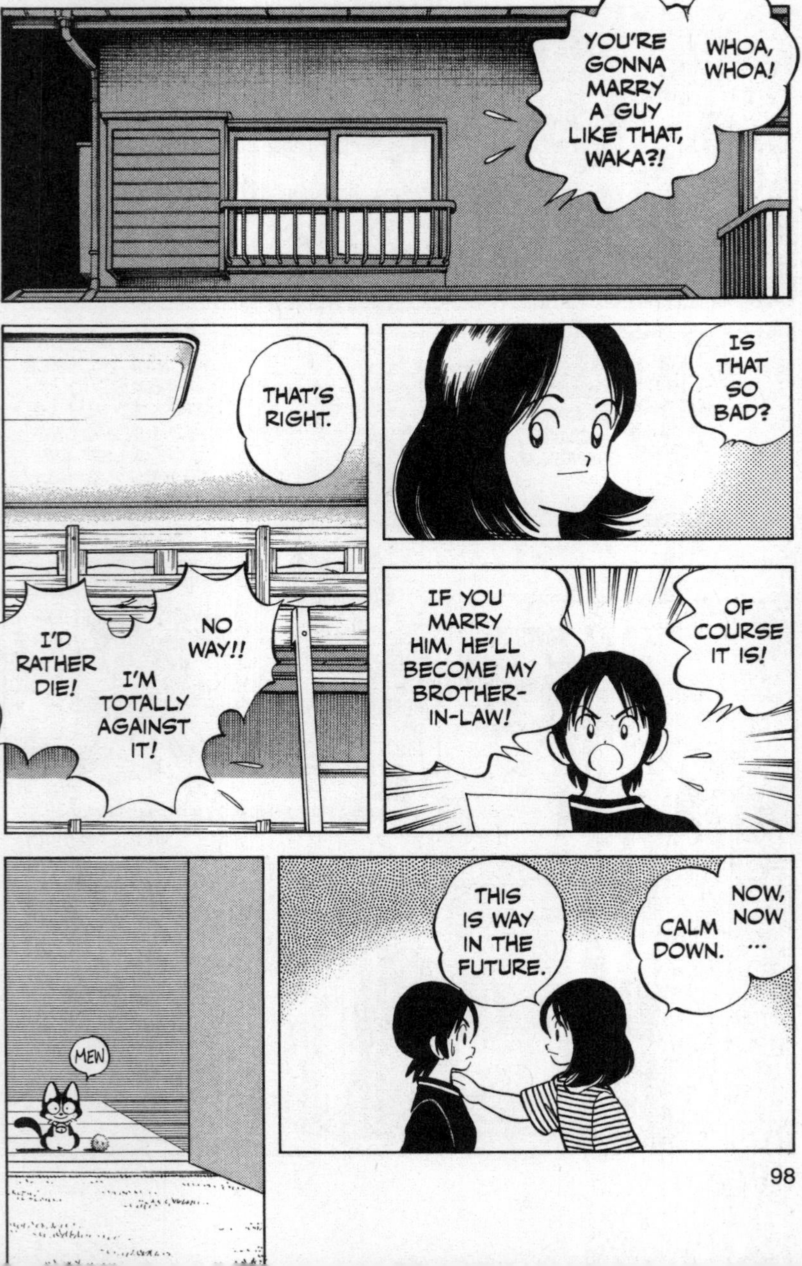
WHOA, WHOA!
YOU'RE GONNA MARRY A GUY LIKE THAT, WAKA?!
IS THAT SO BAD?
OF COURSE IT IS!
IF YOU MARRY HIM, HE'LL BECOME MY BROTHER-IN-LAW!
THAT'S RIGHT.
NO WAY!!
I'M TOTALLY AGAINST IT!
I'D RATHER DIE!
NOW, NOW ...
CALM DOWN.
THIS IS WAY IN THE FUTURE.
MEW

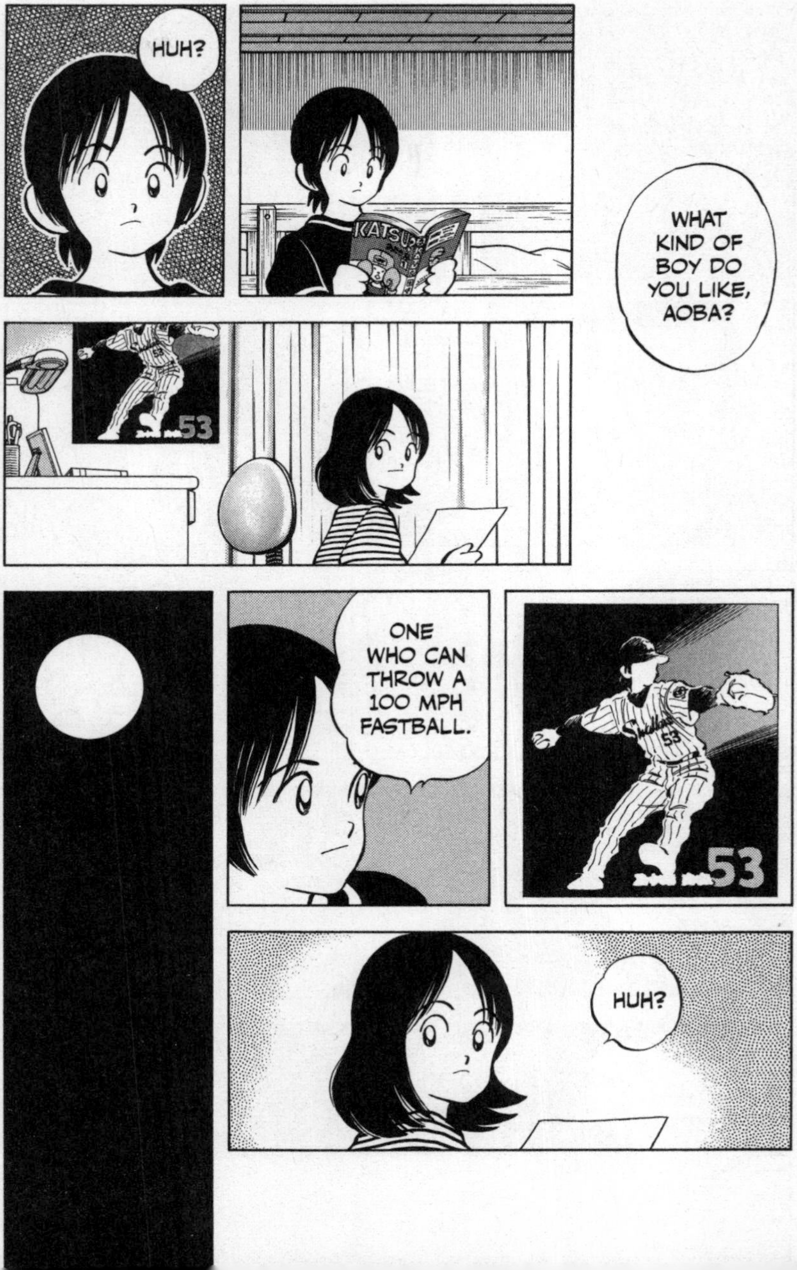
WHAT KIND OF BOY DO YOU LIKE, AOBA?
HUH?
53
ONE WHO CAN THROW A 100 MPH FASTBALL.
53
HUH?

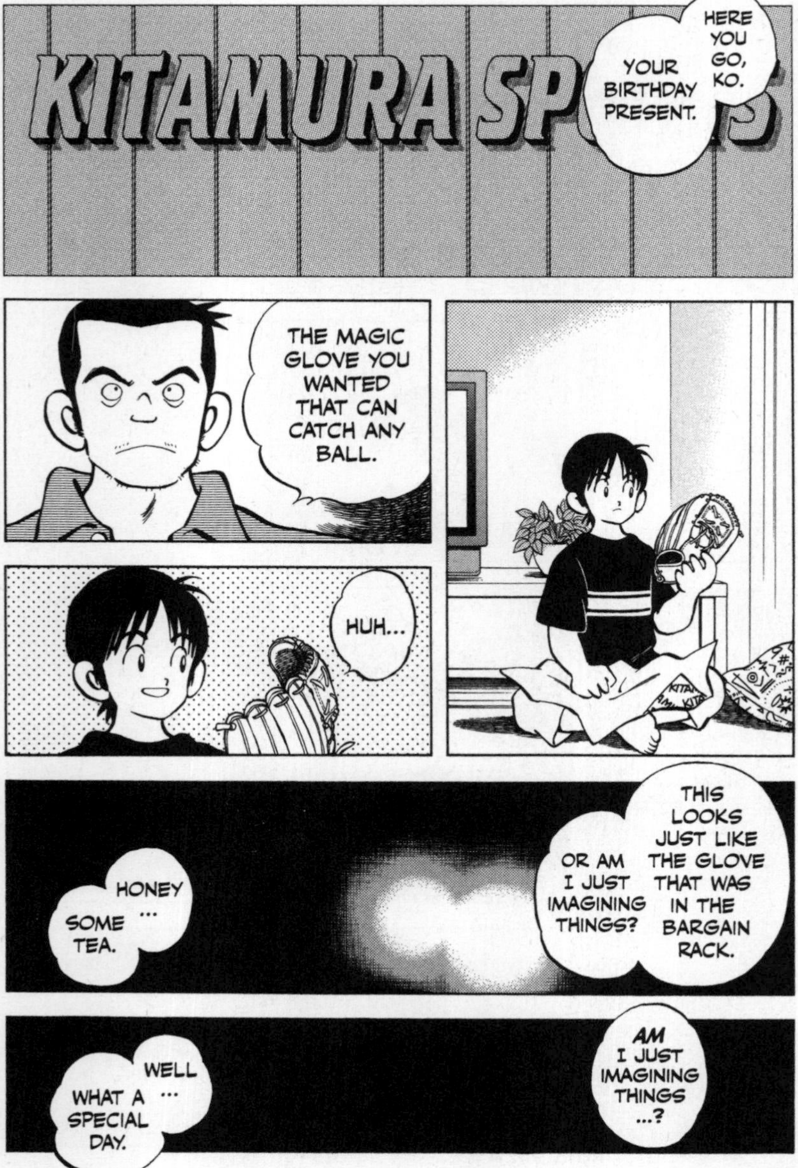
KITAMURA SP
HERE YOU GO, KO.
YOUR BIRTHDAY PRESENT.
THE MAGIC GLOVE YOU WANTED THAT CAN CATCH ANY BALL.
HUH...
THIS LOOKS JUST LIKE THE GLOVE THAT WAS IN THE BARGAIN RACK.
OR AM I JUST IMAGINING THINGS?
HONEY... SOME TEA.
AM I JUST IMAGINING THINGS...?
WELL... WHAT A SPECIAL DAY.

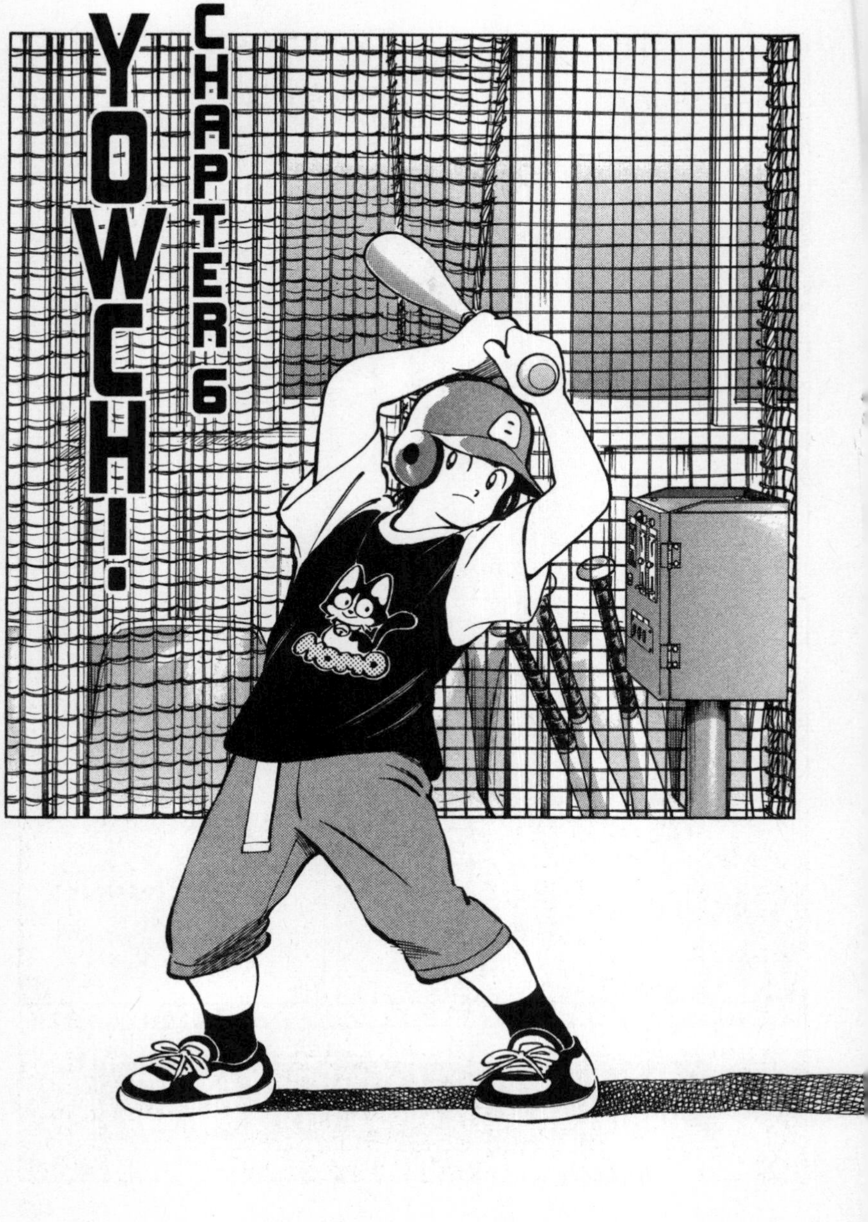
CHAPTER 6
YOWCH!

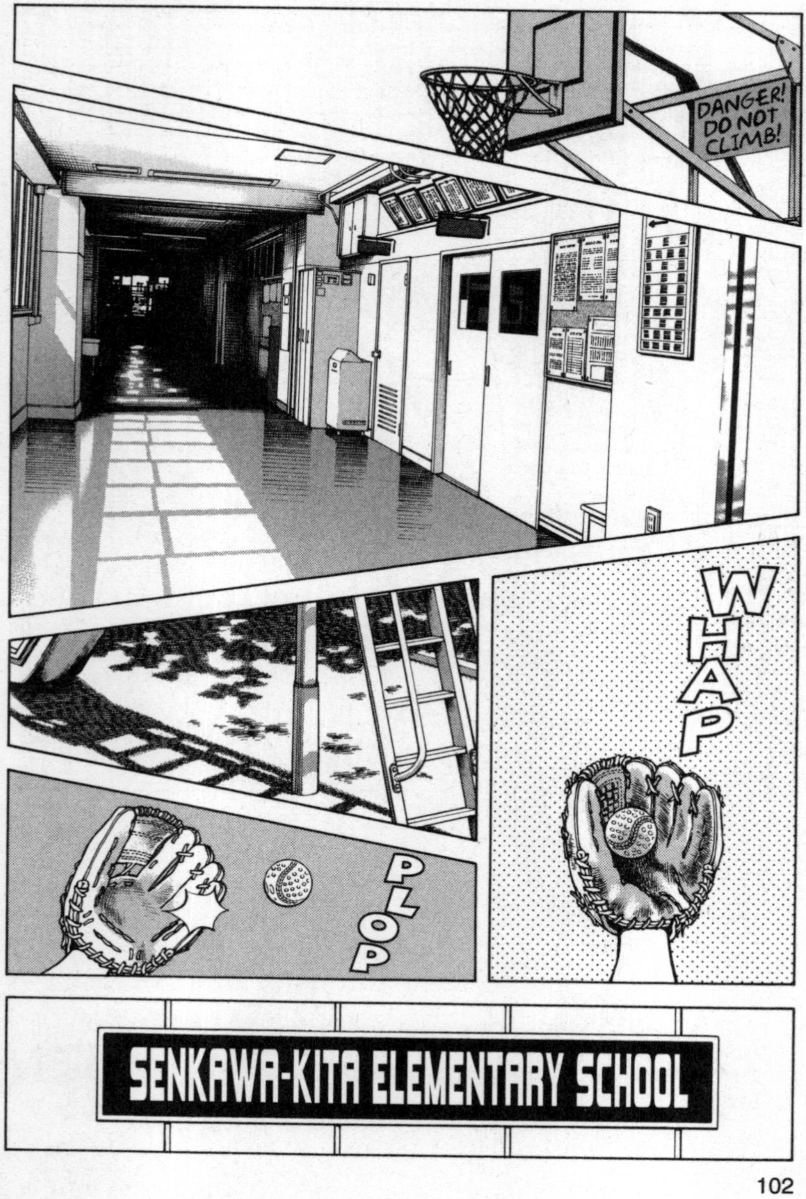
DANGER! DO NOT CLIMB!
WHAP
PLOP
SENKAWA-KITA ELEMENTARY SCHOOL

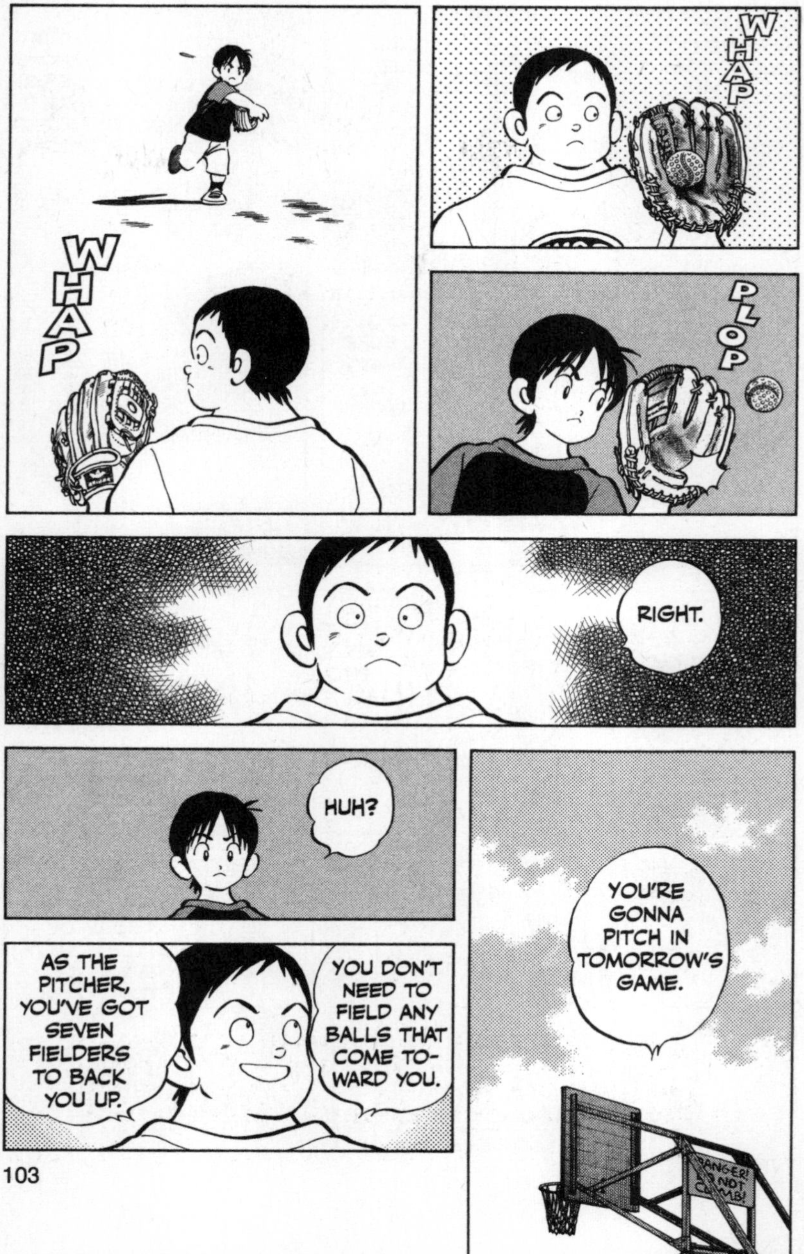
WHAP
PLOP
WHAP
RIGHT.
YOU'RE GONNA PITCH IN TOMORROW'S GAME.
HUH?
YOU DON'T NEED TO FIELD ANY BALLS THAT COME TO-WARD YOU.
AS THE PITCHER, YOU'VE GOT SEVEN FIELDERS TO BACK YOU UP.

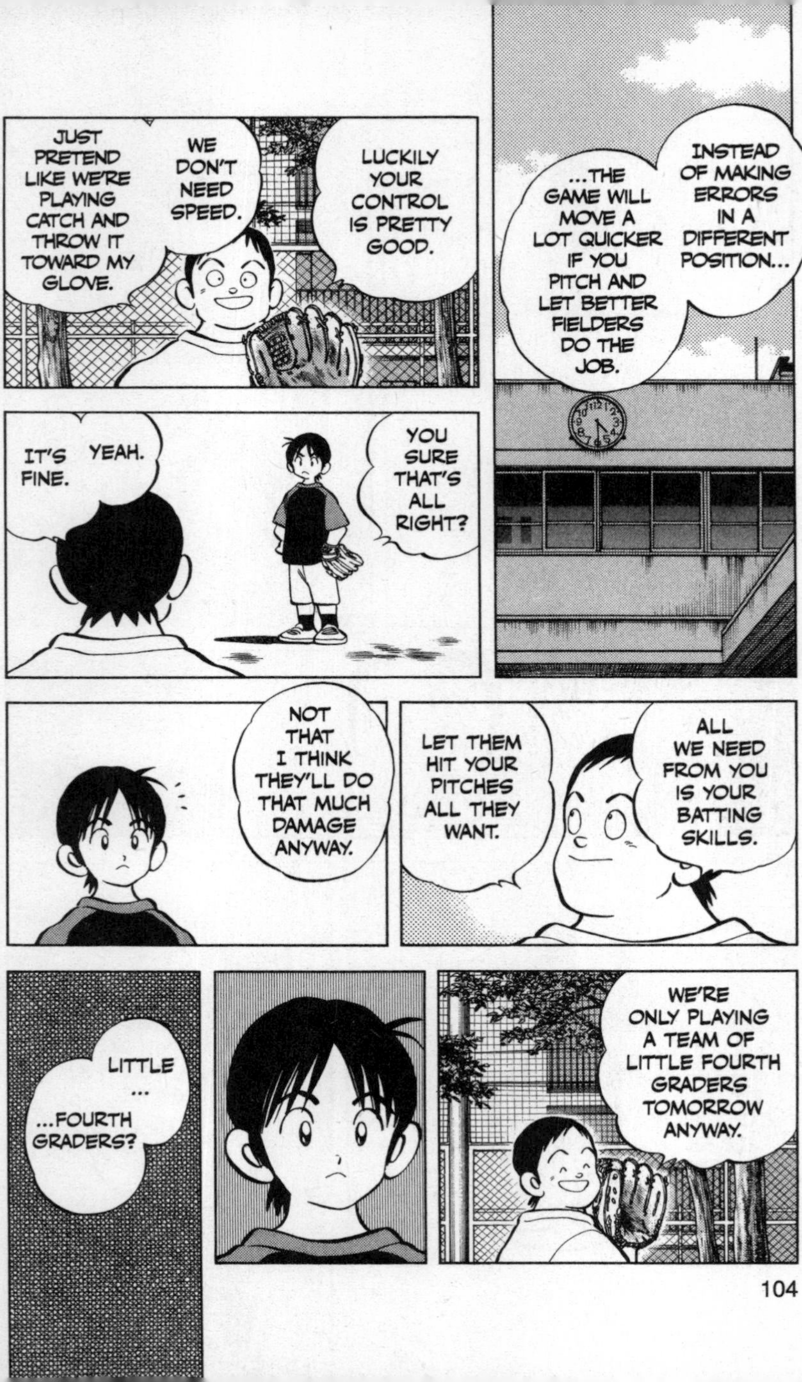
INSTEAD OF MAKING ERRORS IN A DIFFERENT POSITION...
...THE GAME WILL MOVE A LOT QUICKER IF YOU PITCH AND LET BETTER FIELDERS DO THE JOB.
LUCKILY YOUR CONTROL IS PRETTY GOOD.
WE DON'T NEED SPEED.
JUST PRETEND LIKE WE'RE PLAYING CATCH AND THROW IT TOWARD MY GLOVE.
YOU SURE THAT'S ALL RIGHT?
YEAH.
IT'S FINE.
ALL WE NEED FROM YOU IS YOUR BATTING SKILLS.
LET THEM HIT YOUR PITCHES ALL THEY WANT.
NOT THAT I THINK THEY'LL DO THAT MUCH DAMAGE ANYWAY.
WE'RE ONLY PLAYING A TEAM OF LITTLE FOURTH GRADERS TOMORROW ANYWAY.
LITTLE ...
...FOURTH GRADERS?

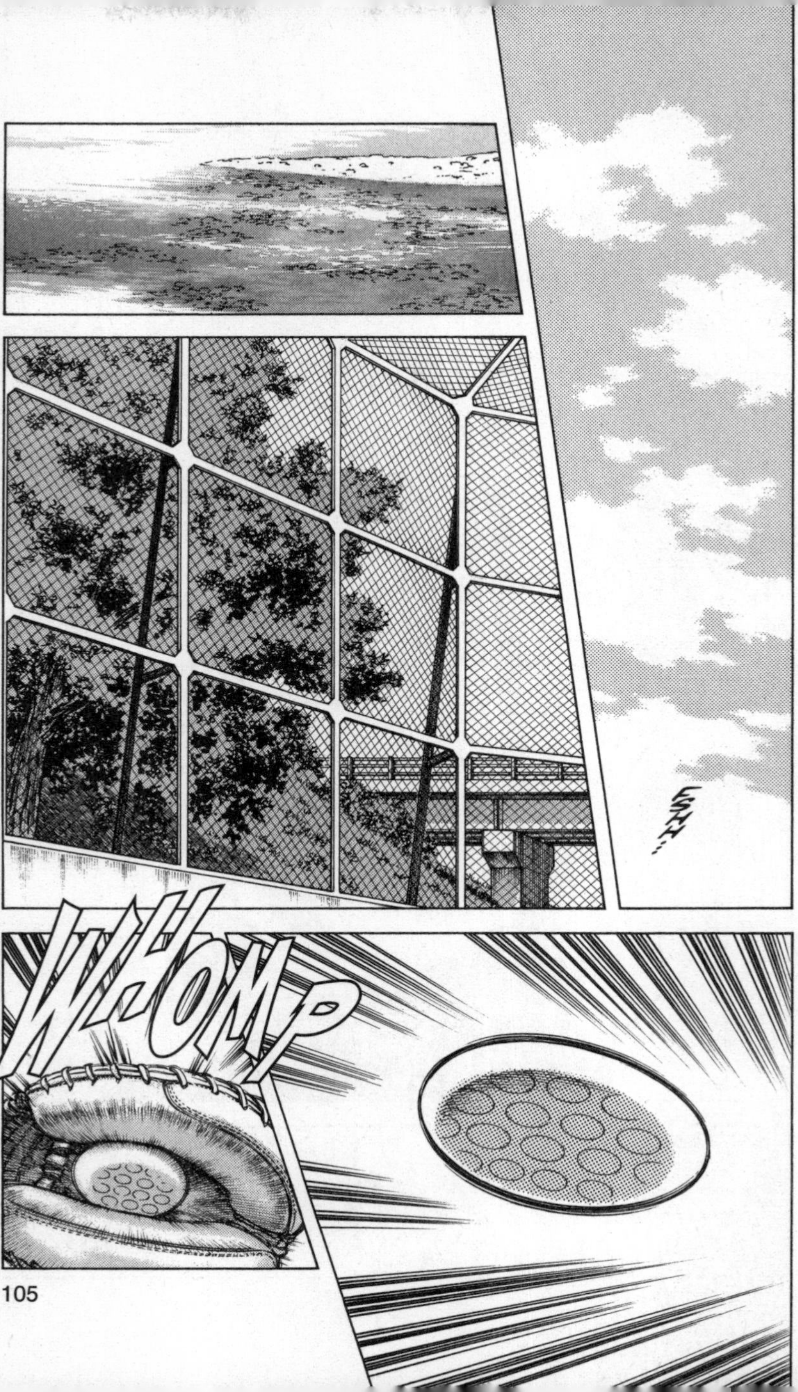
FSHH...
WHOMP

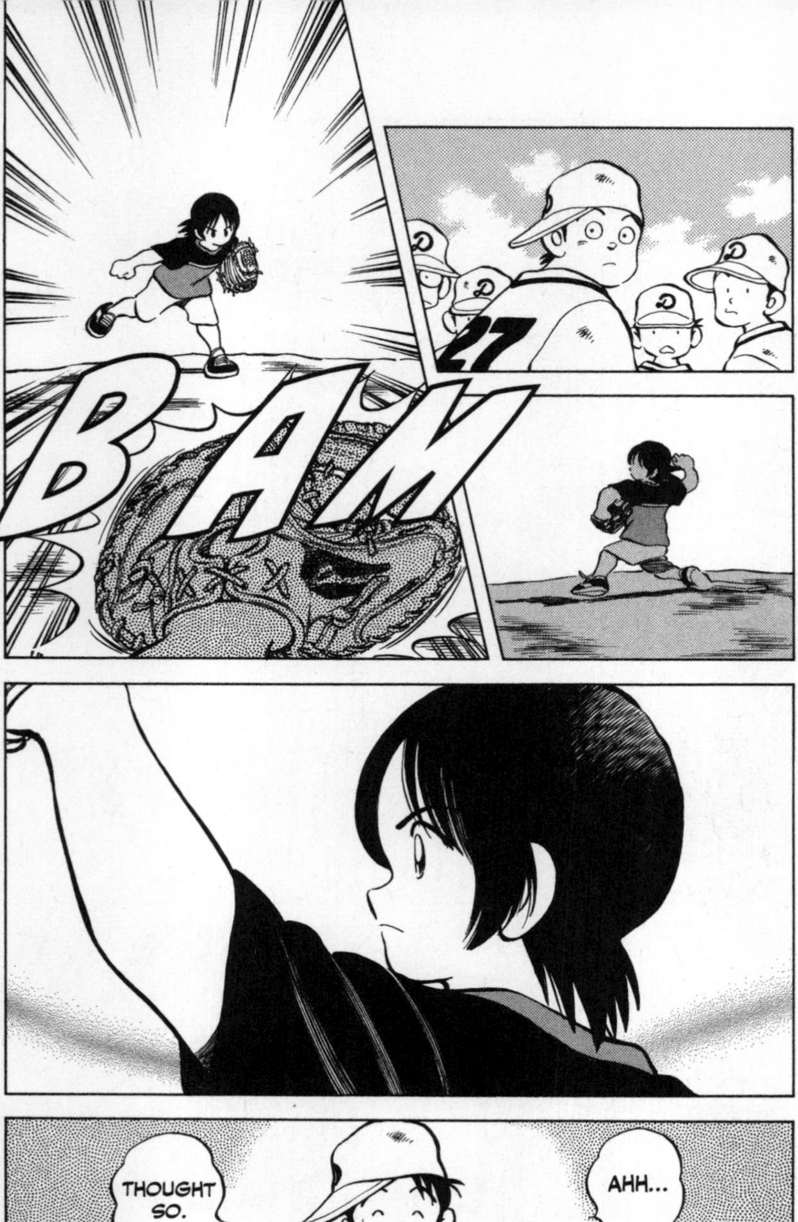
BAM
AHH...
THOUGHT SO.

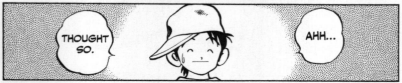

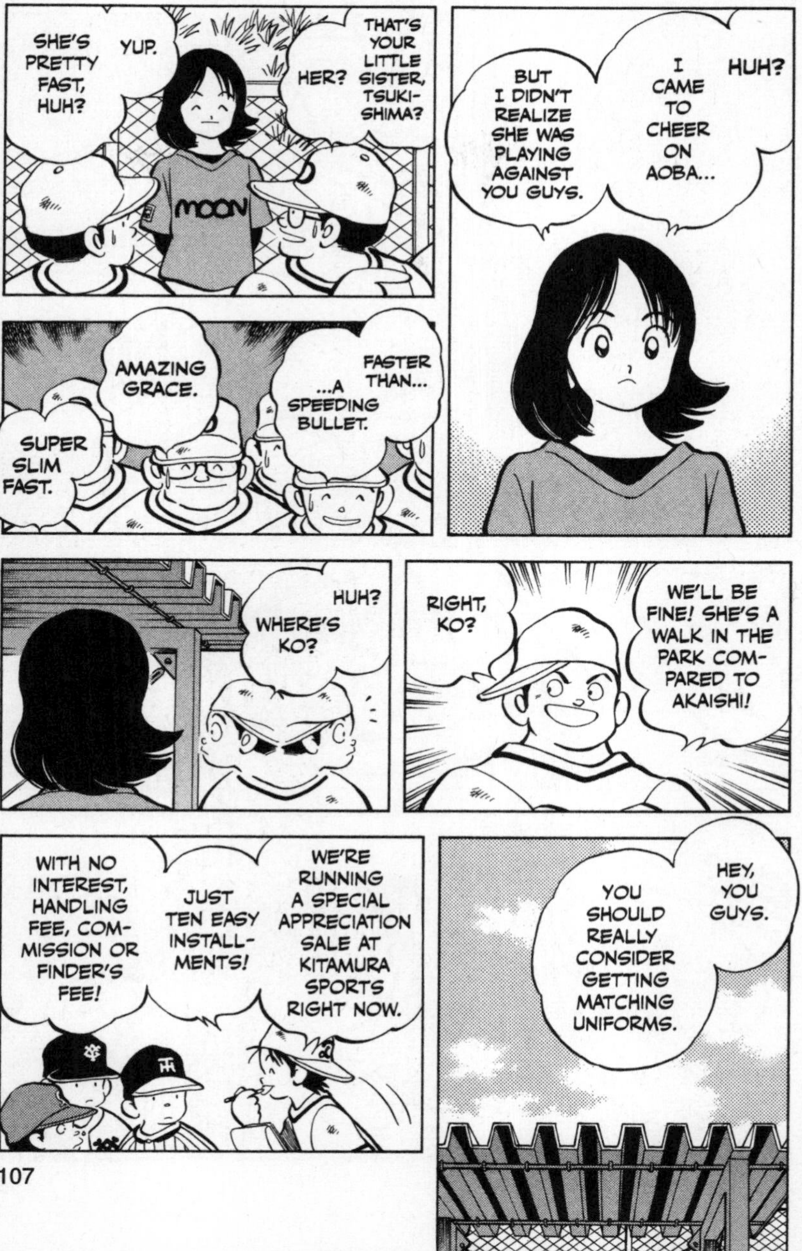
HUH?
I CAME TO CHEER ON AOBA...
BUT I DIDN'T REALIZE SHE WAS PLAYING AGAINST YOU GUYS.
THAT'S YOUR LITTLE SISTER, TSUKISHIMA?
HER?
YUP.
SHE'S PRETTY FAST, HUH?
FASTER THAN...
...A SPEEDING BULLET.
AMAZING GRACE.
SUPER SLIM FAST.
WE'LL BE FINE! SHE'S A WALK IN THE PARK COMPARED TO AKAISHI!
RIGHT, KO?
HUH?
WHERE'S KO?
HEY, YOU GUYS.
YOU SHOULD REALLY CONSIDER GETTING MATCHING UNIFORMS.
WE'RE RUNNING A SPECIAL APPRECIATION SALE AT KITAMURA SPORTS RIGHT NOW.
JUST TEN EASY INSTALLMENTS!
WITH NO INTEREST, HANDLING FEE, COMMISSION OR FINDER'S FEE!

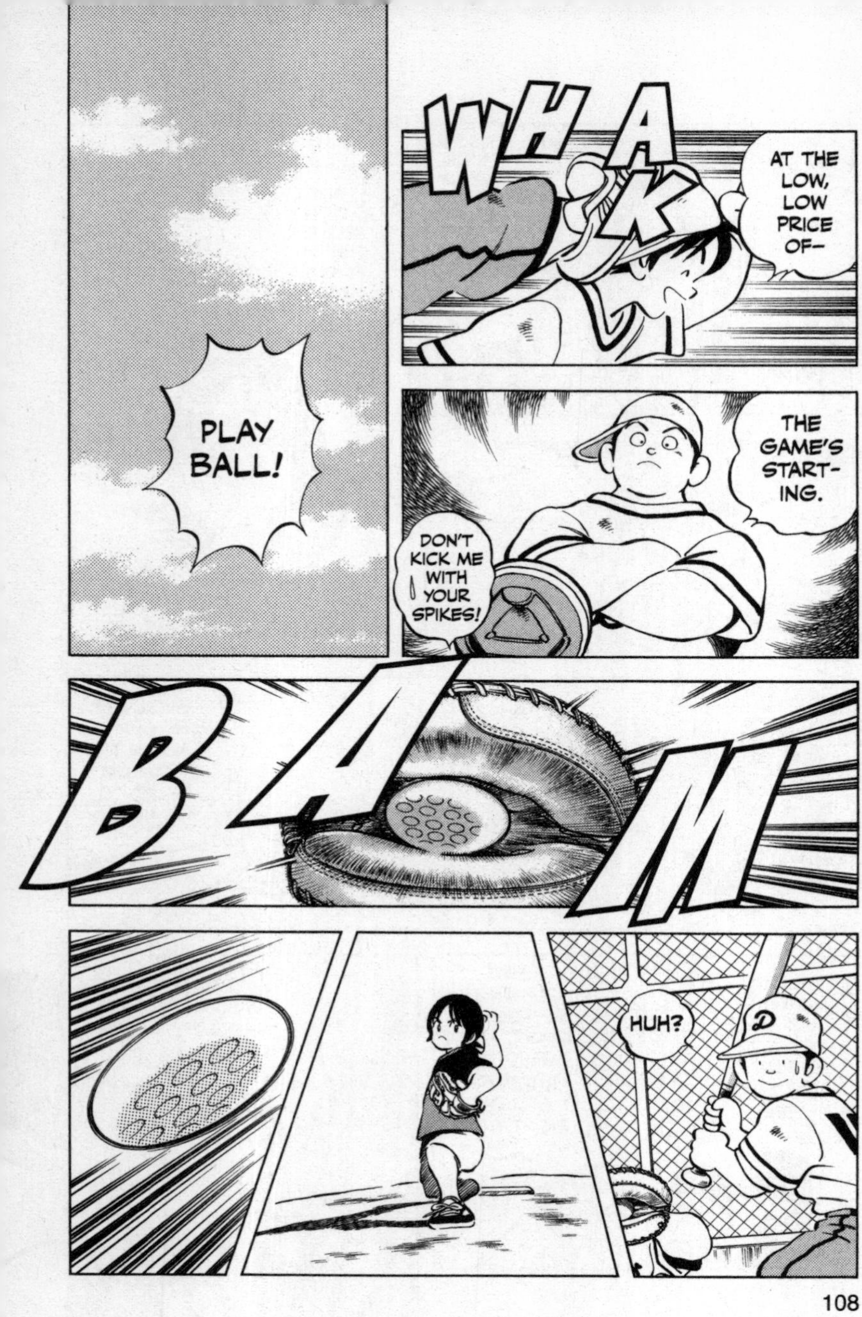
WHAK
AT THE LOW, LOW PRICE OF–
THE GAME'S START-ING.
DON'T KICK ME WITH YOUR SPIKES!
PLAY BALL!
BAM
HUH?

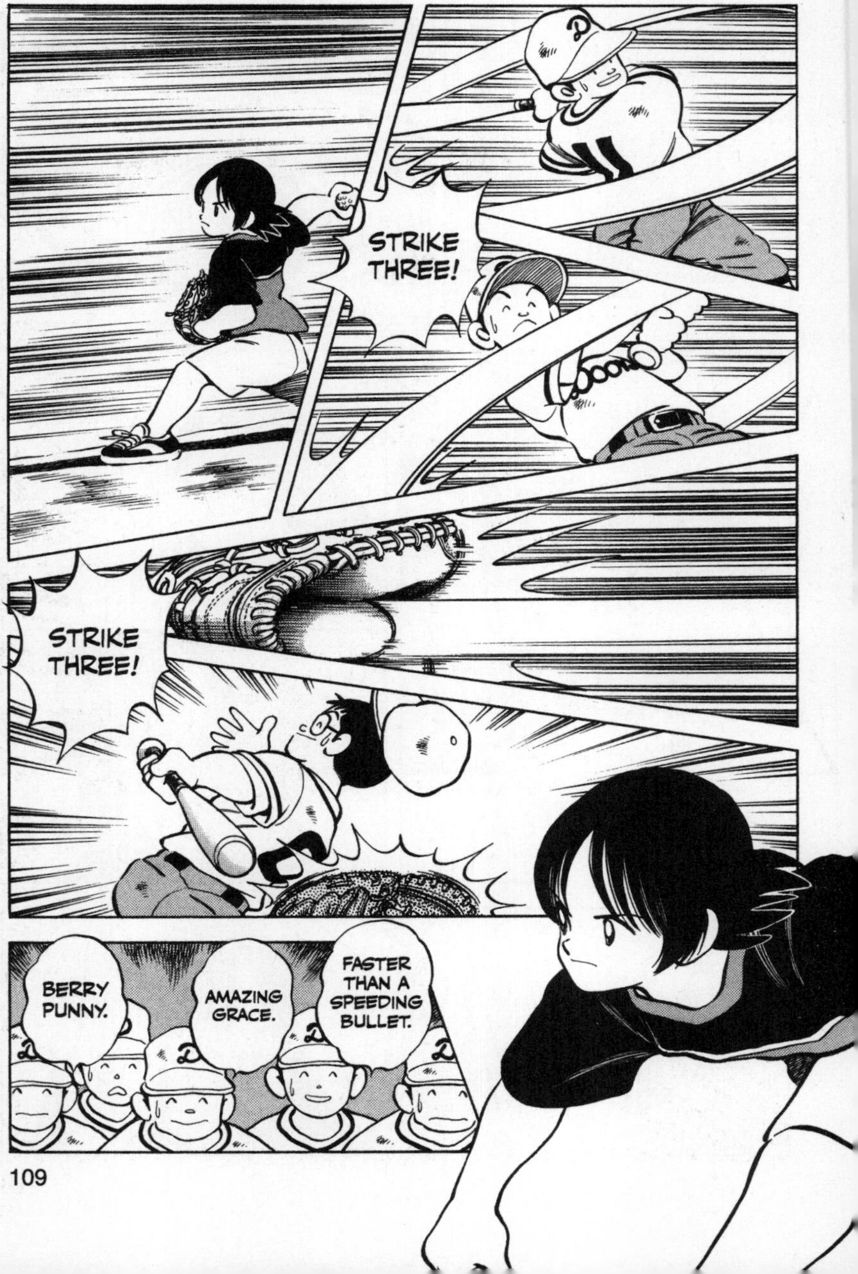
STRIKE THREE!
STRIKE THREE!
FASTER THAN A SPEEDING BULLET.
AMAZING GRACE.
BERRY PUNNY.

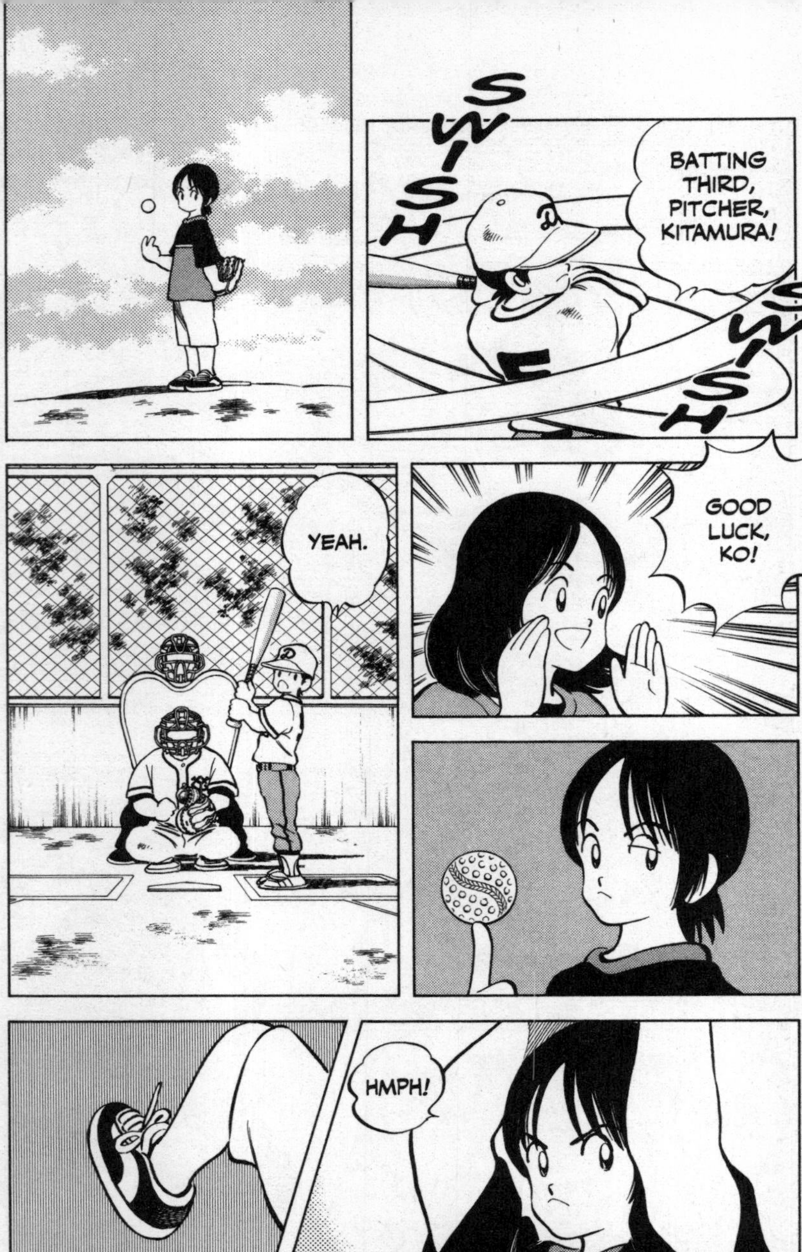
SWISH
BATTING THIRD, PITCHER, KITAMURA!
SWISH
GOOD LUCK, KO!
YEAH.
HMPH!

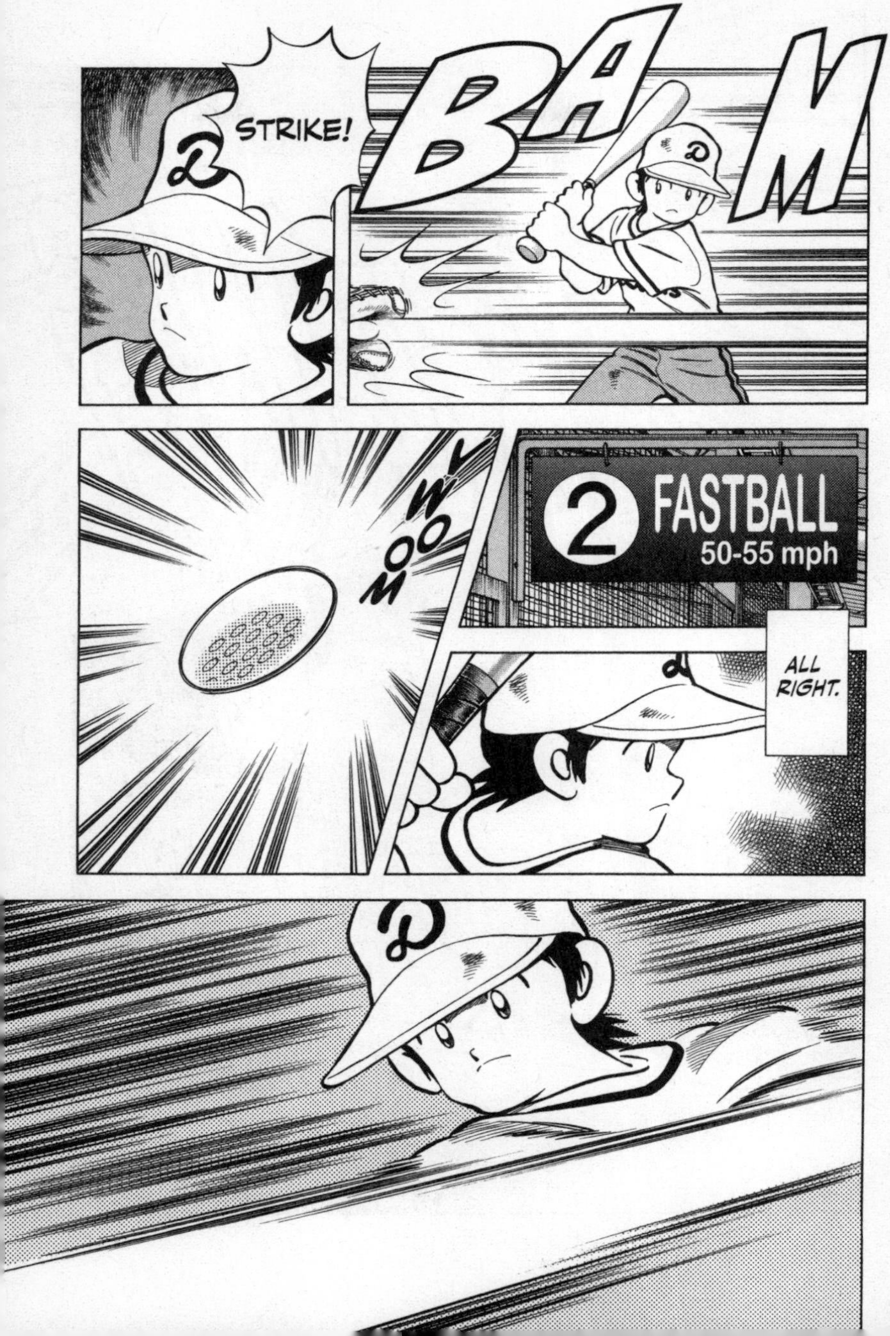
BAM
STRIKE!
2 FASTBALL 50-55 mph
ALL RIGHT.
VWOOM

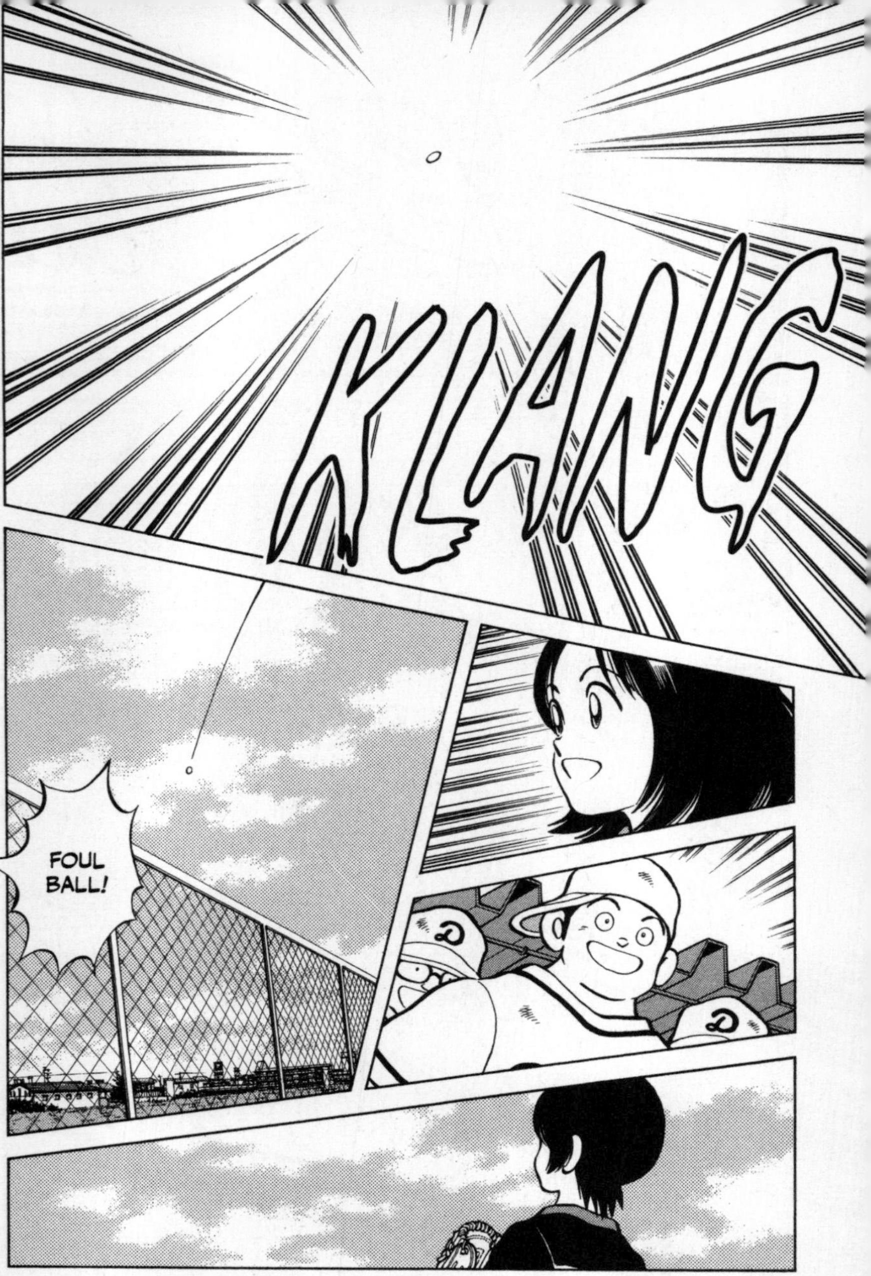
KLANG
FOUL BALL!

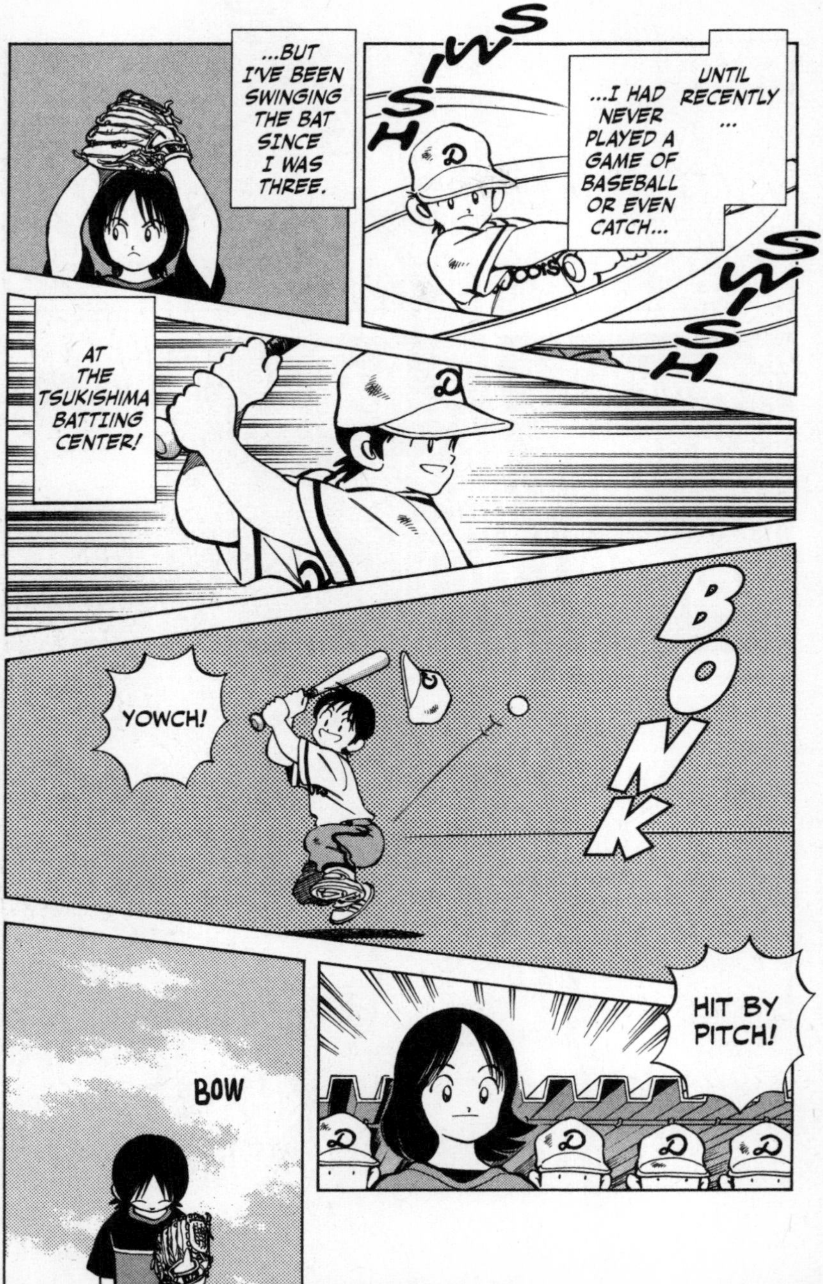
SWISH
UNTIL RECENTLY...
...I HAD NEVER PLAYED A GAME OF BASEBALL OR EVEN CATCH...
SWISH
...BUT I'VE BEEN SWINGING THE BAT SINCE I WAS THREE.
AT THE TSUKISHIMA BATTIING CENTER!
BONK
YOWCH!
HIT BY PITCH!
BOW

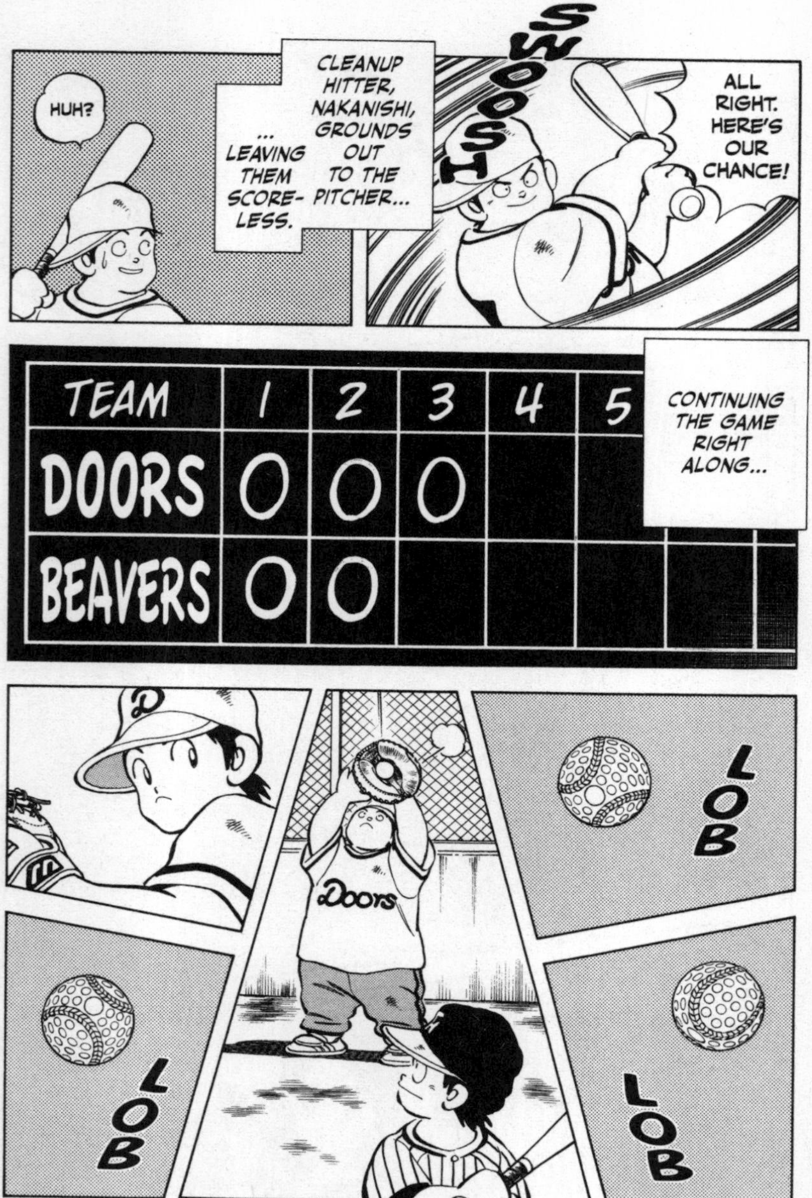
SWOOSH
ALL RIGHT. HERE'S OUR CHANCE!
CLEANUP HITTER, NAKANISHI, GROUNDS OUT TO THE PITCHER...
...LEAVING THEM SCORE-LESS.
HUH?
CONTINUING THE GAME RIGHT ALONG...
TEAM 1 2 3 4 5
DOORS 0 0 0
BEAVERS 0 0
LOB
DOORS
LOB
LOB
LOB

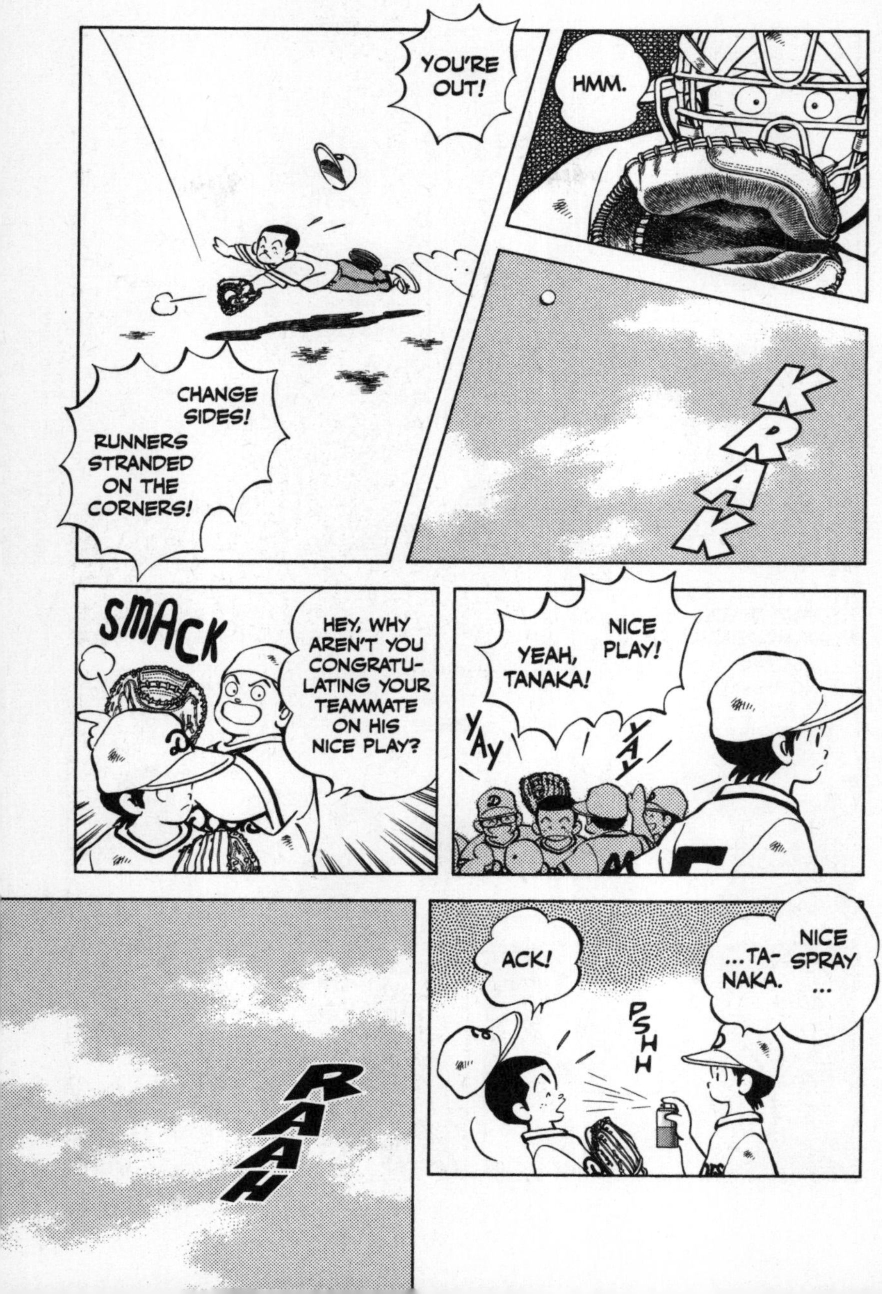
HMM.
KRAK
YOU'RE OUT!
CHANGE SIDES!
RUNNERS STRANDED ON THE CORNERS!
NICE PLAY!
YEAH, TANAKA!
YAY
YAY
HEY, WHY AREN'T YOU CONGRATU-LATING YOUR TEAMMATE ON HIS NICE PLAY?
SMACK
NICE SPRAY ...
...TA-NAKA.
PSHH
ACK!
RAAH

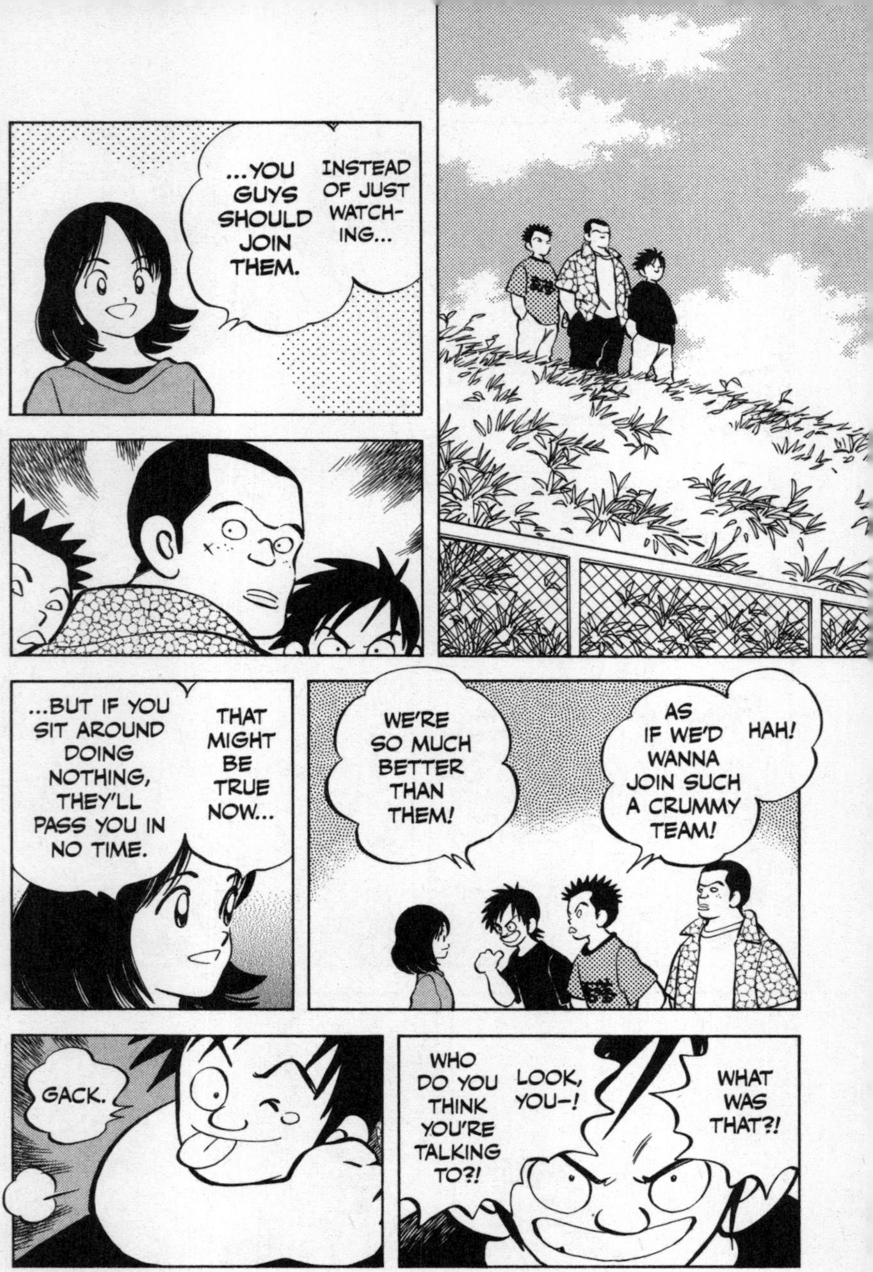
INSTEAD OF JUST WATCHING...
...YOU GUYS SHOULD JOIN THEM.
HAH!
AS IF WE'D WANNA JOIN SUCH A CRUMMY TEAM!
WE'RE SO MUCH BETTER THAN THEM!
THAT MIGHT BE TRUE NOW...
...BUT IF YOU SIT AROUND DOING NOTHING, THEY'LL PASS YOU IN NO TIME.
WHAT WAS THAT?!
LOOK, YOU-!
WHO DO YOU THINK YOU'RE TALKING TO?!
GACK.

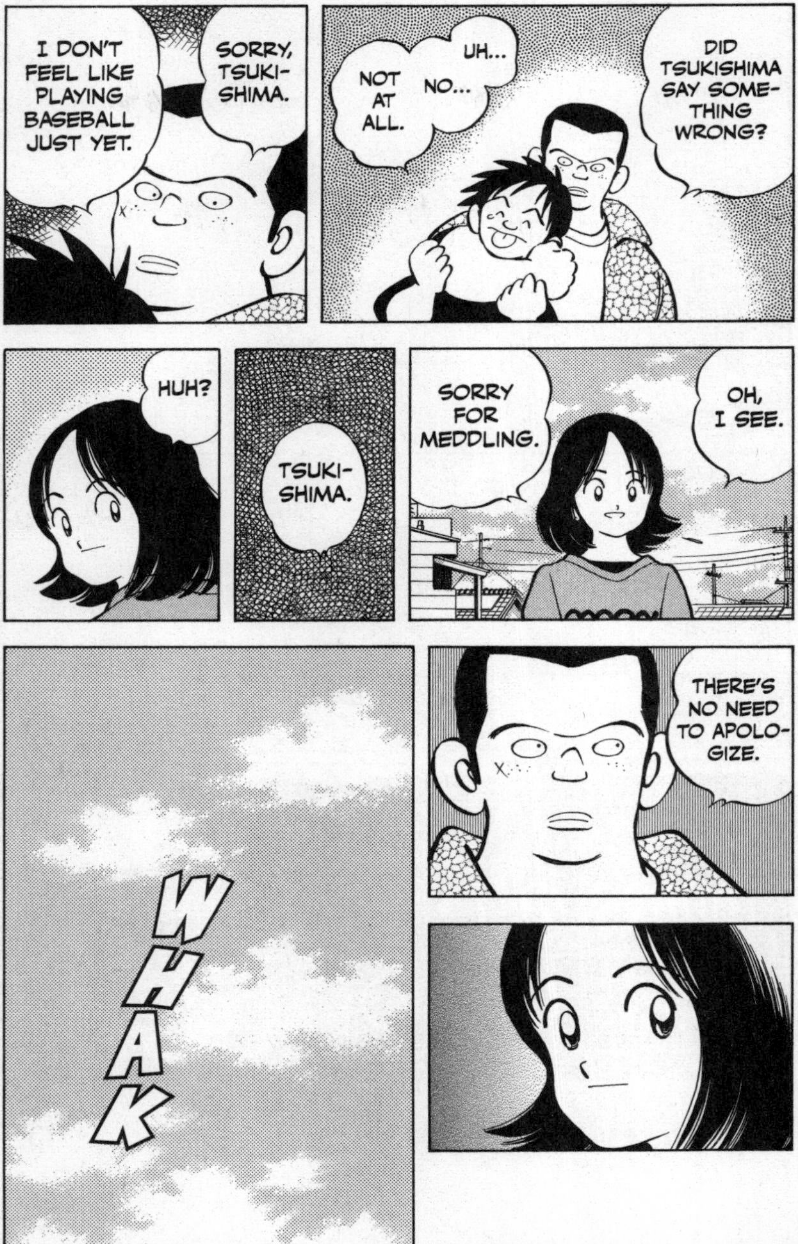
DID TSUKISHIMA SAY SOME-THING WRONG?
UH... NO...
NOT AT ALL.
SORRY, TSUKI-SHIMA.
I DON'T FEEL LIKE PLAYING BASEBALL JUST YET.
OH, I SEE.
SORRY FOR MEDDLING.
TSUKI-SHIMA.
HUH?
THERE'S NO NEED TO APOLO-GIZE.
WHAK

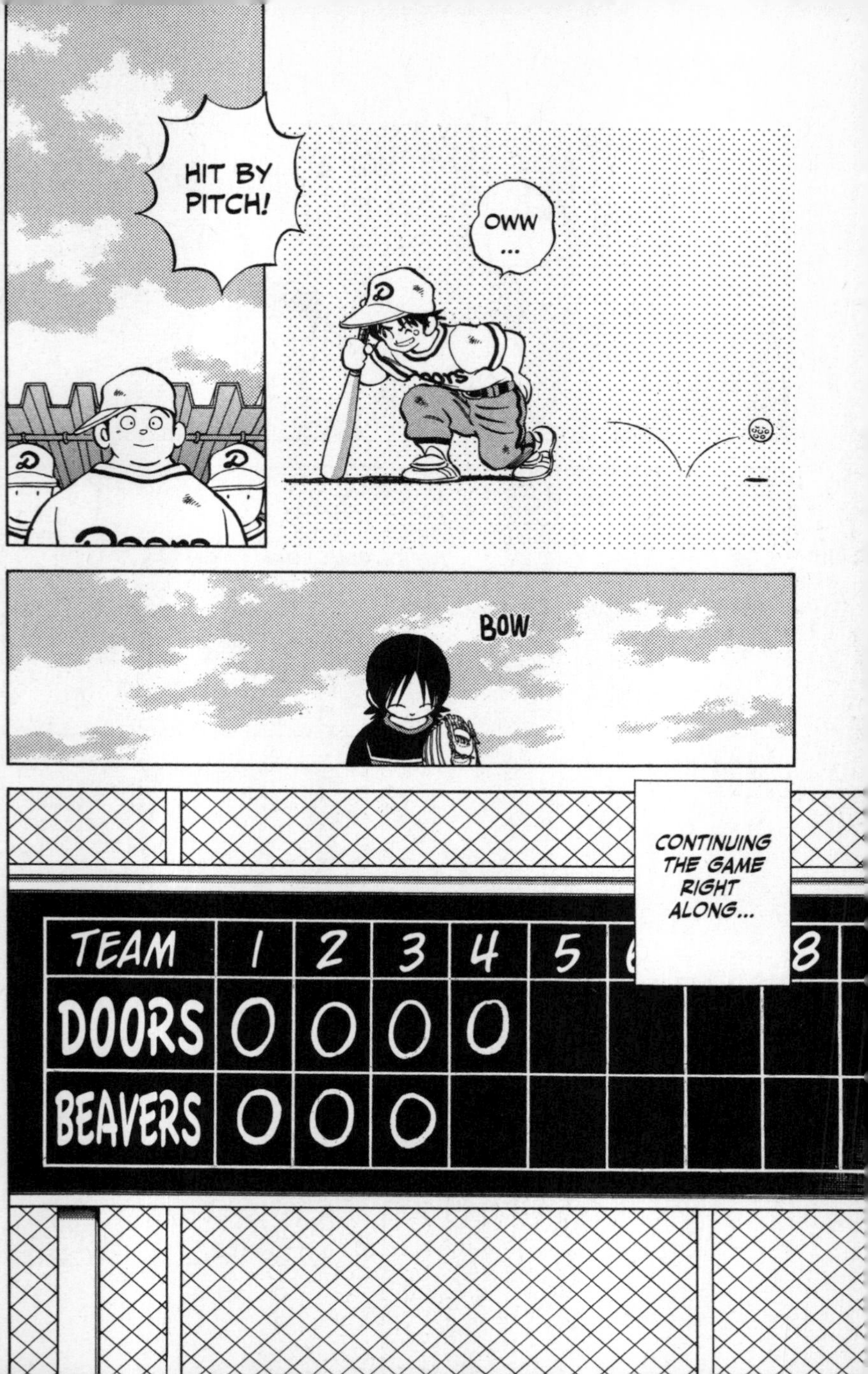
OWW ...
HIT BY PITCH!
BOW
CONTINUING THE GAME RIGHT ALONG...
TEAM 1 2 3 4 5 8
DOORS 0 0 0 0
BEAVERS 0 0 0

CHAPTER 7 WHY, YOU-!

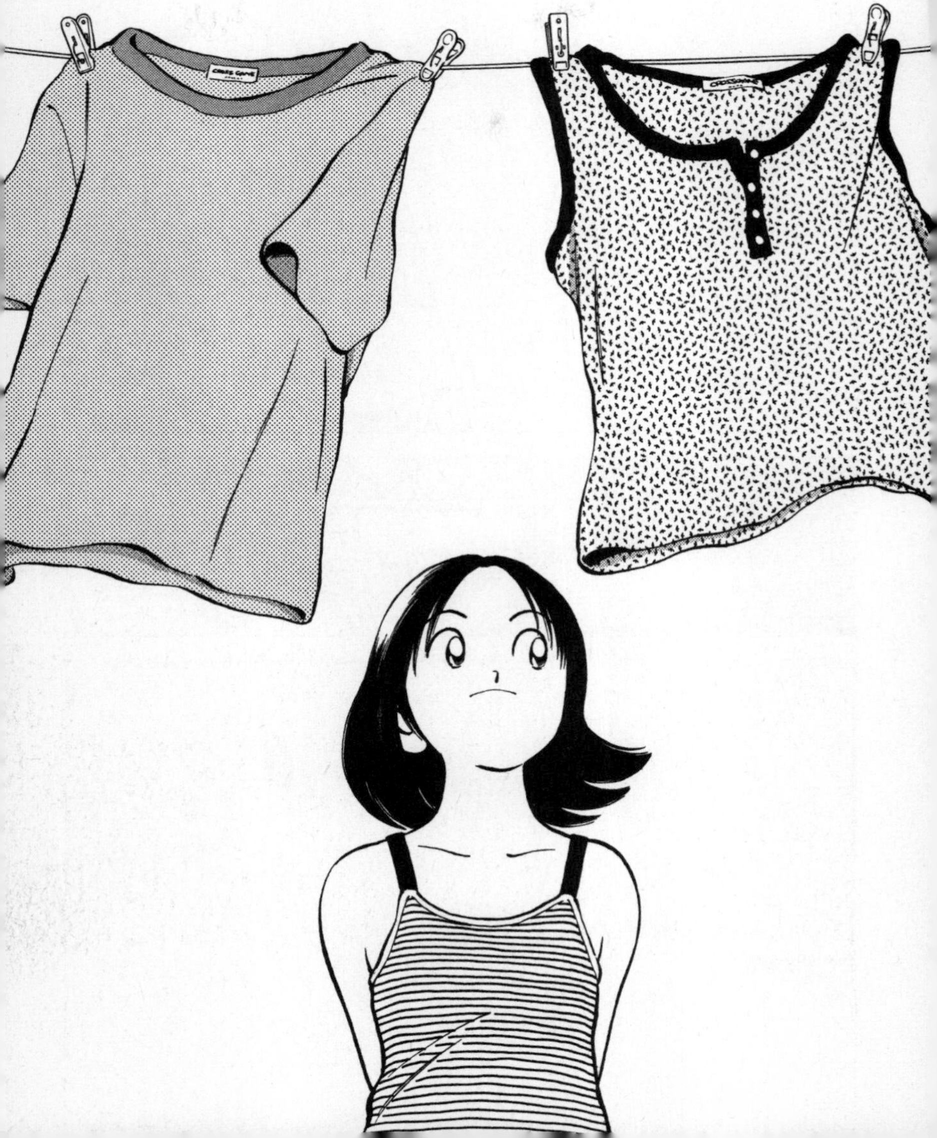

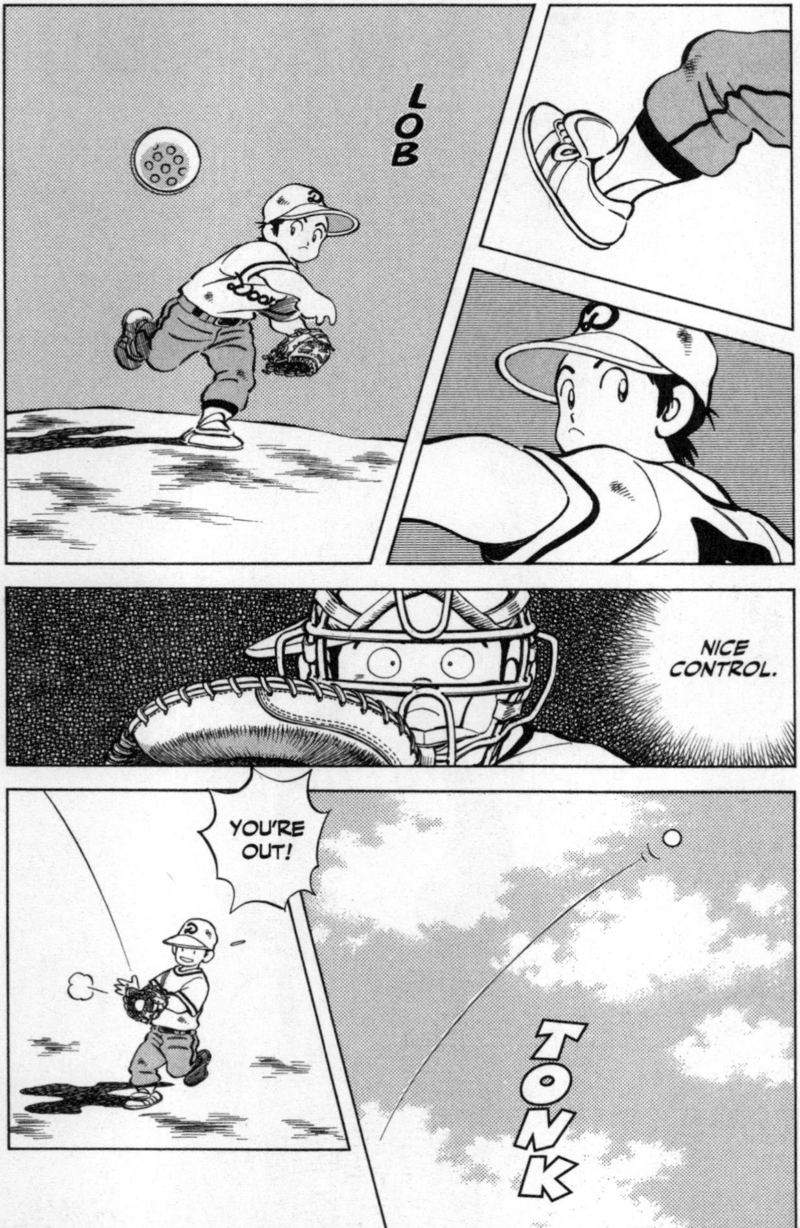
LOB
NICE CONTROL.
TONK
YOU'RE OUT!

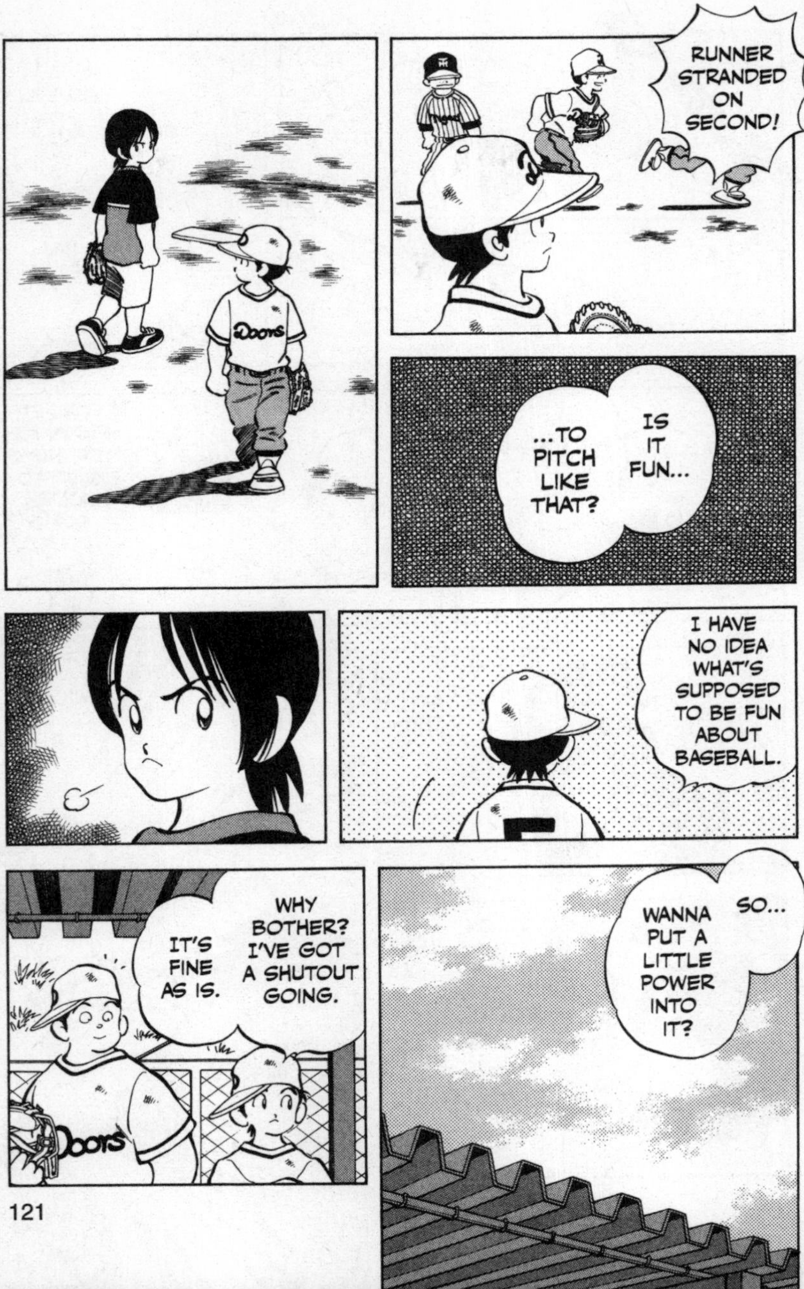
RUNNER STRANDED ON SECOND!
IS IT FUN...
...TO PITCH LIKE THAT?
I HAVE NO IDEA WHAT'S SUPPOSED TO BE FUN ABOUT BASEBALL.
SO...
WANNA PUT A LITTLE POWER INTO IT?
WHY BOTHER? I'VE GOT A SHUTOUT GOING.
IT'S FINE AS IS.

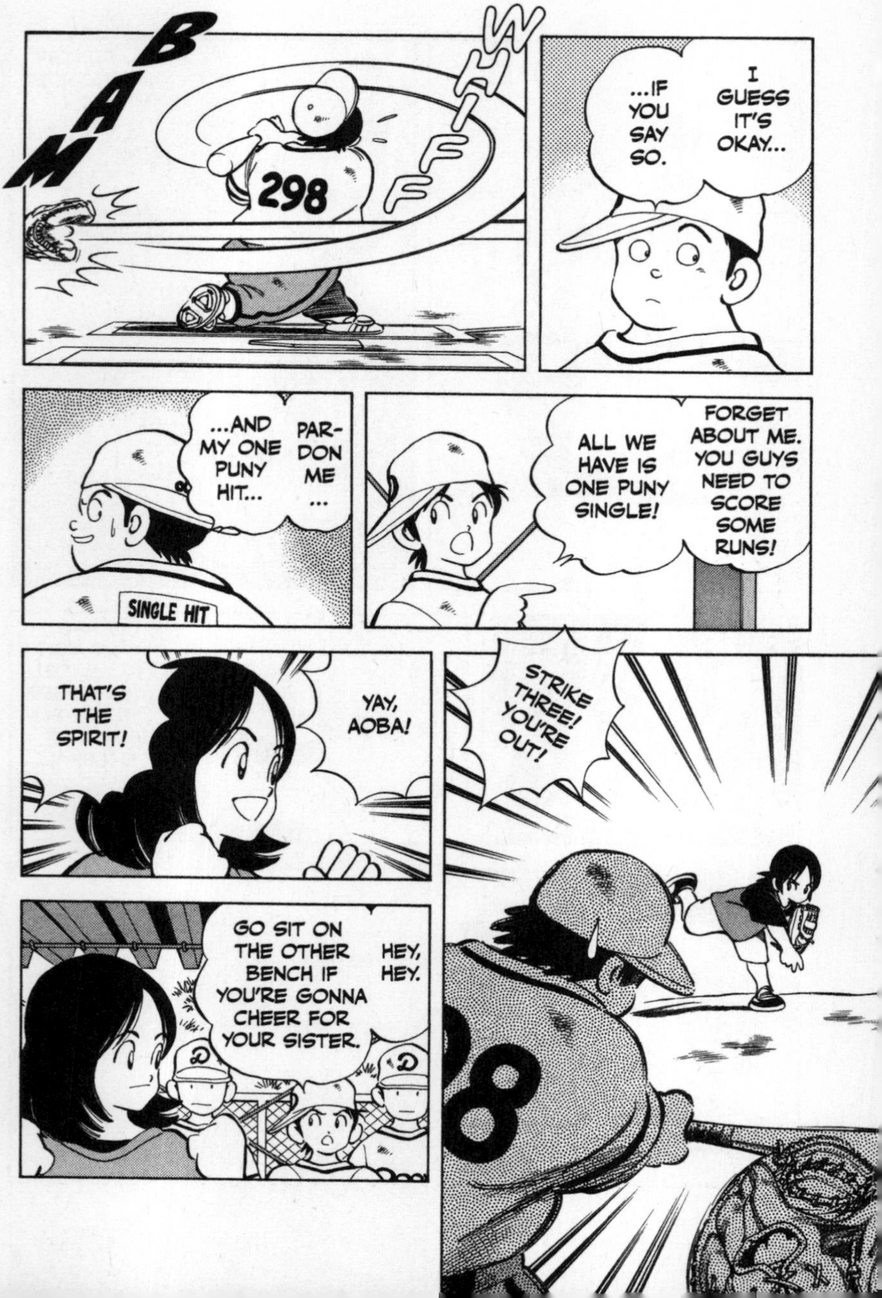
I GUESS IT'S OKAY...
...IF YOU SAY SO.
BAM
WHIFF
298
FORGET ABOUT ME. YOU GUYS NEED TO SCORE SOME RUNS!
ALL WE HAVE IS ONE PUNY SINGLE!
PARDON ME...
...AND MY ONE PUNY HIT...
SINGLE HIT
STRIKE THREE! YOU'RE OUT!
YAY, AOBA!
THAT'S THE SPIRIT!
HEY, HEY.
GO SIT ON THE OTHER BENCH IF YOU'RE GONNA CHEER FOR YOUR SISTER.

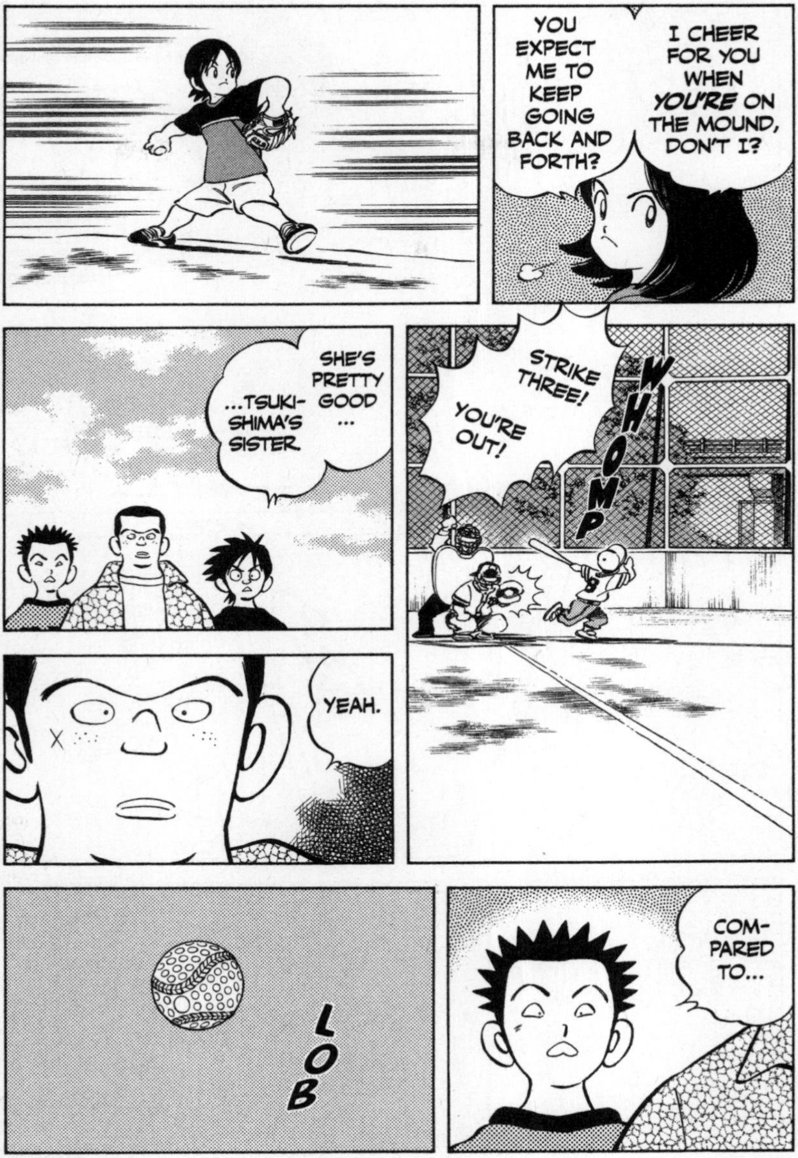
I CHEER FOR YOU WHEN YOU'RE ON THE MOUND, DON'T I?
YOU EXPECT ME TO KEEP GOING BACK AND FORTH?
STRIKE THREE!
YOU'RE OUT!
WHOMP
SHE'S PRETTY GOOD ...
...TSUKI-SHIMA'S SISTER
YEAH.
COM-PARED TO...
LOB

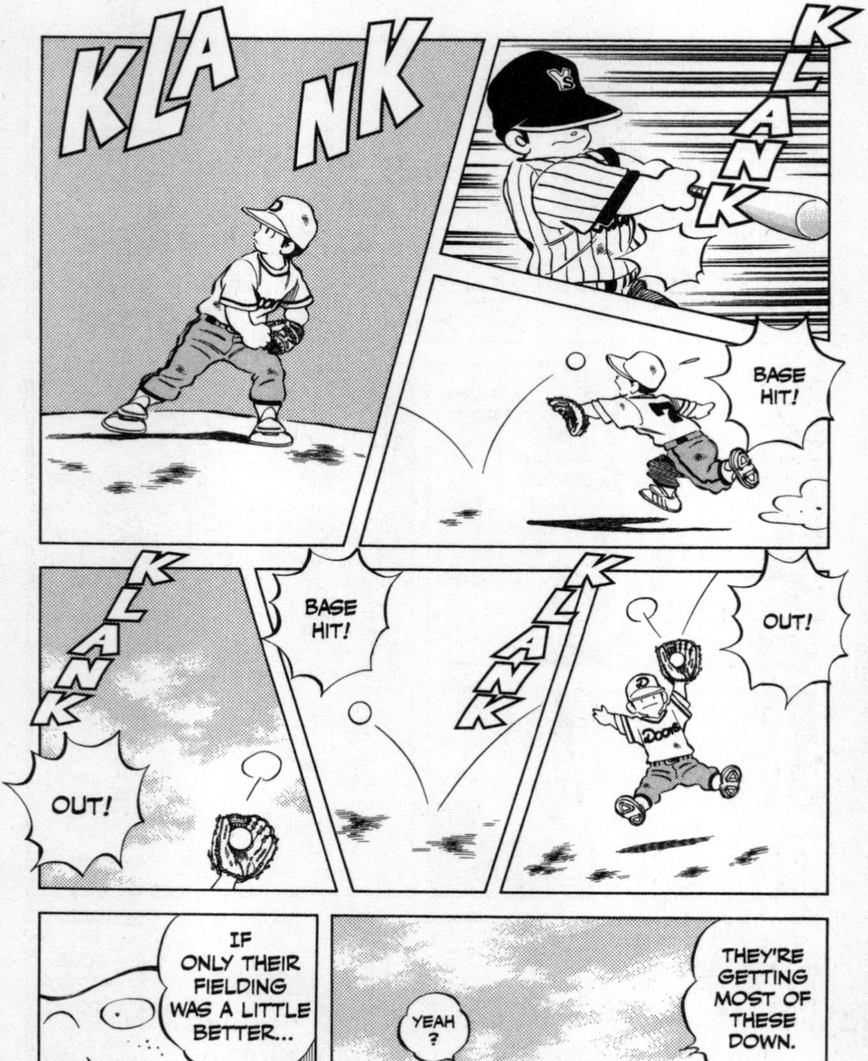
KLANK
BASE HIT!
KLANK
OUT!
KLANK
BASE HIT!
KLANK
OUT!
THEY'RE GETTING MOST OF THESE DOWN.
YEAH?
IF ONLY THEIR FIELDING WAS A LITTLE BETTER...

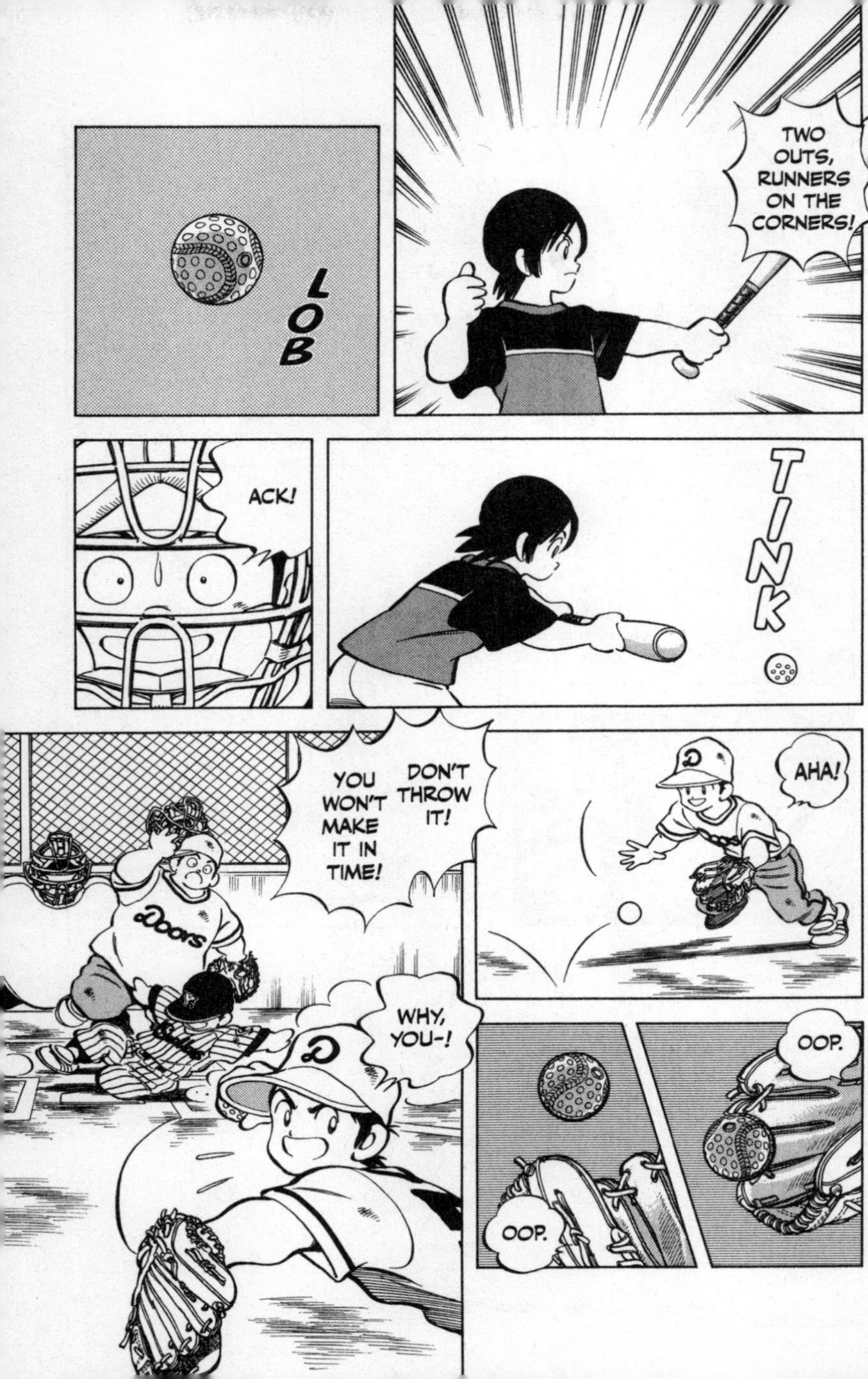
TWO OUTS, RUNNERS ON THE CORNERS!
LOB
TINK
ACK!
AHA!
OOP.
OOP.
DON'T THROW IT!
YOU WON'T MAKE IT IN TIME!
WHY, YOU-!

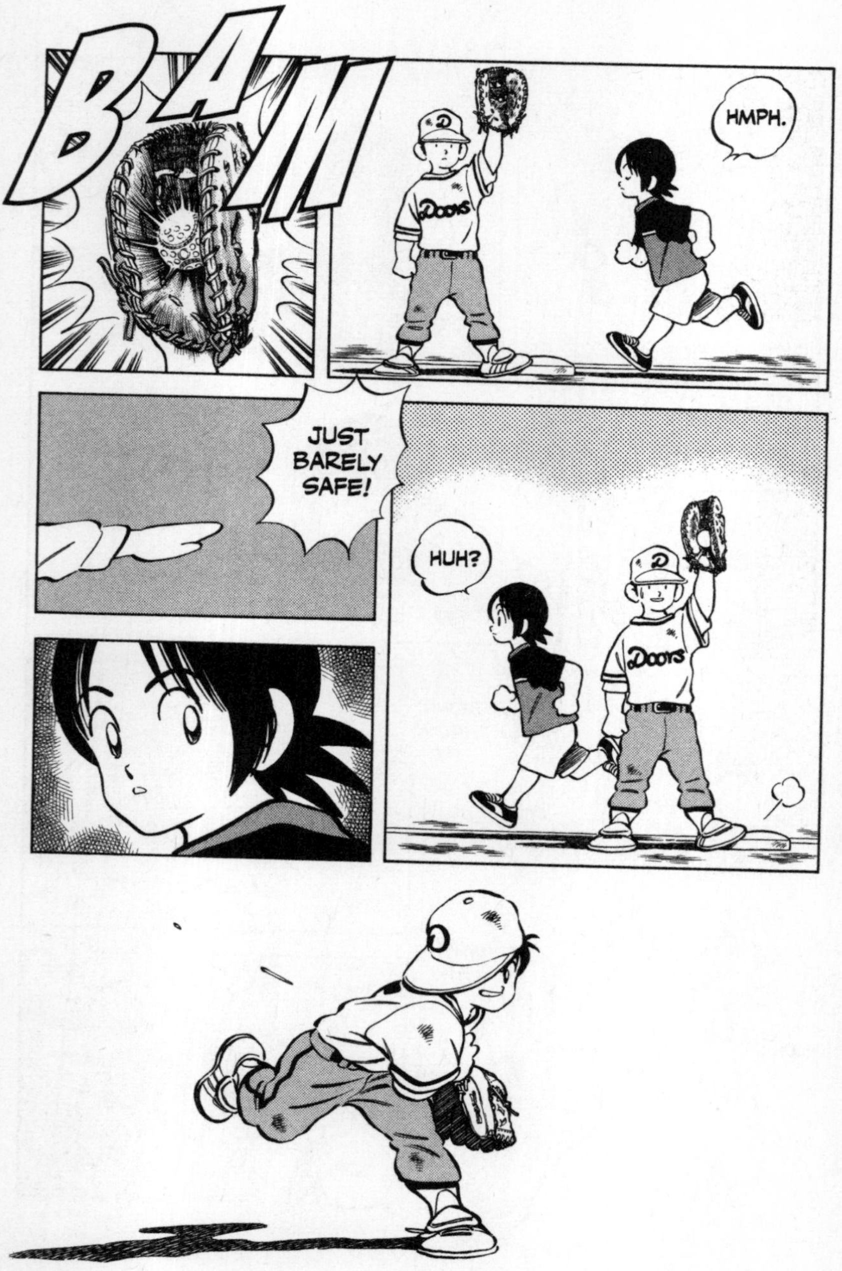
HMPH.
BAM
HUH?
JUST BARELY SAFE!

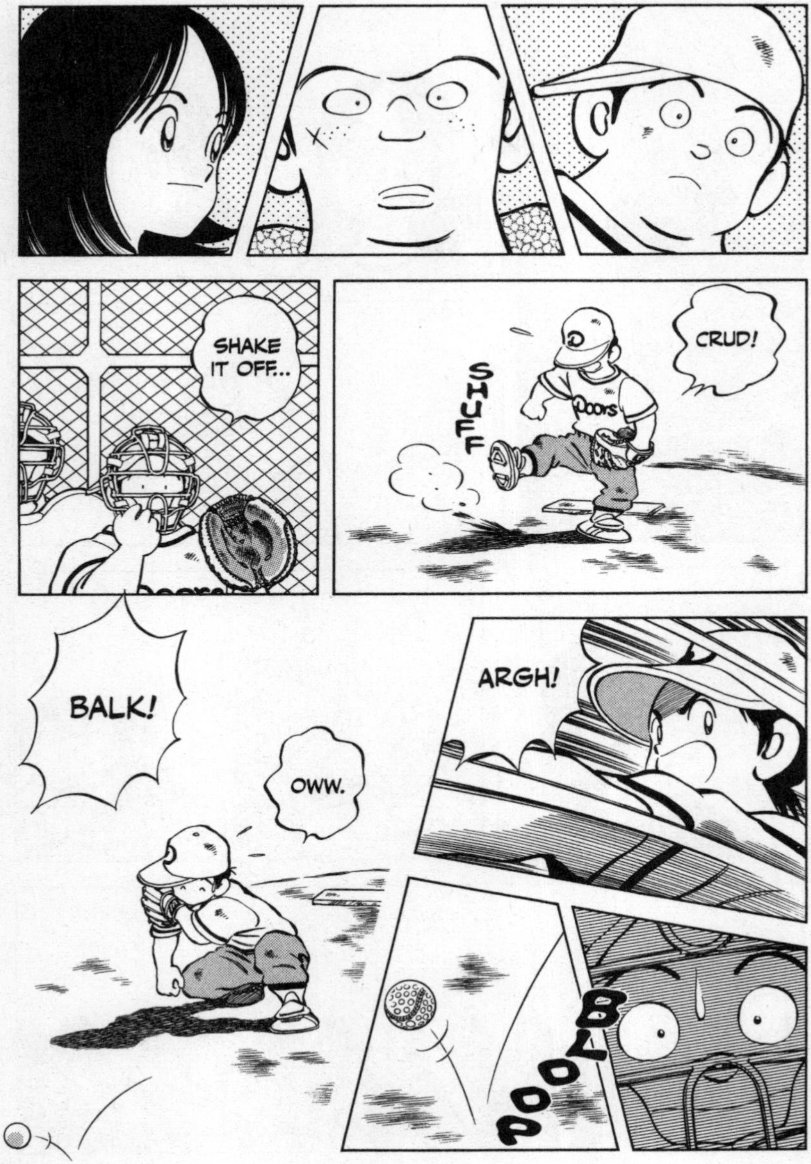
SHUFF
CRUD!
SHAKE IT OFF...
ARGH!
BLOOP
BALK!
OWW.

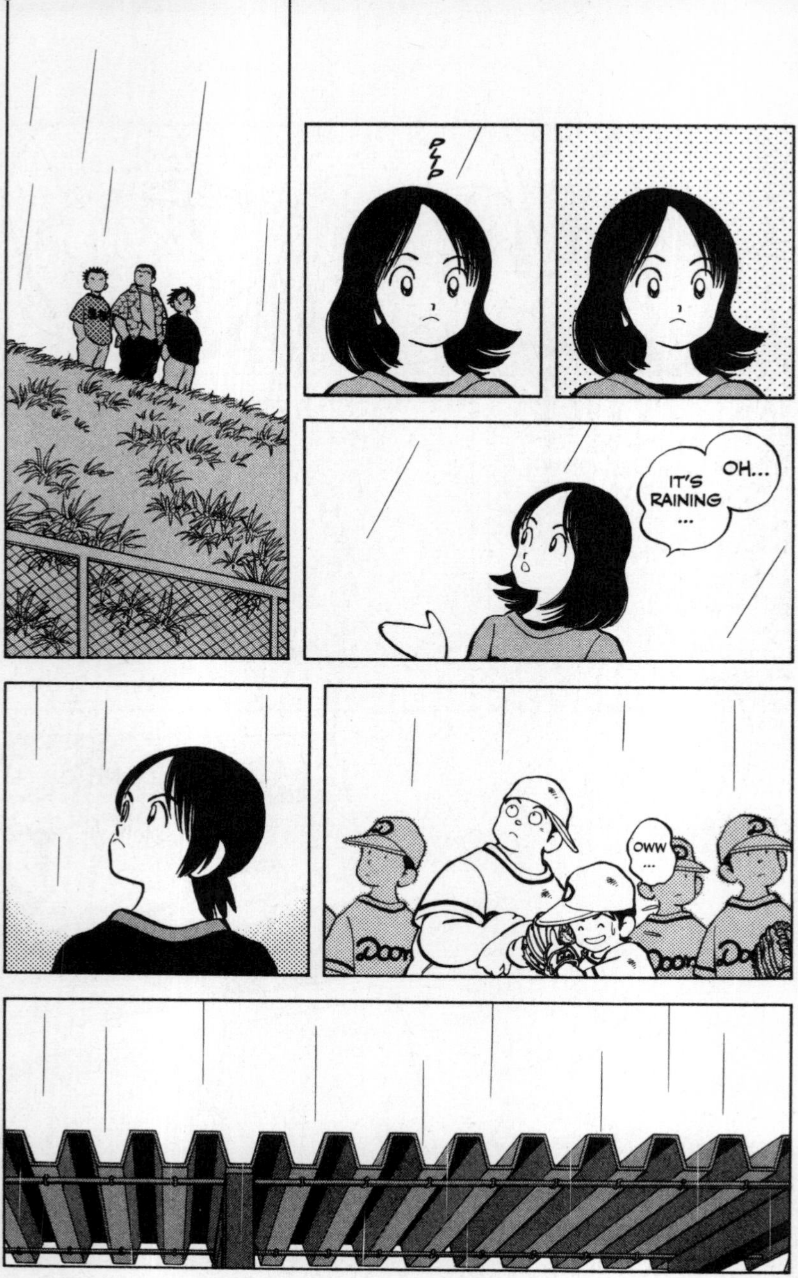
DRIP
OH... IT'S RAINING ...
OWW ...

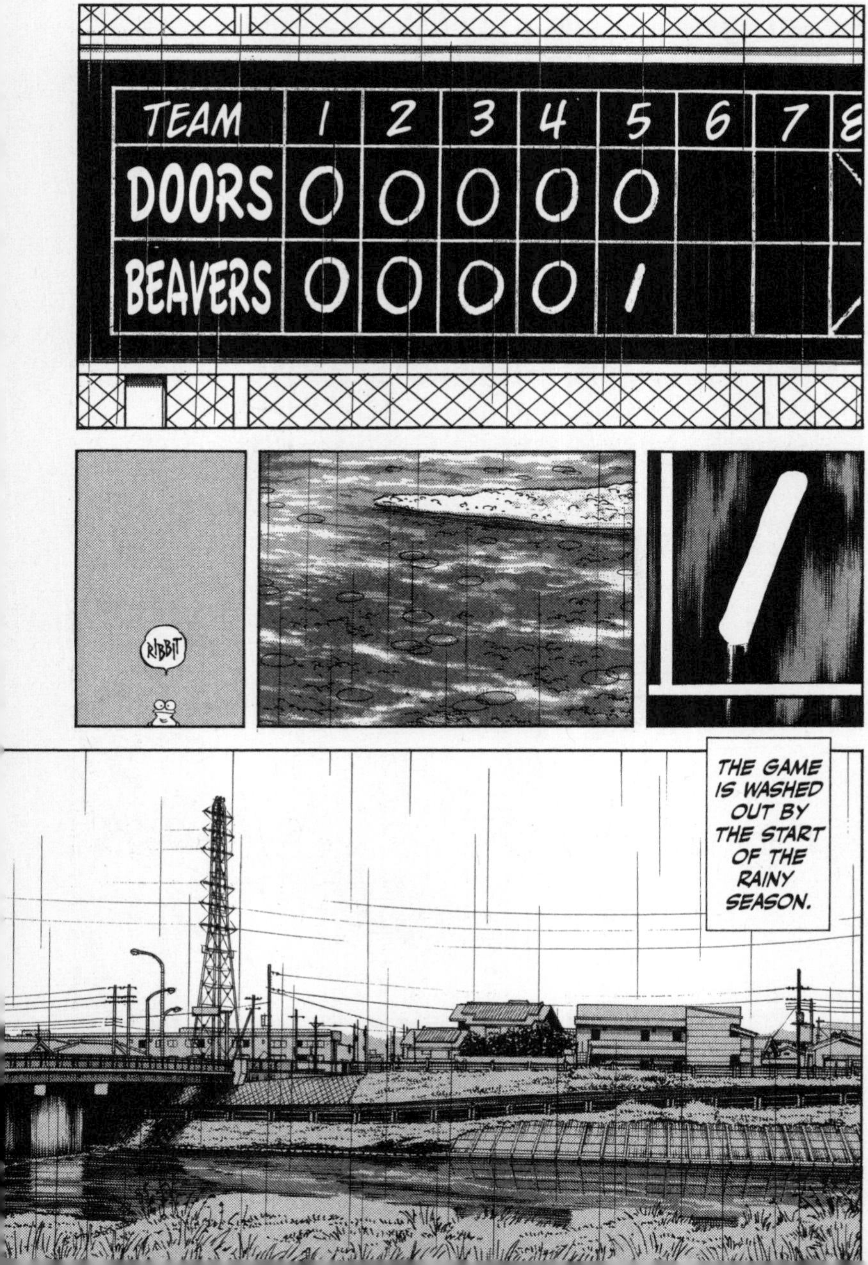
TEAM 1 2 3 4 5 6 7 8
DOORS 0 0 0 0 0
BEAVERS 0 0 0 0 1
1
RIBBIT
THE GAME IS WASHED OUT BY THE START OF THE RAINY SEASON.

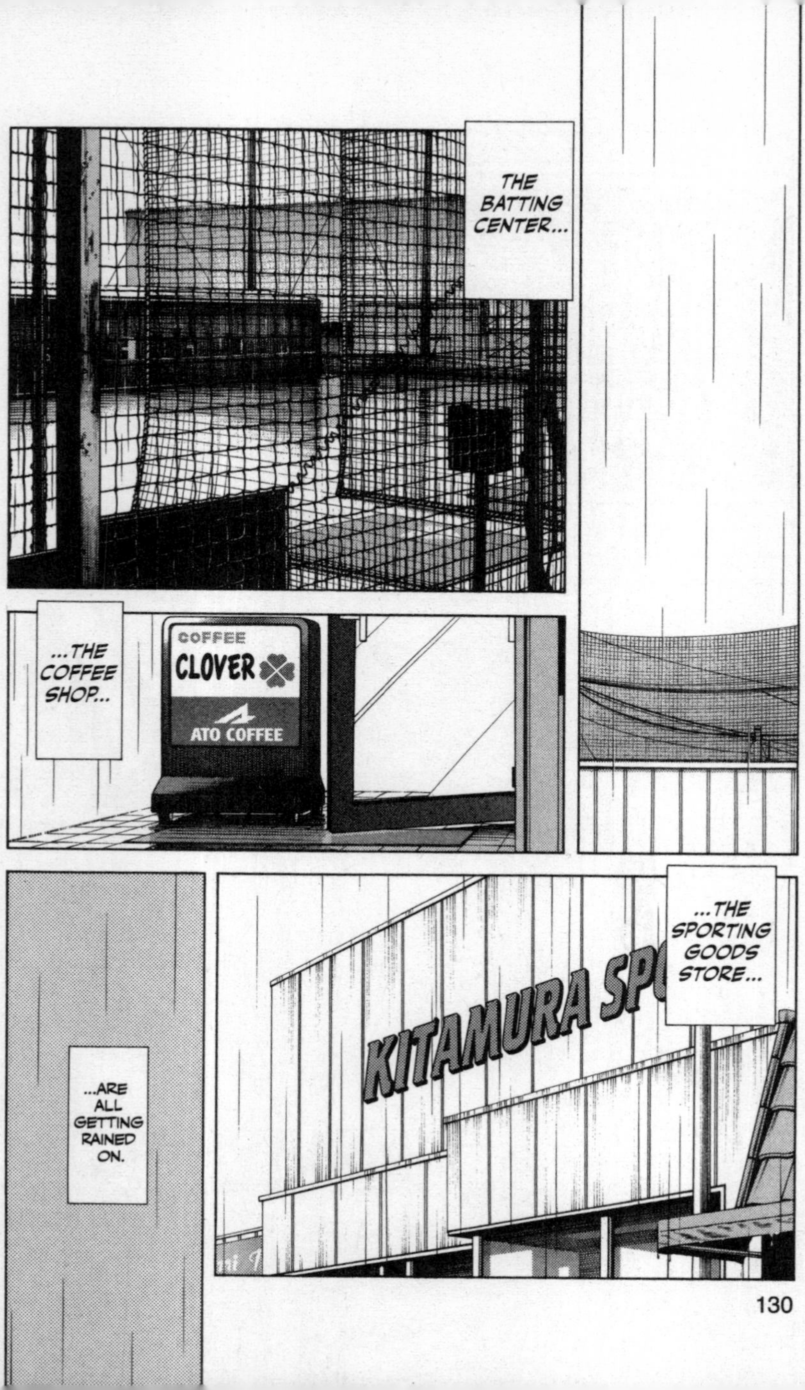
THE BATTING CENTER...
...THE COFFEE SHOP...
COFFEE
CLOVER
ATO COFFEE
...THE SPORTING GOODS STORE...
KITAMURA SP
...ARE ALL GETTING RAINED ON.

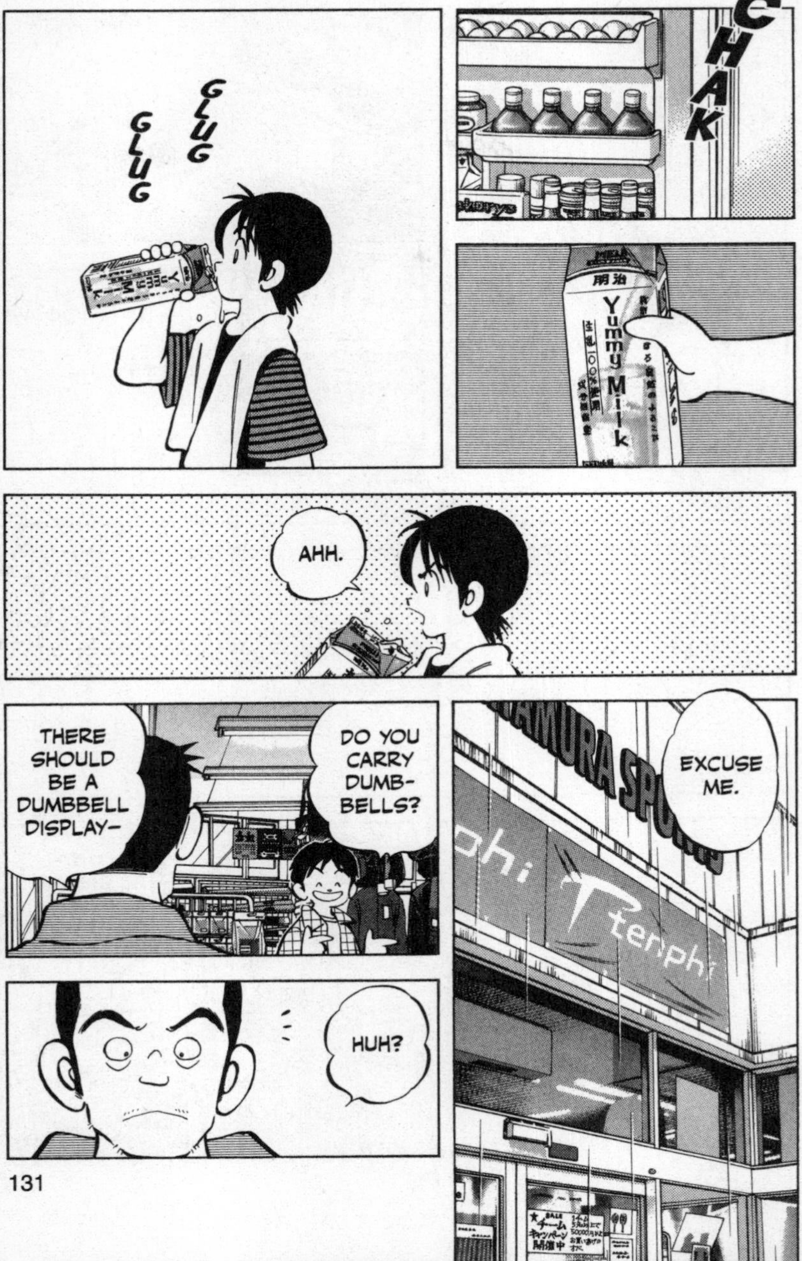
CHAK
明治
Yummy Milk
GLUG
GLUG
AHH.
EXCUSE ME.
tenphi
DO YOU CARRY DUMB-BELLS?
THERE SHOULD BE A DUMBBELL DISPLAY–
HUH?

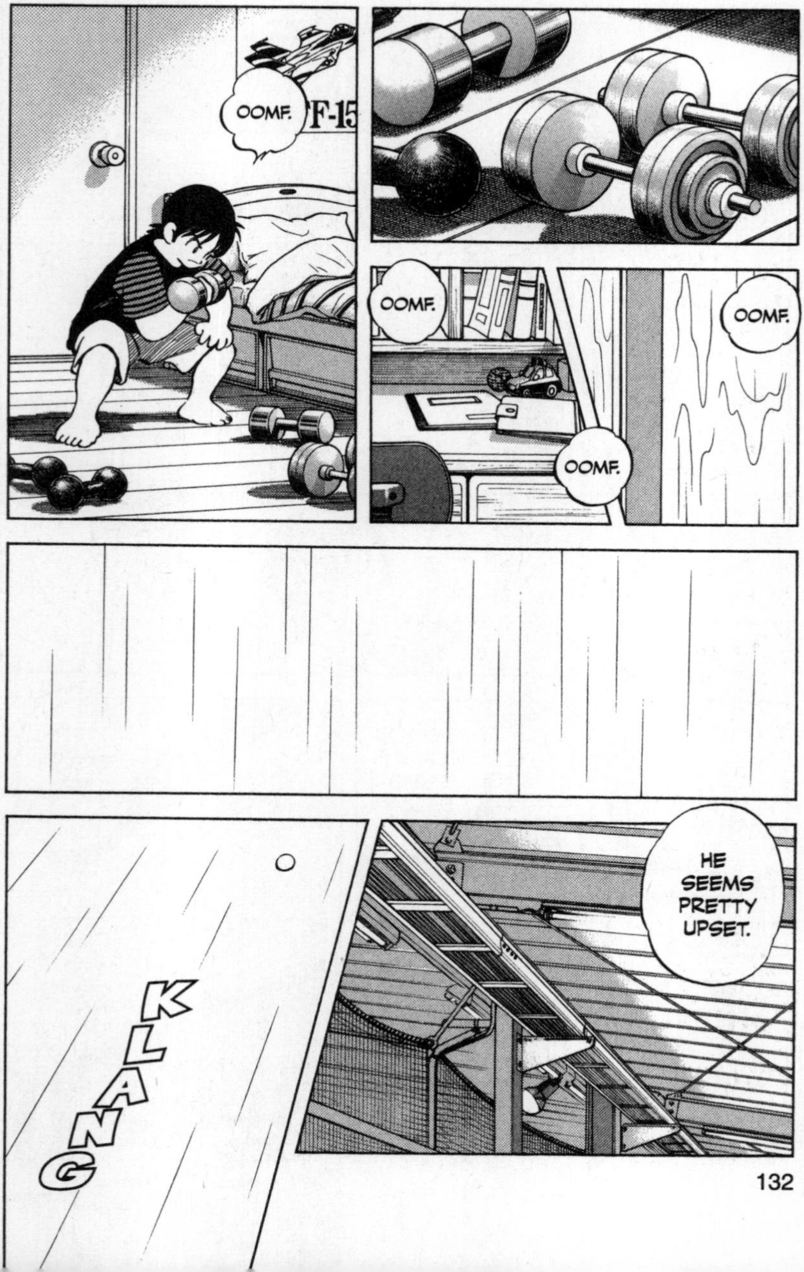
OOMF.
OOMF.
OOMF.
OOMF.
HE SEEMS PRETTY UPSET.
KLANG

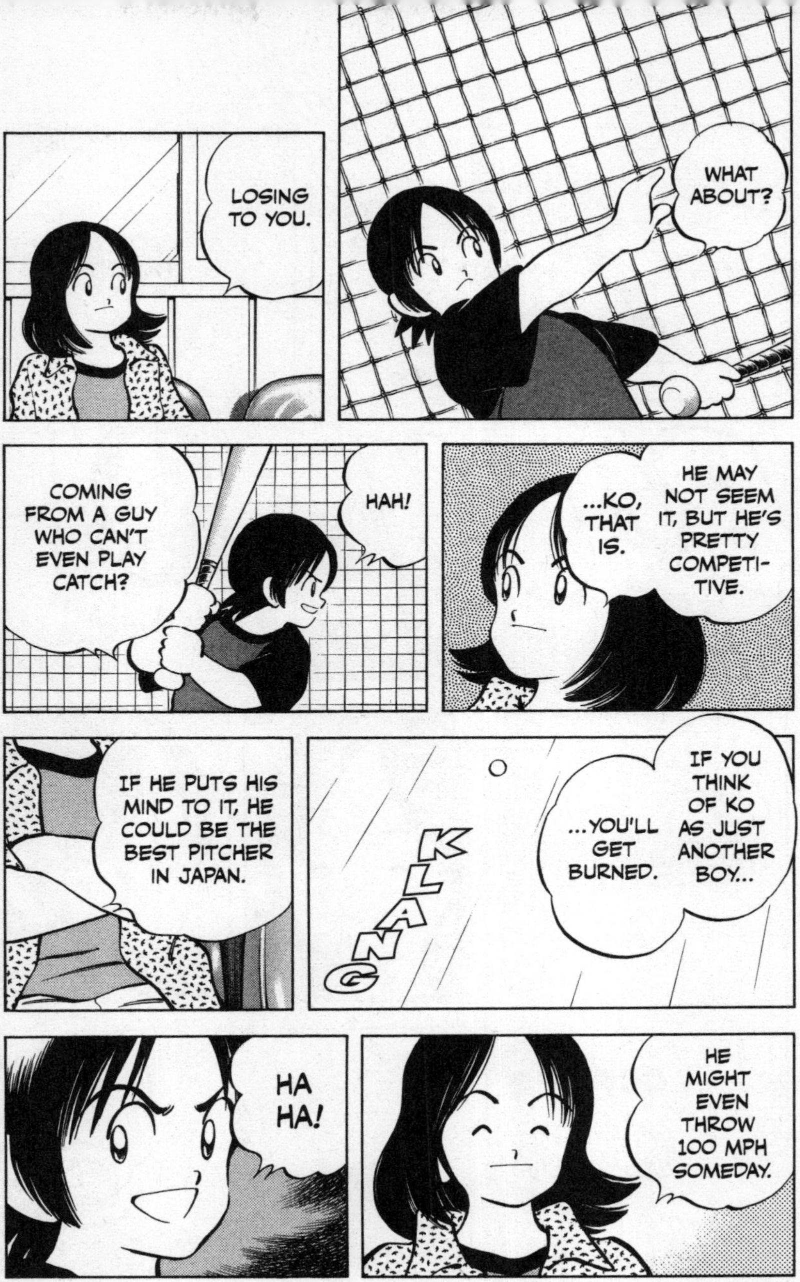
WHAT ABOUT?
LOSING TO YOU.
HE MAY NOT SEEM IT, BUT HE'S PRETTY COMPETI-TIVE.
...KO, THAT IS.
HAH!
COMING FROM A GUY WHO CAN'T EVEN PLAY CATCH?
IF YOU THINK OF KO AS JUST ANOTHER BOY...
...YOU'LL GET BURNED.
KLANG
IF HE PUTS HIS MIND TO IT, HE COULD BE THE BEST PITCHER IN JAPAN.
HE MIGHT EVEN THROW 100 MPH SOMEDAY.
HA HA!

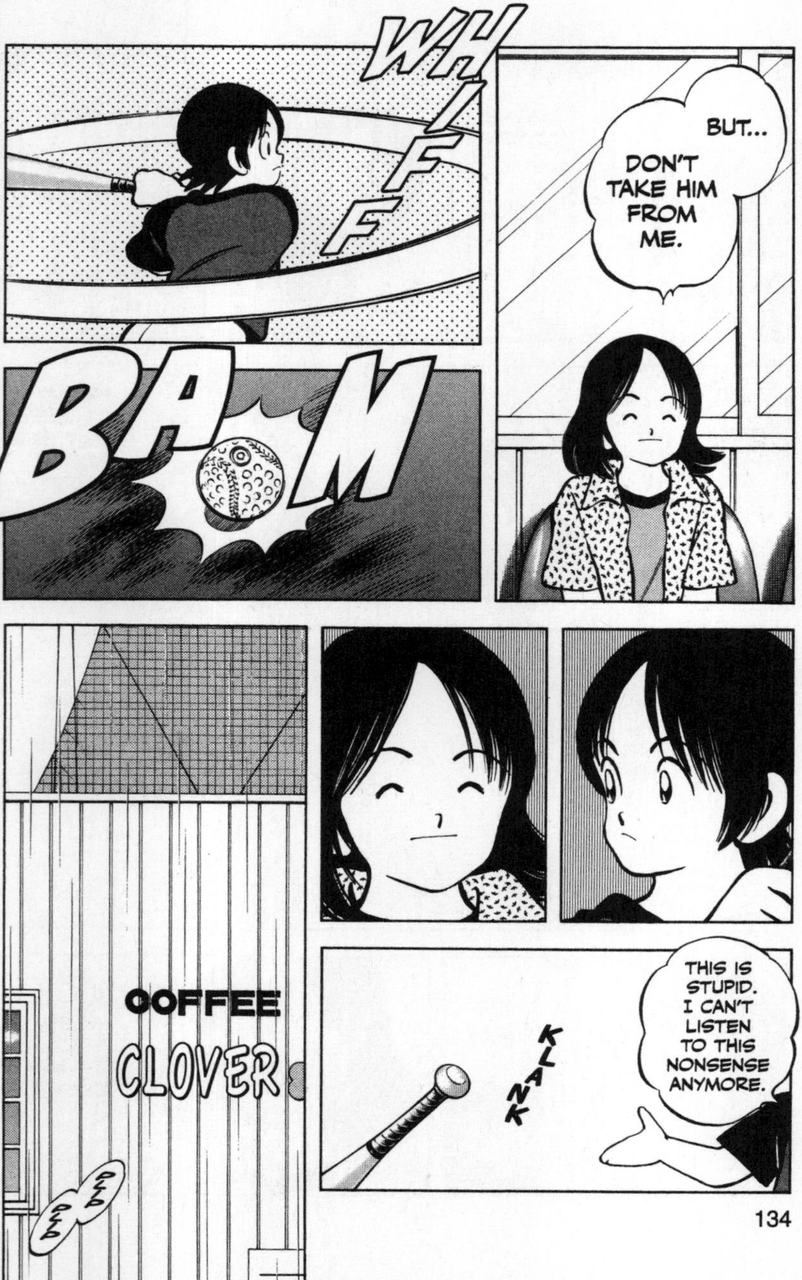
BUT... DON'T TAKE HIM FROM ME.
WHIFF
BAM
KLANK
THIS IS STUPID. I CAN'T LISTEN TO THIS NONSENSE ANYMORE.
COFFEE
CLOVER

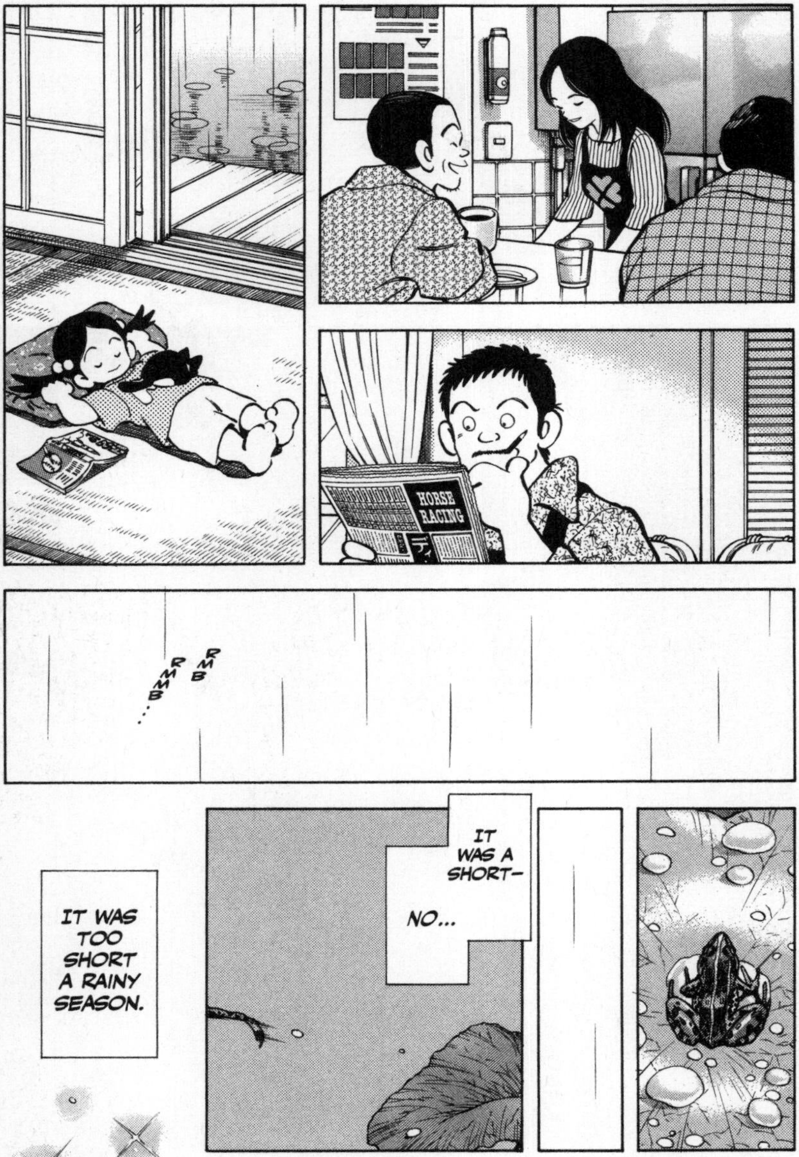
HORSE RACING
ディ
RMB
RMMB...
IT WAS A SHORT—
NO...
IT WAS TOO SHORT A RAINY SEASON.

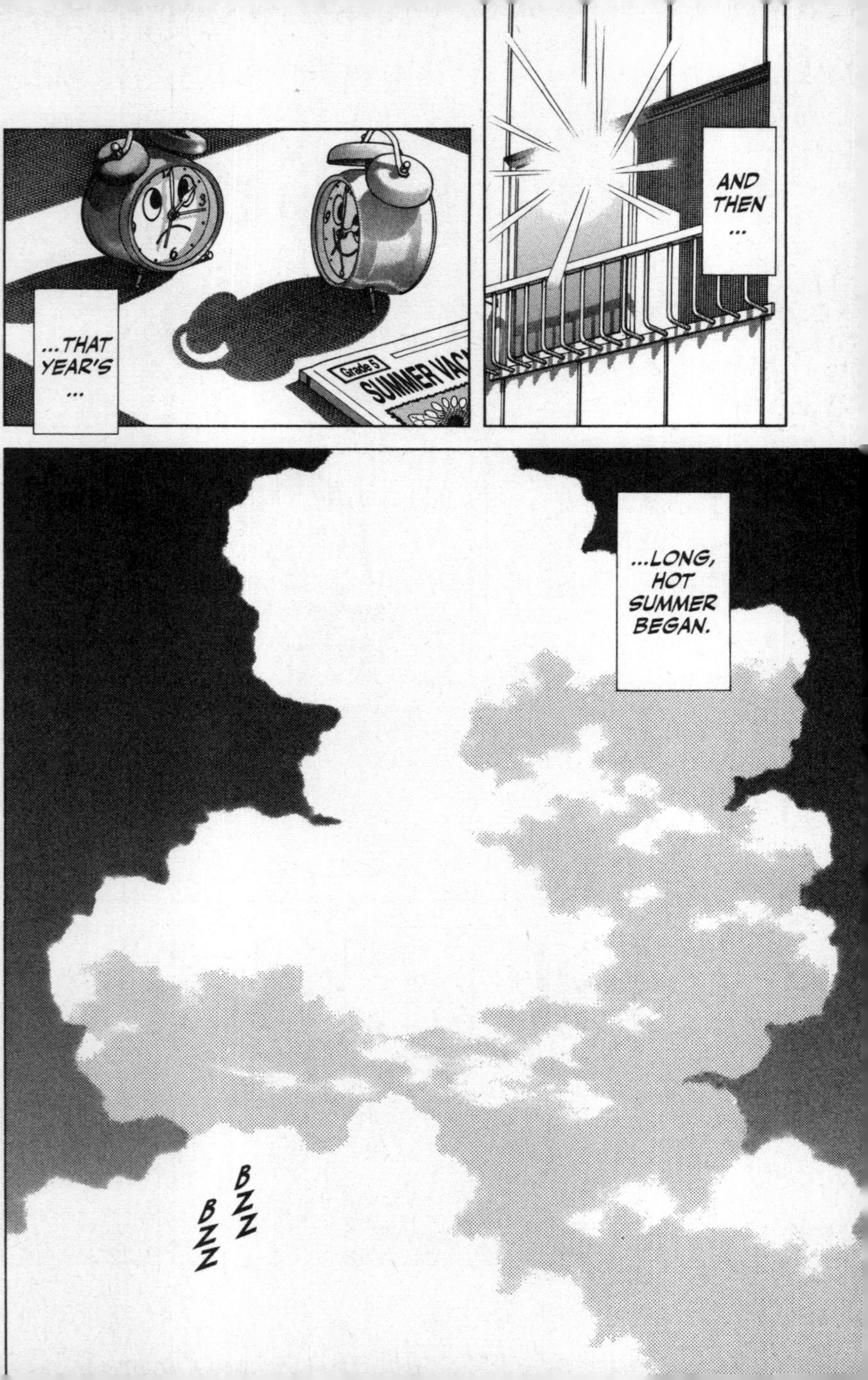
AND THEN ...
...THAT YEAR'S ...
Grade 5
SUMMER VAC
...LONG, HOT SUMMER BEGAN.
BZZ
BZZ

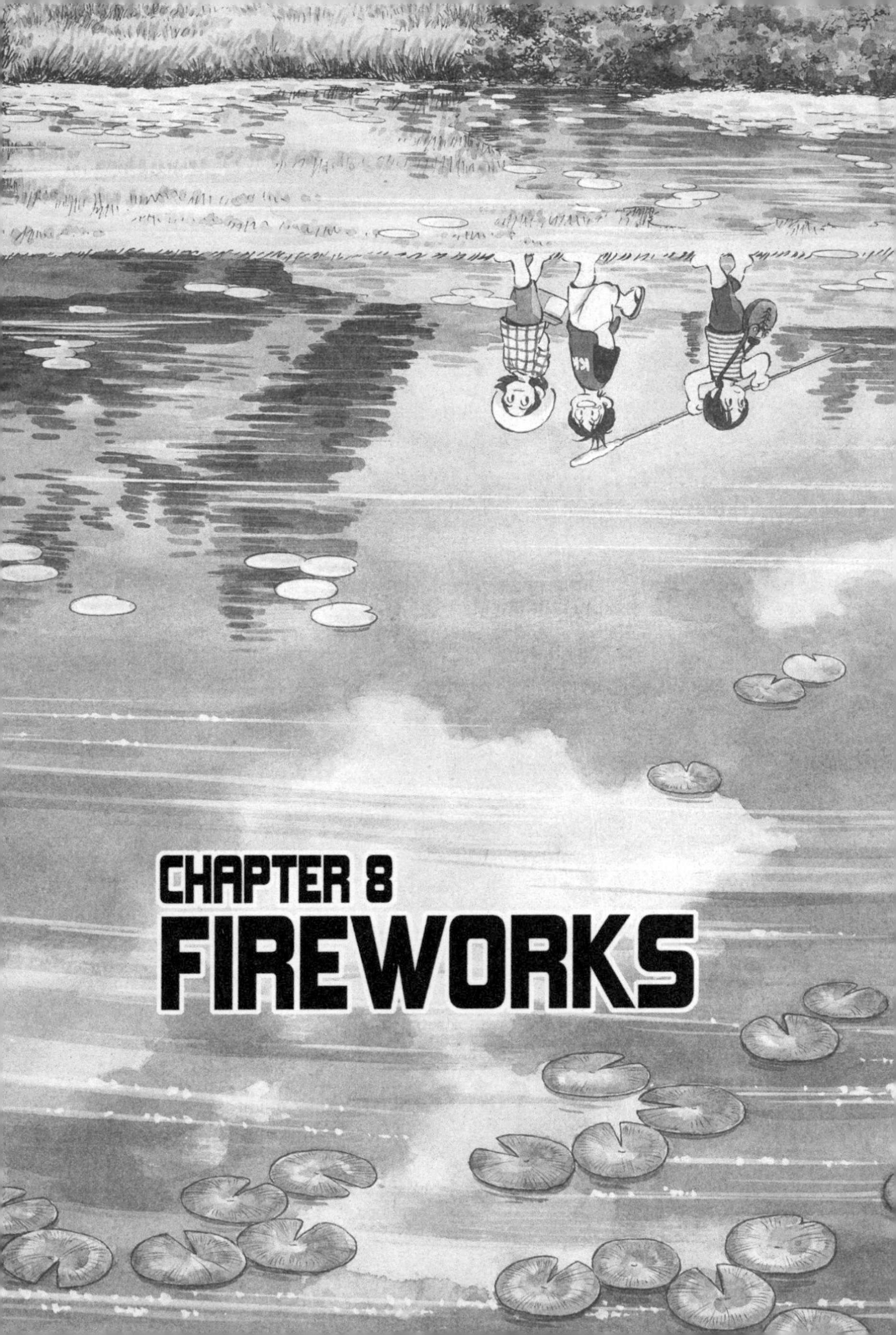

CHAPTER 8
FIREWORKS

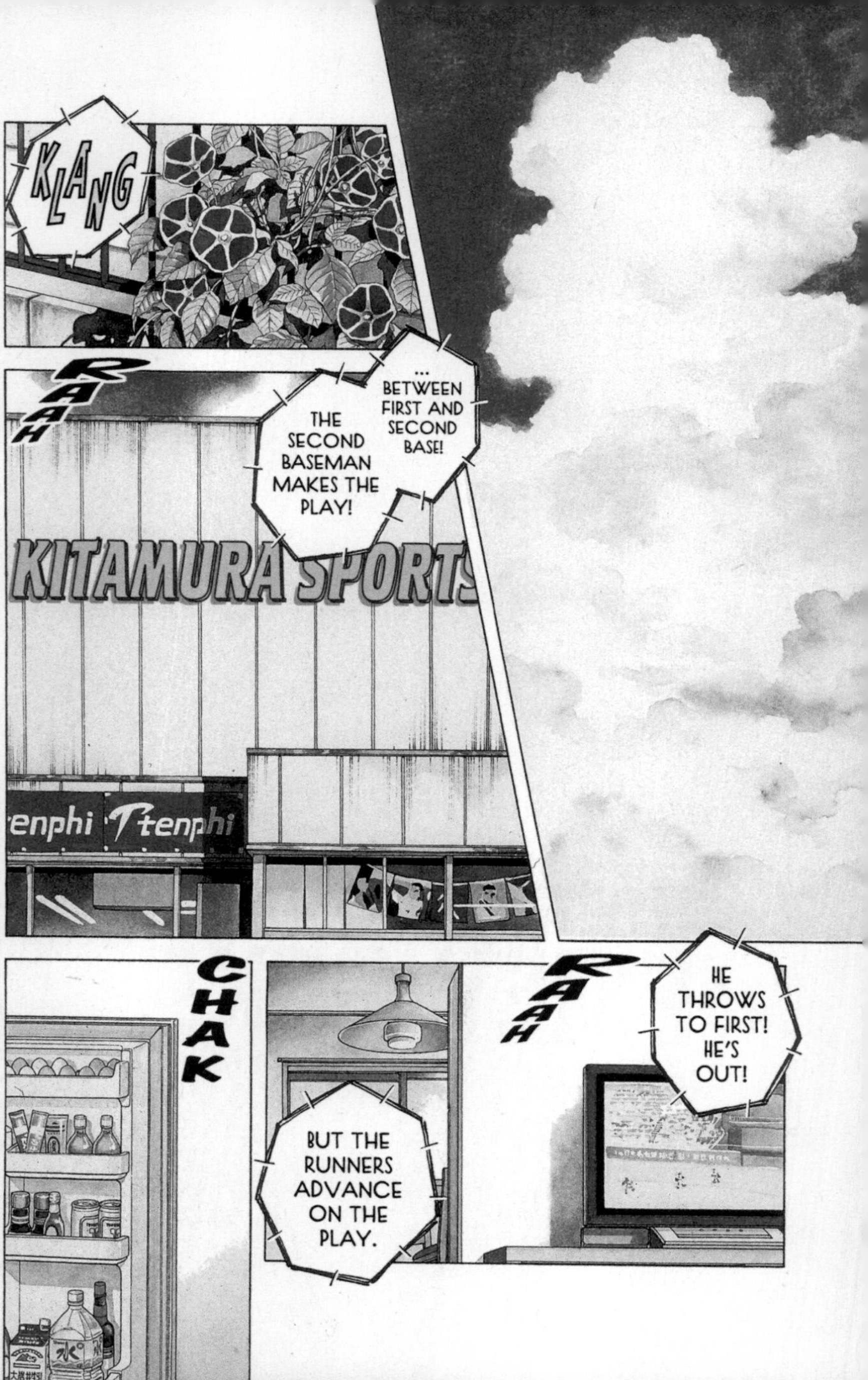
KLANG
RAAH
... BETWEEN FIRST AND SECOND BASE!
THE SECOND BASEMAN MAKES THE PLAY!
KITAMURA SPORTS
tenphi tenphi
RAAH
HE THROWS TO FIRST! HE'S OUT!
BUT THE RUNNERS ADVANCE ON THE PLAY.
CHAK

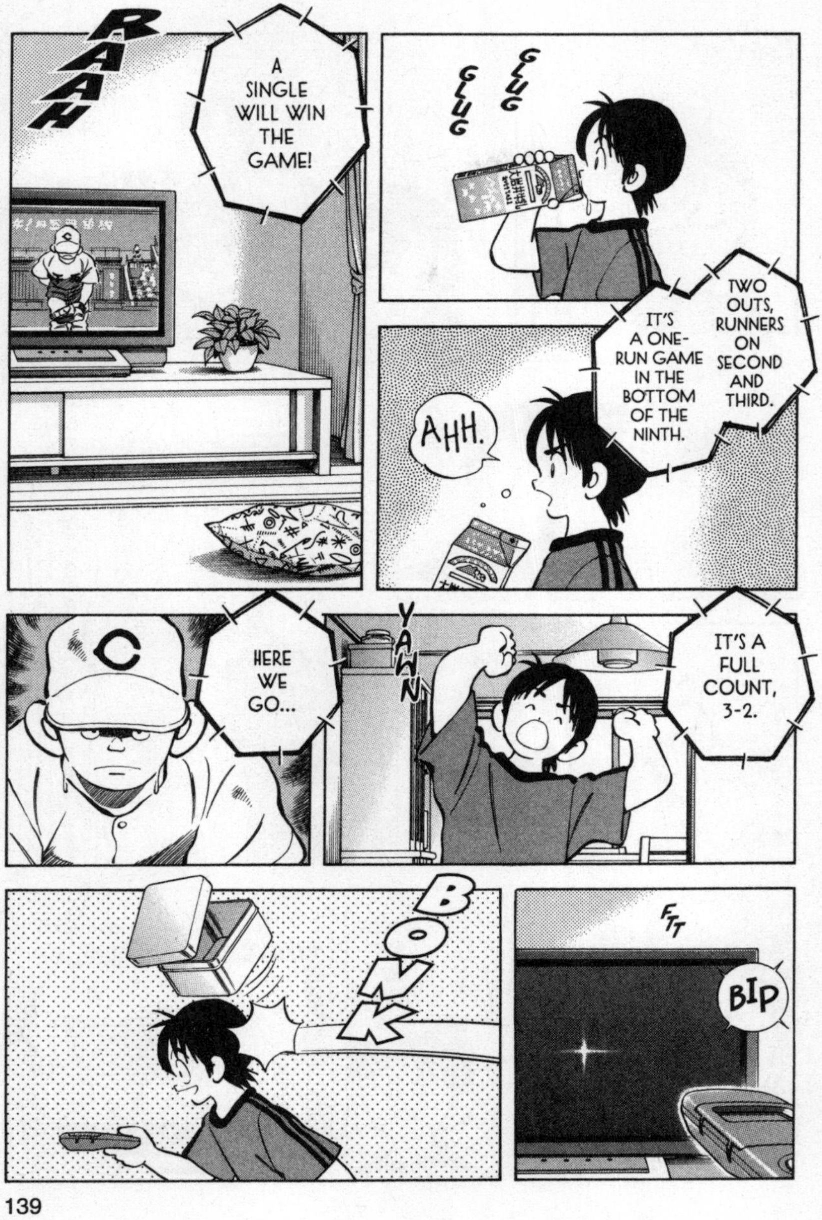
GLUG
GLUG
GLUG
TWO OUTS, RUNNERS ON SECOND AND THIRD.
IT'S A ONE-RUN GAME IN THE BOTTOM OF THE NINTH.
AHH.
RAAAH
A SINGLE WILL WIN THE GAME!
IT'S A FULL COUNT, 3-2.
YAWN
HERE WE GO...
FTT
BIP
BONK

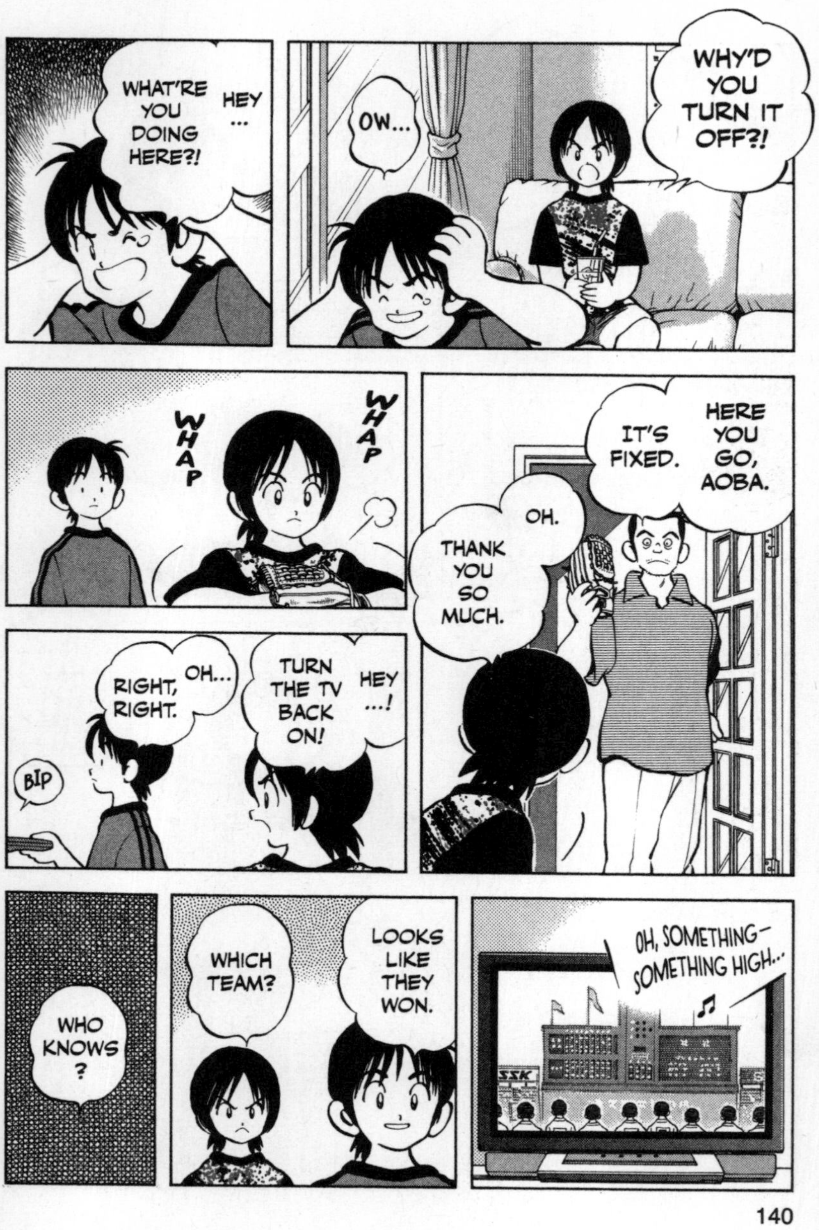
WHY'D YOU TURN IT OFF?!
OW...
HEY ...
WHAT'RE YOU DOING HERE?!
HERE YOU GO, AOBA.
IT'S FIXED.
OH.
THANK YOU SO MUCH.
WHAP
WHAP
HEY ...!
TURN THE TV BACK ON!
OH...
RIGHT, RIGHT.
BIP
OH, SOMETHING-SOMETHING HIGH... ♪
LOOKS LIKE THEY WON.
WHICH TEAM?
WHO KNOWS?

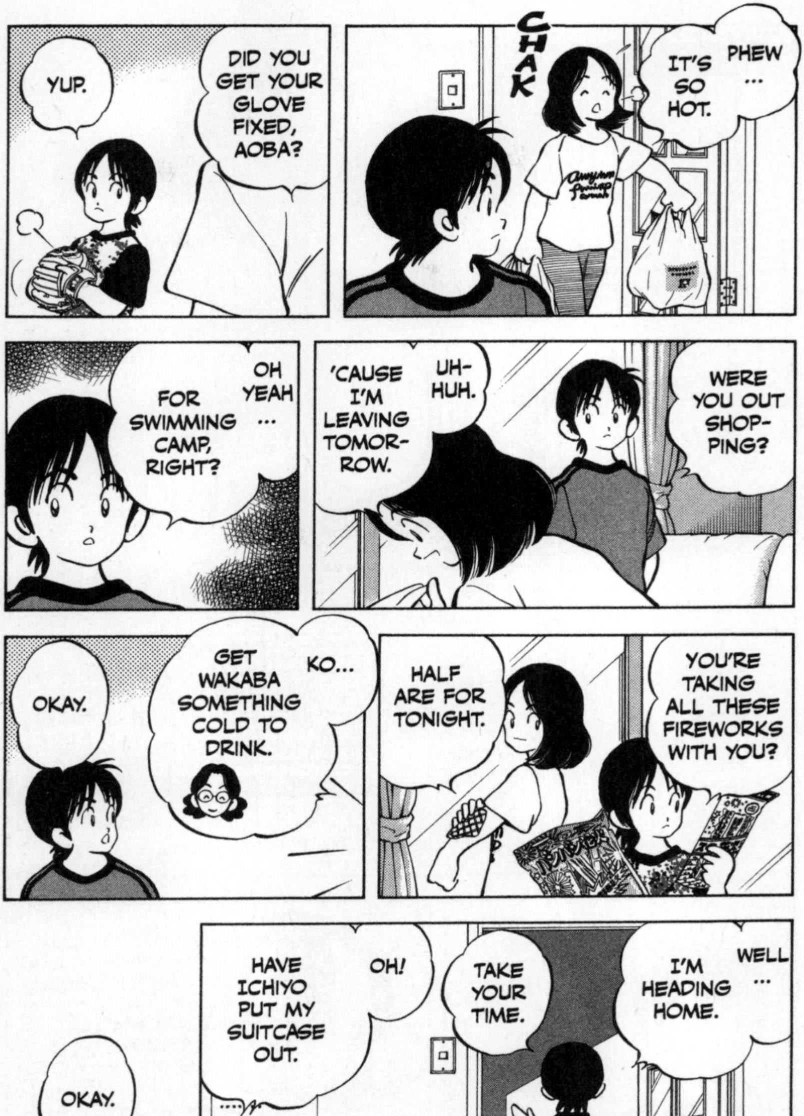
CHAK
PHEW...
IT'S SO HOT.
DID YOU GET YOUR GLOVE FIXED, AOBA?
YUP.
WERE YOU OUT SHOP-PING?
UH-HUH.
'CAUSE I'M LEAVING TOMOR-ROW.
OH YEAH...
FOR SWIMMING CAMP, RIGHT?
YOU'RE TAKING ALL THESE FIREWORKS WITH YOU?
HALF ARE FOR TONIGHT.
KO...
GET WAKABA SOMETHING COLD TO DRINK.
OKAY.
WELL...
I'M HEADING HOME.
TAKE YOUR TIME.
OH!
HAVE ICHIYO PUT MY SUITCASE OUT.
OKAY.

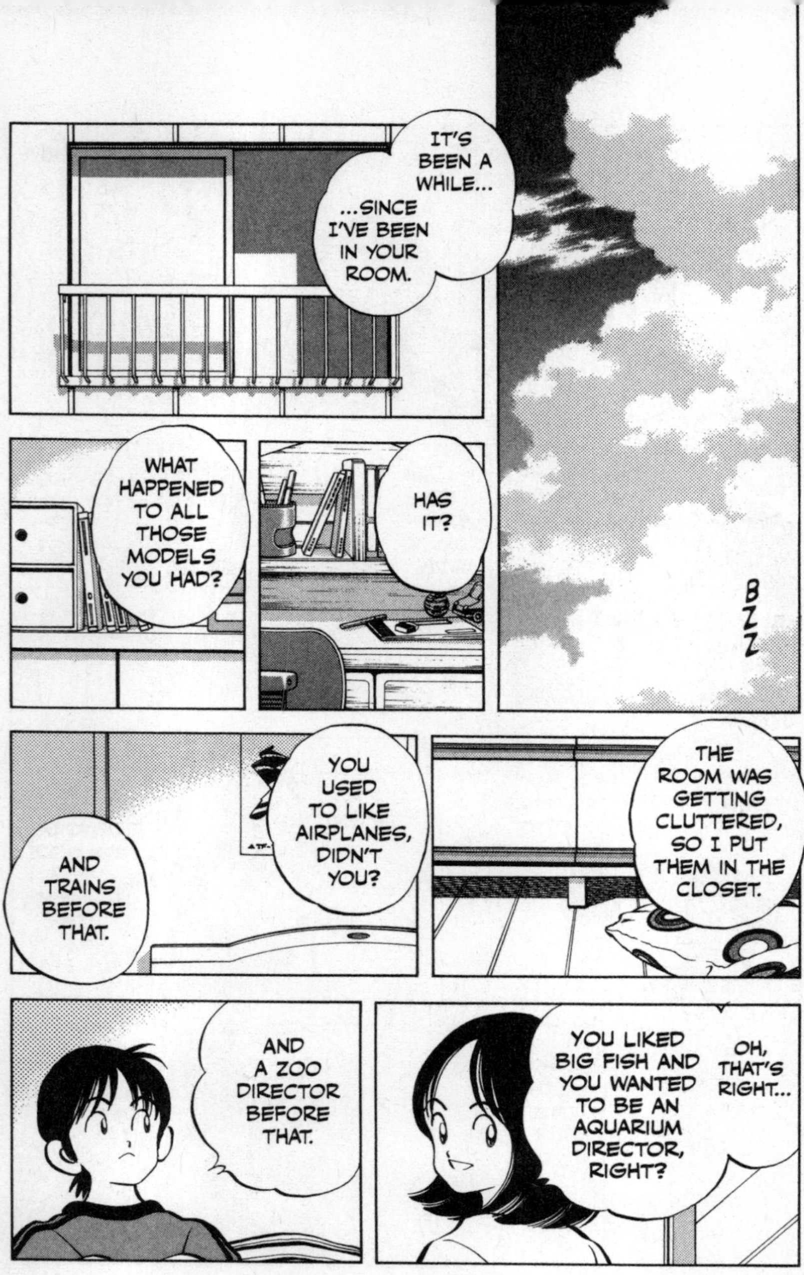
BZZ
IT'S BEEN A WHILE...
...SINCE I'VE BEEN IN YOUR ROOM.
HAS IT?
WHAT HAPPENED TO ALL THOSE MODELS YOU HAD?
THE ROOM WAS GETTING CLUTTERED, SO I PUT THEM IN THE CLOSET.
YOU USED TO LIKE AIRPLANES, DIDN'T YOU?
AND TRAINS BEFORE THAT.
OH, THAT'S RIGHT...
YOU LIKED BIG FISH AND YOU WANTED TO BE AN AQUARIUM DIRECTOR, RIGHT?
AND A ZOO DIRECTOR BEFORE THAT.

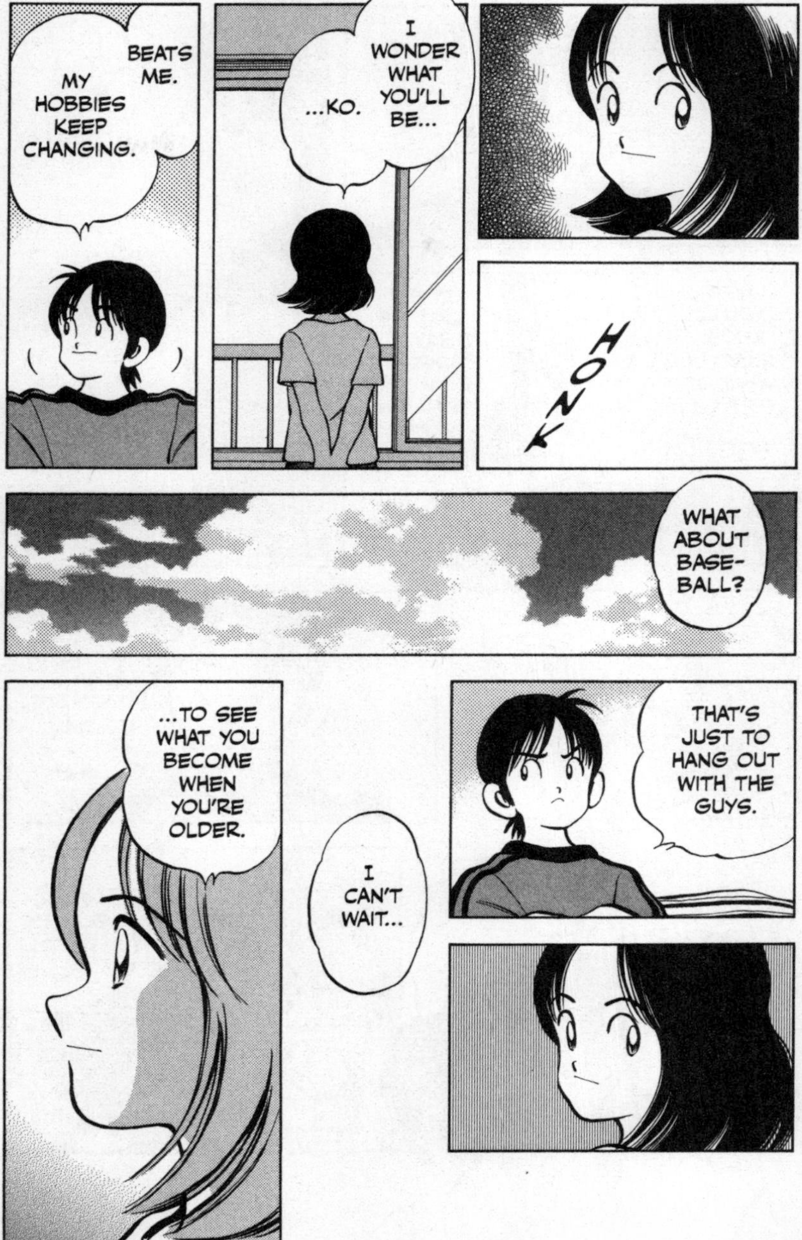
HONK
I WONDER WHAT YOU'LL BE...
...KO.
BEATS ME.
MY HOBBIES KEEP CHANGING.
WHAT ABOUT BASE-BALL?
THAT'S JUST TO HANG OUT WITH THE GUYS.
I CAN'T WAIT...
...TO SEE WHAT YOU BECOME WHEN YOU'RE OLDER.

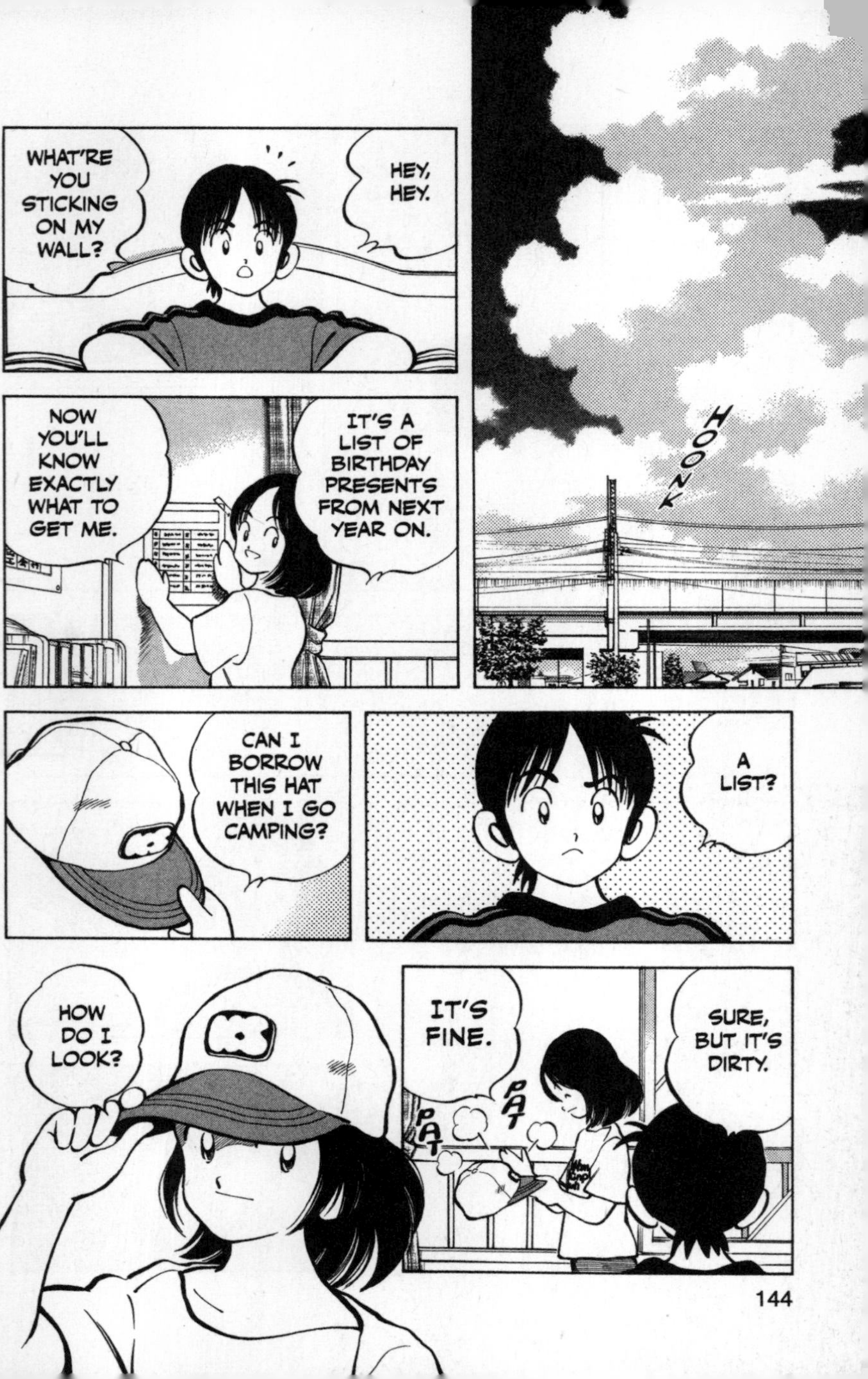
HOONK
HEY, HEY.
WHAT'RE YOU STICKING ON MY WALL?
IT'S A LIST OF BIRTHDAY PRESENTS FROM NEXT YEAR ON.
NOW YOU'LL KNOW EXACTLY WHAT TO GET ME.
A LIST?
CAN I BORROW THIS HAT WHEN I GO CAMPING?
SURE, BUT IT'S DIRTY.
IT'S FINE.
PAT
PAT
HOW DO I LOOK?

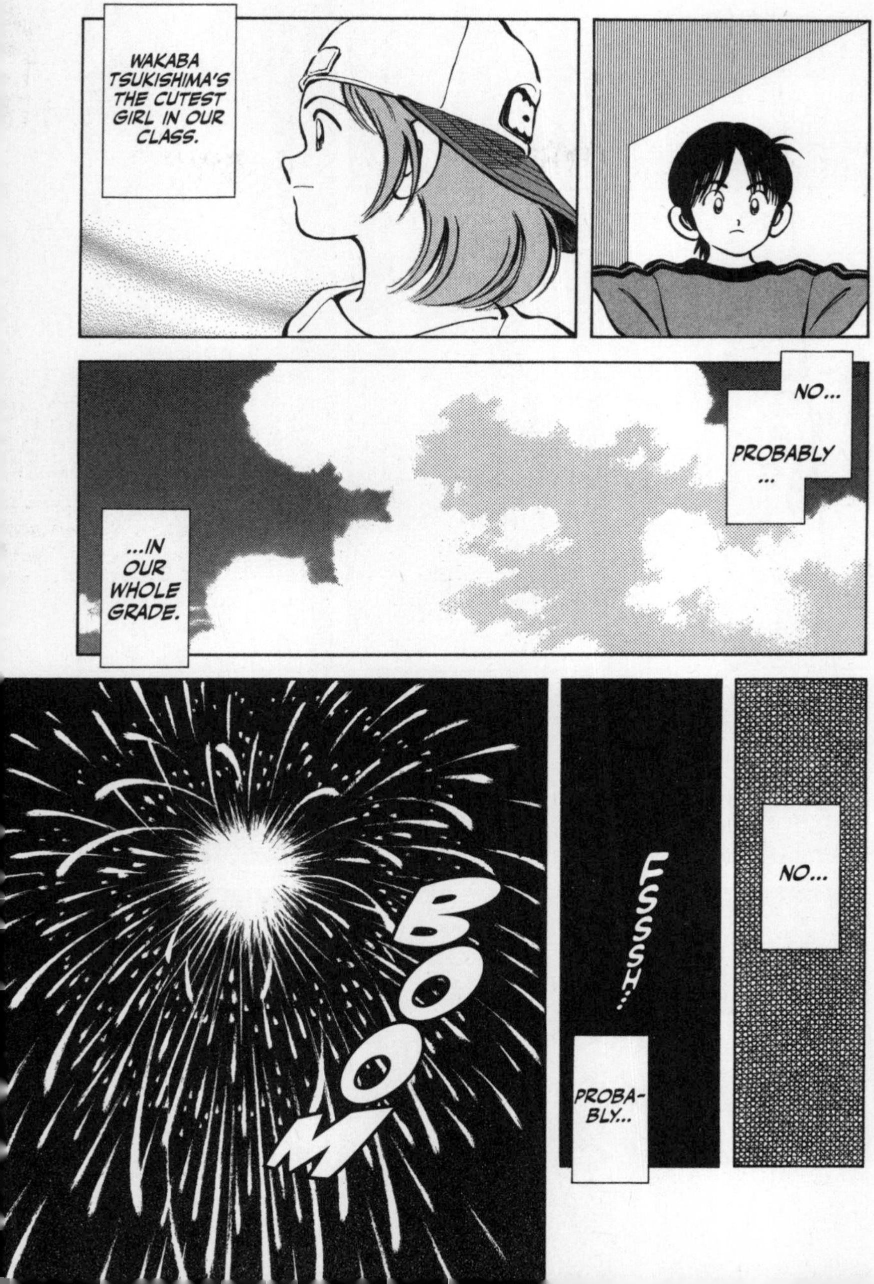
WAKABA TSUKISHIMA'S THE CUTEST GIRL IN OUR CLASS.
NO...
PROBABLY...
...IN OUR WHOLE GRADE.
NO...
FSSSH...
PROBA-BLY...
BOOOM

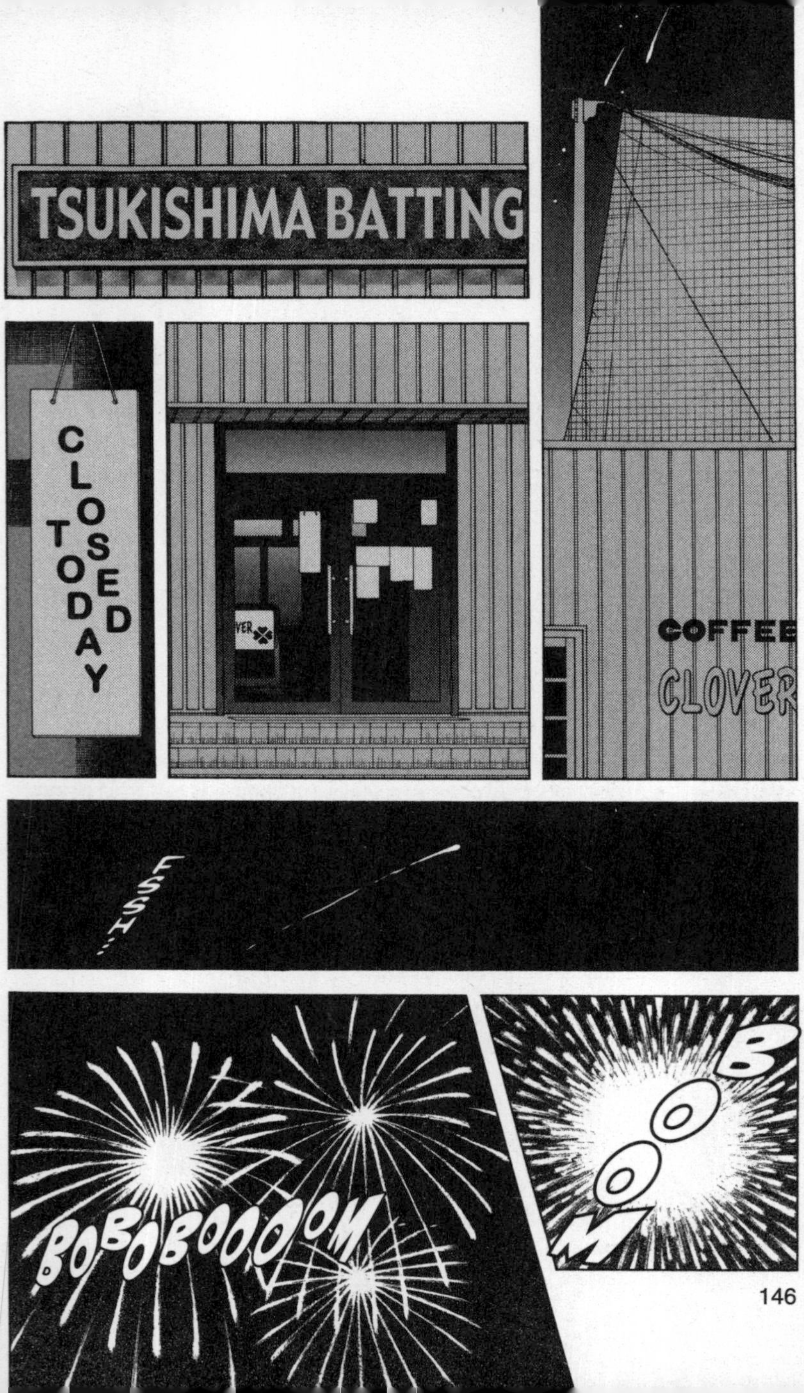
COFFEE
CLOVER
TSUKISHIMA BATTING
VER
CLOSED TODAY
FSSH...
BOOOM
BOBOBOOOOM

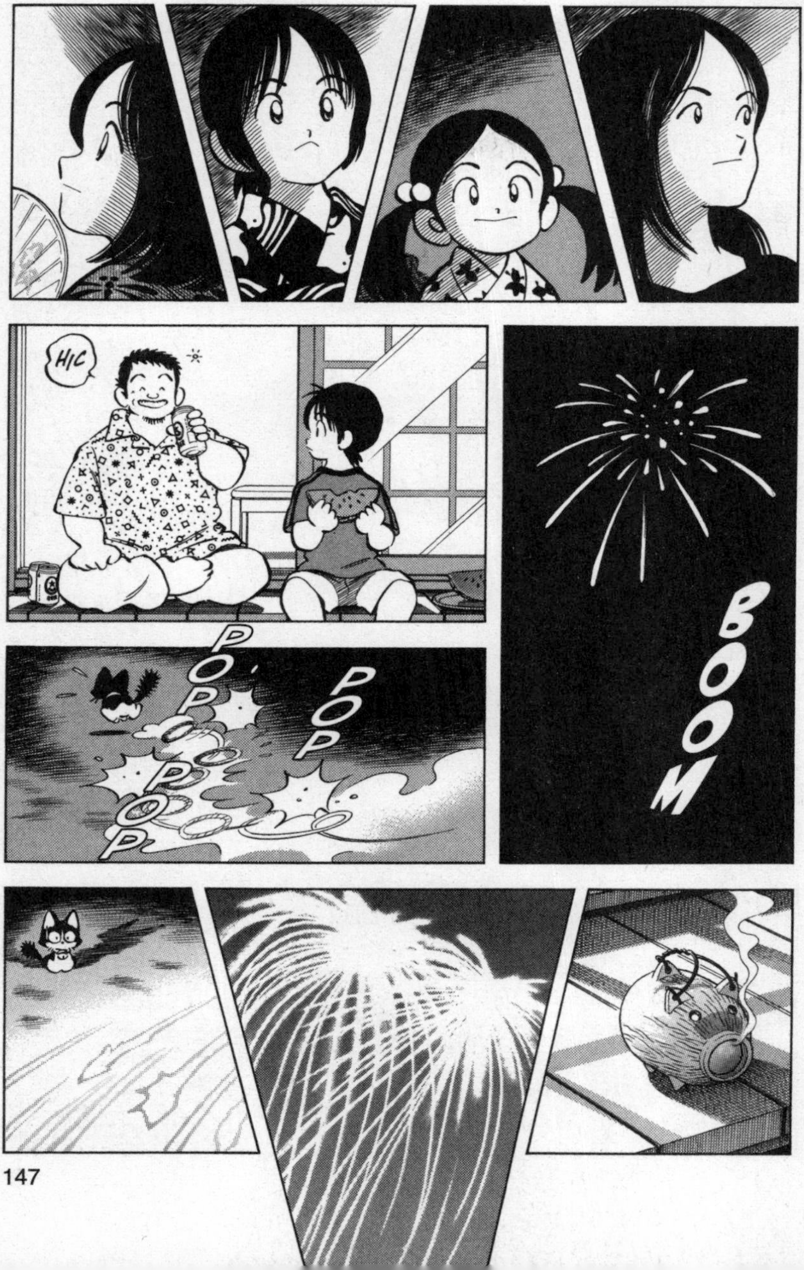
BOOM
HIC
POP
POP
POP

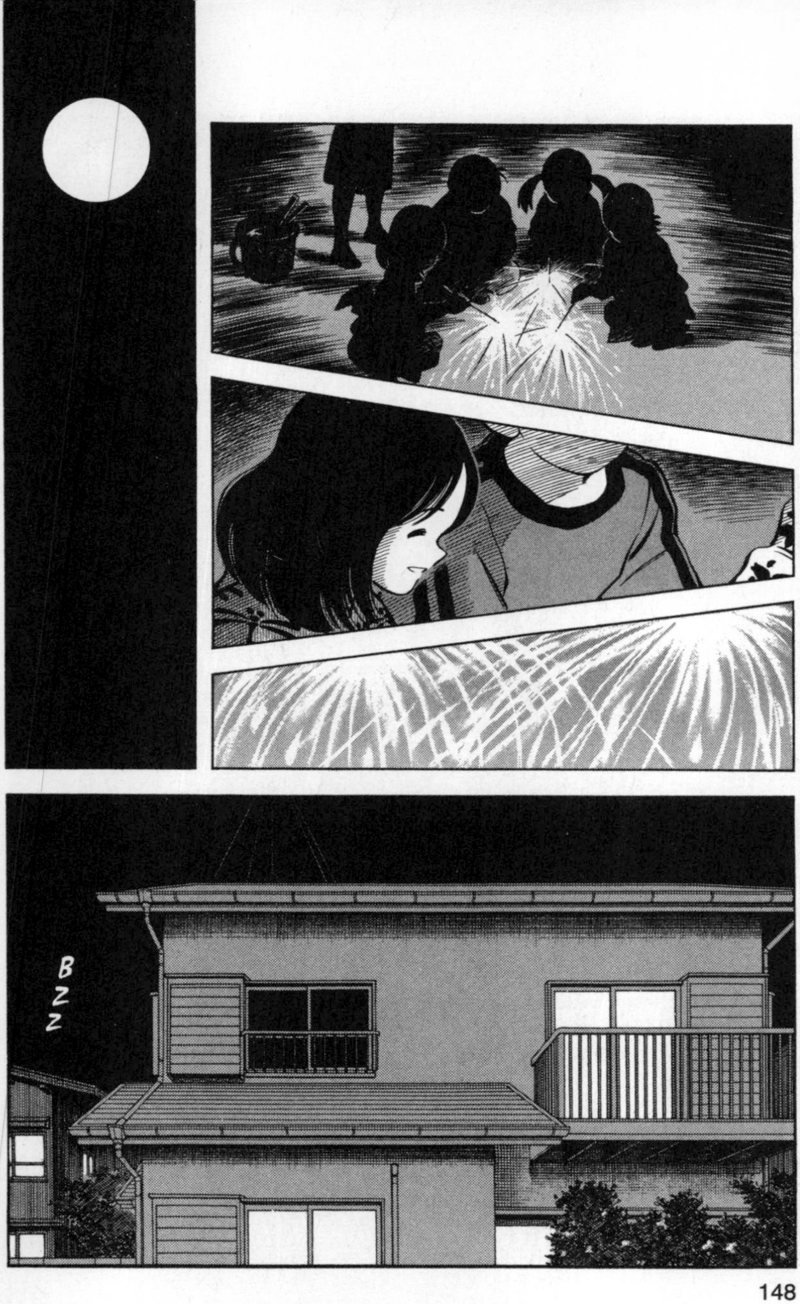
BZZ

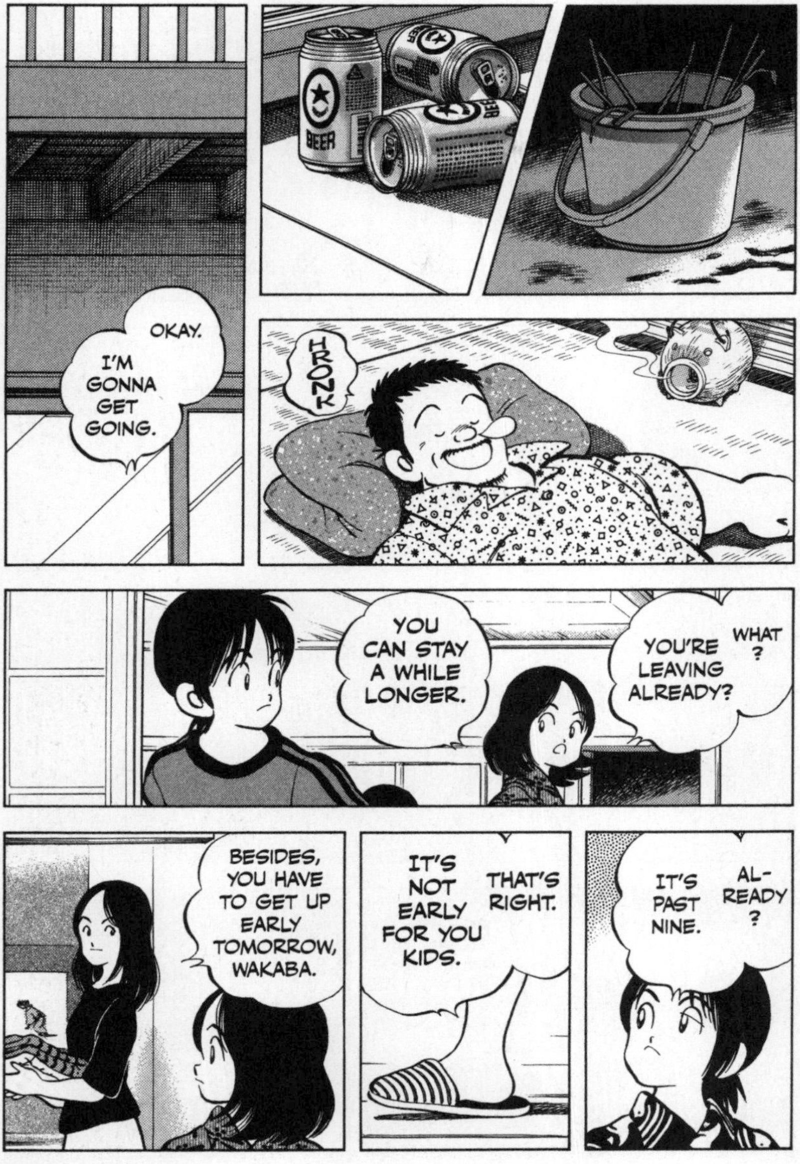
HRONK
OKAY. I'M GONNA GET GOING.
WHAT?
YOU'RE LEAVING ALREADY?
YOU CAN STAY A WHILE LONGER.
AL-READY?
IT'S PAST NINE.
THAT'S RIGHT.
IT'S NOT EARLY FOR YOU KIDS.
BESIDES, YOU HAVE TO GET UP EARLY TOMORROW, WAKABA.

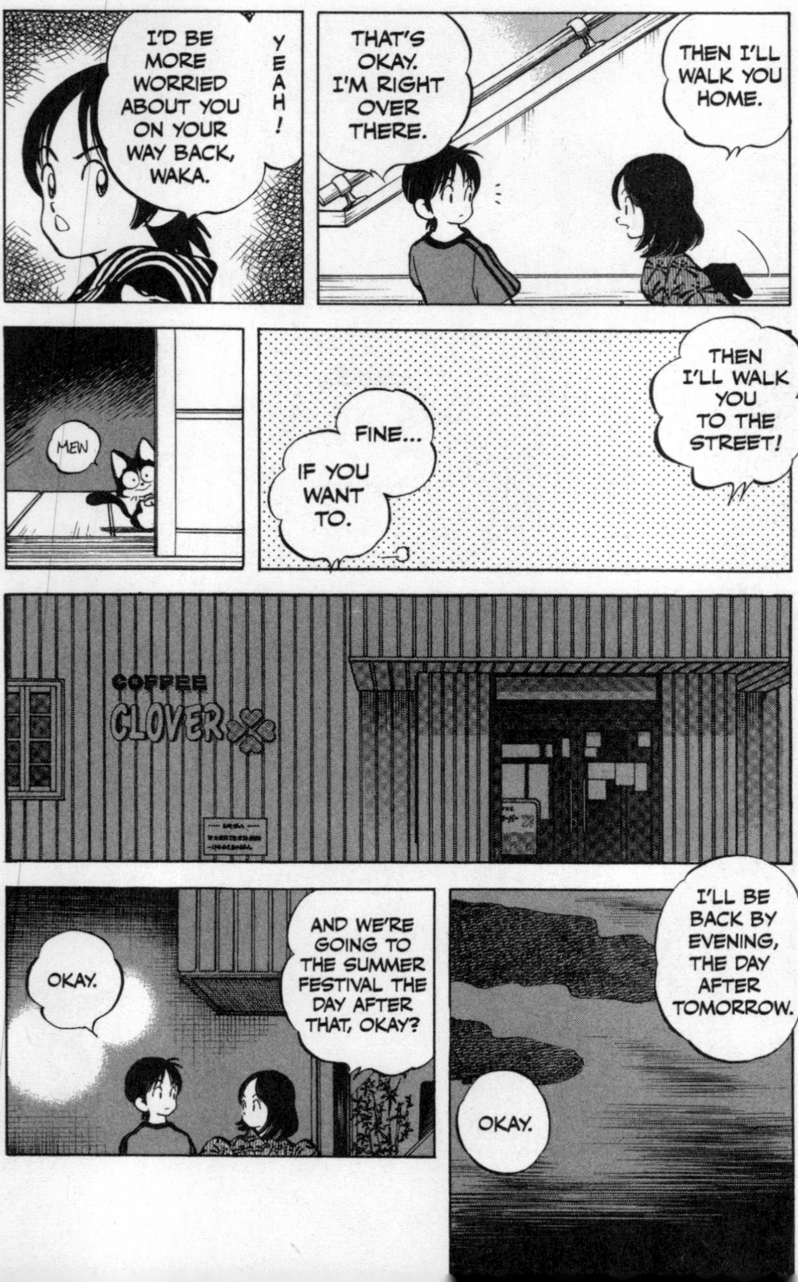
THEN I'LL WALK YOU HOME.
THAT'S OKAY. I'M RIGHT OVER THERE.
YEAH!
I'D BE MORE WORRIED ABOUT YOU ON YOUR WAY BACK, WAKA.
THEN I'LL WALK YOU TO THE STREET!
FINE... IF YOU WANT TO.
MEW
COFFEE
CLOVER
I'LL BE BACK BY EVENING, THE DAY AFTER TOMORROW.
OKAY.
AND WE'RE GOING TO THE SUMMER FESTIVAL THE DAY AFTER THAT, OKAY?
OKAY.

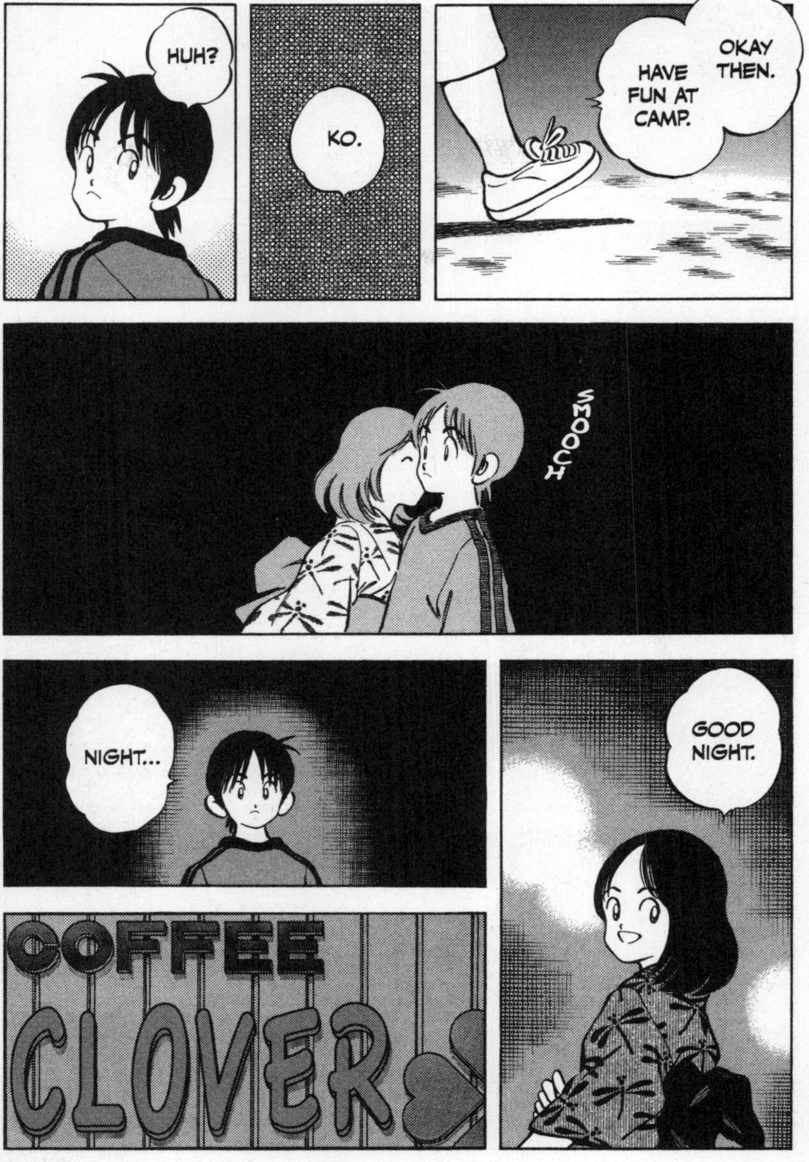
OKAY THEN.
HAVE FUN AT CAMP.
KO.
HUH?
SMOOCH
GOOD NIGHT.
NIGHT...
COFFEE
CLOVER

TOMORROW'S GOING TO BE ANOTHER HOT ONE.

WEATHER REPORT

20% OFF

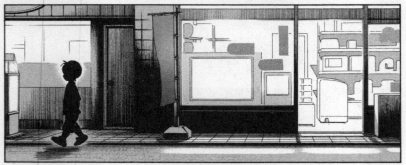

VROOOOM

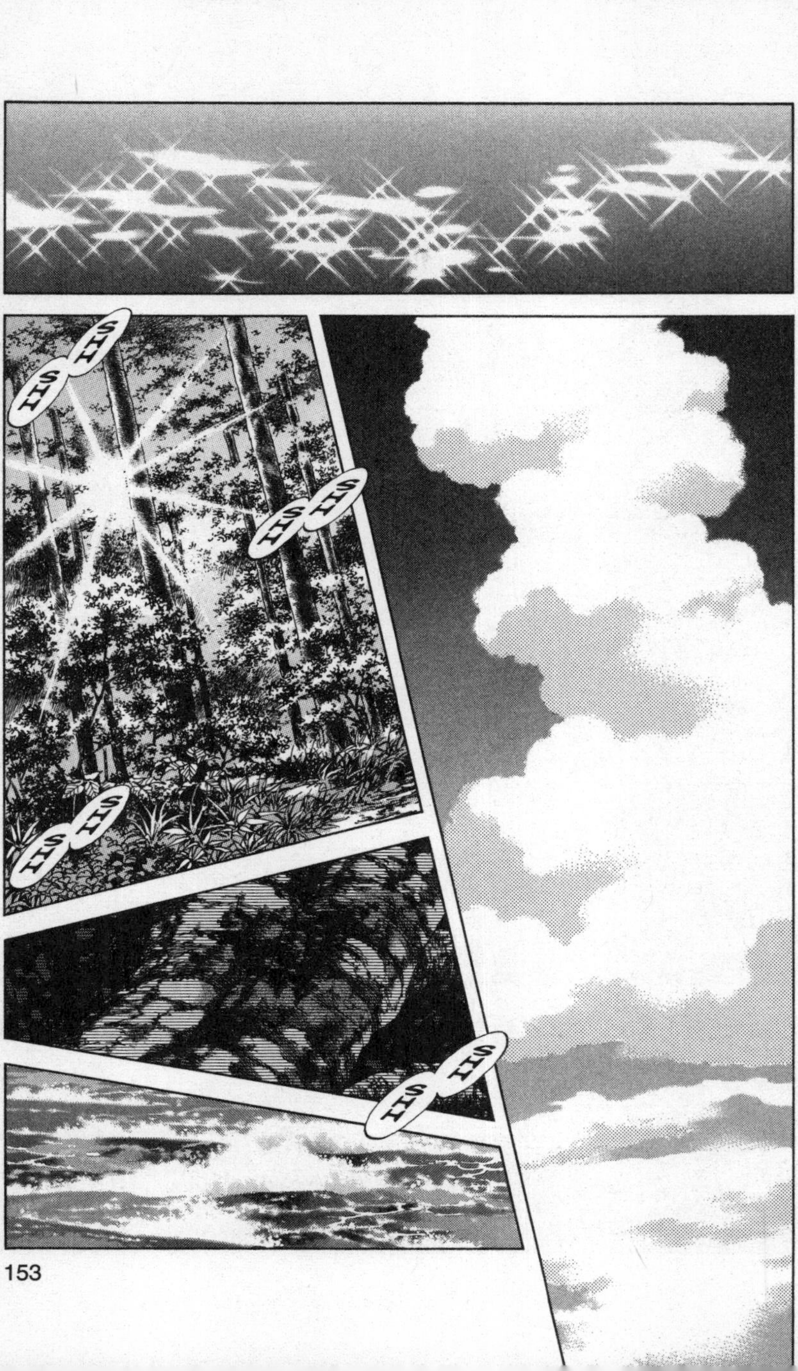
SHH SHH
SHH SHH
SHH SHH
SHH SHH

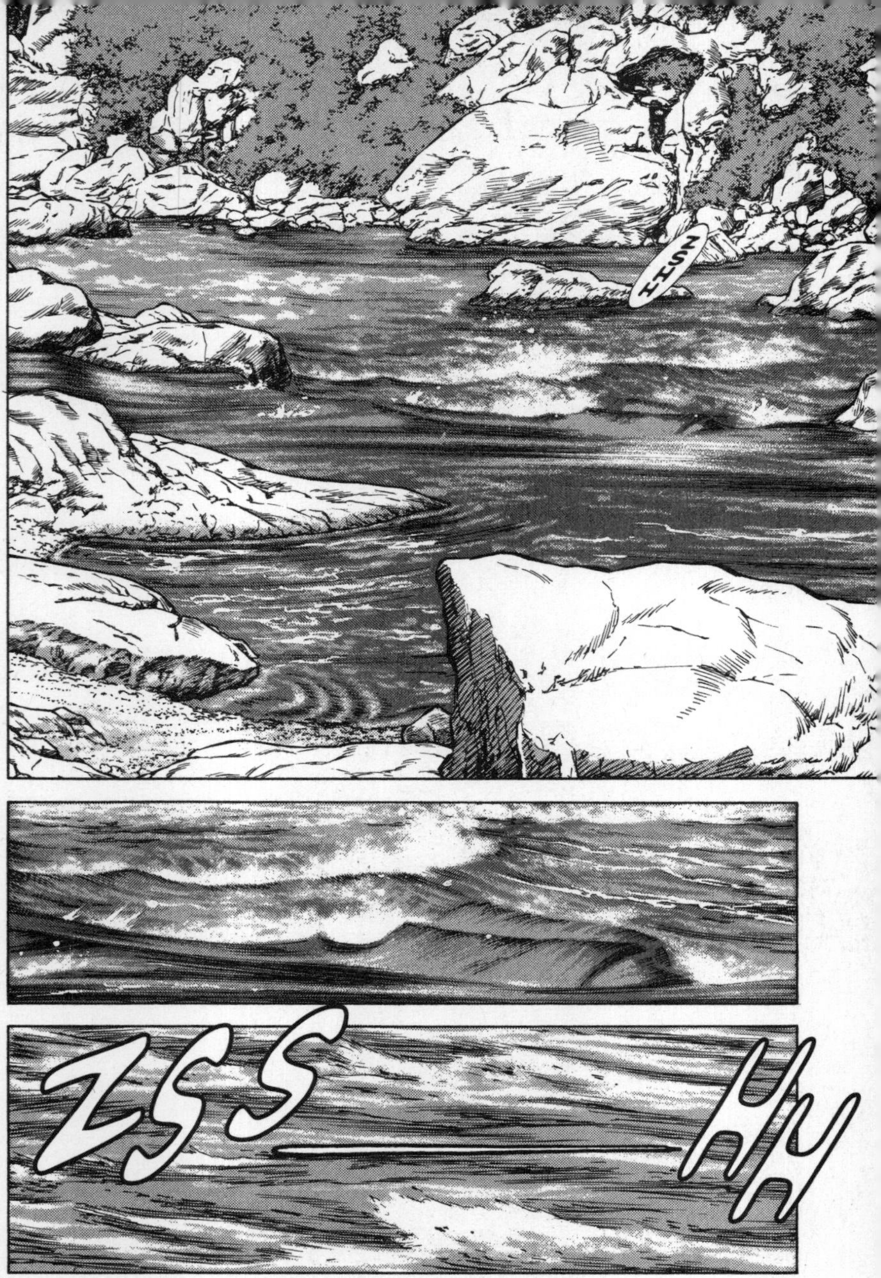
ZSHH
ZSS—HH

CHAPTER 9
SHE SAID BY EVENING

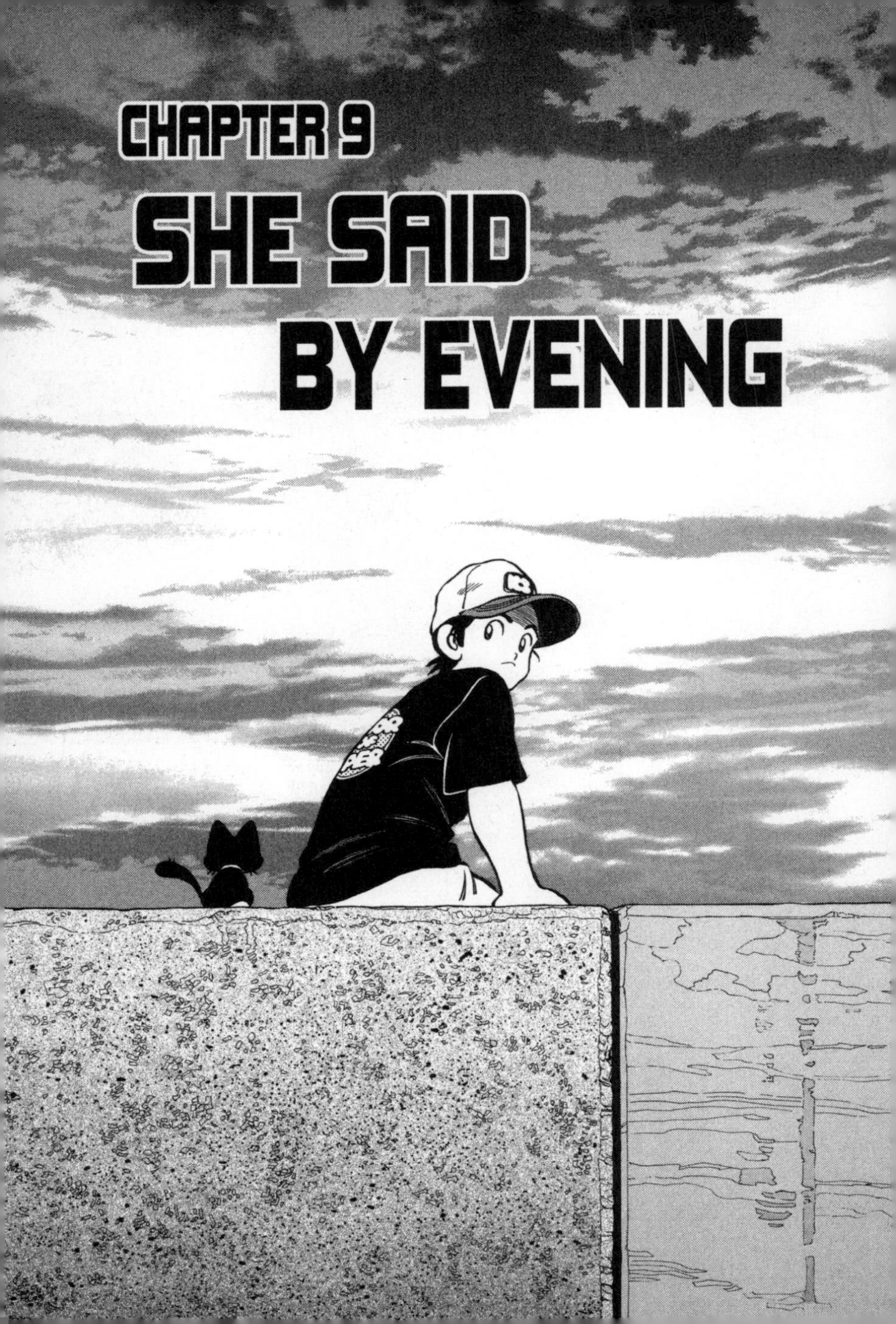

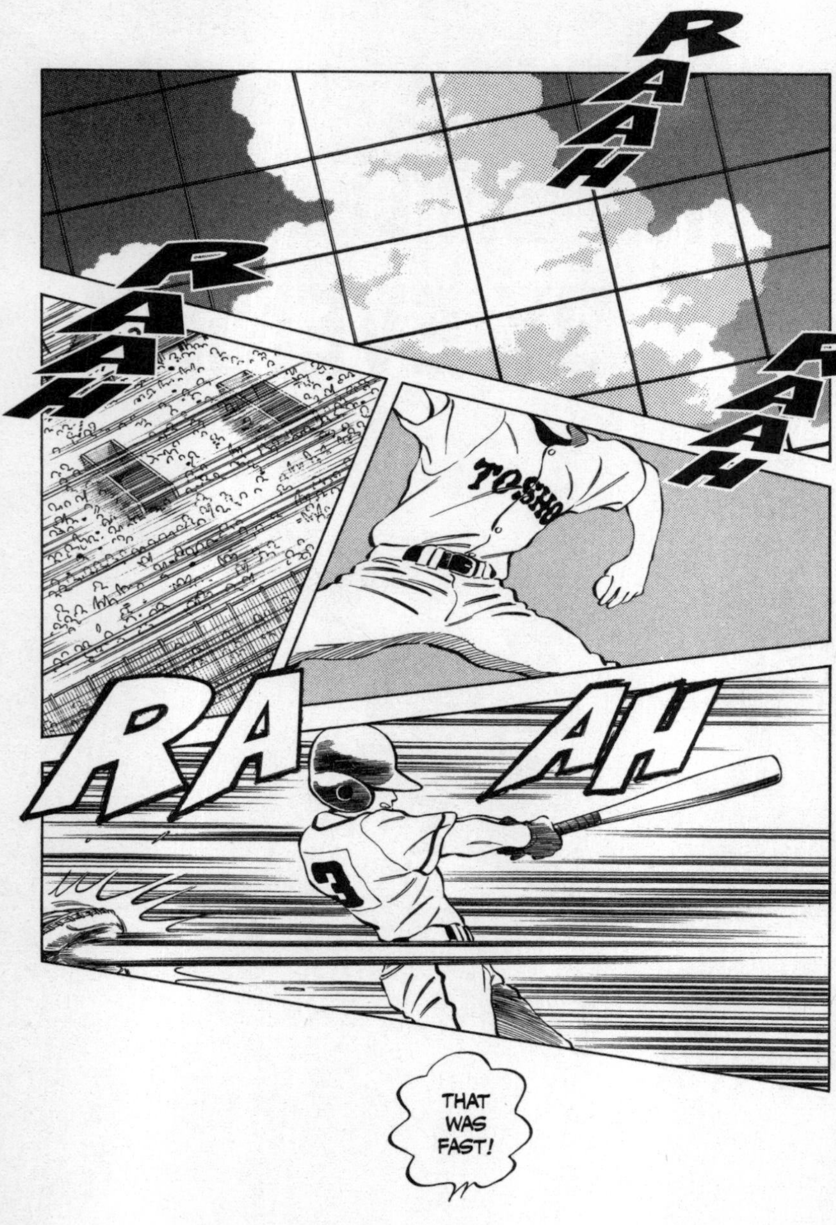
RAAH
RAAH
RAAH
TOSHO
RA AH
3
THAT WAS FAST!

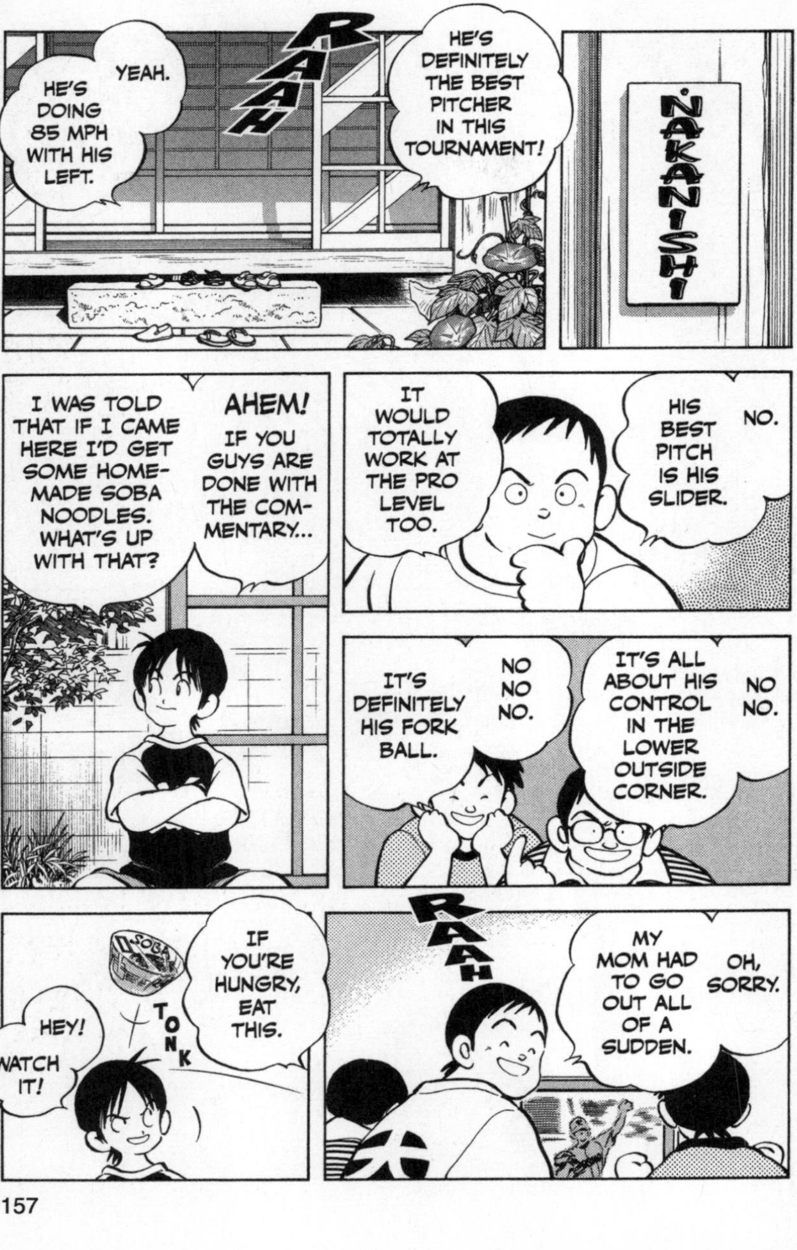
NAKANISHI
HE'S DEFINITELY THE BEST PITCHER IN THIS TOURNAMENT!
RAAH
YEAH.
HE'S DOING 85 MPH WITH HIS LEFT.
NO.
HIS BEST PITCH IS HIS SLIDER.
IT WOULD TOTALLY WORK AT THE PRO LEVEL TOO.
NO NO.
IT'S ALL ABOUT HIS CONTROL IN THE LOWER OUTSIDE CORNER.
NO NO NO.
IT'S DEFINITELY HIS FORK BALL.
AHEM!
IF YOU GUYS ARE DONE WITH THE COMMENTARY...
I WAS TOLD THAT IF I CAME HERE I'D GET SOME HOME-MADE SOBA NOODLES. WHAT'S UP WITH THAT?
RAAH
OH, SORRY.
MY MOM HAD TO GO OUT ALL OF A SUDDEN.
IF YOU'RE HUNGRY, EAT THIS.
SOBA
TONK
HEY!
WATCH IT!

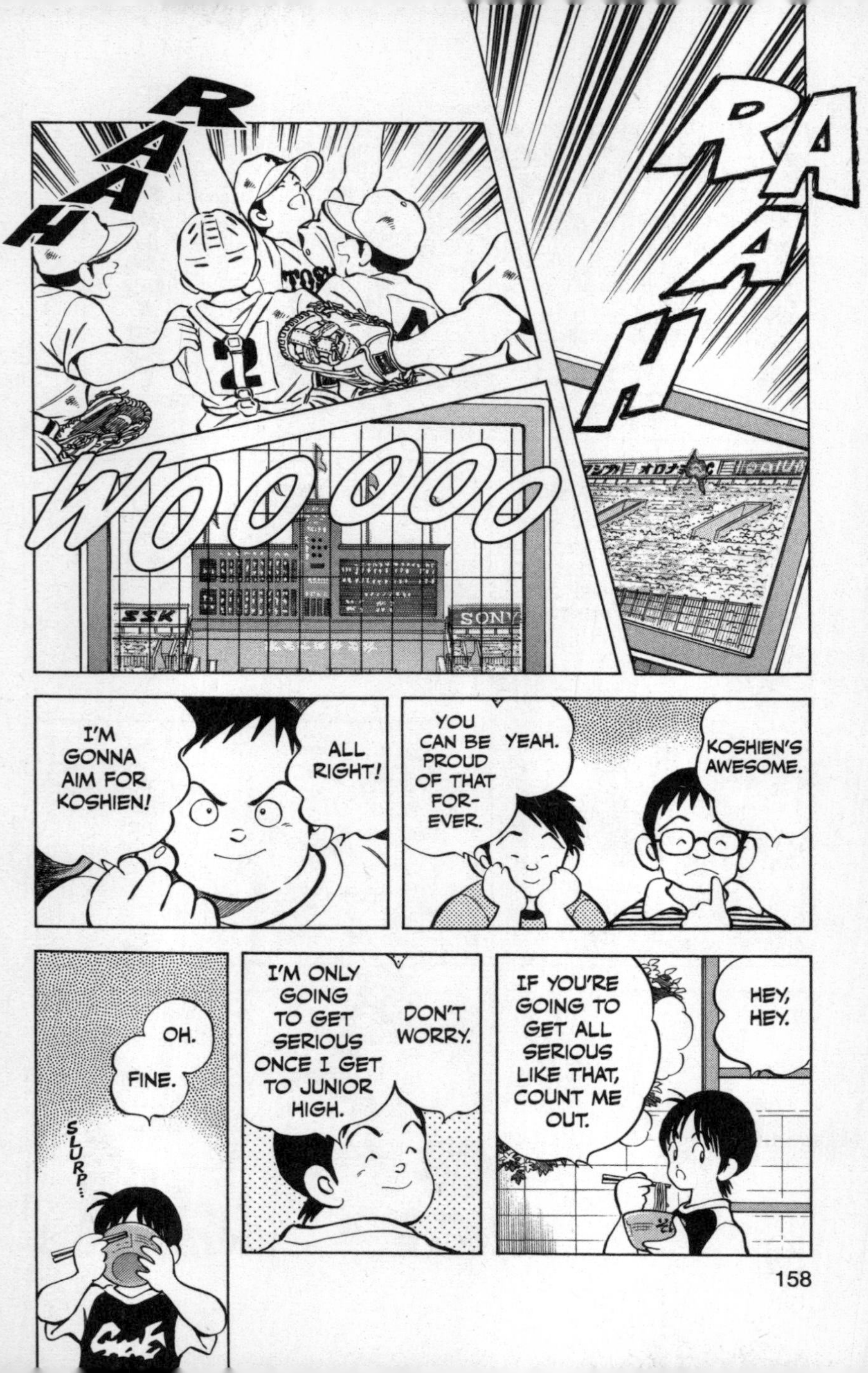
RAAH
RAAH
WOOOOO
KOSHIEN'S AWESOME.
YEAH.
YOU CAN BE PROUD OF THAT FOR-EVER.
ALL RIGHT!
I'M GONNA AIM FOR KOSHIEN!
HEY, HEY.
IF YOU'RE GOING TO GET ALL SERIOUS LIKE THAT, COUNT ME OUT.
DON'T WORRY.
I'M ONLY GOING TO GET SERIOUS ONCE I GET TO JUNIOR HIGH.
OH.
FINE.
SLURP...

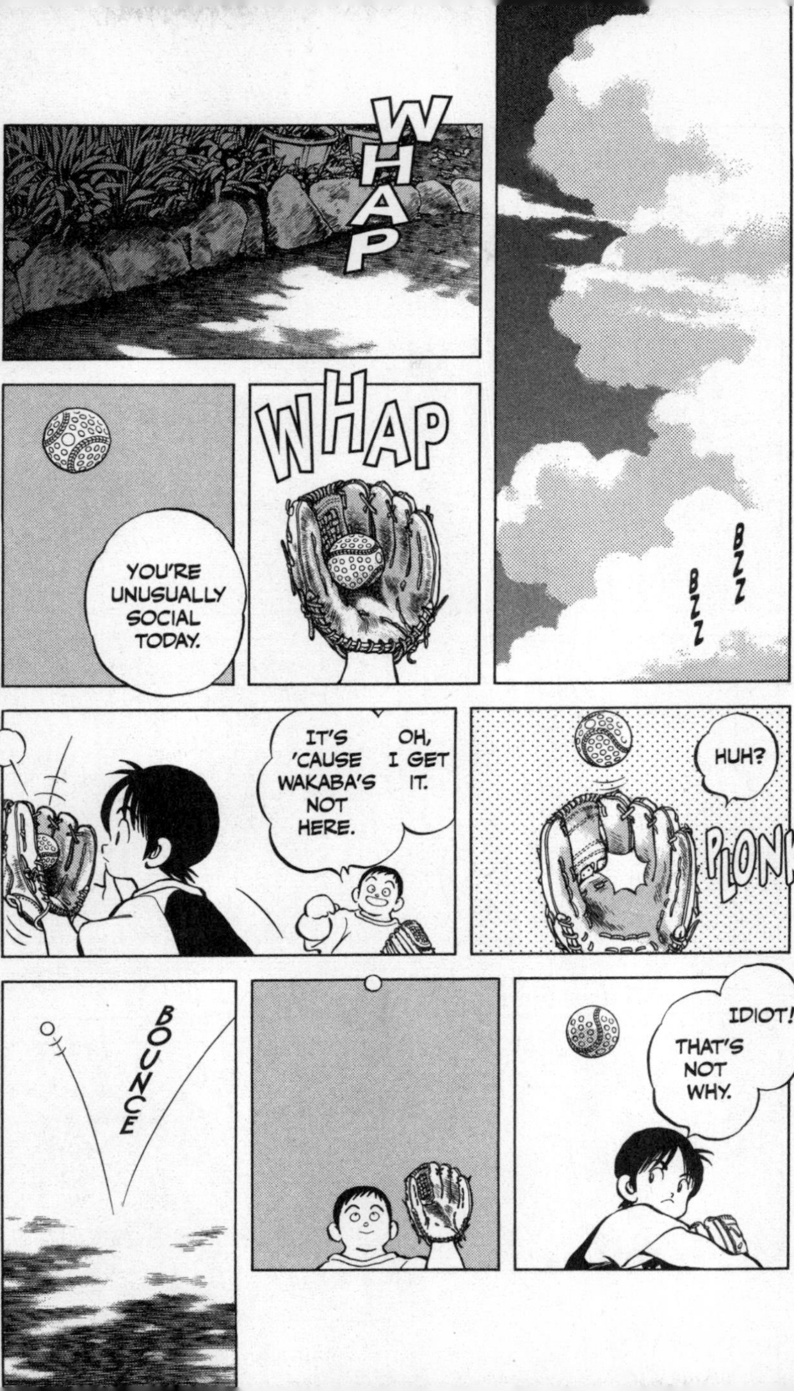
BZZ
BZZ
WHAP
WHAP
YOU'RE UNUSUALLY SOCIAL TODAY.
HUH?
PLONK
OH, I GET IT.
IT'S 'CAUSE WAKABA'S NOT HERE.
IDIOT! THAT'S NOT WHY.
BOUNCE

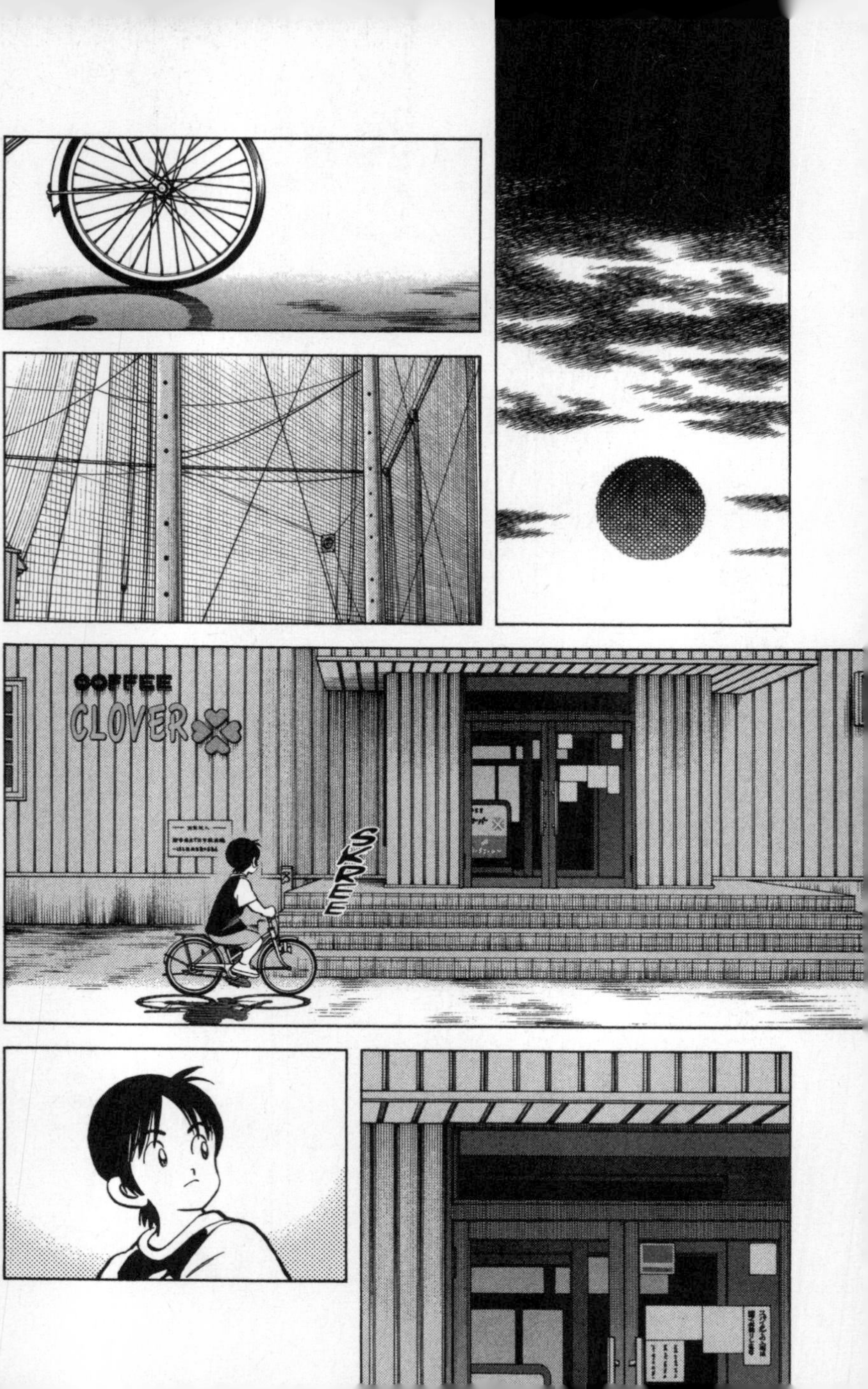
COFFEE
CLOVER
SKREE

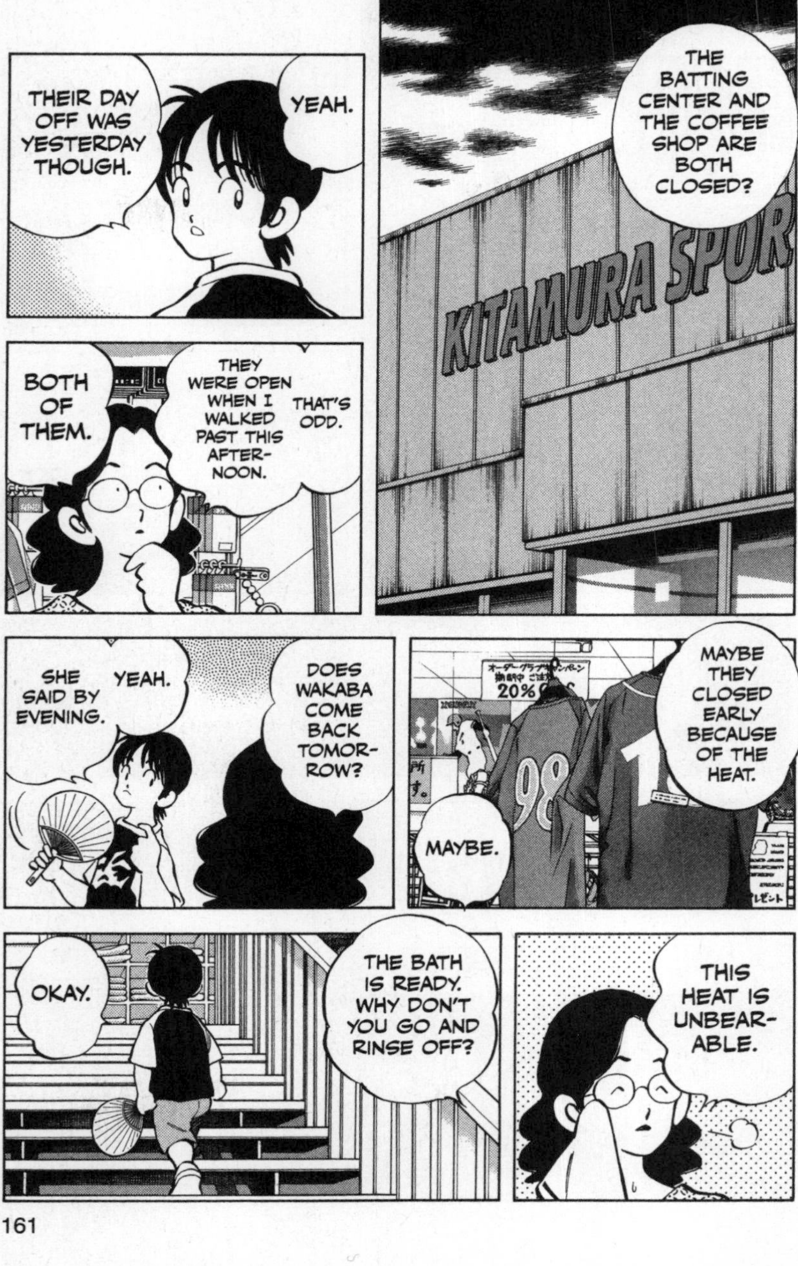
THE BATTING CENTER AND THE COFFEE SHOP ARE BOTH CLOSED?
KITAMURA SPOR
YEAH.
THEIR DAY OFF WAS YESTERDAY THOUGH.
THAT'S ODD.
THEY WERE OPEN WHEN I WALKED PAST THIS AFTER-NOON.
BOTH OF THEM.
MAYBE THEY CLOSED EARLY BECAUSE OF THE HEAT.
MAYBE.
DOES WAKABA COME BACK TOMOR-ROW?
YEAH.
SHE SAID BY EVENING.
THIS HEAT IS UNBEAR-ABLE.
THE BATH IS READY. WHY DON'T YOU GO AND RINSE OFF?
OKAY.

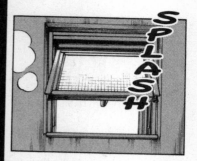

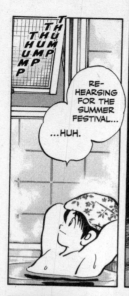

SPLASH
PHEW.
TWEET TWEET
THUMP THUMP THUMP
RE-HEARSING FOR THE SUMMER FESTIVAL...
...HUH.
Wakaba Tsukishima's Birthday Present List
12th Cute pin
18th Earrings
TICK
TICK
TICK

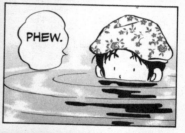

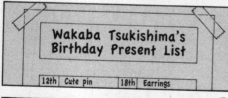

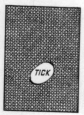

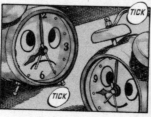

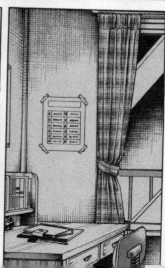

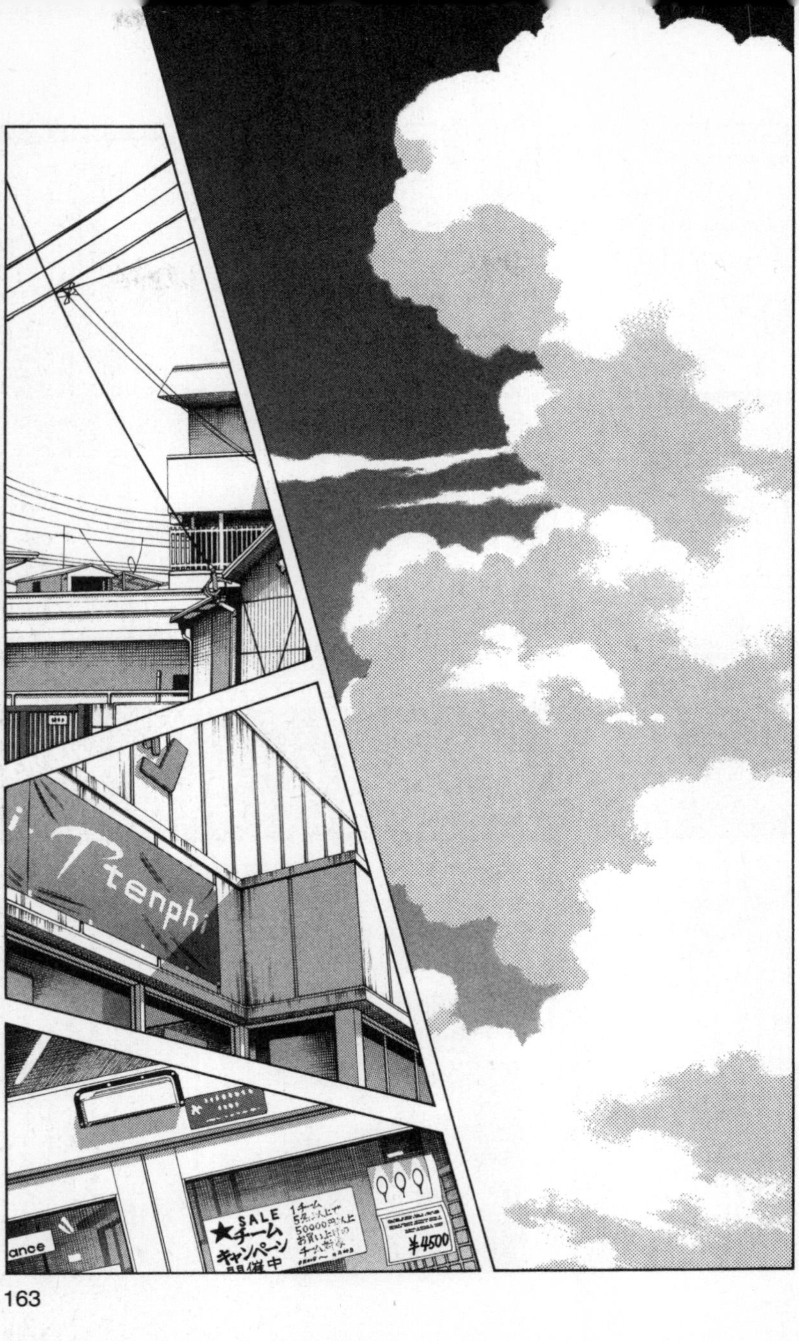
tenphi
SALE
★チーム
キャンペーン
¥4500
ance

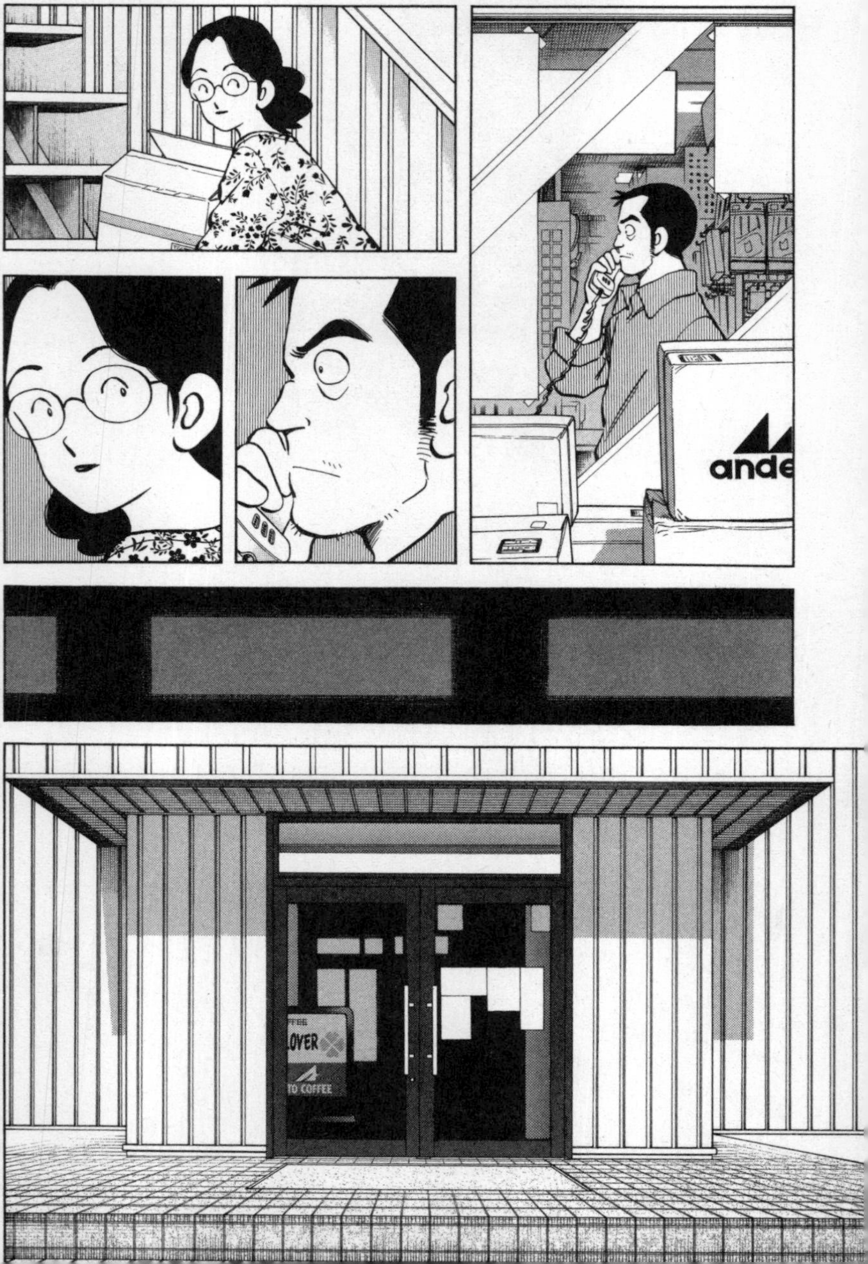
ande
OFFEE
LOVER
TO COFFEE

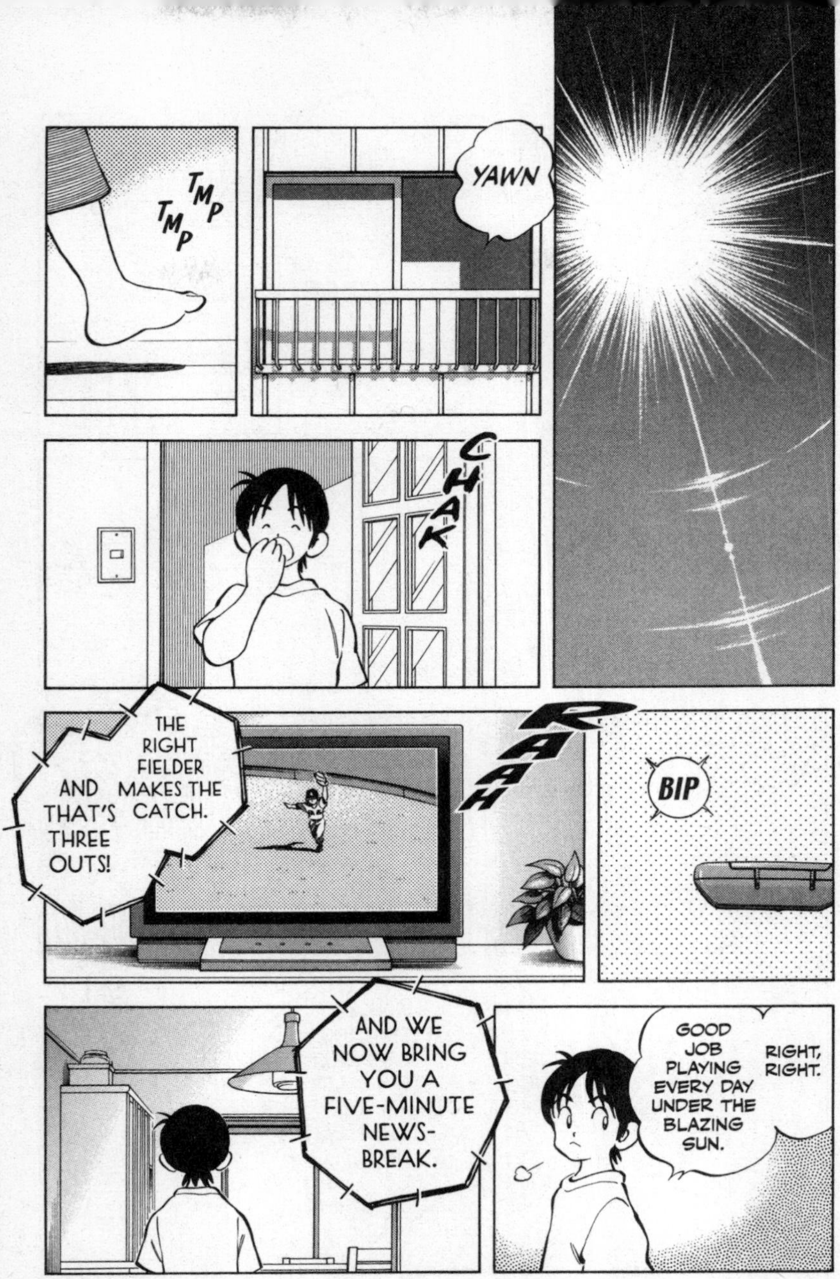
YAWN
TMP TMP
CHAK
BIP
RAAH
THE RIGHT FIELDER MAKES THE CATCH.
AND THAT'S THREE OUTS!
RIGHT, RIGHT.
GOOD JOB PLAYING EVERY DAY UNDER THE BLAZING SUN.
AND WE NOW BRING YOU A FIVE-MINUTE NEWS-BREAK.

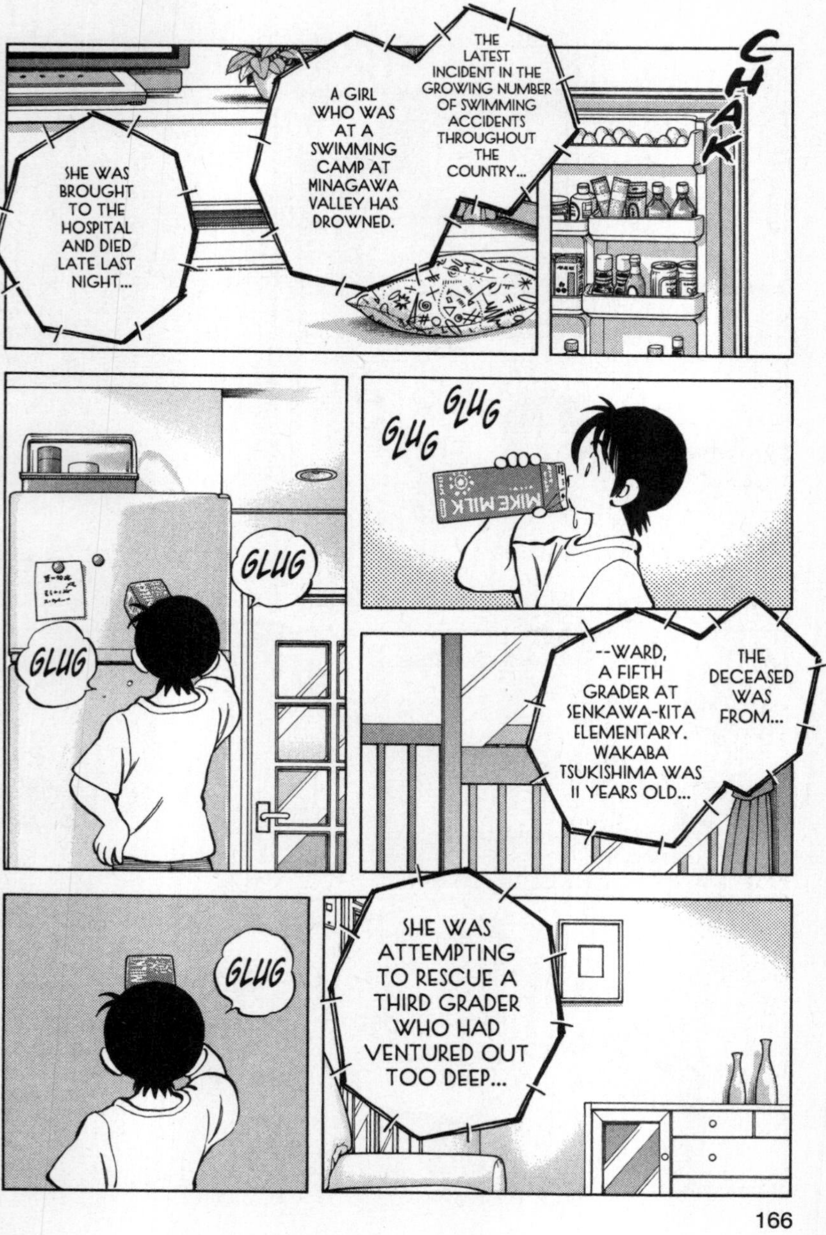
CHAK
THE LATEST INCIDENT IN THE GROWING NUMBER OF SWIMMING ACCIDENTS THROUGHOUT THE COUNTRY...
A GIRL WHO WAS AT A SWIMMING CAMP AT MINAGAWA VALLEY HAS DROWNED.
SHE WAS BROUGHT TO THE HOSPITAL AND DIED LATE LAST NIGHT...
GLUG
GLUG
MIKE MILK
THE DECEASED WAS FROM...
--WARD, A FIFTH GRADER AT SENKAWA-KITA ELEMENTARY. WAKABA TSUKISHIMA WAS 11 YEARS OLD...
GLUG
GLUG
SHE WAS ATTEMPTING TO RESCUE A THIRD GRADER WHO HAD VENTURED OUT TOO DEEP...
GLUG

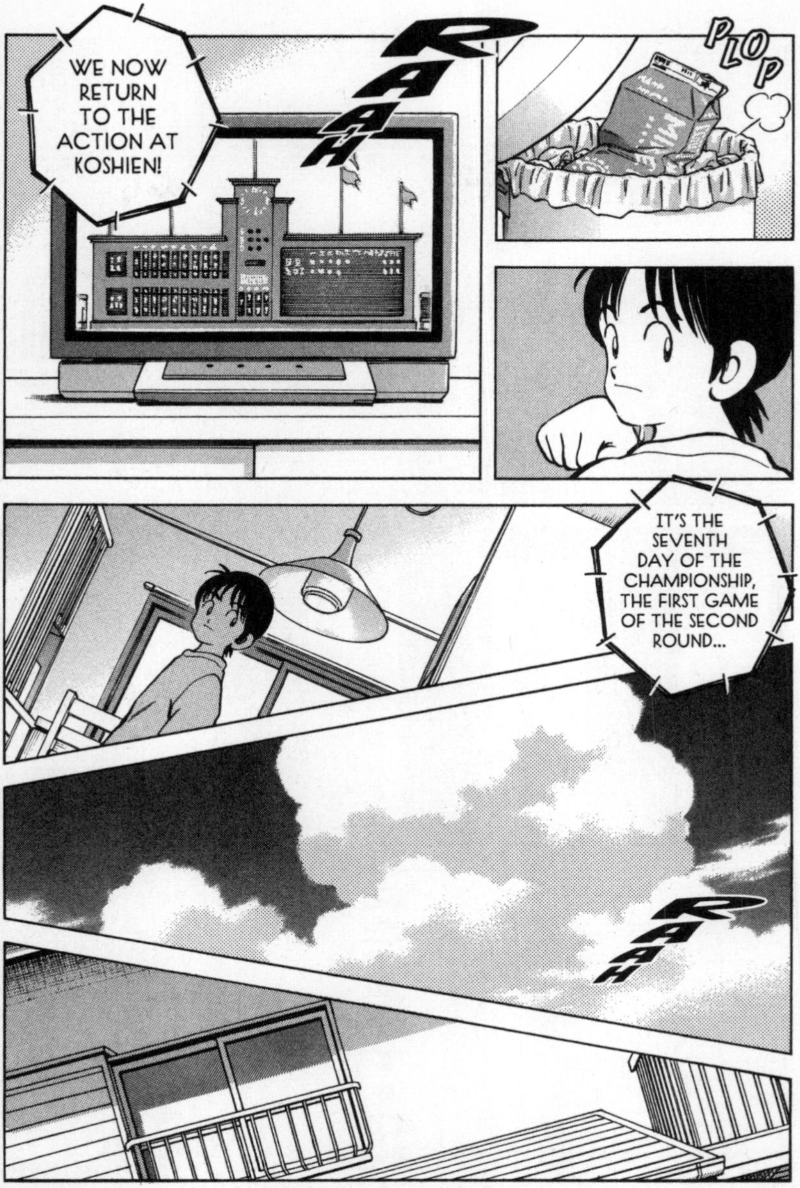
PLOP
RAAH
WE NOW RETURN TO THE ACTION AT KOSHIEN!
IT'S THE SEVENTH DAY OF THE CHAMPIONSHIP, THE FIRST GAME OF THE SECOND ROUND...
RAAH

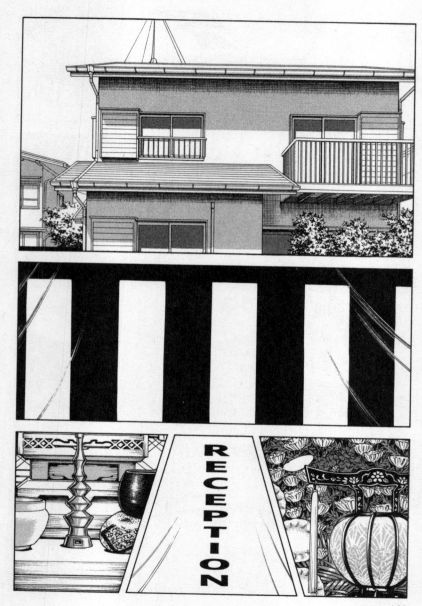

RECEPTION

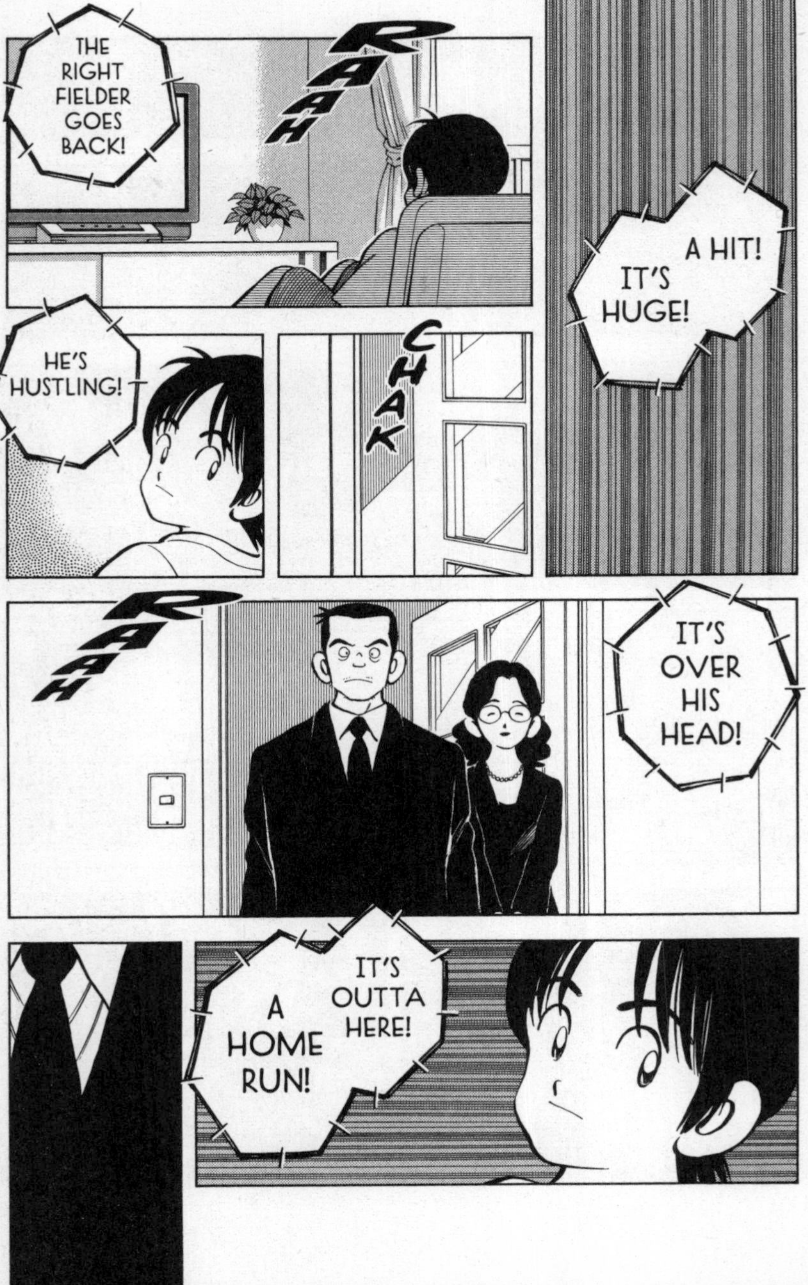
A HIT! IT'S HUGE!
RAAH
THE RIGHT FIELDER GOES BACK!
CHAK
HE'S HUSTLING!
IT'S OVER HIS HEAD!
RAAH
IT'S OUTTA HERE!
A HOME RUN!

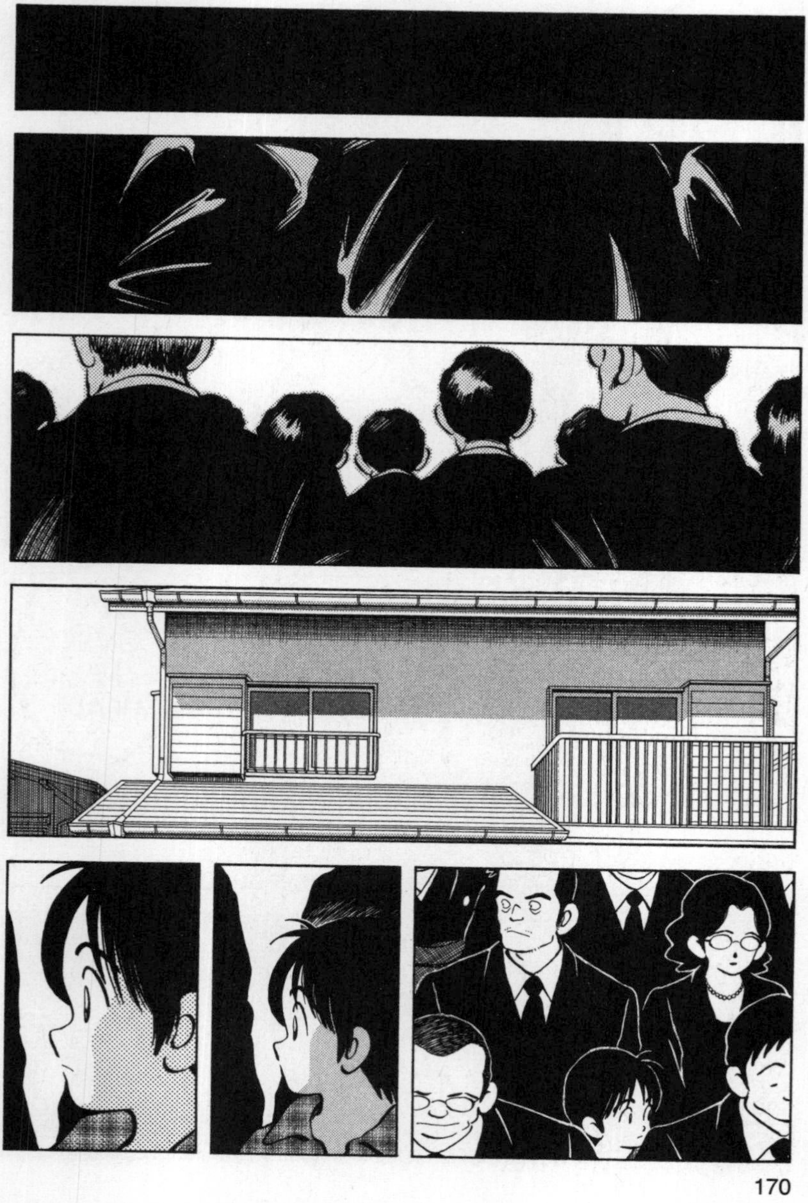

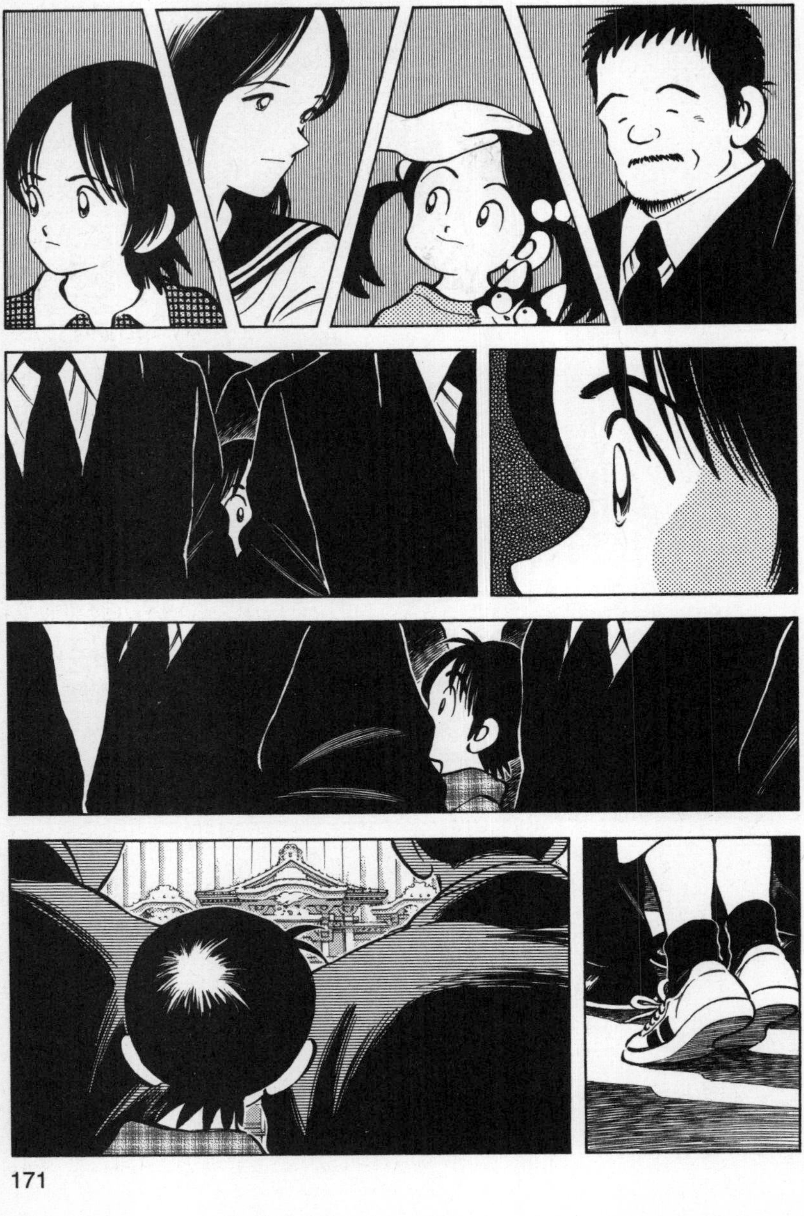

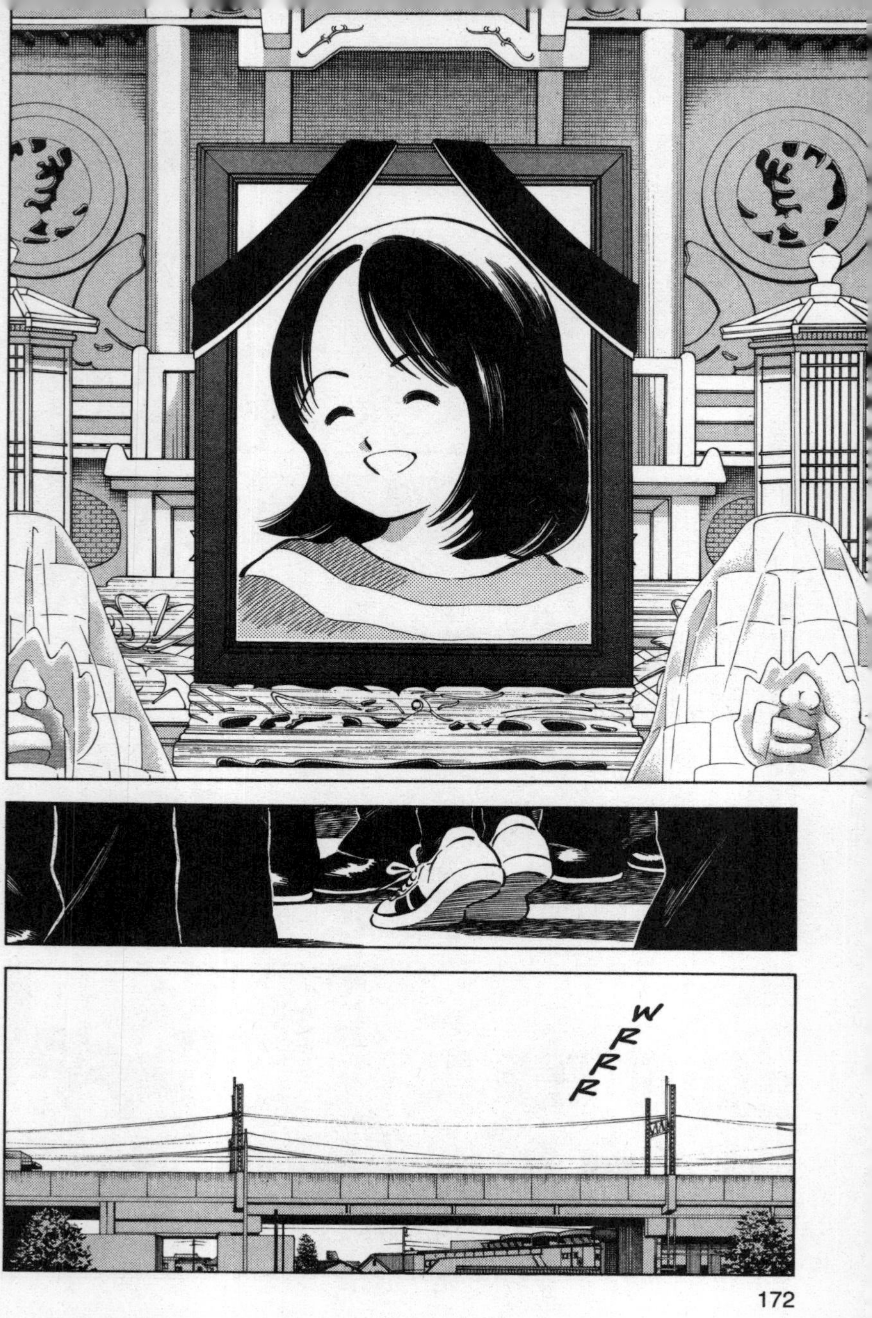
WRRR

CHAPTER 10
IT'S SIMPLE

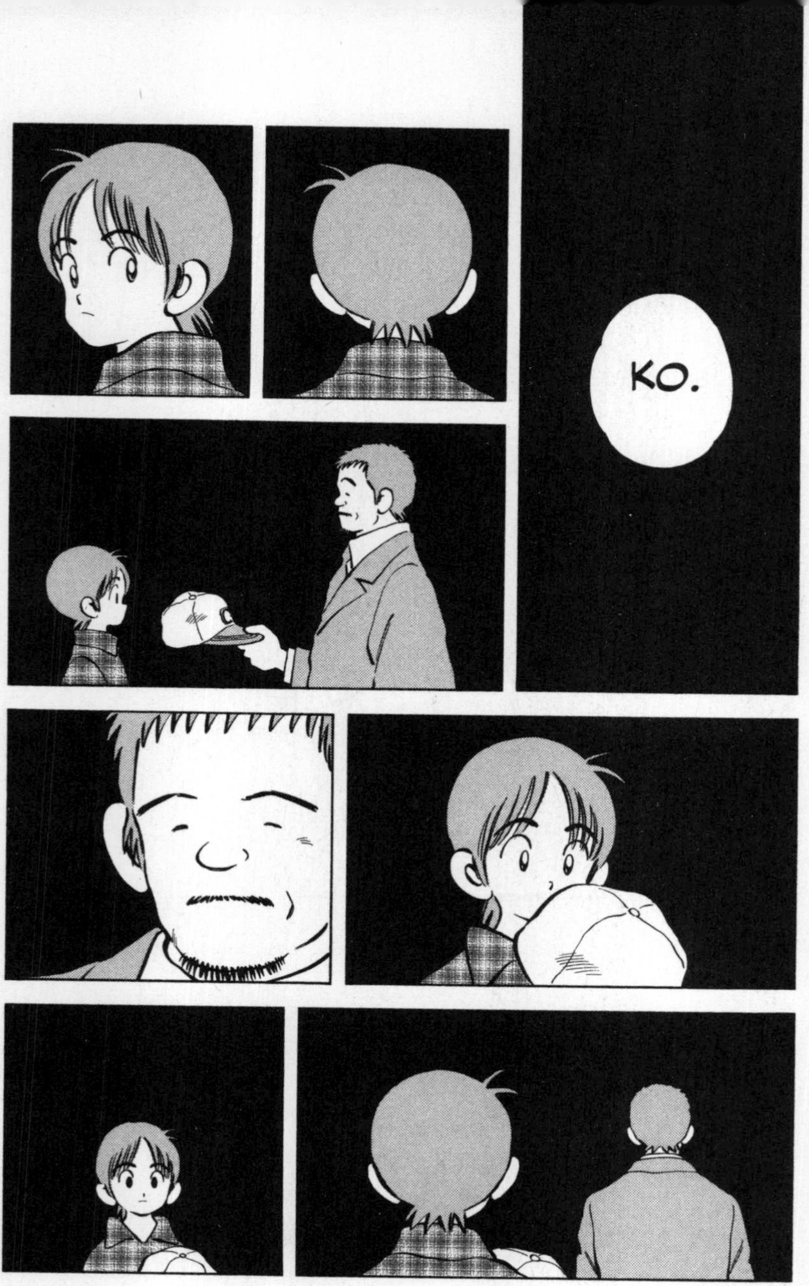
KO.

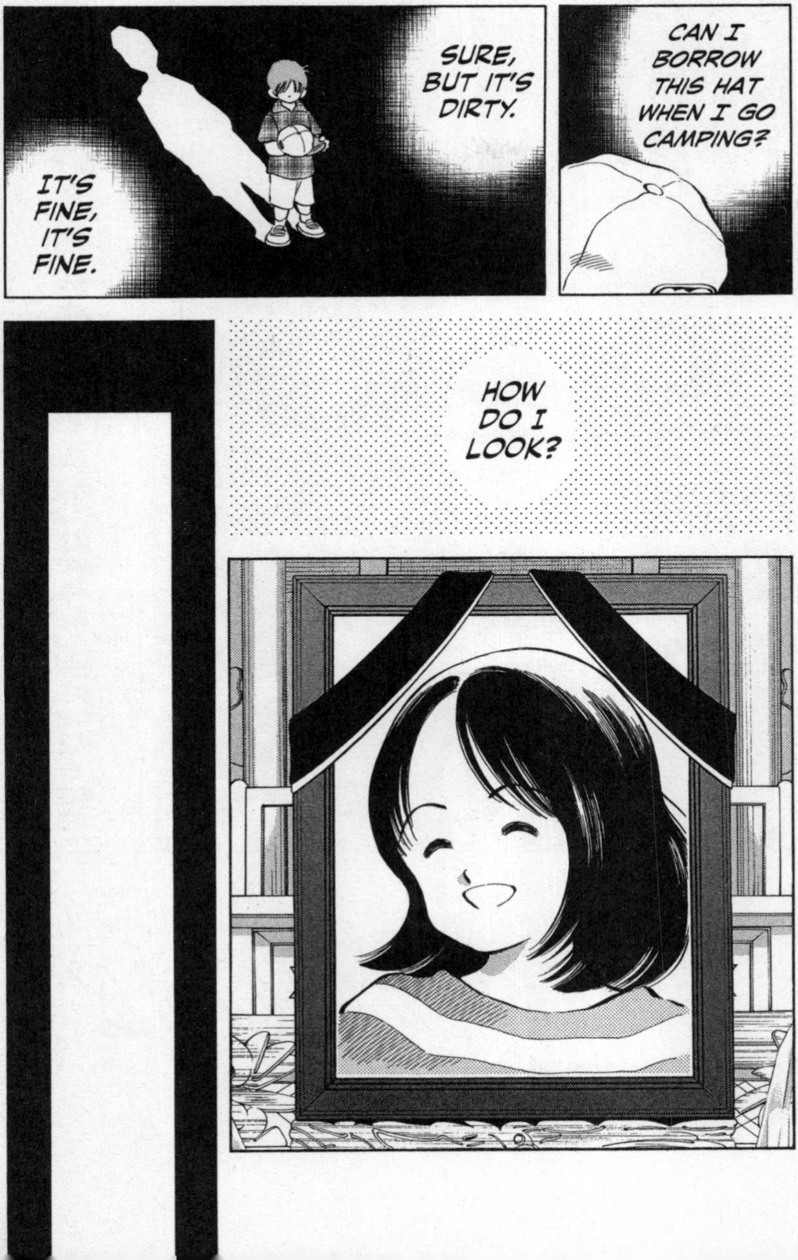
CAN I BORROW THIS HAT WHEN I GO CAMPING?
SURE, BUT IT'S DIRTY.
IT'S FINE, IT'S FINE.
HOW DO I LOOK?

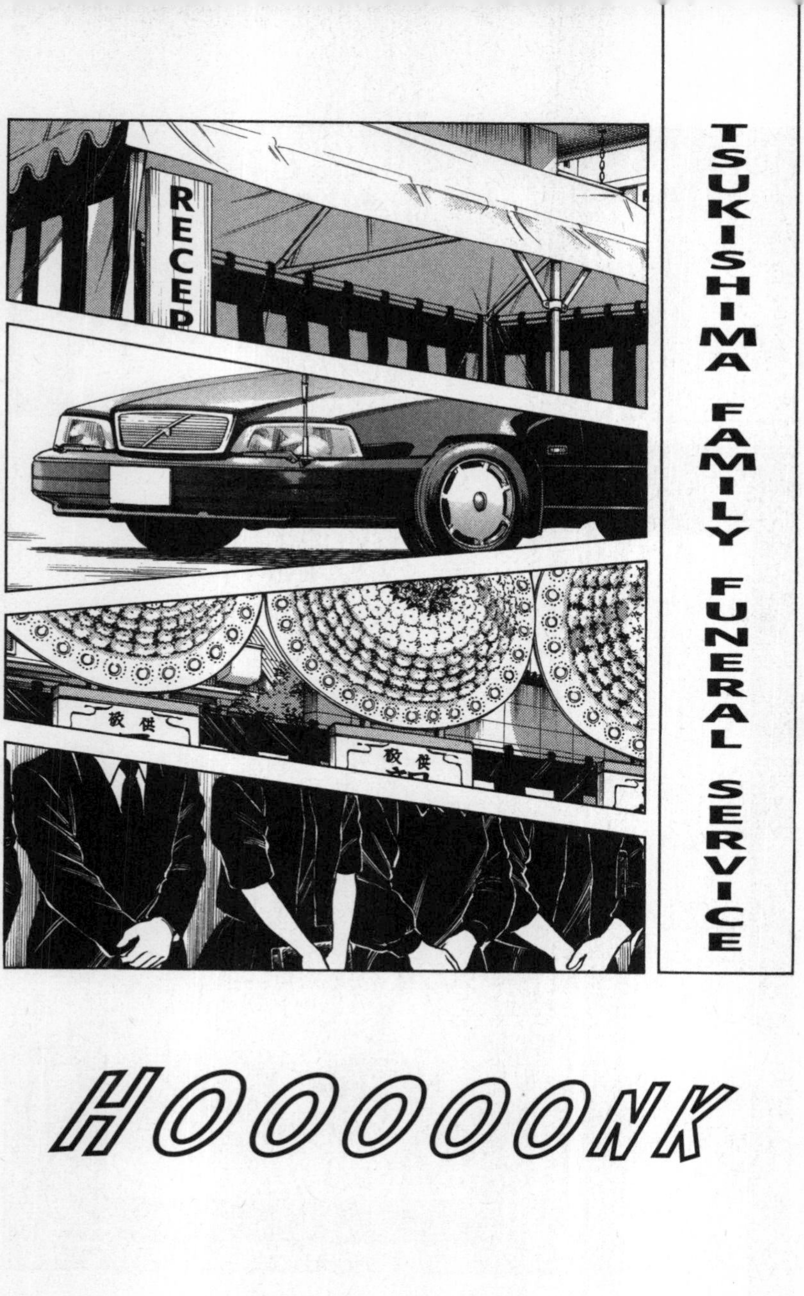
TSUKISHIMA FAMILY FUNERAL SERVICE
RECEP
HOOOOONK

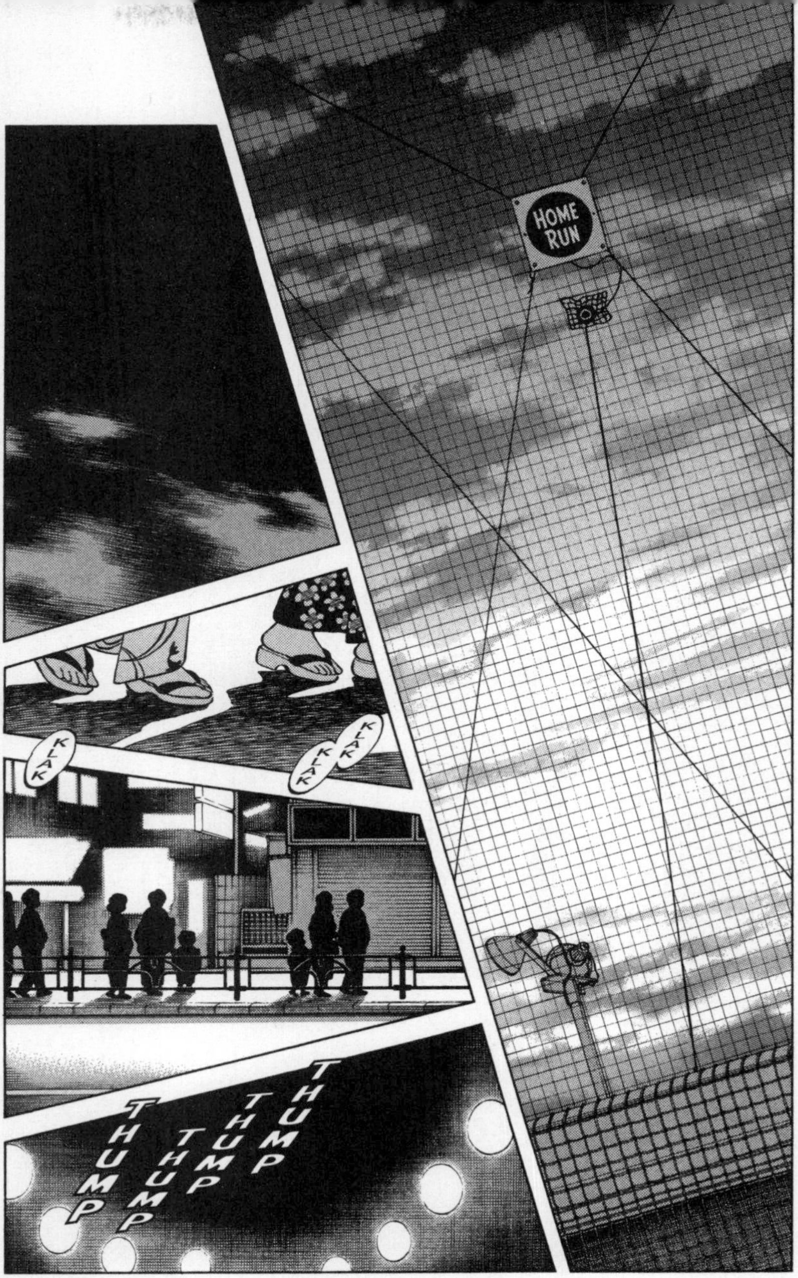
HOME RUN
KLAK
KLAK
KLAK
THUMP
THUMP
THUMP
THUMP

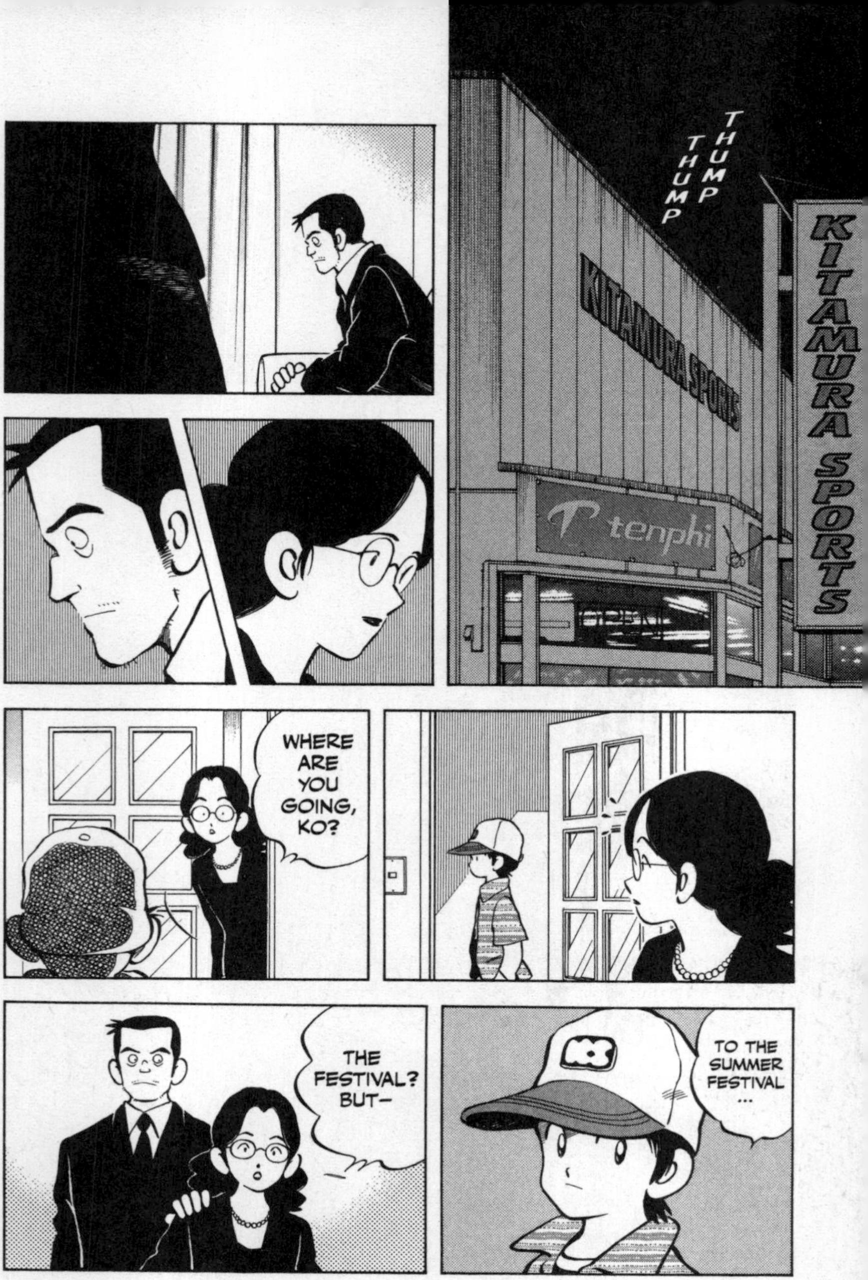
THUMP THUMP
KITAMURA SPORTS
KITAMURA SPORTS
tenphi
WHERE ARE YOU GOING, KO?
TO THE SUMMER FESTIVAL ...
THE FESTIVAL? BUT–

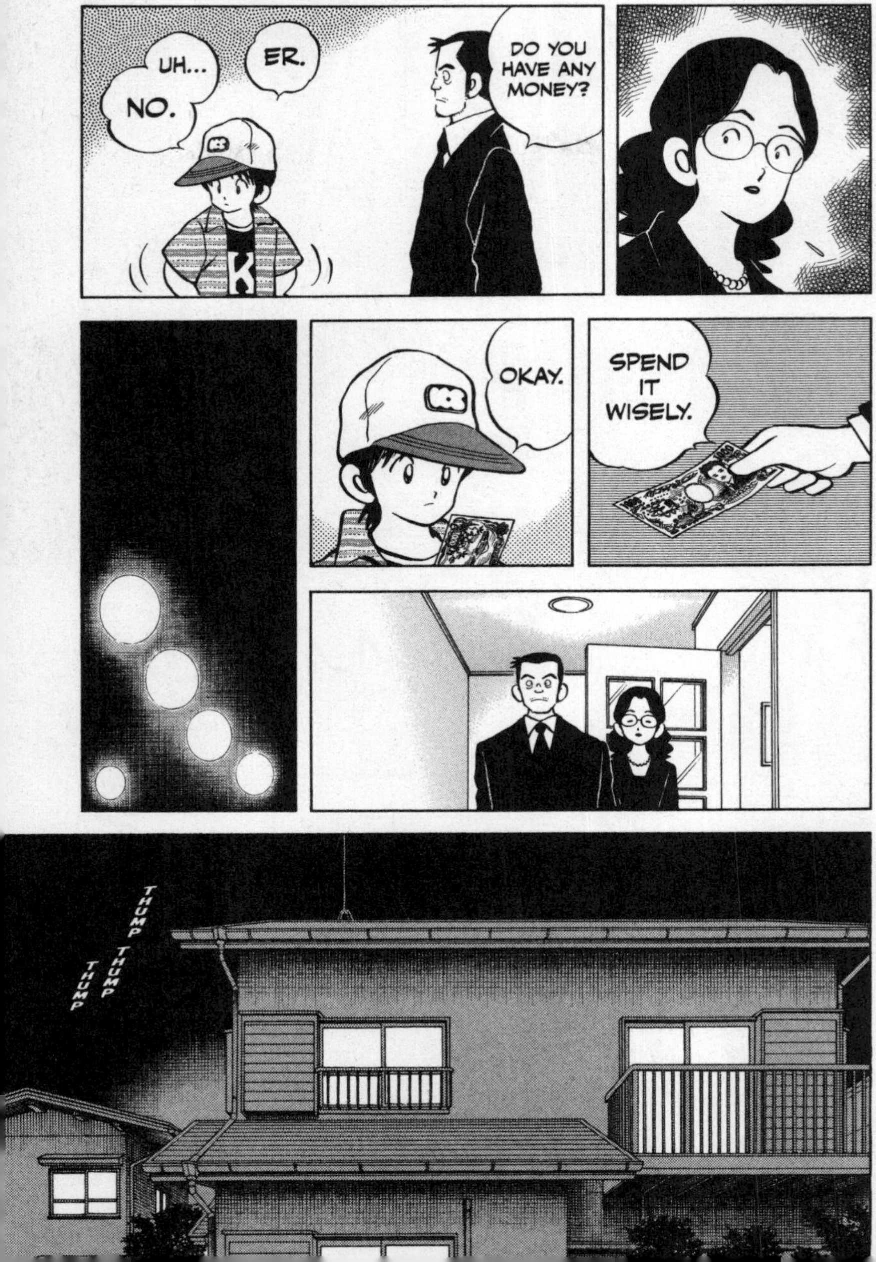
DO YOU HAVE ANY MONEY?
ER.
UH... NO.
SPEND IT WISELY.
OKAY.
THUMP THUMP THUMP

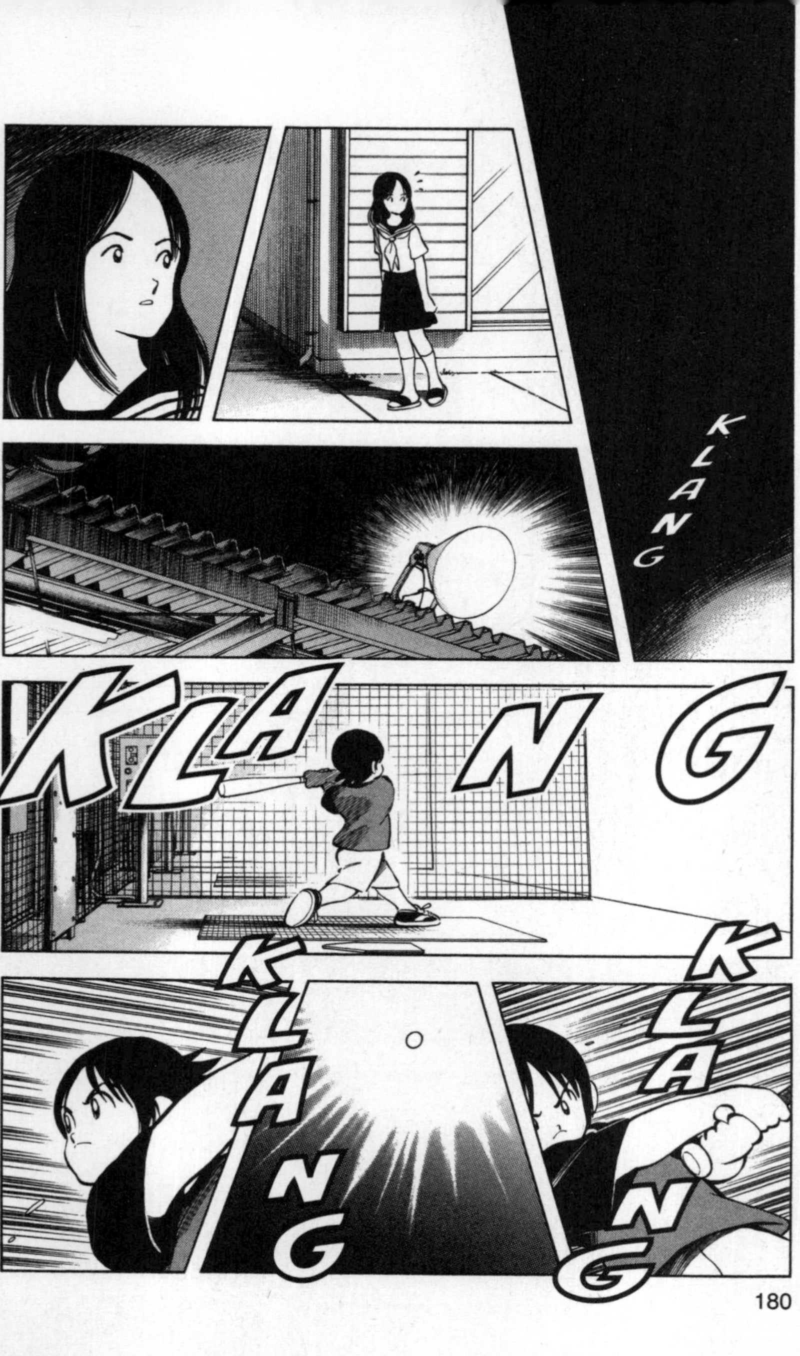
KLANG
KLANG
KLANG
KLANG

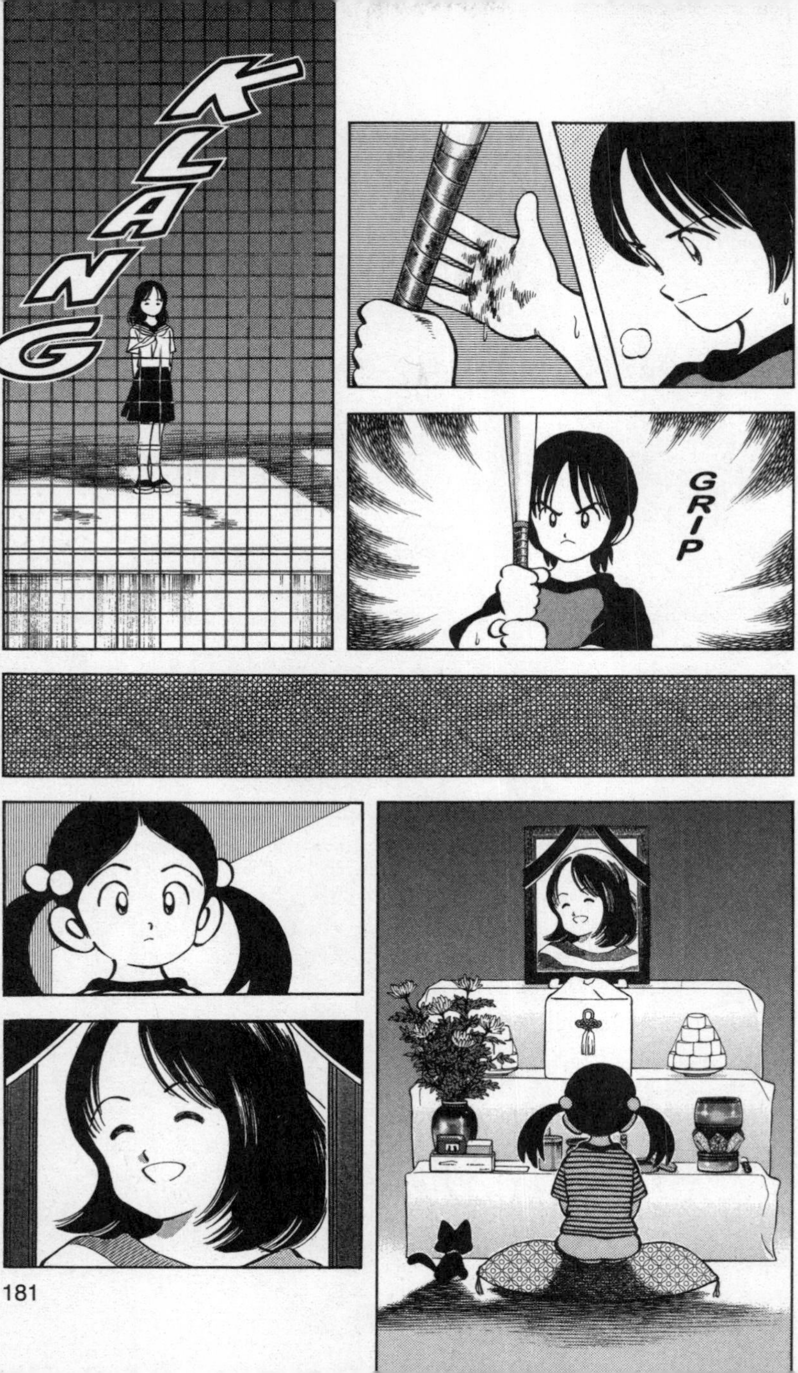
GRIP
KLANG

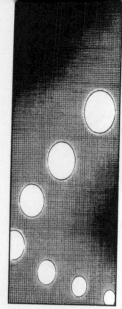

TWEET TWEET TWEET

祭 祭 祭 祭

ラムネ

THUMP
THUMP
THUMP
THUMP
THUMP
THUMP
THUMP

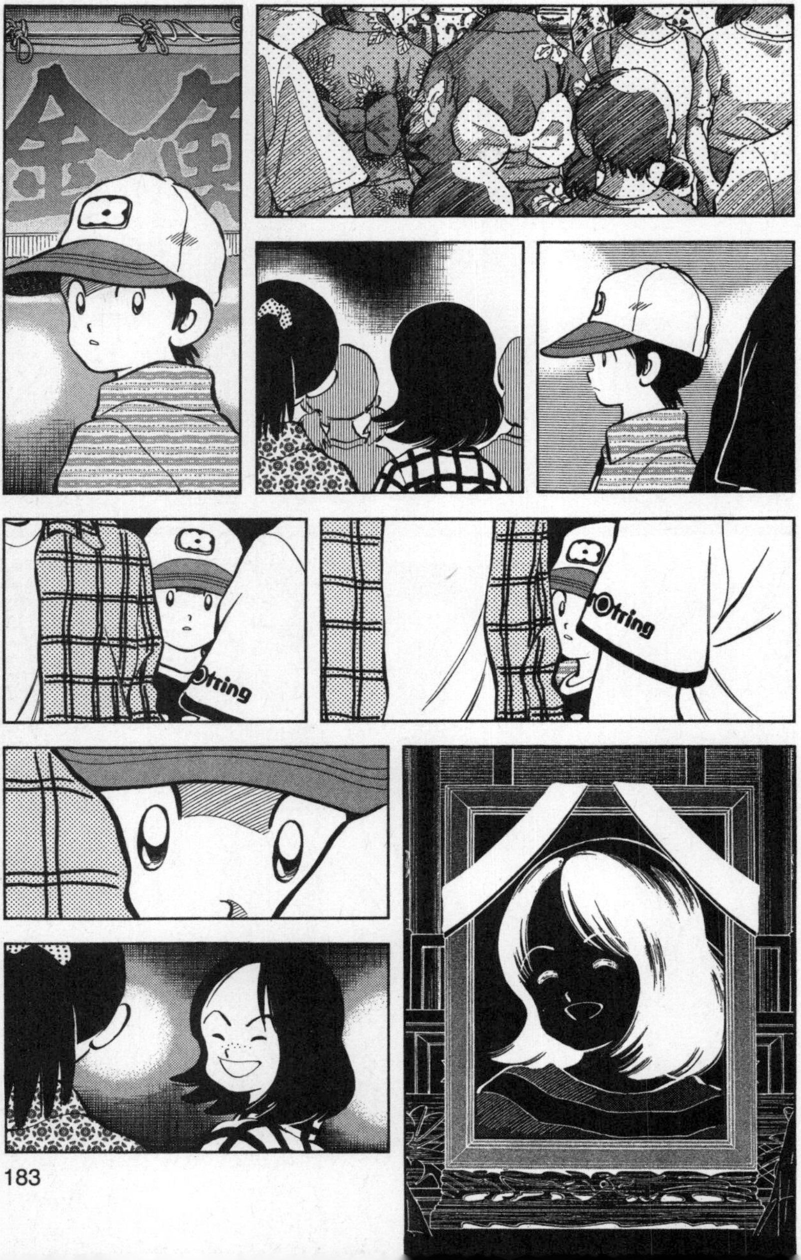

I'LL BE BACK BY EVENING, THE DAY AFTER TOMORROW.

AND WE'RE GOING TO THE SUMMER FESTIVAL THE DAY AFTER THAT, OKAY?

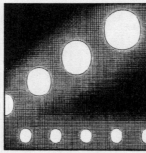

KO.

KO.

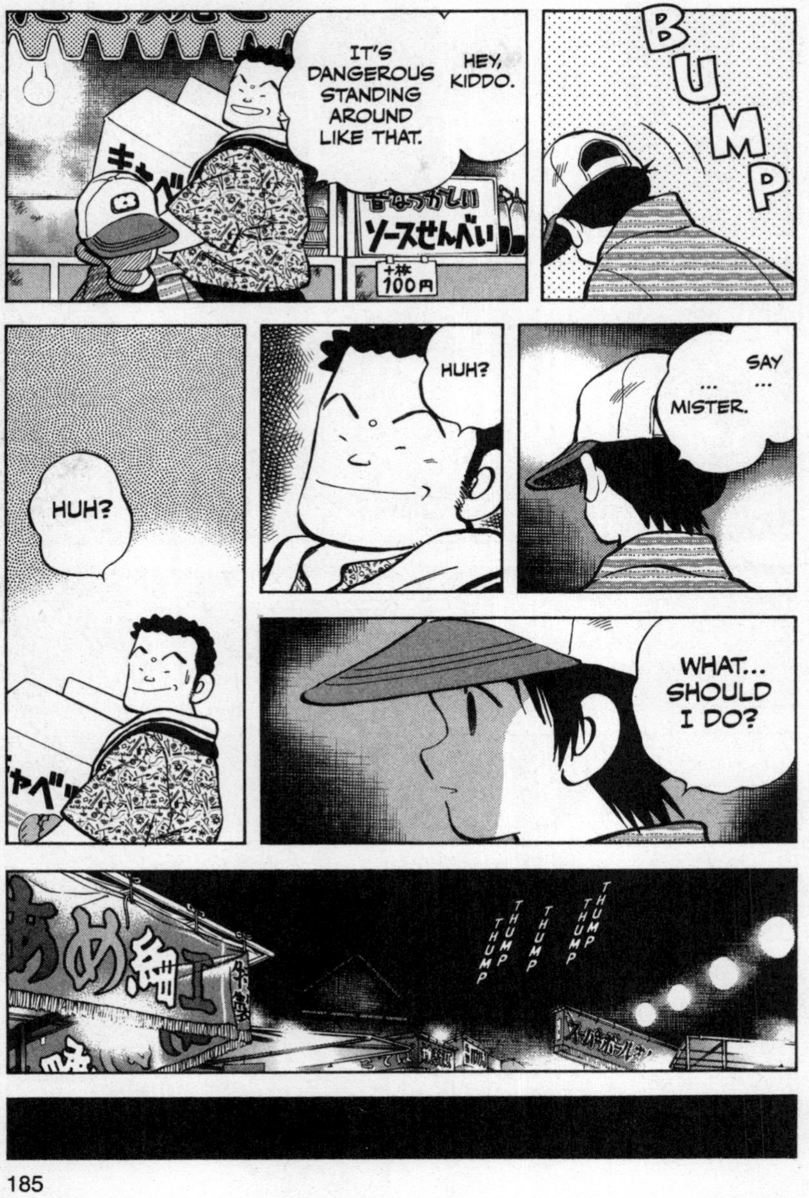
BUMP
HEY, KIDDO.
IT'S DANGEROUS STANDING AROUND LIKE THAT.
ソースせんべい
十枚 100円
SAY... ...MISTER.
HUH?
WHAT... SHOULD I DO?
HUH?
THUMP THUMP THUMP THUMP THUMP
あめ細工

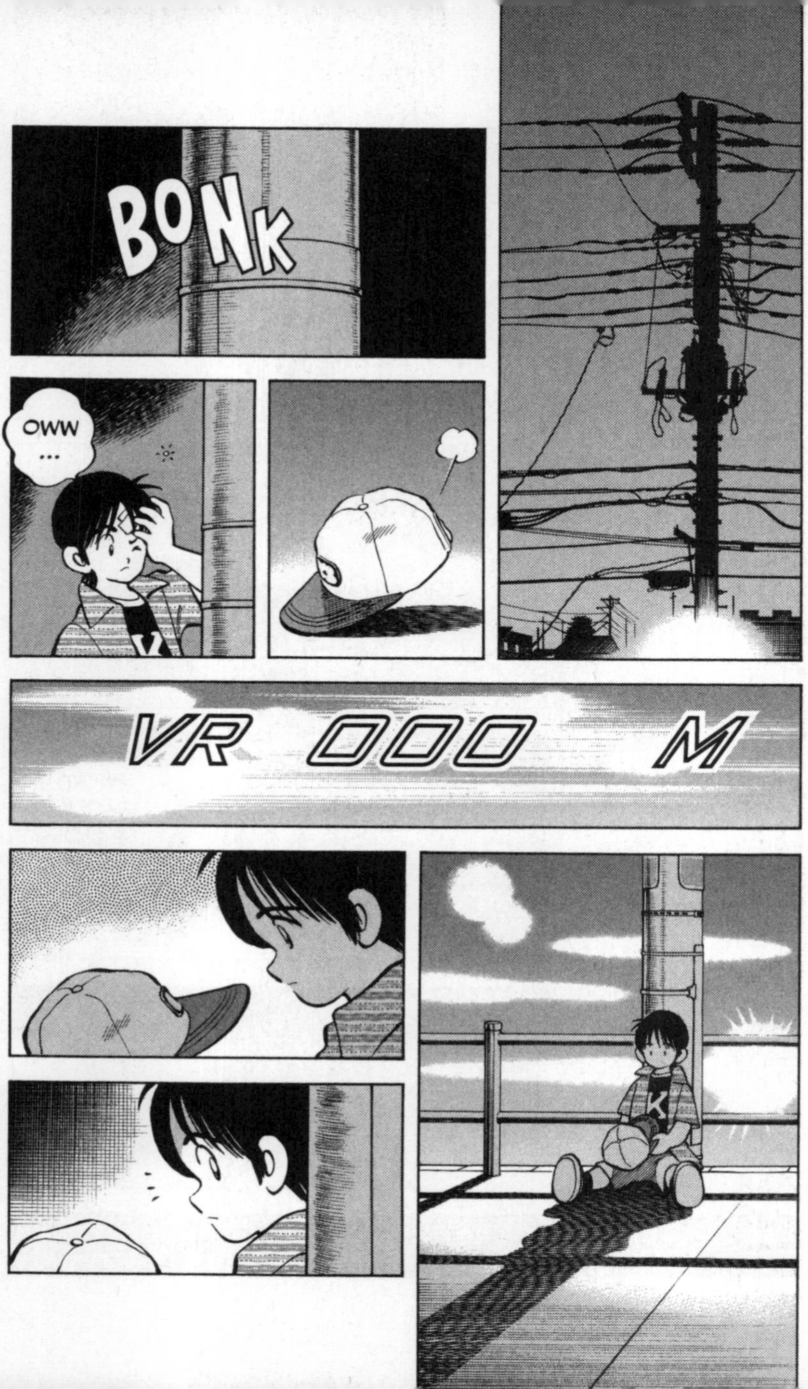
BONK
OWW ...
VR OOO M

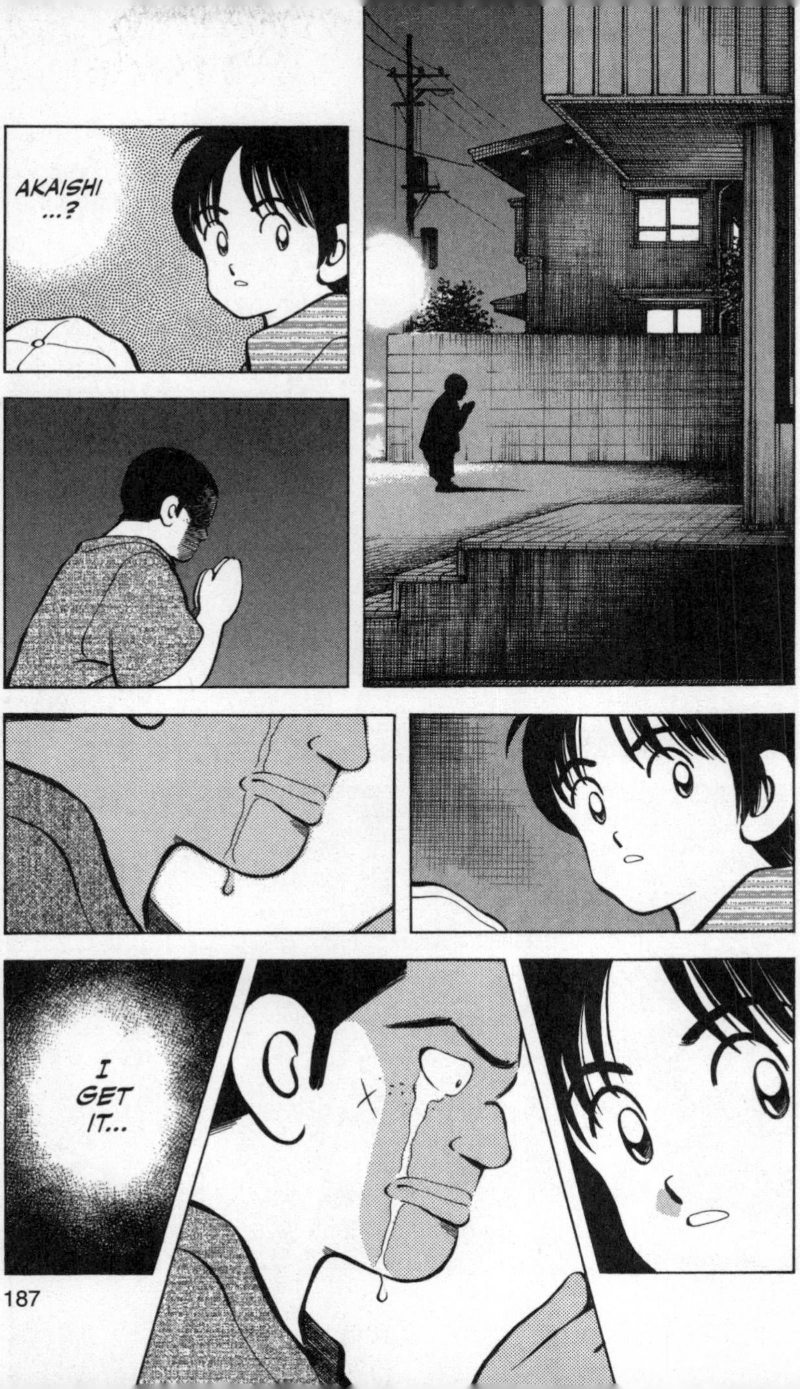
AKAISHI ...?
I GET IT...

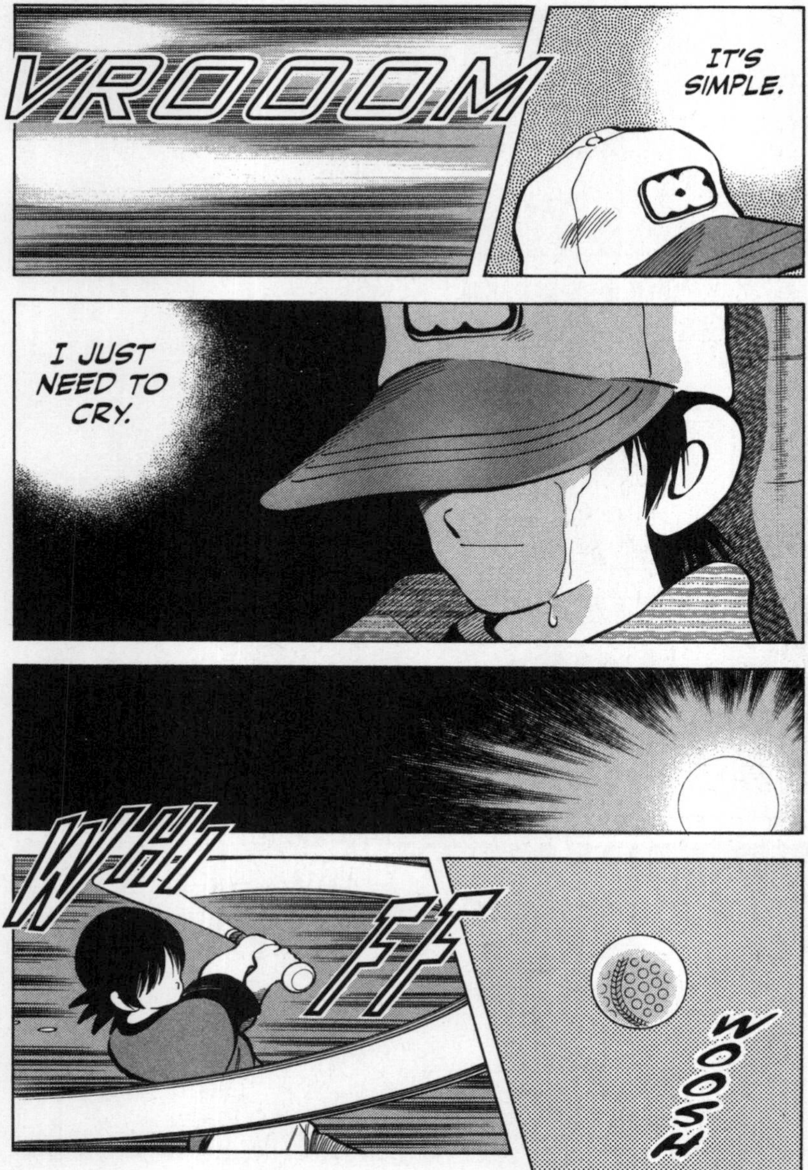
IT'S SIMPLE.
VROOOM
I JUST NEED TO CRY.
WOOSH
WHIFF

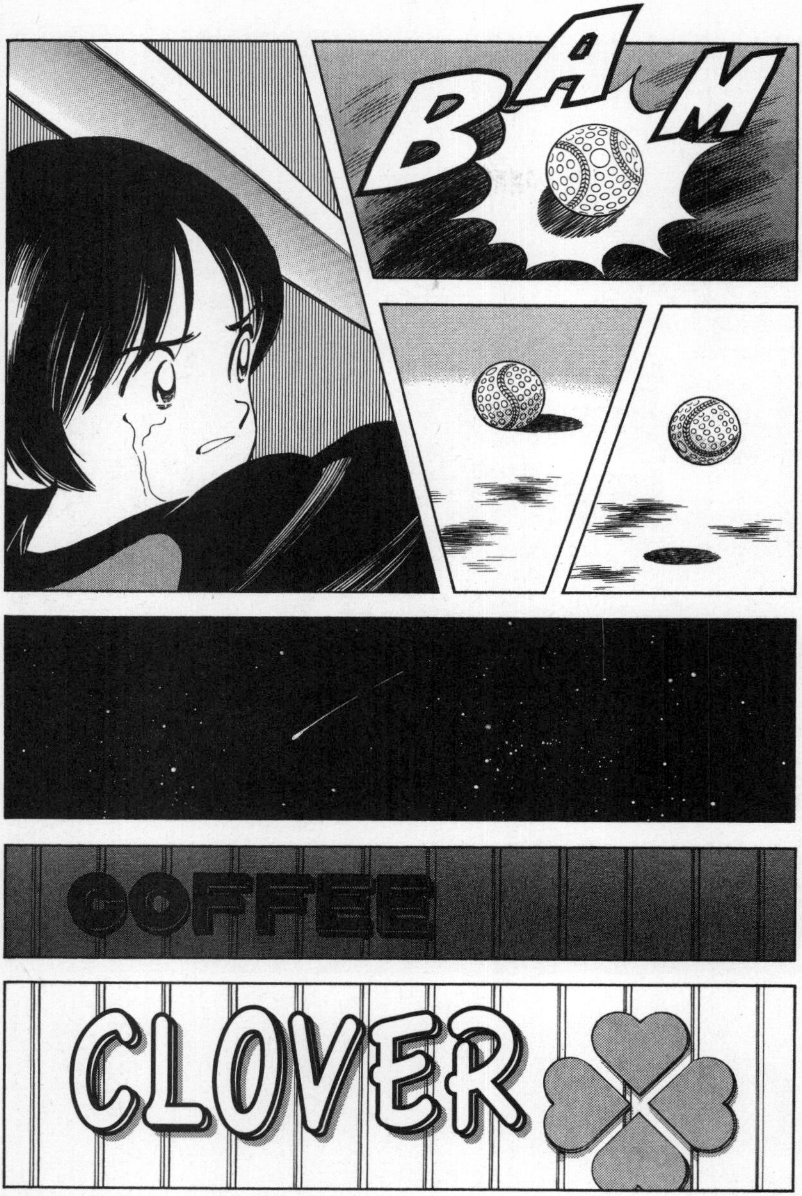
BAM
COFFEE
CLOVER

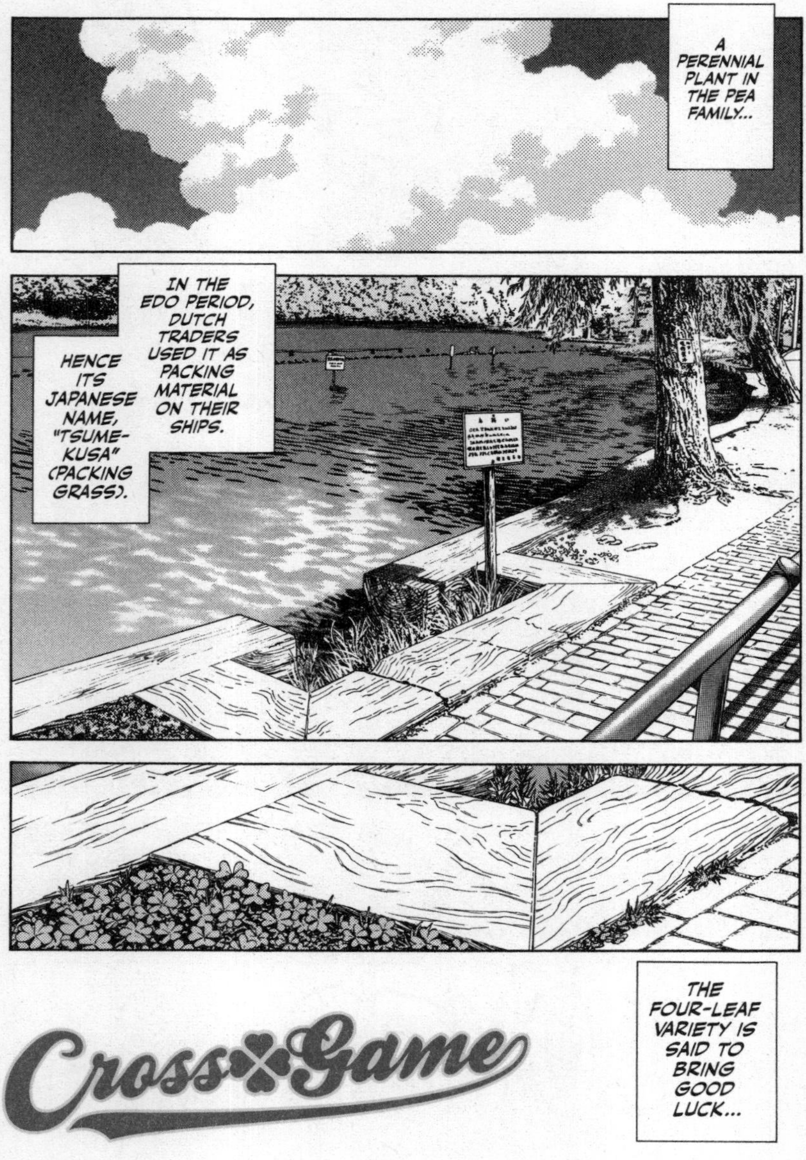
A PERENNIAL PLANT IN THE PEA FAMILY...
IN THE EDO PERIOD, DUTCH TRADERS USED IT AS PACKING MATERIAL ON THEIR SHIPS.
HENCE ITS JAPANESE NAME, "TSUME-KUSA" (PACKING GRASS).
THE FOUR-LEAF VARIETY IS SAID TO BRING GOOD LUCK...
Cross Game

Cross×Game

2

Story & Art by
Mitsuru Adachi

CHAPTER 1
I'M FREE

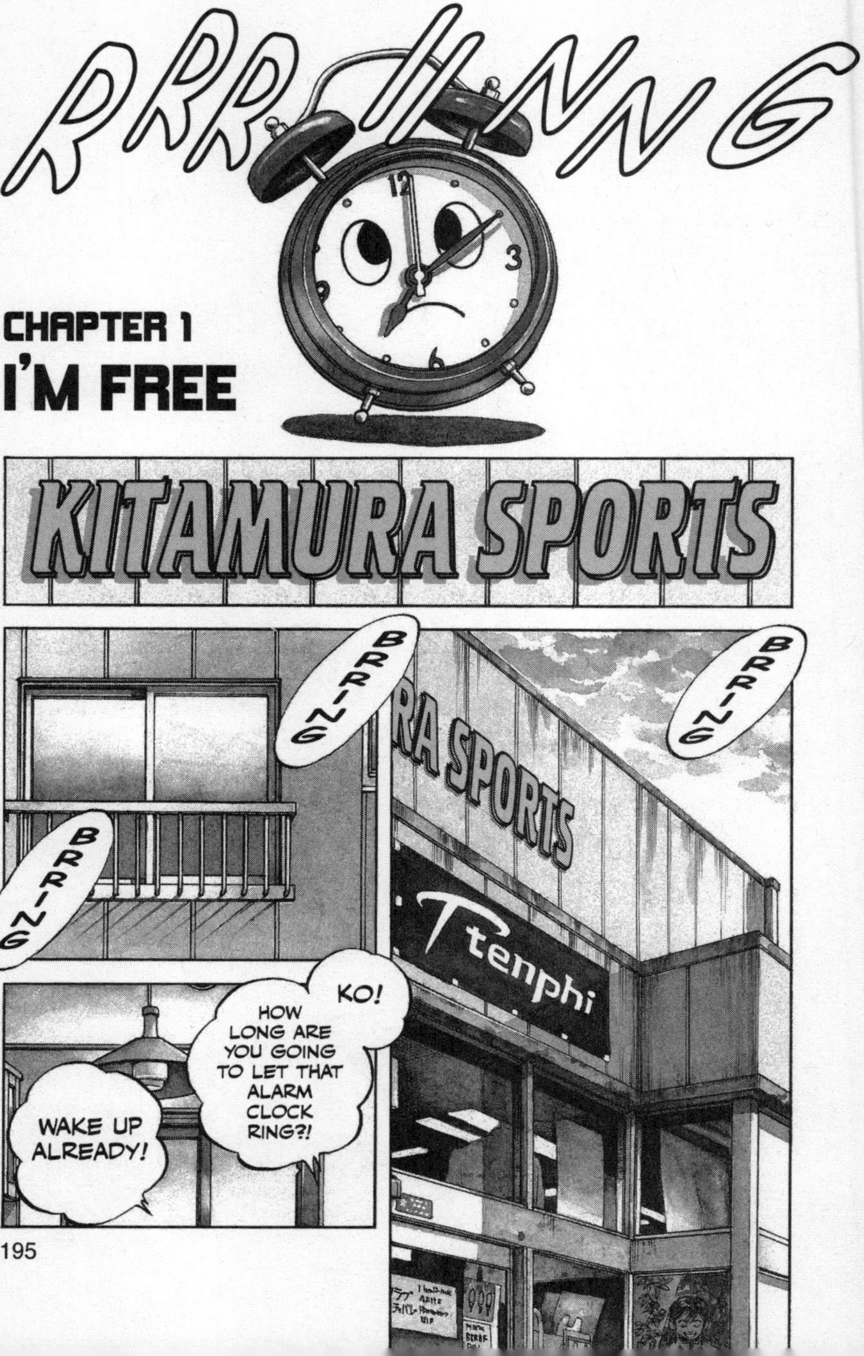
RRRIINNG
KITAMURA SPORTS
BRRING
RA SPORTS
tenphi
BRRING
BRRING
KO! HOW LONG ARE YOU GOING TO LET THAT ALARM CLOCK RING?!
WAKE UP ALREADY!

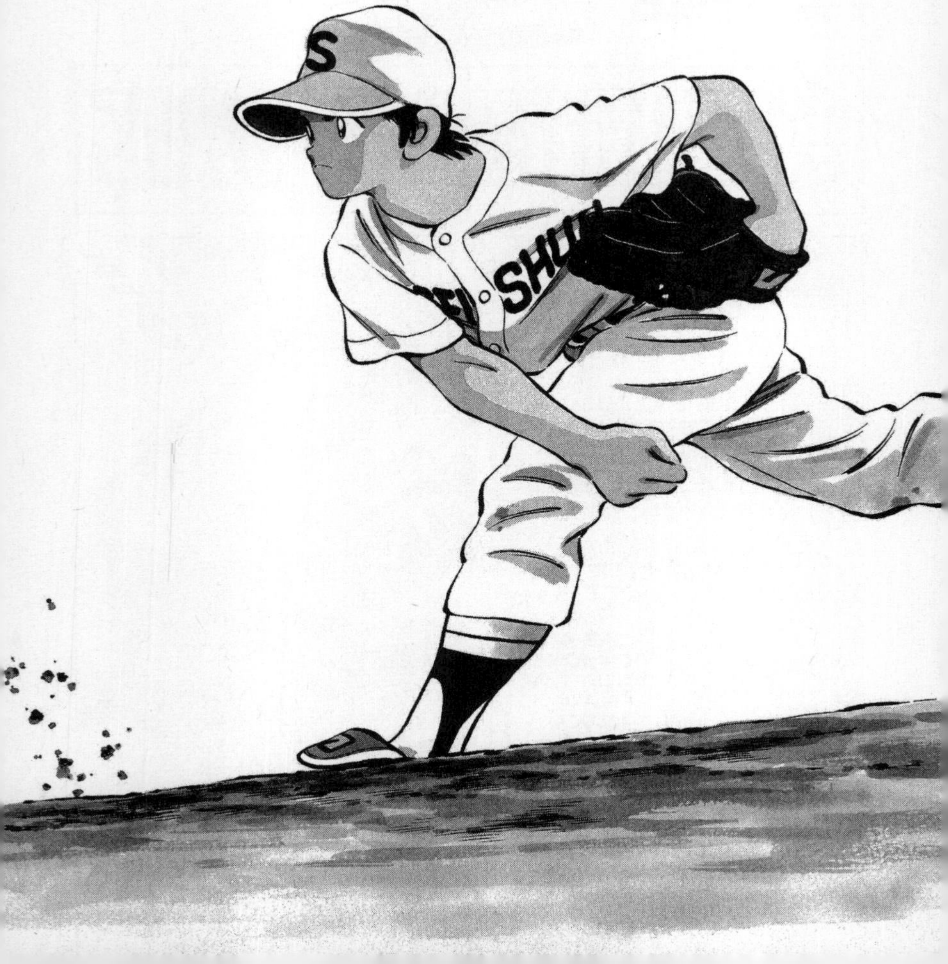

CHAPTER 1
I'M FREE

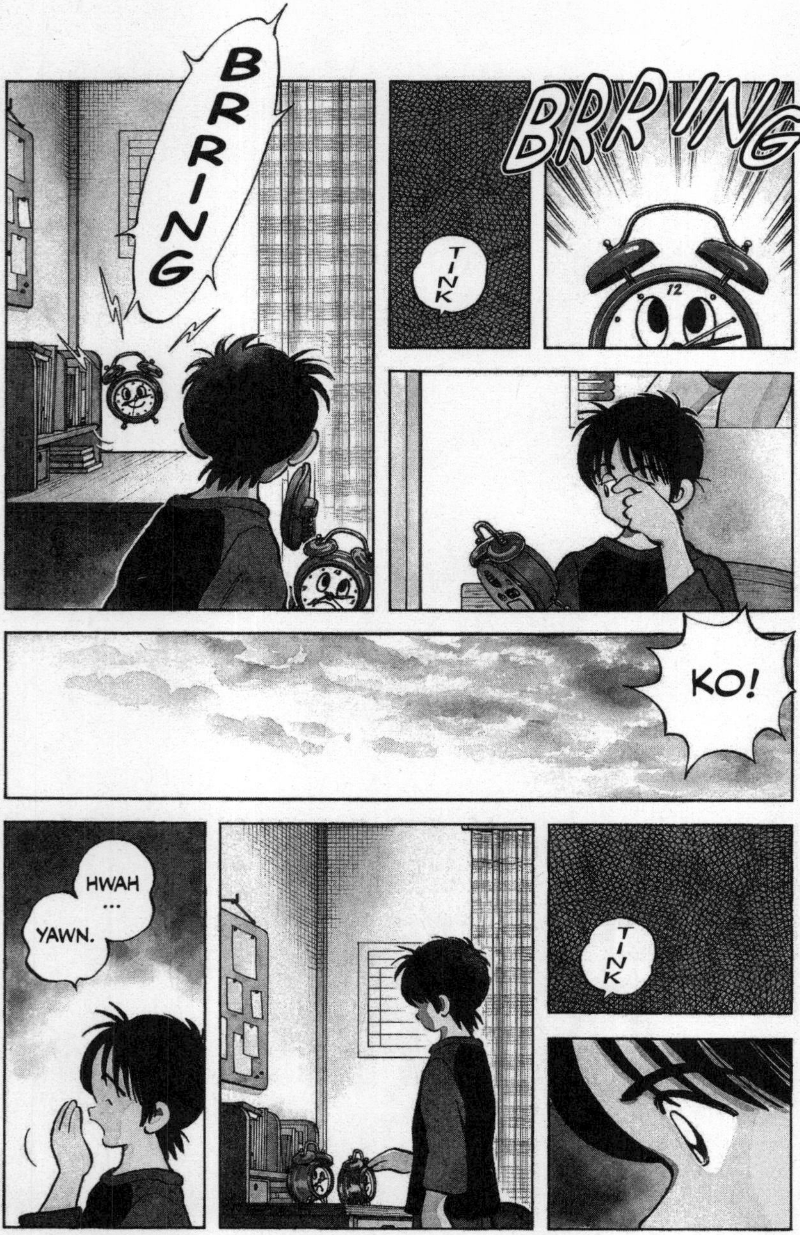
BRRING
TINK
BRRING
KO!
TINK
HWAH ...
YAWN.

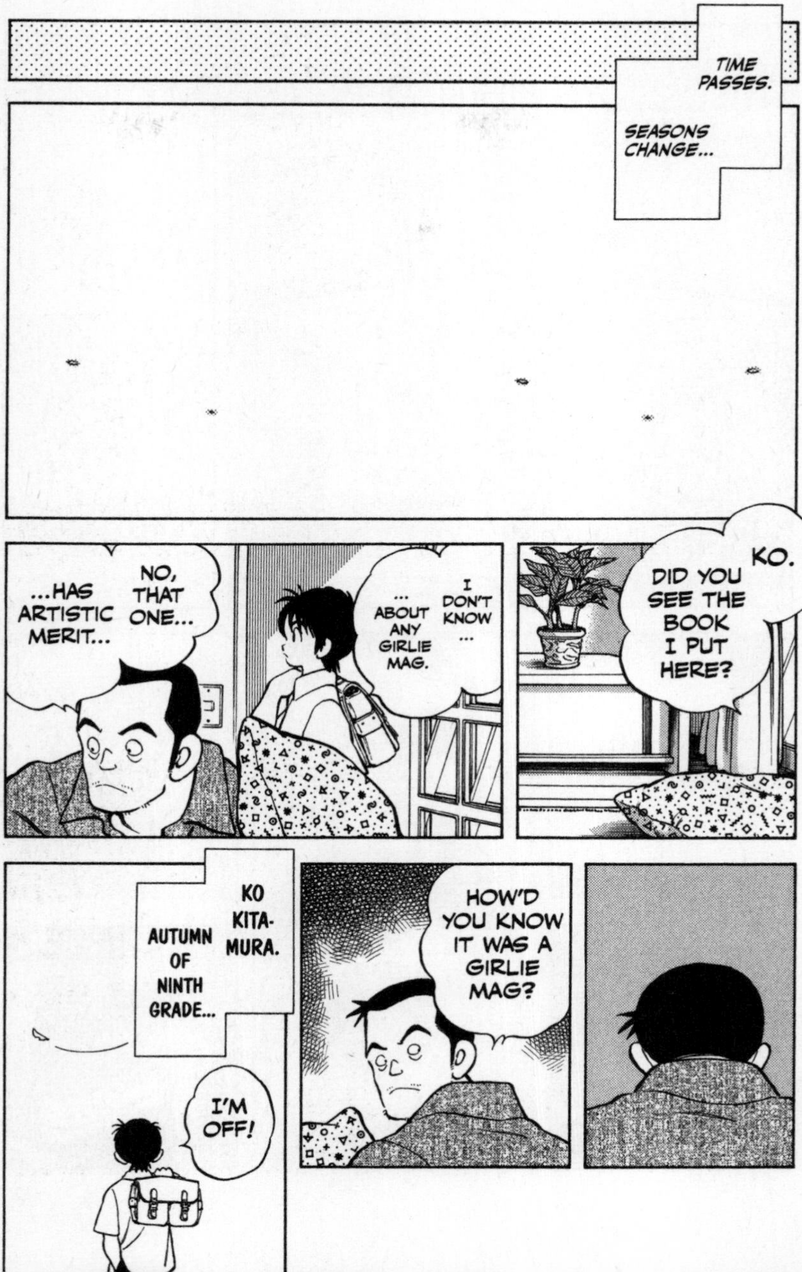
TIME PASSES.
SEASONS CHANGE...
KO.
DID YOU SEE THE BOOK I PUT HERE?
I DON'T KNOW...
...ABOUT ANY GIRLIE MAG.
NO, THAT ONE...
...HAS ARTISTIC MERIT...
HOW'D YOU KNOW IT WAS A GIRLIE MAG?
KO KITA-MURA.
AUTUMN OF NINTH GRADE...
I'M OFF!

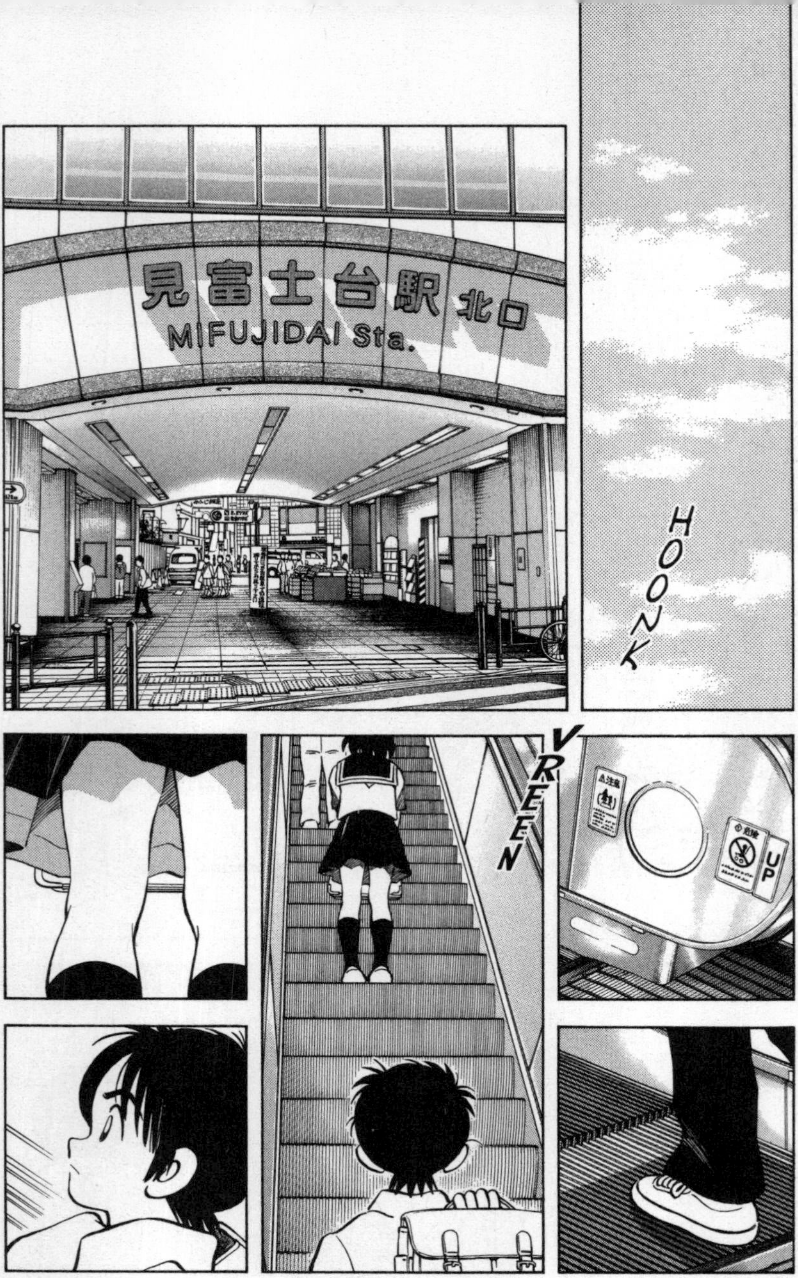
HOOONK
見富士台駅
北口
MIFUJIDAI Sta.
VREEEN
UP

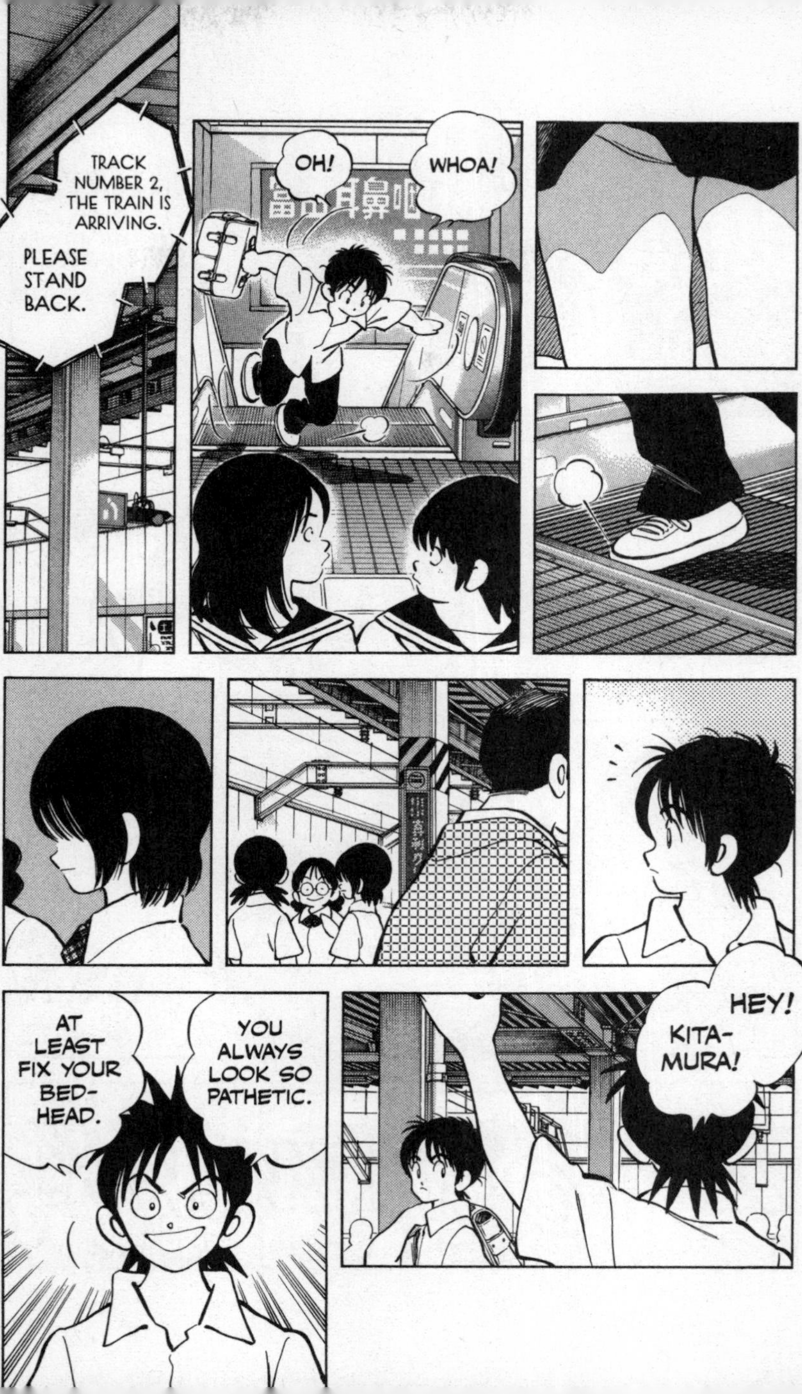
WHOA!
OH!
TRACK NUMBER 2, THE TRAIN IS ARRIVING.
PLEASE STAND BACK.
HEY!
KITA-MURA!
YOU ALWAYS LOOK SO PATHETIC.
AT LEAST FIX YOUR BED-HEAD.

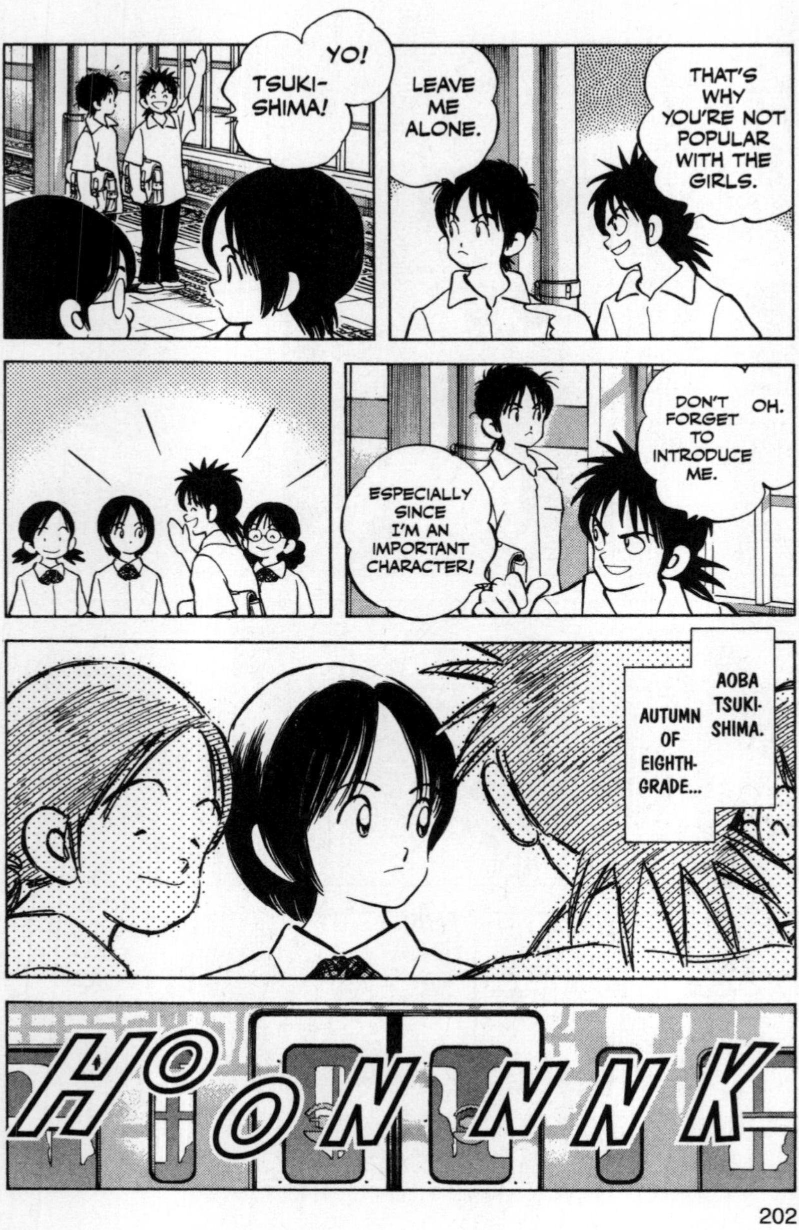
LEAVE ME ALONE.
THAT'S WHY YOU'RE NOT POPULAR WITH THE GIRLS.
YO! TSUKISHIMA!
OH.
DON'T FORGET TO INTRODUCE ME.
ESPECIALLY SINCE I'M AN IMPORTANT CHARACTER!
AOBA TSUKISHIMA.
AUTUMN OF EIGHTH-GRADE...
HONNNK

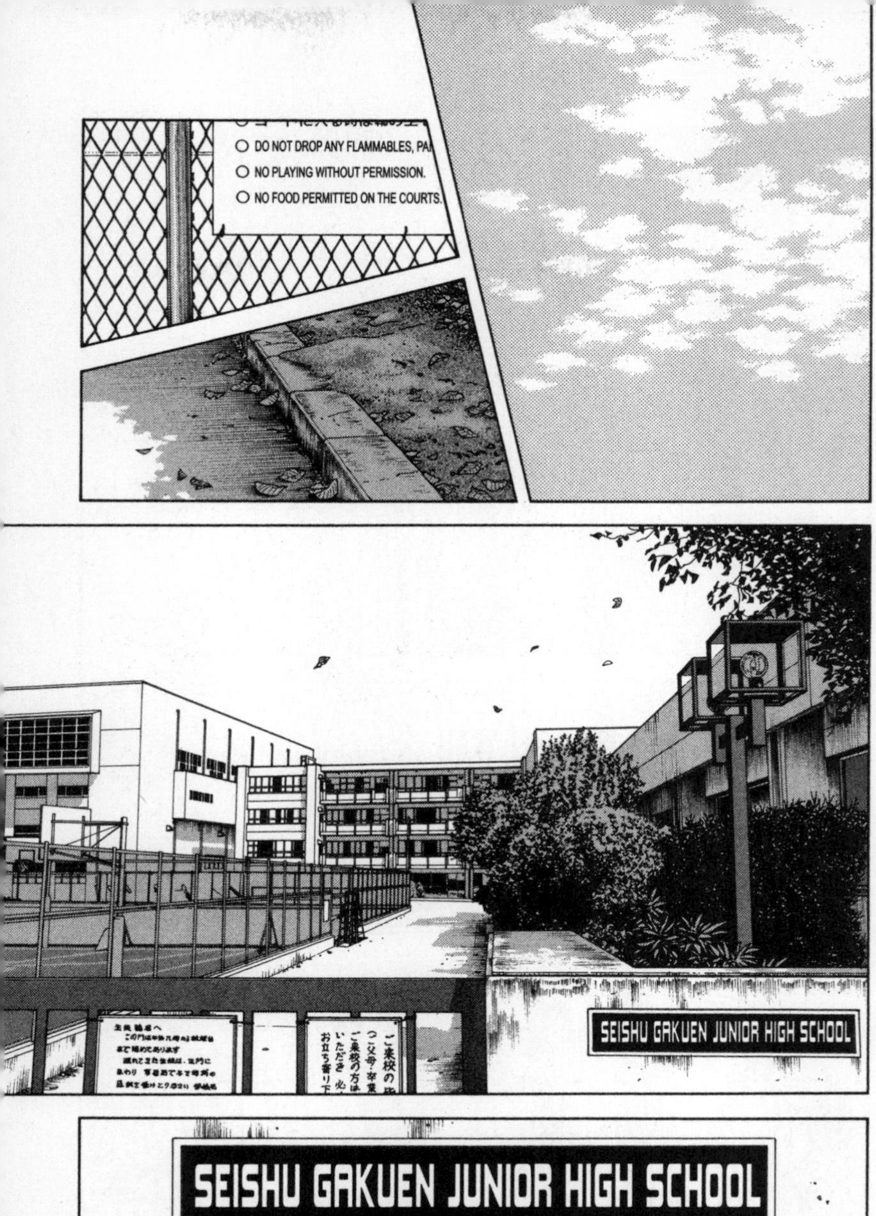
DO NOT DROP ANY FLAMMABLES, PA
NO PLAYING WITHOUT PERMISSION.
NO FOOD PERMITTED ON THE COURTS.
SEISHU GAKUEN JUNIOR HIGH SCHOOL
SEISHU GAKUEN JUNIOR HIGH SCHOOL

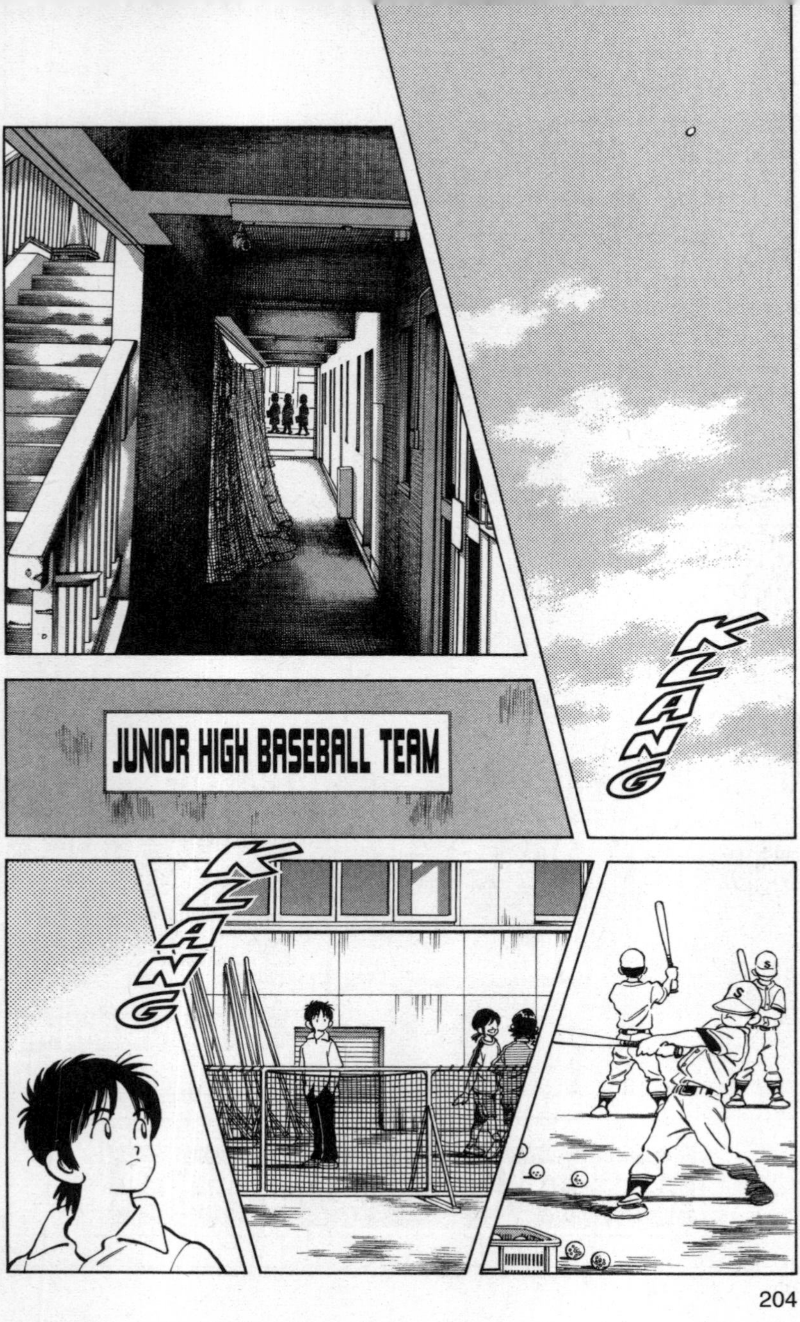
KLANG
JUNIOR HIGH BASEBALL TEAM
KLANG

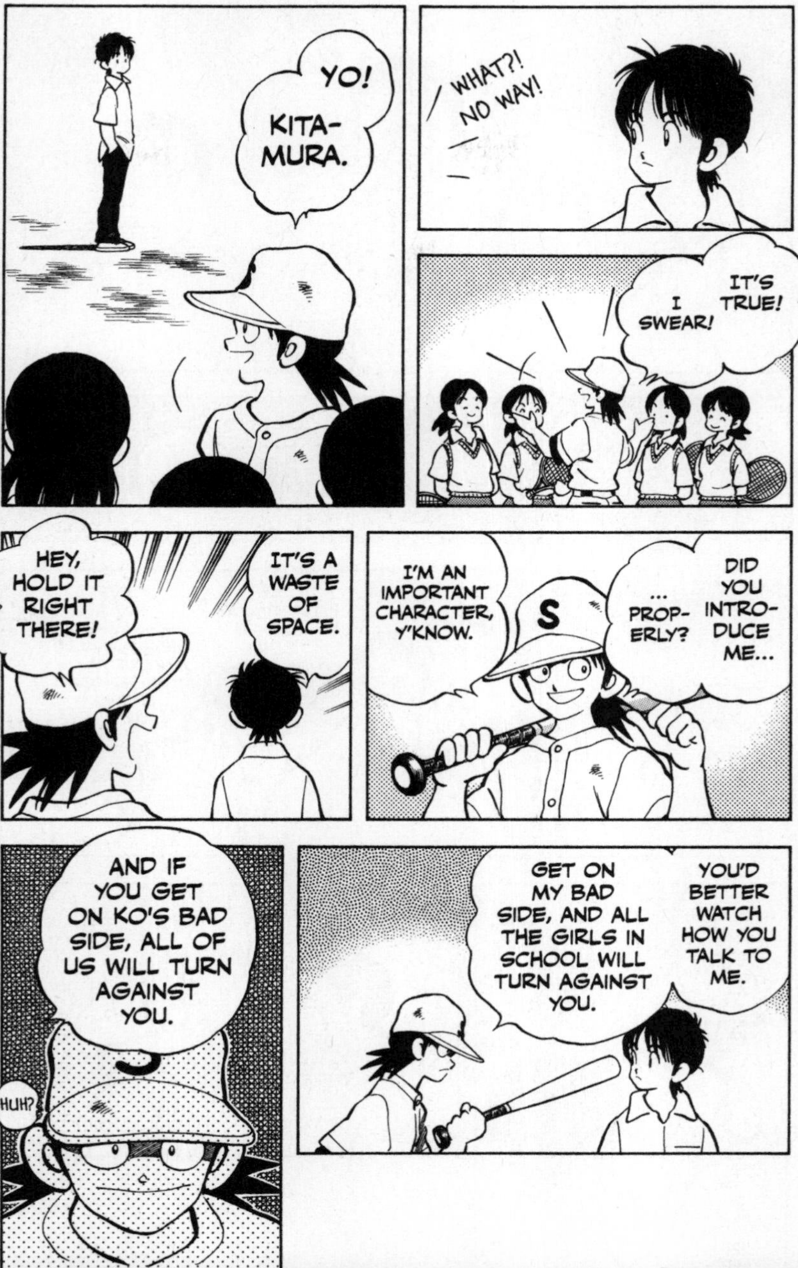
WHAT?! NO WAY!
IT'S TRUE!
I SWEAR!
YO!
KITA-MURA.
DID YOU INTRODUCE ME...
... PROPERLY?
I'M AN IMPORTANT CHARACTER, Y'KNOW.
IT'S A WASTE OF SPACE.
HEY, HOLD IT RIGHT THERE!
YOU'D BETTER WATCH HOW YOU TALK TO ME.
GET ON MY BAD SIDE, AND ALL THE GIRLS IN SCHOOL WILL TURN AGAINST YOU.
AND IF YOU GET ON KO'S BAD SIDE, ALL OF US WILL TURN AGAINST YOU.
HUH?

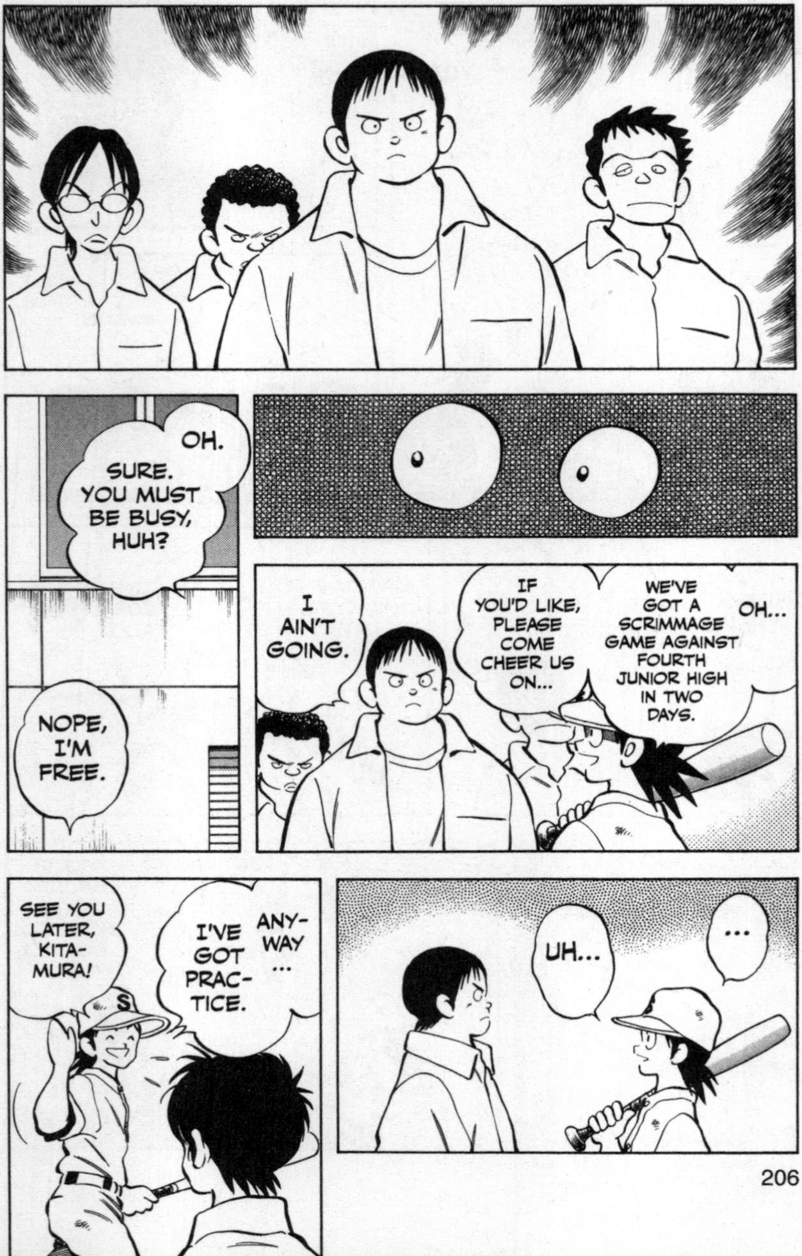
OH...
WE'VE GOT A SCRIMMAGE GAME AGAINST FOURTH JUNIOR HIGH IN TWO DAYS.
IF YOU'D LIKE, PLEASE COME CHEER US ON...
I AIN'T GOING.
OH. SURE. YOU MUST BE BUSY, HUH?
NOPE, I'M FREE.
...
UH...
ANY-WAY...
I'VE GOT PRAC-TICE.
SEE YOU LATER, KITA-MURA!

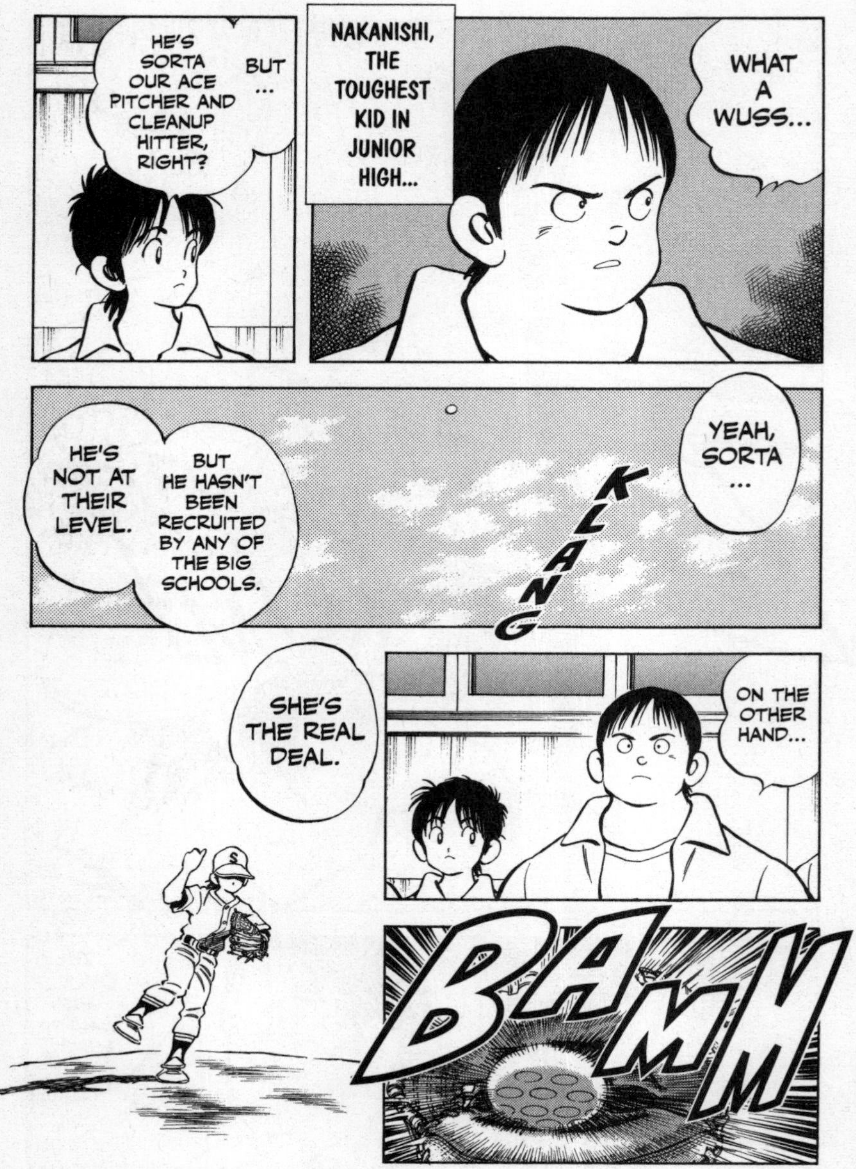
WHAT A WUSS...
NAKANISHI, THE TOUGHEST KID IN JUNIOR HIGH...
HE'S SORTA OUR ACE PITCHER AND CLEANUP HITTER, RIGHT?
BUT ...
YEAH, SORTA ...
KLANG
BUT HE HASN'T BEEN RECRUITED BY ANY OF THE BIG SCHOOLS.
HE'S NOT AT THEIR LEVEL.
ON THE OTHER HAND...
SHE'S THE REAL DEAL.
BAMM

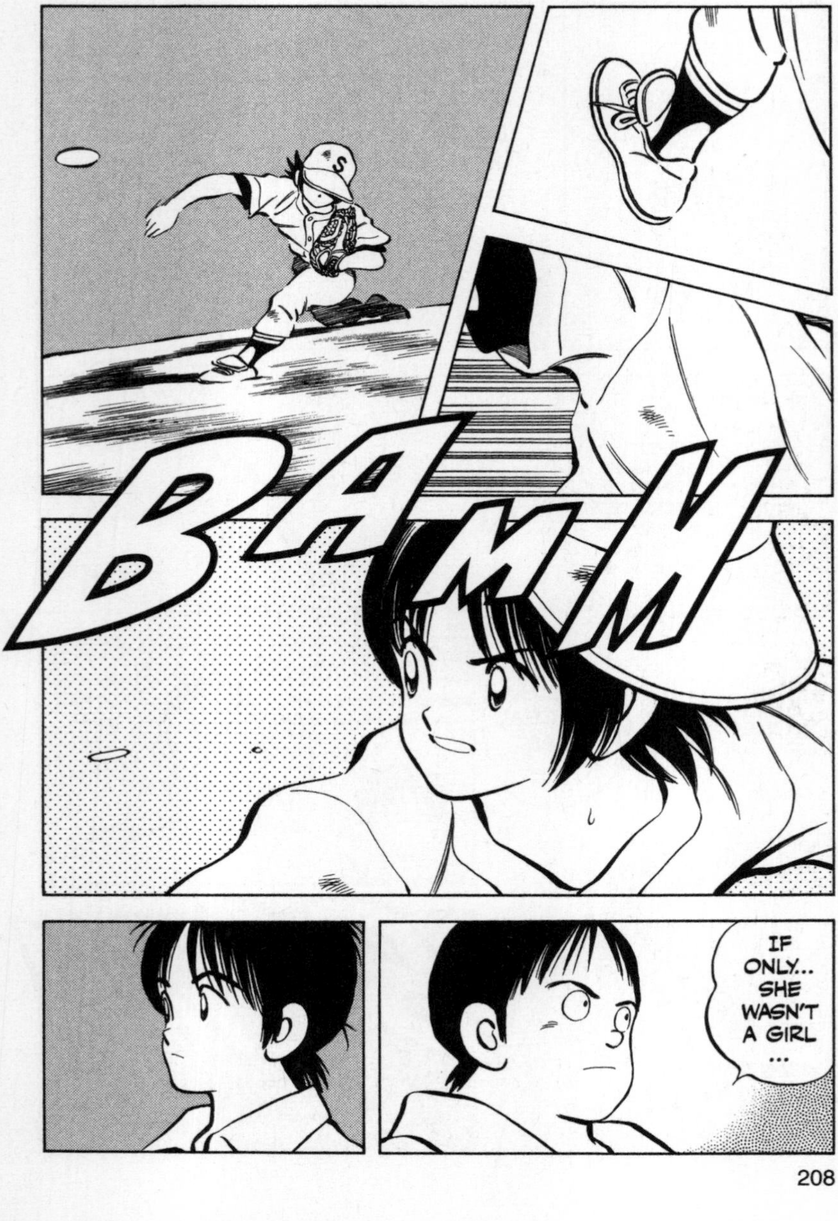
BAMM
IF ONLY... SHE WASN'T A GIRL ...

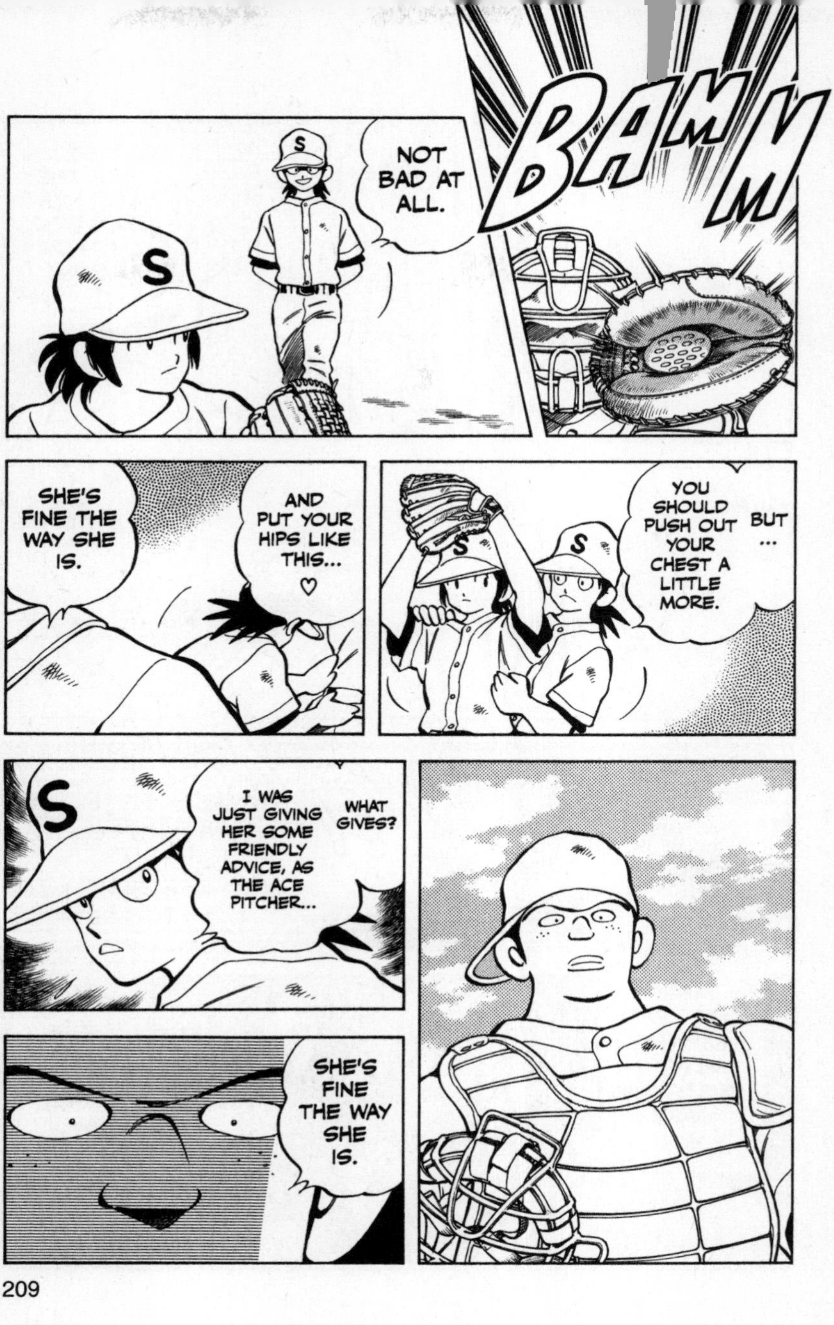
BAMM
NOT BAD AT ALL.
BUT ...
YOU SHOULD PUSH OUT YOUR CHEST A LITTLE MORE.
AND PUT YOUR HIPS LIKE THIS... ♡
SHE'S FINE THE WAY SHE IS.
WHAT GIVES?
I WAS JUST GIVING HER SOME FRIENDLY ADVICE, AS THE ACE PITCHER...
SHE'S FINE THE WAY SHE IS.

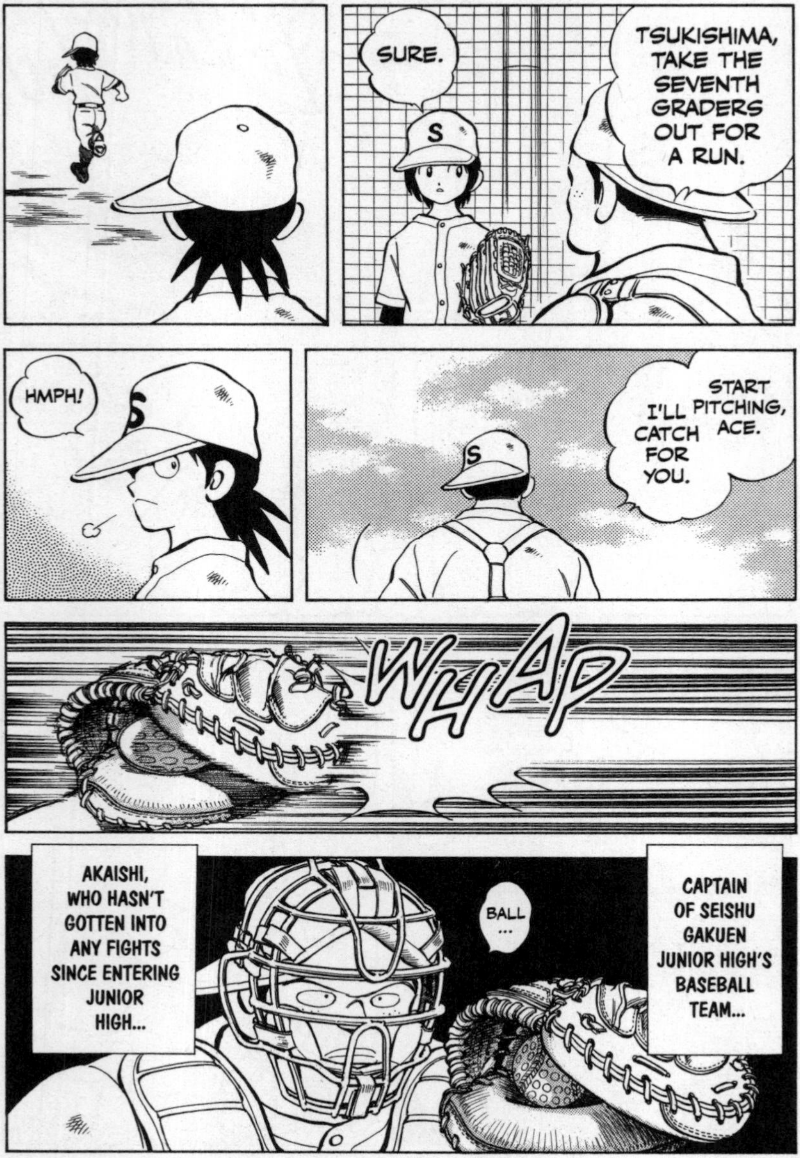
TSUKISHIMA, TAKE THE SEVENTH GRADERS OUT FOR A RUN.
SURE.
START PITCHING, ACE.
I'LL CATCH FOR YOU.
HMPH!
WHAP
CAPTAIN OF SEISHU GAKUEN JUNIOR HIGH'S BASEBALL TEAM...
BALL...
AKAISHI, WHO HASN'T GOTTEN INTO ANY FIGHTS SINCE ENTERING JUNIOR HIGH...

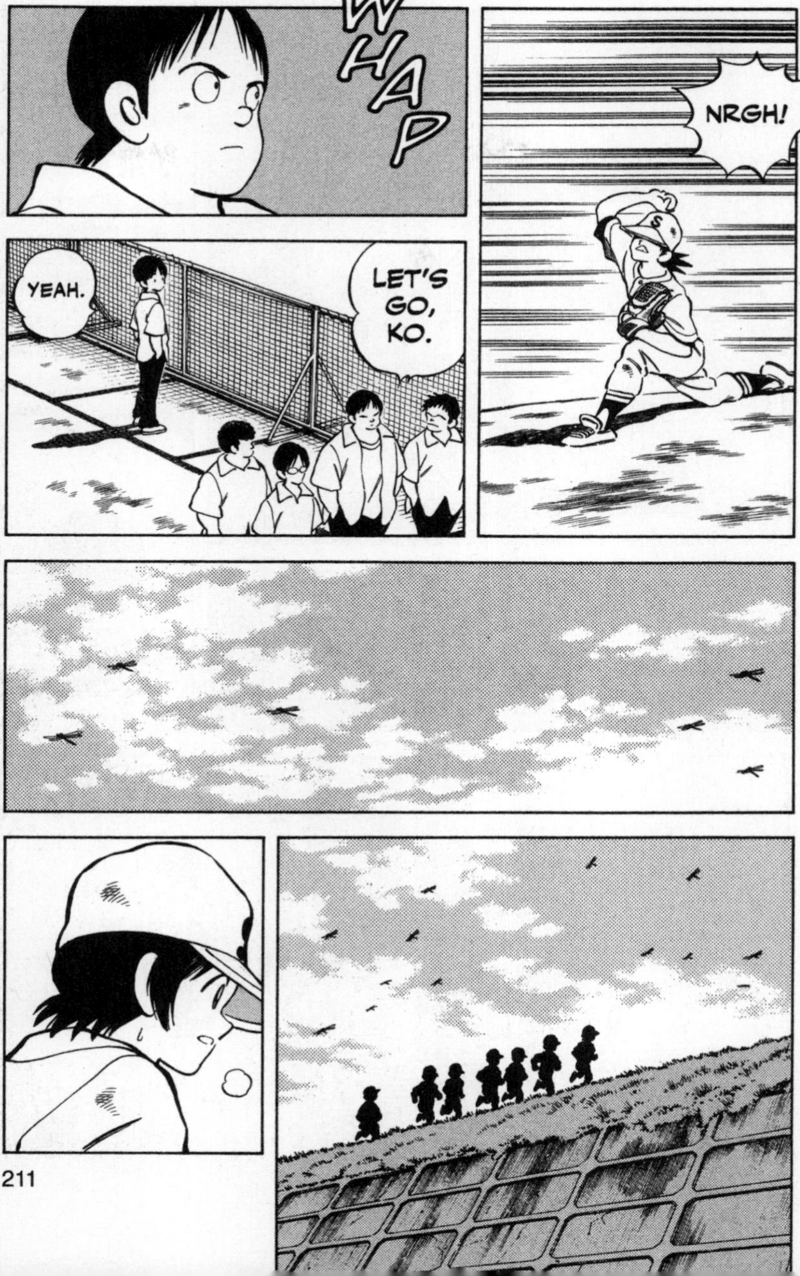
NRGH!
WHAP
LET'S GO, KO.
YEAH.

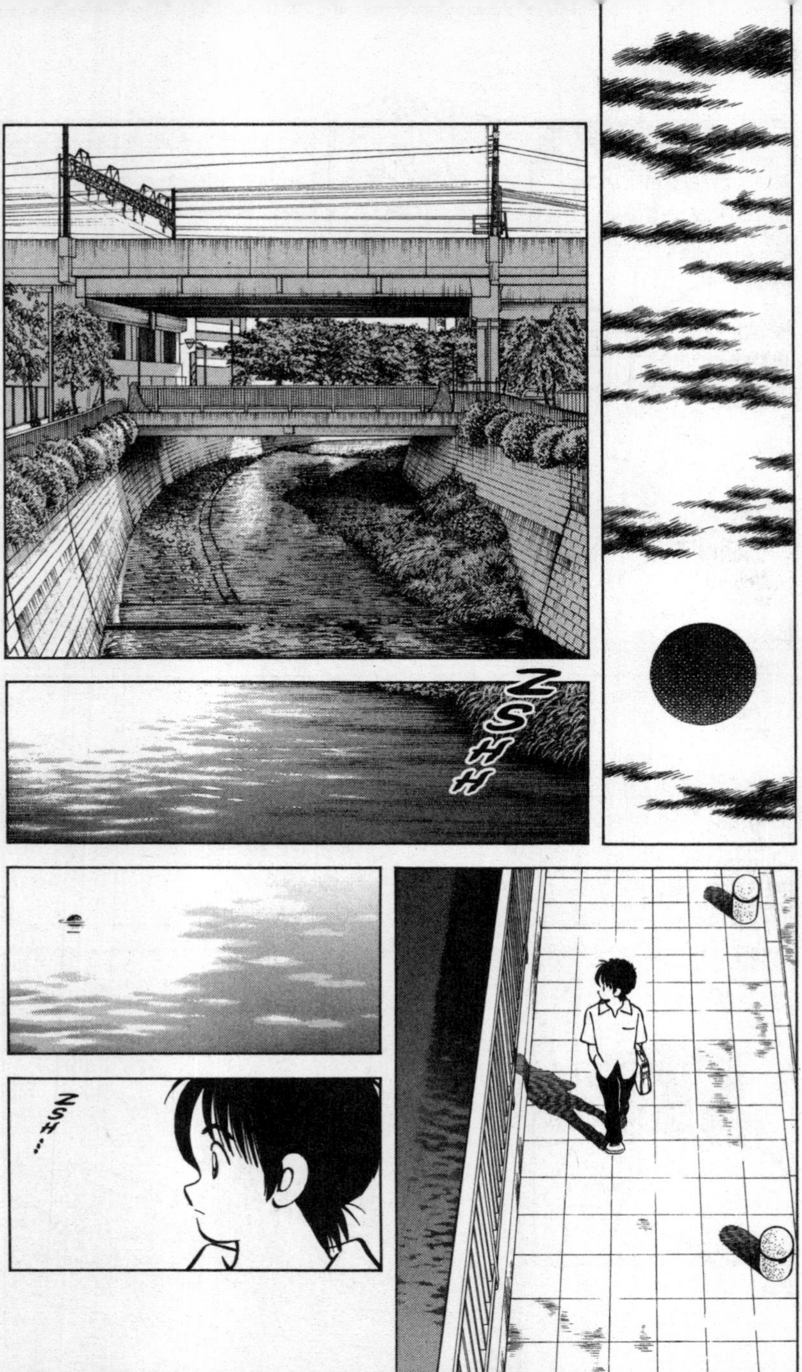
ZSHH
ZSH...

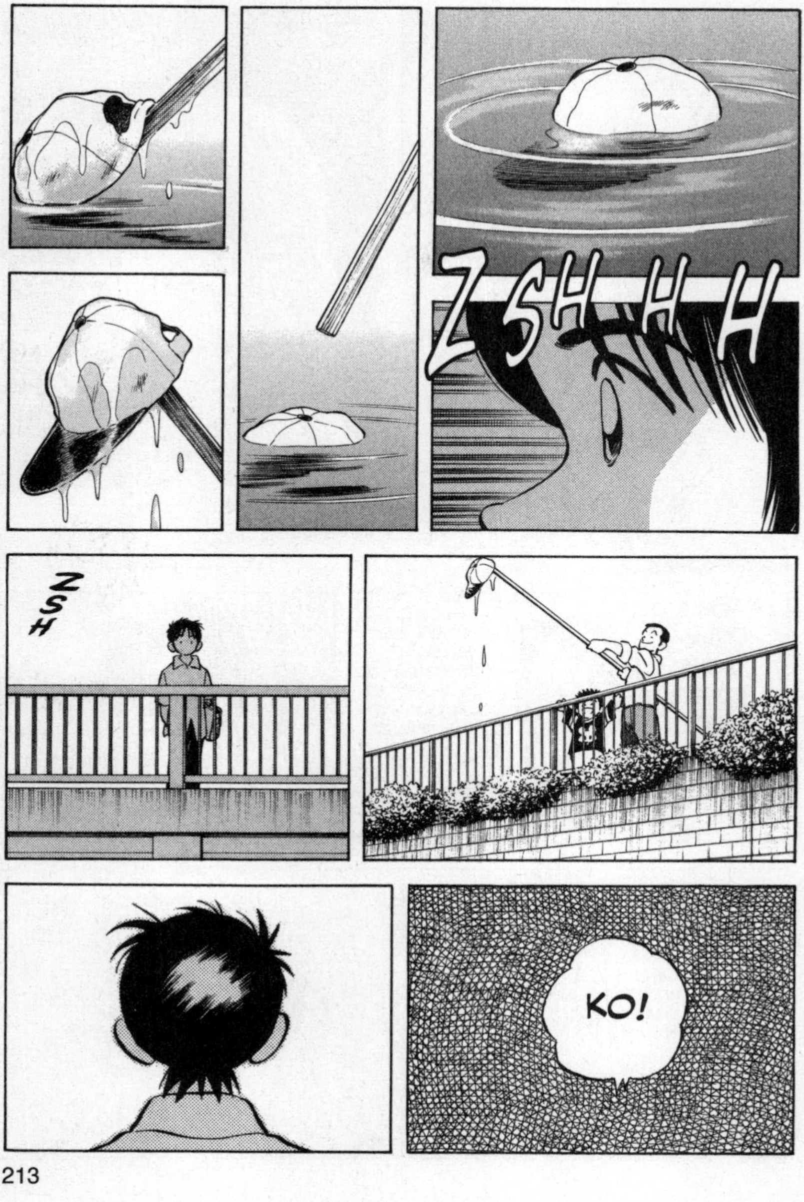
ZSHHH
ZSH
KO!

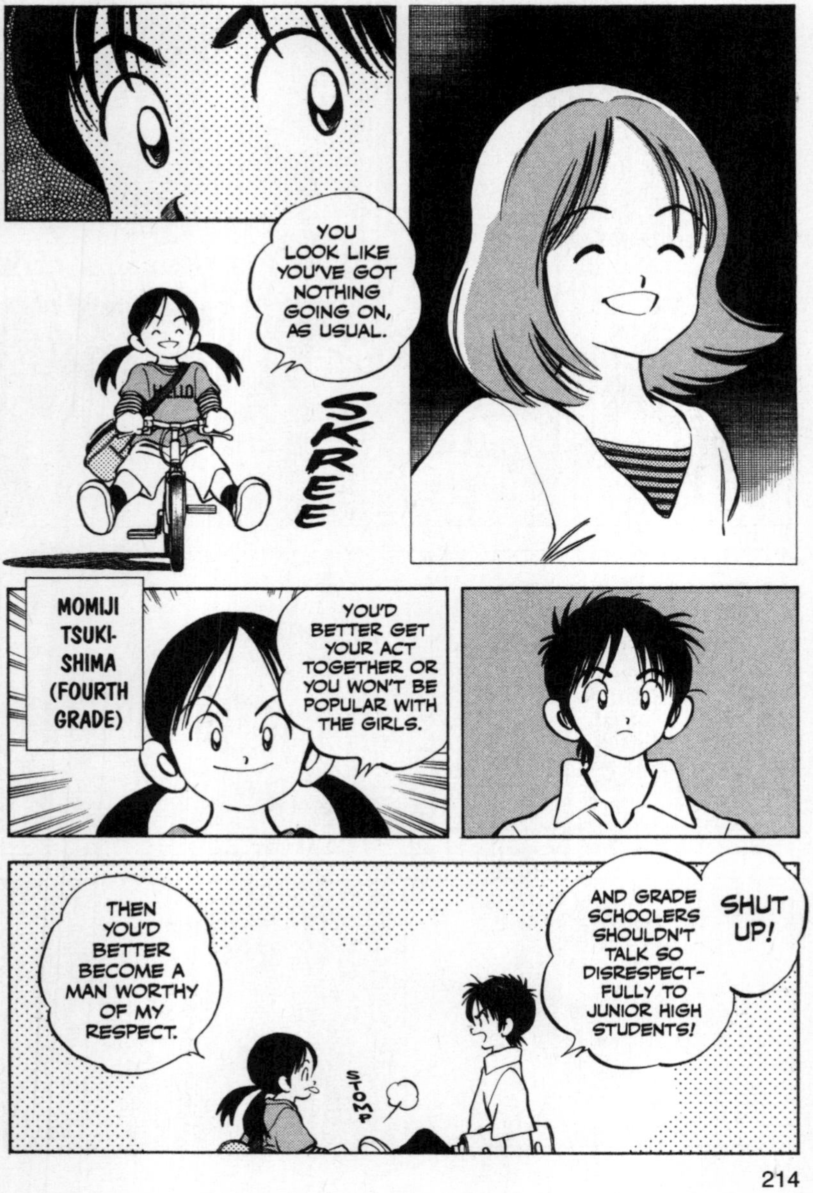
YOU LOOK LIKE YOU'VE GOT NOTHING GOING ON, AS USUAL.
SKREE
YOU'D BETTER GET YOUR ACT TOGETHER OR YOU WON'T BE POPULAR WITH THE GIRLS.
MOMIJI TSUKI-SHIMA (FOURTH GRADE)
SHUT UP!
AND GRADE SCHOOLERS SHOULDN'T TALK SO DISRESPECT-FULLY TO JUNIOR HIGH STUDENTS!
STOMP
THEN YOU'D BETTER BECOME A MAN WORTHY OF MY RESPECT.

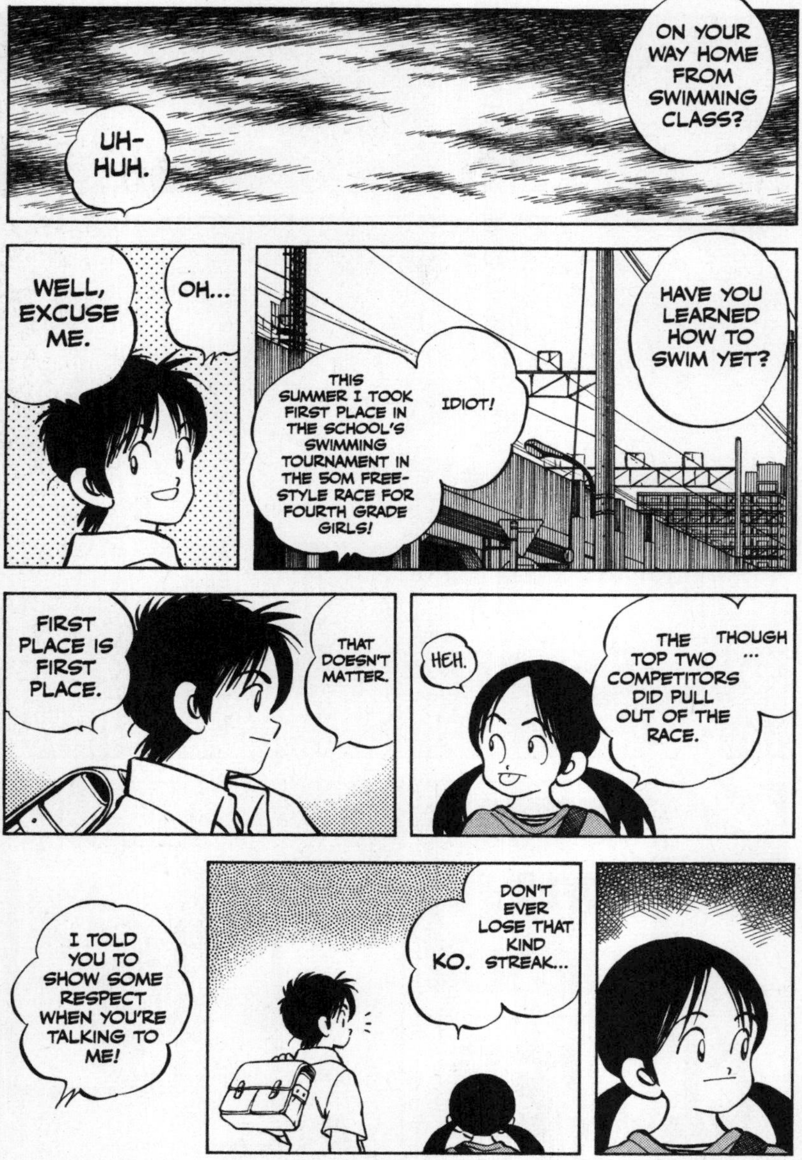
ON YOUR WAY HOME FROM SWIMMING CLASS?
UH-HUH.
HAVE YOU LEARNED HOW TO SWIM YET?
IDIOT!
THIS SUMMER I TOOK FIRST PLACE IN THE SCHOOL'S SWIMMING TOURNAMENT IN THE 50M FREE-STYLE RACE FOR FOURTH GRADE GIRLS!
OH...
WELL, EXCUSE ME.
THE TOP TWO COMPETITORS DID PULL OUT OF THE RACE. THOUGH...
HEH.
THAT DOESN'T MATTER.
FIRST PLACE IS FIRST PLACE.
DON'T EVER LOSE THAT KIND STREAK... KO.
I TOLD YOU TO SHOW SOME RESPECT WHEN YOU'RE TALKING TO ME!

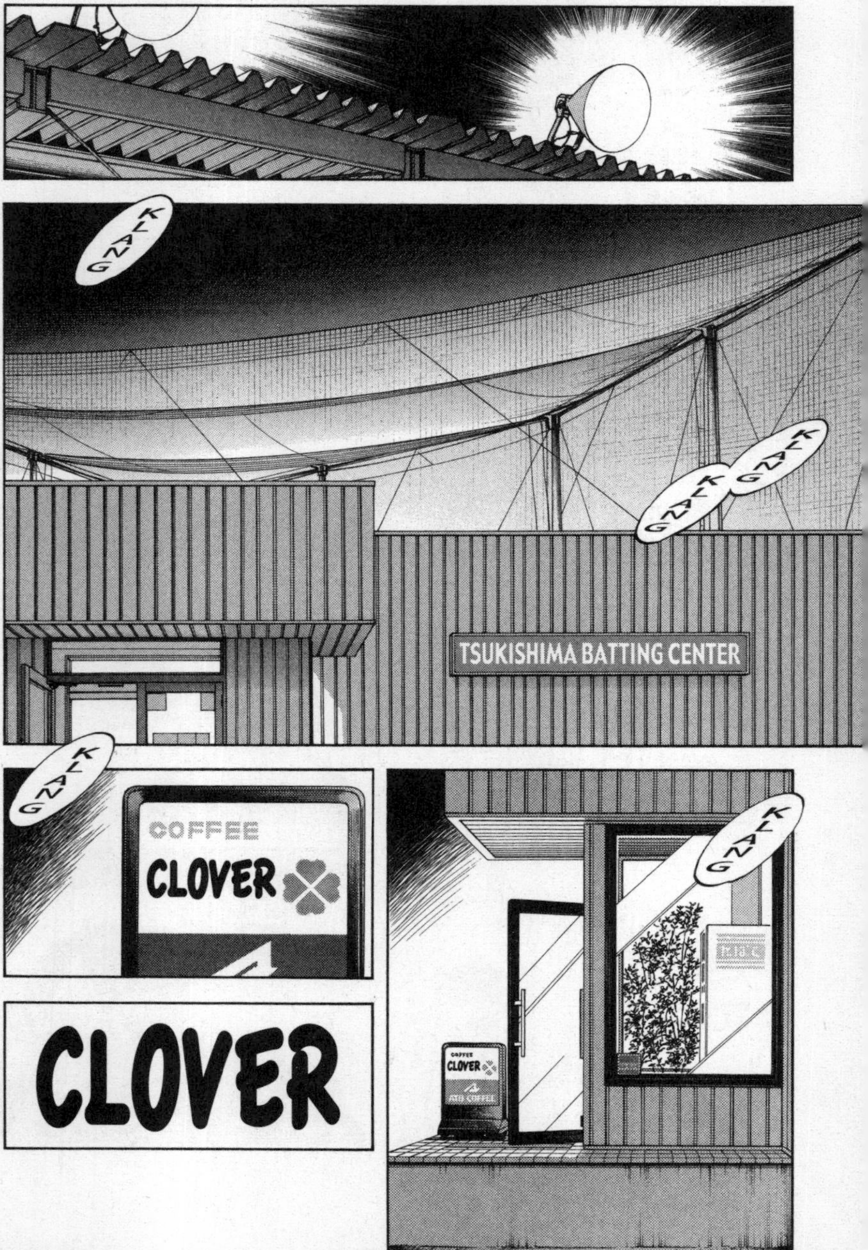
KLANG
KLANG
TSUKISHIMA BATTING CENTER
KLANG
KLANG
COFFEE
CLOVER
KLANG
COFFEE
CLOVER
CLOVER

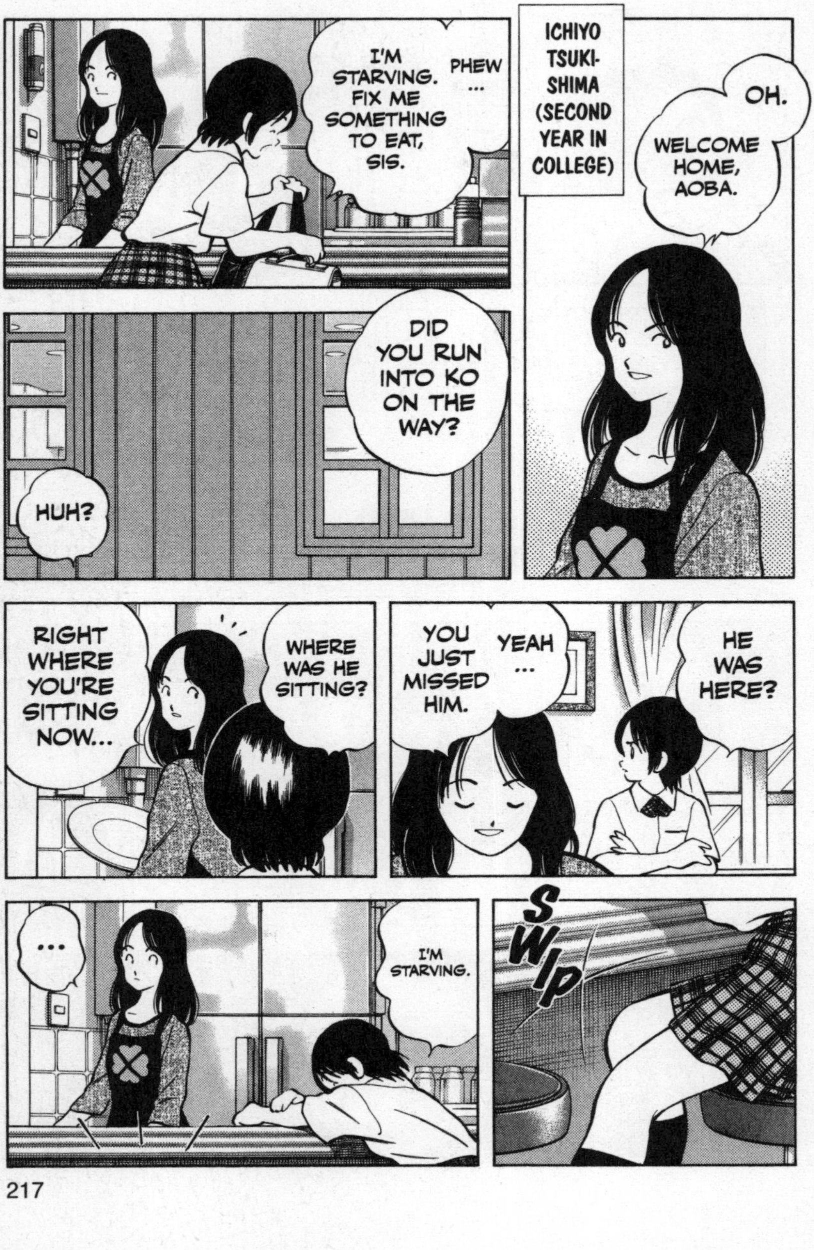
ICHIYO TSUKI-SHIMA (SECOND YEAR IN COLLEGE)
OH.
WELCOME HOME, AOBA.
PHEW ...
I'M STARVING. FIX ME SOMETHING TO EAT, SIS.
DID YOU RUN INTO KO ON THE WAY?
HUH?
HE WAS HERE?
YEAH ...
YOU JUST MISSED HIM.
WHERE WAS HE SITTING?
RIGHT WHERE YOU'RE SITTING NOW...
SWIP
I'M STARVING.
...

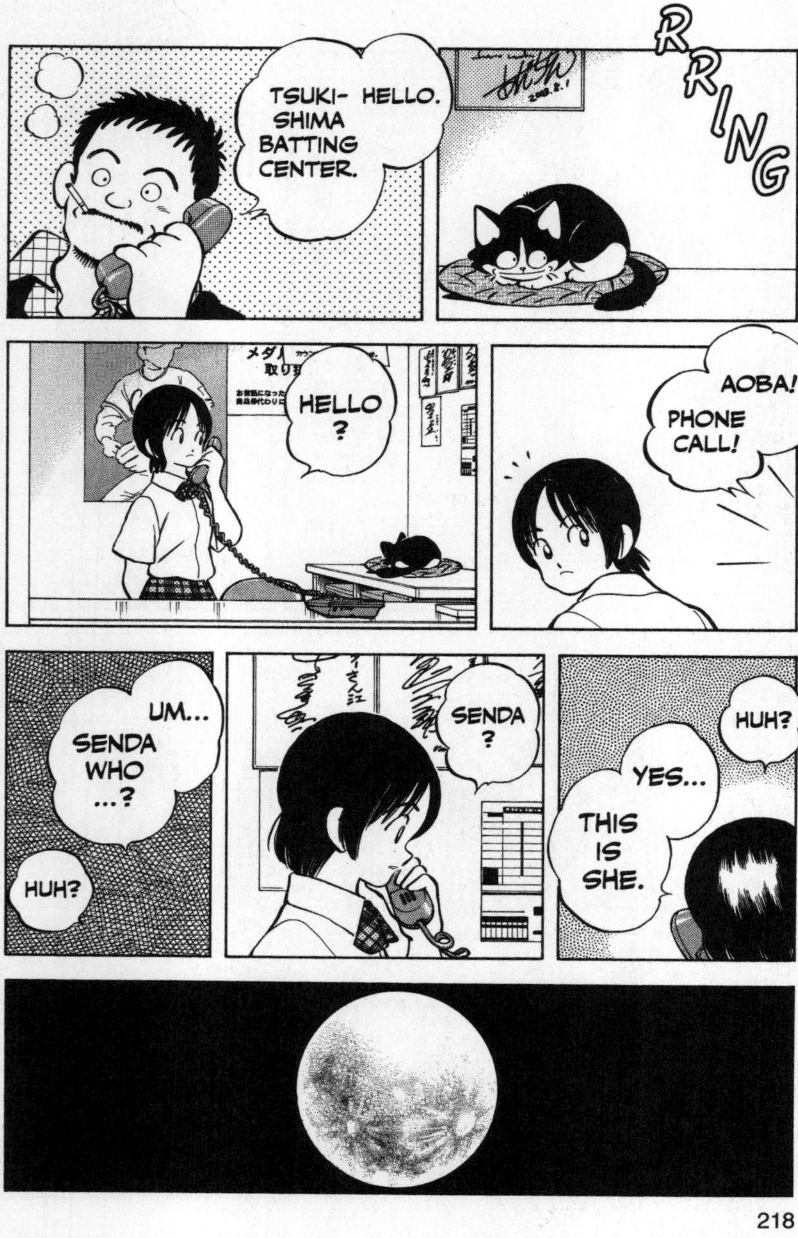
RRING
HELLO.
TSUKI-SHIMA BATTING CENTER.
AOBA! PHONE CALL!
HELLO?
HUH?
YES... THIS IS SHE.
SENDA?
UM... SENDA WHO...?
HUH?

DING

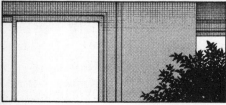

CHIRP
CHIRP
CHIRP

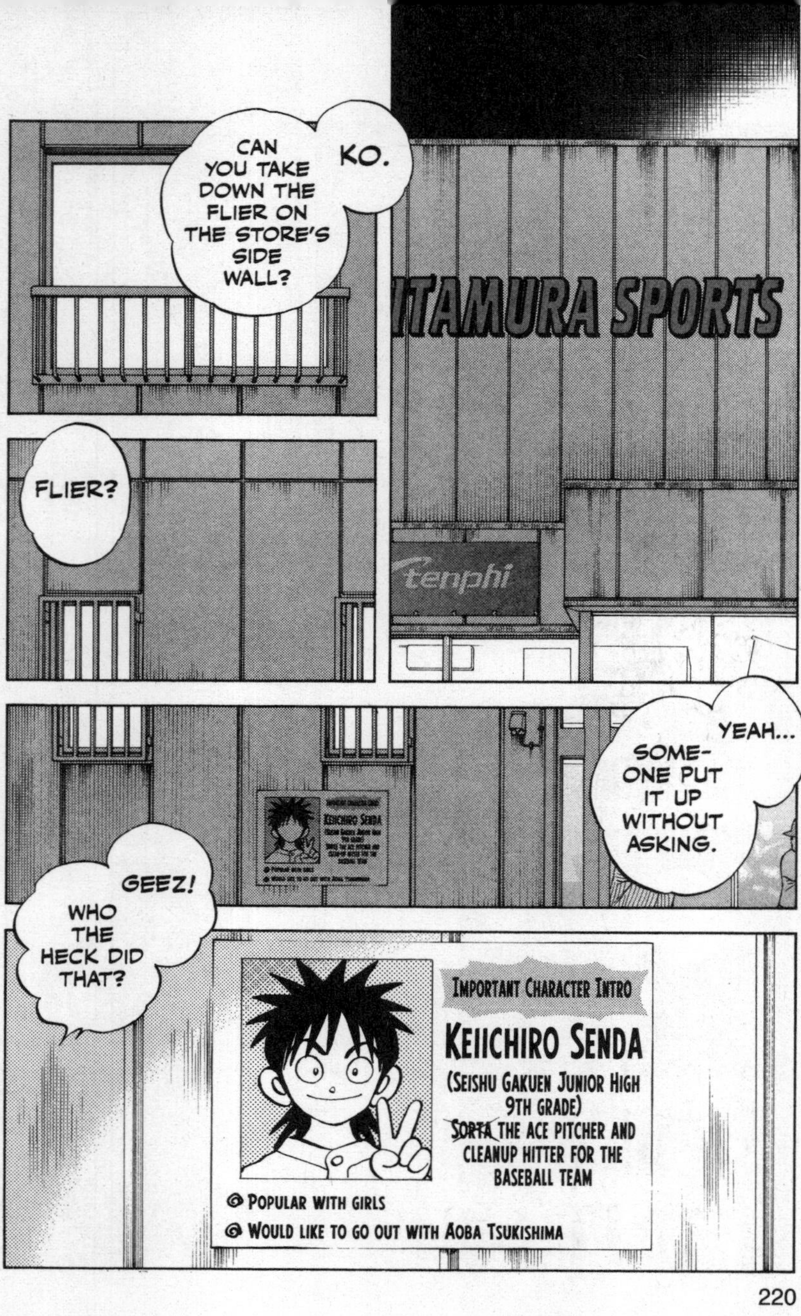
ITAMURA SPORTS
tenphi
KO.
CAN YOU TAKE DOWN THE FLIER ON THE STORE'S SIDE WALL?
FLIER?
YEAH... SOME-ONE PUT IT UP WITHOUT ASKING.
GEEZ!
WHO THE HECK DID THAT?
IMPORTANT CHARACTER INTRO
KEIICHIRO SENDA
(SEISHU GAKUEN JUNIOR HIGH 9TH GRADE)
SORTA THE ACE PITCHER AND CLEANUP HITTER FOR THE BASEBALL TEAM
POPULAR WITH GIRLS
WOULD LIKE TO GO OUT WITH AOBA TSUKISHIMA

CHAPTER 2
JUST A DAILY ROUTINE

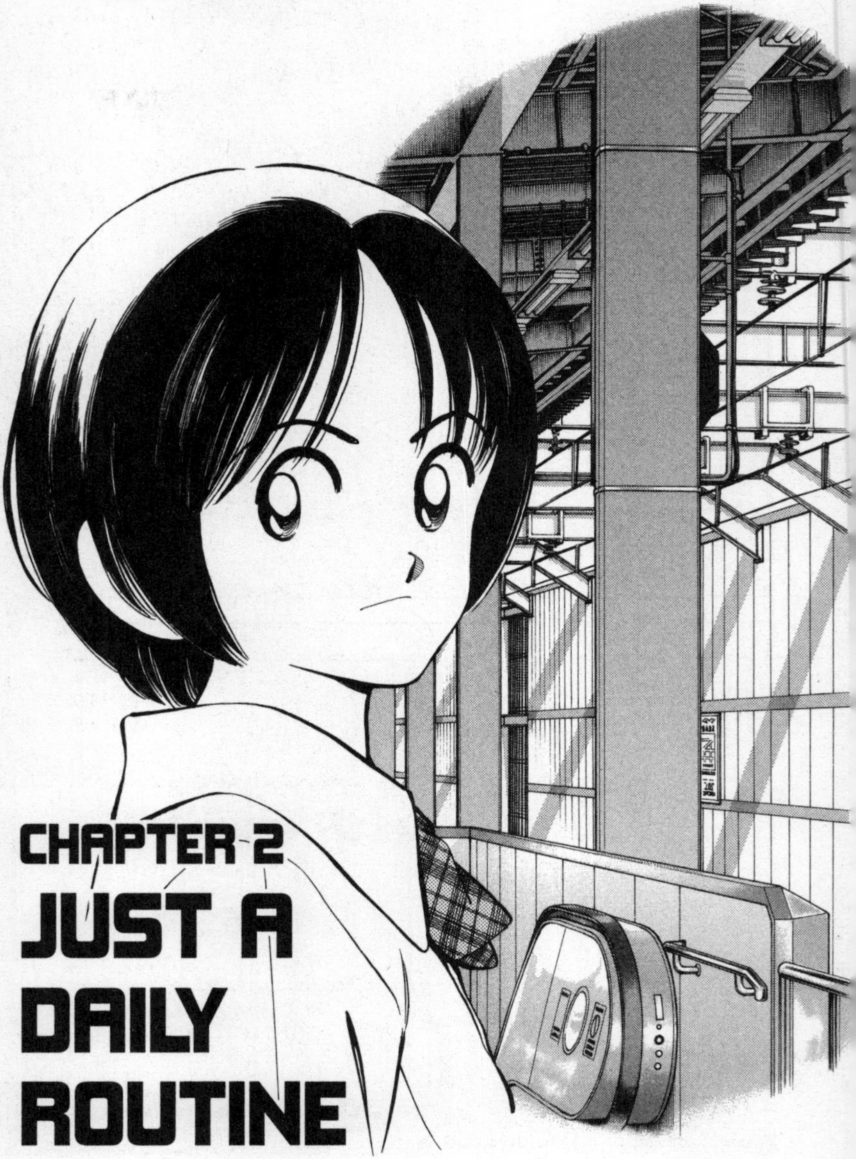

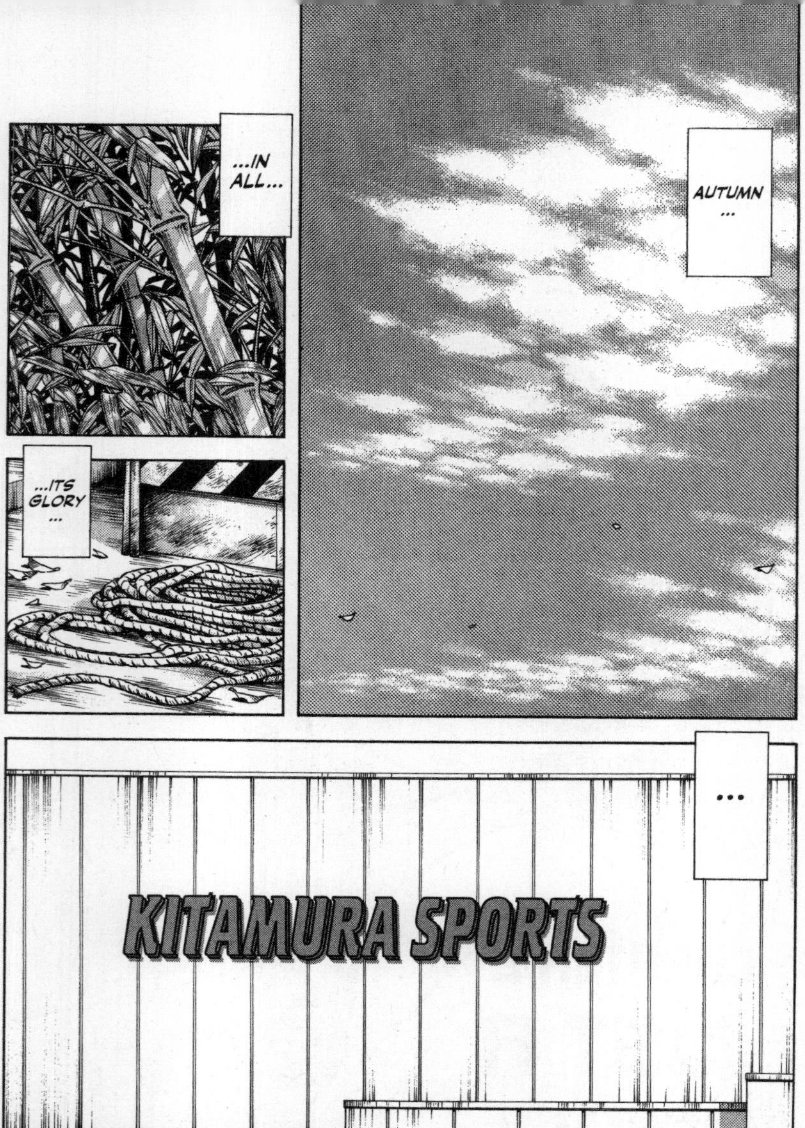
AUTUMN ...
...IN ALL...
...ITS GLORY ...
...
KITAMURA SPORTS
tenphi
tenphi

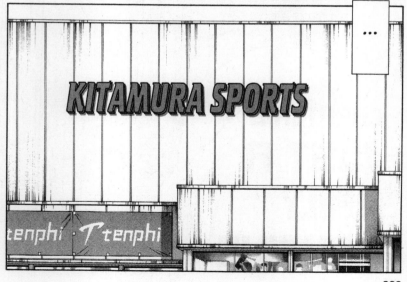

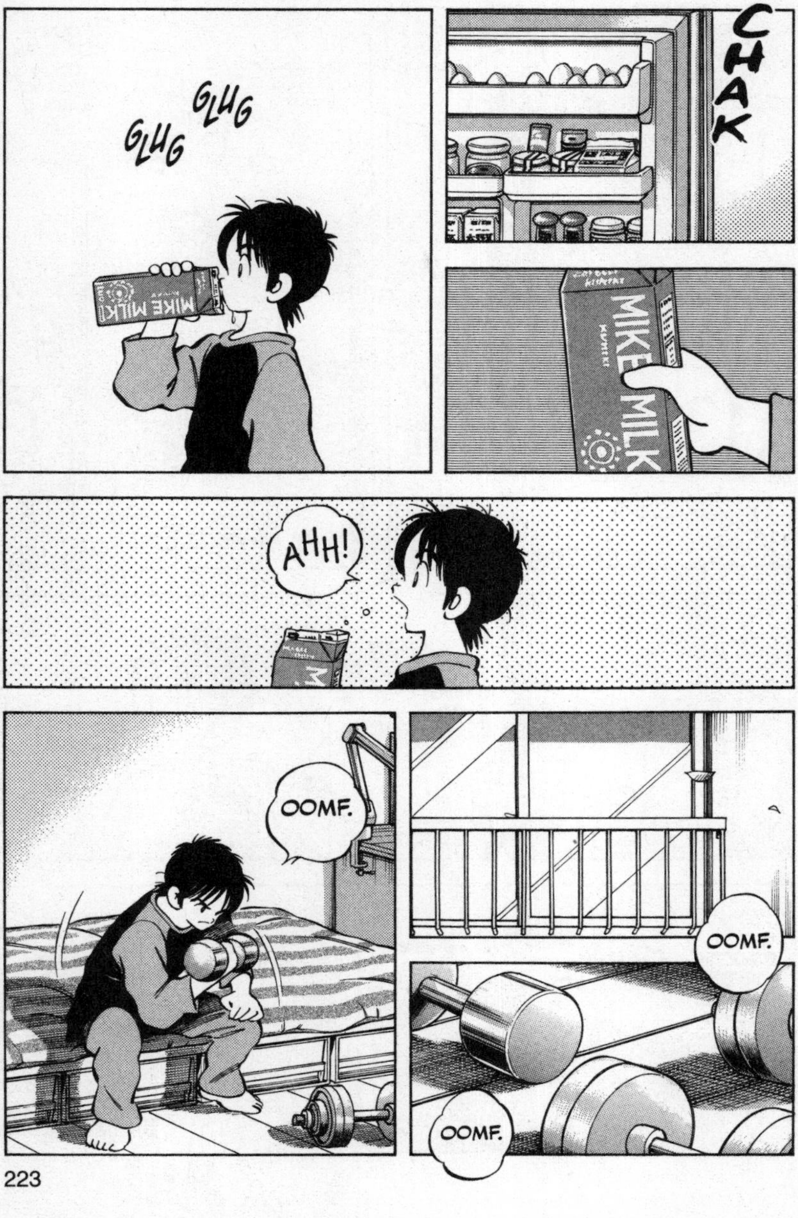
CHAK
MIKE MILK
GLUG GLUG
MIKE MILK
AHH!
OOMF.
OOMF.
OOMF.

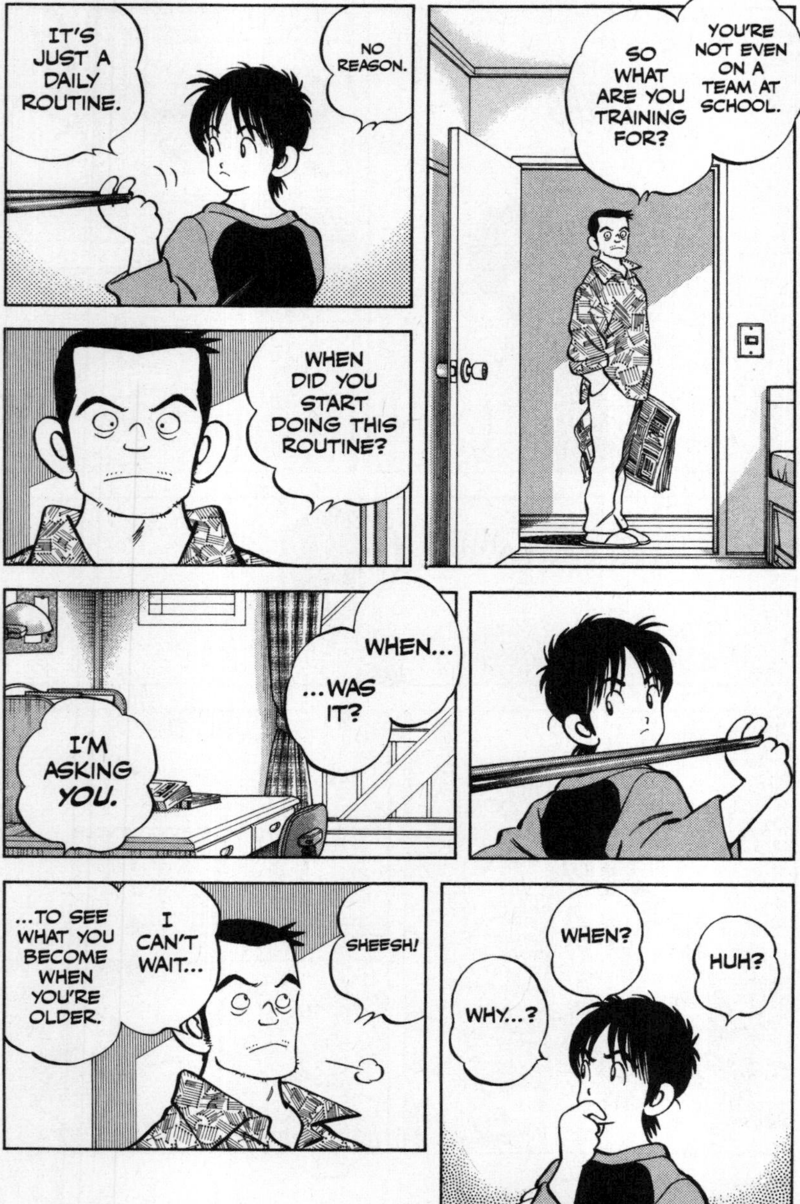
YOU'RE NOT EVEN ON A TEAM AT SCHOOL.
SO WHAT ARE YOU TRAINING FOR?
NO REASON.
IT'S JUST A DAILY ROUTINE.
WHEN DID YOU START DOING THIS ROUTINE?
WHEN...
...WAS IT?
I'M ASKING *YOU.*
HUH?
WHEN?
WHY...?
SHEESH!
I CAN'T WAIT...
...TO SEE WHAT YOU BECOME WHEN YOU'RE OLDER.

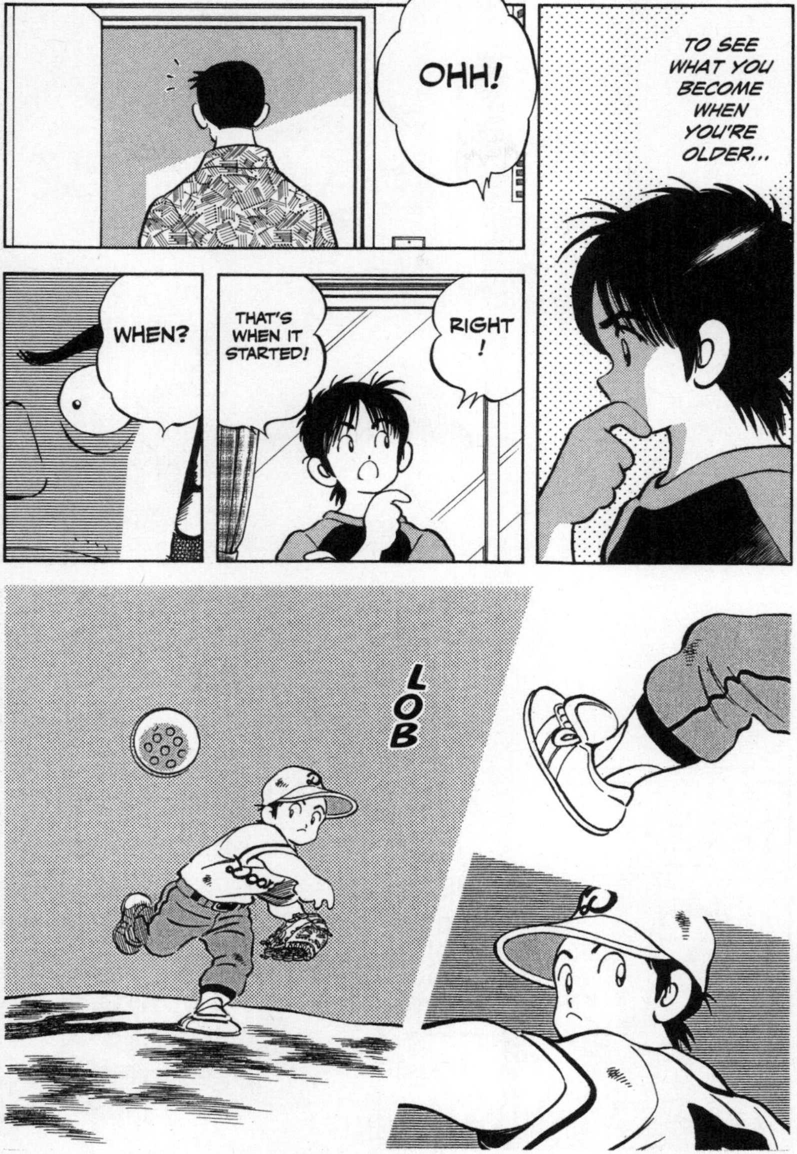
TO SEE WHAT YOU BECOME WHEN YOU'RE OLDER...
OHH!
RIGHT!
THAT'S WHEN IT STARTED!
WHEN?
LOB

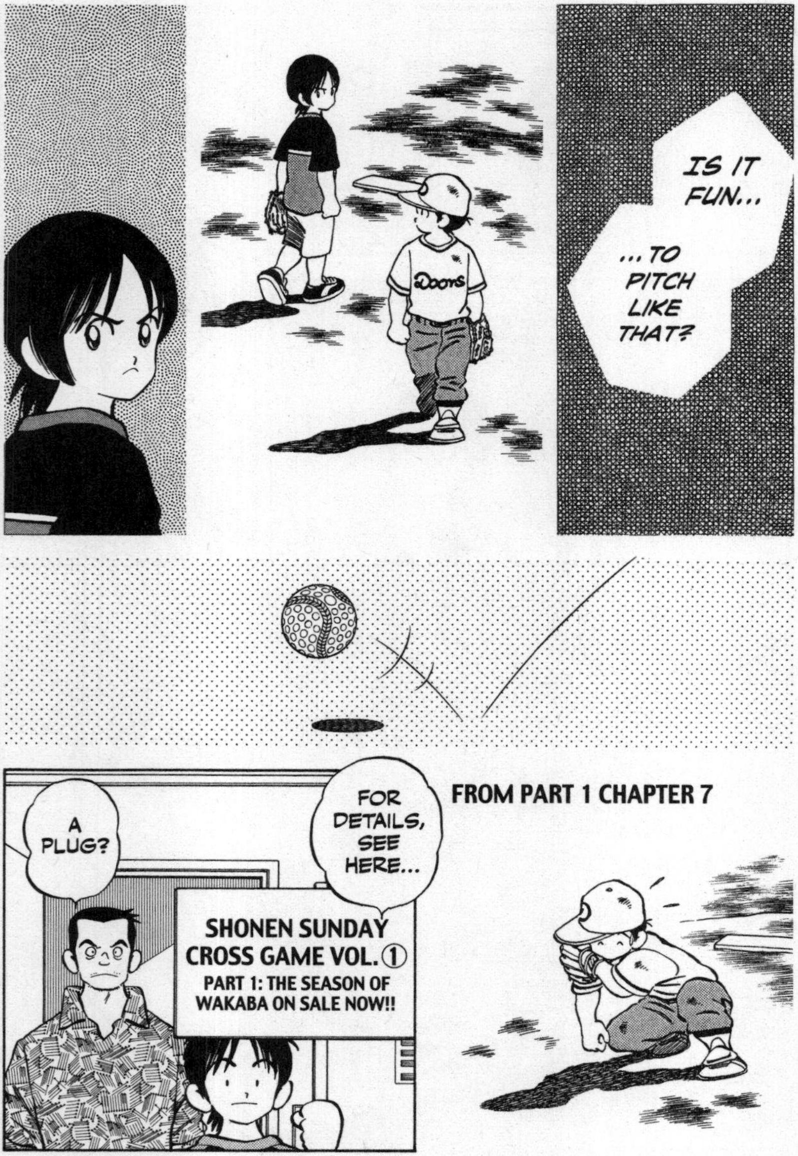

IS IT FUN...
...TO PITCH LIKE THAT?
Doors
FROM PART 1 CHAPTER 7
FOR DETAILS, SEE HERE...
A PLUG?
SHONEN SUNDAY CROSS GAME VOL. ①
PART 1: THE SEASON OF WAKABA ON SALE NOW!!

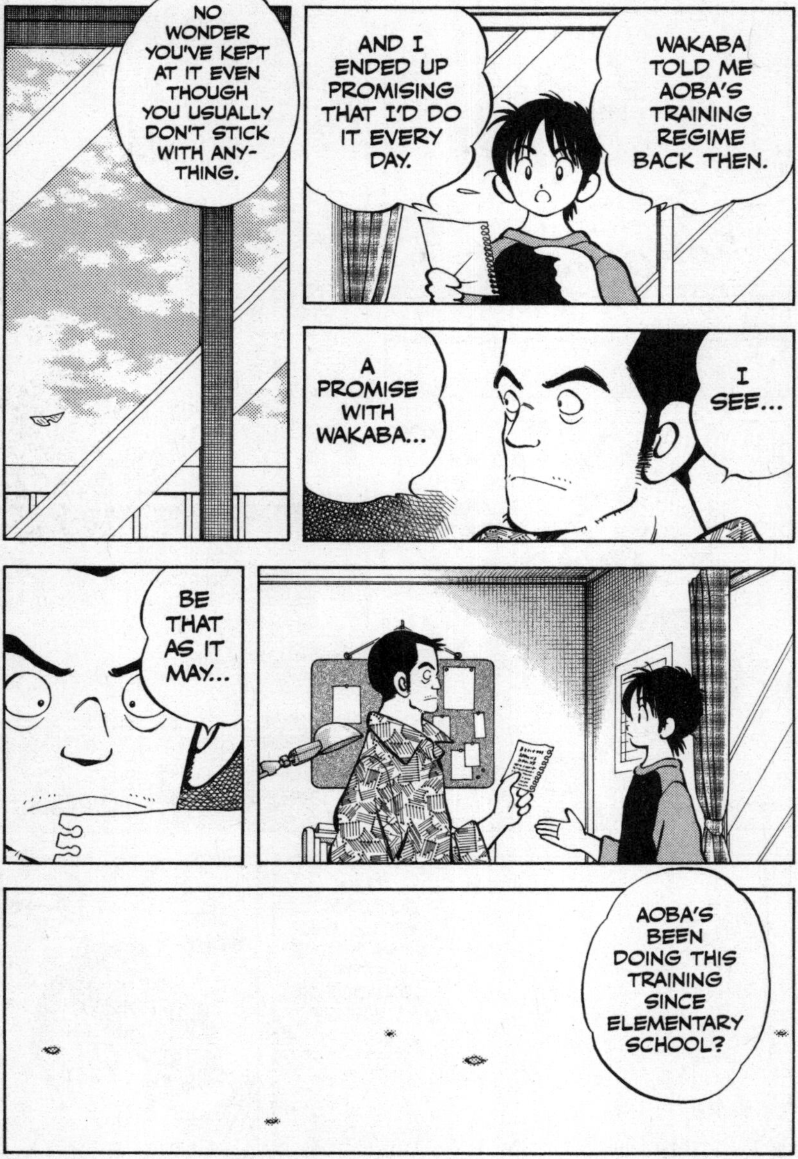
WAKABA TOLD ME AOBA'S TRAINING REGIME BACK THEN.
AND I ENDED UP PROMISING THAT I'D DO IT EVERY DAY.
I SEE...
A PROMISE WITH WAKABA...
NO WONDER YOU'VE KEPT AT IT EVEN THOUGH YOU USUALLY DON'T STICK WITH ANY-THING.
BE THAT AS IT MAY...
AOBA'S BEEN DOING THIS TRAINING SINCE ELEMENTARY SCHOOL?

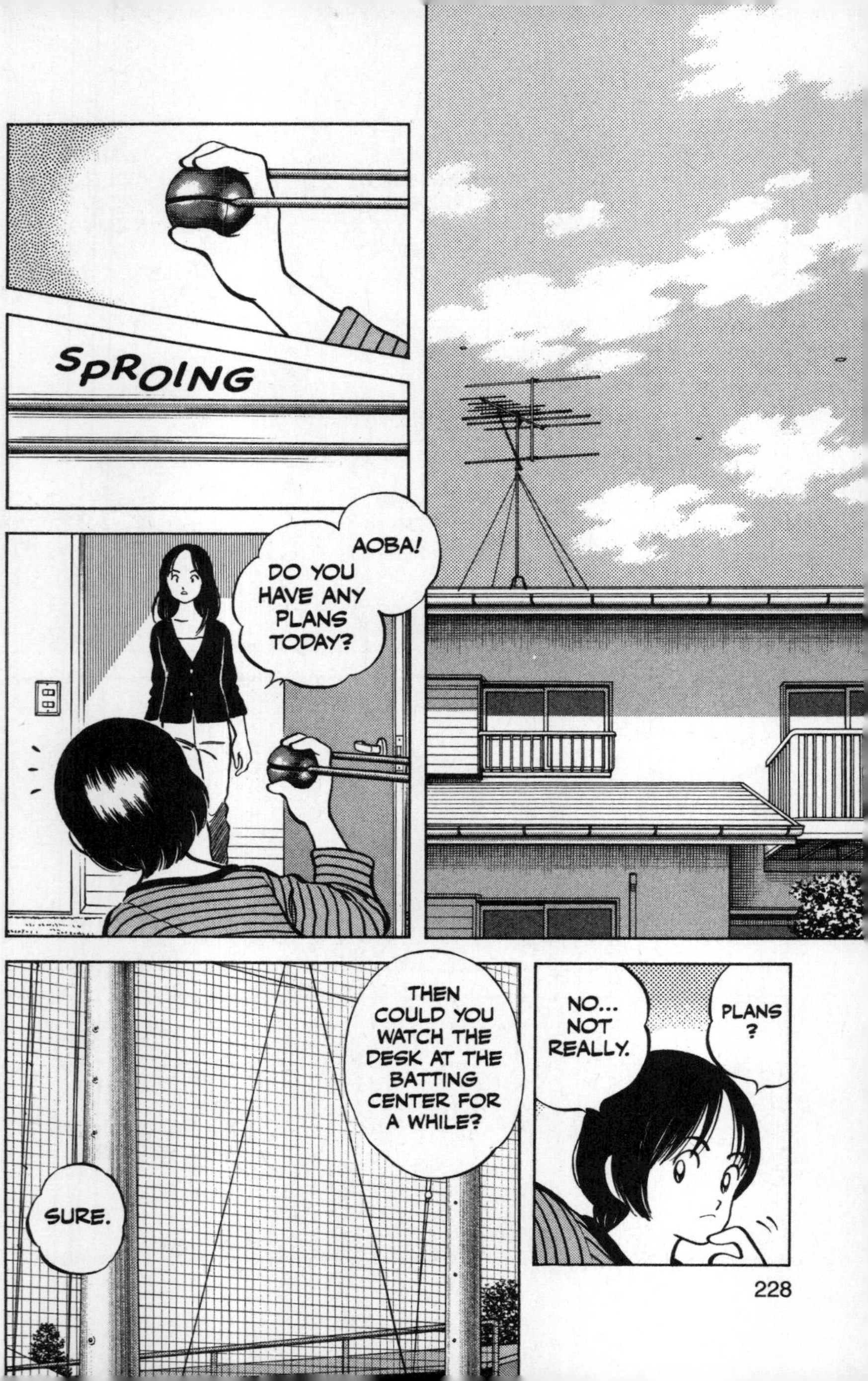
SPROING
AOBA!
DO YOU HAVE ANY PLANS TODAY?
PLANS?
NO... NOT REALLY.
THEN COULD YOU WATCH THE DESK AT THE BATTING CENTER FOR A WHILE?
SURE.

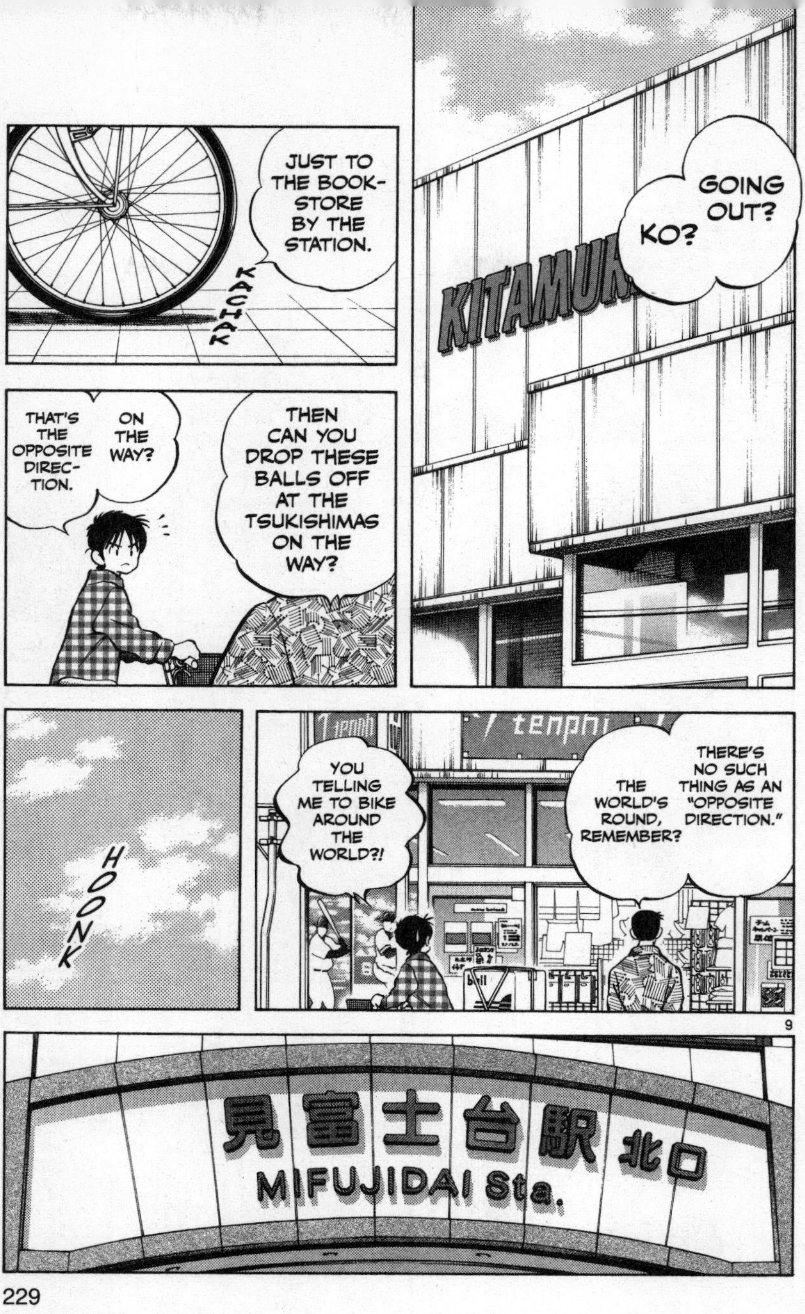
KITAMUR
GOING OUT?
KO?
JUST TO THE BOOK-STORE BY THE STATION.
KACHAK
THEN CAN YOU DROP THESE BALLS OFF AT THE TSUKISHIMAS ON THE WAY?
ON THE WAY?
THAT'S THE OPPOSITE DIRECTION.
THERE'S NO SUCH THING AS AN "OPPOSITE DIRECTION."
THE WORLD'S ROUND, REMEMBER?
YOU TELLING ME TO BIKE AROUND THE WORLD?!
HOONK
9
見富士台駅 北口
MIFUJIDAI Sta.

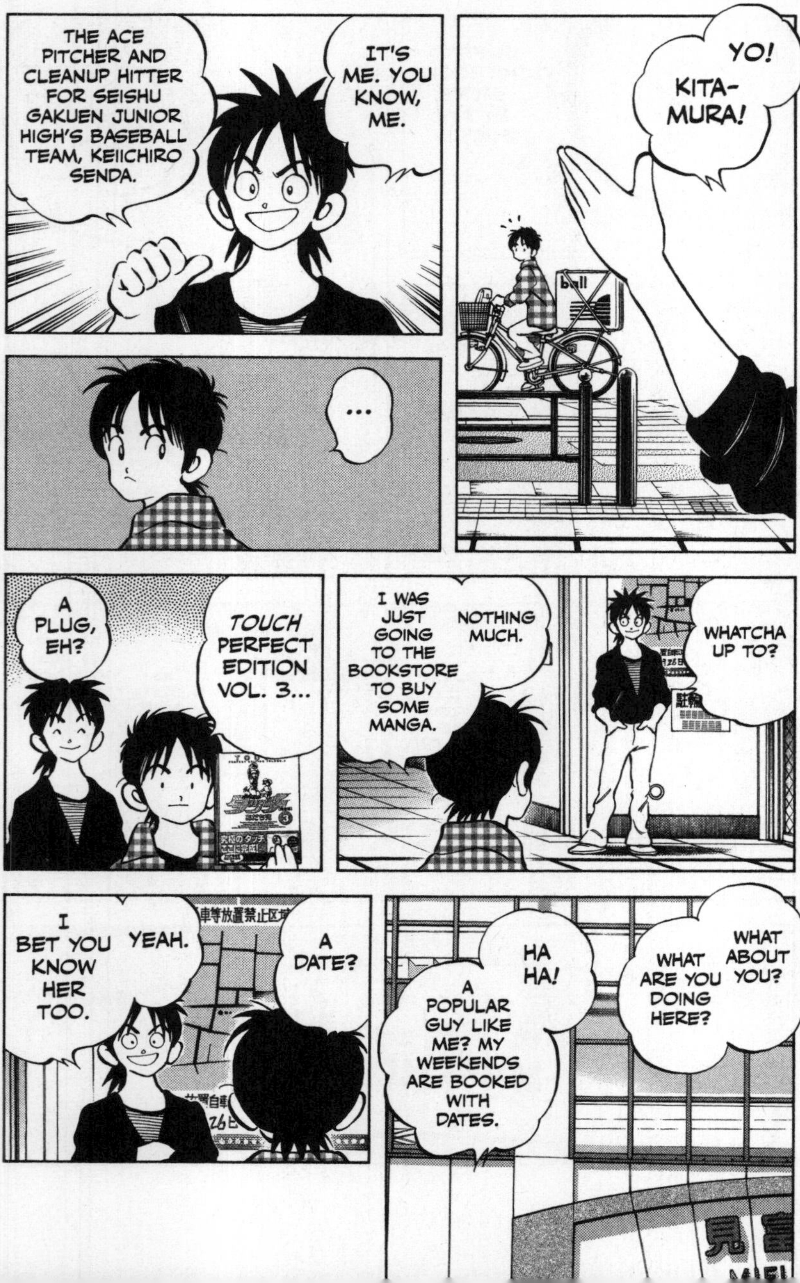
YO!
KITA-MURA!
IT'S ME. YOU KNOW, ME.
THE ACE PITCHER AND CLEANUP HITTER FOR SEISHU GAKUEN JUNIOR HIGH'S BASEBALL TEAM, KEIICHIRO SENDA.
...
WHATCHA UP TO?
NOTHING MUCH.
I WAS JUST GOING TO THE BOOKSTORE TO BUY SOME MANGA.
TOUCH PERFECT EDITION VOL. 3...
A PLUG, EH?
WHAT ABOUT YOU?
WHAT ARE YOU DOING HERE?
HA HA!
A POPULAR GUY LIKE ME? MY WEEKENDS ARE BOOKED WITH DATES.
A DATE?
YEAH.
I BET YOU KNOW HER TOO.

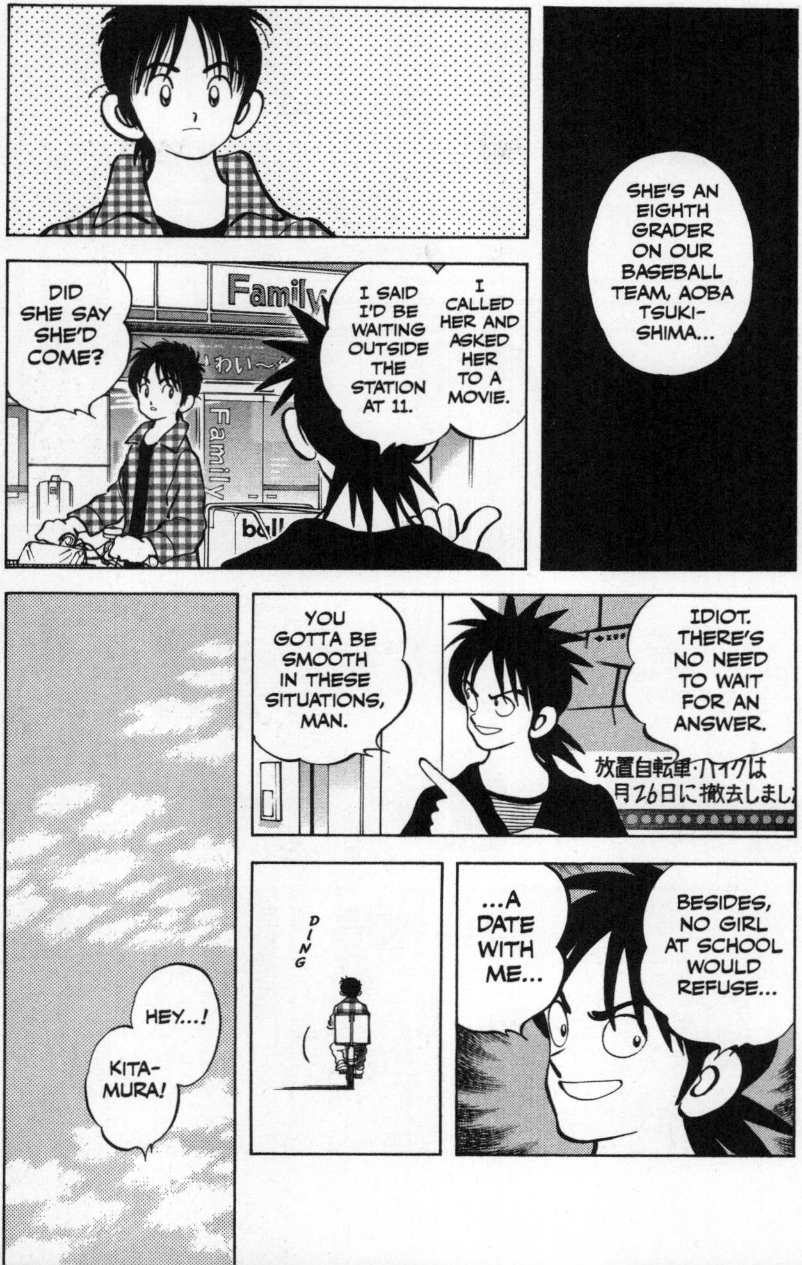
SHE'S AN EIGHTH GRADER ON OUR BASEBALL TEAM, AOBA TSUKI-SHIMA...
I CALLED HER AND ASKED HER TO A MOVIE.
I SAID I'D BE WAITING OUTSIDE THE STATION AT 11.
Family
DID SHE SAY SHE'D COME?
IDIOT. THERE'S NO NEED TO WAIT FOR AN ANSWER.
放置自転車・バイクは
月26日に撤去しまし
YOU GOTTA BE SMOOTH IN THESE SITUATIONS, MAN.
BESIDES, NO GIRL AT SCHOOL WOULD REFUSE...
...A DATE WITH ME...
DING
HEY...!
KITA-MURA!

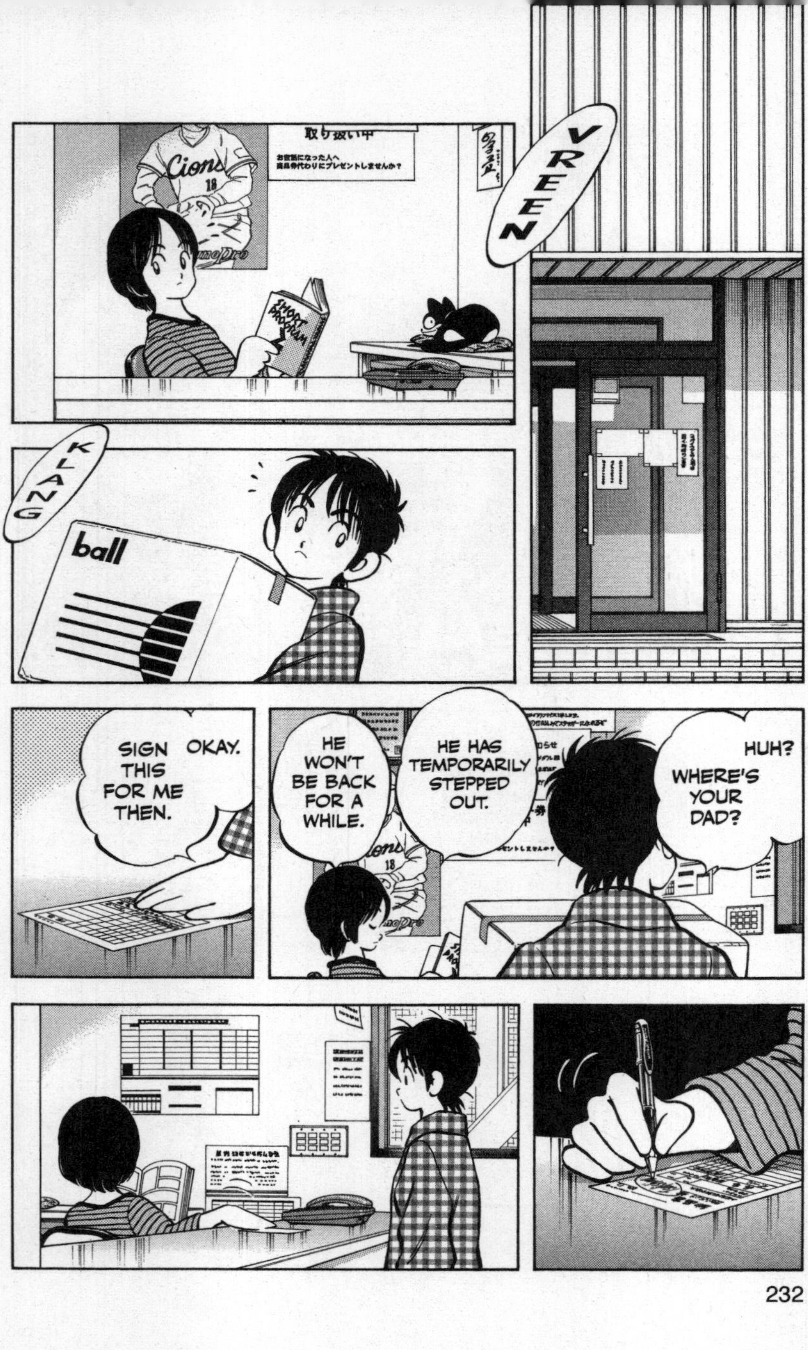
VREEN
取り扱い中
お世話になった人へ
商品券代わりにプレゼントしませんか？
Cions
SHORT PROGRAM
KLANG
ball
HUH? WHERE'S YOUR DAD?
HE HAS TEMPORARILY STEPPED OUT.
HE WON'T BE BACK FOR A WHILE.
OKAY. SIGN THIS FOR ME THEN.

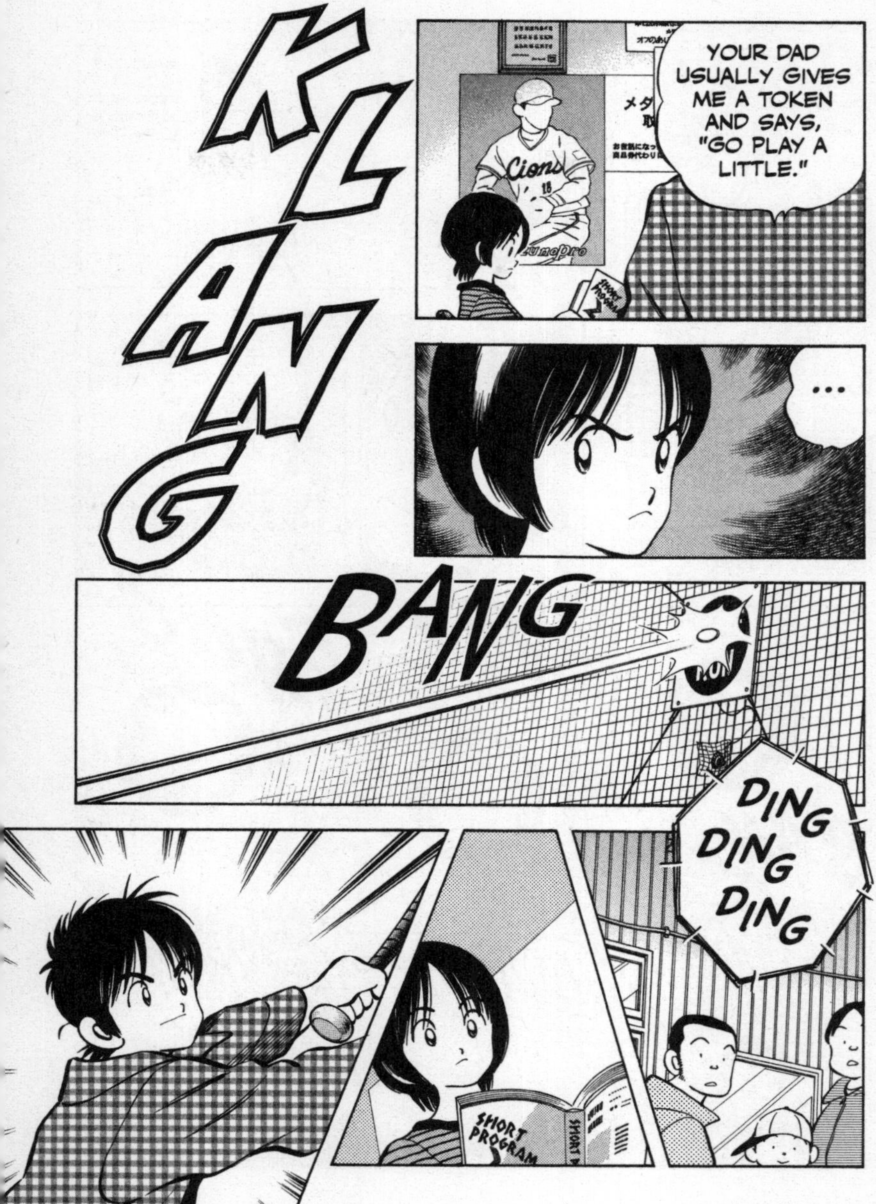
YOUR DAD USUALLY GIVES ME A TOKEN AND SAYS, "GO PLAY A LITTLE."
Cions
...
KLANG
BANG
DING DING DING
SHORT PROGRAM

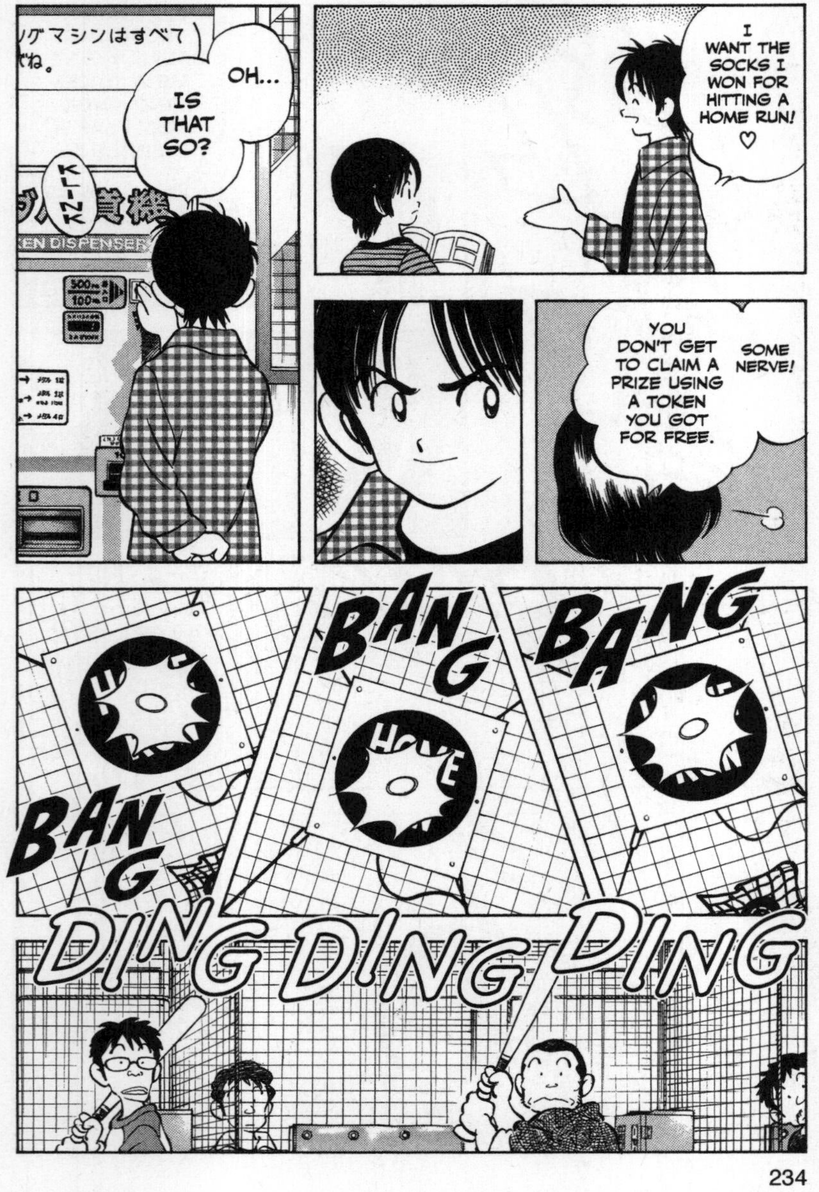
I WANT THE SOCKS I WON FOR HITTING A HOME RUN! ♡
SOME NERVE!
YOU DON'T GET TO CLAIM A PRIZE USING A TOKEN YOU GOT FOR FREE.
OH...
IS THAT SO?
KLINK
BANG
BANG
BANG
DING DING DING

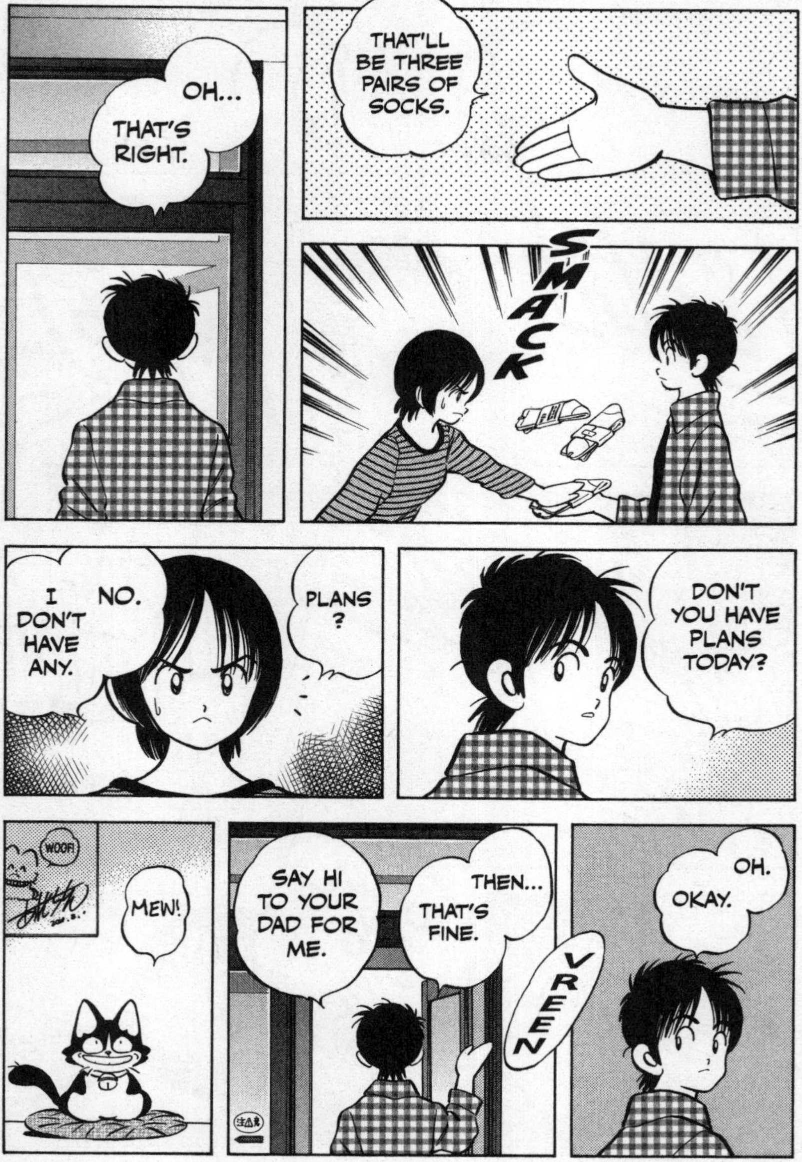
THAT'LL BE THREE PAIRS OF SOCKS.
SMACK
OH... THAT'S RIGHT.
DON'T YOU HAVE PLANS TODAY?
PLANS?
NO. I DON'T HAVE ANY.
OH. OKAY.
THEN... THAT'S FINE.
VREEN
SAY HI TO YOUR DAD FOR ME.
WOOF!
MEW!

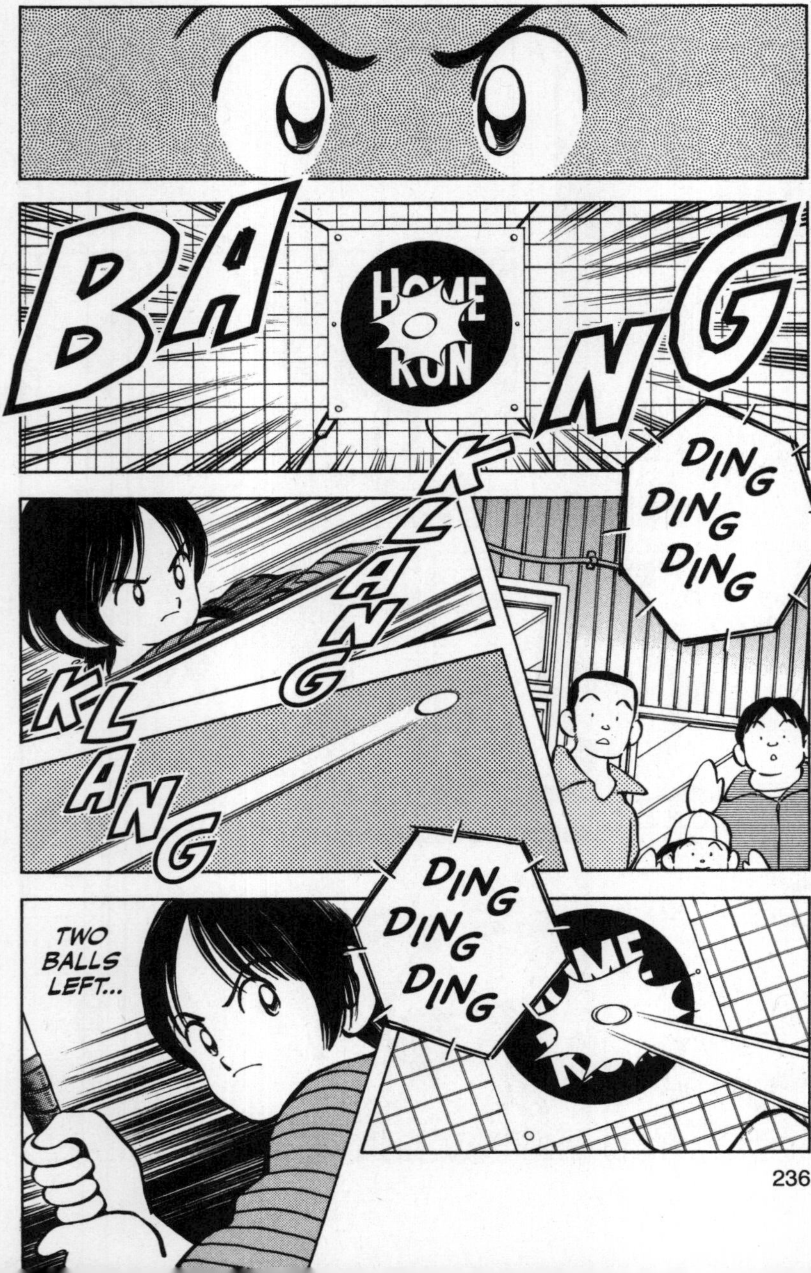
BANG
HOME RUN
KLANG
KLANG
DING DING DING
DING DING DING
TWO BALLS LEFT...

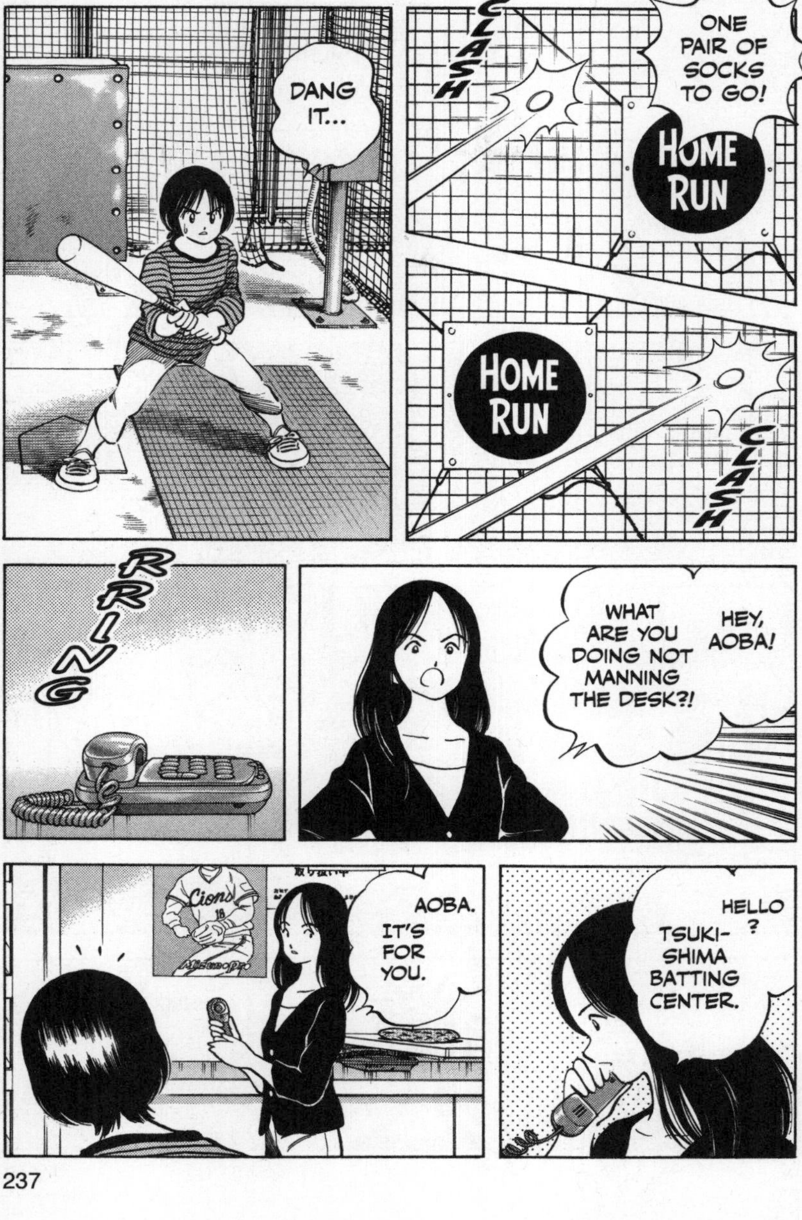
ONE PAIR OF SOCKS TO GO!
CLASH
HOME RUN
HOME RUN
CLASH
DANG IT...
HEY, AOBA!
WHAT ARE YOU DOING NOT MANNING THE DESK?!
RRING
HELLO?
TSUKI-SHIMA BATTING CENTER.
AOBA.
IT'S FOR YOU.

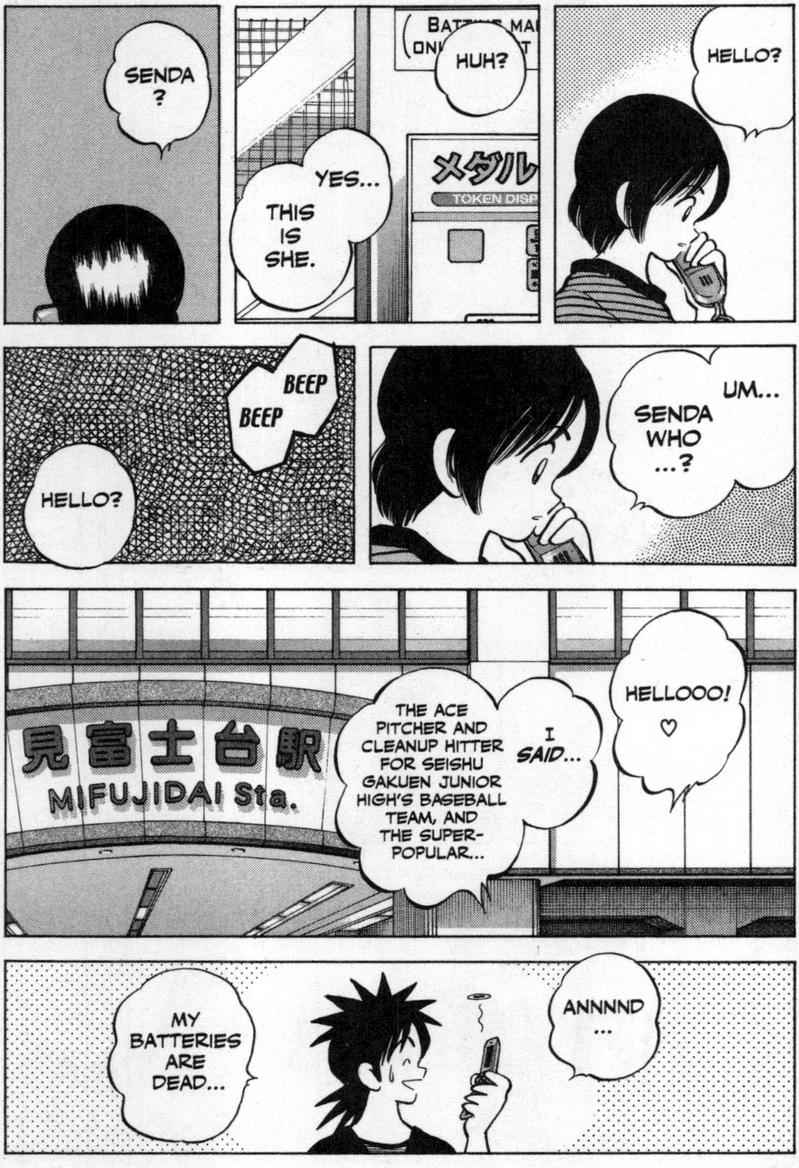
HELLO?
HUH?
YES... THIS IS SHE.
SENDA ?
UM... SENDA WHO ...?
BEEP BEEP
HELLO?
HELLOOO! ♡
I SAID...
THE ACE PITCHER AND CLEANUP HITTER FOR SEISHU GAKUEN JUNIOR HIGH'S BASEBALL TEAM, AND THE SUPER-POPULAR...
見富士台駅
MIFUJIDAI Sta.
ANNNND ...
MY BATTERIES ARE DEAD...

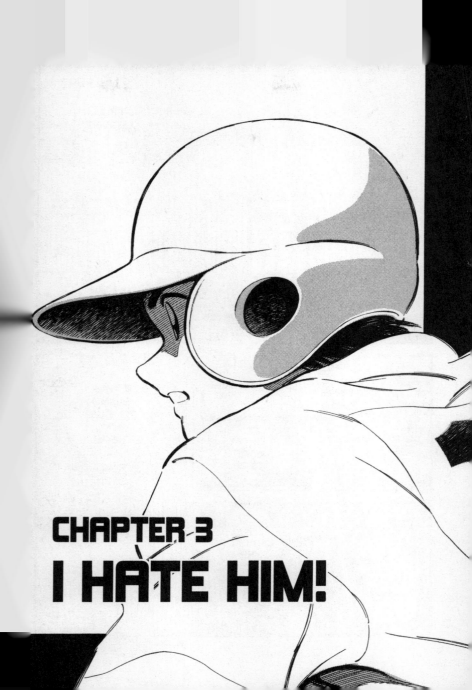

CHAPTER 3
I HATE HIM!

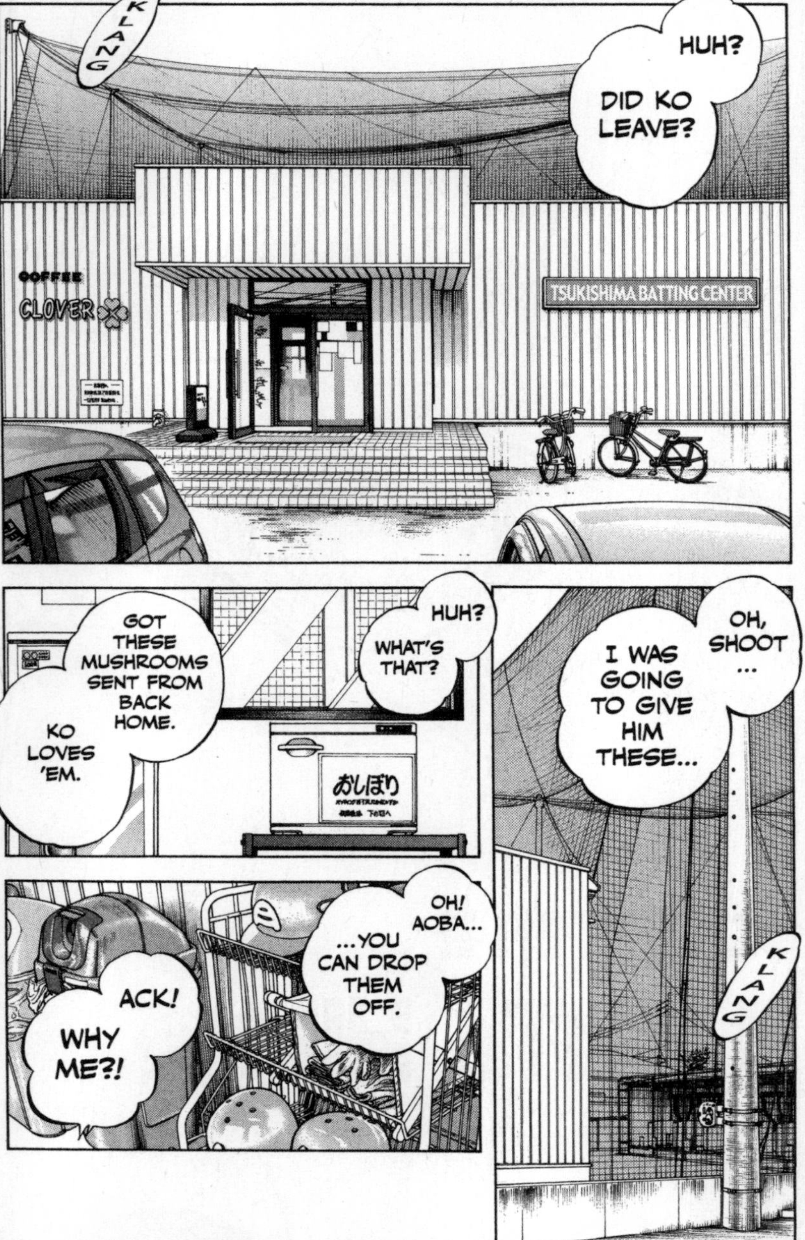
HUH?
DID KO LEAVE?
KLANG
TSUKISHIMA BATTING CENTER
COFFEE
CLOVER
OH, SHOOT...
I WAS GOING TO GIVE HIM THESE...
KLANG
HUH?
WHAT'S THAT?
GOT THESE MUSHROOMS SENT FROM BACK HOME.
KO LOVES 'EM.
おしぼり
OH! AOBA...
...YOU CAN DROP THEM OFF.
ACK!
WHY ME?!

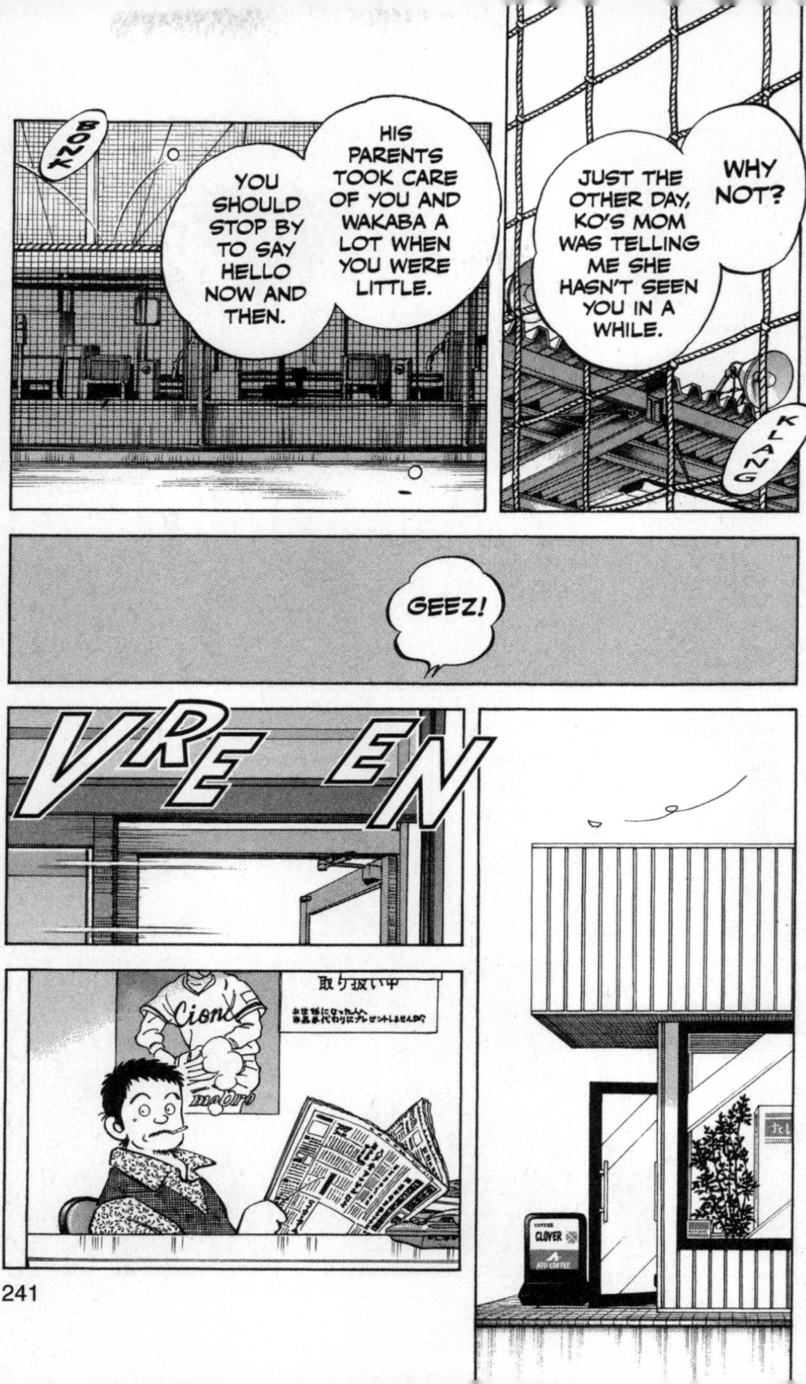
WHY NOT?
JUST THE OTHER DAY, KO'S MOM WAS TELLING ME SHE HASN'T SEEN YOU IN A WHILE.
KLANG
HIS PARENTS TOOK CARE OF YOU AND WAKABA A LOT WHEN YOU WERE LITTLE.
YOU SHOULD STOP BY TO SAY HELLO NOW AND THEN.
BONK
GEEZ!
CLOVER
VREEEN
取り扱い中

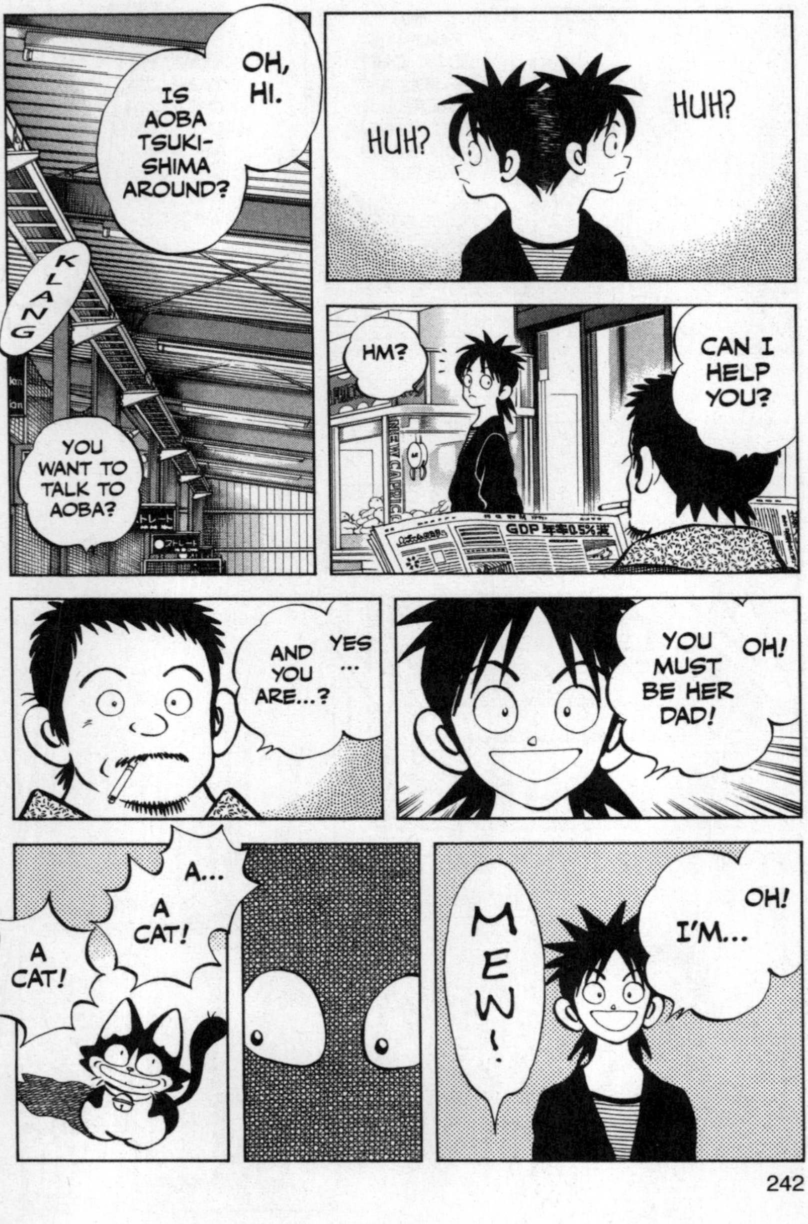
HUH?
HUH?
CAN I HELP YOU?
HM?
OH, HI.
IS AOBA TSUKISHIMA AROUND?
KLANG
YOU WANT TO TALK TO AOBA?
OH!
YOU MUST BE HER DAD!
YES...
AND YOU ARE...?
OH!
I'M...
MEW!
A...
A CAT!
A CAT!

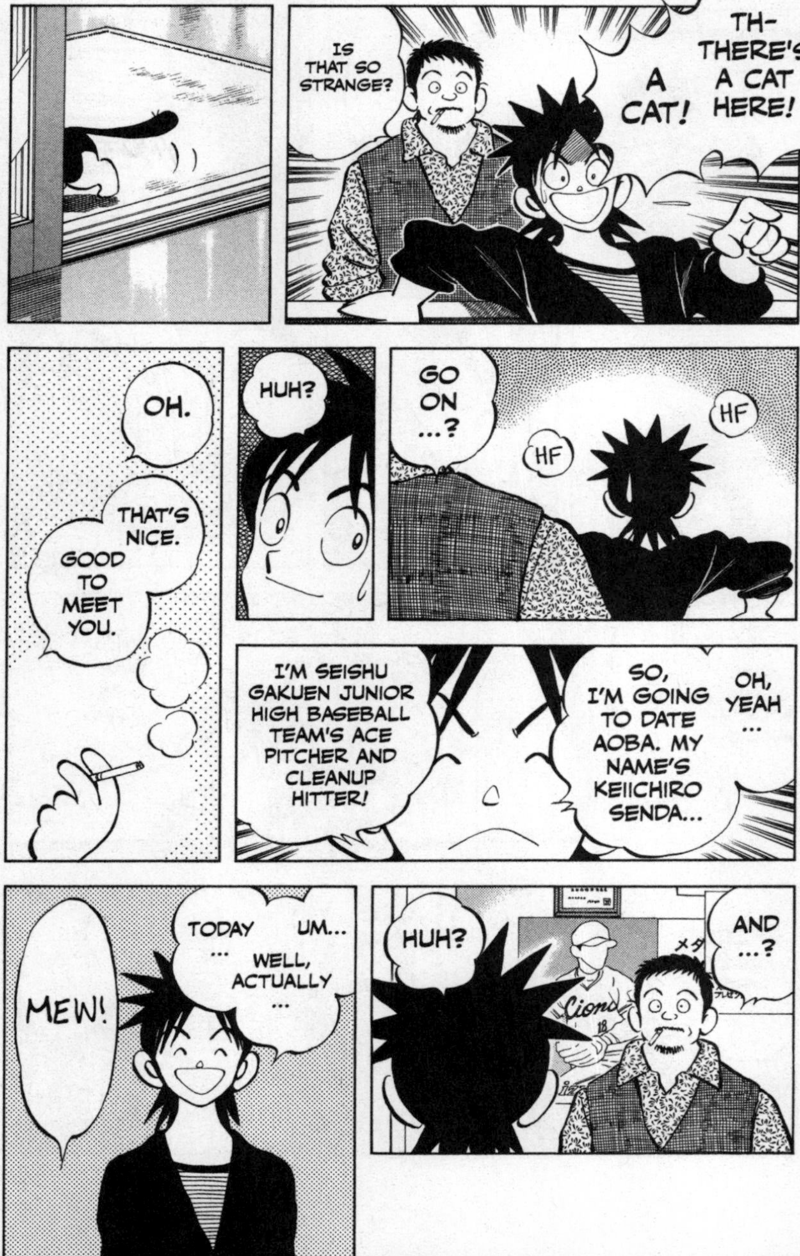
TH- THERE'S A CAT HERE!
A CAT!
IS THAT SO STRANGE?
HF
HF
GO ON ...?
HUH?
OH, YEAH ...
SO, I'M GOING TO DATE AOBA. MY NAME'S KEIICHIRO SENDA...
I'M SEISHU GAKUEN JUNIOR HIGH BASEBALL TEAM'S ACE PITCHER AND CLEANUP HITTER!
OH.
THAT'S NICE.
GOOD TO MEET YOU.
AND ...?
HUH?
UM... WELL, ACTUALLY ...
TODAY ...
MEW!

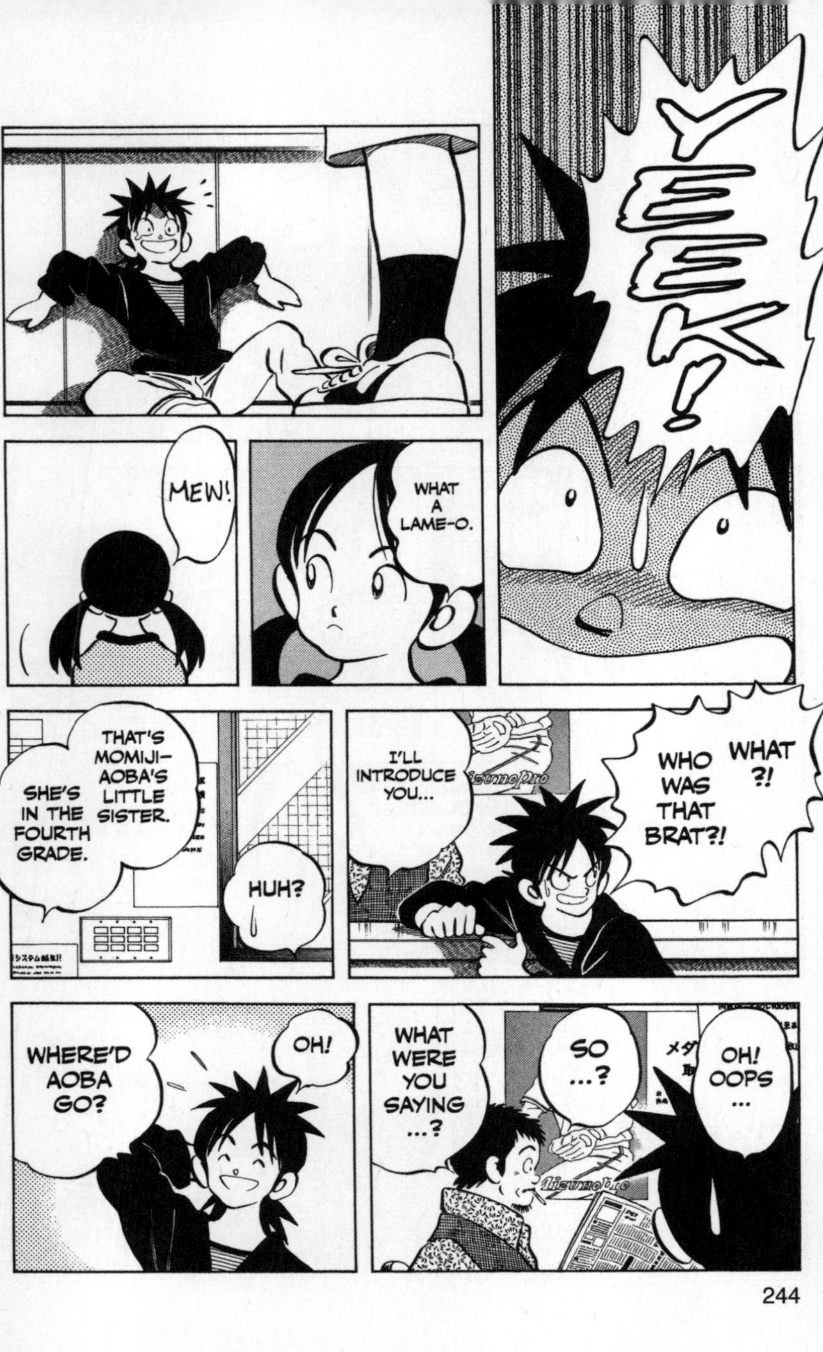
YEEK!
WHAT A LAME-O.
MEW!
WHAT ?!
WHO WAS THAT BRAT?!
I'LL INTRODUCE YOU...
HUH?
THAT'S MOMIJI—AOBA'S LITTLE SISTER.
SHE'S IN THE FOURTH GRADE.
OH! OOPS ...
SO ...?
WHAT WERE YOU SAYING ...?
OH!
WHERE'D AOBA GO?

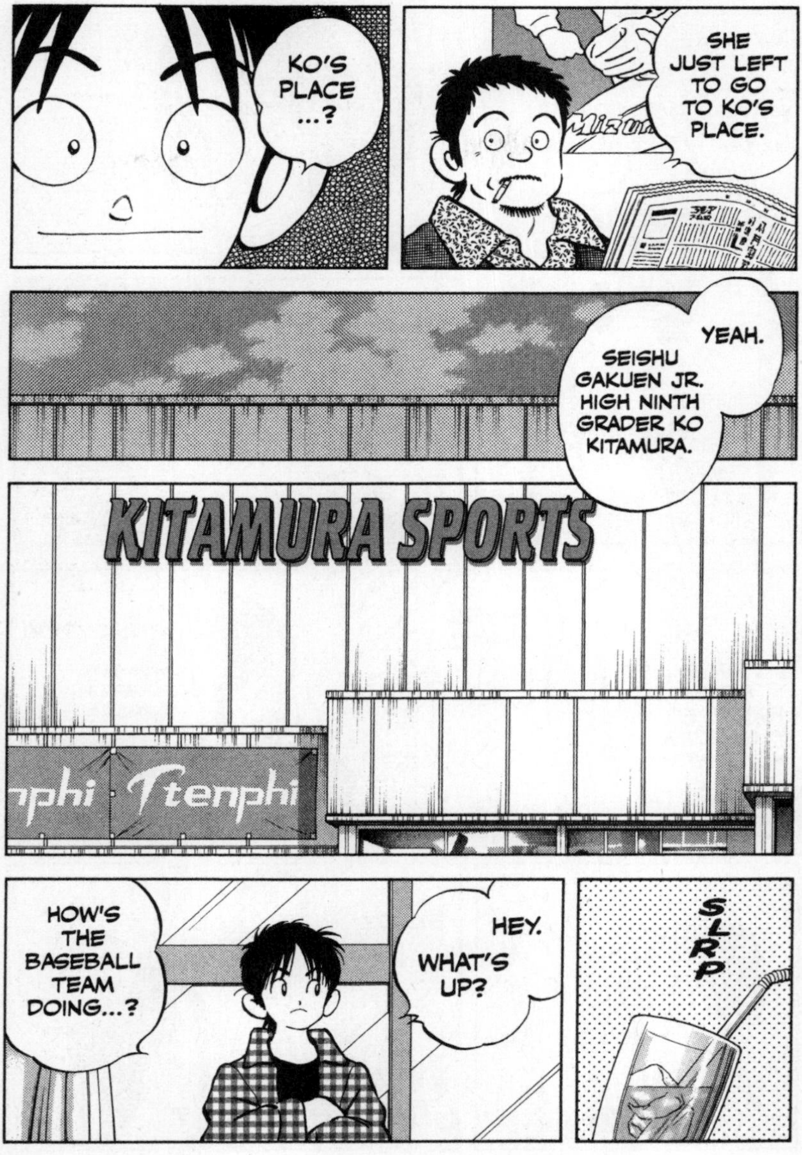
SHE JUST LEFT TO GO TO KO'S PLACE.
KO'S PLACE ...?
YEAH.
SEISHU GAKUEN JR. HIGH NINTH GRADER KO KITAMURA.
KITAMURA SPORTS
tenphi
SLRP
HEY.
WHAT'S UP?
HOW'S THE BASEBALL TEAM DOING...?

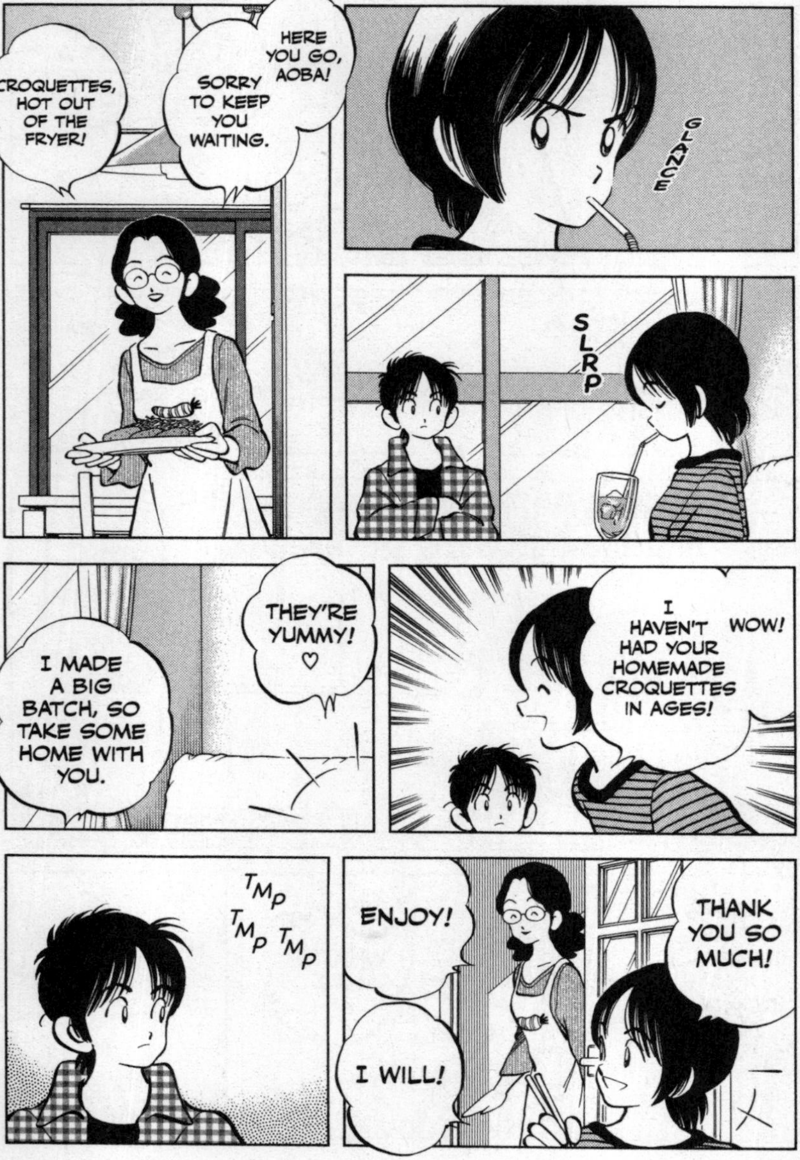
GLANCE
SLRP
HERE YOU GO, AOBA! SORRY TO KEEP YOU WAITING.
CROQUETTES, HOT OUT OF THE FRYER!
WOW!
I HAVEN'T HAD YOUR HOMEMADE CROQUETTES IN AGES!
THEY'RE YUMMY! ♡
I MADE A BIG BATCH, SO TAKE SOME HOME WITH YOU.
THANK YOU SO MUCH!
ENJOY!
I WILL!
TMP TMP TMP

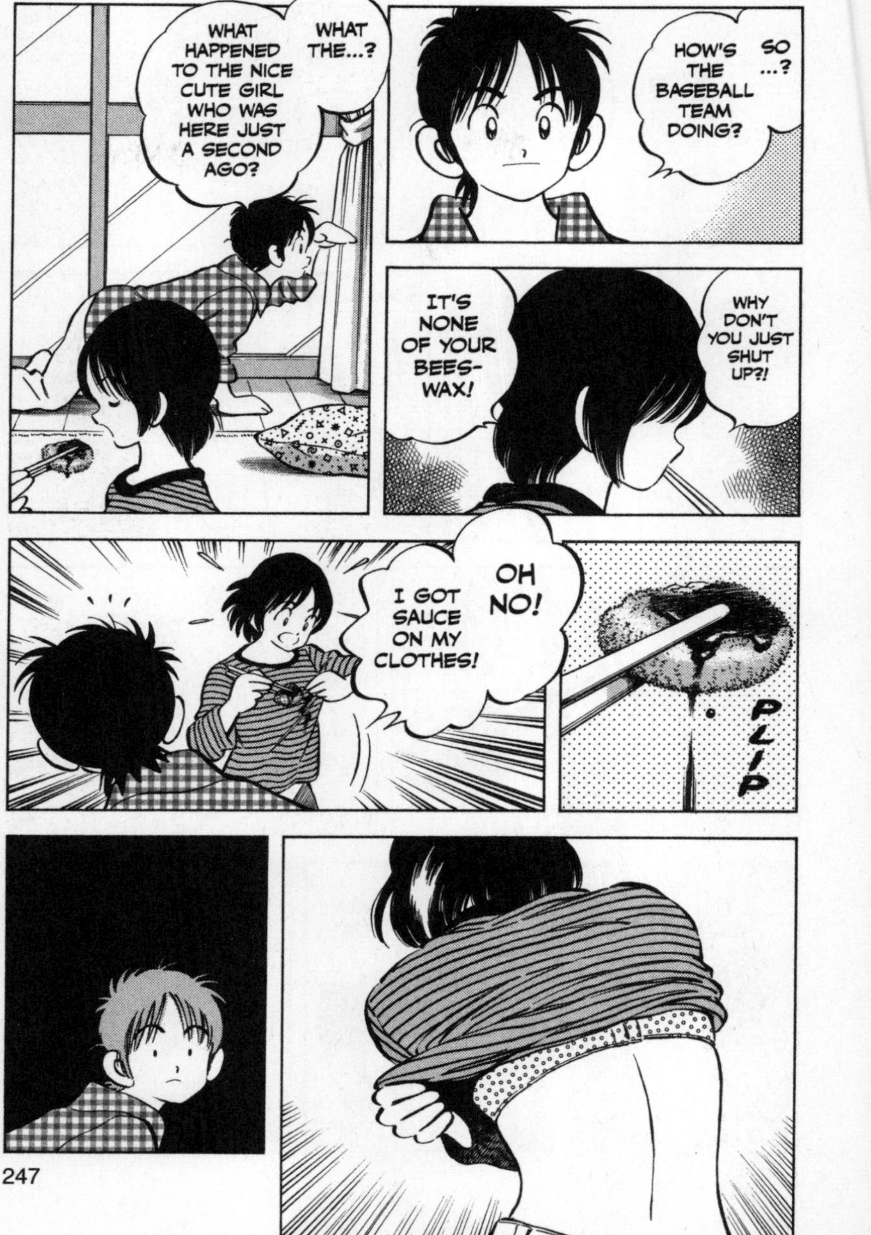
SO ...? HOW'S THE BASEBALL TEAM DOING?
WHY DON'T YOU JUST SHUT UP?! IT'S NONE OF YOUR BEES-WAX!
WHAT THE...? WHAT HAPPENED TO THE NICE CUTE GIRL WHO WAS HERE JUST A SECOND AGO?
PLIP
OH NO! I GOT SAUCE ON MY CLOTHES!

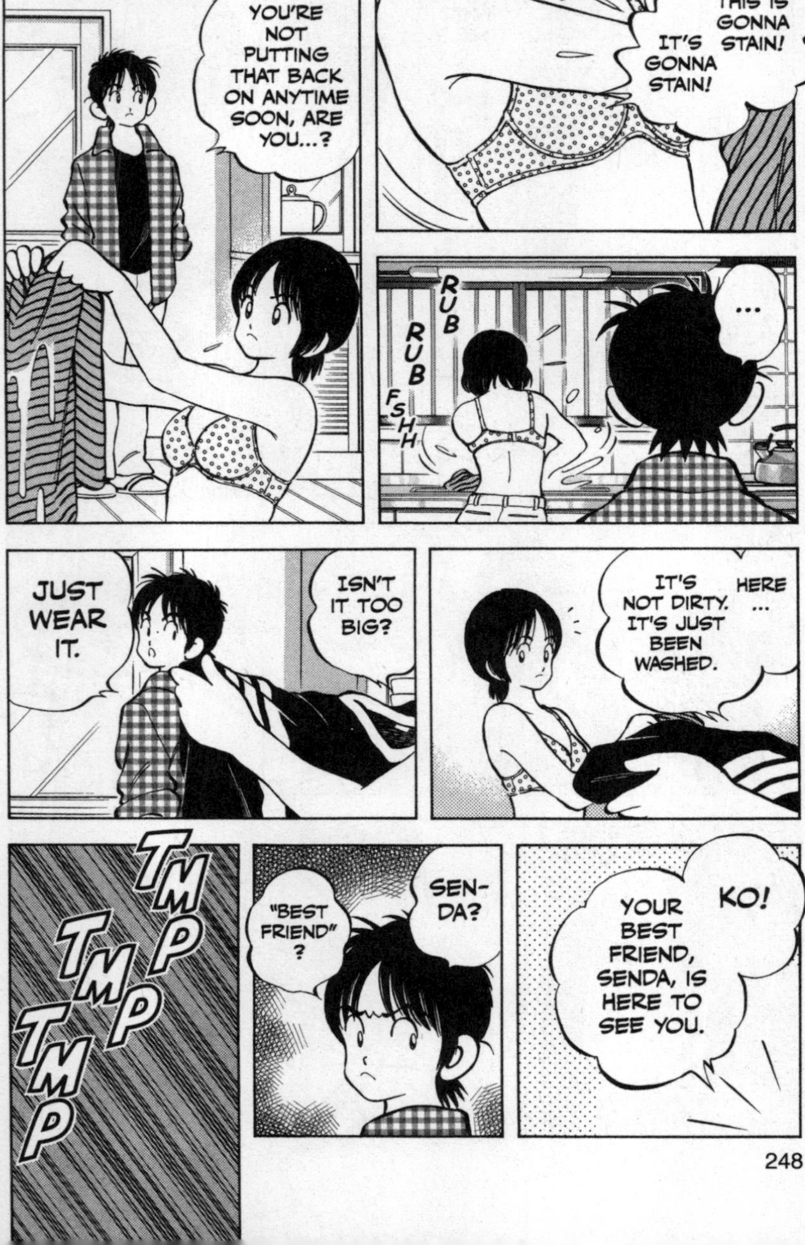
THIS IS GONNA STAIN!
IT'S GONNA STAIN!
...
RUB RUB FSHH
YOU'RE NOT PUTTING THAT BACK ON ANYTIME SOON, ARE YOU...?
HERE...
IT'S NOT DIRTY. IT'S JUST BEEN WASHED.
ISN'T IT TOO BIG?
JUST WEAR IT.
KO!
YOUR BEST FRIEND, SENDA, IS HERE TO SEE YOU.
SEN-DA?
"BEST FRIEND"?
TMP TMP TMP

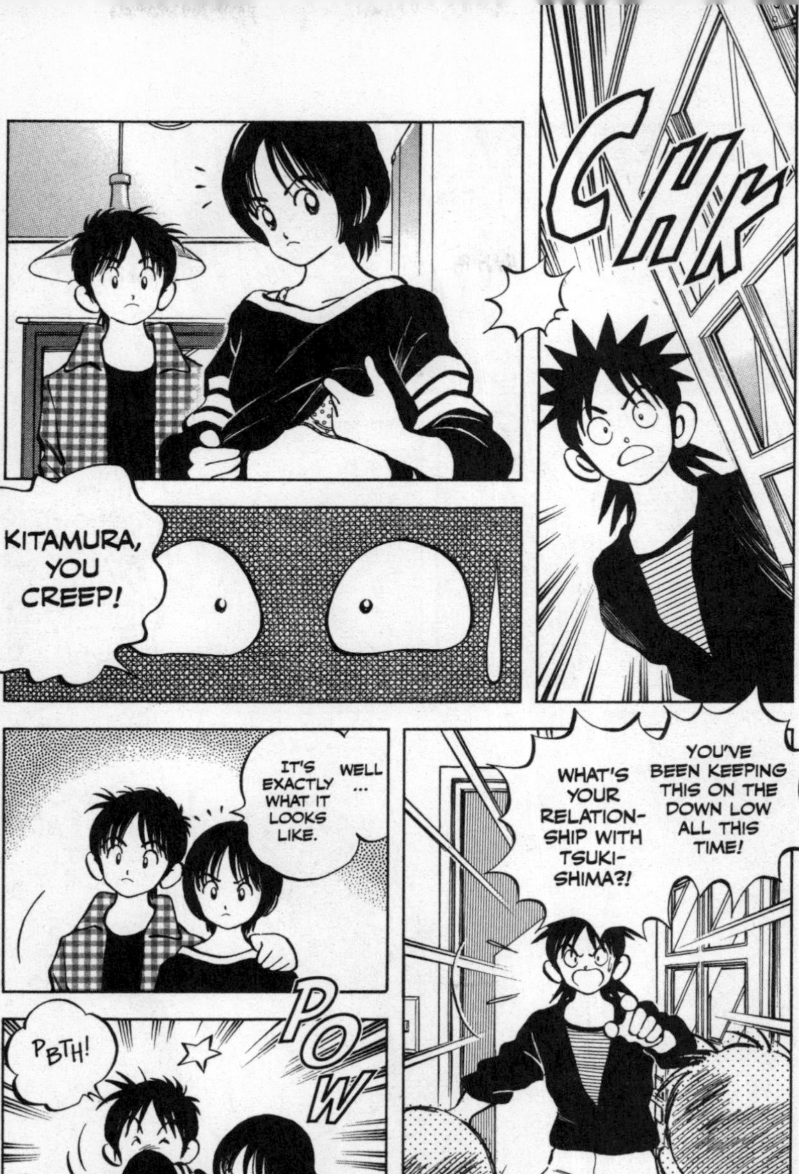
CHK
KITAMURA, YOU CREEP!
YOU'VE BEEN KEEPING THIS ON THE DOWN LOW ALL THIS TIME!
WHAT'S YOUR RELATIONSHIP WITH TSUKI-SHIMA?!
WELL ...
IT'S EXACTLY WHAT IT LOOKS LIKE.
POW
PBTH!

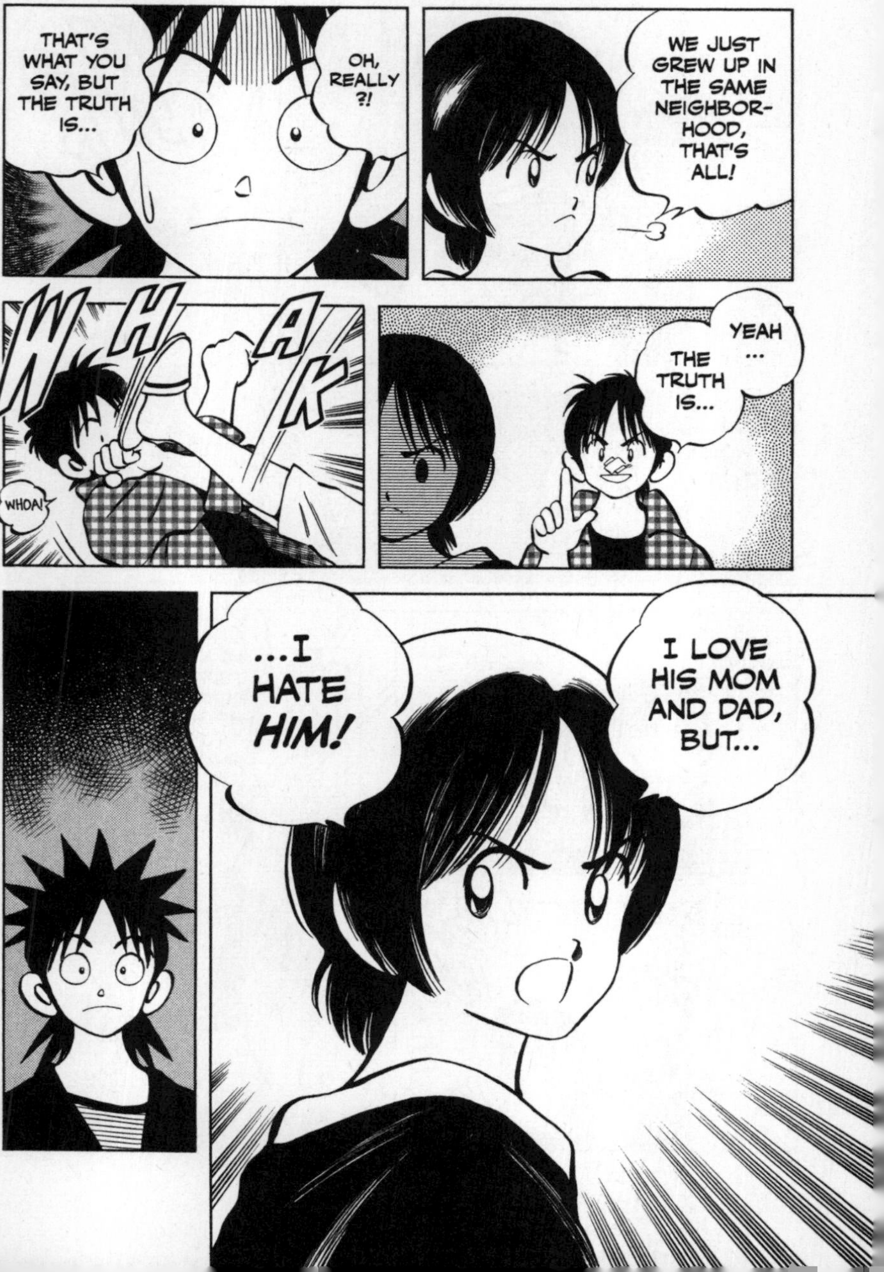
WE JUST GREW UP IN THE SAME NEIGHBOR-HOOD, THAT'S ALL!
OH, REALLY ?!
THAT'S WHAT YOU SAY, BUT THE TRUTH IS...
YEAH ...
THE TRUTH IS...
WHAK
WHOA!
I LOVE HIS MOM AND DAD, BUT...
...I HATE HIM!

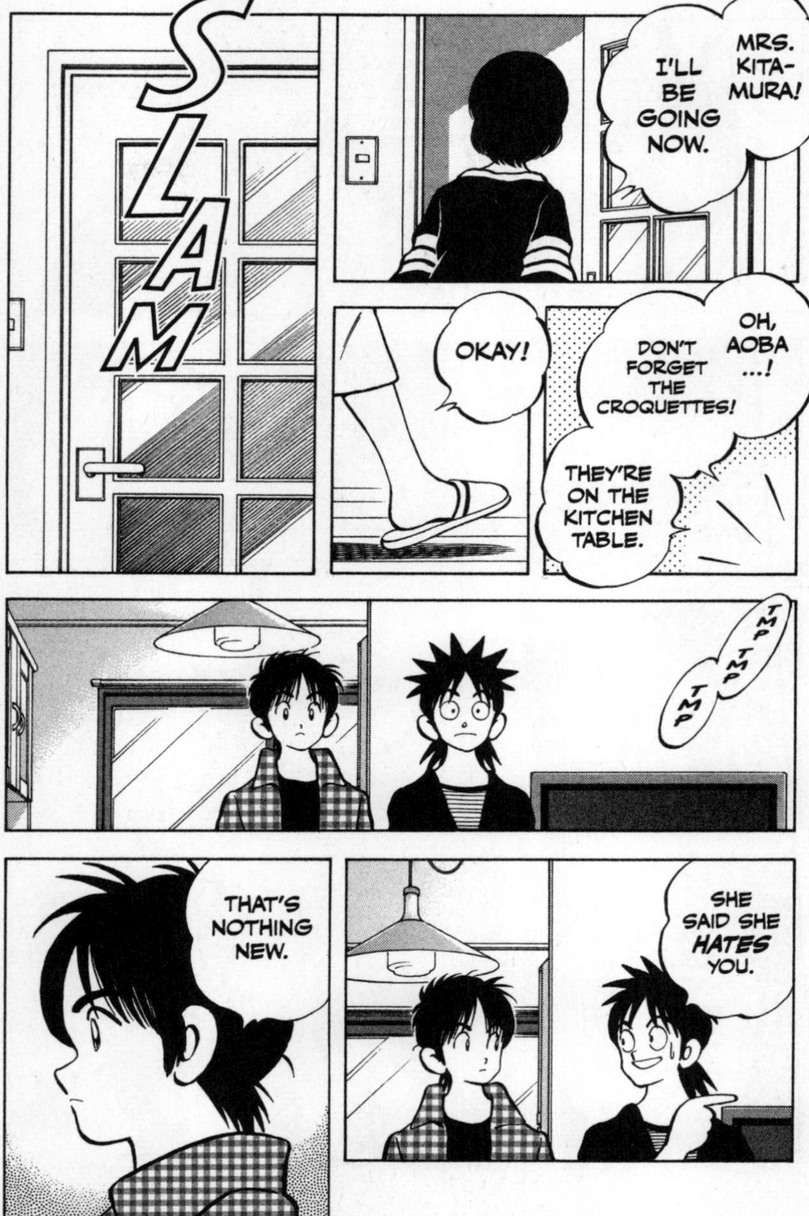
MRS. KITA-MURA! I'LL BE GOING NOW.
OH, AOBA ...! DON'T FORGET THE CROQUETTES!
THEY'RE ON THE KITCHEN TABLE.
OKAY!
SLAM
TMP TMP TMP
SHE SAID SHE *HATES* YOU.
THAT'S NOTHING NEW.

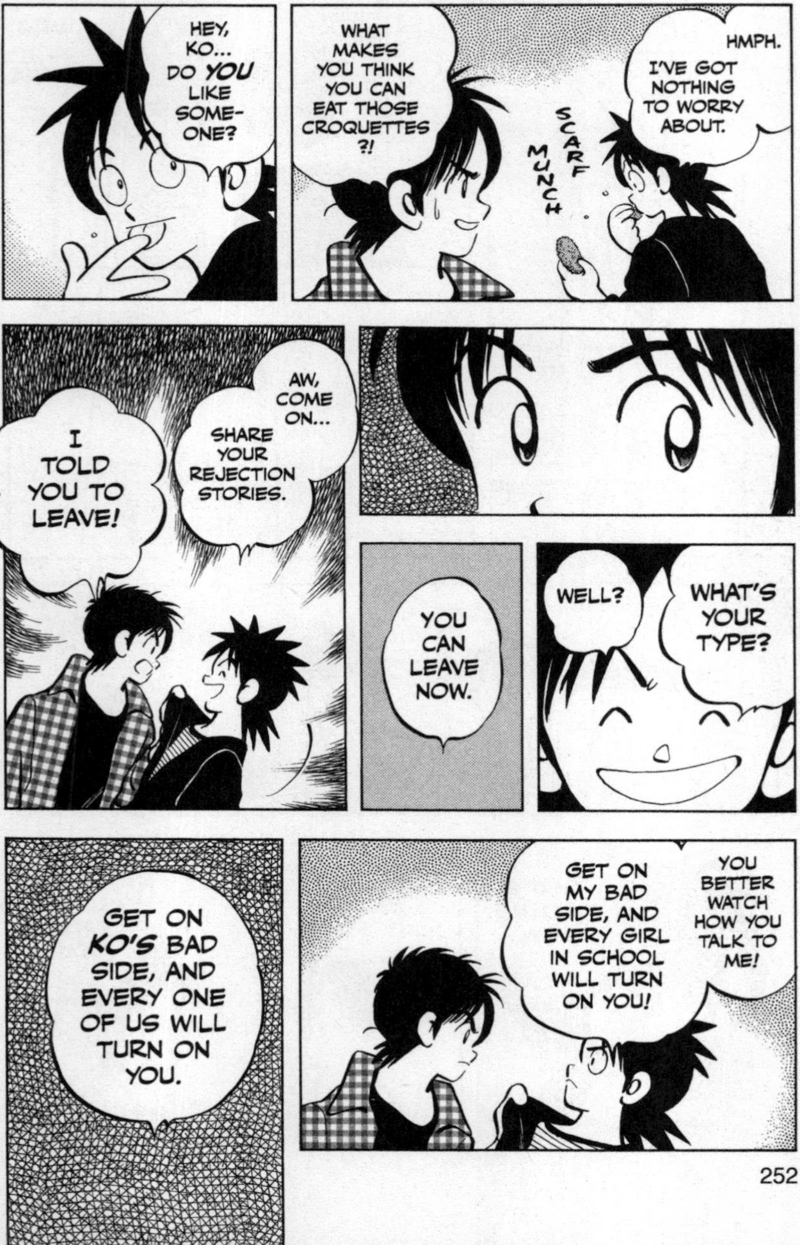
HMPH.
I'VE GOT NOTHING TO WORRY ABOUT.
SCARF
MUNCH
WHAT MAKES YOU THINK YOU CAN EAT THOSE CROQUETTES?!
HEY, KO... DO YOU LIKE SOME-ONE?
WHAT'S YOUR TYPE?
WELL?
YOU CAN LEAVE NOW.
AW, COME ON... SHARE YOUR REJECTION STORIES.
I TOLD YOU TO LEAVE!
YOU BETTER WATCH HOW YOU TALK TO ME!
GET ON MY BAD SIDE, AND EVERY GIRL IN SCHOOL WILL TURN ON YOU!
GET ON KO'S BAD SIDE, AND EVERY ONE OF US WILL TURN ON YOU.

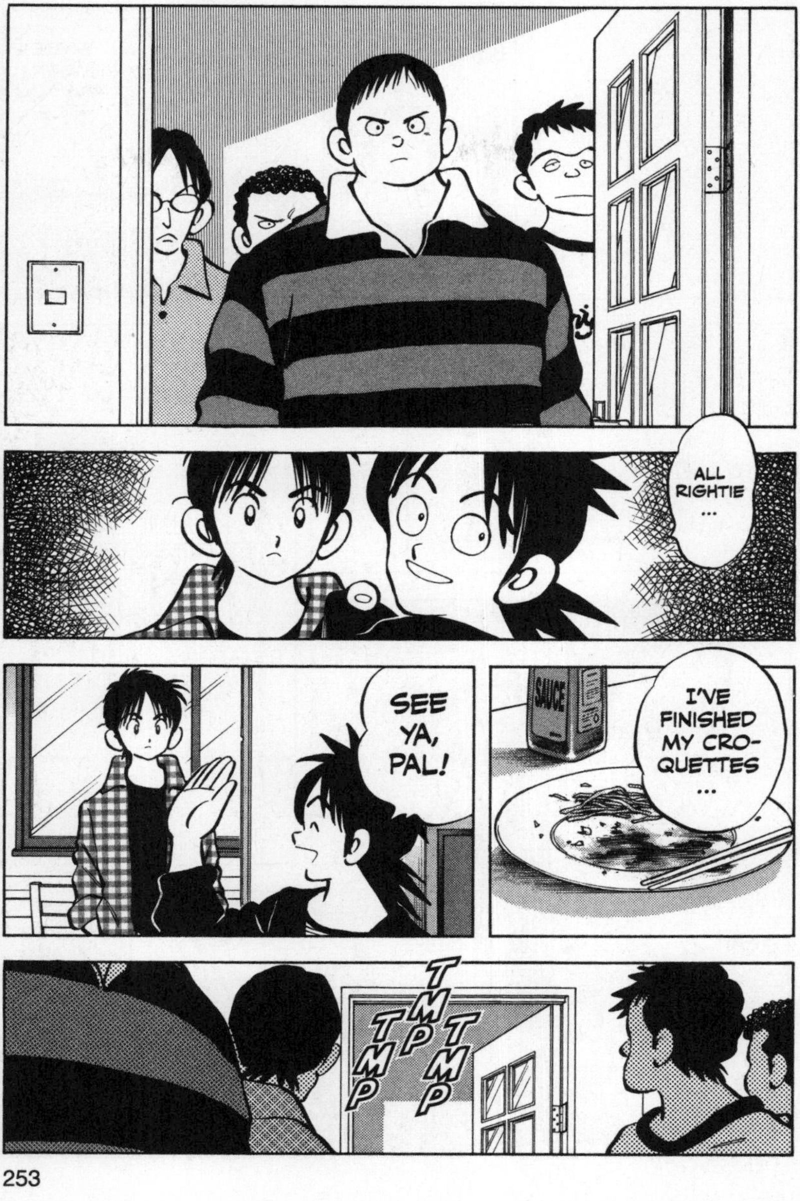
ALL RIGHTIE ...
I'VE FINISHED MY CRO-QUETTES ...
SEE YA, PAL!
TMP
TMP
TMP

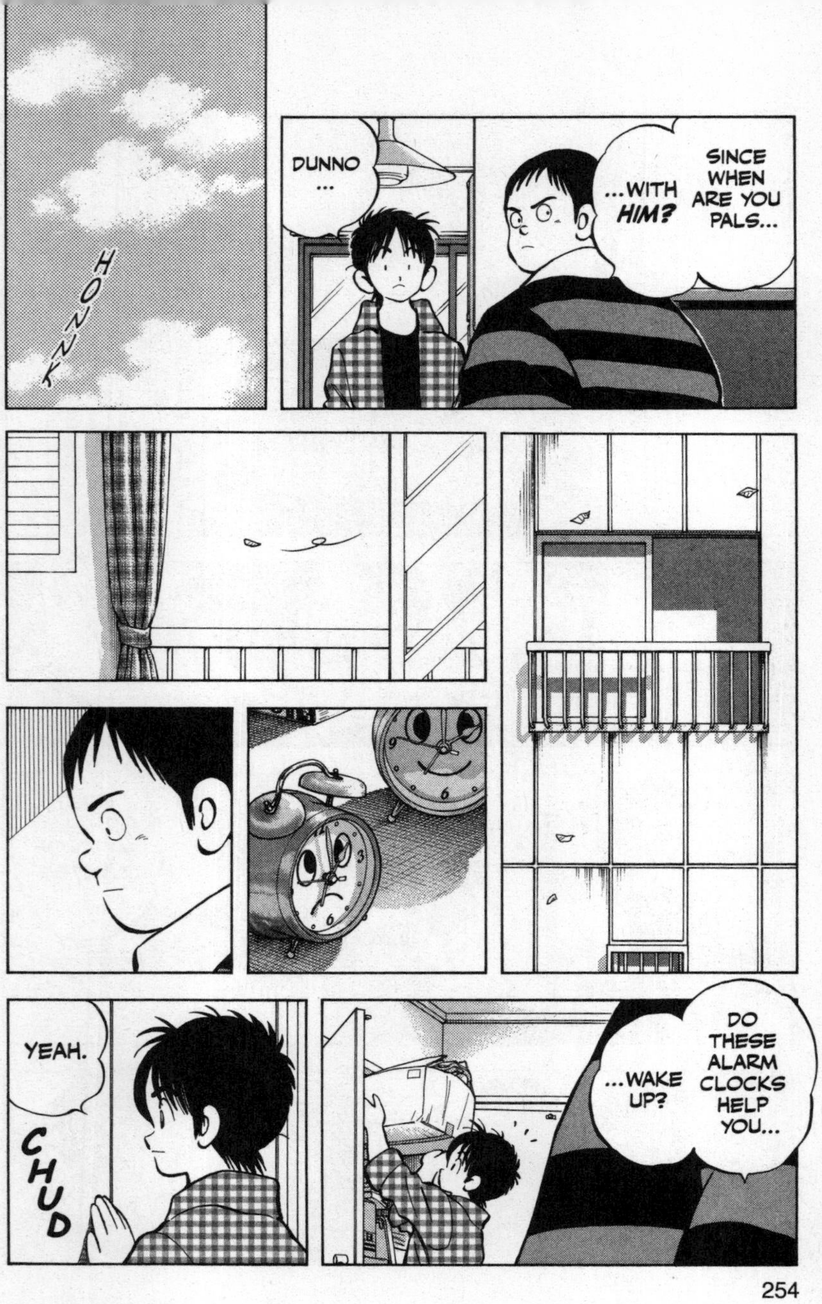
SINCE WHEN ARE YOU PALS...
...WITH *HIM?*
DUNNO ...
HONNK
DO THESE ALARM CLOCKS HELP YOU...
...WAKE UP?
YEAH.
CHUD

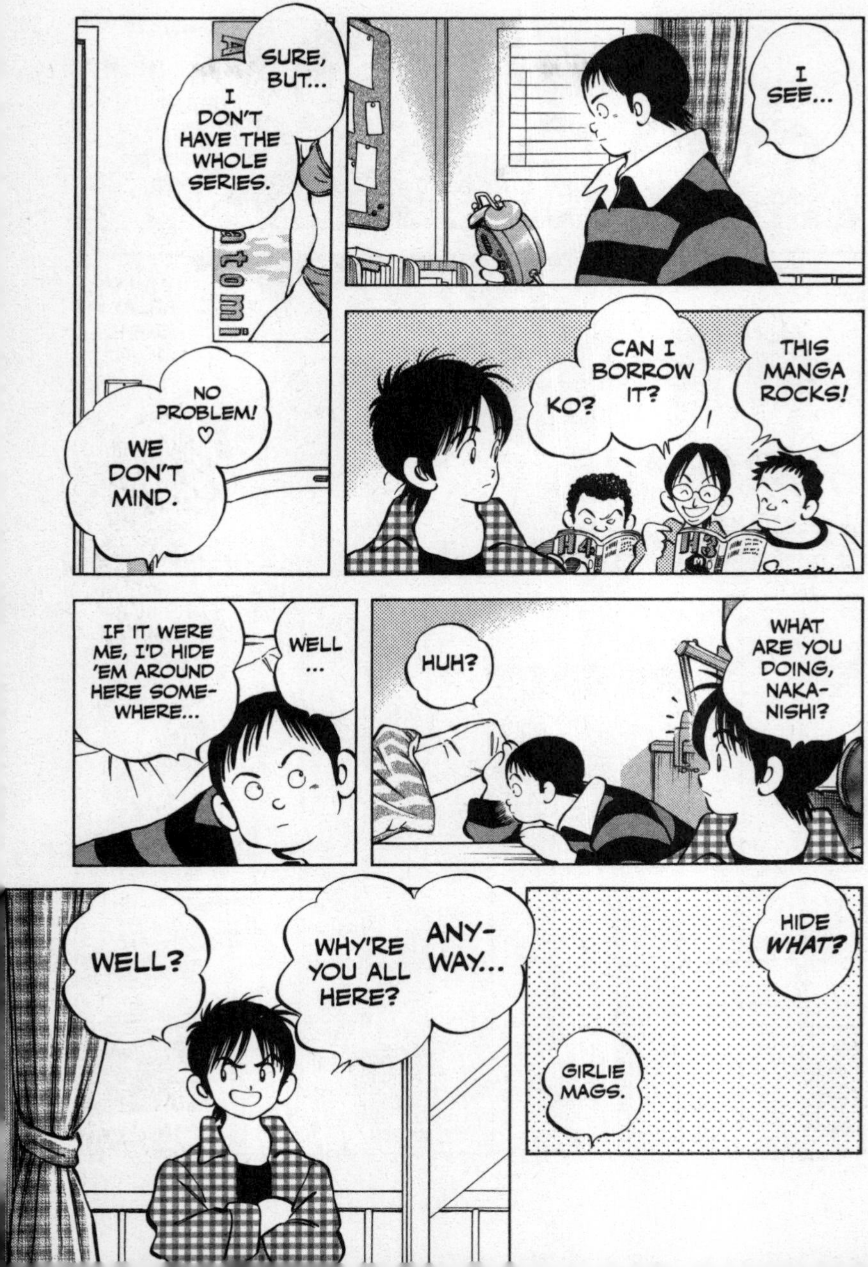
I SEE...
THIS MANGA ROCKS!
CAN I BORROW IT?
KO?
SURE, BUT...
I DON'T HAVE THE WHOLE SERIES.
NO PROBLEM! ♡
WE DON'T MIND.
WHAT ARE YOU DOING, NAKA-NISHI?
HUH?
WELL ...
IF IT WERE ME, I'D HIDE 'EM AROUND HERE SOME-WHERE...
HIDE *WHAT?*
GIRLIE MAGS.
ANY-WAY...
WHY'RE YOU ALL HERE?
WELL?

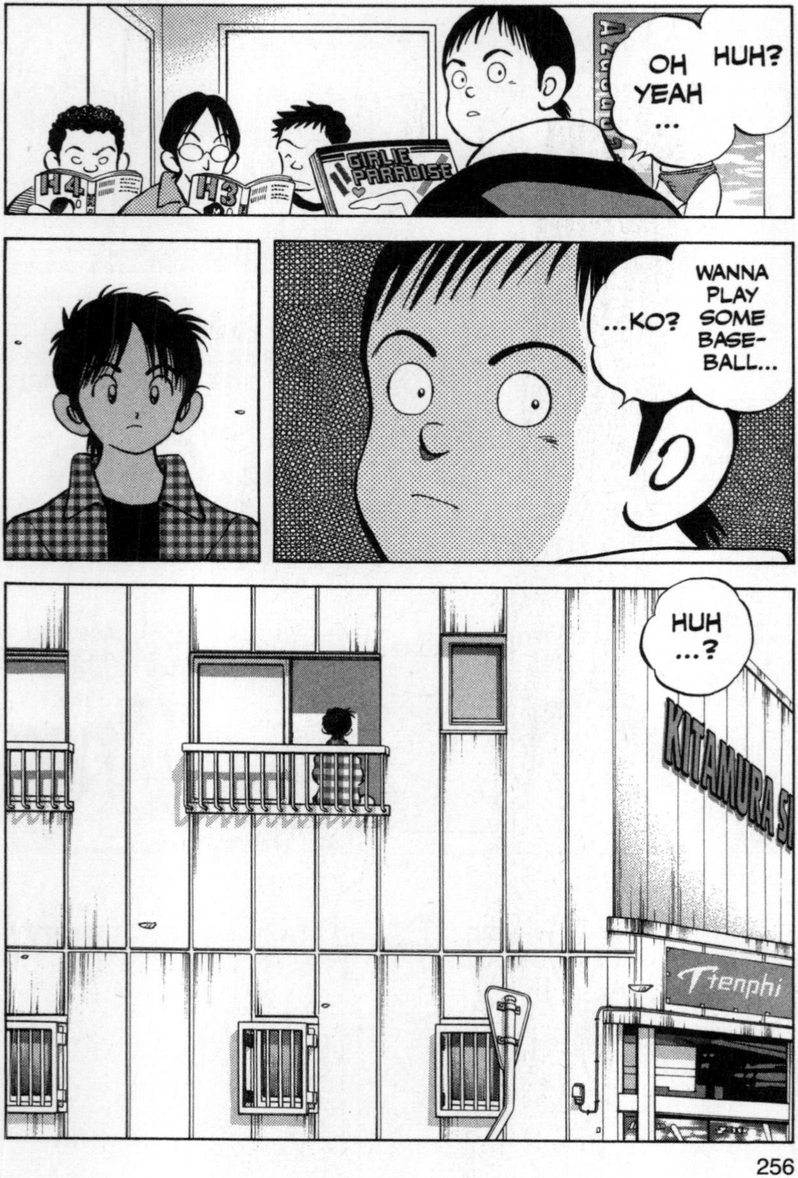
HUH?
OH YEAH ...
GIRLIE PARADISE
H3
H4
WANNA PLAY SOME BASE-BALL...
...KO?
HUH ...?
KITAMURA
tenphi

CHAPTER 4
CHANGE PITCHERS!

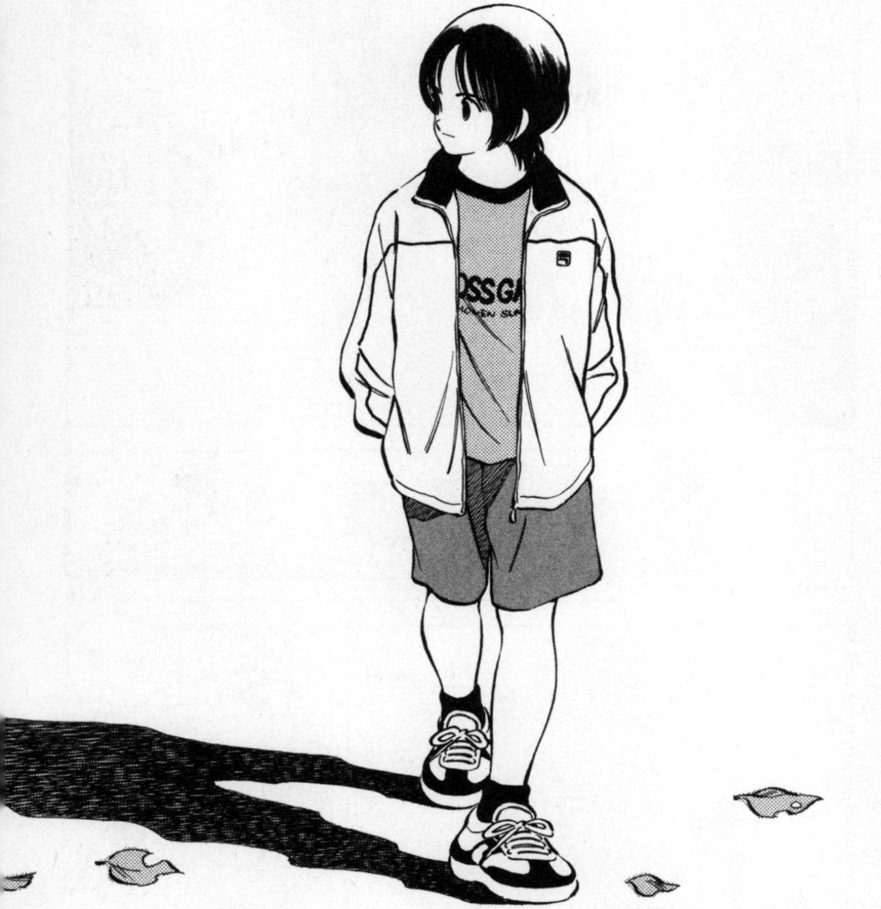

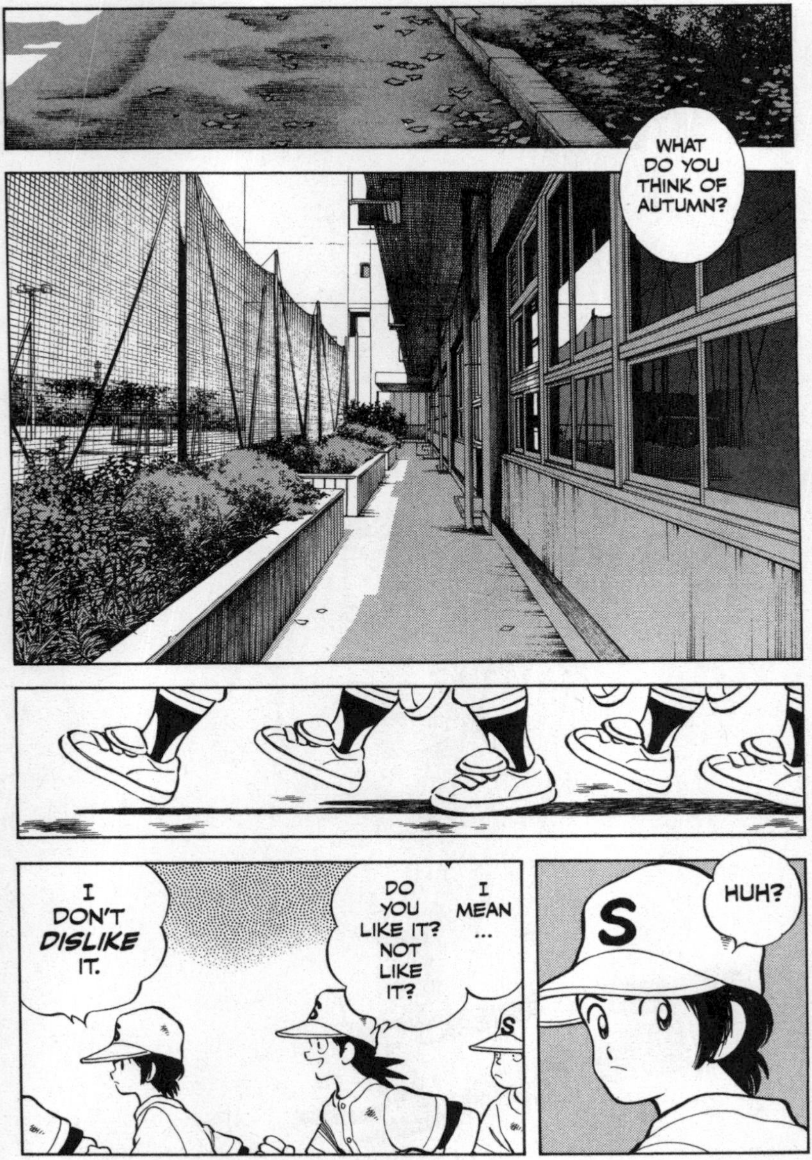
WHAT DO YOU THINK OF AUTUMN?
HUH?
I MEAN ...
DO YOU LIKE IT? NOT LIKE IT?
I DON'T *DISLIKE* IT.

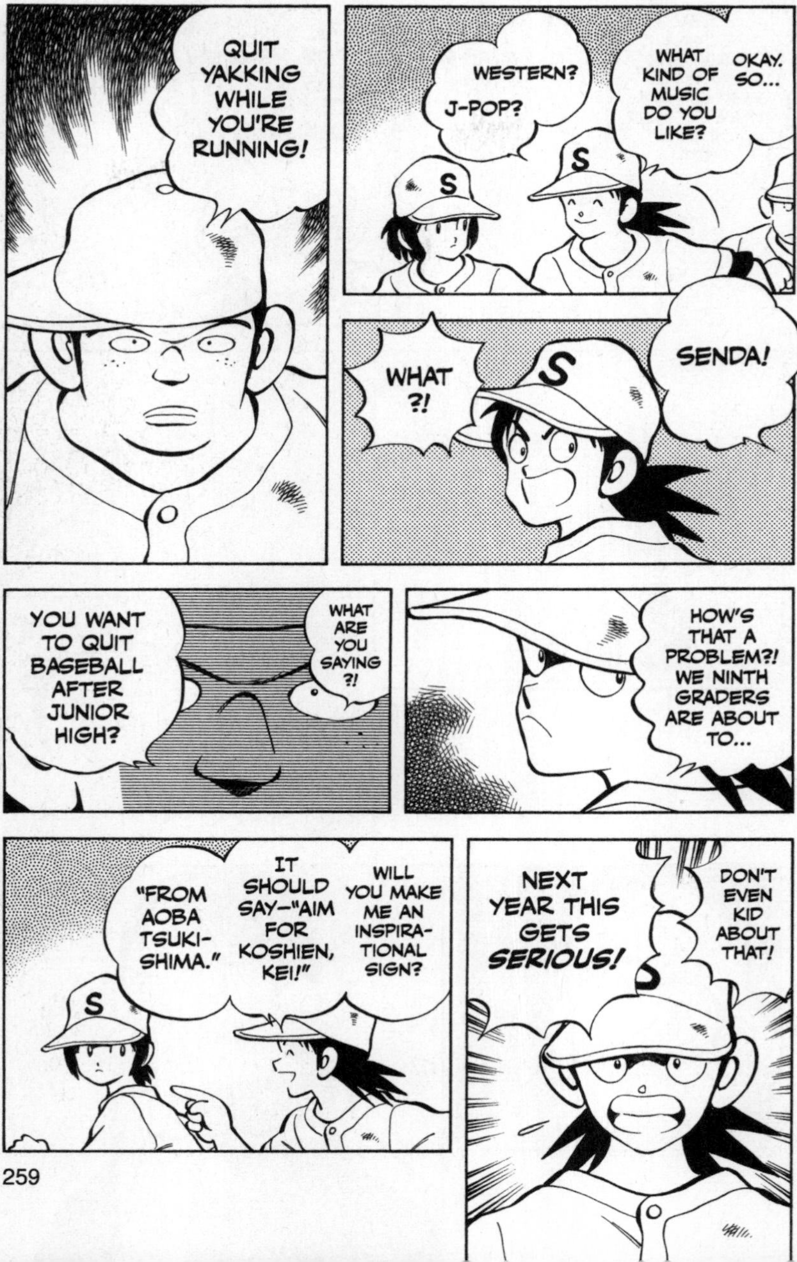
OKAY. SO... WHAT KIND OF MUSIC DO YOU LIKE?
WESTERN? J-POP?
SENDA!
WHAT ?!
QUIT YAKKING WHILE YOU'RE RUNNING!
HOW'S THAT A PROBLEM?! WE NINTH GRADERS ARE ABOUT TO...
WHAT ARE YOU SAYING ?!
YOU WANT TO QUIT BASEBALL AFTER JUNIOR HIGH?
DON'T EVEN KID ABOUT THAT!
NEXT YEAR THIS GETS *SERIOUS!*
WILL YOU MAKE ME AN INSPIRA-TIONAL SIGN?
IT SHOULD SAY—"AIM FOR KOSHIEN, KEI!"
"FROM AOBA TSUKI-SHIMA."

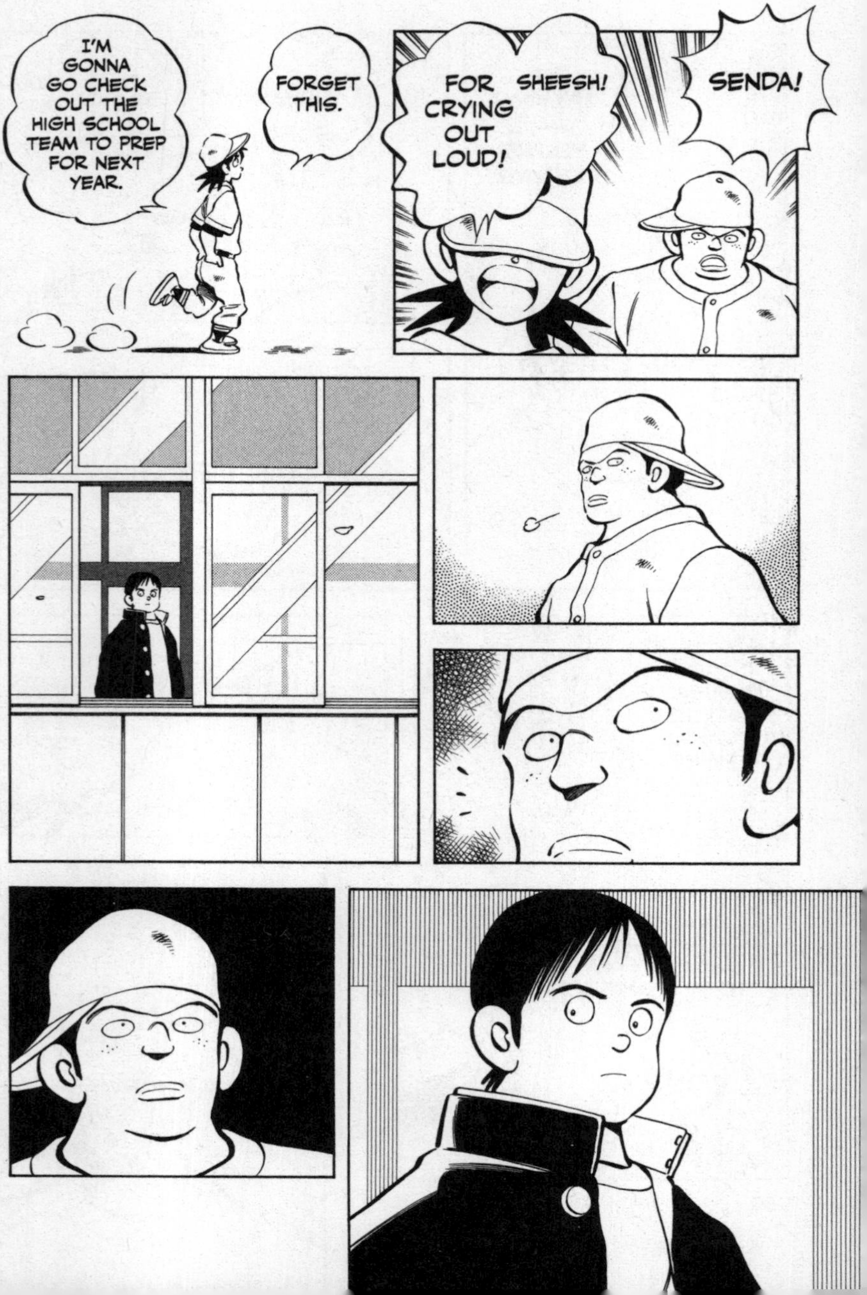
SENDA!
SHEESH! FOR CRYING OUT LOUD!
FORGET THIS.
I'M GONNA GO CHECK OUT THE HIGH SCHOOL TEAM TO PREP FOR NEXT YEAR.

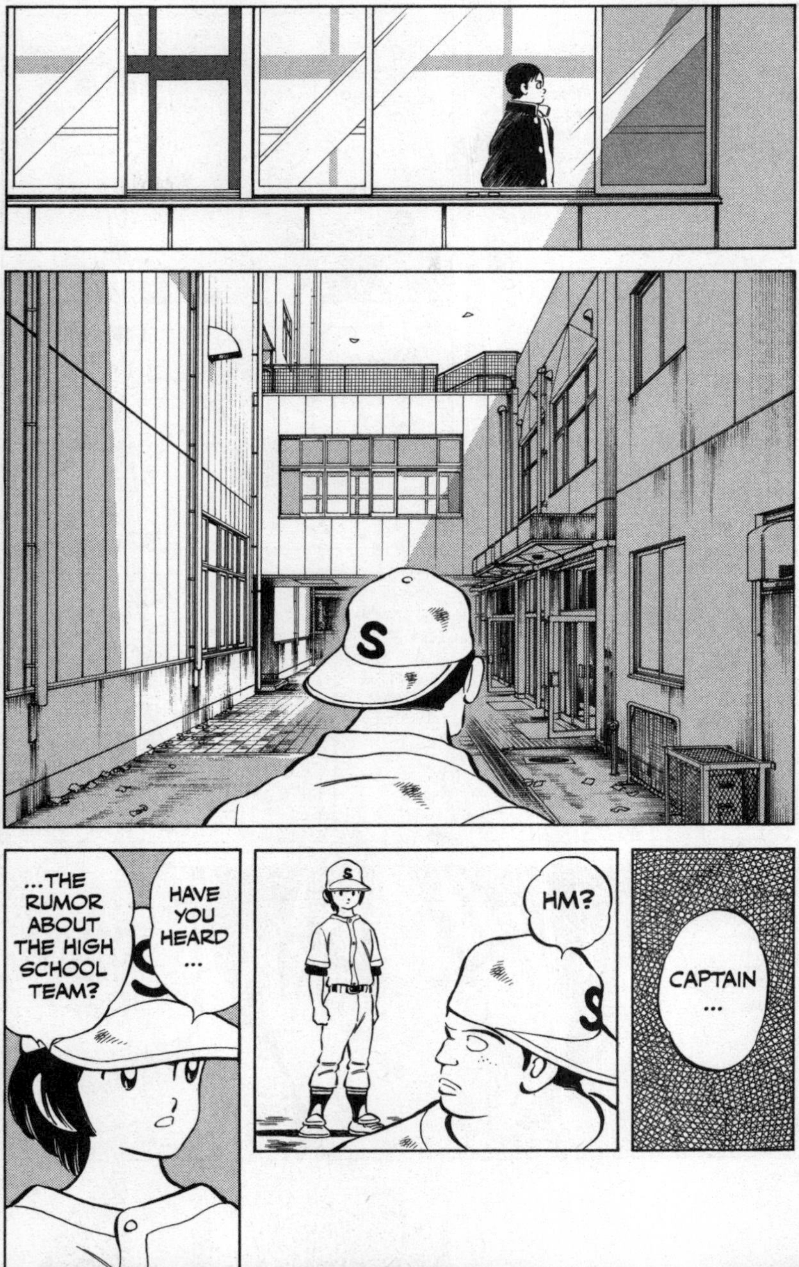
CAPTAIN ...
HM?
HAVE YOU HEARD ...
...THE RUMOR ABOUT THE HIGH SCHOOL TEAM?

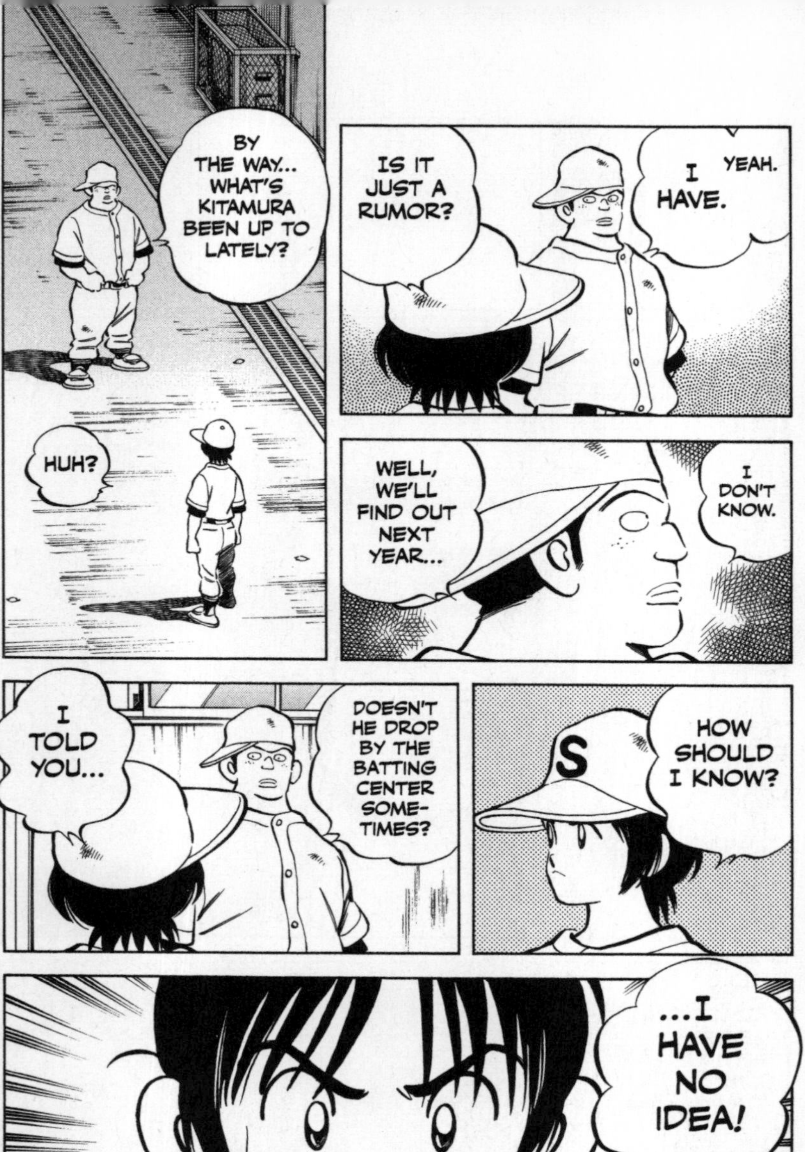
YEAH. I HAVE.
IS IT JUST A RUMOR?
I DON'T KNOW.
WELL, WE'LL FIND OUT NEXT YEAR...
BY THE WAY... WHAT'S KITAMURA BEEN UP TO LATELY?
HUH?
HOW SHOULD I KNOW?
DOESN'T HE DROP BY THE BATTING CENTER SOME-TIMES?
I TOLD YOU...
...I HAVE NO IDEA!

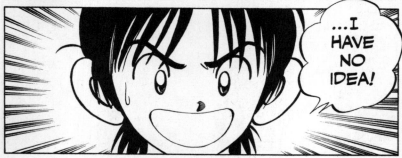

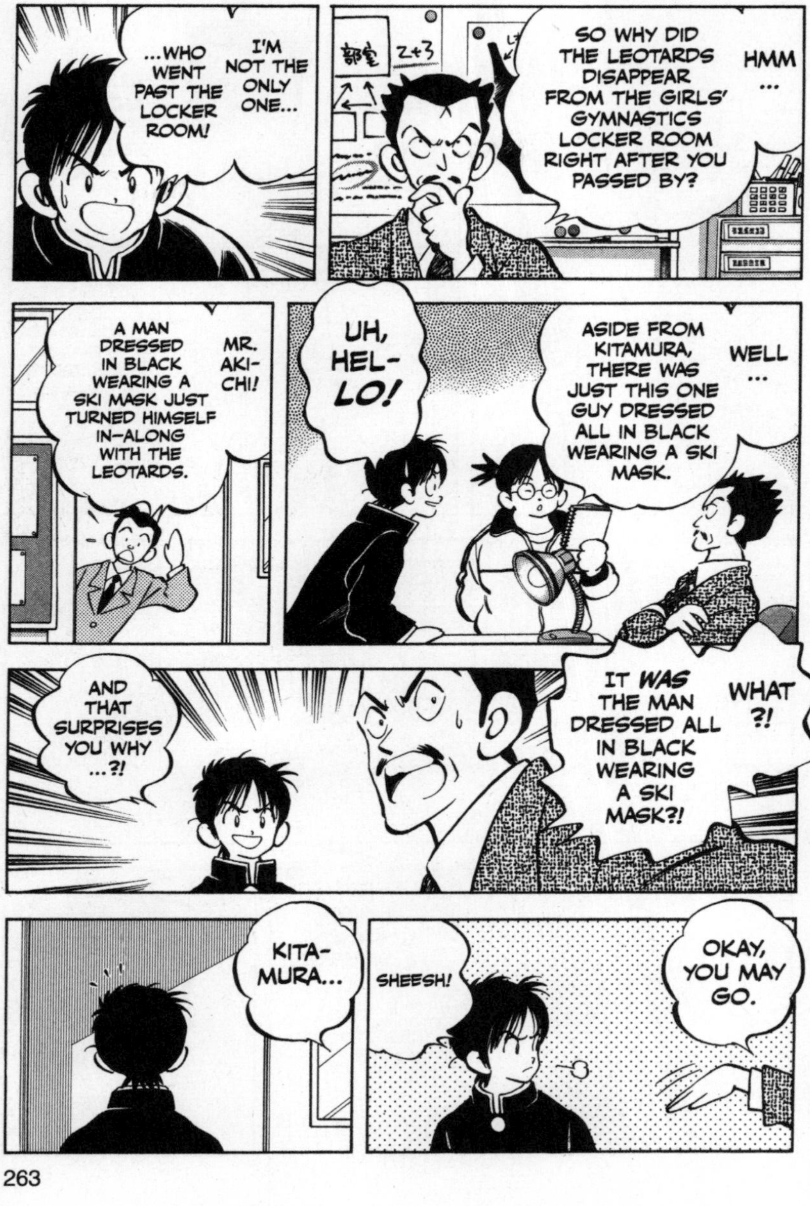
HMM ...
SO WHY DID THE LEOTARDS DISAPPEAR FROM THE GIRLS' GYMNASTICS LOCKER ROOM RIGHT AFTER YOU PASSED BY?
I'M NOT THE ONLY ONE...
...WHO WENT PAST THE LOCKER ROOM!
WELL ...
ASIDE FROM KITAMURA, THERE WAS JUST THIS ONE GUY DRESSED ALL IN BLACK WEARING A SKI MASK.
UH, HEL-*LO!*
MR. AKI-CHI!
A MAN DRESSED IN BLACK WEARING A SKI MASK JUST TURNED HIMSELF IN—ALONG WITH THE LEOTARDS.
WHAT ?!
IT *WAS* THE MAN DRESSED ALL IN BLACK WEARING A SKI MASK?!
AND THAT SURPRISES YOU WHY ...?!
OKAY, YOU MAY GO.
SHEESH!
KITA-MURA...

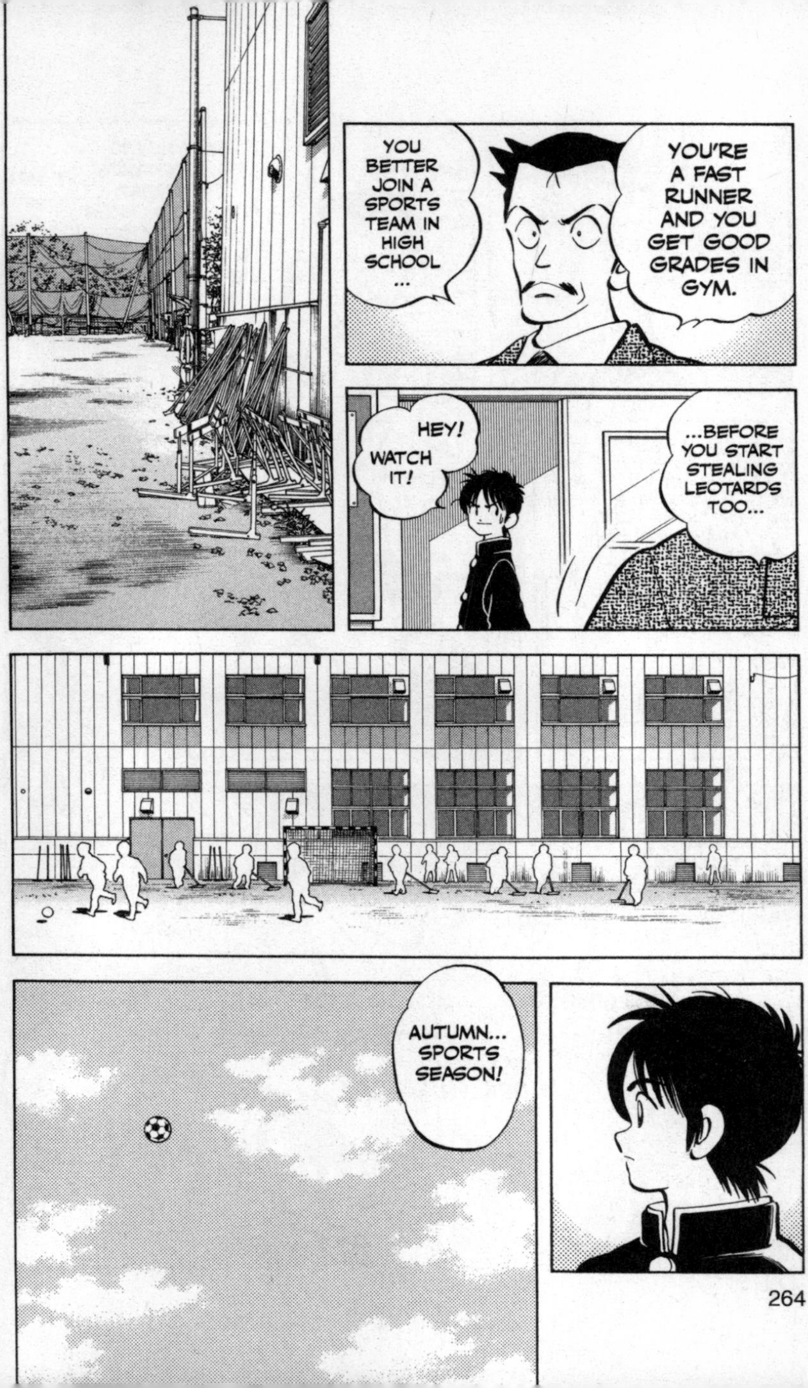
YOU'RE A FAST RUNNER AND YOU GET GOOD GRADES IN GYM.
YOU BETTER JOIN A SPORTS TEAM IN HIGH SCHOOL ...
...BEFORE YOU START STEALING LEOTARDS TOO...
HEY! WATCH IT!
AUTUMN... SPORTS SEASON!

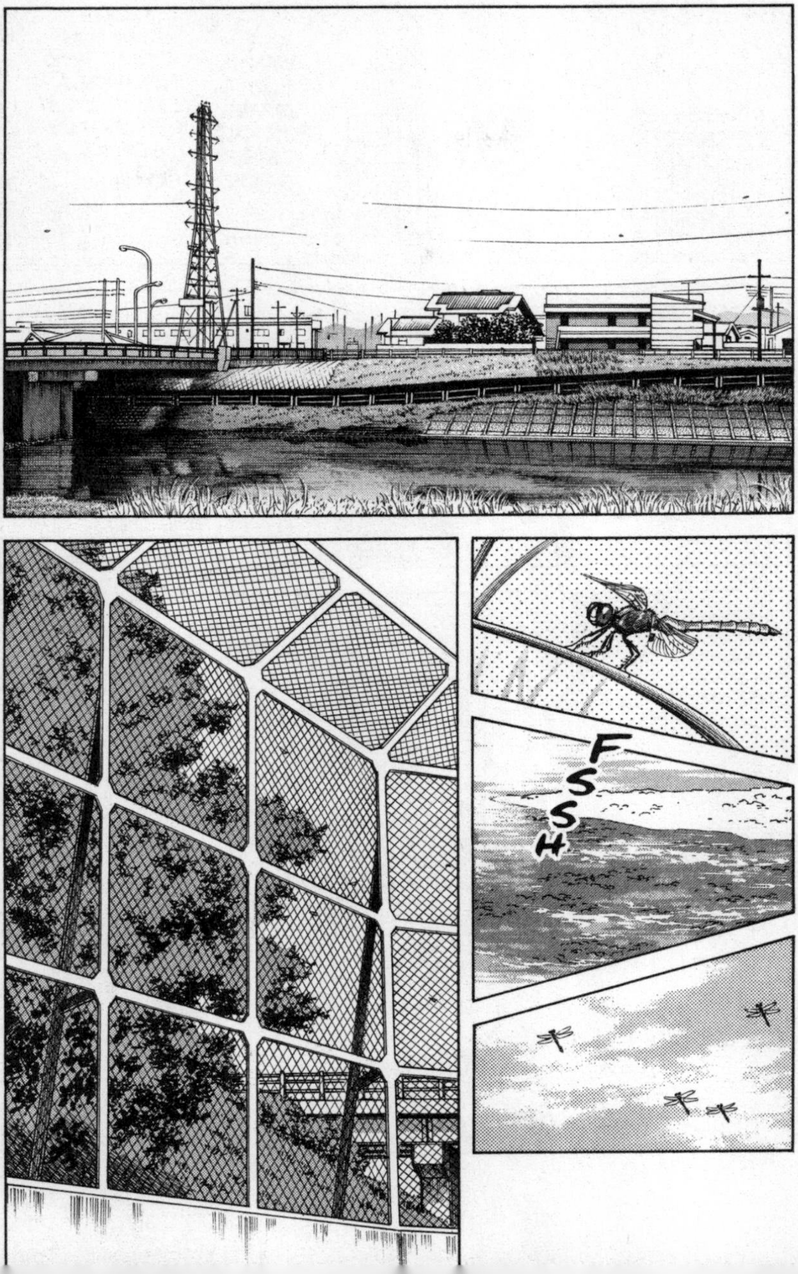
FSSH

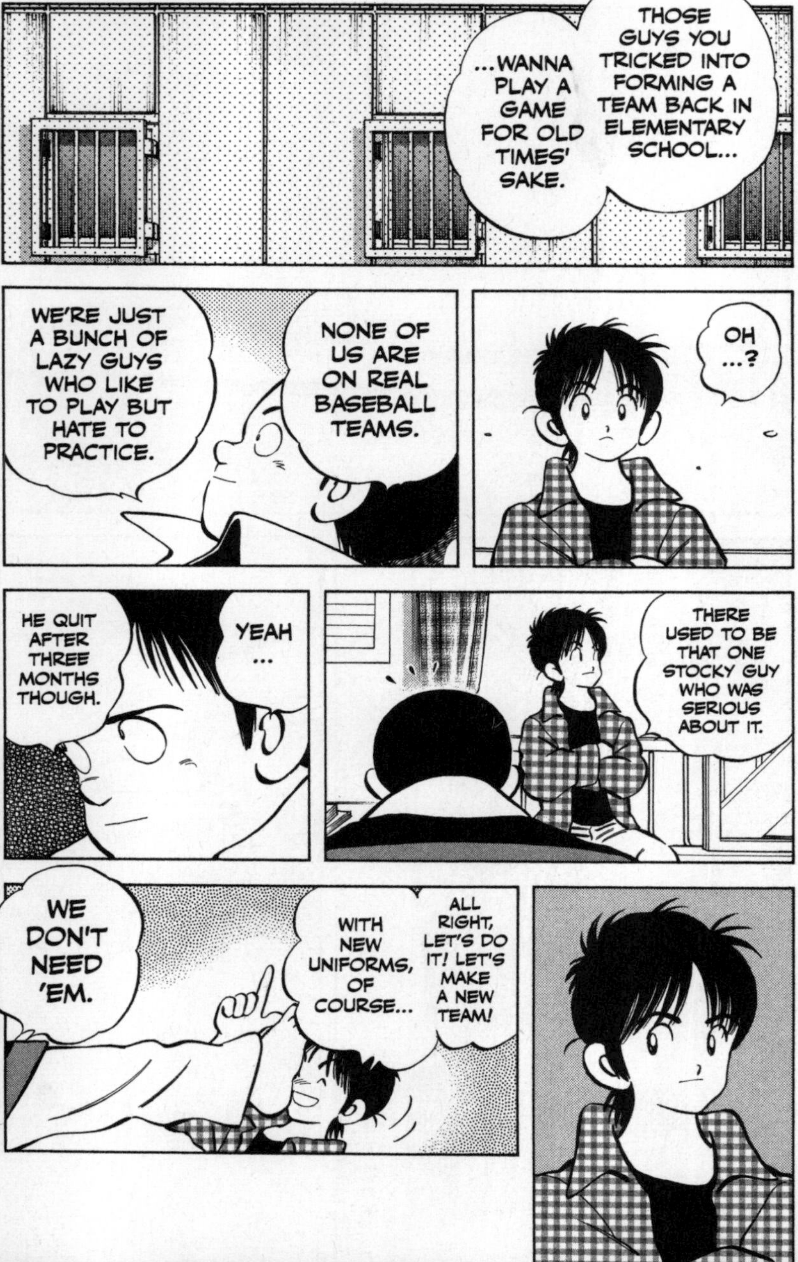
THOSE GUYS YOU TRICKED INTO FORMING A TEAM BACK IN ELEMENTARY SCHOOL...
...WANNA PLAY A GAME FOR OLD TIMES' SAKE.
OH ...?
NONE OF US ARE ON REAL BASEBALL TEAMS.
WE'RE JUST A BUNCH OF LAZY GUYS WHO LIKE TO PLAY BUT HATE TO PRACTICE.
THERE USED TO BE THAT ONE STOCKY GUY WHO WAS SERIOUS ABOUT IT.
YEAH ...
HE QUIT AFTER THREE MONTHS THOUGH.
ALL RIGHT, LET'S DO IT! LET'S MAKE A NEW TEAM!
WITH NEW UNIFORMS, OF COURSE...
WE DON'T NEED 'EM.

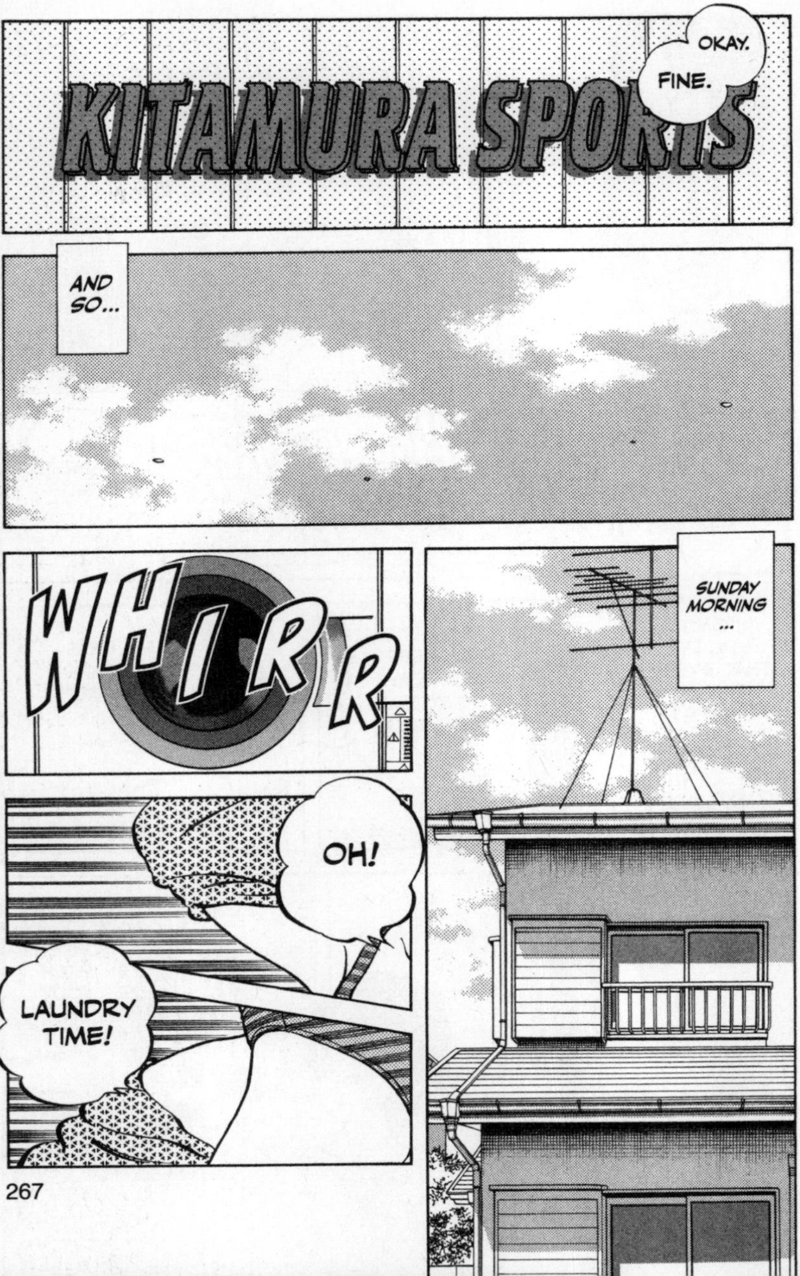
OKAY.
FINE.
KITAMURA SPORTS
AND SO...
SUNDAY MORNING ...
WHIRR
OH!
LAUNDRY TIME!

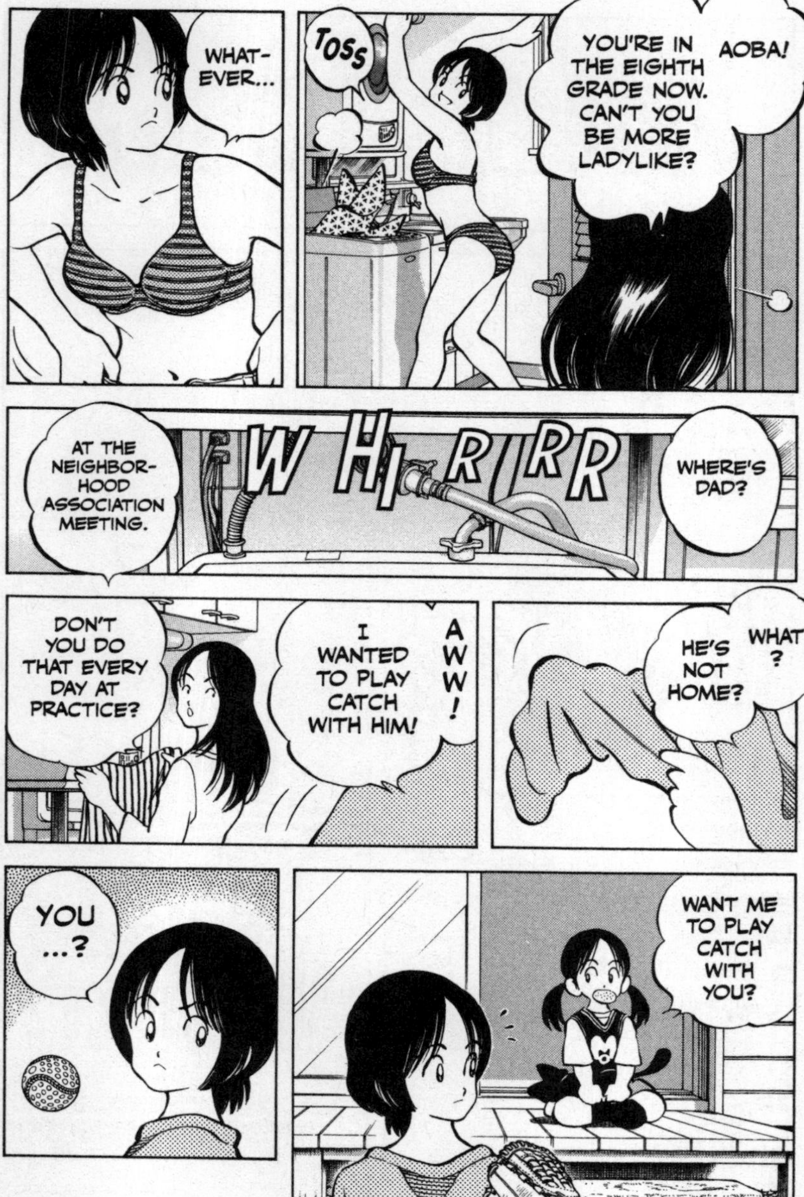
AOBA!
YOU'RE IN THE EIGHTH GRADE NOW. CAN'T YOU BE MORE LADYLIKE?
TOSS
WHAT-EVER...
WHERE'S DAD?
WHIRRR
AT THE NEIGHBOR-HOOD ASSOCIATION MEETING.
WHAT?
HE'S NOT HOME?
AWW!
I WANTED TO PLAY CATCH WITH HIM!
DON'T YOU DO THAT EVERY DAY AT PRACTICE?
WANT ME TO PLAY CATCH WITH YOU?
YOU ...?

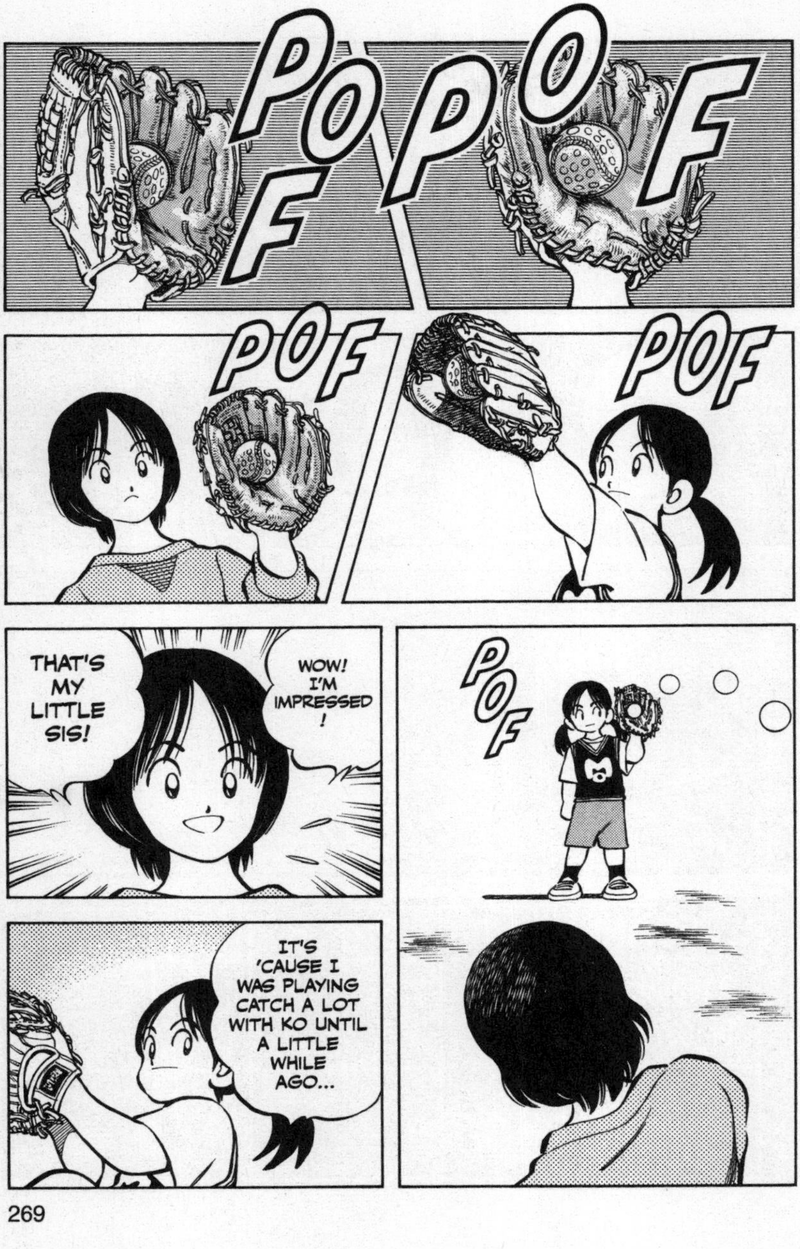
POF
POF
POF
POF
POF
WOW! I'M IMPRESSED!
THAT'S MY LITTLE SIS!
IT'S 'CAUSE I WAS PLAYING CATCH A LOT WITH KO UNTIL A LITTLE WHILE AGO...

WITH...
KO?

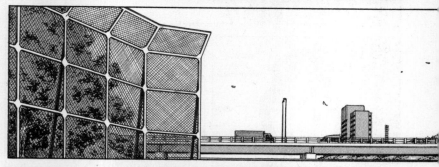

TEAM	1	2	3	4	5	6
RANDOM BUNCH OF GUYS TEAM						
FORMER SENKAWA-KITA ELEMENTARY GRADE 5, CLASS 2 TEAM						

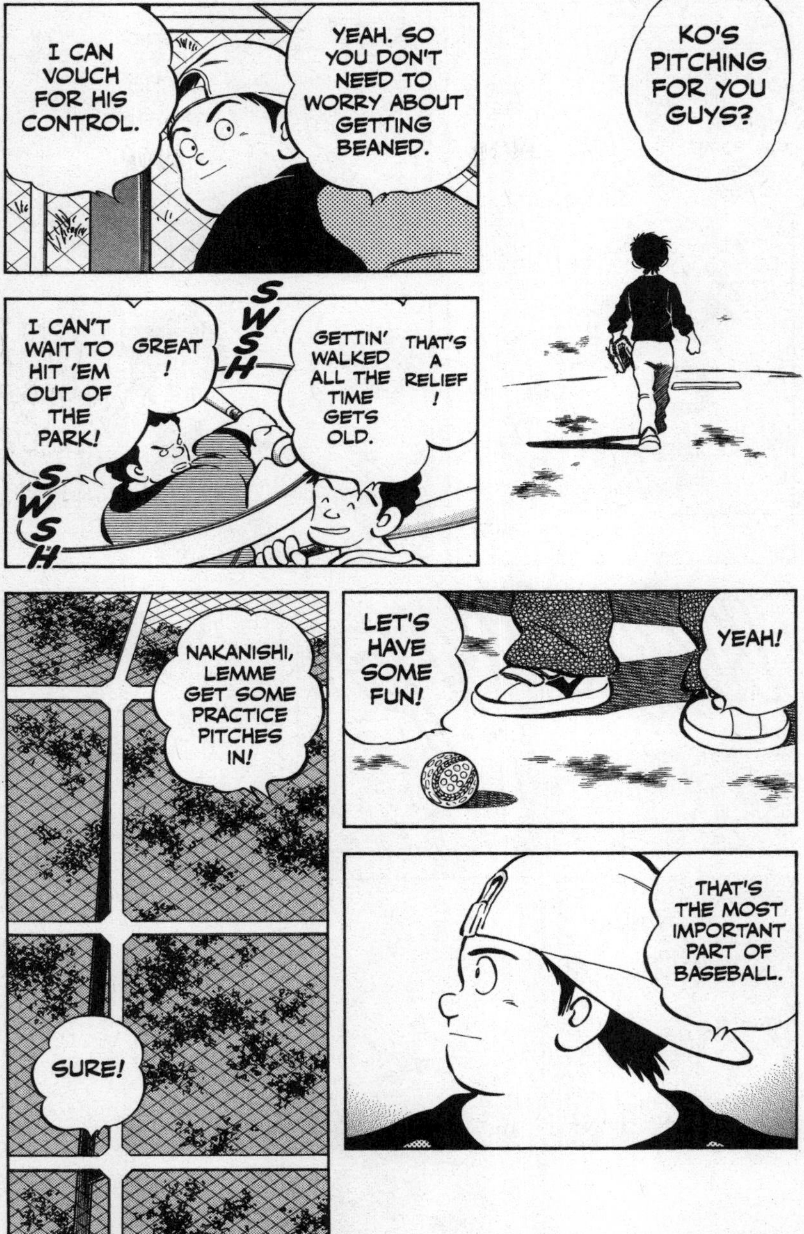
KO'S PITCHING FOR YOU GUYS?
YEAH. SO YOU DON'T NEED TO WORRY ABOUT GETTING BEANED.
I CAN VOUCH FOR HIS CONTROL.
THAT'S A RELIEF!
GETTIN' WALKED ALL THE TIME GETS OLD.
SWSH
GREAT!
I CAN'T WAIT TO HIT 'EM OUT OF THE PARK!
SWSH
YEAH!
LET'S HAVE SOME FUN!
THAT'S THE MOST IMPORTANT PART OF BASEBALL.
NAKANISHI, LEMME GET SOME PRACTICE PITCHES IN!
SURE!

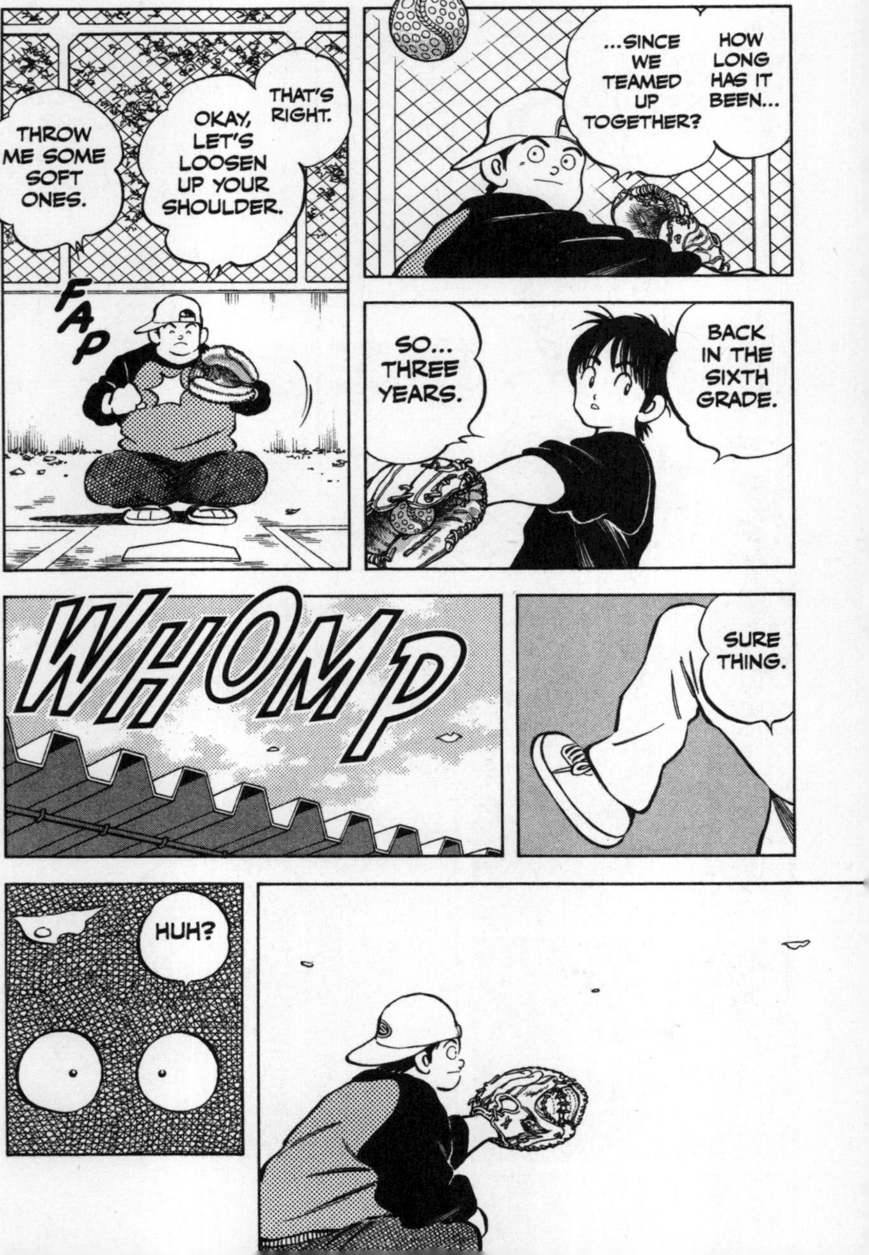
HOW LONG HAS IT BEEN...
...SINCE WE TEAMED UP TOGETHER?
THAT'S RIGHT.
OKAY, LET'S LOOSEN UP YOUR SHOULDER.
THROW ME SOME SOFT ONES.
BACK IN THE SIXTH GRADE.
SO... THREE YEARS.
FAP
SURE THING.
WHOMP
HUH?

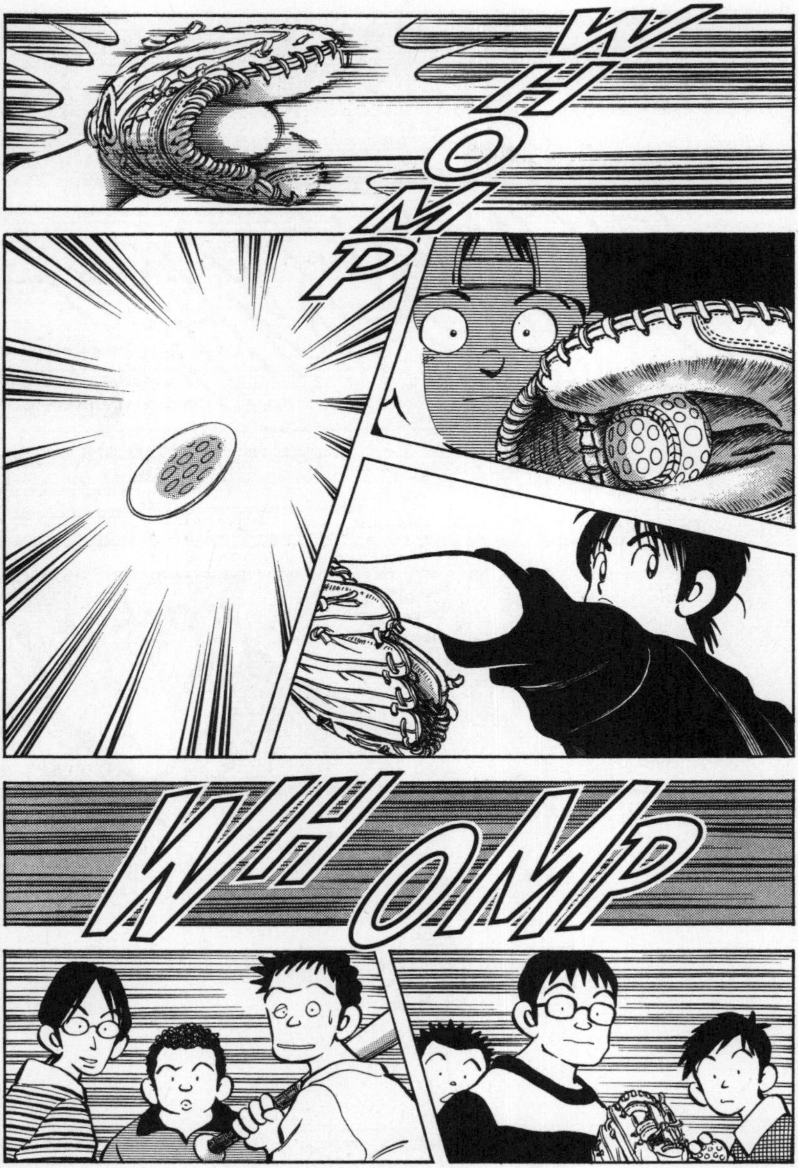
WHOMP
WHOMP

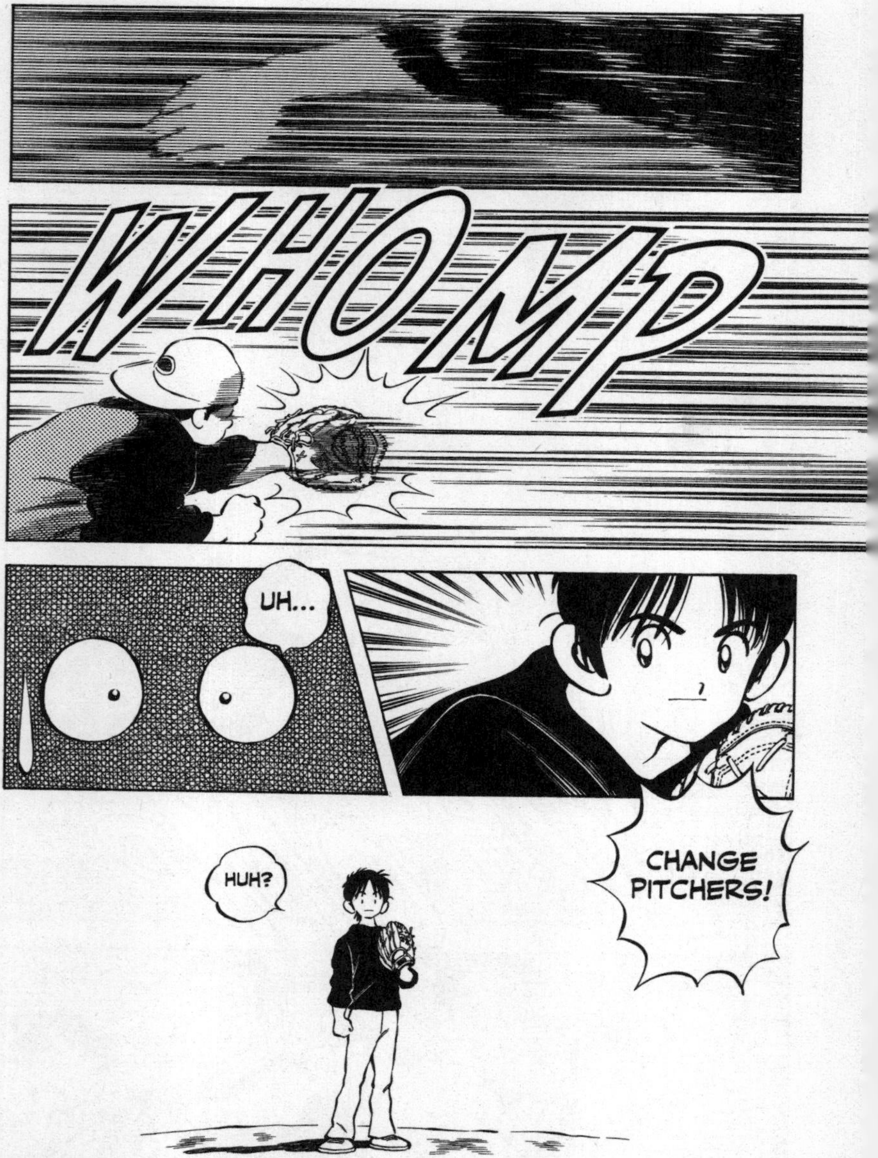
WHOMP
UH...
CHANGE PITCHERS!
HUH?

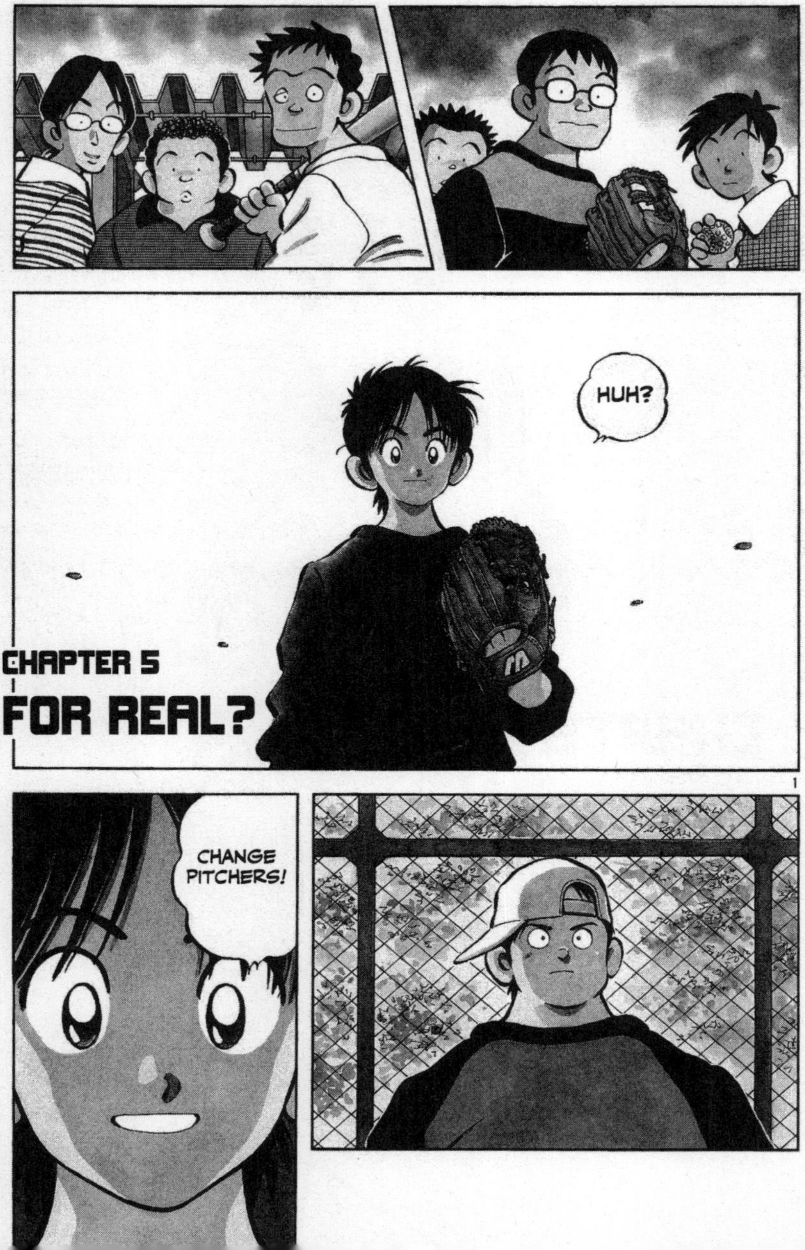
HUH?
CHAPTER 5
FOR REAL?
1
CHANGE PITCHERS!

CHAPTER 5
FOR REAL?

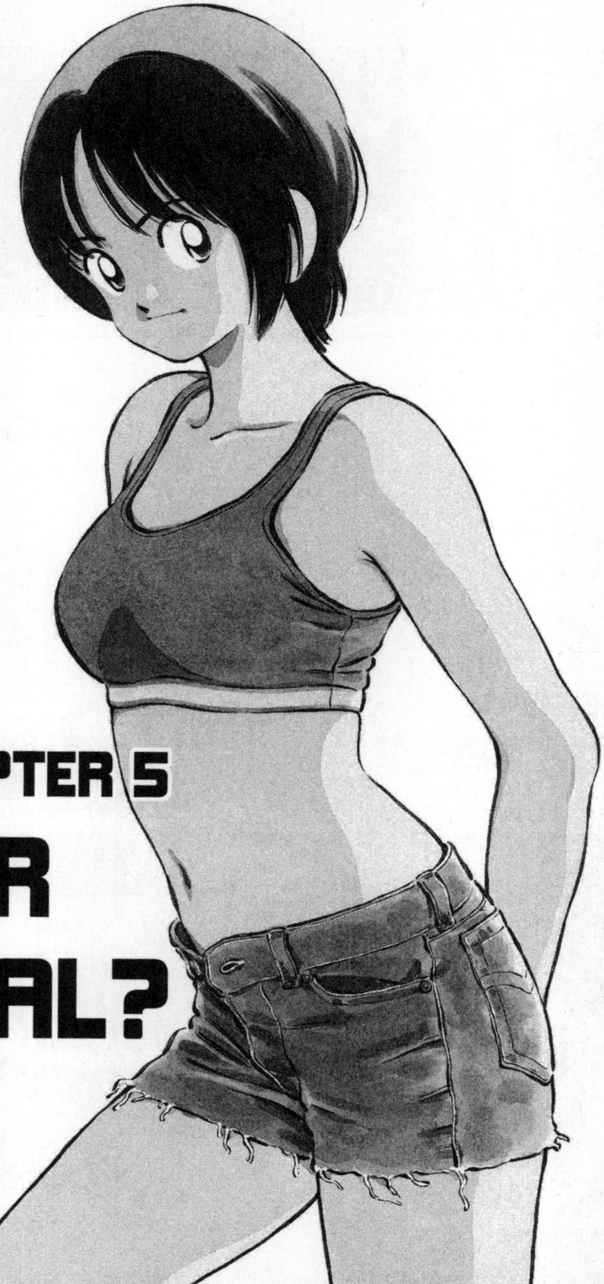

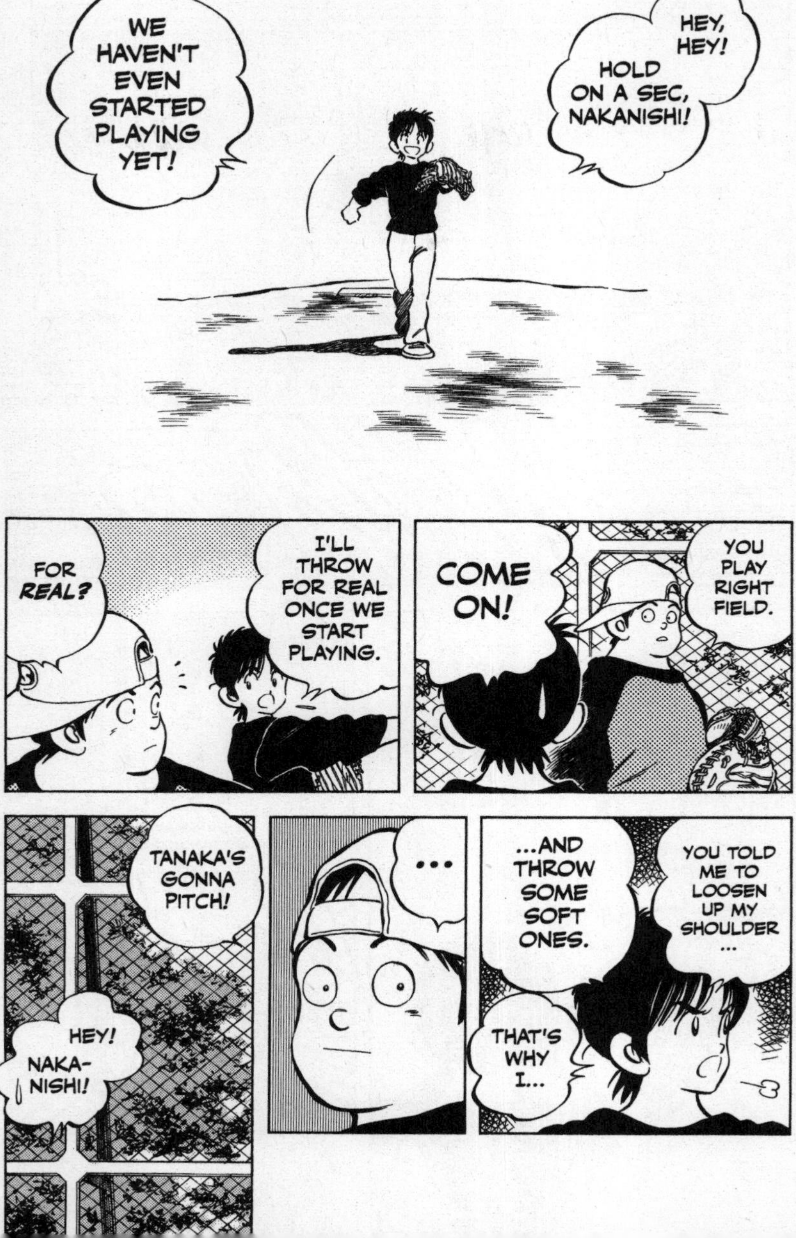
HEY, HEY! HOLD ON A SEC, NAKANISHI!
WE HAVEN'T EVEN STARTED PLAYING YET!
YOU PLAY RIGHT FIELD.
COME ON!
I'LL THROW FOR REAL ONCE WE START PLAYING.
FOR *REAL?*
YOU TOLD ME TO LOOSEN UP MY SHOULDER ...
...AND THROW SOME SOFT ONES.
THAT'S WHY I...
...
TANAKA'S GONNA PITCH!
HEY! NAKA-NISHI!

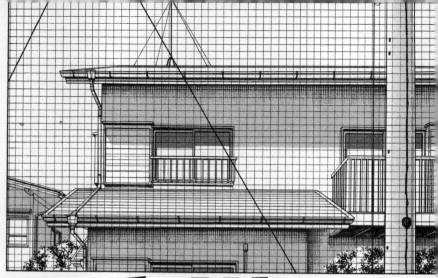

MEW!

WE CAN STOP IF YOUR HAND'S GETTING SORE.

MO-MIJI...

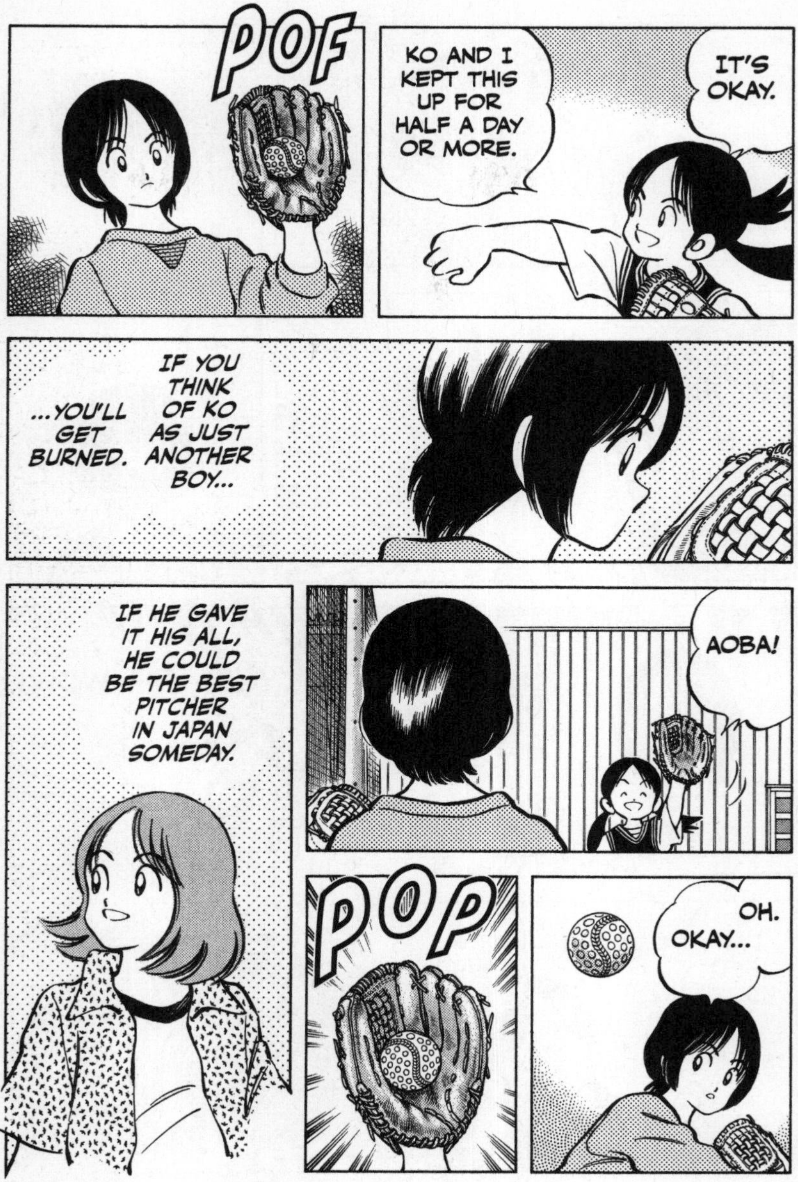
IT'S OKAY.
KO AND I KEPT THIS UP FOR HALF A DAY OR MORE.
POF
IF YOU THINK OF KO AS JUST ANOTHER BOY...
...YOU'LL GET BURNED.
AOBA!
OH. OKAY...
POP
IF HE GAVE IT HIS ALL, HE COULD BE THE BEST PITCHER IN JAPAN SOMEDAY.

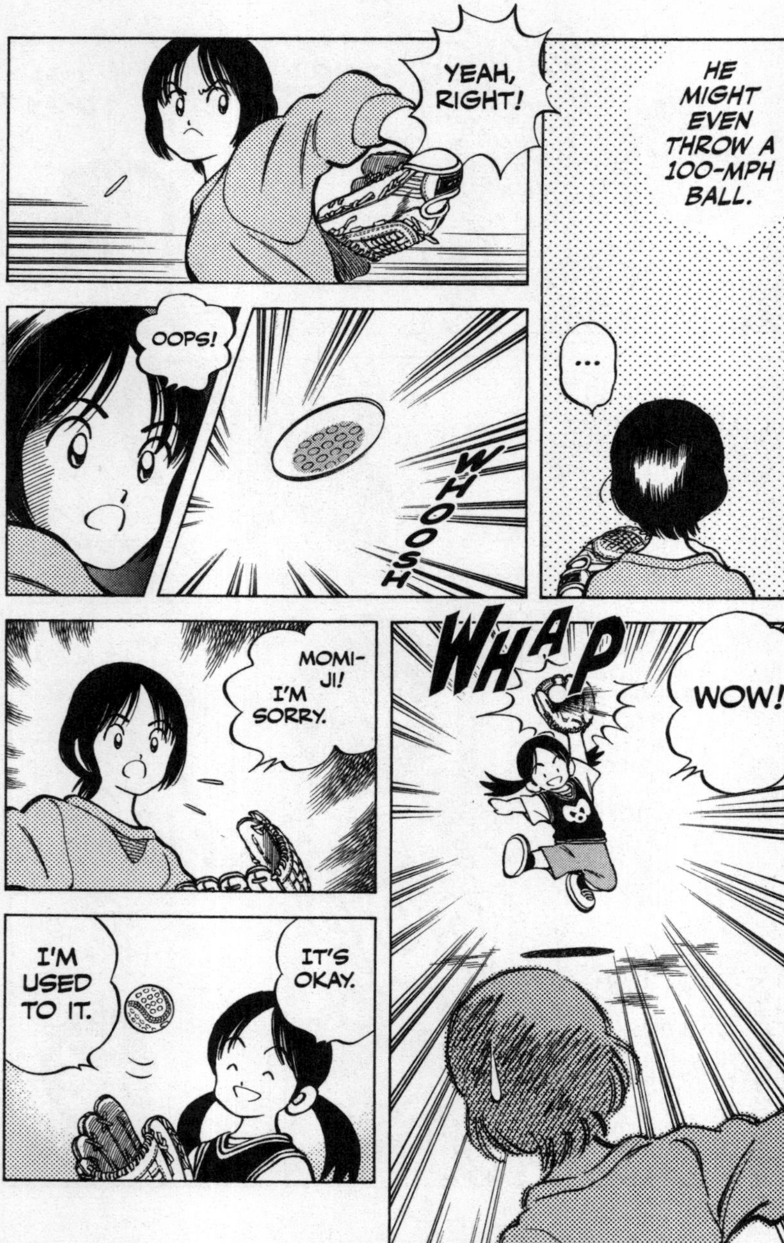
HE MIGHT EVEN THROW A 100-MPH BALL.
...
YEAH, RIGHT!
WHOOSH
OOPS!
WHAP
WOW!
MOMIJI! I'M SORRY.
IT'S OKAY.
I'M USED TO IT.

ZZ

...

POF

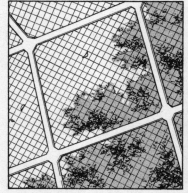

RANDOM BUNCH OF GUYS TEAM

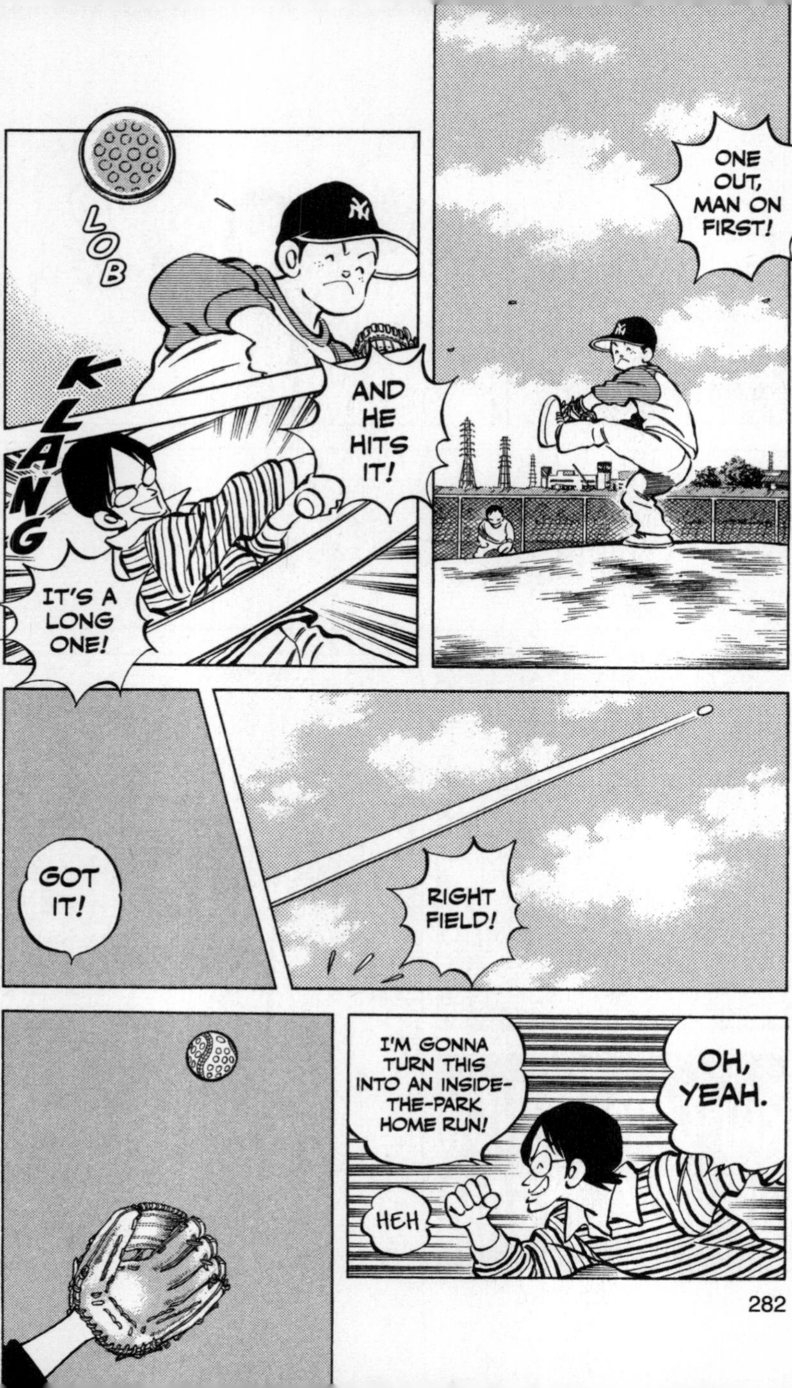
ONE OUT, MAN ON FIRST!
LOB
AND HE HITS IT!
KLANG
IT'S A LONG ONE!
RIGHT FIELD!
GOT IT!
OH, YEAH.
I'M GONNA TURN THIS INTO AN INSIDE-THE-PARK HOME RUN!
HEH

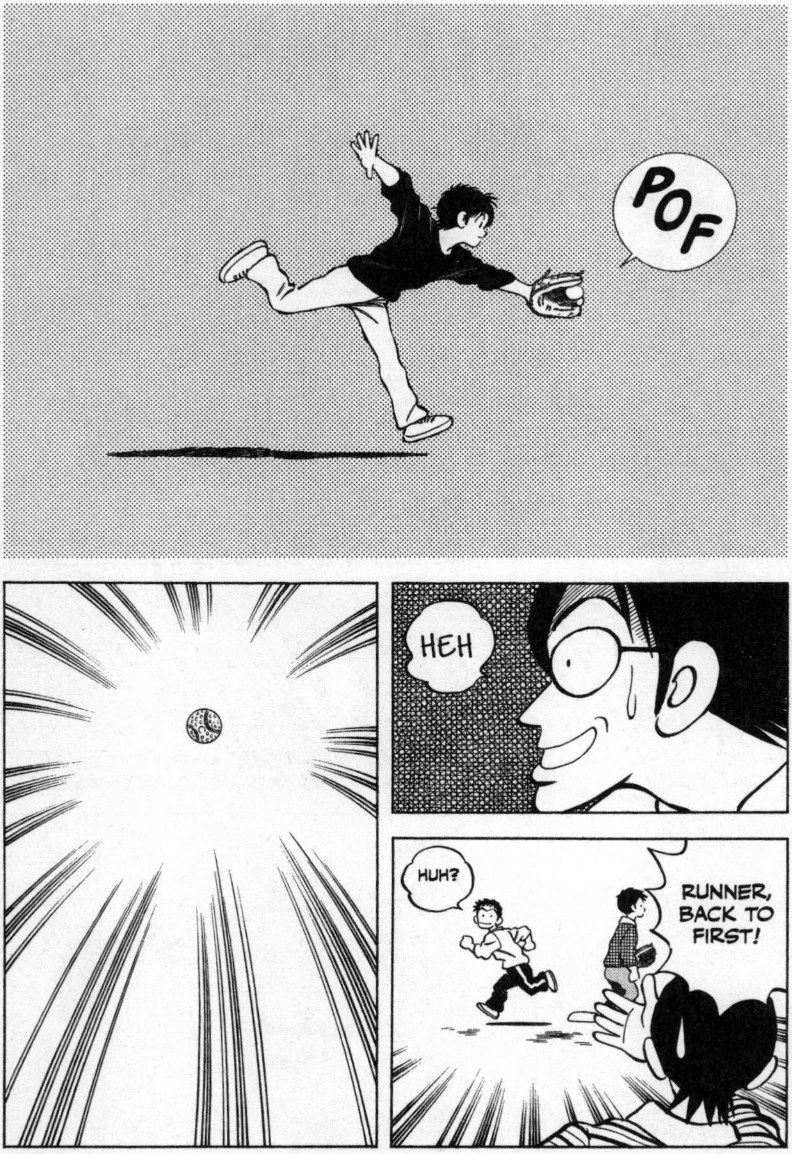
POF
HEH
RUNNER, BACK TO FIRST!
HUH?

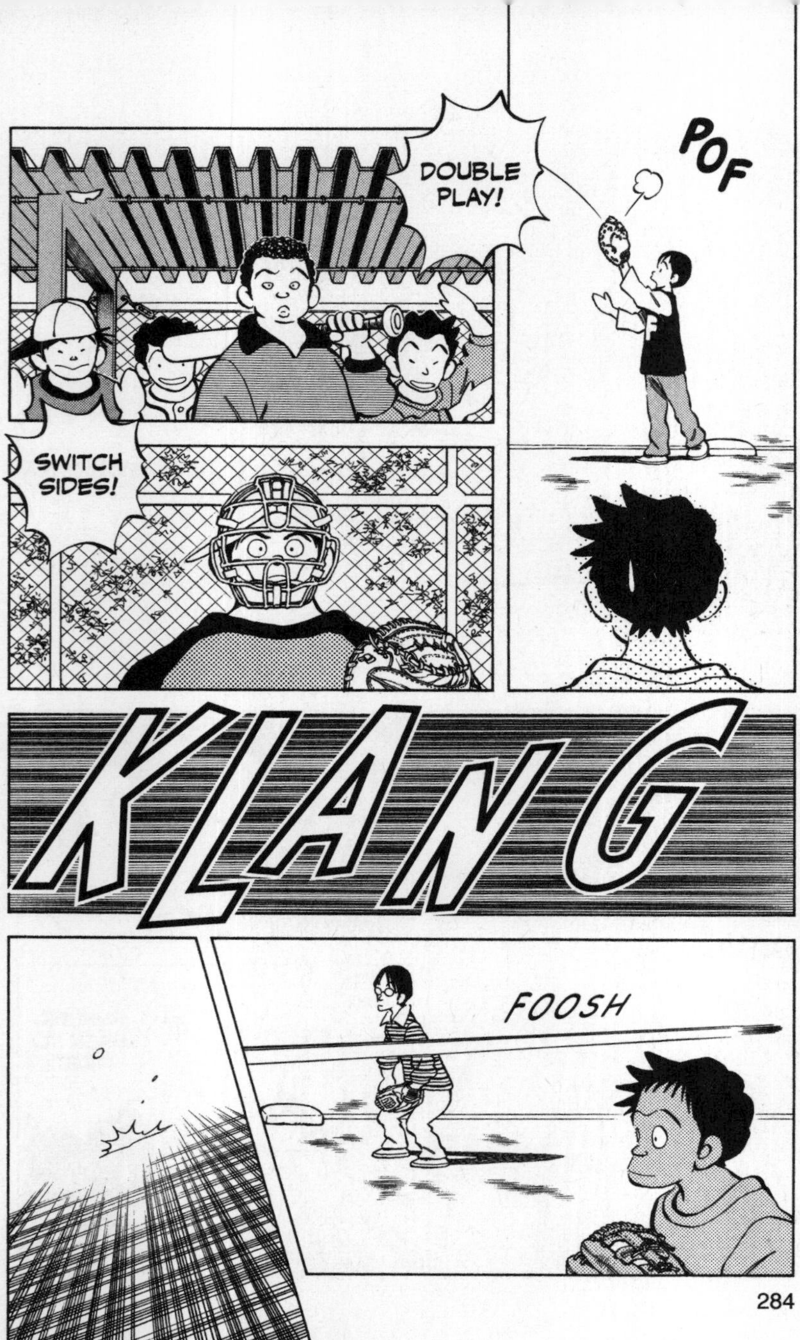
POF
DOUBLE PLAY!
SWITCH SIDES!
KLANG
FOOSH

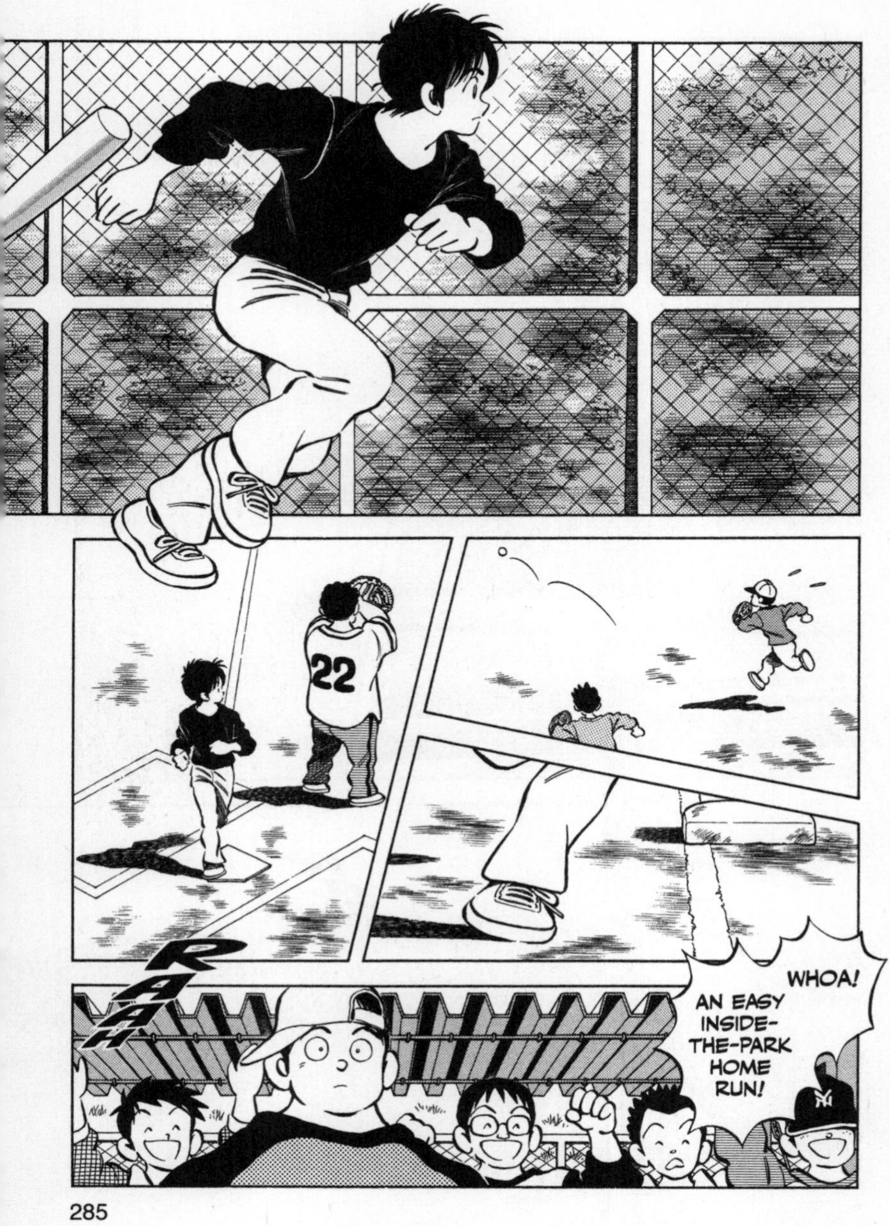
WHOA!
AN EASY INSIDE-THE-PARK HOME RUN!
RAAAH

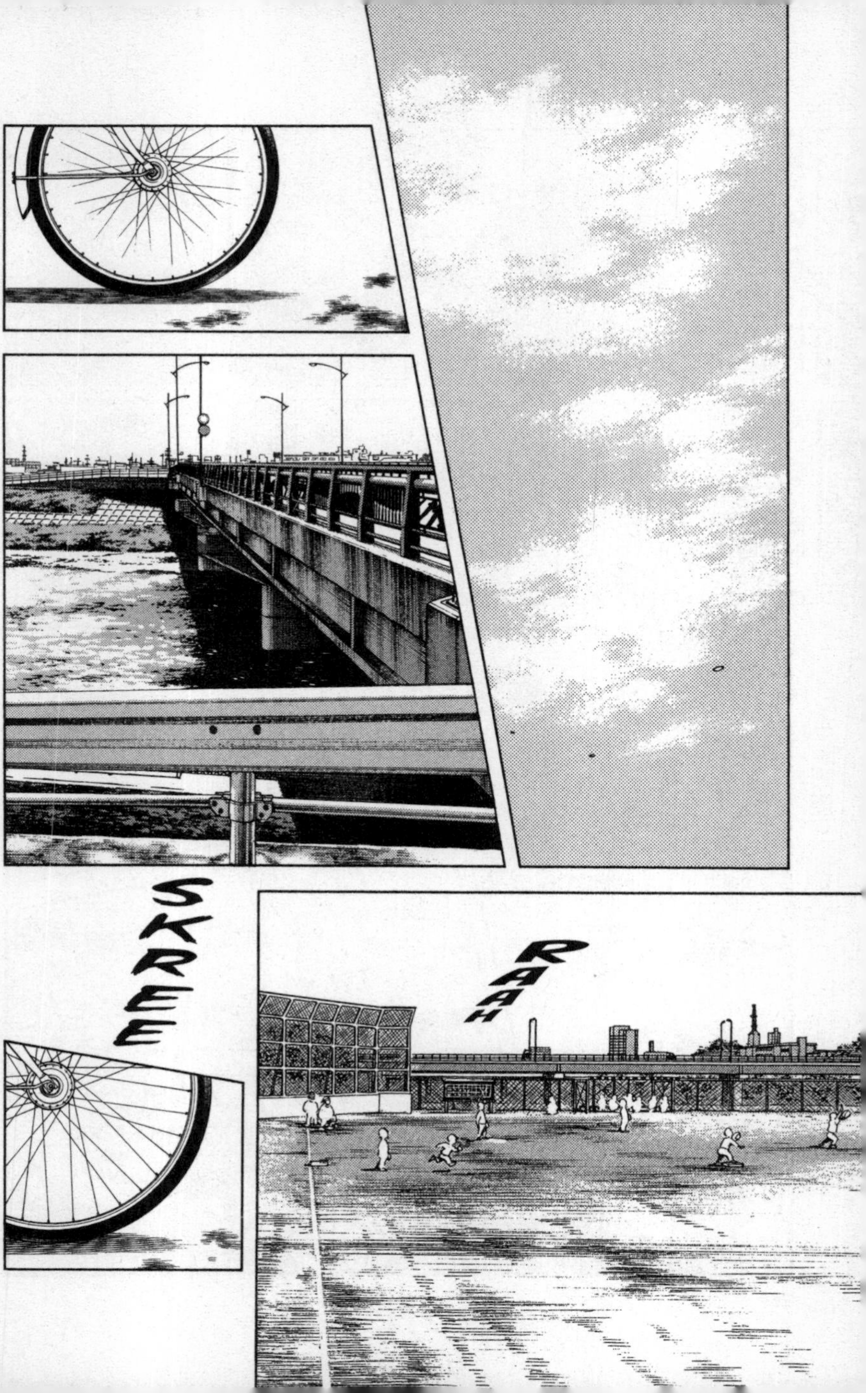
RAAH
SKREE

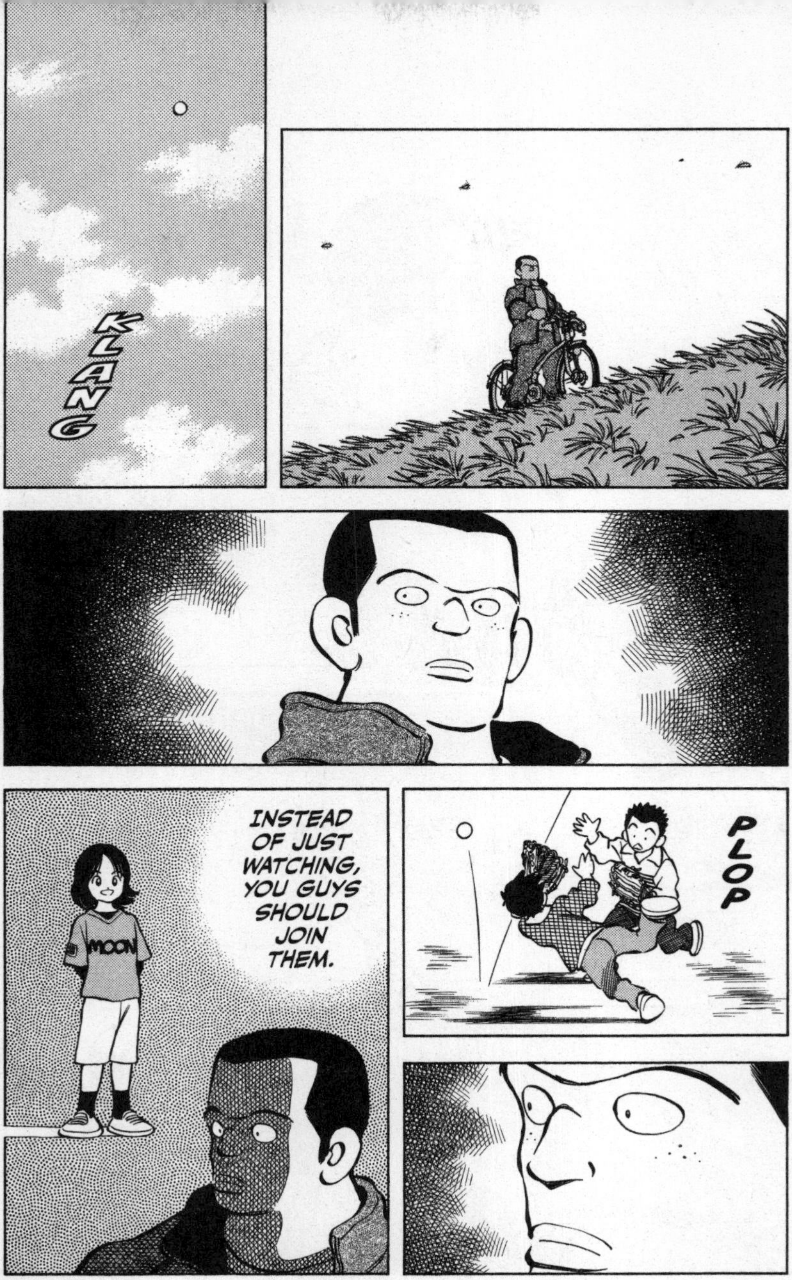
KLANG
PLOP
INSTEAD OF JUST WATCHING, YOU GUYS SHOULD JOIN THEM.

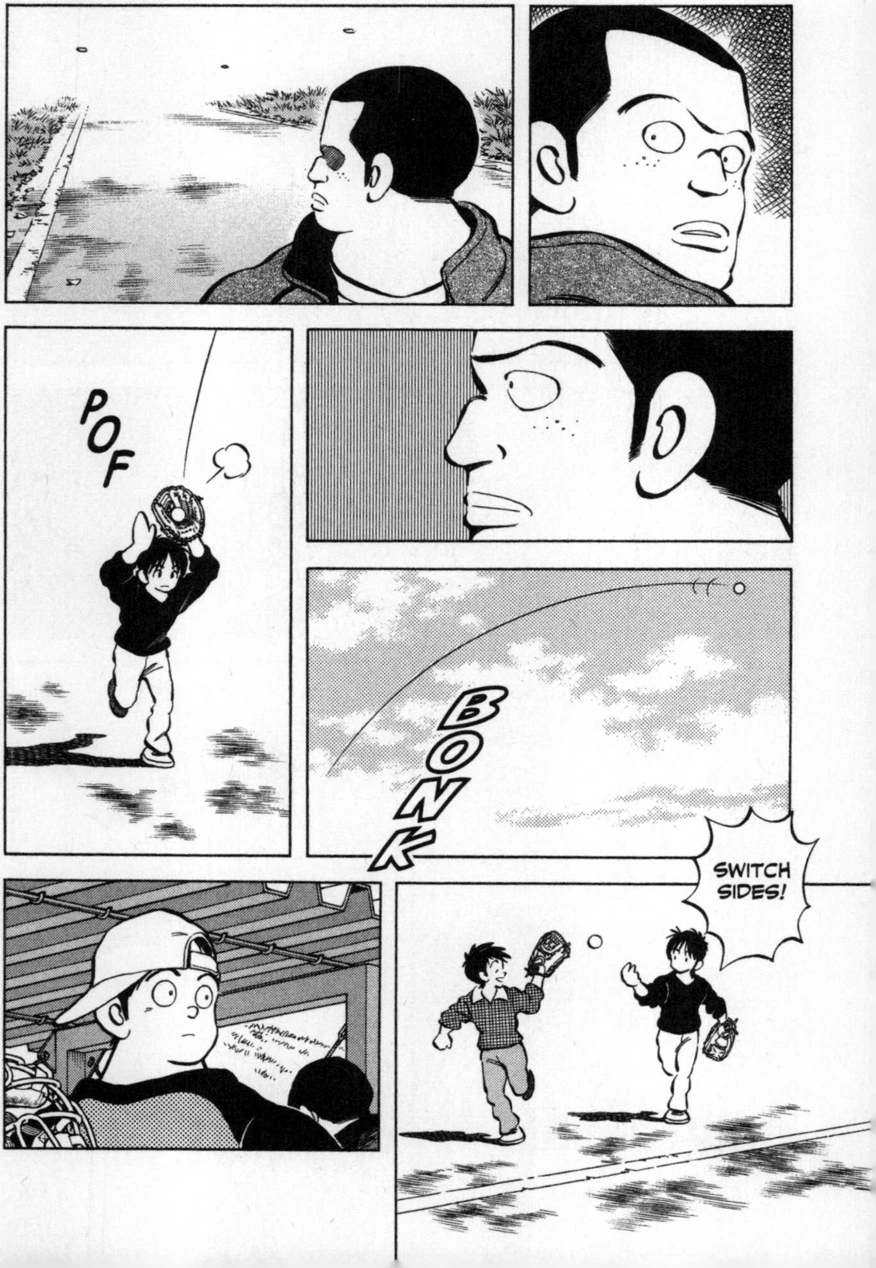
BONK
POF
SWITCH SIDES!

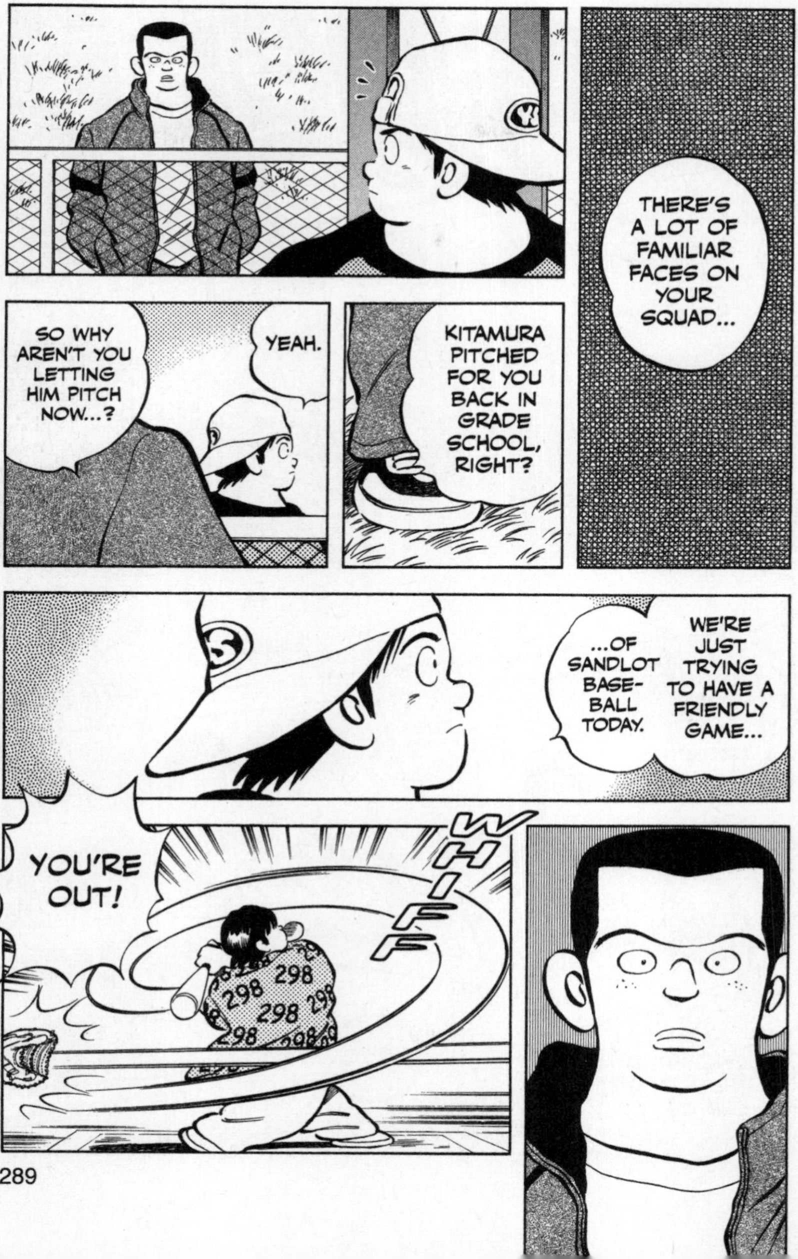
THERE'S A LOT OF FAMILIAR FACES ON YOUR SQUAD...
KITAMURA PITCHED FOR YOU BACK IN GRADE SCHOOL, RIGHT?
YEAH.
SO WHY AREN'T YOU LETTING HIM PITCH NOW...?
WE'RE JUST TRYING TO HAVE A FRIENDLY GAME...
...OF SANDLOT BASE-BALL TODAY.
WHIFF
YOU'RE OUT!

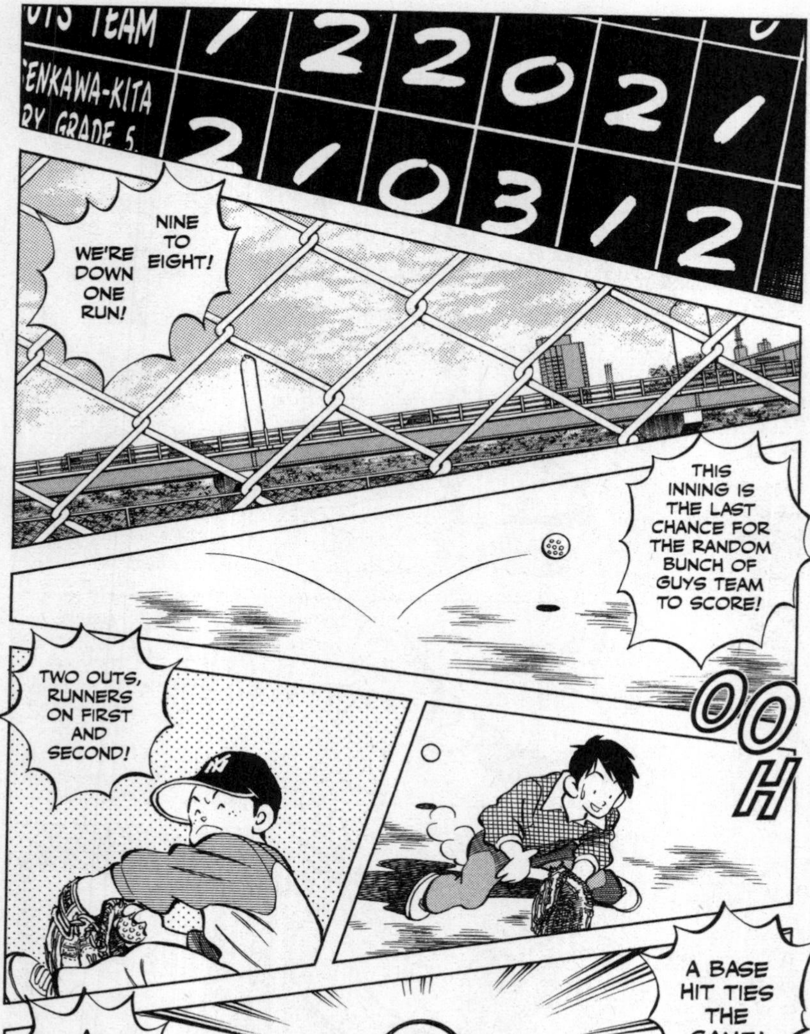
NINE TO EIGHT!
WE'RE DOWN ONE RUN!
THIS INNING IS THE LAST CHANCE FOR THE RANDOM BUNCH OF GUYS TEAM TO SCORE!
OOH
TWO OUTS, RUNNERS ON FIRST AND SECOND!
A BASE HIT TIES THE GAME!
A LONG HIT SHOULD WIN IT!

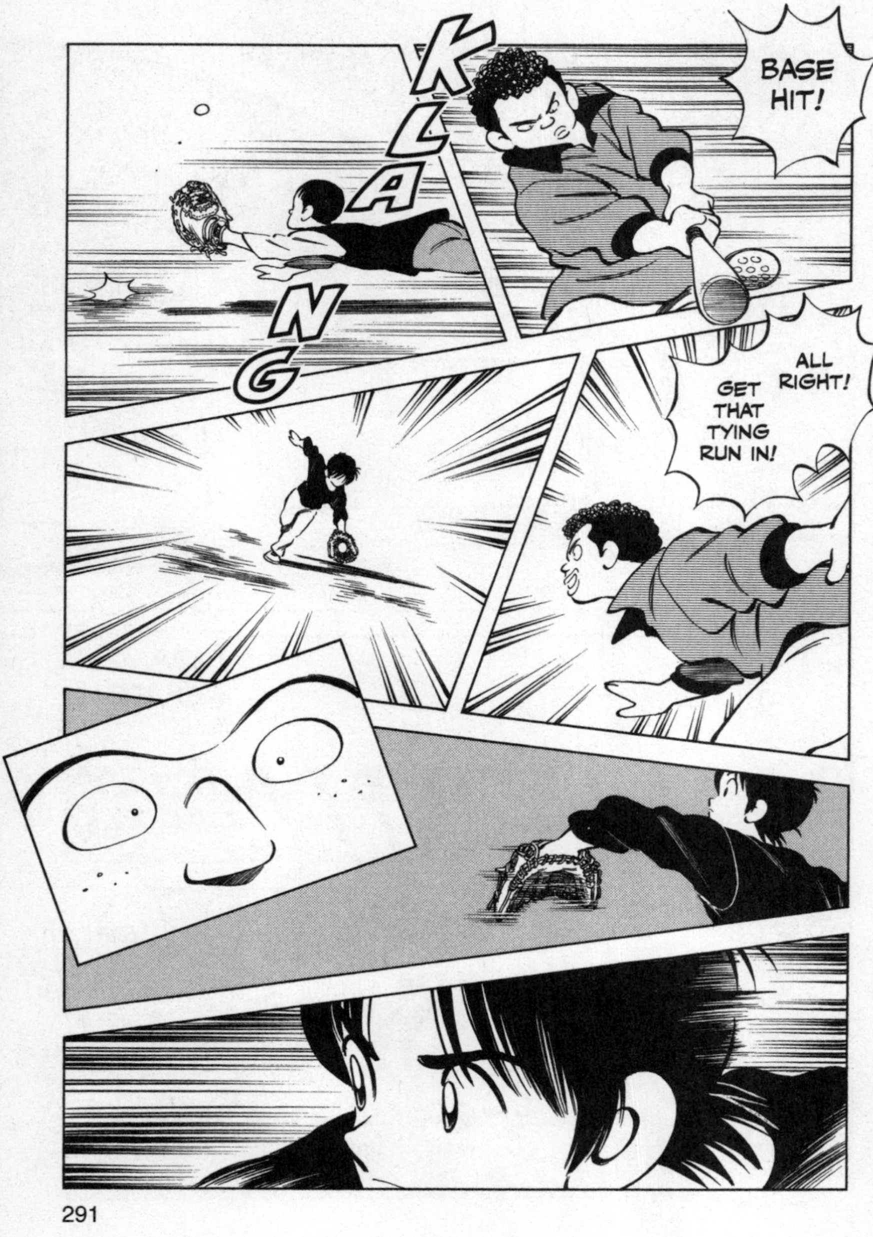
BASE HIT!
KLANG
ALL RIGHT! GET THAT TYING RUN IN!

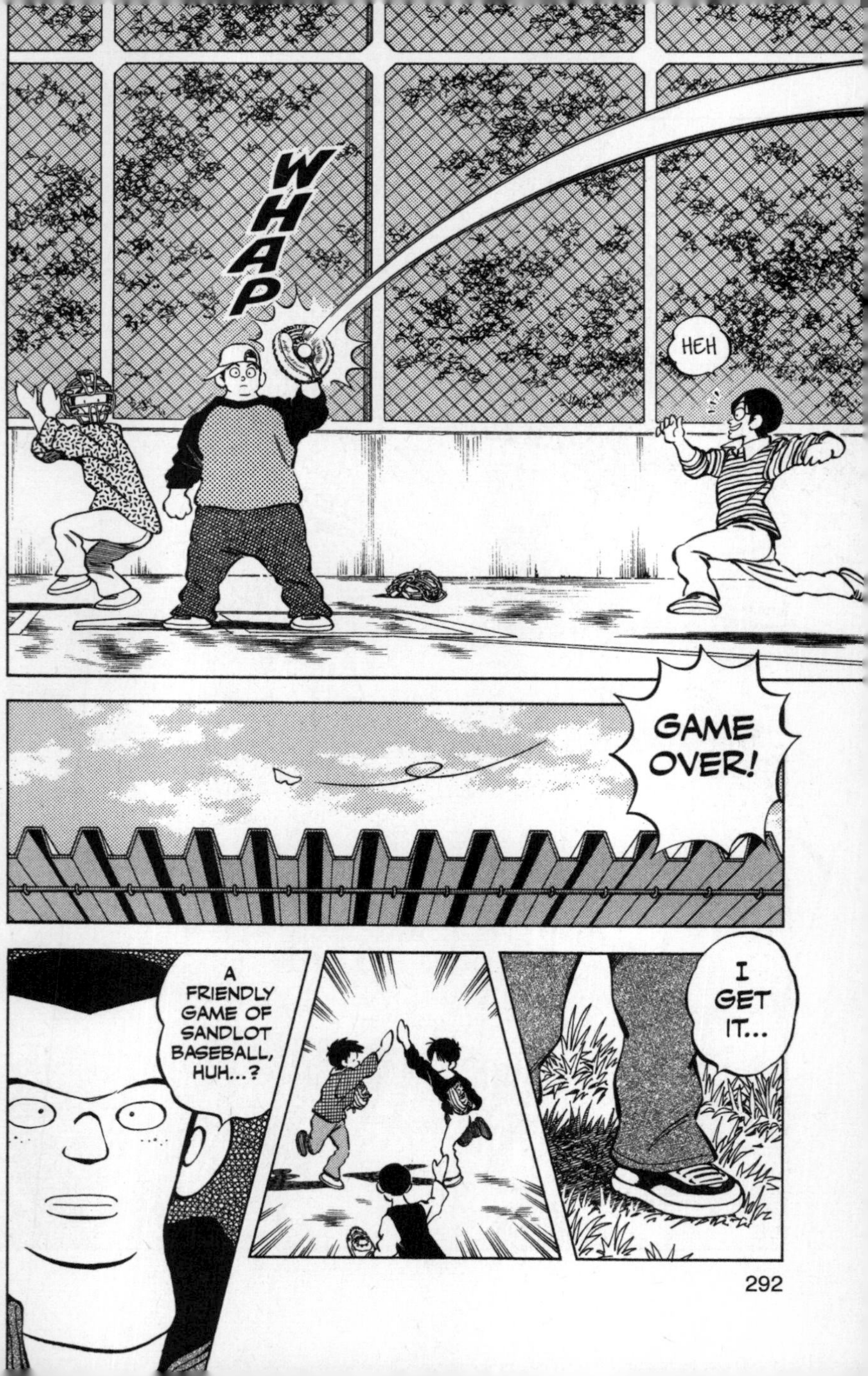
HEH
WHAP
GAME OVER!
I GET IT...
A FRIENDLY GAME OF SANDLOT BASEBALL, HUH...?

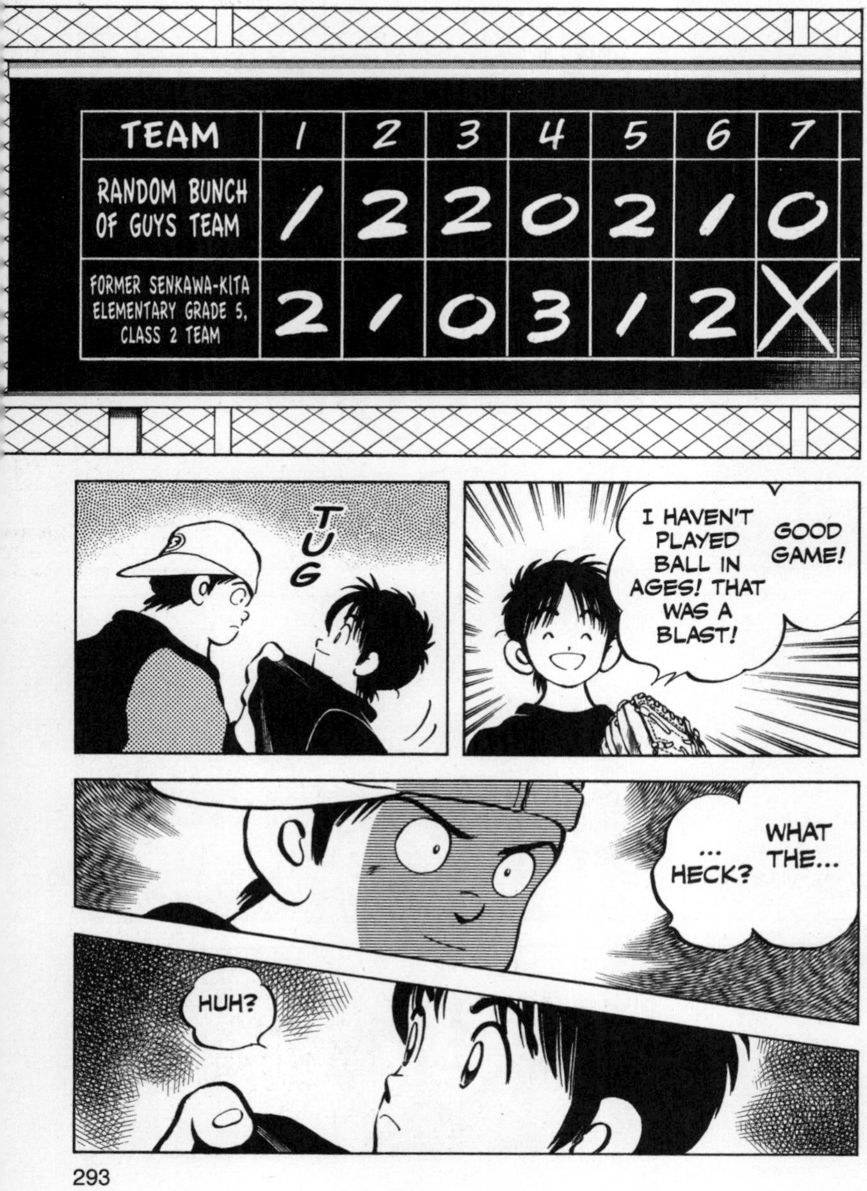
TEAM 1 2 3 4 5 6 7
RANDOM BUNCH OF GUYS TEAM 1 2 2 0 2 1 0
FORMER SENKAWA-KITA ELEMENTARY GRADE 5, CLASS 2 TEAM 2 1 0 3 1 2 X
GOOD GAME!
I HAVEN'T PLAYED BALL IN AGES! THAT WAS A BLAST!
TUG
WHAT THE...
... HECK?
HUH?

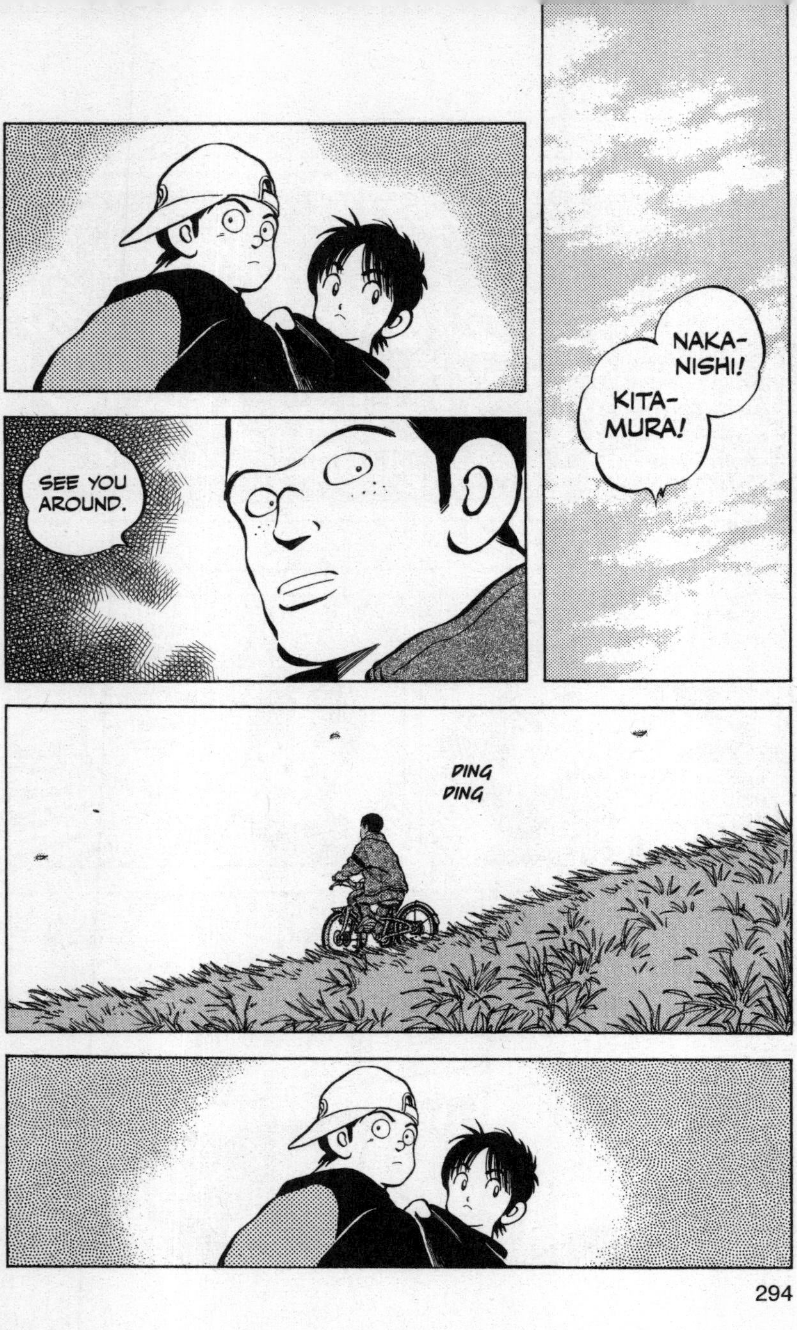
NAKA-NISHI!
KITA-MURA!
SEE YOU AROUND.
DING DING

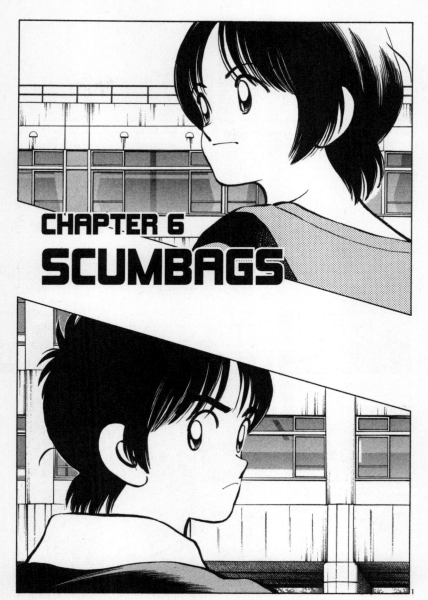

CHAPTER 6
SCUMBAGS

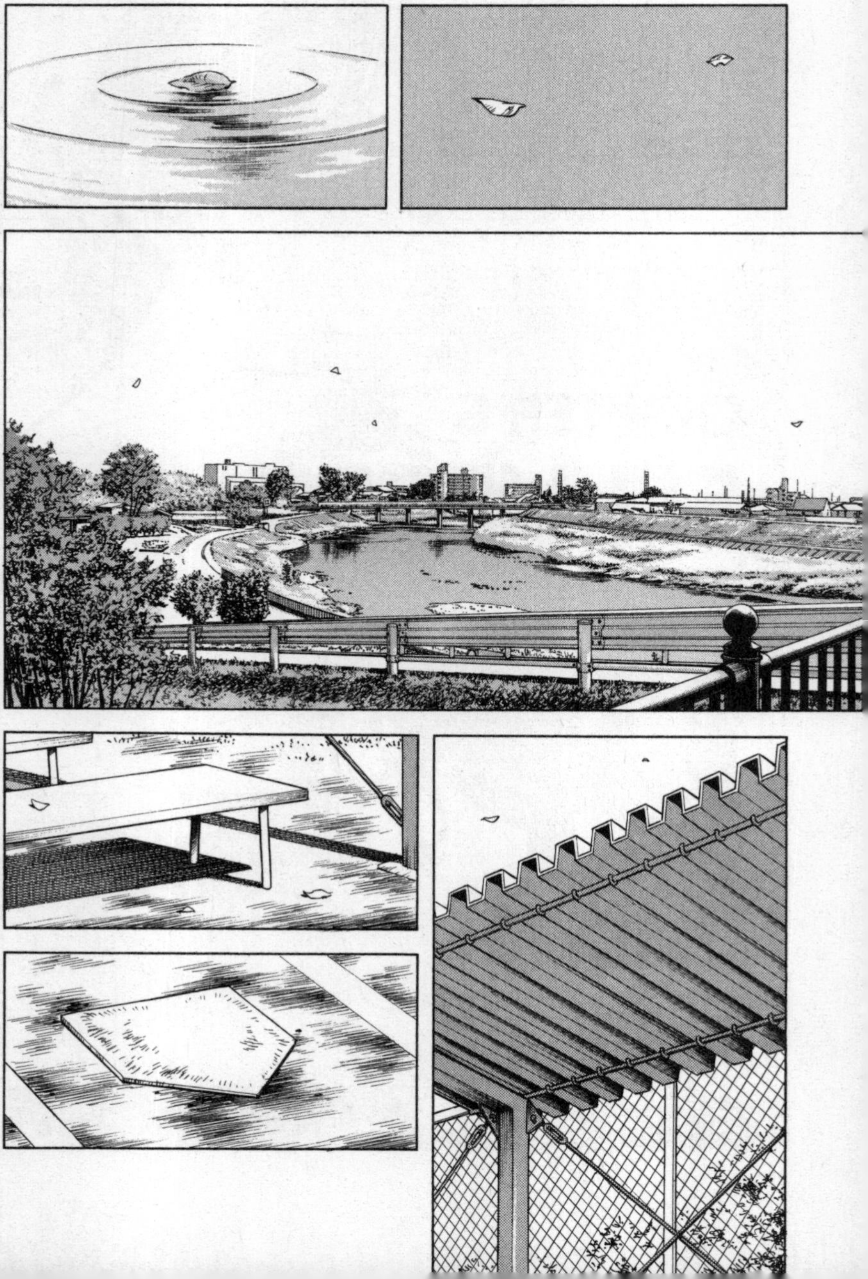

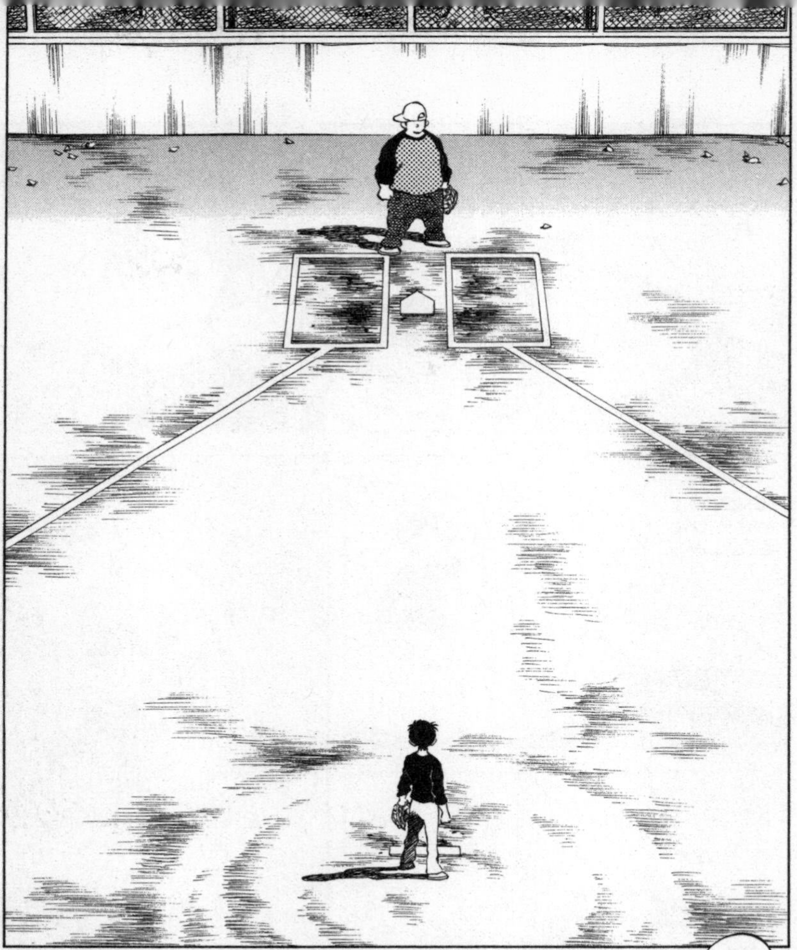

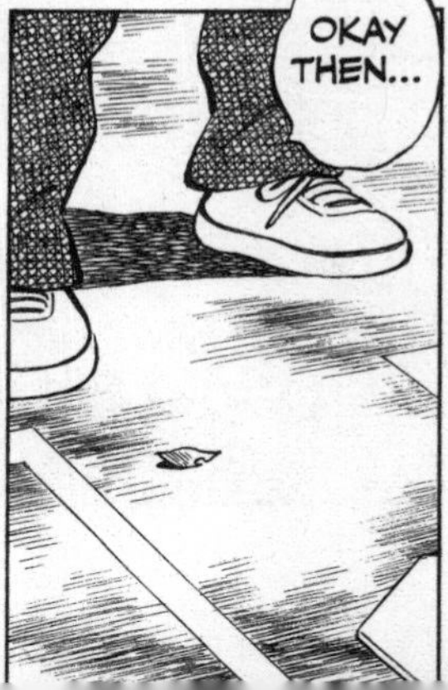
OKAY THEN...

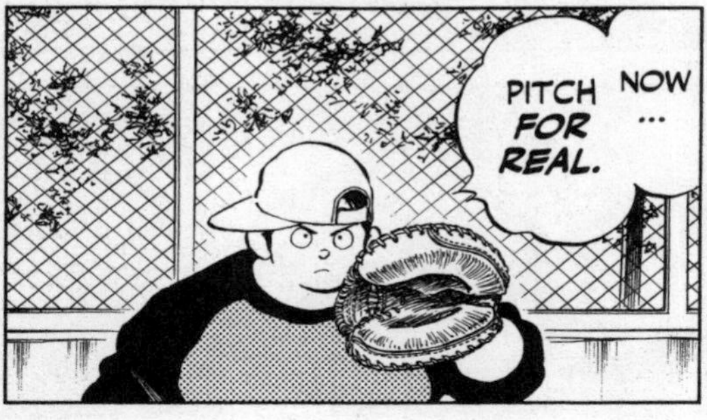
NOW ...
PITCH FOR REAL.

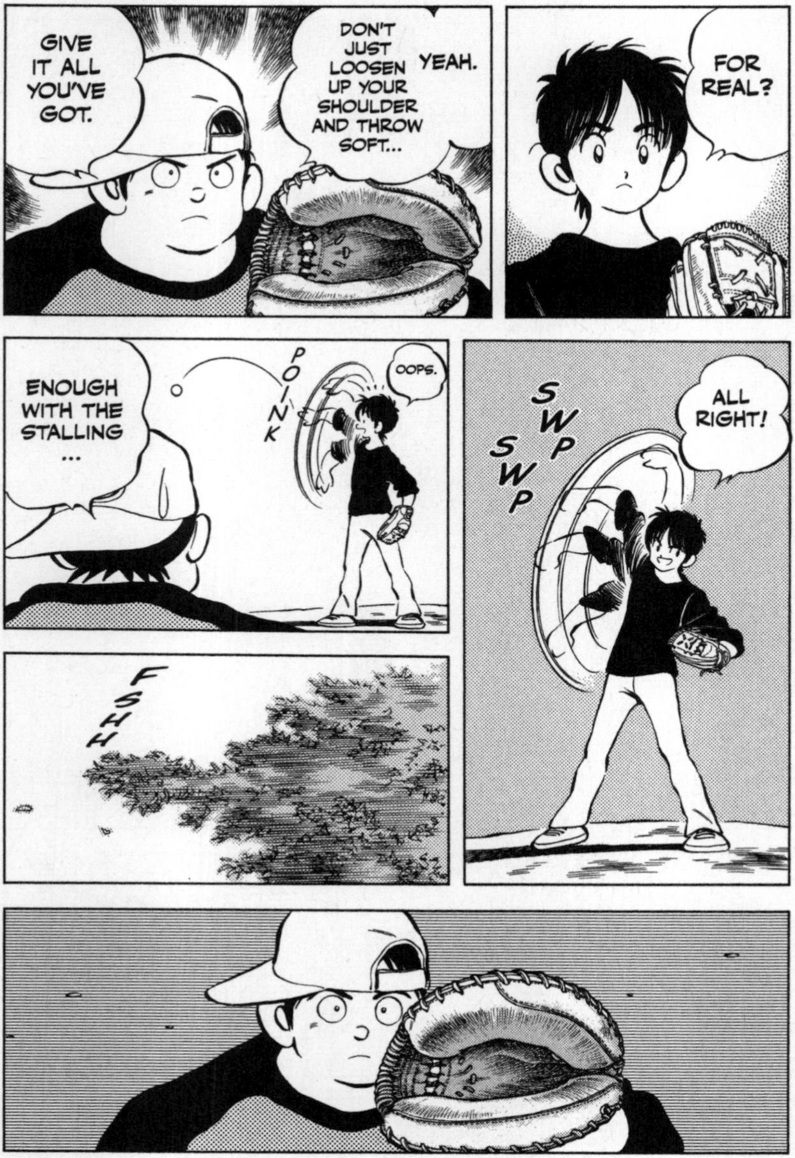
FOR REAL?
YEAH.
DON'T JUST LOOSEN UP YOUR SHOULDER AND THROW SOFT...
GIVE IT ALL YOU'VE GOT.
ALL RIGHT!
SWP SWP
SWP
OOPS.
POINK
ENOUGH WITH THE STALLING ...
FSHH

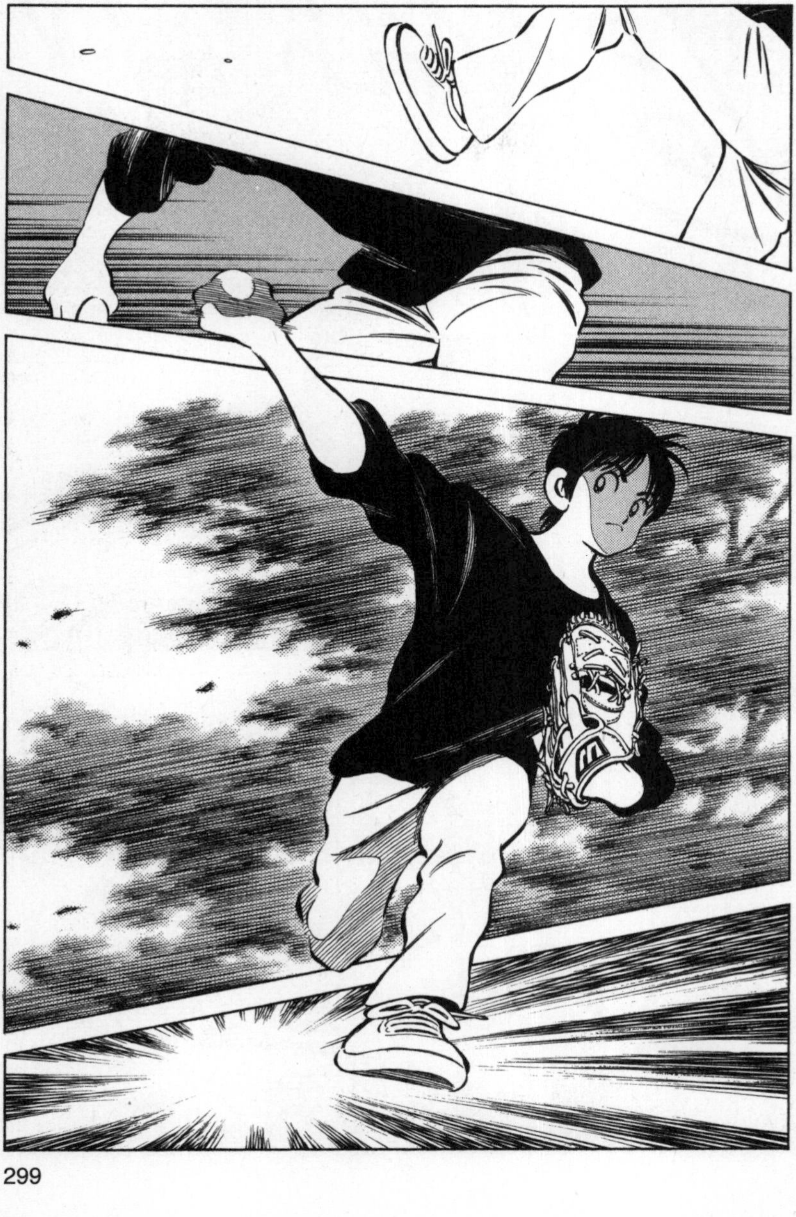

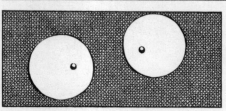

OOPS.

I TENSED UP TOO MUCH.

SORRY ...

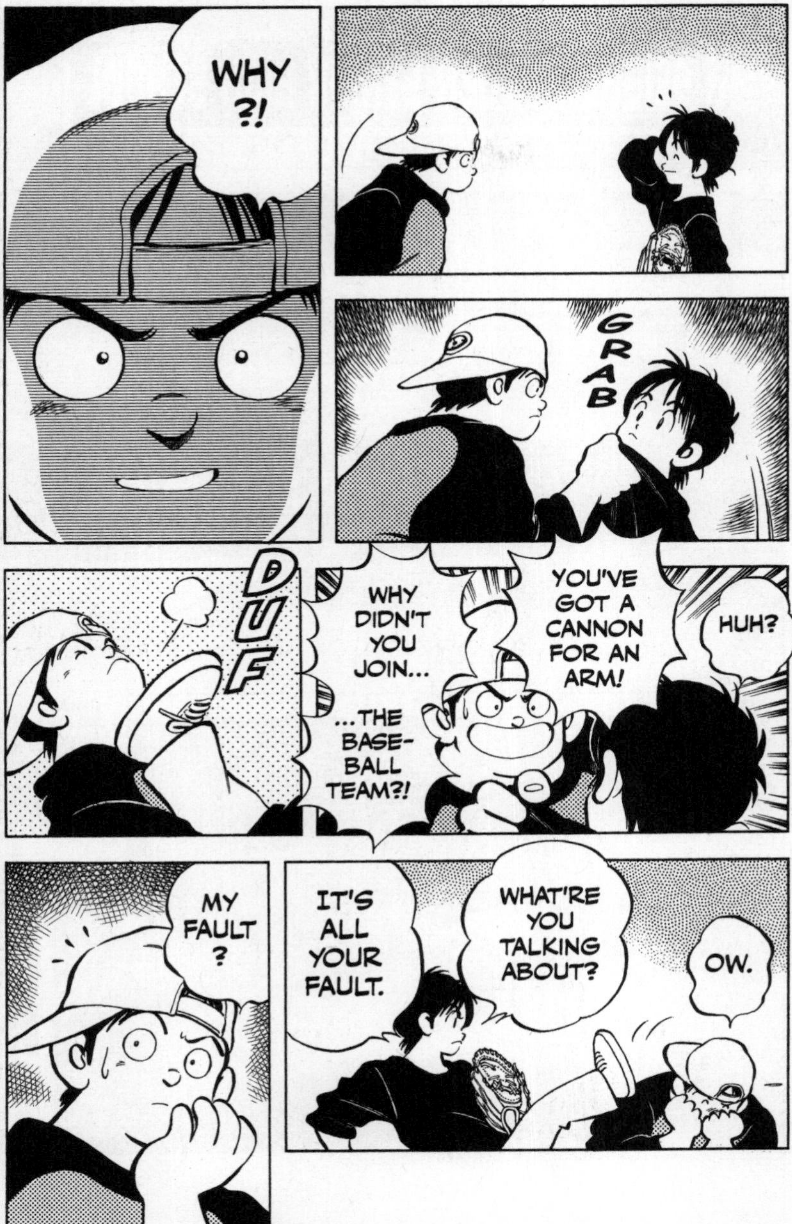
GRAB
WHY ?!
HUH?
YOU'VE GOT A CANNON FOR AN ARM!
WHY DIDN'T YOU JOIN...
...THE BASE-BALL TEAM?!
DUF
OW.
WHAT'RE YOU TALKING ABOUT?
IT'S ALL YOUR FAULT.
MY FAULT ?

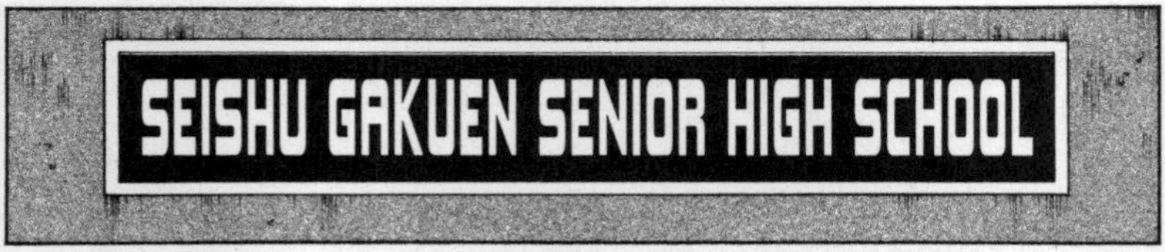
SEISHU GAKUEN SENIOR HIGH SCHOOL

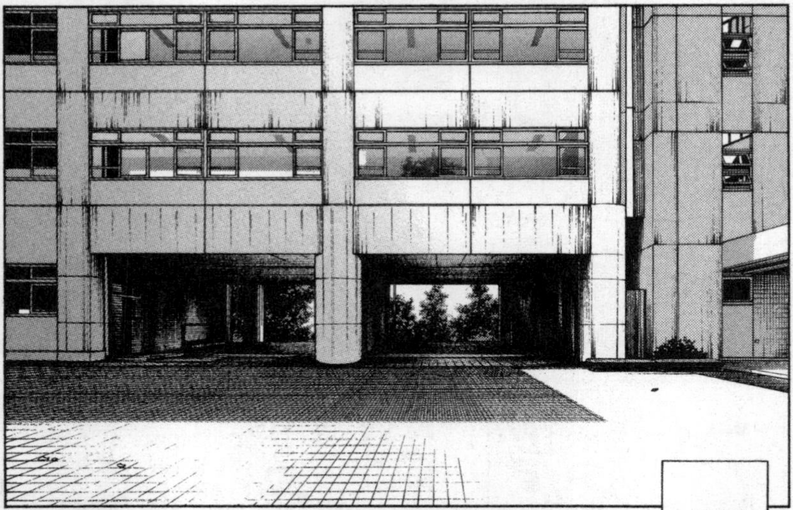

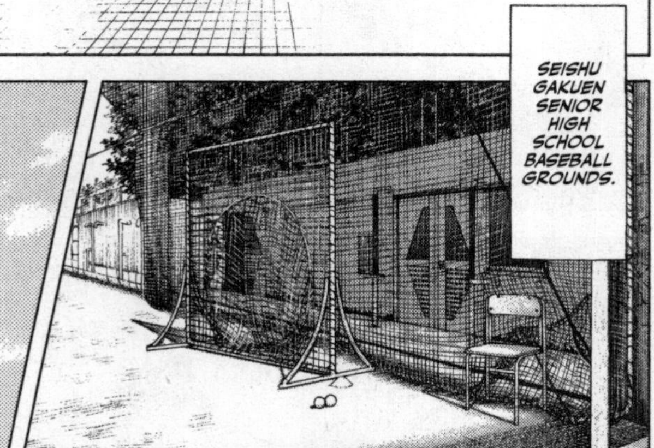
SEISHU GAKUEN SENIOR HIGH SCHOOL BASEBALL GROUNDS.

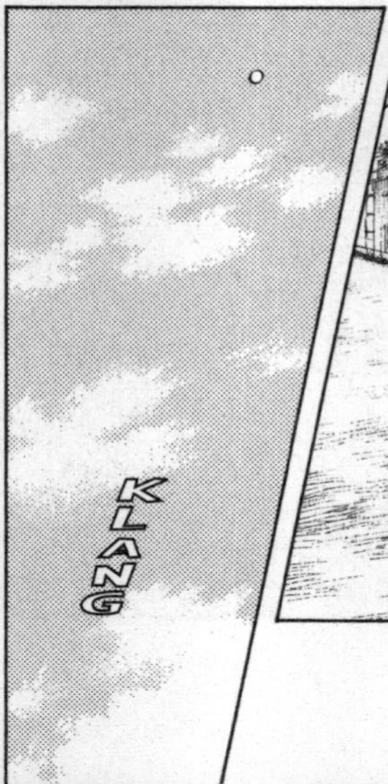
KLANG

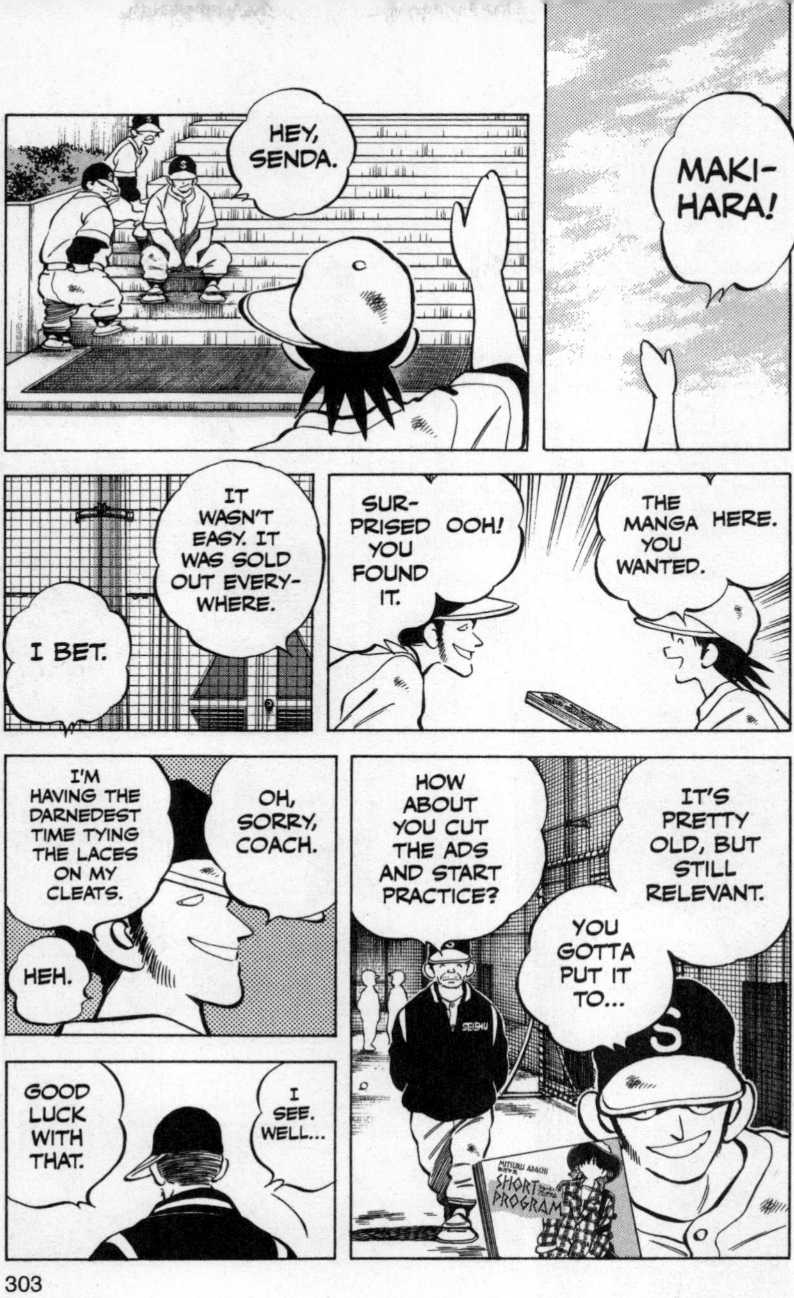
MAKI-HARA!
HEY, SENDA.
HERE. THE MANGA YOU WANTED.
OOH! SUR-PRISED YOU FOUND IT.
IT WASN'T EASY. IT WAS SOLD OUT EVERY-WHERE.
I BET.
IT'S PRETTY OLD, BUT STILL RELEVANT.
YOU GOTTA PUT IT TO...
HOW ABOUT YOU CUT THE ADS AND START PRACTICE?
MITSURU ADACHI
SHORT PROGRAM
SEISHU
OH, SORRY, COACH.
I'M HAVING THE DARNEDEST TIME TYING THE LACES ON MY CLEATS.
HEH.
I SEE. WELL...
GOOD LUCK WITH THAT.

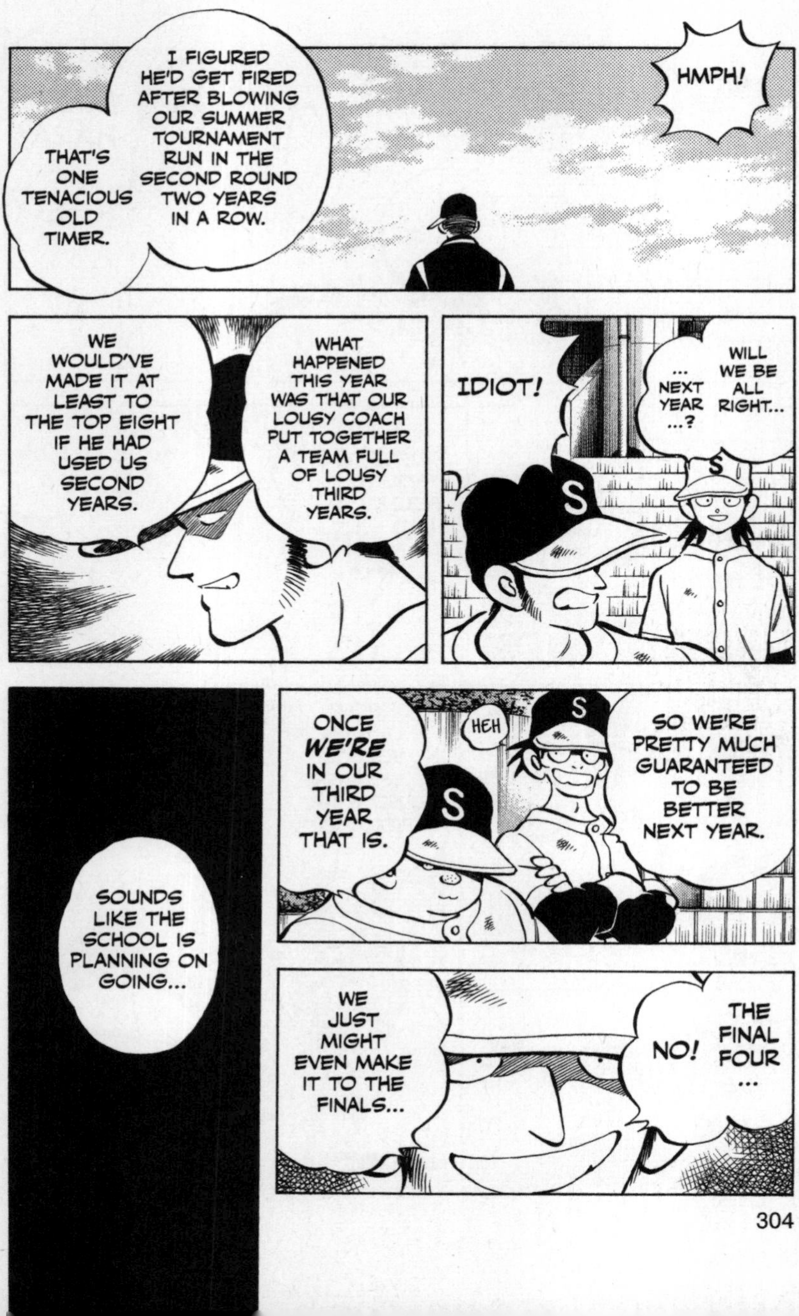
HMPH!
I FIGURED HE'D GET FIRED AFTER BLOWING OUR SUMMER TOURNAMENT RUN IN THE SECOND ROUND TWO YEARS IN A ROW.
THAT'S ONE TENACIOUS OLD TIMER.
WILL WE BE ALL RIGHT...
...NEXT YEAR...?
IDIOT!
WHAT HAPPENED THIS YEAR WAS THAT OUR LOUSY COACH PUT TOGETHER A TEAM FULL OF LOUSY THIRD YEARS.
WE WOULD'VE MADE IT AT LEAST TO THE TOP EIGHT IF HE HAD USED US SECOND YEARS.
SO WE'RE PRETTY MUCH GUARANTEED TO BE BETTER NEXT YEAR.
HEH
ONCE *WE'RE* IN OUR THIRD YEAR THAT IS.
THE FINAL FOUR...
NO!
WE JUST MIGHT EVEN MAKE IT TO THE FINALS...
SOUNDS LIKE THE SCHOOL IS PLANNING ON GOING...

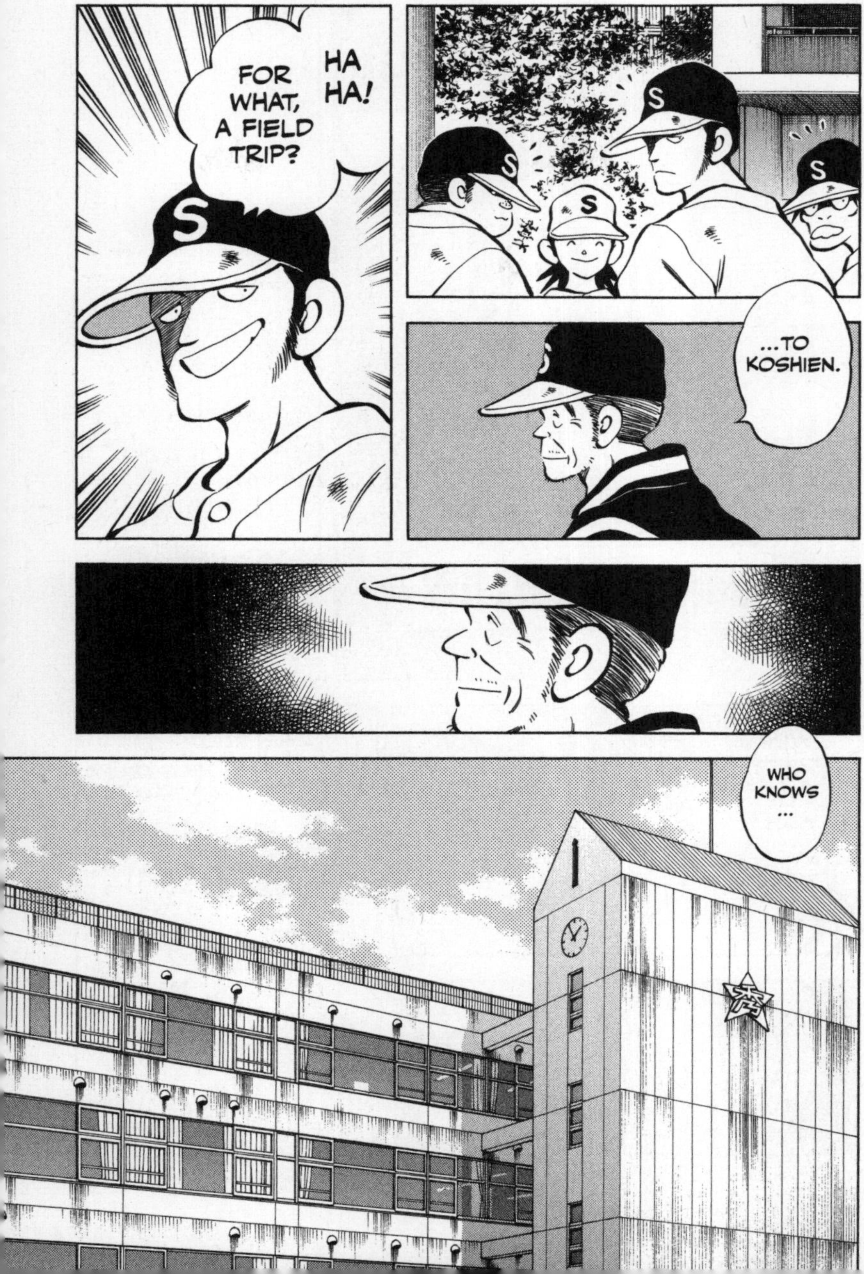
...TO KOSHIEN.
HA HA!
FOR WHAT, A FIELD TRIP?
WHO KNOWS ...

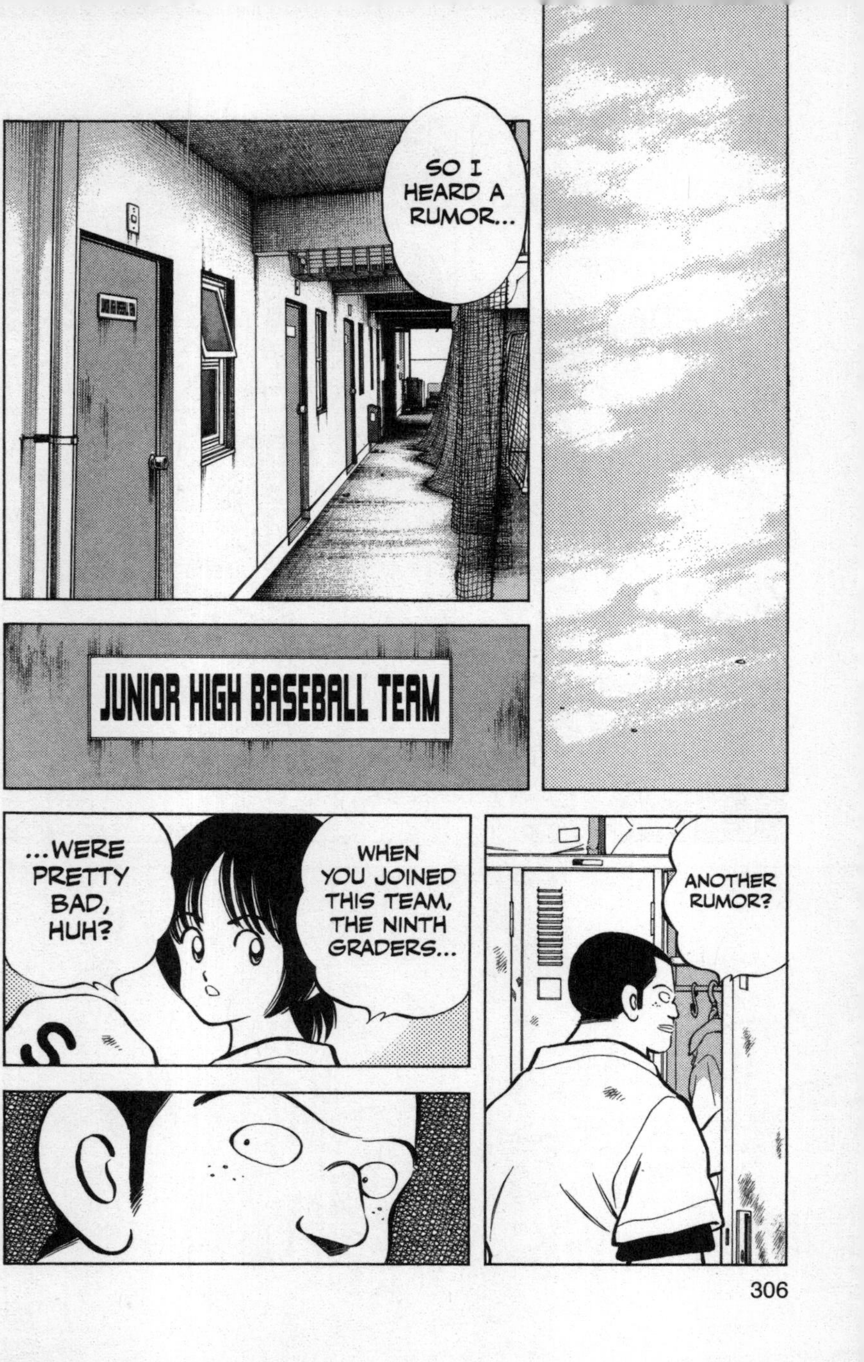
SO I HEARD A RUMOR...
JUNIOR HIGH BASEBALL TEAM
ANOTHER RUMOR?
WHEN YOU JOINED THIS TEAM, THE NINTH GRADERS...
...WERE PRETTY BAD, HUH?

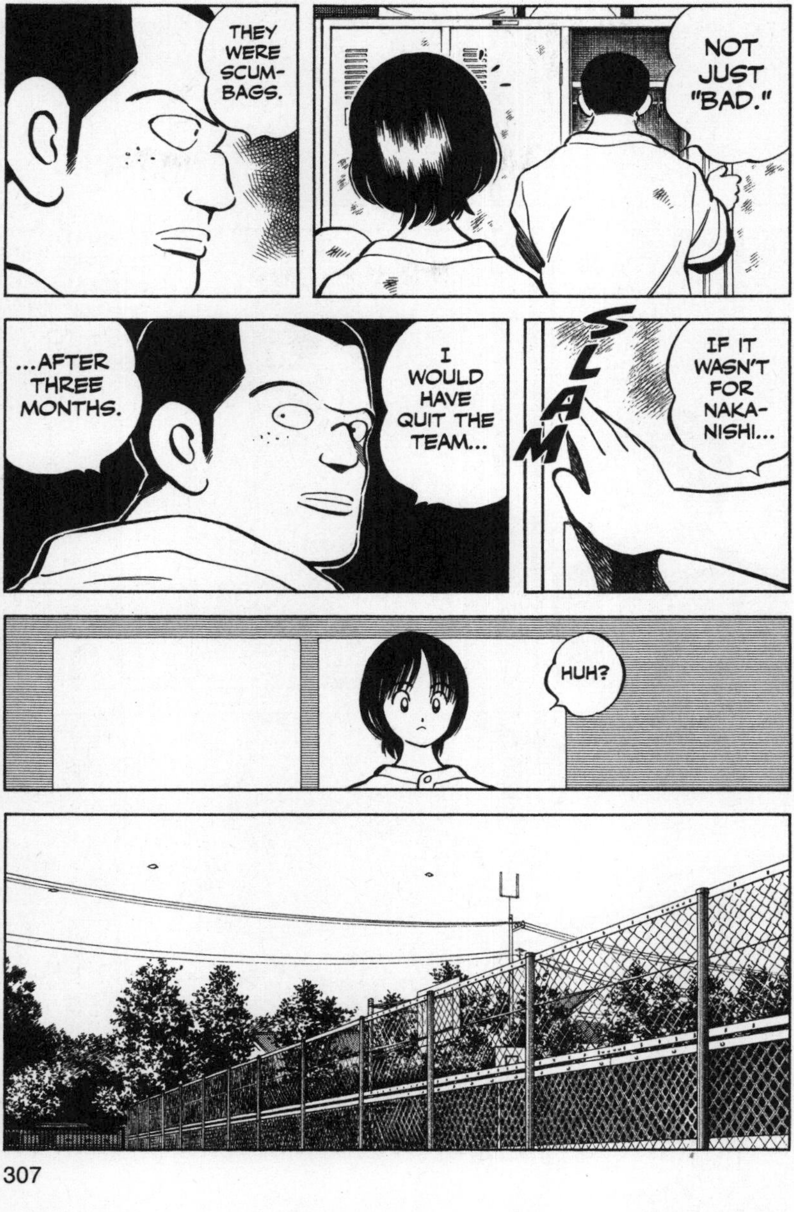

NOT JUST "BAD."
THEY WERE SCUM-BAGS.
IF IT WASN'T FOR NAKA-NISHI...
SLAM
I WOULD HAVE QUIT THE TEAM...
...AFTER THREE MONTHS.
HUH?

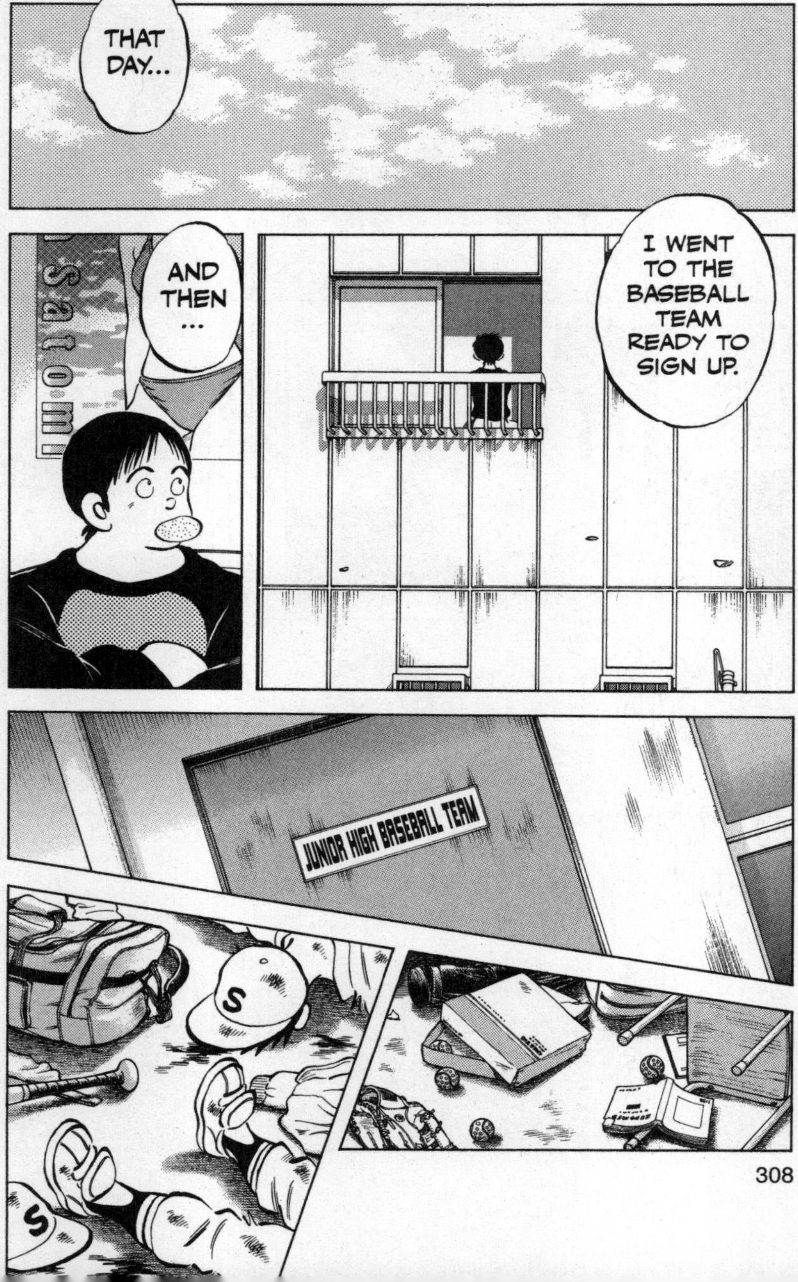
THAT DAY...
I WENT TO THE BASEBALL TEAM READY TO SIGN UP.
AND THEN ...
JUNIOR HIGH BASEBALL TEAM

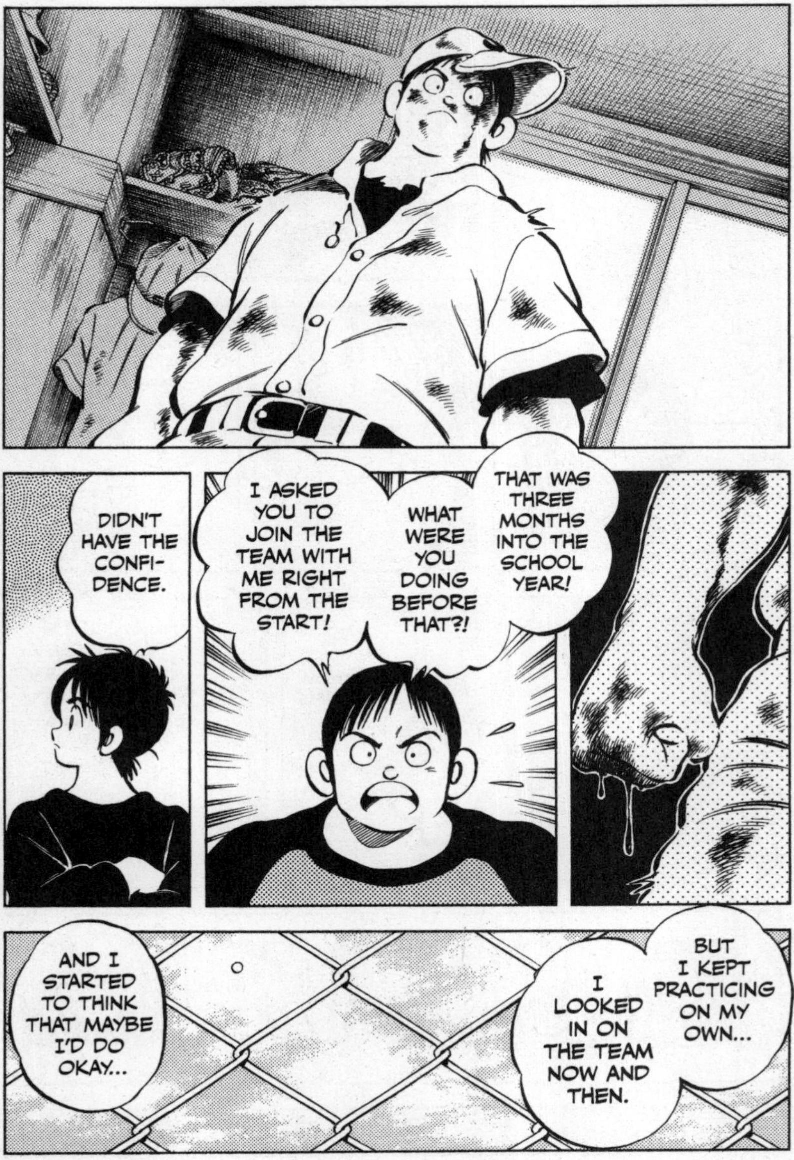
THAT WAS THREE MONTHS INTO THE SCHOOL YEAR!
WHAT WERE YOU DOING BEFORE THAT?!
I ASKED YOU TO JOIN THE TEAM WITH ME RIGHT FROM THE START!
DIDN'T HAVE THE CONFI- DENCE.
BUT I KEPT PRACTICING ON MY OWN...
I LOOKED IN ON THE TEAM NOW AND THEN.
AND I STARTED TO THINK THAT MAYBE I'D DO OKAY...

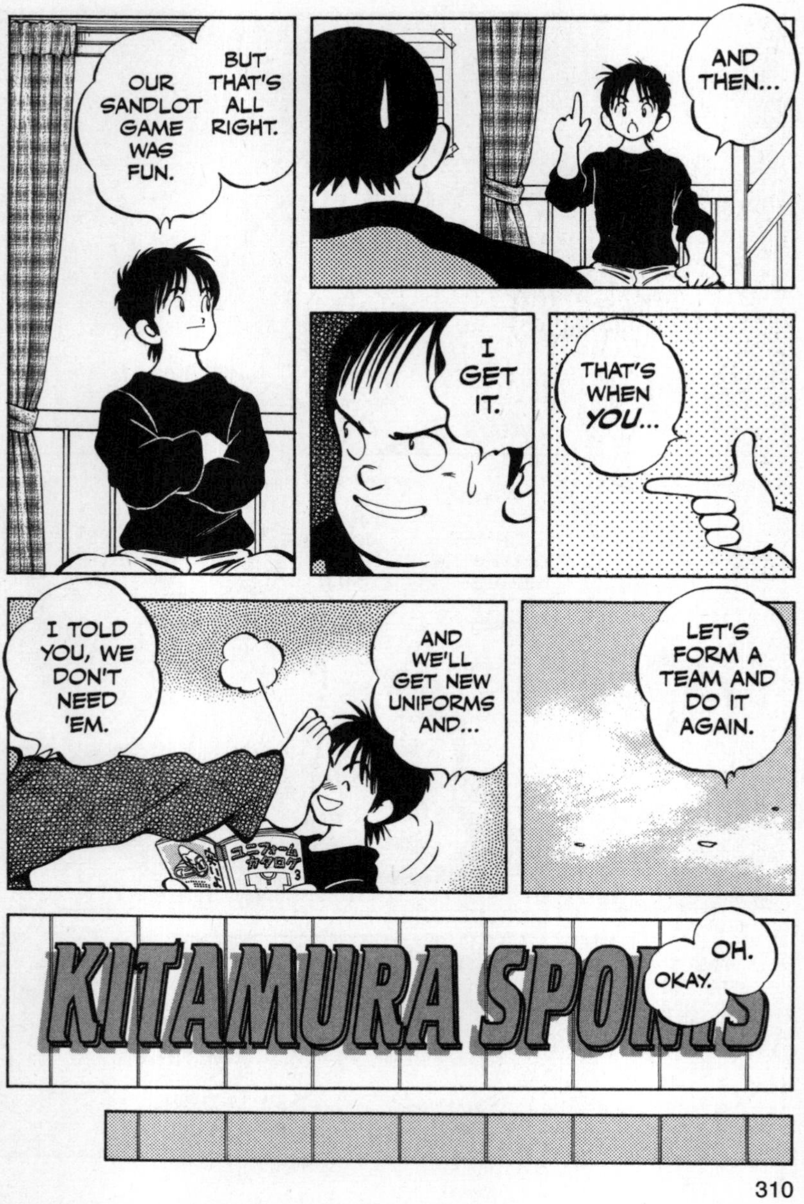
AND THEN...
THAT'S WHEN YOU...
I GET IT.
BUT THAT'S ALL RIGHT.
OUR SANDLOT GAME WAS FUN.
LET'S FORM A TEAM AND DO IT AGAIN.
AND WE'LL GET NEW UNIFORMS AND...
I TOLD YOU, WE DON'T NEED 'EM.
ユニフォームカタログ
KITAMURA SPORTS
OH. OKAY.

SO NEXT YEAR...

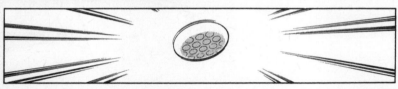

...WHEN YOU START HIGH SCHOOL, THOSE SCUMBAGS ARE GONNA BE WAITING, HUH?

W⁴AP

I'M LOOKING FORWARD TO IT.

YEAH...

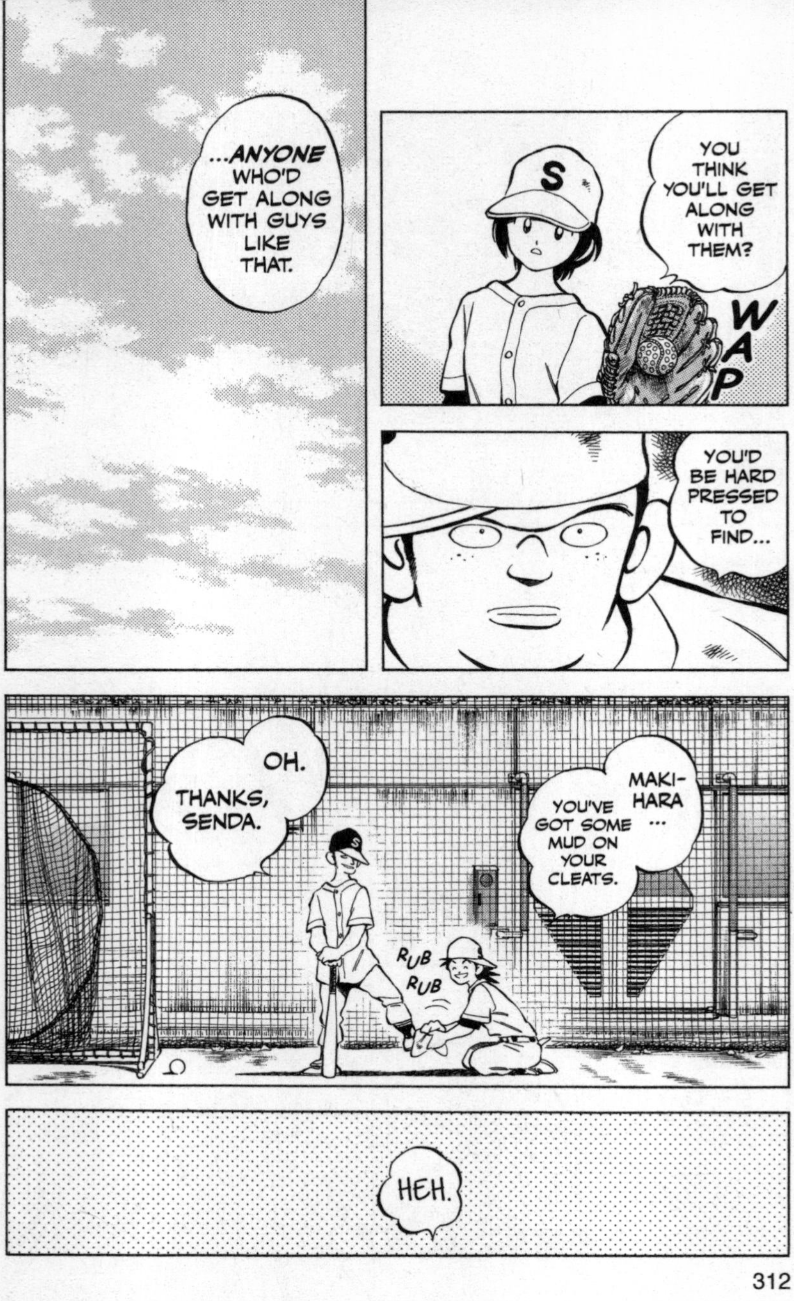
YOU THINK YOU'LL GET ALONG WITH THEM?
WAP
YOU'D BE HARD PRESSED TO FIND...
...ANYONE WHO'D GET ALONG WITH GUYS LIKE THAT.
MAKI-HARA ...
YOU'VE GOT SOME MUD ON YOUR CLEATS.
OH.
THANKS, SENDA.
RUB RUB
HEH.

Hope it's worth the wait! MEOW

K.K

CHAPTER 7
AMAZING
JR. HIGH STUDENT

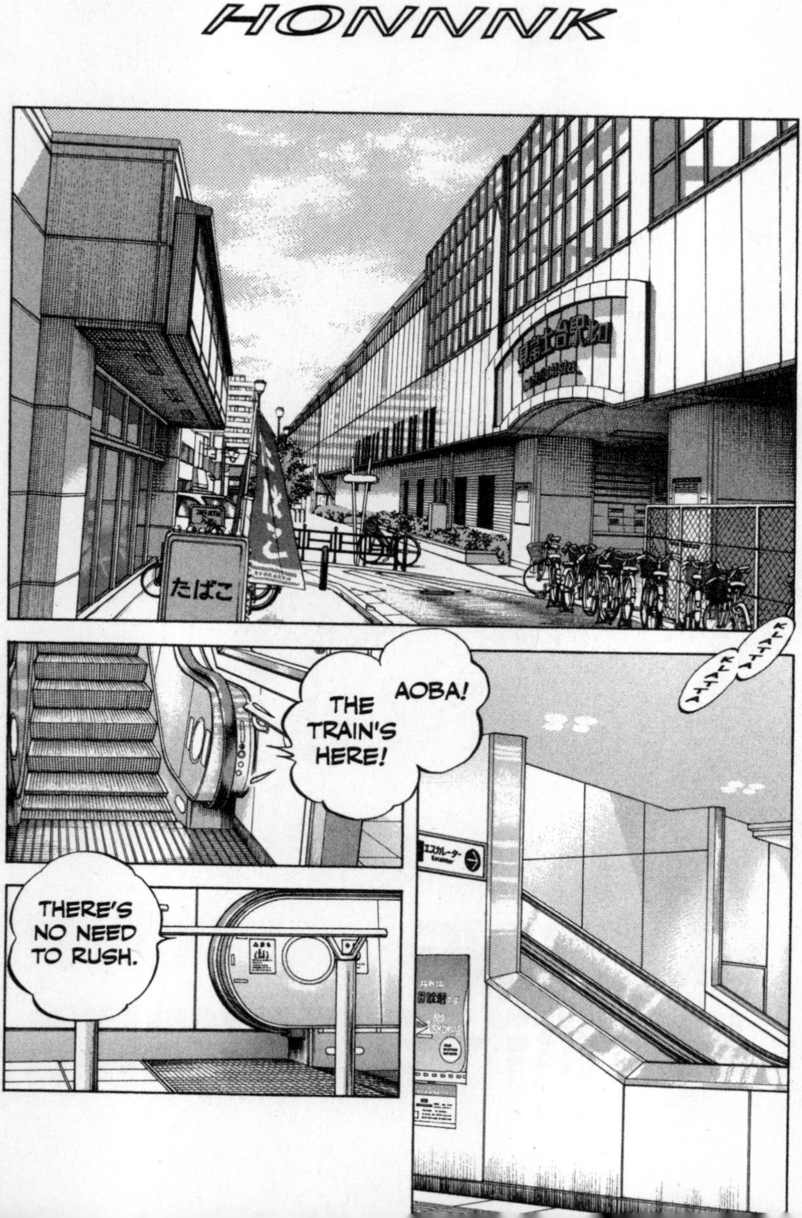
HONNNK
たばこ
KLATTA KLATTA
エスカレーター
AOBA! THE TRAIN'S HERE!
THERE'S NO NEED TO RUSH.

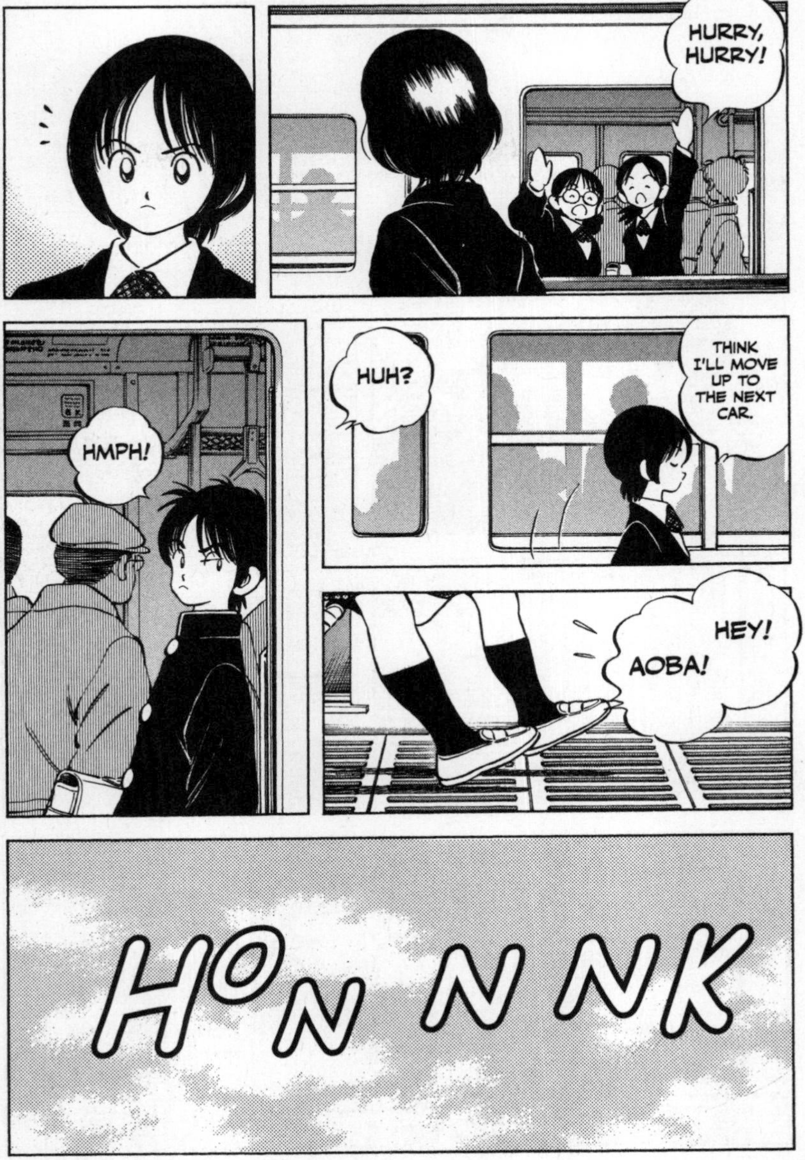
HURRY, HURRY!
THINK I'LL MOVE UP TO THE NEXT CAR.
HUH?
HEY! AOBA!
HMPH!
HONNNK

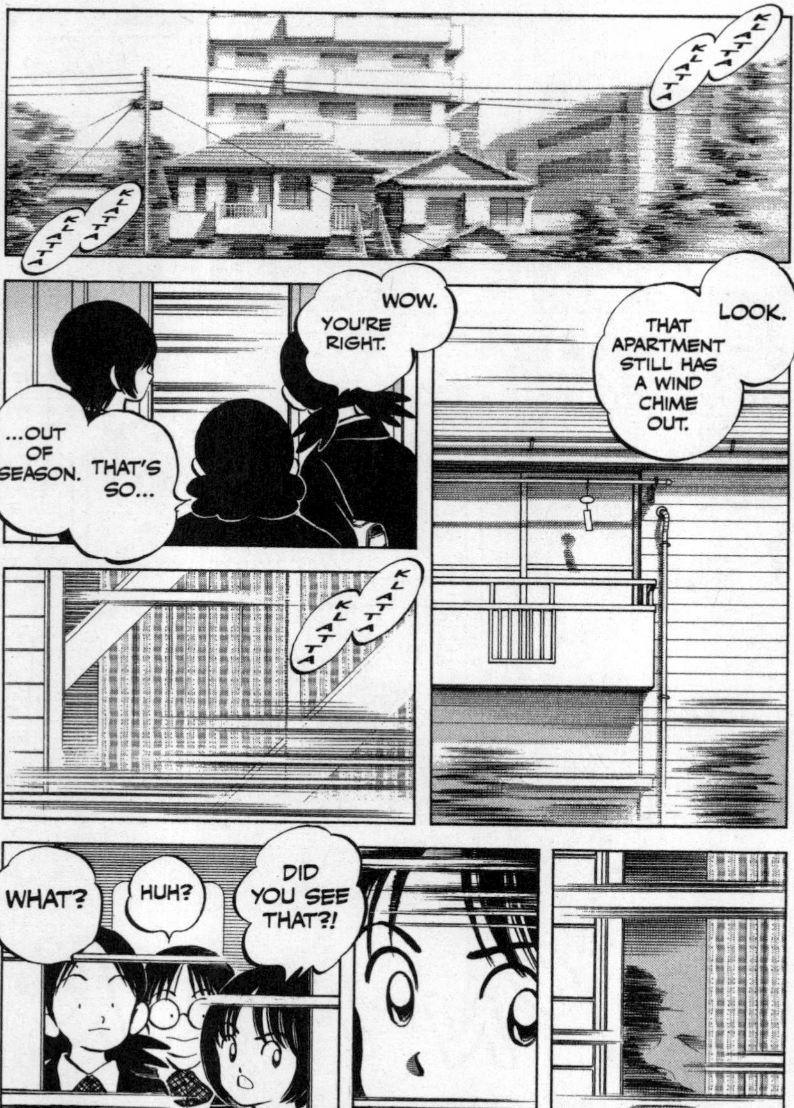
KLATTA KLATTA
KLATTA KLATTA
LOOK.
THAT APARTMENT STILL HAS A WIND CHIME OUT.
WOW. YOU'RE RIGHT.
THAT'S SO...
...OUT OF SEASON.
KLATTA KLATTA
DID YOU SEE THAT?!
HUH?
WHAT?

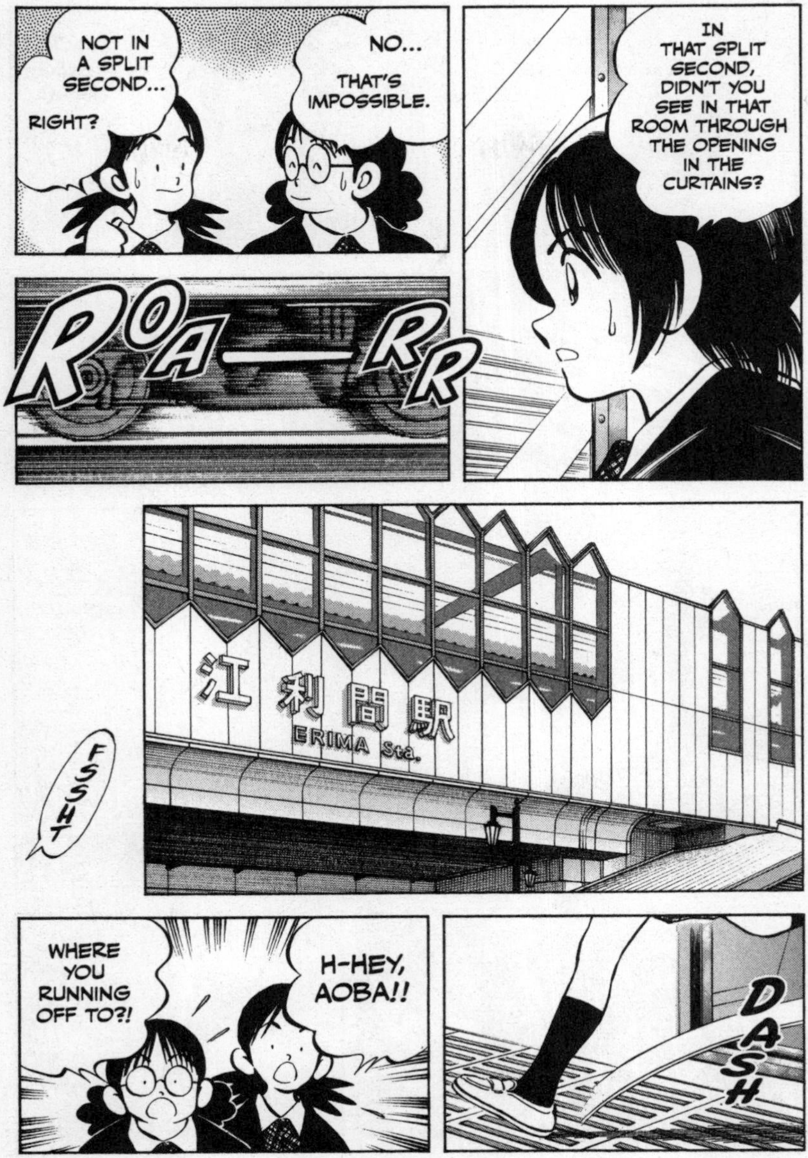
IN THAT SPLIT SECOND, DIDN'T YOU SEE IN THAT ROOM THROUGH THE OPENING IN THE CURTAINS?
NO...
THAT'S IMPOSSIBLE.
NOT IN A SPLIT SECOND...
RIGHT?
ROA—RR
江利間駅
ERIMA Sta.
FSSHT
DASH
H-HEY, AOBA!!
WHERE YOU RUNNING OFF TO?!

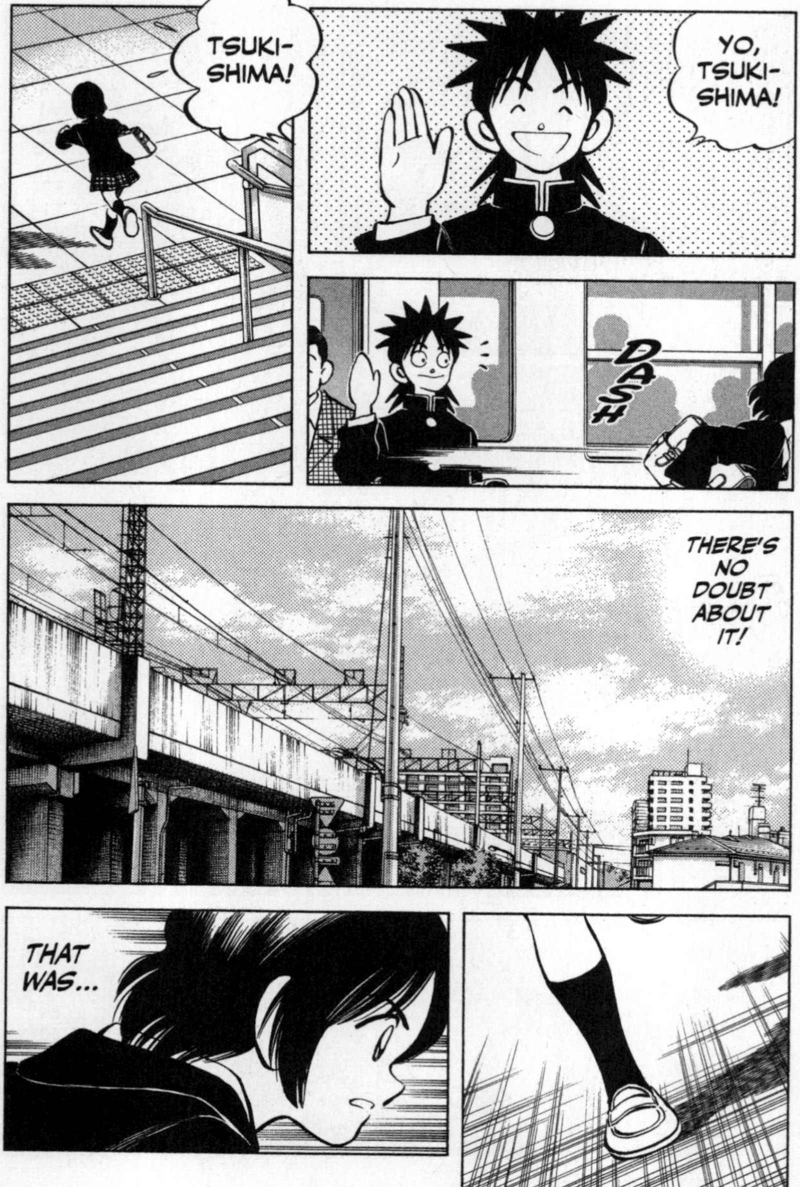
YO, TSUKI-SHIMA!
DASH
TSUKI-SHIMA!
THERE'S NO DOUBT ABOUT IT!
THAT WAS...

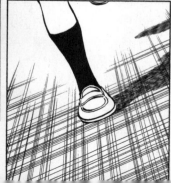

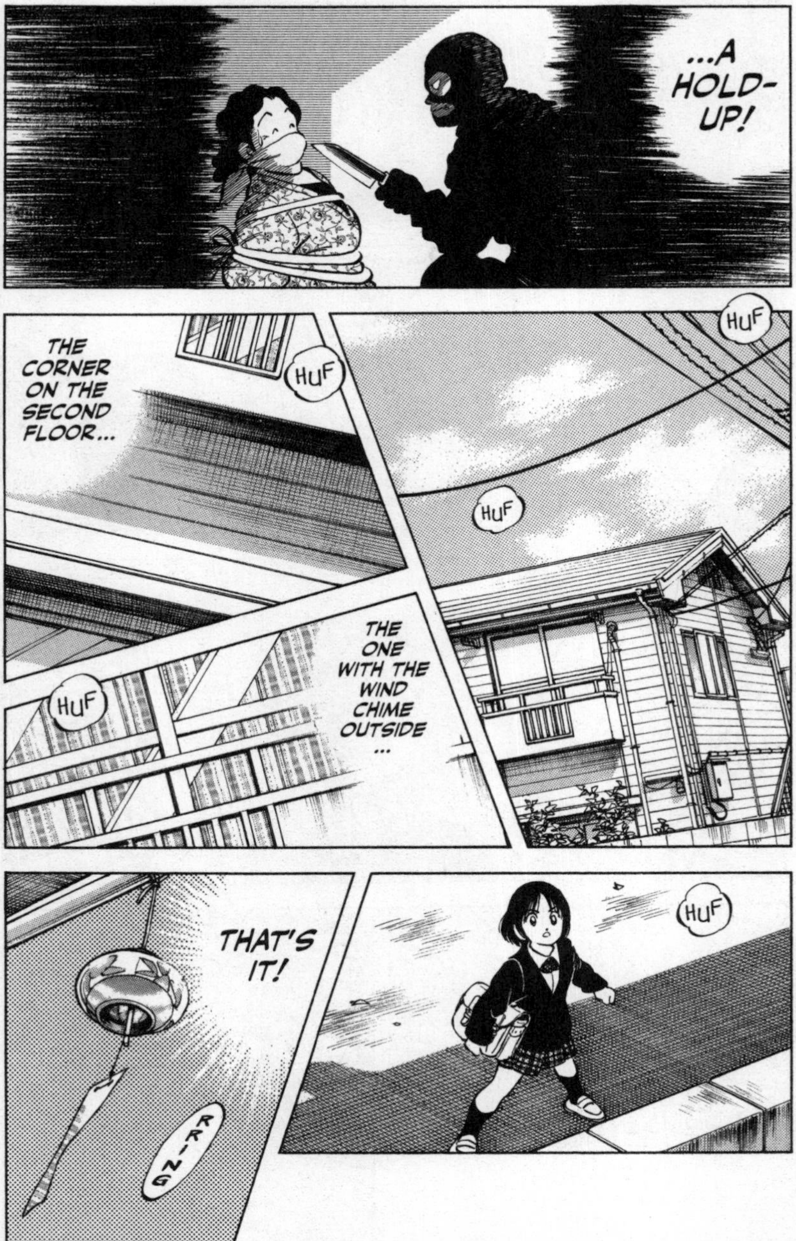

...A HOLD-UP!
HUF
HUF
THE CORNER ON THE SECOND FLOOR...
HUF
THE ONE WITH THE WIND CHIME OUTSIDE...
HUF
HUF
THAT'S IT!
RRING

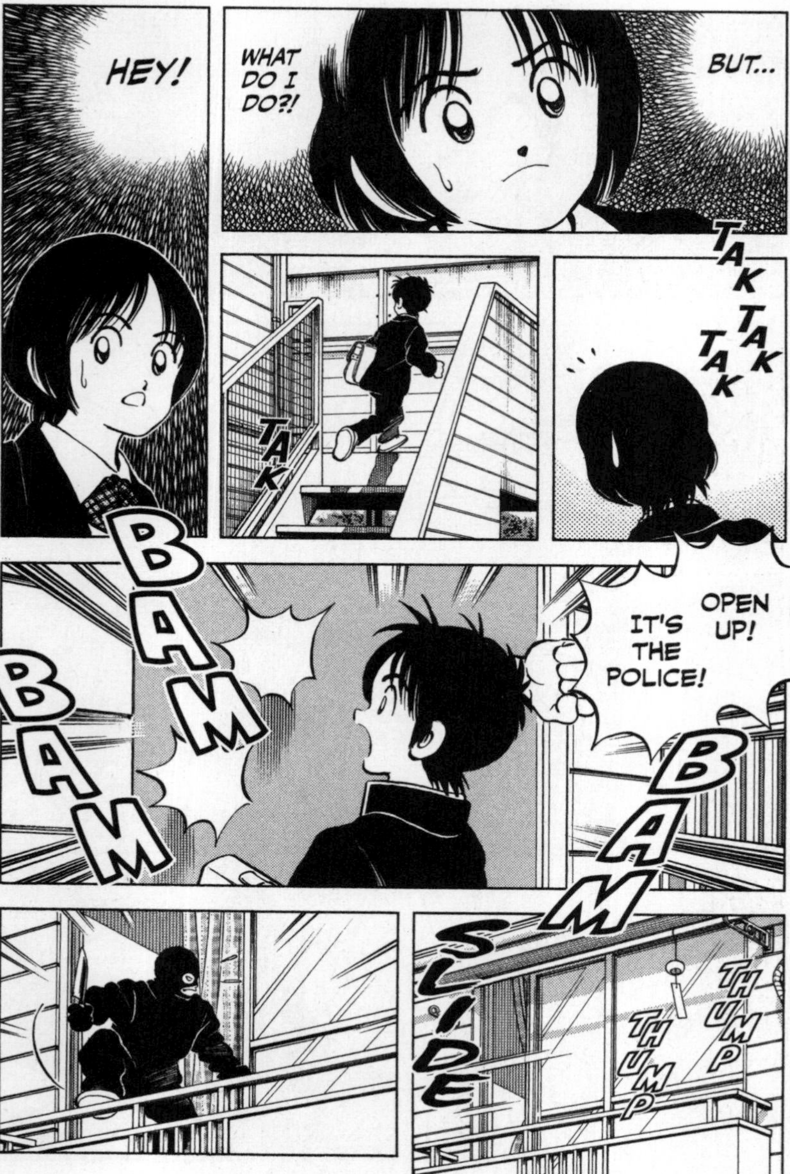
BUT...
WHAT DO I DO?!
TAK TAK TAK TAK
TAK
HEY!
OPEN UP! IT'S THE POLICE!
BAM BAM
BAM BAM
BAM BAM
SLIDE
THUMP THUMP

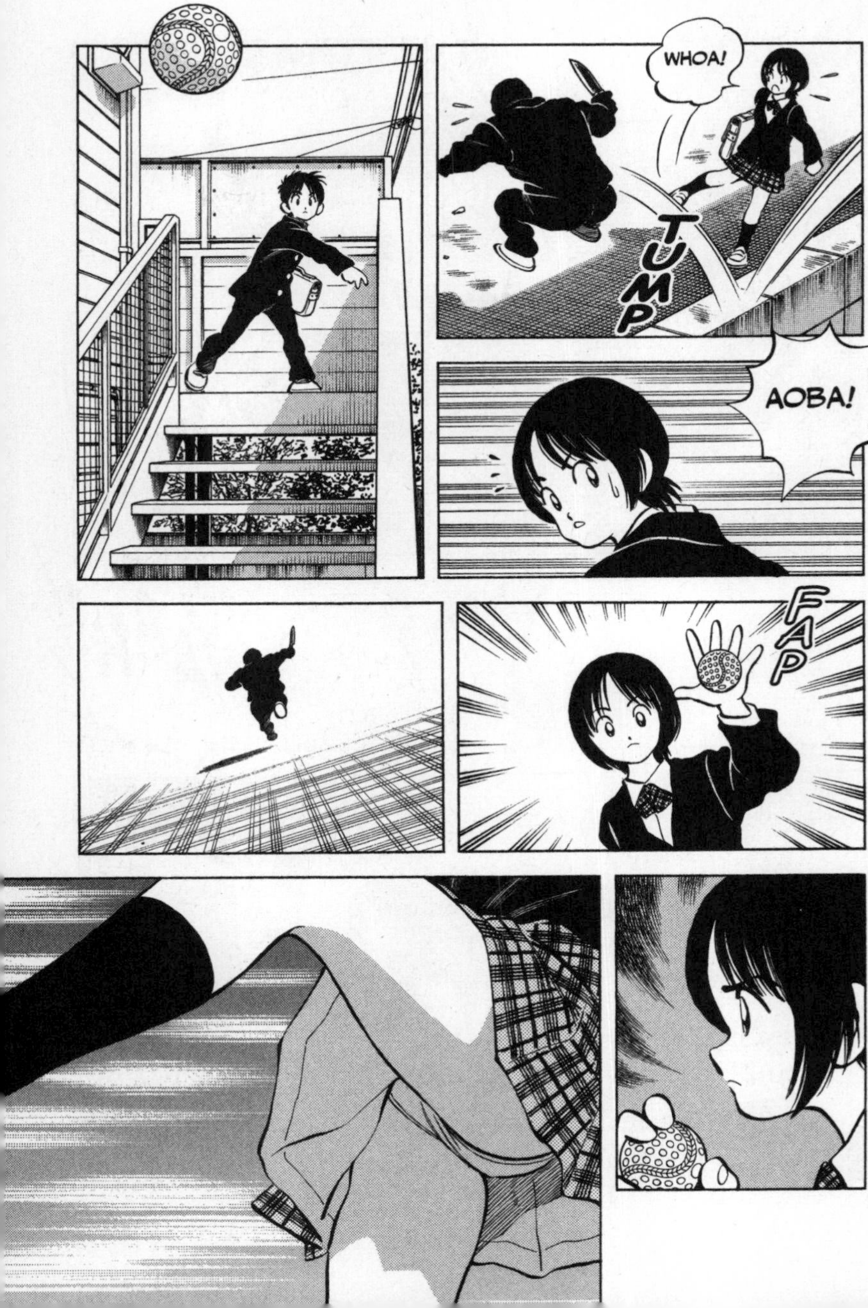
WHOA!
TUMP
AOBA!
FAP

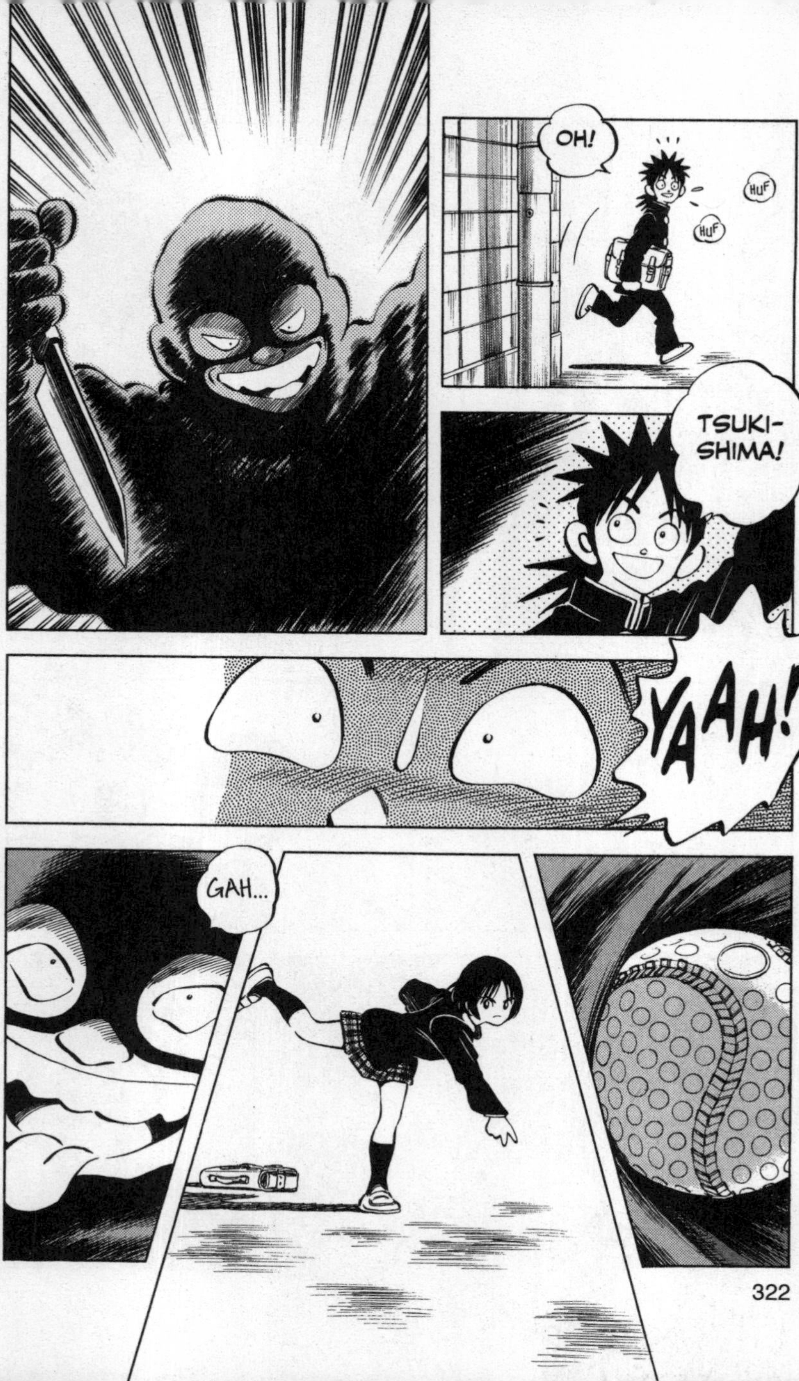

OH!
HUF
HUF
TSUKI-SHIMA!
YAAH!
GAH...

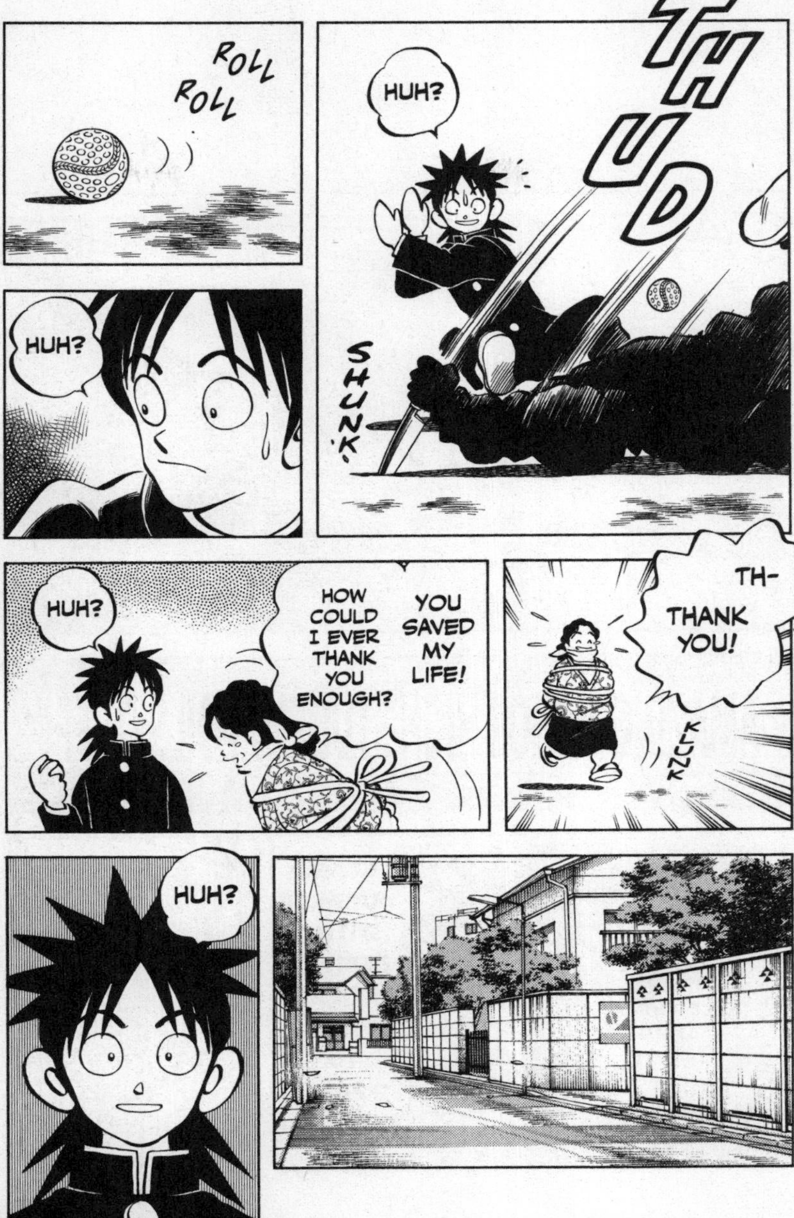
THUD
HUH?
SHUNK
ROLL ROLL
HUH?
TH- THANK YOU!
KLUNK
YOU SAVED MY LIFE!
HOW COULD I EVER THANK YOU ENOUGH?
HUH?
HUH?

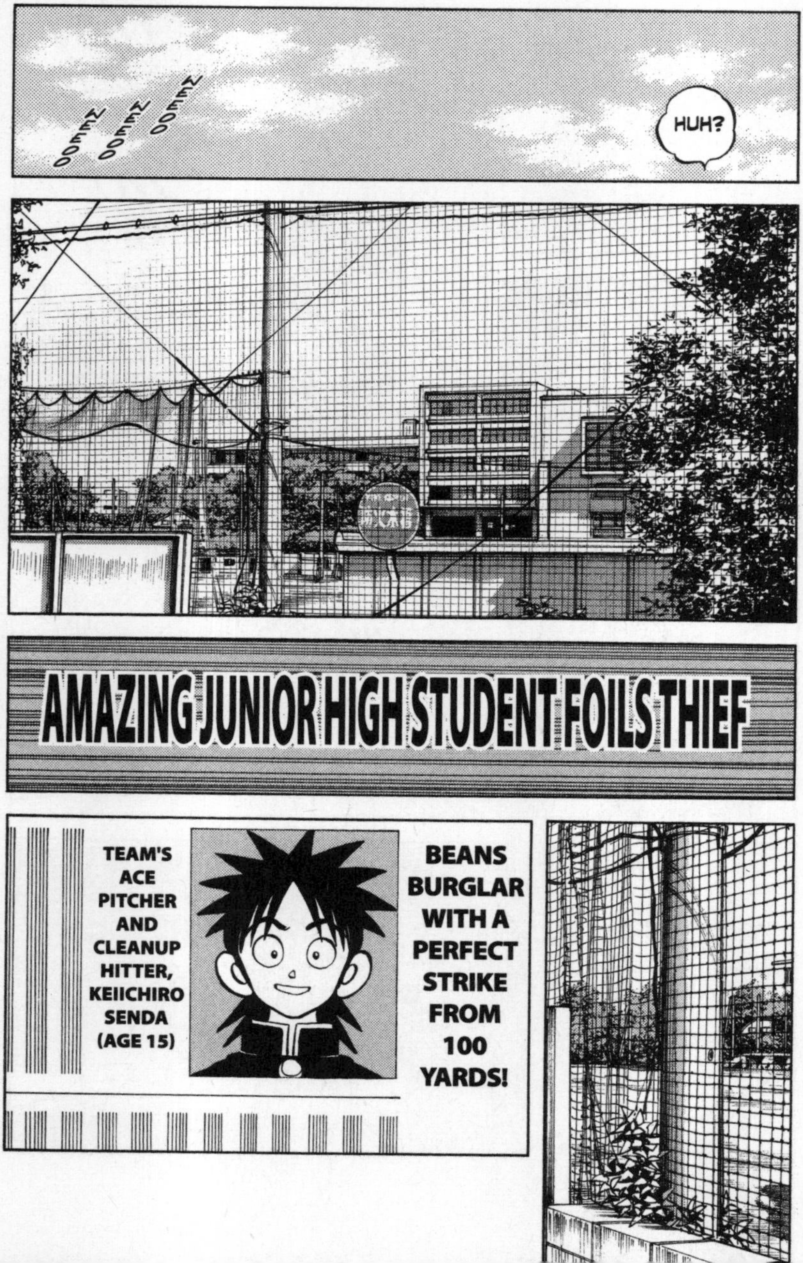
HUH?
WEEOO WEEOO WEEOO
AMAZING JUNIOR HIGH STUDENT FOILS THIEF
TEAM'S ACE PITCHER AND CLEANUP HITTER, KEIICHIRO SENDA (AGE 15)
BEANS BURGLAR WITH A PERFECT STRIKE FROM 100 YARDS!

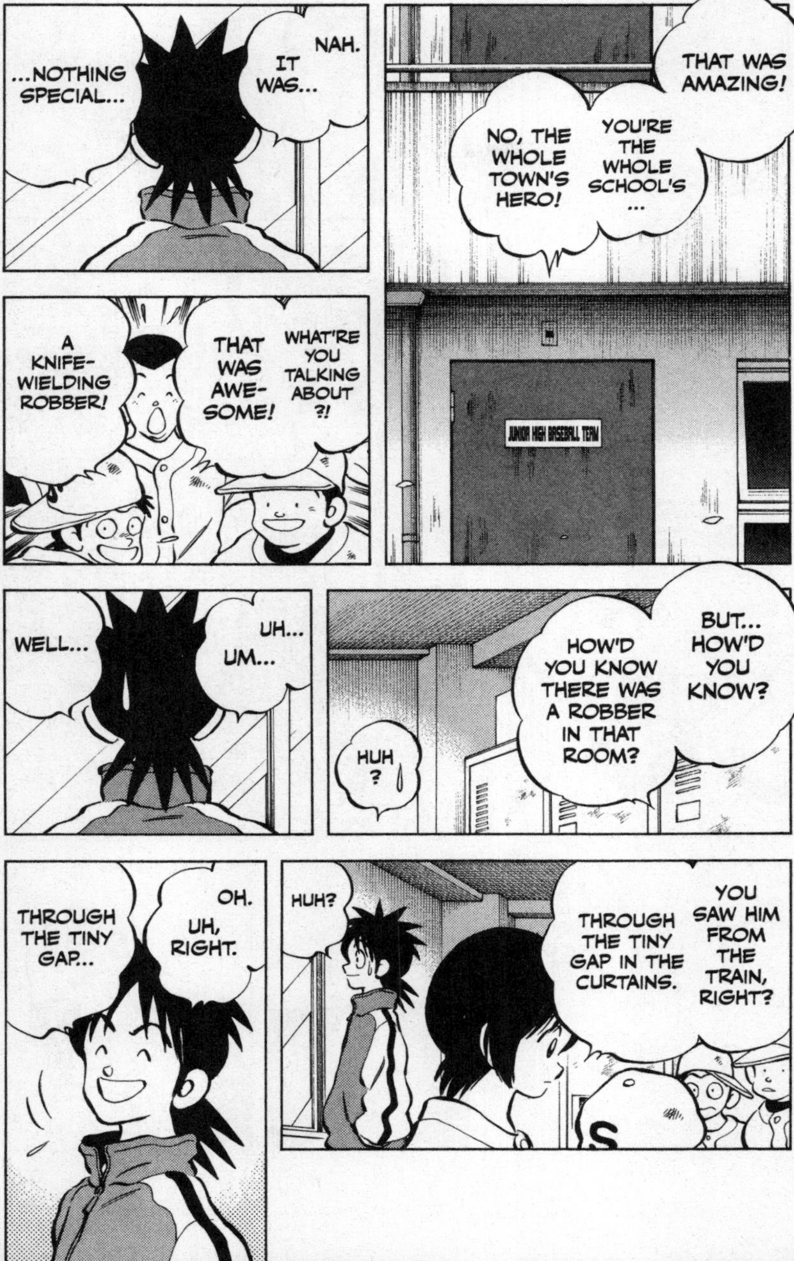
THAT WAS AMAZING!
YOU'RE THE WHOLE SCHOOL'S ...
NO, THE WHOLE TOWN'S HERO!
NAH. IT WAS...
...NOTHING SPECIAL...
JUNIOR HIGH BASEBALL TEAM
WHAT'RE YOU TALKING ABOUT ?!
THAT WAS AWE-SOME!
A KNIFE-WIELDING ROBBER!
BUT... HOW'D YOU KNOW?
HOW'D YOU KNOW THERE WAS A ROBBER IN THAT ROOM?
HUH ?
UH... UM...
WELL...
YOU SAW HIM FROM THE TRAIN, RIGHT?
THROUGH THE TINY GAP IN THE CURTAINS.
HUH?
OH. UH, RIGHT.
THROUGH THE TINY GAP...

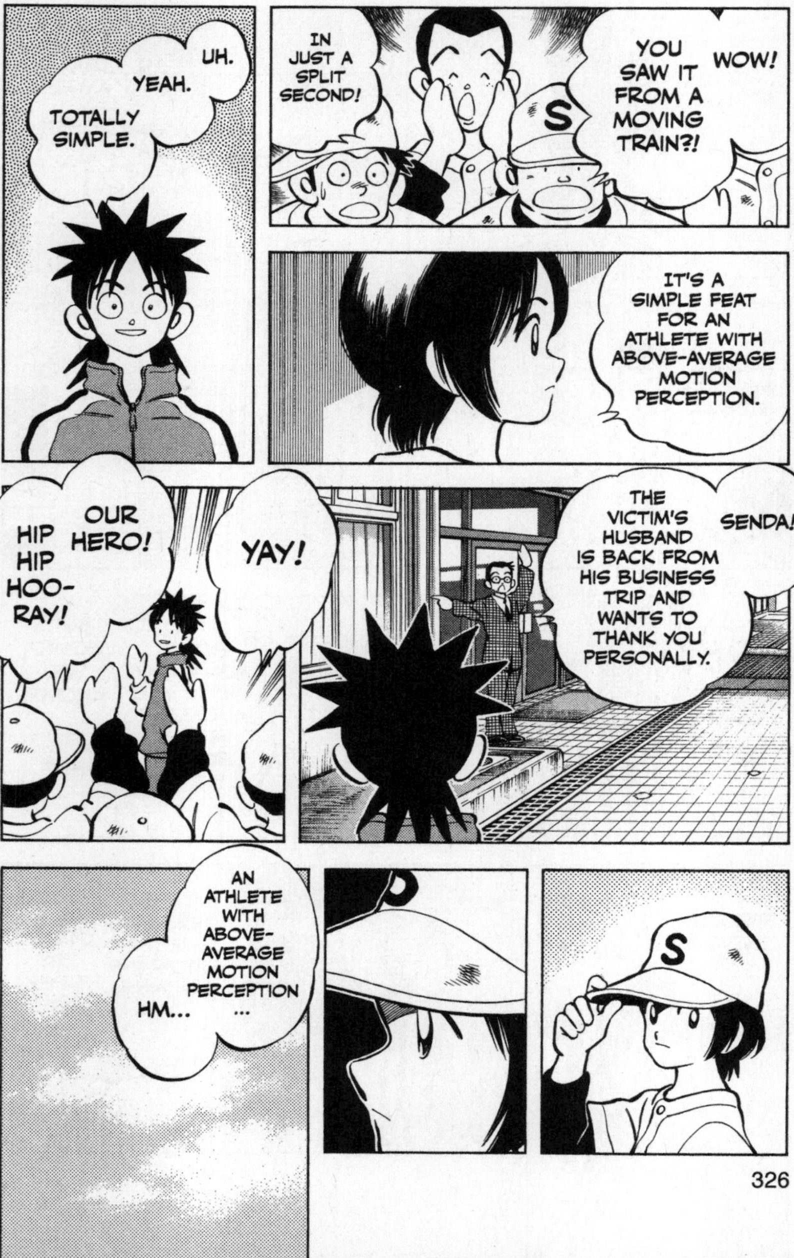
WOW!
YOU SAW IT FROM A MOVING TRAIN?!
IN JUST A SPLIT SECOND!
IT'S A SIMPLE FEAT FOR AN ATHLETE WITH ABOVE-AVERAGE MOTION PERCEPTION.
UH. YEAH. TOTALLY SIMPLE.
SENDA!
THE VICTIM'S HUSBAND IS BACK FROM HIS BUSINESS TRIP AND WANTS TO THANK YOU PERSONALLY.
YAY!
OUR HERO! HIP HIP HOO-RAY!
AN ATHLETE WITH ABOVE-AVERAGE MOTION PERCEPTION ...
HM...

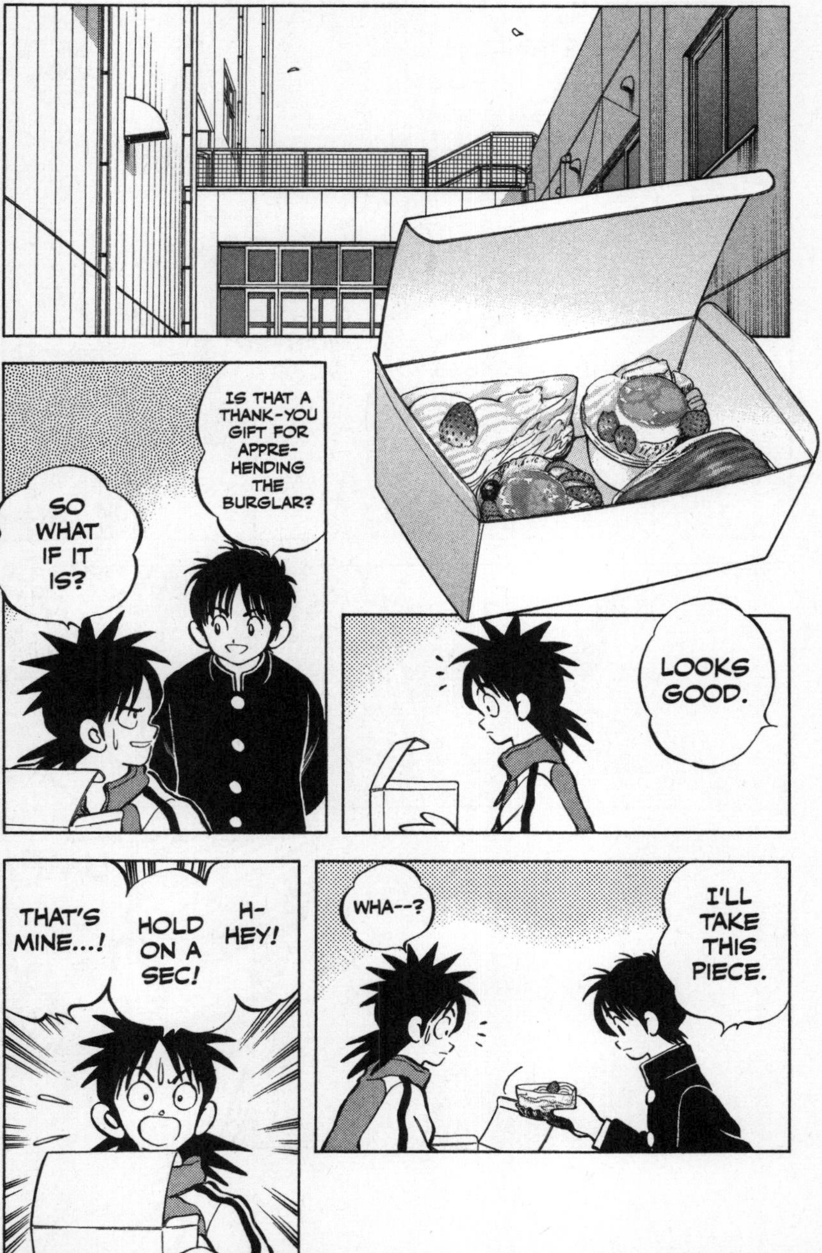
LOOKS GOOD.
IS THAT A THANK-YOU GIFT FOR APPRE-HENDING THE BURGLAR?
SO WHAT IF IT IS?
I'LL TAKE THIS PIECE.
WHA--?
H-HEY!
HOLD ON A SEC!
THAT'S MINE...!

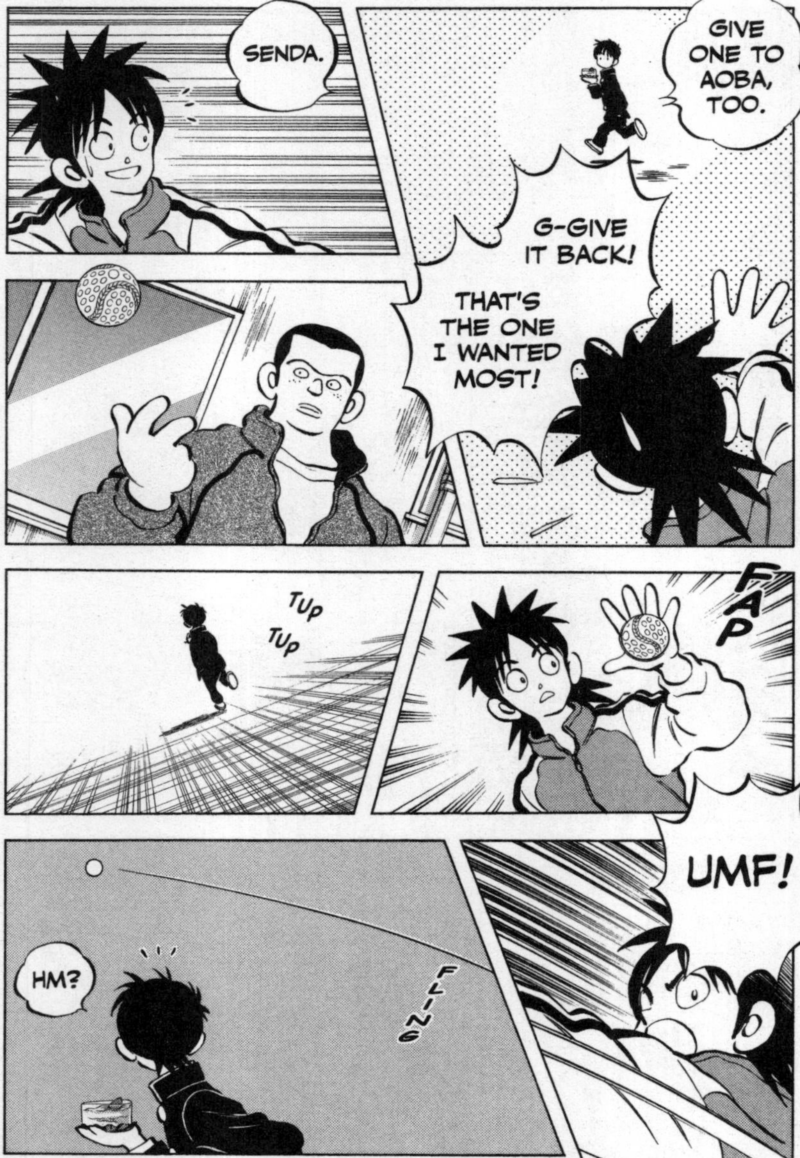
GIVE ONE TO AOBA, TOO.
SENDA.
G-GIVE IT BACK!
THAT'S THE ONE I WANTED MOST!
FAP
TUP
TUP
UMF!
FLING
HM?

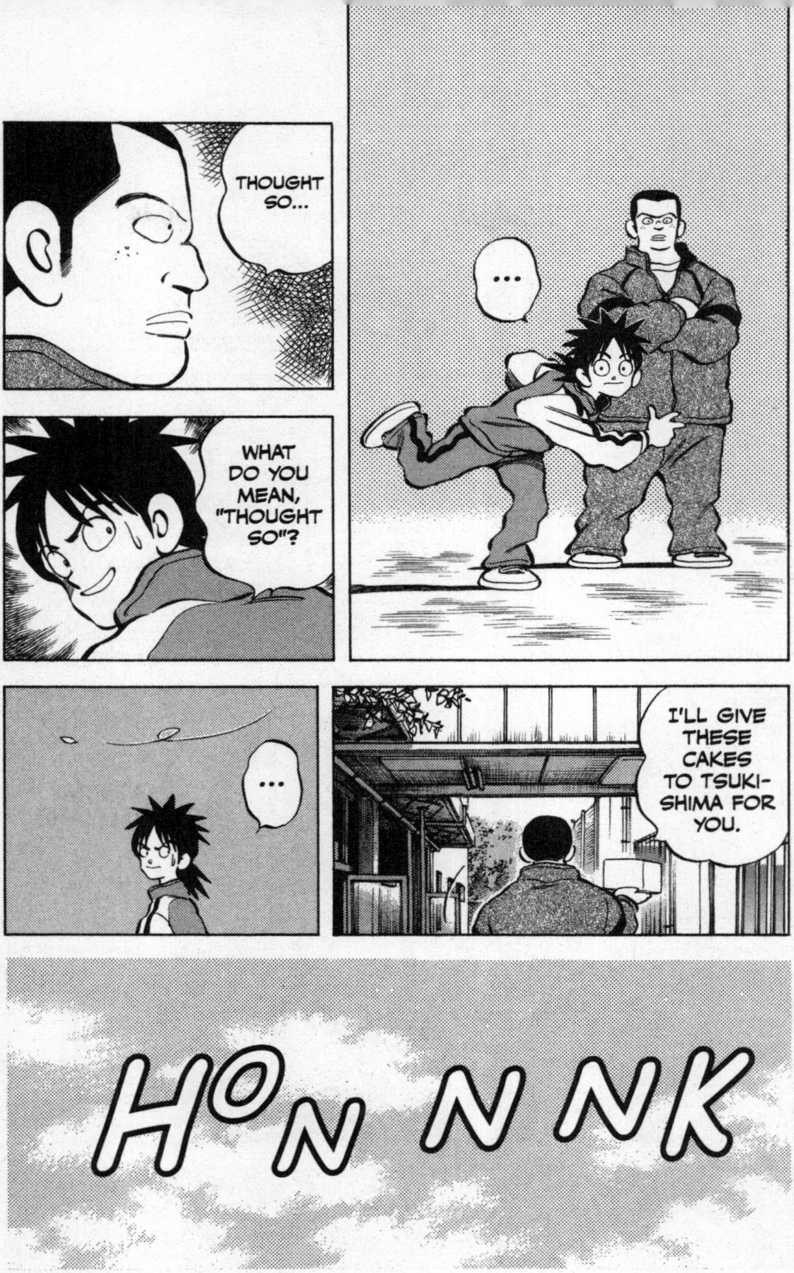
...
THOUGHT SO...
WHAT DO YOU MEAN, "THOUGHT SO"?
I'LL GIVE THESE CAKES TO TSUKI-SHIMA FOR YOU.
...
HONNNK

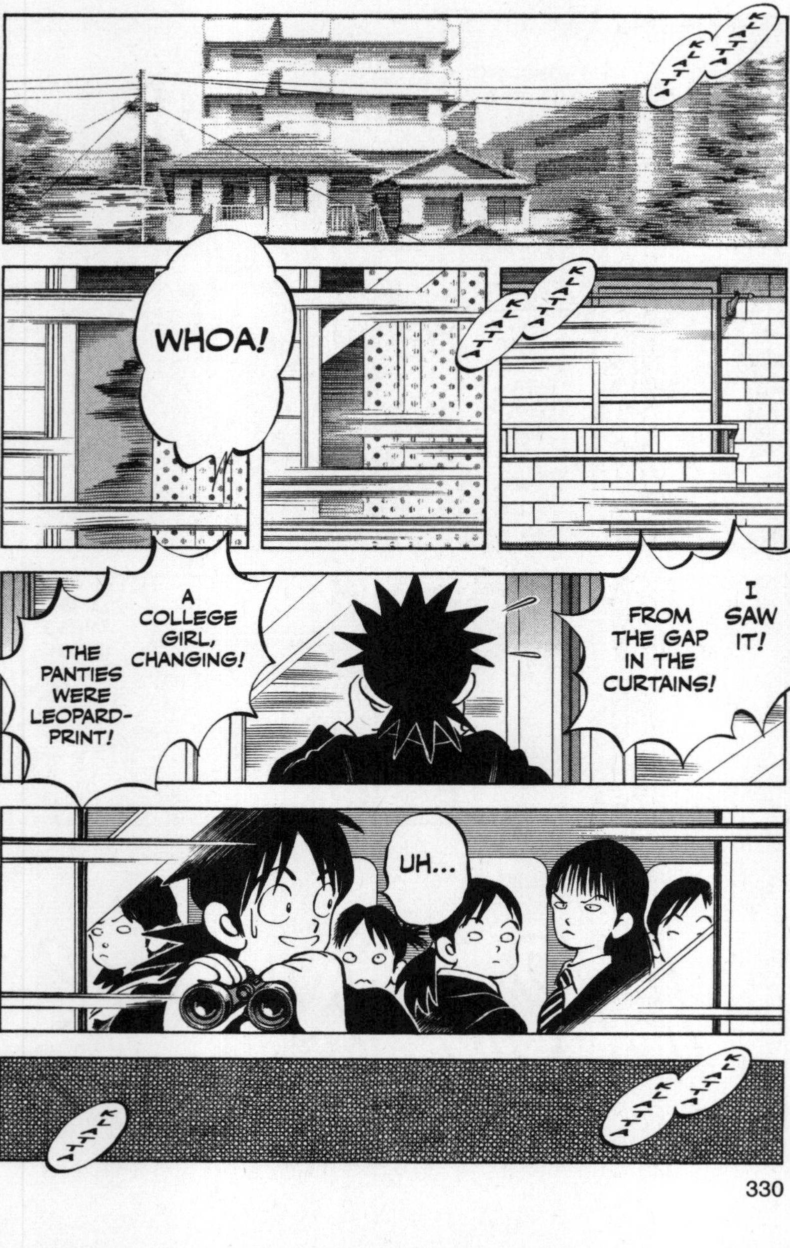
KLATTA KLATTA
KLATTA KLATTA
WHOA!
I SAW IT!
FROM THE GAP IN THE CURTAINS!
A COLLEGE GIRL, CHANGING!
THE PANTIES WERE LEOPARD-PRINT!
UH...
KLATTA KLATTA
KLATTA

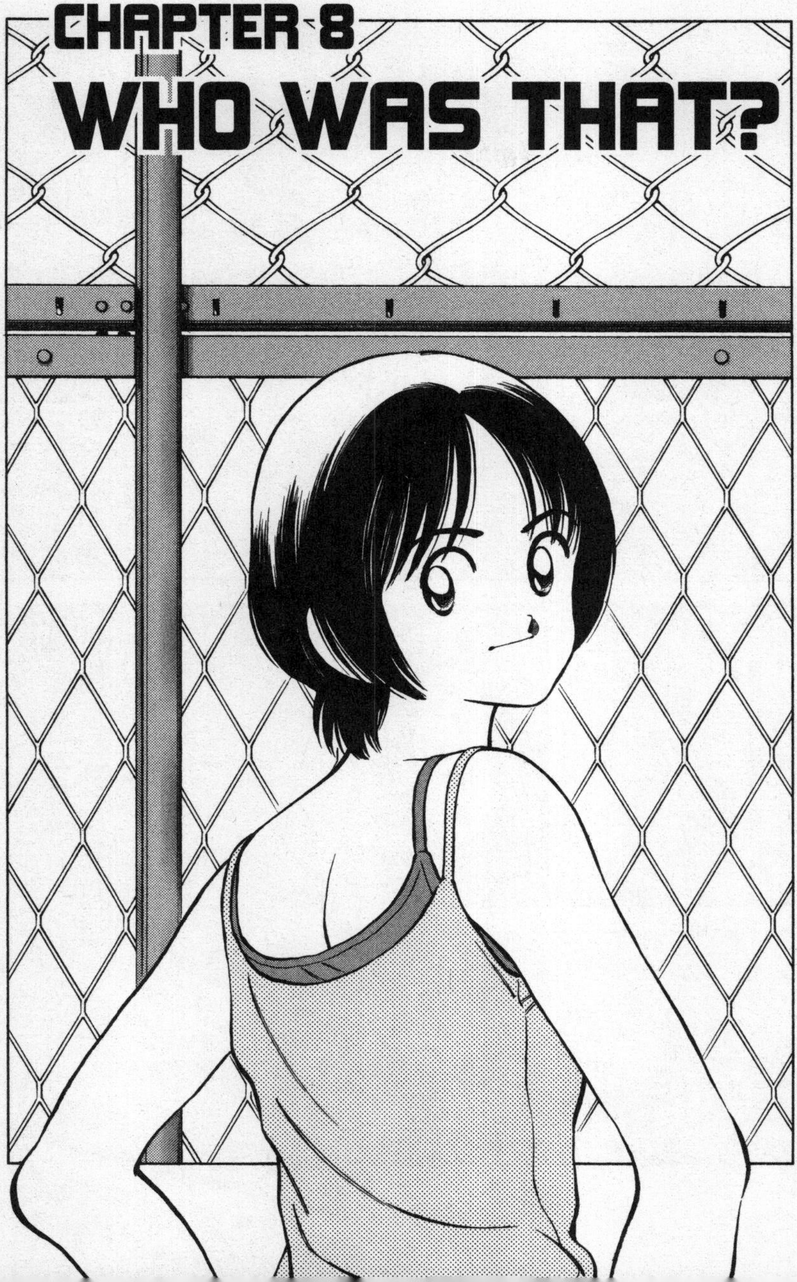
CHAPTER 8
WHO WAS THAT?

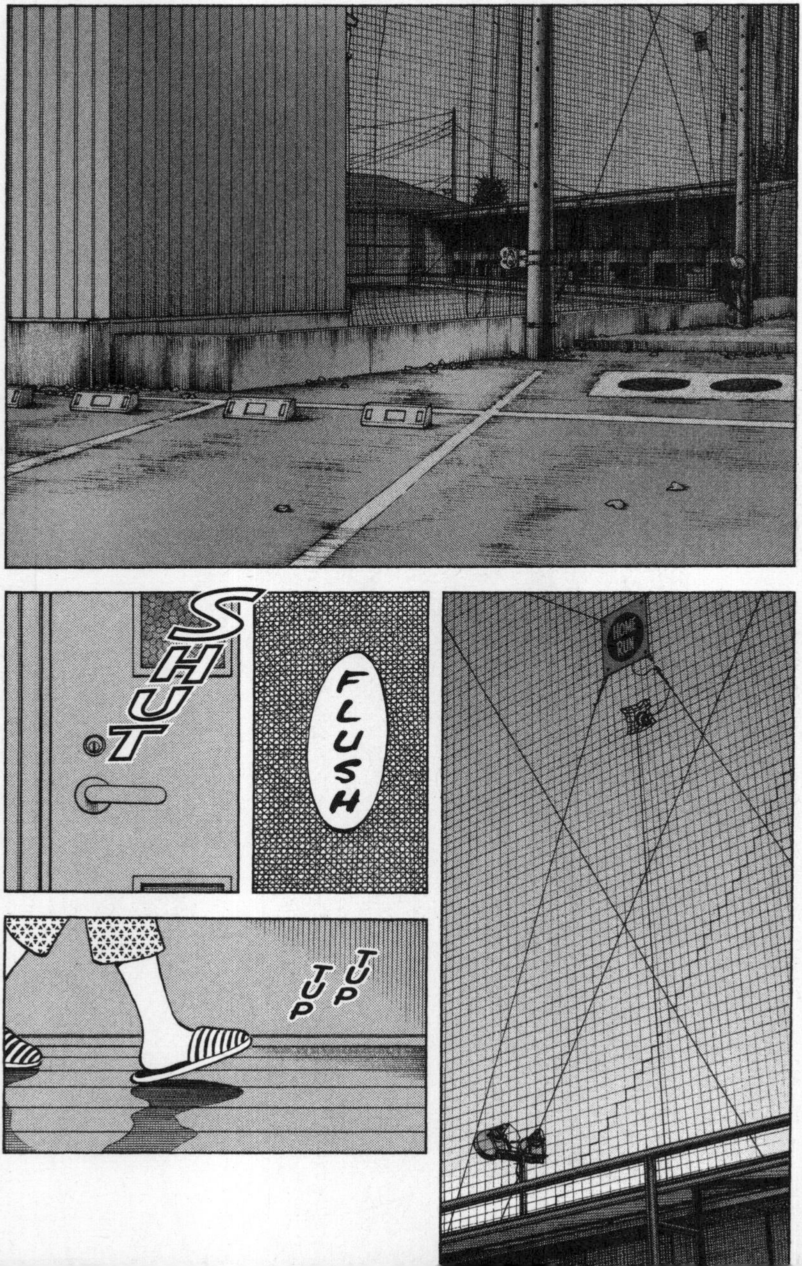
HOME RUN
FLUSH
SHUT
TUP TUP

YAWN.

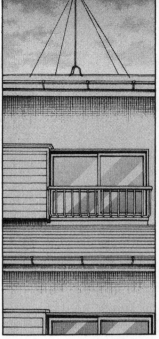

WAKABA & AOBA

SHUT

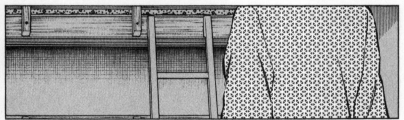

HEY, AOBA!

YOU'VE GOT THE TOP BUNK!

WHY DO I ALWAYS FIND YOU SLEEPING IN MY BED EVERY MORNING?!
BECAUSE IT'S SO COZY AND...
...WARM SLEEPING NEXT TO YOU...
SNIFF ...

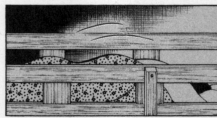

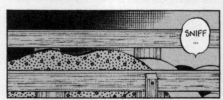

TWEET
TWEET
KLANG
KLANG
KLANG
MNCH
MNCH
ONE
TWO

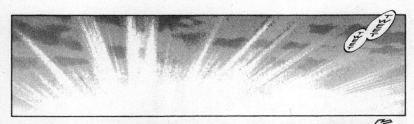

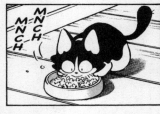

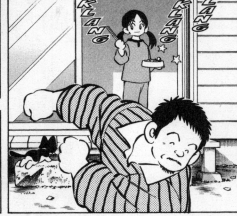

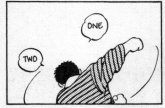

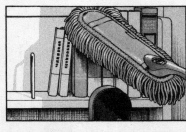

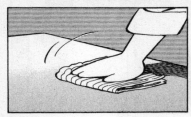

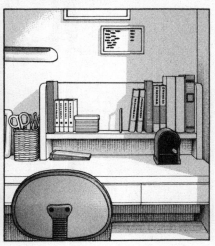

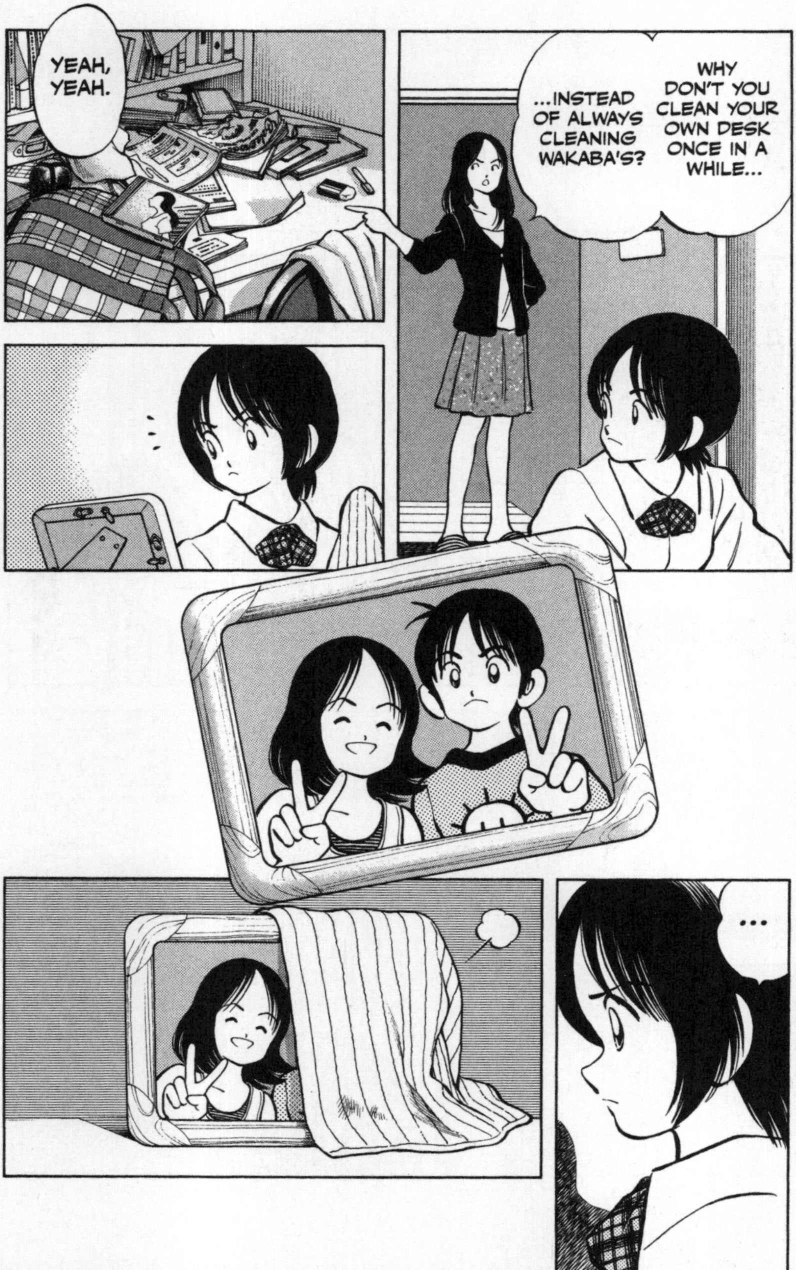
WHY DON'T YOU CLEAN YOUR OWN DESK ONCE IN A WHILE...
...INSTEAD OF ALWAYS CLEANING WAKABA'S?
YEAH, YEAH.
...

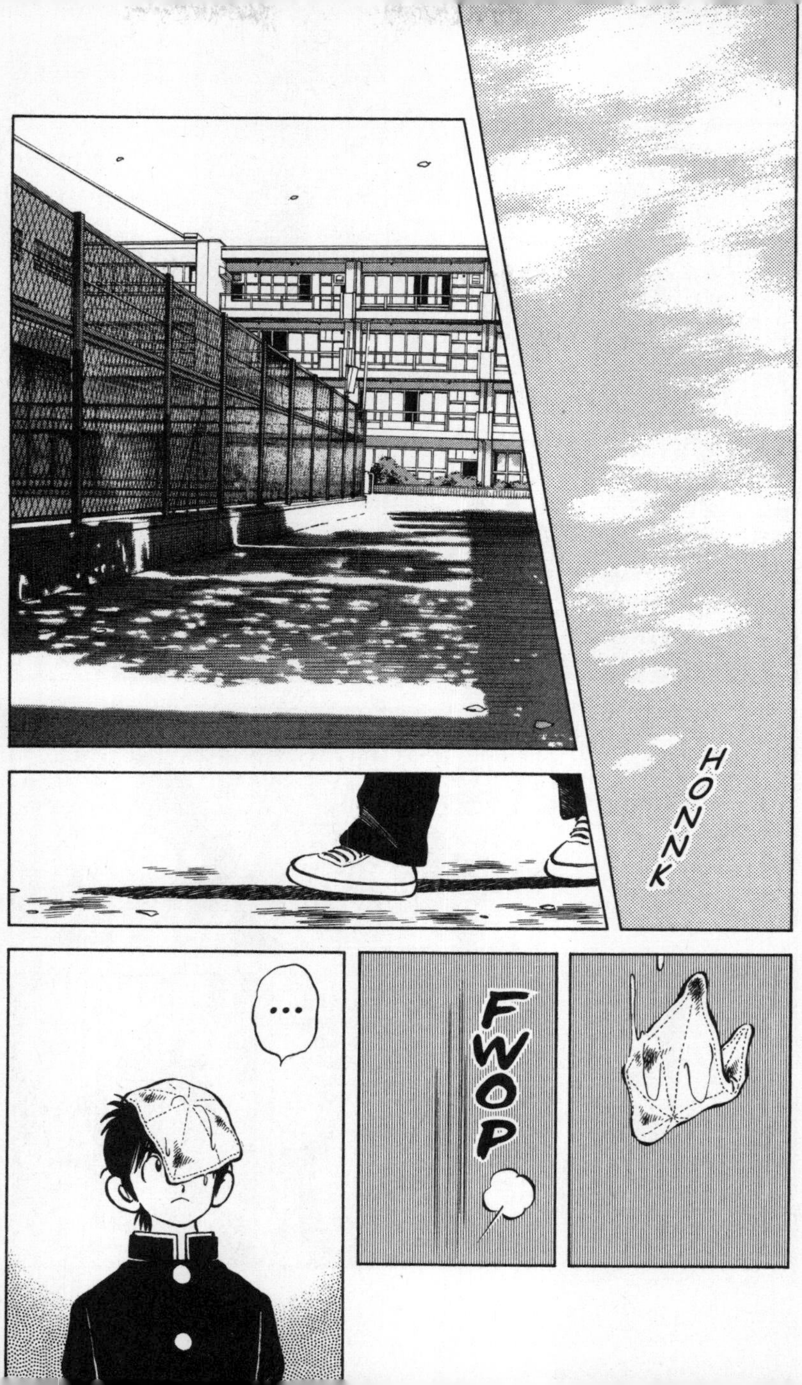
HONNK
FWOP
...

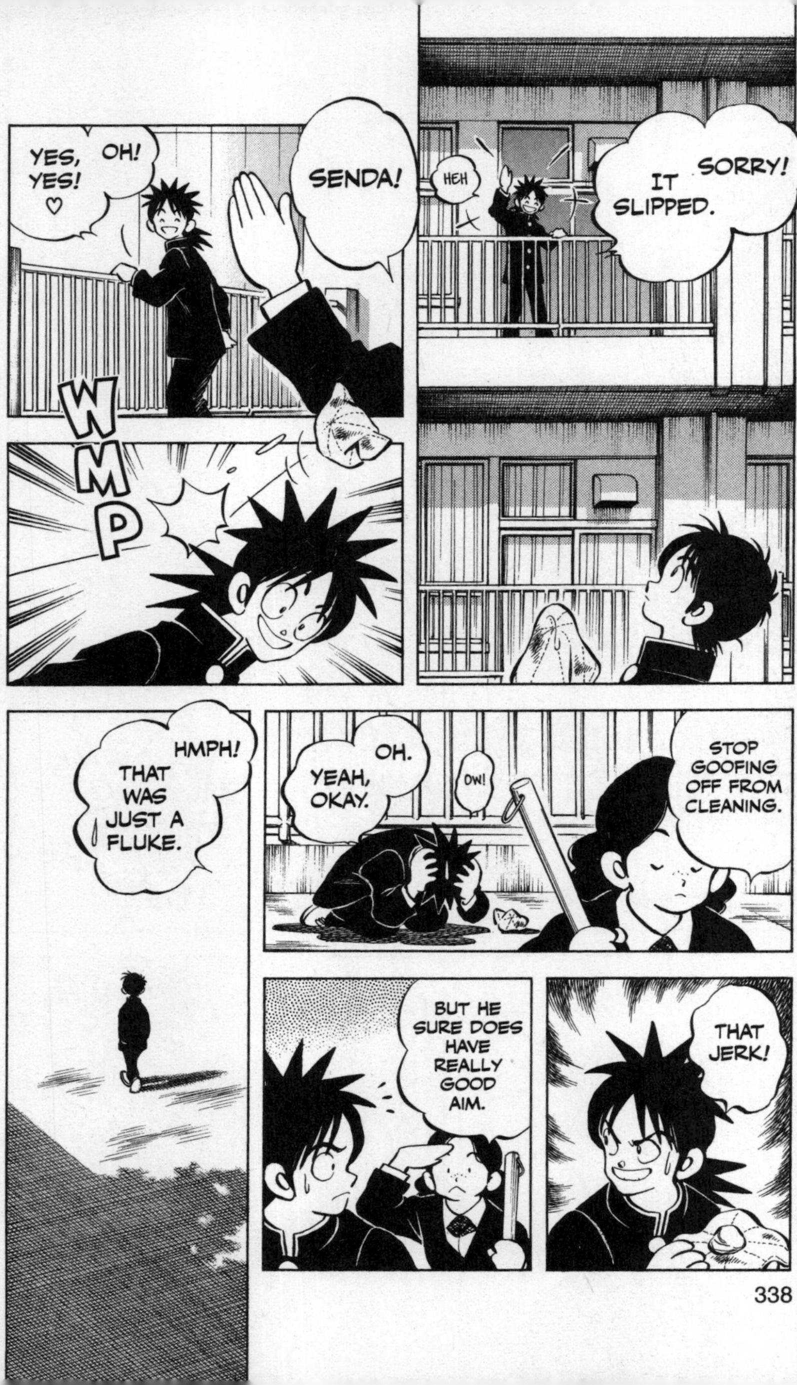
SORRY! IT SLIPPED.
HEH
SENDA!
OH!
YES, YES! ♡
WMP
STOP GOOFING OFF FROM CLEANING.
OW!
OH. YEAH, OKAY.
THAT JERK!
BUT HE SURE DOES HAVE REALLY GOOD AIM.
HMPH! THAT WAS JUST A FLUKE.

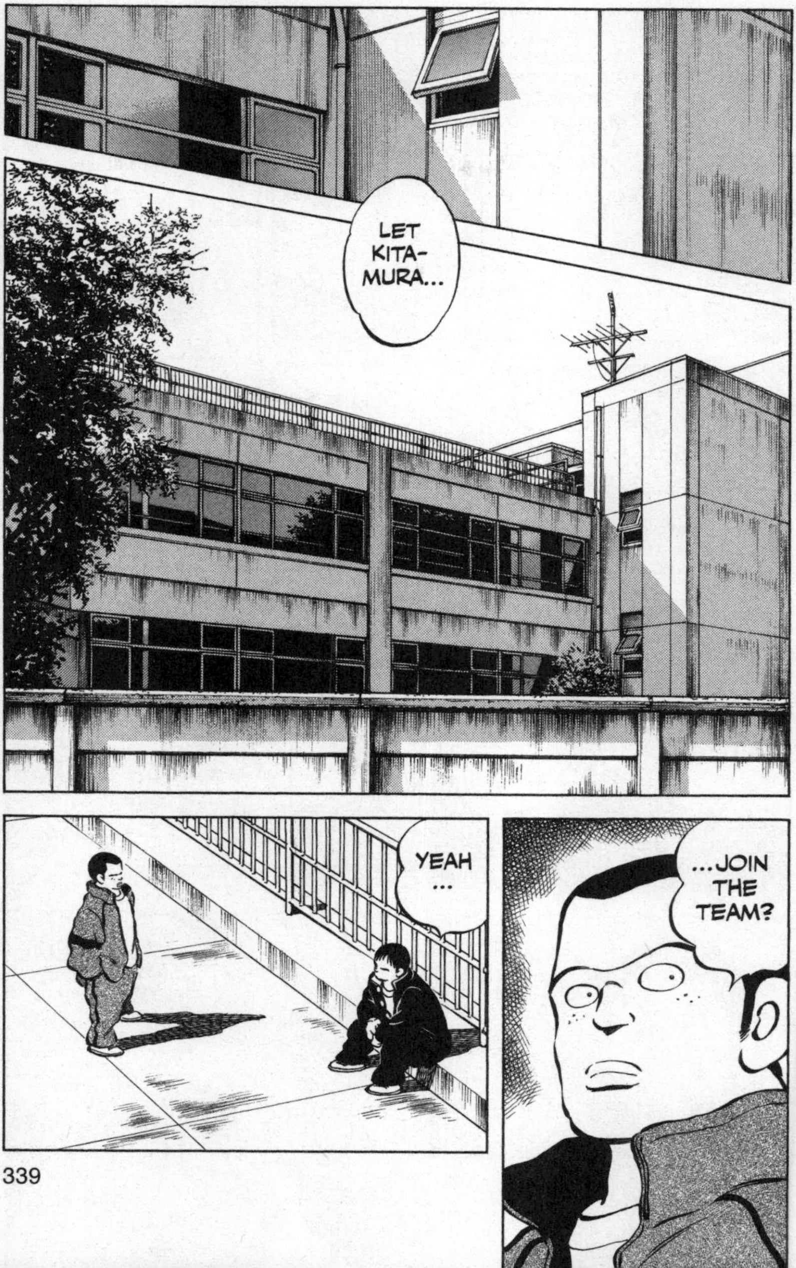
LET KITA-MURA...
...JOIN THE TEAM?
YEAH ...

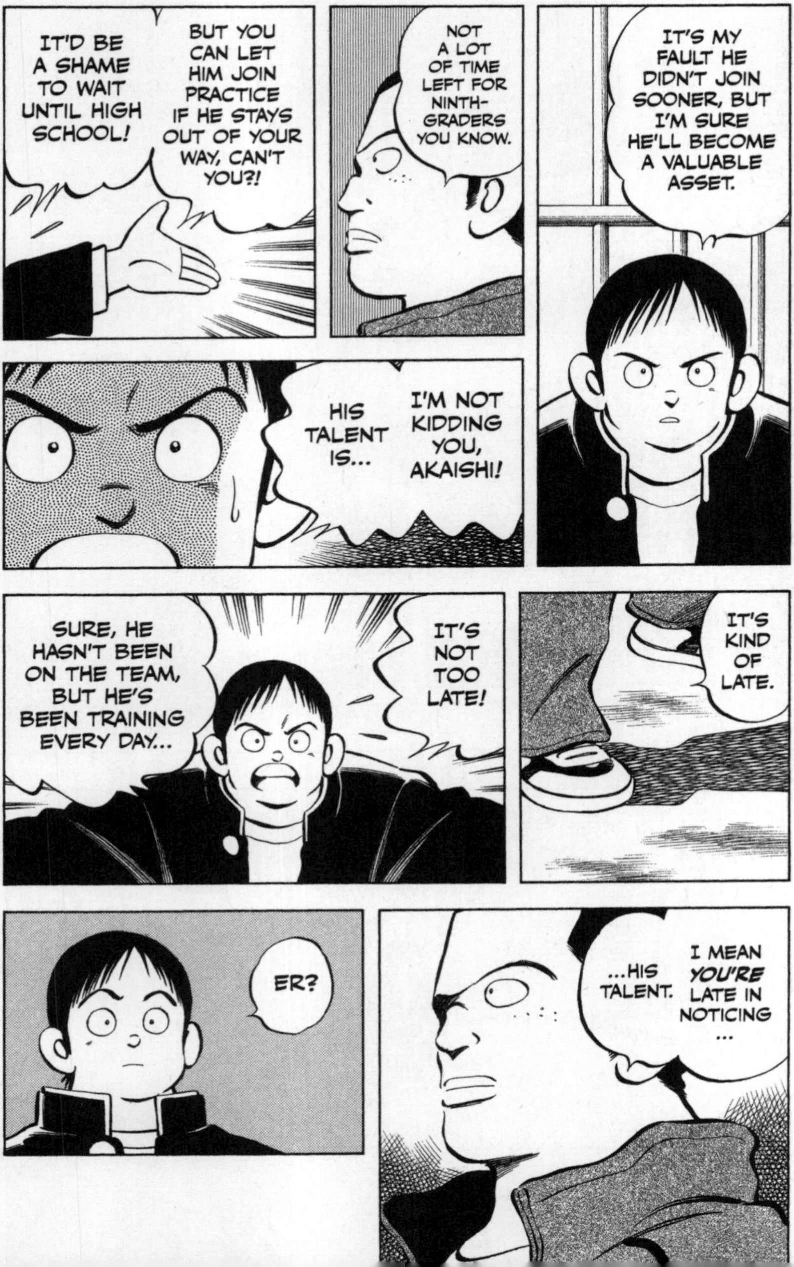
IT'S MY FAULT HE DIDN'T JOIN SOONER, BUT I'M SURE HE'LL BECOME A VALUABLE ASSET.
NOT A LOT OF TIME LEFT FOR NINTH-GRADERS YOU KNOW.
BUT YOU CAN LET HIM JOIN PRACTICE IF HE STAYS OUT OF YOUR WAY, CAN'T YOU?!
IT'D BE A SHAME TO WAIT UNTIL HIGH SCHOOL!
I'M NOT KIDDING YOU, AKAISHI!
HIS TALENT IS...
IT'S KIND OF LATE.
IT'S NOT TOO LATE!
SURE, HE HASN'T BEEN ON THE TEAM, BUT HE'S BEEN TRAINING EVERY DAY...
I MEAN *YOU'RE* LATE IN NOTICING ...
...HIS TALENT.
ER?

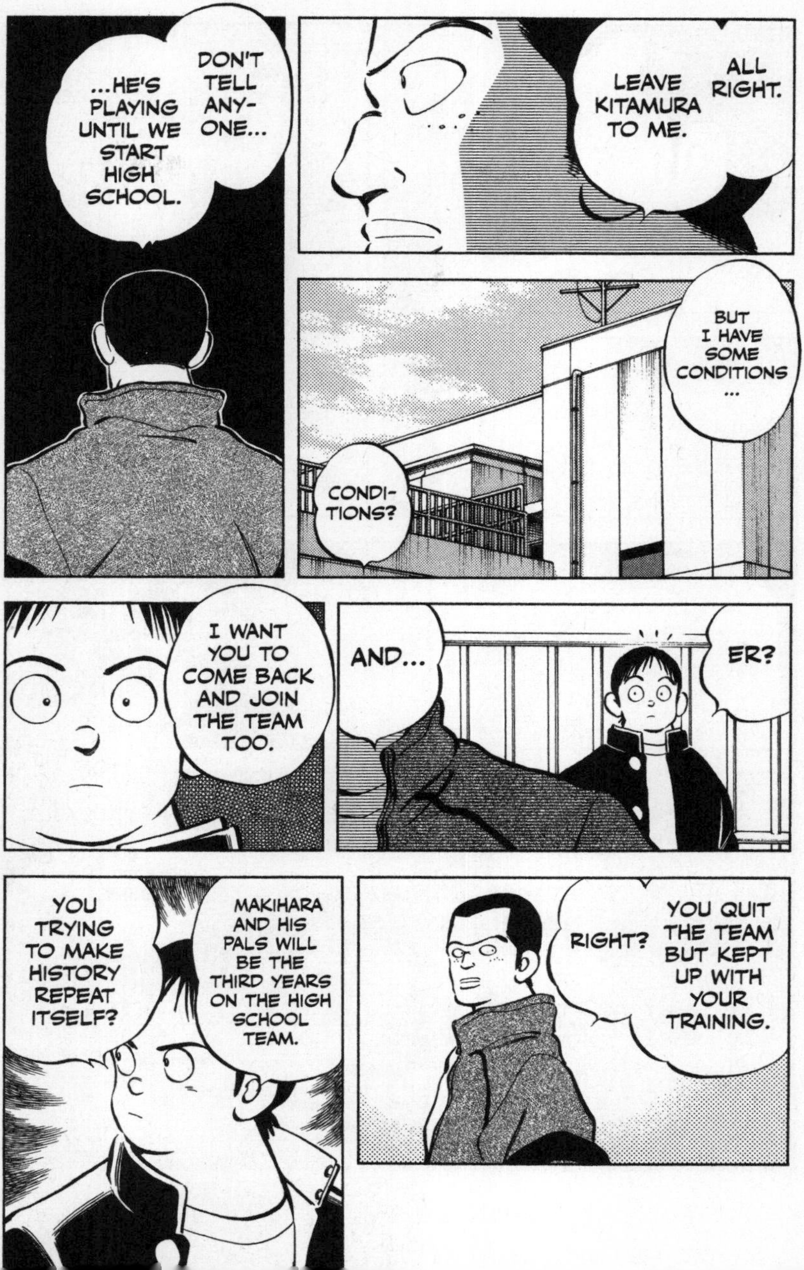
ALL RIGHT.
LEAVE KITAMURA TO ME.
BUT I HAVE SOME CONDITIONS ...
CONDITIONS?
DON'T TELL ANY-ONE...
...HE'S PLAYING UNTIL WE START HIGH SCHOOL.
ER?
AND...
I WANT YOU TO COME BACK AND JOIN THE TEAM TOO.
YOU QUIT THE TEAM BUT KEPT UP WITH YOUR TRAINING.
RIGHT?
MAKIHARA AND HIS PALS WILL BE THE THIRD YEARS ON THE HIGH SCHOOL TEAM.
YOU TRYING TO MAKE HISTORY REPEAT ITSELF?

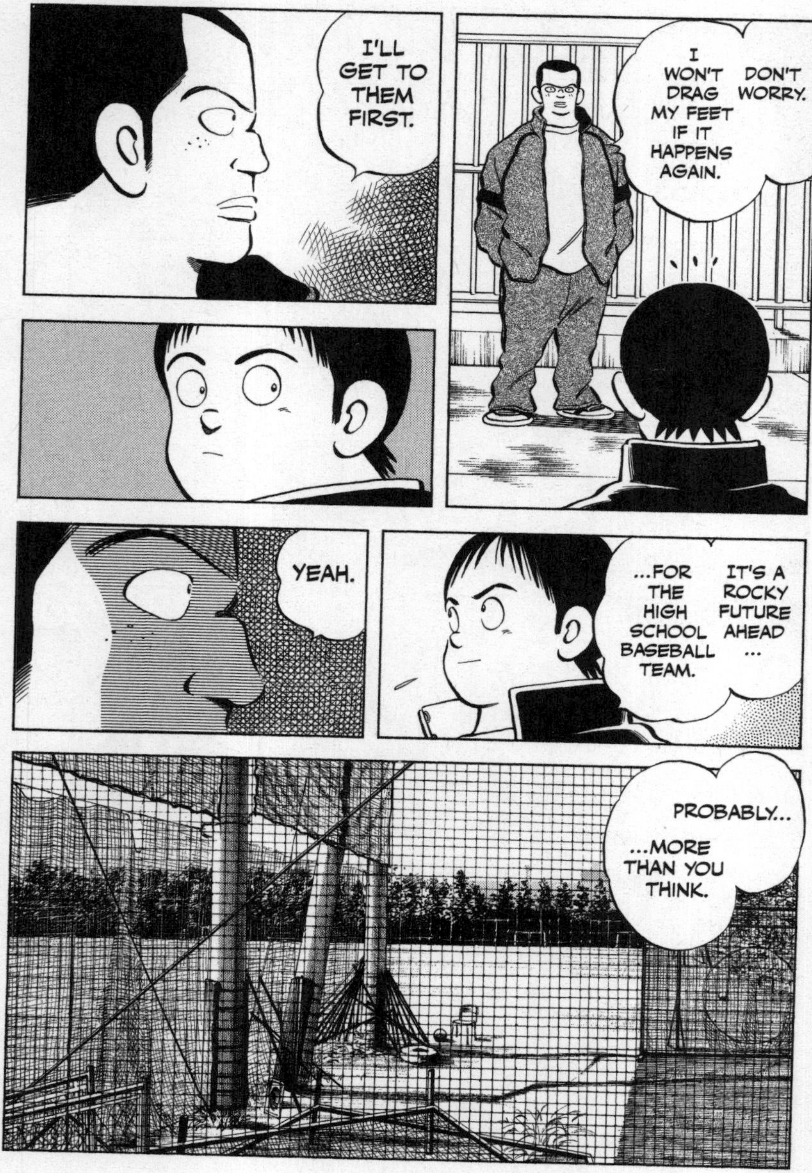
DON'T WORRY.
I WON'T DRAG MY FEET IF IT HAPPENS AGAIN.
I'LL GET TO THEM FIRST.
IT'S A ROCKY FUTURE AHEAD...
...FOR THE HIGH SCHOOL BASEBALL TEAM.
YEAH.
PROBABLY...
...MORE THAN YOU THINK.

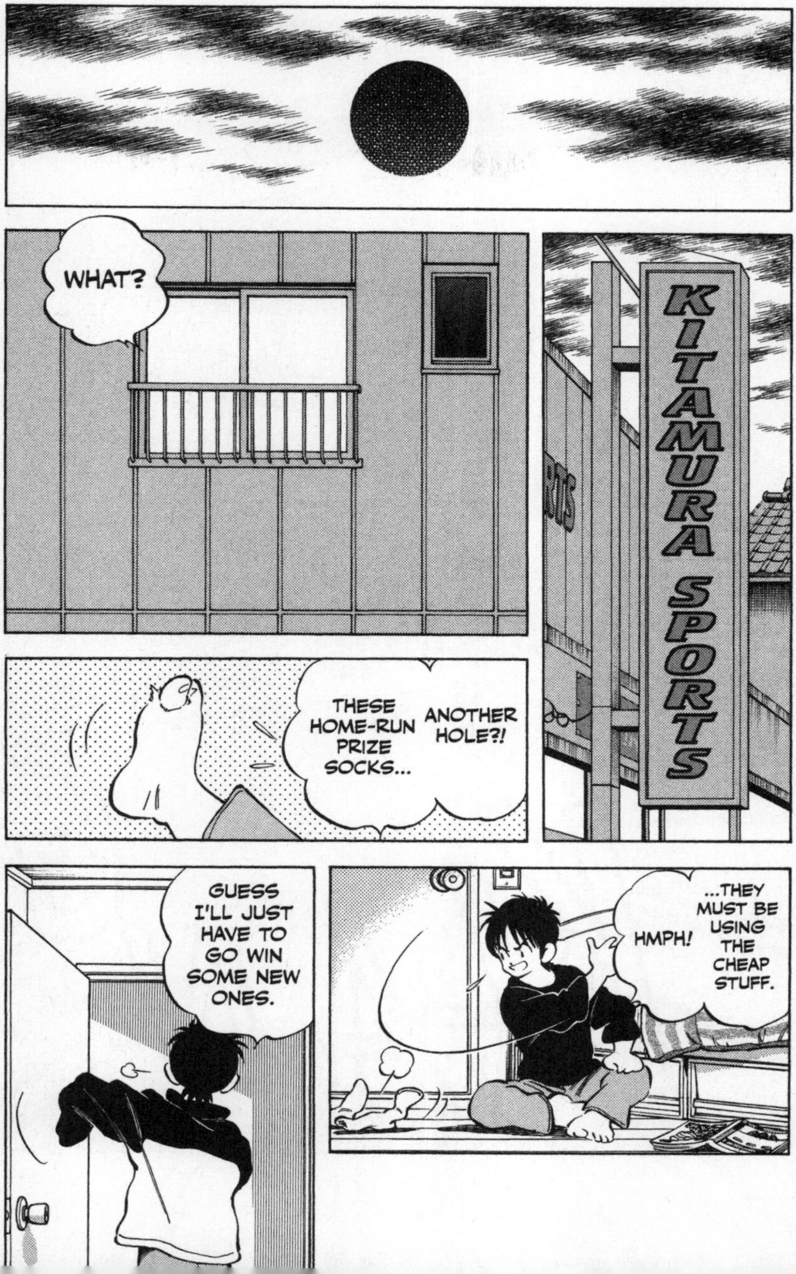
KITAMURA SPORTS
WHAT?
ANOTHER HOLE?!
THESE HOME-RUN PRIZE SOCKS...
...THEY MUST BE USING THE CHEAP STUFF.
HMPH!
GUESS I'LL JUST HAVE TO GO WIN SOME NEW ONES.

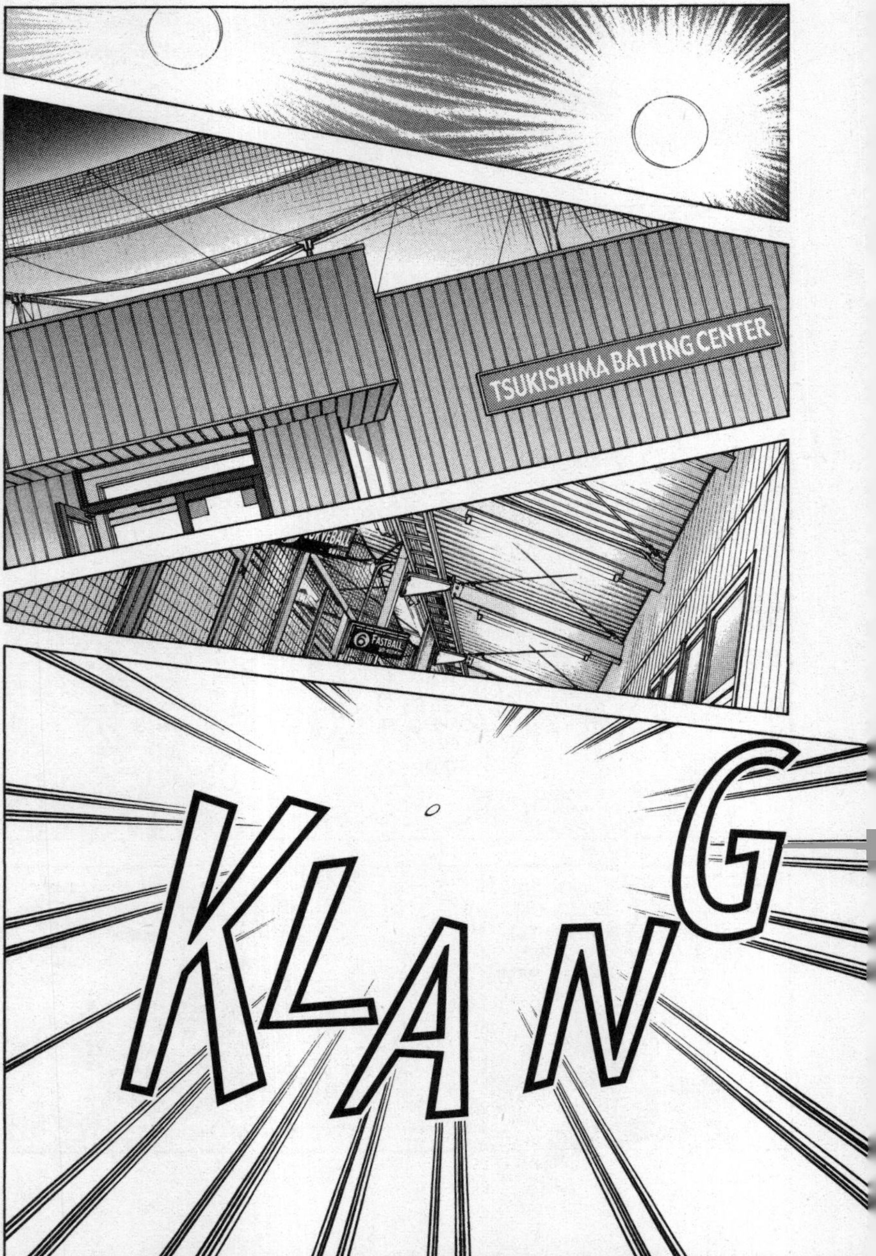
TSUKISHIMA BATTING CENTER
6 FASTBALL
KLANG

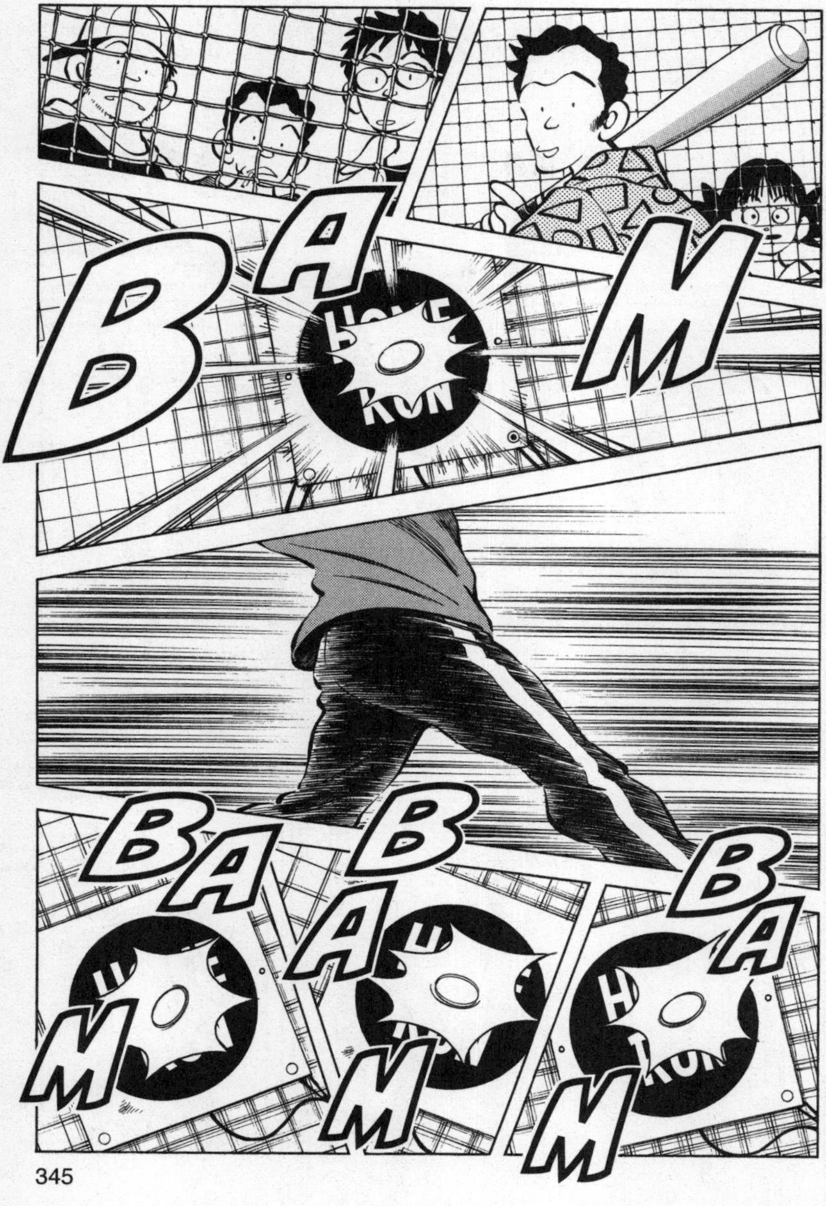
BAM
BAM
BAM
BAM

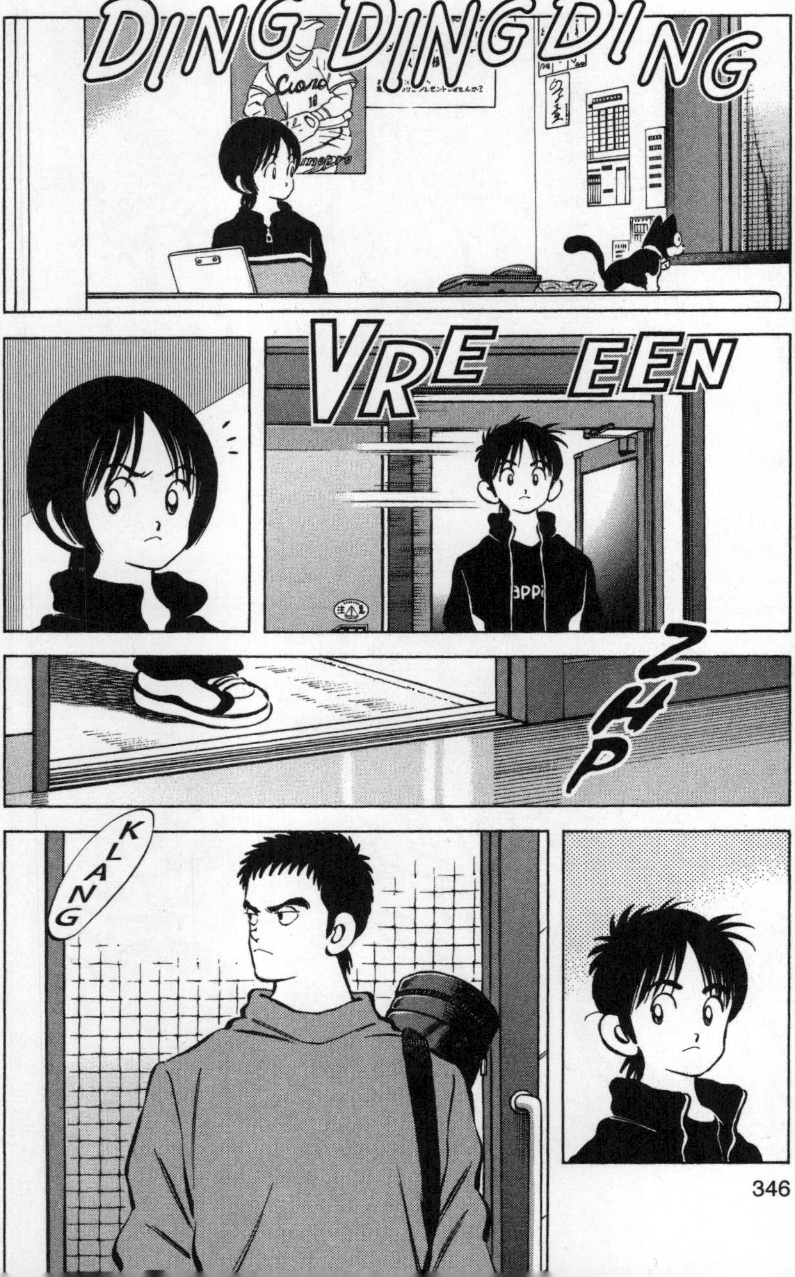
DING DING DING DING
VREEEEN
ZHP
KLANG

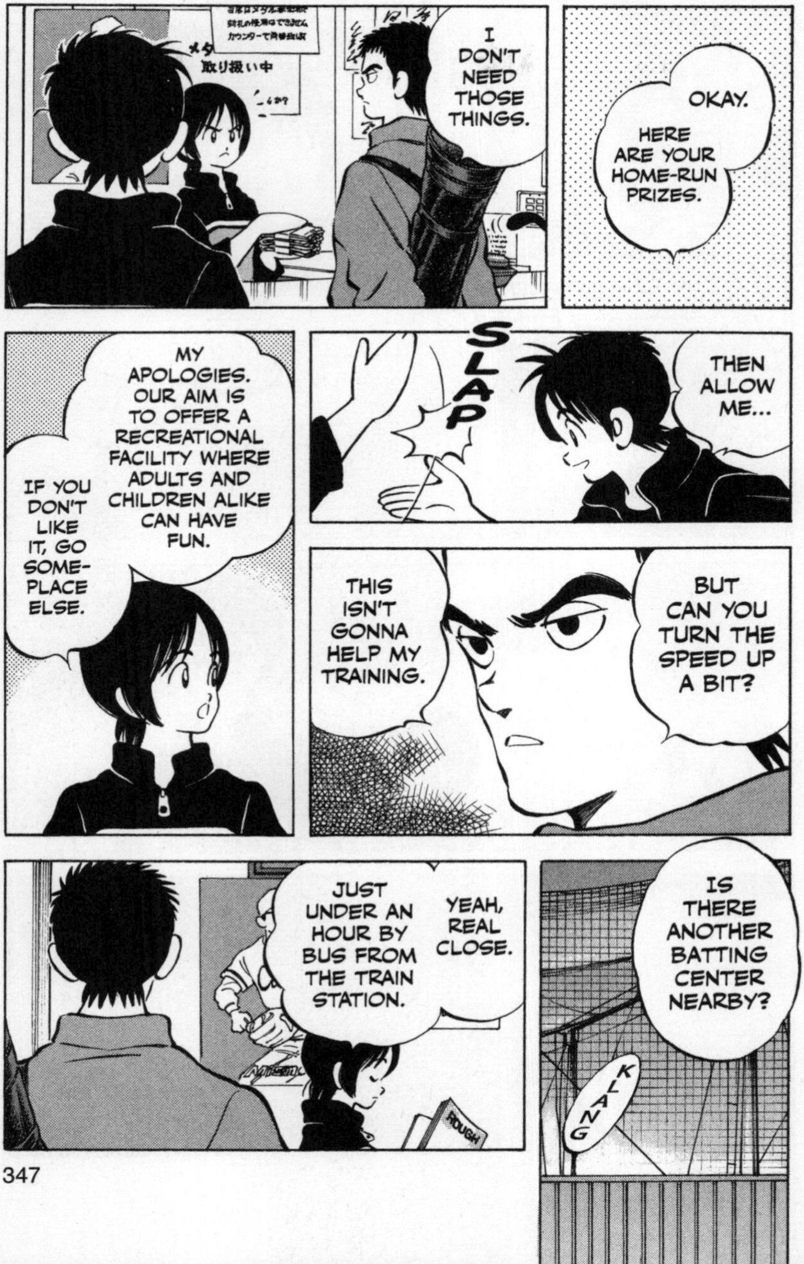
OKAY.
HERE ARE YOUR HOME-RUN PRIZES.
I DON'T NEED THOSE THINGS.
THEN ALLOW ME...
SLAP
BUT CAN YOU TURN THE SPEED UP A BIT?
THIS ISN'T GONNA HELP MY TRAINING.
MY APOLOGIES. OUR AIM IS TO OFFER A RECREATIONAL FACILITY WHERE ADULTS AND CHILDREN ALIKE CAN HAVE FUN.
IF YOU DON'T LIKE IT, GO SOME-PLACE ELSE.
IS THERE ANOTHER BATTING CENTER NEARBY?
KLANG
YEAH, REAL CLOSE.
JUST UNDER AN HOUR BY BUS FROM THE TRAIN STATION.
ROUGH

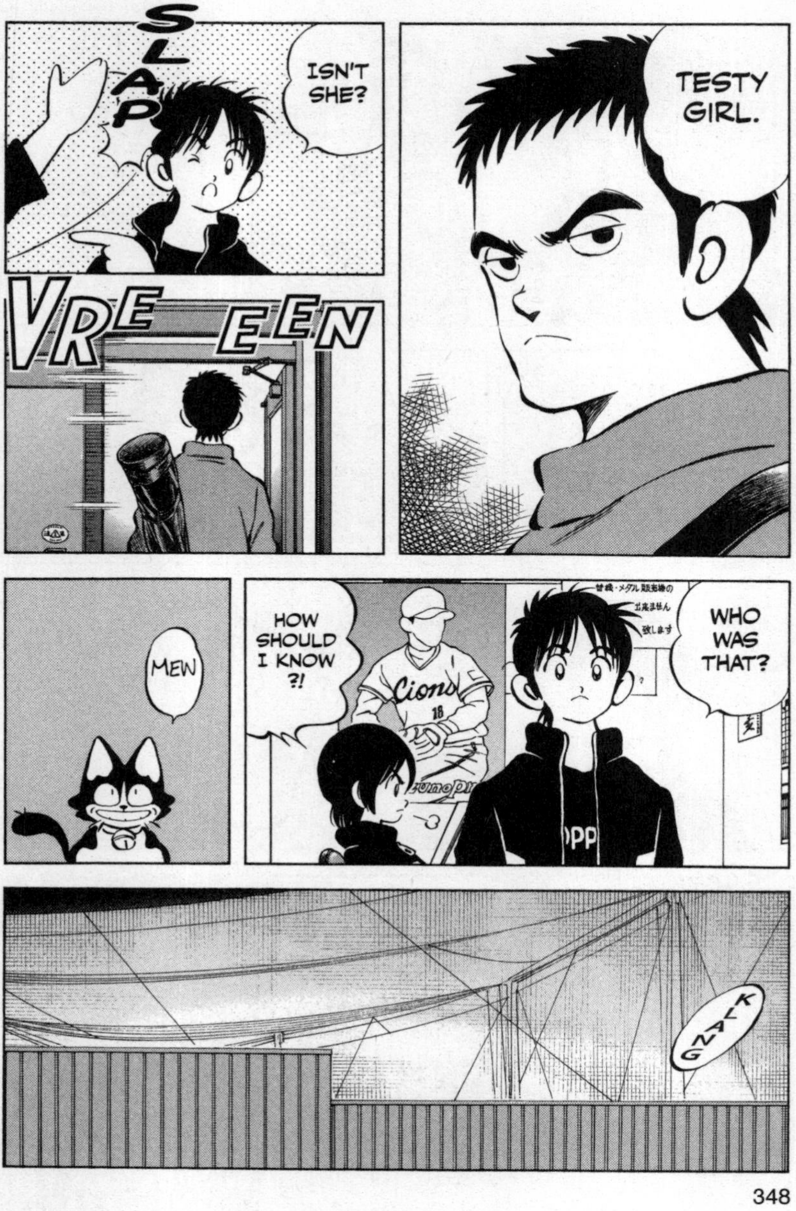
TESTY GIRL.
SLAP
ISN'T SHE?
VREEEEN
WHO WAS THAT?
HOW SHOULD I KNOW ?!
MEW
KLANG

CHAPTER 9
SECRET WEAPON

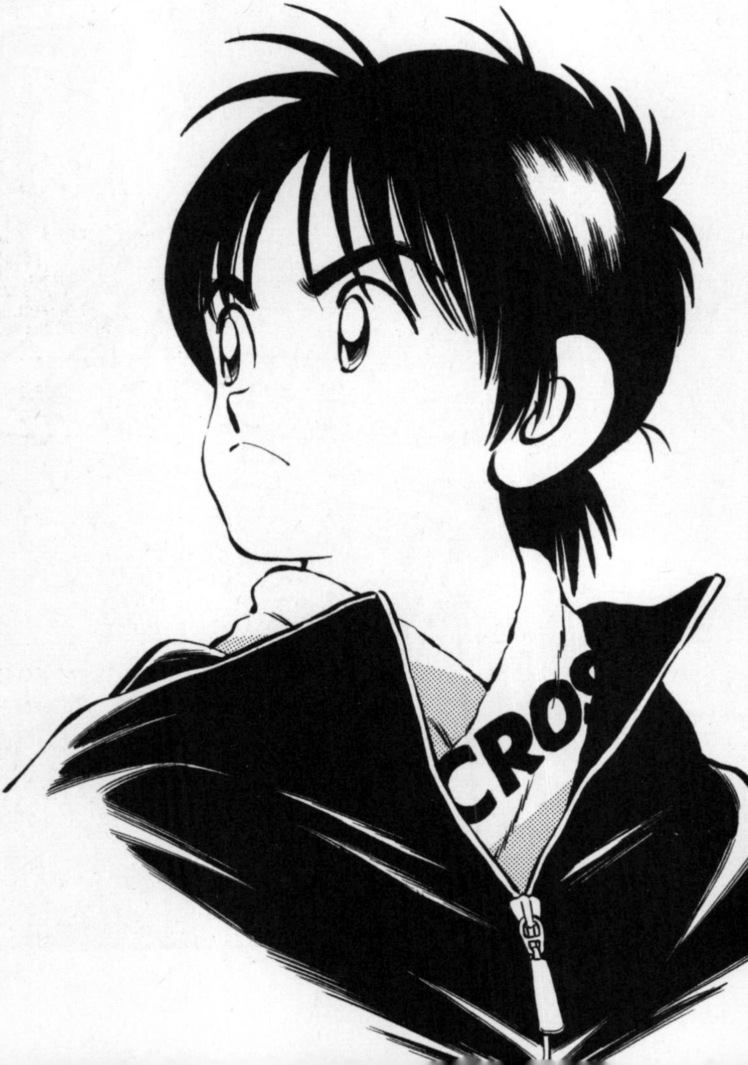
CROS

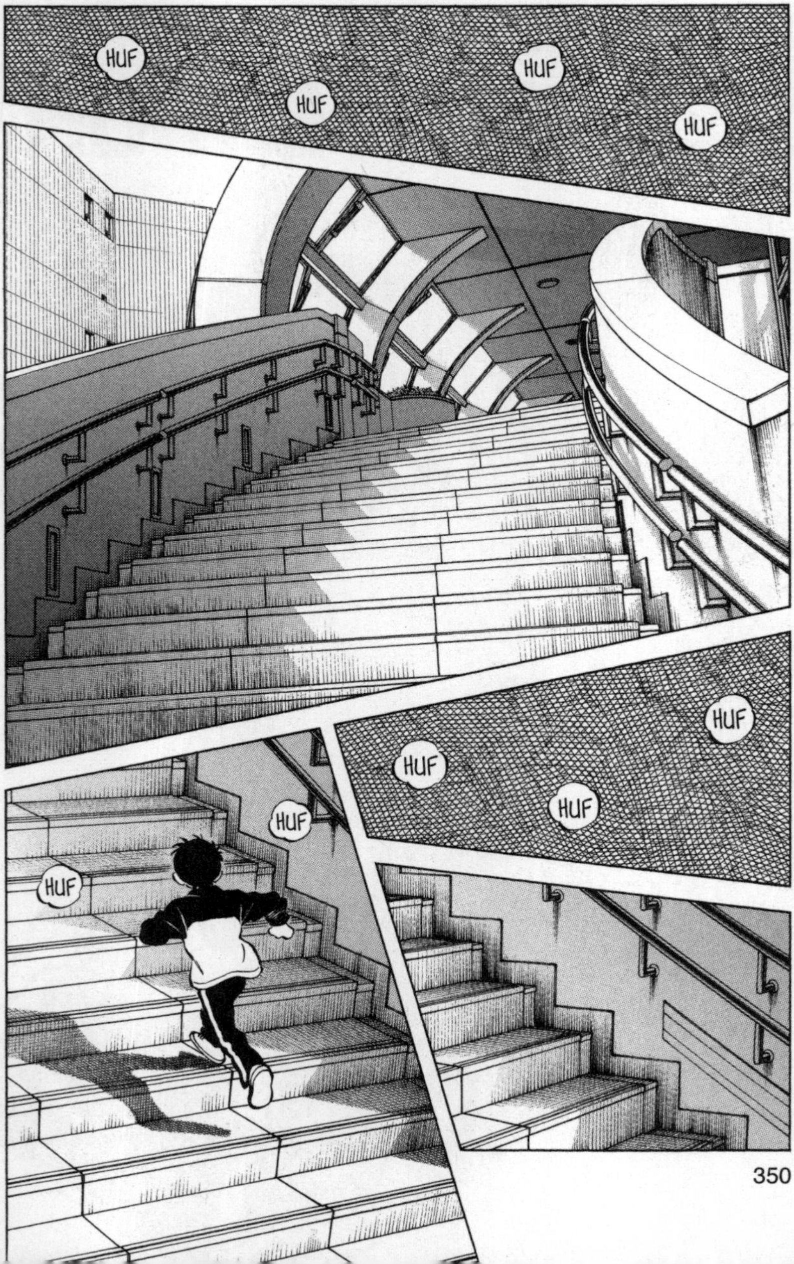
HUF
HUF
HUF
HUF
HUF
HUF
HUF
HUF
HUF

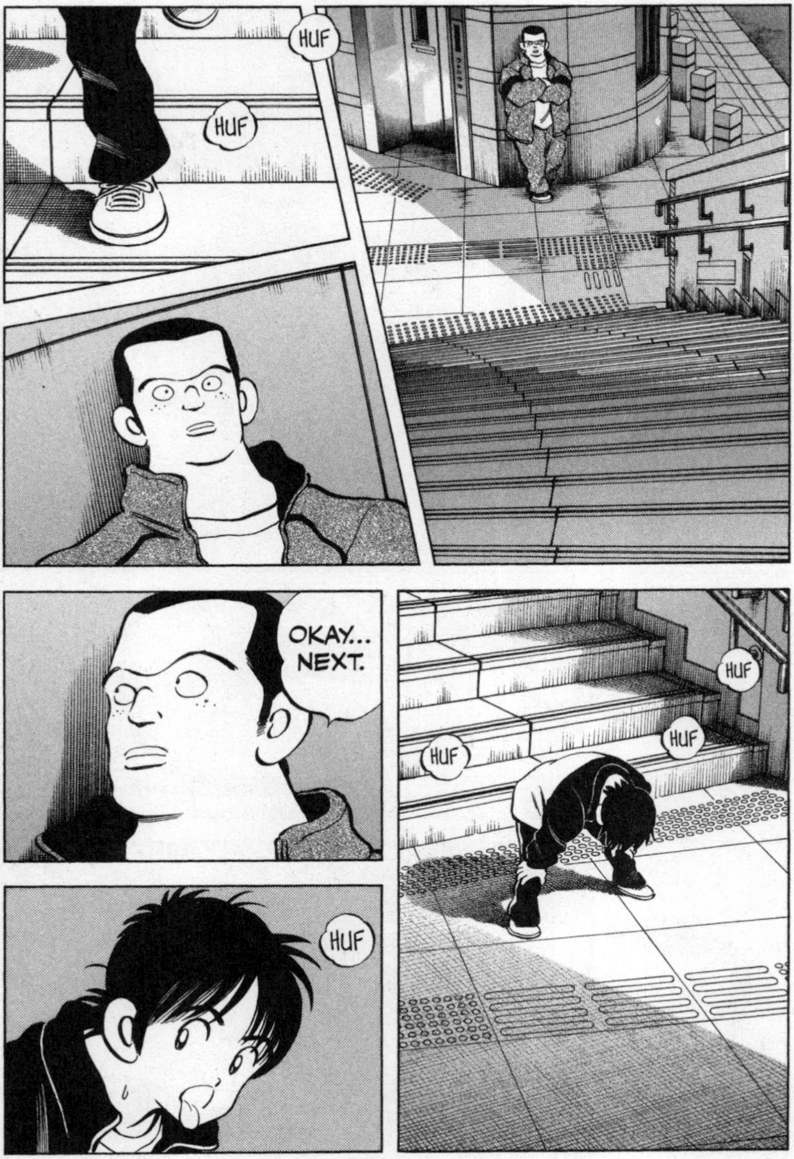
HUF
HUF
HUF
HUF
HUF
OKAY... NEXT.
HUF

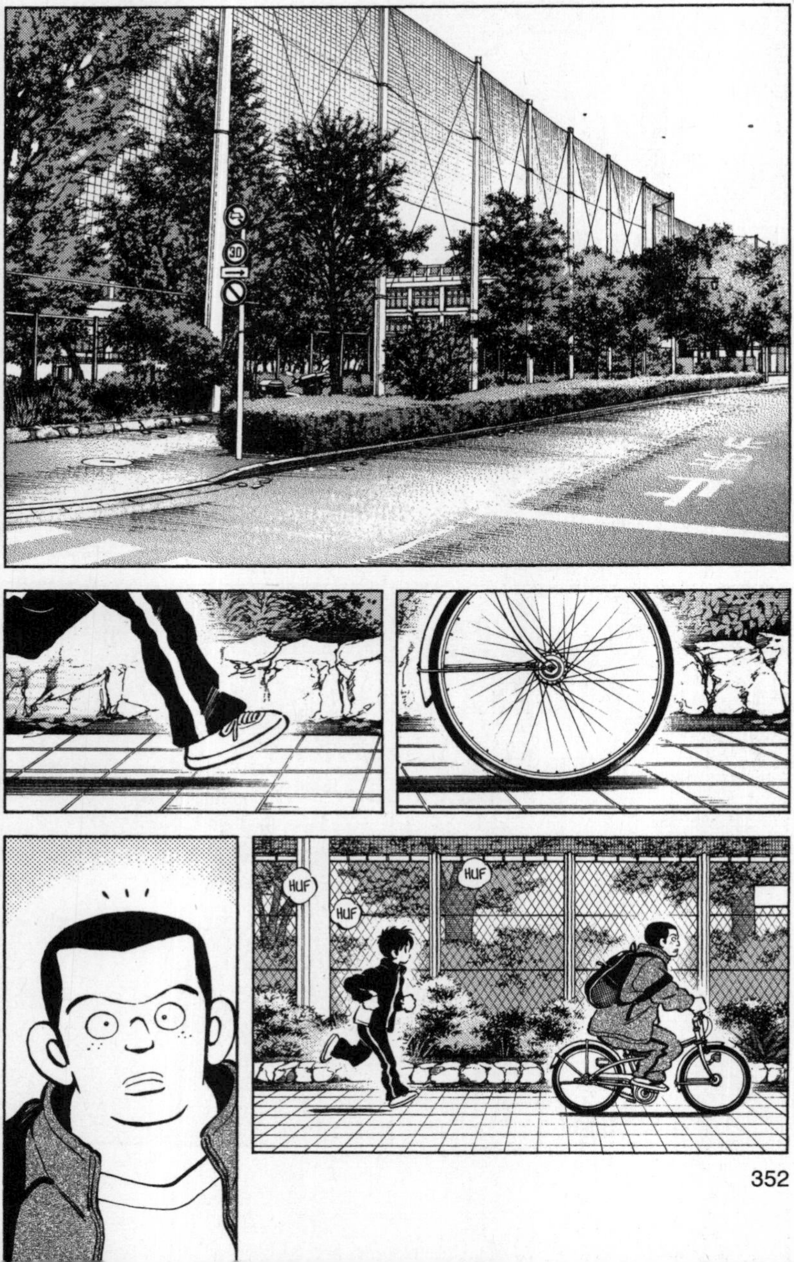
HUF
HUF
HUF

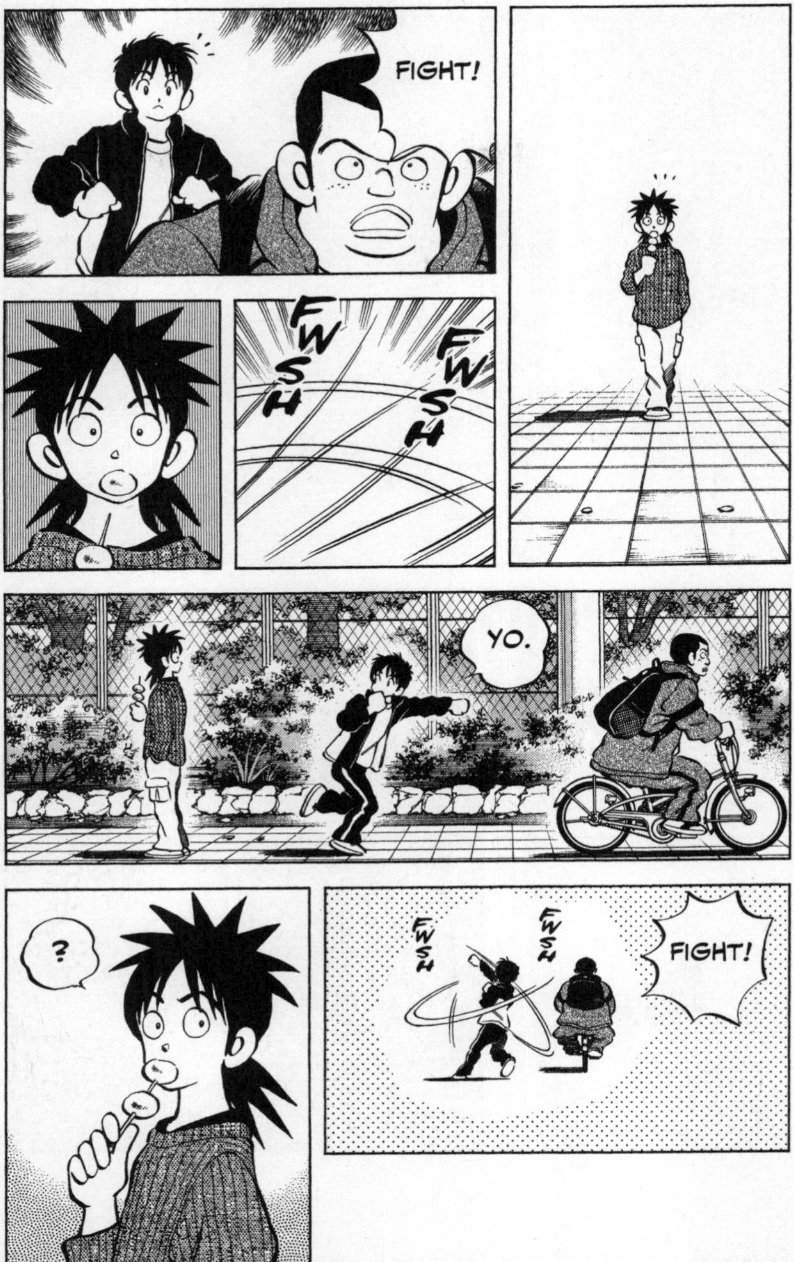
FIGHT!
FWSH
FWSH
YO.
FIGHT!
FWSH
FWSH
?

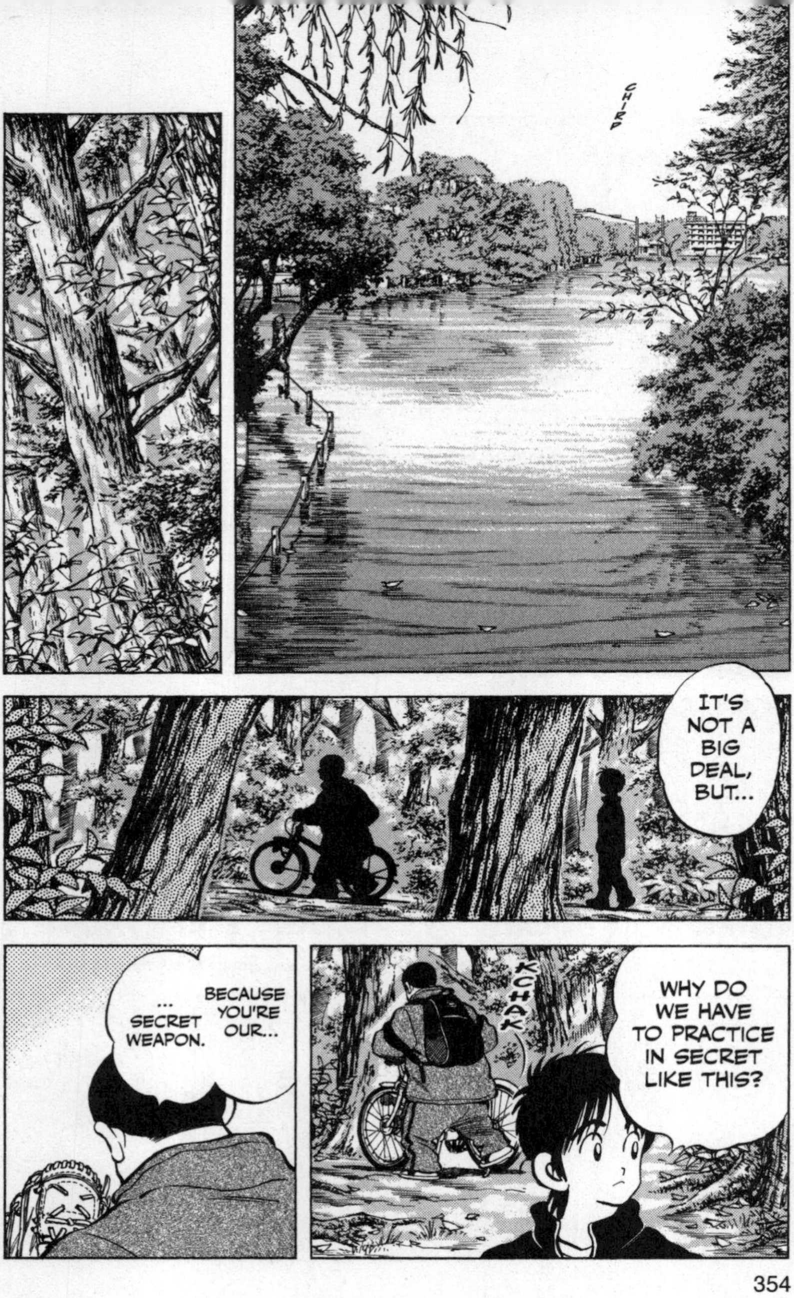
CHIRP
IT'S NOT A BIG DEAL, BUT...
WHY DO WE HAVE TO PRACTICE IN SECRET LIKE THIS?
KCHAK
BECAUSE YOU'RE OUR...
... SECRET WEAPON.

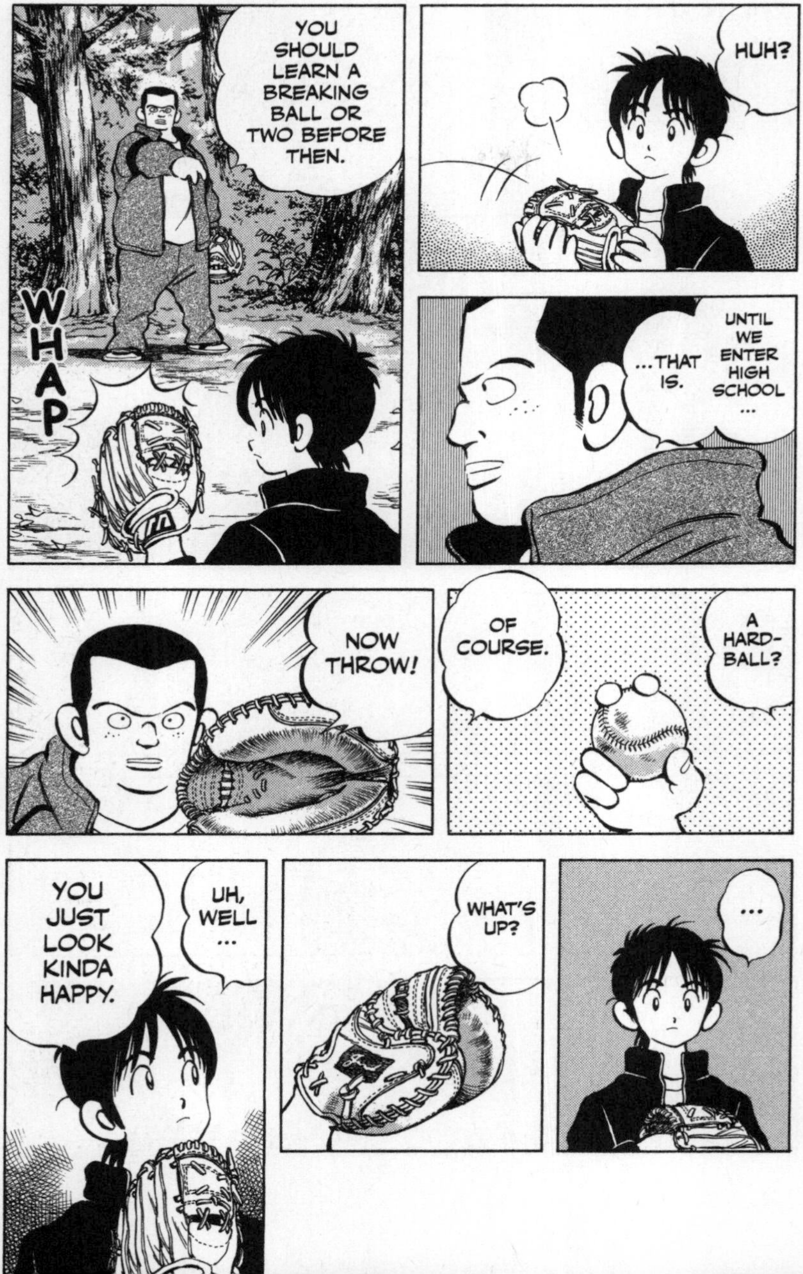
HUH?
UNTIL WE ENTER HIGH SCHOOL ...
...THAT IS.
YOU SHOULD LEARN A BREAKING BALL OR TWO BEFORE THEN.
WHAP
A HARD-BALL?
OF COURSE.
NOW THROW!
...
WHAT'S UP?
UH, WELL ...
YOU JUST LOOK KINDA HAPPY.

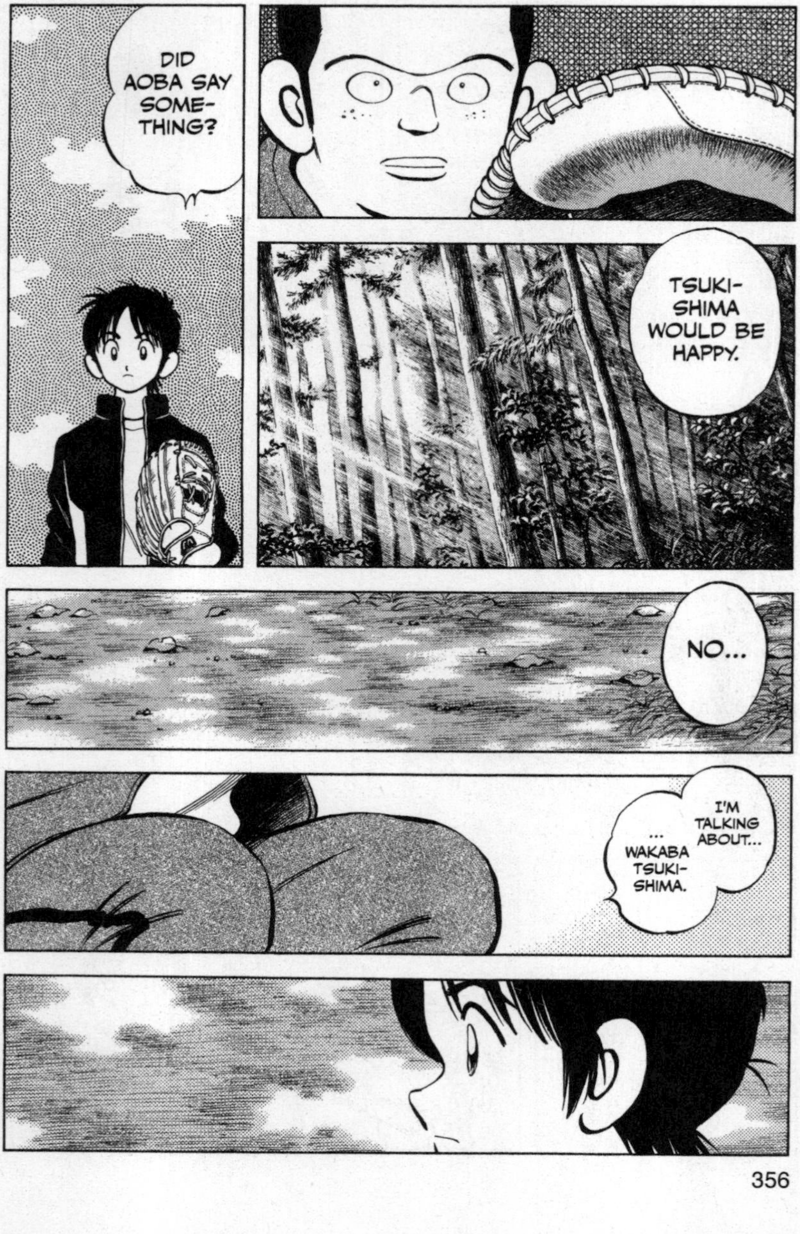
TSUKI-SHIMA WOULD BE HAPPY.
DID AOBA SAY SOME-THING?
NO...
I'M TALKING ABOUT...
...WAKABA TSUKI-SHIMA.

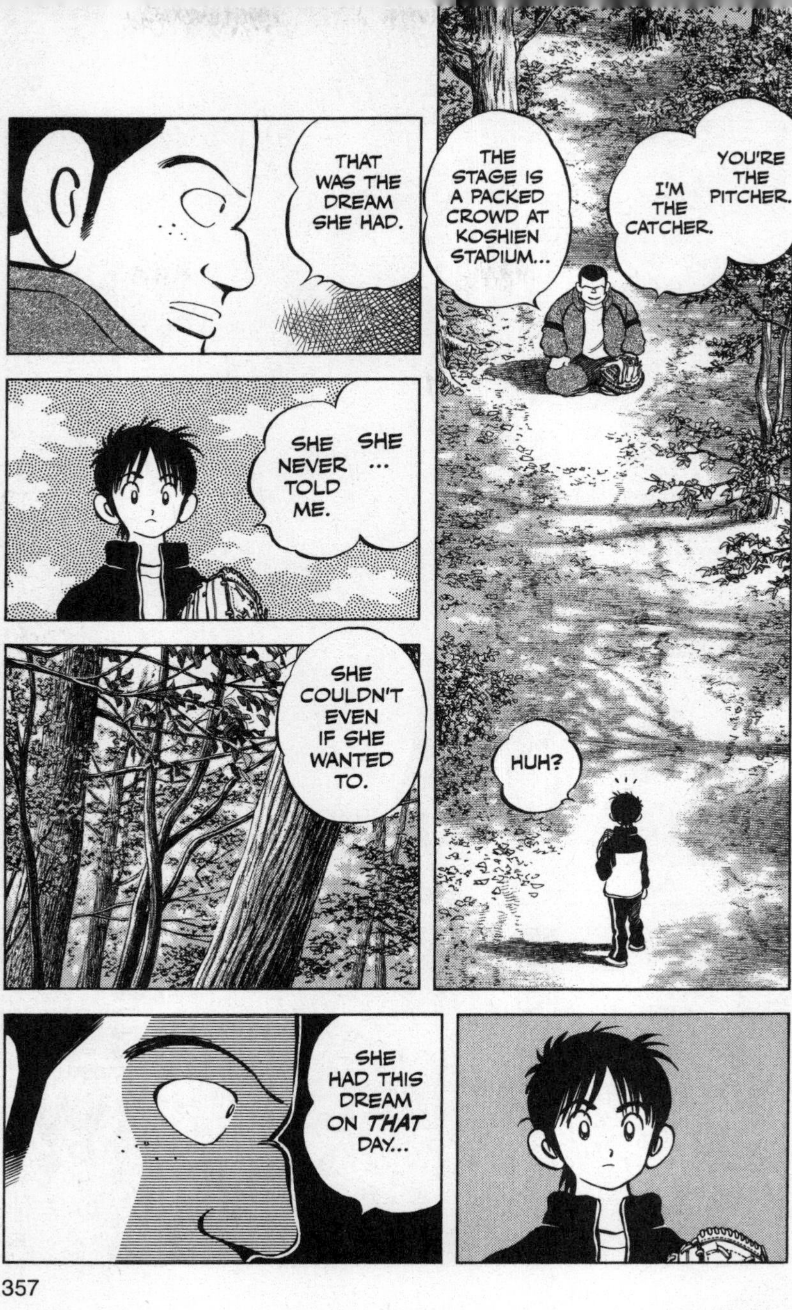
YOU'RE THE PITCHER.
I'M THE CATCHER.
THE STAGE IS A PACKED CROWD AT KOSHIEN STADIUM...
HUH?
THAT WAS THE DREAM SHE HAD.
SHE...
SHE NEVER TOLD ME.
SHE COULDN'T EVEN IF SHE WANTED TO.
SHE HAD THIS DREAM ON *THAT* DAY...

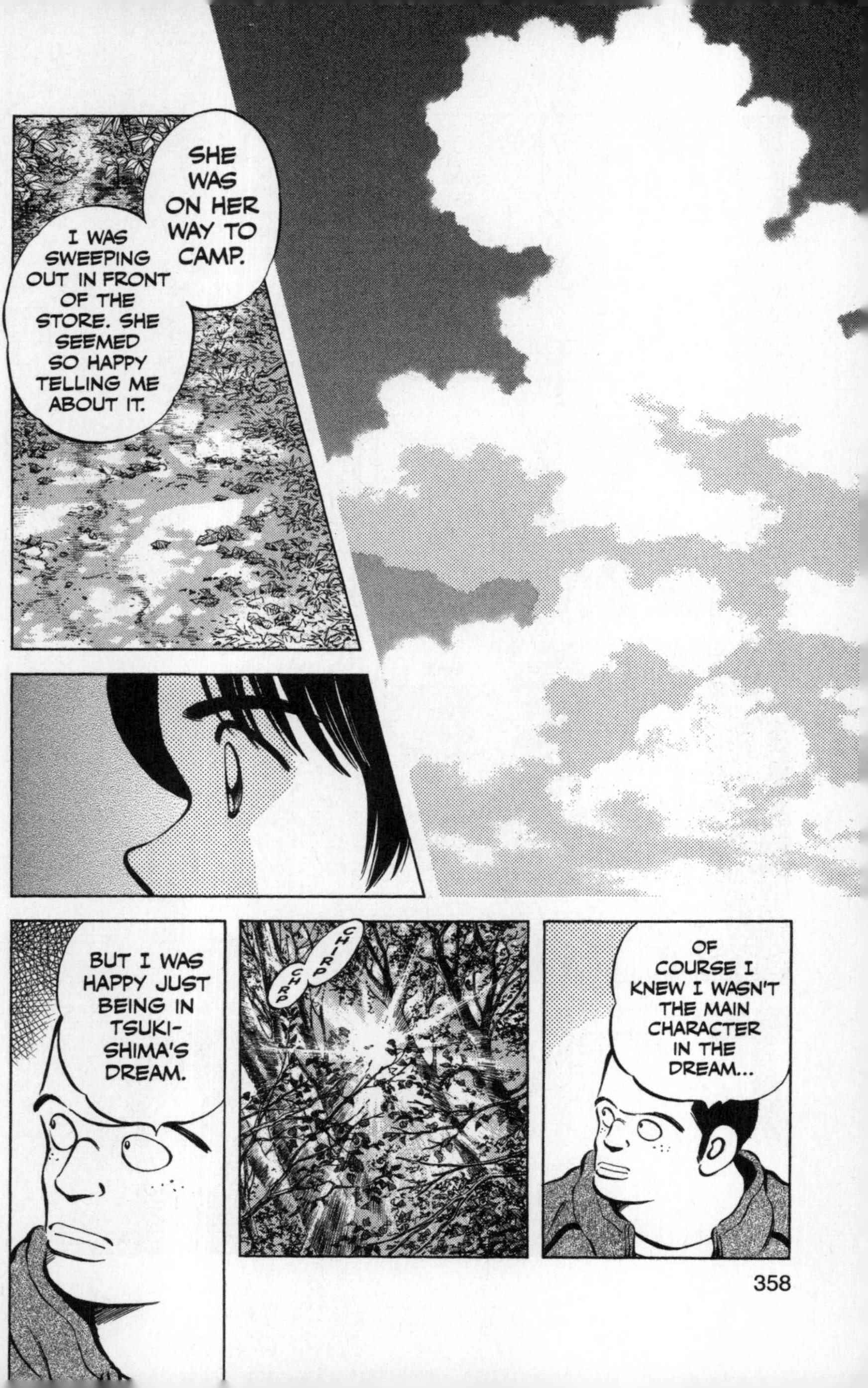
SHE WAS ON HER WAY TO CAMP.
I WAS SWEEPING OUT IN FRONT OF THE STORE. SHE SEEMED SO HAPPY TELLING ME ABOUT IT.
OF COURSE I KNEW I WASN'T THE MAIN CHARACTER IN THE DREAM...
CHIRP
CHIRP
BUT I WAS HAPPY JUST BEING IN TSUKI-SHIMA'S DREAM.

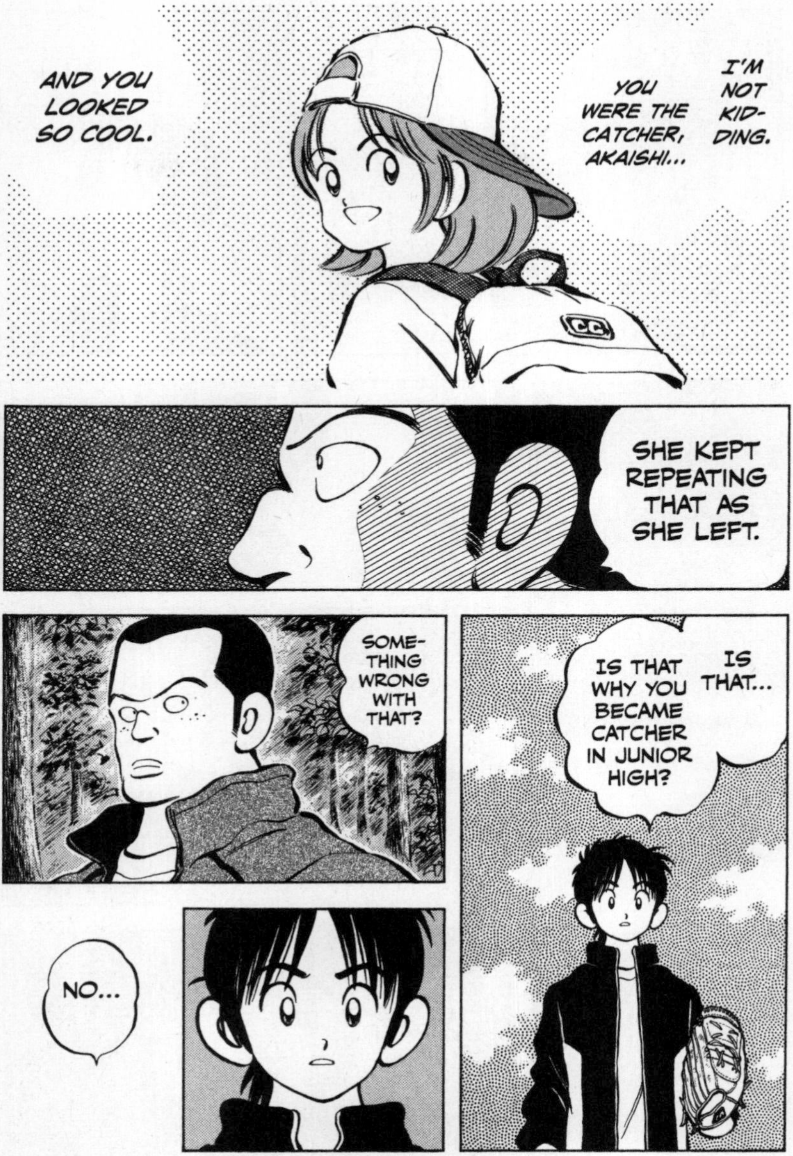
I'M NOT KID-DING.
YOU WERE THE CATCHER, AKAISHI...
AND YOU LOOKED SO COOL.
SHE KEPT REPEATING THAT AS SHE LEFT.
IS THAT...
IS THAT WHY YOU BECAME CATCHER IN JUNIOR HIGH?
SOME-THING WRONG WITH THAT?
NO...

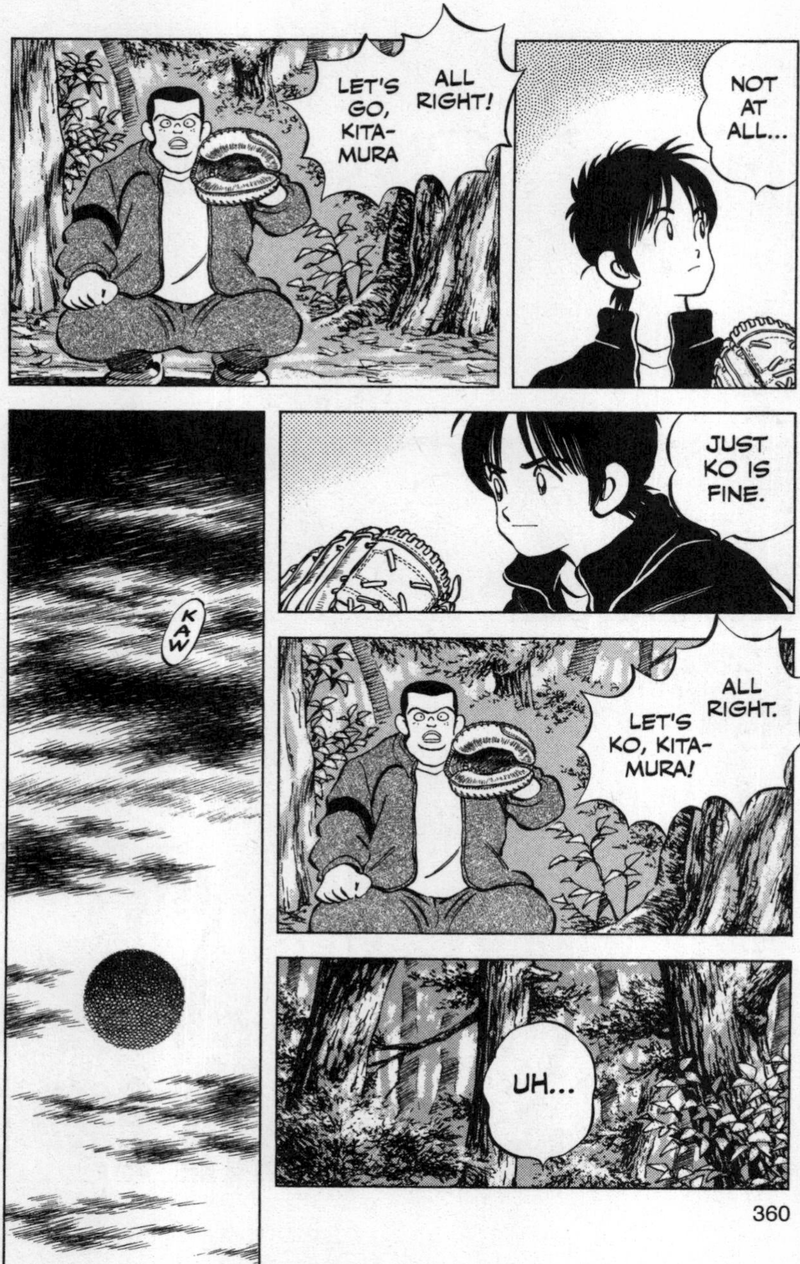
NOT AT ALL...
ALL RIGHT! LET'S GO, KITA-MURA
JUST KO IS FINE.
ALL RIGHT. LET'S KO, KITA-MURA!
UH...
KAW

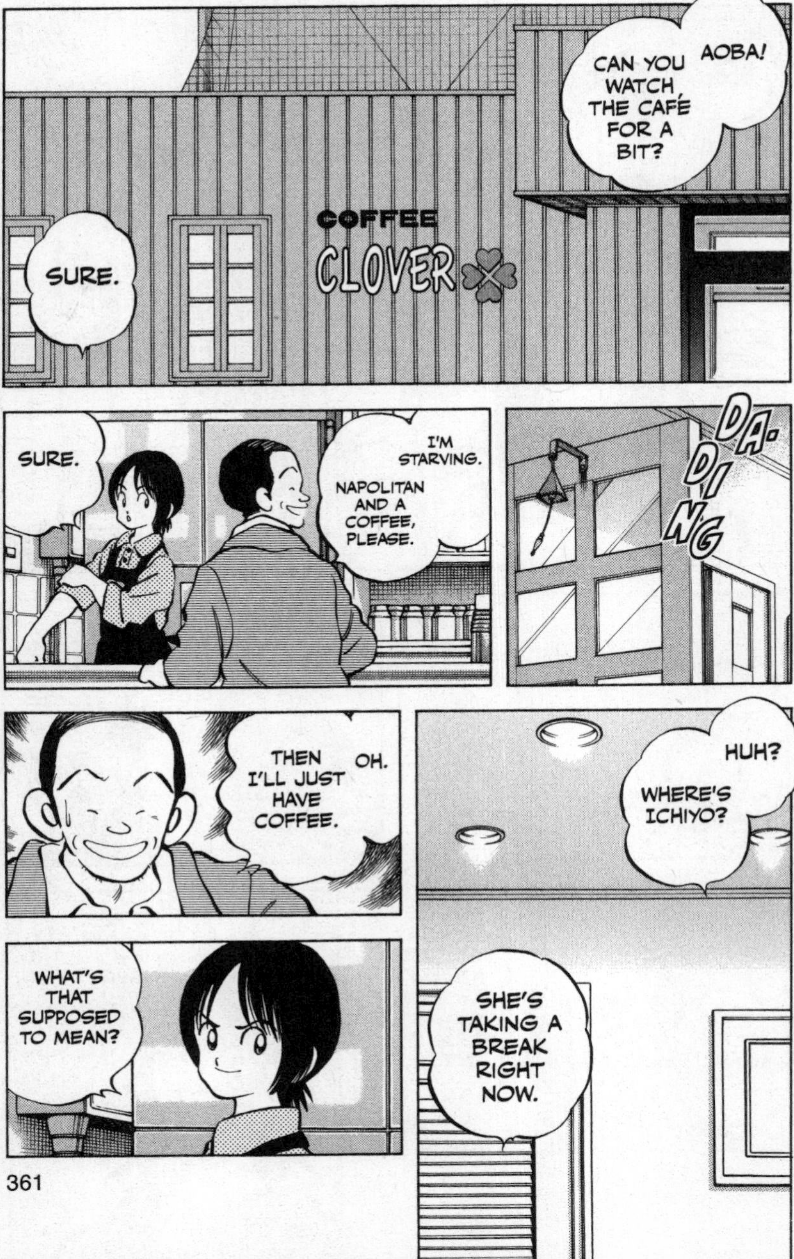
AOBA!
CAN YOU WATCH, THE CAFÉ FOR A BIT?
COFFEE
CLOVER
SURE.
DA-DING
I'M STARVING.
NAPOLITAN AND A COFFEE, PLEASE.
SURE.
HUH?
WHERE'S ICHIYO?
SHE'S TAKING A BREAK RIGHT NOW.
OH.
THEN I'LL JUST HAVE COFFEE.
WHAT'S THAT SUPPOSED TO MEAN?

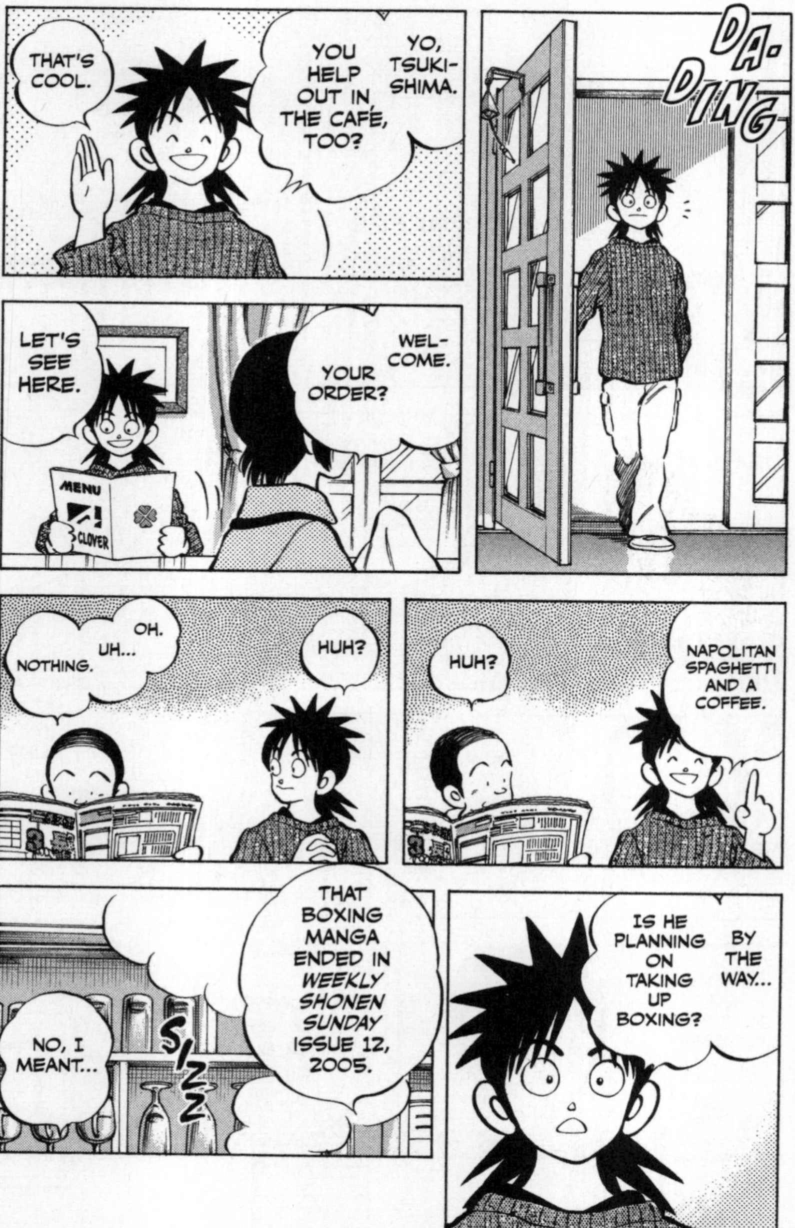
DA-DING
YO, TSUKISHIMA.
YOU HELP OUT IN THE CAFÉ, TOO?
THAT'S COOL.
WELCOME.
YOUR ORDER?
LET'S SEE HERE.
MENU
CLOVER
NAPOLITAN SPAGHETTI AND A COFFEE.
HUH?
HUH?
OH.
UH...
NOTHING.
BY THE WAY...
IS HE PLANNING ON TAKING UP BOXING?
THAT BOXING MANGA ENDED IN WEEKLY SHONEN SUNDAY ISSUE 12, 2005.
SIZZ
NO, I MEANT...

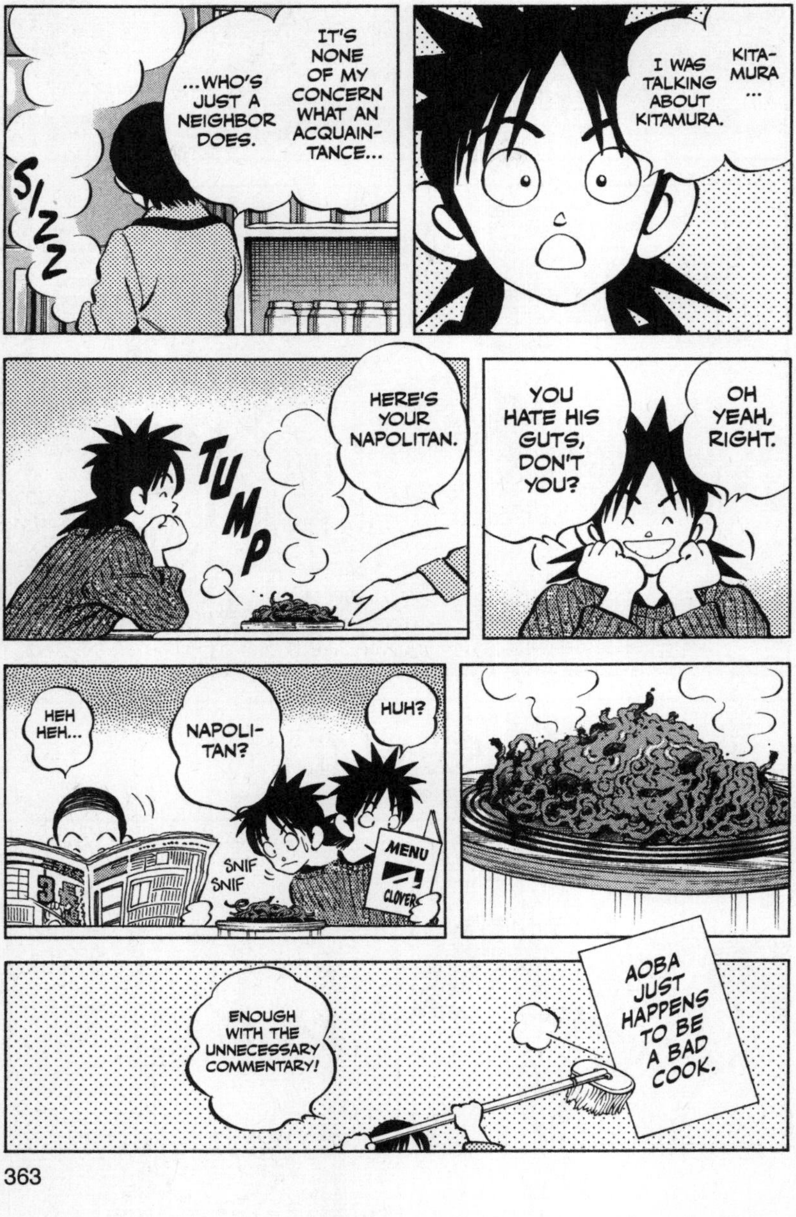
KITA-MURA ...
I WAS TALKING ABOUT KITAMURA.
IT'S NONE OF MY CONCERN WHAT AN ACQUAINTANCE...
...WHO'S JUST A NEIGHBOR DOES.
SIZZ
OH YEAH, RIGHT.
YOU HATE HIS GUTS, DON'T YOU?
HERE'S YOUR NAPOLITAN.
TUMP
HUH?
NAPOLI-TAN?
HEH HEH...
SNIF SNIF
MENU
CLOVERS
AOBA JUST HAPPENS TO BE A BAD COOK.
ENOUGH WITH THE UNNECESSARY COMMENTARY!

SEISHU GAKUEN SENIOR HIGH SCHOOL

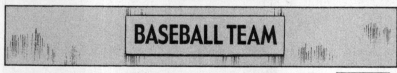

BASEBALL TEAM

BASE-BALL TEAM LOCKER ROOM...

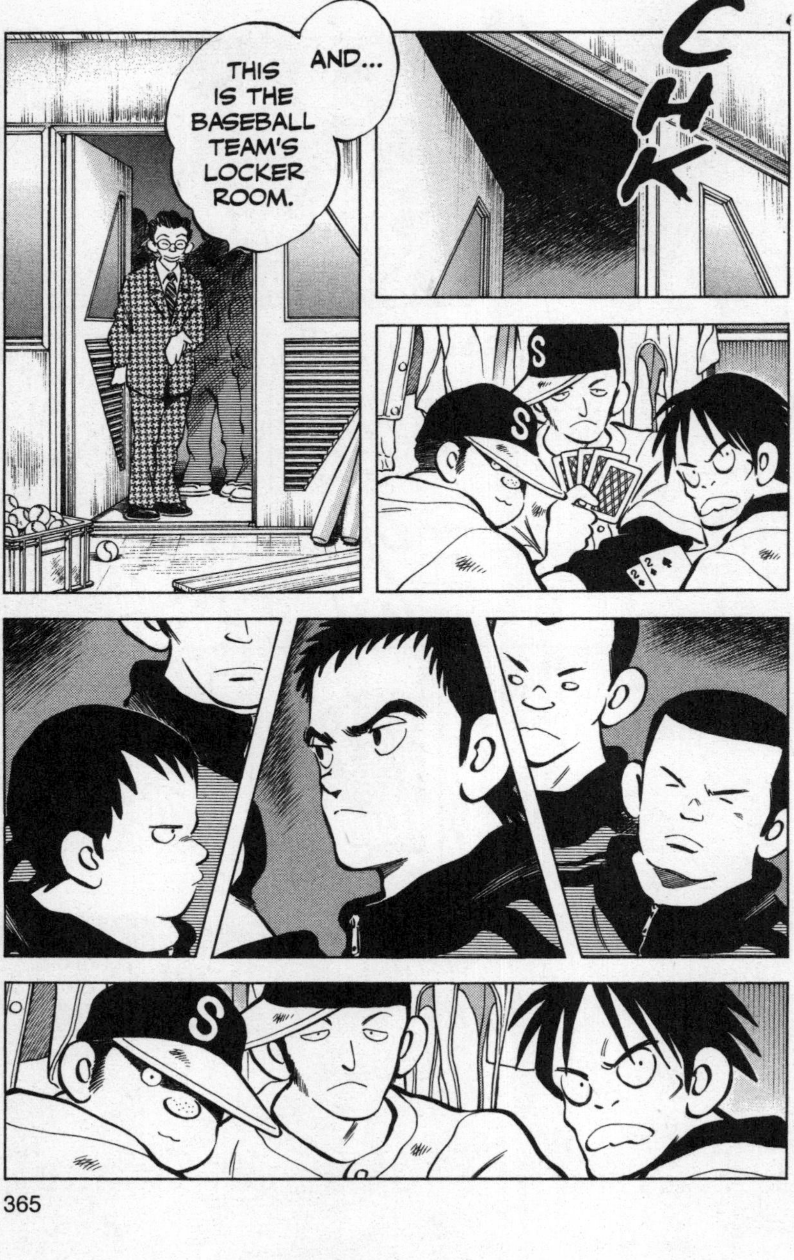
CHK
AND...
THIS IS THE BASEBALL TEAM'S LOCKER ROOM.

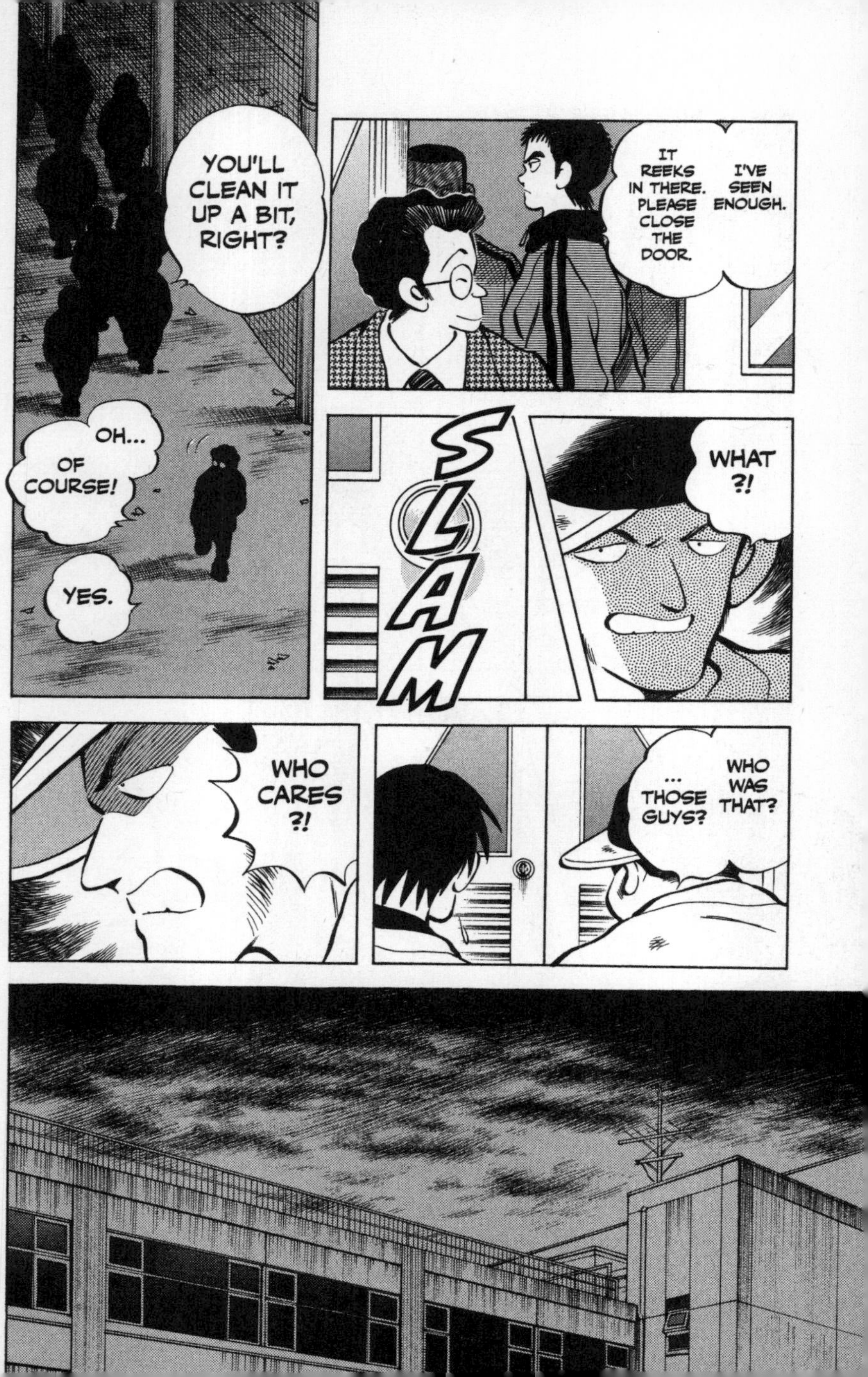
I'VE SEEN ENOUGH.
IT REEKS IN THERE. PLEASE CLOSE THE DOOR.
WHAT ?!
SLAM
YOU'LL CLEAN IT UP A BIT, RIGHT?
OH... OF COURSE!
YES.
WHO WAS THAT?
... THOSE GUYS?
WHO CARES ?!

CHAPTER 10
CAN I BORROW A POT?

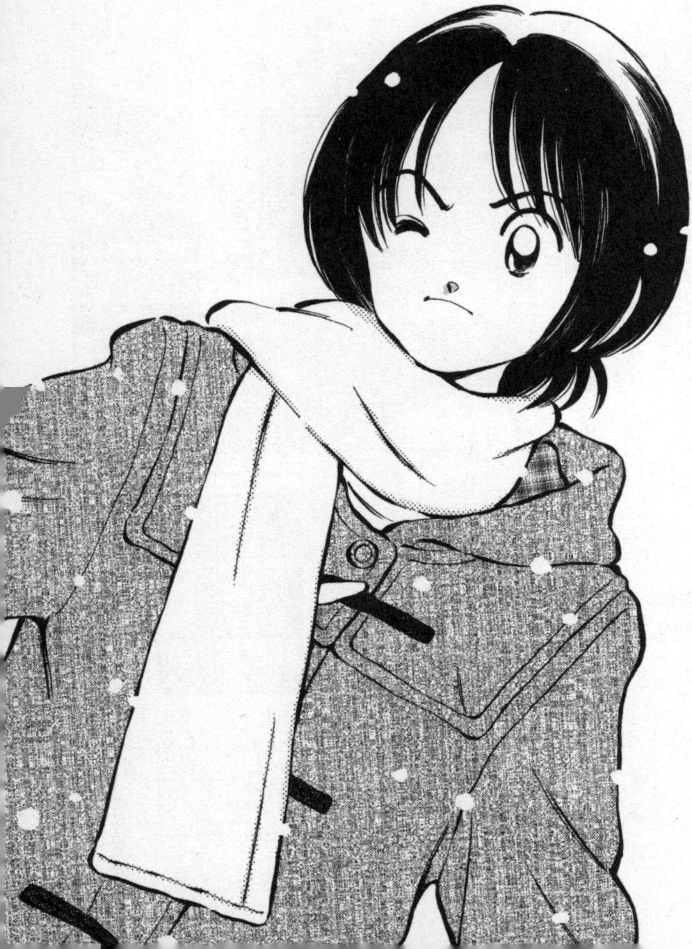

END OF YEAR SALE

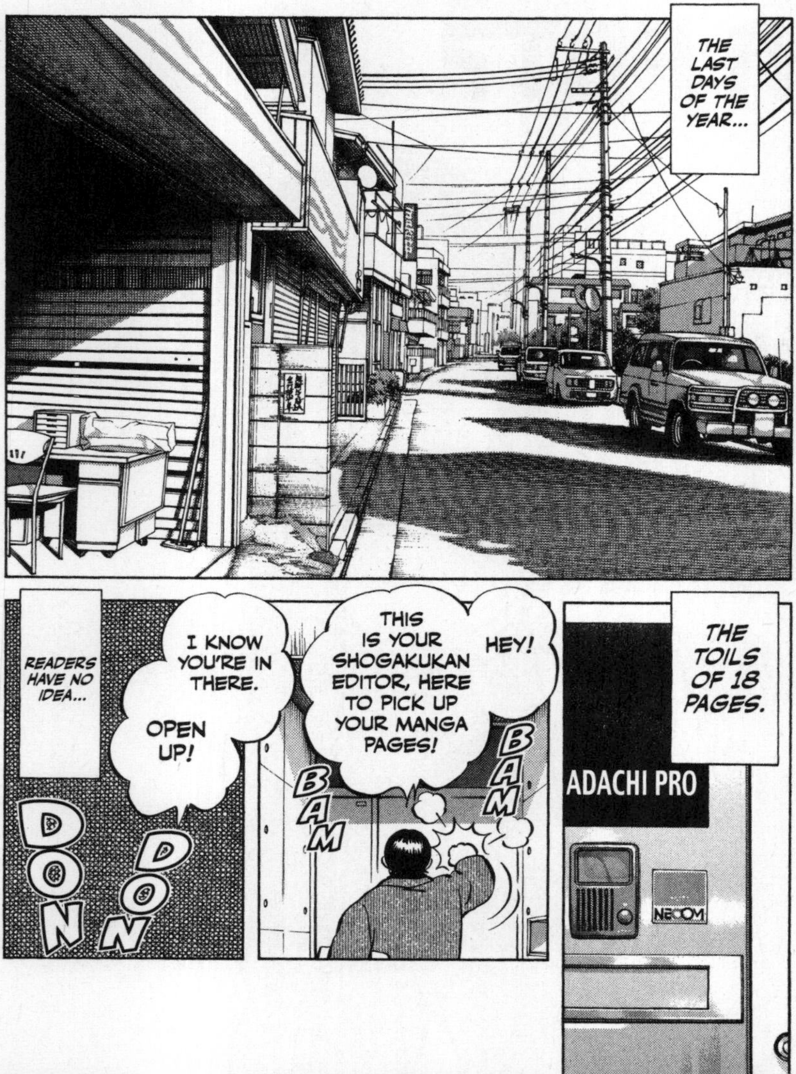
THE LAST DAYS OF THE YEAR...
THE TOILS OF 18 PAGES.
ADACHI PRO
NECOM
HEY!
THIS IS YOUR SHOGAKUKAN EDITOR, HERE TO PICK UP YOUR MANGA PAGES!
BAM
BAM
I KNOW YOU'RE IN THERE.
OPEN UP!
READERS HAVE NO IDEA...
DON
DON

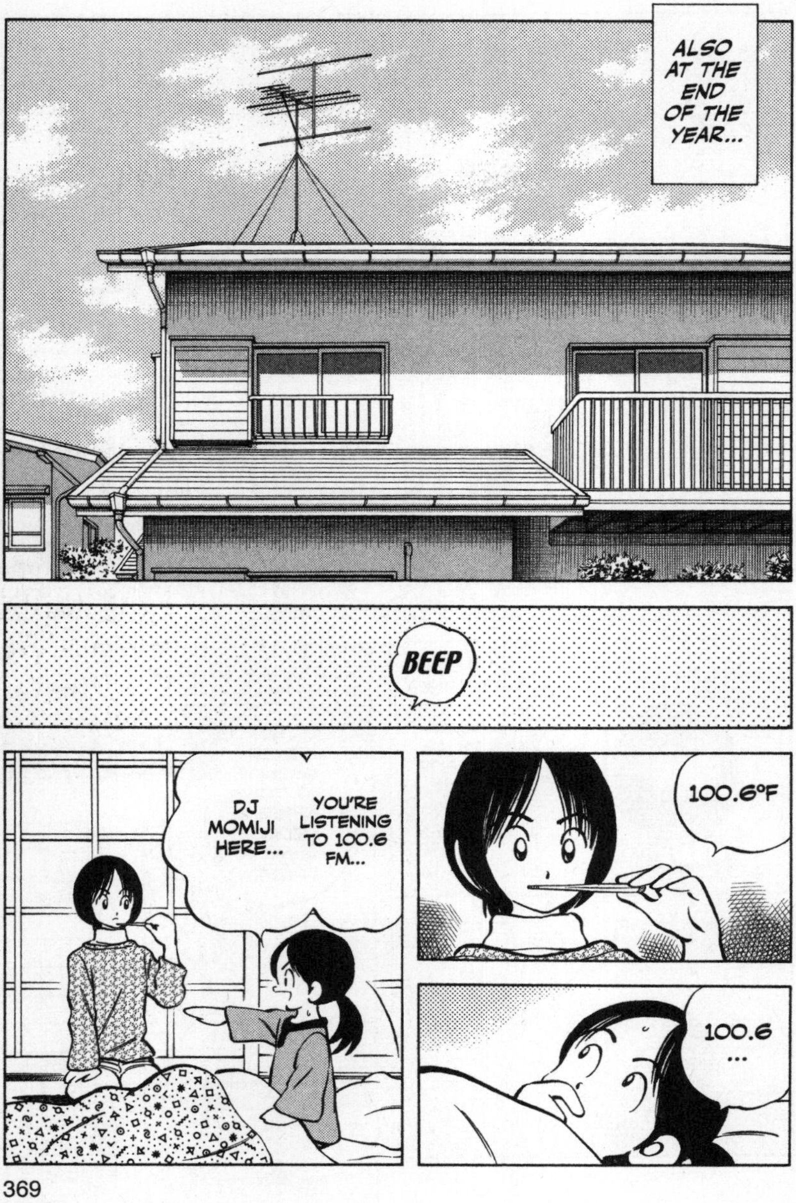
ALSO AT THE END OF THE YEAR...
BEEP
100.6°F
100.6 ...
DJ MOMIJI HERE... YOU'RE LISTENING TO 100.6 FM...

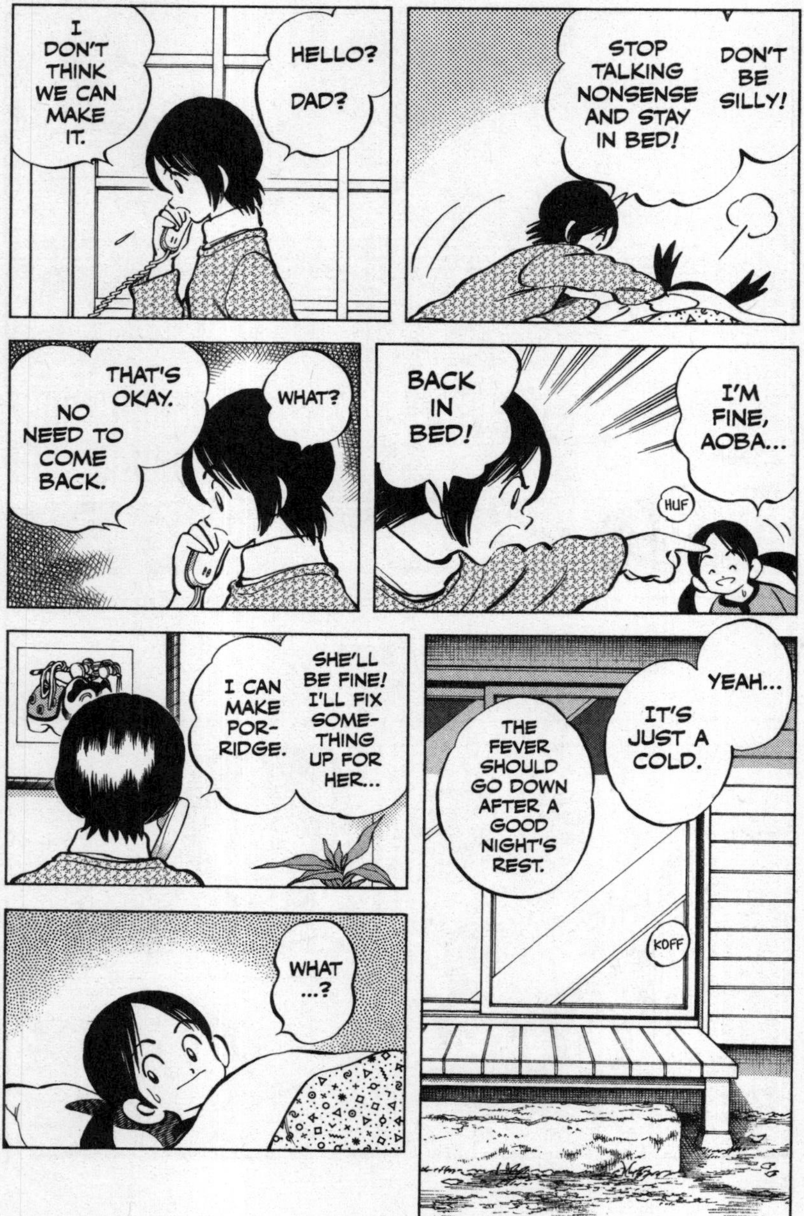
DON'T BE SILLY!
STOP TALKING NONSENSE AND STAY IN BED!
HELLO? DAD?
I DON'T THINK WE CAN MAKE IT.
I'M FINE, AOBA...
HUF
BACK IN BED!
WHAT?
THAT'S OKAY. NO NEED TO COME BACK.
YEAH... IT'S JUST A COLD.
THE FEVER SHOULD GO DOWN AFTER A GOOD NIGHT'S REST.
KOFF
SHE'LL BE FINE! I'LL FIX SOME-THING UP FOR HER...
I CAN MAKE POR-RIDGE.
WHAT ...?

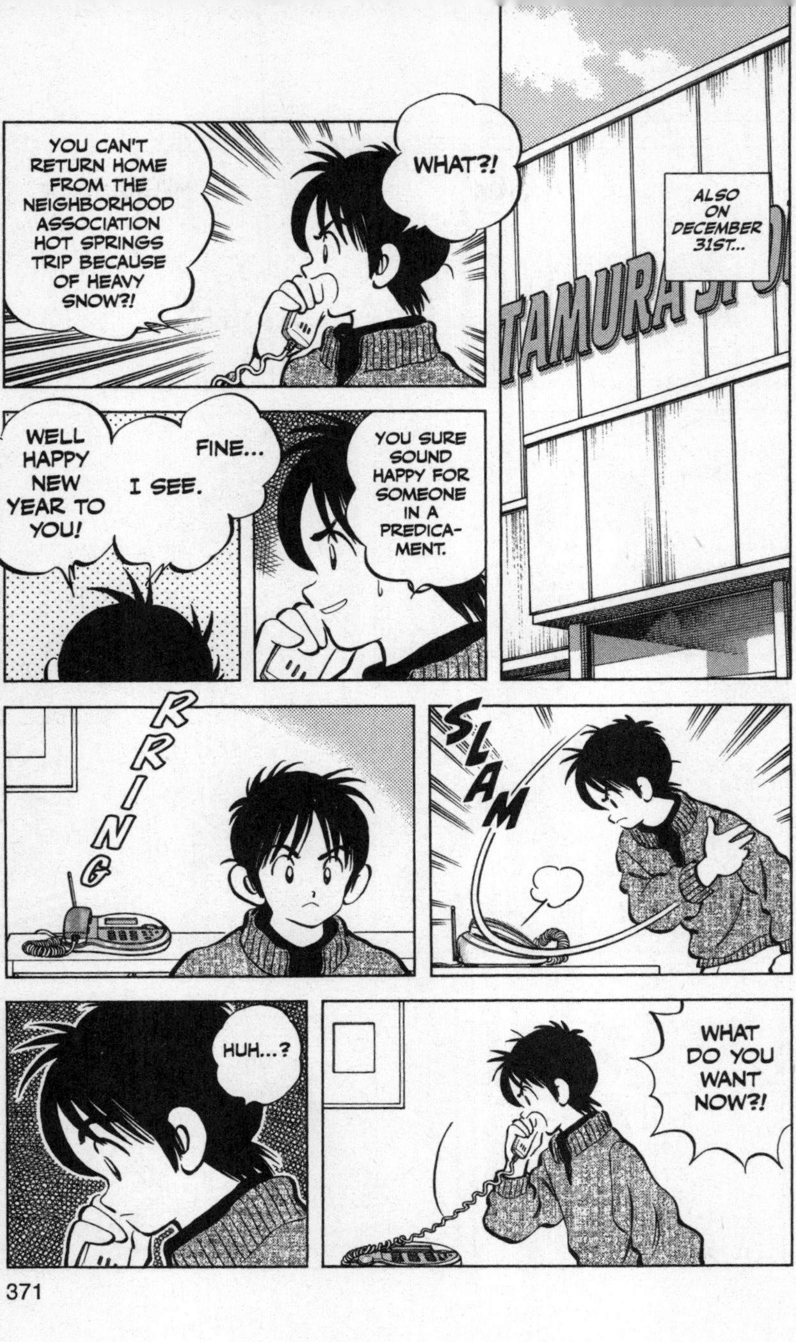
ALSO ON DECEMBER 31ST...
WHAT?!
YOU CAN'T RETURN HOME FROM THE NEIGHBORHOOD ASSOCIATION HOT SPRINGS TRIP BECAUSE OF HEAVY SNOW?!
YOU SURE SOUND HAPPY FOR SOMEONE IN A PREDICA-MENT.
FINE...
I SEE.
WELL HAPPY NEW YEAR TO YOU!
SLAM
RRING
WHAT DO YOU WANT NOW?!
HUH...?

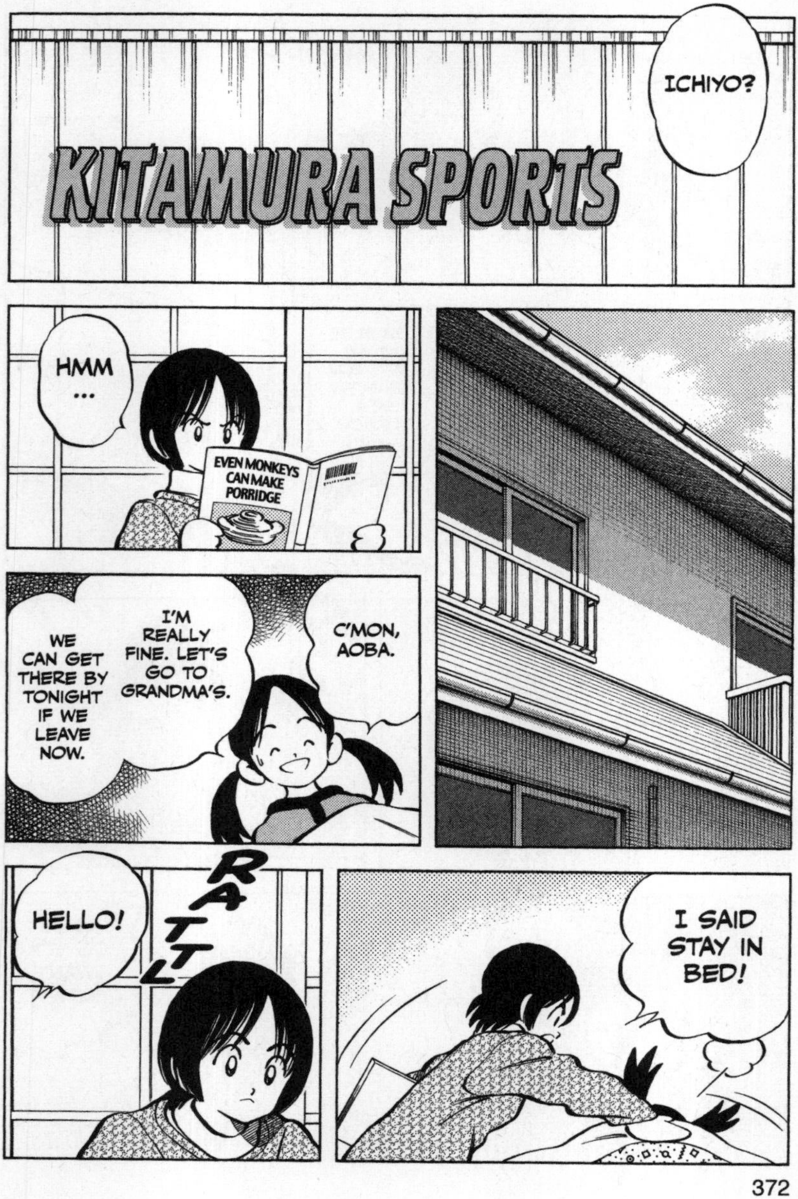
ICHIYO?
KITAMURA SPORTS
HMM ...
EVEN MONKEYS CAN MAKE PORRIDGE
C'MON, AOBA.
I'M REALLY FINE. LET'S GO TO GRANDMA'S.
WE CAN GET THERE BY TONIGHT IF WE LEAVE NOW.
I SAID STAY IN BED!
RATTL
HELLO!

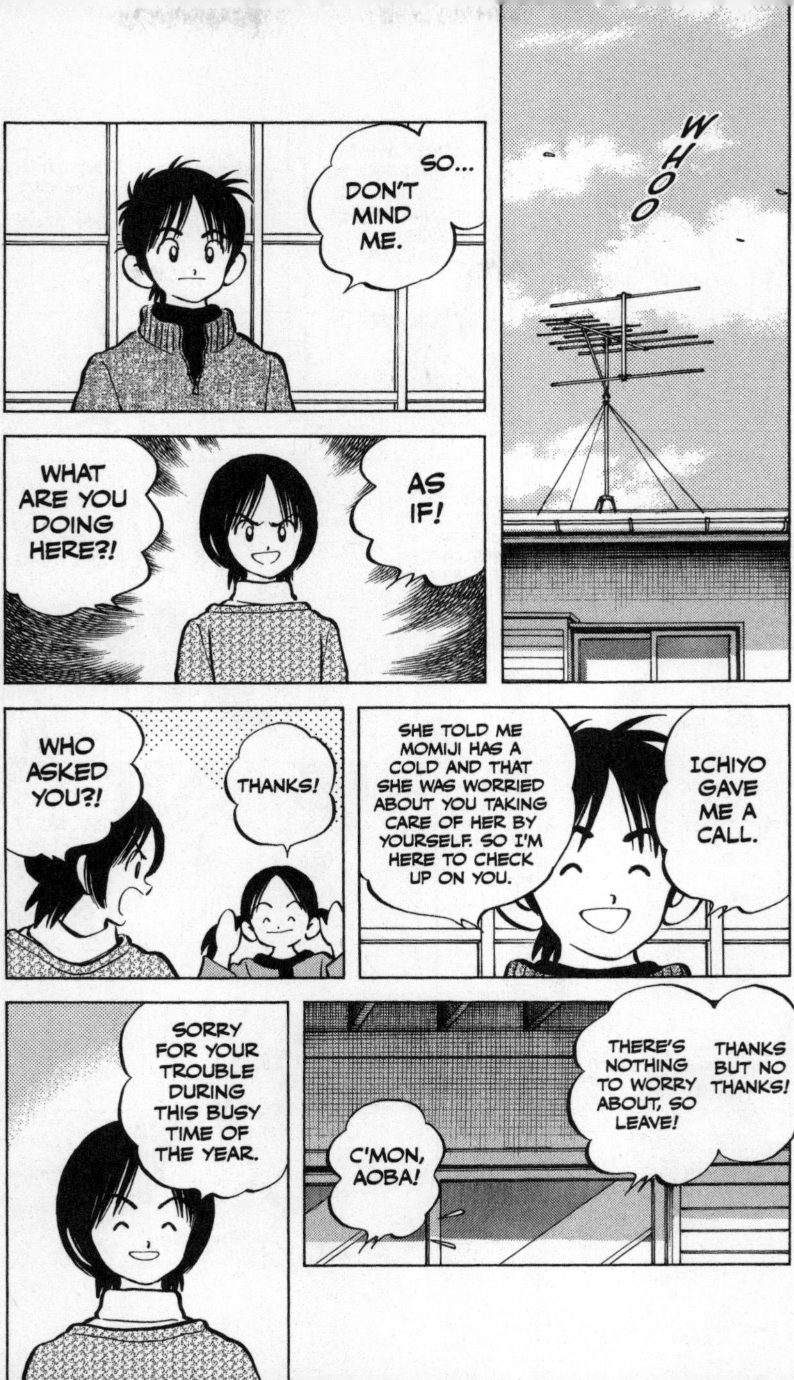
WHOOO
SO... DON'T MIND ME.
AS IF!
WHAT ARE YOU DOING HERE?!
ICHIYO GAVE ME A CALL.
SHE TOLD ME MOMIJI HAS A COLD AND THAT SHE WAS WORRIED ABOUT YOU TAKING CARE OF HER BY YOURSELF. SO I'M HERE TO CHECK UP ON YOU.
THANKS!
WHO ASKED YOU?!
THANKS BUT NO THANKS!
THERE'S NOTHING TO WORRY ABOUT, SO LEAVE!
C'MON, AOBA!
SORRY FOR YOUR TROUBLE DURING THIS BUSY TIME OF THE YEAR.

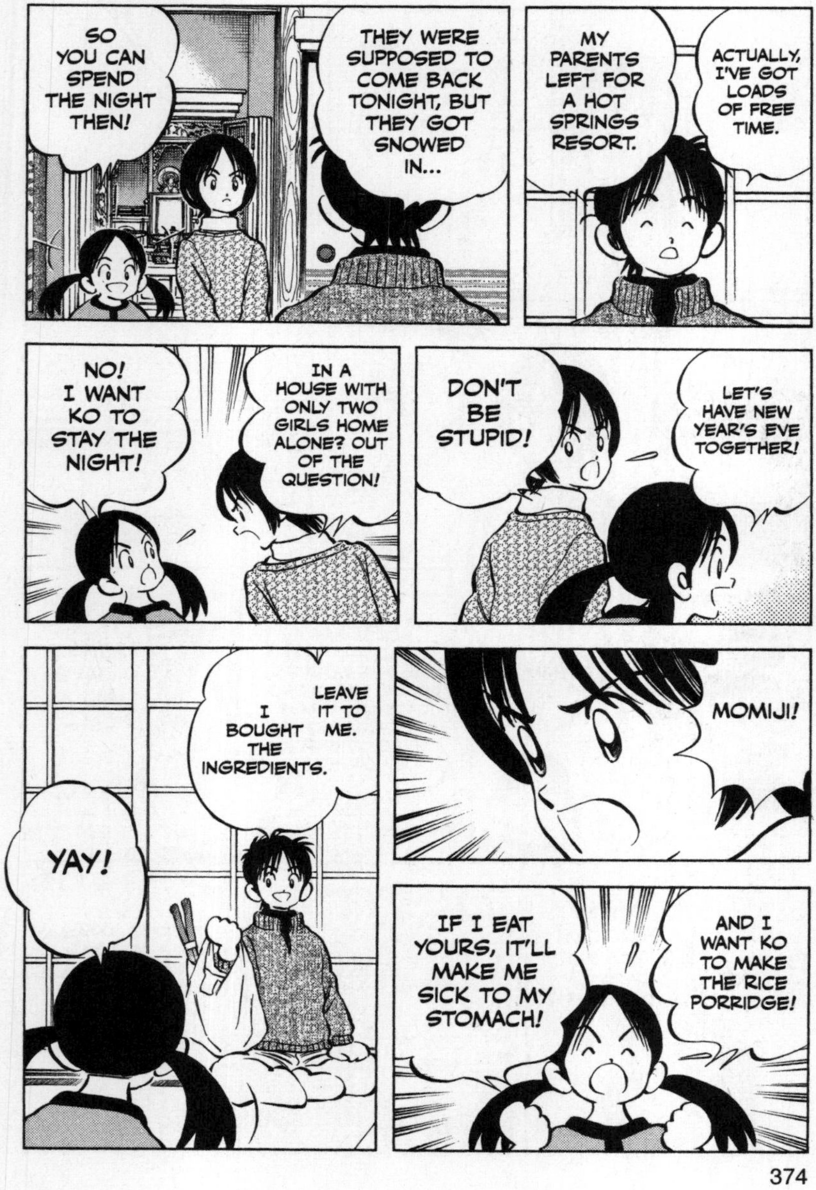
ACTUALLY, I'VE GOT LOADS OF FREE TIME.
MY PARENTS LEFT FOR A HOT SPRINGS RESORT.
THEY WERE SUPPOSED TO COME BACK TONIGHT, BUT THEY GOT SNOWED IN...
SO YOU CAN SPEND THE NIGHT THEN!
LET'S HAVE NEW YEAR'S EVE TOGETHER!
DON'T BE STUPID!
IN A HOUSE WITH ONLY TWO GIRLS HOME ALONE? OUT OF THE QUESTION!
NO! I WANT KO TO STAY THE NIGHT!
MOMIJI!
AND I WANT KO TO MAKE THE RICE PORRIDGE!
IF I EAT YOURS, IT'LL MAKE ME SICK TO MY STOMACH!
LEAVE IT TO ME.
I BOUGHT THE INGREDIENTS.
YAY!

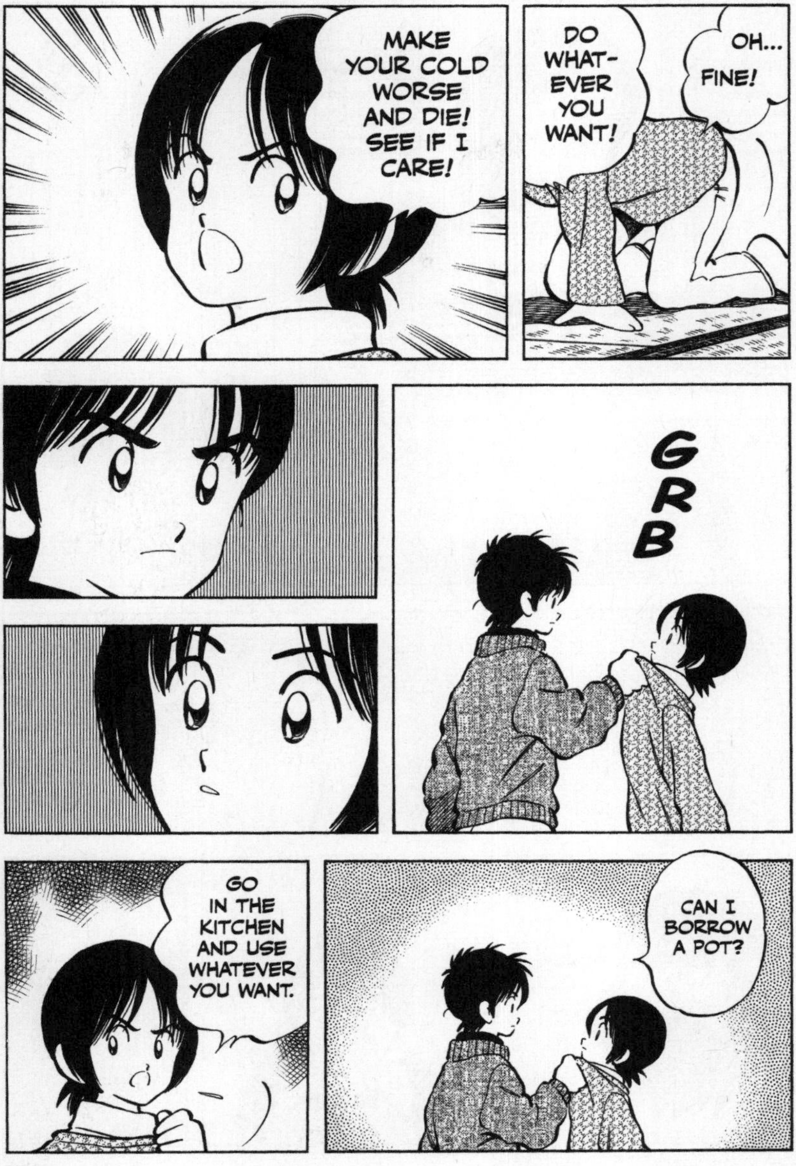
OH... FINE!
DO WHAT-EVER YOU WANT!
MAKE YOUR COLD WORSE AND DIE! SEE IF I CARE!
GRB
CAN I BORROW A POT?
GO IN THE KITCHEN AND USE WHATEVER YOU WANT.

OH, BUT FIRST...

TING

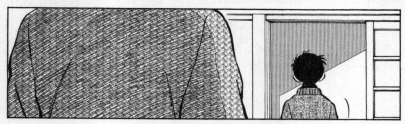

MOMI-JI... I'M SORRY...

SORRY...

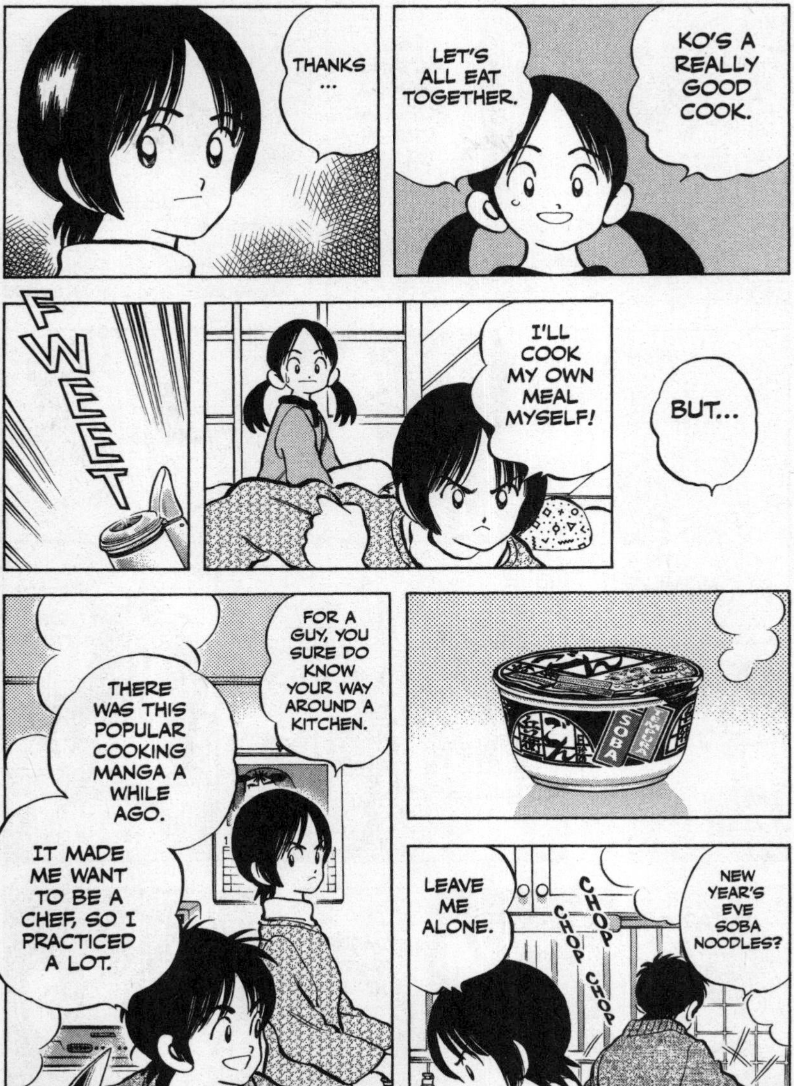
KO'S A REALLY GOOD COOK.
LET'S ALL EAT TOGETHER.
THANKS ...
BUT...
I'LL COOK MY OWN MEAL MYSELF!
FWEET
SOBA
NEW YEAR'S EVE SOBA NOODLES?
CHOP CHOP CHOP CHOP
LEAVE ME ALONE.
FOR A GUY, YOU SURE DO KNOW YOUR WAY AROUND A KITCHEN.
THERE WAS THIS POPULAR COOKING MANGA A WHILE AGO.
IT MADE ME WANT TO BE A CHEF, SO I PRACTICED A LOT.

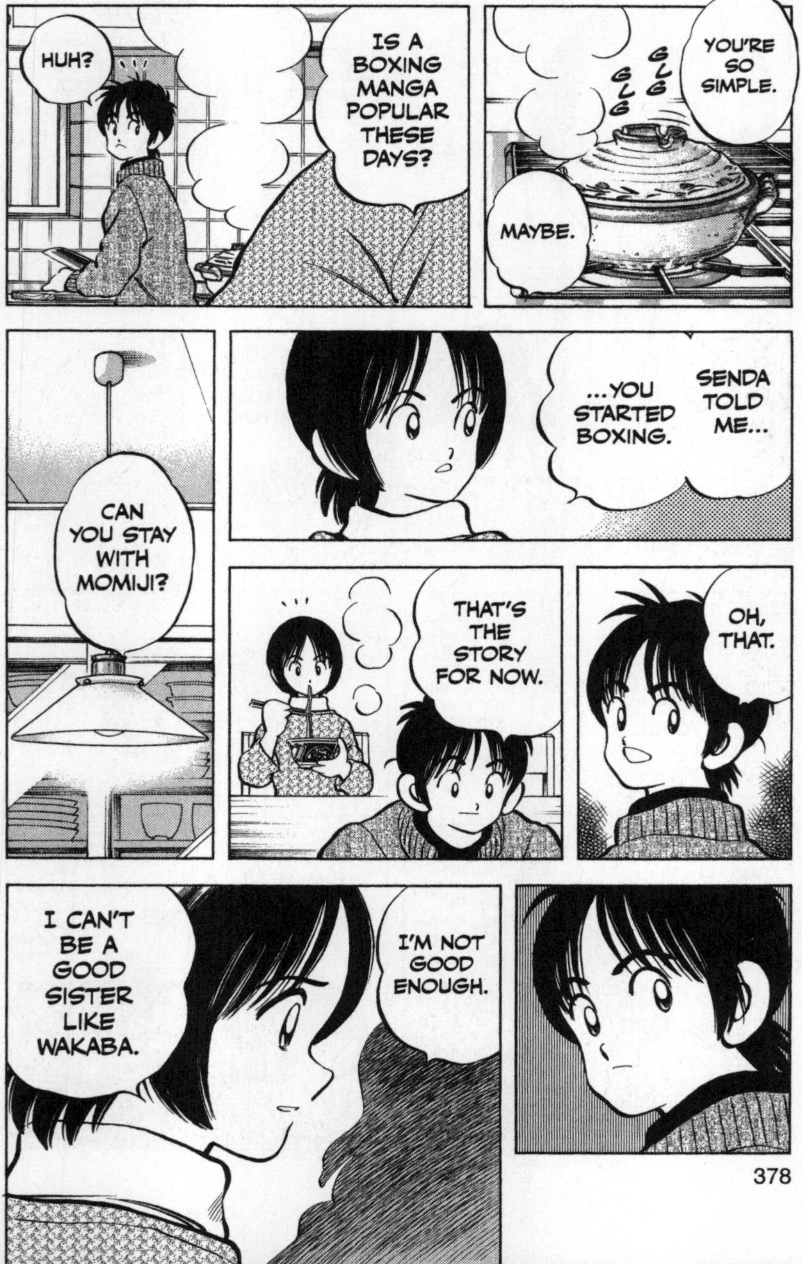
YOU'RE SO SIMPLE.
GLG GLG
MAYBE.
IS A BOXING MANGA POPULAR THESE DAYS?
HUH?
SENDA TOLD ME...
...YOU STARTED BOXING.
OH, THAT.
THAT'S THE STORY FOR NOW.
CAN YOU STAY WITH MOMIJI?
I'M NOT GOOD ENOUGH.
I CAN'T BE A GOOD SISTER LIKE WAKABA.

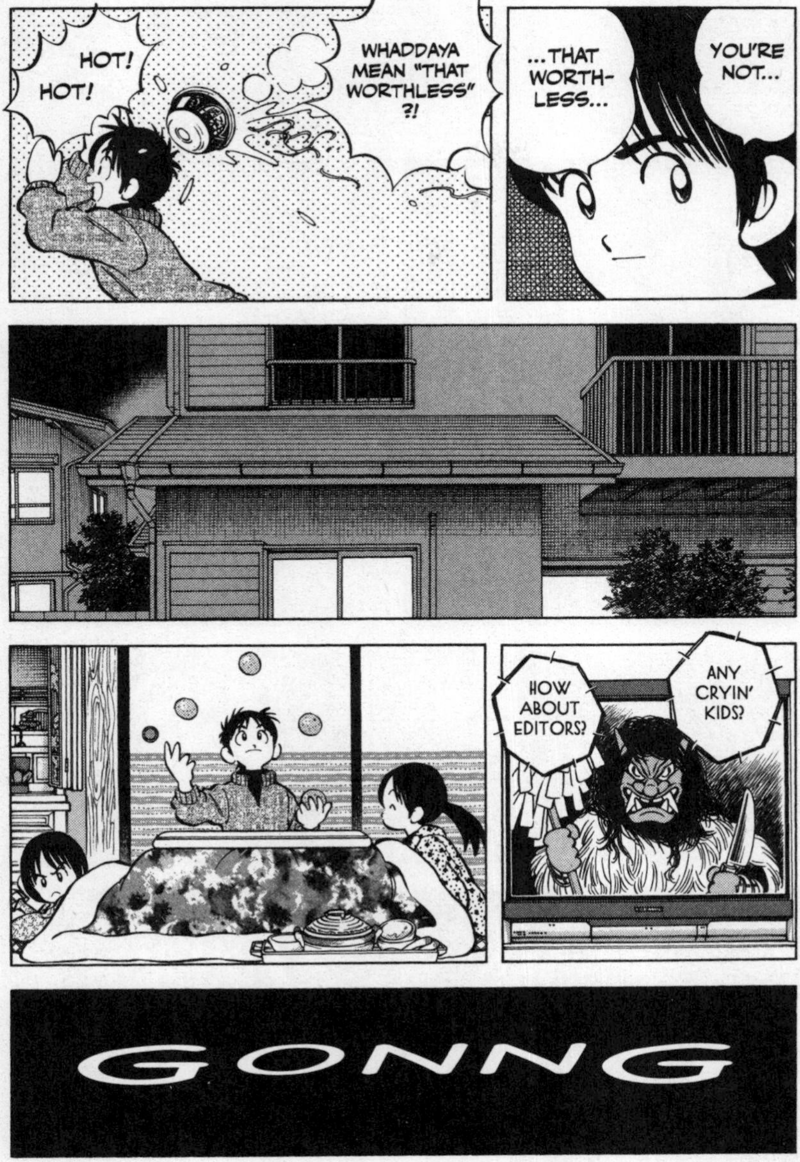
YOU'RE NOT...
...THAT WORTHLESS...
WHADDAYA MEAN "THAT WORTHLESS" ?!
HOT! HOT!
ANY CRYIN' KIDS?
HOW ABOUT EDITORS?
GONNG

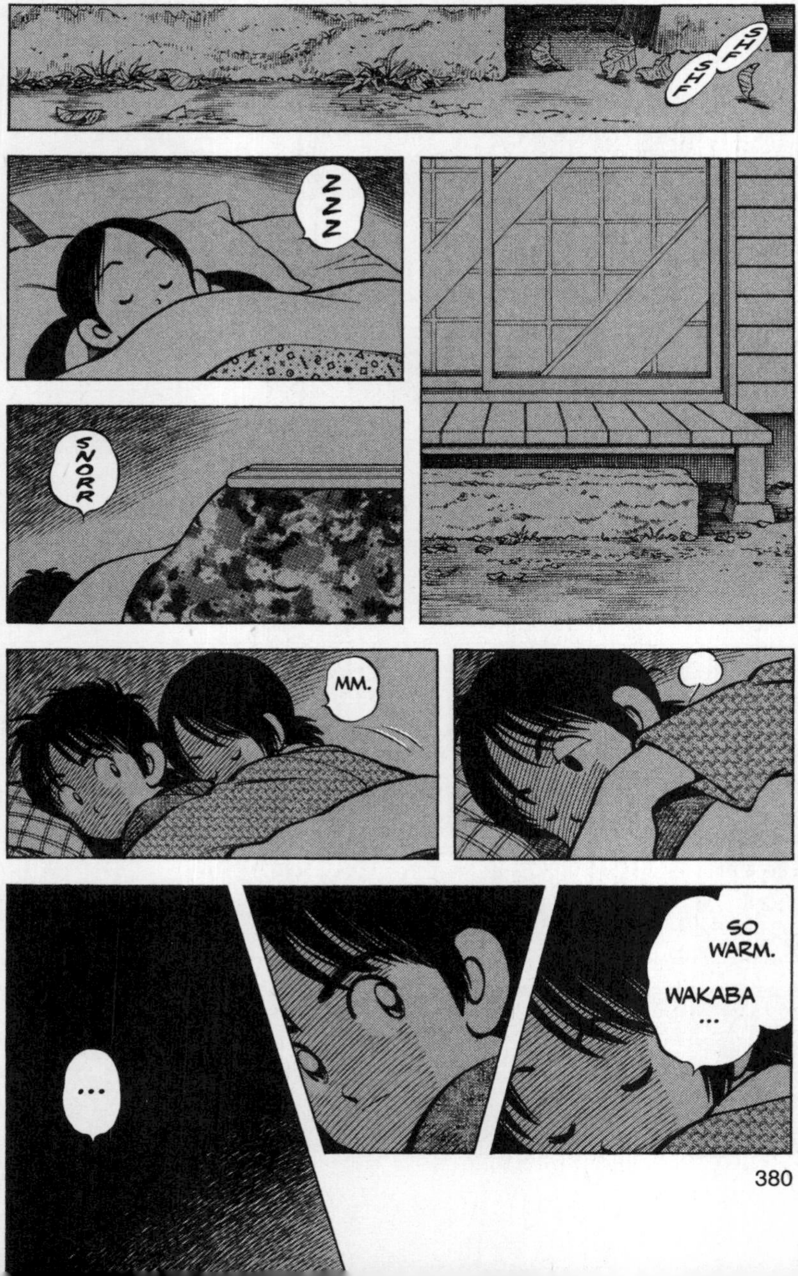
SHF SHF SHF
ZZZ
SNORR
MM.
SO WARM.
WAKABA ...
...

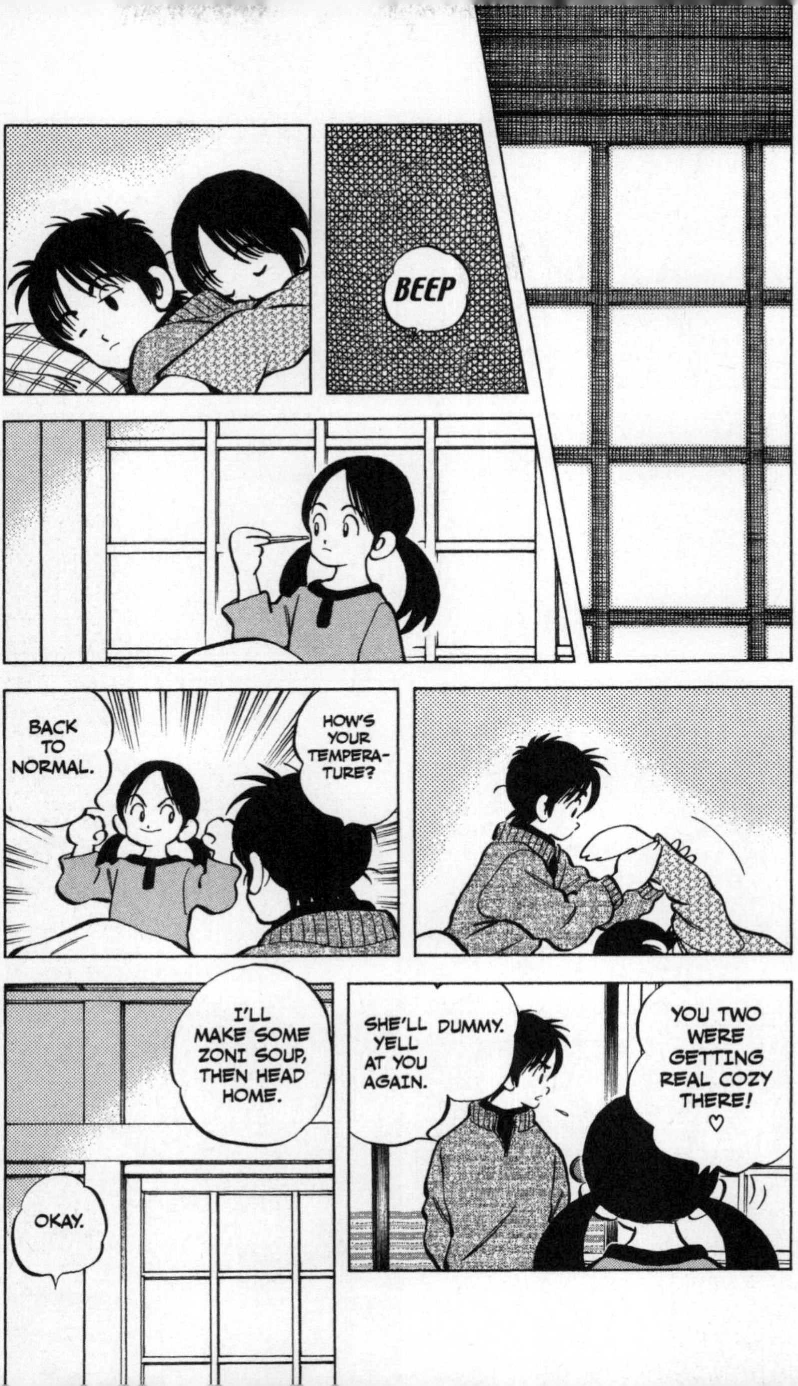
BEEP
HOW'S YOUR TEMPERATURE?
BACK TO NORMAL.
YOU TWO WERE GETTING REAL COZY THERE! ♡
DUMMY.
SHE'LL YELL AT YOU AGAIN.
I'LL MAKE SOME ZONI SOUP, THEN HEAD HOME.
OKAY.

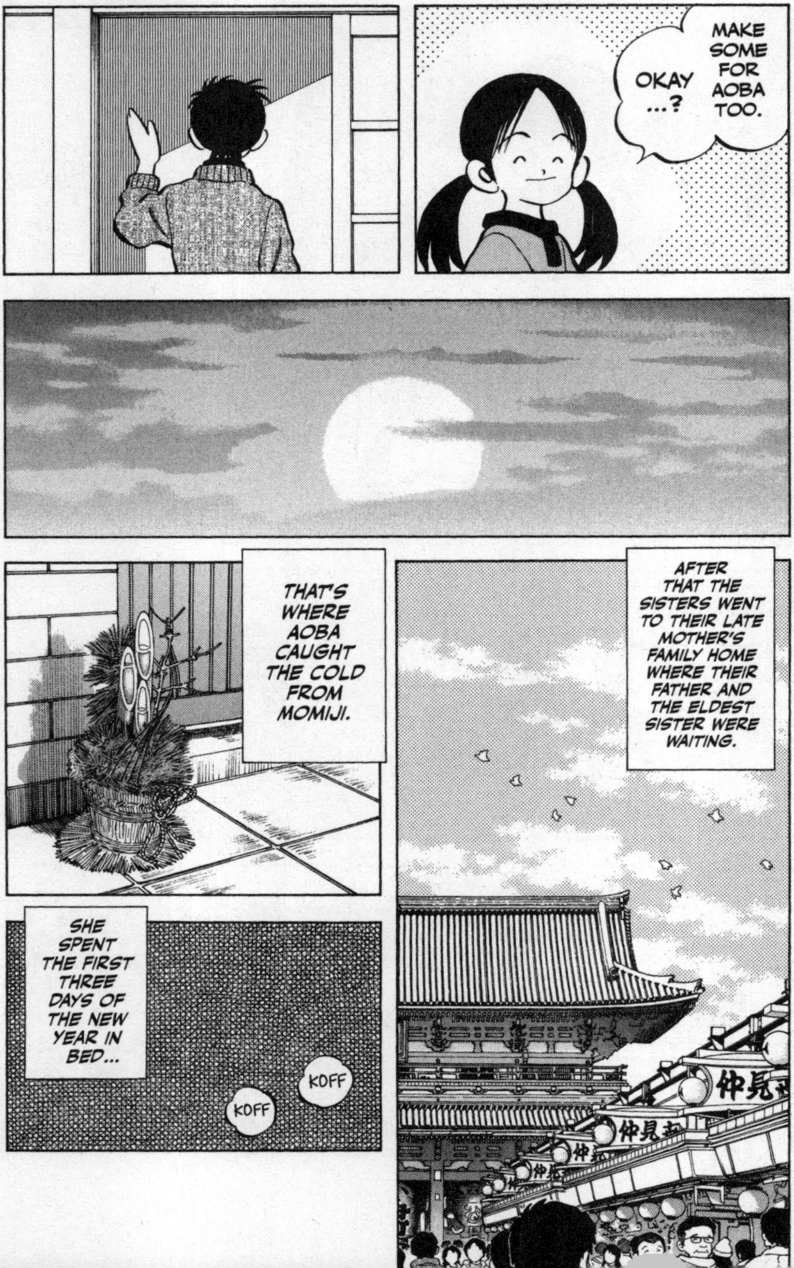
MAKE SOME FOR AOBA TOO.
OKAY ...?
AFTER THAT THE SISTERS WENT TO THEIR LATE MOTHER'S FAMILY HOME WHERE THEIR FATHER AND THE ELDEST SISTER WERE WAITING.
THAT'S WHERE AOBA CAUGHT THE COLD FROM MOMIJI.
SHE SPENT THE FIRST THREE DAYS OF THE NEW YEAR IN BED...
KOFF
KOFF

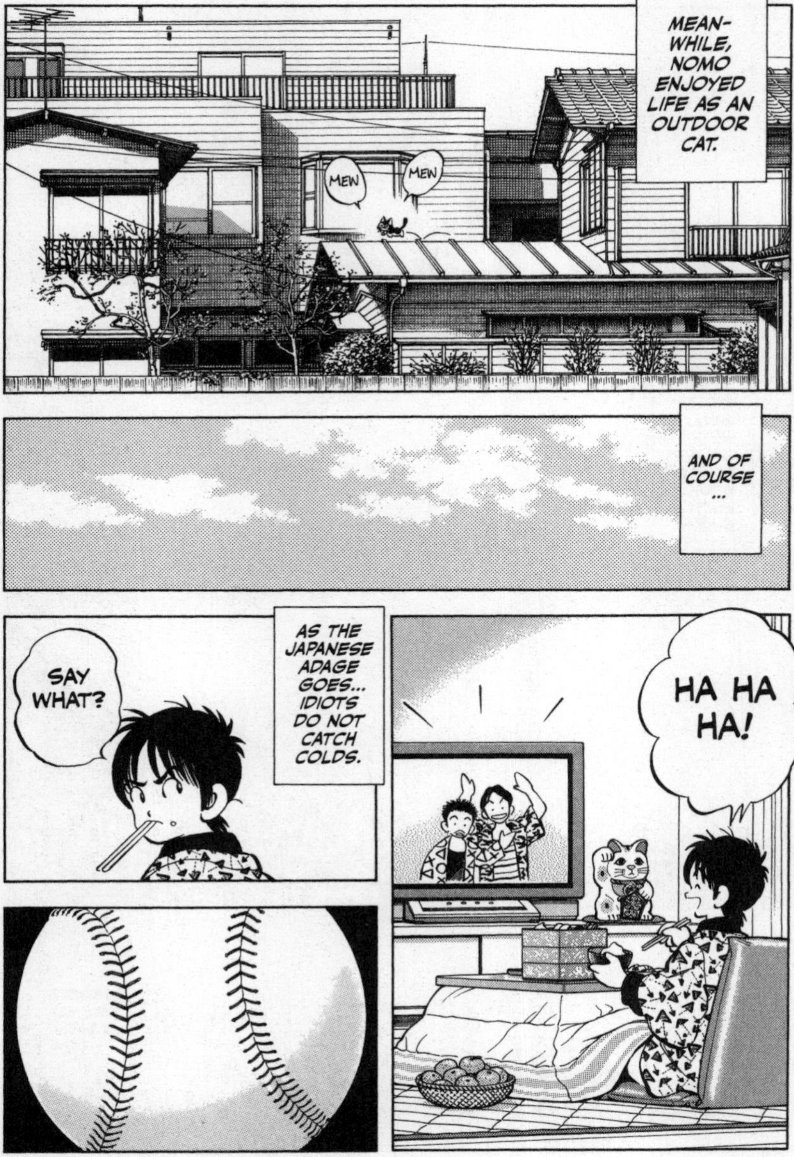
MEAN-WHILE, NOMO ENJOYED LIFE AS AN OUTDOOR CAT.
MEW
MEW
AND OF COURSE ...
HA HA HA!
AS THE JAPANESE ADAGE GOES... IDIOTS DO NOT CATCH COLDS.
SAY WHAT?

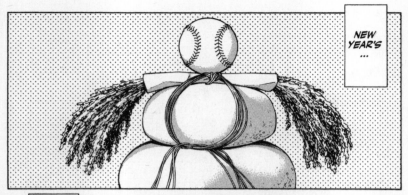

NEW YEAR'S ...

TIME FOR THE ANTICIPATED DOUBLE ISSUE OF WEEKLY SHONEN SUNDAY.

READERS HAVE NO IDEA...

Cross☘Game

Cross Game

③

Story & Art by
Mitsuru Adachi

CHAPTER 11

THE FIRST SPRING OF HIGH SCHOOL

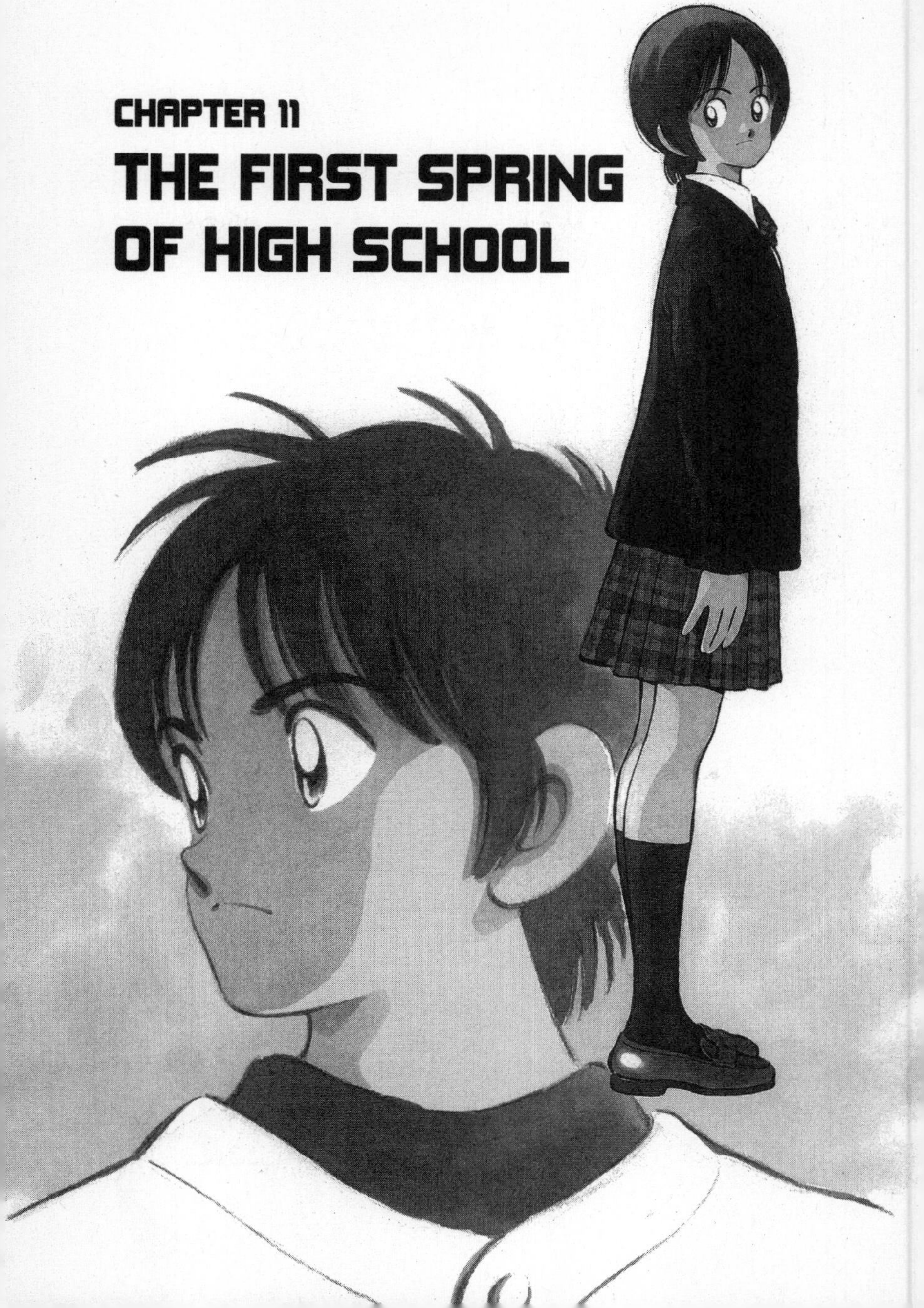

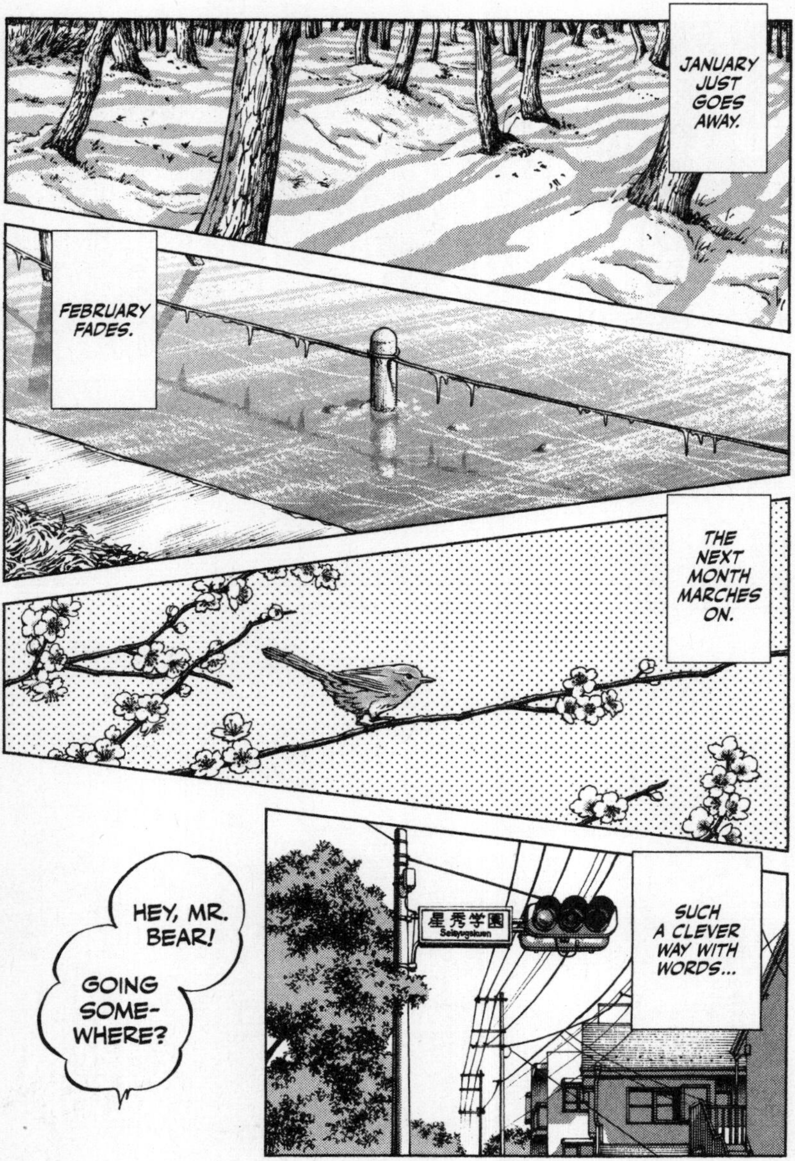
JANUARY JUST GOES AWAY.
FEBRUARY FADES.
THE NEXT MONTH MARCHES ON.
SUCH A CLEVER WAY WITH WORDS...
星秀学園
HEY, MR. BEAR!
GOING SOME-WHERE?

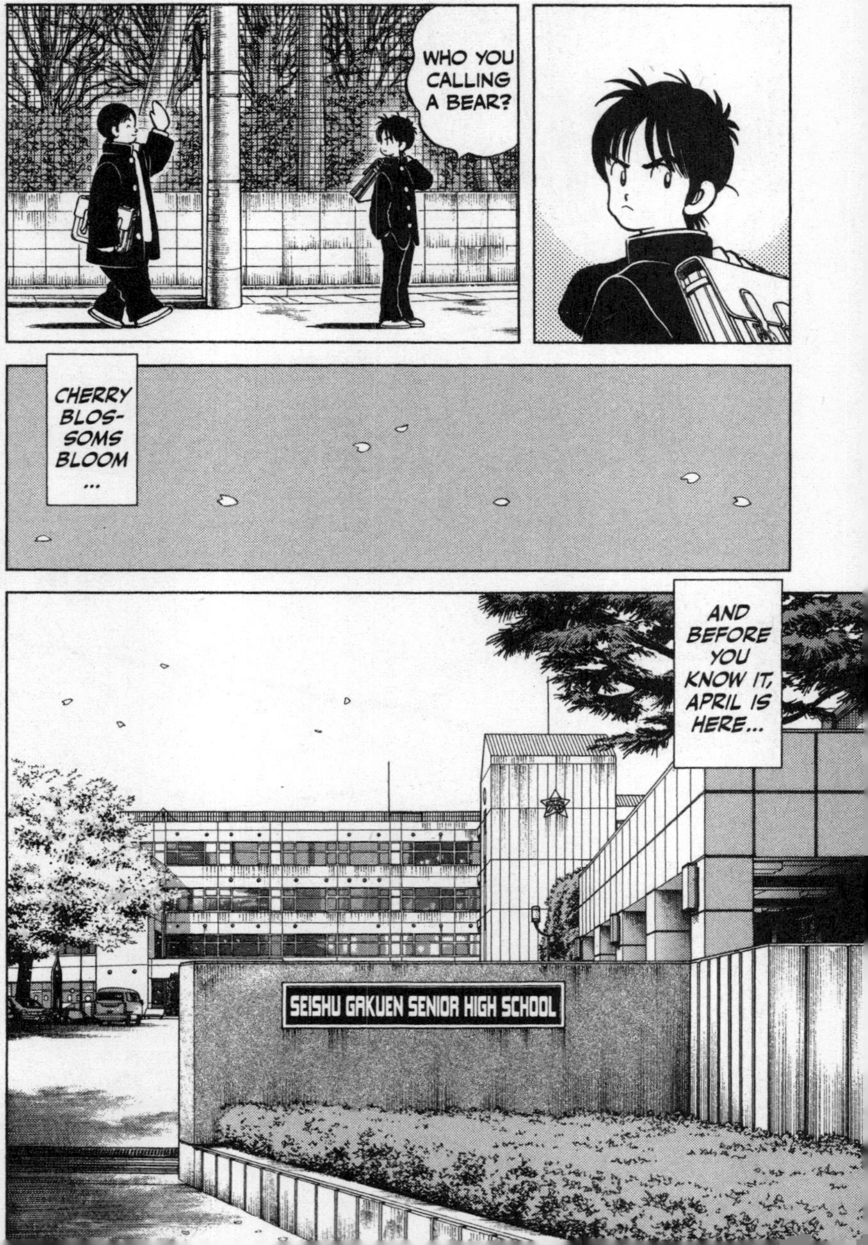
WHO YOU CALLING A BEAR?
CHERRY BLOS-SOMS BLOOM ...
AND BEFORE YOU KNOW IT, APRIL IS HERE...
SEISHU GAKUEN SENIOR HIGH SCHOOL

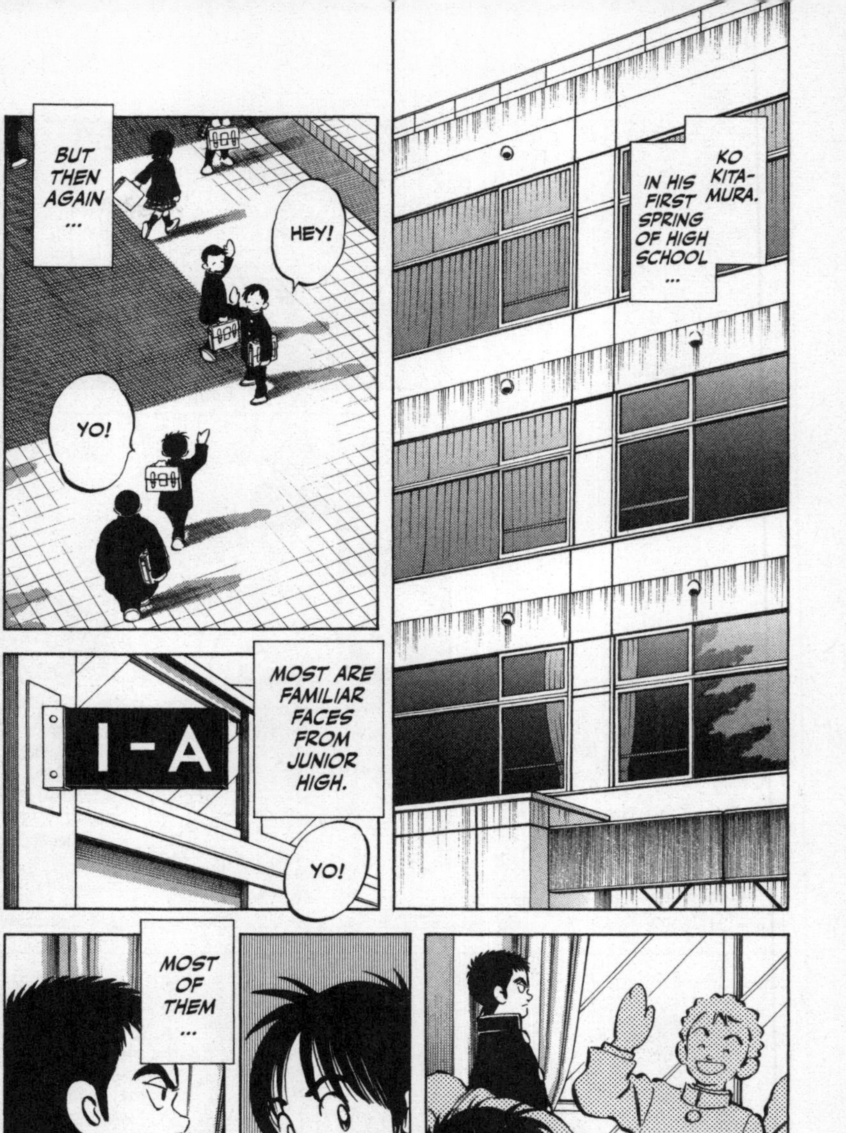
KO KITAMURA.
IN HIS FIRST SPRING OF HIGH SCHOOL...
BUT THEN AGAIN...
HEY!
YO!
I-A
MOST ARE FAMILIAR FACES FROM JUNIOR HIGH.
YO!
MOST OF THEM...

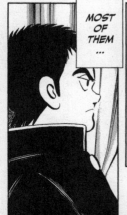

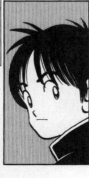

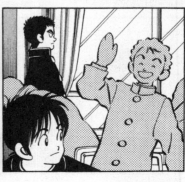

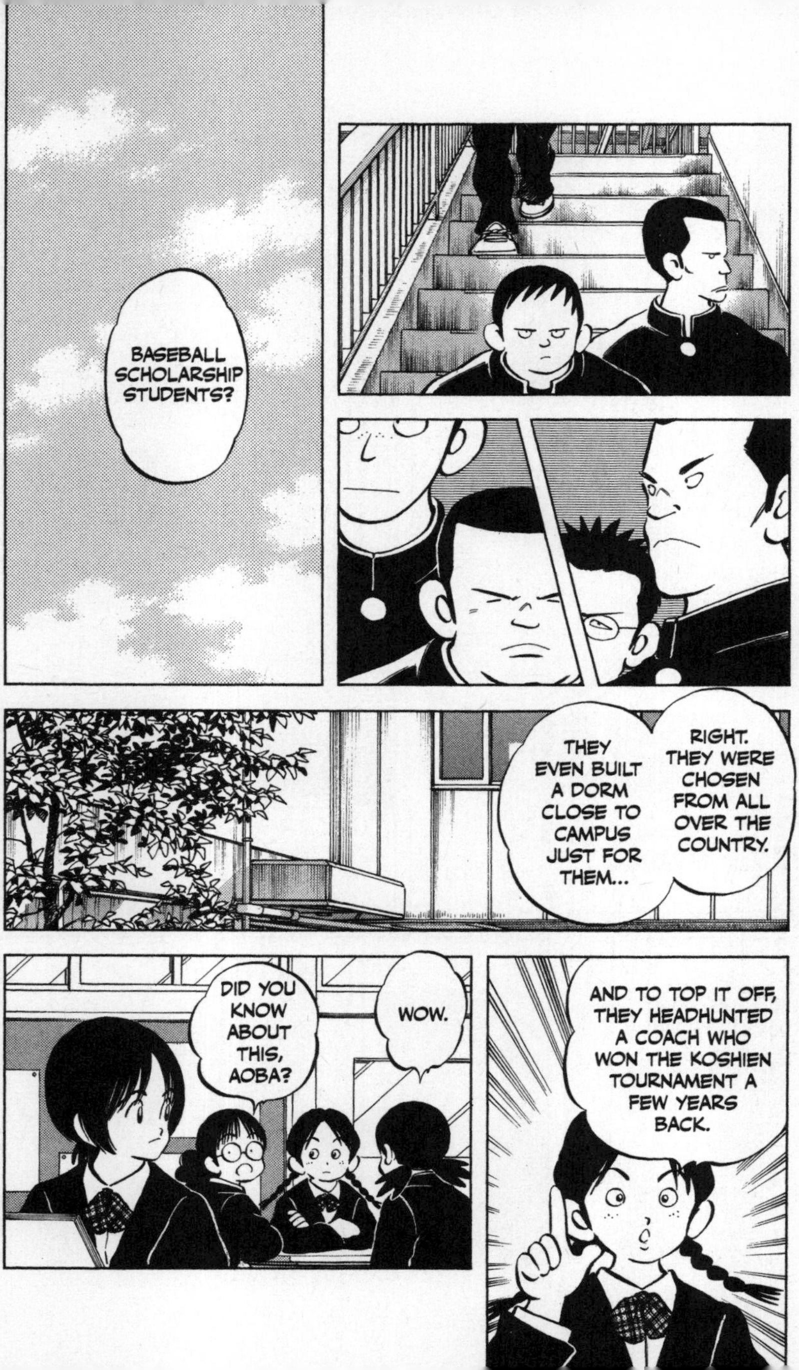
BASEBALL SCHOLARSHIP STUDENTS?
RIGHT. THEY WERE CHOSEN FROM ALL OVER THE COUNTRY.
THEY EVEN BUILT A DORM CLOSE TO CAMPUS JUST FOR THEM...
AND TO TOP IT OFF, THEY HEADHUNTED A COACH WHO WON THE KOSHIEN TOURNAMENT A FEW YEARS BACK.
WOW.
DID YOU KNOW ABOUT THIS, AOBA?

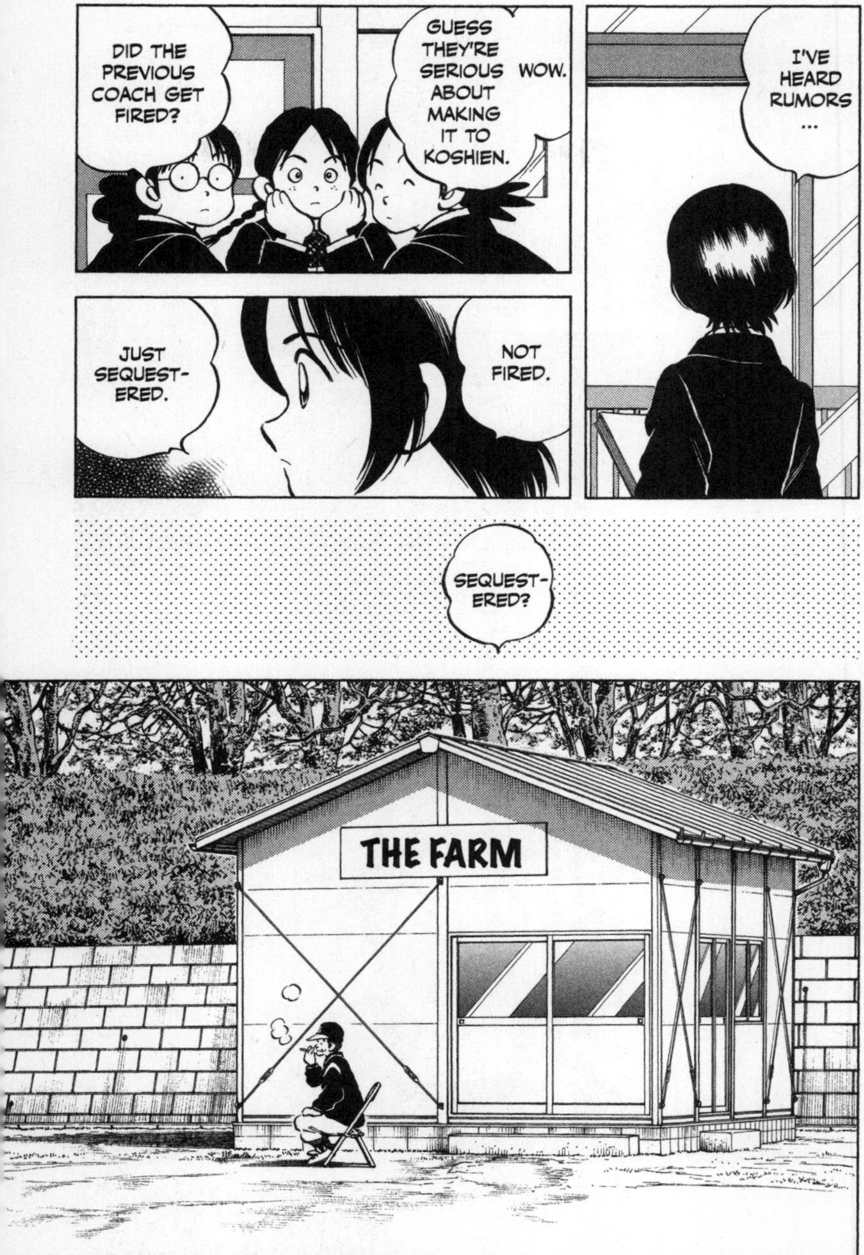
I'VE HEARD RUMORS ...
WOW.
GUESS THEY'RE SERIOUS ABOUT MAKING IT TO KOSHIEN.
DID THE PREVIOUS COACH GET FIRED?
NOT FIRED.
JUST SEQUEST-ERED.
SEQUEST-ERED?
THE FARM

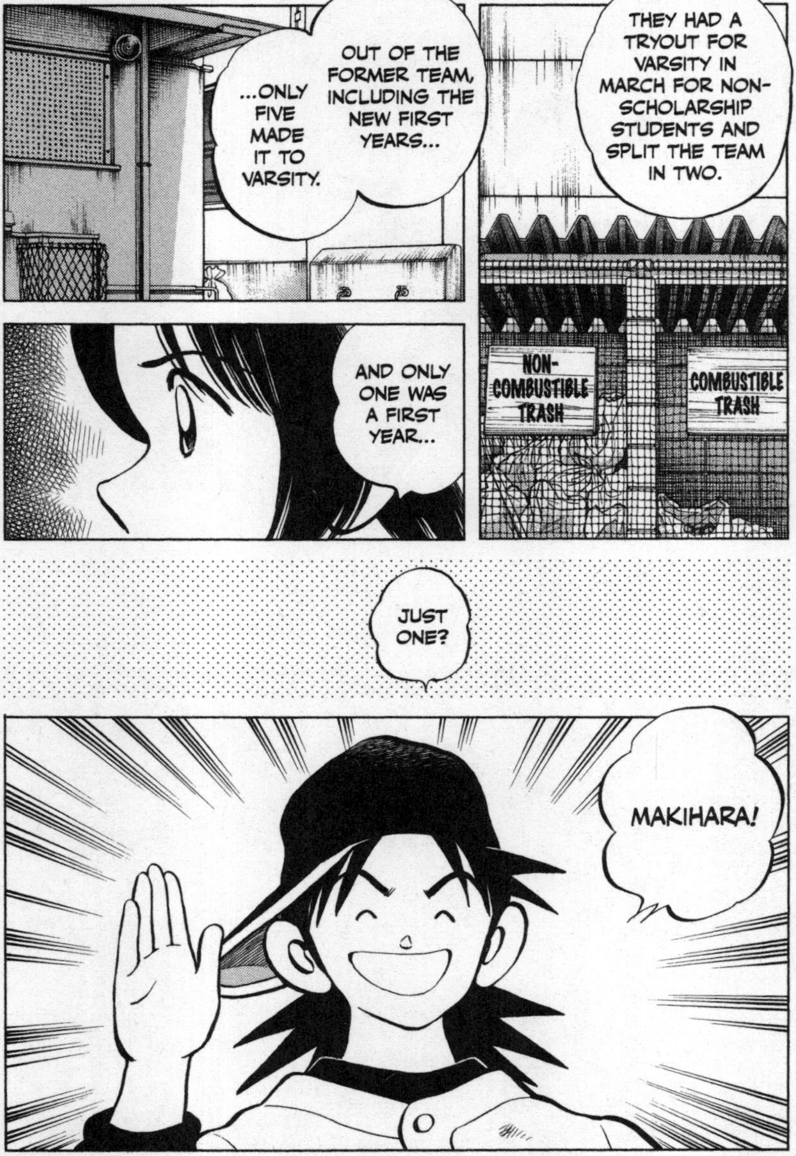
THEY HAD A TRYOUT FOR VARSITY IN MARCH FOR NON-SCHOLARSHIP STUDENTS AND SPLIT THE TEAM IN TWO.
COMBUSTIBLE TRASH
NON-COMBUSTIBLE TRASH
OUT OF THE FORMER TEAM, INCLUDING THE NEW FIRST YEARS...
...ONLY FIVE MADE IT TO VARSITY.
AND ONLY ONE WAS A FIRST YEAR...
JUST ONE?
MAKIHARA!

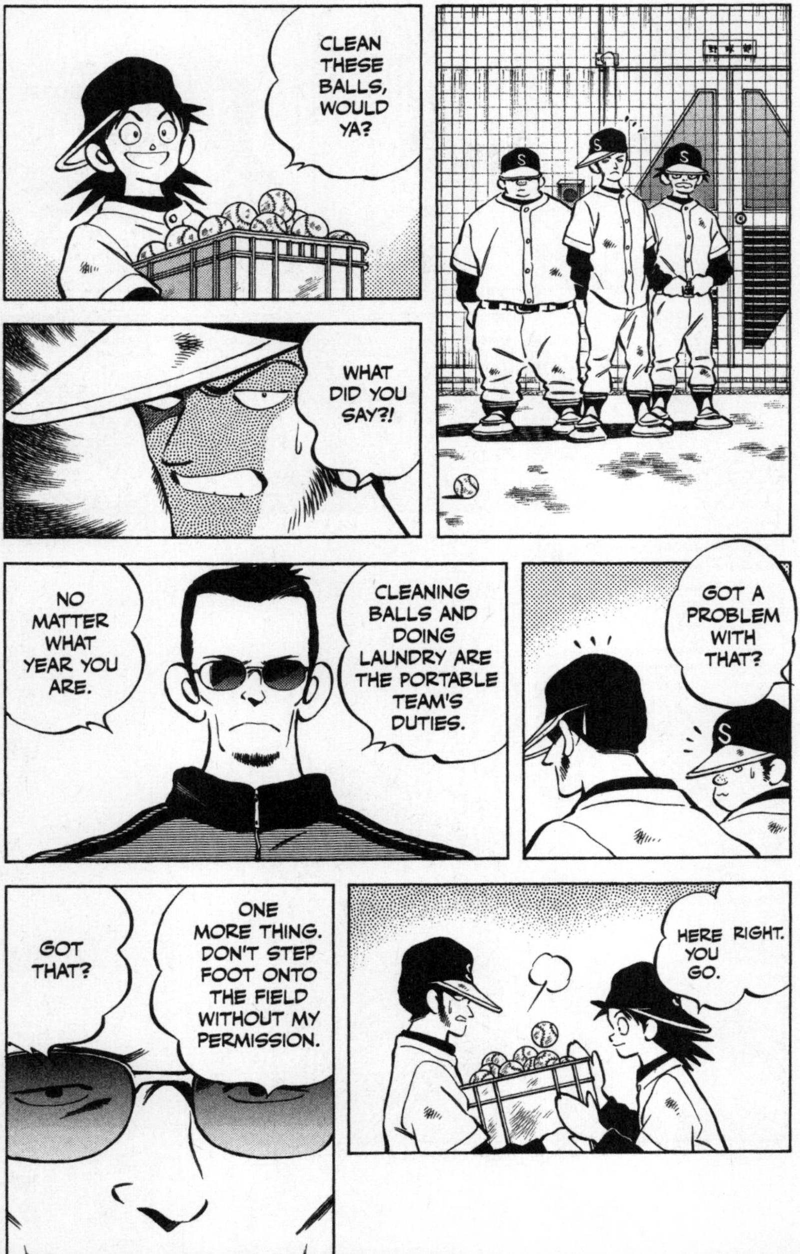
CLEAN THESE BALLS, WOULD YA?
WHAT DID YOU SAY?!
GOT A PROBLEM WITH THAT?
CLEANING BALLS AND DOING LAUNDRY ARE THE PORTABLE TEAM'S DUTIES.
NO MATTER WHAT YEAR YOU ARE.
RIGHT.
HERE YOU GO.
ONE MORE THING. DON'T STEP FOOT ONTO THE FIELD WITHOUT MY PERMISSION.
GOT THAT?

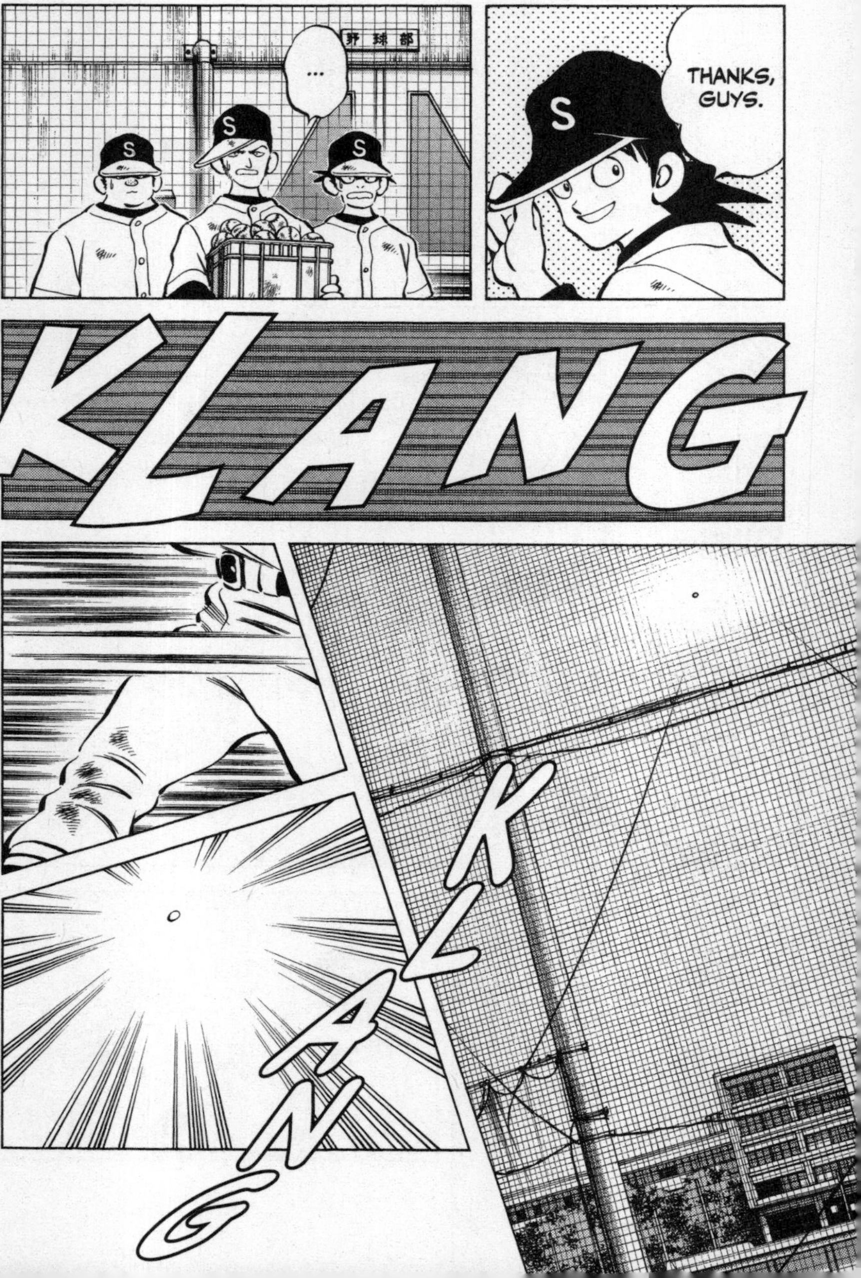
THANKS, GUYS.
野球部
...
KLANG
KLANG

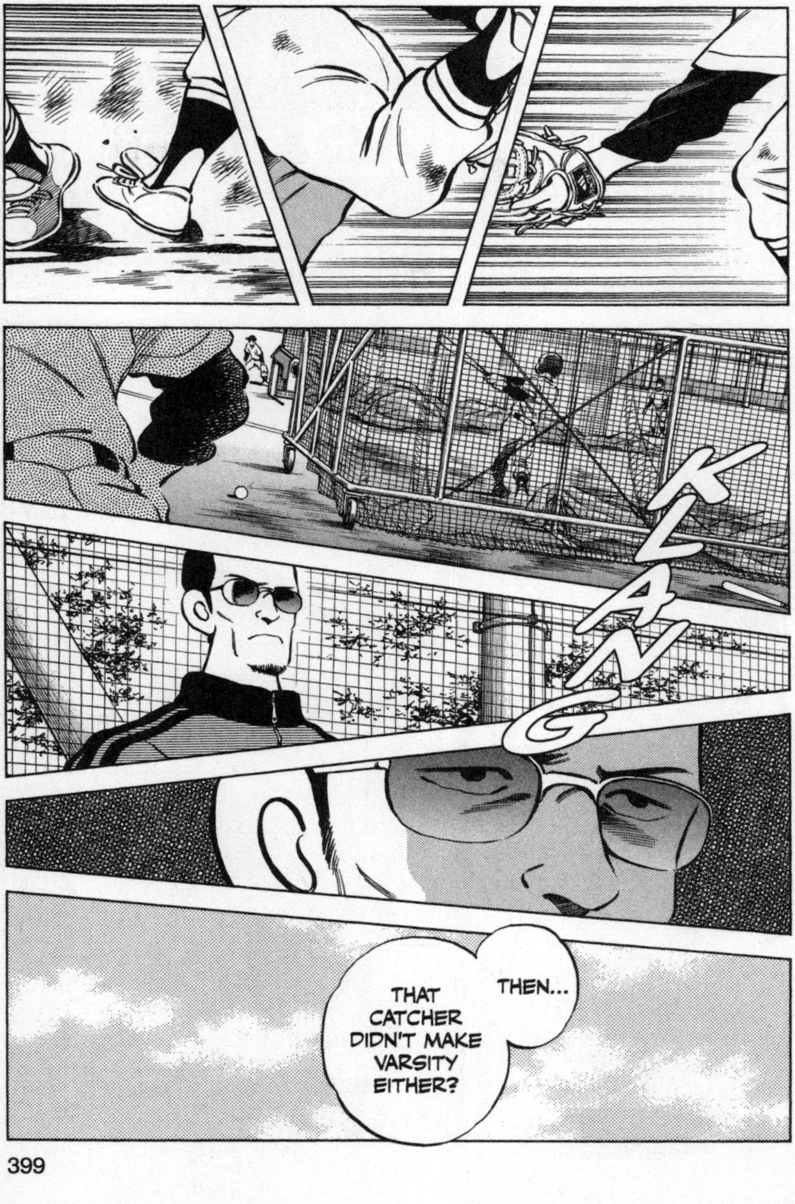
KLANG
THEN...
THAT CATCHER DIDN'T MAKE VARSITY EITHER?

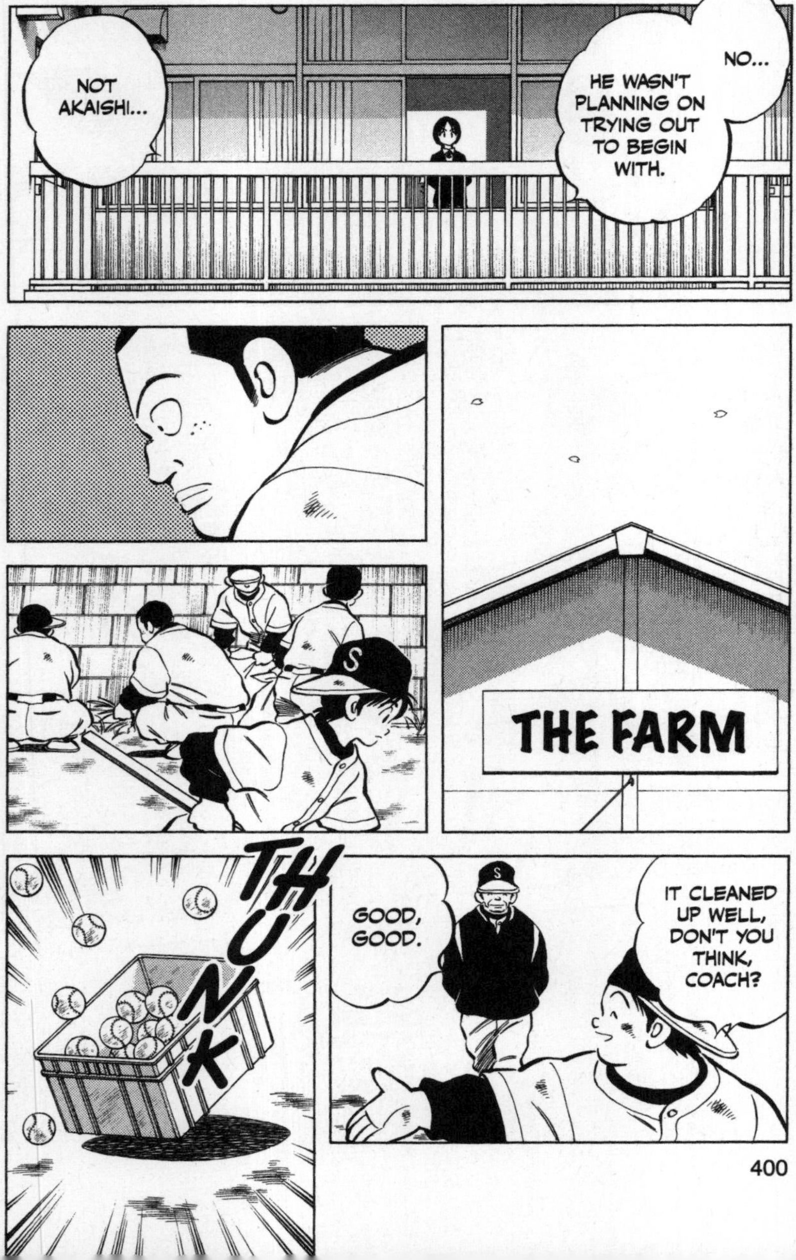
NO...
HE WASN'T PLANNING ON TRYING OUT TO BEGIN WITH.
NOT AKAISHI...
THE FARM
IT CLEANED UP WELL, DON'T YOU THINK, COACH?
GOOD, GOOD.
THUNK

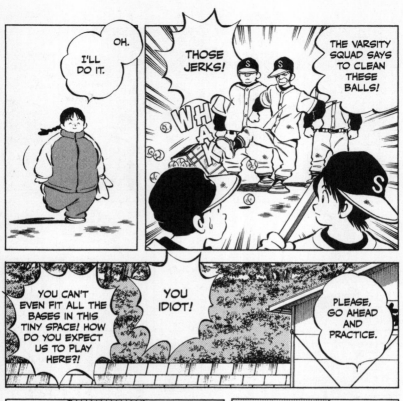

THE VARSITY SQUAD SAYS TO CLEAN THESE BALLS!
THOSE JERKS!
WHAK
OH.
I'LL DO IT.
PLEASE, GO AHEAD AND PRACTICE.
YOU IDIOT!
YOU CAN'T EVEN FIT ALL THE BASES IN THIS TINY SPACE! HOW DO YOU EXPECT US TO PLAY HERE?!
YOU'LL GET ONE MORE CHANCE BEFORE THE SUMMER TOURNAMENT.
IF YOU STAND OUT IN A SCRIMMAGE GAME AGAINST THE VARSITY TEAM, YOU'LL BECOME ONE OF THE ELITES.
KOSHIEN WON'T BE JUST A DREAM ANYMORE.

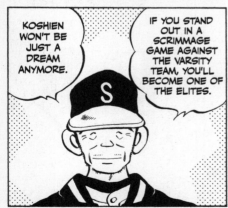

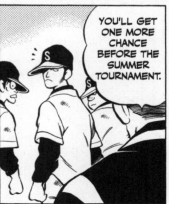

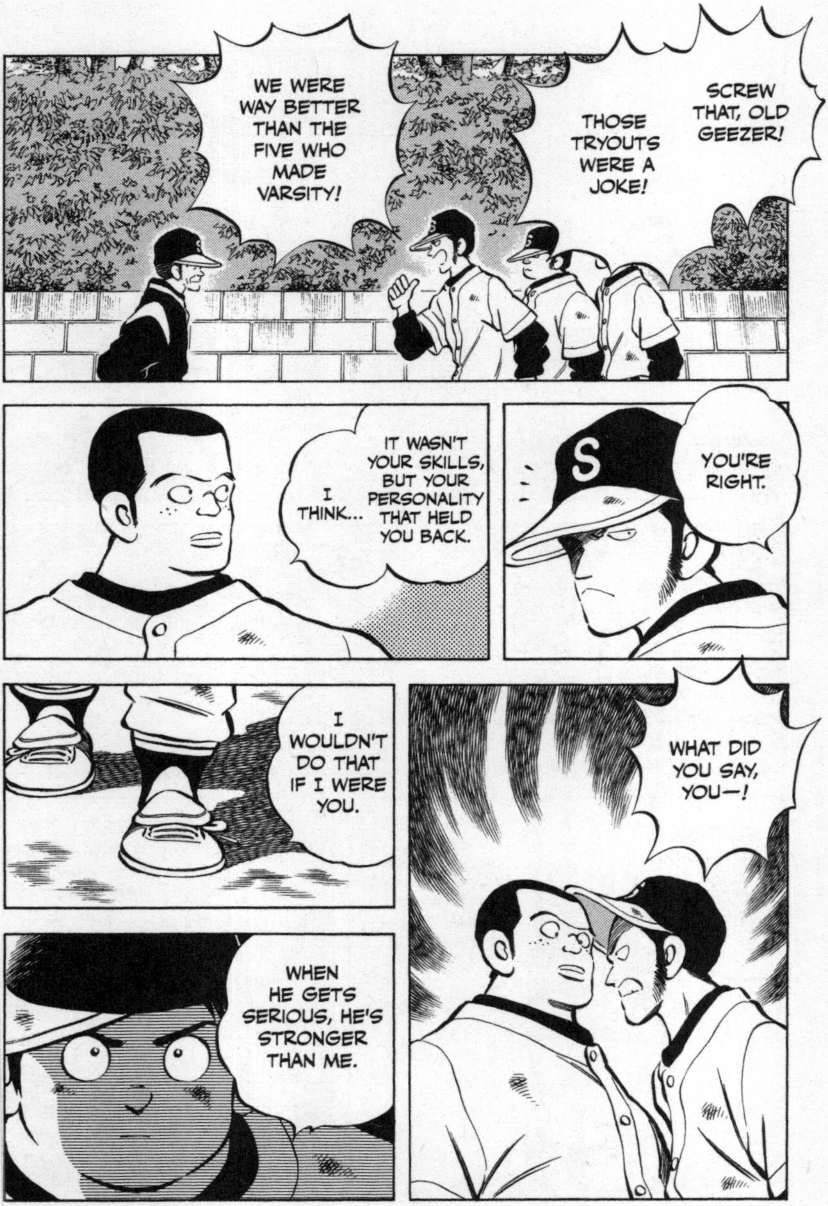
SCREW THAT, OLD GEEZER!
THOSE TRYOUTS WERE A JOKE!
WE WERE WAY BETTER THAN THE FIVE WHO MADE VARSITY!
YOU'RE RIGHT.
I THINK... IT WASN'T YOUR SKILLS, BUT YOUR PERSONALITY THAT HELD YOU BACK.
WHAT DID YOU SAY, YOU—!
I WOULDN'T DO THAT IF I WERE YOU.
WHEN HE GETS SERIOUS, HE'S STRONGER THAN ME.

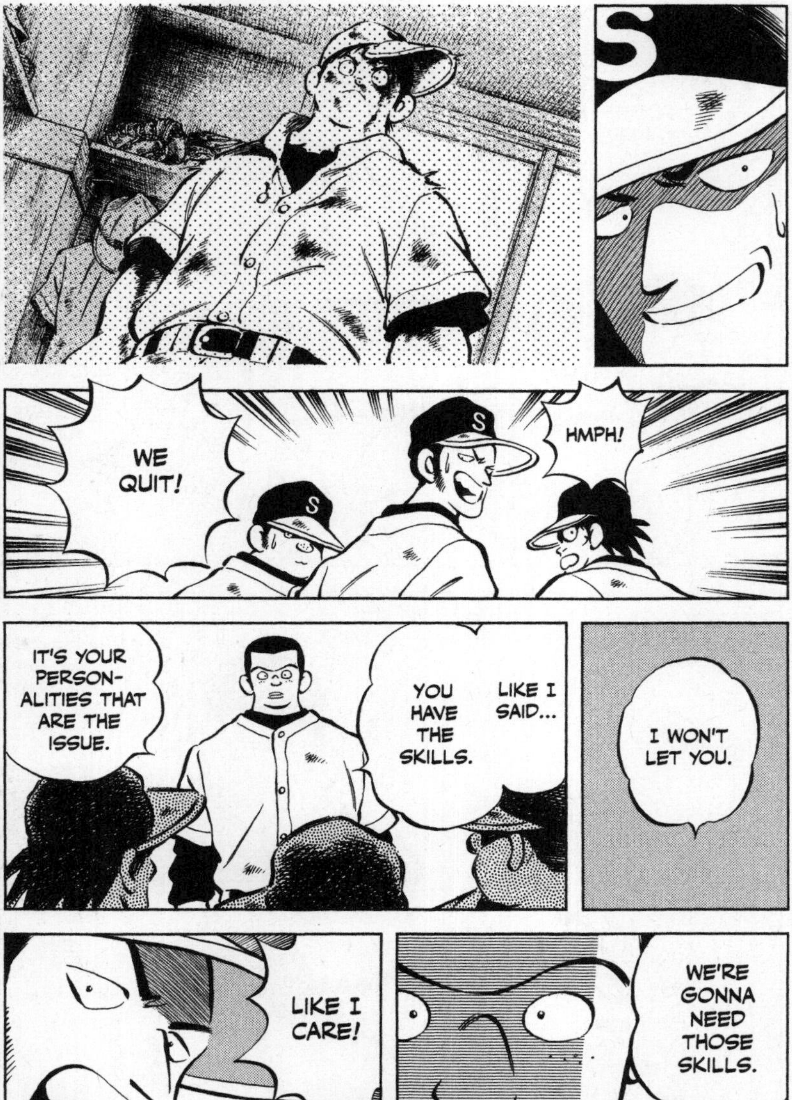
HMPH!
WE QUIT!
I WON'T LET YOU.
LIKE I SAID...
YOU HAVE THE SKILLS.
IT'S YOUR PERSON-ALITIES THAT ARE THE ISSUE.
WE'RE GONNA NEED THOSE SKILLS.
LIKE I CARE!

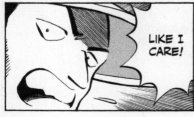

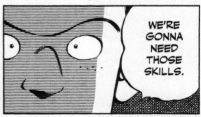

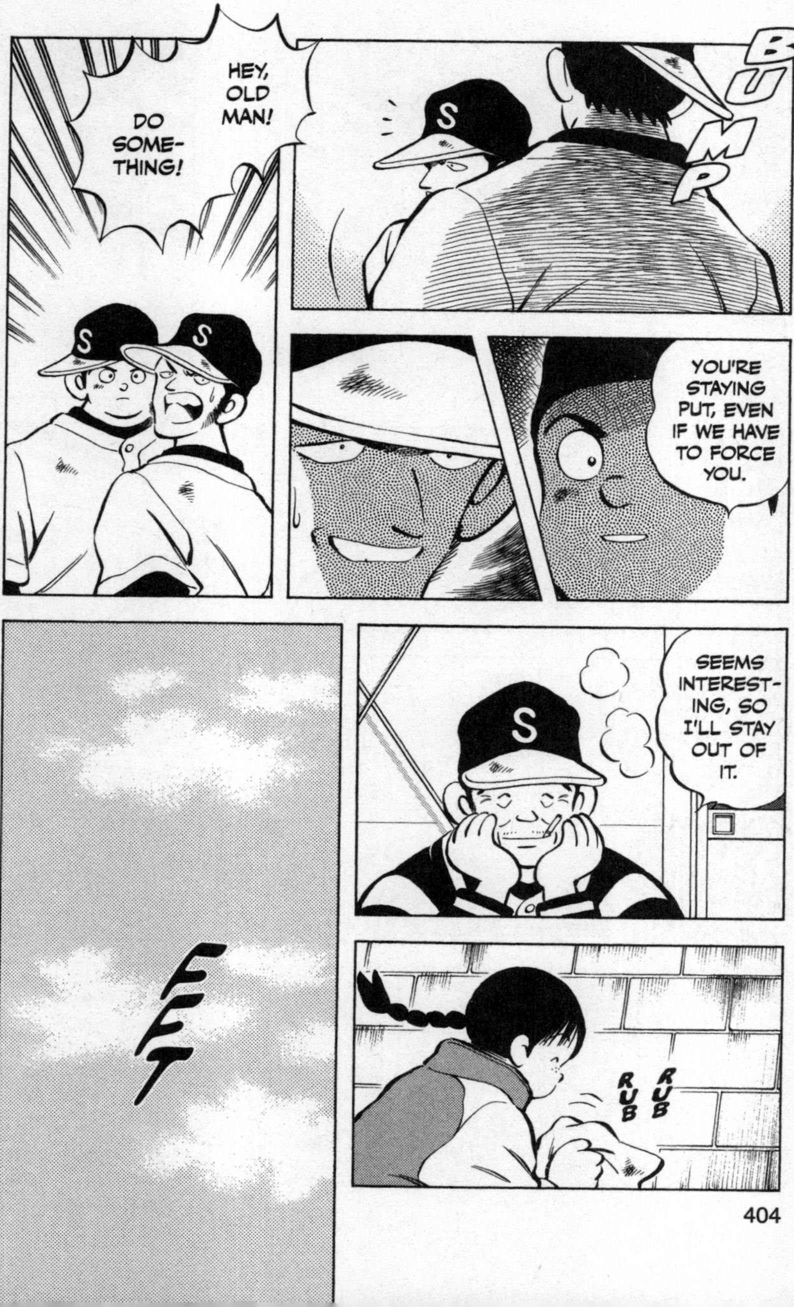
BUMP
YOU'RE STAYING PUT, EVEN IF WE HAVE TO FORCE YOU.
HEY, OLD MAN!
DO SOMETHING!
SEEMS INTERESTING, SO I'LL STAY OUT OF IT.
RUB RUB
FFFT

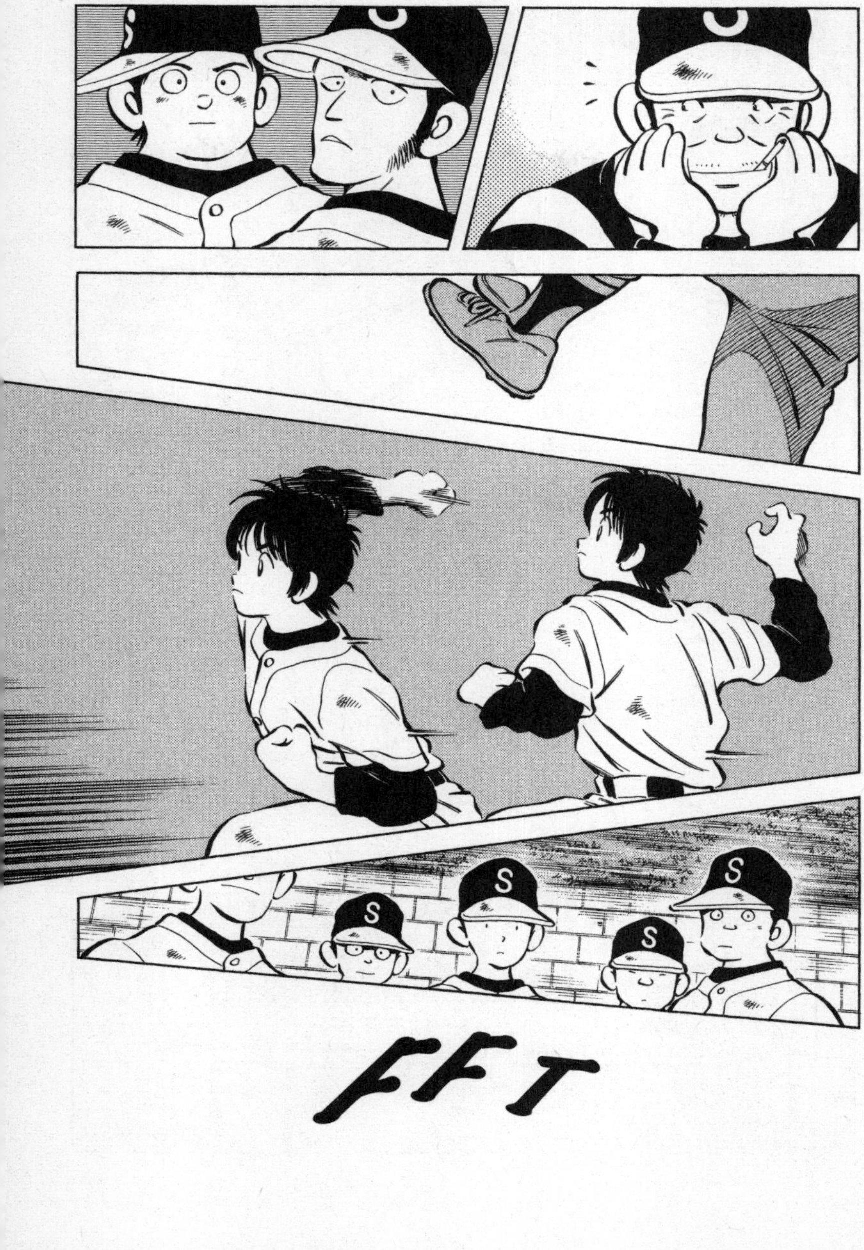
FFT

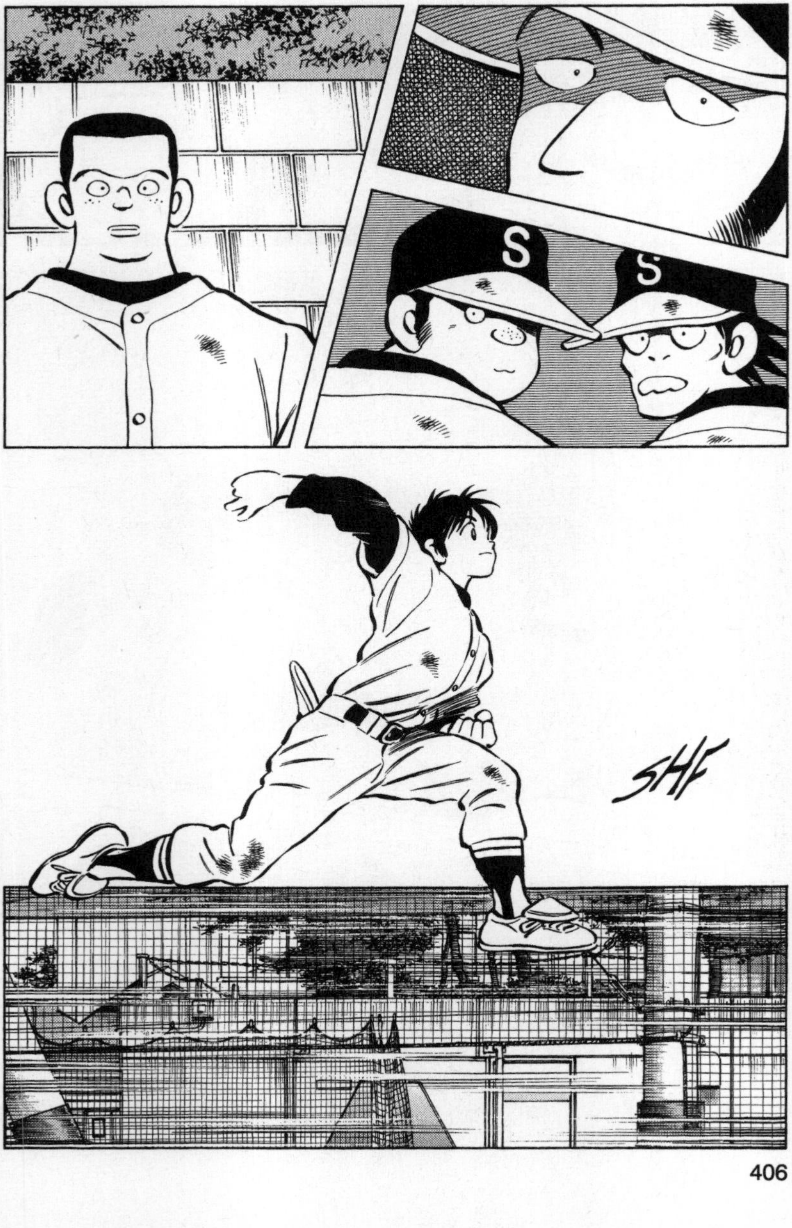
SHF

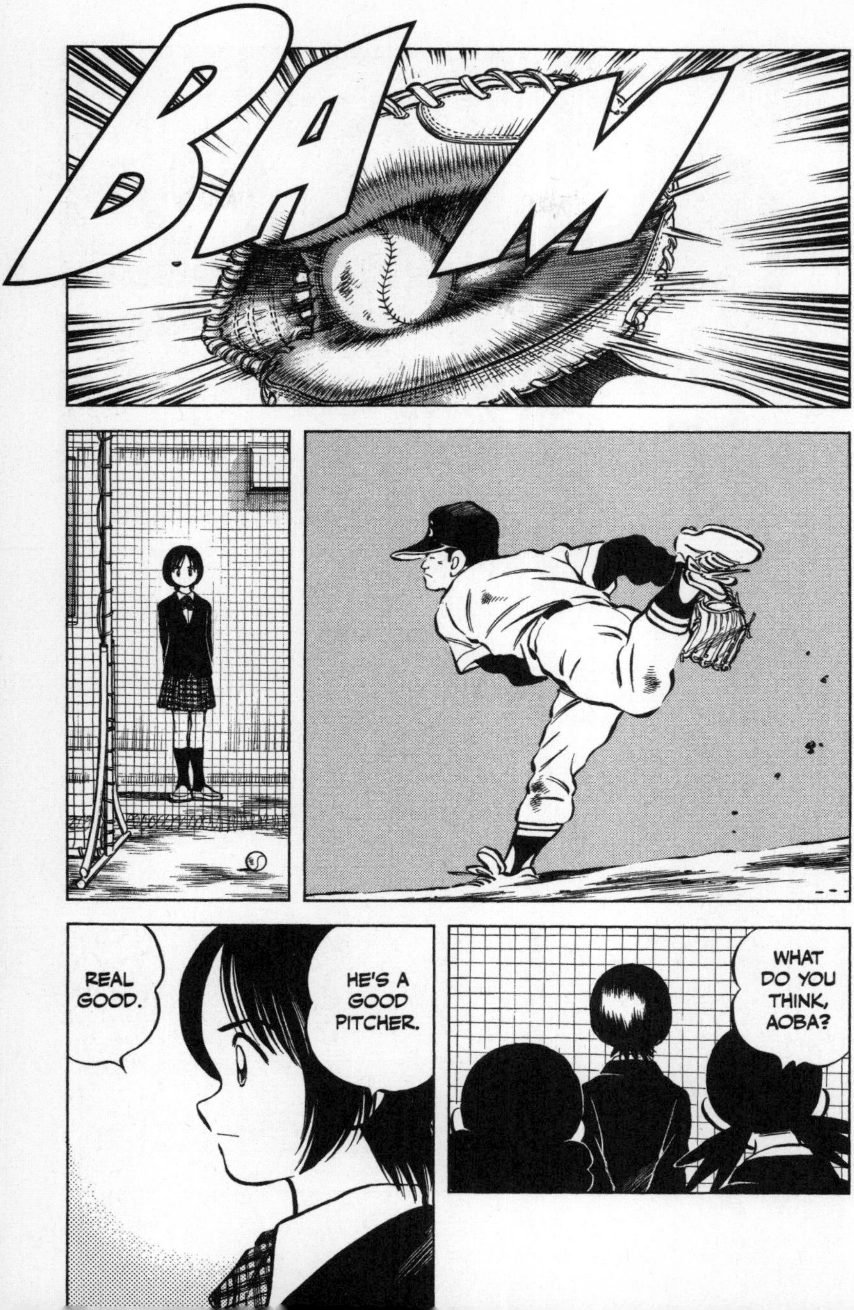
BAM
WHAT DO YOU THINK, AOBA?
HE'S A GOOD PITCHER.
REAL GOOD.

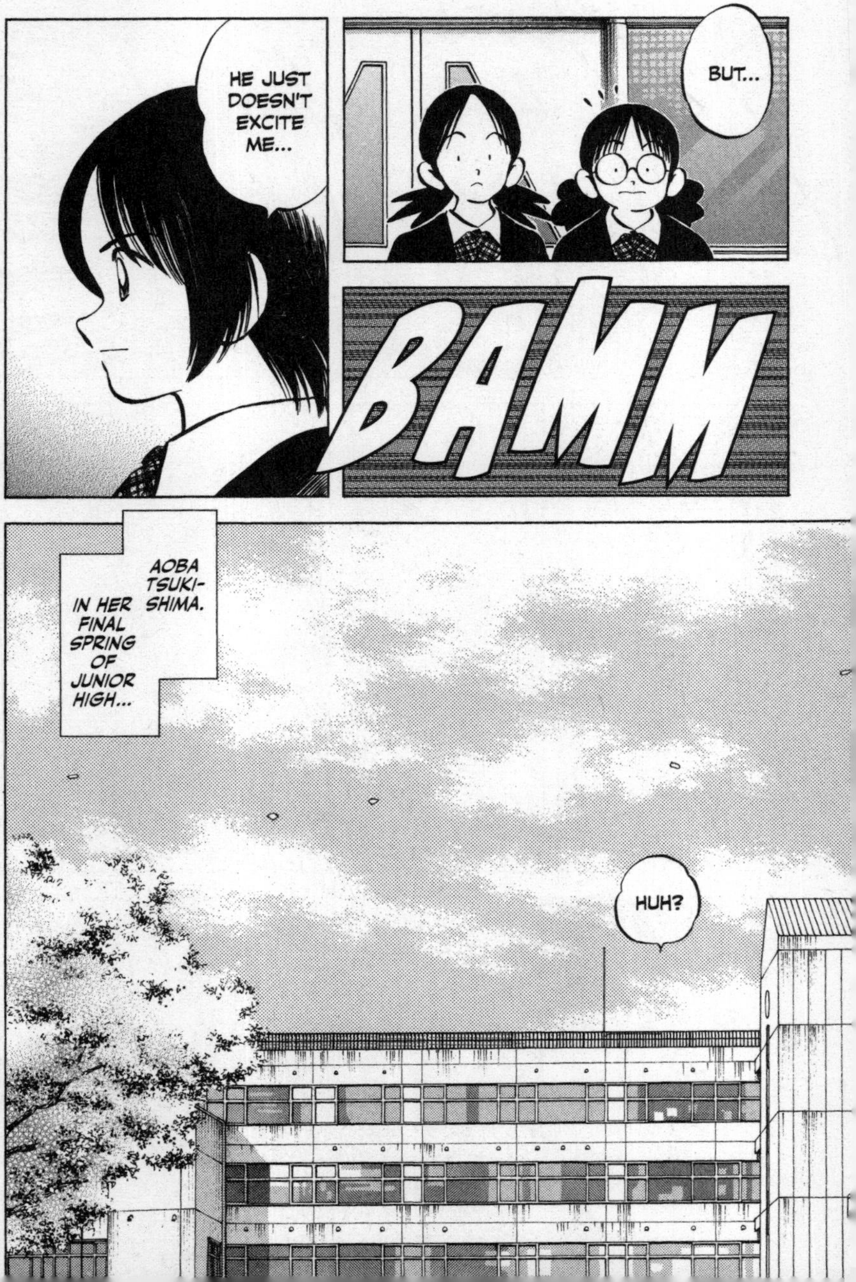
BUT...
BAMM
HE JUST DOESN'T EXCITE ME...
AOBA TSUKISHIMA. IN HER FINAL SPRING OF JUNIOR HIGH...
HUH?

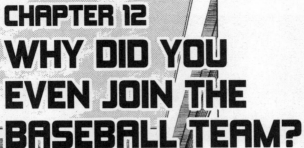

CHAPTER 12
WHY DID YOU EVEN JOIN THE BASEBALL TEAM?

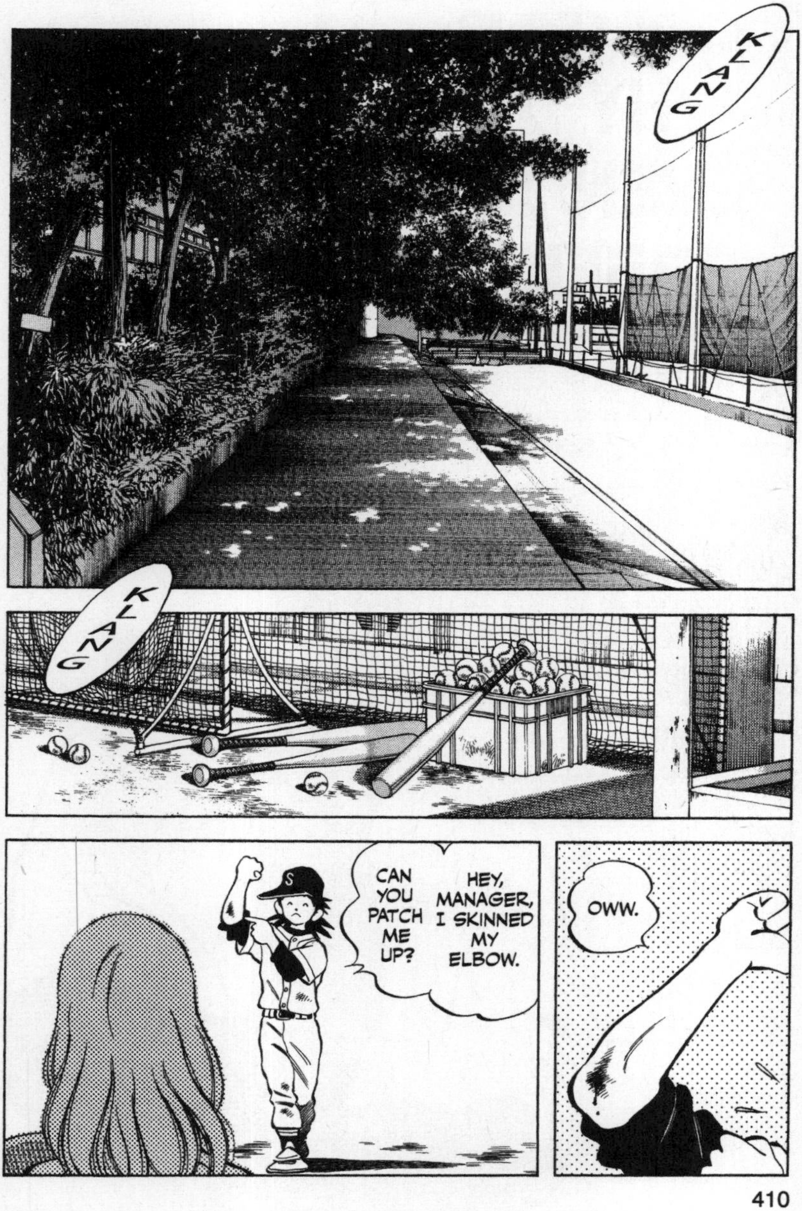
KLANG
KLANG
OWW.
HEY, MANAGER, I SKINNED MY ELBOW.
CAN YOU PATCH ME UP?

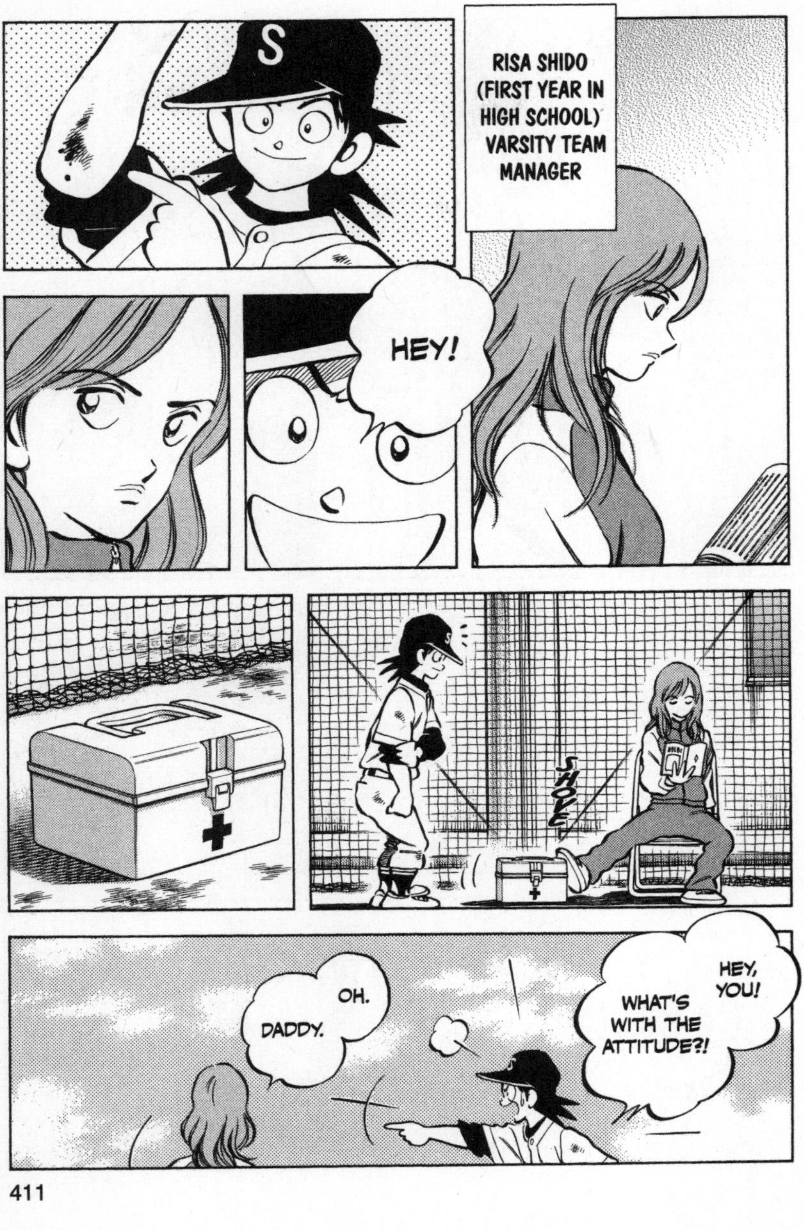
RISA SHIDO (FIRST YEAR IN HIGH SCHOOL) VARSITY TEAM MANAGER
HEY!
SHOVE
HEY, YOU!
WHAT'S WITH THE ATTITUDE?!
OH.
DADDY.

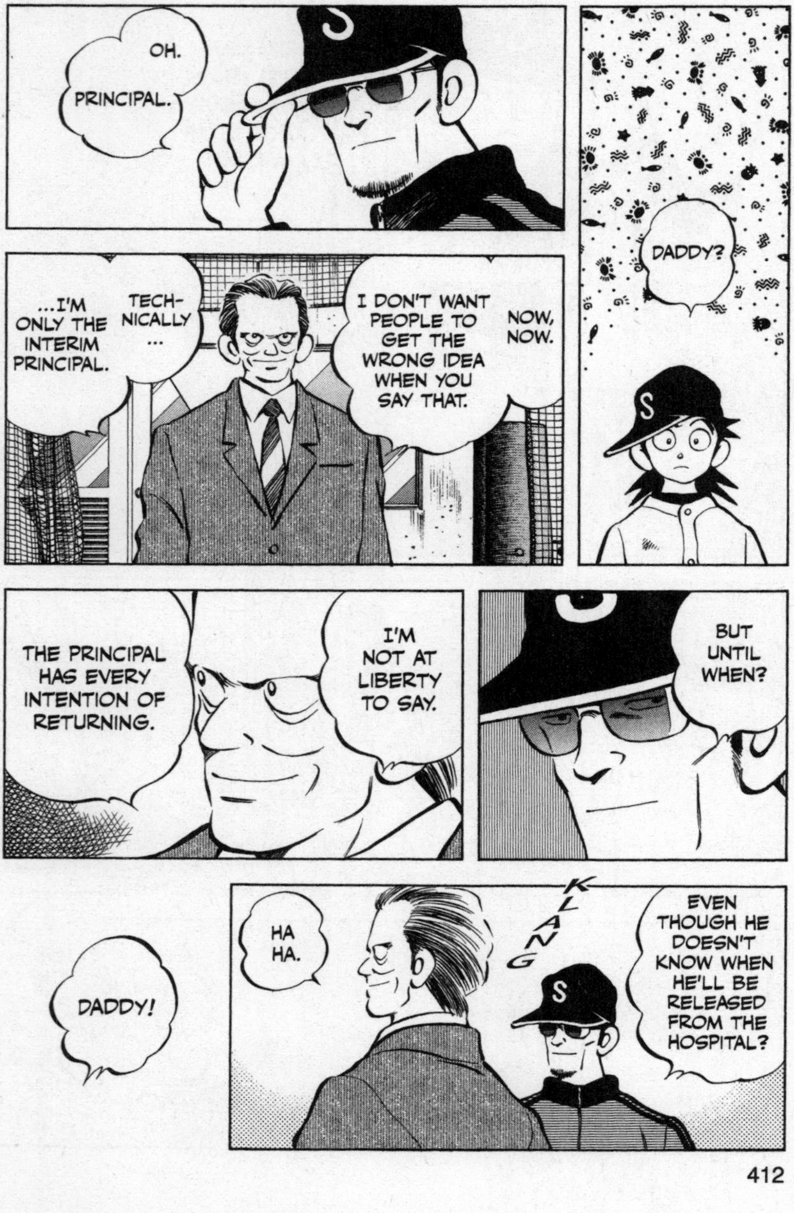
DADDY?
OH.
PRINCIPAL.
NOW, NOW.
I DON'T WANT PEOPLE TO GET THE WRONG IDEA WHEN YOU SAY THAT.
TECH-NICALLY...
...I'M ONLY THE INTERIM PRINCIPAL.
BUT UNTIL WHEN?
I'M NOT AT LIBERTY TO SAY.
THE PRINCIPAL HAS EVERY INTENTION OF RETURNING.
EVEN THOUGH HE DOESN'T KNOW WHEN HE'LL BE RELEASED FROM THE HOSPITAL?
KLANG
HA HA.
DADDY!

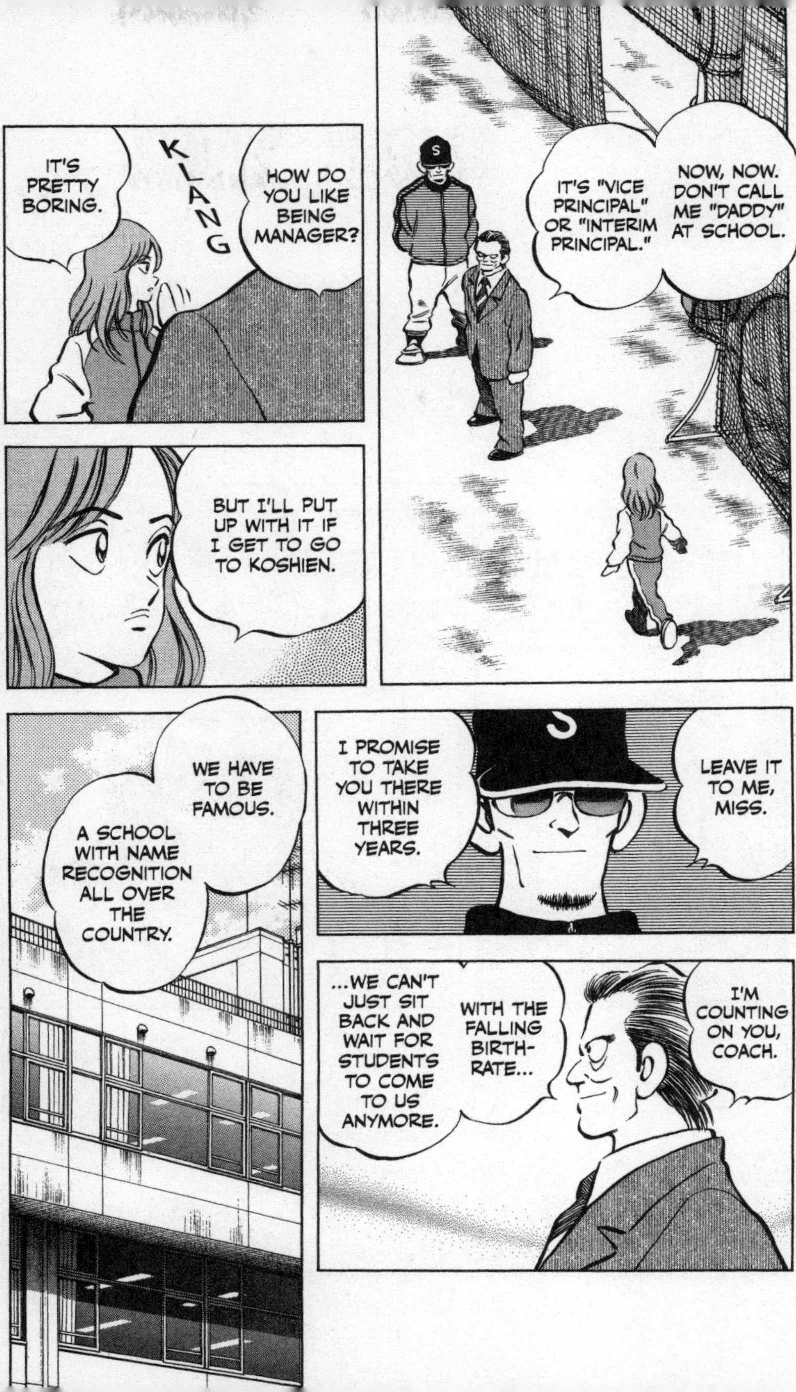
NOW, NOW. DON'T CALL ME "DADDY" AT SCHOOL.
IT'S "VICE PRINCIPAL" OR "INTERIM PRINCIPAL."
HOW DO YOU LIKE BEING MANAGER?
KLANG
IT'S PRETTY BORING.
BUT I'LL PUT UP WITH IT IF I GET TO GO TO KOSHIEN.
LEAVE IT TO ME, MISS.
I PROMISE TO TAKE YOU THERE WITHIN THREE YEARS.
I'M COUNTING ON YOU, COACH.
WITH THE FALLING BIRTH-RATE...
...WE CAN'T JUST SIT BACK AND WAIT FOR STUDENTS TO COME TO US ANYMORE.
WE HAVE TO BE FAMOUS.
A SCHOOL WITH NAME RECOGNITION ALL OVER THE COUNTRY.

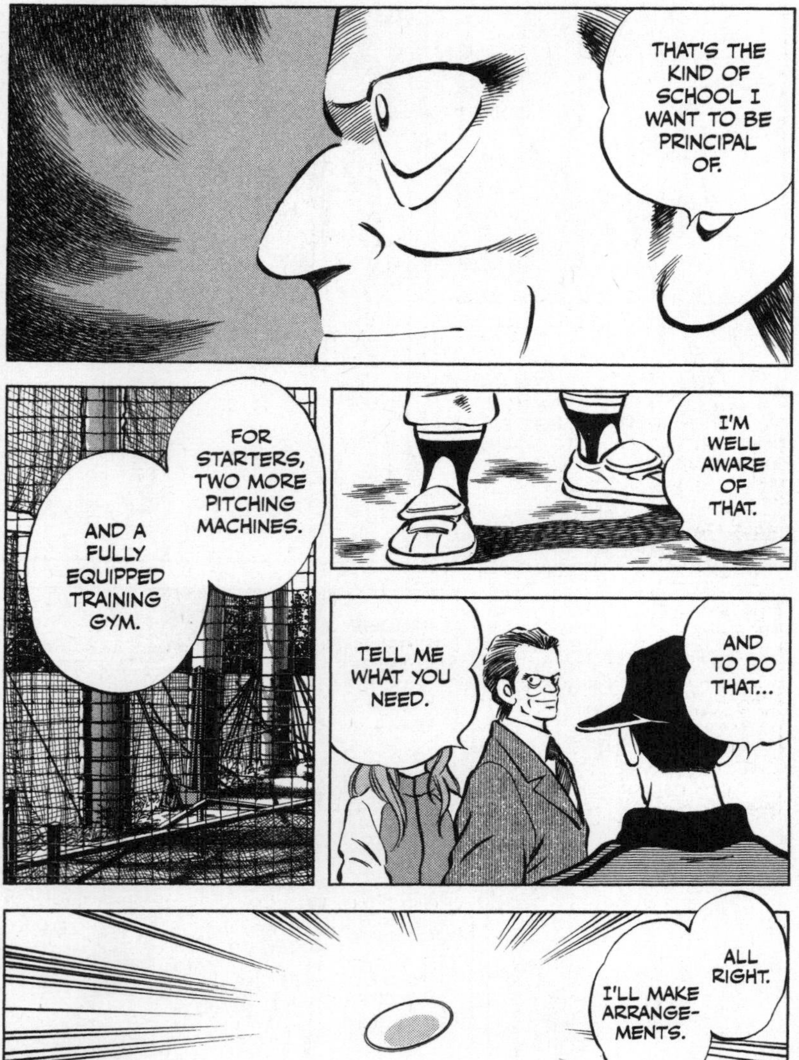
THAT'S THE KIND OF SCHOOL I WANT TO BE PRINCIPAL OF.
I'M WELL AWARE OF THAT.
AND TO DO THAT...
TELL ME WHAT YOU NEED.
FOR STARTERS, TWO MORE PITCHING MACHINES.
AND A FULLY EQUIPPED TRAINING GYM.
ALL RIGHT.
I'LL MAKE ARRANGE-MENTS.

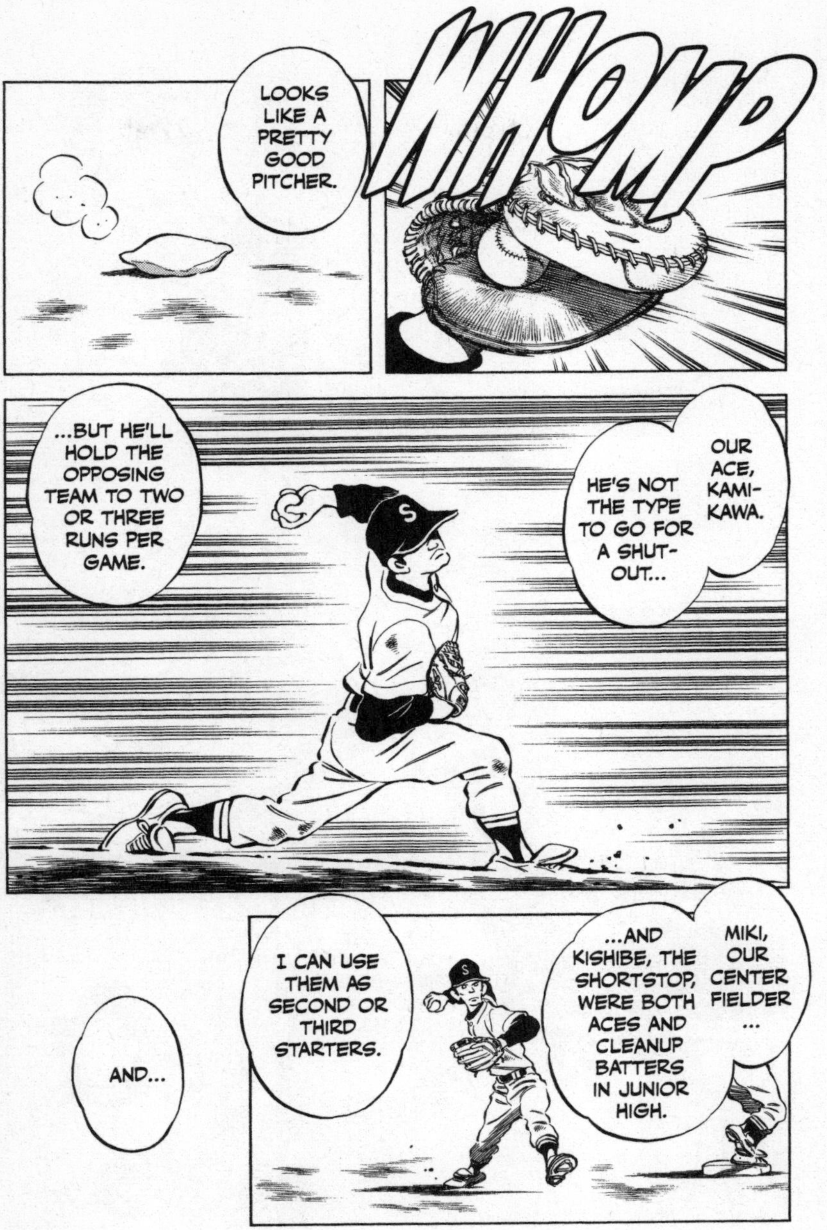
WHOMP
LOOKS LIKE A PRETTY GOOD PITCHER.
OUR ACE, KAMI-KAWA.
HE'S NOT THE TYPE TO GO FOR A SHUT-OUT...
...BUT HE'LL HOLD THE OPPOSING TEAM TO TWO OR THREE RUNS PER GAME.
MIKI, OUR CENTER FIELDER ...
...AND KISHIBE, THE SHORTSTOP, WERE BOTH ACES AND CLEANUP BATTERS IN JUNIOR HIGH.
I CAN USE THEM AS SECOND OR THIRD STARTERS.
AND...

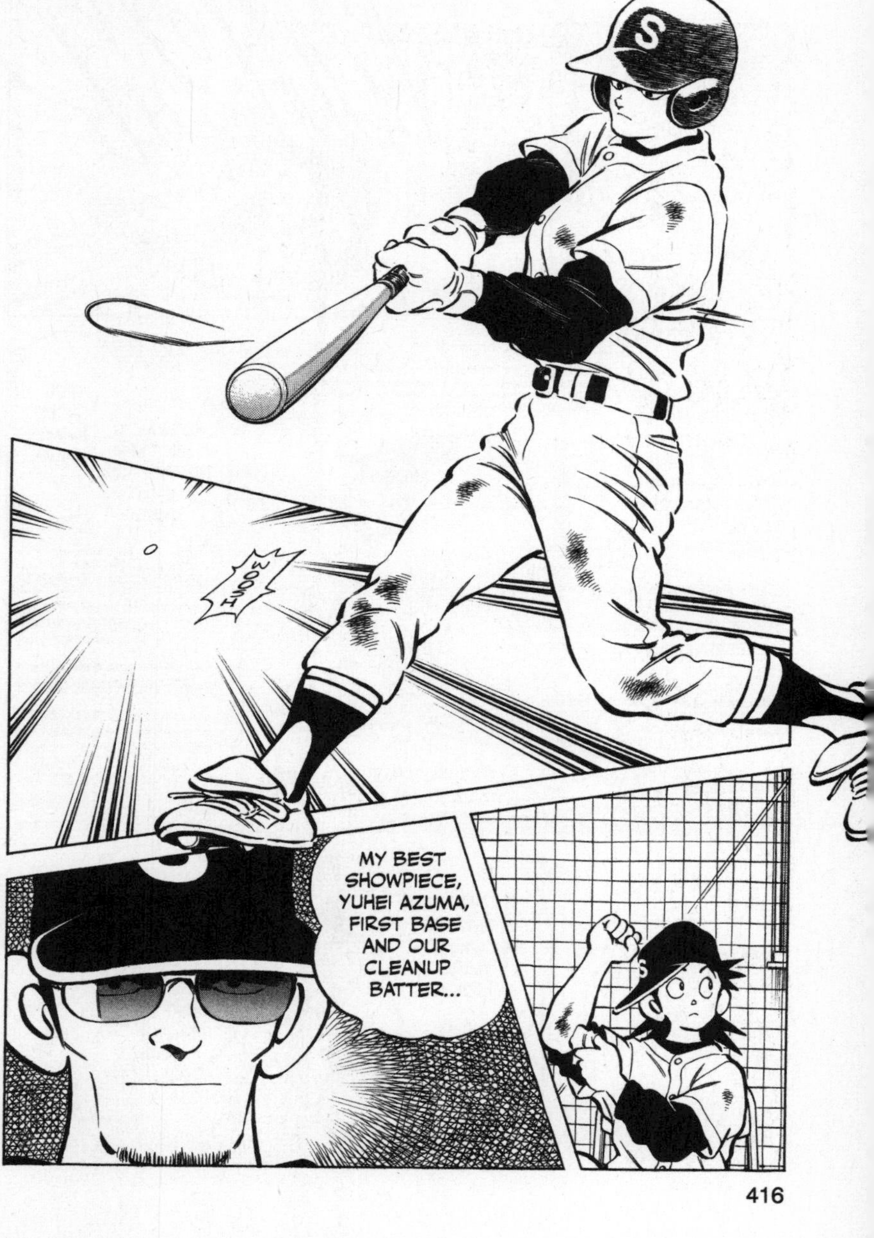
WOOSH
MY BEST SHOWPIECE, YUHEI AZUMA, FIRST BASE AND OUR CLEANUP BATTER...

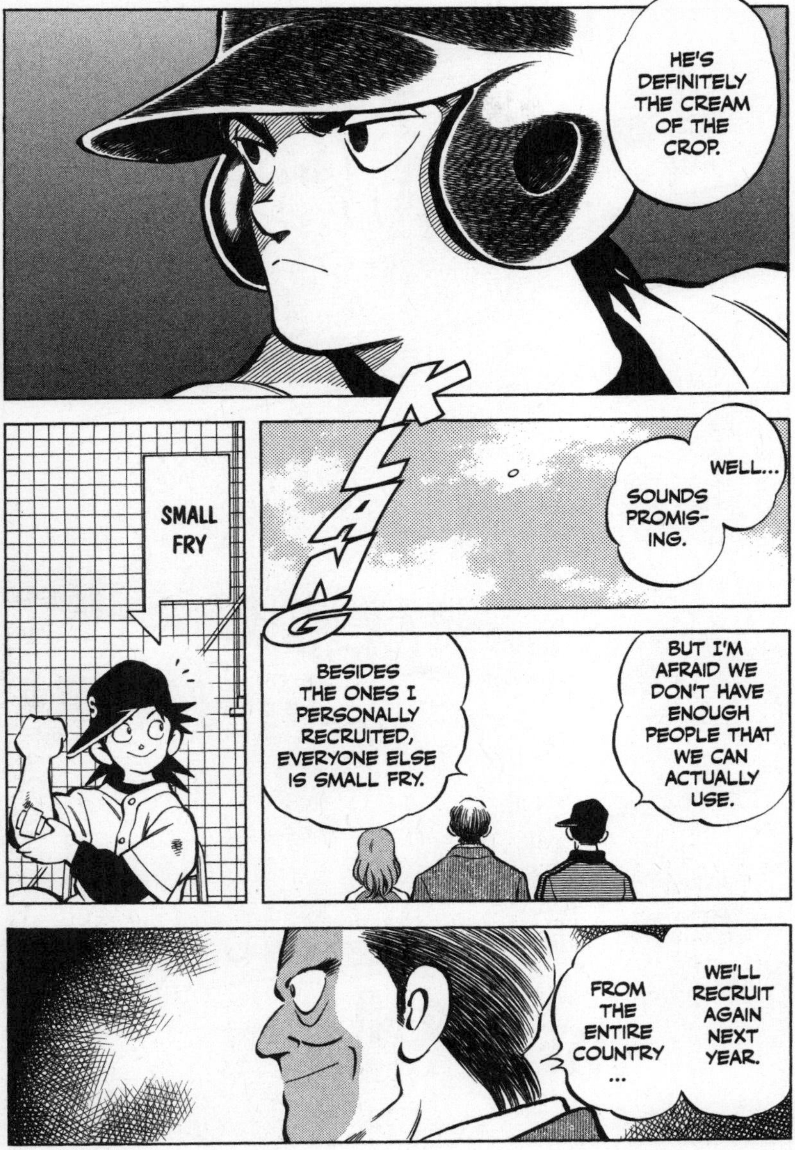
HE'S DEFINITELY THE CREAM OF THE CROP.
WELL...
SOUNDS PROMIS-ING.
KLANG
BUT I'M AFRAID WE DON'T HAVE ENOUGH PEOPLE THAT WE CAN ACTUALLY USE.
BESIDES THE ONES I PERSONALLY RECRUITED, EVERYONE ELSE IS SMALL FRY.
SMALL FRY
WE'LL RECRUIT AGAIN NEXT YEAR.
FROM THE ENTIRE COUNTRY ...

KLAANNNNG

THE FARM

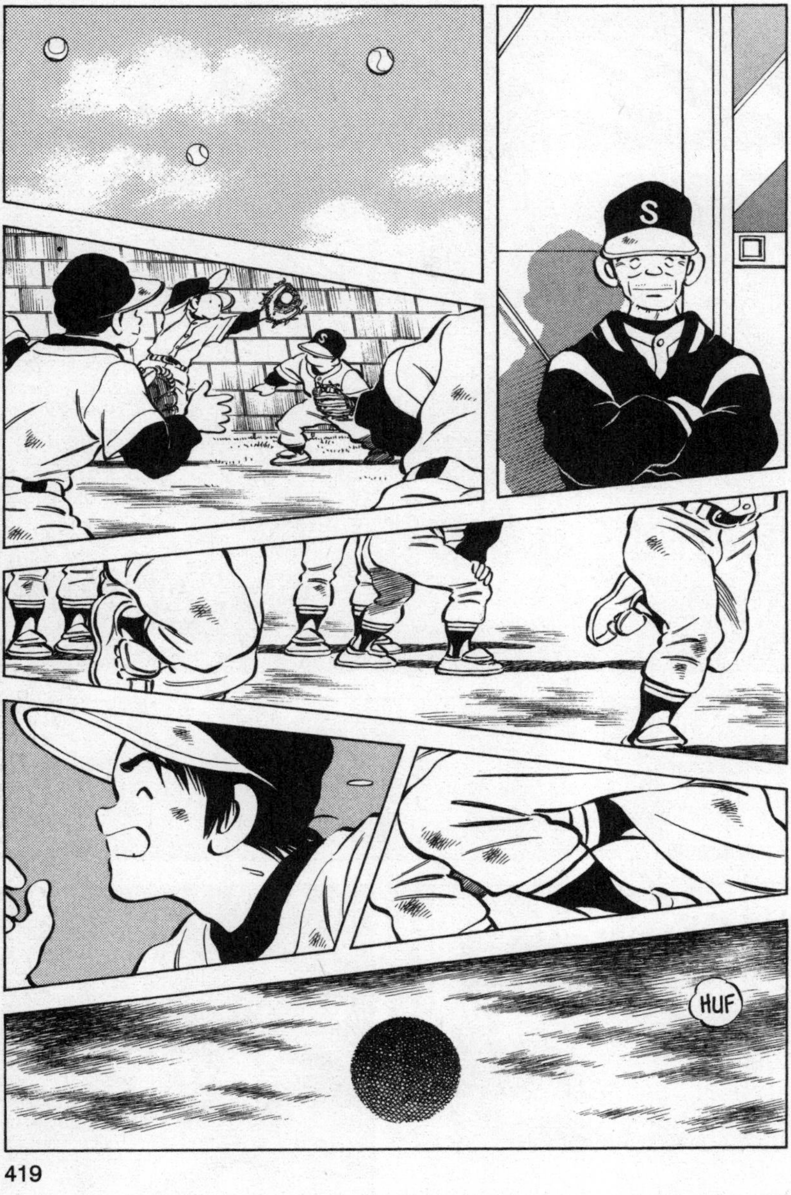
HUF

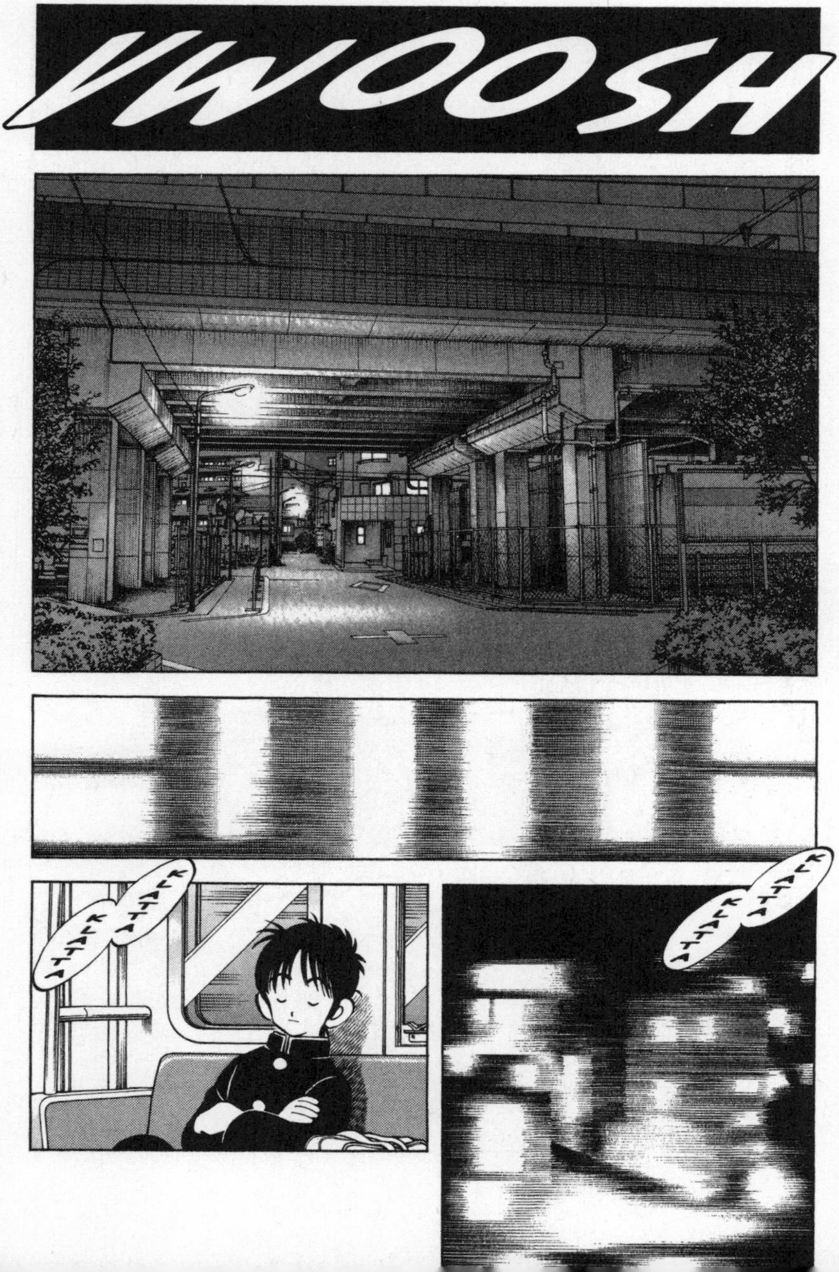
WHOOSH
KLATTA
KLATTA
KLATTA
KLATTA

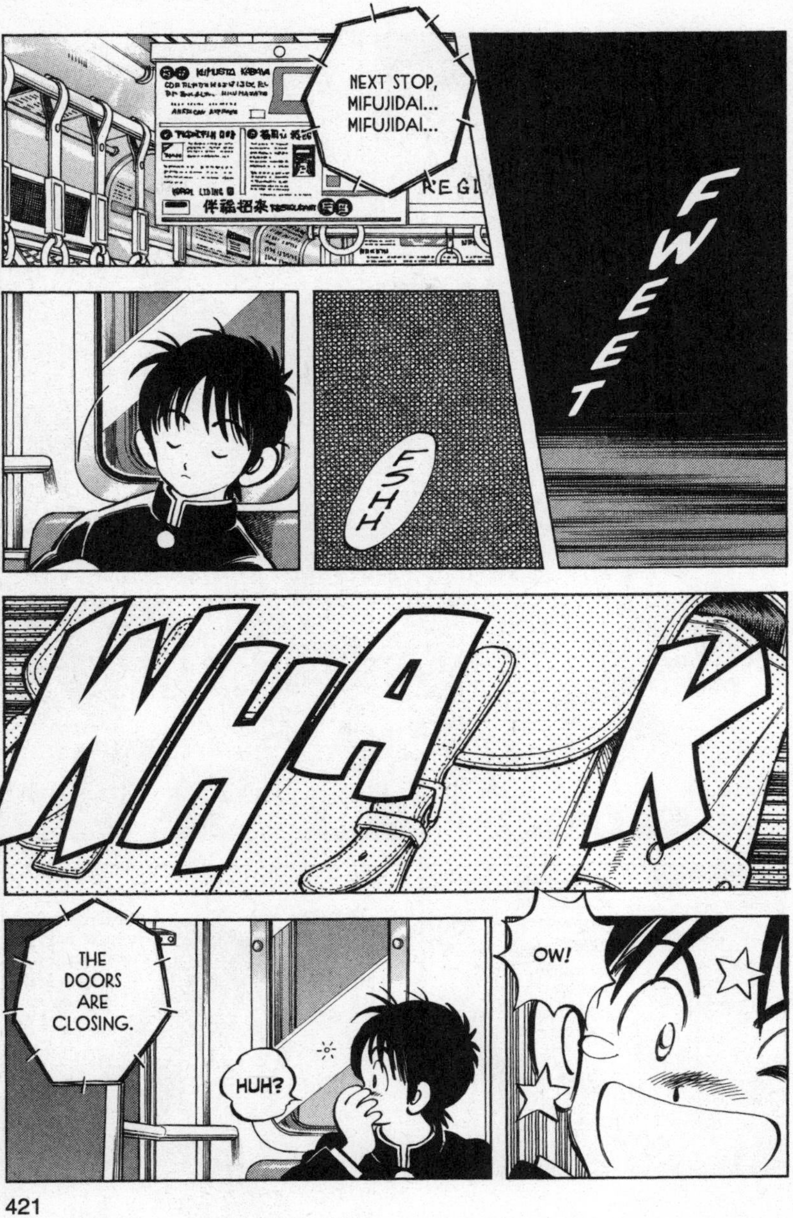
FWEET
NEXT STOP, MIFUJIDAI... MIFUJIDAI...
FSHH
WHAK
OW!
THE DOORS ARE CLOSING.
HUH?

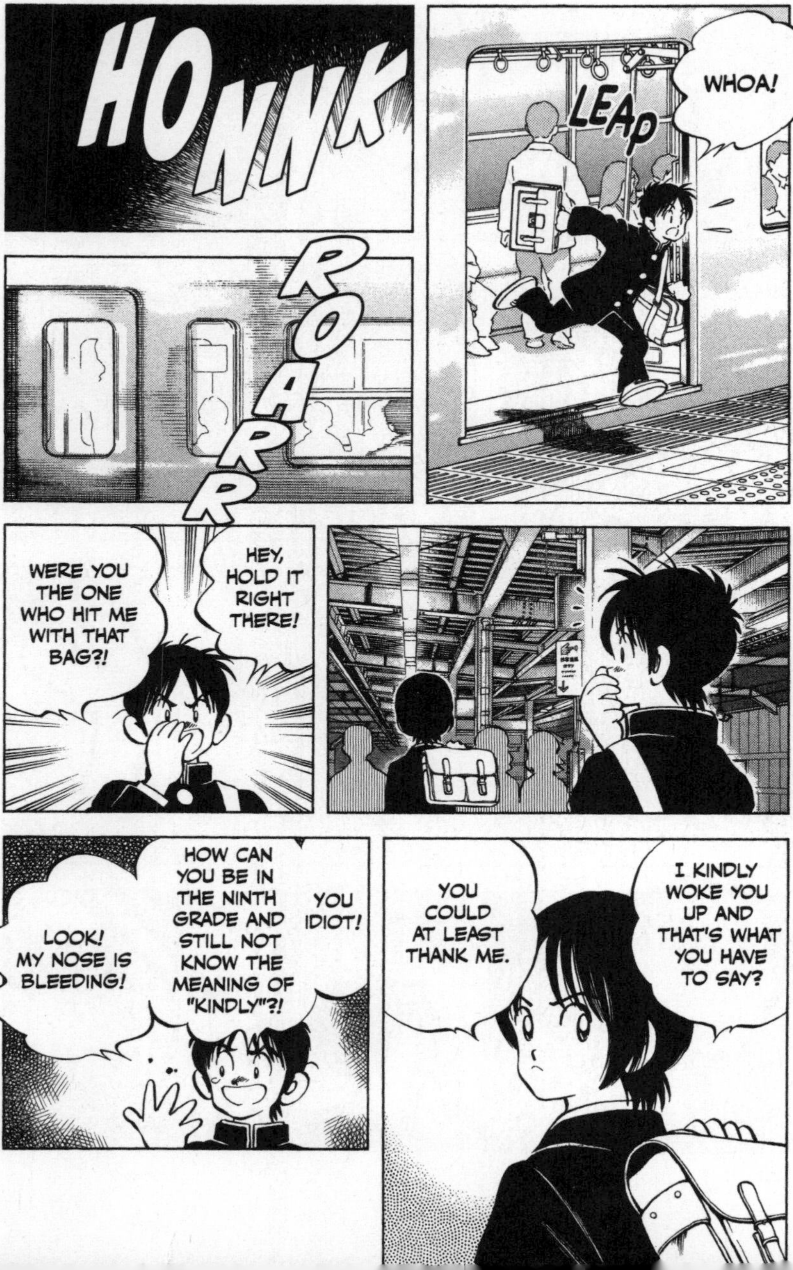
WHOA!
LEAP
HONNK
ROARRR
HEY, HOLD IT RIGHT THERE!
WERE YOU THE ONE WHO HIT ME WITH THAT BAG?!
I KINDLY WOKE YOU UP AND THAT'S WHAT YOU HAVE TO SAY?
YOU COULD AT LEAST THANK ME.
YOU IDIOT!
HOW CAN YOU BE IN THE NINTH GRADE AND STILL NOT KNOW THE MEANING OF "KINDLY"?!
LOOK! MY NOSE IS BLEEDING!

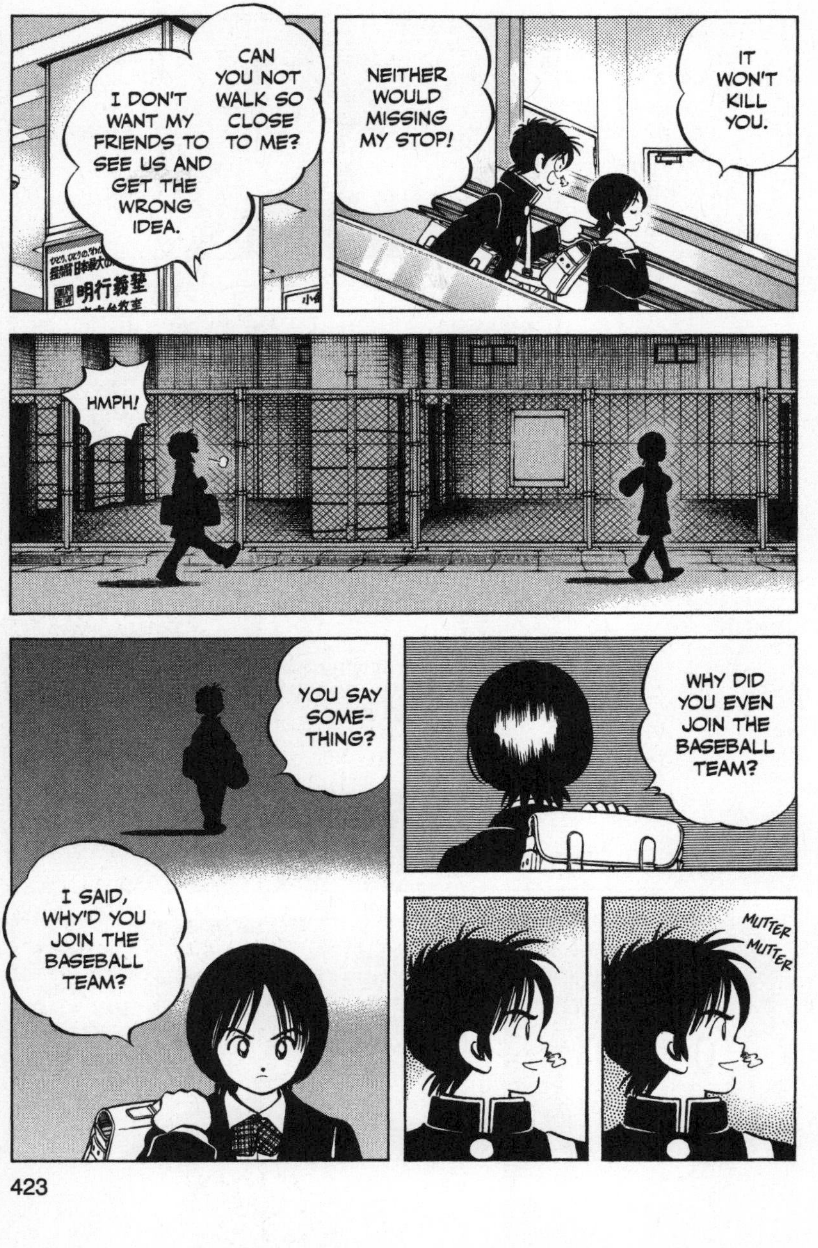
IT WON'T KILL YOU.
NEITHER WOULD MISSING MY STOP!
CAN YOU NOT WALK SO CLOSE TO ME?
I DON'T WANT MY FRIENDS TO SEE US AND GET THE WRONG IDEA.
明行義塾
HMPH!
WHY DID YOU EVEN JOIN THE BASEBALL TEAM?
MUTTER MUTTER
YOU SAY SOME-THING?
I SAID, WHY'D YOU JOIN THE BASEBALL TEAM?

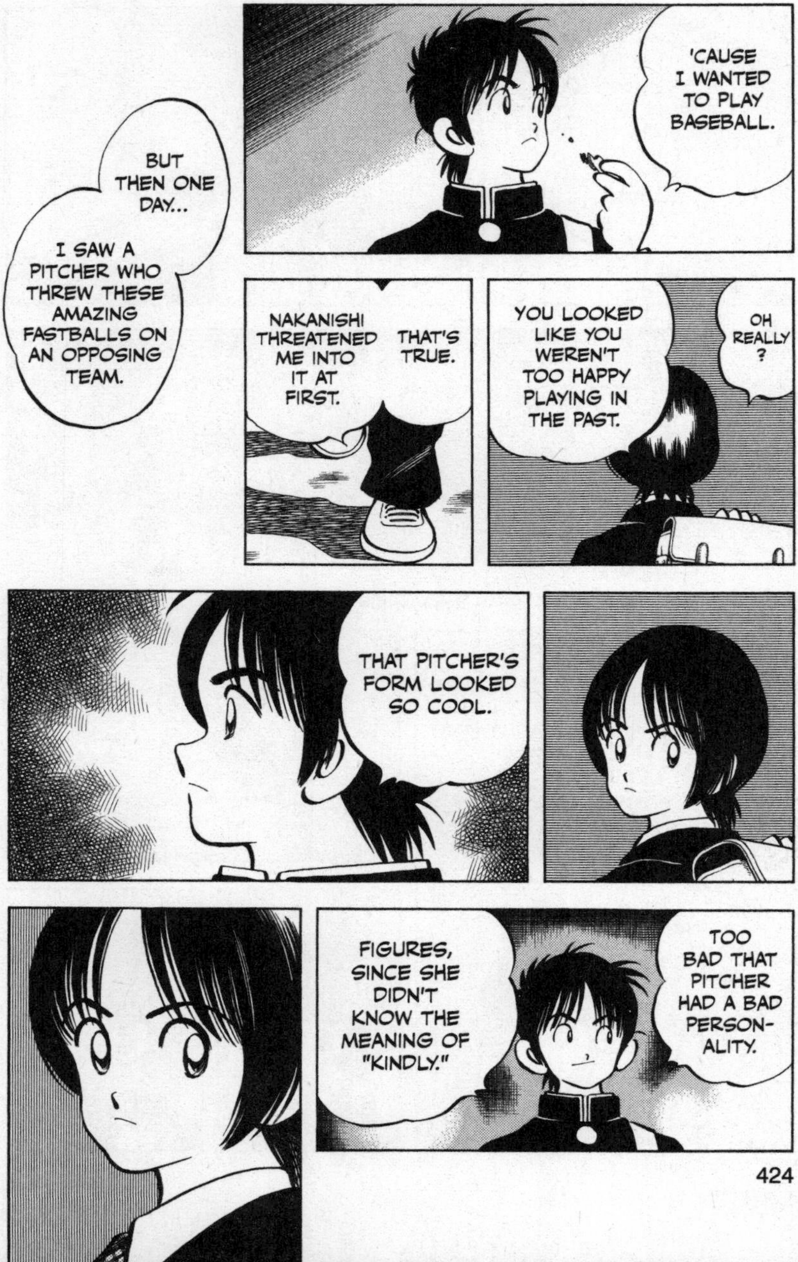
'CAUSE I WANTED TO PLAY BASEBALL.
YOU LOOKED LIKE YOU WEREN'T TOO HAPPY PLAYING IN THE PAST.
OH REALLY?
THAT'S TRUE.
NAKANISHI THREATENED ME INTO IT AT FIRST.
BUT THEN ONE DAY...
I SAW A PITCHER WHO THREW THESE AMAZING FASTBALLS ON AN OPPOSING TEAM.
THAT PITCHER'S FORM LOOKED SO COOL.
TOO BAD THAT PITCHER HAD A BAD PERSON-ALITY.
FIGURES, SINCE SHE DIDN'T KNOW THE MEANING OF "KINDLY."

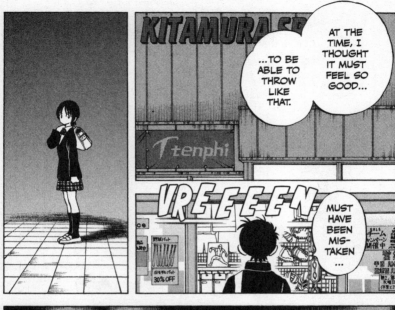

KITAMURA
AT THE TIME, I THOUGHT IT MUST FEEL SO GOOD...
...TO BE ABLE TO THROW LIKE THAT.
tenphi
MUST HAVE BEEN MIS-TAKEN ...
VREEEEN
30% OFF
TSUKISHIMA BATTING CENTER

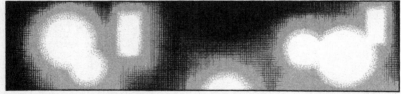

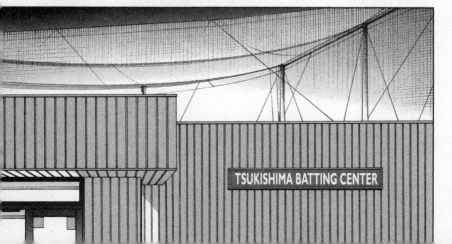

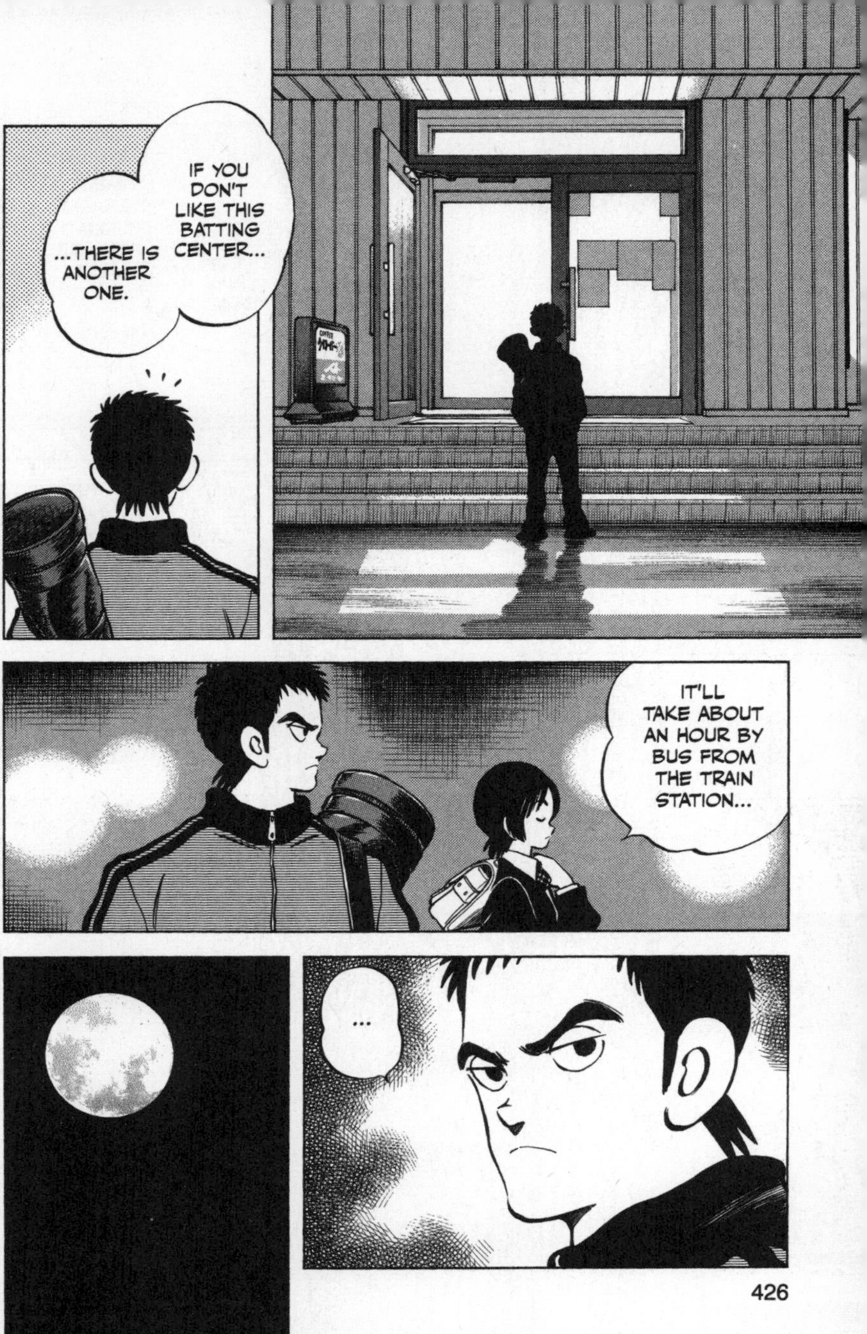
IF YOU DON'T LIKE THIS BATTING CENTER...
...THERE IS ANOTHER ONE.
IT'LL TAKE ABOUT AN HOUR BY BUS FROM THE TRAIN STATION...
...

CHAPTER 13
WHO ARE YOU?

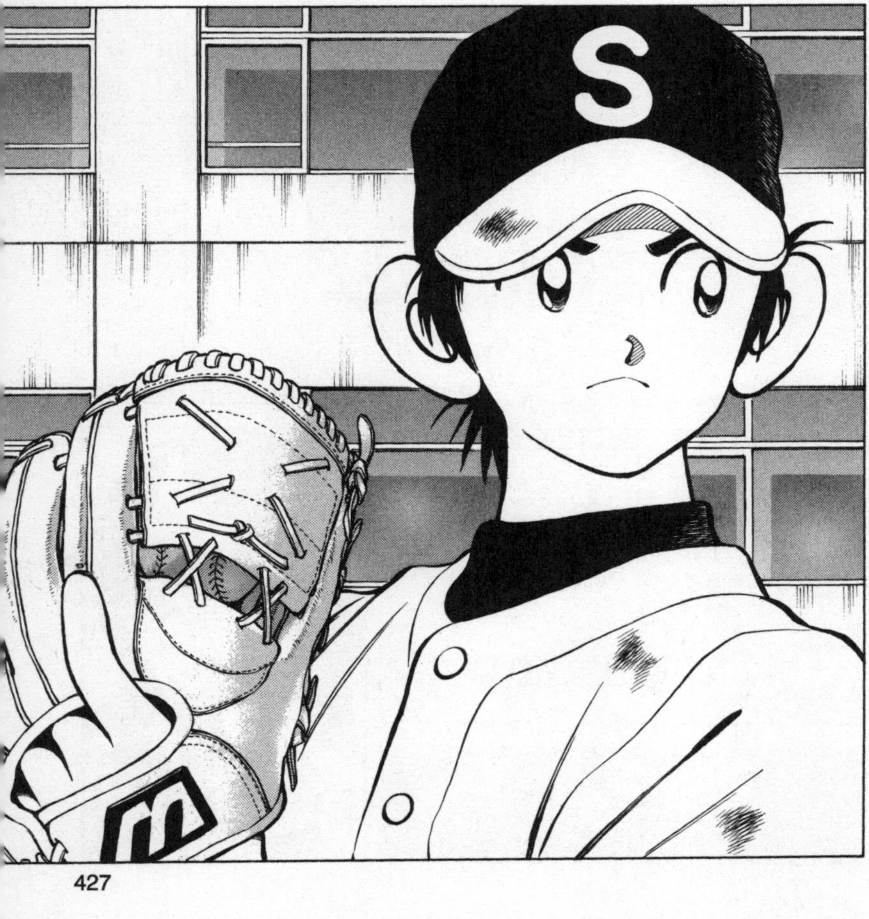

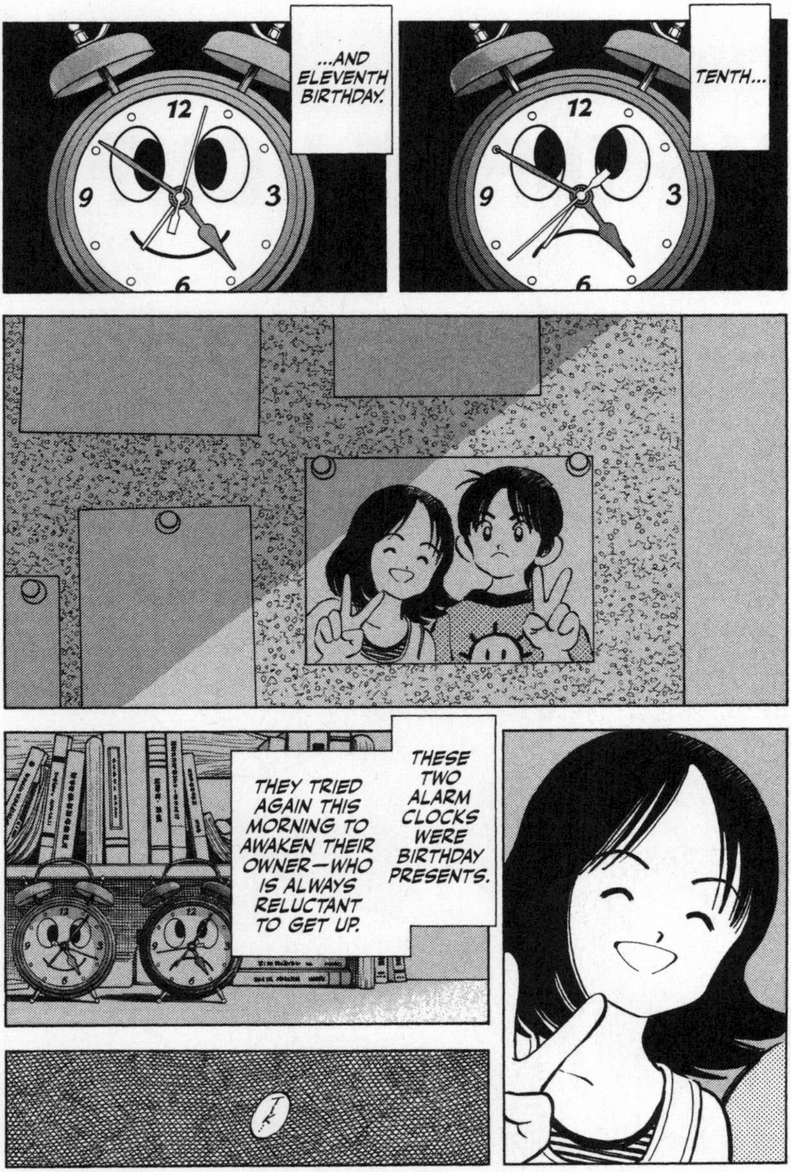
TENTH...
...AND ELEVENTH BIRTHDAY.
THESE TWO ALARM CLOCKS WERE BIRTHDAY PRESENTS.
THEY TRIED AGAIN THIS MORNING TO AWAKEN THEIR OWNER—WHO IS ALWAYS RELUCTANT TO GET UP.
TIK...

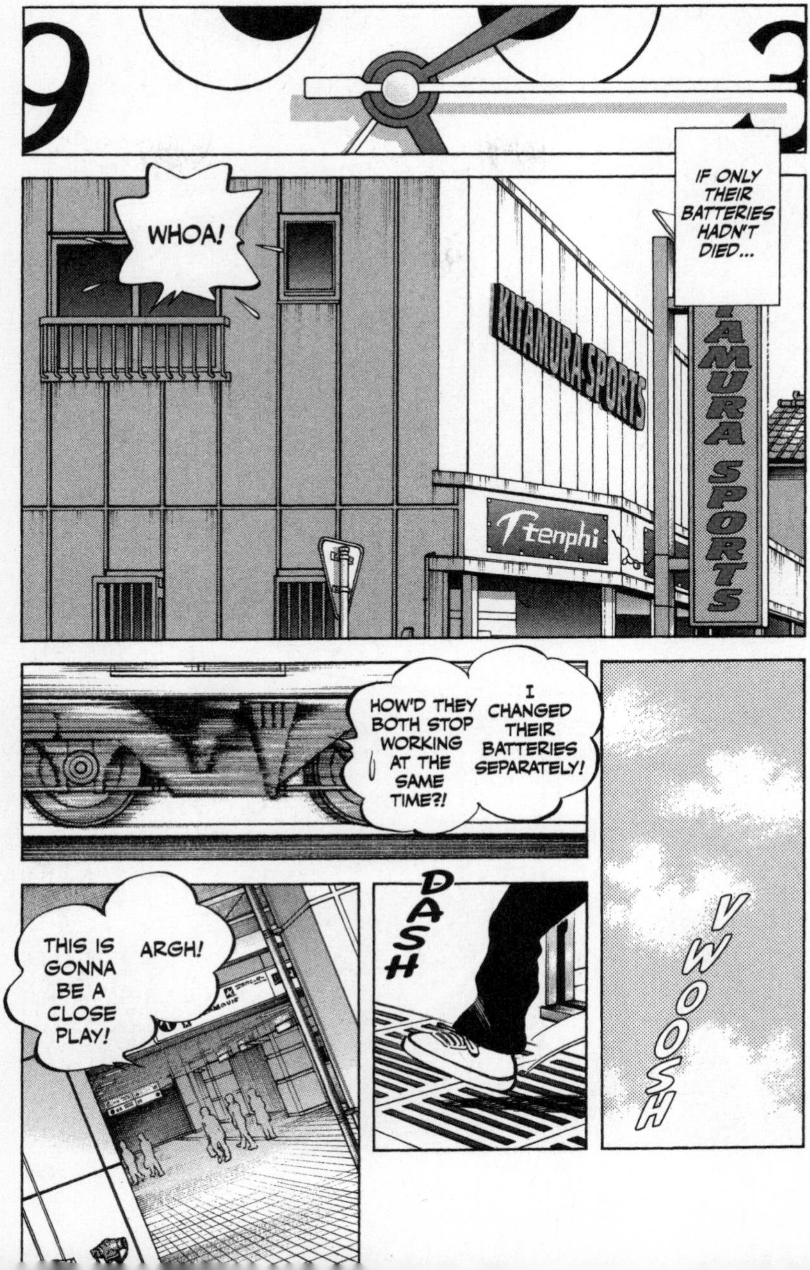
IF ONLY THEIR BATTERIES HADN'T DIED...
WHOA!
KITAMURA SPORTS
KITAMURA SPORTS
tenphi
VWOOSH
I CHANGED THEIR BATTERIES SEPARATELY!
HOW'D THEY BOTH STOP WORKING AT THE SAME TIME?!
DASH
ARGH!
THIS IS GONNA BE A CLOSE PLAY!

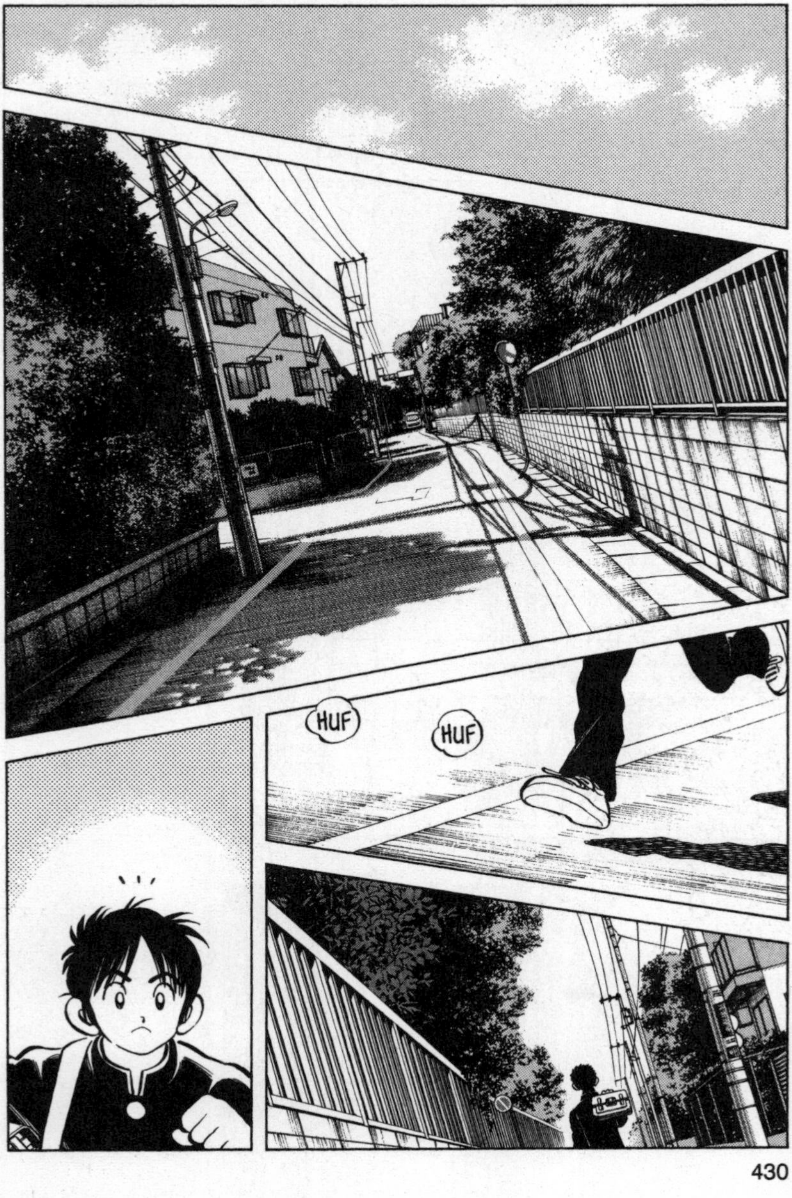
HUF
HUF

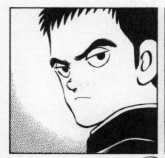

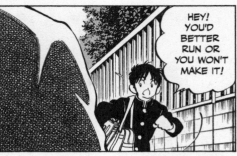

HEY! YOU'D BETTER RUN OR YOU WON'T MAKE IT!
OUR SCHOOL'S STRICT...
...ABOUT TARDINESS!
RRRRIIING...

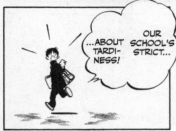

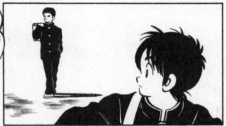

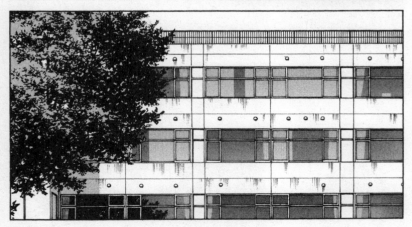

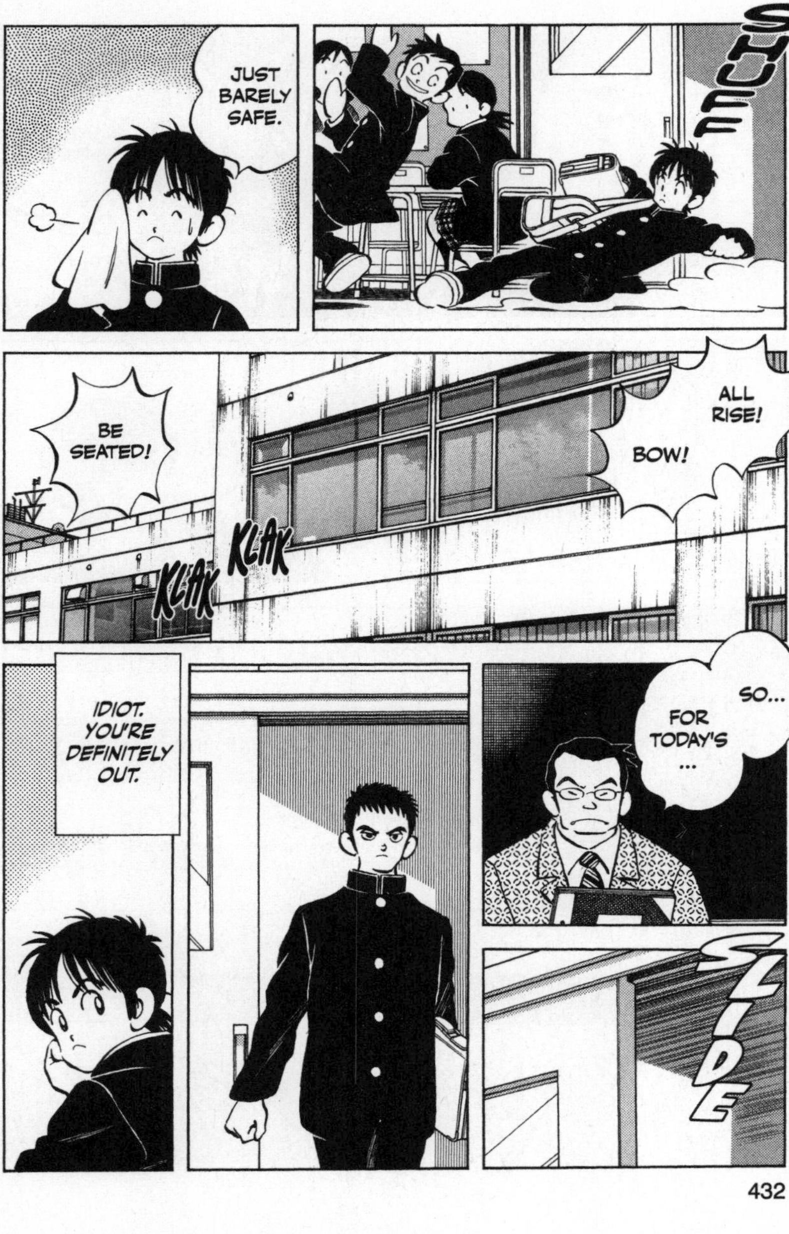
SHUFF
JUST BARELY SAFE.
ALL RISE!
BOW!
KLAK
KLAK
BE SEATED!
SO... FOR TODAY'S ...
SLIDE
IDIOT. YOU'RE DEFINITELY OUT.

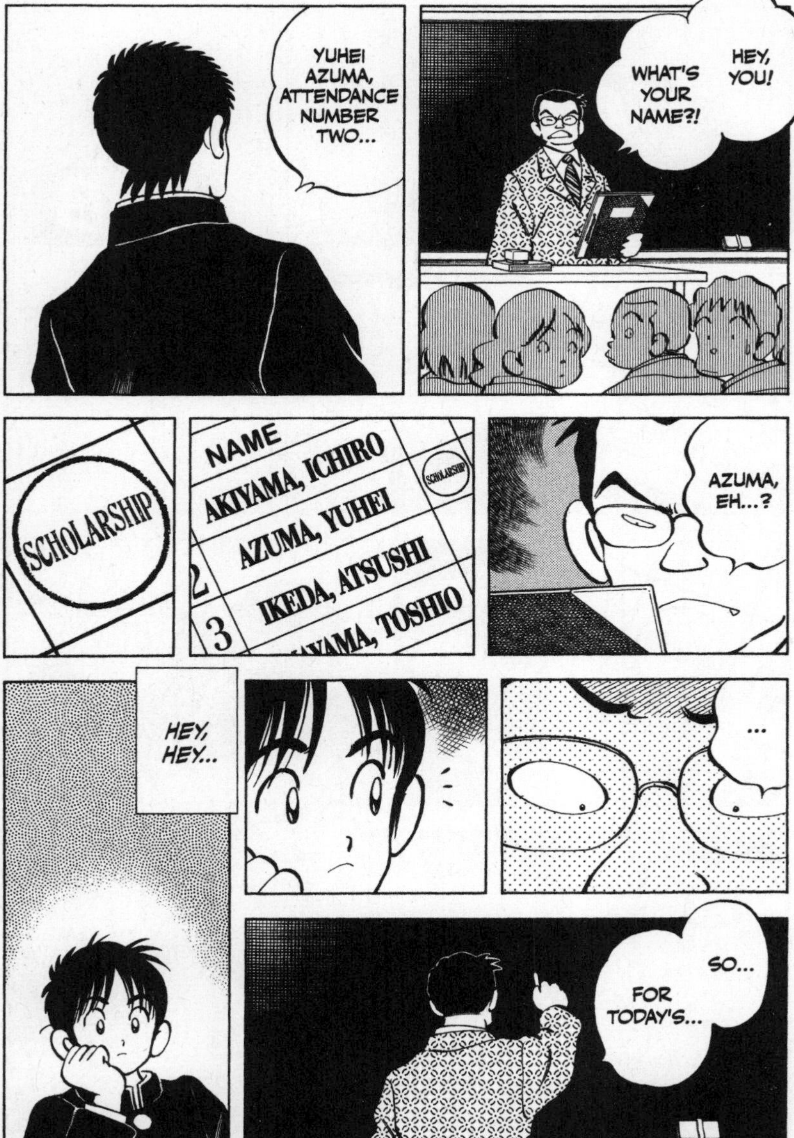
HEY, YOU!
WHAT'S YOUR NAME?!
YUHEI AZUMA, ATTENDANCE NUMBER TWO...
AZUMA, EH...?
NAME
AKIYAMA, ICHIRO
SCHOLARSHIP
AZUMA, YUHEI
2
IKEDA, ATSUSHI
3
SCHOLARSHIP
...
SO...
FOR TODAY'S...
HEY, HEY...

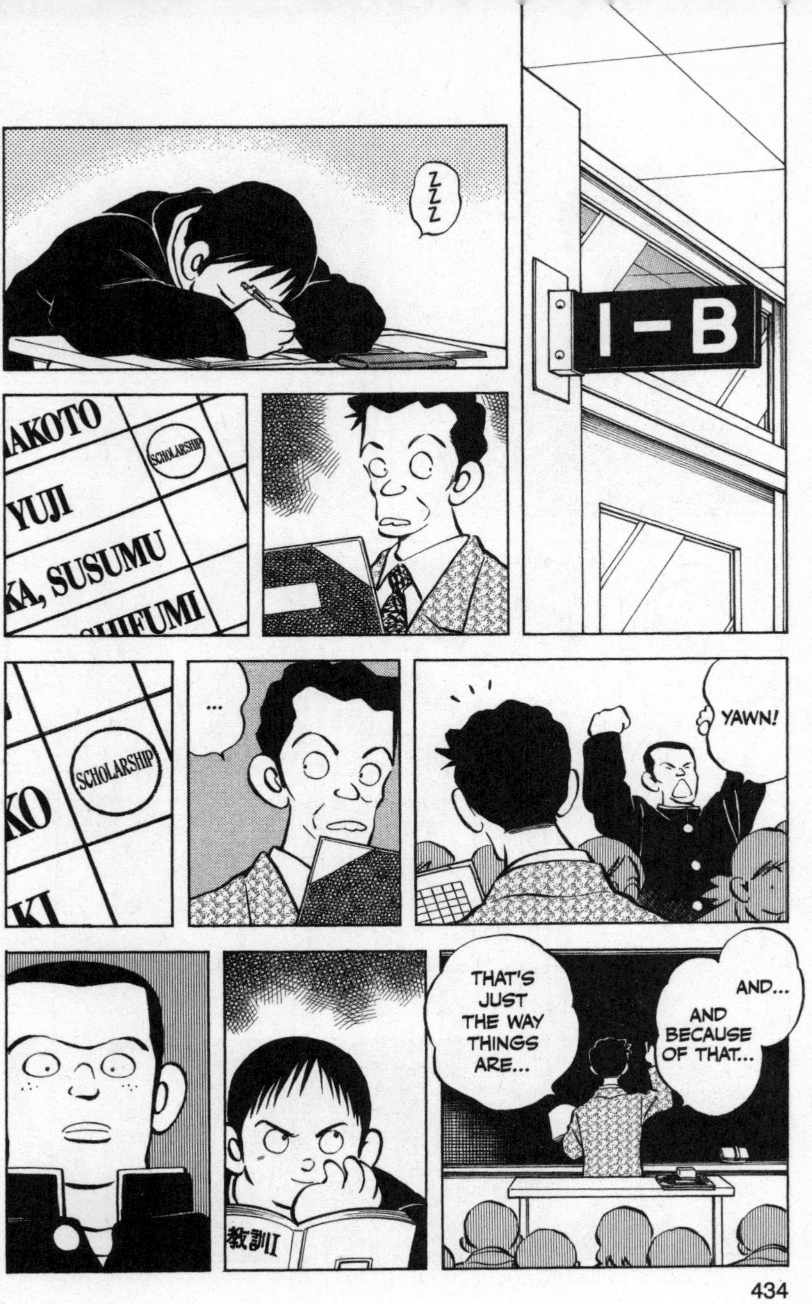
I-B
ZZZ
AKOTO
SCHOLARSHIP
YUJI
KA, SUSUMU
SHIFUMI
YAWN!
...
SCHOLARSHIP
KO
KI
AND... AND BECAUSE OF THAT...
THAT'S JUST THE WAY THINGS ARE...
教訓I

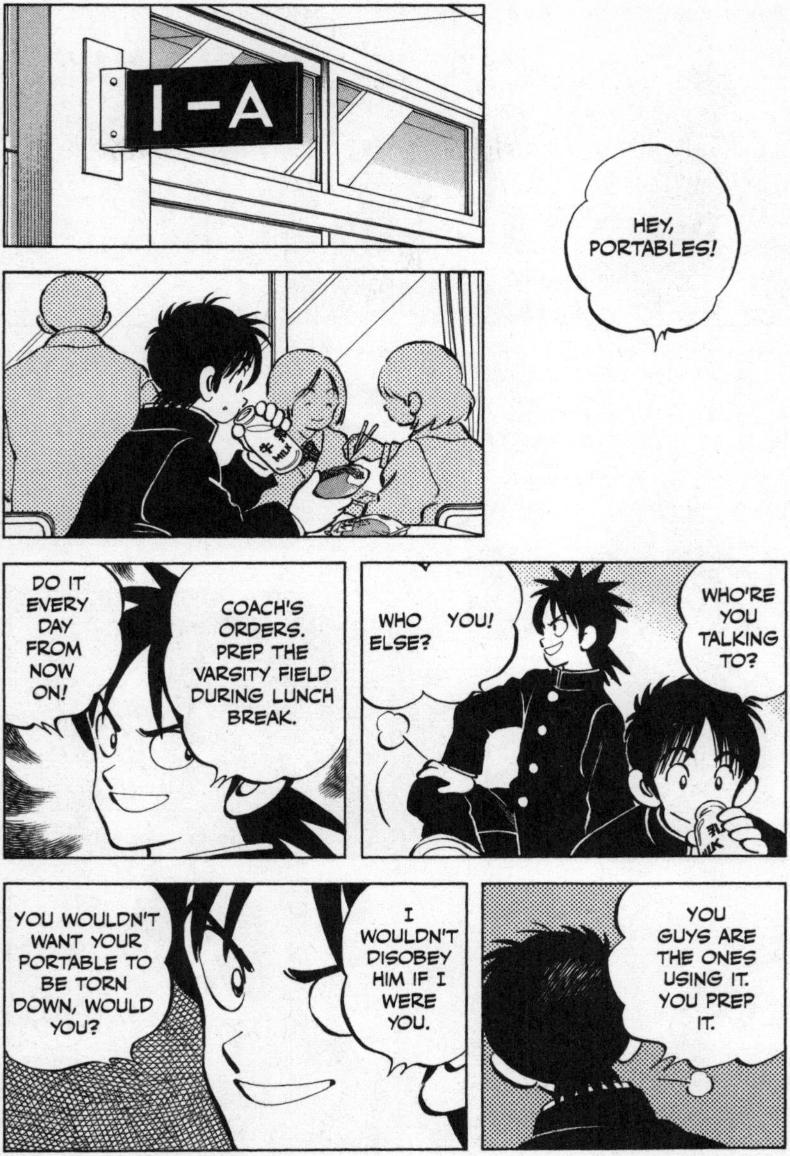
HEY, PORTABLES!
I-A
WHO'RE YOU TALKING TO?
YOU! WHO ELSE?
COACH'S ORDERS. PREP THE VARSITY FIELD DURING LUNCH BREAK.
DO IT EVERY DAY FROM NOW ON!
YOU GUYS ARE THE ONES USING IT. YOU PREP IT.
I WOULDN'T DISOBEY HIM IF I WERE YOU.
YOU WOULDN'T WANT YOUR PORTABLE TO BE TORN DOWN, WOULD YOU?

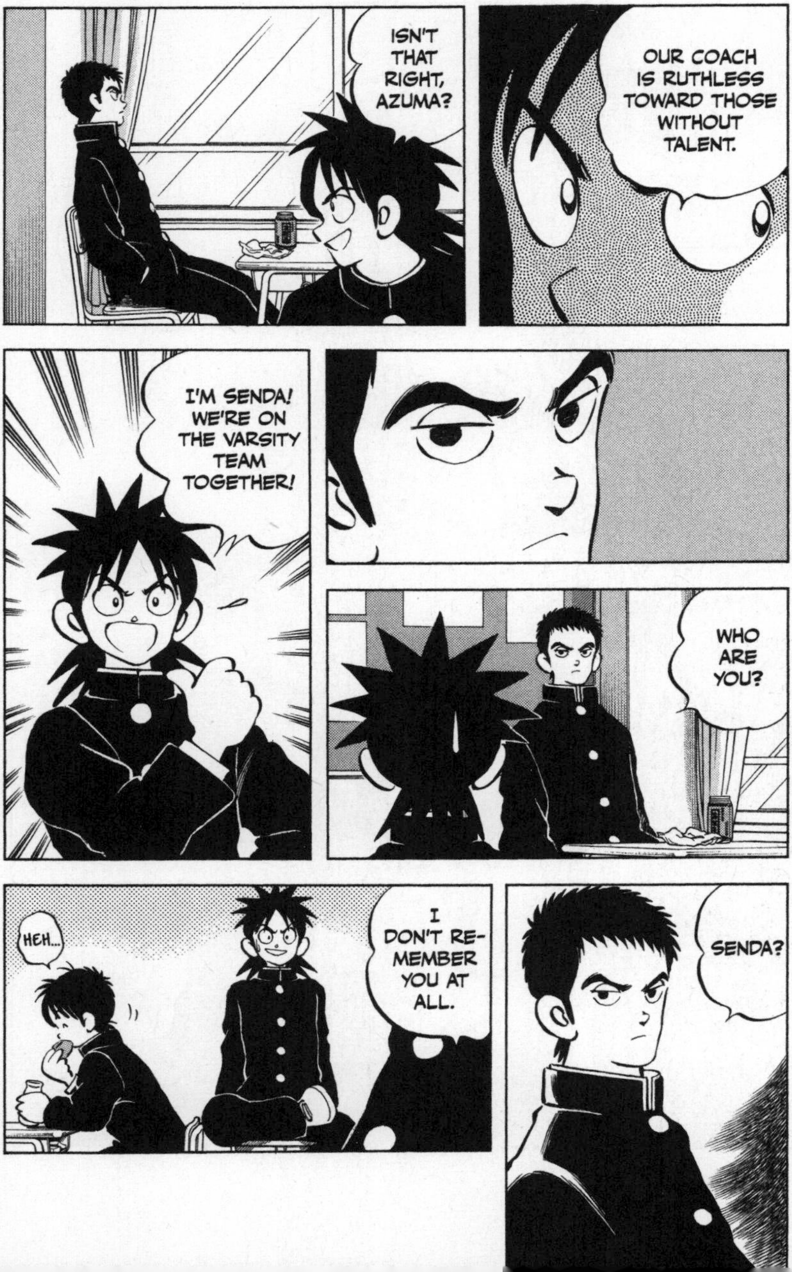
OUR COACH IS RUTHLESS TOWARD THOSE WITHOUT TALENT.
ISN'T THAT RIGHT, AZUMA?
WHO ARE YOU?
I'M SENDA! WE'RE ON THE VARSITY TEAM TOGETHER!
SENDA?
I DON'T RE-MEMBER YOU AT ALL.
HEH...

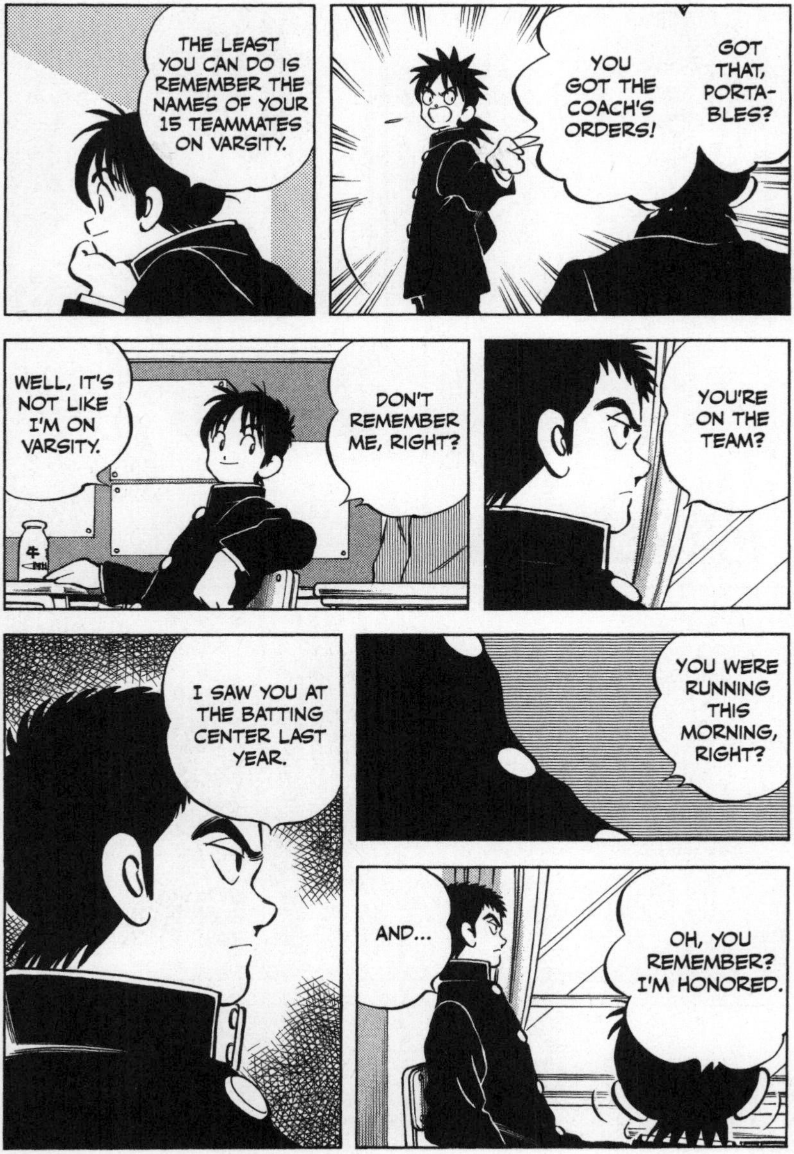
GOT THAT, PORTA-BLES?
YOU GOT THE COACH'S ORDERS!
THE LEAST YOU CAN DO IS REMEMBER THE NAMES OF YOUR 15 TEAMMATES ON VARSITY.
YOU'RE ON THE TEAM?
DON'T REMEMBER ME, RIGHT?
WELL, IT'S NOT LIKE I'M ON VARSITY.
YOU WERE RUNNING THIS MORNING, RIGHT?
OH, YOU REMEMBER? I'M HONORED.
AND...
I SAW YOU AT THE BATTING CENTER LAST YEAR.

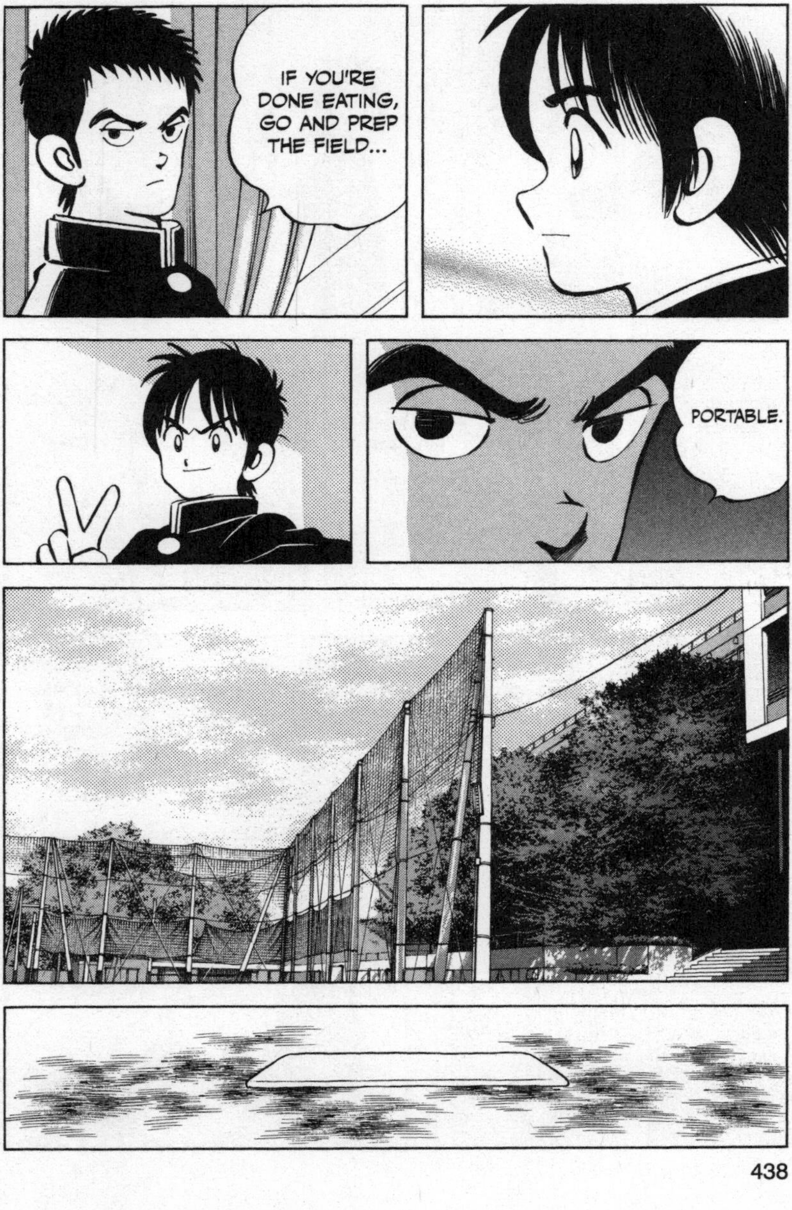
IF YOU'RE DONE EATING, GO AND PREP THE FIELD...
PORTABLE.

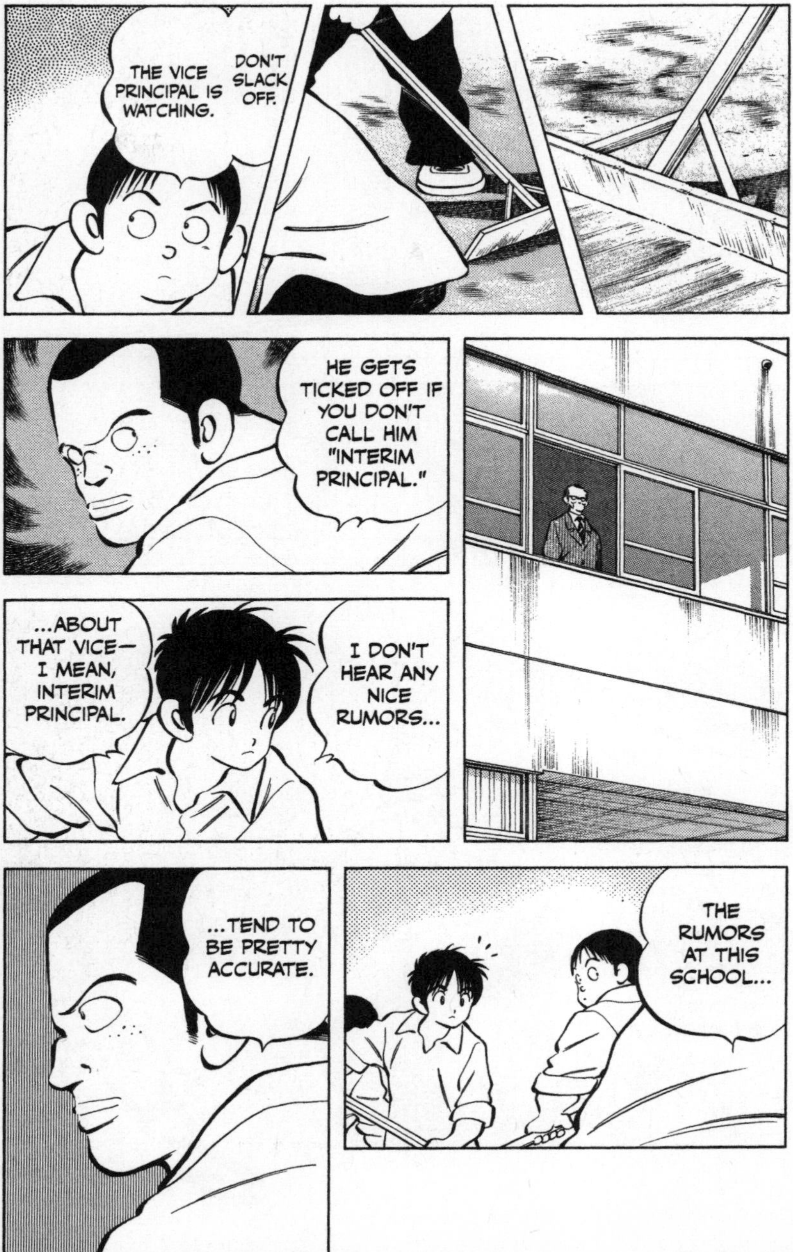
DON'T SLACK OFF.
THE VICE PRINCIPAL IS WATCHING.
HE GETS TICKED OFF IF YOU DON'T CALL HIM "INTERIM PRINCIPAL."
I DON'T HEAR ANY NICE RUMORS...
...ABOUT THAT VICE— I MEAN, INTERIM PRINCIPAL.
THE RUMORS AT THIS SCHOOL...
...TEND TO BE PRETTY ACCURATE.

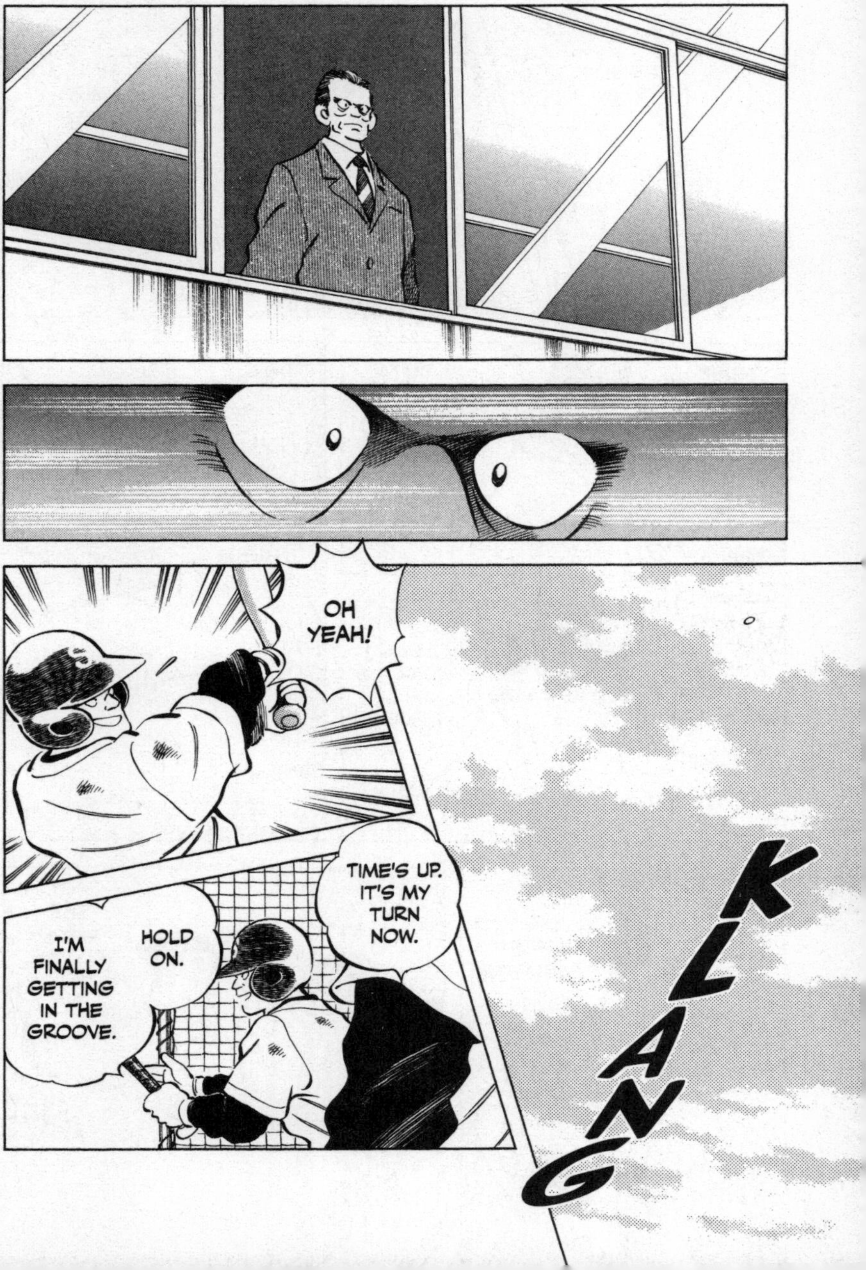
KLANG
OH YEAH!
TIME'S UP. IT'S MY TURN NOW.
HOLD ON.
I'M FINALLY GETTING IN THE GROOVE.

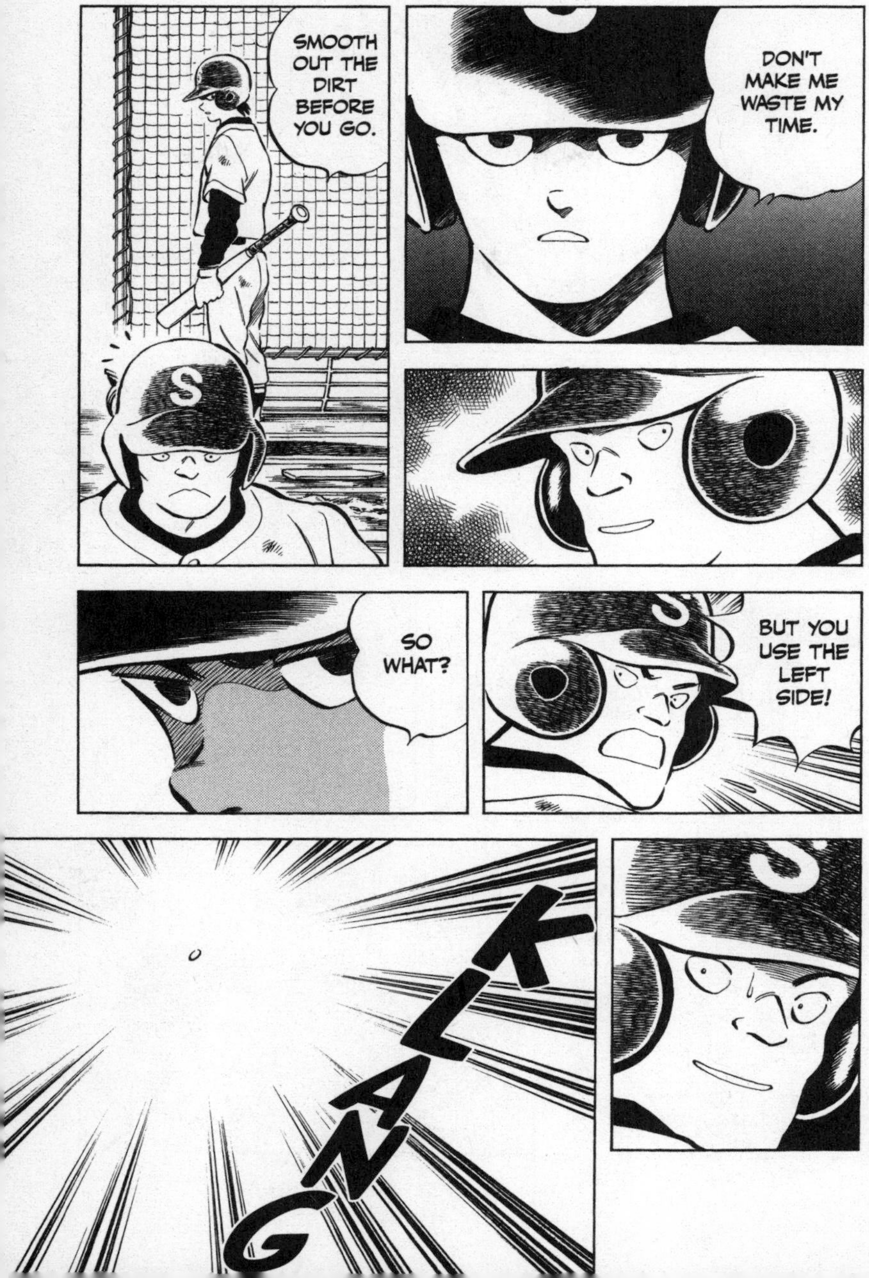
DON'T MAKE ME WASTE MY TIME.
SMOOTH OUT THE DIRT BEFORE YOU GO.
BUT YOU USE THE LEFT SIDE!
SO WHAT?
KLANG

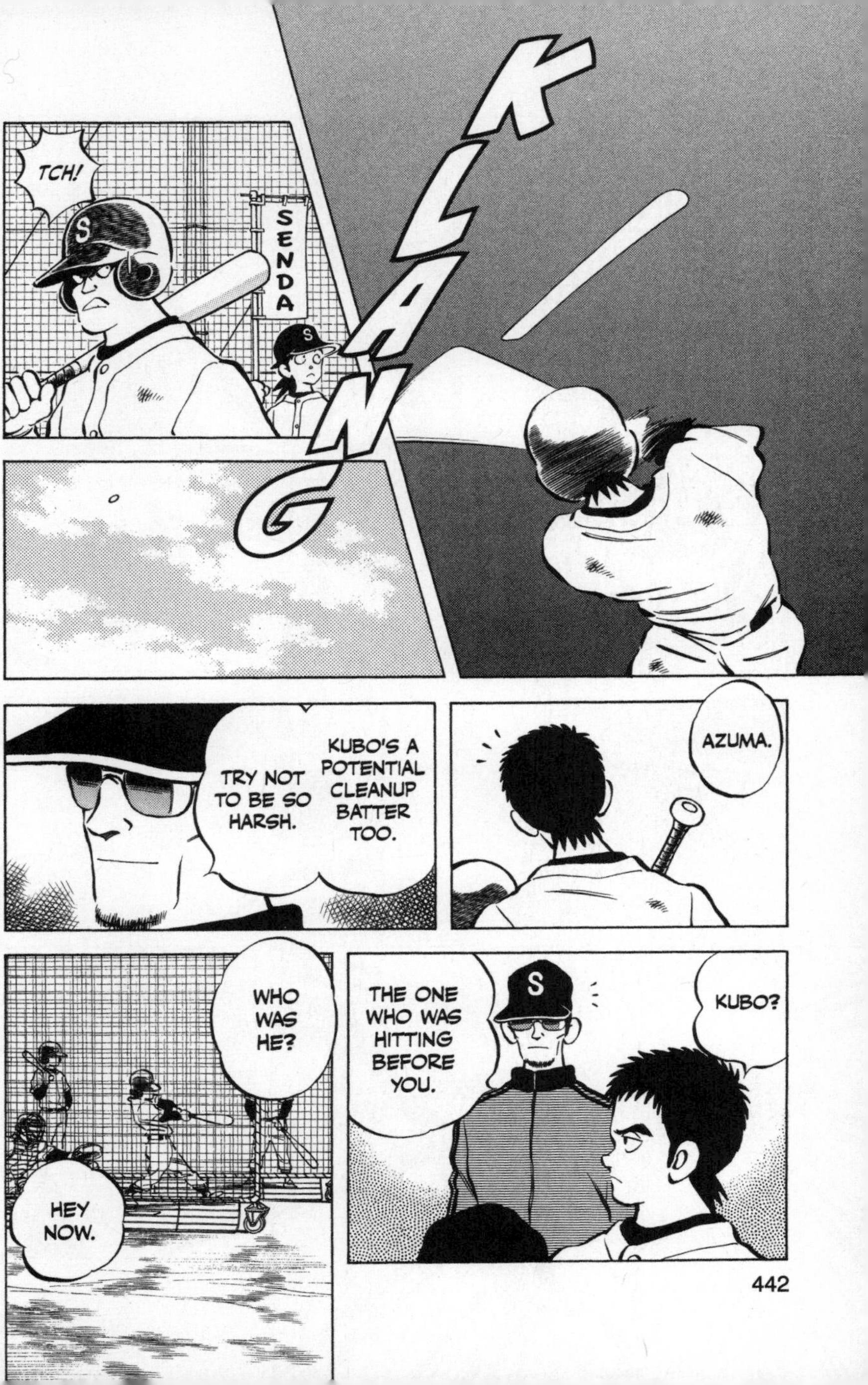
KLANG
TCH!
SENDA
AZUMA.
KUBO'S A POTENTIAL CLEANUP BATTER TOO.
TRY NOT TO BE SO HARSH.
KUBO?
THE ONE WHO WAS HITTING BEFORE YOU.
WHO WAS HE?
HEY NOW.

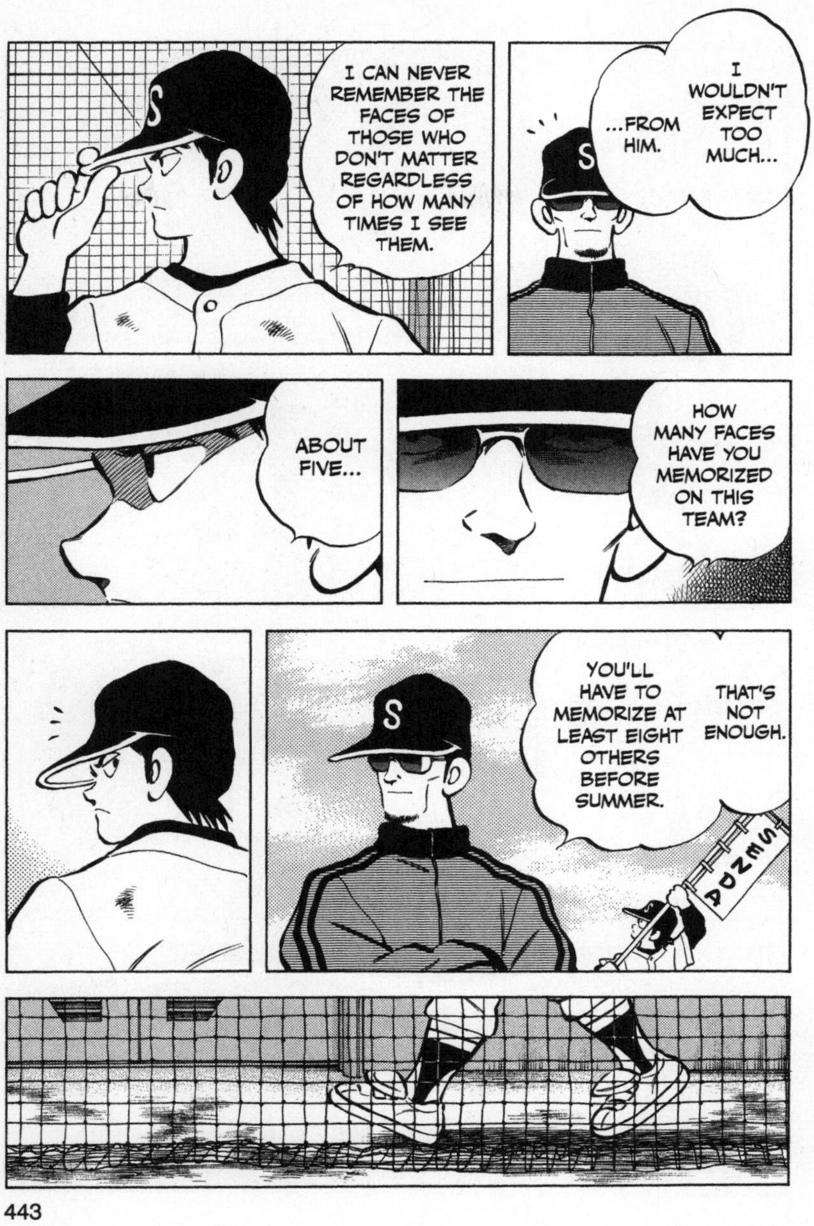
I WOULDN'T EXPECT TOO MUCH...
...FROM HIM.
I CAN NEVER REMEMBER THE FACES OF THOSE WHO DON'T MATTER REGARDLESS OF HOW MANY TIMES I SEE THEM.
HOW MANY FACES HAVE YOU MEMORIZED ON THIS TEAM?
ABOUT FIVE...
THAT'S NOT ENOUGH.
YOU'LL HAVE TO MEMORIZE AT LEAST EIGHT OTHERS BEFORE SUMMER.
SENDA

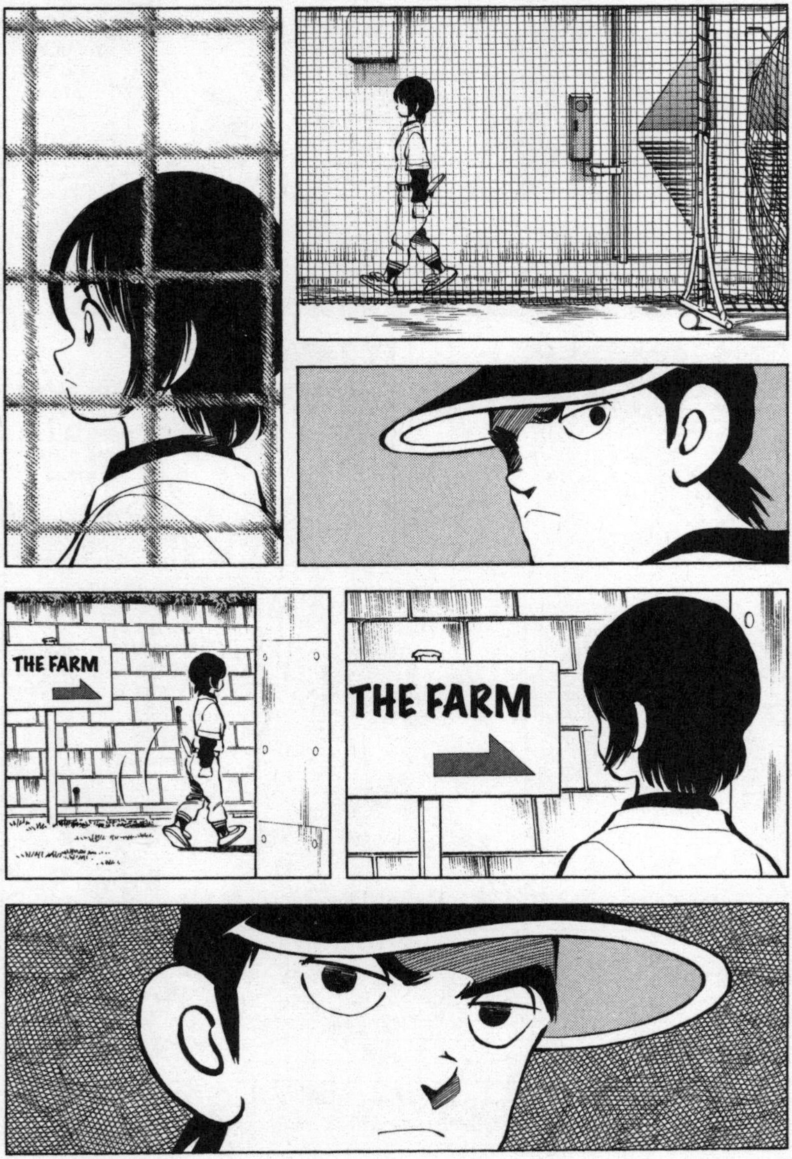
THE FARM
THE FARM

CHAPTER 14
A GOOD DREAM

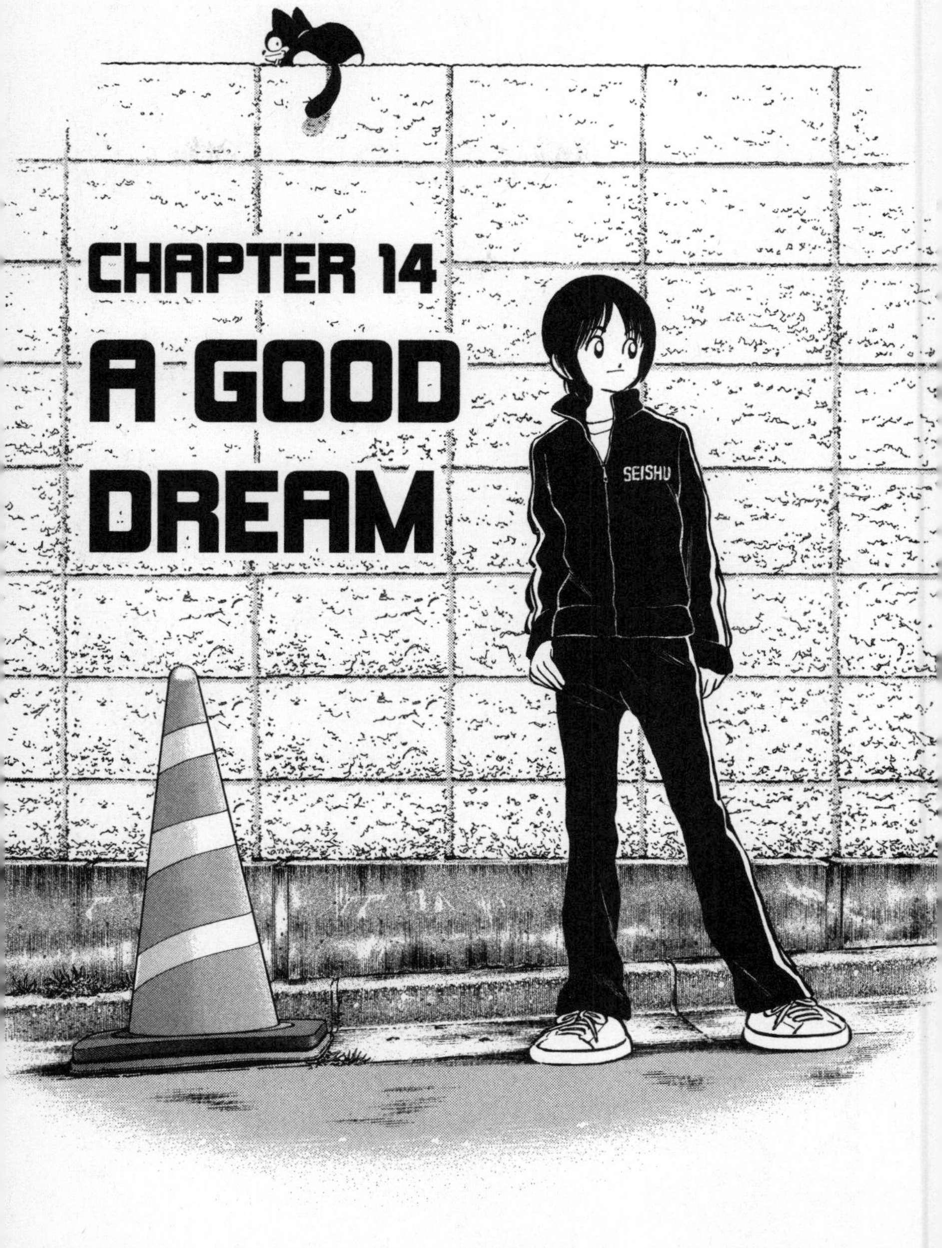
SEISHU

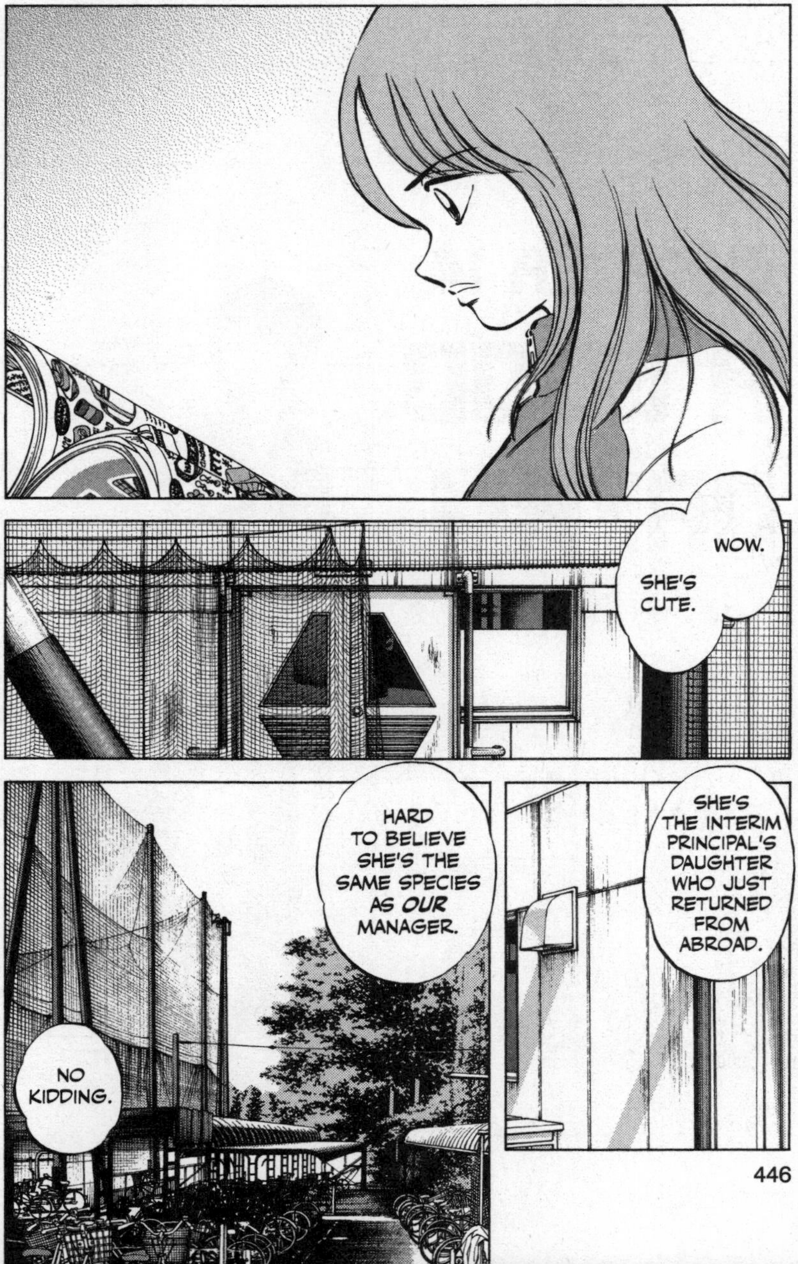
WOW.
SHE'S CUTE.
SHE'S THE INTERIM PRINCIPAL'S DAUGHTER WHO JUST RETURNED FROM ABROAD.
HARD TO BELIEVE SHE'S THE SAME SPECIES AS *OUR* MANAGER.
NO KIDDING.

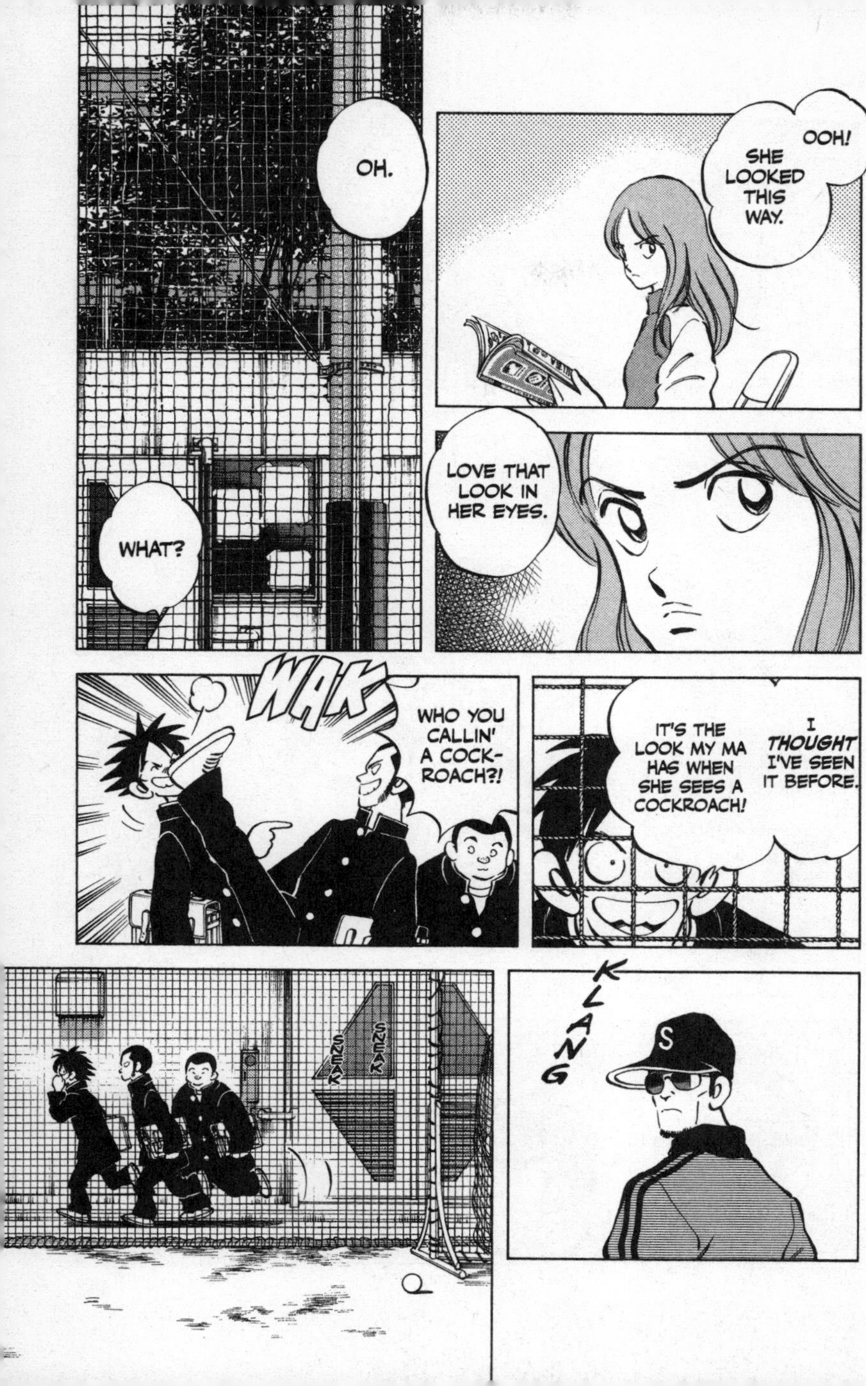
OOH! SHE LOOKED THIS WAY.
LOVE THAT LOOK IN HER EYES.
OH.
WHAT?
I THOUGHT I'VE SEEN IT BEFORE.
IT'S THE LOOK MY MA HAS WHEN SHE SEES A COCKROACH!
WAK
WHO YOU CALLIN' A COCK-ROACH?!
KLANG
SNEAK
SNEAK

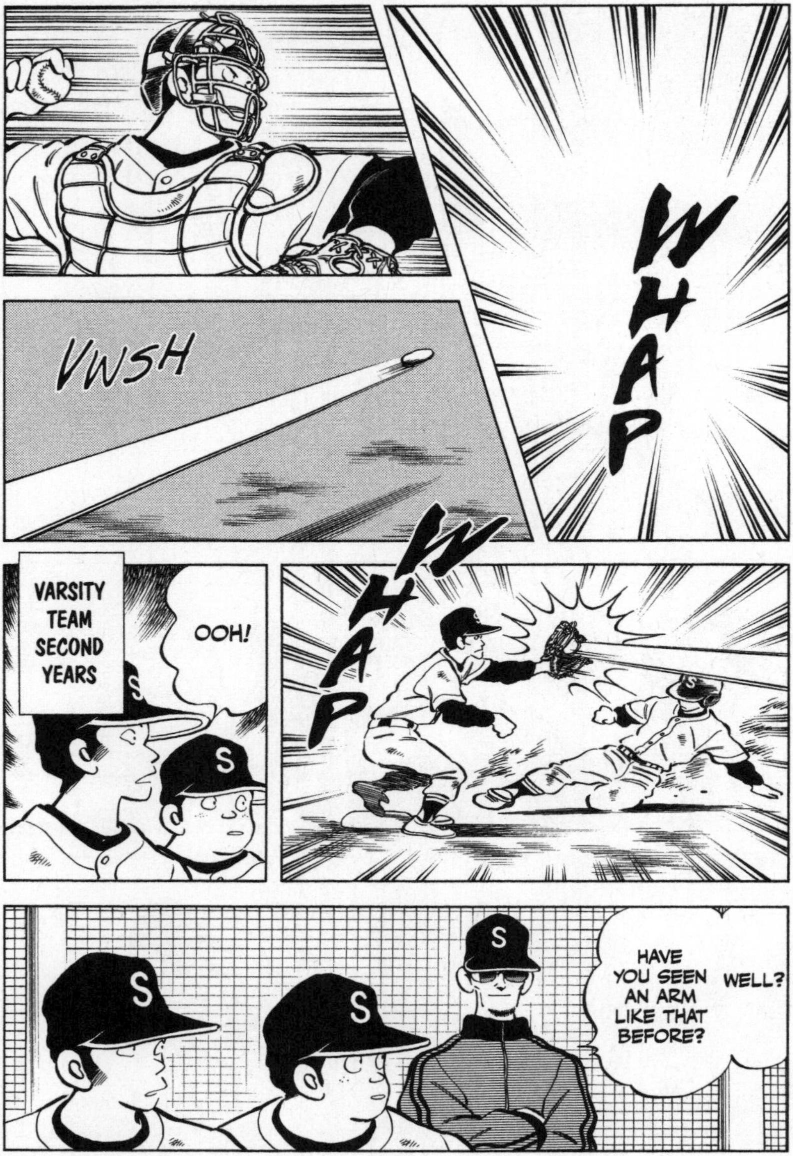
WHAP
VWSH
WHAP
OOH!
VARSITY TEAM SECOND YEARS
WELL?
HAVE YOU SEEN AN ARM LIKE THAT BEFORE?

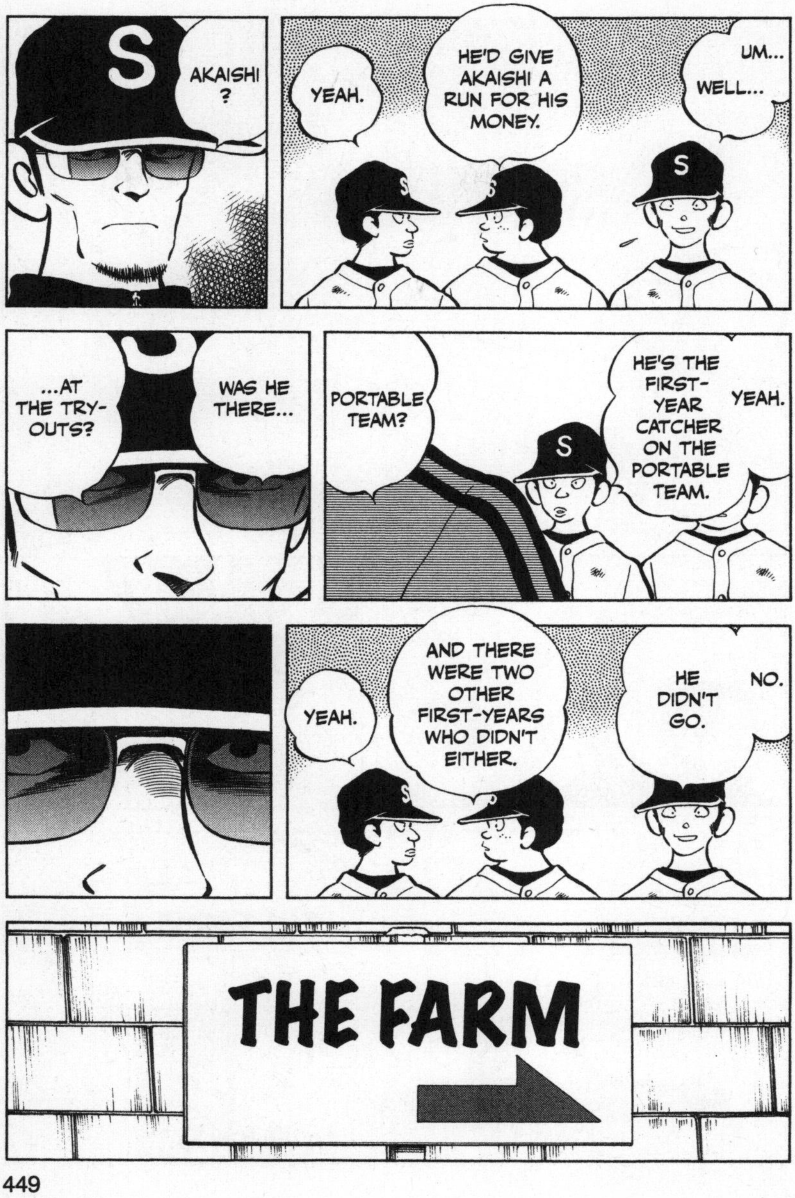
UM... WELL...
HE'D GIVE AKAISHI A RUN FOR HIS MONEY.
YEAH.
AKAISHI ?
YEAH.
HE'S THE FIRST-YEAR CATCHER ON THE PORTABLE TEAM.
PORTABLE TEAM?
WAS HE THERE...
...AT THE TRY-OUTS?
NO.
HE DIDN'T GO.
AND THERE WERE TWO OTHER FIRST-YEARS WHO DIDN'T EITHER.
YEAH.
THE FARM

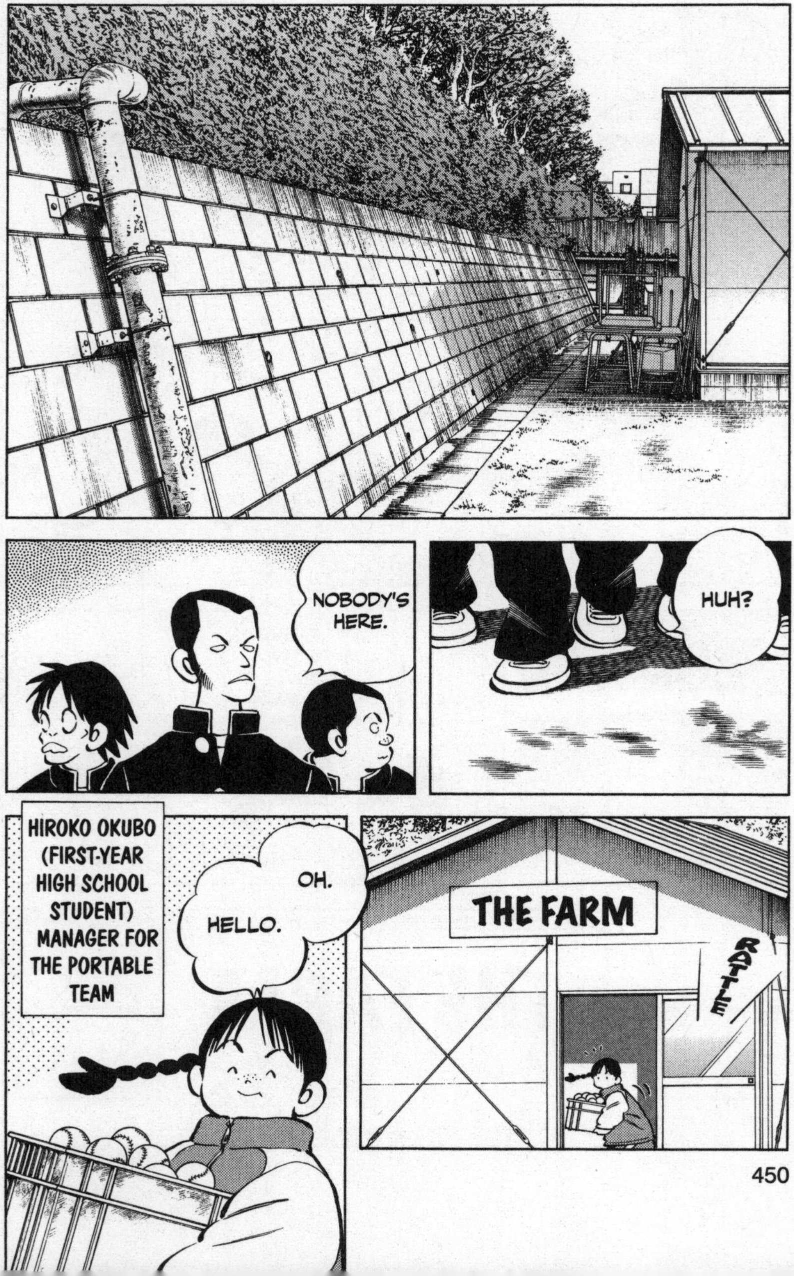
HUH?
NOBODY'S HERE.
THE FARM
RATTLE
OH. HELLO.
HIROKO OKUBO (FIRST-YEAR HIGH SCHOOL STUDENT) MANAGER FOR THE PORTABLE TEAM

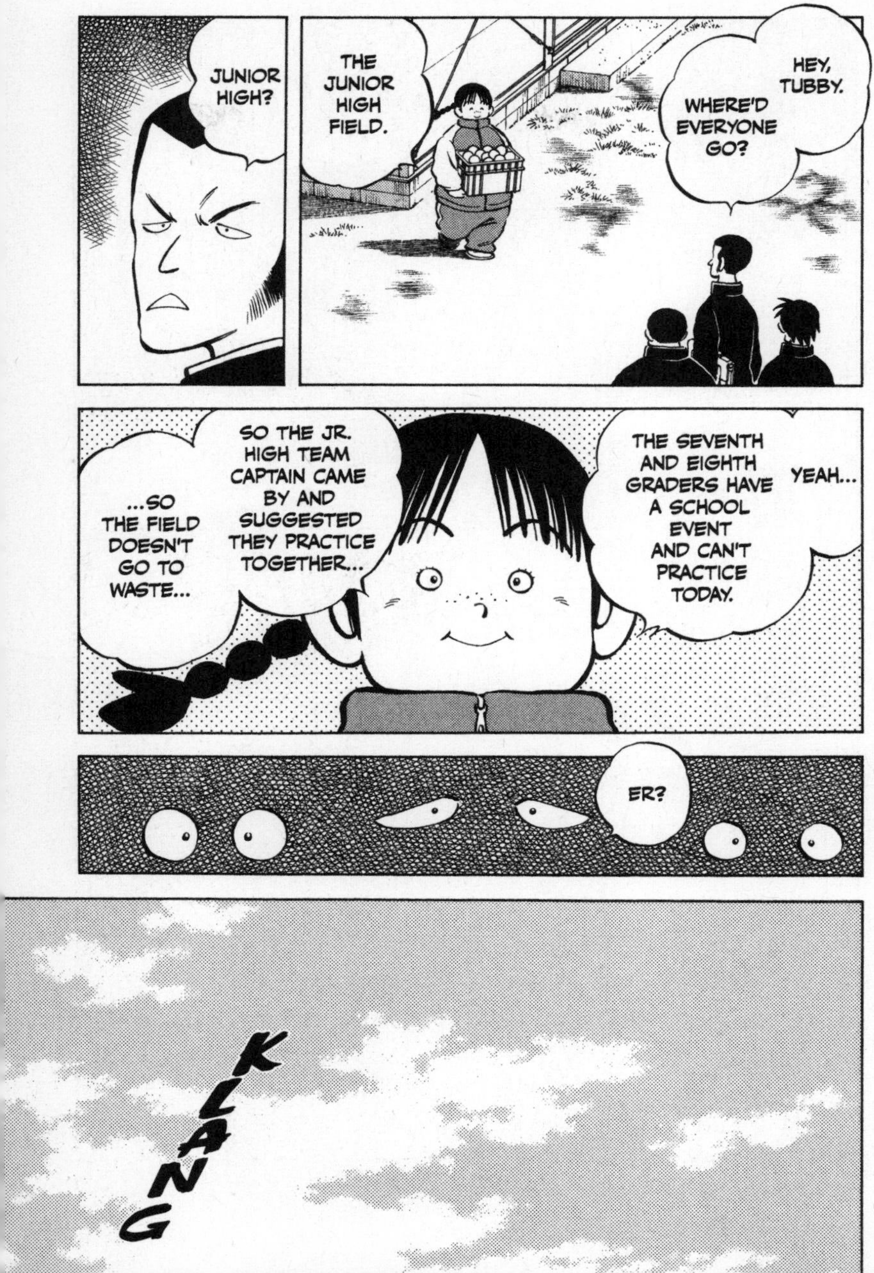
HEY, TUBBY.
WHERE'D EVERYONE GO?
THE JUNIOR HIGH FIELD.
JUNIOR HIGH?
YEAH...
THE SEVENTH AND EIGHTH GRADERS HAVE A SCHOOL EVENT AND CAN'T PRACTICE TODAY.
SO THE JR. HIGH TEAM CAPTAIN CAME BY AND SUGGESTED THEY PRACTICE TOGETHER...
...SO THE FIELD DOESN'T GO TO WASTE...
ER?
KLANG

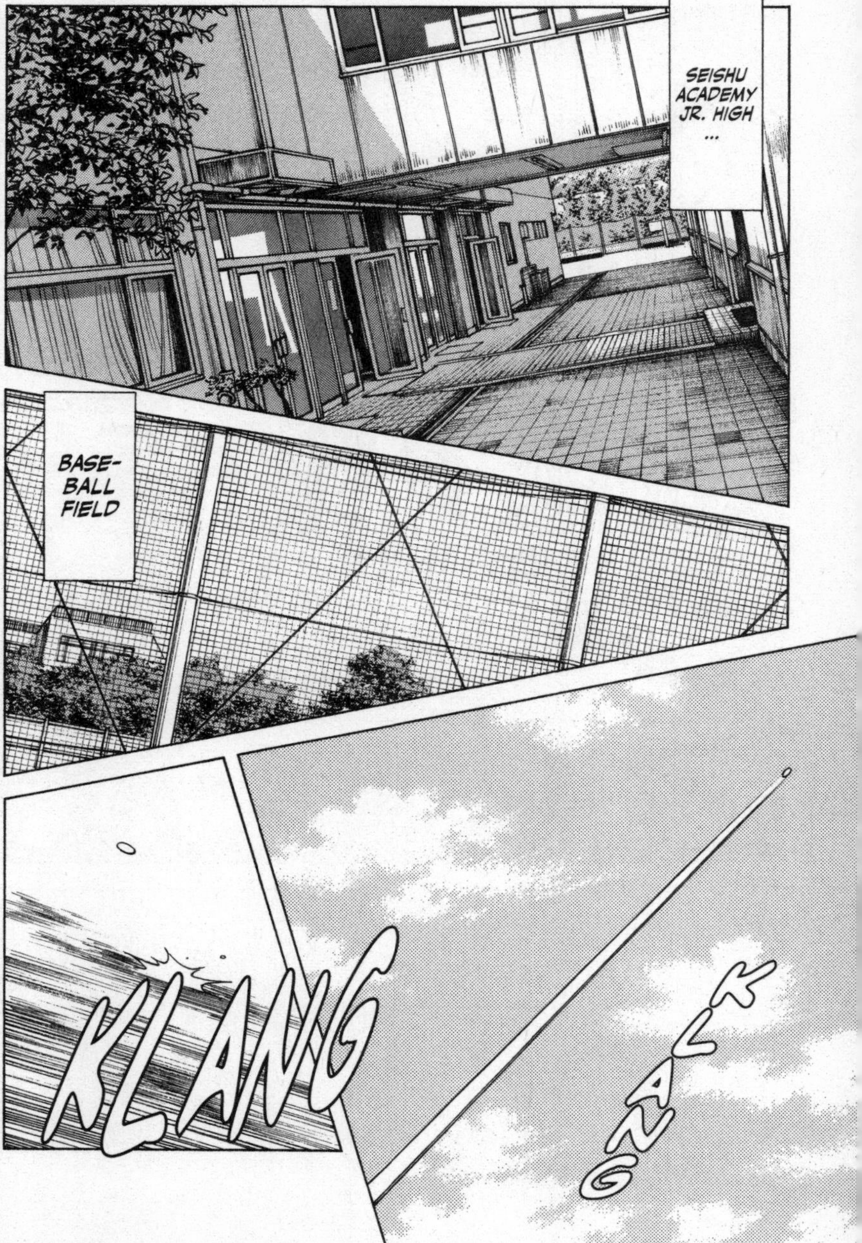
SEISHU ACADEMY JR. HIGH ...
BASE-BALL FIELD
KLANG
KLANG

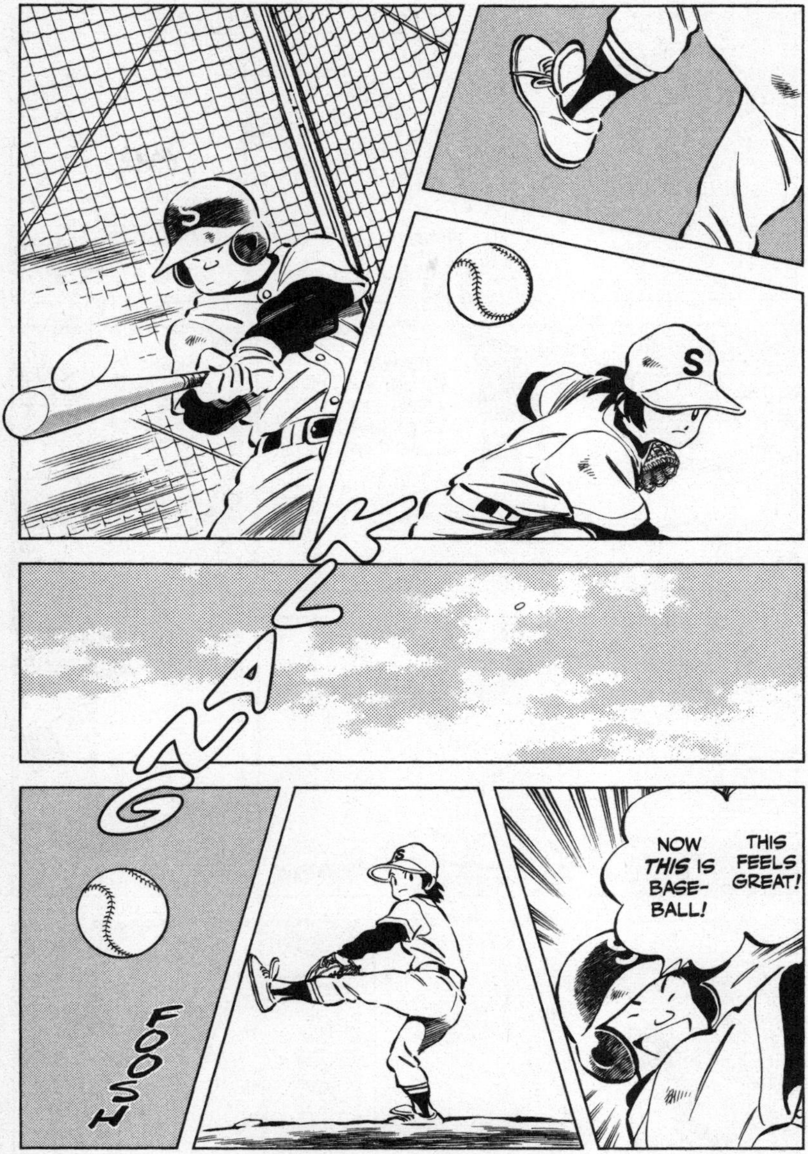
GZALK
FOOSH
NOW THIS IS BASE-BALL!
THIS FEELS GREAT!

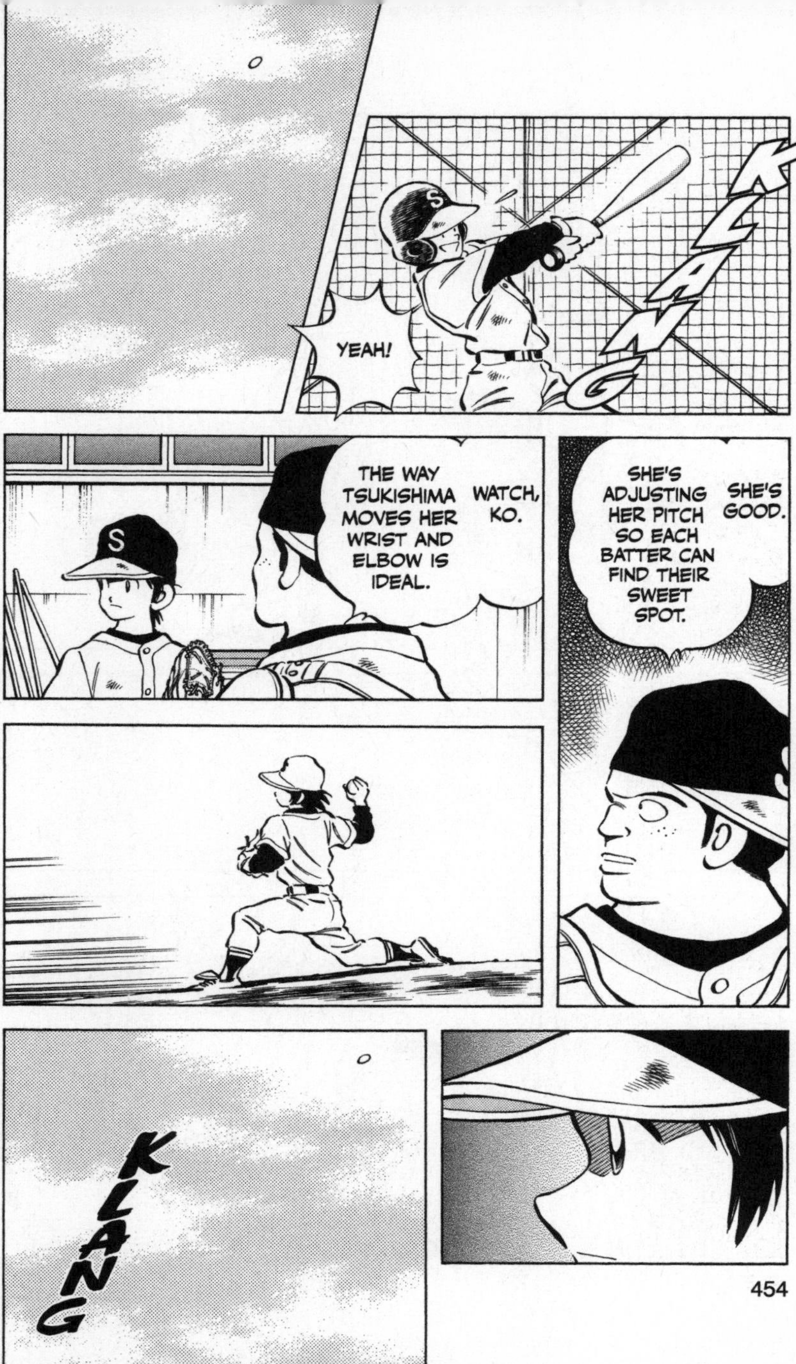
KLANG
YEAH!
SHE'S GOOD.
SHE'S ADJUSTING HER PITCH SO EACH BATTER CAN FIND THEIR SWEET SPOT.
WATCH, KO.
THE WAY TSUKISHIMA MOVES HER WRIST AND ELBOW IS IDEAL.
KLANG

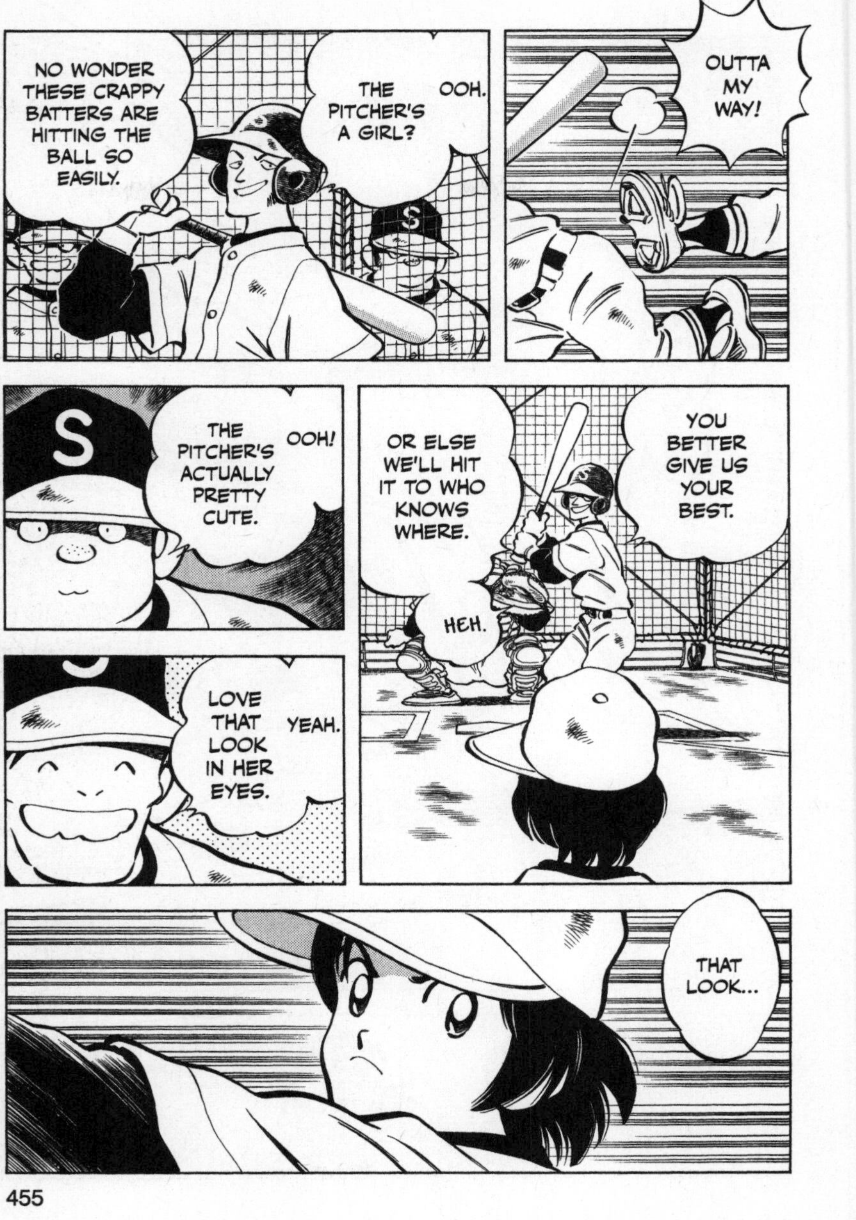
OUTTA MY WAY!
OOH.
THE PITCHER'S A GIRL?
NO WONDER THESE CRAPPY BATTERS ARE HITTING THE BALL SO EASILY.
YOU BETTER GIVE US YOUR BEST.
OR ELSE WE'LL HIT IT TO WHO KNOWS WHERE.
HEH.
OOH!
THE PITCHER'S ACTUALLY PRETTY CUTE.
YEAH.
LOVE THAT LOOK IN HER EYES.
THAT LOOK...

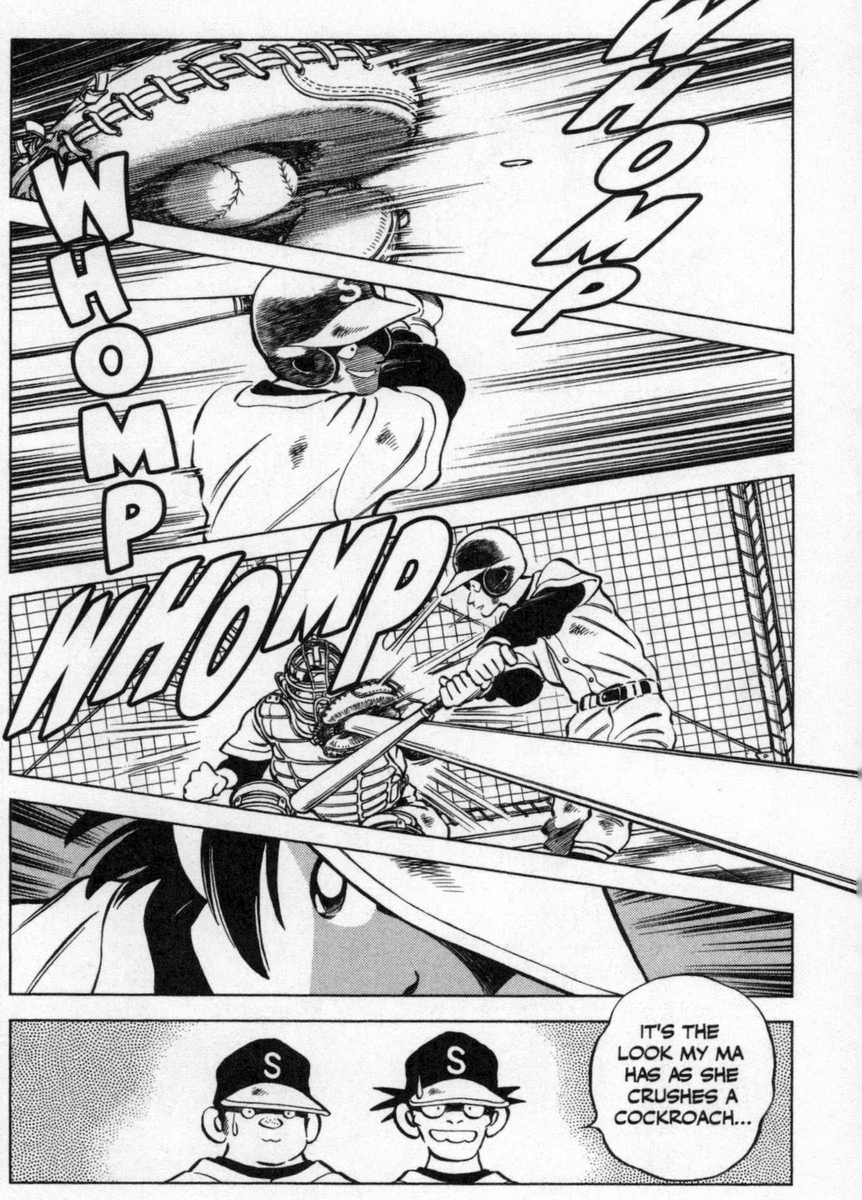
WHOMP
WHOMP
WHOMP
IT'S THE LOOK MY MA HAS AS SHE CRUSHES A COCKROACH...

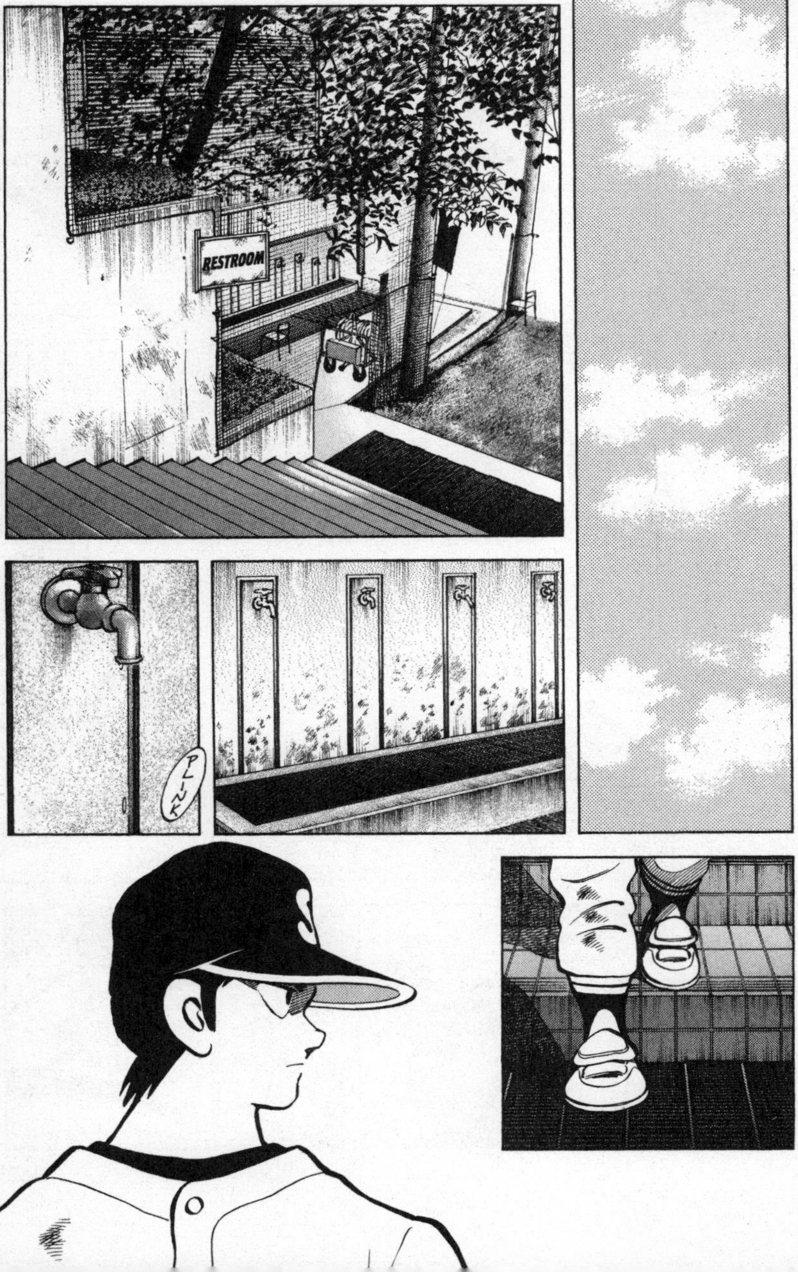
RESTROOM
PLINK

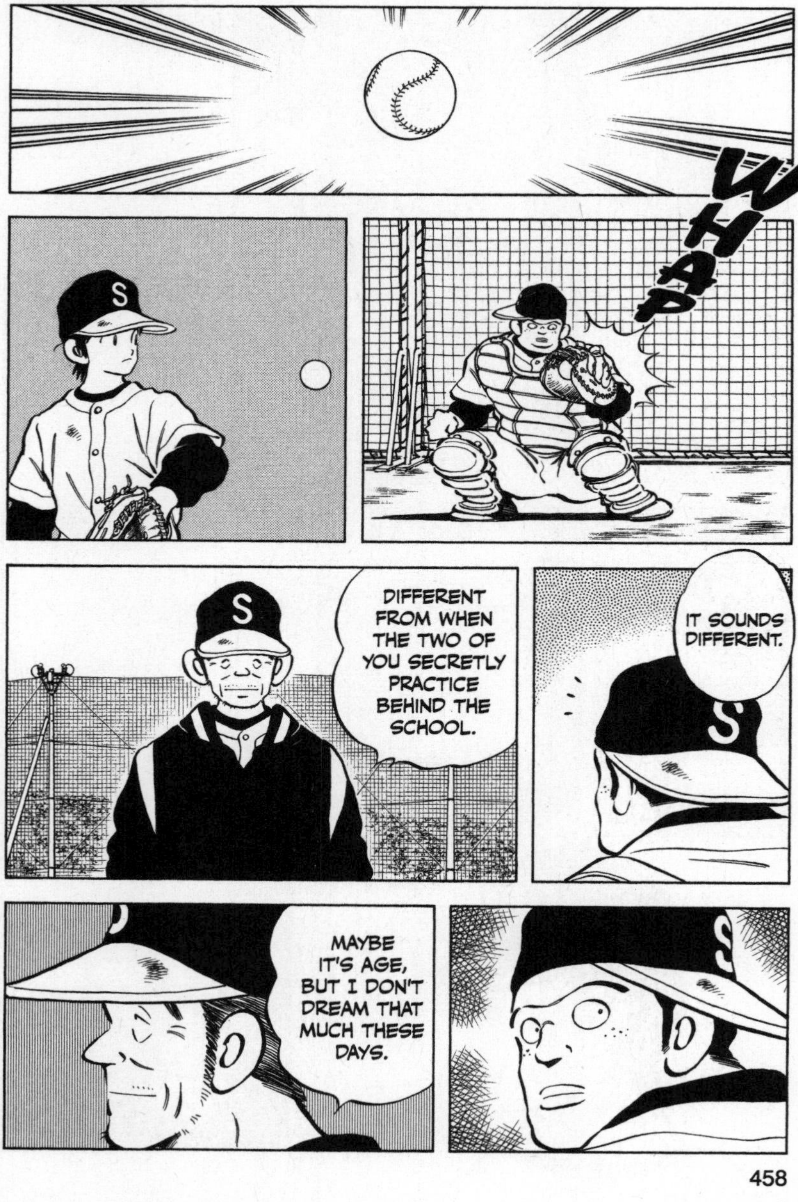
WHAP
IT SOUNDS DIFFERENT.
DIFFERENT FROM WHEN THE TWO OF YOU SECRETLY PRACTICE BEHIND THE SCHOOL.
MAYBE IT'S AGE, BUT I DON'T DREAM THAT MUCH THESE DAYS.

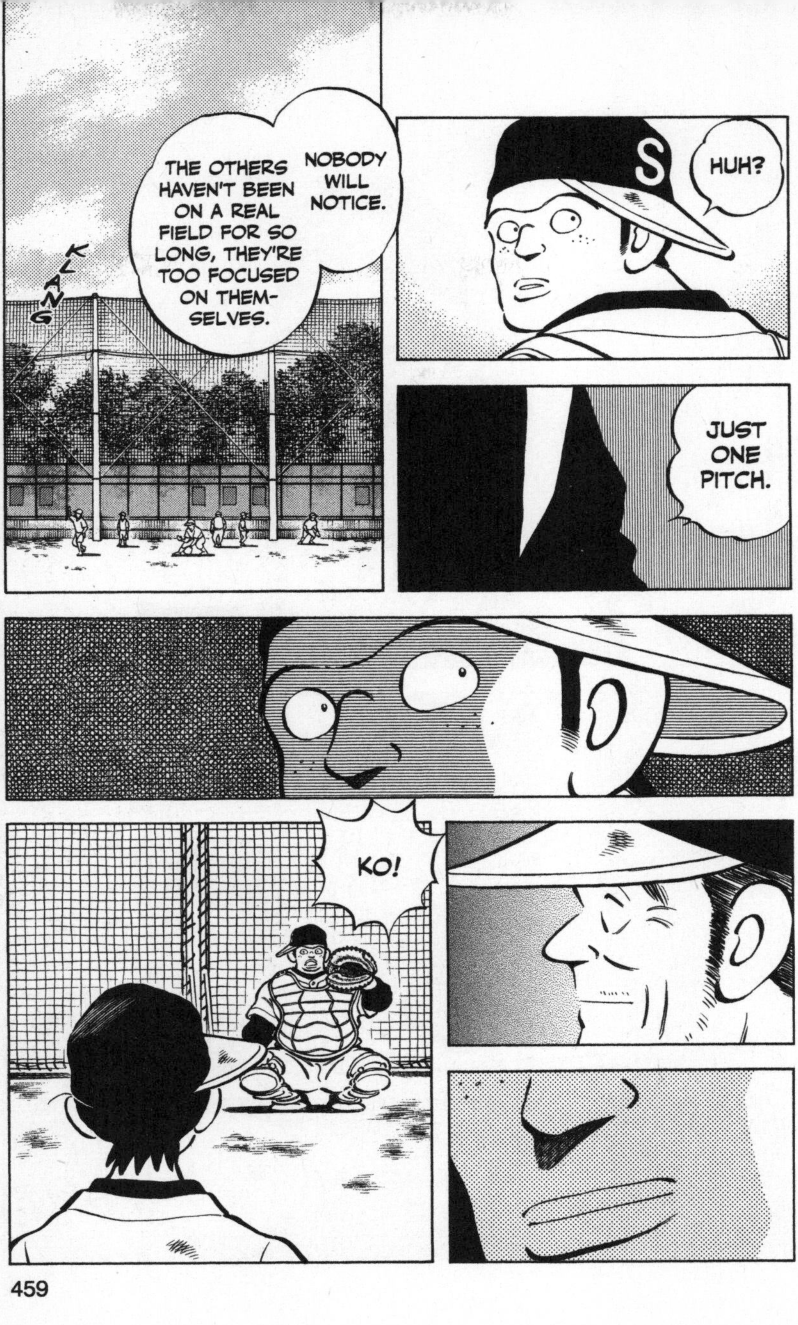
HUH?
JUST ONE PITCH.
NOBODY WILL NOTICE.
THE OTHERS HAVEN'T BEEN ON A REAL FIELD FOR SO LONG, THEY'RE TOO FOCUSED ON THEMSELVES.
KLANG
KO!

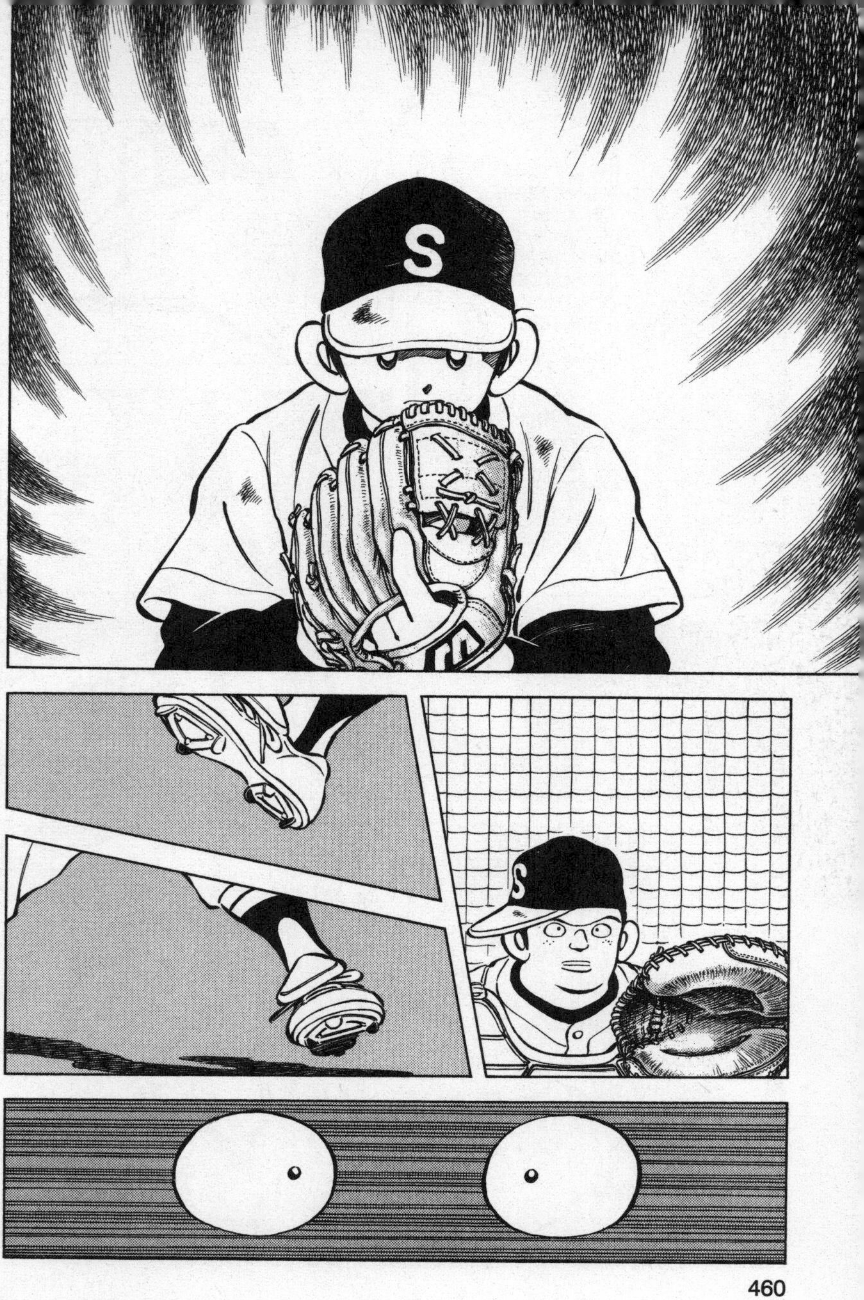

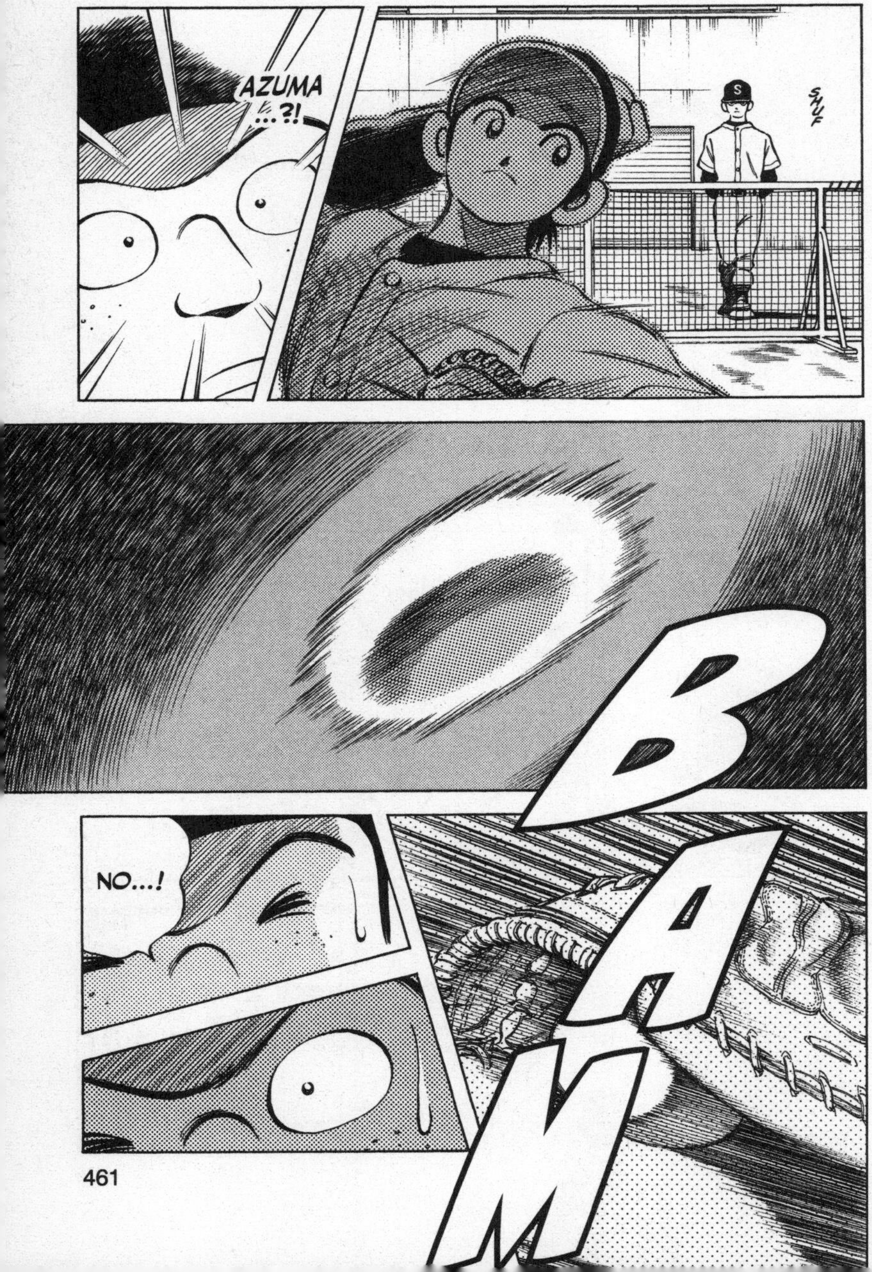
SHUF
AZUMA ...?!
BAM
NO...!

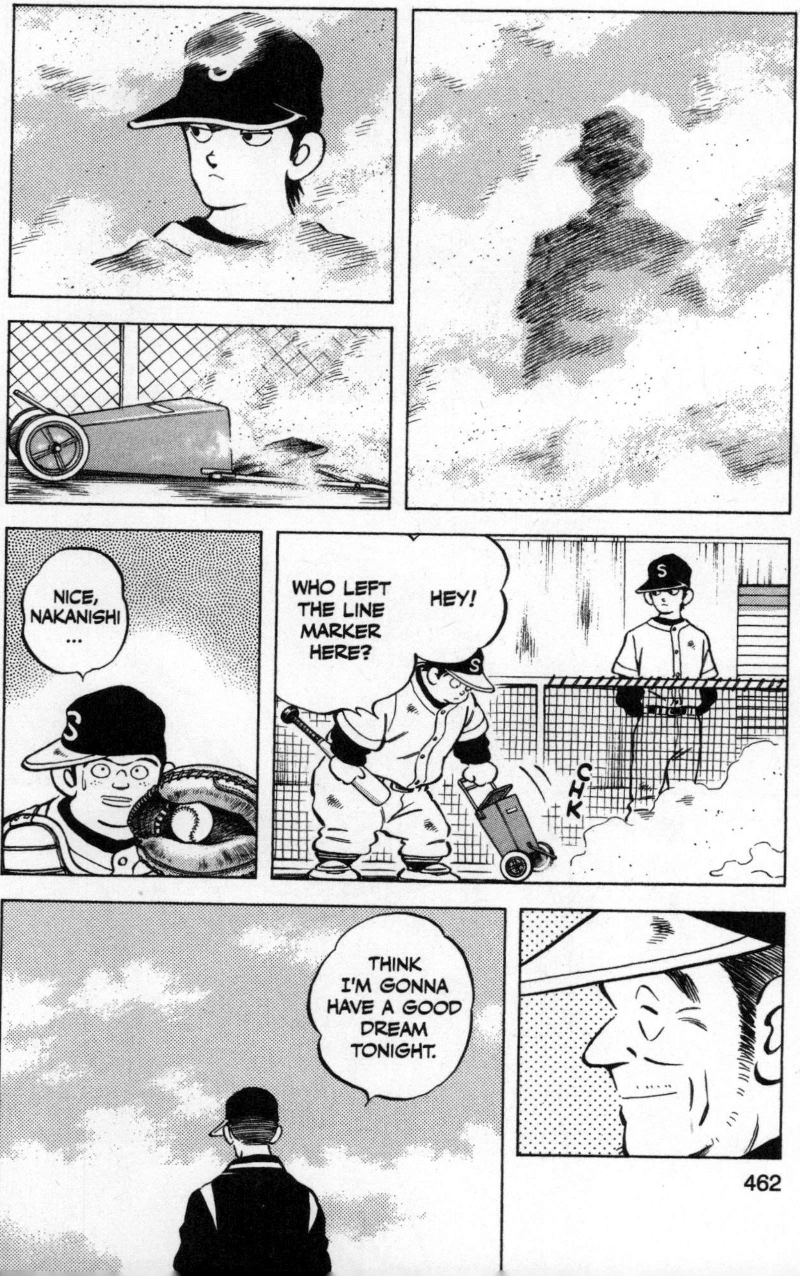
HEY!
WHO LEFT THE LINE MARKER HERE?
CHK
NICE, NAKANISHI ...
THINK I'M GONNA HAVE A GOOD DREAM TONIGHT.

CHAPTER 15

NOPE

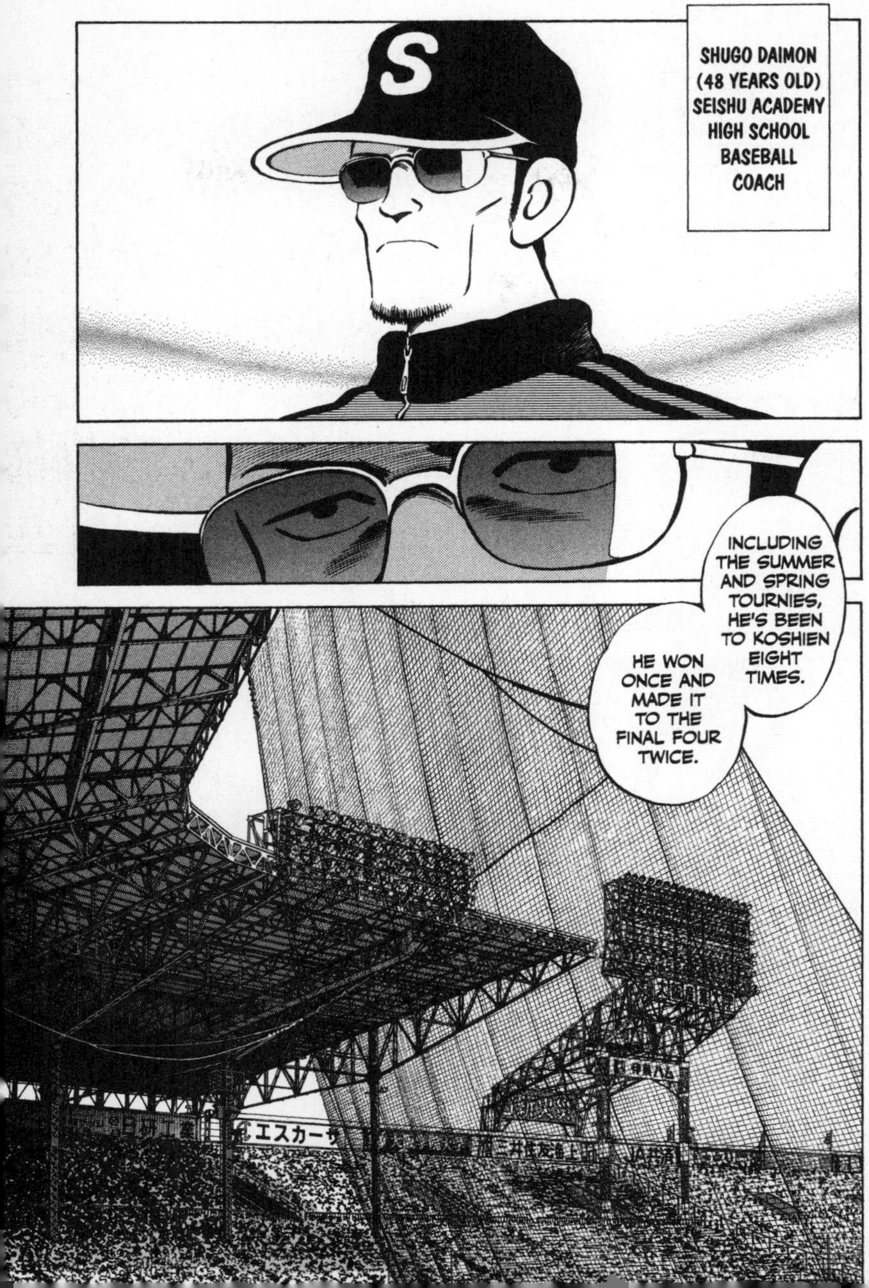
SHUGO DAIMON (48 YEARS OLD) SEISHU ACADEMY HIGH SCHOOL BASEBALL COACH
INCLUDING THE SUMMER AND SPRING TOURNIES, HE'S BEEN TO KOSHIEN EIGHT TIMES.
HE WON ONCE AND MADE IT TO THE FINAL FOUR TWICE.

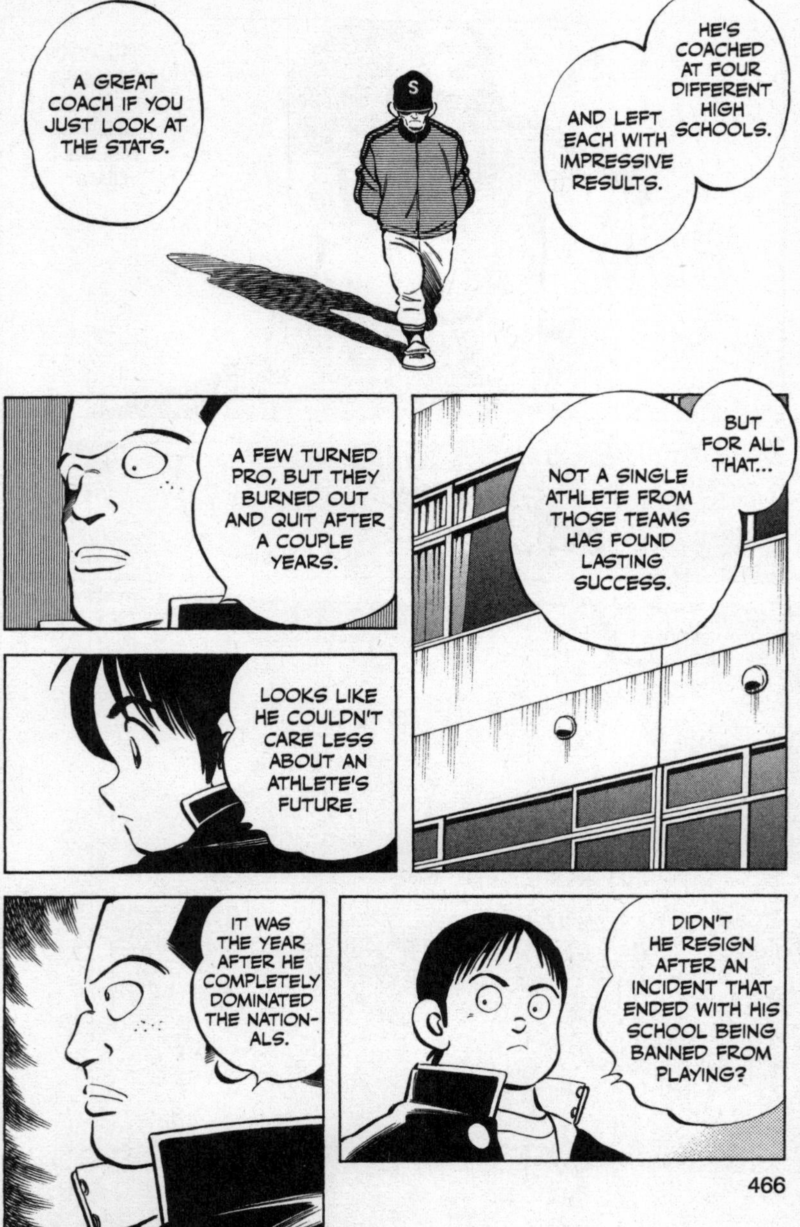
HE'S COACHED AT FOUR DIFFERENT HIGH SCHOOLS.
AND LEFT EACH WITH IMPRESSIVE RESULTS.
A GREAT COACH IF YOU JUST LOOK AT THE STATS.
BUT FOR ALL THAT...
NOT A SINGLE ATHLETE FROM THOSE TEAMS HAS FOUND LASTING SUCCESS.
A FEW TURNED PRO, BUT THEY BURNED OUT AND QUIT AFTER A COUPLE YEARS.
LOOKS LIKE HE COULDN'T CARE LESS ABOUT AN ATHLETE'S FUTURE.
DIDN'T HE RESIGN AFTER AN INCIDENT THAT ENDED WITH HIS SCHOOL BEING BANNED FROM PLAYING?
IT WAS THE YEAR AFTER HE COMPLETELY DOMINATED THE NATION-ALS.

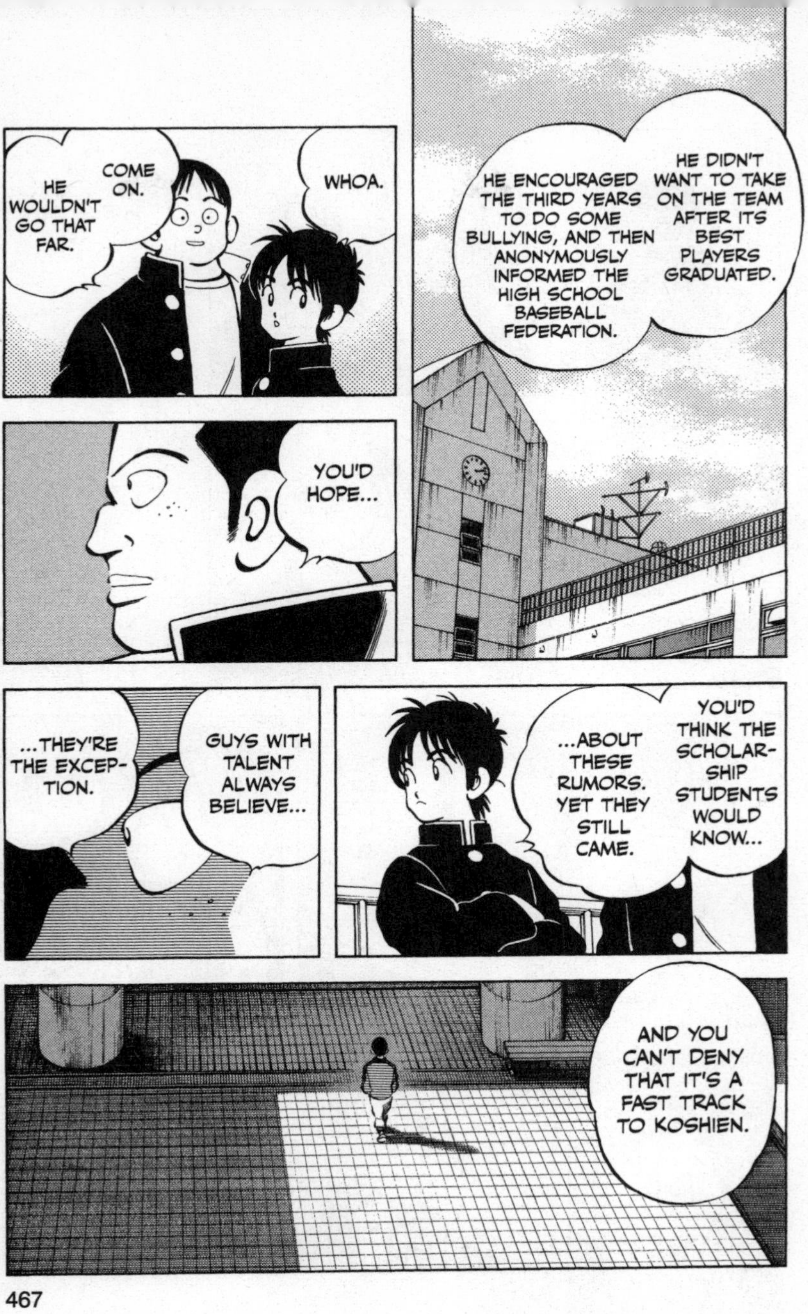
HE DIDN'T WANT TO TAKE ON THE TEAM AFTER ITS BEST PLAYERS GRADUATED.
HE ENCOURAGED THE THIRD YEARS TO DO SOME BULLYING, AND THEN ANONYMOUSLY INFORMED THE HIGH SCHOOL BASEBALL FEDERATION.
WHOA.
COME ON.
HE WOULDN'T GO THAT FAR.
YOU'D HOPE...
YOU'D THINK THE SCHOLAR-SHIP STUDENTS WOULD KNOW...
...ABOUT THESE RUMORS. YET THEY STILL CAME.
GUYS WITH TALENT ALWAYS BELIEVE...
...THEY'RE THE EXCEP-TION.
AND YOU CAN'T DENY THAT IT'S A FAST TRACK TO KOSHIEN.

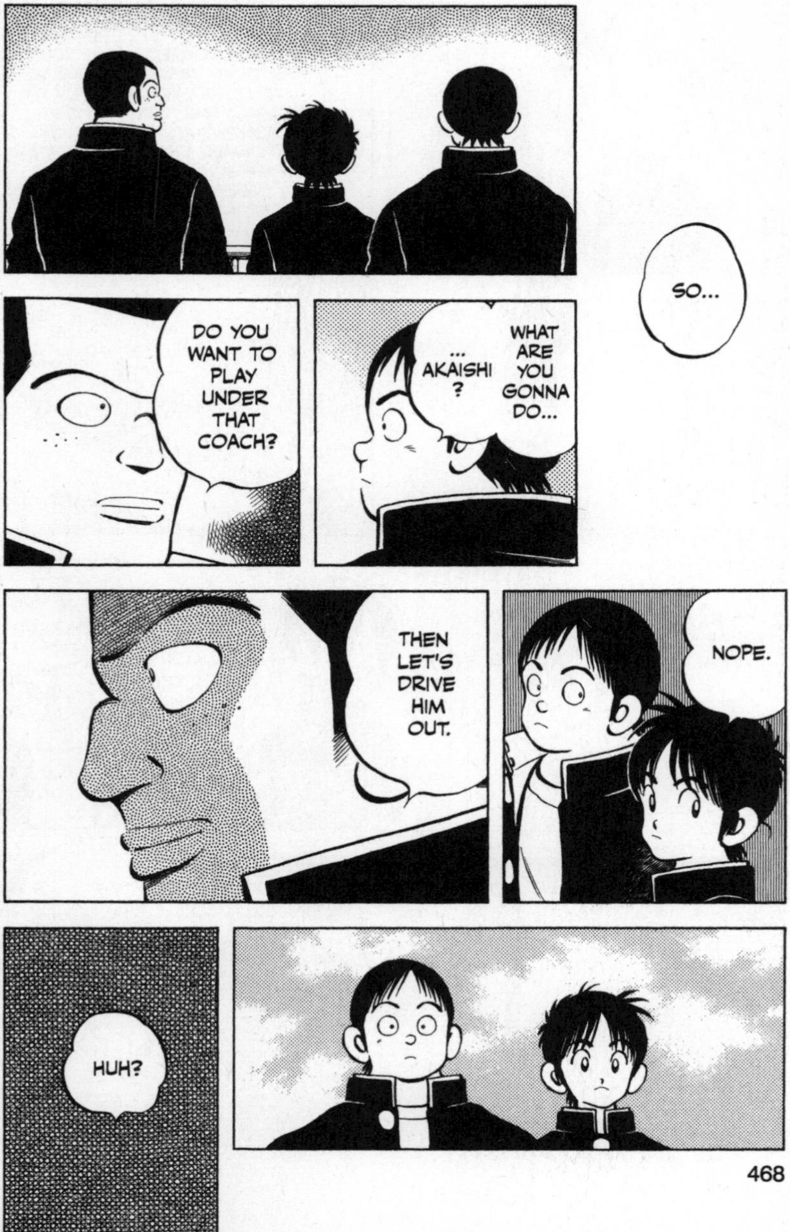
SO...
WHAT ARE YOU GONNA DO...
... AKAISHI ?
DO YOU WANT TO PLAY UNDER THAT COACH?
NOPE.
THEN LET'S DRIVE HIM OUT.
HUH?

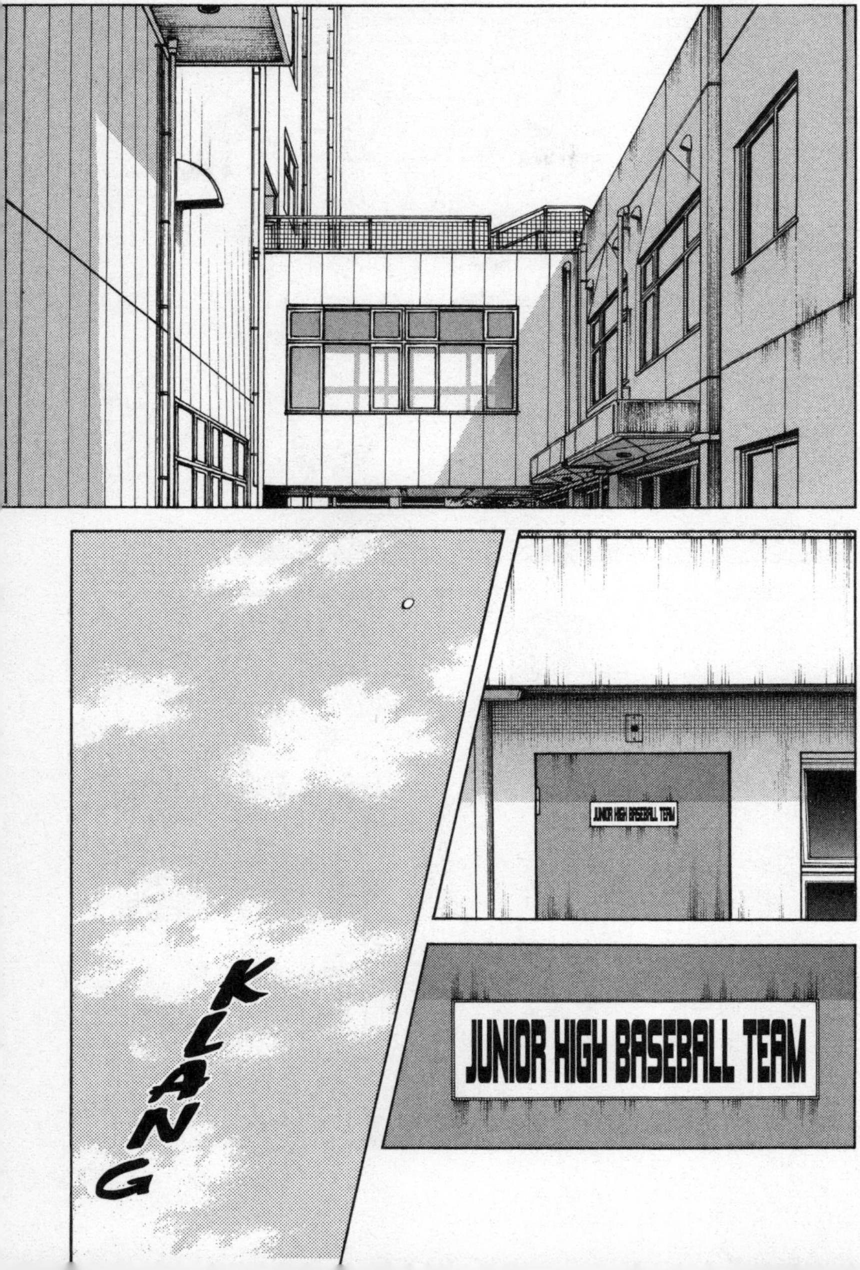
JUNIOR HIGH BASEBALL TEAM
JUNIOR HIGH BASEBALL TEAM
KLANG

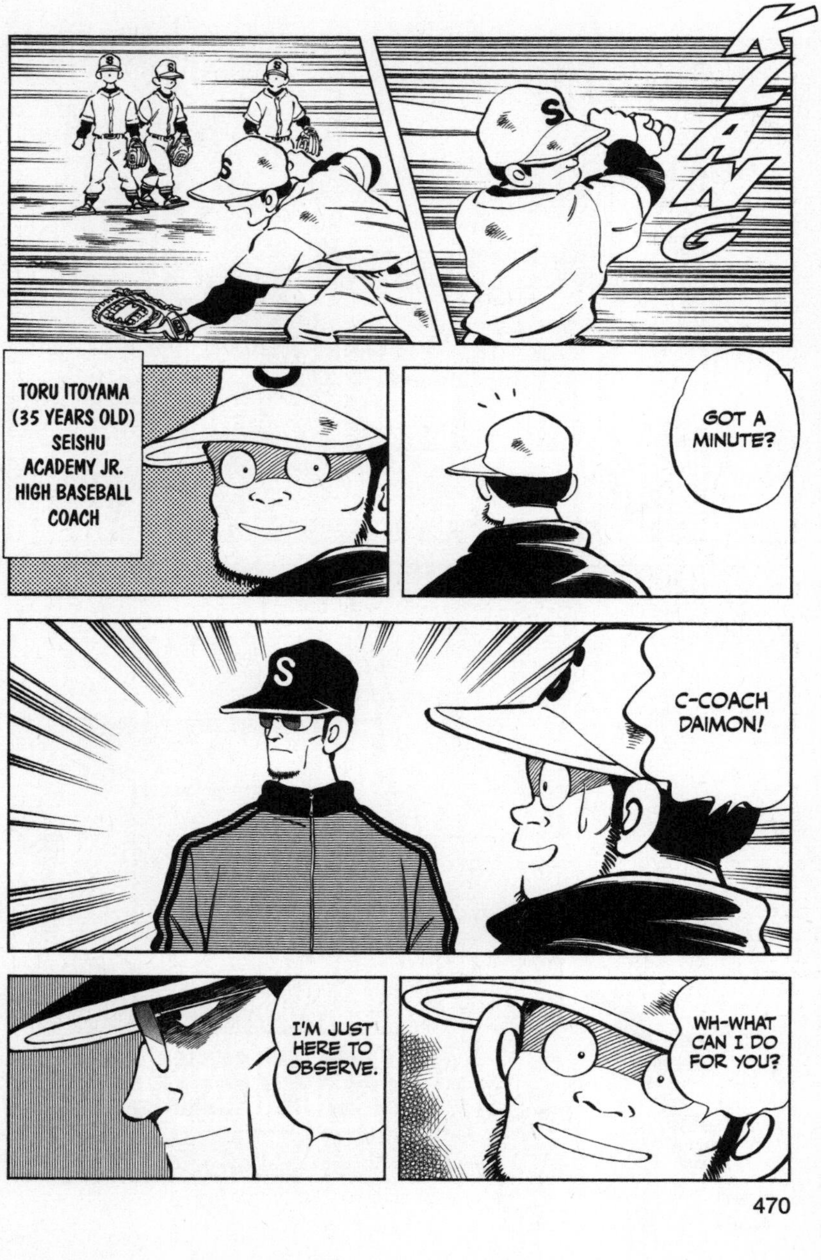
KLANG
GOT A MINUTE?
TORU ITOYAMA (35 YEARS OLD) SEISHU ACADEMY JR. HIGH BASEBALL COACH
C-COACH DAIMON!
WH-WHAT CAN I DO FOR YOU?
I'M JUST HERE TO OBSERVE.

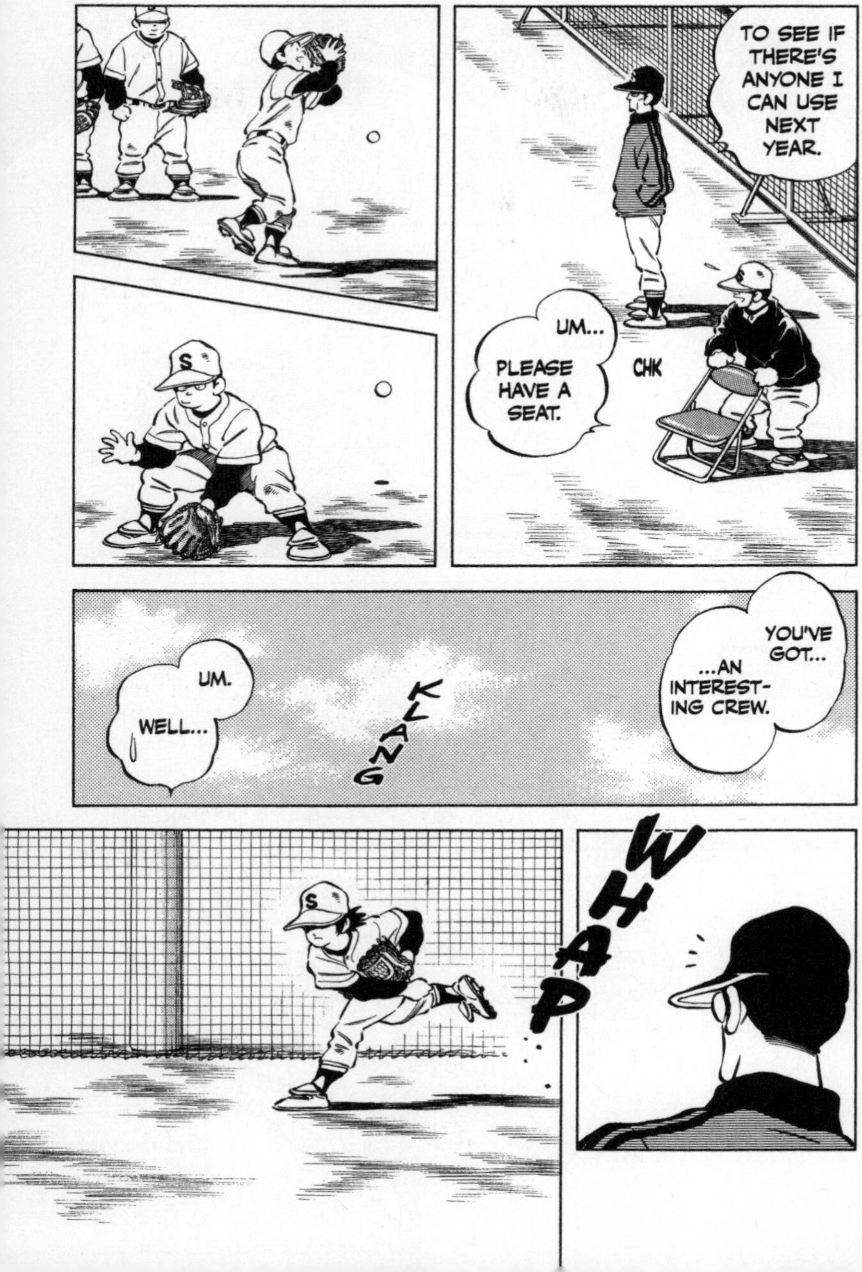
TO SEE IF THERE'S ANYONE I CAN USE NEXT YEAR.
UM... PLEASE HAVE A SEAT.
CHK
YOU'VE GOT... ...AN INTERESTING CREW.
KLANG
UM. WELL...
WHAP

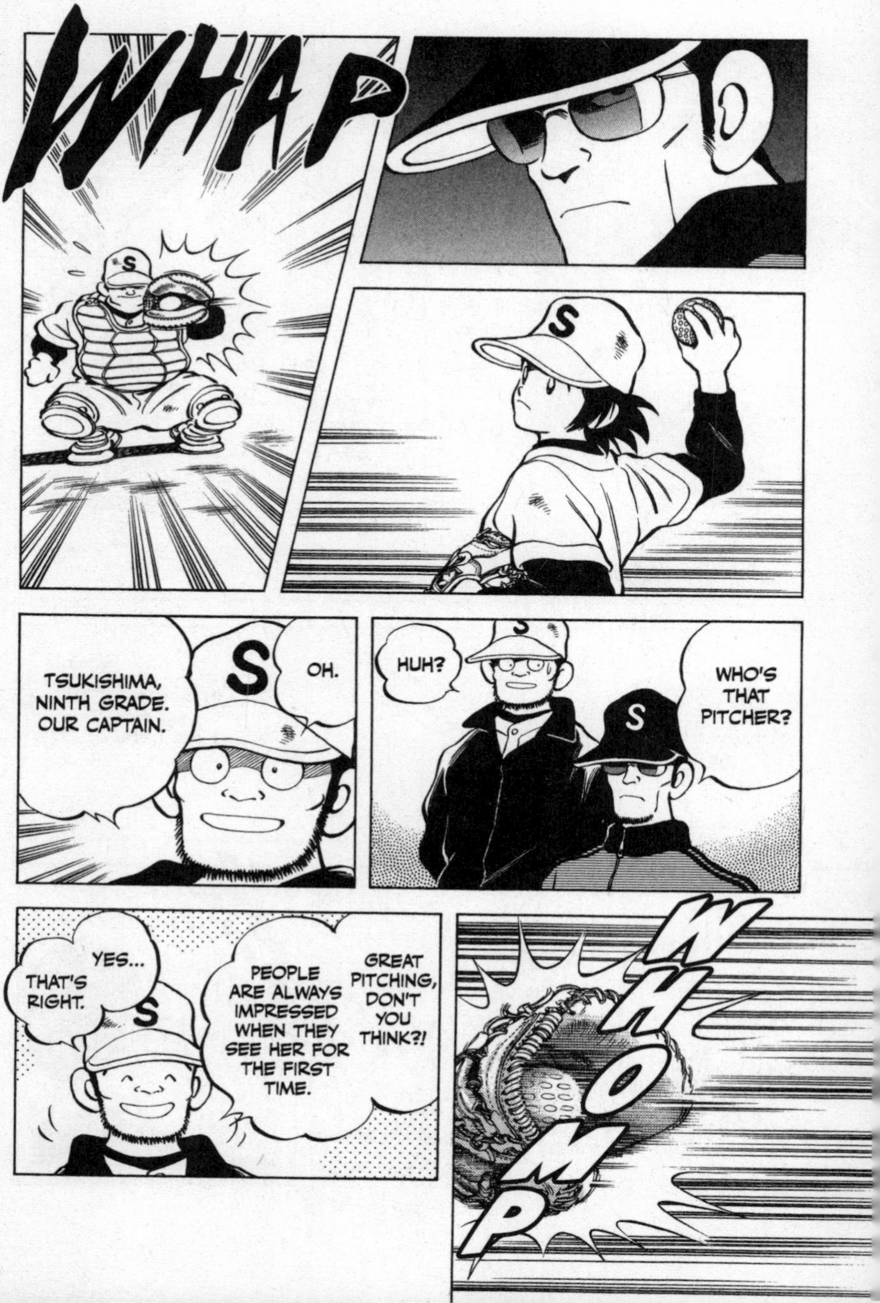
WHAP
WHO'S THAT PITCHER?
HUH?
OH.
TSUKISHIMA, NINTH GRADE. OUR CAPTAIN.
WHOMP
GREAT PITCHING, DON'T YOU THINK?!
PEOPLE ARE ALWAYS IMPRESSED WHEN THEY SEE HER FOR THE FIRST TIME.
YES... THAT'S RIGHT.

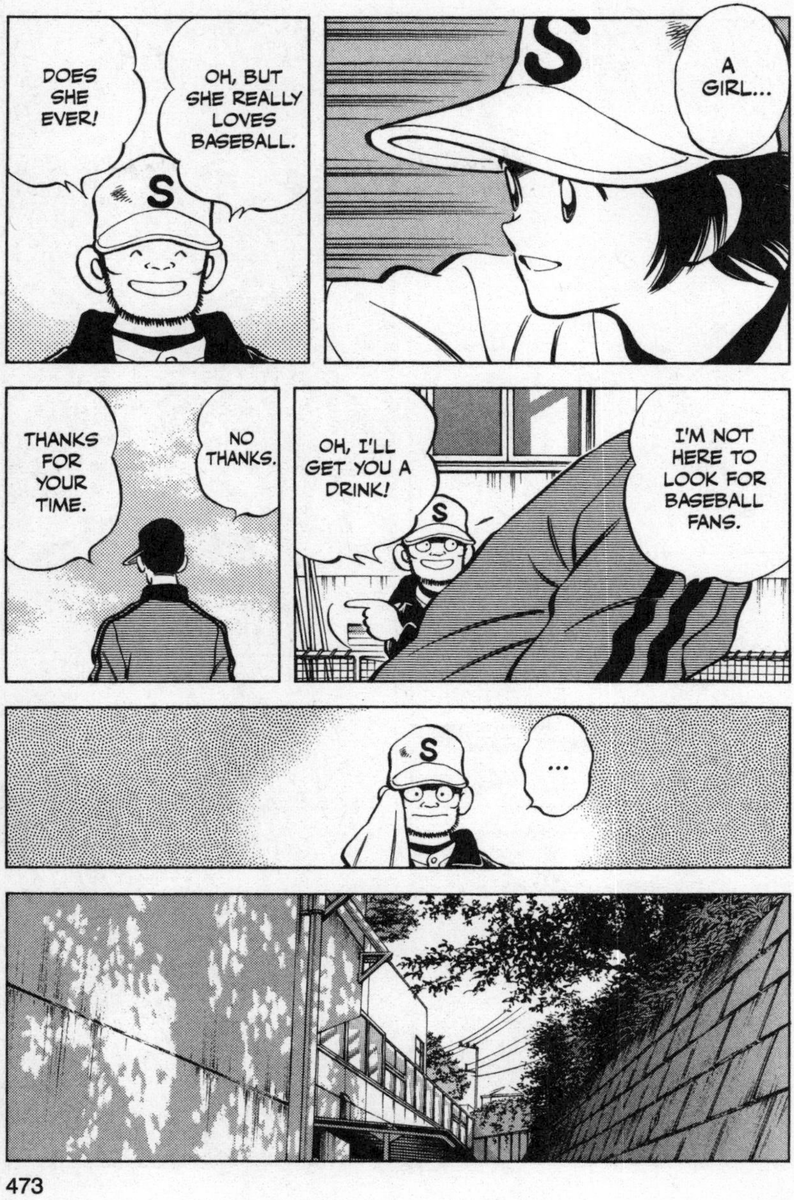
A GIRL...
OH, BUT SHE REALLY LOVES BASEBALL.
DOES SHE EVER!
I'M NOT HERE TO LOOK FOR BASEBALL FANS.
OH, I'LL GET YOU A DRINK!
NO THANKS.
THANKS FOR YOUR TIME.
...

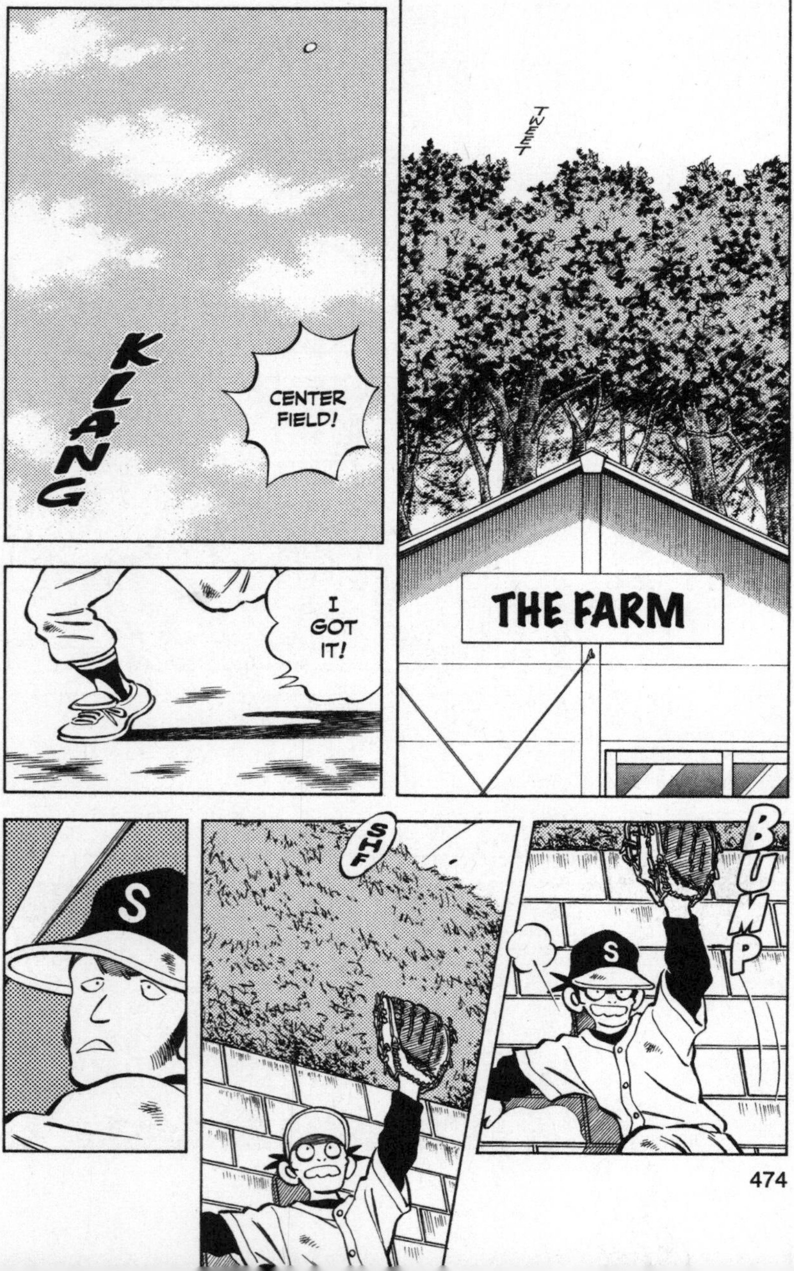
TWEET
THE FARM
KLANG
CENTER FIELD!
I GOT IT!
BUMP
SHF

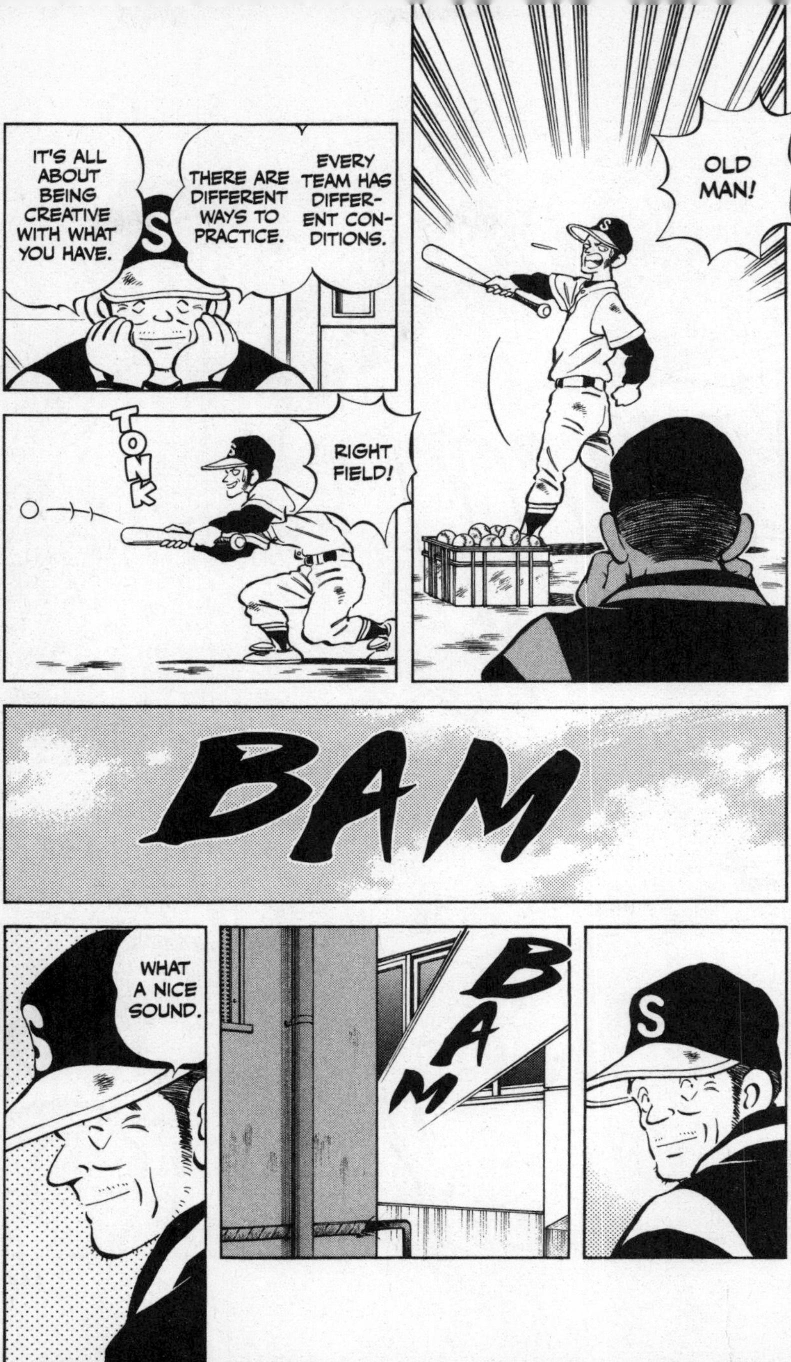
OLD MAN!
EVERY TEAM HAS DIFFER- ENT CON- DITIONS.
THERE ARE DIFFERENT WAYS TO PRACTICE.
IT'S ALL ABOUT BEING CREATIVE WITH WHAT YOU HAVE.
RIGHT FIELD!
TONK
BAM
BAM
WHAT A NICE SOUND.

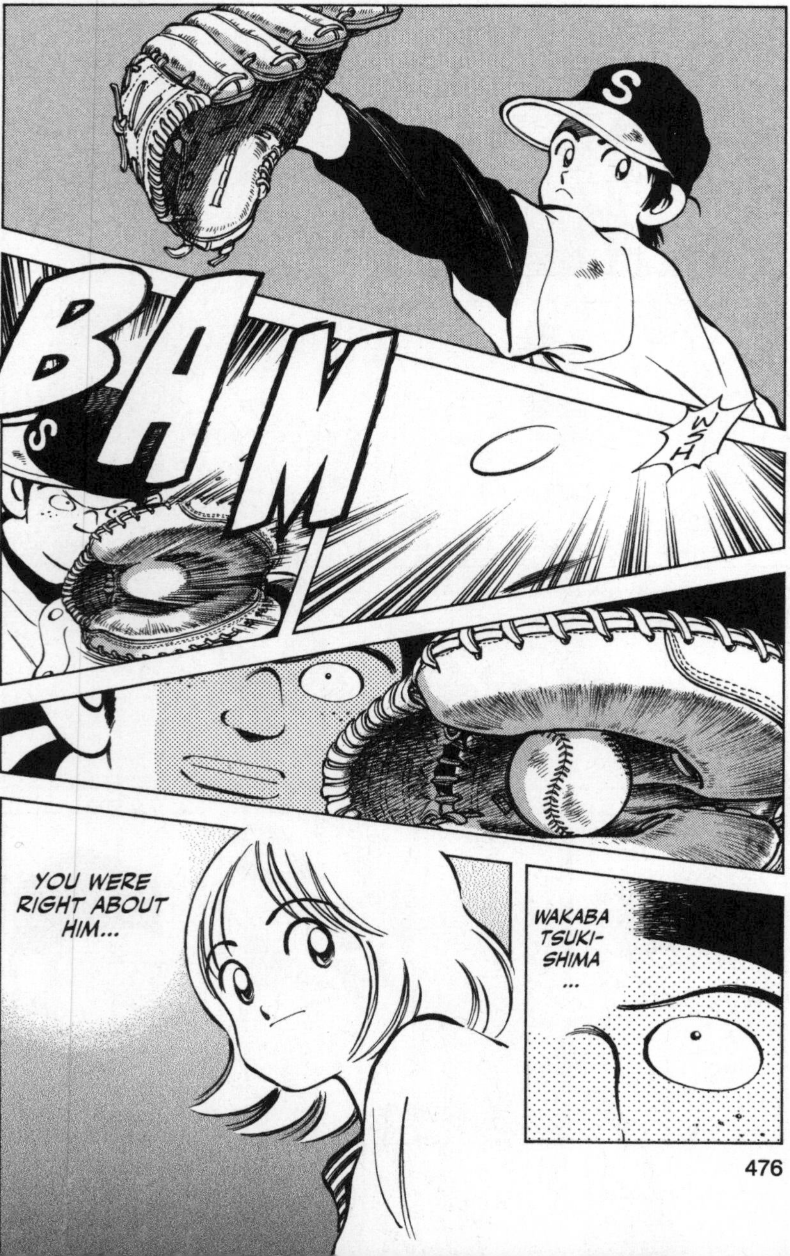
WSH
BAM
WAKABA TSUKI-SHIMA ...
YOU WERE RIGHT ABOUT HIM...

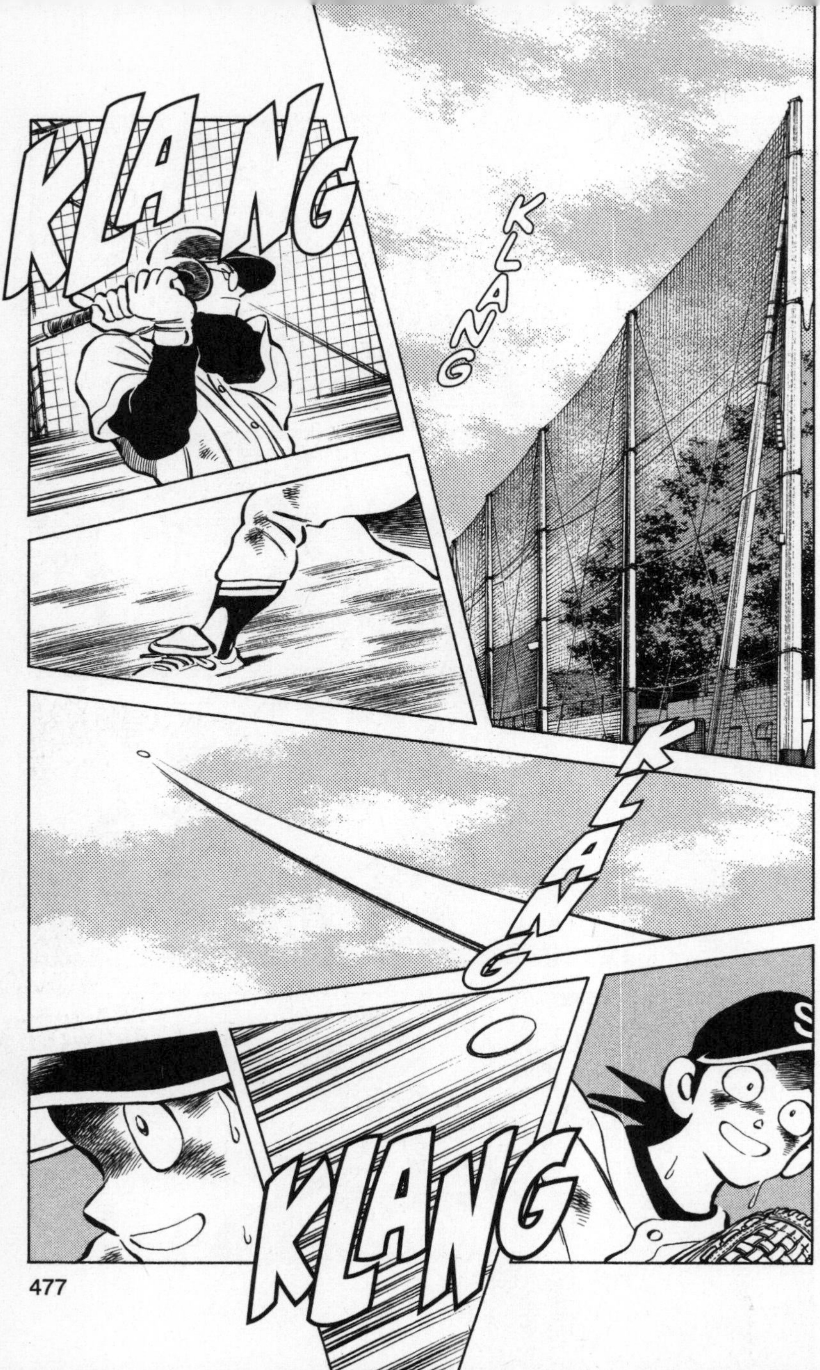
KLANG
KLANG
KLANG
KLANG

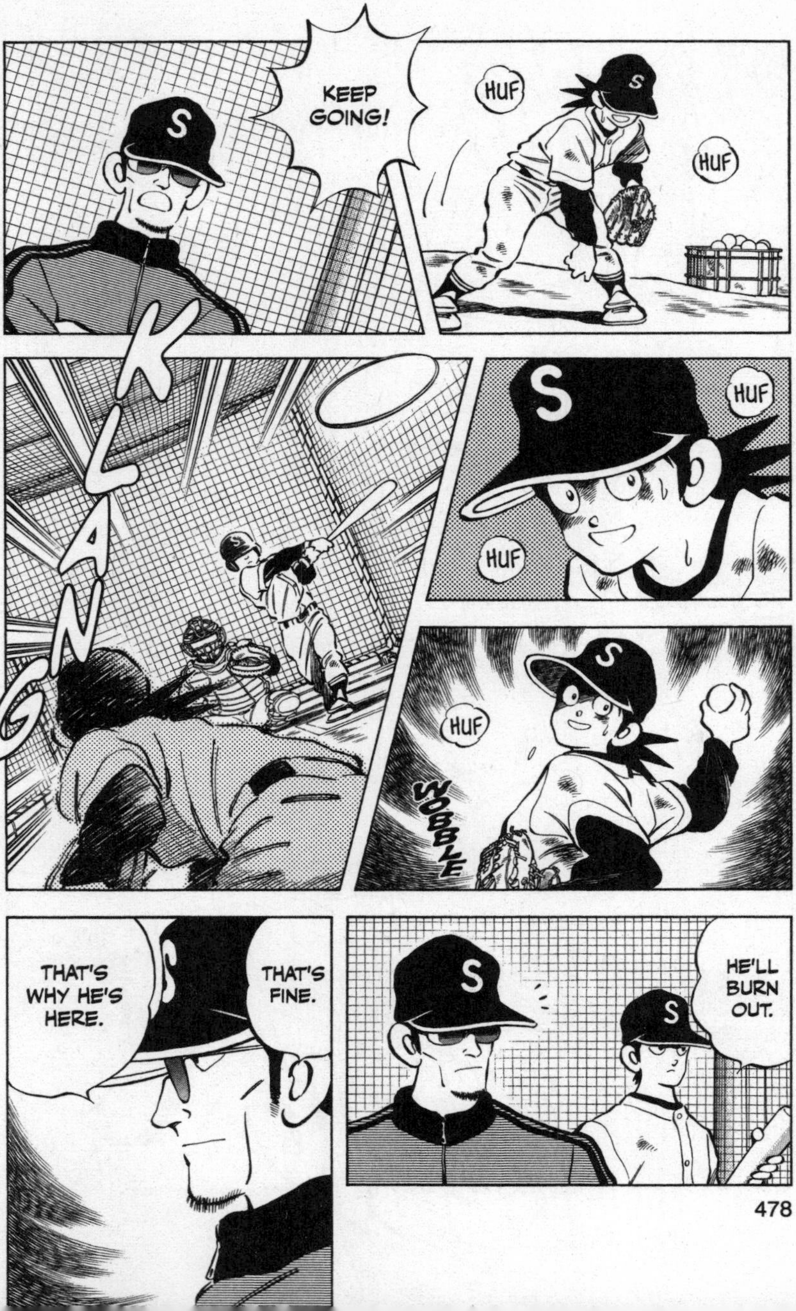
HUF
HUF
KEEP GOING!
HUF
HUF
HUF
WOBBLE
KLANG
HE'LL BURN OUT.
THAT'S FINE.
THAT'S WHY HE'S HERE.

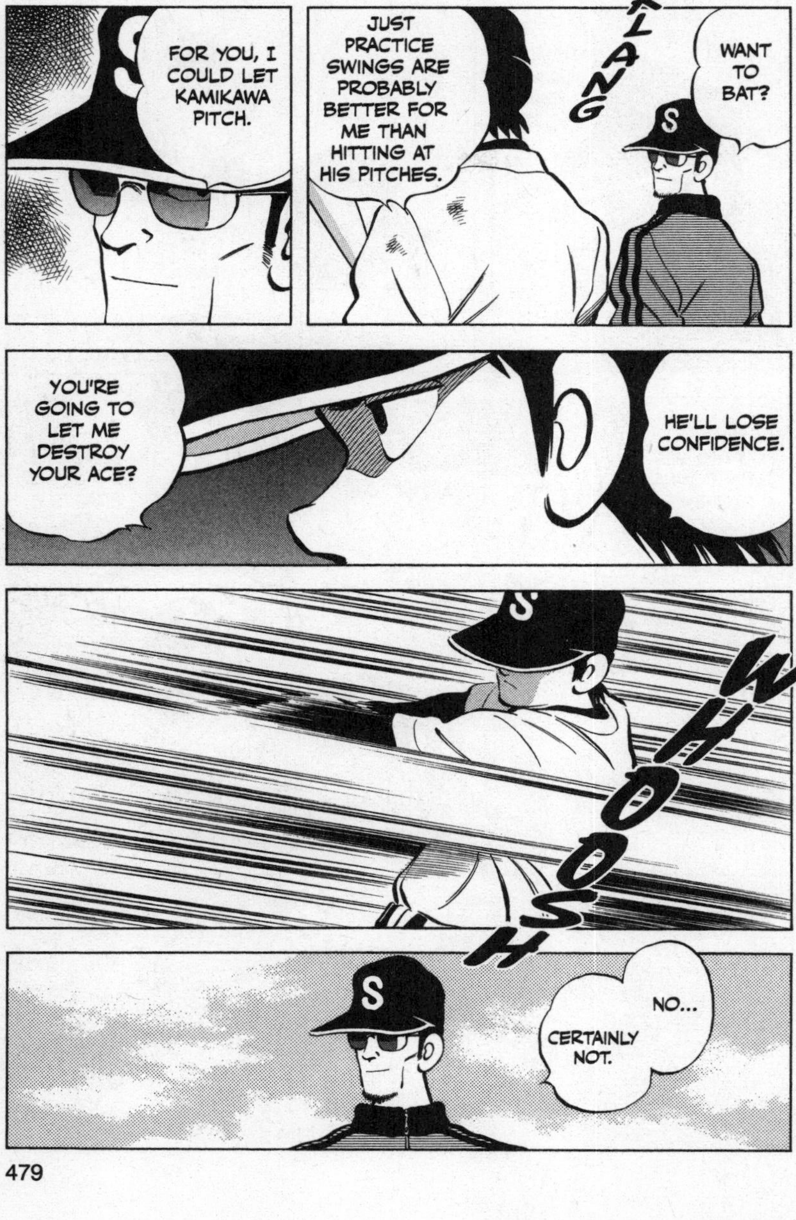
WANT TO BAT?
KLANG
JUST PRACTICE SWINGS ARE PROBABLY BETTER FOR ME THAN HITTING AT HIS PITCHES.
FOR YOU, I COULD LET KAMIKAWA PITCH.
HE'LL LOSE CONFIDENCE.
YOU'RE GOING TO LET ME DESTROY YOUR ACE?
WHOOOSH
NO...
CERTAINLY NOT.

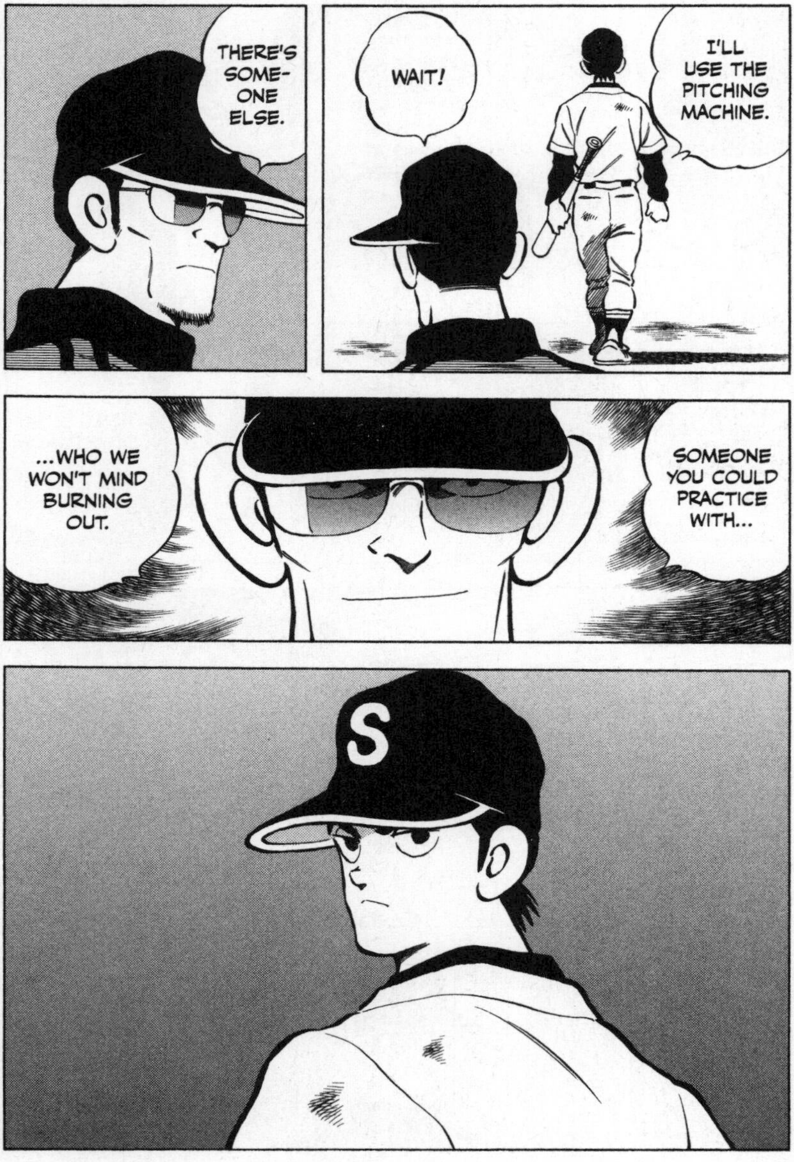
I'LL USE THE PITCHING MACHINE.
WAIT!
THERE'S SOME-ONE ELSE.
SOMEONE YOU COULD PRACTICE WITH...
...WHO WE WON'T MIND BURNING OUT.

CHAPTER 16

AOBA TSUKISHIMA

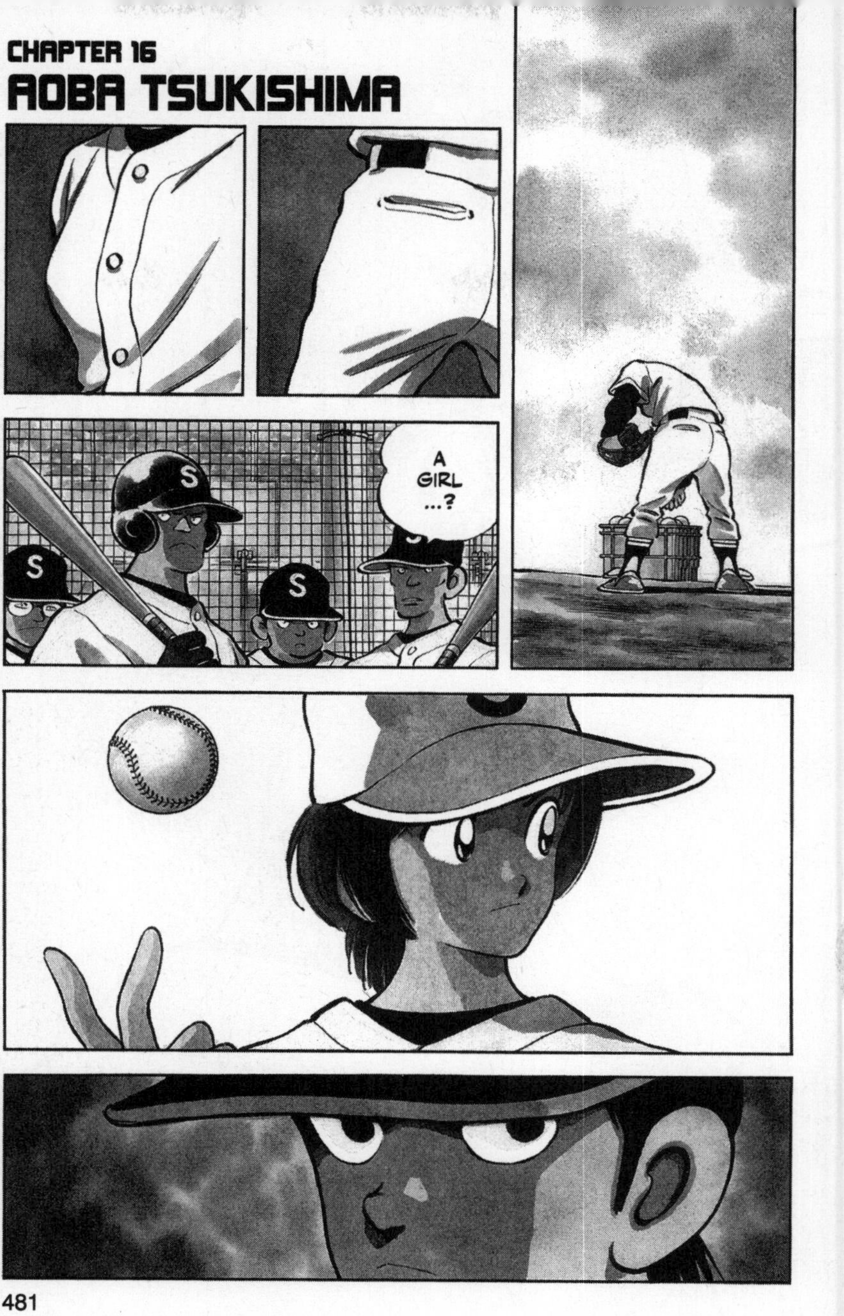
A GIRL ...?

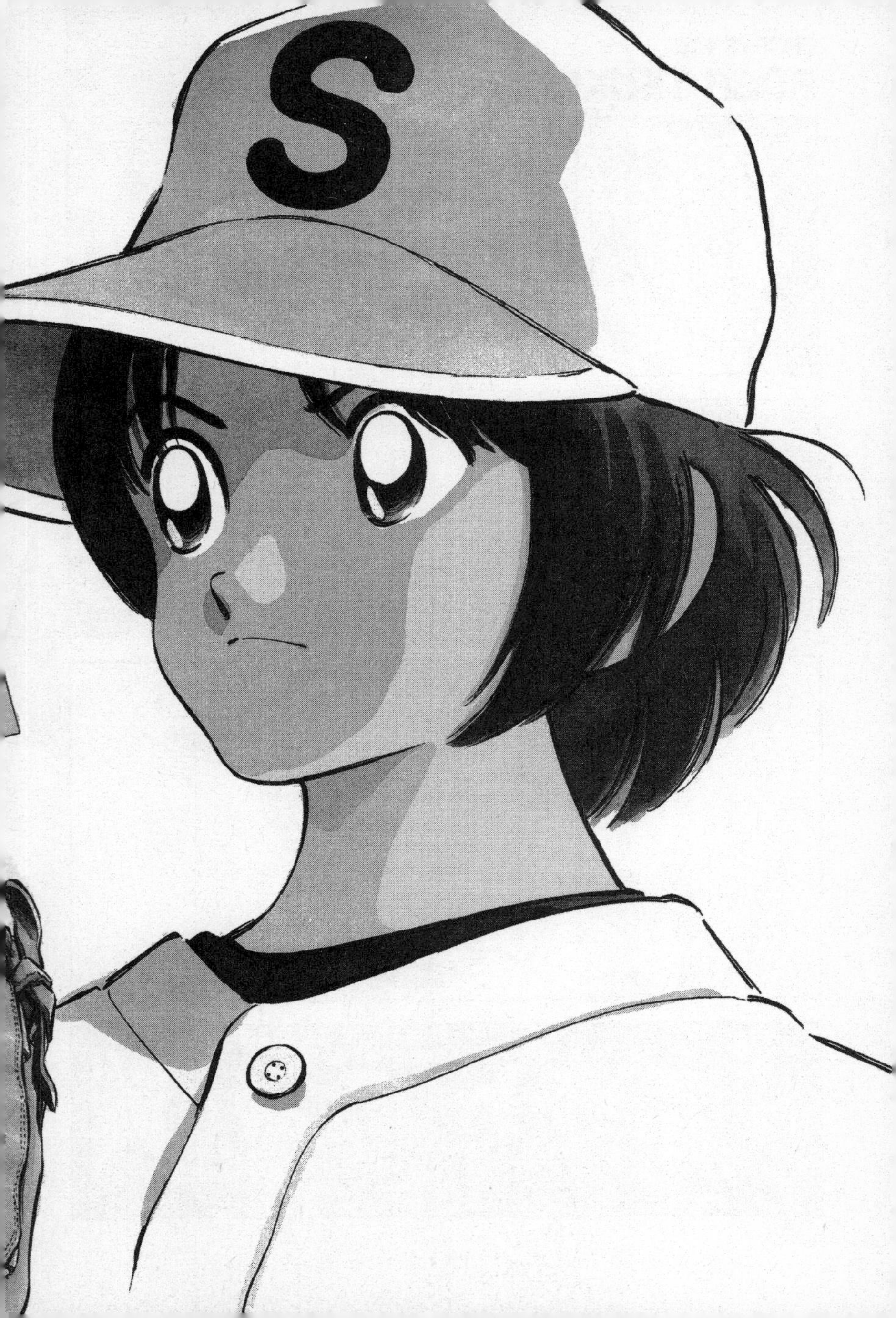

CHAPTER 16
AOBA TSUKISHIMA

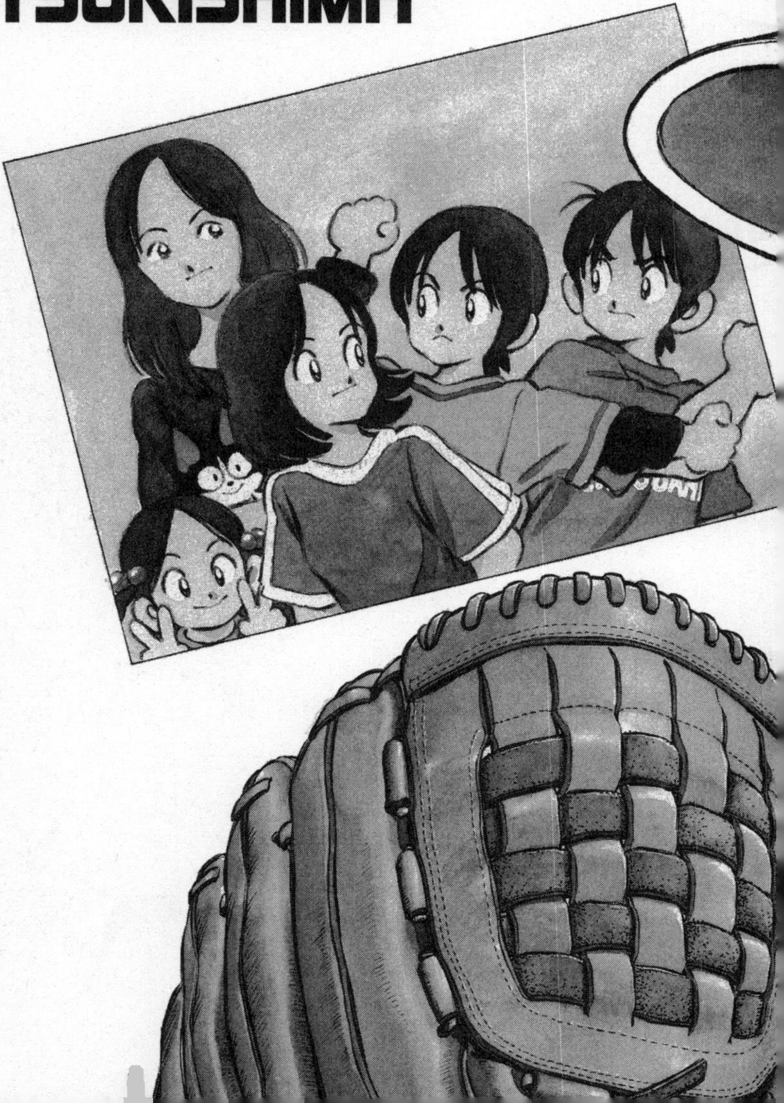

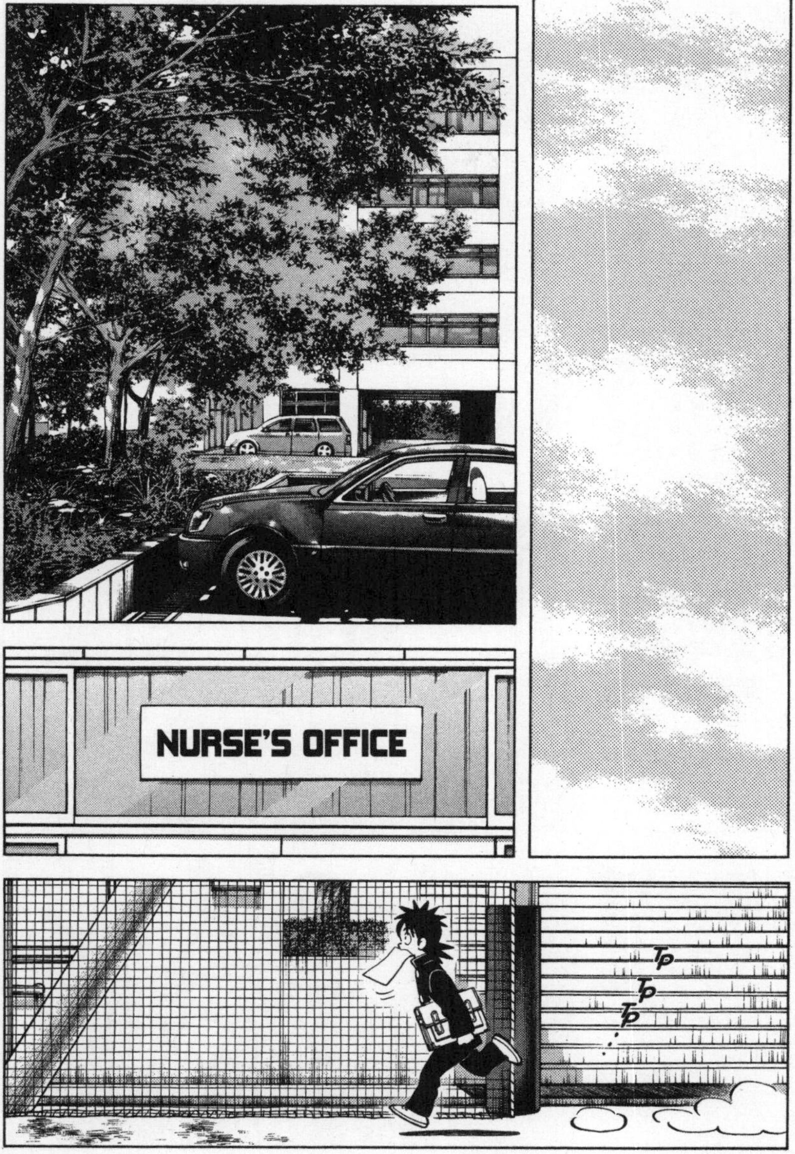
NURSE'S OFFICE
Tp Tp Tp

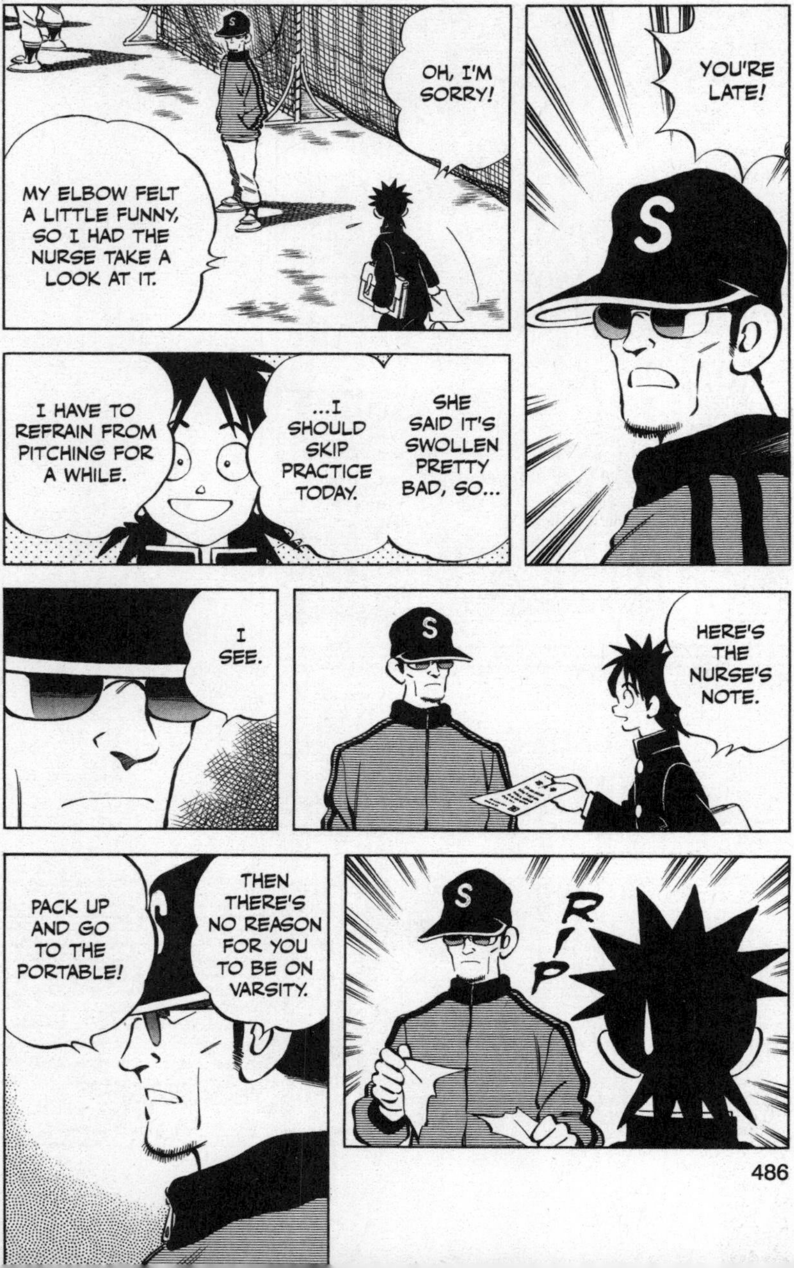
YOU'RE LATE!
OH, I'M SORRY!
MY ELBOW FELT A LITTLE FUNNY, SO I HAD THE NURSE TAKE A LOOK AT IT.
SHE SAID IT'S SWOLLEN PRETTY BAD, SO...
...I SHOULD SKIP PRACTICE TODAY.
I HAVE TO REFRAIN FROM PITCHING FOR A WHILE.
HERE'S THE NURSE'S NOTE.
I SEE.
RIP
THEN THERE'S NO REASON FOR YOU TO BE ON VARSITY.
PACK UP AND GO TO THE PORTABLE!

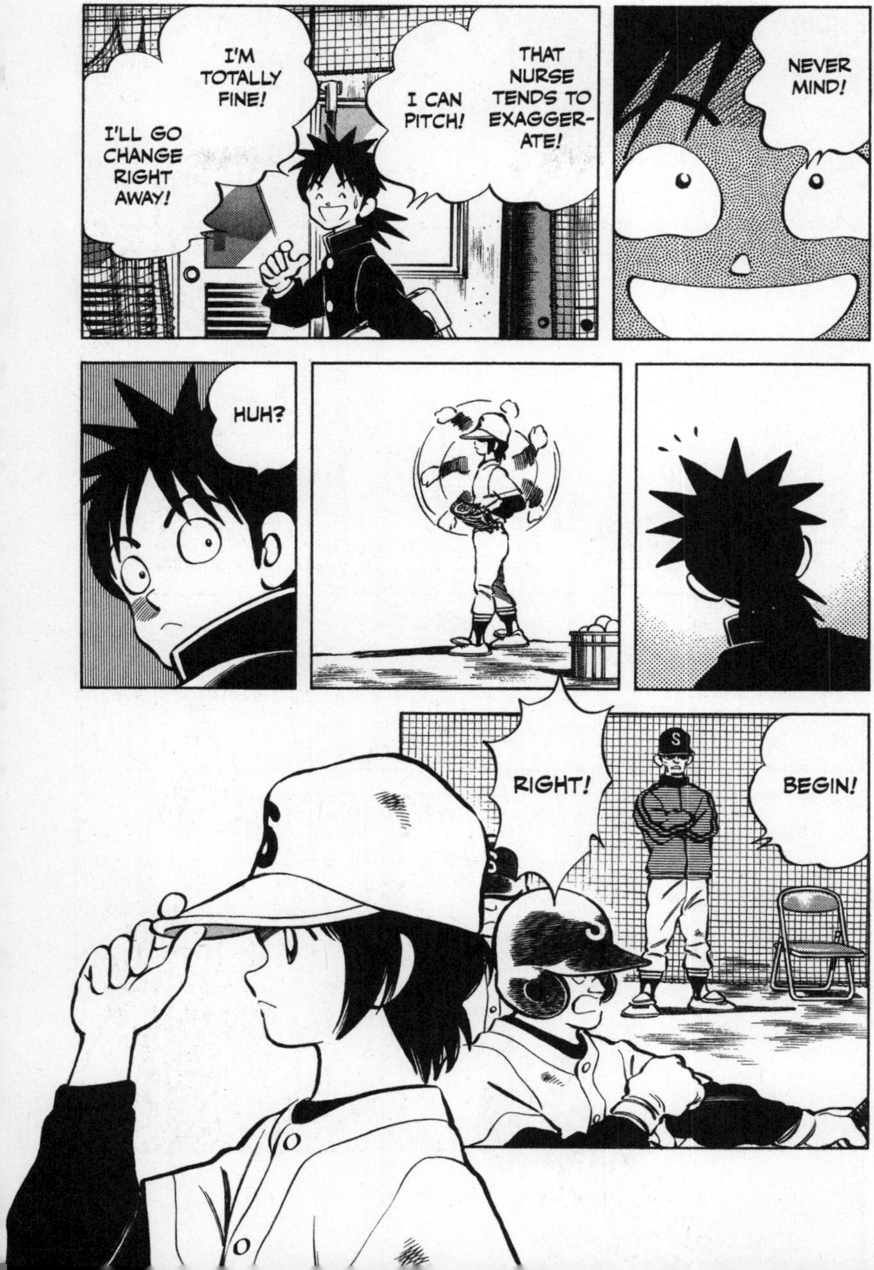
NEVER MIND!
THAT NURSE TENDS TO EXAGGERATE!
I CAN PITCH!
I'M TOTALLY FINE!
I'LL GO CHANGE RIGHT AWAY!
HUH?
BEGIN!
RIGHT!

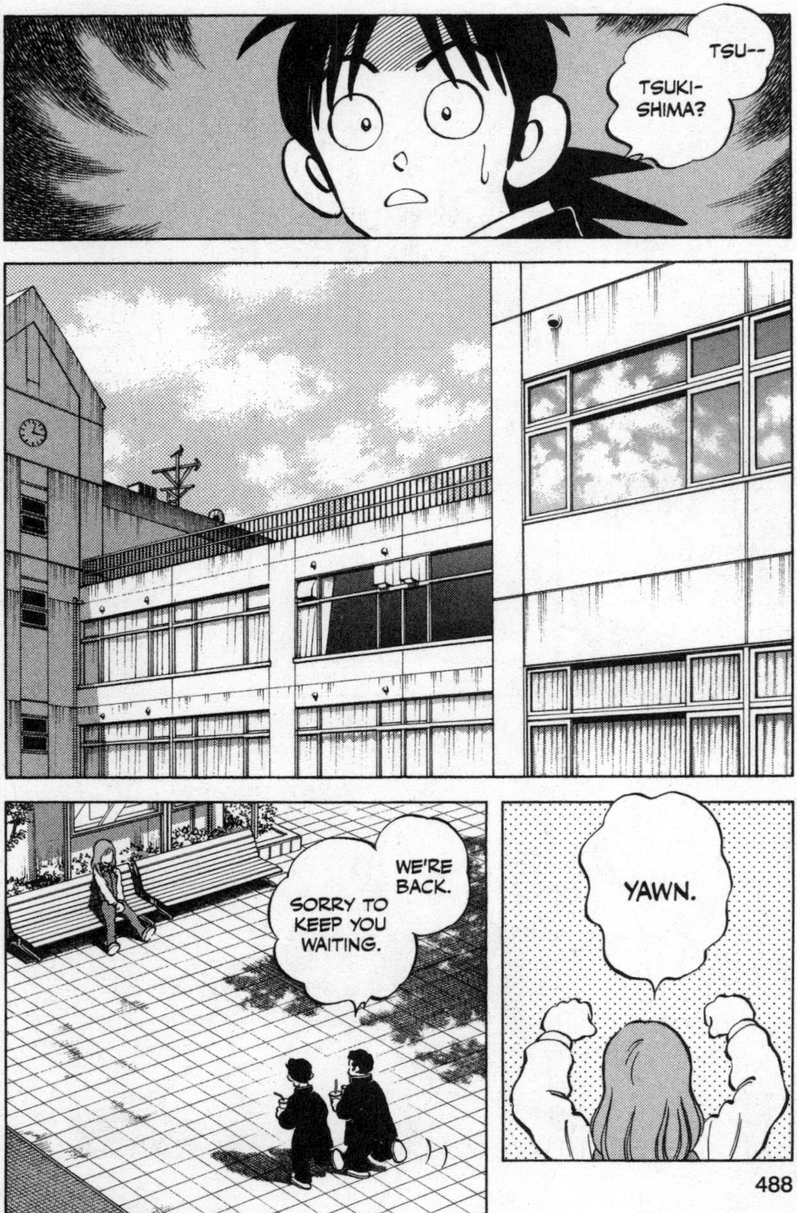
TSU-- TSUKI-SHIMA?
YAWN.
WE'RE BACK.
SORRY TO KEEP YOU WAITING.

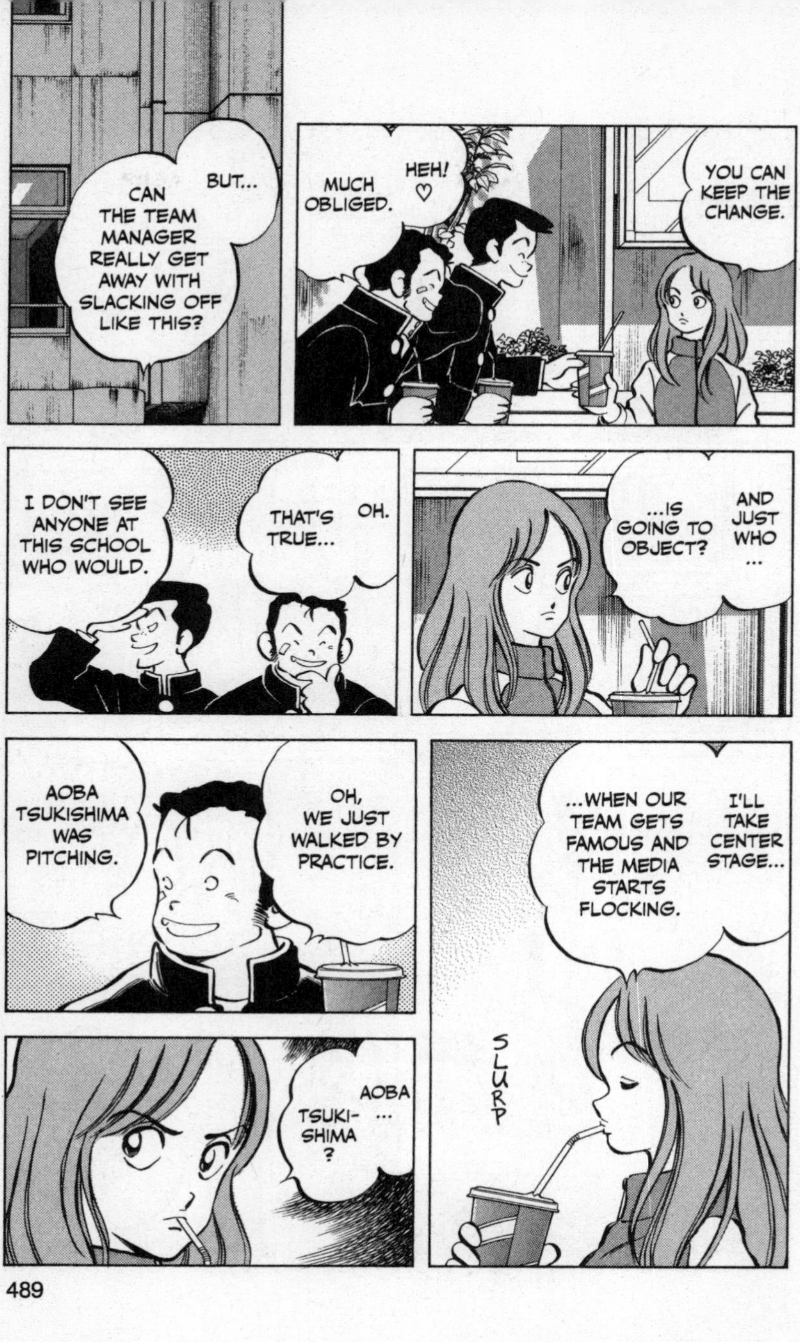
YOU CAN KEEP THE CHANGE.
HEH! ♡
MUCH OBLIGED.
BUT...
CAN THE TEAM MANAGER REALLY GET AWAY WITH SLACKING OFF LIKE THIS?
AND JUST WHO ...
...IS GOING TO OBJECT?
OH.
THAT'S TRUE...
I DON'T SEE ANYONE AT THIS SCHOOL WHO WOULD.
I'LL TAKE CENTER STAGE...
...WHEN OUR TEAM GETS FAMOUS AND THE MEDIA STARTS FLOCKING.
SLURP
OH, WE JUST WALKED BY PRACTICE.
AOBA TSUKISHIMA WAS PITCHING.
AOBA ...
TSUKI-SHIMA ?

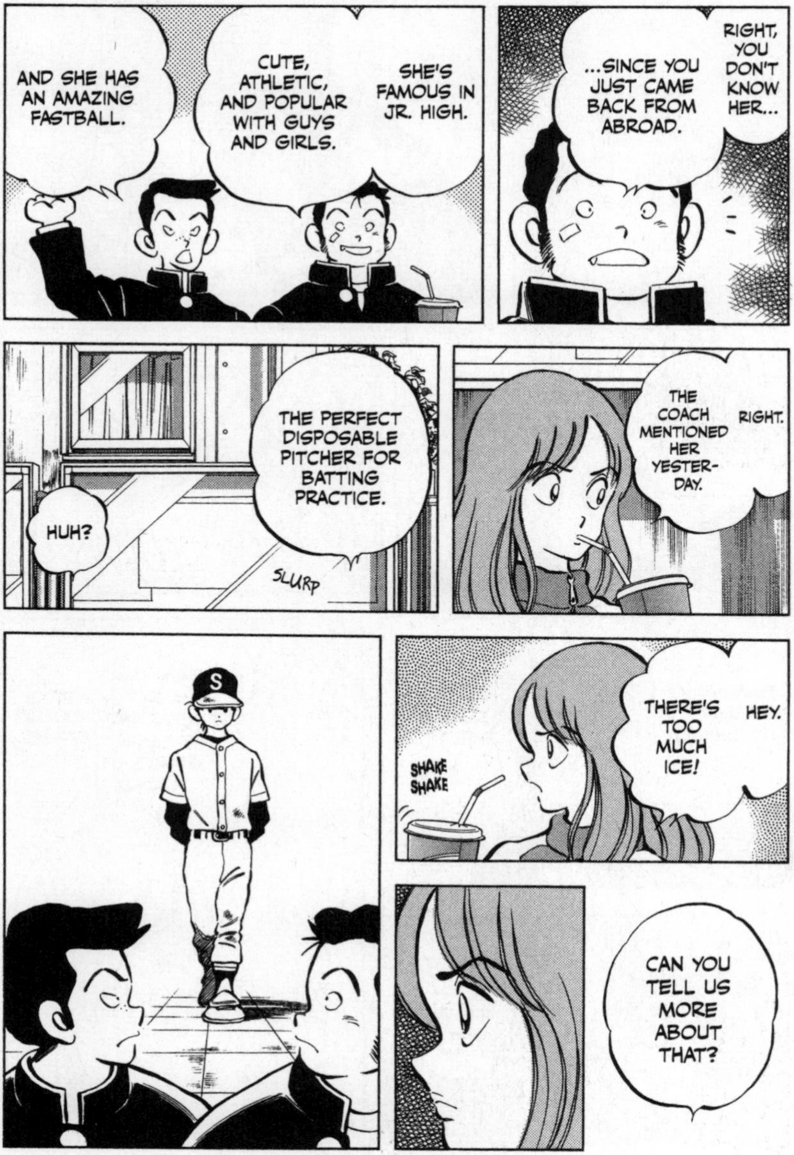
RIGHT, YOU DON'T KNOW HER...
...SINCE YOU JUST CAME BACK FROM ABROAD.
SHE'S FAMOUS IN JR. HIGH.
CUTE, ATHLETIC, AND POPULAR WITH GUYS AND GIRLS.
AND SHE HAS AN AMAZING FASTBALL.
RIGHT.
THE COACH MENTIONED HER YESTER-DAY.
THE PERFECT DISPOSABLE PITCHER FOR BATTING PRACTICE.
SLURP
HUH?
HEY.
THERE'S TOO MUCH ICE!
SHAKE SHAKE
CAN YOU TELL US MORE ABOUT THAT?

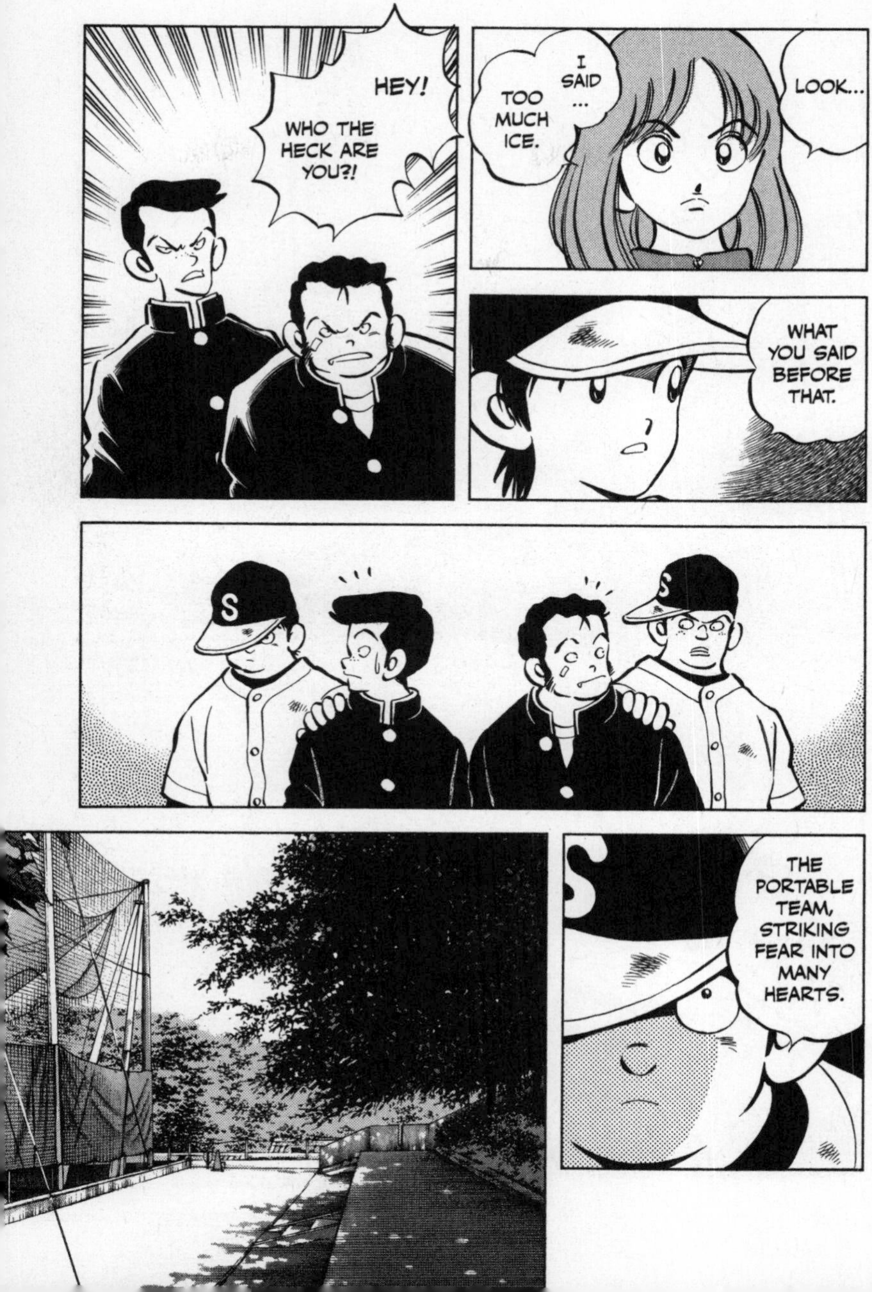
LOOK...
I SAID ...
TOO MUCH ICE.
WHAT YOU SAID BEFORE THAT.
HEY!
WHO THE HECK ARE YOU?!
THE PORTABLE TEAM, STRIKING FEAR INTO MANY HEARTS.

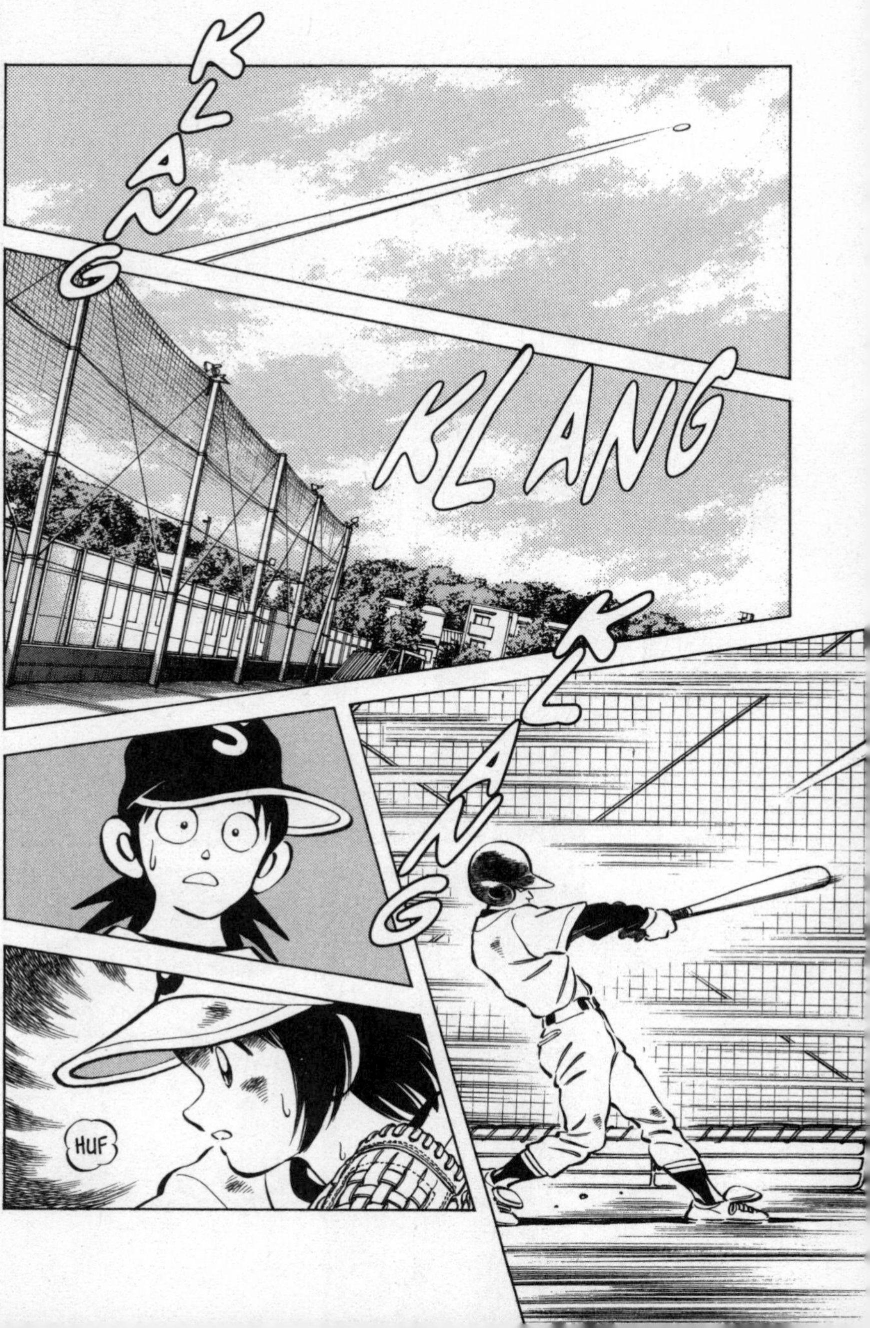
KLANG
KLANG
KLANG
HUF

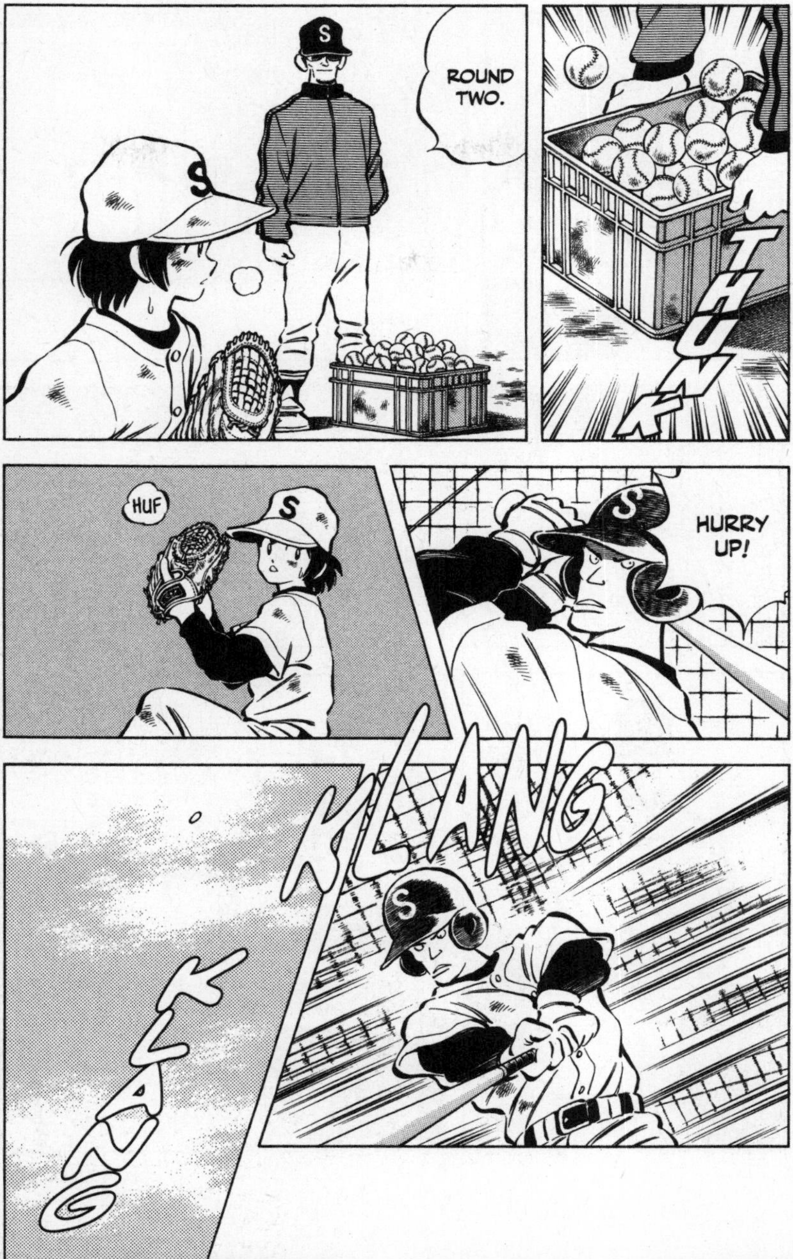
THUNK
ROUND TWO.
HURRY UP!
HUF
KLANG
KLANG

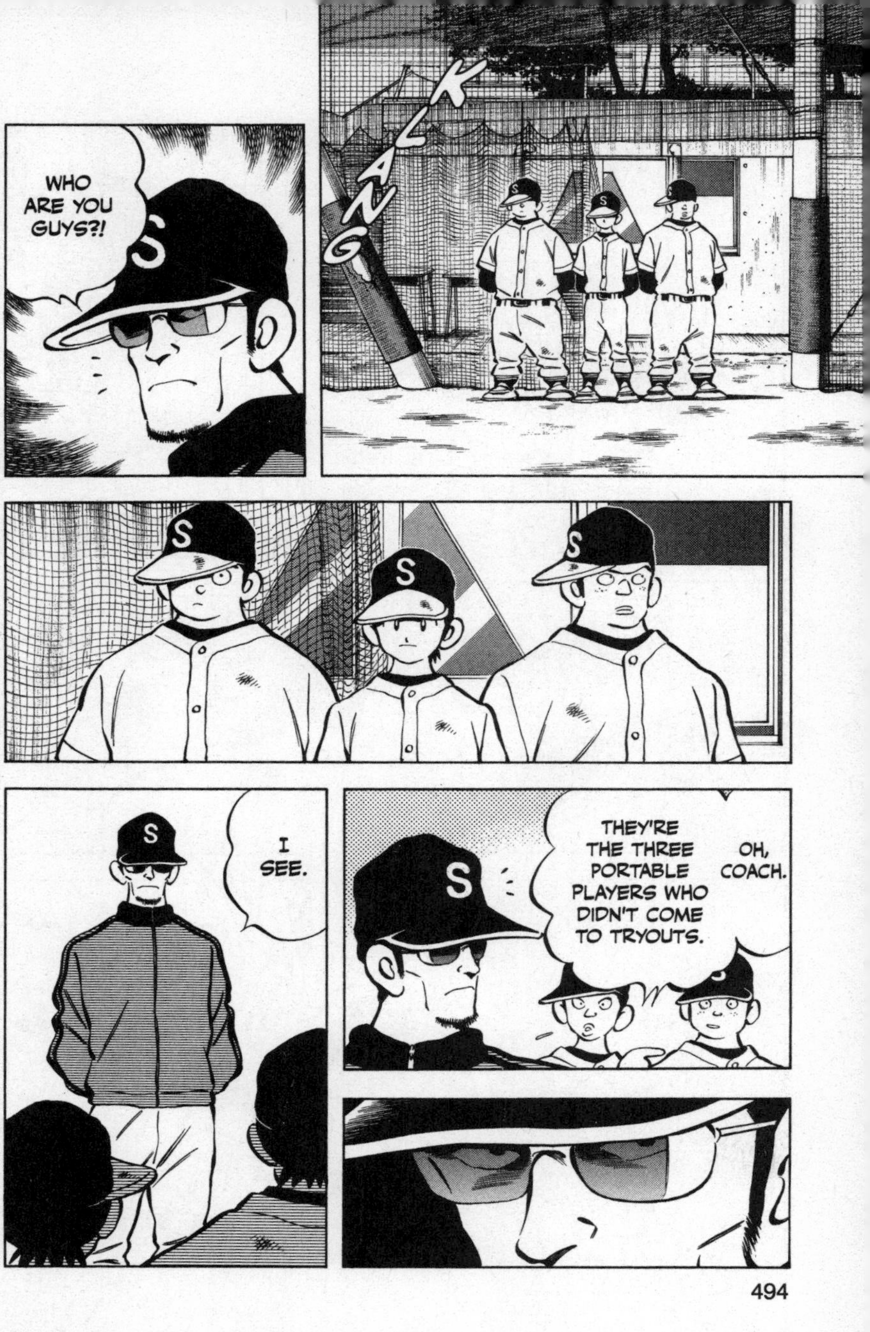
KLANG
WHO ARE YOU GUYS?!
OH, COACH.
THEY'RE THE THREE PORTABLE PLAYERS WHO DIDN'T COME TO TRYOUTS.
I SEE.

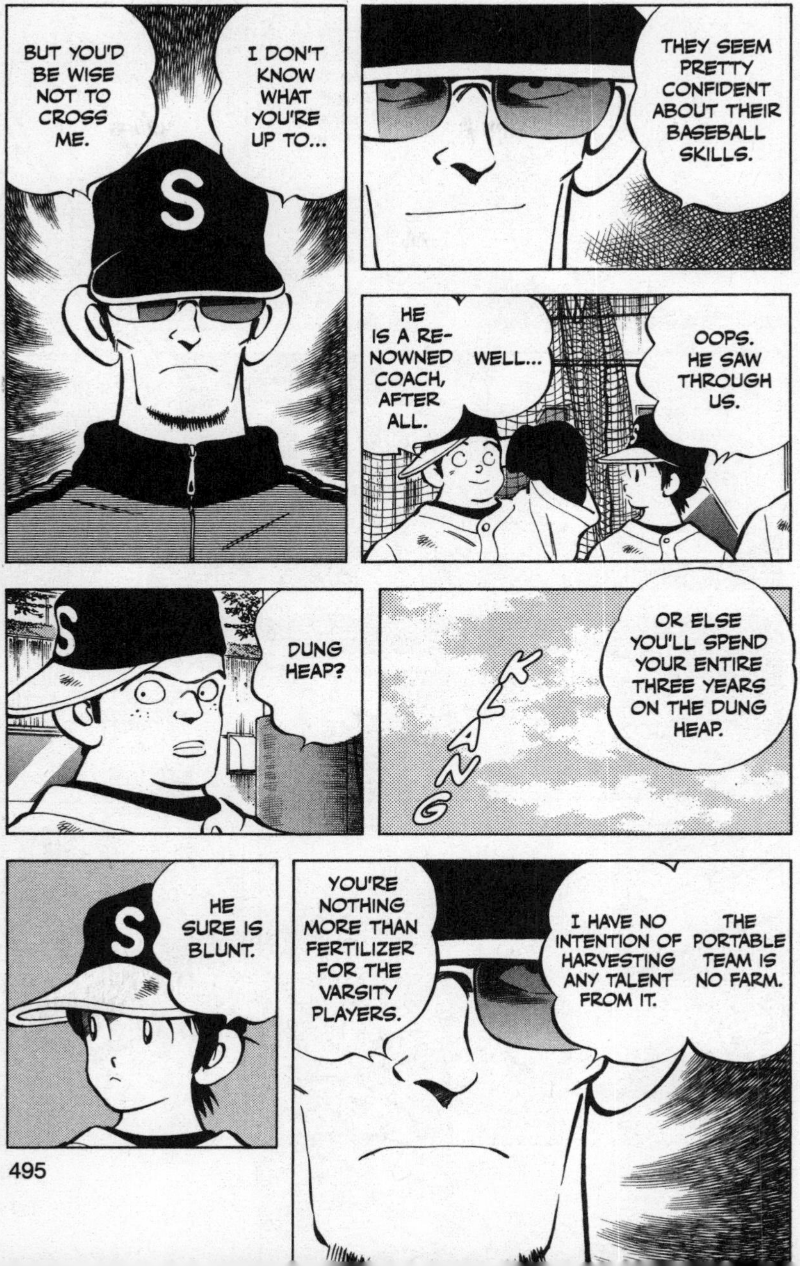
THEY SEEM PRETTY CONFIDENT ABOUT THEIR BASEBALL SKILLS.
OOPS. HE SAW THROUGH US.
WELL...
HE IS A RE-NOWNED COACH, AFTER ALL.
I DON'T KNOW WHAT YOU'RE UP TO...
BUT YOU'D BE WISE NOT TO CROSS ME.
OR ELSE YOU'LL SPEND YOUR ENTIRE THREE YEARS ON THE DUNG HEAP.
KLANG
DUNG HEAP?
THE PORTABLE TEAM IS NO FARM.
I HAVE NO INTENTION OF HARVESTING ANY TALENT FROM IT.
YOU'RE NOTHING MORE THAN FERTILIZER FOR THE VARSITY PLAYERS.
HE SURE IS BLUNT.

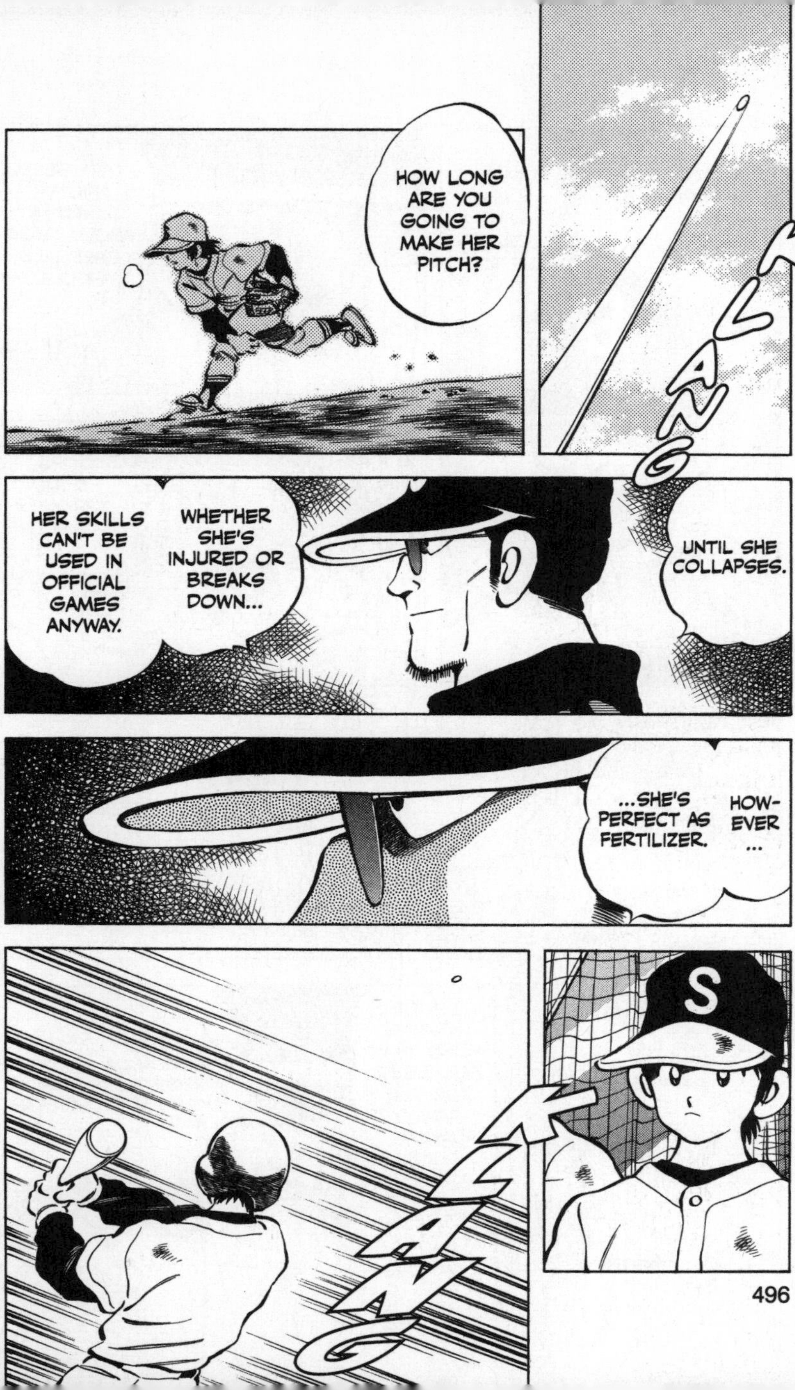
KLANG
HOW LONG ARE YOU GOING TO MAKE HER PITCH?
UNTIL SHE COLLAPSES.
WHETHER SHE'S INJURED OR BREAKS DOWN...
HER SKILLS CAN'T BE USED IN OFFICIAL GAMES ANYWAY.
HOW-EVER...
...SHE'S PERFECT AS FERTILIZER.
KLANG

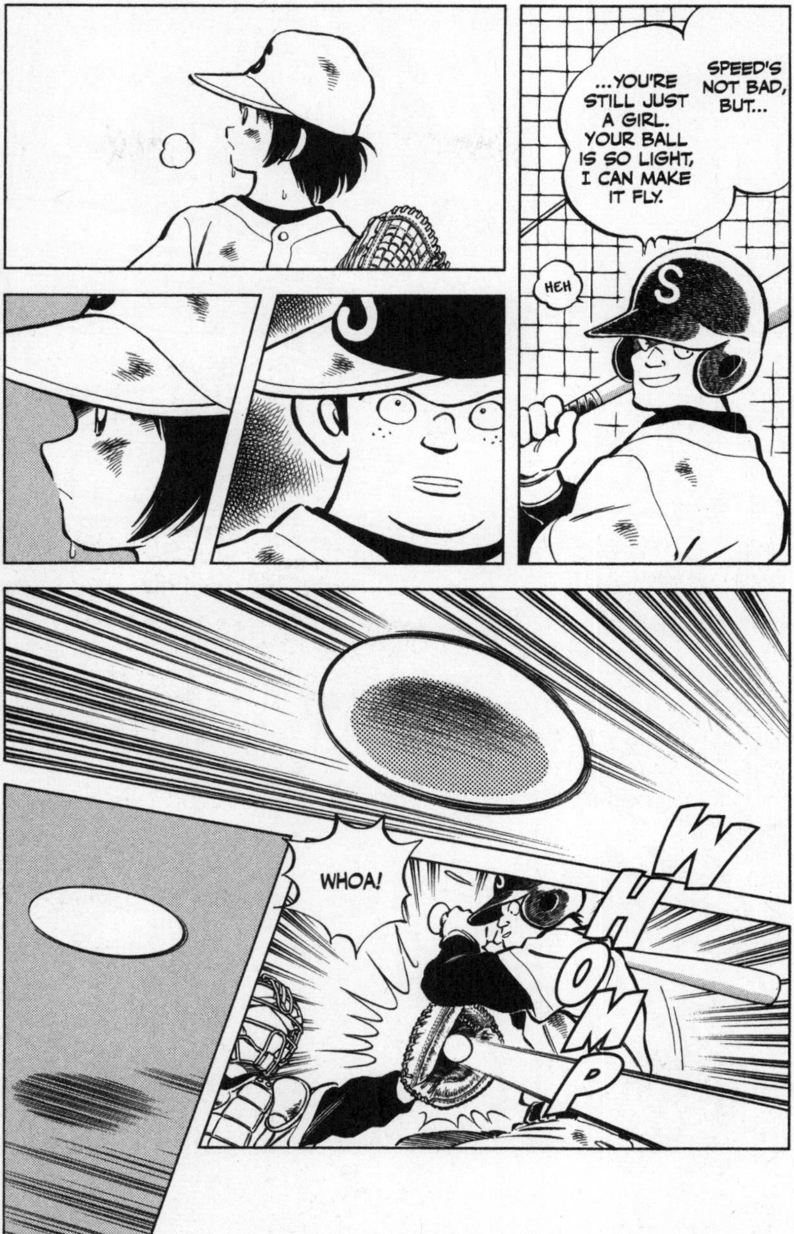
SPEED'S NOT BAD, BUT...
...YOU'RE STILL JUST A GIRL. YOUR BALL IS SO LIGHT, I CAN MAKE IT FLY.
HEH
WHOA!
WHOMP

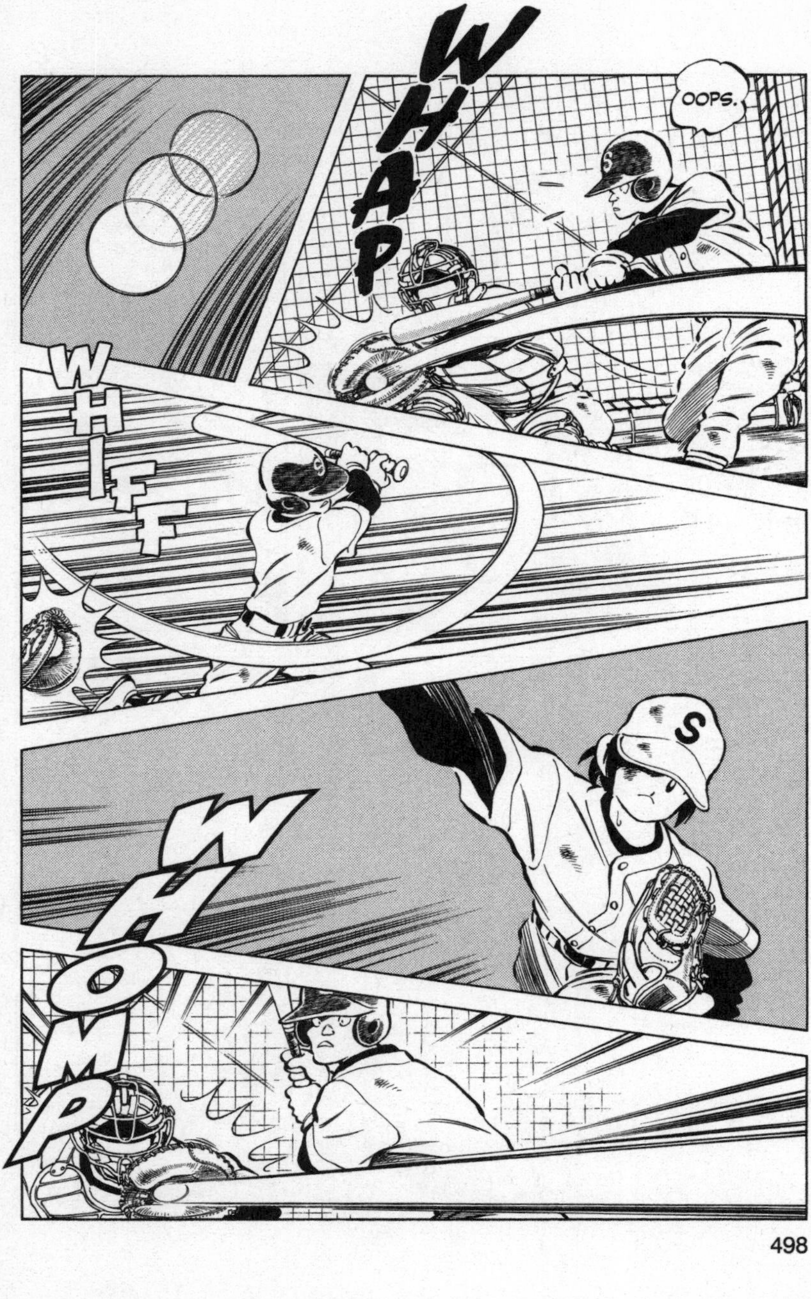
WHAP
OOPS.
WHIFFF
WHOMP

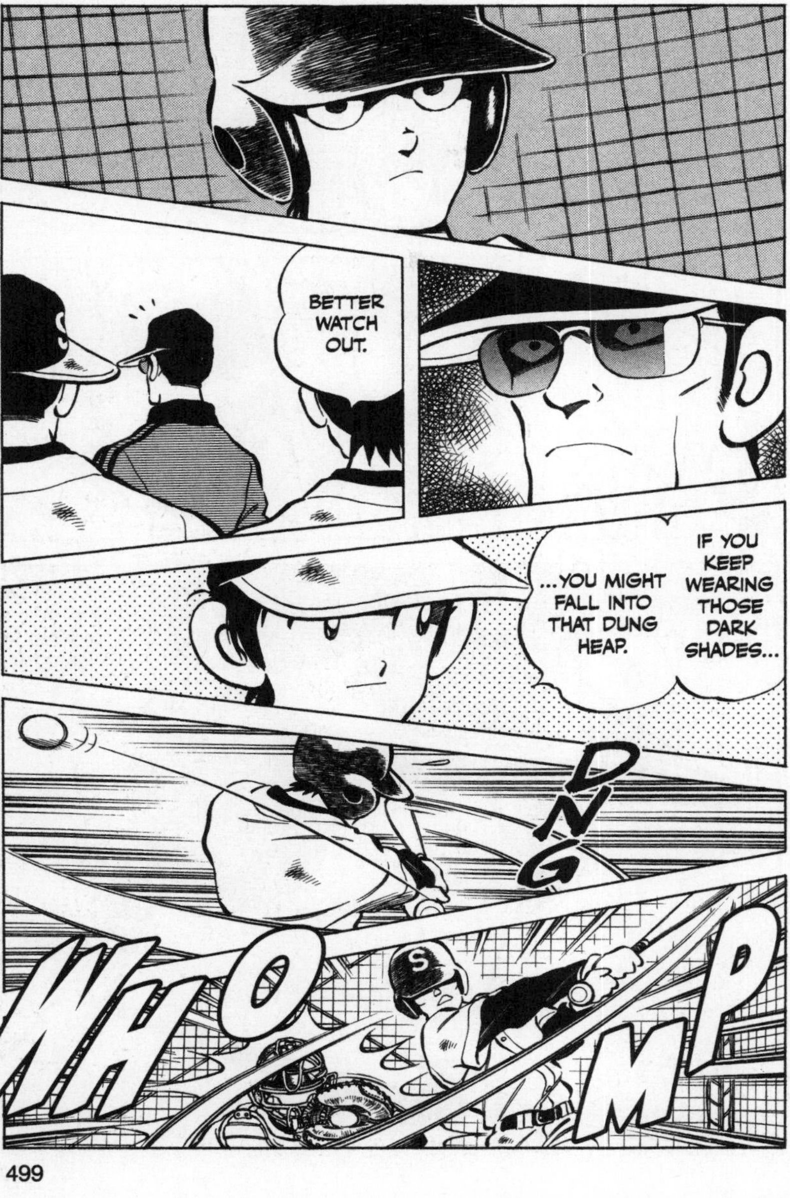
BETTER WATCH OUT.
IF YOU KEEP WEARING THOSE DARK SHADES...
...YOU MIGHT FALL INTO THAT DUNG HEAP.
DNG
WHOMP

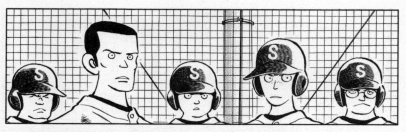

WHY,
THAT--

IT'S MY
TURN,
ISN'T
IT?

CHAPTER 17
A SUCKER FOR A PRETTY FACE

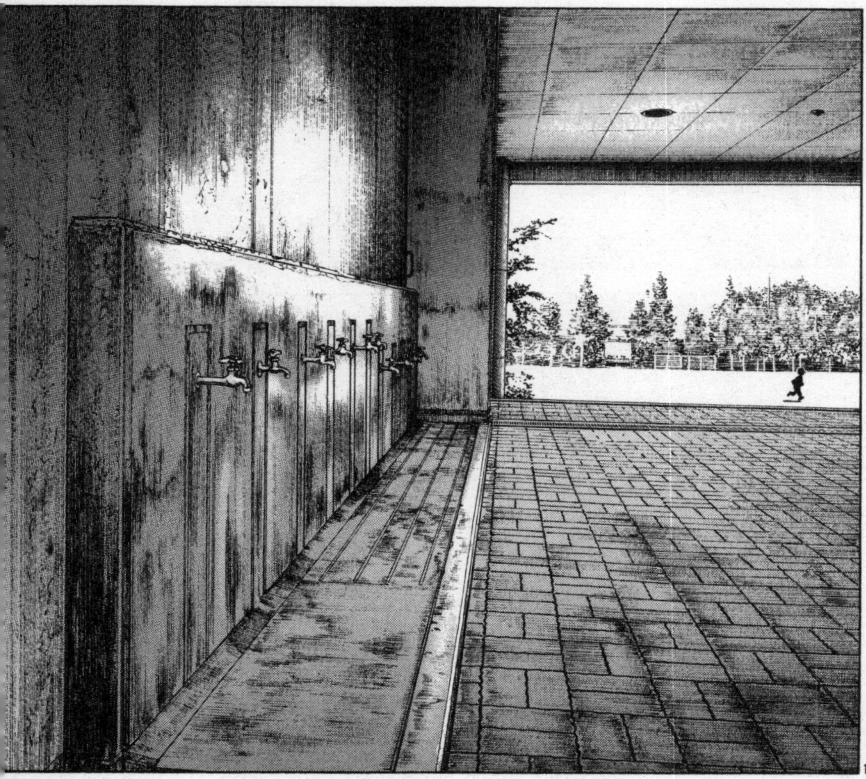

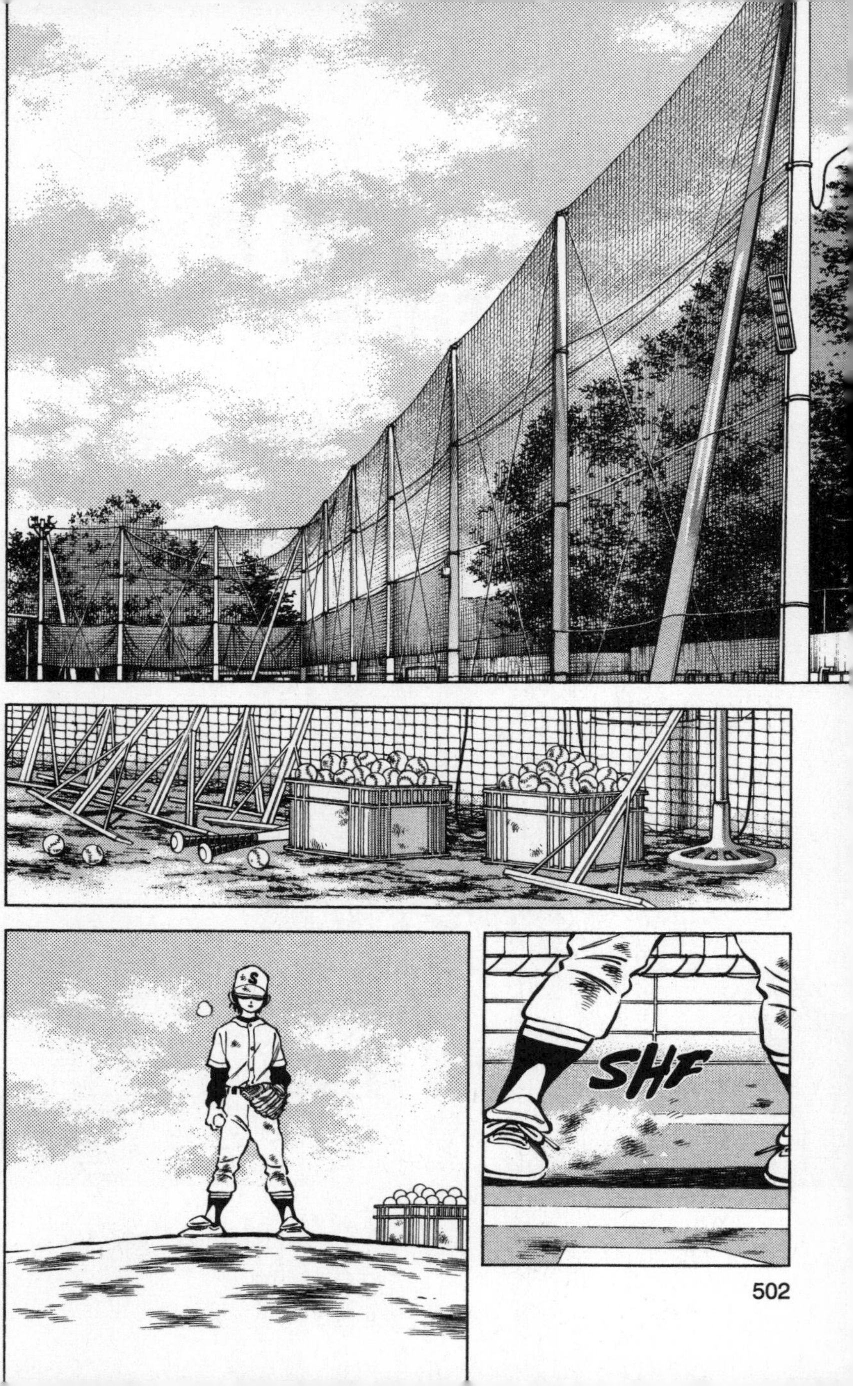
SHF

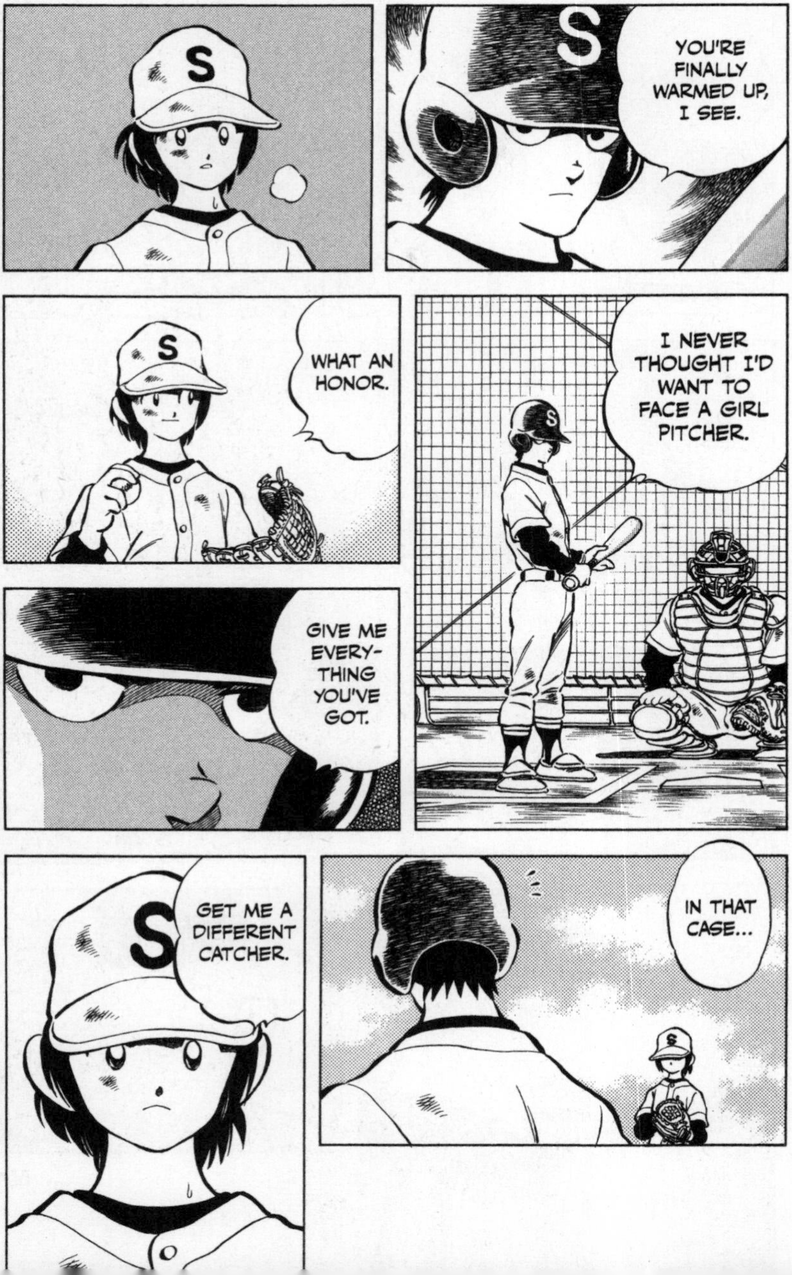
YOU'RE FINALLY WARMED UP, I SEE.
I NEVER THOUGHT I'D WANT TO FACE A GIRL PITCHER.
WHAT AN HONOR.
GIVE ME EVERY-THING YOU'VE GOT.
IN THAT CASE...
GET ME A DIFFERENT CATCHER.

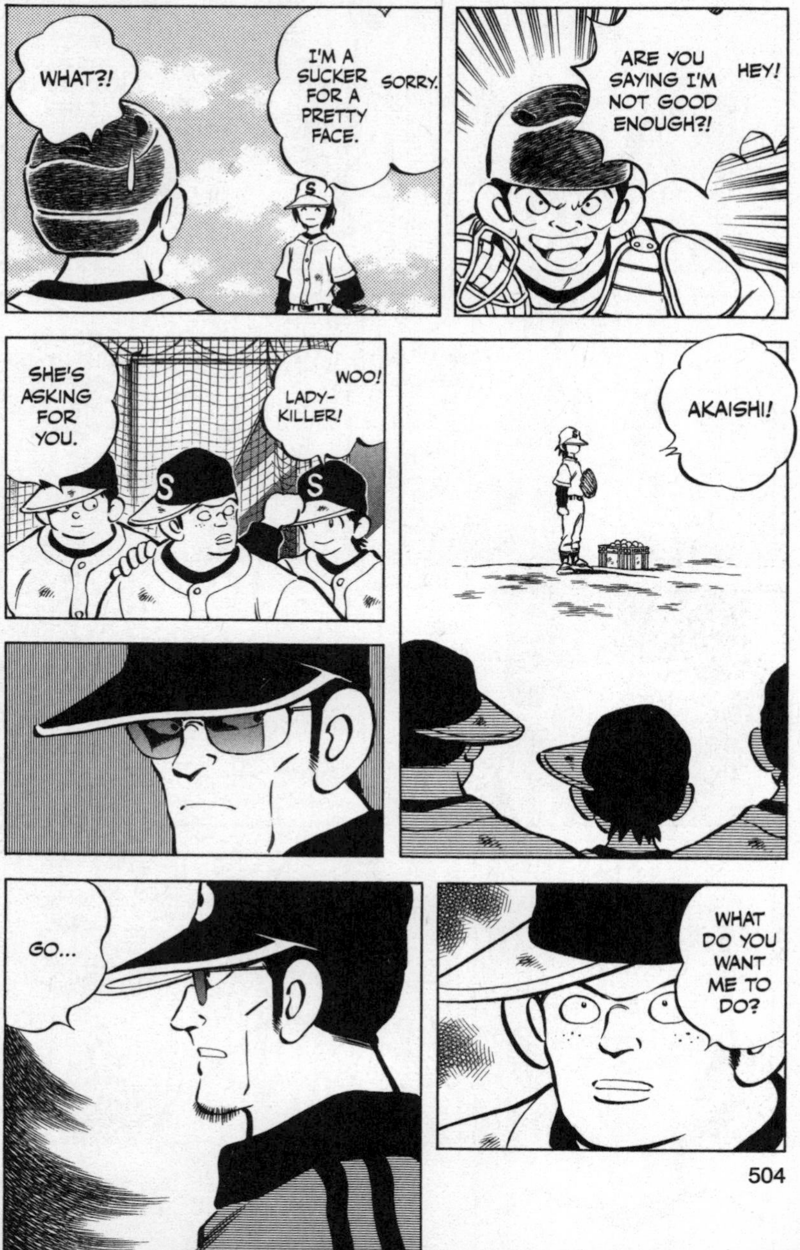
HEY!
ARE YOU SAYING I'M NOT GOOD ENOUGH?!
SORRY.
I'M A SUCKER FOR A PRETTY FACE.
WHAT?!
AKAISHI!
WOO! LADY-KILLER!
SHE'S ASKING FOR YOU.
WHAT DO YOU WANT ME TO DO?
GO...

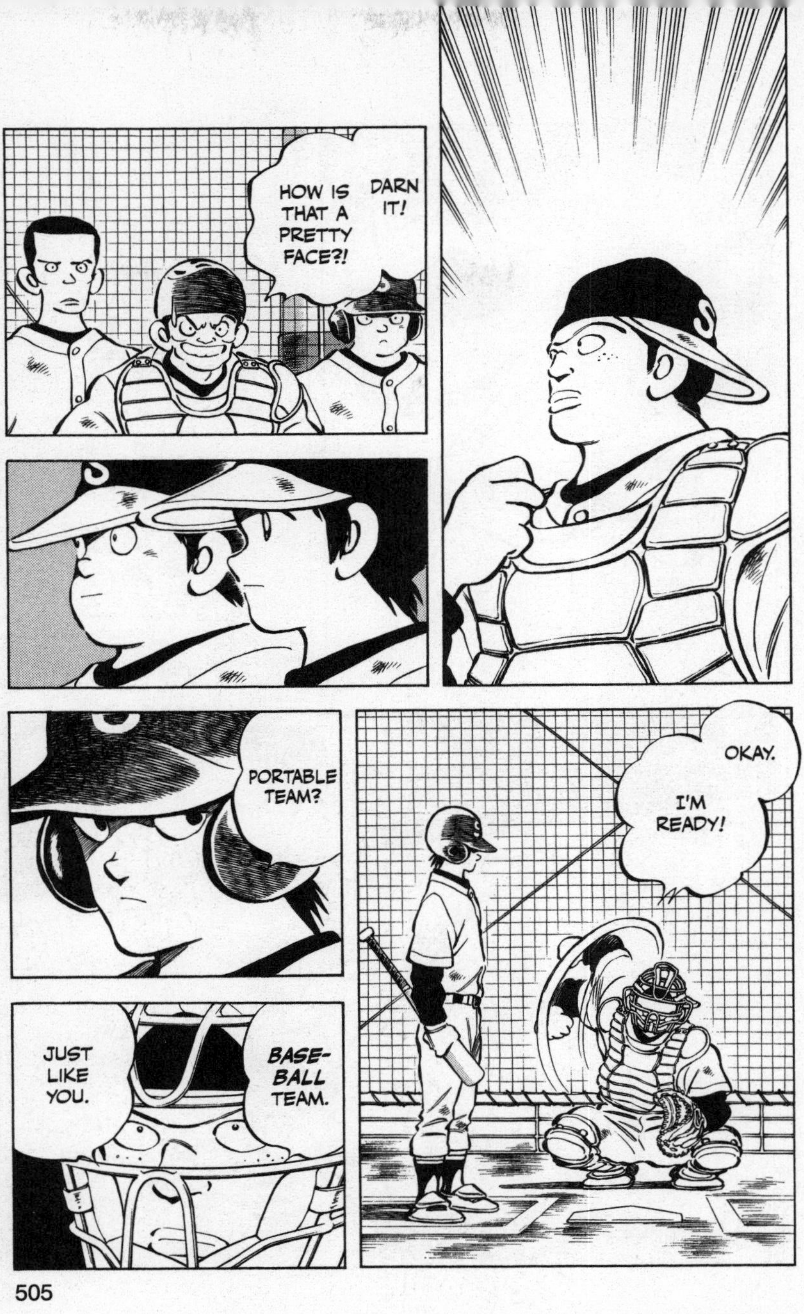
DARN IT!
HOW IS THAT A PRETTY FACE?!
OKAY.
I'M READY!
PORTABLE TEAM?
BASE-BALL TEAM.
JUST LIKE YOU.

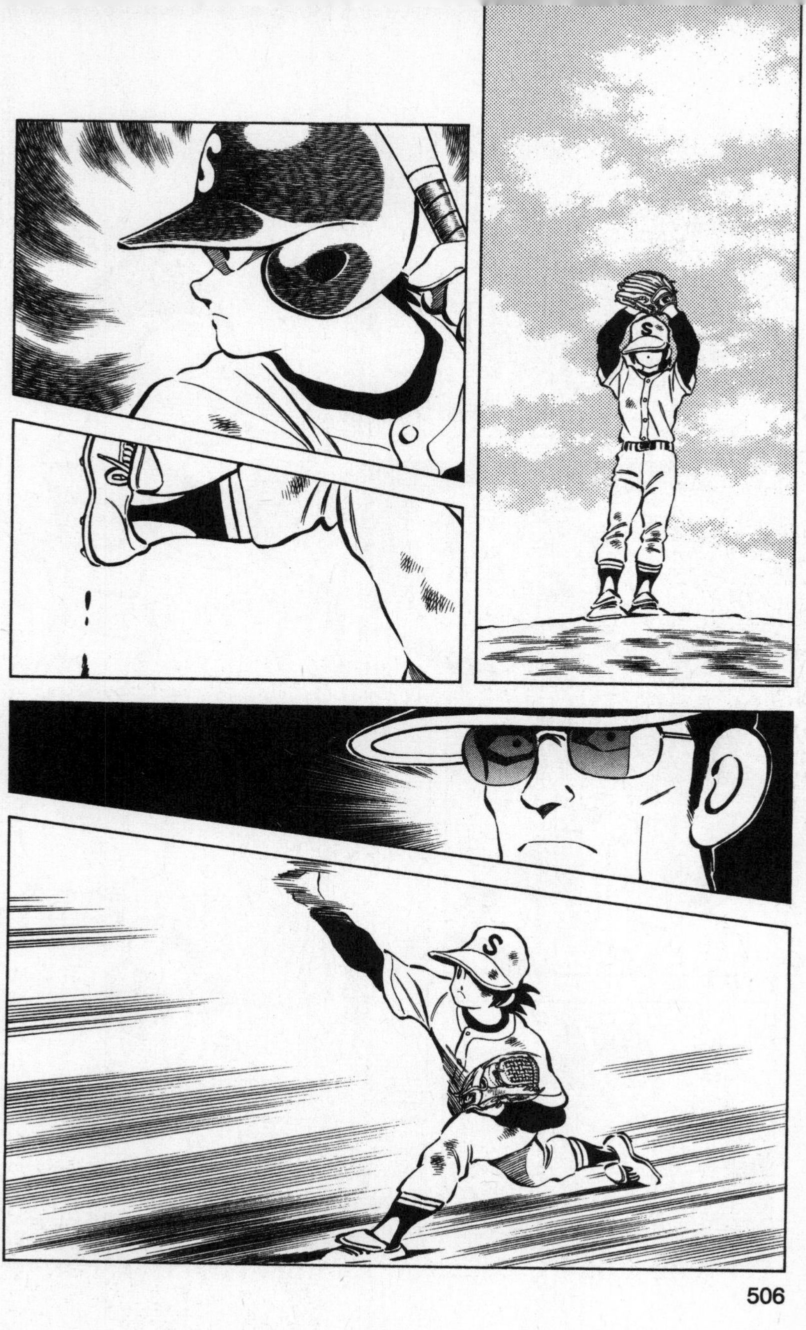

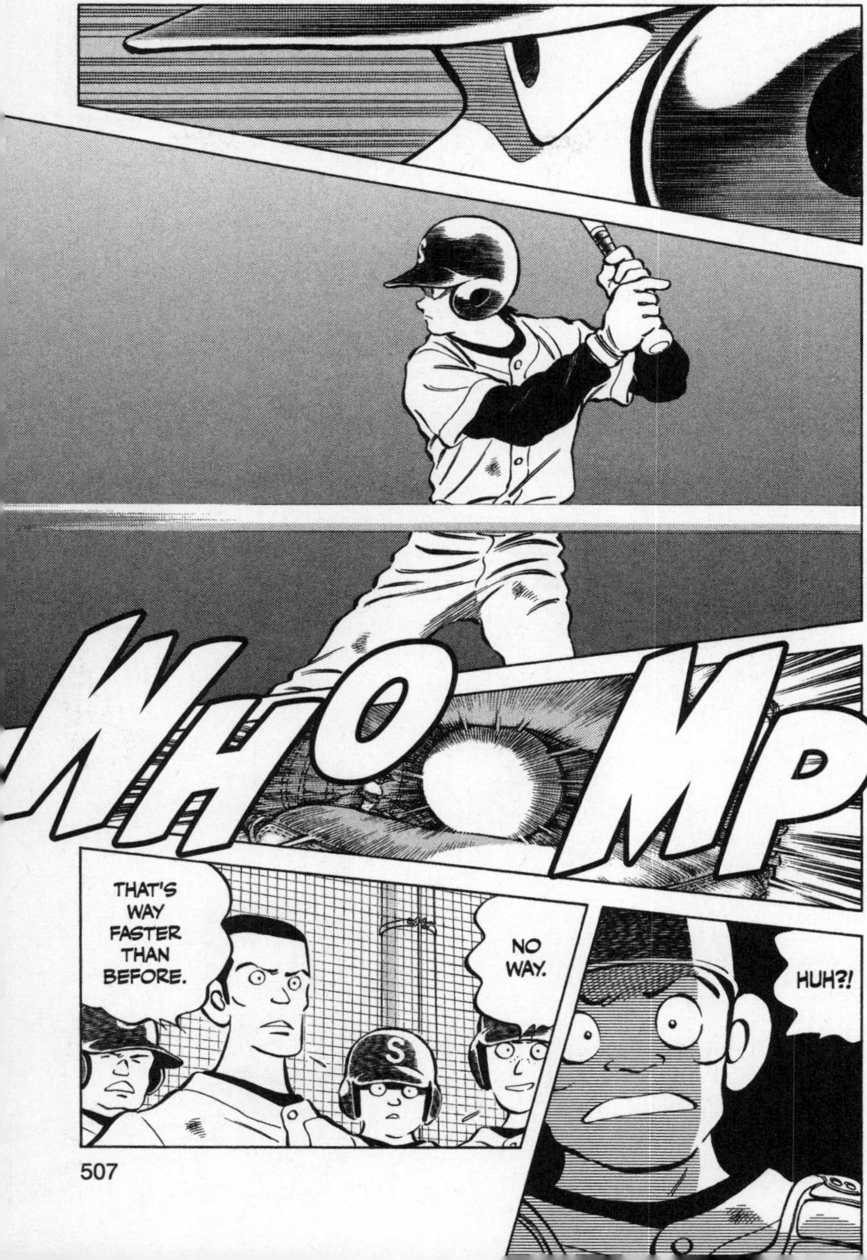
WHOMP
HUH?!
NO WAY.
THAT'S WAY FASTER THAN BEFORE.

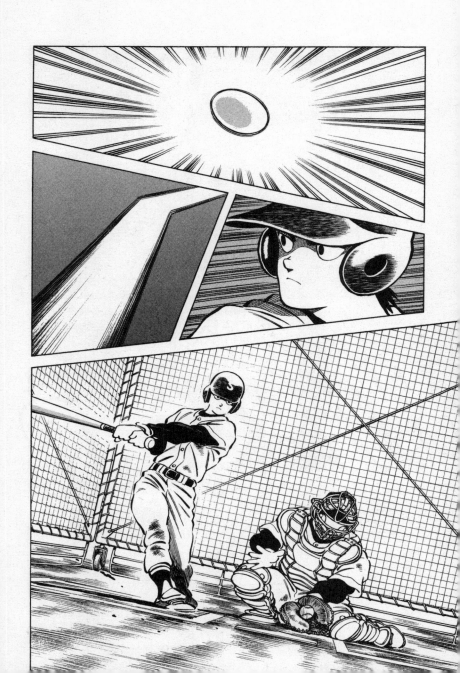

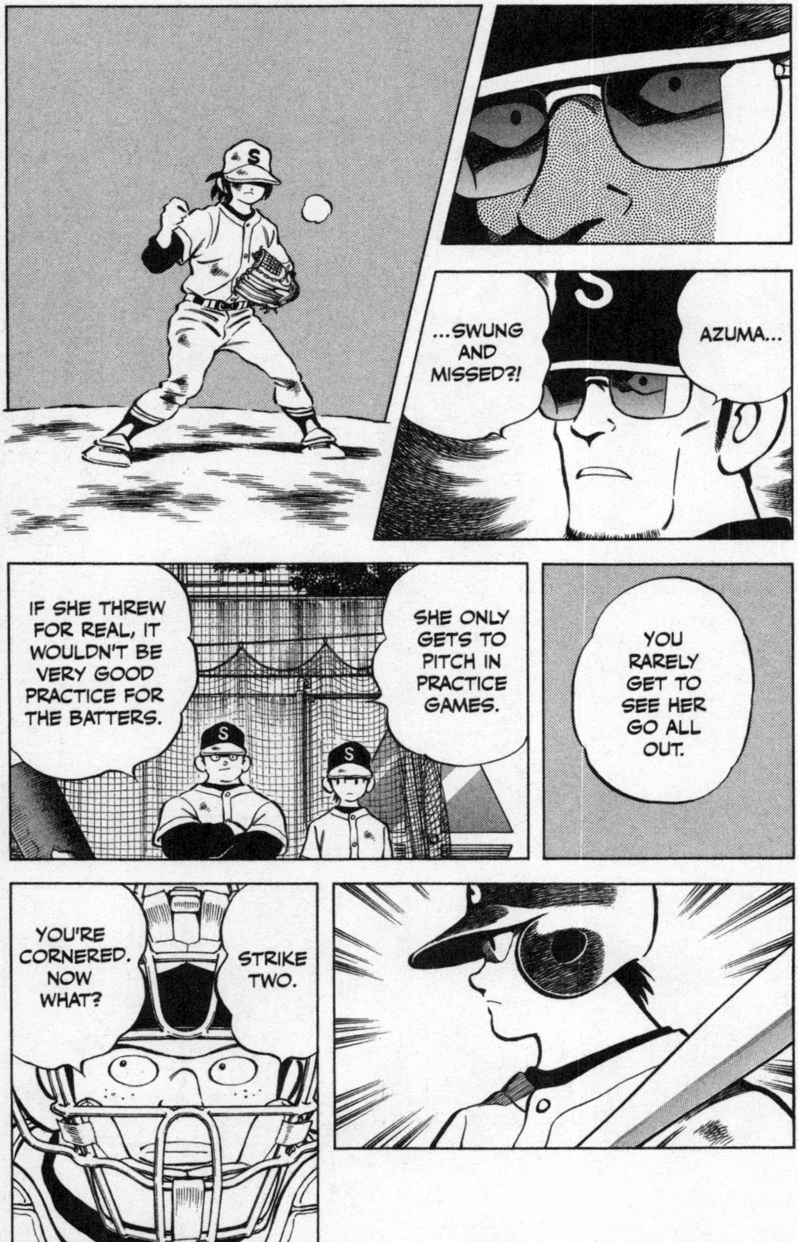
AZUMA...
...SWUNG AND MISSED?!
YOU RARELY GET TO SEE HER GO ALL OUT.
SHE ONLY GETS TO PITCH IN PRACTICE GAMES.
IF SHE THREW FOR REAL, IT WOULDN'T BE VERY GOOD PRACTICE FOR THE BATTERS.
STRIKE TWO.
YOU'RE CORNERED. NOW WHAT?

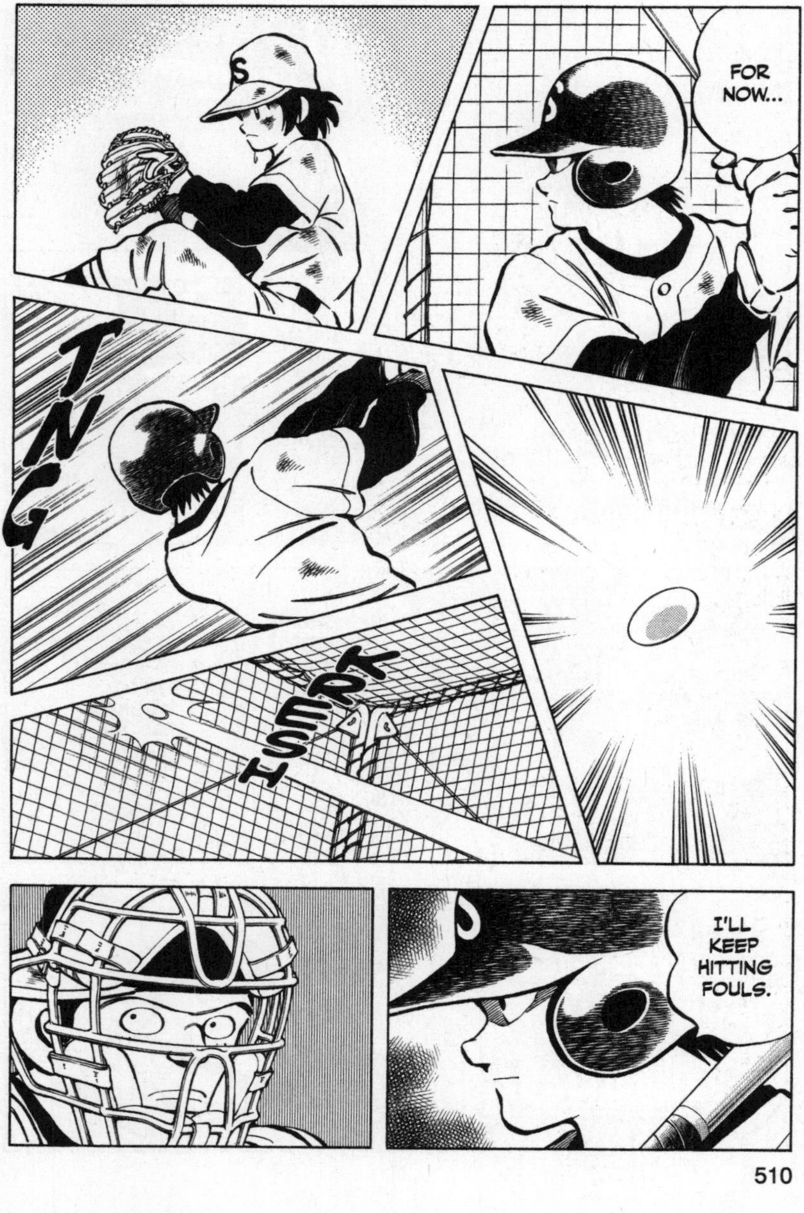
FOR NOW...
TING
KRESH
I'LL KEEP HITTING FOULS.

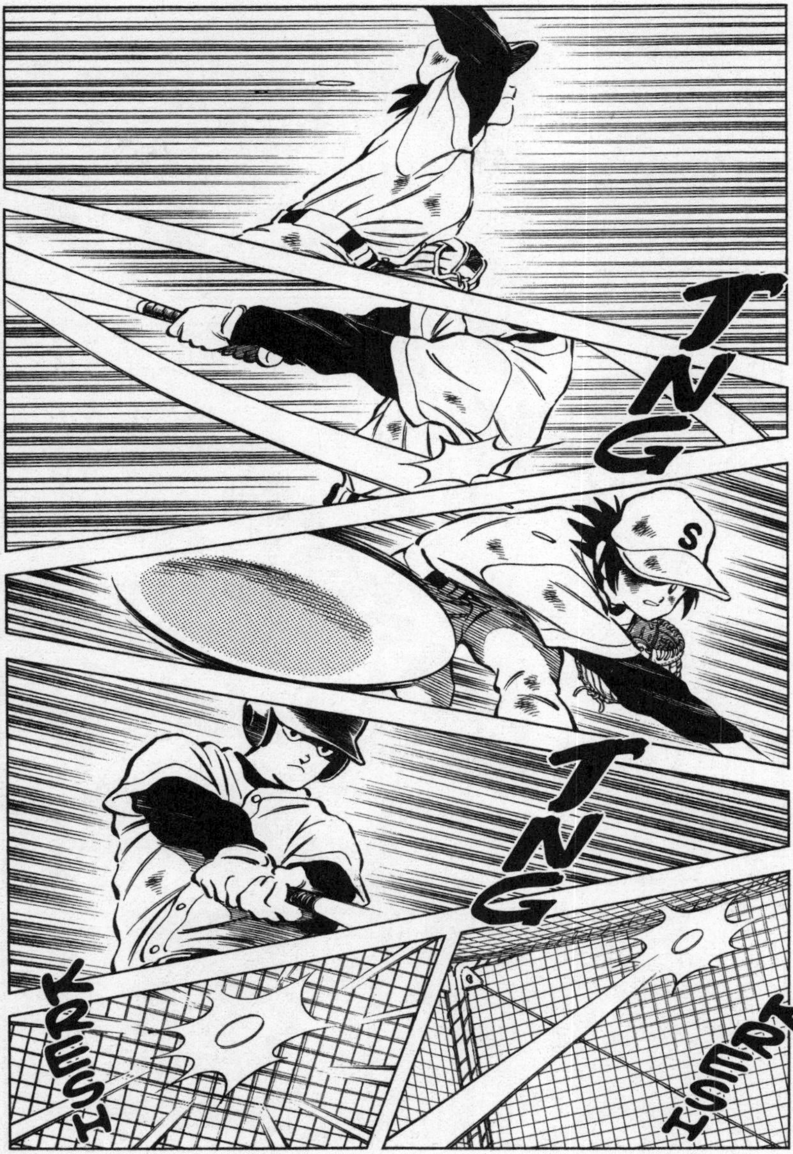
TING
TING
KRESH
KRESH

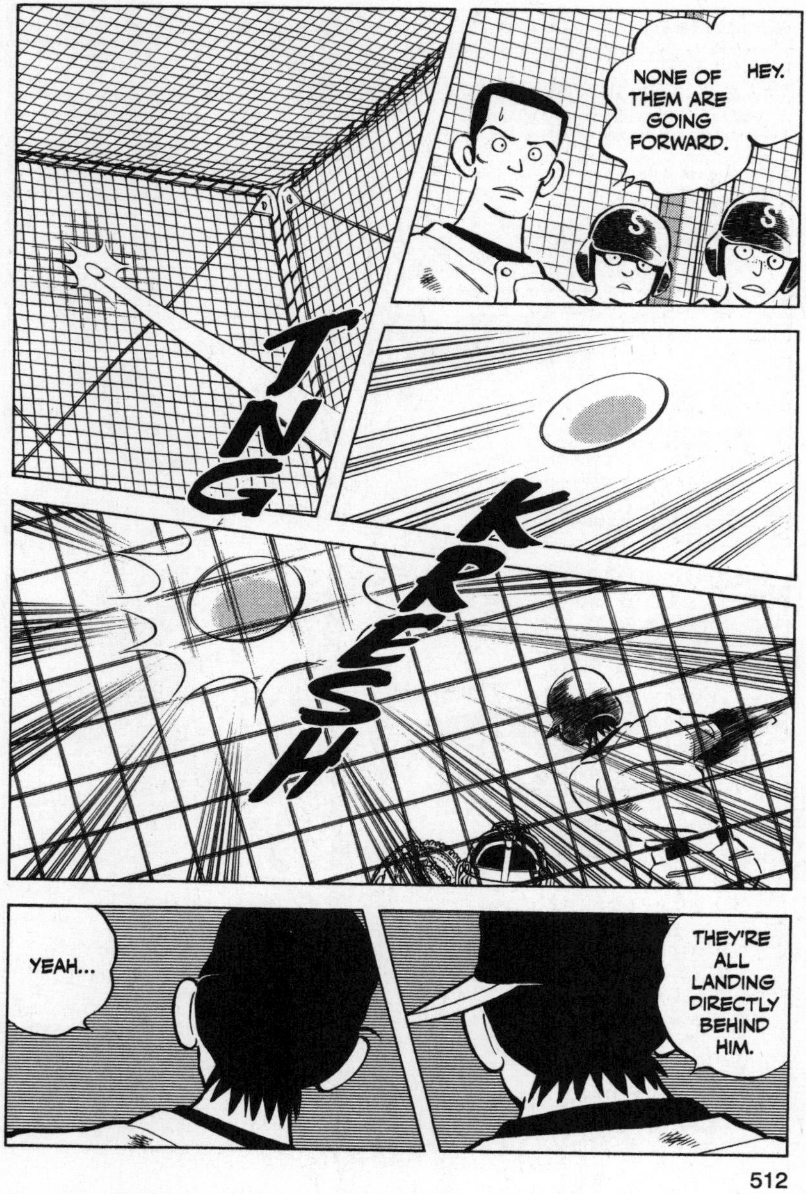
HEY.
NONE OF THEM ARE GOING FORWARD.
TING
KRESH
THEY'RE ALL LANDING DIRECTLY BEHIND HIM.
YEAH...

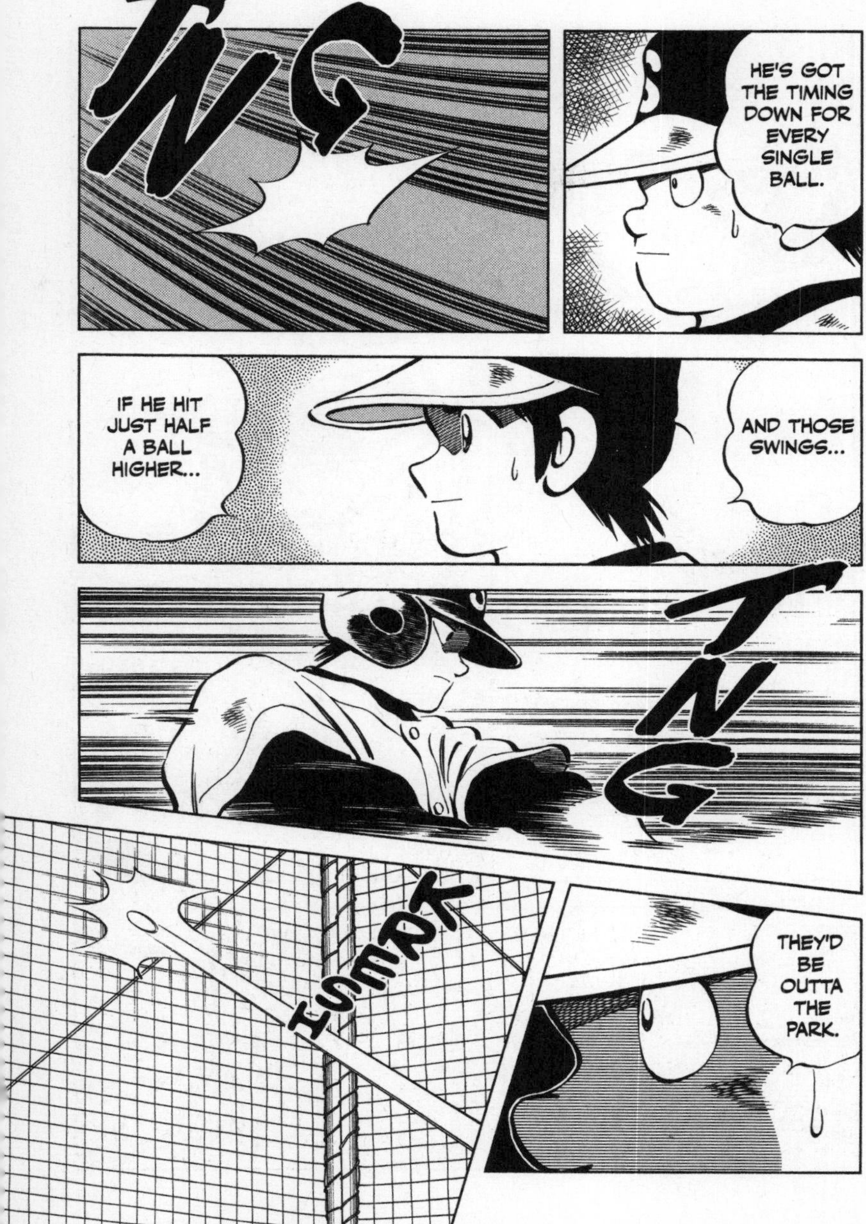
HE'S GOT THE TIMING DOWN FOR EVERY SINGLE BALL.
TING
AND THOSE SWINGS...
IF HE HIT JUST HALF A BALL HIGHER...
TING
THEY'D BE OUTTA THE PARK.
SMAK

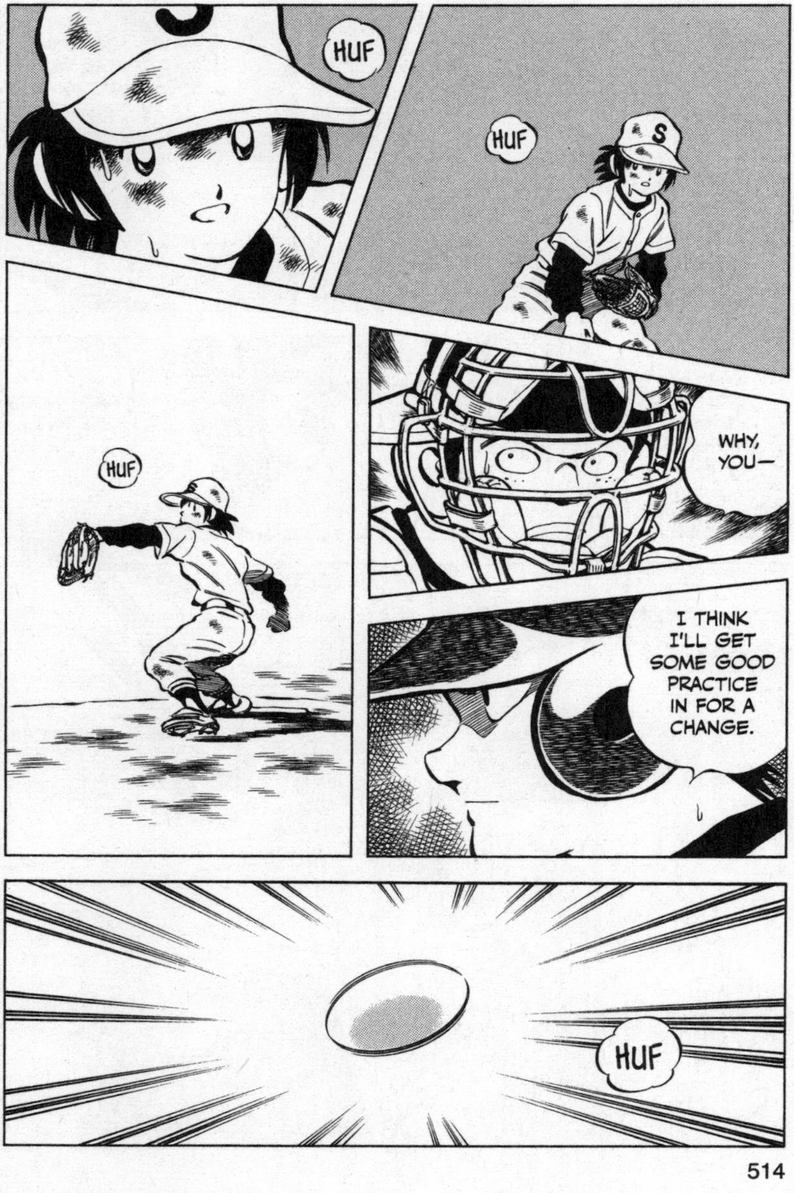
HUF
HUF
WHY, YOU—
I THINK I'LL GET SOME GOOD PRACTICE IN FOR A CHANGE.
HUF
HUF

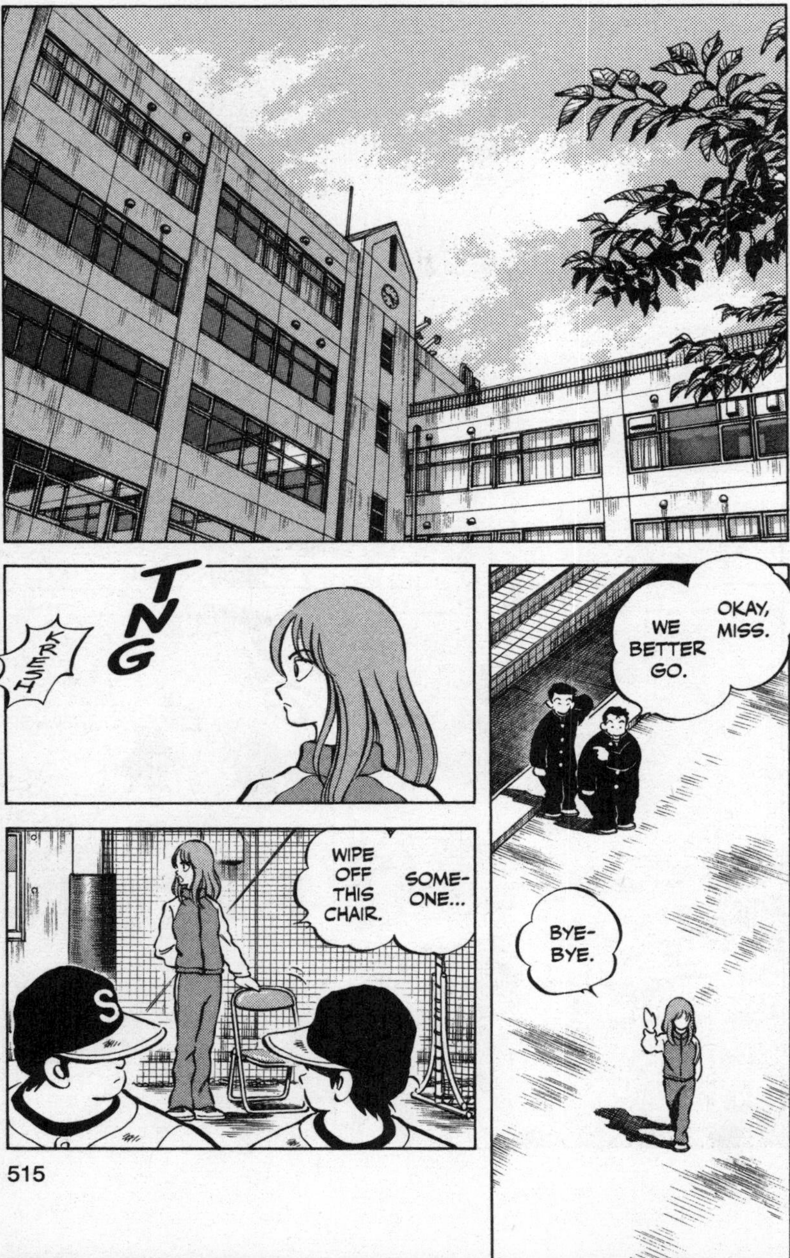
OKAY, MISS. WE BETTER GO.
BYE-BYE.
TNG
KRESH
SOME-ONE... WIPE OFF THIS CHAIR.

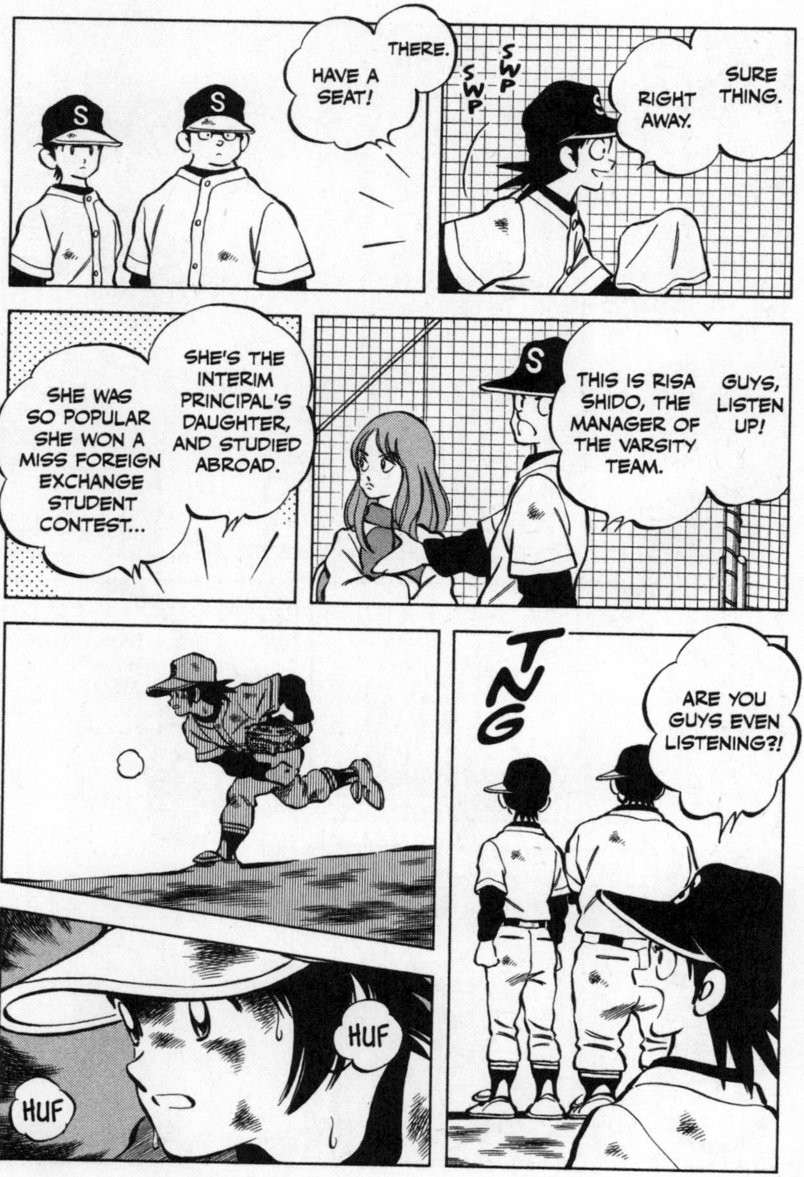
SWP
SWP
SURE THING.
RIGHT AWAY.
THERE.
HAVE A SEAT!
GUYS, LISTEN UP!
THIS IS RISA SHIDO, THE MANAGER OF THE VARSITY TEAM.
SHE'S THE INTERIM PRINCIPAL'S DAUGHTER, AND STUDIED ABROAD.
SHE WAS SO POPULAR SHE WON A MISS FOREIGN EXCHANGE STUDENT CONTEST...
TNG
ARE YOU GUYS EVEN LISTENING?!
HUF
HUF

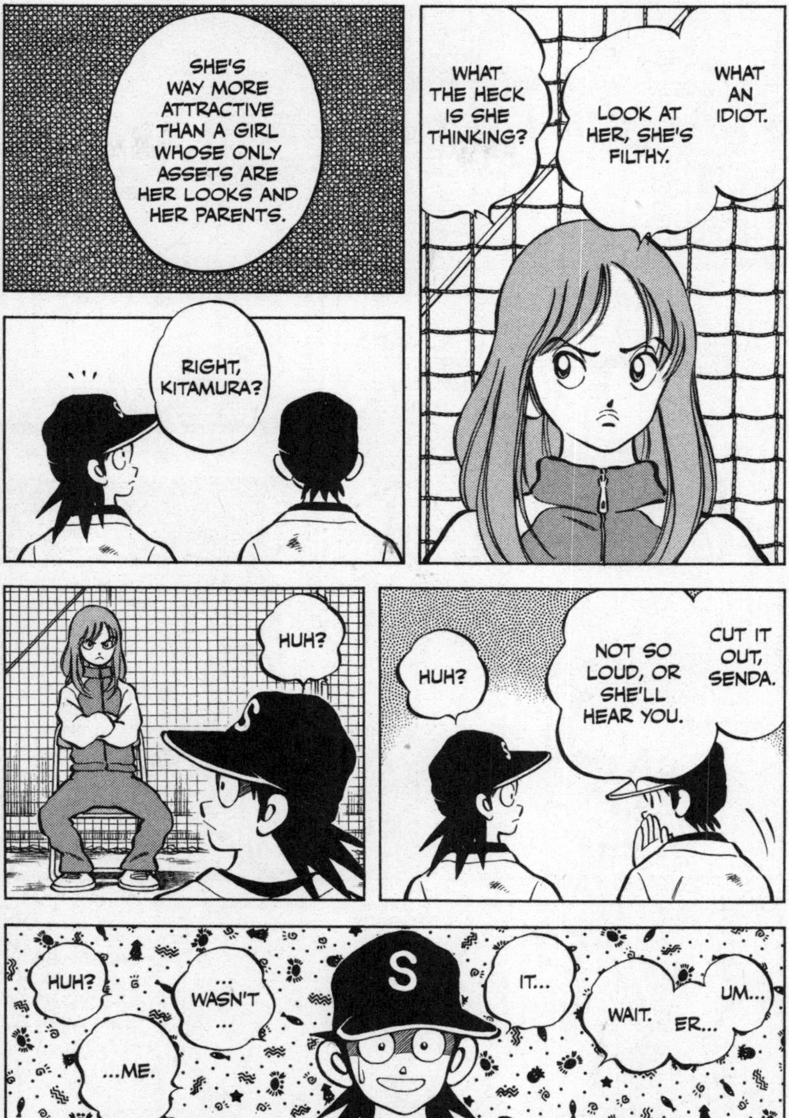
WHAT AN IDIOT.
LOOK AT HER, SHE'S FILTHY.
WHAT THE HECK IS SHE THINKING?
SHE'S WAY MORE ATTRACTIVE THAN A GIRL WHOSE ONLY ASSETS ARE HER LOOKS AND HER PARENTS.
RIGHT, KITAMURA?
CUT IT OUT, SENDA.
NOT SO LOUD, OR SHE'LL HEAR YOU.
HUH?
HUH?
UM...
WAIT.
ER...
IT...
...
WASN'T
...
HUH?
...ME.

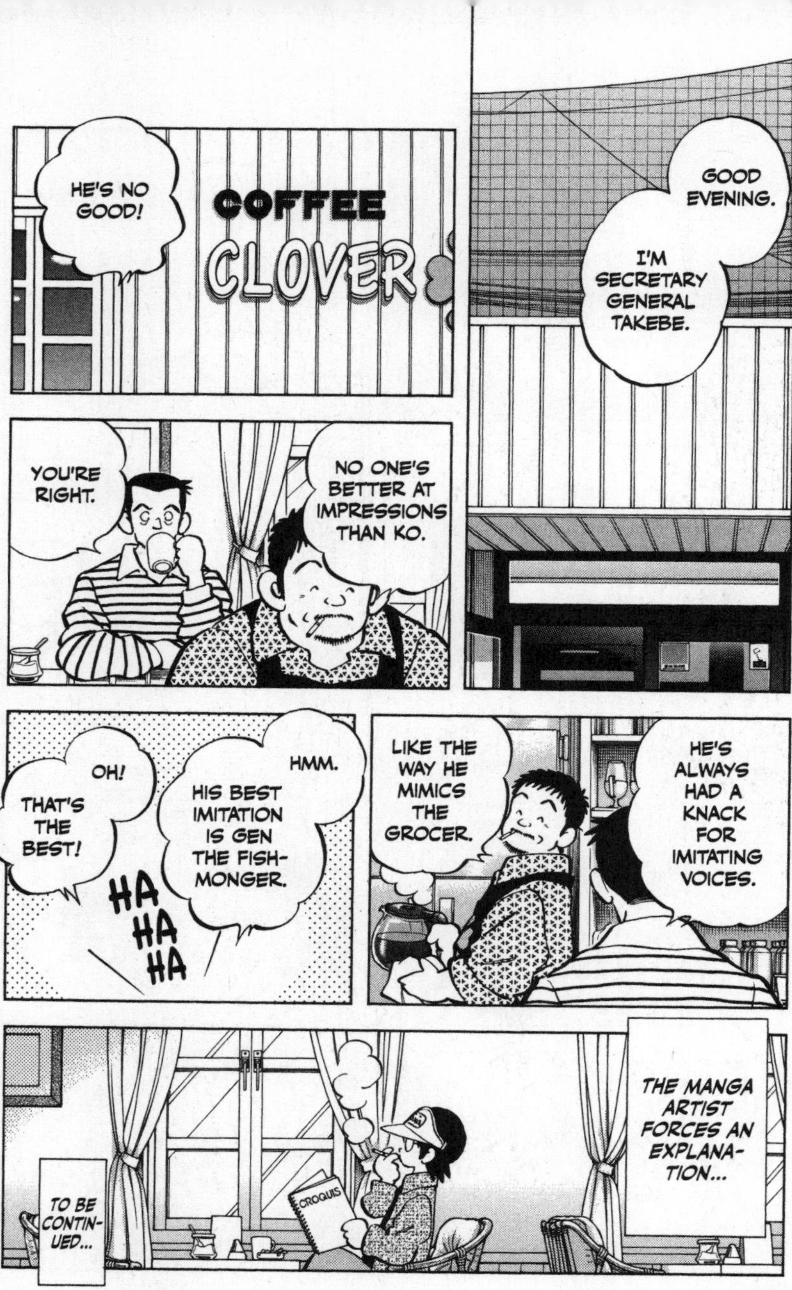
GOOD EVENING.
I'M SECRETARY GENERAL TAKEBE.
COFFEE
CLOVER
HE'S NO GOOD!
NO ONE'S BETTER AT IMPRESSIONS THAN KO.
YOU'RE RIGHT.
HE'S ALWAYS HAD A KNACK FOR IMITATING VOICES.
LIKE THE WAY HE MIMICS THE GROCER.
HMM.
HIS BEST IMITATION IS GEN THE FISH-MONGER.
OH!
THAT'S THE BEST!
HA HA HA
THE MANGA ARTIST FORCES AN EXPLANA-TION...
CROQUIS
TO BE CONTIN-UED...

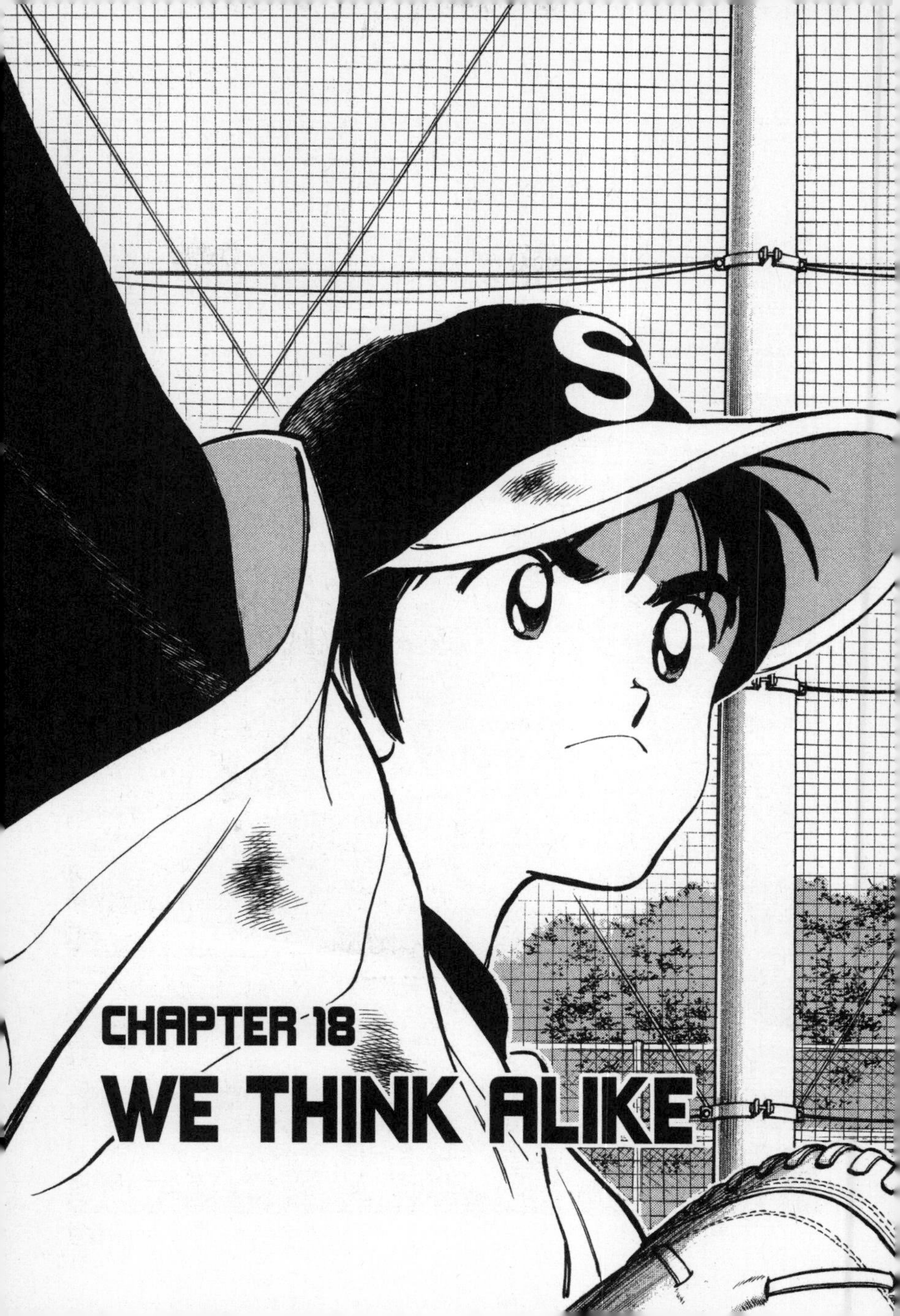
CHAPTER 18
WE THINK ALIKE

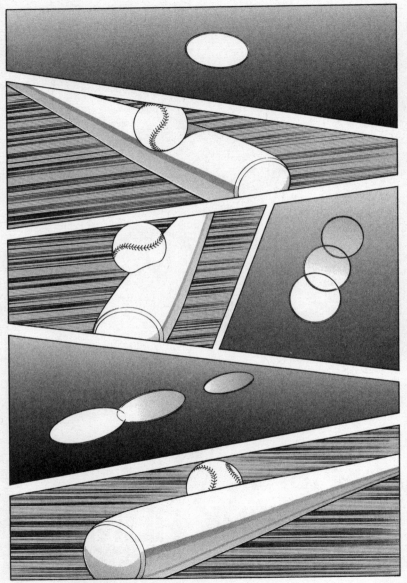

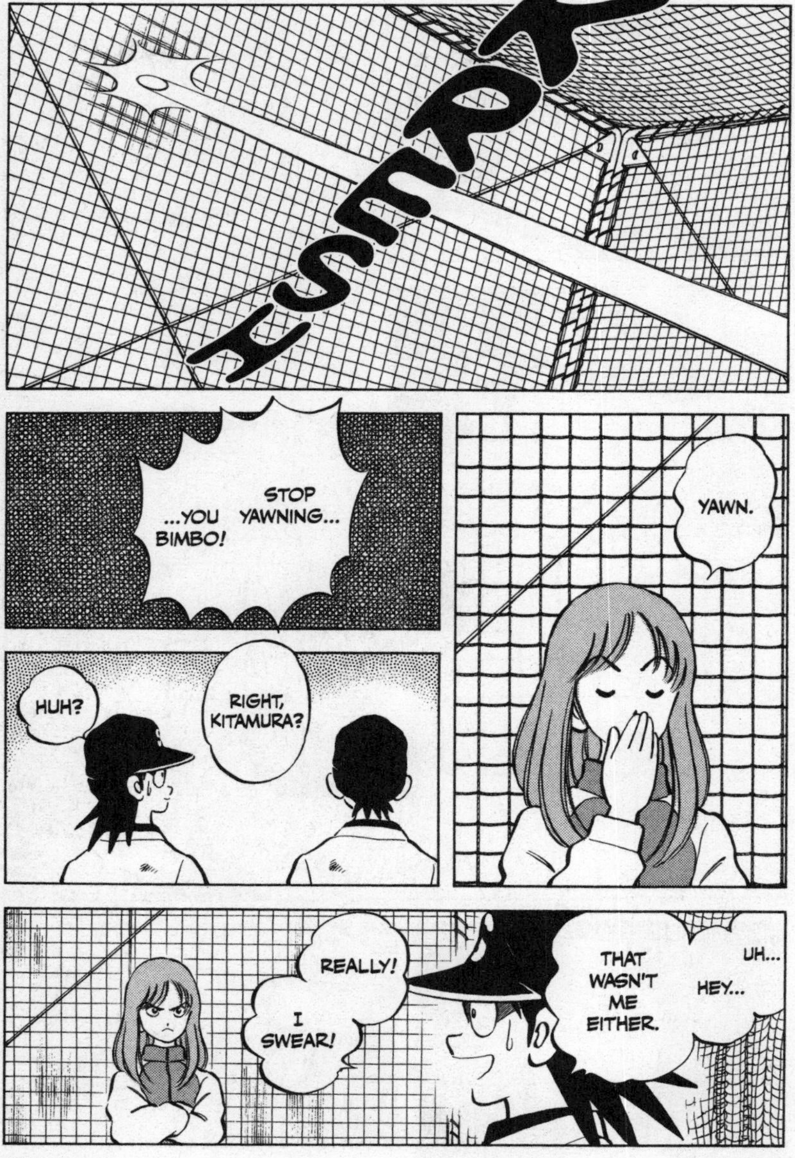
KRESH
YAWN.
STOP YAWNING...
...YOU BIMBO!
RIGHT, KITAMURA?
HUH?
UH... HEY...
THAT WASN'T ME EITHER.
REALLY!
I SWEAR!

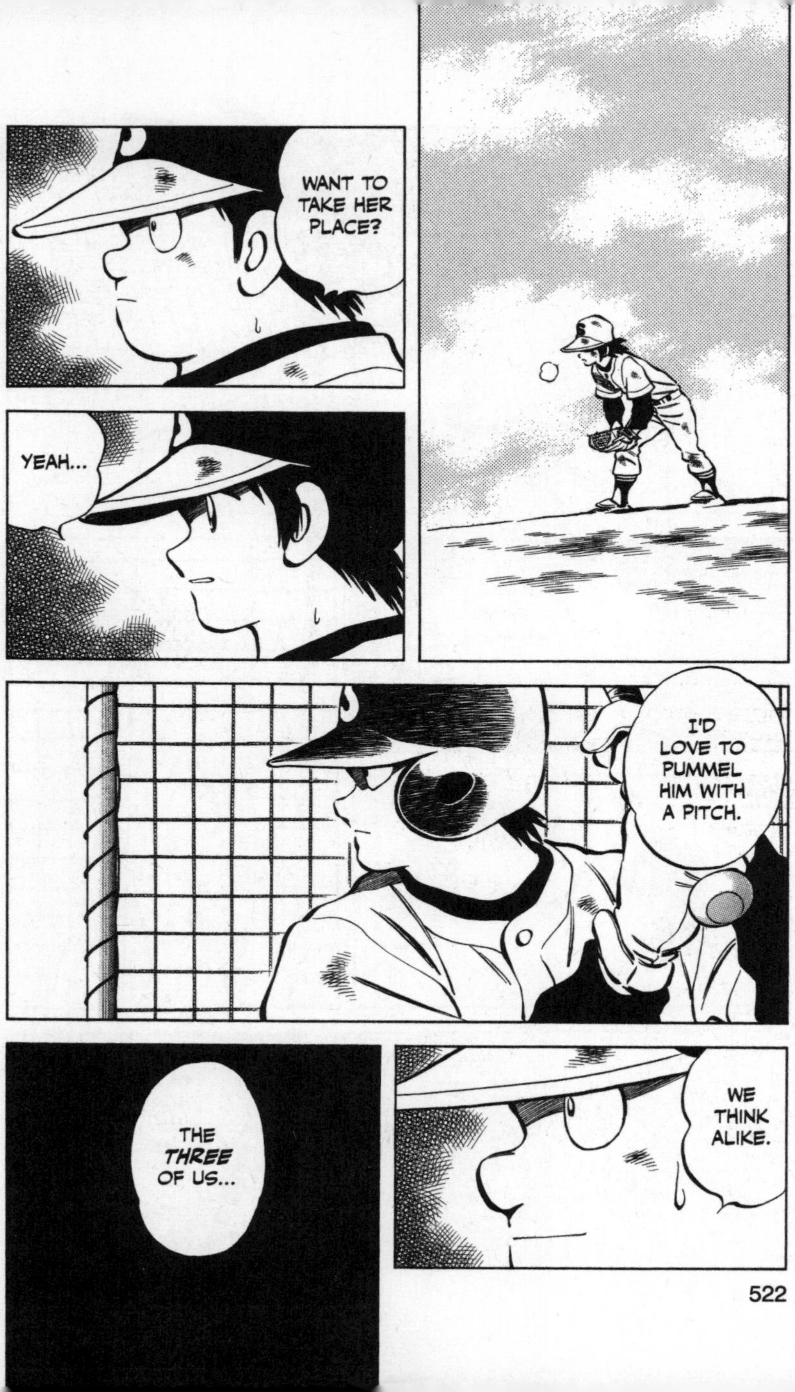
WANT TO TAKE HER PLACE?
YEAH...
I'D LOVE TO PUMMEL HIM WITH A PITCH.
WE THINK ALIKE.
THE *THREE* OF US...

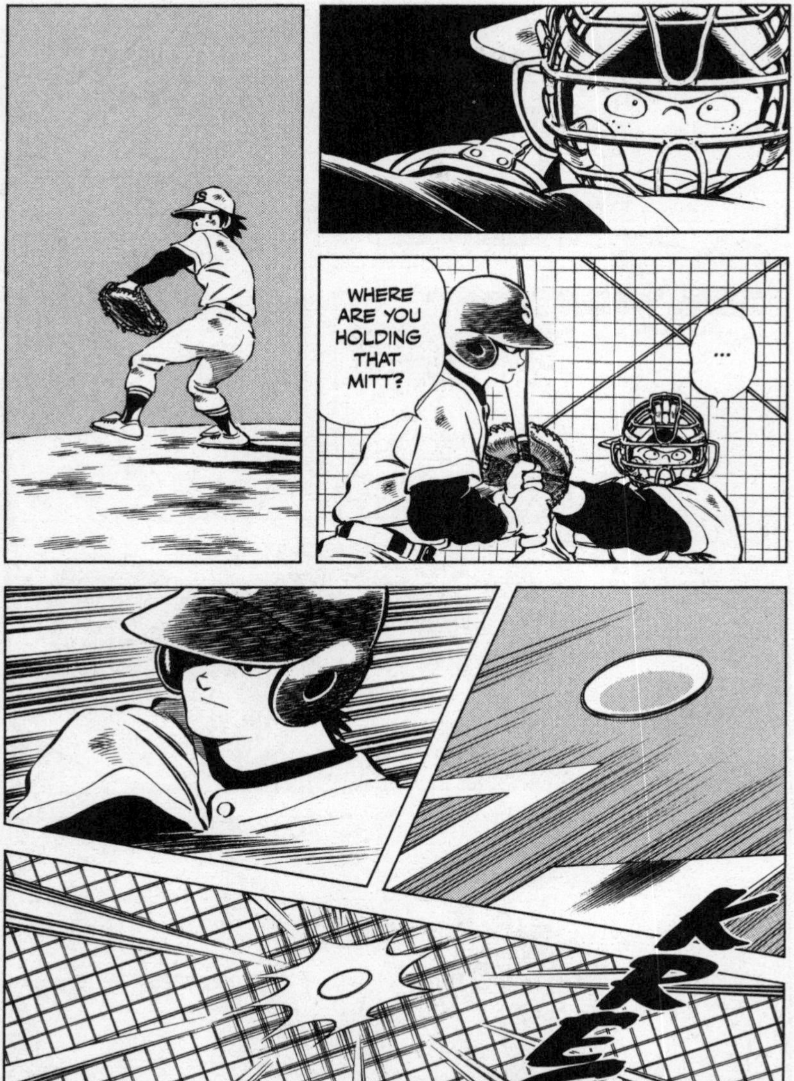
WHERE ARE YOU HOLDING THAT MITT?
...
KRRESH

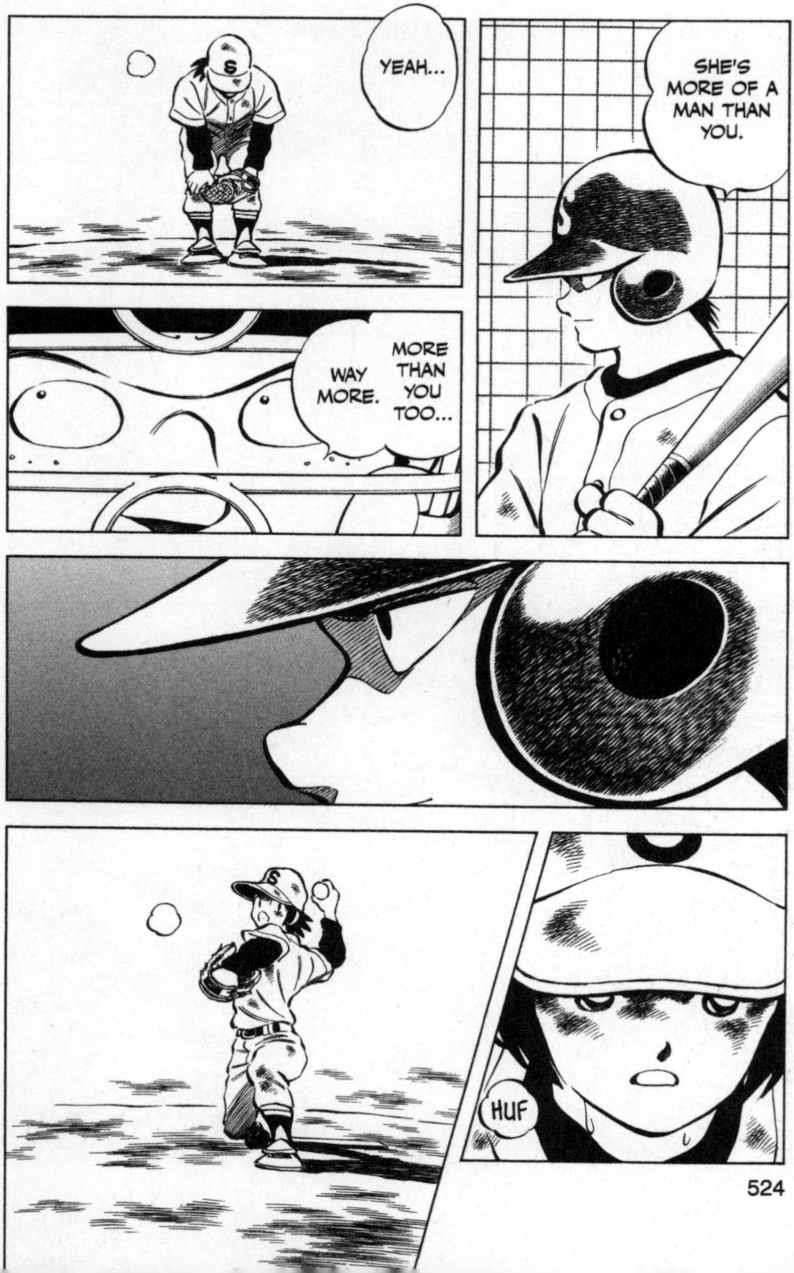
SHE'S MORE OF A MAN THAN YOU.
YEAH...
MORE THAN YOU TOO...
WAY MORE.
HUF

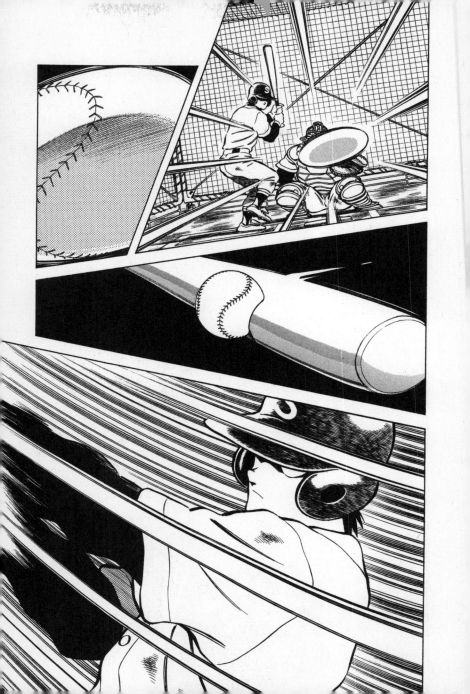

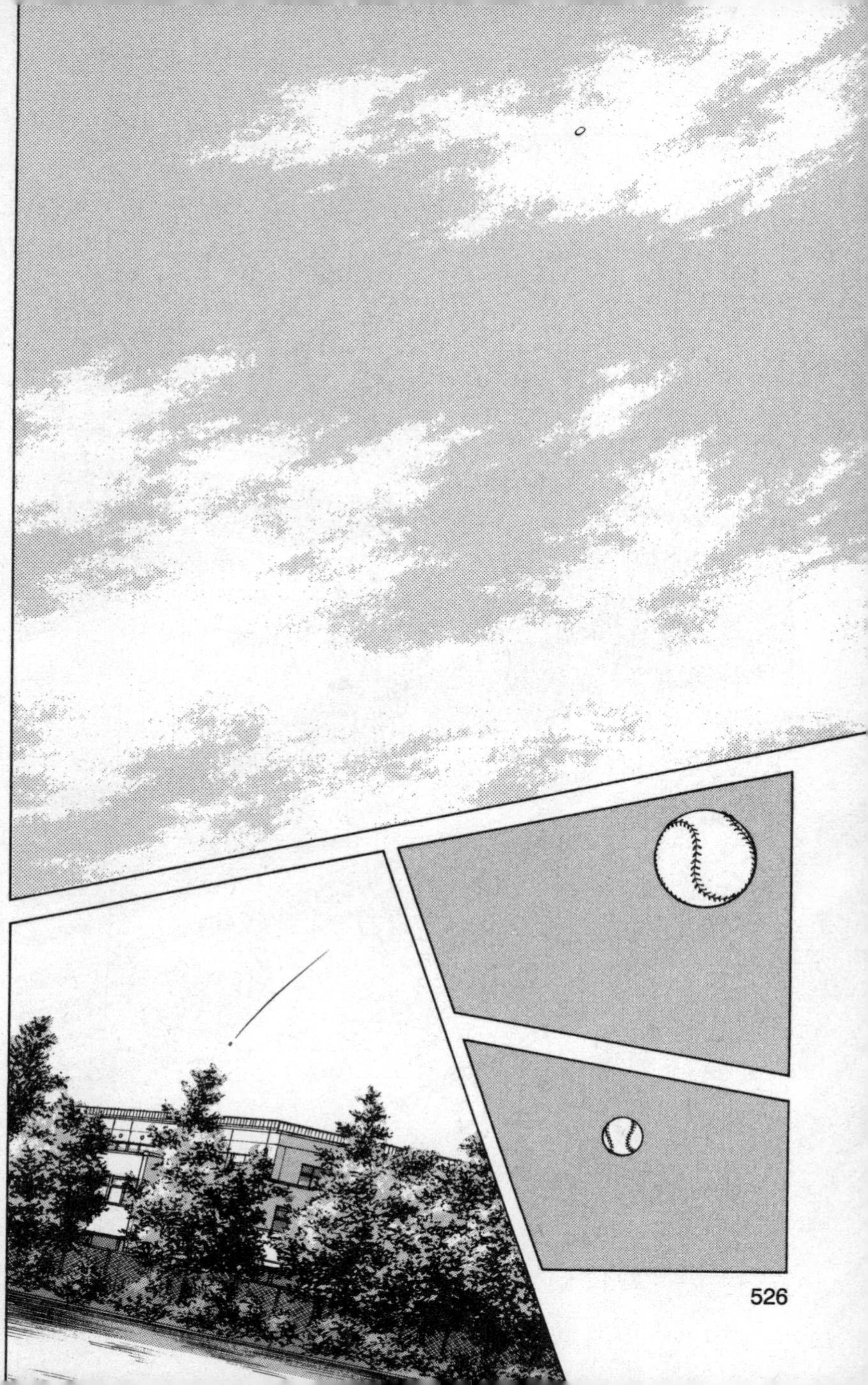

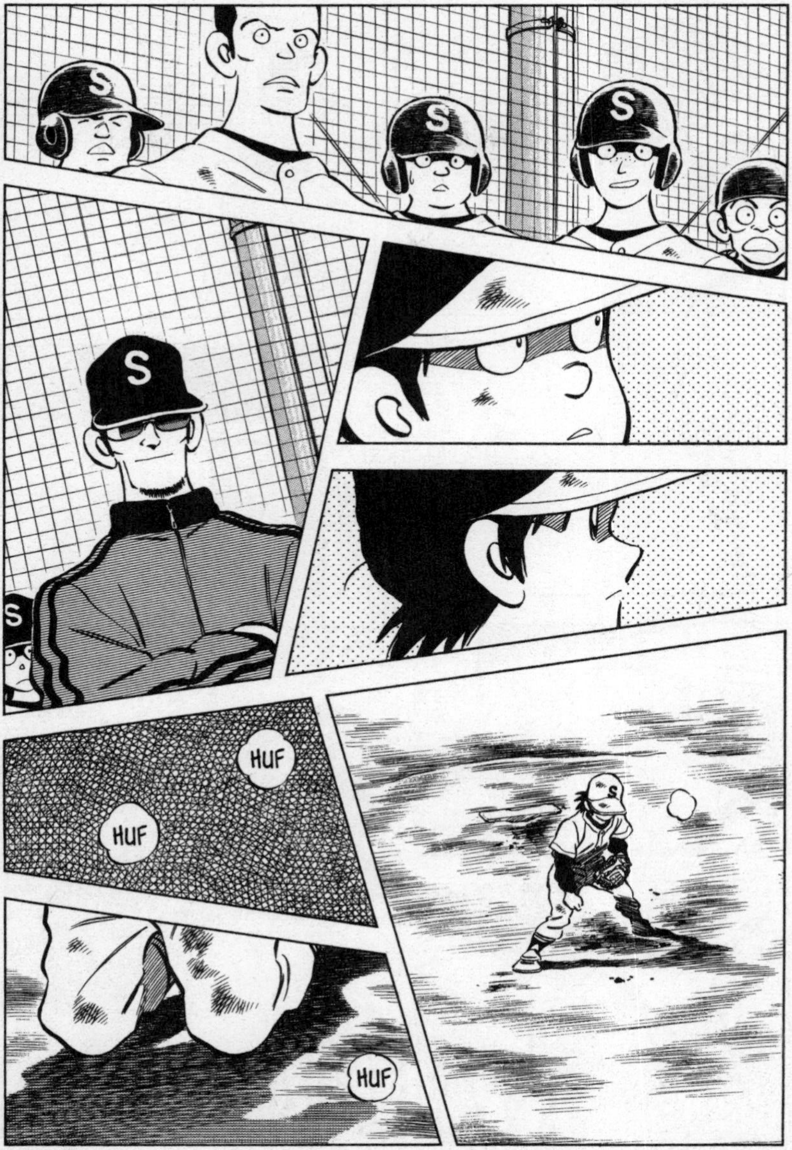
HUF
HUF
HUF

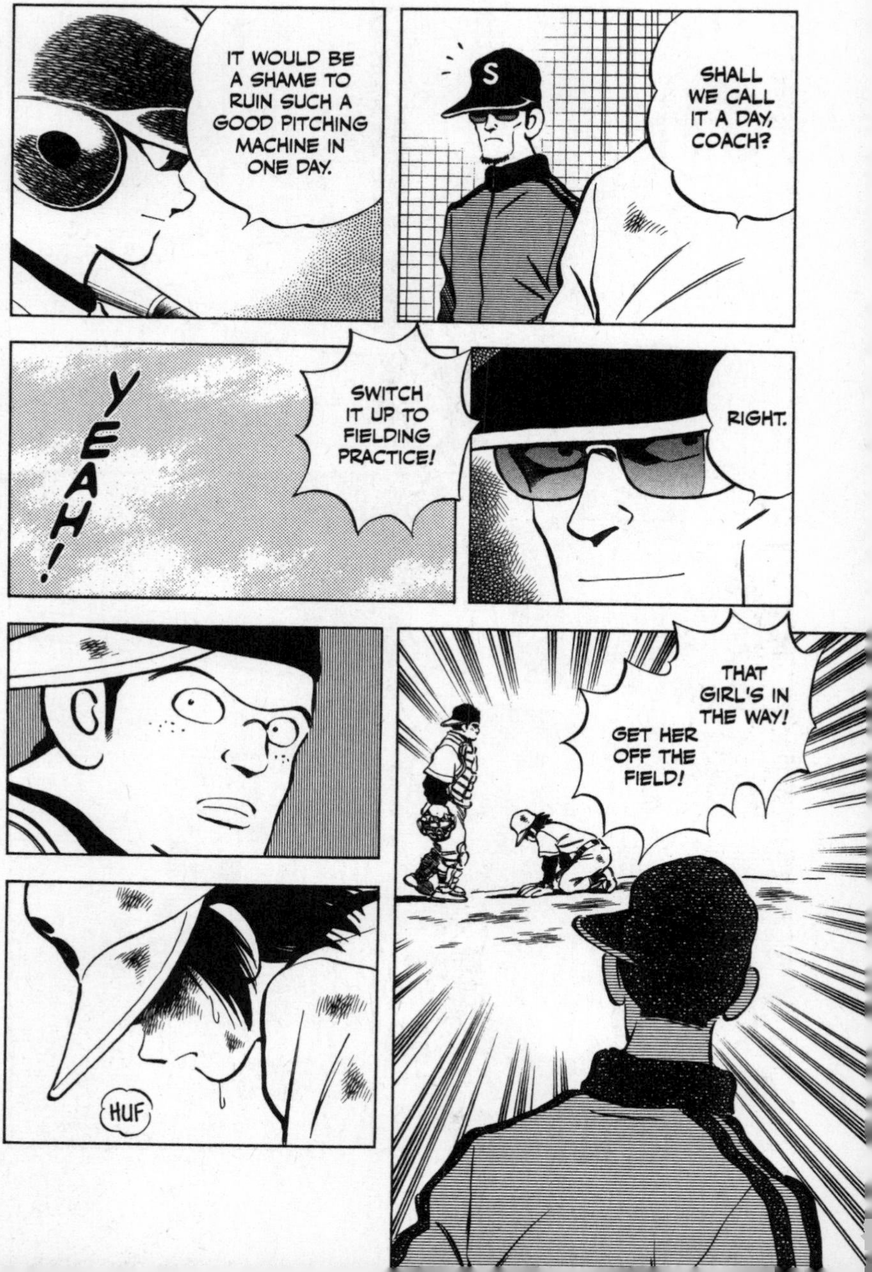
SHALL WE CALL IT A DAY, COACH?
IT WOULD BE A SHAME TO RUIN SUCH A GOOD PITCHING MACHINE IN ONE DAY.
RIGHT.
SWITCH IT UP TO FIELDING PRACTICE!
YEAH!
THAT GIRL'S IN THE WAY!
GET HER OFF THE FIELD!
HUF

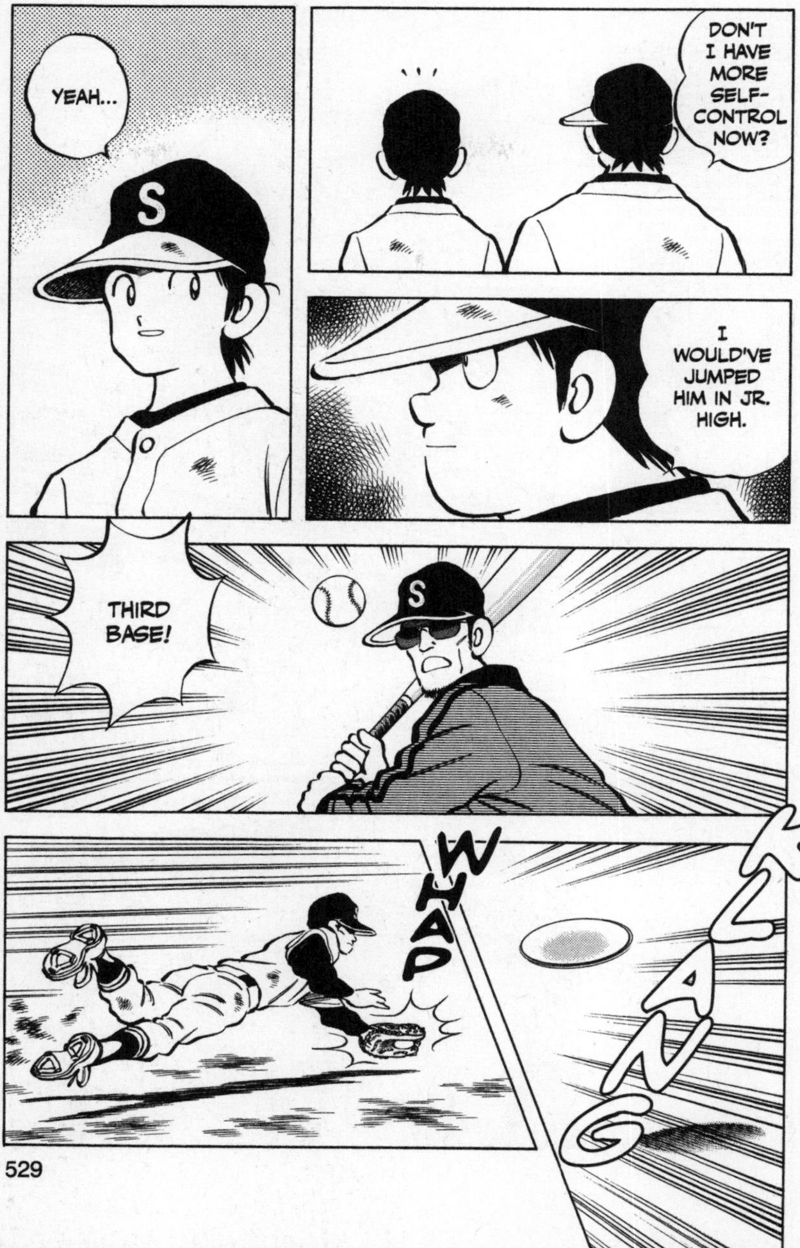
DON'T I HAVE MORE SELF-CONTROL NOW?
I WOULD'VE JUMPED HIM IN JR. HIGH.
YEAH...
THIRD BASE!
KLANG
WHAP

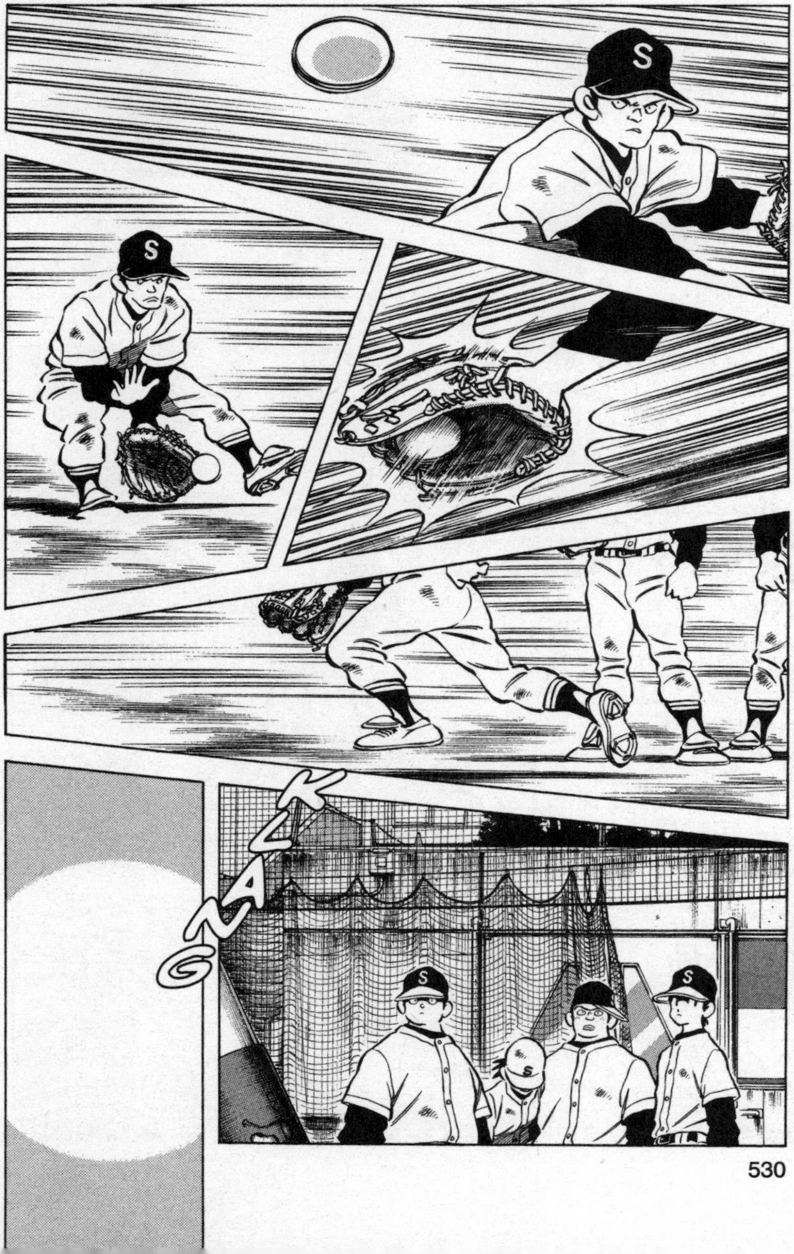
KLANG

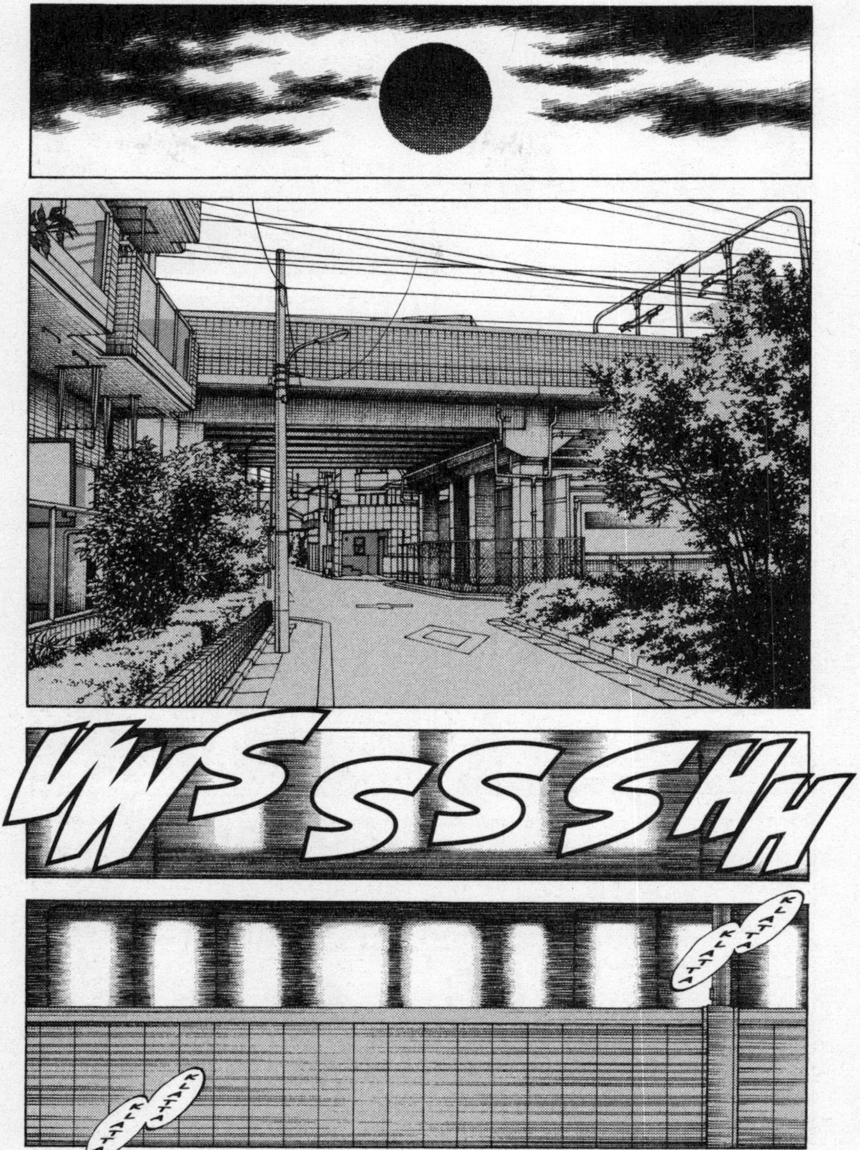
WSSSSH
KLATTA KLATTA
KLATTA KLATTA

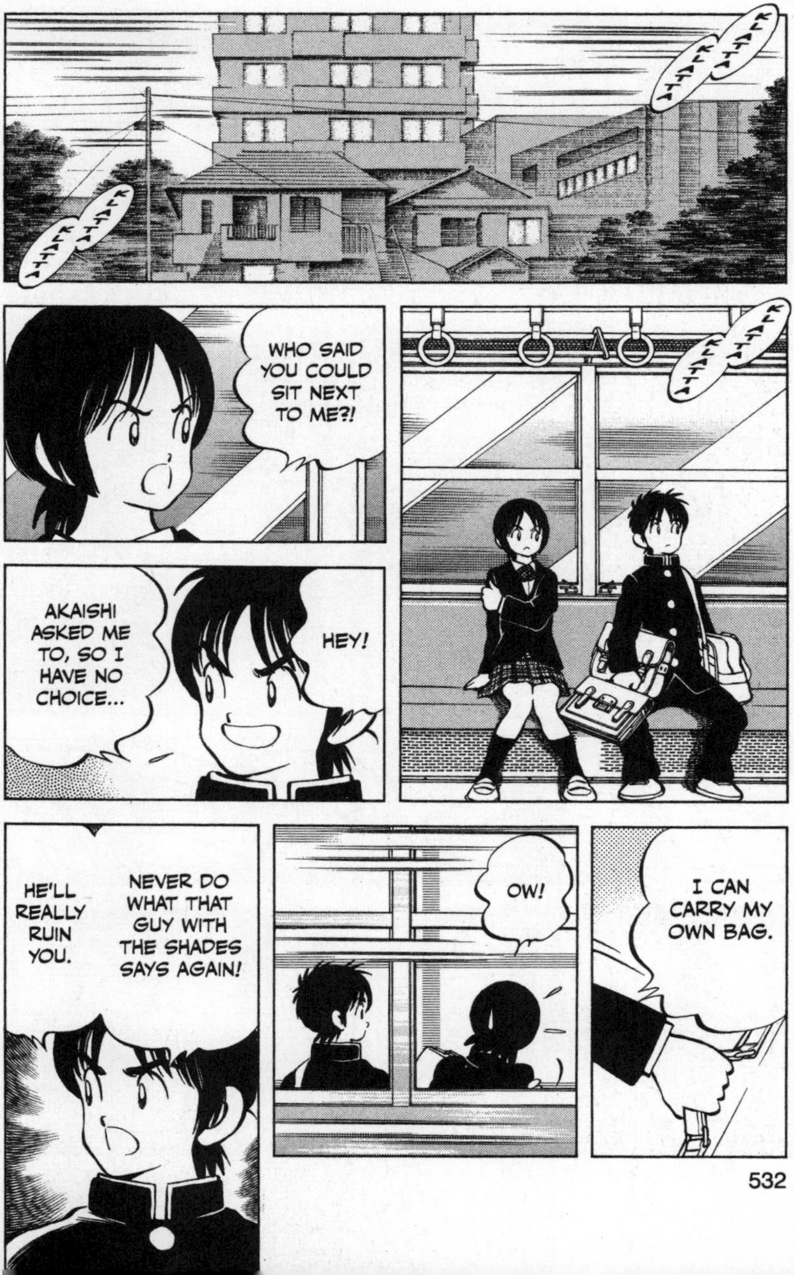
KLATTA KLATTA KLATTA
KLATTA KLATTA KLATTA
KLATTA KLATTA KLATTA
WHO SAID YOU COULD SIT NEXT TO ME?!
HEY!
AKAISHI ASKED ME TO, SO I HAVE NO CHOICE...
I CAN CARRY MY OWN BAG.
OW!
NEVER DO WHAT THAT GUY WITH THE SHADES SAYS AGAIN!
HE'LL REALLY RUIN YOU.

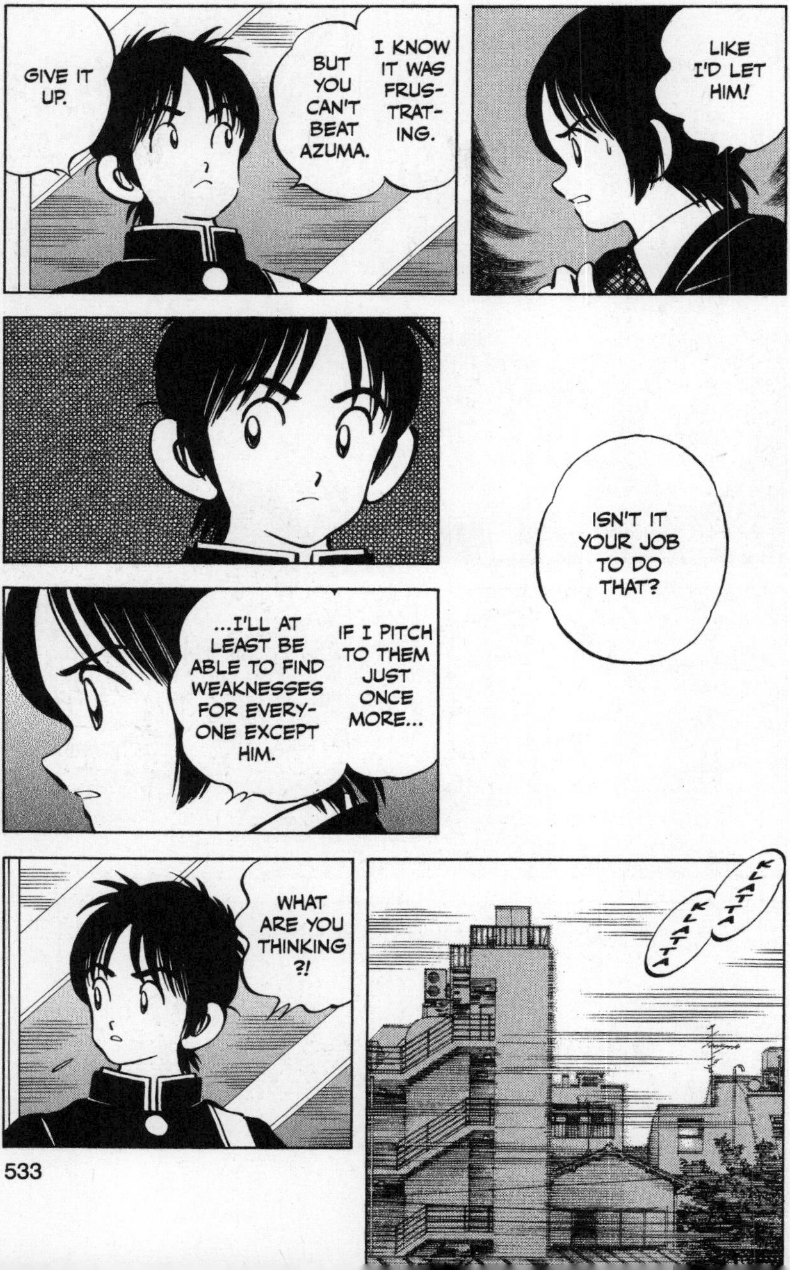
LIKE I'D LET HIM!
I KNOW IT WAS FRUS-TRAT-ING.
BUT YOU CAN'T BEAT AZUMA.
GIVE IT UP.
ISN'T IT YOUR JOB TO DO THAT?
IF I PITCH TO THEM JUST ONCE MORE...
...I'LL AT LEAST BE ABLE TO FIND WEAKNESSES FOR EVERY-ONE EXCEPT HIM.
KLATTA
KLATTA
WHAT ARE YOU THINKING ?!

NOT ONE BIT!

I DON'T HAVE ANY FAITH IN YOU!

IT'S JUST...

WHAT'S WITH YOU?!

MIFUJIDAI STATION, MIFUJIDAI STATION.

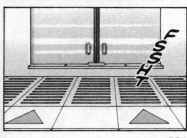

FSSHT

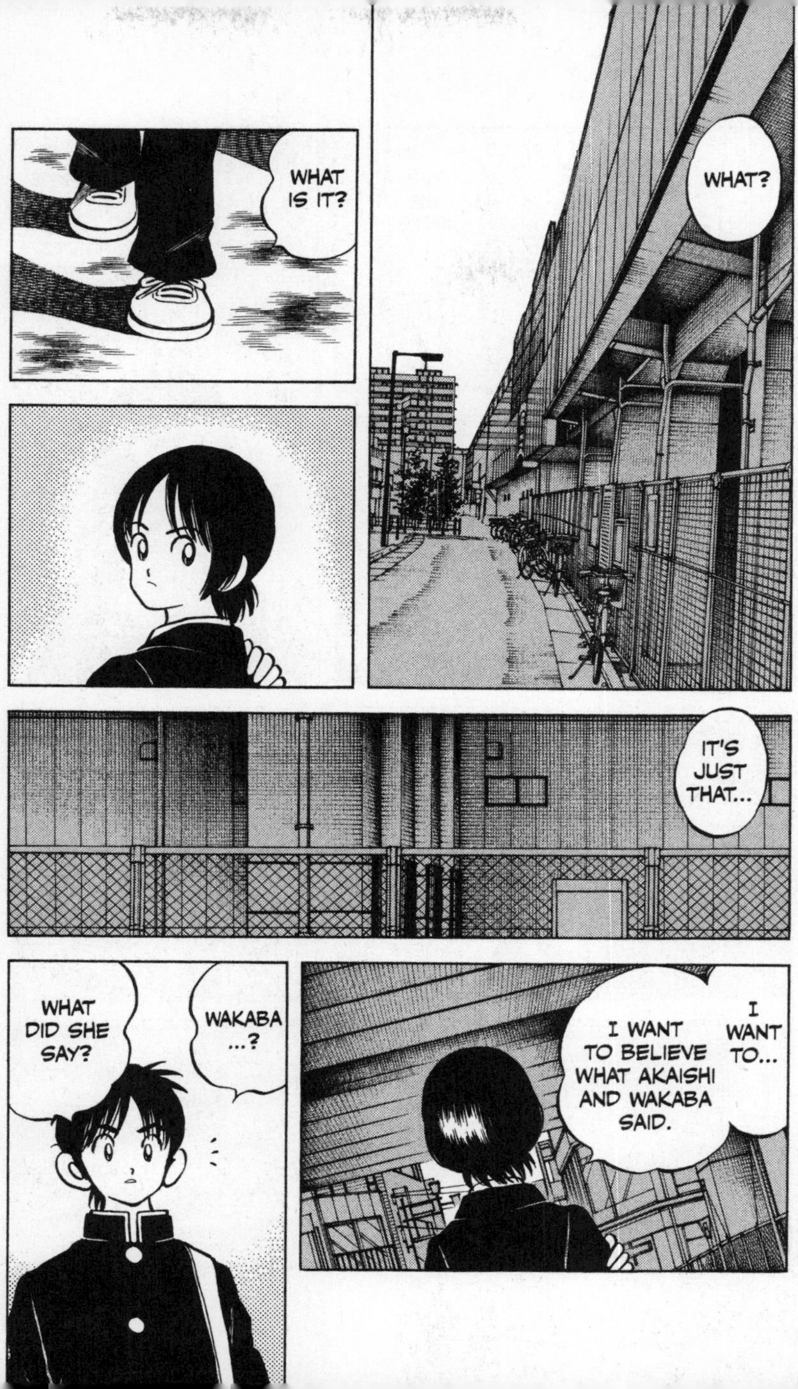
WHAT?
WHAT IS IT?
IT'S JUST THAT...
I WANT TO...
I WANT TO BELIEVE WHAT AKAISHI AND WAKABA SAID.
WAKABA ...?
WHAT DID SHE SAY?

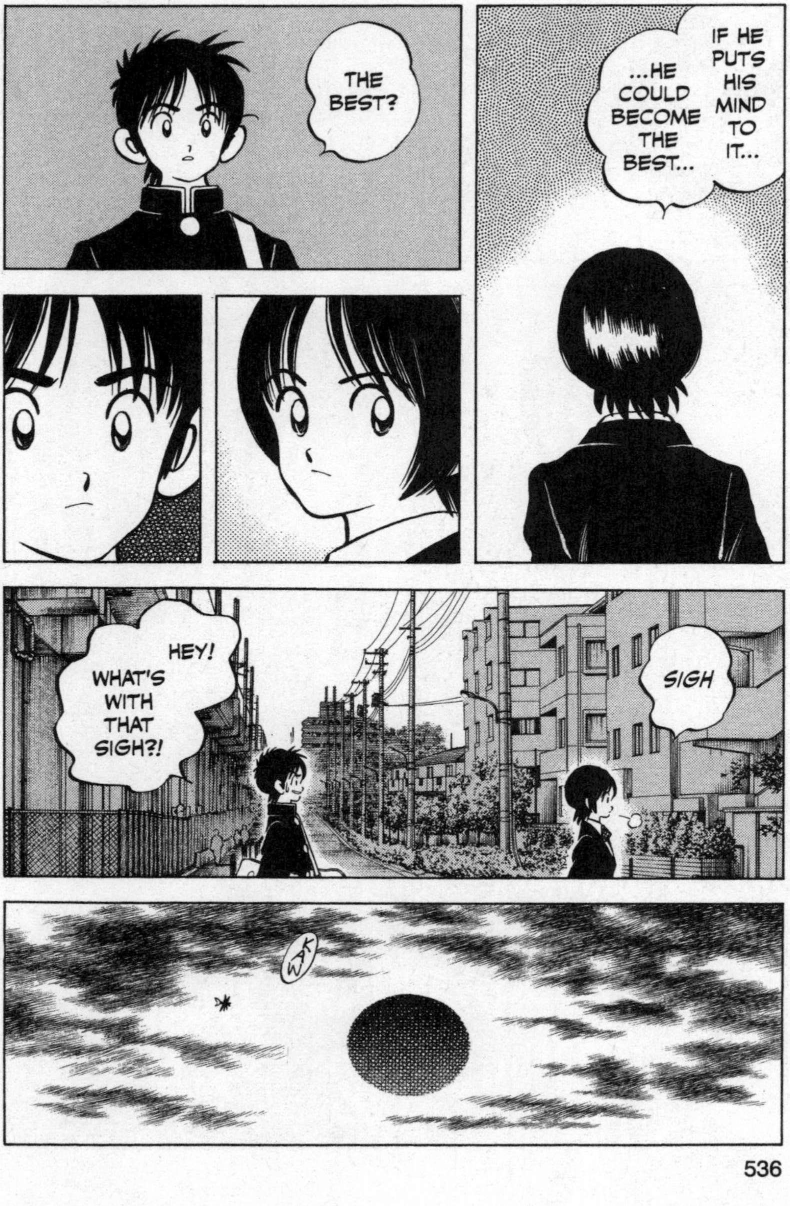
IF HE PUTS HIS MIND TO IT...
...HE COULD BECOME THE BEST...
THE BEST?
SIGH
HEY! WHAT'S WITH THAT SIGH?!
KAW

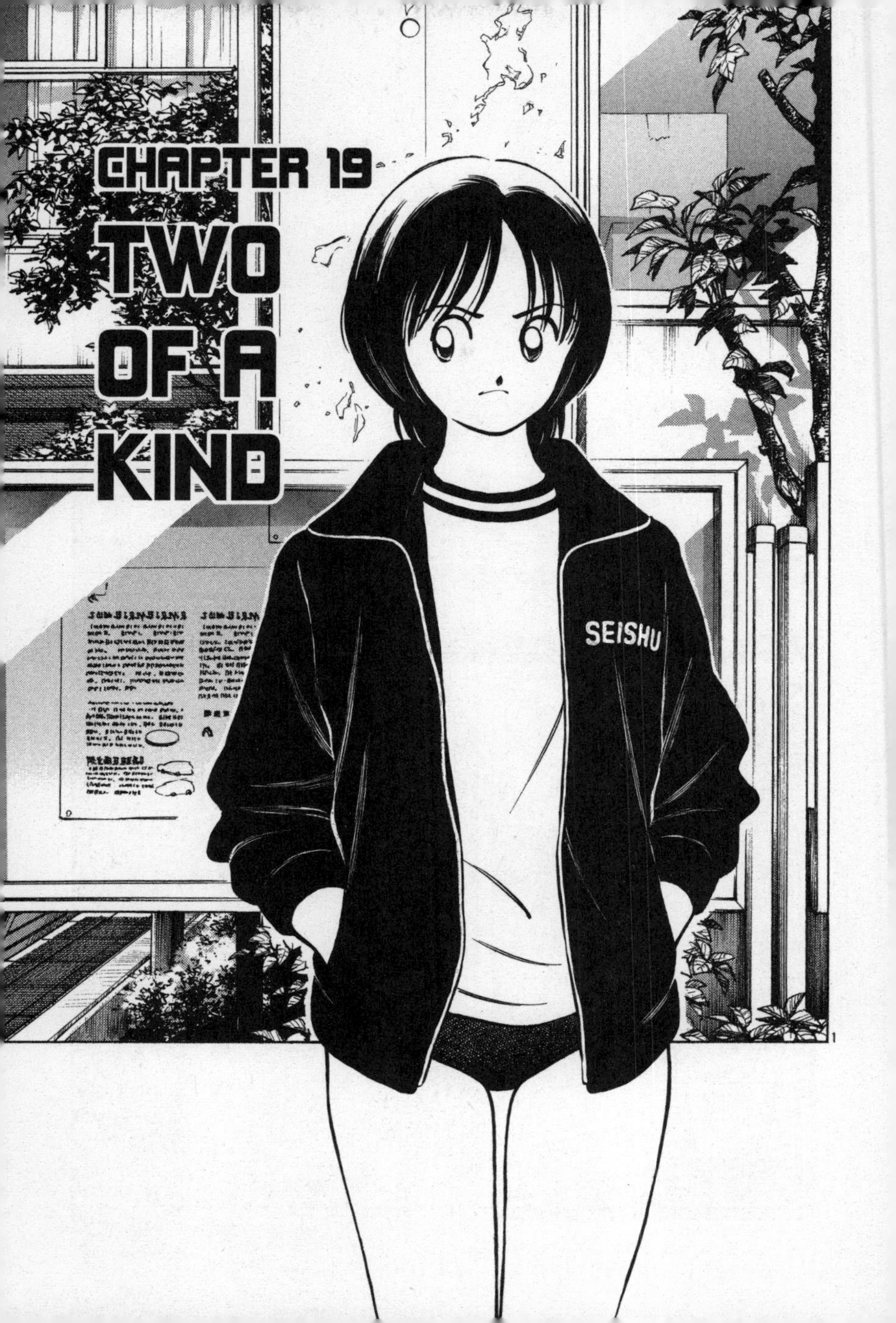
CHAPTER 19
TWO OF A KIND
SEISHU

THE FRAGRANT WIND...

HONNK

サービス工場

THE YOUNG FOLIAGE OF MAY.

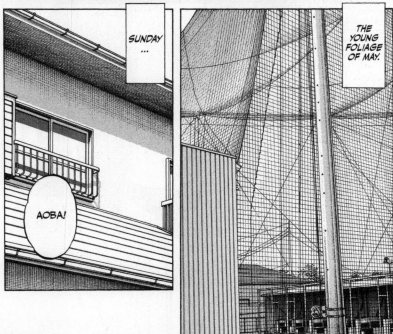

SUNDAY...

AOBA!

IT'S NICE OUT.
LET'S PLAY CATCH!
GIMME A BREAK.
PITCHING PRACTICE DID ME IN.
LEMME SLEEP.
TSK.
TSUKISHIMA BATTING CENTER

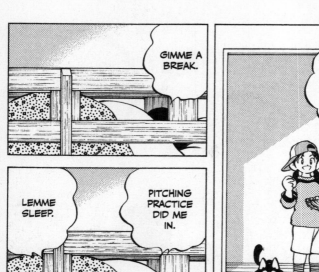

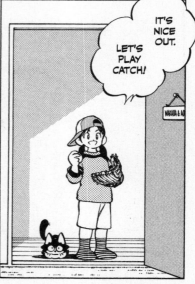

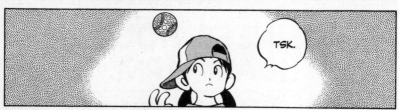

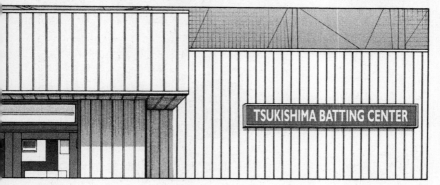

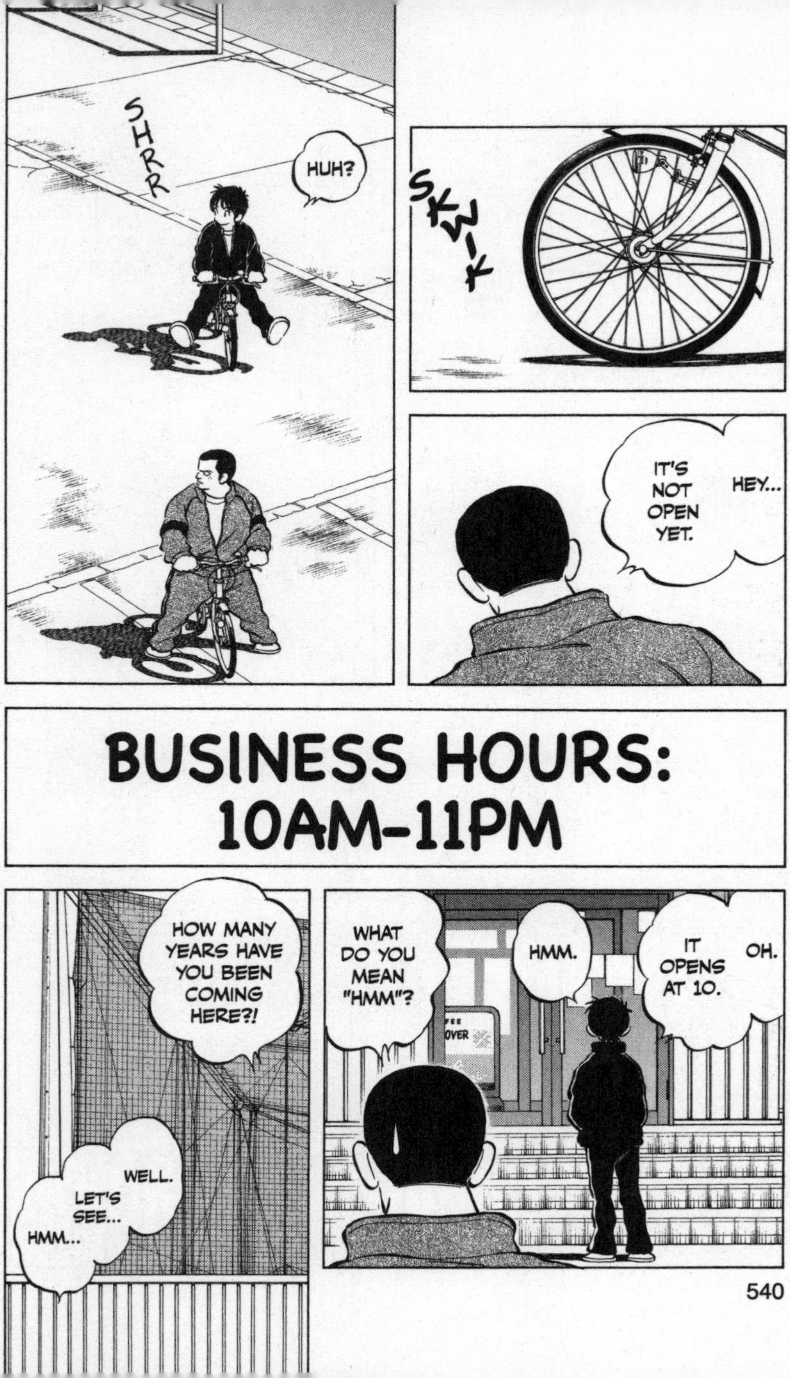
SKWIK
HEY... IT'S NOT OPEN YET.
SHRR
HUH?
BUSINESS HOURS: 10AM-11PM
OH. IT OPENS AT 10.
HMM.
WHAT DO YOU MEAN "HMM"?
HOW MANY YEARS HAVE YOU BEEN COMING HERE?!
WELL. LET'S SEE... HMM...

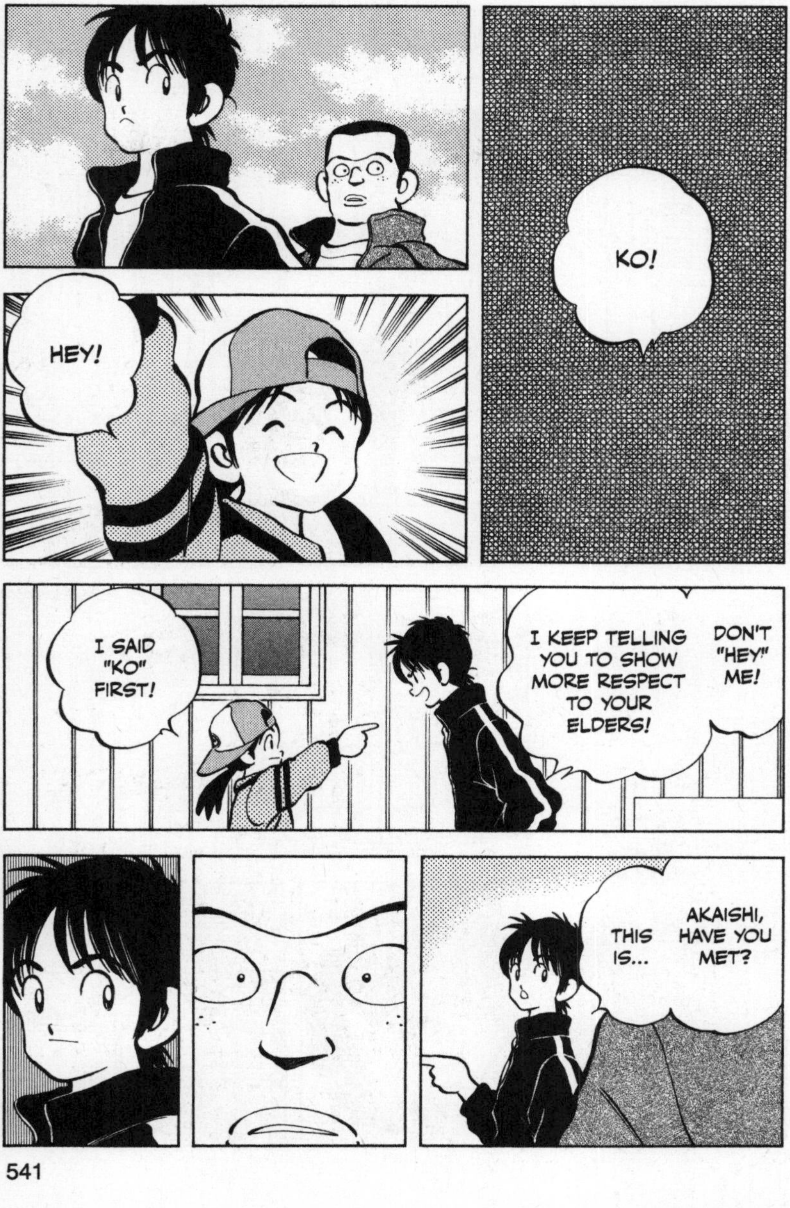
KO!
HEY!
DON'T "HEY" ME!
I KEEP TELLING YOU TO SHOW MORE RESPECT TO YOUR ELDERS!
I SAID "KO" FIRST!
AKAISHI, HAVE YOU MET?
THIS IS...

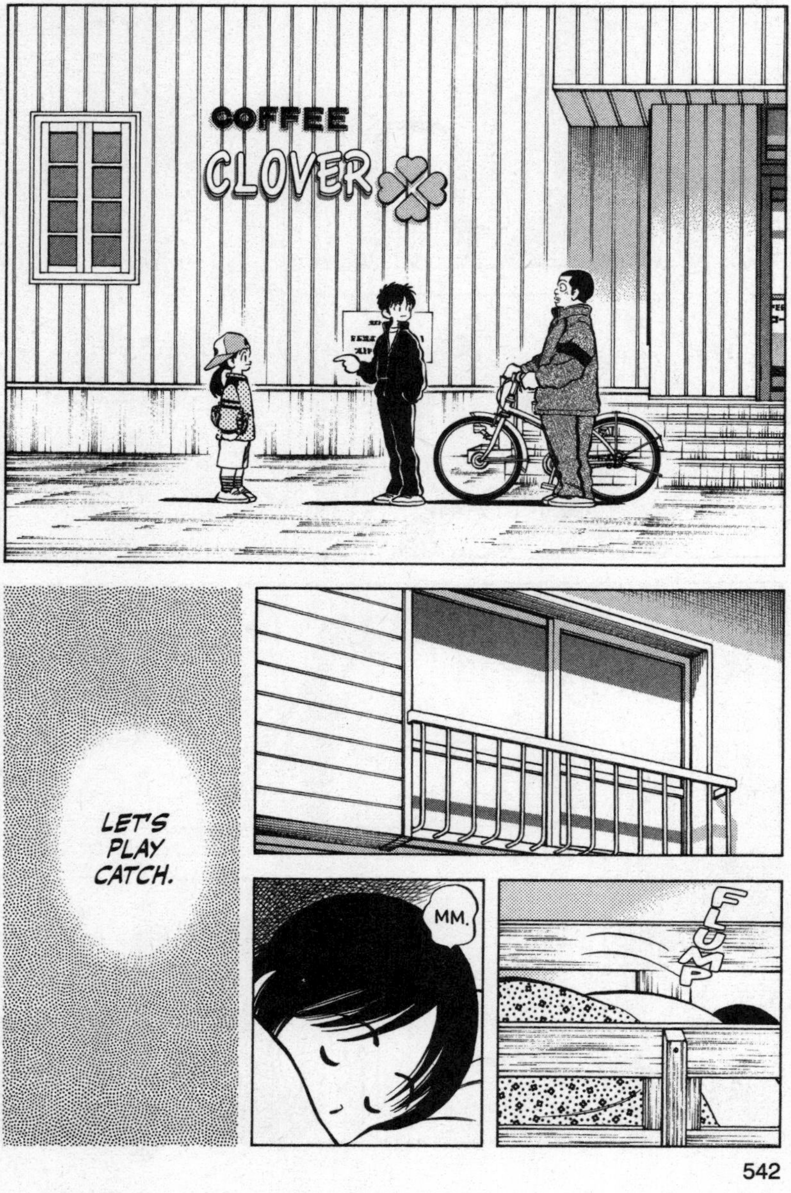
COFFEE
CLOVER
FLUMP
MM.
LET'S PLAY CATCH.

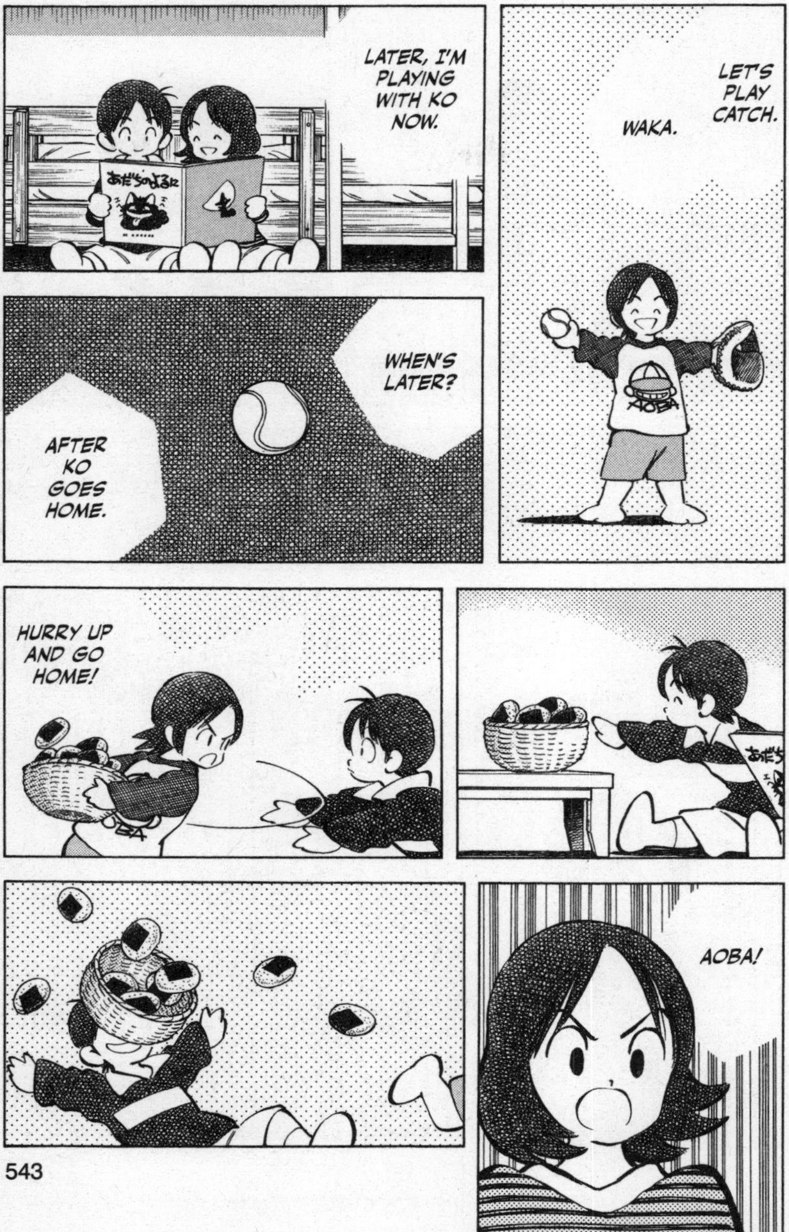
LET'S PLAY CATCH.
WAKA.
LATER, I'M PLAYING WITH KO NOW.
WHEN'S LATER?
AFTER KO GOES HOME.
HURRY UP AND GO HOME!
AOBA!

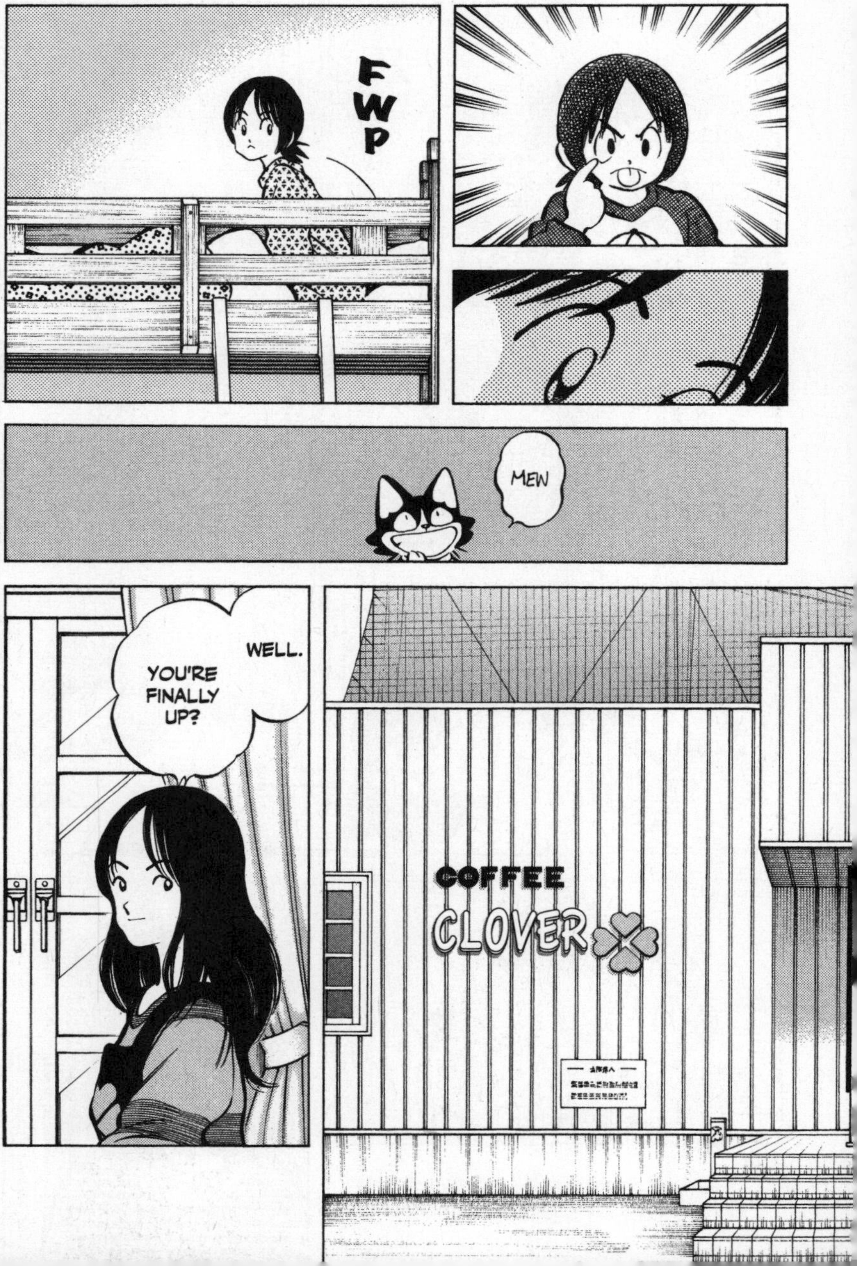
FWP
MEW
COFFEE
CLOVER
WELL.
YOU'RE FINALLY UP?

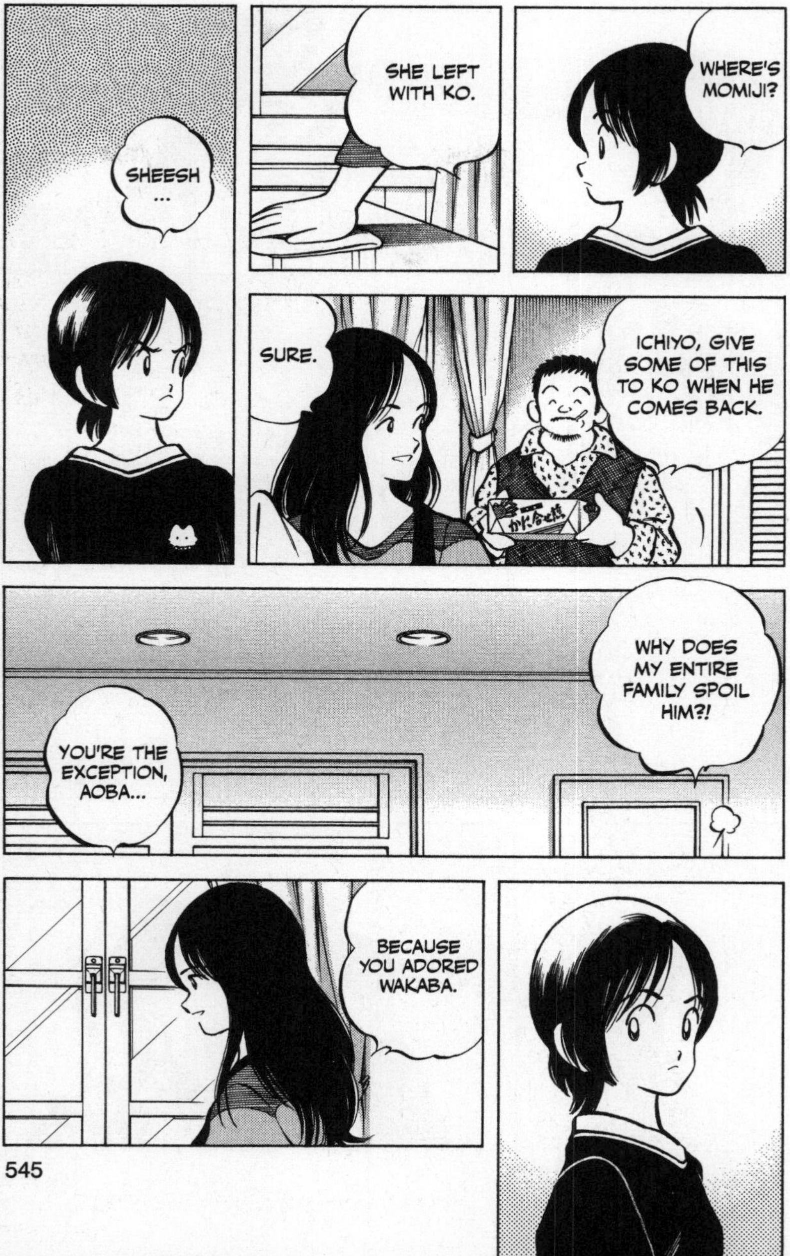
WHERE'S MOMIJI?
SHE LEFT WITH KO.
ICHIYO, GIVE SOME OF THIS TO KO WHEN HE COMES BACK.
SURE.
SHEESH ...
WHY DOES MY ENTIRE FAMILY SPOIL HIM?!
YOU'RE THE EXCEPTION, AOBA...
BECAUSE YOU ADORED WAKABA.

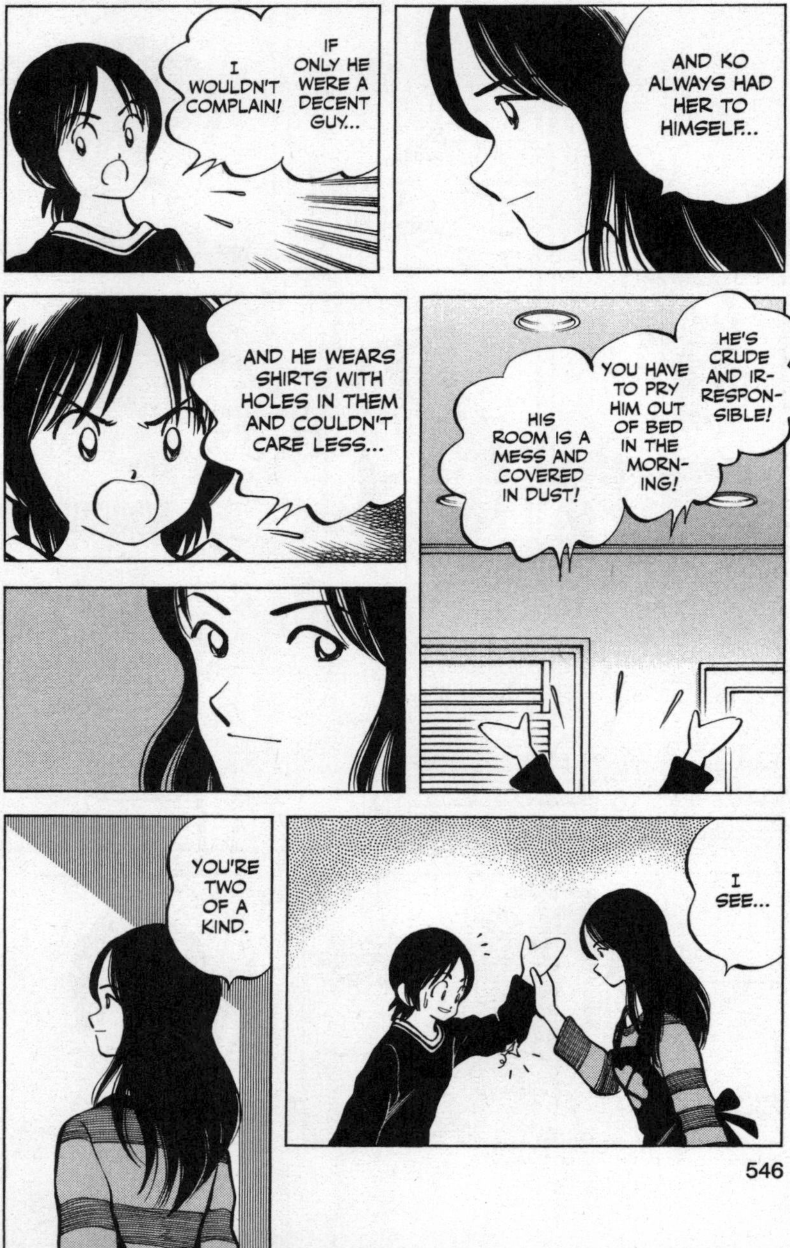
AND KO ALWAYS HAD HER TO HIMSELF...
IF ONLY HE WERE A DECENT GUY...
I WOULDN'T COMPLAIN!
HE'S CRUDE AND IR-RESPON-SIBLE!
YOU HAVE TO PRY HIM OUT OF BED IN THE MORN-ING!
HIS ROOM IS A MESS AND COVERED IN DUST!
AND HE WEARS SHIRTS WITH HOLES IN THEM AND COULDN'T CARE LESS...
I SEE...
YOU'RE TWO OF A KIND.

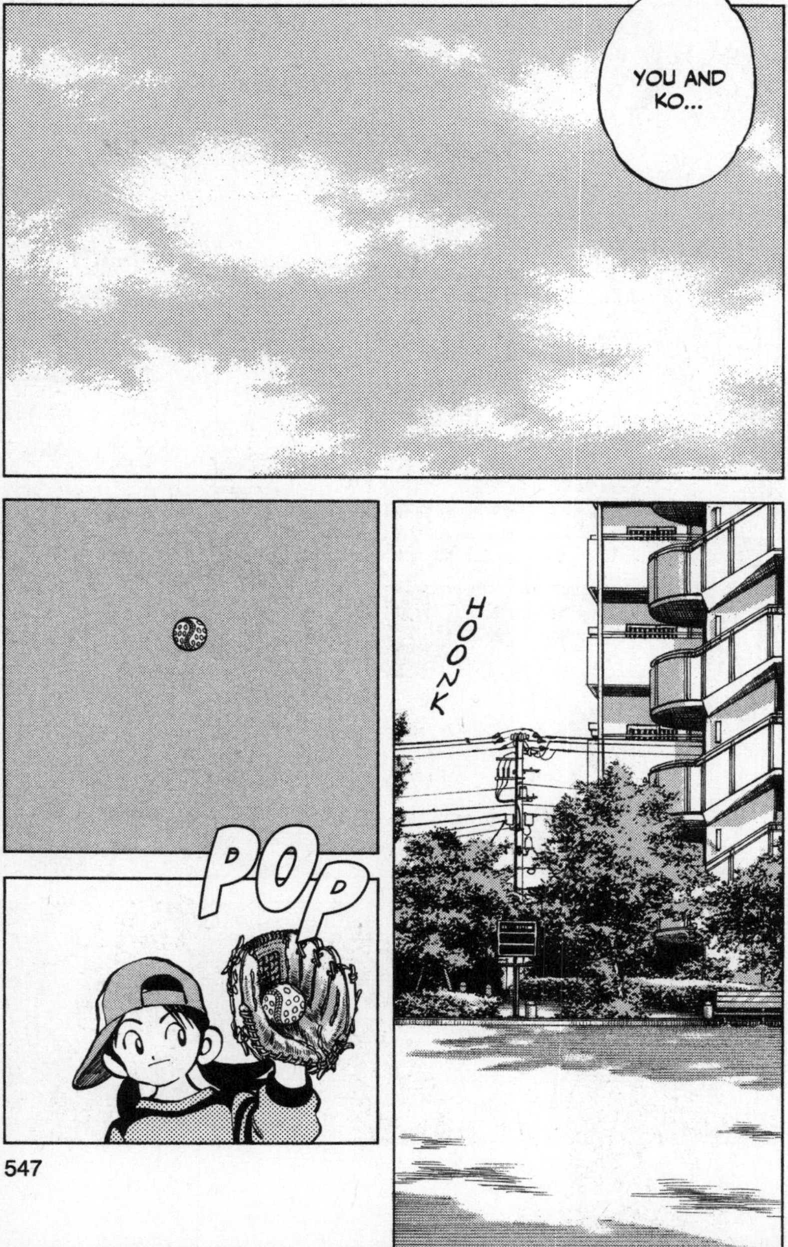
YOU AND KO...
HOONK
POP

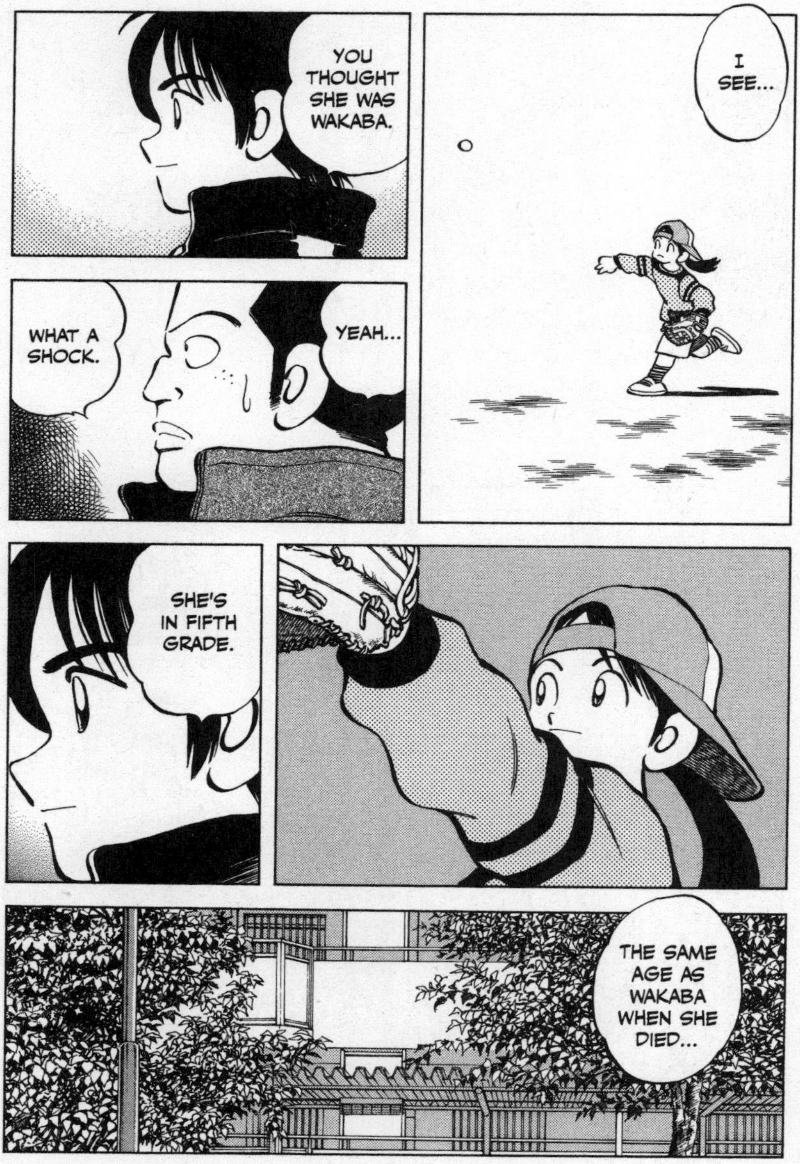
I SEE...
YOU THOUGHT SHE WAS WAKABA.
YEAH...
WHAT A SHOCK.
SHE'S IN FIFTH GRADE.
THE SAME AGE AS WAKABA WHEN SHE DIED...

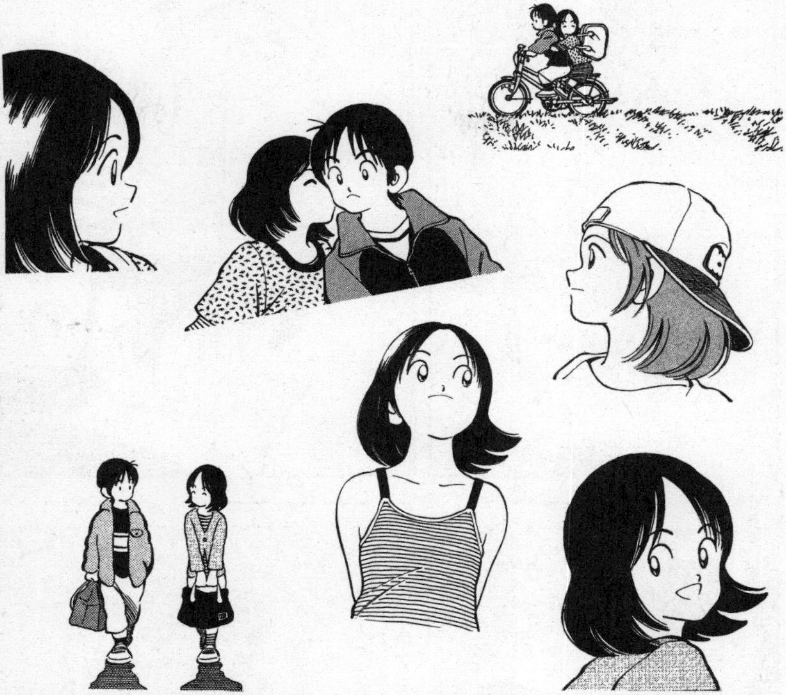

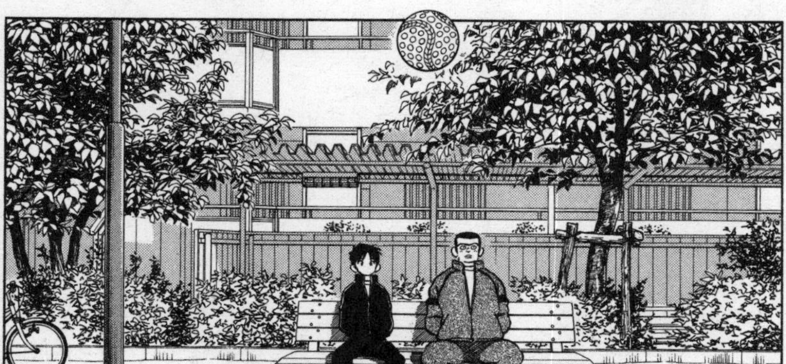

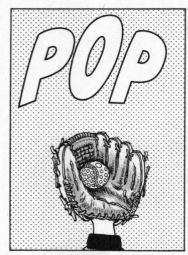

...SO YOUNG... SHE WAS...

YEAH...

SURE.

I'M HUNGRY. LET'S GO HOME. KO!

THANKS, MISTER!

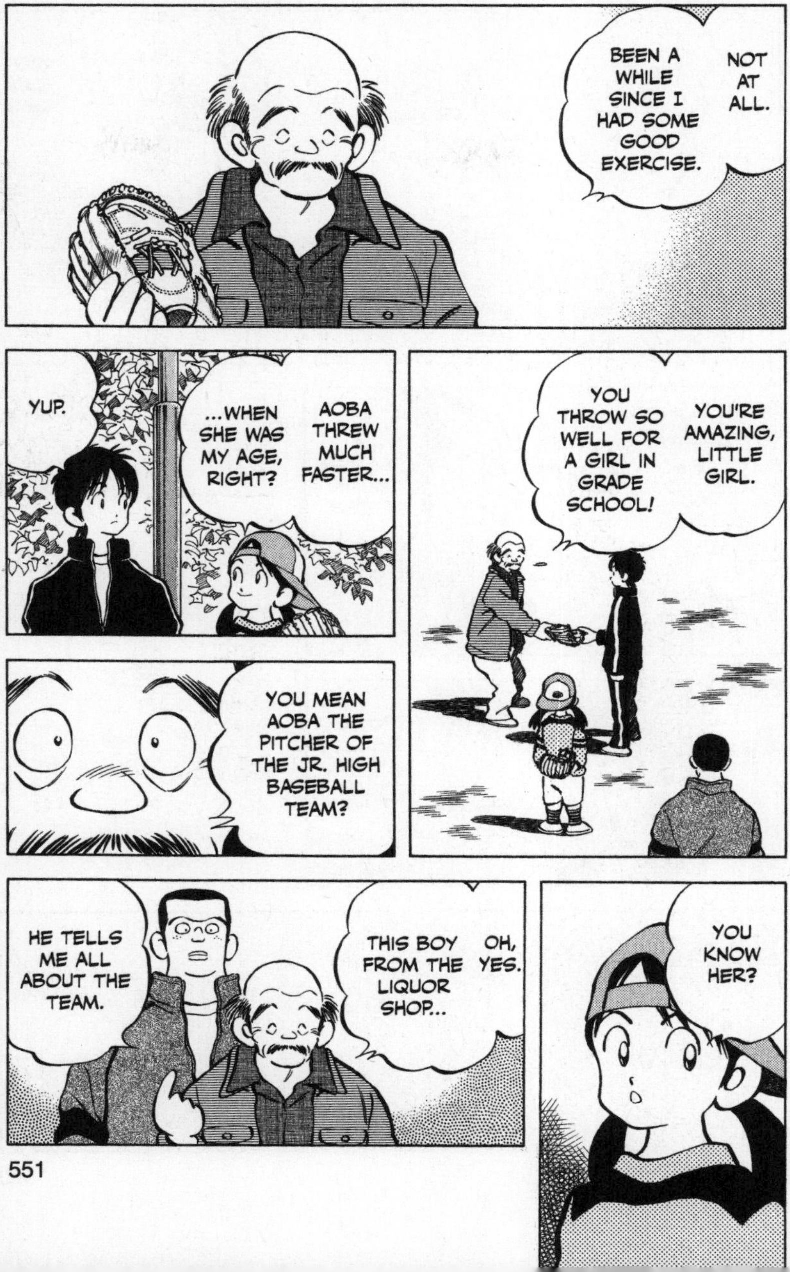
NOT AT ALL.
BEEN A WHILE SINCE I HAD SOME GOOD EXERCISE.
YOU'RE AMAZING, LITTLE GIRL.
YOU THROW SO WELL FOR A GIRL IN GRADE SCHOOL!
AOBA THREW MUCH FASTER...
...WHEN SHE WAS MY AGE, RIGHT?
YUP.
YOU MEAN AOBA THE PITCHER OF THE JR. HIGH BASEBALL TEAM?
YOU KNOW HER?
OH, YES.
THIS BOY FROM THE LIQUOR SHOP...
HE TELLS ME ALL ABOUT THE TEAM.

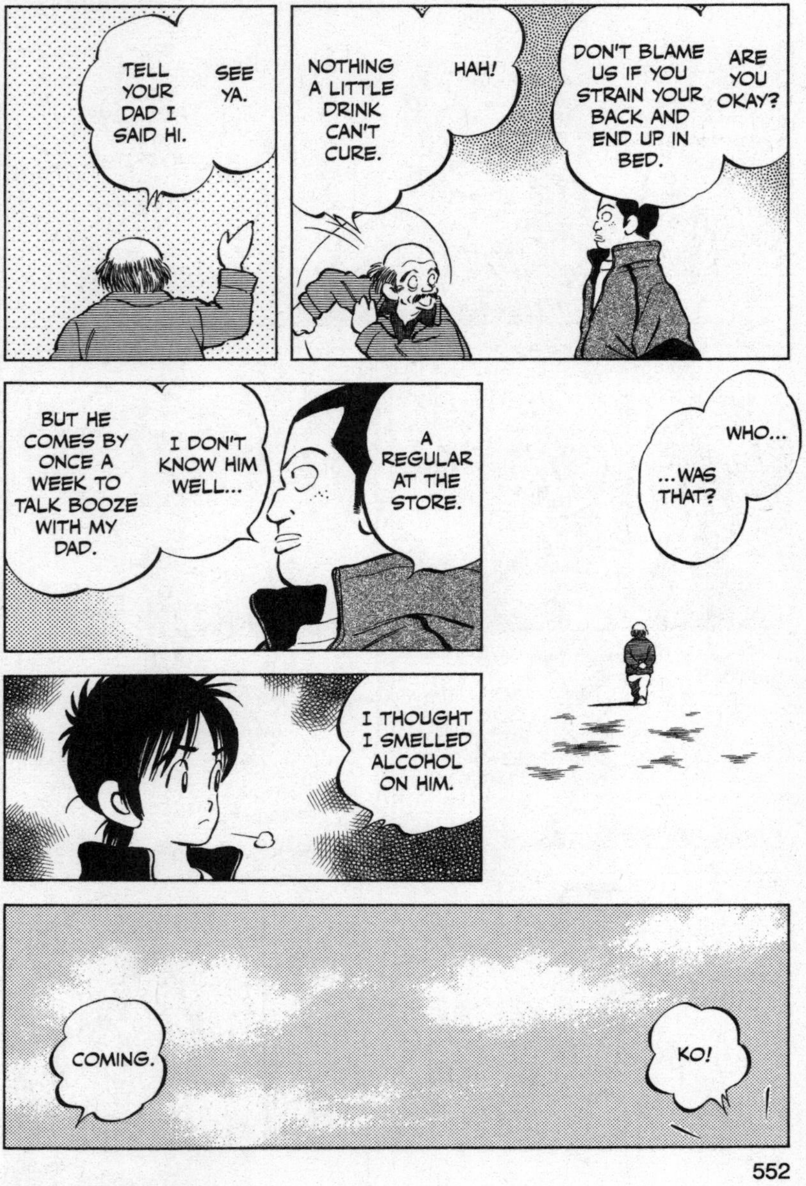
ARE YOU OKAY?
DON'T BLAME US IF YOU STRAIN YOUR BACK AND END UP IN BED.
HAH!
NOTHING A LITTLE DRINK CAN'T CURE.
SEE YA.
TELL YOUR DAD I SAID HI.
WHO...
...WAS THAT?
A REGULAR AT THE STORE.
I DON'T KNOW HIM WELL...
BUT HE COMES BY ONCE A WEEK TO TALK BOOZE WITH MY DAD.
I THOUGHT I SMELLED ALCOHOL ON HIM.
KO!
COMING.

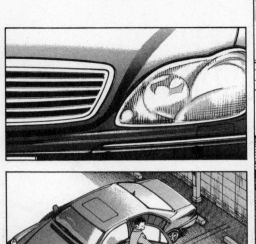

年中無休 **24**時間営業

← **P**

SKNIK

SLAM

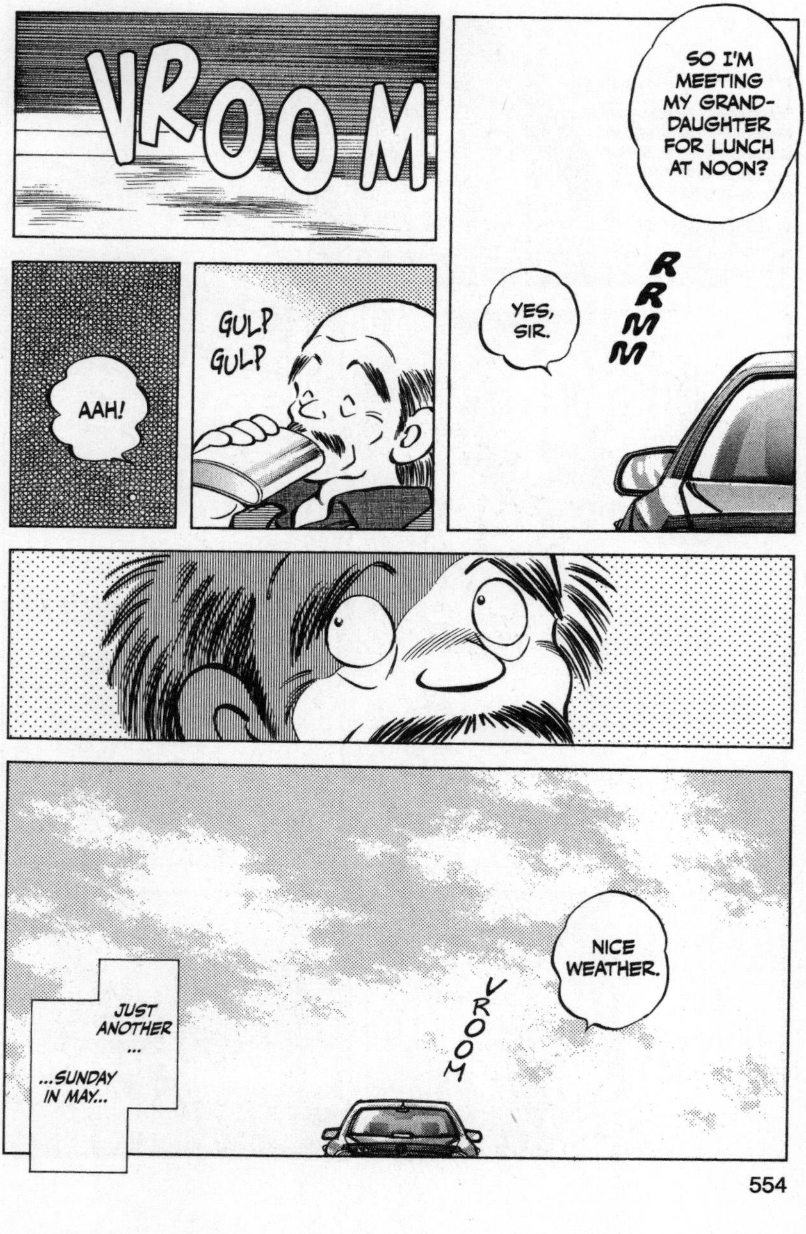
SO I'M MEETING MY GRAND-DAUGHTER FOR LUNCH AT NOON?
YES, SIR.
RRMM
VROOM
GULP GULP
AAH!
NICE WEATHER.
VROOM
JUST ANOTHER ...
...SUNDAY IN MAY...

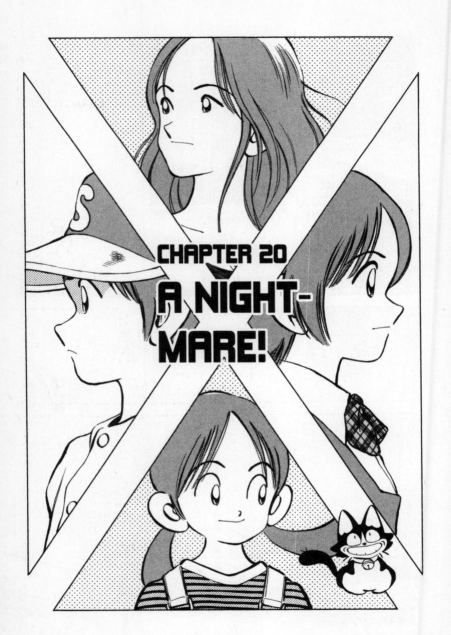

CHAPTER 20
A NIGHT-MARE!

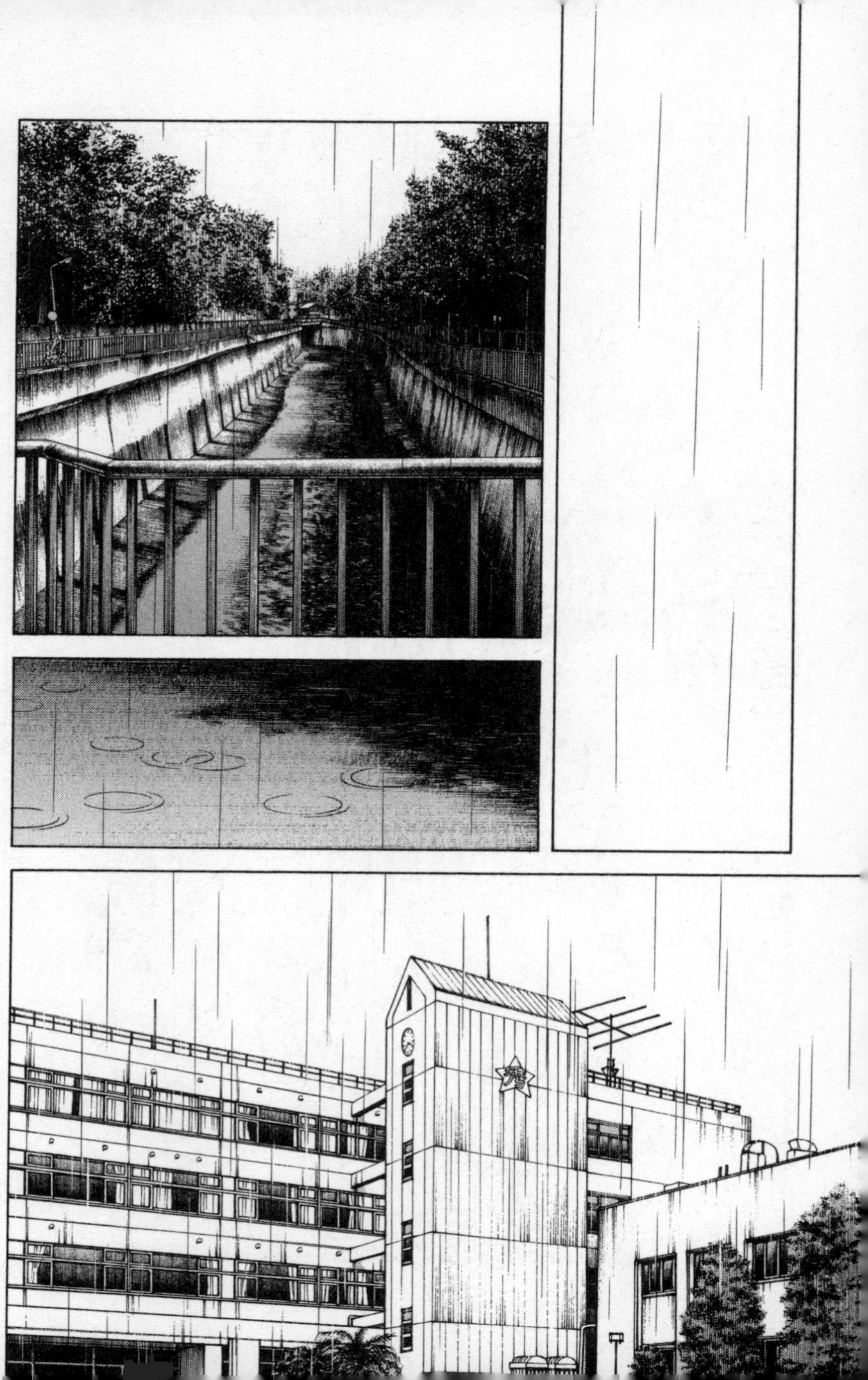

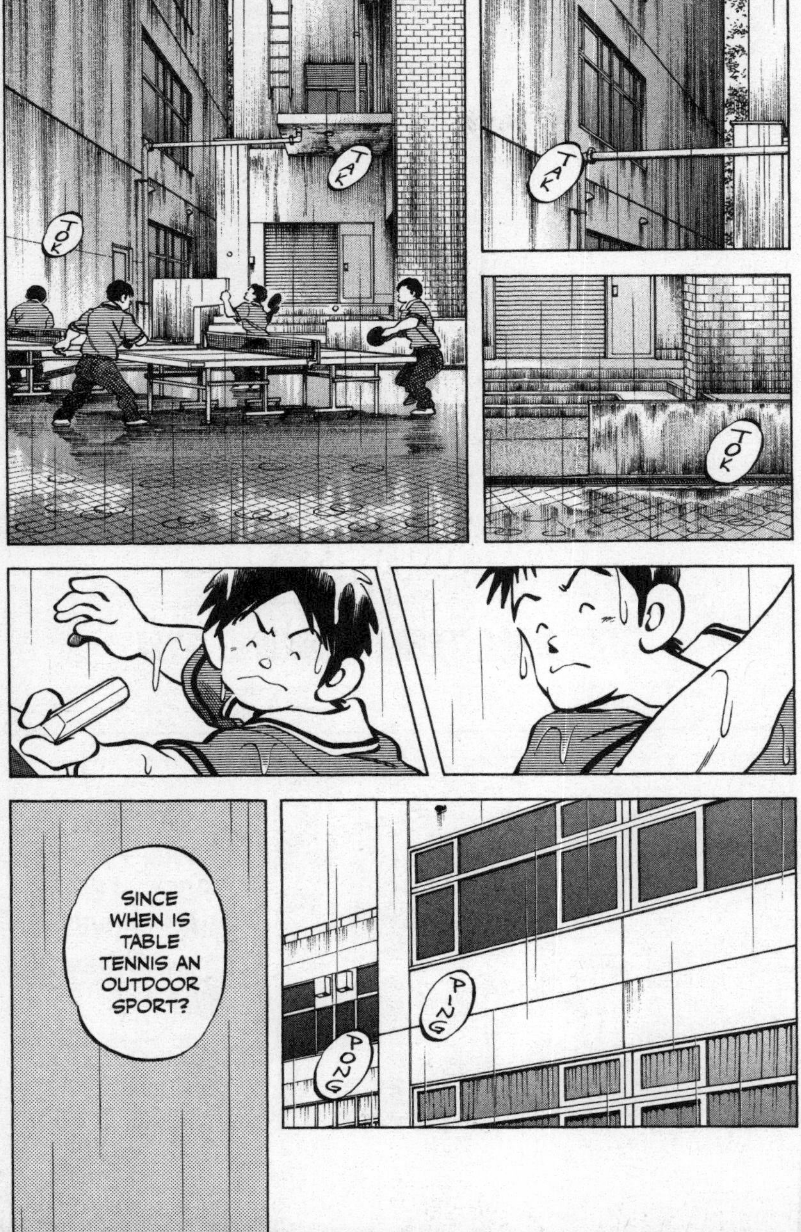
TAK
TOK
TAK
TOK
PING
PONG
SINCE WHEN IS TABLE TENNIS AN OUTDOOR SPORT?

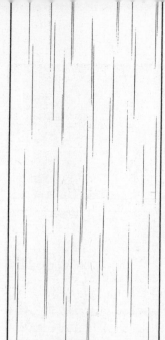

WHAT DO YOU THINK?

THE MINUTE THE INTERIM PRINCIPAL SAYS SO.

BASEBALL TEAM TRAINING GYM

NOTICE: THE PING PONG TEAM HAS MOVED.

GYM

JR. HIGH BUILDING

← HERE

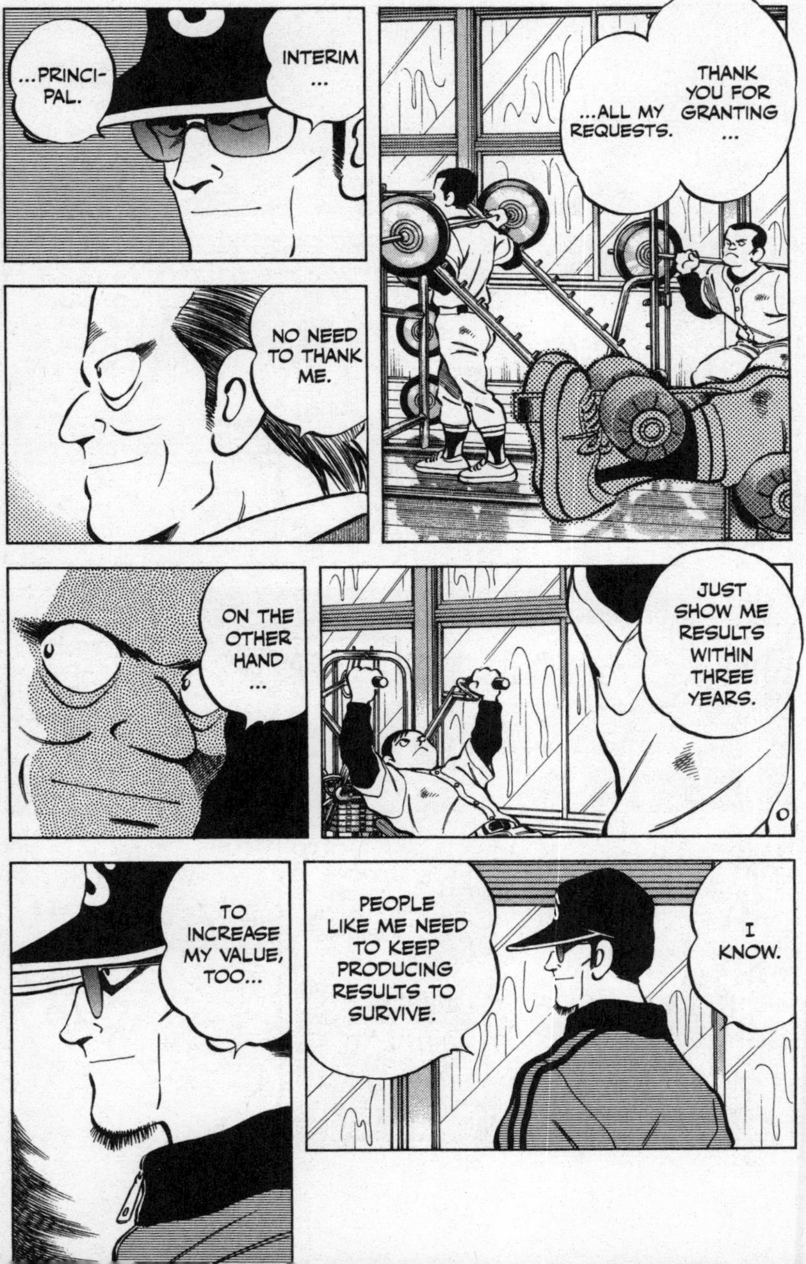
THANK YOU FOR GRANTING ...
...ALL MY REQUESTS.
INTERIM ...
...PRINCI-PAL.
NO NEED TO THANK ME.
JUST SHOW ME RESULTS WITHIN THREE YEARS.
ON THE OTHER HAND ...
I KNOW.
PEOPLE LIKE ME NEED TO KEEP PRODUCING RESULTS TO SURVIVE.
TO INCREASE MY VALUE, TOO...

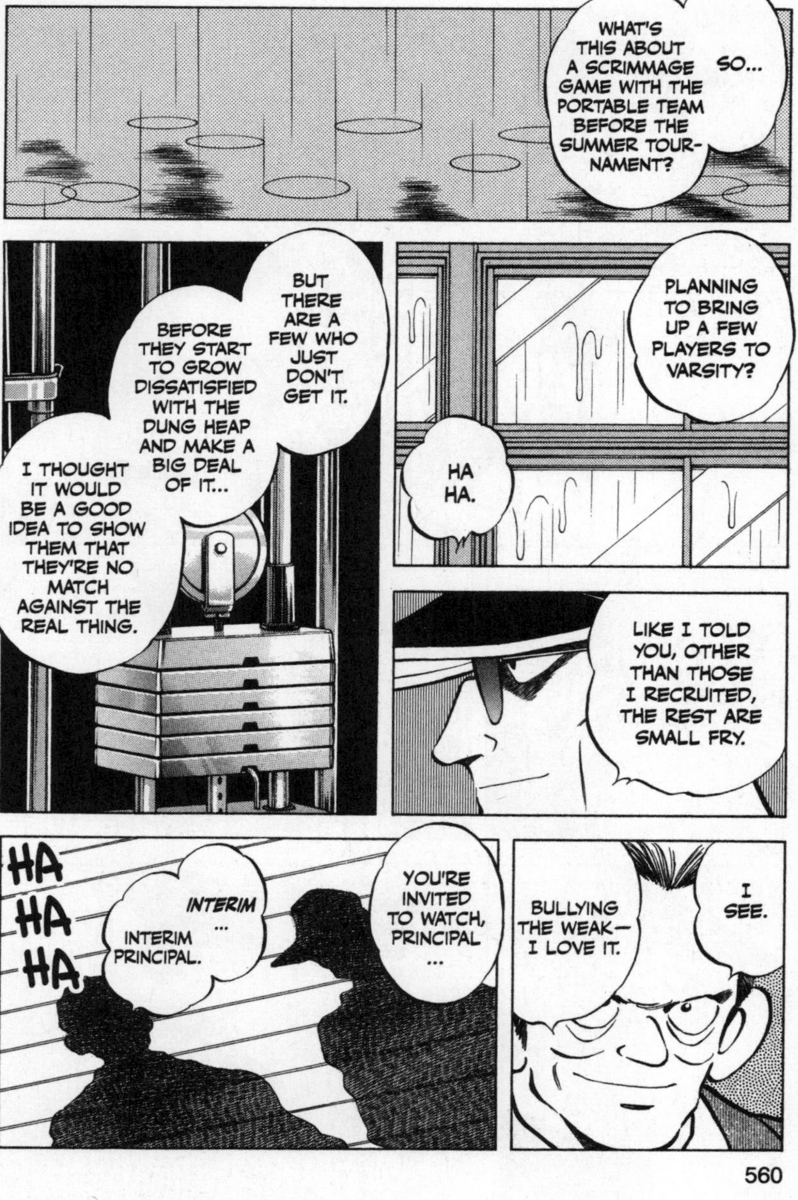
SO...
WHAT'S THIS ABOUT A SCRIMMAGE GAME WITH THE PORTABLE TEAM BEFORE THE SUMMER TOURNAMENT?
PLANNING TO BRING UP A FEW PLAYERS TO VARSITY?
HA HA.
LIKE I TOLD YOU, OTHER THAN THOSE I RECRUITED, THE REST ARE SMALL FRY.
BUT THERE ARE A FEW WHO JUST DON'T GET IT.
BEFORE THEY START TO GROW DISSATISFIED WITH THE DUNG HEAP AND MAKE A BIG DEAL OF IT...
I THOUGHT IT WOULD BE A GOOD IDEA TO SHOW THEM THAT THEY'RE NO MATCH AGAINST THE REAL THING.
I SEE.
BULLYING THE WEAK— I LOVE IT.
YOU'RE INVITED TO WATCH, PRINCIPAL ...
INTERIM ...
INTERIM PRINCIPAL.
HA HA HA

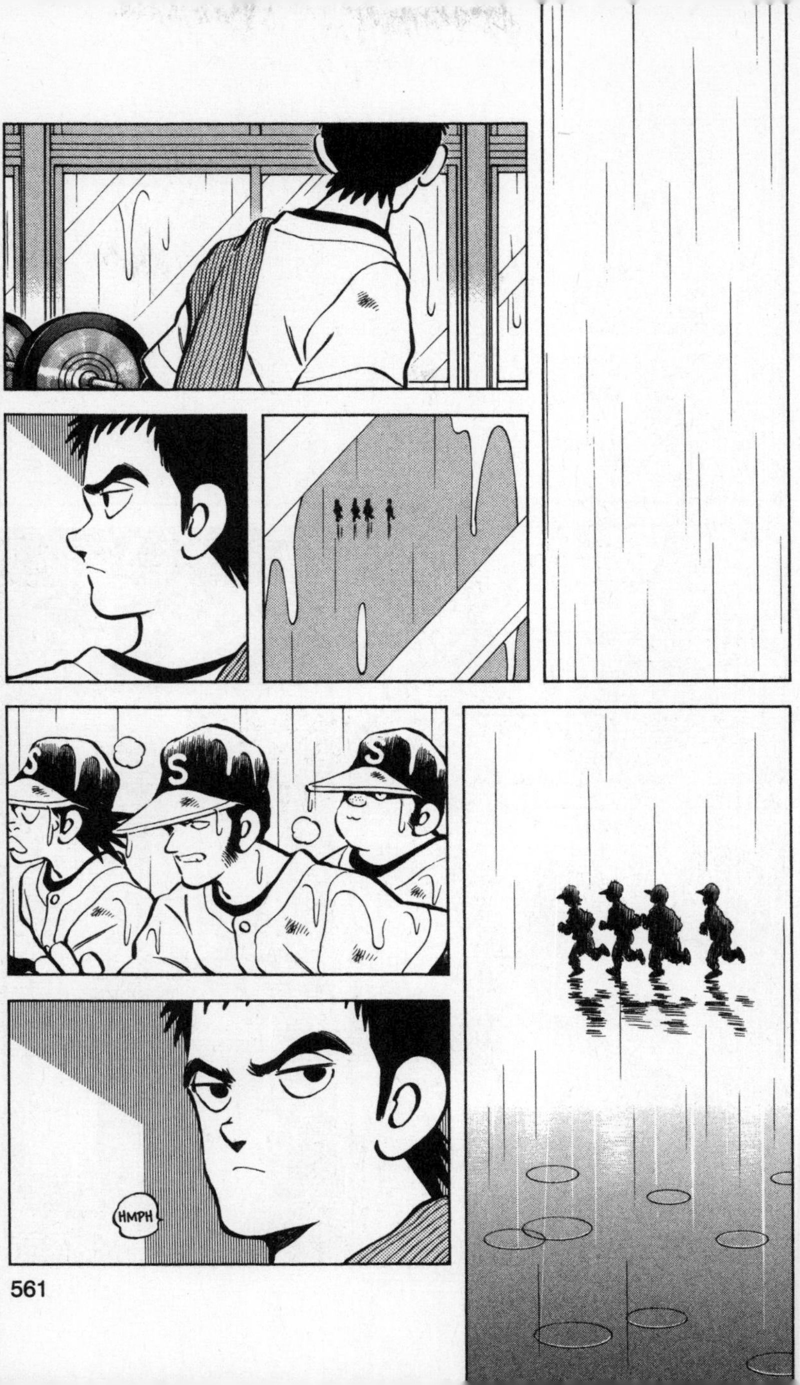
HMPH

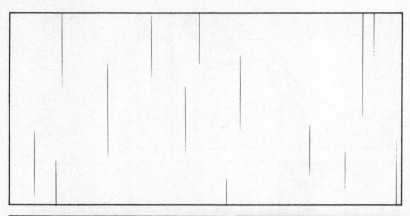

THE THIRD YEARS WENT OUT IN THIS RAIN.

THE FARM

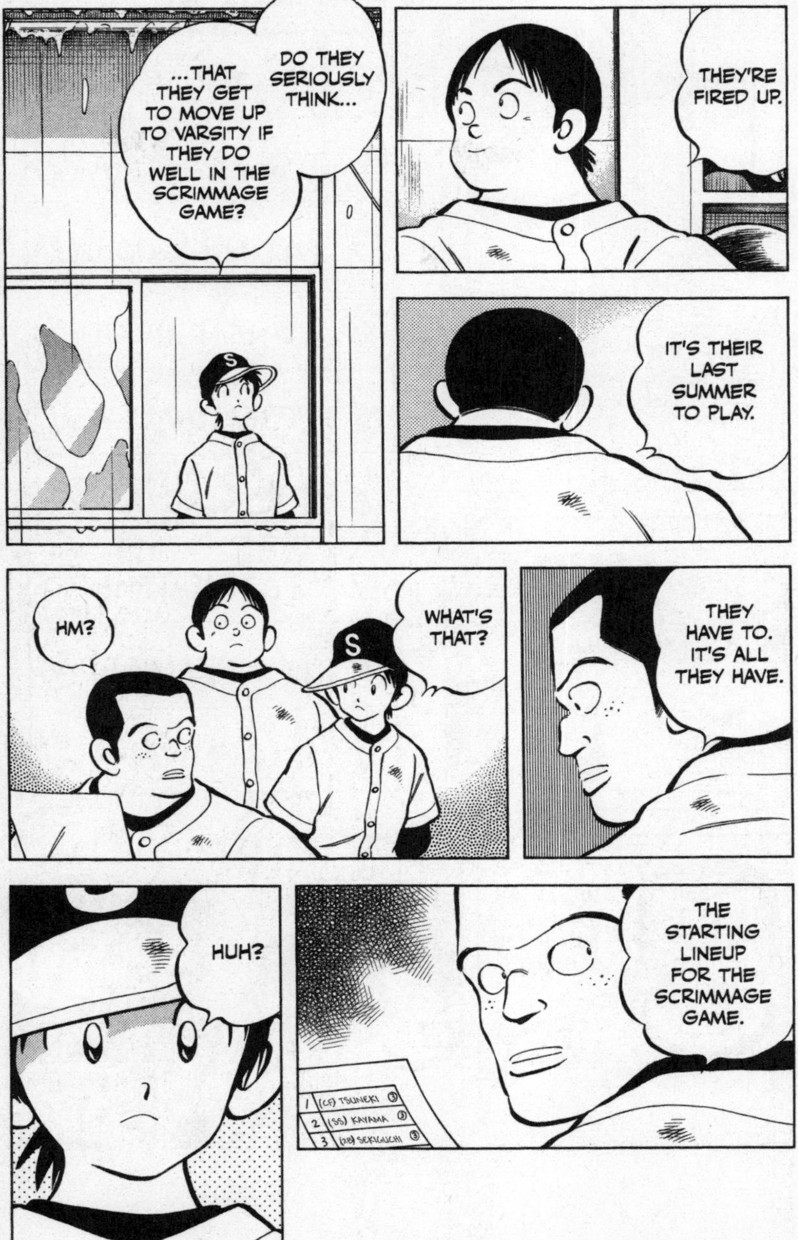
THEY'RE FIRED UP.
IT'S THEIR LAST SUMMER TO PLAY.
DO THEY SERIOUSLY THINK...
...THAT THEY GET TO MOVE UP TO VARSITY IF THEY DO WELL IN THE SCRIMMAGE GAME?
THEY HAVE TO. IT'S ALL THEY HAVE.
WHAT'S THAT?
HM?
THE STARTING LINEUP FOR THE SCRIMMAGE GAME.
1 (CF) TSUNEKI ③
2 (SS) KAYAMA ③
3 (2B) SEKIGUCHI ③
HUH?

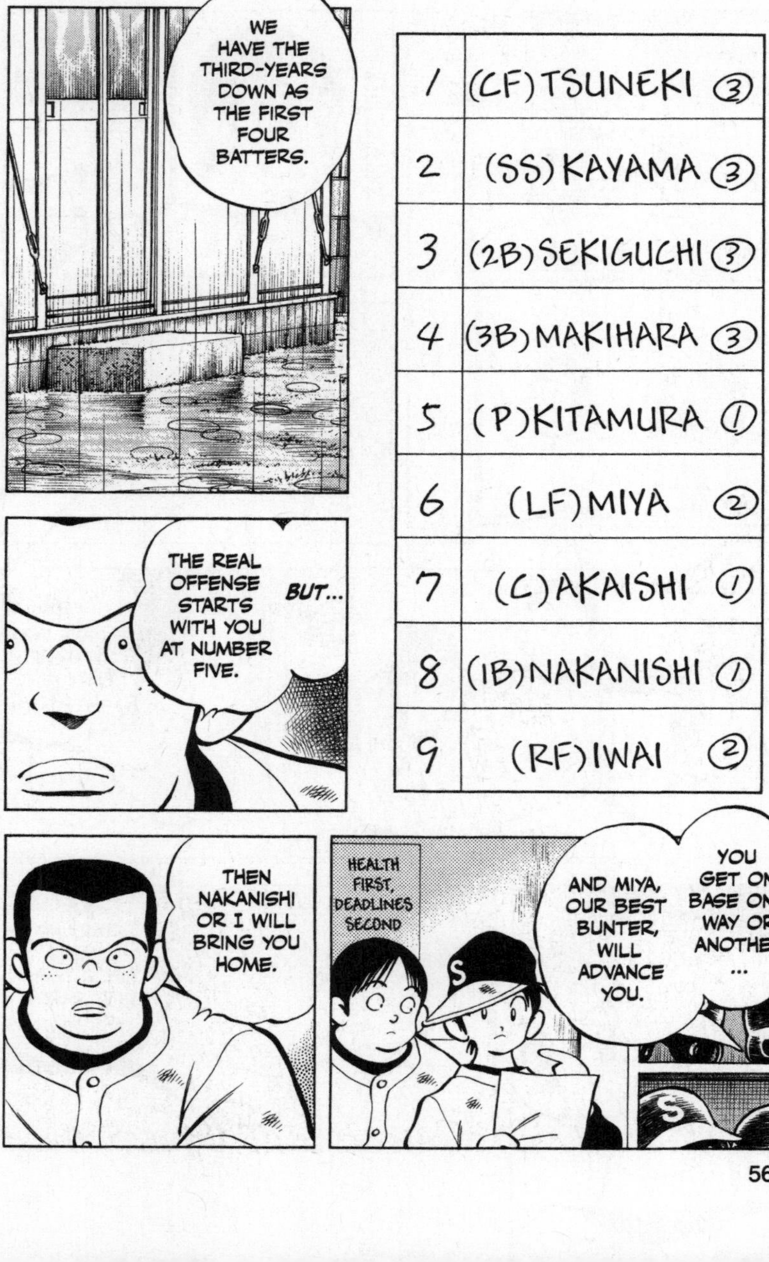
1 (CF) TSUNEKI ③
2 (SS) KAYAMA ③
3 (2B) SEKIGUCHI ③
4 (3B) MAKIHARA ③
5 (P) KITAMURA ①
6 (LF) MIYA ②
7 (C) AKAISHI ①
8 (1B) NAKANISHI ①
9 (RF) IWAI ②
WE HAVE THE THIRD-YEARS DOWN AS THE FIRST FOUR BATTERS.
THE REAL OFFENSE STARTS WITH YOU AT NUMBER FIVE.
BUT...
YOU GET ON BASE ONE WAY OR ANOTHER ...
AND MIYA, OUR BEST BUNTER, WILL ADVANCE YOU.
HEALTH FIRST, DEADLINES SECOND
THEN NAKANISHI OR I WILL BRING YOU HOME.

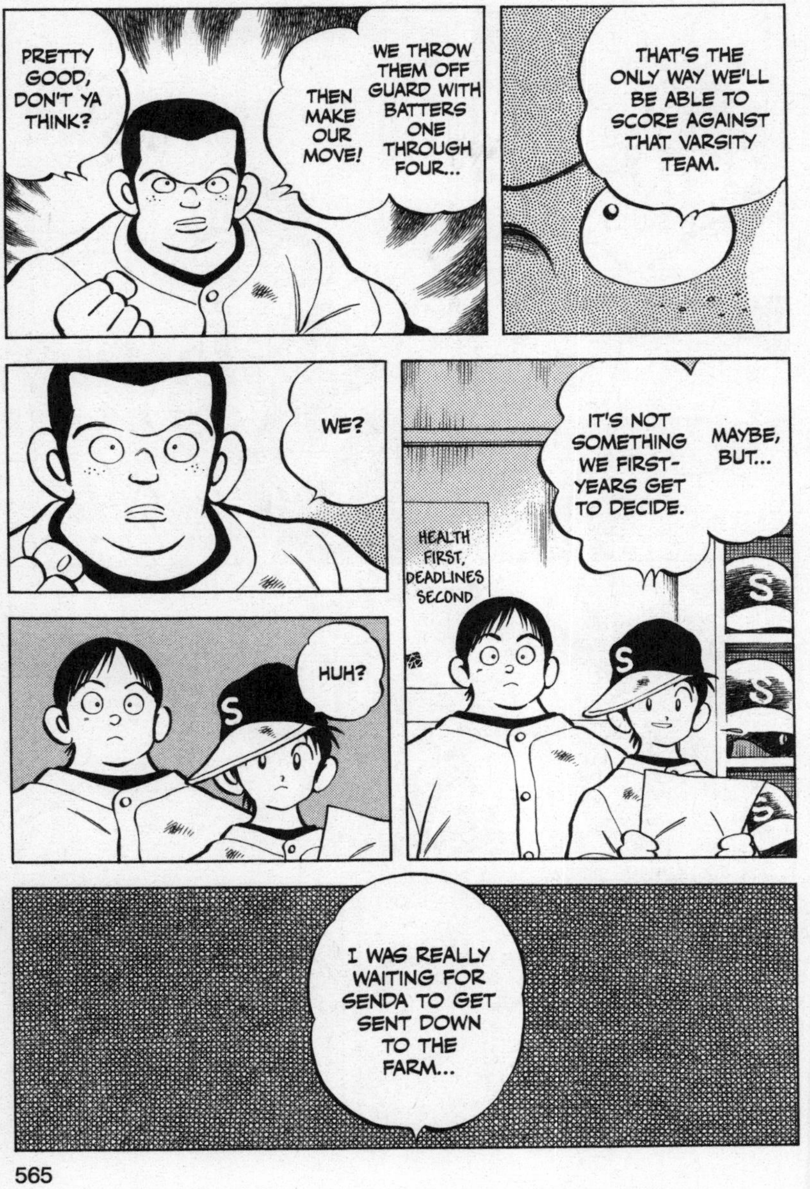
THAT'S THE ONLY WAY WE'LL BE ABLE TO SCORE AGAINST THAT VARSITY TEAM.
WE THROW THEM OFF GUARD WITH BATTERS ONE THROUGH FOUR...
THEN MAKE OUR MOVE!
PRETTY GOOD, DON'T YA THINK?
MAYBE, BUT...
IT'S NOT SOMETHING WE FIRST-YEARS GET TO DECIDE.
HEALTH FIRST, DEADLINES SECOND
WE?
HUH?
I WAS REALLY WAITING FOR SENDA TO GET SENT DOWN TO THE FARM...

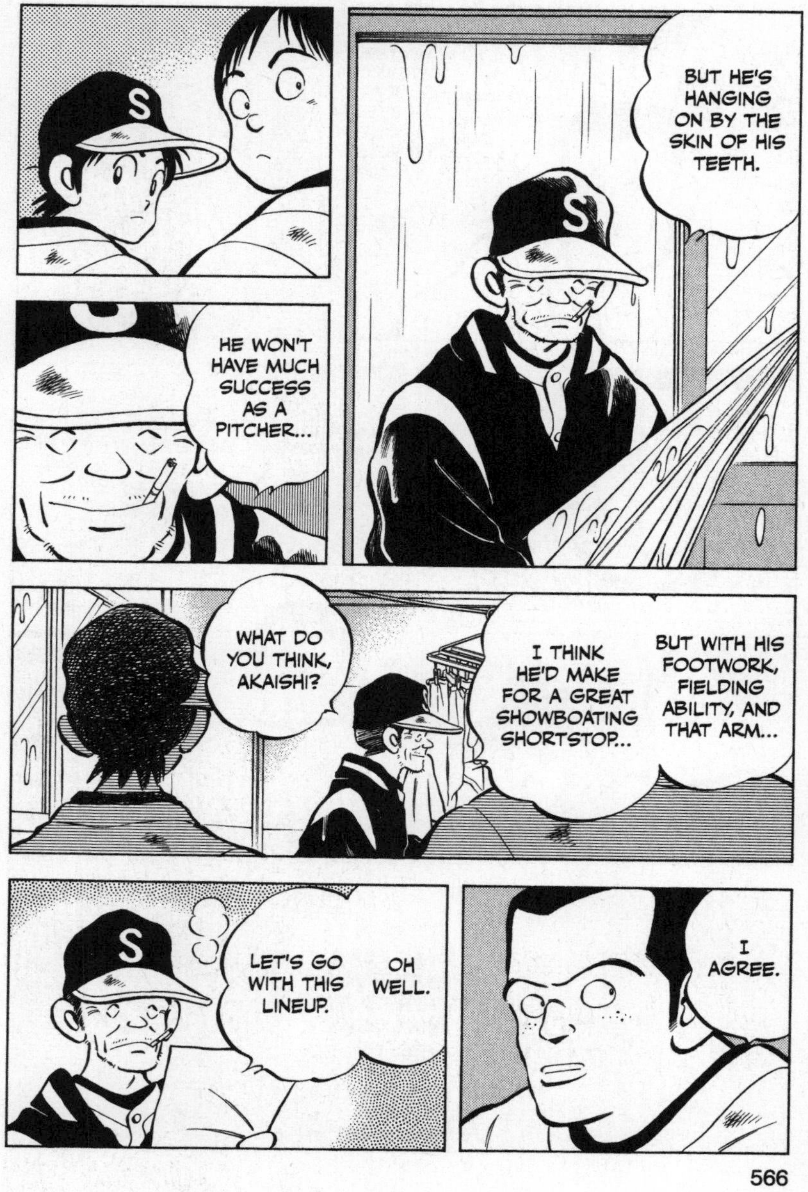
BUT HE'S HANGING ON BY THE SKIN OF HIS TEETH.
HE WON'T HAVE MUCH SUCCESS AS A PITCHER...
BUT WITH HIS FOOTWORK, FIELDING ABILITY, AND THAT ARM...
I THINK HE'D MAKE FOR A GREAT SHOWBOATING SHORTSTOP...
WHAT DO YOU THINK, AKAISHI?
I AGREE.
OH WELL.
LET'S GO WITH THIS LINEUP.

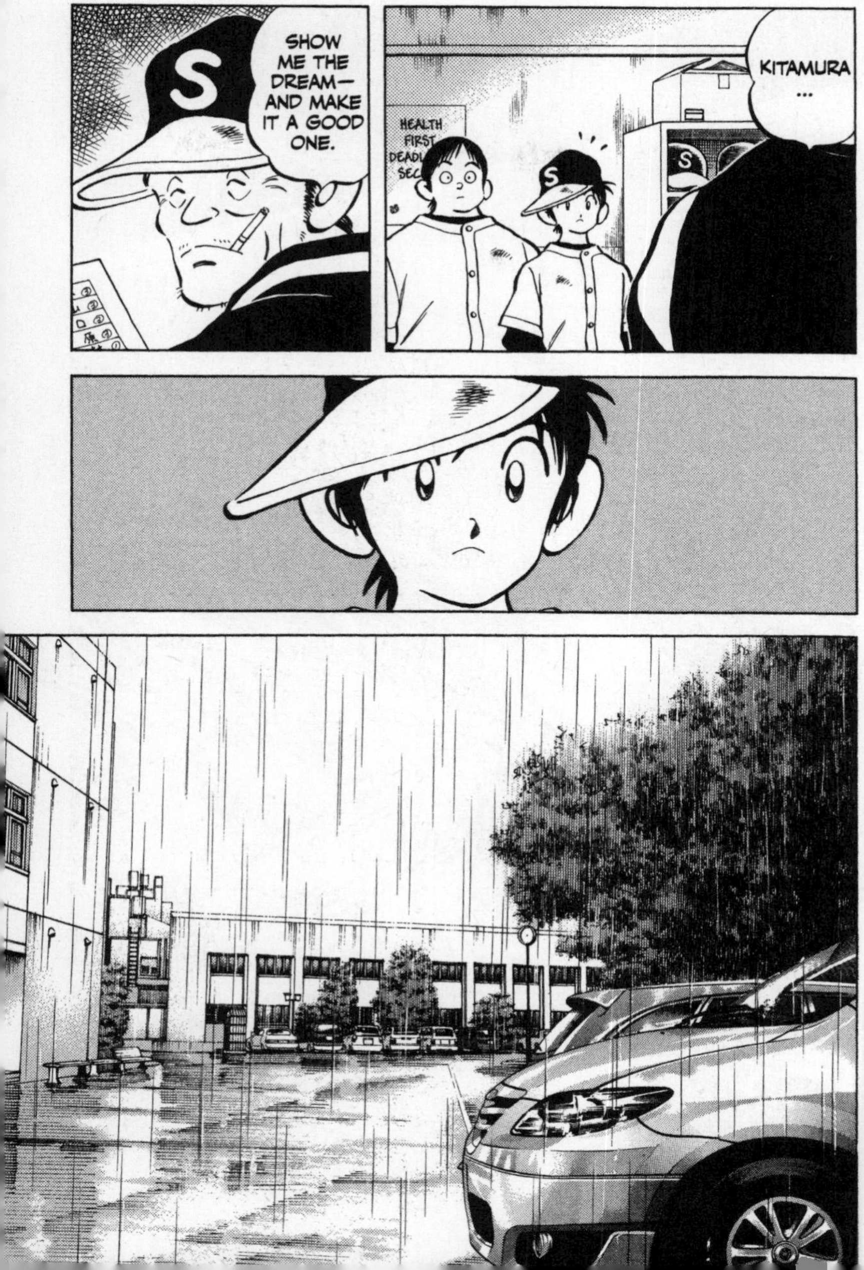
KITAMURA ...
HEALTH FIRST
SHOW ME THE DREAM—AND MAKE IT A GOOD ONE.

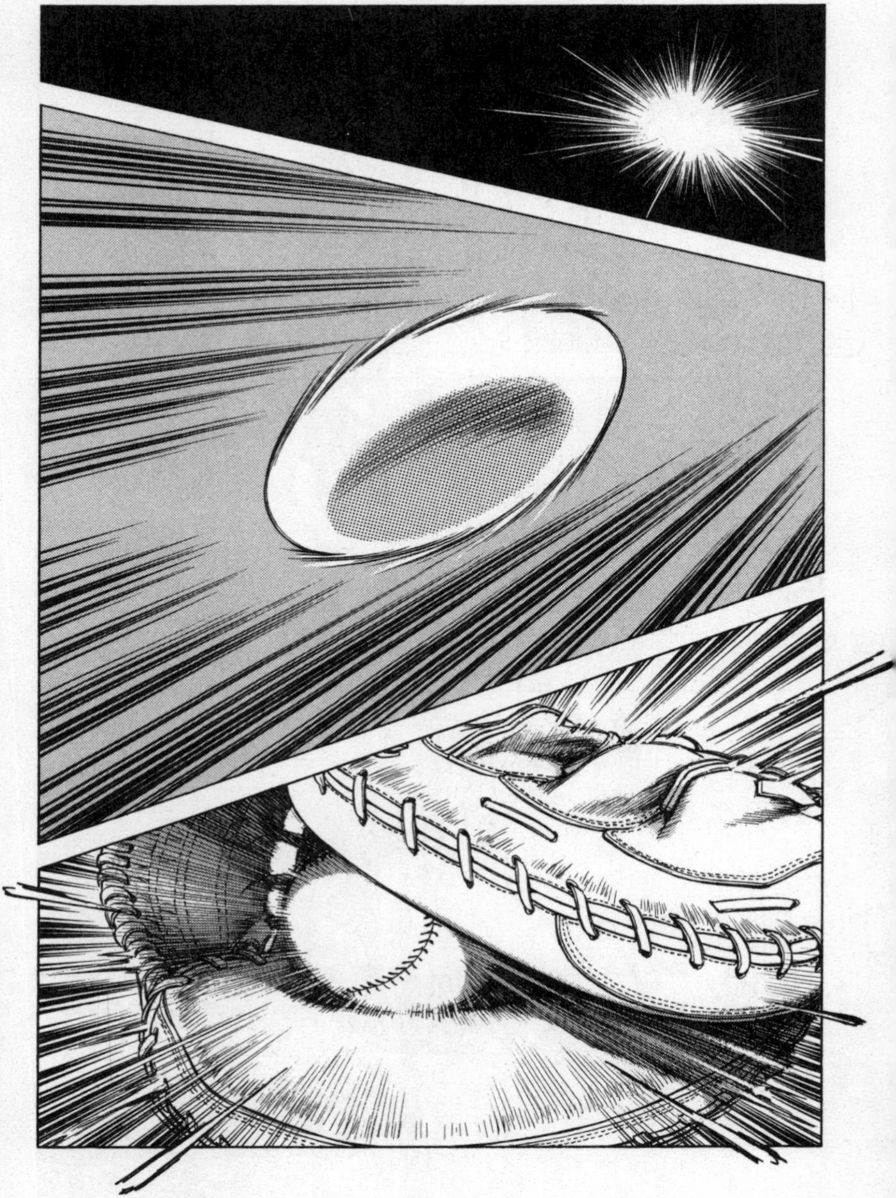

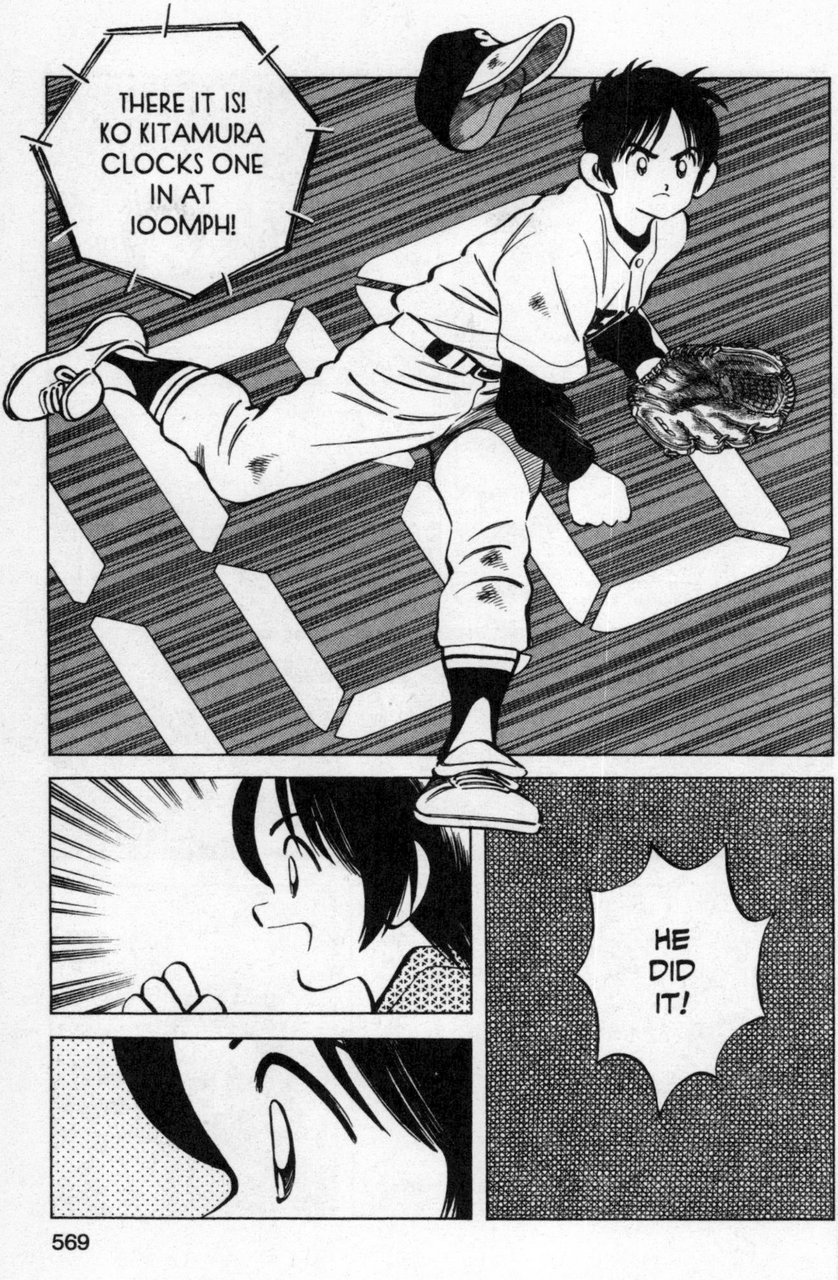
THERE IT IS! KO KITAMURA CLOCKS ONE IN AT 100MPH!
HE DID IT!

MEW
A NIGHT-MARE!
298 MPH.
SPEED
WAIT, THAT CAN'T BE RIGHT!
THAT MUST BE YOUR WEIGHT!
DO IT AGAIN!
SPEED

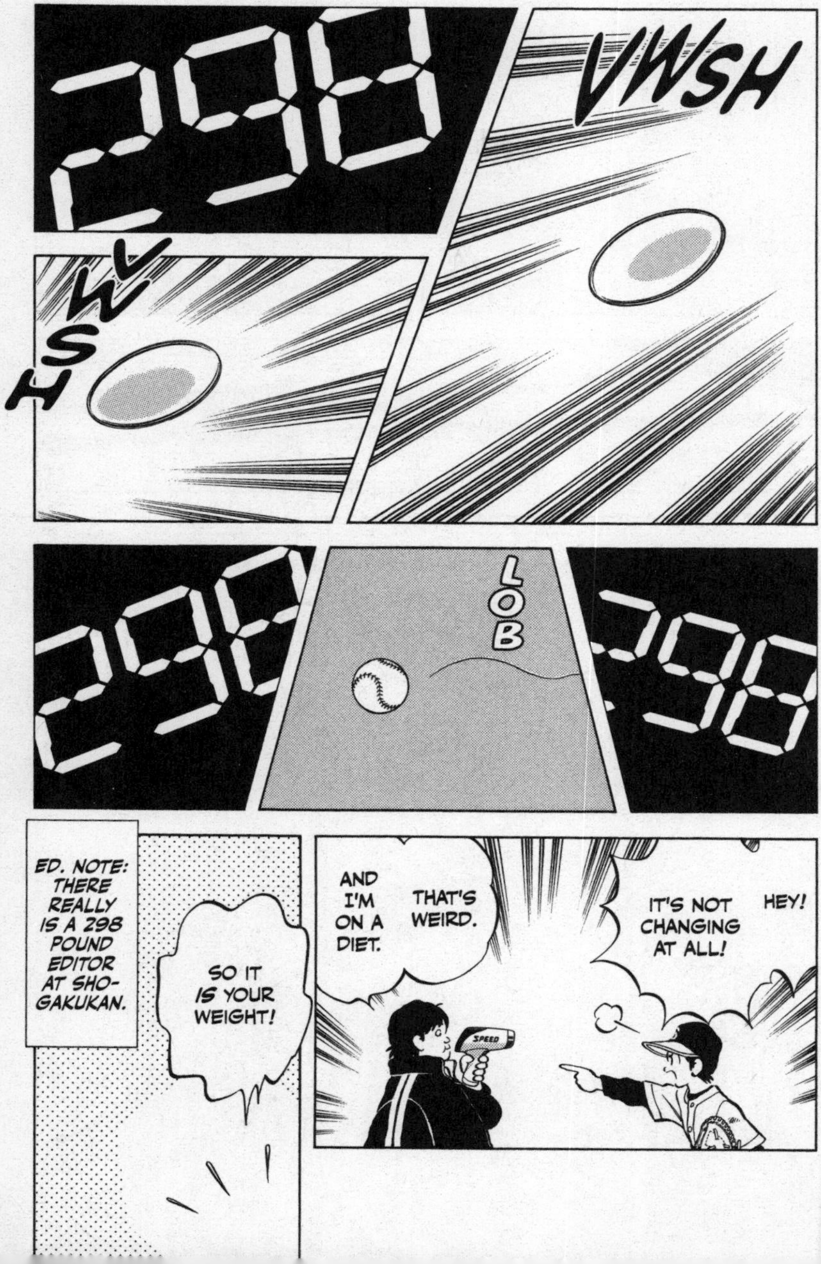
VWSH
298
VWSH
298
LOB
298
HEY!
IT'S NOT CHANGING AT ALL!
THAT'S WEIRD.
AND I'M ON A DIET.
SPEED
SO IT IS YOUR WEIGHT!
ED. NOTE: THERE REALLY IS A 298 POUND EDITOR AT SHO-GAKUKAN.

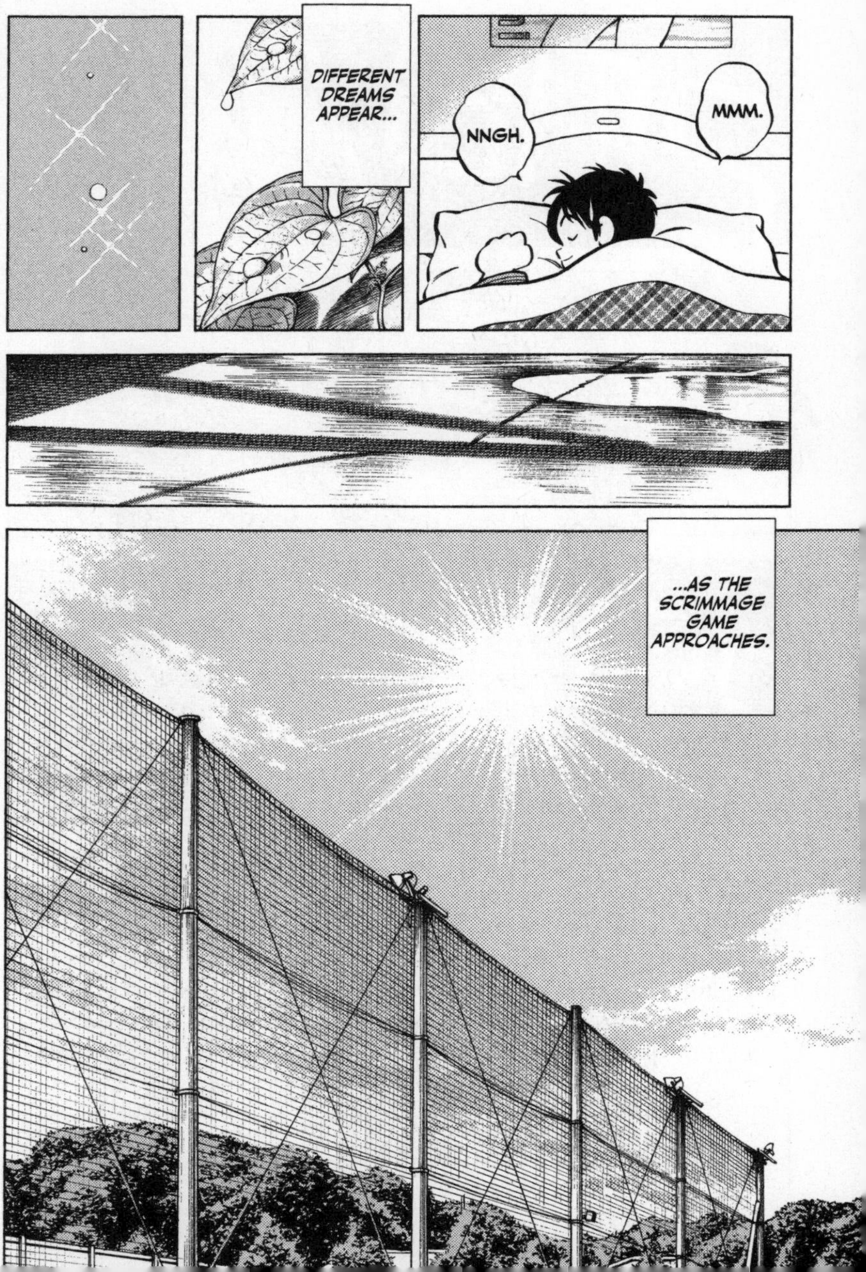
MMM.
NNGH.
DIFFERENT DREAMS APPEAR...
...AS THE SCRIMMAGE GAME APPROACHES.

One of the biggest names in the manga industry today, Mitsuru Adachi made his debut in 1970 with *Kieta Bakuon* in the pages of *Deluxe Shonen Sunday*. The creator of numerous mega-hits such as *Touch*, *Miyuki*, and *Cross Game*, Adachi Sensei received the Shogakukan Manga Award for all three of the aforementioned series. Truly in the top echelon of the manga industry, his cumulative works have seen over 200 million copies sold, and many of his series have been adapted into anime, live-action TV series and film. A master of his medium, Adachi has come to be known for his genious handling of dramatic elements skillfully combined with romance, comedy and sports. He, along with Rumiko Takahashi, has become synonymous with the phenomenal success of *Shonen Sunday* in Japan.

CROSS GAME
VOLUME 1
Shonen Sunday Edition

STORY AND ART BY
MITSURU ADACHI

© 2005 Mitsuru ADACHI/Shogakukan
All rights reserved.
Original Japanese edition "CROSS GAME" published by SHOGAKUKAN Inc.

Translation/Ralph Yamada, Lillian Olsen
Touch-up Art & Lettering/Jim Keefe, Mark McMurray
Cover Design/John Kim, Jodie Yoshioka
Interior Design/Hidemi Sahara, Yukiko Whitley
Editors/Yuki Murashige, Andy Nakatani

Printed in the U.S.A.

Published by VIZ Media, LLC
P.O. Box 77010
San Francisco, CA 94107

10 9 8 7 6 5 4 3 2
First printing, October 2010
Second printing, August 2014

www.viz.com   WWW.SHONENSUNDAY.COM

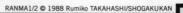